THE SOVIET UNION

THE
SOVIET
UNION
SECOND EDITION

CONGRESSIONAL QUARTERLY INC.
1414 22nd Street, N.W.
Washington, D.C. 20037

Congressional Quarterly Inc., an editorial research service and publishing company, serves clients in the fields of news, education, business, and government. It combines Congressional Quarterly's specific coverage of Congress, government, and politics with the more general subject range of an affiliated service, Editorial Research Reports.

Congressional Quarterly publishes the *Congressional Quarterly Weekly Report* and a variety of books, including college political science textbooks under the CQ Press imprint and public affairs paperbacks designed as timely reports to keep journalists, scholars, and the public abreast of developing issues and events. CQ also publishes information directories and reference books on the federal government, national elections, and politics, including the *Guide to Congress*, the *Guide to the U.S. Supreme Court*, the *Guide to U.S. Elections*, and *Politics in America*. The *CQ Almanac*, a compendium of legislation for one session of Congress, is published each year. *Congress and the Nation*, a record of government for a presidential term, is published every four years.

CQ publishes *The Congressional Monitor*, a daily report on current and future activities of congressional committees, and several newsletters including *Congressional Insight*, a weekly analysis of congressional action, and *Campaign Practices Reports*, a semimonthly update on campaign laws.

An electronic online information system, the Washington Alert Service, provides immediate access to CQ's databases of legislative action, votes, schedules, profiles, and analyses.

Library of Congress Cataloging in Publication Data

Main entry under title:

The Soviet Union.

    Bibliography: p.
    Includes index.
    1. Soviet Union—History. 2. Soviet Union—Relations
—United States. 3. United States—Relations—Soviet
Union. I. Congressional Quarterly, inc.
DK40.S63 1986   947   86-2289
ISBN 0-87187-383-4

Editors: Michelle Parks, John L. Moore

Major Contributor: Daniel C. Diller

Contributors: Barbara de Boinville, Shari Cohen, Mary H. Cooper, Bryan Daves, Brenda Horrigan, Dunbar Lockwood, Carolyn McGovern, Colleen McGuiness, Maria J. Sayers, David R. Tarr, Patrick Towell

Cover: Richard A. Pottern

Credits: Cover photo - Vladimir Vyatkin; p. 7 - Richard L. Worsnop; pp. 21, 22, 26, 28 - Library of Congress; pp. 30, 31, 32, 36 - The Bettmann Archive; p. 38 - National Archive; pp. 49, 50, 63, 65, 76, 108, 146, 148, 150, 221 - AP/Wide World Photos; p. 55 - George Rebh; p. 67 - The White House; pp. 127 (Akhromeev), 167, 199, 200, 201, 202, 203, 204 (Demichev), 205 (Sokolov), 206 (Talyzin), 209, 210, 212 - Novosti; pp. 127 (Ogarkov), 169, 175, 205 (Eltsin) - Tass from Sovfoto; p. 192 - Ray Driver; pp. 213, 217 - United Press International

Graphics: Patrick Murphy, Kathleen A. Ossenfort, Robert Redding

Indexers: Jodean Marks, Jan Danis

Congressional Quarterly Inc.

Eugene Patterson   *Chairman and Chief Executive Officer*

Andrew Barnes   *Editor and President*

Wayne P. Kelley   *Publisher*

Peter A. Harkness   *Deputy Publisher and Executive Editor*

Robert E. Cuthriell   *Director, Research and Development*

Robert C. Hur   *Director, Book Division, and General Counsel*

Jonathan C. Angier   *Business Manager*

Richard A. Shontz   *Marketing Director*

Book Department

David R. Tarr   *Director*

John L. Moore   *Assistant Director*

Joanne D. Daniels   *Director, CQ Press*

Kathryn C. Suárez   *Book Marketing Manager*

Mary W. Cohn   *Associate Editor*

Nola Healy Lynch   *Developmental Editor, CQ Press*

Carolyn Goldinger   *Project Editor*

Carolyn McGovern   *Project Editor*

Colleen McGuiness   *Project Editor*

Susanna Spencer   *Project Editor*

Amy S. Meyers   *Editorial Assistant*

Michelle Parks   *Editorial Assistant*

Linda M. Pompa   *Editorial Assistant*

Renee S. Reiner   *Editorial Assistant*

Maria J. Sayers   *Editorial Assistant*

Linda White   *Secretary*

Production

I. D. Fuller   *Production Manager*

Maceo Mayo   *Assistant Production Manager*

Sydney E. Garriss   *Computer Services Manager*

Table of Contents

Tables, Figures, and Maps

Preface

More than any other country except our own, the Union of Soviet Socialist Republics affects the lives of Americans. *The Soviet Union*, second edition, provides a concise, detailed history of that nation, its relations with other nations — especially the United States — and an assessment of its current social and economic conditions. Beginning with a description of the modern-day Soviet Union — geography, territorial divisions, party and government structure — it charts Russia's transformation into the formidable Soviet empire.

The book covers the power struggles among the top Soviet rulers, the persistent economic problems seemingly endemic to communism, and the Soviet Union's emergence from World War II as the world's second superpower — albeit one whose economic potential has not matched its military might. Also examined are communist expansion into Eastern Europe, the East-West confrontation known as the Cold War, the easing of tensions in the 1960s and early 1970s, and the deterioration of relations since the Soviet invasion of Afghanistan in 1979 and the imposition of martial law in Poland in 1981.

General events and relations between the Soviet Union and the United States, which are central to the foreign and domestic policies of both superpowers, are covered throughout the main text. Selected areas of Soviet foreign policy are detailed in Chapter 5, with separate sections on China, Africa, the Middle East, Afghanistan, and Eastern Europe, and a case study on Poland during the Solidarity labor union events of the early 1980s.

Particular attention is paid to relations between the Soviet Union and the United States after the rule of Nikita Khrushchev, as both sides made halting progress toward accommodation against a background of nuclear arms proliferation, intermittent international tension, and chronic Soviet economic difficulties. Special attention is given to the Soviet military — its composition as well as its role in Soviet society — and to the record of Soviet-U.S. arms control efforts. The policies pursued by the Khrushchev, Brezhnev, Andropov, Chernenko, and Gorbachev regimes are outlined as well as those of the Johnson, Nixon, Ford, Carter, and Reagan administrations. The state of relations with the United States under Mikhail Gorbachev is examined, and his 1985 summit meeting with Ronald Reagan is highlighted.

An attempt is made in Chapter 8 to give a clearer understanding of Soviet society. The multiethnic USSR and the economic conditions of its citizens present Soviet leaders with numerous contradictions and dilemmas that Western observers expect will multiply during the remainder of the 1980s: the Islamic population is growing more quickly than the Russian, the entire population is exposed to more Western influences, and the ratio of defense spending to consumer spending is coming under closer scrutiny than ever before.

In this book we have tried to make proper use of the words *Russian*, which applies to the official language of the Soviet Union and is an ethnic description of about half the nation's population, and *Soviet*, which describes nationality, not ethnicity.

The book contains in the appendix a chronology of events from 1900 to 1986. For the years 1964 to the present it is a unique, nearly day-by-day account that is almost a book in itself. The chronology is largely the work of Daniel C. Diller, exclusively his from 1982 to the present. To compile the accounting he drew on diverse sources such as *Facts on File*, *Foreign Affairs'* America and the World issues, half-a-dozen newspapers, various history books, the *New York Times Index*, and limited chronologies from other books. It should prove useful for quick reference to almost every notable event related to Soviet affairs.

Also in the appendix are biographies of current and past Soviet leaders from revolutionary Russia to the present, including background on leaders who emerged from the 27th Soviet Communist Party Congress of February 1986. A substantial selection of excerpts and texts from key documents related to Soviet, and especially Soviet-U.S., affairs is included. This affords readers easy access to speeches, letters, and announcements such as Winston Churchill's 1946 "Iron Curtain" speech, Nikita Khrushchev's 1956 "Secret Speech," Cuban missile crisis documents, the Brezhnev Doctrine, and the Soviet Constitution of 1977. Texts and excerpts from the Soviet-U.S. summits of the 1970s and the Gorbachev-Reagan summit of 1985 are included, as are excerpts from Gorbachev's address to the 27th Party Congress.

The bibliography, divided by chapter, provides a diverse base for further study. An index is included.

Spelling and Dates

There are several systems available to transliterate Russian words into English. *The Soviet Union*, second edition, has relied for the most part on the Library of Congress (LOC) transliteration system. LOC reference librarian Grant Harris of the European Division provided gracious assistance in our attempt to offer consistent, accurate spellings.

Soviet citizens usually have three names: a first name, a middle name derived from the father's first name (a patronymic), and a surname. In most cases, spellings are consistent with LOC style. However, when spellings differed among individuals, the editors elected to follow the various common usages. For example, Alexander has the following variants: Alexander for tsars Alexander I, II, and III; Aleksander Pushkin; and Aleksandr Kerensky. Aleksandr is the correct LOC style. Kerensky, however, is followed rather than Kerenskii, because he used that spelling when publishing in the West. This exception also applies to the names of others who have published in the West, such as Arkady Shevchenko, which would be Arkadii under the LOC system.

Names that have become widely known to Western readers were rendered in their familiar spellings, such as Leo Tolstoy. An exception has also been made in the case of Yuri Andropov, whose first name would be spelled Iurii under the LOC system. Soviet Jewish dissident Anatolii Shcharanskii is spelled according to LOC style, although various other spellings have been used in the Western media.

Spellings preferred by the People's Republic of China are also used. Thus, it is Beijing, not Peking; Mao Zedong, not Mao Tse-tung, and so on.

Dates in *The Soviet Union* are according to the Gregorian (Western) calendar. Before 1918 Russia used the Julian calendar; as a result, the Bolshevik Revolution (November 7, 1917, in *The Soviet Union*) is referred to in most Soviet sources as the October Revolution because, under the Julian calendar, it occurred in late October.

Sources

Listed in the bibliography are several books and articles useful in compiling *The Soviet Union*, both the first and second editions. Certain books, however, merit special attention: *Expansion and Coexistence; Soviet Foreign Policy, 1917-73; Dangerous Relations: The Soviet Union in World Politics, 1970-1982; A History of Soviet Russia;* and *Russia's Failed Revolutions: From the Decembrists to the Dissidents,* all by Adam B. Ulam; *A History of Russia,* by Nicholas V. Riasanovsky; *USSR: A Concise History,* 4th ed., by Basil Dmytryshyn; *The Brezhnev Politburo and the Decline of Détente,* by Harry Gelman; *The Armed Forces of the USSR,* 3d ed., by Harriet Fast Scott and William F. Scott; and *How the Soviet Union Is Governed,* by Jerry F. Hough and Merle Fainsod. *Problems of Communism* was a particularly useful journal.

John Keegan's 1985 copyrighted article "The Ordeal of Afghanistan" was first published in the *Atlantic Monthly*; a paragraph is reprinted here with permission. Full citations to other books and publications excerpted in this edition are given in the bibliography.

Ellen Jones of the Defense Intelligence Agency reviewed Chapter 1 and the military section of Chapter 6 for accuracy and content and offered several helpful suggestions. Her colleague in the Network for Women in Slavic Studies, Peggy Harlow, also reviewed a portion of Chapter 6. Nevertheless, responsibility for any errors rests with Congressional Quarterly.

Some teachers may need further elaboration of Marxism. The editors found particularly helpful R. N. Carew Hunt's *The Theory and Practice of Communism*. The bibliography contains additional sources on Marxism.

Michelle Parks
John L. Moore

Introduction

Soviet motivations and behavior have become a major political issue in the West because how we picture the Soviets helps to determine our policies toward them. Western scholars of the 1940s and 1950s used totalitarianism as an all-encompassing term to describe the Russian and Soviet systems. Soviet behavior came to be characterized as inherently aggressive and expansionistic.

Geography and a far from ideal climate have been instrumental in shaping the nation's development. Since the seventeenth century the Russian state has been the world's largest territorial entity — its borders hard to defend; its neighbors in Europe and China generally opposed to its ambitions or even existence. Growing enough food has been a perennial problem. Scholars often cited these factors to help explain what they saw as a defensive Soviet posture toward the outside world.

There are other factors Western analysts have used to determine why and how the Soviet Union developed as it has. Throughout the nation's history, tsars and the Soviet regime have used armed forces to support a centralized, authoritarian government. A religion of orthodoxy helped perpetuate feelings of xenophobia while at the same time admiration for and imitation of Western culture developed among the elite. A patrimonial system of rule fostered passivity toward politics and acceptance of a life largely devoid of freedom of choice. Many characterized Soviet defensiveness, bullying, and duplicity in world affairs as manifestations of a serious inferiority complex.

Unavoidable Bond

Since World War II the United States has been forced to link its foreign policy to the Soviet Union, despite the conflicts between the ideology and values of the two countries. Neither Washington nor Moscow can institute a new arms policy, forge a new relationship with another nation, or take any other significant foreign action without considering the impact on its counterpart.

Yet in attempting to formulate U.S. policy toward the Soviet Union, presidents have sometimes received advice that was shortsighted, simplistic, or biased. Assessments of Soviet motivations and predictions of behavior have often been colored by emotional distaste for the Soviet system and a paucity of data caused by Soviet secretiveness. The totalitarian model perpetuated oversimplified images of the Soviet Union.

For its part, the Soviet foreign policy process underwent significant evolution after 1953, with dynamism and pragmatism largely replacing the more irrational posture dictated by Joseph Stalin. During Nikita Khrushchev's tenure the Soviet Union solidified its claims to being a superpower. But this status was primarily one-dimensional because it depended largely on military power. The Soviet domestic economy made gains in the postwar years but the USSR remained a limited player in the international economy. The Soviets viewed America as the principal obstacle to their international ambitions and sought to compete with the United States in areas outside the military realm. The Soviets saw U.S. efforts to "contain" them and deal with them "from a position of strength" as direct challenges to their superpower status and concomitant right to exercise influence internationally.

The United States, besides being the Soviets' foremost opponent, was the yardstick by which they measured their own success. Soviet leaders wanted the United States to consider the USSR as its equal. Khrushchev noted in his memoirs how opposition to the United States was coupled with admiration: "America occupied a special place in our thinking about the world. And why shouldn't it? It was our strongest opponent among the capitalist countries, the leader that called the tune of anti-Sovietism for the rest."

As scholar Dimitri Simes has explained, throughout the 1960s and 1970s there was "fear and competitive impulse" in the U.S. and Soviet images of each other. "But in the American case they were mixed with contempt; in the Russian, with jealousy and respect."

The wily, gregarious Khrushchev vacillated in his policy toward the United States. The Soviet military was quickly and sharply upgraded under his guidance, with emphasis on nuclear forces. Yet Khrushchev's peaceful coexistence became a policy cornerstone, even after his removal from power in 1964. While less emotional and volatile than Khrushchev, Leonid Brezhnev also displayed a need to be reassured of Soviet equality. Brezhnev placed Soviet foreign policy on a more stable, predictable footing, but the Soviet-U.S. relationship seesawed under him as it had under his predecessor. The highs produced by détente during the Nixon years gave way to the post-Afghanistan return to the Cold War that survived into the Yuri Andropov and Konstantin Chernenko years.

The November 1985 summit between Mikhail Gorbachev and Ronald Reagan brought renewed hope that

1

a dialogue between the two leaders would lead to an easing of tensions. But six months later the superpowers had yet to make substantial progress toward improved relations.

The constant competition has affected the domestic policies of both countries, as illustrated by President Reagan's determination to bolster U.S. defenses while dramatically reducing domestic social programs. In the Soviet Union, incessant pursuit of military strength has retarded the availability and quality of consumer goods. The White House blames its painful budget decisions on the Soviet Union's steady buildup. But the Soviets contend that they have had to beef up their arsenal to protect themselves against the United States' "imperialist aggression."

Critics of past U.S. policies toward the Soviet Union, including President Reagan, charge that too often Washington merely reacted to Moscow's aggression. They argue that it is time for the United States to flex its muscles and fashion policies that will circumscribe the Soviets' freedom to challenge the West's interests and security. Opponents of Reagan's strategy contend that it only forces the Soviets into a corner and prompts them to act more defensively.

In mid-1986 it was unlikely that future improvements in the relationship between the superpowers would foster the high hopes and expectations of the earlier era of détente. The feeling remained in the Reagan administration and much of Congress that détente brought benefits to the Soviets at U.S. expense. It appeared doubtful that significant progress in arms control and, consequently, overall superpower relations, would come unless each side made concessions on Reagan's controversial Strategic Defense Initiative (SDI).

Impact of Leadership Changes

When Mikhail Gorbachev was named to replace Chernenko in March 1985, the new generation of leaders finally took the reins. Again the West was called upon to reassess its image of the Soviet Union.

Was Gorbachev truly intent on reform? If so, would he be able to bring it about? Would paying more attention to the domestic economy mean fewer foreign policy adventures? Were Gorbachev's nuclear testing moratorium and his calls for eliminating nuclear weapons merely propaganda ploys — or did these moves indicate truly revised attitudes and a genuine desire to slow down the arms race?

From the beginning Gorbachev has called for fundamental change in the domestic economy. His first year in office he began to alter the bureaucracy's way of thinking and operating. But the "radical" changes he says are neces-

sary to revive the economy, reinvigorate the bureaucracy, and improve worker productivity are not taking place with any great speed. Some Western observers note how seldom his cries for change are accompanied by concrete plans to implement them. To many, it appears that he has simply tinkered with the basic central planning mechanism without effecting true reform.

Others note that accurate judgments cannot be made on the basis of just one year. Moving too rapidly could foster dissatisfaction among many members of the elite and create limitations on Gorbachev's power or even bring about his downfall. Instead, some Western scholars believe his rapid personnel turnovers, his limited but forward-looking economic restructuring, and his foreign policy initiatives should be considered significant in their own right.

Although Gorbachev has largely removed the top leadership remaining from the Brezhnev era, many who benefited from past coddling are widely dispersed in middle and lower levels of the party and government bureaucracy and may still present obstacles to economic reform. Only when policy has been implemented can it be judged a success or failure, and it is here that individuals opposed to radical reforms will have the opportunity to thwart Gorbachev's efforts.

The effect on defense must be addressed in any analysis of Gorbachev's drive toward economic reform. Some Soviet military leaders apparently realize the armed forces will be adversely affected if the economy does not improve.

President Reagan's SDI will likely remain the major source of contention in arms control efforts and, indeed, overall relations between the superpowers. If Reagan refuses to restrain SDI research, Gorbachev will have an even more difficult time convincing the military that defense budget cuts will not seriously affect Soviet security.

In foreign policy, many observers expect the Soviets to try to improve relations with Western Europe and Japan; stabilize relations in the important Asian region, especially by reducing hostility with China; and limit involvement in the faltering economies of the Third World. Lower world oil prices have meant the Soviets earn less hard currency from oil exports; Third World oil-producing nations in turn have less money with which to buy Soviet weapons — thereby further reducing Soviet export earnings.

Despite these assessments the direction the Soviets will take in domestic or foreign policy cannot be predicted with certainty. Who the Soviets are, what they want, and how they will pursue their ambitions will continue for years to be questions at the heart of the debate over U.S. policy toward Moscow.

The Land and State

The Union of Soviet Socialist Republics is the largest country in the world, with an area measuring 8.65 million square miles and stretching across 11 time zones. About two-and-one-half times larger than the United States, the Soviet territory extends from the Baltic Sea to the Bering Strait. Only 53 miles across the Bering Strait lies the Alaskan mainland. The vastness of the USSR is protected on every border — except at the Polish frontier — by natural barriers. This, combined with a history of foreign invasion and Russia's early embrace of the Orthodox Church rather than the Church of Rome, has contributed to the nation's tendency toward xenophobia — a sense of isolation and distrust of the outside world, particularly the West.

This large land mass shares borders with 12 other nations: Afghanistan, China, Czechoslovakia, Finland, Hungary, Iran, Mongolia, North Korea, Norway, Poland, Romania, and Turkey. It opens to the Arctic Ocean, Pacific Ocean, Baltic Sea, Caspian Sea, Black Sea, and the Sea of Azov. And it encompasses Lake Baikal, the largest freshwater basin in Eurasia and the deepest in the world. The principal rivers in the Soviet Union include the Volga, Don, Dnepr, Amu-Darya, Ob, Irtysh, Yenisei, Lena, and Amur. The Yenisei flows north across Siberia, cutting the Soviet Union in half. The Volga, one of the mightiest rivers in the world, and the Oka, one of its tributaries, are typical of many Soviet rivers — they are navigable only about eight months a year. The remaining time they are frozen.

The eastern half of the country is made up of mountains and highlands; the west has two huge flatlands themselves divided in half by the Ural Mountain Range. The Urals, running for 1,500 miles from north to south, form the traditional dividing line between Europe and Asia. West of this mountain range is the broad East European Plain, encompassing all of the so-called European part of the Soviet Union. East of the Urals lies the vastness of Siberia. The Central Siberian Plateau is more elevated than the eastern plain but equally flat.

The Central Asian territory is largely mountainous, including the Caucasus range between the Black and Caspian seas and the Altai range in east Central Asia. There are other, lower, mountain ranges on the Crimean Peninsula and on the borders of Poland, Czechoslovakia, and Hungary.

Much of the Soviet Union lies above 50° north latitude (in North America, some 300 miles north of Montreal). The northernmost part of the Soviet Union is arctic desert and tundra, where moss and low shrubs are the main vegetation. South of the tundra stretch enormous forests, then the steppes (grasslands) and finally the deserts of Central Asia.

The steppes contain the famous black soil of Russia, which is considered among the most fertile in the world. Two-thirds of the Soviet Union's arable land is on the steppes. However, unfavorable weather conditions — insufficient, unreliable rainfall and hot winds — thwart full exploitation of this significant resource. Less than 20 percent of the entire Soviet territory is estimated to be suitable for agricultural cultivation. Agriculture is further hampered, most Western observers agree, by the highly bureaucratic and inefficient decision-making structure imposed by the central government.

The heart of Soviet economic, political, and cultural life extends for a few hundred miles from the capital, Moscow. The area is densely populated and highly industrialized. Numerous rail lines and highways surround it and connect Moscow to several major urban areas. Both Moscow and the surrounding cities rely on energy and food supplies brought from other parts of the country. More than 12 million people live in Moscow and its suburbs.

The Northwest is especially important economically because it is the nation's second-largest industrial base. Subsections include Belorussia, the Baltic states, and the Kola Peninsula on the Soviet-Finnish border. Most of the cities in the Northwest are ports, including Leningrad, the nation's second-largest city and the largest seaport. Because the Northwest territory is so vast, the physical environment has many differences, providing for widely divergent population sizes and agricultural products. There are numerous rivers in the territory and timber is a main natural resource.

The largest city in the southwestern part of the country is Kiev, the ancient capital of Russia. The Ukraine, south of Kiev, is most conducive to agriculture but it is outproduced in wheat and rice by the steppe to the south, just above the Caucasus mountains. Grapes grow in the Crimea and the area is a major summer resort that resembles the Mediterranean in climate.

Central Asia supplies several types of agricultural supplies, including livestock, but most crops, such as cotton and rice, depend heavily on irrigation. The entire area lacks major natural waterways and modern transportation

The Soviet Union

Area	8.65 million square miles.
Population	277,930,000.
Major Ethnic Groups	Russian, 52 percent; Ukrainian, 16 percent; Uzbek, 5 percent; Belorussian, 4 percent.
Religions	Atheist, 70 percent; Russian Orthodox, 18 percent; Moslem, 9 percent; Others, 3 percent (Jewish, Protestant, Georgian Orthodox, Roman Catholic).
Languages	Russian (official); Altaic, 12 percent; other Indo-European, 8 percent; Uralian, 3 percent; Caucasian, 2 percent.
Literacy	99.8 percent.
Work Force	147 million (civilian).
Capital	Moscow.
Government System	Federal Union.
Political Party	Communist Party of the Soviet Union.
Currency	Ruble. Official exchange rate: 0.743 rubles = $1 (1983).
Gross National Product	$1.84 trillion (1983).
National Day	October Revolution Day, November 7.

Source: *The World Fact Book*, CIA (Washington, D.C.: Government Printing Office), 1985.

routes, deficiencies that have hindered economic growth despite rapid population growth. The Caucasus range is the overland route to the Middle East, a difficult journey connecting Georgia, Armenia, and Azerbaidzhan with Turkey and Iran. Soviet ports on the climatically pleasant Black and Caspian seas also make these two countries relatively accessible.

Westerners usually think of Siberia as the vast, arctic territory where political malcontents have been sent for centuries. For the Soviets, it is the "giant construction site of the USSR." Yet the economic development hoped for because of its natural resources has been significantly hindered because of Siberia's inhospitable climate and size. Roads are few and far between; there is but one rail line, the Trans-Siberian Railway. The region's largest cities are along the rail line and include Novosibirsk and Krasnoyarsk. Most evidence points to vast mineral supplies but Siberia's steppe zone is limited agriculturally. Fish are plentiful, and hunting of furred animals is extensive.

The Soviet Far East differs in many ways from the rest of Siberia. It is humid, relatively mild, and has several large cities, including Vladivostok. Because the area is so far from Moscow, the economy has become somewhat self-contained, according to some Soviet experts. The area's climate and location on the Pacific Ocean have long attracted settlers from throughout the Soviet Union. Economic development is considerable. There are also numerous sensitive military bases in the area, particularly near Sakhalin Island.

Part of the Soviet Union roughly corresponds to the Arctic Circle. The Far North is primarily a maritime territory and not well suited for humans. Murmansk is one of the larger urban areas and has a substantial fishing industry. There are other ports providing navigation between Europe and Asia for a few months each year and, despite the near isolation, population in the Far North is slowly growing.

Geography has played a particularly significant role in Soviet history and culture. Russia's isolation contributed to its backwardness compared with Western Europe. Foreign invaders found the orginal Russian territory lacking in natural barriers such as large bodies of water or mountain ranges; this factor has long been cited as justification for Russian and Soviet desires to secure the nation's borders. In the search for security, the Russian and Soviet states invaded other territories, making the nation rich in resources yet difficult to manage in its enormity. The severe climate has helped when the Soviet Union was being invaded yet has hindered development and largely determined population and economic distribution.

Resources

Within its enormous territory, the Soviet Union contains at least 25 percent of the world's energy resources and hydroelectric power, according to the U.S. State Department. The Soviet Union currently is the world's largest producer of petroleum, leading all members of the Organization of Petroleum Exporting Countries and the United States.

How much longer the Soviets can continue producing large amounts of oil is the subject of much debate. The Soviets' first oil production declines since World War II came in 1984 and 1985. Most analysts projected the downward trend to continue through the 1980s. In the mid-1970s, the U.S. Central Intelligence Agency predicted that the Soviets soon would find themselves in an energy squeeze, but production levels climbed impressively until the end of the decade. It was not until 1981 that the Eastern bloc faced some reductions in petroleum supplies from the Soviet Union. By the winter of 1984, Moscow canceled some oil shipments to West European customers.

Most analysts maintained that to sustain current production levels the Soviets would need to devote considerable funding to exploration and drilling in inhospitable regions, notably Siberia. The technology required for such operations had to be imported from the West. The continued availability of advanced drilling equipment posed a potential serious problem for the Soviets throughout the 1980s. Additionally, many Western analysts believed the important Volga-Urals and Siberian oil fields began drying up sooner than the Soviets expected. A few major oil fields in Siberia have provided the bulk of oil for years. Labor shortages in the rugged oil regions also limited production levels. *(Map, Chapter 7, p. 168)*

Publications and Definitions

Publications

Following are brief descriptions of some major Communist Party and Soviet government publications (with 1985-86 circulation figures taken from journals unless otherwise noted):

Newspapers: *Pravda* (Truth) — Daily organ of Central Committee with more than 12 million circulation; considered most important newspaper; emphasizes party affairs and general news. Slightly different versions appear in more than 20 cities.

Izvestiia (News) — Daily organ of government with 8-10 million circulation; emphasizes official information and general news; considered most influential daily after *Pravda*. Sunday supplement includes news analysis, features.

Trud (Labor) — Six-day-a-week trade union publication with 14 million circulation (1983); emphasizes labor and economic information.

Krasnaya Zvezda (Red Star) — Ministry of Defense daily publication; of major importance as publisher of official thinking on strategic matters.

Literaturnaya Gazeta (Literary Gazette) — Weekly of writers' union; circulation 3.1 million (1983); carries most authoritative opinions on literary life, stage, screen, and other cultural areas.

Sovetskaya Rossiya (Soviet Russia) — Central Committee daily serving RSFSR; circulation 3.3 million (1983). (Each Union Republic has a jointly published party-government daily.)

Komsomolskaya Pravda (Communist Youth League Truth) — Six-day-a-week daily of Komsomol for younger readers; circulation 9 million (1983).

Sovetsky Sport (Soviet Sport) — Daily with illustrated coverage of major sporting events; circulation 4.6 million (1983).

Magazines and Monthlies: *Kommunist* (Communist) — Party central organ; 18 issues a year; the most important political journal of ideology; circulation 976,000 (1983).

Kommunist Vooruzhennykh Sil (Communist of the Armed Forces) — Semimonthly of Main Political Administration.

Krokodil (Crocodile) — Weekly popular satirical; circulation 5 million.

Ogonyok (Flame or Little Light) — Weekly popular illustrated socio-political and literary journal about life in Soviet Union; circulation 1.5 million (down from more than 2 million).

Partiinaya Zhizn (Party Life) — Semimonthly of Central Committee; circulation 1.1 million.

SShA (USA) — Monthly of Academy of Sciences' Institute of the USA and Canada; circulation 30,000.

Vedomosti Verkhovnovo Soveta SSSR (Collections of USSR Supreme Soviet and Presidium) — Weekly.

Voprosy Ekonomiki (Problems of Economics) — Monthly of Academy of Sciences' Economics Institute; circulation 70,000.

Zhurnalist (Journalist) — Monthly of journalists' union; circulation 120,000 (1984).

Molodaya Gvardia (Young Guard) — Central Committee periodical; book, film, and play reviews; circulation 220,000 (1984).

Neva (The Neva) — Leningrad; book, film, play reviews; circulation 292,000.

Novy Mir (New World) and *Oktyabr* (October) — Circulations 160,000 and 195,000, respectively; these are often called "thick journals"; the most important of numerous such literary reviews, providing exposure for wide range of poets and writers.

Definitions

Apparat: Full-time administrative apparatus (bureaucracy) of the Communist Party or the Soviet government.

Apparatchik: Member of the apparat.

Cadres: Party term for personnel.

Central Committee (CC) Plenum: Meeting of the entire CC; usually occurs twice annually.

Collegia: Decision-making or advisory committees at any administrative level that bring together party and government officials and outside experts.

Combine: Enterprises linked by common location, functions, or needs; overseen by a director.

Enterprise: A state-owned company involved in production or trade.

Gorod: City.

Intelligentsia: Soviet term for stratum (not class) of society that includes white-collar administrators, professionals, and students.

Kolkhoz: Collective farm; statutorily a self-governing agricultural cooperative but in reality limited by state controls.

Krai: Territory. Administrative unit larger than an oblast. Found only in the RSFSR.

Kraikom, Obkom, Raikom, Gorkom: Party committee of given krai, oblast, raion, or gorod.

Kremlinology: Study of Soviet internal politics using evidence "hidden" in diverse sources such as personnel changes, pronouncements, and ceremonial procedures.

Nomenklatura: List of positions over which a designated party body has the power of appointment.

Oblast: Province. About 160 in the USSR.

Primary Party Organization (PPO): The smallest party organizational unit at the local level.

Raion: District. Subdivision of oblast.

Samizdat: Underground dissident literature.

Sovkhoz: State-owned and -managed farm.

Energy plays a critical role in the Soviet economy, as in all highly industrialized societies. Western oil exports account for more than 60 percent of Moscow's hard-currency earnings, which Moscow requires to finance purchases of much-needed grain and technology. Moscow has been hard pressed to maintain high levels of Western oil exports in the face of stagnant oil prices worldwide on top of the domestic production declines.

Since Mikhail Gorbachev became party general secretary in March 1985, the official position has been that the drop in oil production is the fault of poor management. Several industrial ministers have been replaced. Party plans for the rest of the decade include significant increases in oil production, primarily through conservation and import of Western technology.

Natural gas production has increased since 1980 more rapidly than oil production has fallen. The much-publicized contracts with the West were quickly acted on as pipelines were laid and gas fields tapped. To continue high levels of oil exports to the West, Moscow has begun exploring ways to substitute gas for oil at home and in Eastern Europe.

Besides its energy wealth, the Soviet Union contains great reserves of other natural resources. Its supplies of timber and manganese are the largest in the world, and it has ample reserves of lead, zinc, nickel, mercury, potash, and phosphate. According to the Office of Technology and Assessment, the Soviet Union supplies the United States with 17 percent of its chromite and 16 percent of its platinum metal group needs. Both groups have important industrial and defense uses. Soviet reserves in platinum metals, cobalt, and manganese are among the world's largest. Of the major minerals, the USSR lacks large amounts only of tin and uranium, according to the State Department.

Years of emphasis on heavy industry have brought the Soviet Union unwelcome environmental problems, just as in other parts of the industrial world. By most accounts environmental protection has not progressed much beyond mitigating past damage, as rapid industrialization continues to be the highest policy priority. Several significant environmental problems have implications that could continue for years. The level of the Caspian Sea has been lowered by more than 15 feet because of the extensive use of the Volga River for irrigation and hydroelectricity, disrupting the ecological chain and threatening with extinction several varieties of fish. Baikal Lake's purity and delicate ecological balance have been severely damaged because of hydroelectric power plants, wood pulp mills, and chemical plants. The lake has thousands of species of animal life known nowhere else in the world. Acid rain and irreparable soil erosion due to deforestation are said to be problems of major consequence in several industrial areas. And some Soviet experts say rumors are persistent about nuclear facility disasters in the Urals and Ukraine that have caused both human and lasting environmental damage. *(Details on energy, industry, Chapter 7)*

The Kremlin

The Kremlin — a contemporary symbol of Soviet power — is a walled fortress built on a hill in the center of Moscow. The walls, 40 feet in height and 12 feet thick, enclose several cathedrals and government buildings, including the mid-nineteenth century Grand Palace. Built as the tsar's residence, the Grand Palace housed the Supreme Soviet until 1961, when that body moved to new quarters within the Kremlin. The Grand Palace is used today for Communist Party meetings and other party and state functions.

Moscow's Kremlin (other cities, such as Novgorod and Rostov, also had kremlins) was built in the twelfth century. The original wooden towers and battlements were replaced by oak and earthen fortifications in 1296. In 1367 the first stone walls were built. They enclosed the palaces of the grand duke and the nobility, government offices, churches, and monasteries. The brick walls surrounding the triangular Kremlin were built in the late fifteenth century. The striking cathedrals within the Kremlin were built around a central square in the fifteenth and sixteenth centuries by Italian artisans working for the tsars. Other buildings within the Kremlin are the Moscow Senate building, which today houses the offices of the Council of Ministers, and the Armory Palace, which is used as a museum.

Along the northeastern wall of the Kremlin lies Red Square, the site of military parades and other state celebrations. Red Square also is the site of the tomb of V.I. Lenin and the multicolored Cathedral of St. Basil the Blessed, built by Tsar Ivan the Terrible. The square's name is not an allusion to communism. The Russian adjective for "beautiful" also may be translated as "red."

Population

The approximately 278 million population of the Soviet Union is the world's third largest, containing more than 170 ethnic groups, speaking some 130 languages, and practicing several religions (although most claim to be atheists). Ethnic Russians traditionally have made up most of the population but demographers predict that by the year 2000 ethnic Russians will make up less than half the population. As non-Russian ethnic groups increase in size, problems of nationalism likely will grow.

Russian is the official language of the country, and for the non-Russian population it is considered politic to master and use Russian. The emphasis on Russian is one part of the central government's attempt to assimilate the disparate Soviet population. The government also has developed programs to "Russify" the republics, dispatching thousands of ethnic Russians to work in, and sometimes to keep an eye on, ethnically distinct areas. *(Details regarding population, Chapter 8)*

Religion

The Soviet state and the religious establishment maintain an uneasy relationship. Because the party dominates government, religious organizations are circumscribed and religion is not a large part of the population's consciousness.

The Kremlin as Seen From Bridge Over the Moscow River

Of the numerous religions, Moslems and Jews are the most visible groups of concern to Soviet leaders, primarily because of their "outside" centers of gravity. Russian Orthodoxy is the largest religious bloc, although 70 percent of the total population is described as atheist. Particularly important in the eyes of policy makers is the increased monitoring of Soviet human rights and religious conditions by internal and international groups. *(Details regarding religion, Chapter 8)*

The Republics

The Soviet Union is divided into 15 union republics, which, under the Constitution, are sovereign states. In fact, Moscow maintains firm control over the entire system. Each republic has the trappings of sovereignty: a constitution (that conforms to the USSR Constitution), national anthem, flag, supreme court, and government and party hierarchy paralleling the USSR structure. The republics theoretically have the authority to conduct relations with other nations and the right to secede from the USSR. Two of the republics — the Ukraine and Belorussia — have their own representation in the United Nations, an arrangement worked out at the end of World War II by Western leaders to obtain Soviet backing of the world organization.

The largest and most important union republic is the Russian Soviet Federated Socialist Republic (RSFSR). At 6.5 million square miles, it contains about 75 percent of the Soviet land mass and 52 percent of the population (143.1 million, according to 1985 Soviet figures). Its capital is Moscow, which, of course, is also the capital of the USSR. The RSFSR is divided into 16 autonomous republics (comparable to states in the United States), 5 autonomous regions (ethnic territories), 10 autonomous areas (smaller territories inhabited by particular nationalities), and 55 krais and oblasts. *(Definitions, box, p. 5)*

The other union republics (and their 1985 populations according to the *Soviet Annual Statistical Handbook*) are:

● Armenian Soviet Socialist Republic. Population, 3.317 million; religious heritage, predominantly Armenian Apostolic; capital, Yerevan. Nationalist sentiment among Armenians is strong.

● Azerbaidzhan Soviet Socialist Republic. Population, 6.614 million; religious heritage, predominantly Moslem; capital, Baku. The republic historically has had strong ties to the Shi'ite Moslems of Iran.

● Belorussian Soviet Socialist Republic. Population, 9.942 million; religious heritage, predominantly Russian Orthodox; capital, Minsk.

● Estonian Soviet Socialist Republic. Population, 1.466 million; religious heritage, predominantly Lutheran; capi-

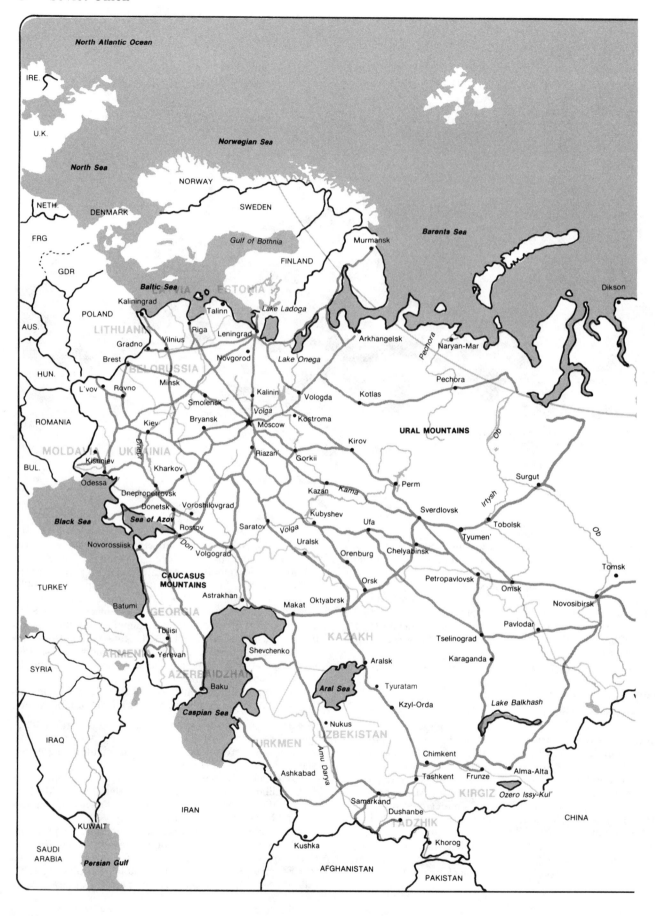

Soviet Union

International boundary
Railroad
Republic

| 0 | 400 | 800 | Kilometers |

| 0 | 400 Miles | 800 |

tal, Tallin. Along with Latvia and Lithuania, Estonia is one of the three formerly independent Baltic nations overrun by the Red Army in 1940.

● Georgian Soviet Socialist Republic. Population, 5.201 million; religious heritage, predominantly Orthodox; capital, Tiflis. The homeland of Joseph Stalin, Georgia attempted to establish an independent state after the Bolshevik Revolution in 1917, but the movement was crushed by Moscow. Separatist feelings in Georgia still run high.

● Kazakh Soviet Socialist Republic. Population, 15.842 million; religious heritage, predominantly Moslem; capital, Alma-Ata. Kazakhstan is the second-largest republic and the scene of the largely disappointing "virgin lands" agricultural scheme of the 1950s.

● Kirgiz Soviet Socialist Republic. Population, 3.967 million; religious heritage, predominantly Moslem; capital, Frunze.

● Latvian Soviet Socialist Republic. Population, 2.604 million; religious heritage, predominantly Lutheran; capital, Riga. Latvia was taken over by the Soviets in 1940; it enjoys a standard of living well above that in the RSFSR.

● Lithuanian Soviet Socialist Republic. Population, 3.570 million; religious heritage, predominantly Roman Catholic; capital, Vilnyus. Annexed by the Soviets in 1940, Lithuania also has a standard of living far above that in other parts of the Soviet Union.

● Moldavian Soviet Socialist Republic. Population, 4.111 million; religious heritage, predominantly Orthodox; capital, Kishinev. It is the smallest of the republics — 13,012 square miles — and formerly was part of Romania.

● Tadzhik Soviet Socialist Republic. Population, 4.499 million; religious heritage, predominantly Moslem; capital, Dushanbe. The capital was renamed Stalinabad to honor Joseph Stalin, but was changed back to the original name in 1961 as part of the government's efforts to destroy the Stalin "personality cult."

● Turkmen Soviet Socialist Republic. Population, 3.189 million; religious heritage, predominantly Moslem; capital, Ashkhabad.

● Ukrainian Soviet Socialist Republic. Population, 50.840 million; religious heritage, predominantly Russian Orthodox; capital, Kiev. The Ukraine has been the scene of much nationalist agitation throughout Russian history.

● Uzbek Soviet Socialist Republic. Population, 17.974 million; religious heritage, predominantly Moslem; capital, Tashkent.

Party Structure

Power in the Soviet Union is centered in and controlled by the Communist Party. The government structure parallels the party hierarchy. The party and governmental structures can best be described as pyramids, with policy making centralized in several key decision-making committees. Party members have ultimate control over decisions. (Charts, pp. 14 and 15)

The party's domination of society and the government is stated directly in Article 6 of the Soviet Constitution:

> The leading and guiding force of Soviet society and the nucleus of its political system, of all state organizations and public organizations, is the Communist Party of the Soviet Union. The CPSU exists for the people and serves the people.

The Communist Party, armed with Marxism-Leninism, determines the general perspectives of the development of society and the course of the home and foreign policy of the USSR, and imparts a planned, systematic, and theoretically substantiated character to the struggle for the victory of communism.

Membership in the Communist Party is restricted. Only about 7 percent of the population — 19 million citizens as of 1986 — were full members of the CPSU, according to Soviet statistics. While not required legally, party membership in reality is required for any position of importance. For example, virtually all top government, military, educational, and scientific officials are party members. At every level of the party hierarchy, these select positions and the lists of authorized nominees for these posts are known as the *nomenklatura*. Thus it is not surprising that approximately half of all college-educated males between the ages of 30 and 60 are party members. It is accepted that party membership brings certain rewards. Party members, it is said, are assigned the best housing (including dachas — country houses ranging in size from simple shacks to palatial mansions), drive the newest cars, go to the best universities, and shop in specially stocked stores for provisions that are not available to the ordinary citizen.

Joining the party is challenging. The party is meant to be an elite corps of dedicated activists. A prospective member must be 23 years old (18 if he or she is a member of the Komsomol, the Communist Youth League). Membership requires recommendations from three CPSU members who have been in the party at least five years and who have known the applicant for at least one year. Individuals selected for membership are made probationary members for one year before being granted full membership.

The Komsomol admits members aged 14 through 28. Younger Soviet citizens, age 10 through 15, join the All-Union Youth Pioneers, a kind of Communist Boy or Girl Scouts.

Women comprise almost 25 percent of the party membership, according to official Soviet statistics, but few women hold party positions of power. Women are especially being encouraged to join the party. The Soviet Communist Party claims that most party members are workers. But statistics concerning occupations of party members are misleading because members are categorized according to their occupation when they first joined the party.

Whether or not to join the party is one of the most important choices a young person makes in the Soviet Union. Along with the privileges that come with membership come many extra responsibilities. Party members are supposed to be a minority group, although they are to maintain close ties with nonmembers.

Democratic centralism is one of the main guiding principles of the Soviet Communist Party. It means, simply put, that all executive party organs are to be elected from the lowest to the highest; theoretically meaning that the lowest party workers are to choose the individuals who run the party at the highest levels. Democratic centralism calls for majority rule and periodic accountability to the people of all party organizations. Democratic centralism also requires "the obligation of lower bodies to observe the decisions of higher ones," which means in effect that lower bodies receive their orders from superiors (including the names of those to be elected) and cannot be questioned. This obligation makes moot the other provisions of democratic centralism.

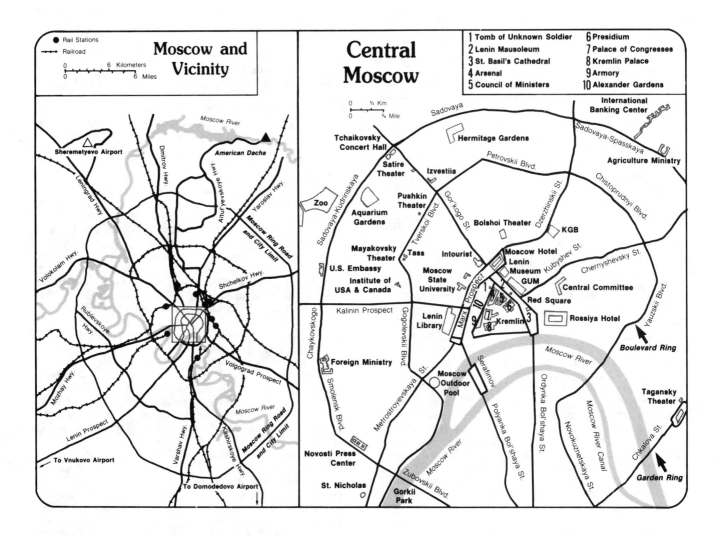

Moscow and Vicinity

Rail Stations
Railroad

0 6 Kilometers
0 6 Miles

Sheremetyevo Airport

Moscow River

American Dacha

Leningrad Hwy.
Dmitrov Hwy.
Altufyevskoye Hwy.
Yaroslav Hwy.
Moscow Ring Road and City Limit
Volokolam Hwy.
Shchelkov Hwy.
Rublevskoye Hwy.
Mozhay Hwy.
Lenin Prospect
Varshav Hwy.
Kashirskoye Hwy.
Volgograd Prospect
Moscow River
Moscow Ring Road and City Limit
To Vnukovo Airport
To Domodedovo Airport

Central Moscow

1 Tomb of Unknown Soldier
2 Lenin Mausoleum
3 St. Basil's Cathedral
4 Arsenal
5 Council of Ministers
6 Presidium
7 Palace of Congresses
8 Kremlin Palace
9 Armory
10 Alexander Gardens

0 ¼ Km
0 ¼ Mile

Sadovaya
International Banking Center
Sadovaya-Spasskaya
Tchaikovsky Concert Hall
Hermitage Gardens
Petrovskii Blvd.
Agriculture Ministry
Satire Theater
Izvestiia
Chistoprudnyi Blvd.
Pushkin Theater
Zoo
Sadovaya-Kudrinskaya
Aquarium Gardens
Gor'kogo St.
Bolshoi Theater
Dzerzhinskii St.
KGB
Tverskoi Blvd.
Mayakovsky Theater
Tass
Intourist
Moscow Hotel
Kubyshev St.
Chernyshevsky St.
U.S. Embassy
Lenin Museum
Institute of USA & Canada
Moscow State University
GUM
Central Committee
Marx Prospect
Red Square
Kalinin Prospect
Rossiya Hotel
Yauzskii Blvd.
Chaykovskogo
Gogolevskii Blvd.
Lenin Library
Kremlin
Moscow River
Boulevard Ring
Foreign Ministry
Moscow Outdoor Pool
Seralimov
Tagansky Theater
Smolensk Blvd.
Metrostroyevskaya St.
Polyanka Bol'shaya St.
Ordynka Bol'shaya St.
Moscow River Canal
Chkalova St.
Novokuznetskaya St.
Novosti Press Center
Zubovskii Blvd.
Moscow River
Garden Ring
St. Nicholas
Gorkii Park

Party Congress, Party Program. Theoretically, the party's highest authority is the Party Congress. Every party organ is constitutionally accountable to this body, which meets every five years. The Congresses are now held to coincide generally with the unveiling of the latest Five-Year Plan. Before 1971, Party Congresses were supposed to be held every four years, but that schedule was not strictly kept. The most recent Congress was held February 25-28, 1986.

An important function of the Party Congress is to elect the new party leadership. Theoretically, delegates to the Congress name the Central Committee (CC) members who will run the party until the next Congress and the chairman of the Central (or Party) Control Commission, which oversees behavior of party members and expulsions. (According to Sovietologist Jerry F. Hough, the commission acts similarly to a party supreme court.) In practice, however, the approximately 5,000 delegates to the Congress ratify a previously selected slate of the most important party figures to be members of the CC. The delegates themselves are technically elected at regional and republic party conferences; however, the central party leadership has much say over delegate composition. The Congress hears the CC report, delivered by the general secretary, and the report on the new Five-Year Plan.

At the 1986 Congress, the new program to guide the party to the year 2000 was expected to be ratified. The party program is the primary theoretical document on goals and strategies. Gorbachev's party program revised the 1961 program put forth by Nikita Khrushchev, which promised that "the present generation of Soviet people shall live in communism." Khrushchev's program was only the third program used by the party. In mid-October 1985, the Central Committee approved the revisions, predicting the next five years would be the turning point for the country's faltering economy. The draft was to be debated across the country until the Congress in February 1986, although it was expected that the draft would be adopted largely intact.

Gorbachev's draft program implicitly criticized all his predecessors except Lenin and reflected a major departure from the party's traditional goals. He made it clear that the exaggerated claims of the previous program would be dropped in favor of more practical goals. It asserted, for example, that the party "does not set itself the aim of forseeing in detail the features of full communism," and that efforts to move too quickly in introducing communism, "without due account taken of the level of material and spiritual maturity of society, are, as experience shows, doomed to failure." Gorbachev's program termed the economic projections of the past guide as "groundless fantasies." Nonetheless, Gorbachev called for a doubling of production potential by the end of the century and an increase of labor productivity by as much as 150 percent in 15 years. The draft stated that "the basic issue in the Party's economic strategy is the acceleration of scientific and technological progress," and that improving the situation "calls for serious structural changes in the economy." Recognizing the need to import Western technology, the draft said the party would "improve foreign economic strategy and more fully utilise the possibilities offered by mutually advantageous international division of labour.... Foreign economic, scientific and technical contacts will be extended, and progressive structural changes will be introduced in the sphere of exports and imports...."

Where Khrushchev expressed certainty about capitalism's imminent collapse, the Gorbachev draft stated that the free enterprise system, while still doomed, is "constantly manoeuvering to adjust itself to the changing situation."

Central Committee. The members of the Central Committee meet about every six months at special sessions called plenums. The CC is technically charged with directing the party's work between Congresses. The Politburo often issues resolutions in the name of the CC or as joint CC-government decrees. The CC itself, however, normally has no real decision-making authority. "Its mission is more one of mobilization and socialization than actual policy making," one expert has said.

Since the 1981 Congress, the CC contained 319 full members and 151 candidate members. The composition of the CC is representative of the entire party: predominantly male Russians. CC membership confers considerable status to both the individual and the institution he represents. Virtually all major officials in the party or state hierarchies are members or candidate members. Of the state side, the Ministry of Defense has the most members.

Although not central to the decision-making process, the CC can wield considerable power. For example, when a majority of CPSU First Secretary Nikita Khrushchev's colleagues in the party Presidium tried to depose him in 1957, Khrushchev argued his case to the CC. The CC supported Khrushchev and enabled him to remain as head of the party.

The CC membership changed little during the course of Leonid Brezhnev's, Yuri Andropov's, and Konstantin Chernenko's tenures but changed considerably in February 1986. Membership in the CC traditionally has considerable turnover just after a succession.

CC Secretariat. Above the CC is the CC Secretariat, the CC's executive body and the executive branch of the party. The CC theoretically delegates the day-to-day operation of the party to both the CC Secretariat and the Politburo. Simply put, the Secretariat is the administrative end of the party, operating (some experts say) much like a subcommittee of the Politburo. The Secretariat meets once a week or so and according to party statutes is charged with overseeing party and government appointments and implementation of high-level party decrees.

There were 11 CC secretaries as of May 1986. The general secretary is Mikhail Gorbachev, who leads both the Secretariat and the Politburo. From 1952 to 1966 this position was referred to as first secretary. The other secretaries are divided along both functional and geographic lines. Unlike Politburo members, Secretariat members are all full-time Moscow-based party officials. There is some

overlap of Secretariat members and Politburo members (see below), in keeping with the interlocking nature of the system. The CC ostensibly selects Secretariat members, but, as throughout the Soviet party and government hierarchies, the selections are actually made by the next higher level of authority — in this case, the general secretary and members of the Politburo — and merely ratified by the CC.

The Secretariat is broken down into various departments, each concerned with a particular topic; for example, defense, heavy industry, propaganda, and relations with communist parties in other socialist countries. There are approximately 21 departments, with varying degrees of importance and influence. The departments and sections make up the party apparatus (*apparat*). The bureaucrats who work in the apparatus are known as the *apparatchiki*. It has been estimated that the Secretariat apparat numbers in the several thousands, and the careers and job duties of the apparatchiki are quite specialized.

Some party secretaries head one department, others may head several; Western experts often refer to these as "informal portfolios of responsibilities." These responsibilities are seldom officially acknowledged and have often been inferred in the West from the secretaries' public activities. *(Chart, p. 15)*

Through these portfolios, Secretariat members play a vital role in the policy-making process. The departments the secretaries head often form the drafts of decisions later reviewed and approved by the Secretariat and Politburo. The nearly two-dozen departments support the Secretariat by monitoring organizations within their areas of responsibility and intervening when necessary to ensure that plans are fulfilled. Each department is further broken down into several specialized sections.

There are also numerous consultants in the apparat. Some departments have standing groups of consultants, others apparently have none. According to Jerry Hough, these consultants are considered important. They are generally freed from day-to-day responsibilities and instead concentrate on major projects.

Politburo. At the top of the CPSU hierarchy is the Politburo (Political Bureau). The Politburo (called the party Presidium from 1952 to 1966) sets policy for the Soviet Union. While theoretically chosen by the CC to run the country between CC plenums, in reality it is the only true policy-making body in the Soviet Union. In October 1985 it had 18 members, 12 of whom were full (voting) members. The remaining men were candidate (nonvoting) members. Though little is known about the workings of the Politburo, it is known that it meets weekly (on Thursdays) and discusses an extremely wide range of items. Indications are that discussions are frank and often argumentative. During the last part of Brezhnev's tenure, and for most of the time since then, the Politburo has published a selected list of agenda items in the Soviet media.

An adjunct body to the Politburo, the Defense Council, apparently exerts considerable influence. It is made up of a select group of Politburo members representing both civilian and military sides and is formally part of the government structure. *(Details, Chapters 4, 6)*

The members of the Politburo and Secretariat comprise an interlocking directorate of Soviet party power; members of these bodies also intersect with high governmental positions. As of March 1986, three full members of the Politburo (Gorbachev, Egor Ligachev, and Lev Zaikov) and one candidate member (Vladimir Dolgikh) were also members of the Secretariat. Four full Politburo members

(Geidar Aliev, Viktor Chebrikov, Nikolai Ryzhkov, and Eduard Shevardnadze) and three candidates (Petr Demichev, Sergei Sokolov, and Nikolai Talyzin) were members of the Council of Ministers.

These groups reflect the Soviets' professed dedication to the principle of collective leadership, which in theory is designed to guarantee that power is shared. In practice, power usually lies with one man, who emerges as the first among equals. In the past, this was Stalin (who exercised dictatorial control), Khrushchev, and Brezhnev (who were thought of more as chairmen of a collective leadership). When Brezhnev died in November 1982, Yuri Andropov replaced him for about one year. When he died in February 1984, Konstantin Chernenko became the general secretary. One year later, in March 1985, he died. Neither Andropov nor Chernenko was in office long enough to truly command first-among-equal status, many experts conclude. Today, Mikhail Gorbachev, as head of the CPSU, is the acknowledged leader of the Soviet Union. He rapidly worked to consolidate his power by making numerous personnel changes in both the Politburo and other party and government organizations in the first several months of his regime.

For much of Brezhnev's term, the general secretary also had held the formal government post of chairman of the Presidium of the Supreme Soviet (in Western terms, the president), though this was not a dual position prescribed by any written regulations. After Chernenko died, this largely ceremonial post of president was left vacant for long periods — perhaps an indication of its relative nonimportance, many experts have said.

In July 1985 Gorbachev surprisingly did not take the position himself but named longtime foreign minister Andrei Gromyko to the post. (*Details, government structure, below*)

None of these organizations — the Central Committee, the Secretariat, the Defense Council, nor the Politburo — is guided by institutionalized regulations regarding size of the organization, length of tenure for members, or specific duties. There is no legal method to pass power from one individual or organization to another. This has led to bitter, often lengthy, power struggles over both individual positions and relative importance of certain organizations, such as the CC itself or departments within the CC (such as the Information Department).

Each union republic (except for the RSFSR) also has its own party, presidium, secretariat, central committee, and party congress, in keeping with the constitutionally declared autonomy of each republic. But republic communist parties are not independent; they are key components of the CPSU and work under the guidelines of democratic centralism. First secretaries of republics are becoming increasingly better known as the USSR tries to promote younger leaders into party positions of responsibility. Gorbachev has drawn heavily from regional leaders in replacing members of the Secretariat, Politburo, and Council of Ministers.

At the bottom of the party structure is the primary organization, a group of party members (as few as three) usually formed at a place of work. According to Soviet data, there are 414,000 primary organizations. Their organization reflects the hierarchy of the top party bodies. Each primary organization has a general meeting at which a secretary is named to run the group. Above primary party organizations are party groups of districts, cities, national areas, provinces, territories, and republics.

Soviet Leaders, 1917-86

Chairmen of the Presidium of the Supreme Soviet (Presidents)

Mikhail L. Kalinin	1923-46
Nikolai M. Shvernik	1946-53
Kliment E. Voroshilov	1953-60
Leonid I. Brezhnev	1960-64
Anastas I. Mikoian	1964-65
Nikolai V. Podgornyi	1965-77
Leonid I. Brezhnev	1977-82
Konstantin U. Chernenko	1984-85
Andrei A. Gromyko	1985-

Chairmen of the Council of Ministers (Prime Ministers)

V. I. Lenin	1917-24
Aleksei I. Rykov	1924-30
Viacheslav M. Molotov	1930-41
Joseph Stalin	1941-53
Georgi M. Malenkov	1953-55
Nikolai A. Bulganin	1955-58
Nikita S. Khrushchev	1958-64
Aleksei N. Kosygin	1964-80
Nikolai A. Tikhonov	1980-85
Nikolai I. Ryzhkov	1985-

Communist Party Heads

V. I. Lenin*	1917-24
Joseph Stalin*	1922-53
Nikita S. Khrushchev	1953-64
Leonid I. Brezhnev	1964-82
Yuri V. Andropov	1982-84
Konstantin U. Chernenko	1984-85
Mikhail S. Gorbachev	1985-

* As chairman of the Council of People's Commissars, Lenin was the de facto head of the party and the government; although Stalin was named general secretary of the party in 1922, he was unable to assert unquestioned control over the party until after Lenin's death in 1924.

The party publishes the daily newspaper, *Pravda* (Truth), considered the most authoritative organ on Soviet party policy and politics, as well as other newspapers and publications. (*Publications, box, p. 5*)

Government Structure

According to the 1977 Constitution, the highest government body in the Soviet Union is the Supreme Soviet, the legislature. The word soviet is Russian for "council." The Supreme Soviet is divided into two chambers: the

Organization of Soviet Union ...

PARTY STRUCTURE:

Politburo

Central Committee Secretariat

Central Committee

Republic committees

Regional committees

District and large city committees

Primary organizations (approx. 420,000)

Politburo Members:

Geidar A. Aliev
Viktor M. Chebrikov
Mikhail S. Gorbachev
Andrei A. Gromyko
Dinmukhamed A. Kunaev
Egor K. Ligachev

Nikolai I. Ryzhkov
Vladimir V. Shcherbitskii
Eduard A. Shevardnadze
Mikhail S. Solomentsev
Vitalii I. Vorotnikov
Lev N. Zaikov

Candidate Politburo Members:

Petr N. Demichev
Vladimir I. Dolgikh
Boris N. Eltsin
Nikolai N. Sliunkov

Sergei L. Sokolov
Iurii Solovev
Nikolai V. Talyzin

Central Committee Secretariat:

General Secretary: Mikhail S. Gorbachev
Other Secretaries: Alexandra Biriukova — Light Industry, Consumer Goods, Trade Unions
Anatolii F. Dobrynin — Foreign Policy
Vladimir I. Dolgikh — Heavy Industry, Energy, Transportation
Aleksandr N. Iakolev — Propaganda, Culture
Egor K. Ligachev — Cadres, Ideology, Internal Party Affairs
Vadim A. Medvedev — Bloc Relations
Viktor P. Nikonov — Agriculture
Georgii P. Razumovskii — Cadres
Lev N. Zaikov — Defense Industry
Mikhail V. Zimianin — Science and Education

Central Committee Departments:

Administrative Organs — Nikolai I. Savinkin
Agricultural Machine Building — (department may have been eliminated)
Agriculture and Food Industry — Vladimir A. Karlov
Cadres Abroad — Stepan V. Chervonenko
Chemical Industry — Veniamin G. Afonin
Construction — Aleksandr G. Melnikov
Culture — Iurii P. Voronov
Defense Industry — Oleg S. Beliakov
Economics — (no identification known)
General Department — Anatolii I. Lukianov
Heavy Industry and Power Engineering — Ivan P. Iastrebov
International — Anatolii F. Dobrynin
International Information — (department may have been eliminated)
Letters — (department may have been eliminated)
Liaison with Communist and Workers' Parties of Socialist Countries — possibly Vadim A. Medvedev
Light Industry and Consumer Goods — Leonid F. Bobykin
Machine Building — Arkadii Volskii
Organizational Party Work — Georgii P. Razumovskii
Propaganda — Aleksandr N. Iakovlev
Science and Educational Institutions —
Trade and Domestic Services — Nikolai Stashenkov
Transport and Communications — Viktor S. Pasternak

... Communist Party and Government

GOVERNMENT STRUCTURE:

Legislative | *Executive*

USSR Supreme Soviet, Presidium	USSR Council of Ministers
Union Republic Supreme Soviets, Presidium	Union Republic Councils of Ministers
Autonomous Republic Supreme Soviets, Presidiums	Autonomous Republic Councils of Ministers
Province and regional soviets, presidiums	Province and regional soviets' executive committees
Large city and district soviets, presidiums	Large city and district soviets' executive committees
Smaller city and village soviets	Smaller city and village soviets' executive committees

Supreme Soviet of the USSR:
Last elections 1984
Next elections 1989

Presidium of the Supreme Soviet of the USSR:
President: *Andrei Gromyko*
First Deputy Chairman:
Vice Presidents: *presidents of the supreme soviets of the union republics are ex officio vice presidents of this body*

Council of Nationalities:
Chairman: *Avgust Voss*
Total members elected: *750*
Distribution of members: *32 deputies from each union republic, 11 from each autonomous republic, 5 from each autonomous region, and 1 from each national area*

Chairman of Defense Council:
Mikhail Gorbachev

Council of Union:
Chairman: *Lev Tolkunov*
Total members elected: *750*

Soviets of Working Peoples' Deputies:
Delegates represent all sections of the population, attending sessions to discuss legislation and participate in state and public affairs

Council of Ministers:
Chairman (Prime Minister): *Nikolai I. Ryzhkov*
First Deputy Chairmen: *Geidar A. Aliev, Ivan V. Arkhipov, Vsevolod S. Murakhovskii, Nikolai V. Talyzin*
Selected Other Ministers and State Committee Chairmen:
Minister of Communications: *Vasilii A. Shamshin*
Minister of Construction: *Vladimir I. Reshetilov*
Minister of Construction Materials Industry: *Sergei F. Voenushkin*
Minister of Culture: *Petr N. Demichev*
Minister of Defense: *Sergei L. Sokolov*
Minister of Electrical Equipment Industry: *Gennadii Voronovskii*
Minister of Ferrous Metallurgy: *Serafim Kolpakov*
Minister of Finance: *Boris I. Gostev*
Minister of Foreign Affairs: *Eduard A. Shevardnadze*
Minister of Foreign Trade: *Boris I. Aristov*
Minister of Higher and Secondary Specialized Education: *Gennadii Iagodin*
Minister of Internal Affairs: *Aleksandr V. Vlasov*
Minister of Land Reclamation and Water Resources: *Nikolai F. Vasil'ev*
Minister of Light Industry: *Vladimir G. Kliuev*
Minister of Power and Electrification: *Anatolii I. Maiorets*
Minister of Public Health: *Sergei P. Burenkov*
Minister of Railways: *Nikolai S. Konarev*
Minister of Transport Construction: *Vladimir Brezhnev*
Chairman of State Planning Committee (Gosplan): *Nikolai V. Talyzin*
Chairman of State Security Committee (KGB): *Viktor M. Chebrikov*
Chairman of State Agro-Industrial Committee: *Vsevolod S. Murakhovskii*
Chairman of State Committee for Computer Equipment and Information Technology: *Nikolai V. Gorshkov*
Chairman of State Committee for Inventions and Discoveries: *Ivan S. Naiashkov*
Chairman of State Committee for Material and Technical Supply: *Nikolai V. Martynov*
Chairman of State Committee for Prices: *Nikolai T. Glushkov*
Chairman of State Committee for Science and Technology: *Gurii I. Marchuk*

Council of the Union, with 750 members elected on the basis of population, and the Council of Nationalities, with 750 members representing the republics. During its semi-annual two-to-four-day sessions, the Supreme Soviet adopts general legal codes embodying basic principles, to be administered by the republics, and statutes (*zakony*), which are similar to laws passed by the U.S. Congress. Most of the work of the Supreme Soviet is devoted to transforming the edicts (*ukazy*) issued by the Supreme Soviet Presidium into statutes, such as ratifiying five-year plans and state budgets. In reality it merely rubber-stamps party policies. Elections to the Supreme Soviet are held every five years. Deputies elected to the Supreme Soviet are not professional legislators; they have other full-time jobs. The delegates are more representative of the rank-and-file workers than are other party or government organizations. For example, 31 percent of the deputies are women. Suffrage is universal for citizens 18 and over, but only one candidate, selected by local party bosses, runs for election in each district. While Supreme Soviet membership is varied, it is still dominated by the most important political figures in the country. CC members and other high-status officials comprise well over half the membership.

Presidium of Supreme Soviet. The Supreme Soviet has a presidium, whose chairman also is considered the head of state (the president). Andrei A. Gromyko is the current chairman of the Presidium, breaking with recent past practice of having the party general secretary occupying both posts. Brezhnev, for example, was chairman of the Presidium from 1977 to his death in 1982, apparently to permit the actual leader of the country — the head of the party — to have the proper status according to international standards of protocol. The Gorbachev leadership named Gromyko to this post July 2, 1985.

The Presidium of the Supreme Soviet has the constitutional power to issue *ukazy*, which have the force of law. In addition, the Presidium, according to Article 122 of the Soviet Constitution, is authorized to take the following actions, subject to later ratification by the Supreme Soviet:

1. amend existing legislative acts of the USSR when necessary;
2. approve changes in the boundaries between Union Republics;
3. form and abolish Ministries and State Committees of the USSR on the recommendation of the Council of Ministers of the USSR;
4. relieve individual members of the Council of Ministers of the USSR of their responsibilities and appoint persons to the Council of Ministers on the recommendation of the Chairman of the Council of Ministers of the USSR.

According to Jerry Hough, the 1977 Soviet Constitution specified for the first time that the Presidium of the Supreme Soviet should have 39 members: a chairman; a first deputy chairman (formerly Vasilii Kuznetsov); 15 deputy chairmen (one from each of the republics); a secretary; and 21 other members.

The Supreme Soviet has numerous standing committees whose work has expanded in recent years — although not to a degree having significant impact on the policy-making process. There are at least 15 standing committees in each house, including agriculture, consumer goods, education, science and culture, transportation-communication, and legislative proposals. It is believed that the Presidium of the Supreme Soviet has a coordinating role regarding the standing committees. The standing committees meet infrequently, but some experts believe their preparatory role, especially in the budgetary planning process, is meaningful to some extent.

Council of Ministers. The head of the vast Soviet government bureaucracy is the USSR Council of Ministers. It implements party decisions. Many key legal acts are passed not by the Supreme Soviet but by the Council of Ministers, often jointly with the CC.

There are more than 100 members of the Council of Ministers, making this another rather unwieldy body. The Council of Ministers is officially selected by the Supreme Soviet and is subordinate to it and its presidium, according to the Constitution. In practice, membership is determined by the party leadership. It is made up of a chairman, vice chairmen, ministers, chairmen of state committees, and chairmen of the Council of Ministers of the union republics. The power of the Council of Ministers lies in its authority to issue decrees that have the force of law. Sovietologists assume that decrees generally guide the country's economic and social policies. Decrees are sometimes published and presumably take shape during deliberations of the Council's Presidium.

The Council's steering (or executive) committee is the Presidium of the USSR Council of Ministers. This should not be confused with the Presidium of the Supreme Soviet. The chairman of the USSR Council of Ministers, currently Nikolai Ryzhkov, is the head of the government, or prime minister. General Secretary Gorbachev appointed Ryzhkov chairman in September 1985, replacing Nikolai A. Tikhonov, who was 80. Tikhonov had replaced Aleksei N. Kosygin in the post in 1980. Kosygin had been prime minister since 1964, which shows how little turnover there has been in this position.

In addition to Ryzhkov, the Council presidium is comprised of first deputy chairmen Geidar Aliev, Ivan Arkhipov, Vsevolod S. Murakhovskii, and Nikolai Talyzin. In keeping with the interlocking nature of the leadership, Ryzhkov and Aliev are full Politburo members and Talyzin is a candidate member. These presidium deputies are the chairman's closest government advisers who coordinate and oversee ministry activity and plan fulfillment. Because Tikhonov was a senior Politburo member during the time he headed the large government bureaucracy, experts presume he had considerable influence over how party policy was executed. It is likely Ryzhkov will garner similar influence. Additionally, it should be noted that the Council and its presidium do not preside only over civilian matters. Because defense matters are so closely involved with the civilian economy, the Council is an important link in coordinating and mediating between the two sides. Tikhonov, for example, was probably a Defense Council member and was so because of his civilian job as Council chairman.

Other Units. Below the Council of Ministers in the governmental hierarchy are the ministries and state committees that make up the Soviet governmental bureaucracy. These are designated either Union Republic or All-Union. The former direct the work of corresponding bodies at the republic level, the latter have national responsibility. The difference between a ministry and a state committee can be obscure. As Hough writes in *How the Soviet Union Is Governed*:

The distinction between a ministry and a state committee generally revolves around the in-

USSR Government Organizations

**Supreme Soviet
Presidium
Council of Ministers**

Ministries

Automotive Industry†
Aviation Industry†
Bread Products*
Chemical Industry†
Chemical and Petroleum
   Machine Building†
Civil Aviation†
Coal Industry*
Communications*
Communications
   Equipment Industry†
Construction*
Construction of Heavy
   Industry Enterprises*
Construction Materials
   Industry*
Construction of Petroleum
   and Gas Industry
   Enterprises†
Construction, Road and
   Municipal Machine
   Building†
Culture*
Defense†
Defense Industry†
Education*
Electrical Equipment
   Industry†
Electronics Industry†
Ferrous Metallurgy*
Finance*
Fish Industry*
Foreign Affairs*
Gas Industry†
General Machine Building†
Geology*
Health*
Heavy and Transport
   Machine Building†
Higher and Secondary
   Specialized Education*

Industrial Construction*
Installation and Special
   Construction Work*
Instrument Making,
   Automation Equipment
   and Control Systems†
Internal Affairs*
Justice*
Land Reclamation and
   Water Resources*
Light Industry*
Machine Building†
Machine Building for
   Animal Husbandry and
   Fodder Production†
Machine Building for Light
   and Food Industry and
   Household Appliances†
Machine Tool and
   Toolbuilding Industry†
Maritime Fleet†
Medical Industry†
Medium Machine Building†
Nonferrous Metallurgy*
Petroleum Industry†
Petroleum Refining and
   Petrochemical Industry*
Power and Electrification
Power Machine Building†
Public Health*
Pulp and Paper Industry†
Radio Industry†
Railways†
Shipbuilding Industry†
Timber and Wood
   Processing Industry*
Tractor and Agricultural
   Machine Building†
Trade*
Transport Construction†

State Committees

Cinematography*
Construction Affairs*
Foreign Economic Relations†
Forestry*
Hydrometerology and
   Environmental Control†
Inventions and Discoveries†
Labor and Social Problems*
Material Reserves†
Material and Technical
   Supply*
Planning (Gosplan)*
Prices*
Publishing Houses, Printing
   Plants and the Book Trade*
Science and Technology†
Standards†
Committee for State Security
   (KGB)*
State Agro-Industrial
   Committee
Television and Radio
   Broadcasting*
Vocational and Technical
   Education*

Agencies

With Ministerial Status
Administration of Affairs
Board of the State Bank
   (Gosbank)
Central Statistical
   Administration
Committee of People's
   Control

Without Ministerial Status
All-Union Bank for Financing
   Capital Investment
Commission for the
   Establishment of Personal
   Pensions
Committee for Lenin and
   State Prizes in Literature,
   Art and Architecture
Committee for Lenin and
   State Prices in Science and
   Technology
Committee for Physical
   Culture and Sports
Council for Religious Affairs
Main Administration for
   Foreign Tourism
Main Administration of
   Geodesy and Cartography
Main Administration of the
   Microbiology Industry
Main Administration for
   Safeguarding State Secrets
   in the Press (Glavlit)
Main Archives
   Administration
State Board of Arbitration
State Commission for
   Stockpiling Useful Minerals
State Committee for the
   Supervision of Safe
   Working Practices in Indus-
   try and for Mine
   Construction
State Committee for the
   Utilization of Atomic Energy
Telegraphic Agency of the
   USSR (Tass)
Higher Certification
   Commission

† All-Union

* Union Republic

Note: Union Republic organizations operate locally through corresponding organizations on the republic level. All-Union organizations have no such regional counterparts.

stitution's responsibilities. A ministry is usually in charge of a single branch, and its orders usually are binding only on its own subunits. Examples are the Ministry of [Education and] the Ministry of Defense.... A state committee is an agency whose responsibilities normally cut across a number of branches and whose decrees often relate to other ministries. Examples are the State Committee for Prices, the State Committee for Science and Technology and the State Committee for Labor and Social Questions. However, there are exceptions to this rule (for example, the State Committee for Television and Radio), and it is most unclear why the People's Control Committee is called a committee instead of a state committee and why the Committee for State Security [KGB] is listed simply as "attached to"... the Council of Ministers instead of being a regular state committee. Soviet scholars themselves are often at a loss to explain these irregularities.

The People's Control Committee has responsibility for monitoring the work of government administrators and receiving complaints of government ineptitude and corruption.

Each republic has a government structured along lines identical to the central government: a supreme soviet, presidium, and council of ministers. Beneath the republic level are territorial, regional, and local soviets. Soviets, on all levels, are elected, representative councils empowered to implement and administer the law. In addition, "people's control" groups flourish at the local level. According to the Soviet press agency Novosti, the locally elected controllers, like the People's Control Committee staffers at the national level, "check up on the fulfillment of state plans [and] combat violations of state discipline, parochial tendencies and instances of excessive attention to departmental interests, bad management and squandering, lovers of red-tape and bureaucrats."

The central government publishes the daily newspaper *Izvestiia* (news) and numerous others.

Judiciary

The judicial branch of the Soviet government is made up of people's courts, regional courts, republic supreme courts, and the Supreme Court of the USSR. People's courts are presided over by a judge, elected to a term of five years, and two "people's assessors," who are Soviet citizens elected by their colleagues at their place of work. The judges and assessors hear cases and hand down decisions; findings are based on majority rule. People's assessors are elected to terms of two and one-half years. Each year they devote two weeks to these duties.

The Supreme Court of the USSR is made up of judges appointed by the Supreme Soviet for a term of five years. Chairmen of the republics' supreme courts are ex officio members of the Supreme Court of the USSR. In addition to the ex officio members, the Supreme Court includes "a Chairman, Vice-Chairmen, members and people's assessors." *(Article 153, Soviet Constitution)* The Supreme Court hears appeals from the republic supreme courts and supervises the administration of justice. The nation's chief prosecutor in 1985 was Alexander Rekunkov.

Punishments for criminal offenses range from public censure and fines to exile, banishment, imprisonment (with and without hard labor), commitment to a mental institution (usually for political criminals), and death. Capital punishment is "for persons who have committed an exceptionally heinous crime, such as taking life or encroaching upon the foundations of the socialist system," according to the Soviets' Novosti Press Agency *'81 Yearbook USSR*.

The same publication lists the rights enjoyed by Soviet citizens. These include: the right to work, the right to rest and leisure, the right to health protection, social security and education, freedom of speech and conscience, freedom of artistic, scientific and technical work, and the right to choose one's place of residence. But the yearbook notes that "the exercise by citizens of their rights and freedoms must not, however, be to the detriment of other citizens, of society and state. For instance, the law forbids the exercise of the freedom of speech for purposes of defamation and slander and for carrying out anti-Soviet agitation, propaganda of war, of racial and national exclusiveness, and so on." The notion of "anti-Soviet agitation" has been employed to block the official publication of novels ranging from Boris Pasternak's *Doctor Zhivago* to Alexander Solzhenitsyn's *The Gulag Archipelago 1918-1956* and to justify the arrest or imprisonment of critics of the state.

Imperial Russia and the Revolution

The early history of Russia — from 1000 B.C. to the mid-fifteenth century A.D. — was a chronicle of foreign invasion and domination. The Slavic agricultural tribes that inhabited the southern Russian steppes lived on the border between East and West, between the civilized nations of Europe and Asian lands peopled by barbarous nomads.

From about 1000 B.C. to 700 B.C. the Cimmerians (about whose origins little is known) ruled southern Russia. They were replaced by the Scythians, a central Asian nomad tribe, who held sway until the end of the third century B.C. Scythian dominion gave way to other Asian nomads, the Sarmatians. Around 200 A.D. the Goths, a Germanic tribe, replaced the Sarmatians; the Goths were defeated by the Huns around 370 A.D., reinstituting the pattern of Asian domination. The Huns were ousted by yet another Asian tribe, the Avars, in 558 A.D. Avar rule lasted about 100 years.

The centuries of invasion caused considerable migration among the Slavs, breaking up the original tribe into three groups. These were the West Slavs: Poles, Czechs, Slovaks, and Lusatians; the South Slavs: Serbs, Croats, Macedonians, Slovenes, Montenegrins, and Bulgars; and the East Slavs: the Russians, Ukrainians, and Belorussians.

Although they suffered centuries of invasion, the Slavs were adept at assimilating the ways of their foreign masters. They benefited from exposure to foreign influences, notably trade with Greek colonies in southern Russia. By the mid-eighth century A.D. the East Slavs had established several independent city-states that were attractive targets for roving bands of Viking and Asian warriors. The need for joint protection led to consolidation under Scandinavian rulers and the establishment of the first Russian state.

The Kievan State

Historians disagree over whether the East Slavic merchants and commercial traders asked the Scandinavians to be their rulers or whether the Danes were invaders. Similar disagreements surround the name "Russia." It is derived from a tribe known as the Rus, but its origin is a hotly debated topic among historians and philologists. At any rate, around 862 A.D. a Dane named Rurik (details concerning his life lack historical certainty) assumed control and settled in Novgorod, a trading town about 300 miles northeast of present-day Moscow. His successor, Oleg,

transferred the seat of power south to Kiev, located on the Dnepr River. Oleg established himself as a prince, brought the neighboring eastern Slavic tribes under his sway, and extracted tribute from them. Trade and culture flourished in the relatively liberal Kievan state as subsequent princes expanded the boundaries of their domain until the eleventh century, when the state reached from the Baltic Sea to the Black Sea and from near the town of Gorkii to the present-day Romania.

The Scandinavian rulers, instead of imposing a foreign culture upon their subjects, assumed the name Rus and adopted the local language and customs. Kievan Russia witnessed a tremendous growth of culture, art, architecture, language, and law. Cultural and social development was strongly influenced by the state's relations with the Byzantine Empire (although contacts also were developed with western states). Prince Vladimir (c. 980-1015), whose father had warred against the Byzantine Empire, made peace with his powerful neighbor and adopted Byzantine Christianity for himself and his pagan subjects around 988.

The establishment of the Russian Orthodox Church turned Russia away from Western Europe and the influence of the Roman Church, a development that would contribute greatly to Russia's sense of isolation. The conversion of the country gave rise to a written language, based on the Cyrillic alphabet developed (if not perfected) by St. Cyril and his brother, St. Methodius. Both were holy men from Moravia (now in central Czechoslovakia) who ministered to the Slavs in the second half of the ninth century. The institution of a uniform religion, language, and customs and the consolidation of an empire created the idea of a separate Russian state and a sense of national identity that could withstand the subsequent years of disintegration and domination.

Appanage Period

The Kievan state survived until the Mongol invasion, which began in 1236. However, the central authority of the grand prince of Kiev was weakened by a process of inheritance established by Yaroslav (1019-54) under which the state was divided into principalities, each headed by one of his sons.

The most important princedom was Kiev and, according to Yaroslav's awkward system, it was to be ruled by each of his sons on a rotating basis. The system soon created tension and acrimony among the various uncles and nephews and gave rise to Appanage Russia, a period during which princes ruled their individual lands (appanages). Civil war characterized the 200 years following the death of Yaroslav. Kiev declined also because changing East-West trade routes sapped its commercial strength while continual foreign aggression — culminating in the Mongol invasion — undermined its tenuous cohesion.

Among the greatest of the appanage princes was Alexander Nevski of Novgorod, who warded off attacks on Russia from the West. In 1240 he defeated Swedish invaders on the banks of the Neva River; from this battle he took the name Nevski. Alexander also fought the Teutonic Knights, Germanic crusaders dedicated to expansion and Roman Catholicism. They were routed by Alexander's troops April 5, 1242, at a battle on the ice of Lake Peipus in Estonia. This defeat of European invaders has long been enshrined in Russian folklore, most recently in Russian film maker Sergei Eisenstein's 1938 movie, *Alexander Nevski*.

Mongol Period

The composition of thirteenth-century Russia — consisting of dozens of informally related city-states — contributed to the Mongols' victory. Skilled and experienced soldiers, the invaders overcame the various Russian princes, who failed to fashion a joint defense. By 1242 all of Russia was under Mongol domination. The Mongols (called Tatars by Russian historians) secured the loyalty of the grand prince and through him collected tribute from the other appanage princes.

During the Mongol domination of Russia, Moscow was established as the center of the state. Kiev had been destroyed during the invasion and by 1315 the grand prince ruled from Tver (now Kalinin), located about 100 miles northwest of Moscow. In the early fourteenth century, Yuri, the prince of Moscow, undertook a campaign to win the title of grand prince. After several years of battle and intrigue, Ivan Kalita, the younger brother of Yuri (who was killed by a Tver enemy), was named grand prince by the Mongol khan in 1328. Ivan expanded his territory by buying up appanages and villages from bankrupt princes. He also convinced the Metropolitan Theognost, the head of the Russian Church, to live in Moscow, making it the religious capital of the state.

Ivan's grandson, Grand Prince Dmitri, attempted to overthrow the Mongol lords; on September 8, 1380, his army defeated Mongol forces at the battle of Kulikovo field. From then on, the Mongols' authority in Russia steadily weakened, even though they regained control of Russia in 1382. Finally, in 1480, Ivan III, also known as Ivan the Great, refused to recognize the authority of the Mongols and, with their empire falling apart, they failed in a half-hearted effort to keep the Russians in line.

Muscovite Russia

Under Ivan the Great and his son Basil III, the last appanages were brought under Moscow's control. Ivan in 1472 married Sophia, a niece of the last Byzantine emperor, and began to refer to himself as tsar (from Caesar).

The power and authority of the Moscow tsar was established definitively under Basil III's son Ivan IV, better known as Ivan the Terrible. Crowned tsar in 1547 at the age of 16, Ivan for several years relied on the advice of a group of liberal-minded advisers, the Chosen Council. He also sought the approval of the *zemskii sobor,* an assembly of landholders. As he grew older, however, he began to suspect the boyars — the descendants of the appanage princes, who now formed the hereditary nobility — of plotting against him. Ivan established in 1565 his personal domain, the *oprichnina* (from the Russian word for "apart"), and gave land to trusted followers, the *oprichniki.* The oprichniki, described by some historians as the first political police force, were assigned the task of eliminating anyone who opposed the tsar. In the reign of terror that lasted until 1572, thousands perished and whole towns — Novgorod, for example — were leveled.

Relative calm was restored under Ivan's son Fëdor I, who ruled from 1584 to 1598. Russia was again thrown into turmoil, however, when Fëdor died without an heir and his brother-in-law and close adviser, Boris Godunov, seized power, ushering in the Time of Troubles.

Boris Godunov was elected tsar by a special session of the zemskii sobor. His rule was soon beset with crises. In 1601-1603, drought and famine decimated the population. At the same time, it was rumored that Godunov had had a hand in the death of Prince Dmitri, the younger brother of Tsar Fëdor; moreover, some suspected that another child had been murdered in Dmitri's place and that the "real" Dmitri would reappear and claim the throne. A young man claiming to be Prince Dmitri gathered an army (with Polish assistance) and invaded Russia in October 1604. His campaign gained popular support and, after Godunov died in April 1605 and his wife and son Fëdor II were murdered, the False Dmitri ascended the throne. His disdain for the Russian people and reliance on Polish advisers eroded his support among the nobility and he was overthrown in May 1606. The leader of the coup, Basil Shuiski, a boyar prince, named himself tsar. A second False Dmitri arose during Basil's reign and almost succeeded in gaining the throne. Basil was overthrown in 1610 and during the next three years the country was ruled by a group of seven boyars.

Basil Shuiski's attempt to defeat the second False Dmitri involved an alliance with Sweden in which Basil agreed to join the Swedes in opposing the Poles. In retaliation, the king of Poland, Sigismund III, attacked Russia in 1609. After Basil Shuiski's death, the Muscovites invited the Polish king's son Ladislas to become tsar and allowed Polish troops to enter Moscow. The deal fell through and finally, in late 1612, the Russians drove the Poles from the city of Moscow. A special zemskii sobor was convened and elected Michael Romanov as tsar in early 1613. He was crowned, at the age of 16, on July 21, 1613. Related to the dynastic family — Ivan the Terrible's first wife was Anastasia Romanovna — Michael Romanov was the first member of the Romanov line that would rule Russia until the Bolshevik Revolution.

RISE AND FALL OF THE ROMANOVS

Michael Romanov took the throne of a country in dire trouble. As historian Nicholas V. Riasanovsky wrote in *A History of Russia:*

The treasury was empty, and financial collapse of the state appeared complete. In Astrakhan,

Zarutsky [a cossack leader] . . . rallied the cossacks and other malcontents, continuing the story of pretenders and social rebellion so characteristic of the Time of Troubles. Many roaming bands, some of them several thousand strong, continued looting the land. Moreover, Muscovy remained at war with Poland and Sweden, which had seized respectively Smolensk and Novgorod as well as other Russian territory and promoted their own candidates to the Muscovite throne. . . .

Tsar Michael moved quickly to quiet domestic unrest. His armies broke the rebel movement in the countryside. He reached an agreement with the Swedes in 1617 (Sweden having declared war after Moscow denounced the treaty promising an alliance against Poland) and made a truce with Poland in 1618. The truce gave the Poles control over the town of Smolensk and other areas in western Russia. After the truce expired in 1632 the war began anew, but it ended in 1634 with a treaty that again recognized Polish authority in western Russia.

To restore Moscow's finances, Tsar Michael levied new taxes and arranged loans generating sufficient funds to keep the country from bankruptcy. Money troubles were to plague the tsars for several decades.

Michael's successor, his son Alexis, ruled from 1645 to 1676. He oversaw the Ukraine's unification with Moscow in 1654 after the Ukrainians broke with their Polish rulers. His armies put down a large peasant rebellion, led by Stepan Razin in 1670. Tsar Fëdor III, Alexis's elder son from his first marriage, assumed the throne in 1676 and died six years later at the age of 20, leaving no heir.

Peter the Great

Peter the Great, who transformed Russia into a leading European power, was Alexis's son from his second marriage. The boyar assembly named the 10-year-old Peter tsar after the death of his half-brother, Fëdor III. But the followers of Ivan, Fëdor's brother, rebelled and forced the boyars to appoint Ivan senior tsar and Peter junior tsar, with Ivan's sister Sophia as regent. An ambitious woman, Sophia attempted to claim the throne for herself in 1689, but the church hierarchy and the boyars backed Peter and Sophia's coup failed. Peter, then aged 17, handed power over to his mother, Natalia Narishkina (Alexis's second wife), who ran the government for five years. Finally, after his mother's death, Peter, aged 22, took charge.

Taking Western Europe as his model, Peter proceeded to modernize Russian society. He reorganized the army and created a navy, updated the Russian calendar, modified the Cyrillic alphabet, introduced Roman numerals, mandated compulsory education for gentry children, and oversaw the publication of Russia's first newspaper. The tsar also introduced Western dress and attracted European teachers and technicians to his court.

Peter the Great also reformed Russia's system of government by dividing the country into 50 provinces and establishing a Senate to handle state financial, legal, and administrative matters. Government ministries *(collegia)* were created to administer commerce, income, war, manufacturing, and other activities. But the tsar had no interest in sharing power with his subjects; no government plan could be implemented without his approval. His power extended to the church as well; in 1721 he decreed that the head of the church would be a layman. He restructured the traditional system of service to the state by introducing the Table of Ranks (the *chin*) under which a member of the gentry entered service (in the military or the government) at the bottom and worked his way up through 14 levels, instead of receiving a certain rank based on family influence. Nongentry Russians who entered service were made members of the gentry class for life if they reached the fifth rank.

Peter pursued an active foreign policy designed to defeat Russia's old enemies and expand its territory. "The Great Northern War," waged against Sweden from 1700 until 1721, resulted in the acquisition of territories bordering the Gulf of Finland, including the site of Russia's future capital city, St. Petersburg (now Leningrad), as well as Estonia and Latvia. After the defeat of the Swedes, the Senate conferred upon Peter the title of emperor (which subsequently was used interchangeably with tsar) and the Russian Empire formally was established. The capital was moved from Moscow to St. Petersburg in 1712.

Peter the Great died February 8, 1725, without designating a successor. Over the next 37 years, Russia was governed by six monarchs. During this period, the gentry's position was strengthened while the rights of serfs, peasants who farmed the gentry's fields, underwent continual restriction. In 1736 the lifetime term of gentry service to the crown was reduced to 25 years and in 1762 service was canceled. Serfs, on the other hand, became in effect the personal property of their gentry masters.

Catherine the Great

A princess from the small German state of Anhalt-Zerbst, Catherine married Peter III in 1745 and spent the next 17 years carefully forming alliances among members of the imperial court. Backed by the court's elite guards

Peter the Great

corps, she ousted her husband and was named empress. Although she was well versed in democratic thought associated with the Enlightenment (she carried on a celebrated correspondence with Voltaire), Catherine the Great remained a staunch supporter of absolute monarchy in Russia. She contributed to the continuing degradation of the serfs by giving away to her supporters thousands of acres of state land; the peasants working the lands were included in the gifts. The serf rebellion of 1773-75, led by Emelyan Pugachev, frightened Catherine and her gentry supporters and brought about stronger gentry rights and privileges and stricter control over the serfs. Gentry privilege was broadened by the 1785 Charter of the Nobility, which guaranteed a trial by a jury of noble peers and freed the gentry from taxation, conscription, and corporal punishment. It also reiterated the 1762 exemption from military or civil service to the state.

Catherine's foreign policy was designed to expand Russia's southern and western boundaries. In the south, the empress's army and navy defeated the Turks in 1774 and won control over part of the Black Sea coastline. Catherine, however, had larger plans and attempted to take over the Crimea; by 1792, she achieved her goal.

To the west, Catherine shared in the partition of Poland. Weakened by years of internal strife and civil war, Poland was a likely prospect for domination by her powerful neighbors. In 1772 Russia, Prussia, and Austria divided among themselves about one-third of Poland's territory, Russia gaining 1.3 million new citizens. The formulation of a new Polish constitution in 1791 provoked the second partition; it awarded Russia most of Belorussia and the western Ukraine and 3 million inhabitants. The Poles rose in rebellion but were defeated by the Russian and Prussian

Catherine the Great

armies in 1795. To punish the rebels, the remaining parts of their homeland were divided among Russia, Prussia, and Austria. Poland, as a state, no longer existed.

Catherine's long reign ended in 1796 and her son, Emperor Paul, took control of one of the world's mightiest powers. During his five years on the throne, Paul codified the law of succession to require primogeniture in the male line (Peter the Great had declared that the emperor had the right to name his successor) and displayed a liberal attitude toward the serfs, reducing the number of days each week a serf was required to work his master's lands. In foreign affairs, he made war against revolutionary France and later entered into a Russian-French coalition. His extreme disdain for the gentry, who had supported his mother's claims to a throne he considered rightfully his, resulted in a palace coup in 1801. Paul was murdered and his son, the 23-year-old Alexander I, was made emperor.

Alexander I

The early years of Alexander's reign seemed to portend broad changes in Russian society. The emperor increased the powers of the Senate, which had been moribund for several years, tightened and improved the administration of the ministerial departments, and promoted education. His advisers devised a scheme to permit the gentry to release serfs from bondage, although few serf owners took advantage of it.

Alexander's reforms, however, took a back seat to developments in Europe, particularly in France. His apprehension over Napoleon's aggressive empire building caused Alexander to break the treaty his father had negotiated with France. The resulting war — with Russia allied with Great Britain, Sweden, Prussia, and Austria against France and Spain — ended in a victory for the French. The Treaty of Tilsit (now known as Sovetsk), signed in 1807, severely weakened Prussia and left France and Russia as the only two continental superpowers. Tensions between the two simmered for five years, culminating in Napoleon's ill-fated invasion of Russia.

Although the Russians put up a stiffer defense than Napoleon expected (at the battle of Borodino on September 7, 1812, nearly half the French army of 130,000 were killed or wounded), French forces entered Moscow just three months after the invasion. Backed by his subjects, Alexander declined to make peace. With the onset of winter and their supply lines overextended, the French retreated, followed by the Russian army, which engaged the invaders in repeated skirmishes. After forming a coalition with Austria, Sweden, and Great Britain, the Russians pursued Napoleon's army into France. Paris was occupied March 31, 1814, and Napoleon banished to Elba.

Alexander represented Russia at the Congress of Vienna, the momentous gathering of 1814-15 that redrew the map of Europe in the wake of Napoleon's defeat. (Napoleon retook the French throne in March 1815 and finally was defeated at the Battle of Waterloo, June 18, 1815.) Out of the Congress came a smaller, recreated Poland with Tsar Alexander as constitutional monarch. Prussia emerged from the Congress of Vienna as a restored major power, Austria received much of northern Italy, Belgium and Holland were joined in a kingdom, and Switzerland and Germany were awarded constitutions. In addition, Norway was taken from Denmark and given to Sweden. The Danes were compensated with German lands.

Although Alexander was preoccupied with Napoleon

Serfdom: Bondage to the Landed Gentry

The establishment of serfdom in Russia was a prolonged process that had its roots in the Kievan period. At the dawn of Kievan Russia in the ninth century, most peasants were free, engaged in widespread agriculture on land for the most part owned by the nobility. Economic pressures on peasants — drought, poor harvest, famine — compelled agricultural workers to turn to landlords for assistance, primarily in the form of loans. Inability to repay loans resulted in a form of bondage, under which the peasant's obligation to the landlord took one of two forms: *barshchina*, direct work for the landlord, or *obrok*, payment to the landlord in money or goods. Over the centuries, landlords' control of the peasants grew; by the fifteenth century, a peasant could leave his master's service only on a specified day each year — some time near the feast of St. George, late in the fall — if he had paid off his debts.

Treated as Property

Serfs' rights were circumscribed further during the Muscovite period (fifteenth, sixteenth, and seventeenth centuries). The serfs fell victim to the tsars' practice of awarding vast tracts of state lands *(pomesties)* to the service gentry, the men who performed administrative chores for the ruler and served in his armies. Included in the land grants were the peasants occupying them. To ensure the loyalty of the gentry, landlords were empowered to govern and tax their subjects. When the peasants resisted by escaping to outlying regions, the government outlawed peasant migration.

The legal code of 1649, the *Ulozhenie,* lengthened to an indefinite time the period during which an escaped serf had to be returned to his master (it had been five years) and stiffened penalties for providing refuge for fugitive serfs. By the end of the seventeenth century buying and selling serfs was common.

In the eighteenth century the position of the serfs continued to deteriorate as the power of the gentry grew. Millions of peasants passed into serfdom as the emperors and empresses expanded on the practice of giving state land to their supporters. Decrees prohibited serfs from owning land, signing government contracts, or joining the army (thus escaping servitude). Landlords, in contrast, were given authority to exile errant serfs to Siberia and to shift serfs from one estate to another. In 1741 serfs were not among the Russians required to pledge loyalty to the tsar and a criminal code of 1754 designated serfs as gentry property. Catherine the Great (1762-96) established serfdom in the Ukraine, continued the practice of giving generous grants of land and peasants to her favorites, and prohibited serfs from complaining to the empress or her government about their treatment by landlords.

The abolition of serfdom on March 3, 1861, failed to resolve Russia's social ills. Serfs who tilled the soil were granted lands to work, but in many instances the most productive fields remained under gentry control. Household serfs — domestic servants in gentry homes — received no land.

Servant and Master

A portrait of the landlord-serf relationship is contained in the Russian classic, *The Family Chronicle,* by Sergei Aksakov, originally published in 1856. The hero of the novel, Stepan Michailovich Bagrov, gladdened by the impending birth of a grandchild, decides to "reward his tea-and-coffee handmaiden, Aksiutka" by arranging a marriage for her. He summons the peasant and says, " 'You stupid girl, why do you always go about in that dirty old smock? Be off, and dress yourself decently: put on your holiday clothes and I will find you a husband.' " The servant girl dismissed, the master calls for another serf, Ivan Malisch: "Ivan Malisch made his appearance before his master, who observed his good looks with great satisfaction, and addressed him in such a kind and friendly tone, that the young man's heart faintly throbbed with joy: 'Malisch, I am going to have you married.' 'Your gracious will be done, little father Stepan Michailovich!' replied the young man, who was devoted, body and soul, to his master. 'Run away and dress yourself nicely and come back to me as quickly as you can.' Off dashed Malisch to do as he was told."

And, although the bridegroom objected to his prospective mate, "No resistance was possible. The wedding took place immediately."

during the first 15 years of his reign, he also engaged in wars on his empire's southern boundaries. His response to a request for help from the small nation of Georgia led to the 1804-13 war against Georgia's neighbor, Persia, and the 1806-12 Russo-Turkish war. In both, the Russian armies won and Russian rule was extended over Georgia. In the north, a war with Sweden in 1809 resulted in the occupation of Finland, which Alexander ruled as grand duke.

The domestic liberalism that characterized Alexander's early rule did not extend to his later years, however. The emperor investigated (and, according to some historians, gave his approval to) a proposal for a Russian constitutional monarchy but the plan was never implemented. Moreover, his progressive educational policies were overturned after he became enamored of a kind of religious fundamentalism that eschewed modern ideas.

The Romanov Dynasty

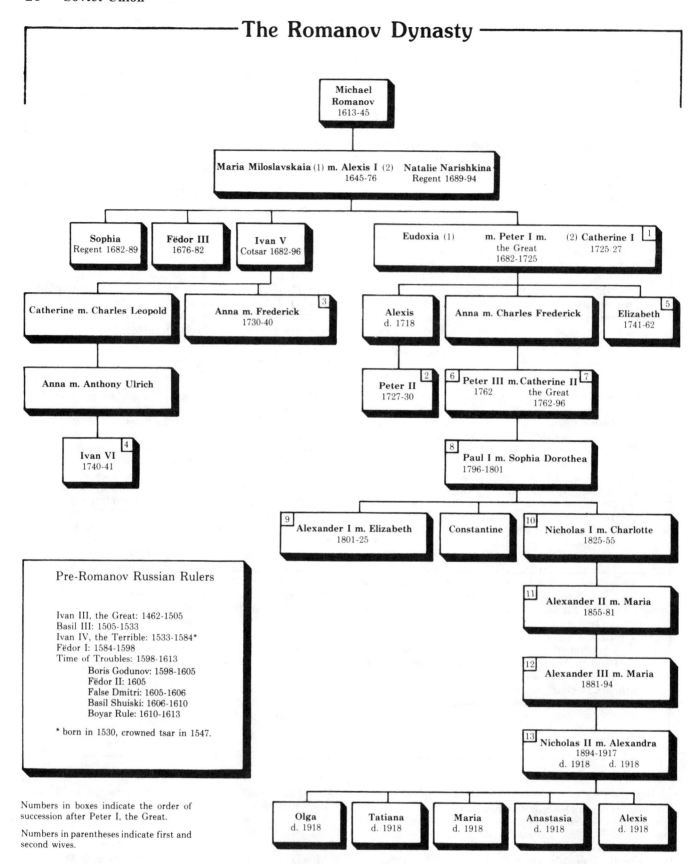

Michael Romanov 1613-45

Maria Miloslavskaia (1) m. **Alexis I** (2) **Natalie Narishkina** 1645-76 Regent 1689-94

Sophia Regent 1682-89

Fëdor III 1676-82

Ivan V Cotsar 1682-96

Eudoxia (1)   m. **Peter I** m.   (2) **Catherine I** [1] the Great 1725-27 1682-1725

Catherine m. Charles Leopold

Anna m. Frederick [3] 1730-40

Alexis d. 1718

Anna m. Charles Frederick

Elizabeth [5] 1741-62

Anna m. Anthony Ulrich

Peter II [2] 1727-30

Peter III m. **Catherine II** [6] [7] 1762 the Great 1762-96

Ivan VI [4] 1740-41

Paul I m. Sophia Dorothea [8] 1796-1801

[9] **Alexander I m. Elizabeth** 1801-25

Constantine

[10] **Nicholas I m. Charlotte** 1825-55

[11] **Alexander II m. Maria** 1855-81

[12] **Alexander III m. Maria** 1881-94

[13] **Nicholas II m. Alexandra** 1894-1917 d. 1918   d. 1918

Olga d. 1918

Tatiana d. 1918

Maria d. 1918

Anastasia d. 1918

Alexis d. 1918

Pre-Romanov Russian Rulers

Ivan III, the Great: 1462-1505
Basil III: 1505-1533
Ivan IV, the Terrible: 1533-1584*
Fëdor I: 1584-1598
Time of Troubles: 1598-1613
    Boris Godunov: 1598-1605
    Fëdor II: 1605
    False Dmitri: 1605-1606
    Basil Shuiski: 1606-1610
    Boyar Rule: 1610-1613

* born in 1530, crowned tsar in 1547.

Numbers in boxes indicate the order of succession after Peter I, the Great.

Numbers in parentheses indicate first and second wives.

Source: Adapted from Nicholas V. Riasanovsky, *A History of Russia,* 3d ed. (New York: Oxford University Press, 1977)

The emperor's disavowal of his earlier liberal tendencies provoked animosity among a small group of aristocratic army officers who, familiar with the democratic changes sweeping Europe, wished to establish a constitutional monarchy in their homeland. When Alexander died suddenly in December 1825 without an heir, the country temporarily was left leaderless while the late emperor's brothers, Constantine and Nicholas, attempted to decide who should assume the throne. (Although Constantine was the older brother, he had renounced his claim to the throne when he married a commoner.) In the ensuing confusion, the army officers decided to seize power. They gathered their few followers in St. Petersburg, but they were quickly dispersed by government troops. The leaders of the rebels, thereafter known as the Decembrists, were tried and executed by the government of the new emperor, Nicholas I.

The Decembrists failed because they had little or no public support. Their abortive uprising had two results: It ushered in an era of repression under the new emperor, and it served as an important symbolic event for the generations of revolutionaries who matured during the nineteenth and early twentieth centuries.

Nicholas I

The Decembrist revolt, led and staffed by members of the nobility and gentry, chilled relations between Emperor Nicholas and the upper classes. In reaction to the failed rebellion, Nicholas sought to reassert complete control over the lives of his subjects. George Vernadsky wrote in his book, *A History of Russia:*

All manifestations of liberalism were mercilessly suppressed. The press was limited; the universities were placed under strict supervision; a special "third" division of the Imperial Chancellery was organized for the secret police. This was reinforced by the newly created Corps of Gendarmes. The slightest suspicion of political untrustworthiness terminated the career of any civil or military official, however talented. As a result, the proportion of capable officers and civil servants in higher posts decreased considerably. Arrest and exile threatened anyone having independent political views.... The system of Nicholas I was enforced harshly and without right of appeal.

Nicholas adopted a similarly conservative outlook toward international affairs. A staunch monarchist and defender of the status quo, he ordered his armies to put down revolutions in Poland (1830-31) and Hungary (1849). Russian troops also intervened in 1848 to curb increasing Romanian nationalist activities. He even considered dispatching his armed forces to restore order during two French revolutions, those of 1830 and 1848.

Nicholas's aggressive foreign policy led to disaster in the Crimean War (1853-56). Ignited by a dispute over religious rights in the Holy Land, war between Russia and Turkey broke out in October 1853. Turkey soon was joined by two powerful allies, Great Britain and France, whose forces laid siege to Sevastopol, Russia's naval base in the Crimea. After nearly a year, the Russians were forced to forsake Sevastopol in September 1855 and accept defeat. The Treaty of Paris, signed March 30, 1856, codified Russia's military weakness: among other terms, the treaty forced Moscow to withdraw all its forces from the Black Sea and abandon its claim as the protector of the Orthodox peoples in the Ottoman Empire.

Despite the generally repressive atmosphere that prevailed in Russia during Nicholas's reign, the cultural life of the nation flourished. The years 1820 to 1860 are known as Russia's "Golden Age." The early years of the Golden Age were marked by the writings of Aleksander Pushkin and Nikolai Gogol, as well as the work of several lesser poets and novelists. In later years, the leading lights of the Golden Age included Ivan Turgenev, Fëdor Dostoevsky, and Leo Tolstoy. *(Box, Chapter 8, p. 177)*

Alexander II

Emperor Nicholas I died in March 1855, before the end of the Crimean War. The conclusion to that disastrous foreign exercise was presided over by his son Alexander II, who then proceeded to hasten his nation's development into a modern, less repressive state.

Alexander attempted, with some success, to improve Russia's tarnished international image. He entered a military alliance with Germany and Austria-Hungary in the early 1870s and improved Russia's standing as a military power by scoring a victory over the Turks in 1878, although the resulting peace treaty forced Russia to make concessions to Britain, Austria-Hungary, and Germany. In the East, however, Russia's expansion was unhampered by European political considerations. The emperor's armies established Moscow's dominion over the Caucasus and central Asia and his diplomats received land concessions from the Chinese, including the area around Vladivostok, which was founded in 1860.

Alexander's most pressing concerns were domestic. Serfdom was on its last legs. Few members of the gentry could afford to maintain vast numbers of serfs. For their part, the serfs in the early nineteenth century began to seek freedom. Between 1800 and 1860, there were more than 1,500 peasant rebellions.

An imperial order freeing the estimated 23 million serfs was signed by Alexander II on March 3, 1861. Under the terms of their emancipation, serfs received parcels of land to work as their own, although legal title to this land was held collectively by the village commune (or *mir*). The gentry gave up about half the land it controlled, for which it was reimbursed by the government. The serfs were granted long-term credits to pay (through their communes) for the lands they, in effect, had been forced to purchase. The financial burden imposed by emancipation led to a wave of peasant revolt that swept the country the following year, but soon died down.

Additional reforms followed on the heels of the serfs' emancipation. In 1864 elected county representatives were assigned responsibility for public health, roads, and education. The legal system was reformed the same year. The administration of justice was made a separate branch of government and equal treatment before the law was guaranteed for all citizens. Alexander's reforms extended to the military as well; general conscription was extended to all Russians (it previously had applied only to peasants) and the term of service was lowered from 25 years to 6.

Unrest Leads to Radicalism

Rather than stem the radical movements growing in Russia, Alexander's reforms encouraged calls for additional change. Since the failed Decembrist revolt of 1825, the Russian revolutionary movement had developed into several distinct branches. It remained, however, an upper-class movement, centered in the universities and the drawing rooms of Moscow and St. Petersburg. Indeed, Tibor Szamuely, in *The Russian Tradition*, has pointed out that the paradox of Russian radicalism was the

> conviction that the much-loved people were too backward to be able to understand their own good, and that they therefore had to be forced into the Elysian Fields by beings of a superior intelligence — a self-appointed intellectual elite or a single leader of superhuman stature. . . .

By the 1840s two main strands of radicalism had appeared, the Slavophiles and the Westerners. As their name implies, the Slavophiles sought a return to the Russian state as it existed before the introduction of Western ideas and structures under Peter the Great and his successors. Their ideal was an isolated nation whose main characteristics were the communal system, the Orthodox Church, and the autocracy. The Westerners, on the other hand, advocated greater reliance on Western-style development, though they rejected capitalism. Their hero was Peter the Great during the early days of the Western movement. Eventually, however, the leader of the Westerners, literary critic Vissarion Belinsky, turned against the monarchy and argued for its overthrow.

A third radical group that rose to prominence in the 1840s was the Petrashevskists. Named after Mikhail Petrashevskii, at whose home they met secretly, the Petrashevskists followed the teachings of the French utopian socialist, Charles Fourier. They were responsible for the spread of socialist literature among the intelligentsia, an activity that, coupled with their general opposition to the government of Nicholas I, led to the arrest and sentencing to death of some of the group's members, including Dostoevsky. The death sentences were reduced to prison terms at the last minute.

These movements of the 1840s were superseded by the rise in the following decade of Populism *(Narodnichestvo)*. Its high priest was Aleksandr Ivanovich Herzen. Herzen embraced socialism but adapted it to Russian conditions, arguing that socialism would spring from the traditional Russian communal villages. Herzen's views, contained in *Kolokol* (The Bell), a journal he published during his exile in Europe from 1857 until 1867, found an eager audience among the educated class. As the tide of revolution rose in his homeland, Herzen's ideas were taken over by men and women bent on overthrowing the state to implement them.

Herzen's Populism was taken up by Nikolai Gavrilovich Chernyshevsky, a critic whose novel *What Is to Be Done?* outlined his vision of socialist Russia. In it, he postulated the existence of the "new men," an elite corps of intellectuals who selflessly would strive to improve conditions for the people. Borrowing from Herzen, Chernyshevsky argued that Russia should forgo capitalist development and step directly into socialism. But unlike Herzen, who expected that the change to socialism would come about peacefully, Chernyshevsky exhorted his followers to pull down the existing system. Chernyshevsky's ideas enjoyed wide popularity among Russian radicals and made a lasting impression on the generations of revolutionaries who followed him. One telling example: Lenin in 1902 wrote a pamphlet bearing the title, "What Is to Be Done?"

Also contributing to the political discussions of the period was the nihilist philosophy. In brief, it postulated that anything — art, literature, ideas — that failed to improve the lot of the people was worthless. The nihilists, like the "new men," would have no time for pleasurable pursuits until they radically altered society.

A welter of conspiratorial groups and radical cliques of every description engaged in endless discussion of the problems of Russia and the ways to resolve them. But there was very little direct action until 1873, when thousands of young adults decided to work among the peasants in a movement known as "going to the people." Lasting for several years, the exercise was a failure. Most of the students hoped to convert the peasants to socialism and radicalism. In most cases, the students met with indifference; in others, the student propagandists were handed over to the police. By 1877 the disillusioned students had returned to the cities.

The failure of "going to the people" turned many radicals back to the idea that the revolutionary movement required an elite group of leaders to tear down the tsarist system and recreate Russian society in the name of the "people." In the autumn of 1876, several disparate radical groups formed a central organization, Land and Liberty *(Zemlya i Volya)*, dedicated to the violent overthrow of the government. Quoting Szamuely:

> The party's basic strategy and tactical principles were set forth in its first program, adopted in 1876. It stated that the party's final aim was the achievement of the full anarchist ideal, i.e., the abolition of the state, but recognized that this

Alexander II

would be a task for the distant future. The immediate aims of the revolution were threefold: (1) the abolition of private ownership of land, and its distribution among the peasants; (2) the restructuring of the social system on the basis of the village communes; (3) the right of self-determination, including independence, of the national minorities. This, the program went on, was what the party meant by "Land and Liberty."

In January 1878 the pace of radical activity quickened. A revolutionary named Vera Zasulich failed at her attempt to assassinate the governor of St. Petersburg; though she was caught red-handed, the jury at her trial refused to convict her. The stunned government ordered immediately afterward that all political crimes would be tried by special tribunals.

By 1879 Land and Liberty had split into two groups, one that wanted to prepare the people for revolution and another dedicated to an immediate reign of terror. The latter group, The Will of the People *(Narodnaya Volya)*, decided to throw the government into disarray by killing the tsar. After several unsuccessful attempts on the tsar's life — including a February 5, 1880, bomb blast that destroyed the dining room in the Winter Palace — the terrorists achieved their goal March 1, 1881.

Alexander III

The son of Alexander II, Tsar Alexander III, quickly moved to destroy Russian revolutionary activity. A series of measures gave police the authority to arrest and imprison troublemakers. The tsar's government also lent its support to traditional Russian social structures, bolstering the power of the gentry and the Orthodox Church. These measures — combined with martial law — reduced the level of political activity considerably. The period of domestic peace permitted the tsar and his advisers to concentrate on improving the national economy.

Industrialization

Industrialization began slowly in Russia. During Kievan Russia, the commercial emphasis was on trade in raw materials and the traditional occupations of farming and cattle raising. Metals, pottery, textile, and fur products were manufactured on a small scale. When Peter the Great assumed the throne, Russia had some 20 factories; by the time of his death, there were more than 200, about 40 percent of which were state owned. Peter promoted the establishment of metallurgical and textile factories to furnish guns and clothing to his armed forces. Beyond these pressing needs, the new manufacturing concerns also aided the development of the economy and increased Russia's exports.

Industrialization after Peter progressed steadily. Metallurgy and textile production continued to dominate. The pace of industrial growth began to accelerate in the nineteenth century. In 1800 there were about 1,200 Russian factories; by midcentury, their number had more than doubled. And between 1850 and 1860 the number of factories to construct machines rose fivefold.

Under Alexander III, Russia developed into an industrial nation, some years behind its European counterparts. In the 1890s Russia's growth rate averaged 8 percent a year. Alexander's government witnessed the enlargement of the railroad system by about 40 percent (it would double in size between 1895 and 1905) and a tremendous growth in the amount of foreign industrial investment — from 100 million rubles in 1880 to 900 million by 1900. Riasanovsky wrote:

> Toward the end of the century Russia possessed eight basic industrial regions.... The Moscow industrial region, comprising six provinces, contained textile industries of every sort, as well as metal-processing and chemical plants. The St. Petersburg region specialized in metal-processing, machine-building and textile industries. The Polish region, with such centers as Lodz and Warsaw, had textile, coal, iron, metal-processing and chemical industries. The recently developed south Russian Ukrainian region supplied coal, iron ore and basic chemical products. The Ural region continued to produce iron, non-ferrous metals and minerals. The Baku sector in Transcaucasia contributed oil. The southwestern region specialized in beet sugar. Finally, the Transcaucasian manganese-coal region supplied substantial amounts of its two products.

Government protection for industrial workers was mandated by a series of labor laws enacted in the 1880s. The legislation outlawed the use of women and children for night work in the textile industry, limited to eight hours the working days of 12- to 15-year-old factory hands and established regulations guaranteeing regular pay for employees. By 1900 the estimated 2 million Russian workers received additional protection: Factories with more than 20 employees could not require adults to work more than 11-½ hours daily or 10 hours nightly on Saturdays and on the day before holidays. Work was forbidden on Sundays and holidays. Adolescents were permitted to work only 10 hours a day, children only 9. In 1903 employers were made liable for workplace injuries.

Alliance With France

In foreign affairs, Alexander III made one major move. Russia's three-part alliance with Austria-Hungary and Germany, formed in the early 1870s, dissolved over conflicts between Moscow and Vienna in the Balkans. Germany attempted to maintain a secret Berlin-Moscow connection to offset growing French power, but this arrangement fell apart in 1890. Casting about for new European allies, Russia selected France. By 1894 Russia and France faced an alliance among Austria-Hungary, Germany, and Italy.

Nicholas II

Tsar Alexander III died in 1894 and was succeeded by his son, Nicholas II, the last Russian monarch. He continued his father's conservative policies and enlarged upon them, restricting further the authority of local governments, imposing widepread press censorship, and curbing the education system. Religious persecution, begun under Alexander III in an attempt to "Russify" the populace, reached new heights, resulting in Jewish pogroms and violent harassment of other non-Orthodox denominations.

Nicholas's attempts to maintain order won him few friends. Faith in the monarchy had been undermined by the famine of 1891, an event that rallied the disparate radical movements decimated by the repression of the

1880s. By the early 1900s the liberals, composed of members of the rising professional class, had established the Union of Liberation and, in 1905, set up the Constitutional Democratic Party (Cadet), a group devoted to constitutional reform. The radicals established two units, the Marxist-oriented Russian Social Democratic Labor Party and the Socialist Revolutionaries, a group that derived from the radical populists.

At its 1903 gathering, the Social Democratic Labor Party split into two branches, the "Men of the Majority" (Bolsheviks) and the "Men of the Minority" (Mensheviks). The Bolsheviks, led by V. I. Lenin (whose real name was Vladimir Ilich Ulyanov), preferred a concentrated party made up of dedicated revolutionaries; the Mensheviks envisioned a more broadly based organization.

Nicholas's foreign adventures in the Far East increased domestic opposition to his rule. The Russo-Japanese War of 1904-05, begun over conflicts in China, resulted in a Russian rout. The unpopular war added to the unrest in Russia, and demands mounted for the establishment of a legislative assembly and civil rights as workers went on strike and students demonstrated in the cities.

Revolution of 1905

The series of events known as the Revolution of 1905 began on "Bloody Sunday," January 22, 1905. A large group of workers, demonstrating peacefully in front of St. Petersburg's Winter Palace, was fired upon by the police. Hundreds were killed and wounded. The violent police reaction stunned the liberals and turned the traditionally loyal working people away from the tsar and into the arms of the socialists. Strikes and disturbances continued until August, when Nicholas announced the creation of an elective *Duma* (representative assembly) to advise the tsar. The proposal satisfied few in the opposition and the revolutionaries organized a general strike that brought the country to a standstill from October 20 to October 30. The strike forced the Tsar Nicholas II and his ministers to issue on October 30 a manifesto guaranteeing full civil rights for all Russians and mandating a Duma empowered to propose and enact legislation. This program won the approval of the liberals and the disdain of the radicals. The opposition was split.

During the October strike, workers in St. Petersburg formed the Soviet (Council) of Workers' Deputies. One of the leaders of this first soviet was Leon Trotsky (whose real name was Bronstein). After the general strike, the government arrested the members of the St. Petersburg Soviet. Trotsky was banished to Siberia, but escaped to Europe.

The tsar in May 1906 released a declaration outlining the powers and responsibilities of the Duma. Although its powers were limited — for example, it controlled only 60 percent of the state budget — the first Duma met May 10, 1906. Neither it nor its successor lasted long. Not until after it modified the electoral law did the tsarist government allow the Duma to remain in session for a full term. Jerry F. Hough and Merle Fainsod wrote in *How the Soviet Union Is Governed:*

> The history of the *dumas* is largely a record of the frustration of parliamentary hopes. The first *duma* (1906) was quickly dissolved after a bitter struggle in which the Cadet [liberal] majority re-

Tsar Nicholas II and Tsarina Alexandra with Their Entourage

Father of Marxism Was Skeptical Of Russia's Potential for Revolution

Karl Marx, the political philosopher who gave his name to the social system embraced by Russian radicals, initially put Russia low on his list of European countries ripe for socialist revolution. Marx, assisted by his colleague and frequent financial supporter Friedrich Engels, proposed a theory of history based on the struggle between social classes over control of the "means of production." Adapting an idea developed by the German philosopher Georg Wilhelm Friedrich Hegel (1770-1831), Marx and Engels argued that class struggle occurred in cycles: an existing situation, the thesis, inevitably was challenged by a new idea, the antithesis, and the exchange, the dialectic, between thesis and antithesis resulted in something new, the synthesis. Throughout history, the continuous cycle of thesis, antithesis, and synthesis spurred the evolution of social organization from slavery to feudalism to capitalism, in Marx's view. He believed that a fully developed capitalist state would be overturned by the oppressed mass of workers, the proletariat, who would then establish the final (and to Marx the purest) form of society, the socialist state. As a result, he looked to the industrialized nations — Germany, France, Britain — for signs of impending revolution. Russia, backward and largely agricultural, was to Marx an unlikely candidate for socialist revolution.

Call to Workers

Born May 5, 1818, in Trier in the German Rhineland, Marx studied history and philosophy at the universities of Bonn and Berlin. In school, Marx was exposed to key aspects of Hegelianism. His developing political views were expressed in the Cologne-based journal *Rheinische Zeitung*, which he edited in 1842-43. The publication was closed by the authorities in 1843 and Marx settled in Paris to work as an editor of *Deutsch-Franzosische Zeitung*. In 1845 his radical ideas led to his expulsion by the French; Marx and his wife, Jenny von Westphalen, took refuge in Brussels. While there he and Engels, his constant collaborator, wrote the *Communist Manifesto*. A blueprint for the Communist League, a small group of European radicals, the *Manifesto* outlined the philosophy of dialectical materialism and called on the proletariat to liberate itself from capitalist enslavement.

Shortly after publication of the *Manifesto* in 1848, Marx returned to Cologne and again published a newspaper, retitled the *Neue Rheinische Zeitung*. In 1849 Germany expelled him once more. He settled in London, where he spent the rest of his life.

The radical revolutions that swept Europe in 1848 were not communist inspired, a fact that disappointed Marx. But he continued to promote revolution from London, helping to establish with the radical Russian émigré Mikhail Bakunin the First International Workingmen's Association in 1864 and maintaining a network of revolutionary contacts. Marx also devoted himself to his major scholarly effort, *Das Kapital*, the first volume of which was published in 1867. He was kept aware of revolutionary movements in Russia but continued to doubt that his program could be implemented successfully in that underdeveloped nation. Marx reportedly was amused at the news that the first foreign language edition of *Das Kapital* was the Russian translation published in 1872.

Despite Marx's seeming indifference, the establishment of communism was a hotly debated topic among radical Russians. The revolutionary Populists, members of *Narodnaya Volya*, argued that socialism was uniquely suited to Russia because Russian society was based on the village commune, a primitive communist organization. Under this favorable circumstance, Russia could skip over the capitalist development phase and directly proceed to socialism. In the preface to a new Russian edition of the *Communist Manifesto* published in 1882, Marx and Engels finally agreed with this analysis of Russia's revolutionary potential. The following year, on March 14, Marx died in London. Engels died in 1895.

Marxist Economic Doctrine

R. N. Carew Hunt in *The Theory and Practice of Communism* summarizes Marx's economic doctrine this way:

Labour alone creates value. All profits are derived from unpaid labour time. Capitalists are driven by competition to accumulate capital, which becomes concentrated in fewer and fewer hands, with the result that smaller businesses disappear and their owners are driven back into the working class. The accumulation of capital in the form of labour-saving devices reduces the use of human labour and at the same time the profits of the capitalists, who are therefore compelled to offset their losses by intensifying the exploitation of their workers, over whom the increase of unemployment has given them an even stronger hold and who are now prepared to work on any terms. Hence the misery of the workers, eventually almost the entire population, will progressively become more and more unendurable. This will lead them to combine for their own protection, and so create a force which will eventually destroy the whole system.

Rasputin: Royal Adviser and Rake

Grigori Rasputin, the strange mystic who wielded enormous influence over Tsarina Alexandra, was a peasant. Born around 1872 in Pokrovokoe, a village in Siberia, Rasputin's original surname was Novykh. He was given the name Rasputin — in Russian, "dissolute" — by villagers who witnessed his early lecherous behavior. After his marriage to a local woman, Rasputin spent his early adulthood in religious wandering.

During these travels across Russia he fashioned a personal brand of religion, which included his belief  that sexual indulgence was part of the process of religious rapture. Most commentators believe that Rasputin's endorsement of uninhibited sexual activity was a convenient justification for indulging his prodigious sexual appetite.

In 1903 Rasputin arrived in St. Petersburg, where he soon became a spiritual adviser to members of the royal circle. In 1905 he was introduced to the royal family. Presenting himself simply as a holy man, a *starets,* Rasputin won the admiration and respect of the tsarina through his reported ability to improve the health of the Tsarevitch Alexis, a hemophiliac.

Over the next several years he became one of the tsarina's favorites, advising her on spiritual and, eventually, political matters.

He considered himself the voice of the Russian peasantry; the tsarina, some think, considered him the voice of God.

As Rasputin's influence grew, he was besieged by petitioners seeking to curry favor with the royal family and the government. The constant flow of visitors to his home in St. Petersburg facilitated his debauchery; he allegedly seduced many of the more attractive female petitioners. Reports of his sexual exploits were circulated widely in St. Petersburg, but when they reached the tsarina she dismissed them as gossip.

Opposition to Rasputin grew among conservatives after Tsar Nicholas II in September 1915 assumed field command of his troops fighting in World War I. Nicholas's departure from St. Petersburg left the tsarina, with Rasputin at her side, in virtual control of the country. As reports of Rasputin's scandalous excesses and fear of his hold over the tsarina increased, a group of conservatives hatched a plot to assassinate him in the hope of preserving the monarchy.

According to historical accounts, the conspirators included Vladimir Purishkevich, a conservative Duma member; Prince Feliks Yusupov, a wealthy nobleman; and Grand Duke Dmitri Pavlovich, the tsar's first cousin. On the night of December 30, 1916, while he was visiting Yusupov's home, Rasputin was poisoned and, when the poison seemed to have no effect, shot.

---

fused to bow before the will of the government. The second *duma* (1907), with strengthened radical representation, proved even less tractable than its predecessor, and it too was soon dissolved. Repression replaced concession as the reactionary "ruling spheres" around the throne consolidated their dominant position. The new electoral law proclaimed on the occasion of the dissolution of the second *duma* greatly increased the influence of the wealthier categories of the electorate, and the composition of the third and fourth *dumas* reflected their increased power. The reconstruction of the *duma* provided a pliant and accommodating majority for the government, and the third *duma* was permitted to serve out its full term (1907-12). The elections to the fourth *duma* (1912-16) resulted in a victory for the conservative nationalist groups, but even these groups were pushed into opposition to the government by the incompetence of the autocracy in grappling with the problems presented by the first World War.

World War I

Popular dissatisfaction with the imperial government simmered from 1905 until 1914. Radicals continued to agitate, workers struck, and some acts of terror occurred, including assassinations of government officials. The tsar's agents were active, infiltrating and disrupting revolutionary societies. But the burgeoning political, economic, and cultural transformation of Imperial Russia was interrupted when World War I broke out in August 1914. Initially the people rushed to support the tsar and his army, believing unprovoked Austro-German aggression called for a national defense. The people were encouraged by early successes but a series of military disasters on the German front dashed morale. Many of the casualties were blamed on the government's ineptitude.

Arms and munitions were in short supply or completely unavailable. Food was scarce and the people again turned against the government. The tsar had left St. Petersburg to take personal charge of his armies. In his absence, the government was run by the tsarina, who heavily relied on the counsel of Grigori Rasputin, a strange peasant whom the tsarina credited with relieving her son's hemophilia. *(Rasputin, box, p. 30)*

Rasputin and the tsarina successfully alienated all members of the Duma, on the left and the right. Rasputin, "the mad monk," was assassinated December 30, 1916, by a group of conservatives in the hope that his removal would restore calm to the government. Instead, the tsar did nothing until March 1917.

The Revolution of 1917

The Russian Revolution began in March 1917 in Petrograd (renamed from the Germanic St. Petersburg during the war). Women demonstrated on March 8 against bread shortages; others joined the disruption over the next two days. The government sent in troops March 11 to restore order, but, instead of putting down the riots, the soldiers joined them. The next day, the leaders of the Duma proclaimed a Provisional Government. Tsar Nicholas II abdicated March 15 in favor of his brother, Michael, who handed power over to the Provisional Government.

While the Duma leaders were forming a government led by Prince Georgi Lvov, the radicals were organizing the Petrograd Soviet of Workers' and Soldiers' Deputies. The Soviet lent support to the Provisional Government in return for some say in the running of the state. Asserting its authority, the Soviet independently issued a statement directing soldiers to assume control of the army, a move that led to the eventual collapse of the armed forces.

The Provisional Government immediately proclaimed liberal measures: Full equality before the law was granted to all Russians and the regime guaranteed freedom of speech, assembly, press, and religion. Unions and strikes were permitted. Local government underwent modifications to make it more egalitarian. New labor laws inaugurated eight-hour days for some workers. Poland was declared independent and ethnic minorities were granted autonomy.

Despite such steps, the Provisional Government failed to assert control over the country or resolve its most pressing problems. The economy continued its decline. Perhaps more important, the government decided to continue the war, despite the dismal state of morale, the lack of supplies, and the decimated transportation system.

Lenin arrived in Petrograd in April 1917 and immediately called for the end of the war, an increasingly popular position. Meanwhile, the government, headed by the socialist Aleksandr Kerensky, resisted the growing power of the radicals, dispersing a two-day riot in July and arresting some Bolshevik leaders (Lenin escaped to Finland).

Kornilov Affair

Gen. Lavr Kornilov, the recently appointed commander in chief of the Russian Army, made the most forceful challenge to the revolution in what came to be known as the Kornilov Affair. A simple, hard-working man with little capacity for political nuance, Kornilov was convinced the Soviet was the source of all Russia's problems. He initiated what most historians now term a comedy of errors that led to the complete disintegration of the military and the Provisional Government.

Kornilov insisted on evacuating Petrograd after the Germans occupied Riga. Kornilov dispatched troops to the capital ostensibly to protect the government but in reality to ensure that both the government and especially the Soviet were removed. After an intermediary urged Kerensky to cede to Kornilov, Kerensky became convinced that

Soldiers Firing Rifles in the Courtyard of the Winter Palace, St. Petersburg, During the Russian Revolution

Kornilov's efforts were really a conspiracy. He dismissed Kornilov, who refused to leave and instead appealed to the people against the government. Kornilov ordered more troops to the capital.

In the meantime, the Soviet and other socialist organizations acted quickly by mobilizing and arming the generally sympathetic workers in Petrograd and the nearby sailors from Kronstadt naval base. It took little effort to disband the arriving Kornilov soldiers once they were convinced their efforts were actually helping to restore the former regime. Many refused to fight at all. Kornilov and other officers were arrested and several government ministers were dismissed.

Reorganizing the government proved difficult. Kerensky organized a five-man cabinet that attempted to placate the left-wingers; the State Duma was formally dissolved; and moderate right-wing politicians were arrested. Purges and other moves against men and groups within the army that had been favorable to Kornilov caused the front to deteriorate further. Desertions increased; men were embittered, disillusioned, and physically incapable of continuing the war.

In Kerensky's desperation at the height of the Kornilov crisis, he appealed to the Bolsheviks for help and released Trotsky and other imprisoned leaders. The Bolsheviks wasted no time in taking charge of the disorganized situation. They obtained 50 percent of the seats in the Petrograd Soviet in September, and by October, Trotsky became its chairman. Lenin secretly returned to Petrograd October 23 and urged his followers to seize power. "History will not forgive us if we do not take power now," he pleaded.

Lenin's longtime lieutenants Grigori Zinoviev and Lev Kamenev wanted to postpone the coup, but after some initial hesitation the Bolsheviks occupied government offices November 7, 1917. The next day they took over the Winter Palace and placed under arrest those members of the Provisional Government who remained behind after the hasty departure of Kerensky and other government leaders. (The Soviet government often refers to the Bolshevik takeover as the "Great October Revolution" because in 1917 the Julian calendar was still in use in Russia, making the date of the revolution October 25 instead of November 7. The Gregorian, or Western, calendar was adopted January 31, 1918.)

Peasant Reaction

According to Western historian Basil Dmytryshyn, the Kornilov Affair shortened the Provisional Government's life span but was "not the decisive cause of its downfall." Instead, the decisive cause was the "great social upheaval which engulfed all of Russia," and was precipitated not by the peasant population's desire for voting rights but for land. In his book *USSR: A Concise History*, Dmytryshyn explains:

> As was everyone else, the peasants were surprised by the swift collapse of the old regime .... To the Russian peasants, both in and out of the armed forces, the collapse of the old regime revived their centuries-old aspiration.... They understood not such schemes neatly devised by intellectuals as nationalization, or socialization, but simple partition of nearby estates. Illiterate, backward, and never reconciled to the land settlement of the 1860's ... the Russian peasants sincerely believed that only through the enlargements of their plots of land would they be able to improve their wretched and, even by Russian standards, miserable condition.

Peasants formed an overwhelming majority in the armed forces, and with the promise of coming land redistribution, more than 1 million men simply left the army between March and October to ensure they got their share of the land. Peasants often took action against landowners because they felt the Provisional Government was moving too slowly. If owners could not be persuaded to sell, peasants burned down the manors, pillaged, and murdered. The government was besieged by owners' pleas for help. Little was forthcoming.

Industrial workers were also rapidly joining the revolutionary ranks. Because they were centered in urban areas and better organized, these workers had aided the revolution and were among the first to see benefits from it. But things were still not moving fast enough for them and, as the economic picture rapidly declined, many were forced

Soldiers Sitting in the "Auto Sledge" Confiscated From Tsar Nicholas II in the 1917 Russian Revolution

out of work. With increasing hunger came increasing violence. According to Dmytryshyn, "They were ready to listen and to follow any demagogue who would promise a change, and Lenin, the realist, did not allow this opportunity to slip away."

ESTABLISHING THE BOLSHEVIK GOVERNMENT

The Bolsheviks on November 9, 1917, established the Council of People's Commissars to rule the country. Lenin assumed the chairmanship. Other prominent Bolsheviks in the government included Leon Trotsky, commissar for foreign affairs, and Joseph Stalin, who was assigned responsibility for national minority groups. The Bolsheviks capitalized on the mistakes of their opponents' policies and, at the same time, appropriated popular policies of other parties. They translated their program into simple language the peasants understood: land, bread, peace, workers' control.

Acting through its network of local soviets, the party spread its influence throughout the nation. It gained popular support by announcing that it would delay no longer the distribution of gentry land, establish worker control of industry in keeping with Marxist doctine (which Lenin did within 20 days), and arrange a settlement with the Germans.

The peace terms laid down by Germany were harsh. Trotsky and other leaders initially refused to accept the enemy's demands; they were overruled by Lenin. The Treaty of Brest-Litovsk, signed on March 3, 1918, forced Russia to grant independence to Estonia, Latvia, Lithuania, Poland, and the Ukraine. The Soviet government had encouraged independence movements in these and other nations; Stalin, in his official capacity as commissar for nationalities, had announced the independence of Finland in November 1917. The hope was that the newly independent states would embrace Bolshevism. The demands of consolidating power permitted the development of Finland, Estonia, Latvia, Lithuania, and Poland without Soviet domination (until World War II). However, independence movements in Ukrainia, Georgia, Armenia, and other regions were put down.

Politically, the new government asserted its power by disbanding the Constituent Assembly. This legislative body created by the Provisional Government had been elected in late 1917. It met for the first time on January 18, 1918. Of the 707 elected representatives, only 170 were Bolsheviks. As a result, Bolshevik troops January 19 dispersed the assembly.

Other actions designed to consolidate Bolshevik power included nationalization of banks, foreign trade, and all land, seizure of private property, dissolution of all political parties except the Bolsheviks, and establishment of a political police force, the Extraordinary Commission to Combat Counterrevolution, Sabotage, and Speculation (the Cheka).

Civil War

The most pressing problems facing the new regime

Kronstadt Rebellion

The Kronstadt rebellion in early 1921 was a dramatic climax to the anti-Bolshevik rural and urban unrest. Strikes and demonstrations in Petrograd over food shortages sparked sympathy among men stationed at the nearby Kronstadt naval base. The sailors were renowned for their revolutionary zeal, and the base had once been a Bolshevik stronghold. But in the face of nationwide anti-Bolshevik sentiment, the sailors apparently believed their own rebellion supporting the workers would succeed in drawing workers throughout the country. Their platform included establishment of civil rights, secret-ballot elections, release of political prisoners, peasant freedom to use their land however they wished, and an end to discriminatory food rationing.

The chairman of the Soviet's Central Executive Committee, Mikhail I. Kalinin, went to Kronstadt but was unable to settle the situation. The sailors did little to garner strength for their position, expecting the rest of Russia to revolt and join them. The revolution failed to materialize. The government had meanwhile mobilized its forces and made its assault on the naval base. Some 15,000 people were killed; no trials were held. The rebellion had failed, but it had carried a message — of possible popular rebellion — that the communist leaders heard.

were the Civil War and the state of the economy. The war pitted the Bolshevik Red Army against various anti-Bolshevik forces, including liberals, members of the bourgeoisie, officers from the tsar's army, and cossacks. Begun in the summer of 1918, the war almost destroyed the Bolshevik state. Among the many casualties were the members of the royal family. Nicholas II, his wife, and his four children were imprisoned in Ekaterinburg (renamed Sverdlovsk in 1924) in Russian Asia. On July 16, 1918, as forces loyal to the tsar approached the town, local Bolsheviks killed the family. By October, anti-Bolshevik armies were threatening Petrograd and Moscow (the capital had been moved back to Moscow in March 1918). But the Red Army held and took the offensive, driving back the enemy forces. One of the decisive factors in the Bolsheviks' success was their hold over the railroad lines. By the end of 1920, most of the major fighting had ended.

The civil conflict was accompanied by a war with Poland, armed intervention by Russia's erstwhile World War I allies, and independence movements among Russian minorities. The April-October 1918 war with Poland resulted in Polish territorial gains in western Ukrainia. British and American troops entered several Russian ports, including the northern cities of Archangel and Murmansk, to block German attempts to seize stored Allied war supplies. They, with other Allied regiments, also provided

The KGB and Its Predecessors ...

The Soviet security organ, today known as the KGB, is almost as old as the Bolshevik regime. While known by different names over the decades, its consistent purpose has been to keep the Soviet regime in power. In less than 70 years, the Soviet security service has had about a dozen different chiefs. A few are held in esteem in official Soviet history. Some were victims of the terror they helped propagate. The fate of others is still in question.

Feliks Edmundovich Dzerzhinskii, the first head of the Soviet security police, was born in Vilnius (now in Lithuania) in 1877. The son of Polish aristocracy, he became a terrorist and revolutionary at an early age for reasons not entirely clear. He established his revolutionary credentials by leading a series of unsuccessful raids against the tsar's security forces, the Okhrana. He was arrested for the first time in 1897, two months before he turned 20, for these raids and for distributing pamphlets demanding release of political prisoners. Sentenced to five years' hard labor in Siberia, he escaped within two years.

As William Corson and Robert Crowley describe in *The New KGB: Engine of Soviet Power,* Dzerzhinskii became a "convict celebrity" by the time he was recaptured. He escaped several more times from the Okhrana, until his final release after the 1917 revolution. In 1906, during one period of freedom, he had a fateful meeting in Stockholm with two other revolutionaries — Lenin and Stalin. Dzerzhinskii earned their trust and admiration and lived to serve both as head of the Soviet security service. (Dzerzhinskii's statue still stands in front of the KGB headquarters building in Moscow in the well-known square that bears his name.) It was Dzerzhinskii, in fact, who urged the Bolsheviks to establish the "Extraordinary Commission to Combat Counterrevolution." (He also proposed that they empty the tsar's wine cellars into the Neva River to help stem the wave of drunkenness that overcame the people in the first chaotic weeks following the revolution.) The Bolsheviks' Council of People's Commissars established the security service on December 20, 1917, just six weeks after taking over the state. Its acronym, VChK, was quickly shortened to ChK, or "Cheka," which means "linchpin" in Russian. Dzerzhinskii celebrated the Cheka's birth with two Americans, Louise Bryant and John Reed.

The Cheka's powers were immense: the new Bolshevik regime had to battle tsarists and other revolutionary factions. During the Russian Civil War the Chekists were free to arrest, imprison, torture, and execute those they judged to be enemies of the revolution. By 1921 the Cheka was 30,000 strong, had its own armed force, was responsible for protecting Soviet borders and maintaining domestic peace, and had begun to set up an international spy network.

The Stalin Era

After the war ended, the Cheka was replaced February 6, 1922 by the State Political Administration (GPU), part of the People's Commissariat of Internal Affairs (NKVD). In 1932 the GPU became a separate organization, the United State Political Administration (OGPU). Dzerzhinskii retained his place as security chief. In 1924 Stalin also gave him responsibility for the Soviet economic program. Dzerzhinskii became a candidate member of the Politburo and he backed Stalin in his succession fight with Trotsky.

Dzerzhinskii died in 1926 and Viacheslav Rudolfich Menzhinskii, another Pole, succeeded him. Menzhinskii oversaw the brutal collectivization of 14 million peasant holdings. He died while still in office and was replaced by his chief assistant, Genrikh Grigoriyevich Yagoda, who in 1930 had headed the Main Administration of Corrective Labor Camps (the notorious GULAG).

In 1934 Yagoda was made head of the NKVD, which had absorbed the OGPU. In *KGB: Inside the World's Largest Intelligence Organization,* Brian Freemantle asserts that Yagoda, a trained pharmacist, first developed the security service's facilities and research on "methods of extermination." Stalin directed Yagoda to arrange the murder of Sergei Kirov, a potential rival of Stalin's. After Kirov's "assassination" in 1934, which Stalin passed off to the public as a tragic conspiracy, Yagoda was charged with finding the culprits. Dozens of men were arrested, charged with the crime, and executed. For one day Yagoda himself was under arrest, while Stalin weighed the merits of sacrificing him to quiet the public's outrage. The execution of Kirov's "murderers" marked the first wave of the Stalinist purges. Yagoda did eventually become a victim. He was dismissed in 1936, charged with "abusing his office," and shot in 1938.

Yagoda's successor, Nikolai Ivanovich Yezhov, directed the bloodiest phase of the Great Purges. While publicly charged with curbing the NKVD's "excesses," he reigned over the greatest period of terror in Soviet history. The period, in fact, bears his name — the Yezhovshchina. Less than five feet tall, Yezhov became known as the "bloody dwarf." Accounts of his fate differ. Stalin removed him from office in 1938. Freemantle claims he was shot. Others say he was first sent to a mental hospital where he either committed suicide or was murdered.

An ally of Stalin and a fellow Georgian, Lavrentii Beria, the new security chief, held onto his position longer than his predecessor. An early Chekist, he joined under Dzerzhinskii with Stalin's personal recommendation. His first assignment in the Cheka was

... Feared Tool of the Soviet Regime

to infiltrate émigré groups; Beria spoke fluent French, German, and Czech. He was also one of the security officers who trailed Leon Trotsky to Mexico, where Stalin's former rival was axed to death.

Yezhov had terrorized his officers and decimated their ranks. Beria tempered the internal purges, though he did not stop them, and reinitiated intelligence work abroad. Though his equal in ruthlessness, Beria was, at least superficially, more polished and more intelligent than Stalin.

During World War II Beria's secret police were assigned additional responsibilities, including deportation and destruction of ethnic groups living in the Soviet Union, and guarding the front-line Russian troops to prevent retreat and desertion. Beria became a candidate Politburo member in 1939, deputy premier in 1941, and a full Politburo member in 1946.

By the time Stalin died in 1953, Beria controlled Soviet espionage activities, the labor camps, the militia, and more than a quarter-million troops. A likely replacement for Stalin, until other Politburo members turned on him, Beria was shot in 1953. Over the next three years at least 18 of his associates suffered a similar fate.

Establishment of KGB

During Beria's tenure, the security service underwent its final name changes. The People's Commissariat of State Security (NKGB) was established in February 1941 but was dismantled that June, after the German invasion. It was reestablished in April 1943 and in 1946 it became the Ministry of State Security (MGB).

An associate of Beria, V. S. Abakumov, was named head of the MGB. He was succeeded by S. D. Ignatiev in 1951. Beria replaced Ignatiev when the MGB and Ministry of Internal Affairs (MVD) merged in 1953. The present-day Committee for State Security (KGB) was established in March 1954.

After Beria's execution the security organs became directly responsible to the Politburo and trial and sentencing rights were given to the Ministry of Justice. Terrorized by its own security organs, the party wished to ensure its control in the future.

Ivan Aleksandrovich Serov became KGB chief in 1954 but Khrushchev dismissed him in 1958. His replacement, Alexander Nikolaevich Shelepin, held the position until 1961. Shelepin spent his career in the Komsomol before joining the KGB. In 1961 he returned to party work in the Central Committee.

From 1961 to 1967 Vladimir Yefimovich Semichastnyi headed the KGB. His term was marked by several "embarrassments," such as the defection of Svetlana Alliluyeva, Stalin's daughter, to the West

and a failed attempt to frame a visiting Yale professor as a spy so that he could be exchanged for a Soviet charged with spying in the United States.

Yuri Vladimirovich Andropov headed the KGB from 1967 until 1982. He was the first security organs chief to be elected general secretary, though not the first to try. Corson and Crowley attribute Andropov's success to "the avoidance of the kind of internecine bureaucratic warfare that in the past had dominated the resource allocations to intelligence and internal security elements." They also credit Andropov with setting up, while with the KGB, the complex system through which the Soviets illegally acquire Western technology for their military.

Born in 1914, Andropov worked as a Komsomol organizer for many years. He began his party career in 1944 as second secretary of a city party committee. He later worked in the Central Committee in Moscow before being sent to the embassy in Budapest in 1953. The following year he was promoted to ambassador. Andropov became a full Politburo member in 1973. In May 1982 he moved to the Secretariat and became general secretary following Brezhnev's death.

Andropov is compared by many experts, Soviet and American, to the intelligent and well-read Dzerzhinskii. While general secretary, Andropov worked to improve the KGB's public image. The KGB and Cheka began to be likened to each other in Soviet literature, movies, and public speeches. KGB personnel today refer to themselves as "Chekists."

Andropov rewarded the most intelligent and capable of his personnel; that is, he "promoted up." (Andropov's predecessors, Freemantle states, tended to "promote down," that is, promote the less threatening, and less capable, officers.) Viktor Chebrikov, the current KGB chief, benefited from Andropov's patronage; he was a deputy KGB chief under Andropov for many years.

Vitalii Fedorchuk, a career security service man and another Andropov protégé, replaced Andropov as KGB head in May 1982. The former KGB head in the Ukraine, Fedorchuk has been known for his brutal treatment of dissenters. In December 1982 Fedorchuk was transferred to head the Ministry of Internal Affairs. In January 1986 he was removed amid numerous other high-level political shake-ups and later joined the Inspector General's office. Fedorchuk's successor, Alexander V. Vlasov, 55, is a longtime party official with no police experience.

KGB chief since December 1982, Viktor Chebrikov became a candidate Politburo member in 1973 and a full member in April 1985. A metallurgical engineer by training, Chebrikov did party work in Dnepropetrovsk during Brezhnev's term there as party chief. Like Andropov, Chebrikov avoided the political intrigues rampant under Brezhnev.

material support to some of the anti-Bolshevik forces in the Civil War. Japan sent a large contingent of soldiers to occupy parts of Siberia, with an eye toward expanding its own empire in the Far East. Smaller groups of British, American, French, and Italian soldiers also entered Siberia. Except for the Japanese, the foreign troops left Russian territory by the end of 1920.

Independence movements among various Russian minority groups applied additional pressure on the Bolshevik regime. Estonia, Latvia, Finland, Poland, and Lithuania — declared independent by the Treaty of Brest-Litovsk — remained free of Russian domination after the Allied defeat of the Germans, despite Bolshevik pressure to bring them back into the Russian fold. The Red Army prevailed, however, in the Ukraine and in southern Russia, where it assumed control over several self-proclaimed independent states, including Georgia, Armenia, and Azerbaidzhan.

War Communism

Another important contribution to the Bolsheviks' victory in 1917 and their maintenance of control afterward was the use of War Communism. First, War Communism attempted to establish a communist society. The blueprint for achieving that goal was spelled out in the Program of the Eighth Party Congress in March 1919. Among other lofty goals, women were to be liberated "from all the burdens of antiquated methods of housekeeping"; the government was to move closer to the people; all nationalities were to be equal; and there was to be an all-out struggle against backwardness.

A second characteristic of War Communism, according to Dmytryshyn's description, was its "heavy contribution to economic chaos, both in industry and in agriculture." The deteriorating economy inherited by the Bolsheviks worsened with their nationalization and workers'-control decisions. This state capitalism theory of Lenin's only accelerated "economic disorganization." The Allied blockade of the country exacerbated the economic paralysis; the loss of much of the food-producing Ukraine exacerbated food shortages.

War Communism was also characterized, according to Dmytryshyn, by all production and distribution being controlled by the government. This was initially designed to mobilize all available resources and to ensure military priority for them, and to prevent sabotage. This meant also a drastic increase in the size of the bureaucracy and in confusion. Finally, War Communism brought about a direct, violent struggle between the new regime and the peasants. The Marxist Bolsheviks wanted to transform the peasants into agricultural workers under a large-scale, centralized system of agricultural production. Peasants had no interest in this and the government temporarily acceded to some of their wishes. But as the food situation grew more desperate, the government took action. When the peasants refused to cooperate with the collective farming plans, and refused to give up their food production for urban consumption, the government initiated Food Requisition Detachments to get food any way they could. These detachments are often now mentioned as a first step toward common government acceptance of the use of violence against its citizenry.

There were numerous other changes the Bolsheviks initiated, including separation of church and state, compulsory military training, and free education. Yet the growing estrangement between the peasants and the government over food, housing, and jobs was manifested in passive resistance to the regime's programs. Two popular methods were absenteeism among industrial workers and leaving large areas of land uncultivated among rural workers; riots and strikes also became more common. The government realized War Communism had not worked as a regular

People Running From Machine-Gun Fire Directed at Revolutionists in Petrograd, 1917

program. Years of war, the crop failure of 1920-21, and worker discontent slowed production almost to a halt. Lenin called a retreat with his New Economic Policy (NEP).

New Economic Policy

In the face of a serious threat to his rule, Lenin proclaimed the New Economic Policy as a way to ease the nation's financial woes. The New Economic Policy, declared in the spring of 1921, was a dose of free enterprise. In announcing it, Lenin said that "We are in a condition of such poverty, ruin and exhaustion of the productive powers of the workers and the peasants, that everything must be set aside to increase production." Under NEP, compulsory surrender of agricultural produce was replaced by a tax, leaving farmers free to sell the surplus on the open market. In industry, control of small factories reverted to private individuals. Individuals also were allowed to engage in retail trade and economic and market incentives substituted for coercion. The government also made substantial efforts to induce foreign capitalists to invest in the country's industrializtion process. Lenin was careful, however, in his liberalization program to maintain party control of the country's most important elements: heavy industry, transportation, foreign trade, and banks.

NEP succeeded in stabilizing the country and revitalizing the economy. After the shock of the 1920-21 famine dissipated (it was estimated that the famine caused the deaths of 5 million Russians), the economy began to move forward, equaling pre-World War I levels by 1928.

The Party

The victory of Bolshevism — later communism — in Russia is generally attributed to the climate of national unrest against tsarist absolutism, Russian military losses in World War I, and Lenin's organizational brilliance. The communists were able to remain in power mainly because they were far better organized than their opponents and because their totalitarian rule was little different from the absolutism Russia had known for centuries.

The American historian George Barr Carson, Jr., has noted that "perhaps it makes little difference whether Marxism took such deep root in Russia because the Russian tradition offered a uniquely fertile environment for the ideas of social ownership and management found in Marx or because revolutionaries steeped in the Russian heritage took Marxism as a weapon ... and gave it the peculiar cast it has by warping its growth to make it viable in a Russian society.... The Russian populace was conditioned by Russian history to be receptive to socialism."

The men who led the Russian Revolution considered themselves the vanguard of a socialist movement that would soon sweep the rest of the industrialized world. In March 1918 the party changed its name from the Russian Social Democratic Labor Party, Bolshevik, to the Communist Party, Bolshevik. The Russian Soviet Federated Socialist Republic was created by the first Soviet constitution, which the Fifth All-Russian Congress of Soviets adopted July 10, 1918. The Union of Soviet Socialist Republics was declared December 30, 1922. In March 1919 the first meeting of the Communist International (Comintern) was held in Moscow. Made up of communists from around the world, the Comintern existed to foment worldwide revolution. George Vernadsky noted in his *History of Russia* that

Terror and the KGB

Terror's role in Soviet society is as old as the Soviet regime itself. The Soviet Union's first leaders, of course, were professional terrorists and revolutionaries. The use of terror was legitimized by Lenin, who wrote in a letter on the Soviet criminal code:

> The law should not abolish terror.... The paragraph on terror should be formulated as widely as possible, since only revolutionary consciousness of justice and revolutionary conscience can determine the conditions of its application in practice.

Where terror was the most noticeable tool of the Soviet security organs under Lenin and Stalin, today increasing emphasis appears to be placed on positive public relations.

In May 1984 the State Security Committee (KGB) offered prizes for the best works on the KGB in literature, film, and television. The competition is part of the KGB's plans for its 70th anniversary celebration in 1987. Jerry F. Hough, in *How the Soviet Union Is Governed*, remarks on the KGB's current "educational role," with KGB officers trying to dissuade dissidents from their activities before arresting them. But the KGB still uses coercion and terror.

According to Brian Freemantle in *The KGB: Inside the World's Largest Intelligence Organization*, the "Red Terror," the period when the Soviet security organs first fought for control of the country, resulted in about a half-million deaths. A. Myagov, in *Rossiski Democrat*, alleges that 20 million Soviet citizens were executed by the Cheka's "Special Department."

Terror had its greatest use under Stalin. However, as Adam B. Ulam put it in *Russia's Failed Revolutions*:

> To look for an explanation of the terror of the 1930s in just Stalin's irrational characteristics is to postulate that he was entirely mad, an assumption that his ability to retain absolute power for twenty-five years renders quite absurd.... It is more reasonable to assume that terror on such a scale was the product of a deliberate design.

Thus, the Soviet security organs have evolved and developed, but they cannot be said to have changed. Dissidents and other "enemies of the regime" are still harassed, imprisoned, and murdered. Party leaders cannot be differentiated as "hardliners" or "closet liberals" because they are all products and supporters of the Soviet system. Similarly, the purpose of the Soviet security organs has consistently been to control the Soviet people. Terror has continually been used to ensure the survival of the Soviet regime.

Uprisings did actually occur in a few nations, but their achievements were short-lived: the Communist government of Bela Kun in Hungary lasted from March 21 until August 1, 1919, and a Bavarian Soviet government, founded on April 7, 1919, held power for an even shorter period. Revolutions were also planned for England and the United States, though in these countries the "plans" could hardly have been more than vague hopes.

By 1922 it was clear to the Soviet leaders that widespread revolution in the capitalist states was not likely to occur. The Comintern backed away from revolutionary agitation and embraced communist propaganda as its program. Propaganda activities, of course, did little to win friends for the Soviets in the community of nations.

The international position of the Soviet Union in the early 1920s was precarious. On the one hand, it encouraged the overthrow of its capitalist neighbors; on the other, it sought recognition as a legitimate state, though it refused to pay tsarist-era debts and canceled treaties. Putting aside world revolution, Moscow settled for relations with the other black sheep of Europe, Germany. The two nations signed the Treaty of Rapallo on April 16, 1922, establishing commercial ties. In 1924 diplomatic recognition was extended to the Soviet state by several nations — Great Britain, France, China, Mexico, Greece, Austria, Denmark, Sweden, Norway, and Italy. The United States did not offer diplomatic recognition to the communist regime until November 1933.

The Soviets established relations with their southern and eastern neighbors as well, negotiating treaties with Afghanistan, Persia, and Turkey. In China, the Soviets urged the local communists to support Chiang Kai-shek's nationalist forces. Once Chiang had the upper hand, however, he purged the Chinese communists and sent the Russian advisers back to Moscow.

Lenin's Death

Unlike his successors, Lenin never held the official title of party leader. But his need to safeguard communism required him to control the party, and this he did without serious challenge during his six years in power. It was not Lenin's intention to establish a "militarily powerful bureaucratic Russian state under a new tsar-autocrat," Robert C. Tucker wrote. But "by the seizure and monopolizing of power and the establishment of a party dictatorship, Lenin and the Bolsheviks had, however, created a medium in which a dynamic resurgence of statism could occur."

Lenin, the man most responsible for guiding the Russian Revolution through its most dangerous years, died January 21, 1924. The state honored him by building a mausoleum in Red Square to house his embalmed remains and by changing the name of the former capital from Petrograd to Leningrad. His death left the nation without a strong central leader.

When Lenin died there were no rules on how a successor should be chosen and no definite proof of whom Lenin favored to follow him. It was revealed later that in a letter to the Party Congress, dated December 22, 1922, he had praised Leon Trotsky's "exceptional abilities" while criticizing Joseph Stalin as "too rude" to hold high office.

Trotsky had been Lenin's right-hand man during the revolution and had organized the Red Army's victory in the Civil War. Trotsky also, however, had clashed bitterly with Lenin at times and was a Jew — both factors that became weapons against him. In fact, Stalin alone among the contenders for power had never had a major public conflict

British Prime Minister Winston Churchill, U.S. President Franklin D. Roosevelt, and Soviet Premier Joseph Stalin at the 1945 Summit Conference at Yalta, the Soviet Union

with Lenin. Stalin, named party general secretary in 1922, also had the advantage of having the strongest institutional hold. Because of his roles in government, Stalin had cultivated innumerable contacts throughout the country. After Lenin died, Stalin realized he had the opportunity to build those contacts into a powerful political tool. According to Jerry Hough, Lenin's later comments on Stalin's personality were indicative of Stalin's major obstacle in taking over the leadership. The "darker side to Stalin's personality" had caused a long history of uneasy relations with other party members.

Grigori Zinoviev and Lev Kamenev, the influential party leaders in Petrograd and Moscow, respectively, were the other top leaders in contention after Lenin died. Both had had major disagreements with Lenin but were nonetheless party leaders. Lenin had mentioned one other man, Nikolai Bukharin, as a possible successor. Bukharin, the party's leading theoretician and editor of *Pravda*, however, was never seriously considered by the other leaders.

To fill the vacuum after Lenin's death, a triumvirate was formed, composed of Stalin, Zinoviev, and Kamenev. All were members of the Politburo. The three-man rule effectively froze out Trotsky, who attacked the regime's policies, charging that the NEP was a retreat from socialism and claiming that he and his followers, the "left" faction, embodied the true spirit of communism. The "right" group, led by Bukharin, supported the NEP as a way to gain the trust of the peasantry. In the center were Stalin and his followers; they sought to use the NEP as a repugnant but necessary tool to further socialism in the Soviet Union.

In the power struggle of the 1920s, Zinoviev and Kamenev sided with Trotsky but their position failed to gain the support of party members. Stalin, on the other hand, had worked long and hard to extend his personal control over the party membership. A master of the political switch, Stalin sided first with Zinoviev and Kamenev, supporting their position but freezing out Trotsky. He backed the right, discredited Zinoviev and Kamenev, then attacked his new allies of the right wing. By 1927 Stalin's position was unequaled. He engineered the expulsion of his main rivals from the party and assumed personal control of the country. Trotsky was thrown out of the party in 1927 and banished from the Soviet Union in 1929.

THE SOVIET UNION UNDER JOSEPH STALIN

Stalin established dictatorial authority over every aspect of Soviet society, exercising unrestrained power in party and government affairs. Externally, he sought to protect his nation's interests in the face of rising threats in Germany and Japan. Internally, Stalin oversaw the forced industrialization of the Soviet economy and the brutal destruction of his domestic enemies.

Foreign Policy

The trend begun after the Civil War — developing Soviet contacts abroad — continued under Stalin's one-man rule. Originally intended to lend legitimacy to the regime, the policy in the late 1920s and early 1930s was designed to preserve peace while Moscow engaged in a widespread transformation of Russian society. The Soviets feared an alliance among the capitalist powers directed against the Kremlin; at the same time, they eagerly anticipated the demise of the capitalist structure. In *Expansion and Coexistence*, Adam B. Ulam wrote:

> The historical irony of the situation facing Soviet policymakers at the end of 1933 consisted in the fact that the fulfillment of many long-standing Soviet hopes in international politics promised not successes but a terrible danger to the Soviet Union. The League of Nations and the Versailles settlement had been the object of unremitting Soviet propaganda attacks ever since 1919. Now the League had been rendered even more ineffective since Japan and Germany were turning their backs on it. The Versailles settlement was crumbling, with Germany openly rearming and advancing far-reaching claims in other directions. The great crisis of the world economy had come to pass, but its political consequences were seen in the growth and successes of fascist movements rather than communist ones. The rising level of international tension threatened new wars, but the targets of Japanese and German militarism might become not the other capitalist powers but the Soviet Union. Seldom has an ideology played a comparable trick on its devotees as did communism in 1933: all the major desiderata of its philosophy of international relations were fulfilled, and their sum total promised disaster for the Soviet Union.

In the Far East, Japan embarked on a program of expansion, occupying southern Manchuria in 1929. China could do little more than protest to the powerless League of Nations. Emboldened, the Japanese in 1932 seized northern Manchuria, threatening the Soviet-controlled Chinese Eastern Railway. Moscow, preoccupied with collectivization and industrialization, had no desire for a war with the Japanese and, in 1935, sold the railroad to the Tokyo-controlled Manchurian government. To prevent Japanese expansion into Mongolia and Siberia, however, the Soviets patched up their differences with China's nationalist leader, Chiang Kai-shek, and supplied his armies with materiel and advisers. Soviet-Japanese tensions continued to build through the 1930s, resulting in clashes in 1938 and 1939 on the Manchurian-Mongolian border.

In Europe, Stalin faced the prospect of a rearmed Germany led by a virulently anticommunist dictator, Adolf Hitler. In 1932 Moscow signed nonaggression agreements with France, Finland, Estonia, Latvia and Poland. In 1934 the Soviet Union joined the League of Nations. The following year, Moscow concluded military alliances with France and Czechoslovakia. The Soviets' fears of fascist animosity were confirmed in November 1936 when Germany and Japan signed an "Anti-Comintern Pact" warning of the dangers of international communism; Italy and Spain signed the pact in 1937 and 1939, respectively.

Moscow's alliance with Czechoslovakia required the Soviet Union to aid the Czechs, provided France also offered assistance. French acquiescence in Hitler's seizure of the Sudetenland, a section of Czechoslovakia densely populated by Germans, relieved the Soviets of any responsibility to defend their Czech allies. However, the French (and British) capitulation to Hitler — the Soviets had not been invited to participate at the September 1938 Munich conference that sealed Czechoslovakia's fate — made Stalin and his colleagues question the value of the Soviet-French alliance.

The overriding desire of Stalin and his followers to avoid or at least postpone involvement in a war allowed the Soviets to engage in negotiations in 1939 with both the Germans and the nations lined up against Germany — Britain and France. The Western democracies sought to include Moscow in a united front against Hitler; the Germans sought a pledge of strict neutrality, which they received from Stalin August 23, 1939. With the threat of Russian aggression temporarily relieved, the Nazis attacked Poland September 1 and the British and French declared war September 3.

Under the terms of the 10-year German-Soviet agreement, Moscow was permitted to occupy eastern Poland. In July 1940 the Red Army occupied the independent states of Latvia, Estonia, and Lithuania; Finland, invaded in November 1939, was conquered by March 1940. To protect its eastern flank, the Soviet Union concluded a nonaggression treaty with Japan, Germany's ally, in 1941.

Stalin's treaty with Hitler delayed a confrontation between the Russian and German forces until June 1941. Concentrating his war effort in Western Europe, Hitler quickly dominated most of that region. Nearly two years after the invasion of Poland, the Germans turned east, catching their Soviet allies off guard.

Domestic Policy

Stalin's reign in the years leading up to World War II was marked by two widely felt programs — forced collectivization and industrialization and the great purges. By 1928 the successes of the New Economic Policy raised fears among government officials that private enterprise was gaining a foothold in Soviet society.

Five-Year Plan

In response, the government announced the first Five-Year Plan, calling for large-scale industrial projects to be financed by the production of agricultural collectives.

The plan met with widespread opposition from peasants working private plots of land. It was estimated that 5 million peasants who resisted collectivization were killed or dispatched to prison camps. By the end of the first Five-Year Plan, which was declared completed December 31, 1932, nine months ahead of schedule, 78 percent of Soviet land was controlled by the government.

In addition to the radical reconstruction of agriculture, the first Five-Year Plan sought to establish Russia's industrial capacity. Industries created or greatly enlarged included machine building, electric power, automobile production, chemicals, agricultural machines, and aviation. The advances achieved were dramatic, with industrial growth rates averaging 12 percent annually. The sacrifices imposed on Russian citizens, however, included scarcity of consumer goods, rationing of most available products, and significantly stepped-up government control of the economy.

The Purges

While his government was extending control over the lives of its citizens, Stalin moved against his enemies, real and imagined. The purge of the Communist Party began in 1934 when some 100 members were executed for their alleged involvement in the assassination of Sergei Kirov, the party leader in Leningrad (formerly Petrograd; the name was changed after Lenin's death). Over the ensuing four years, an estimated 8 million citizens were arrested on suspicion of disloyalty to the state. The main events of the purge era were the so-called "show trials" held to disgrace former high-ranking government and party officials. In 1936, 16 Bolshevik leaders, including Zinoviev and Kamenev, Stalin's former enemies in the Politburo, were convicted of treasonous activities; in 1937, 17 others were found guilty; and in 1938 an additional 21 former leaders were convicted. Of the 54 men tried, 50 received the death sentence.

The countrywide purge was carried out by the NKVD, the political police, headed by Nikolai Yezhov. Yezhov himself disappeared in 1938 and was replaced by Lavrentii Beria. The purge spread from party circles to include most branches of government. The military was decimated: three of the five Soviet marshals, including Mikhail Tukhachevskii, a Civil War hero, were removed, as well as 13 of the army's 15 commanders, 57 of its 85 corps commanders, and 110 of its 195 division commanders. But by far the effects of the purge were felt most severely at the top levels of government. By 1939 only Stalin and the exiled Trotsky were left of the original members of Lenin's Politburo. (Trotsky was assassinated in 1940 in Mexico, presumably on Stalin's orders.) Stalin was in complete control and even the mildest opposition voices had been stilled.

In 1936 the government formulated a new constitution to replace the document adopted in 1924. It guaranteed civil rights for all Soviet citizens, including the right to work, rest, medical care and education, religious freedom and "anti-religious propaganda," and the right to vote, but it declared that only one political organization, the Communist Party, was allowed to exist. The 1936 constitution also guaranteed equal rights to women and members of minority groups.

World War II

Stalin was stunned by Hitler's massive invasion of the Soviet Union on June 22, 1941. The premier (Stalin had named himself head of the government in 1941) reportedly went into seclusion for several days after the German attack. Nicholas Riasanovsky wrote:

> The blow was indeed staggering. Hitler threw into the offensive some 175 divisions, including numerous armored formations. A huge and powerful air force closely supported the attack.... The Germans aimed at another *Blitzkrieg*, intending to defeat the Russians within two or three months or in any case before winter. Although it encountered some determined resistance, the German war machine rolled along the entire front, particularly in the north towards Leningrad, in the center towards Moscow and in the south towards Kiev and Rostov-on-Don. Entire Soviet armies were

smashed and taken prisoner at Bialystok, Minsk and Kiev, which fell in September. The southern wing of the invasion swept along the Ukraine. In the north, Finnish troops [which had joined the German attack] pushed to the Murmansk railroad, and German troops reached, but could not capture, Leningrad. The city underwent a two-and-a-half year siege, virtually cut off from the rest of the country; its population was decreased by starvation, disease and war from four to two and a half million. Yet the city would not surrender, and it blocked further German advance north.

Soviet defenses and the onset of the Russian winter slowed the German attack, though not before Nazi troops reached the suburbs of Moscow. In the summer of 1942 the Germans directed their forces against industrial regions in the Ukraine and the Caucasus. By August they were at Stalingrad. The battle at Stalingrad lasted until February 1943, when the exhausted German troops surrendered to the Russians. The Russian victory at Stalingrad marked a turning point in the war. Aided by $11 billion in British and U.S. aid, the Soviets during the next two years drove back the overextended Germans.

Grand Alliance

Germany's attack created the Grand Alliance among the Soviet Union, Great Britain, (and after the December 7, 1941, Japanese attack on Pearl Harbor), the United States. The war years witnessed three summit meetings — at Tehran in December 1943, at Yalta in February 1945, and at Potsdam in July and August 1945. For Stalin, premier and generalissimo of the Soviet forces, the most pressing issue at the first meeting was the establishment of a second front in France, a proposal he urged on his allies at every opportunity after the German invasion. He got his wish June 6, 1944, when Allied forces invaded Normandy on the French coast, relieving pressure on the Soviet forces.

The subsequent summit sessions dealt with the joint war effort and the administration of a liberated Europe. Soviet-Allied relations resulted in several measures endorsed by all parties, including the Atlantic Charter in 1941 guaranteeing self-determination for all nations and the Declaration of the United Nations of 1942. To appease its allies, the Soviet Union disbanded the Comintern in 1943.

The war in Europe ended May 8, 1945, after Soviet troops, according to an Allied agreement, entered Berlin and overwhelmed the German defenders. The focus of the Allied war effort switched to the Far East. Japan surrendered formally September 2, 1945, after suffering atomic bomb attacks on Hiroshima August 6 and Nagasaki August 9. The Soviet Union entered the war against Japan August 8 and its forces proceeded to occupy Manchuria, the Kuril Islands, and the Japanese section of the island of Sakhalin.

Effects of the War

Estimates of the Russian casualties suffered during World War II range as high as 20 million. In addition to lives lost, the war caused widespread destruction. The Red Army practiced a scorched-earth policy during its retreats; the German forces followed similar practices when they quit Soviet territory. Riasanovsky described the devastation:

Much of the Soviet Union became an utter waste-land. According to official figures — probably somewhat exaggerated as all such Soviet figures tend to be — Soviet material losses in the war included the total or partial destruction of 1,700 towns, 70,000 villages, 6,000,000 buildings, 84,000 schools, 43,000 libraries, 31,000 factories and 1,300 bridges. Also demolished were 98,000 kolkhozes [collective farms] and 1,876 sovkhozes [agricultural factories]. The Soviet economy lost 137,000 tractors and 49,000 combine-harvesters as well as 7,000,000 horses, 17,000,000 head of cattle, 20,000,000 hogs and 27,000,000 sheep and goats.

Stalin and the Communist Party emerged from the war more powerful than ever. The war evoked a strong wave of nationalist feeling whose main beneficiary was the strong man himself. Stalin, during the war, came to be directly associated with the war effort, leading the Red Army to victory over the invaders in what became known in the Soviet Union as the "Great Patriotic War."

Postwar Developments

When World War II ended in Europe, the Red Army occupied the East European nations that were to become Moscow's satellites in the postwar era — Albania, Czechoslovakia, Poland, Yugoslavia, Bulgaria, Romania, and Hungary. Soviet troops also occupied East Germany. By 1948 all the occupied countries had established communist regimes based on the Soviet model. In most cases, communist governments were led by local insurgents, rather than directly from Moscow, although the Kremlin threw its weight behind the indigenous communists in the power struggles that followed the liberation of Europe.

The Soviet domination of Eastern Europe — in clear violation of pledges of noninterference made by Stalin at the Yalta Conference — was accomplished with relative ease after the rapid demobilization of Allied troops in Europe. Although U.S. leaders were alarmed by the rise of communist states in Eastern Europe, there was little popular sentiment for sending the recently returned troops back overseas to guarantee the development of democratic governments. To the Soviets, the sympathetic governments on their borders represented the creation of a long-desired buffer zone between the communist monolith and the capitalist world.

The Soviet expansion of influence brought on an era of Allied-USSR animosity, the so-called Cold War. Relations among the United States, Great Britain, and the USSR had begun to chill shortly after the end of hostilities. The Soviets refused to join the newly established United Nations Atomic Energy Commission and only reluctantly agreed to remove their forces from Iran after application of substantial pressure from the West. Winston Churchill, Britain's wartime prime minister, warned of the hazards of growing Soviet domination of Europe in a March 5, 1946, speech at Westminster College in Fulton, Missouri. In the speech, Churchill popularized the term "iron curtain," which he said had "descended across the continent." *(Churchill speech excerpts, p. 277)*

President Harry S Truman proposed March 12, 1947, that the United States take over from impoverished Great Britain responsibility for aiding the democratic governments in Greece and Turkey. At the time, the Greeks were engaged in a civil war that pitted government troops against communist forces and the Turks were facing mounting Soviet pressure. In proposing the aid plan, the president outlined to Congress what became known as the Truman Doctrine. He said:

> I believe that it must be the policy of the United States to support free peoples who are resisting attempted subjugation by armed minorities or by outside pressures.... The seeds of totalitarian regimes are nurtured by misery and want.... The free peoples of the world look to us for support in maintaining their freedoms. If we falter in our leadership, we may endanger the peace of the world — and we shall surely endanger the welfare of this Nation....

Despite fears in Congress that direct U.S. aid would undercut the United Nations and provoke a clash with Moscow, a $400 million program was approved.

To bolster European economies, the United States in June 1947 proposed the European Recovery Program, known as the Marshall Plan after its chief architect, Secretary of State George C. Marshall. The original plan included $17 billion in grants and loans to rebuild industry and agriculture in war-torn Europe; aid totaled $10.25 billion over three years. Although Marshall Plan assistance was offered to all European states, the Soviet Union and its satellites declined to participate. Instead, the Soviet-bloc countries in October 1947 formed the Communist Information Bureau (Cominform), the successor to Comintern, the propaganda organization abolished in 1943. Dominated by Moscow, Cominform was designed to orchestrate communist policy in Europe. Its early cohesion was shattered in 1948 when Marshal Josip Broz Tito, the Yugoslav leader, refused to toe the Cominform's Stalinist line.

'Containment' Policy

The Truman administration's Soviet policy was set forth in an article in the July 1947 issue of *Foreign Affairs*. Signed "X," the article was written by George F. Kennan, a State Department Soviet expert who became U.S. ambassador to Moscow in 1952. Kennan declared that "we are going to continue for a long time to find the Russians difficult to deal with" and argued that "the main element of any United States policy toward the Soviet Union must be that of a long-term, patient but firm and vigilant containment of Russian expansive tendencies." The term "containment" came to describe longstanding U.S. policy toward the Soviet Union.

Western opposition to the Soviet Union was consolidated by the April 4, 1949, signing of the North Atlantic Treaty, establishing a mutual defense pact among the United States and its Western allies: Belgium, Canada, Denmark, France, Great Britain, Iceland, Italy, Luxembourg, the Netherlands, Norway, and Portugal. A sense of urgency was added to plans for an anti-Soviet alliance with the announcement September 23, 1949, that the Soviets successfully had exploded an atomic bomb.

East-West tensions peaked in June 1948 when the Soviets blocked land transport of Allied supplies into Berlin, the former German capital jointly administered by the Soviet Union, Britain, France, and the United States. Rather than abandon the city, as the Soviets hoped, the Allies mounted an airlift to supply the estimated 2.5 million West Berliners under their jurisdiction. Thwarted, the Soviets lifted the blockade in May 1949. The Allies established the Federal Republic of Germany in May 1949. The seat of the new government was in Bonn. The Soviets responded with the establishment in Berlin of the German Democratic Republic in October 1949.

Additional worldwide tension was created in 1949 by the victory of Chinese communist forces, led by Mao Zedong, over the nationalist followers of Chiang Kai-shek. The Soviet Union welcomed the creation of a new communist state and signed a 30-year Sino-Soviet mutual aid pact February 14, 1950. The United States refused to recognize Red China, preferring to deal with the nationalist government headquartered on Formosa (now Taiwan).

The Cold War turned hot in Korea in 1950. The Southeast Asian nation had been divided between occupying forces at the end of World War II, the Red Army in the North and U.S. forces in the South. As in Germany, reunification failed and separate governments were established. The Soviet-backed North Koreans attacked South Korea June 25, 1950. President Truman ordered U.S. troops into Korea June 27, the same day that the United Nations requested military assistance from its members to halt North Korean aggression. The fighting quickly bogged down following China's entry into the conflict in November 1959. The war continued until the signing of an armistice July 27, 1953, four months after the death of Joseph Stalin.

While directing Soviet expansion in the postwar years, Stalin also had overseen the reconstruction of his damaged country. In 1946 the government revealed the terms of the fourth Five-Year Plan, a blueprint for the rebuilding of Soviet industry, particularly the production of farm machinery and trucks, iron and steel, coal, electrical power, timber, and cement. Moscow declared the plan was overfulfilled in four years and three months. The fifth Five-Year Plan, 1951 to 1955, similarly emphasized development of heavy industry.

3

Khrushchev Years: 1953-64

Stalin died March 5, 1953. Georgii Malenkov (Stalin's heir apparent) and Lavrentii Beria (chief of the secret police) led the succession battle. Malenkov emerged as both chairman of the Council of Ministers (or prime minister) and secretary of the Central Committee. Only a few weeks later, however, *Pravda* announced that Malenkov's "request" to resign his Secretariat duties had been granted at a Central Committee plenum. This made Nikita S. Khrushchev the de facto first (or general) secretary because he was the only Presidium member also in the Central Committee Secretariat. He moved quickly to expand his base of power.

Most Presidium members agreed after Stalin's death that considerably more attention had to be paid to consumer needs. The military had had priority over monetary and material resources not only during World War II but before and after it as well. Food shortages had been common in the years surrounding the war and livestock herds had been nearly wiped out. Most leaders were concerned that continued food problems would lead to unrest; a few, however, worried that paying too much attention to consumer issues would impair the military's ability to rebuild.

If the Soviet Union was to recover quickly from the war, the leaders had to get the people fed and industry on its feet. Civilian housing, especially in the cities, was scarce. Elementary and secondary education required extensive attention just to keep reducing the nation's high illiteracy rates. Skilled industrial workers were in limited supply. Additionally, the war had claimed the lives of vast numbers of men who would ordinarily be in the middle of their working lives, which meant there was also a shortage of knowledgeable midcareer workers and managers.

Only conservatives Lazar Kaganovich and Viacheslav Molotov were significantly opposed to consumer reforms that might impinge on military needs. Kaganovich, also a deputy prime minister in the Council of Ministers who dealt primarily with transportation and heavy industry, had been one of Stalin's top deputies. Molotov was Stalin's top foreign policy lieutenant during the 1930s and 1940s. These two men would play important roles in the continuing leadership struggle. The postwar battle over resource allocation really became an issue only after Stalin's death. Once Stalin died and other men moved to take over, it soon became evident that a system of governing other than Stalin's terror mechanism would be both necessary and desired to solve the nation's overwhelming problems.

Jerry Hough comments in *How the Soviet Union Is Governed* that four factors were uppermost in the minds of the Presidium members when they decided Khrushchev would be the man to emerge on top: his personality, his policy positions, his knowledge and expertise, and the fears his rivals — especially Beria — provoked.

Khrushchev poured into any new idea or initiative all available resources, seeking a panacea for each problem. Many of his programs were begun not because of their soundness but because of his hard lobbying work and an outwardly jovial personality that masked what some have called a violent cleverness. Western observers have said Khrushchev was the last "true believer." He took Marxism-Leninism seriously and was convinced of the likelihood of a great leap forward. He believed in the possibility of perfecting a "New Soviet Man" and of the Soviet Union's ability to overtake the West economically in a matter of decades.

The Thaw

The first few years after Stalin's death became known as "the thaw." This was widely perceived as a period when the political process gradually returned to more normal operation and daily life for the citizenry became less repressive. Khrushchev declared that government organizations must operate during traditional business hours, a departure from the secretive midnight rendezvous common during Stalin's regime.

Most important in the thawing process, however, was the repudiation of terror. Secret police chief Beria was arrested and executed, thereby eliminating not only other Presidium members' fears that Beria's wide-reaching terror apparatus would act against them, but also eliminating one of Khrushchev's opponents for power. Additionally, hundreds of prisoners held in Stalin's forced labor camps — the GULAG — were released and "rehabilitated." The new leaders began focusing on improving the country's living standards and ameliorating the legacy of strained relations with the West, particularly the United States.

In policy, Malenkov advocated spending more resources on consumer goods and developing a moderate stance toward relations with the West. Khrushchev leaned much the same way but emphasized agricultural reform.

Most celebrated of his early agricultural efforts was

the virgin lands program begun in 1954. Khrushchev chose Leonid I. Brezhnev to carry out the risky venture of cultivating for grain 32 million acres of previously unplanted ("virgin") land in Central Asia and Siberia. By 1960 more than 101 million acres had been opened for planting. After several years of famines and poor harvests, the program succeeded in temporarily relieving the agrarian crisis, but for long-term needs it was a failure. The Soviets were forced in the early 1960s to buy large quantities of grain from Canada and the United States.

Khrushchev and Malenkov continued battling over policy control. Each began ranking priorities differently. Khrushchev took a harder line toward the production of consumer goods and the increasing debate over resource priorities came to a head in late 1954. Shortly after Khrushchev castigated Malenkov's views at a Central Committee meeting, Malenkov was accused of administrative inexperience and was forced out as chairman of the Council of Ministers.

Malenkov's removal marked Khrushchev's opening for realigning the leadership. Nikolai Bulganin replaced Malenkov and Marshal Georgii Zhukov replaced Bulganin as minister of defense. At the July 1955 Central Committee plenum, two more of Khrushchev's allies were named to the Presidium — A.I. Kirichenko, from Khrushchev's Ukrainian stronghold; and Mikhail Suslov, a party apparat in charge of ideological matters. By most accounts, Suslov rose quickly, becoming in effect Khrushchev's "second secretary."

Khrushchev next acted against the conservatives he thought most dangerous to his rule — Kaganovich and Molotov. Kaganovich's power was diluted first when Anastas Mikoian (an "Old Bolshevik" Presidium member), M. G. Pervukhin, and M. Z. Saburov (both younger, less powerful Presidium members allied with Khrushchev) joined Kaganovich on the Council of Ministers. Then, in 1955, Kaganovich was removed and placed in a minor governmental position, although he remained a Presidium member. Molotov's demise did not come about all at once. Instead, it followed a pattern similar to the removal of many of Khrushchev's opponents — a gradual erosion of position and influence partly due to Khrushchev's lobbying efforts.

Khrushchev, apparently more confident of his position, began speaking and acting against Stalin's foreign policy. Khrushchev decried the philosophy of the two-camp world and the practice of shunning international organizational involvement, policies with which Molotov had been involved for decades. Already, in 1954, Khrushchev had shown his determination to pursue more friendly international relations by joining the United Nations International Labor Organization and UNESCO. The following year, the Soviets agreed to remove their forces occupying Austria, thus recognizing Austria's neutrality and independence. Neutrality for the Soviets had long been an ideological nonoption: A nation could not be neutral; it was either friendly or an enemy, socialist or imperialist. In return for these moves by the Soviets, leaders of the United States, France, and Great Britain assented to a week-long summit with the Soviets at Lake Geneva, Switzerland. Khrushchev and Bulganin — not Molotov — attended, meeting President Dwight D. Eisenhower of the United States. It was the first trip to the West by any top Soviet leader.

The week-long summit began July 18, 1955. Four items were on the agenda: the reunification of Germany, Euro-pean security, disarmament, and improvement of East-West relations. An overriding external objective of Khrushchev's was to rid West Berlin of the continued Allied military presence.

During the meeting, President Eisenhower made an "open skies" proposal to the Soviets, "to give to each other a complete blueprint of our military establishments" and "to provide within our countries facilities for aerial photography to the other country." Although the Soviets refused to rise to Eisenhower's bait, the meeting did result in the "spirit of Geneva," generally equated with a desire on both sides to seek accommodation and avoid confrontation. The four powers directed their foreign ministers to continue the talks in October, though the ministers' talks ended in a deadlock.

Khrushchev took his next step in revising Stalinist foreign policy at the July 1955 Central Committee session. Khrushchev made known his intent to reconcile with Yugoslavia's Tito and to use foreign aid to make advances toward Third World countries. This was in marked opposition to Molotov, who believed concessions to Tito would undermine bloc unity. Molotov's views found little support in the Central Committee and his influence began declining.

Also in 1955, the Soviets formed the Warsaw Pact to offset the North Atlantic Treaty Organization (NATO) and the rearming of West Germany. While Yugoslavia did not join the pact, relations between the countries did improve, with past animosity between the two blamed on Stalin.

Khrushchev brought to an abrupt, official halt the public adoration of Stalin when he gave his February 1956 speech to the 20th Communist Party Congress. Khrushchev had developed a strong contingent of allies among the delegates to the congress, primarily through numerous party personnel replacements in the republics and regions since Stalin's death. This was to prove crucial when the stunning nature of Khrushchev's speech became known.

The 'Secret Speech'

Khrushchev gave the main Central Committee report at the congress, an honored responsibility. He renounced bedrock Marxist-Leninist doctrines such as the inevitability of war among capitalist states and eventual revolutionary overthrow of those systems. He declared international socialist goals could be achieved peaceably and the danger of nuclear war dictated the prudent strategy of peaceful coexistence.

These central party doctrines could be renounced only by a man believing his control and power were secure. Yet, these were not the most striking aspects of Khrushchev's report. Instead, it was his so-called "Secret Speech," which, although never published in the Soviet Union, was distributed to party members there and abroad. In the speech, Khrushchev portrayed Stalin as a ruthless tyrant responsible for the deaths of thousands of innocent Russians and communists. Stalin put the country into jeopardy by liquidating high-ranking military officers during the war, Khrushchev charged. In Jerry Hough's words, Khrushchev depicted the post-1934 Stalin as "a morbidly suspicious man who suffered from a persecution phobia, saw enemies and spies in his closest associates and demanded servility and obsequiousness from all who served him."

The thawing process became one of "de-Stalinization." Khrushchev dramatically emphasized his intent by removing Stalin's remains from Lenin's mausoleum in the Krem-

Western Schools of Thought
On Khrushchev's Power Structure

Nikita Khrushchev's tenure as the party's first secretary was characterized by policy inconsistency and ambiguity. The frequent shifting of priorities between competing programs such as agrarian reform and building military strength made coherent policy impossible. While Khrushchev ostensibly supported agricultural reform, capital investments for farming lagged far behind those for heavy industry. In cultural areas, official leniency one day was offset by suppression of dissidents the next.

Khrushchev's statements on defense and foreign policy issues were less inconsistent with his actions than in other areas. But they changed often from steps toward détente with the West to steps certain to provoke confrontation, which made Soviet international conduct volatile and unpredictable.

Pressure Factor

Did changes in Khrushchev's individual priorities adequately explain these reversals and inconsistencies? Were the decisions Khrushchev's alone to make, or was he forced to bend to pressures applied by his colleagues and influential institutions? There are two broad schools of thought among Western analysts with regard to these questions, though in recent years distinctions between the two have blurred somewhat.

The first is generally referred to as the "conflict school." Carl Linden and certain other early Kremlinologists believed Khrushchev was a reformer who fought an uphill battle against powerful bureaucrats opposed to major reforms or concessions to the citizenry that might unleash uncontrollable consequences. Policy decisions, according to this school, resulted either from Khrushchev's defeat on certain issues or his attempts to outmaneuver or compromise with his opponents to ward off defeat. Accordingly, inconsistent, ambivalent policy flowed from Khrushchev's battles to implement at least parts of his reforms. Scholars of this view argued that the events of 1960 — particularly the U-2 spy incident — were evidence of Khrushchev's weakening position. When several men allied to Khrushchev were removed in 1960-61 from their posts on the Presidium (Politburo) and Central Committee, the conflict school said this indicated that serious division existed among the top leaders.

The opposing school of thought said Khrushchev was not inherently a reformer. According to Merle Fainsod, Khrushchev was an "essentially conservative transitional figure," willing to experiment with reforms but without necessarily calculating their consequences. Fainsod viewed Khrushchev as a typical national leader who sought to escape making hard choices by reacting to events rather than cogently responding to them. Khrushchev was willing not only to try new directions, but also to reverse those that no longer seemed to work.

This school viewed Khrushchev's inconsistency as being similar to Lenin's. Policy ambivalence was not the result of political battles; rather it was largely attributed to Khrushchev's changing perceptions of his own policies and the needs of the Soviet Union. Accordingly, this school did not see the 1960-61 Presidium and Central Committee personnel changes as a political move against Khrushchev engineered by his rivals. Khrushchev himself may have had a hand in removing his own Presidium allies. According to Jerry Hough, this school of thought interprets the "reduction in the number of Central Committee secretaries on the Presidium . . . as an attempt to prevent the Secretariat from dominating the Presidium and thereby to strengthen the position of the one individual (Nikita Khrushchev) who headed the three major collective institutions below the level of the Presidium — the Central Committee Secretariat, the Council of Ministers, and the Bureau of the Central Committee for the RSFSR [Russian Soviet Federated Socialist Republic]."

Role of Majority

In synthesizing the views of the two schools, Hough asserts that the real issue was whether Khrushchev had to have a majority in the Presidium to push through his policies. The abrupt changes in those policies may have indicated that Khrushchev was not always forced to act according to the wishes of a collective leadership. In *How the Soviet Union Is Governed*, Hough said:

> In judging the structure of power in the Khrushchev period, we must ultimately rely upon our sense of the nature of committee politics and the meaning of different patterns of policy outcomes that emerge. . . . The natural outcome of a divided collective committee is deference to the key individual interests of most of the respective members (logrolling, if you will), compromise on the major issues dividing the committee, and (except in rare cases), gradualism and even conservatism in the change of major policy.

The leadership was not divided in 1964 when it engineered a major policy shift: Khrushchev's removal.

lin's Red Square. Nearly 30 years of Soviet history became inexplicably absent from rewritten schoolbooks. Towns and streets bearing Stalin's name were renamed; Stalingrad became Volograd, for example.

Scholars still debate Khrushchev's motives for making these sensational revelations at the congress. Khrushchev later explained that he was trying to preclude recurrence of "such phenomena in the future" and to reinvigorate Leninist "norms" in the party. Subsequent events make other motivations more likely, for the speech had two significant effects. (Excerpts from "Secret Speech," Appendix, p. 279)

First, Molotov, Kaganovich, Malenkov, and Kliment Voroshilov were accused of attempting to thwart Khrushchev's proposal to disclose Stalin's crimes and of opposing his efforts to halt the so-called cult of the individual. Khrushchev's control was greatly strengthened — and his opponents' guard raised further — when the Party Congress named the 133 members of the Central Committee. More than one-third were newly elected, and many could directly trace their elevation to earlier associations with Khrushchev. Full Presidium membership did not change, though five new candidate members were chosen who appeared to owe their promotions to Khrushchev.

Following the congress, Stalin's "Old Guard" came under attack. Dmitri Shepilov replaced Molotov as foreign affairs minister. Kaganovich was relieved from his minor post as chairman of the State Committee on Labor and Wages and named to a still lower ministerial post. Molotov and Kaganovich remained, however, on the Presidium.

Polish and Hungarian Rebellions

Second, the speech had severe unintended consequences outside the USSR. Party control broke down in 1956 in Poland and Hungary. In late June, Polish workers rioted, demanding eased restrictions and a degree of autonomy. A delegation including Molotov, Kaganovich, Khrushchev, and Mikoian went hurriedly to Warsaw. After negotiations, the Poles were granted some concessions.

Similar demonstrations in Hungary in late October developed into a revolution that placed a liberal communist, Imre Nagy, at the head of the government. Soviet troops entered Budapest October 23 but withdrew seven days later. Subsequently, however, Nagy appealed for the support of Hungary's "fighters for freedom," pledged an end to the one-party system, and called for Hungary's withdrawal from the Warsaw Pact. This meant the Hungarian revolt was going far beyond the limited change that the Soviets had decided to permit in Poland.

Eight Soviet military divisions struck at Budapest and other Hungarian cities November 4, launching a ruthless repression of the rebellion. Organized resistance collapsed quickly and thousands of Hungarians fled into Austria. Janos Kadar, who succeeded Nagy, was faced with crippling strikes and the Soviets came under worldwide attack for their display of Stalinist brutality. The United States, while declining to intervene directly in Hungary, mounted a massive propaganda campaign in the United Nations and elsewhere against the Soviet actions. Yet widespread condemnation was tempered by the Suez Canal crisis that competed with the Hungarian revolution for worldwide attention.

Egypt had nationalized the canal in July. In late October, Israeli, French, and British forces attacked Egypt, a move condemned by the United States. Bickering among the Western allies prevented a united rebuke to the Soviet repression in Hungary.

Eisenhower Doctrine and Suez Crisis

The Suez crisis created a power vacuum in the Middle East because of the withdrawal of the British and French. The Eisenhower administration concluded that the U.S. commitment to resist communism in the region had to be fortified. Accordingly, on January 5, 1957, President Eisenhower went before a joint session of Congress to urge support for a declaration that was promptly dubbed the Eisenhower Doctrine.

The Joint Resolution to Promote Peace and Stability in the Middle East (H J Res 117) declared that "if the President determines the necessity . . . [the United States] is prepared to use armed forces to assist . . . any nation or groups of nations requesting assistance against armed aggression *from any country controlled by international communism.*" [Emphasis supplied.]

The resolution did not draw a precise geographical line around the area to which it was intended to apply. The Senate and House committee reports on the resolution accepted the administration's view and defined the Middle East as the area bounded by Libya on the west, Pakistan on the east, Turkey in the north, and the Sudan in the south. The Senate report said that no precise listing of nations was included in the resolution because this "would restrict the freedom of action of the United States in carrying out the purposes of the resolution."

The first test of the Eisenhower Doctrine came in 1958 following a coup in Iraq in which the pro-Western government of King Faisal II was overthrown and replaced with a regime favorable to the Soviet Union and the United Arab Republic (UAR). The new Iraqi government immediately withdrew from the Baghdad Pact — the 1955 mutual defense treaty among Britain, Iran, Iraq, Pakistan, and Turkey.

When the government of Lebanon came under similar pressures and its president requested U.S. assistance, Eisenhower ordered U.S. Marines from the 6th Fleet in the Mediterranean to land in Lebanon to protect the government. Citing the Eisenhower Doctrine, the president said July 15, 1958, that Lebanon's territorial integrity and independence were "vital to United States national interests and world peace." The UAR and the Soviet Union, Eisenhower charged, were trying to overthrow the constitutional government of Lebanon and "install by violence a government which subordinates the independence of Lebanon to . . . the United Arab Republic."

Iraq's withdrawal from the Baghdad Pact convinced the Eisenhower administration that the three remaining "northern tier" members of the organization needed an additional pledge of U.S. support in resisting communism. With the Middle East resolution as a basis, the United States initiated negotiations with Turkey, Iran, and Pakistan on defense arrangements, bringing the United States into closer cooperation with the Baghdad Pact, which was renamed the Central Treaty Organization (CENTO). Three identically worded executive agreements were signed in March 1959 between the United States and each of the three nations. Washington pledged to come to the defense of the three countries in the event of communist aggression or subversion.

The Cold War, McCarthy, and the 'Red Scare'

Shortly after the close of World War II, rising tensions between the United States and the Soviet Union, coupled with the disclosure that a communist espionage ring had been operating in Canada, prompted a wave of concern over espionage and subversion within the United States.

Few movements in U.S. history have so pervaded the fabric of national life as the anticommunist movement of the late 1940s and early 1950s. Not only did states have their own anticommunist statutes and legislatures their own un-American activities committees, but loyalty oaths and investigations became commonplace both in public and private employment. Some veterans and patriotic organizations became involved in the movement to expose and eliminate alleged communist influence in various aspects of American life.

There were widespread efforts to weed out communists and communist sympathizers in the legal profession, on college and university faculties, in the mass communications field (especially motion pictures and radio), and in areas of industry not directly involved in the nation's security.

Fear of communist infiltration of the federal government first focused on the State Department. The revelations in the *Amerasia* case, involving the discovery of secret U.S. records in that allegedly procommunist magazine's files, began a series of congressional investigations of communist subversion that continued for years. They also figured in President Truman's initiation of a comprehensive loyalty program for all government employees in 1947.

The same year, Congress reached out beyond the government in its anticommunist crusade. It moved against communist labor leaders by attaching a noncommunist affidavit requirement to the Taft-Hartley Act, and the House Un-American Activities Committee (HUAC) undertook a controversial probe of the motion picture industry. Ronald Reagan, then the newly elected president of the Screen Actors Guild, testified as a friendly witness before the Un-American Activities Committee in October 1947. He supported the blacklist, which Hollywood producers created to deny work to actors and writers suspected of having communist ties.

But it was the committee's investigation in 1948 of State Department official Alger Hiss, and Hiss's subsequent conviction for perjury, that established internal communism as a leading political issue and the committee as an important political force. The case against Hiss was based on testimony by Whittaker Chambers and Elizabeth Bentley, members of the Communist Party, who alleged that at least 75 government officials had been involved in spying during the 1930s. The charges against Hiss, which at one point appeared flimsy to other committee members, were vigorously developed by Richard Nixon, then a young member of the committee. Truman characterized the investigation as a "red herring."

Between 1950 and 1954 Congress enacted a wide variety of restrictive legislation. High priests of the anticommunist movement were congressional investigators — members of the HUAC, the Senate Internal Security Subcommittee, and, briefly, the Senate Permanent Investigations Subcommittee headed by Joseph R. McCarthy, R-Wis. Viewed as heroes by their supporters, as witch-hunters and character assassins by opponents, these men were largely responsible for the Internal Security Act of 1950, the Communist Control Act of 1954, and other laws.

With the return of Congress to Republican control in 1953, McCarthy assumed chairmanship of the Senate Permanent Investigations Subcommittee, and under him that group became a headline forum for anticommunist charges.

On June 19, 1953, Julius and Ethel Rosenberg, a married couple convicted of conspiracy to commit espionage by passing atomic information to the Soviets, died in the electric chair. The Rosenbergs were the first civilians to be executed for spying, and their case aroused considerable — and lingering — controversy.

Prior to the 1954 midterm elections, Republicans and Democrats traded charges with abandon. McCarthy accused the Democrats of "20 years of treason," and the Democrats, hoping to embarrass the Eisenhower administration, countered with legislation to outlaw the Communist Party. The result was the Communist Control Act, most disputed of the assortment of antisubversive legislation enacted in 1954. The CCA was a patchwork law of doubtful impact.

Anticommunist fervor reached its peak in 1954, but the movement began to wane after the Senate censured McCarthy late in the year. In ensuing years the courts and Congress curbed some of the most extreme laws and regulations. Some others never were enforced completely or were quietly repealed. The demise in January 1975 of HUAC, renamed the Internal Security Committee in 1969, ended 30 years of controversy over its zealous pursuit of subversives.

A new measure of anticommunist sentiment developed in the early 1960s. The Supreme Court in 1961 upheld an order requiring the Communist Party to register under the Internal Security Act. Congress tightened antisubversion acts and tried to curb the flow of communist propaganda into the United States. New anticommunist organizations, notably the John Birch Society, also emerged — to the accompaniment of widespread criticism and with marked lack of political success.

Domestic Difficulties

After the Hungarian problems, Tito again broke with Moscow. This further discredited Khrushchev and his attempts to reconcile with Yugoslavia. It also kept the opposition (namely, Molotov) in a better position from which to maintain or rekindle support.

Other series of events undermining Khrushchev's control of the leadership came from the domestic economic front. Industrial difficulties led, at the December 1956 Central Committee meeting, to a reorganization of the country's economic planning "machinery." The industrial management specialist on the Presidium was named chairman of the State Economic Commission and was given broad new powers to run the national economy. Khrushchev was opposed to these moves, but the Supreme Soviet nonetheless approved them February 12, 1957. The next day, Khrushchev counterattacked with a plan to decentralize economic power.

Western analysts have questioned why, if Khrushchev controlled the leadership and opposed the changes, he waited until February to move against his detractors. Three possible reasons stand out: the satellite countries were, by February, under control; the virgin lands program had brought in a good harvest; and Khrushchev had developed a program behind which he believed the Central Committee would rally. In short, Khrushchev was in a much better position in February to launch his attack.

Khrushchev's counterprogram was designed to temper the power of the highly centralized economic ministries that had flourished under Stalin by abolishing most of them and placing much of their industrial responsibilities in the hands of new regional economic councils — or sovnarkhozes. Khrushchev employed the Supreme Soviet in his effort to line up program support among regional officials. It was not a difficult task because decentralization would directly benefit these men at the expense of entrenched urban industrial administrators. Khrushchev apparently did not fully comprehend the power of these bureaucrats. They joined with Khrushchev's opponents on the Presidium in a direct effort to overthrow him.

The men who became known as the "antiparty" group moved against Khrushchev in June 1957. When it came time for the showdown, the antiparty group had grown to the point where Mikoian, Suslov, and Kirichenko were the only full Presidium members openly supporting Khrushchev. Spearheaded by Malenkov, Molotov, and candidate member Shepilov (and to a somewhat lesser degree Bulganin, in whose office the group met), the men called for Khrushchev's resignation. The group tried to announce the resignation immediately, so as to present the Central Committee with a fait accompli. Khrushchev maneuvered quickly and refused to resign. He cleverly demanded a Central Committee meeting to decide the issue. The Presidium met in almost continuous session for several days hoping to forestall such a meeting, but regional officials swarmed upon Moscow, rallied behind Khrushchev, and demanded a plenum.

Firm support for Khrushchev among both the Central Committee and candidate Presidium members blocked the "resignation." The rising young Central Committee members from the republics likely saw themselves as beneficiaries if Khrushchev retained his position and as direct losers if he did not.

After the situation settled, Khrushchev returned fire toward his opponents. Malenkov, Kaganovich, Molotov,

and Shepilov were accused of "antiparty, factional methods in an attempt to change the composition of the party's leading bodies" and of fighting the party line, according to Soviet announcements. All four lost their Presidium and Central Committee memberships and their governmental posts. Other conspirators were demoted or removed immediately, but Bulganin was not ousted from the Presidium until 1958 and Voroshilov did not resign his posts until 1960.

Khrushchev's real triumphs came when he reconstructed the Presidium leadership, Hough and other experts have said. Full membership expanded to 15. Khrushchev rewarded not only numerous lower level supporters but also Marshal Zhukov, who was promoted from candidate status. Zhukov, however, lasted only four months. The strong-willed military leader was removed from both the Presidium and as defense minister amidst accusations of political deficiency and of "surrounding himself with sycophants and flatterers." The charges were largely spurious. His removal marked yet another instance of a Soviet leader doing away (through terror or other means) with any perceived source of competition for power.

Expanding the Presidium also increased Khrushchev's potential power on the Central Committee Secretariat. Now, eight other Presidium members were also Central Committee secretaries. By giving these men additional power, he also made them more "his men." In 1958 Khrushchev donned another hat: chairman of the Council of Ministers. The man who had been a party worker all his career now was head of the government as well.

Khrushchev did not slow down his efforts to bring about a thoroughly industrialized, equally competitive superpower after his 1957 successes. In fact, after 1957 Khrushchev was able to pursue his policies more freely. He abolished the machine tractor stations and pushed educational reform to benefit working-class children and peasants. For the most part, however, his domestic initiatives failed; and, as with many of his foreign adventures, they became known as Khrushchev's "hare-brained schemes."

U.S.-Soviet Summitry

The Soviets announced August 26, 1957, that they successfully had tested an intercontinental ballistic missile (ICBM). And Moscow disclosed October 4 that it had placed into orbit Sputnik I, a 184-pound satellite. Sputnik II, weighing more than 1,100 pounds and carrying a dog named Laika, was launched November 3. Not until January 31, 1958, did the United States launch its first satellite, a 30-pound cylinder. Besides stirring alarm in the United States that it was falling behind in education and technological advances, the successful Soviet space shots lent credence to Moscow's claims that it had developed ICBMs capable of carrying nuclear warheads.

Meanwhile, Khrushchev's political intrigues permitted his assumption of complete power in 1958, after he engineered the removal of his prime minister, Bulganin. Khrushchev juggled the two conflicting themes of Soviet foreign policy: coexistence and pursuit of Soviet interests. As Adam Ulam wrote:

> Thus between 1957 and 1962 Khrushchev's regime pursued two apparently contradictory policies: one of militant communist expansionism designed

The Nixon-Khrushchev 'Kitchen Debate'

An unlikely public give-and-take session between Soviet leader Nikita Khrushchev and U.S. vice president Richard Nixon made worldwide headlines when Nixon visited Moscow July 22-August 2, 1959.

The trip was a follow-up to a June 28-July 13 visit to the United States by Nixon's Soviet counterpart, First Deputy Premier Frol R. Kozlov. After arriving in the Soviet capital, Nixon quickly found himself defending actions of his government at home; the previous week Congress had passed a "Captive Nations" resolution and President Dwight D. Eisenhower had issued a declaration calling on Americans to "study the plight of the Soviet-dominated nations and to recommit themselves to the support of the just aspirations of those captive nations." Khrushchev condemned the resolution as "rude" interference in "our internal affairs" and added that "the camp of the socialist countries has never before been so solid and powerful as now."

But the most publicized event was the informal Nixon-Khrushchev exchange, which took place before reporters and videotape cameras at a U.S. trade exhibition. It was soon dubbed the "Kitchen Debate" because part of the colloquy took place near a display of an American home, complete with a kitchen. Viewing the model home, Khrushchev said, "You think the Russian people will be dumbfounded to see this? But I tell you all our modern homes have equipment of this sort, and to get a flat you have only to be a Soviet visitor, not a citizen."

To which Nixon replied: "We do not claim to astonish the Russian people. We hope to show our diversity and our right to choose. We do not wish to have decisions made at the top by government officials who say that all homes should be built in the same way. Would it not be better to compete in the relative merits of washing machines than in the strength of rockets? Is this the kind of competition you want?" Khrushchev: "Yes, that's the kind of competition we want, but your generals say we must compete in rockets...." *(Debate excerpts, p. 290)*

Khrushchev and Nixon during the Kitchen Debate, with Leonid I. Brezhnev at right.

to weaken the West's position or to push it out of Berlin, the Middle East, Africa and even Latin America; and the other a strenuous search for accommodation (or more) with the United States.

Khrushchev's overriding interest in foreign affairs was winning the removal of the continuing Allied presence in West Berlin, 110 miles within East Germany. West Berlin and the status of the Eastern bloc nations were discussed during Vice President Richard Nixon's July 22-August 2, 1959, visit to the Soviet Union. Nixon and Khrushchev also publicly debated the quality of life in the United States and the Soviet Union. *(Kitchen Debate, box, this page)*

In September 1959 Khrushchev made a cordial visit to the United States, though little came out of his meetings with Eisenhower except the intangible "spirit of Camp David." However, the two leaders agreed to a summit meeting scheduled for May 1960, to be followed by an Eisenhower visit to the Soviet Union.

The summit meeting was marred, however, by the May 5, 1960, disclosure that the Soviets had shot down a U.S. spy plane, a U-2, over their territory. The routine flights had been made since 1956, the planes flying at 70,000 feet to elude Soviet air defenses. But in May a recently developed Soviet ground-to-air missile hit the U-2, forcing the pilot, Francis Gary Powers, to bail out. Powers, an ex-Air Force flyer employed by the Central Intelligence Agency, was captured and the Soviets retrieved the wreckage of the spy plane.

After some initial denials of responsibility, the Eisenhower administration admitted May 9 that the flights occurred with the full knowledge and support of the government. The reaction from Moscow was threatening. Khrushchev warned Turkey, Pakistan, and Norway that "if they allow others to fly from their bases to our territory we shall hit at those bases." He added May 11 that Powers would be tried "severely as a spy" for his "gangster and bandit raid." And as for his invitation to Eisenhower to visit the USSR June 10, he said, "The Russian people would say I was mad to welcome a man who sends spy planes over here like that."

The summit meeting in Paris, attended by Eisenhower, Khrushchev, British prime minister Harold Macmillan, and French president Charles de Gaulle, opened May 16 and quickly broke down into mutual recrimination. Khrushchev condemned the surveillance missions. In reply, Eisenhower defended the overflights as an essential precaution against surprise attack. Nevertheless, he said,

The shoe he used to pound the desk sits in front of Premier Nikita S. Khrushchev at the United Nations in October 1960. To Khrushchev's left is Foreign Minister Andrei Gromyko.

"These flights were suspended after the recent incident and are not to be resumed."

The conference ended in deadlock. The Soviets brought Powers to trial and, on August 9, sentenced him to 10 years in prison. He was released February 10, 1962, in exchange for the Soviet "master spy" Rudolph Abel, apprehended by the United States in 1957 and sentenced to 30 years.

Khrushchev returned to the United States in September to attend a Soviet-proposed meeting of the heads of government of the 82 members of the United Nations. Ostensibly there to help reopen disarmament negotiations, Khrushchev used the gathering to promote a plan to replace UN General Secretary Dag Hammarskjöld, whom the Soviets charged was a "willing tool" of the Western powers. The plan called for replacing Hammarskjöld with a three-member executive committee representing, according to Khrushchev, three UN groups: "the military blocs of the Western powers, socialist states, and neutralist countries." The Soviet proposal garnered little support among the world leaders. The heated debate was punctuated by Khrushchev's shouted interruptions and desk-pounding (with his fists and, in a celebrated incident, his shoe). His plan a failure, Khrushchev returned to Moscow October 13.

Germany and Berlin

Despite the failure of the summit meeting the previous year, Khrushchev was eager to meet and size up the new U.S. president, John F. Kennedy, elected in November 1960. A Kennedy-Khrushchev meeting was arranged for June 3-4, 1961, in Vienna. President Kennedy said afterward on June 6 that their "most somber talks" mainly dealt with Germany and Berlin. Khrushchev had made plain his determination to sign a peace treaty with East Germany, a move long interpreted in Washington as part of the Soviet effort to force Western powers out of West Berlin. Kennedy, in press conferences in June and July,

stressed the "real intent" of the Soviets to dislodge the Western powers and on July 25 called for an immediate buildup of U.S. and NATO forces. Khrushchev replied, in speeches August 7, 9, and 11, with threats of Soviet mobilization and boasts that Moscow could build a 100-megaton nuclear bomb.

Then, with no advance warning, the East German regime August 13 began sealing off the sector border between East and West Berlin to stem the flow of East Germans to the West. (By 1961 nearly 3 million East German citizens had "voted with their feet" by emigrating to the West.) The sealing off virtually was completed before the Western allies agreed on a formal protest, which the Soviets ignored. Within a few months, the East Germans built a mortar and barbed-wire wall running along the entire sector border, effectively stopping the transit of refugees from East to West. But Khrushchev's hopes for Western concessions in response to his actions failed — he announced October 17 that he was withdrawing his year-end deadline for the signing of a German peace treaty — and the Berlin Wall came to symbolize communist oppression.

Cuban Missile Crisis

A more serious confrontation between Washington and Moscow developed in Cuba in 1962. Since the successful revolution in 1959, Cuban leader Fidel Castro had moved his government ever further into the Soviet sphere of influence. In January 1962, at Washington's urging, Cuba was expelled from the Organization of American States. Cuba's economic isolation in the West led to increased Soviet shipments of arms and goods.

The steady stream of Soviet supplies to Cuba was viewed with increasing alarm in Washington. Finally, on October 22, 1962, President Kennedy broadcast to the nation an address in which he announced that aerial reconnaissance photos revealed that the Soviets secretly were building launching sites in Cuba for medium- and intermediate-range ballistic missiles capable of reaching many U.S. cities. The "secret, swift and extraordinary buildup" of a nuclear capability in Cuba, the president said, "is a deliberately provocative and unjustified change in the status quo which cannot be accepted by this country...."

Kennedy announced the imposition of "a strict quarantine of all offensive military equipment under shipment to Cuba," adding that "ships of any kind bound for Cuba, from whatever nation or port, will, if found to contain cargoes of offensive weapons, be turned back." "Any nuclear missile launched from Cuba against any nation in the Western Hemisphere" would be regarded, Kennedy said, "as an attack by the Soviet Union on the United States requiring a full retaliatory response upon the Soviet Union." And the president called on Khrushchev "to halt and eliminate this clandestine, reckless and provocative threat to world peace."

An estimated 25 Soviet-bloc vessels were moving toward Cuba as the Navy quarantine officially began October 24. But the Soviets recalled several ships that might have been challenged and on October 27 Kennedy received two letters from Khrushchev broaching a compromise. The first letter was conciliatory, offering to remove the weapons from Cuba. The second letter proposed in return the removal of U.S. intermediate-range ballistic missiles from bases in Turkey, an offer Kennedy refused to consider. Khrushchev wrote again October 28, agreeing to dismantle the Cuban missiles and failing to mention any reciprocal

U.S. move in Turkey. President Kennedy announced November 20 that "all known offensive missile sites in Cuba have been removed." He declared the quarantine lifted. *(Cuban missile crisis documents, Appendix, p. 291)*

What Kennedy saw as Khrushchev's "statesmanlike decision" to remove the Cuban missiles appeared differently to many communists. They viewed it as the leader of the world's socialists backing down to the leader of the capitalist camp. The Chinese in particular lost whatever little faith they had retained in Moscow's ability to lead the struggle against imperialism. And at home Khrushchev's behavior eroded his support in the party. Khrushchev, Adam Ulam has written, "was too unpredictable and too arbitrary to be tolerated as head of the regime. He had ceased to be respected and trusted and was not feared enough — a fatal combination for the head of a totalitarian state."

Sino-Soviet Relations

Moscow's dealings with its massive Chinese neighbor rarely have been smooth. Present-day animosities date at least to the nineteenth century. When presented with a weak and ineffective government in China, Russia, like other major powers, seized Chinese territory and forced the Chinese emperor to sign treaties legalizing the transfers. The People's Republic of China (PRC) officially does not recognize the legality of these agreements, which it terms "unequal treaties." The Soviets have refused to revise the pacts, and China has been unwilling to drop its claims on the territory in question, leaving most of the Sino-Soviet border in dispute.

In the twentieth century, Soviet aid to the Chinese communists prior to their victory over the nationalists was inconsistent and often came with strings attached. But in 1950, when Chinese Communist Party Chairman Mao Zedong went to Moscow and signed a treaty of friendship and alliance with the Soviet Union, old Sino-Soviet animosities appeared to be buried. Western observers saw the new relationship as a logical union of two communist powers. In fact, the similarities in ideologies obscured fundamental differences and did nothing to halt numerous Soviet efforts to interfere in internal Chinese politics.

Nikita Khrushchev's performance at the 20th Party Congress in 1956 sent shock waves through the communist world; nowhere was the impact of peaceful coexistence and de-Stalinization greater than in Beijing. The Chinese had endorsed a never-ending struggle against the imperialist camp, and they found much to criticize in the unthinkable notion of peaceful coexistence.

Since 1950 Chinese leaders perceived the United States as attempting to surround China, cut it off from the world, and replace its communist regime with the government of Chiang Kai-shek on Taiwan. There were U.S. troops all around China: on Taiwan, in Japan, in the Philippines, and in South Korea. There were U.S. advisers in South Vietnam and British troops in Burma and Malaysia. China's only opening to the outside world was through the Soviet Union, and Mao and his colleagues saw Soviet atomic weapons as the ultimate guarantor of Chinese security against the West.

Khrushchev, eager to maintain the image of a monolithic communist bloc led by the Soviet Union, pacified his radical Asian allies with aid and promises of nuclear pro-

U.S.-Soviet Relations And the 1964 Election

The Republican Party and its presidential nominee, Sen. Barry Goldwater of Arizona, tried to make U.S.-Soviet relations a central issue of the 1964 presidential election. The party platform, which reflected the views of Goldwater supporters, sharply castigated the Democrats for their alleged soft attitude toward the Soviets.

The platform asserted that "this [Johnson] administration has sought accommodations with Communism without adequate safeguards and compensating gains for freedom." This theme was elaborated with criticism of the sale of wheat to the Soviet Union, communist advances in Laos and South Vietnam, and failure to take any action in response to the "wall of shame" in Berlin.

In his nomination acceptance speech Goldwater said, "The Republican cause demands that we brand Communism as the principal disturber of peace in the world today.... And we must make clear that until its goals of conquest are absolutely renounced, and its relations with all nations tempered, Communism and the governments it now controls are enemies of every man on earth who is or wants to be free." In characterizing his political philosophy, Goldwater made the celebrated statement that "extremism in the defense of liberty is no vice" and that "moderation in the pursuit of justice is no virtue."

The Democrats congratulated themselves in their platform for overseeing a world that "is closer to peace today than it was in 1960." Designed to claim the middle ground, the platform stressed the Democratic administration's moderation in relations with the Soviets. Repeating President John F. Kennedy's dictum of never negotiating from fear but never fearing to negotiate, the platform promised to "continue all-out efforts through fully enforceable measures to halt and reverse the arms race and bring to an end the era of nuclear terror."

Seeking to fan allegations that his Republican opponent exhibited a cavalier attitude toward the use of atomic weapons, President Lyndon B. Johnson, accepting the Democratic nomination, said, "There is no place in today's world for weakness, but there is also no place in today's world for recklessness. We cannot act rashly with the nuclear weapons that could destroy us. The only course is to press with all our minds and all our will to make sure, doubly sure, that these weapons are never really used at all."

Johnson won by a landslide.

tection in the event of an attack on China. The Chinese, however, preferred the prospect of relying on their own power and pressed Moscow to supply them with the means to produce atomic weapons. The Soviets complied with this request in 1957 when they signed a secret agreement to aid China in building its own atomic arsenal. But the Kremlin's refusal to risk a nuclear confrontation with the United States during the Quemoy Crisis of 1958 and its repudiation of the secret nuclear weapons technology agreement in 1959 demonstrated to Beijing that it could not depend on Moscow to ensure China's national security.

Khrushchev's "Secret Speech" at the 1956 Party Congress also upset and alarmed the Chinese. His attack on Stalin appeared to be a condemnation of one-man, totalitarian rule. In China, it was viewed as an attack on Mao. The Chinese at first responded to Khrushchev's actions by relaxing censorship, encouraging criticism, and liberalizing their rule. The intensity of the resulting criticism caught the regime unawares, however, and the lid on free expression was quickly slammed down. The Chinese challenged Soviet ideological preeminence by asserting that Moscow was revisionist, that peaceful coexistence with the West was impossible, and that Khrushchev had violated the basic tenets of Leninist orthodoxy.

Some of the trouble between the countries stemmed from the personal animosity that developed between the two leaders. After Stalin's death, Mao saw himself as the successor to the ideological throne in the communist world. It soon became obvious that Khrushchev and the other Soviet leaders were not interested in relinquishing the crown. In addition to their own ideological ideas, the Soviets viewed the Chinese as too backward to represent the cutting edge of international communism.

In 1958 with the decision to launch the Great Leap Forward — "a great revolutionary leap toward the building of socialism" — the Chinese tried to solve all their problems at once. They claimed that Beijing, not Moscow, was the center of true communist ideology. And they asserted that, faced with U.S. encirclement and Soviet abandonment, they would modernize on their own. Announcing that Mao had discovered a shortcut to achieving a communist society, the Chinese espoused the principle of "self-reliance." Mao explained that no longer would the Chinese "lean to one side" (Moscow), but would "walk on two legs."

Moscow reacted harshly. The Soviets heaped scorn on the Great Leap Forward (which soon stumbled) and chided the Chinese for claiming to understand Lenin better than his own countrymen. As the 1960s began, the war of words was confined to ideology and attacks were indirect. The Soviets criticized China's ally Albania, rather than China itself, as "adventurist" and "infantile" for its insistence on direct confrontation with the West. In turn, China castigated Yugoslavia, in place of the Soviet Union, for its "revisionist" views toward peaceful coexistence.

In July 1960 the Soviets retaliated against the Chinese verbal abuse by recalling all their technicians in China and suspending their cooperative scientific and technical ventures. The Chinese continued to accuse Khrushchev of being soft on imperialism. Partially in response to these criticisms in the early 1950s, Khrushchev hardened his approach to East-West relations and eventually reinterred Stalin's body at the foot of the Kremlin wall.

But in 1962 the Soviets refused to help China in its war with India and Khrushchev withdrew the missiles the Soviets had placed in Cuba. The Chinese denounced both moves as "retreats" and said they had made no contribu-

tion to peace. During the last years of Khrushchev's reign, Chinese and Soviet polemics became increasingly direct and accusatory. Khrushchev himself remained the primary focus of Chinese attacks. Western observers finally began to acknowledge that the Sino-Soviet rift was more than a temporary falling out.

Precursors to Ouster

The men surrounding Khrushchev in the Kremlin tired of the inconsistent, overly optimistic plans he concocted. They grew wary of his continuing hold over the organs of power. Amidst plan reversals, perceived foreign policy humiliations, and fears for personal power, party leaders soon joined in an effort to remove Nikita Khrushchev.

The Soviet Communist Party goals of the Seven-Year Plan (so called because the Sixth Five-Year Plan, 1956-60, was scuttled in 1958) proved impossible to achieve. The goals included an 83 percent jump in housing investment, a 70 percent increase in agricultural production, and a 100 percent hike in productivity on collective farms. In the eyes of Khrushchev's opponents, his attempts to increase the supply of consumer goods weakened the two favored segments of the Soviet economy, heavy industry and defense production.

In addition, Kremlin leaders feared that the tangible effects of de-Stalinization at home — particularly reduced censorship and a lessening of restrictions on the flow of information — would provoke unrest, as they had in Hungary. State control over the arts eased after Khrushchev's 1956 "Secret Speech," although the thaw never resulted in more than a modicum of artistic freedom. Relaxed censorship was applied selectively. Khrushchev, for example, personally oversaw the publication in 1962 of Alexander Solzhenitsyn's harsh portrait of Stalin's labor camps, *One Day in the Life of Ivan Denisovich*. On the other hand, in 1958 Khrushchev prevented the publication in the Soviet Union of Boris Pasternak's *Doctor Zhivago*. In late 1962 he attacked abstract artists.

Khrushchev's attempt to reorganize the party and government in 1962 was probably his most damaging domestic initiative. This reorganization was a bifurcation, or split, of most of the lower party and governmental organs into two independent structures. One was industrial (or urban), the other agricultural (or rural). Important regions of the country were given sections of both. The industrial regional party committees and soviets, which had subordinate units in areas roughly equivalent to U.S. cities or counties, supervised nearly all the population in the cities and those involved with industry and construction efforts. The agricultural counterpart supervised rural citizenry and institutions, as well as institutions in cities that were closely related to agriculture. One problem with this arrangement was that the "amalgamations of the economic regions" (created primarily by the sovnarkhozes) severely undercut the plan, Jerry Hough has noted. A Party-State Control Committee was formed with broad powers in an attempt to correct this. Although the committee retained its importance in the years to come, the bifurcation failed largely because of the confusion it created and the number of powerful individuals and groups at which it struck. According to Hough, the bifurcation decision directly affected 30 percent of the Central Committee's voting members —

Khrushchev Reminisces on War and Arms Race

...World War III *is* possible. There are more than enough crazy people around who would like to start one. I know that *our* government doesn't want war ... But anything is possible....

I remember President Kennedy once stated.... that the United States had the nuclear missile capacity to wipe out the Soviet Union two times over, while the Soviet Union [could] wipe out the U.S. only once.... When journalists asked me to comment, ... I said jokingly, "Yes, I know what Kennedy claims, and he's quite right. But I'm not complaining ... We're satisfied to be able to finish off the U.S. the first time around.... We're not a bloodthirsty people." These remarks of mine drew some smiles ...

[T]he capitalist powers are unlikely to risk a world war, [but] they will never miss an opportunity to conduct subversive ideological policies against us. I consider that normal and legitimate.... [But] to speak of ideological compromise would be to betray our Party's first principles.... It was with this conviction in mind that I allowed myself ... to use the expression "We will bury the enemies of the Revolution." I was referring, of course, to America. Enemy propagandists ... blew it all out of proportion: "Khrushchev says the Soviet people want to bury the people of the United States of America!" I said no such thing. Our enemies were purposely distorting a few words I'd just let drop....

The case of the ABMs is a perfect example of how idiotic the arms race is. The spiraling competition is an unending waste of human intellectual and material resources... Naturally, the updating of defenses is necessary, but it can go to absurd extremes.... The reactionary forces in the West know it's expedient for them to force us to exhaust our economic resources in a huge military budget, thus diverting funds which could otherwise be spent on the ... needs of our peoples....

When I was the leader of the Party and the government, ... I think, at the time at least, I was right to concentrate on military spending ... If I hadn't put such a high priority on our military needs, we couldn't have survived.... [But] once we ... had what it took to defend ourselves and deter our enemy ... we began to economize on our military expenditures.... I can't help noticing ... that now money is being wasted ....

Meanwhile, we should keep in mind that it's the size of our nuclear missile arsenal, and not the size of our army, that counts. The infantry has become ... not the muscle but the fat of the armed forces....

We must also press for arms control.... During my political career we reached a partial agreement on nuclear testing.... It was a good beginning, but ... I must also say that the Americans proposed certain arms control measures to which we could not agree.

I'm thinking now about their insistence [on] ... a provision for on-site inspection anywhere in our country.... I agreed in principle to on-site inspection ... but we couldn't allow ... their inspectors crisscrossing around the Soviet Union. They would have discovered that we were in a relatively weak position, [which] ... might have encouraged them to attack us. However, all that has changed.... [W]e no longer lag behind to any significant degree....

Therefore, I think there is no longer any reason for us to resist the idea of international control. If I had any influence ... I would urge that we sign a mutual agreement providing for more extensive inspection.... I would like to see us sign a mutual treaty of nonaggression and inspection.... Naturally, we don't want to undress all the way and stand before NATO inspectors as naked as Adam. Perhaps ... [a] temporary [accord could] give us time to work out other, more far-reaching agreements.... [E]ven if a Soviet-American agreement ... were impossible, we should go ahead and sharply reduce our own expenditures — unilaterally....

Any leadership which conducts a policy of arms control and disarmament must be courageous and wise.... and not let others intimidate them. Who, in our own country, are the "others"...? They are the military. I don't reproach the military for that — they're only doing their job.... However, leaders must be careful not to look at the world through the eyeglasses of the military. Otherwise, ... the government will start spending all its money and the best energies of its people on armaments — [and] ... pretty soon the country will have lost its pants in the arms race.... [T]he government must always keep a bit between the teeth of the military....

A government leader should keep in mind exactly what sort of destruction we're capable of today.... Can you picture what would be left after a few hydrogen bombs fell on Moscow? Forget about "a few" — imagine just one. Or Washington? Or New York? Or Bonn? It staggers the mind....

I know people will say, "Khrushchev is in a panic over the possibility of war." I am not. I've always been against war, but at the same time I've always realized full well that fear of nuclear war on the part of a country's leader can paralyze that country's defenses. And if a country's defenses are paralyzed, then war really is inevitable: the enemy is sure to sense your fright and try to take advantage of it....

Besides, what kind of panic would you expect from a man my age? I'm nearly seventy-seven years old. As they say, I'm no longer on my way to the fair — I started my journey home a long time ago....

—*Khrushchev Remembers: The Last Testament*, ed. and trans. Strobe Talbott (Boston: Little, Brown, 1974), 328–542.

antagonizing the military, local party officials, industrial administrators, diplomats, and educators.

For several years prior to 1964, Khrushchev's supporters as well as opponents became increasingly alarmed over the loss of Soviet international prestige, a loss they attributed to Khrushchev. In relations with the noncommunist world, Khrushchev pursued policies that resulted in Soviet humiliation during the Cuban missile crisis. Within the socialist camp, his opponents charged, he presided over and promoted the Sino-Soviet split, thereby relinquishing Moscow's position as unqualified leader of the communist world and directing widespread attention to the fragmentary nature of what the world had feared was a monolithic communist movement.

Khrushchev Removed

Unlike 1957 when Khrushchev was able to outflank his Presidium opponents by taking his case to the Central Committee, in 1964 the Presidium members prevented him from making a similar appeal.

Khrushchev was forced to surrender leadership of the state and the party at the October 14, 1964, session of the Central Committee of the Communist Party. His actual ouster presumably occurred the day before at a meeting of the Presidium. It was announced October 15 that the Central Committee granted Khrushchev's "request to be relieved of his duties . . . in view of his advanced age and deterioration of his health."

The 70-year-old Khrushchev, who was vacationing at his dacha on the Black Sea coast when he was summoned back to Moscow October 13, dropped from sight. Supported by a government pension, he lived in enforced obscurity outside Moscow until he died September 11, 1971.

World Reaction

American president Lyndon B. Johnson broadcast a message October 18, 1964, in which he said, "We do not know exactly what happened to Nikita Khrushchev. . . . We do know that he has been forced out of power by his former friends and colleagues. Five days ago he had only praise in Moscow. Today we learn only of his faults." Johnson added that the Soviet leader had "learned from his mistakes" in the Berlin and Cuban crises and that "in the last two years, his government has shown itself aware of the need for sanity in the nuclear age." As examples of Soviet willingness to cooperate, Johnson cited the 1963 nuclear test ban treaty, the Moscow-Washington hot line, and the agreement to bar deployment of nuclear or other mass-destructive weapons in outer space.

The president disclosed that at an October 16 White House meeting the Soviet ambassador, Anatoli Dobrynin, assured Johnson the new regime planned "no change in basic foreign policy." Johnson said he pointed out to Dobrynin that "we intend to bury no one, and we do not intend to be buried," referring to Khrushchev's widely reported remark in 1956 that "History is on our side. We will bury you!"

In China, the news of Khrushchev's demise was greeted with delight. Chinese leaders sent the new regime a congratulatory note October 16 wishing it success "in all fields and in the struggle for the defense of world peace." China's ally, Albania, welcomed the change in command, saying it was "a heavy blow" to the United States and to "the modern revisionists."

Western reaction was muted somewhat by the announcement October 16 that China had detonated an atomic bomb.

The Brezhnev Era Opens

Both the United States and the Soviet Union were distracted during the early 1960s by issues not directly related to improving U.S.-Soviet ties. In the United States, Lyndon B. Johnson, who had become president following the November 22, 1963, assassination of John F. Kennedy, greatly expanded America's military commitment in South Vietnam. In the Soviet Union, an oligarchy took over from Nikita S. Khrushchev in October 1964 and presided over a chronically troubled economy, unrest in Czechoslovakia, and an increasingly bitter dispute with the People's Republic of China.

Yet the years 1964-68 witnessed attempts to improve relations between the two powers. Various agreements were signed and a 1967 summit meeting between Johnson and Soviet premier Aleksei Kosygin was considered a symbolic success. Relations were chilled, however, by the Soviet-led invasion of Czechoslovakia in August 1968.

The men who replaced Khrushchev moved quickly to do away with domestic programs instituted during their predecessor's 10 years at the top. They also put their stamp on foreign policy, although their changes here were less drastic than the abrupt reversals they instituted at home in Soviet leadership and in government programs.

While the new leaders deemphasized the kind of individual dominance that Khrushchev personified, one man among them — Leonid I. Brezhnev — gradually emerged as the leading figure in fact as well as title.

During Brezhnev's 18-year regime (1964-82) relations between the United States and the Soviet Union became an increasingly important barometer of the climate of international affairs worldwide. Seemingly little was left outside the reach of superpower involvement. *(Centrality of U.S.-Soviet Relations, box, p. 57)*

Because U.S.-Soviet relations dominated foreign policy issues of the two countries, the general aspects will be discussed in this chapter and specific regions of Soviet involvement will be discussed separately in Chapter 5.

BREZHNEV TAKES REINS, REVISES DOMESTIC POLICY

Khrushchev's regional economic councils, designed to decentralize state authority by allowing local jurisdictions some say over regional matters, were dismantled immediately after his ouster. His programs emphasizing consumer products at the expense of heavy industry (steel and defense) were scaled down.

Although Brezhnev and Kosygin embraced collective leadership in reaction to the excesses of Stalin's "personality cult," the process of de-Stalinization was stemmed. Public criticism of Stalin was curbed. At the ceremony marking the 50th anniversary of the Bolshevik Revolution, Brezhnev referred to Stalin's reign of terror as "temporary setbacks and errors."

'Clerical Mediocrities'

"The dismissal of Khrushchev . . . means a further step in the progressive weakening of personal dictatorial power. It also means a decline in the quality of the men who wield it. Lenin's associates would not have removed him even if they could have, because of his enormous political and ideological stature. Stalin's associates probably would have if they could have, but they were paralyzed by terror. Khrushchev's associates finally could and did, largely because he had neither the personal stature nor the advantage of terror. Bureaucratic politics tends to elevate non-entities, and the non-entities have a stake in making certain that only someone like themselves emerges as the *primus inter pares*. The weakening of personal dictatorial power hence reflects a trend toward government by clerical mediocrities, a trend inherent in the gradual fading in the revolutionary generation and its replacement by a bureaucratic one. Lenin-Stalin-Khrushchev-Brezhnev: the decline in intellectual and personal qualities seems too unilinear and too marked to be merely accidental. . . ."

—Zbigniew Brzezinski, "Victory of the Clerks,"
The New Republic, November 14, 1964, 15-18.

By the time the 23d Party Congress convened in March 1966, Brezhnev and Kosygin were firmly in control. Two potential rivals, Nikolai Podgornyi and Alexander Shelepin, were transferred to posts away from the center of power. As head of the party, Brezhnev was responsible for party matters and relations with other communist countries and parties; Kosygin oversaw relations with the noncommunist world and was in charge of economic planning. By 1972 Brezhnev edged out Kosygin and was clearly the first among equals.

The 23d Party Congress gave its blessing to the moderate course the new regime proposed. The economic program was a mixture of heavy industry and consumer production, with the former reverting to its position as the top economic priority. The needs of consumers were not ignored; rather, they were assigned second place on the economic agenda. *(Details, Chapters 6 and 7)*

The congress also endorsed the leaders' promotion of stricter artistic and ideological controls. The end of the de-Stalinization "thaw" was marked by the trial in February 1966 of two dissident writers, Andrei Siniavskii and Yuli Daniel. *(Chapter 7)* The two were convicted of writing articles critical of the Soviet regime and sentenced to several years of internal exile. The treatment of Siniavskii and Daniel was applauded at the congress and the somewhat relaxed censorship of the Khrushchev years was attacked as harmful to the state and the party.

Perhaps more symbolic of the new regime's desire to put de-Stalinization behind it was the readoption of the Stalin-era titles for the top policy-making group in the party and the party leader. The policy-making Presidium reverted to its former name, the Politburo, and the designation of the party chief was changed from first secretary to general secretary (both titles had been changed at the 19th Party Congress in 1952).

Brezhnev's Early Position

Brezhnev was not able to act independently immediately after Khrushchev's ouster. The Politburo was a heterogeneous group and Brezhnev had just one close ally, Andrei Kirilenko. Mikhail Suslov and Alexsei Kosygin were independent, influential figures, and Nikolai Podgornyi was an outright rival. Other Politburo members had alliances with rivals of Brezhnev, were vulnerable party elders (such as Anastas Mikoian), or were personal protégés of Khrushchev who were on the way out. There were also lesser candidate Politburo members who were waiting to gravitate toward the leader who proved the strongest.

Top Leadership Circle

In the wake of Khrushchev's ouster, Petr Shelest was promoted to the Politburo, a move that benefited his associate Podgornyi. Alexander Shelepin, who had "provided the muscle" for the Khrushchev ouster through his KGB contacts, was also rewarded with a Politburo seat. A third Politburo member, Mikhail Suslov, also had the potential to erode or supersede Brezhnev's authority. Suslov was seen as a defender of the rights of the oligarchy against individual leadership, something uppermost in the leaders' minds. Because of Podgornyi's experience and political base, he was seen as a logical alternative if Brezhnev faltered as general secretary. In time, however, his colleagues came to believe he lacked ideological toughness.

Shelepin, it turned out, was initially the main threat to Brezhnev. He was young and ambitious and had a foothold in both the Council of Ministers (as deputy premier) and the Secretariat. He was chairman of the Party-State Control Commission, which he could use against rivals, and he had well-placed personal associates below him.

Brezhnev had only limited direct influence within the Council of Ministers in his early reign; Kosygin ran the government apparatus. Brezhnev's public role as foreign policy spokesman was also limited because he shared this function with Kosygin. During the first 18 months of his regime, however, Brezhnev managed to extend his power base in a number of ways.

It was inevitable that some of Khrushchev's cronies would be replaced. Although Brezhnev bargained and was forced to accept trade-offs, the removals made room for slots that Brezhnev filled to his advantage. Later he was able to promote more turnover, which secured positions for several of his own associates. Konstantin Chernenko was named secretary of the General Department of the Central Committee and Andrei Kirilenko became a member of the Secretariat.

Brezhnev's power also increased when his rivals Shelepin and Podgornyi were eventually removed. Shelepin's removal came about after rumors surfaced that Brezhnev might be replaced. Shelepin's associates were believed to have started the rumors and the other Politburo members resented this type of "inspired leak . . .

Centrality of U.S.-Soviet Relations

Many experts believe that U.S.-Soviet relations have been the central feature of the foreign policies of each superpower and of all international relations since World War II. Several factors have prompted this situation. The European theater has been the main area of conflict in the postwar years and the United States and Soviet Union have been the main players there. Outside Europe, the United States dominated the global economic and political scene for most of the period, and consequently, it has been able to use its influence to help manage or resolve problems in ways the Soviet Union has not. This has been true in the Middle East, for example. Additionally, each power has perceived the other as its greatest threat.

This centrality, however, is declining, some experts have said, because U.S.-Soviet relations no longer exert exclusive domination over world affairs and American policy. Some major developments, and their consequences, have brought this about. Internal economic problems now have greater impact on the social and political stability of Western countries than during the postwar boom. The international economic order is no longer stable. Economic interdependence among and between Western nations and less-developed countries (LDCs) has increased phenomenally. Because of the decline in colonialism and the rise of national liberation movements, regional powers have emerged that compete economically, politically, and militarily with the superpowers.

Lack of Cohesion

The world communist movement is no longer cohesive, another factor that has contributed to the decline in the centrality of U.S.-Soviet relations. The increasing independence of Western communist parties, the failure of the Soviet system to provide a successful economic and social model for developing nations, and the reformist tendencies in Eastern Europe have all combined to split the communist movement. The split between the People's Republic of China and the USSR diluted the influence of the two largest communist nations. The Soviets generally consider the United States as the main obstacle to improved relations with China. Since the succession of Mikhail Gorbachev to the Soviet leadership, however, relations between those countries have become somewhat friendlier.

The superpower centrality is likely to continue to decline because it is highly doubtful that the Soviets can catch up with the West economically and technologically in the near future. Economic aspects of international relations are more important than ever to the well-being of both industrialized and developing nations. Since the Soviets' impact in the international economic arena is minimal, some Western experts believe this limits their influence over countries in desperate need of economic (rather than military) assistance. Other experts note that the Soviet Union is considered a military superpower but not an economic one.

Although the United States has lost some influence in recent decades, the Soviet Union has not moved in to replace it as the dominant superpower. Many types of interstate relations now exist, with more and more regional alliances, and many problems are of limited relevance to superpower relations, according to experts such as Seweryn Bialer. Conversely, in some cases regional problems may make superpower relations more central in that superpower cooperation is sometimes seen as the only hope for resolving complex disputes, such as in the Middle East.

Some Western experts believe the U.S.-Soviet conflict has become less ideological and more of a "normal traditional great power competition" to protect national interests and to extend influence. Other experts cite President Reagan's ideological rhetoric to counter that.

Superpower Rivalry

The Soviets have long perceived the United States as an obstacle to international political parity. The USSR desires recognition as an equal superpower, not as a "two-thirds superpower," as some members of the media have termed it. Psychologically, the United States is what the Soviet Union wants to be. America has been the measuring rod of Soviet success politically, economically, and technologically. Even Lenin saw the United States as a model for Soviet economic development, and Bialer and other analysts contend this preoccupation has been essential to the West's understanding of the Soviet concern with U.S.-Soviet relations.

At least until the Gorbachev succession, the Soviets expected the United States to treat U.S.-Soviet relations as the most important aspect of world relations. They have been sensitive to indications that U.S. policy makers were giving precedence to non-Soviet foreign issues. But there is some evidence of a slight shift in Soviet perceptions since Gorbachev became general secretary. He and several of his political appointees are believed to encourage a further decline in the U.S.-Soviet centrality by emphasizing improved relations with Western Europe, Japan, and China. Foreign Minister Eduard Shevardnadze, for example, made the highest-level Soviet visit to Japan in more than a decade in January 1986. Also in early 1986, the Soviets named longtime UN diplomat Oleg Troyanovsky as the new ambassador to Beijing.

[which appealed] to the influence of pluralistic outside forces," as Soviet expert Harry Gelman termed it. Especially after Khrushchev's ouster, Shelepin's functions and associations gave him power his colleagues feared. They soon formed a coalition against him. Even some of Brezhnev's other rivals acted with him against Shelepin. Shelepin was stripped of his deputy-premiership, his most important position, and over the next 10 years gradually lost the rest of his power. Despite this erosion, however, Shelepin retained enough influence for some time to help instigate anti-Brezhnev confrontations whenever Brezhnev was vulnerable on an issue. He was not formally removed from the Politburo until 1975.

Brezhnev's other primary rival, Podgornyi, was neutralized in stages at the same time Shelepin was being checked. Podgornyi's ally Vitalii Titov was removed from his key post, and in December of 1965 Brezhnev was able to get Podgornyi appointed to the prestigious but politically unpowerful job of president. In early 1966 Kirilenko replaced Podgornyi on the Secretariat. According to Gelman, each successive move against Podgornyi depended on the pro-Brezhnev coalition on the Politburo. Opportunistic fence-sitters went over to Brezhnev as evidence of his strength grew. Podgornyi's stand on several important issues also had given him a bad image among many colleagues. This was particularly true with the military when he argued for increased spending on consumer goods and publicly attacked the military's priority on resources.

Other personnel changes also reinforced Brezhnev's position during the 1970s. By the April 1973 session of the Central Committee of the Communist Party of the Soviet Union, Brezhnev was firmly in control. The Central Committee on April 27 endorsed "entirely and without reservation" the policy of détente with the West that bore Brezhnev's personal imprint. The "important role played personally by Leonid Brezhnev" also received approval.

Dropped from the Politburo in 1973 were two men thought to be hard-line conservatives critical of Brezhnev's opening to the West — Petr Shelest, former first secretary of the Ukrainian Communist Party, and Gennadi Voronov, former president of the Russian Soviet Federated Socialist Republic.

Most important, however, was the selection of new full members of the Politburo: Yuri V. Andropov, head of the KGB (the first secret police chief in the Politburo since Lavrentii Beria's ouster in 1953), Foreign Minister Andrei Gromyko, and Defense Minister Andrei Grechko. It was thought significant that all the new Politburo members were responsible for some part of the Kremlin's foreign policy apparatus.

Oligarchy's Rules

The Brezhnev oligarchy was self-contained, self-renewing, and conscious of the barriers between itself and the rest of the party. The top leadership maintained great distance between the junior members of the Secretariat who did not have Politburo status and those senior members who did. Politburo members based outside Moscow such as Vladimir Shcherbitskii (in the Ukraine), Grigori Romanov (Leningrad), and Dinmukhamed Kunaev (Kazakhstan) were generally less influential and excluded from some important matters because they were not always able to attend weekly meetings or receive routine information about impending decisions. The simple circumstance of being in Moscow could be a powerful weapon. A leader

could use the bureaucracy to ensure certain rivals did not receive timely information about subjects or meetings, or even to exclude them from initial decision-making processes.

More importantly, the Politburo was informally divided between a changing group of four or five superelite members and the remainder. The top echelon always included the general secretary and head of the Defense Council, the premier, the president, and the leaders of the Secretariat, which included at various times Andropov, Brezhnev, Chernenko, Kirilenko, Kosygin, Podgornyi, Suslov, and Nikolai Tikhonov.

Brezhnev and the post-Khrushchev oligarchs strove for stability, order, routine, and predictability. Their internal sense of political decorum made it unacceptable to publicly air any internal Politburo disputes, as had happened occasionally under Khrushchev. The leaders wanted to protect the exclusivity of the Politburo and Secretariat's decision-making prerogatives and to limit influence and pressure from below. The Politburo leaders usually punished violators of these unwritten rules, such as occurred with Shelepin's removal. Even Brezhnev had difficulties when he took actions his colleagues believed "went beyond the framework of Politburo consensus," according to Gelman. The leadership was suspicious and resentful of members who tried to use public opinion for personal advantage.

Brezhnev-era oligarchs encouraged the development of expertise in the bureaucracy but resisted pressure to use that expertise as influence. Many Western observers have discussed over the past two decades the increased use of specialists in Soviet policy making. Brezhnev, in his quest for scientific decision-making processes, did employ social science experts and other specialists to a greater degree than any other Soviet leader, but their power and influence on the policy-making process was significantly circumscribed. They provided inputs and information, which the leaders then used to formulate decisions. There were no real interest groups to speak of outside the military that commanded power enough to influence foreign policy decisions.

Some institutional groups did gain enough influence over the years under Brezhnev to have impact on domestic policy making, but interest groups were primarily rewarded favorably or unfavorably depending on the level of prestige of their representatives on the Politburo or Central Committee Secretariat. Groups within the Academy of Sciences, for example, developed influence because of their ability to help set Central Committee agendas and those of other politically powerful bodies, but in keeping with democratic centralism their power and influence do not extend from the discussion stage to the decision-making stage.

Brezhnev's Sources of Power

Brezhnev's power came from three primary areas: the Central Committee Secretariat, his chairmanship of the Defense Council, and through the foreign and defense ministries, including the KGB. Through the Secretariat, Brezhnev could direct appointments, set the Politburo's weekly agendas, manage the party, and oversee government ministries and the economy.

Various Central Committee departments had more political power than would normally be indicated by the extraparty organizations they supervised, but the power varied from department to department. The International

Department was the most graphic example. During the Brezhnev era it developed a responsibility much more powerful than that of an institution designed ostensibly for relations with nonruling communist parties. Rather, it dealt with national liberation movements and was charged with nurturing Third World leftist parties. In the early 1970s the department's work spread to include dealings with Western nations, a job previously the special province of the Foreign Ministry and Politburo. Additionally, the International Department developed power under Boris Ponomarev's tutelage because it had institutional advantages over the Foreign Ministry. It was closer to the center of the power structure and some experts contend the department had the central role in coordinating intelligence and keeping the top leadership informed on foreign affairs. To be sure, the Politburo had several other sources of information, including the Institute of USA and Canada Studies; key individuals such as ambassador to the United States Anatolii Dobrynin; and the Foreign Ministry, which became more prominent as Andrei Gromyko became more powerful. It was the International Department, however, that became the most influential source of foreign affairs information and analysis. As such, some Western experts have said, the department protected the leaders' orthodox foreign policy views from contamination by other perspectives. Because Brezhnev had control over the Secretariat, the International Department was particularly responsive to his desires. This department, however, was not involved with military policy.

Evidence suggests that, during most of his era, Brezhnev alone from the Secretariat was a member of the Defense Council (renamed from Khrushchev's Supreme Military Council). This naturally gave him significant power. The foreign and defense ministries and the KGB were answerable to and worked primarily for the Politburo, rather than the Council of Ministers to whom they were ostensibly accountable. Brezhnev further broadened his political support by seeking alliances with personalities who had their own organizational bases outside the Secretariat; in particular, the defense minister, foreign minister, and the premier (after Kosygin).

The Defense Council arrangement worked to Brezhnev's advantage in other ways. It created a separation of authority. The Politburo tacitly agreed to let this small group deal with and dominate military policy. This arrangement segregated information and, therefore, power. It created a subelite. The Politburo as a whole was less able to challenge members of the Defense Council because it lacked information and expertise on most defense issues that did not have to do with broad questions of foreign policy or resource allocation. Furthermore, if Brezhnev's defense policies came under attack, the blame could be spread among all the Defense Council members. One important political disadvantage in the Defense Council arrangement was that other members could potentially bring more leverage against Brezhnev. He had to reach an accommodation with these colleagues before a defense issue was brought to the Politburo. It was to Brezhnev's advantage, then, to change the Defense Council's composition during his tenure, although the changes likely caused temporary discord among the Politburo.

Defense Council members during the first half of the Brezhnev era tried to bring together all the major actors from the various realms of Soviet defense but excluded senior Secretariat members such as Suslov and Kirilenko, a significant change from the Khrushchev-era arrangement.

Moscow's European Strategy

"It might be asked why the USSR was so eager to proclaim by formal agreements what in fact had become an unalterable feature of Europe's political landscape — the division of Germany and, largely because of it, Soviet domination of East and Central Europe. The answer must be that the Kremlin still felt it of great psychological importance to legitimize what in the first instance had been secured by Soviet military power. In the second place, normalization, as they saw it, of the European situation fitted in with the Soviets' long-range diplomatic objectives. If western Europe were to lose most of its fear of the Soviet colossus, it would grow even more independent of the United States, and the impetus toward political unity of the area (originally a function of the fear) would grow weaker. Beyond virtual neutralization of western Europe (admittedly not tomorrow or the day after tomorrow), or even, as it is sometimes described, its 'finlandization,' the Soviets see profitable economic ties with its countries. At the Twenty-fourth Party Congress in 1971, Kosygin drew a vista of vast collaborative projects, such as a united electric grid, joint transportation network, Western credits and expertise already exemplified in the huge Kama automobile plant being built on Soviet soil by a consortium headed by Italian interests. Thus quite apart from similar hopes in respect to the United States, the Soviet Union would like various European countries to provide it with trade and help to improve its somewhat unsatisfactory rate of economic growth."

—Adam B. Ulam, *A History of Soviet Russia* (New York: Praeger Publishers, 1976), 285-286.

In the latter half of the Brezhnev era, Politburo representation on the Defense Council shifted and was broadened to include Premier Tikhonov, Defense Minister Ustinov, Foreign Minister Gromyko, Secretariat member Chernenko, and KGB chief Andropov as well as Brezhnev. Ustinov was appointed defense minister in 1976 when Marshal Andrei Grechko died and Podgornyi was eventually removed in 1977. With the inclusion of Chernenko, Andropov, and Gromyko, the Defense Council returned to the Khrushchev pattern of participation by some key Politburo officials who were not directly involved with defense. Gromyko's appointment was remarkable in one sense because of the Defense Ministry's past reluctance to allow the Foreign Ministry access to defense secrets. The appointments of both Gromyko and Ustinov, however, were widely regarded as political moves by Brezhnev to bring in close allies of long association. Ustinov, although a longtime defense industry supervisor, was not a professional military officer, which may have contributed to his acceptance of Gromyko's presence, Western experts have noted. *(Details, Chapter 6)*

Politburo involvement in defense matters increased during Brezhnev's era because of two primary reasons. First, the ongoing arms control process with the United States assumed higher priority, which meant more Politburo members needed more information. Second, political tension in the leadership increased during the latter part of the Brezhnev era as the impending succession drew closer and the economic costs of defense grew more burdensome. *(Chapters 5, 6)*

Military Funding, Stalinist Ideologues

The emphasis on the military's priority over national resources was renewed after Khrushchev's ouster. This return particularly pleased the conservative leaders who believed Khrushchev had been too liberal. These so-called Stalinist ideologues increased their influence over time, and Soviet foreign policy bore the marks of that influence.

Overall Expansion. In 1965 the leadership decided to expand Soviet military power in all major areas rather than concentrate on the missile, air defense, and submarine programs of Khrushchev's regime. The change in priorities was a sign that the leaders accepted an external rationalization for increased military spending. That is, instability in many parts of the developing world and the danger of nuclear war gave the Soviets an opportunity to explain their military buildup as being in keeping with their international duties and avowed peaceful socialist nature. The decision to build up all aspects of the military had an impact on Soviet foreign policy because it improved the Soviet Union's ability to exert pressure and expand influence abroad. This decision came about, however, only after much debate within both the military and the political leadership. *(Chapter 5)*

Two factors significantly influenced the leaders: American involvement in Vietnam, and the failure to reconcile with China and the resulting decision to build up the Soviet Far Eastern forces. The ideologues among the leadership maintained the premise that the world was divided into two irrevocably opposed camps. They depicted Americans as relentless imperialists in much the same way that conservative U.S. leaders viewed the Soviets as relentless expansionists. Consequently, with increasing U.S. involvement in Vietnam, the Politburo reversed Khrushchev's policy of shunning North Vietnam because of its close ties with the People's Republic of China. The Brezhnev regime sought instead to use Hanoi to cause trouble for the United States and to compete with Beijing on the international revolutionary front.

Ideologues in Policy Making. As a rule, Brezhnev leaned in the direction of supporting the so-called Stalinist ideologues in his policy decisions. He agreed that discussions of Stalinist crimes must end. Particularly since the current leaders had derived their power from Stalin, denigrating Stalin raised questions about the legitimacy of their own rule. Consequently, in early 1966 the leaders made it clear that harsh criticism of the Stalin period was unacceptable. Furthermore, Brezhnev manipulated Stalinist-era symbols for political advantage. He changed the name of the Presidium back to the Politburo and the title of first secretary reverted to general secretary. Still, Brezhnev was cautious not to completely rehabilitate or associate himself

with Stalin, and the oligarchs since that time discouraged any kind of discussion about Stalin, good or bad.

The "contradictory inclinations" of his assistants working in different policy spheres affected Brezhnev's ideological course, Gelman and other Western experts have noted. Some of Brezhnev's old associates in key areas had a reactionary influence on policy; the most notorious being Sergei Trapeznikov, head of the Science and Educational Institutions Department of the Central Committee. Another was Gen. Ivan Pavlovskii, a World War II associate of Brezhnev. Pavlovskii led the 1968 invasion of Czechoslovakia and allegedly planned the 1979 invasion of Afghanistan. Other associates were also ideologically rigid, such as Aleksei Epishev, head of the Main Political Administration. *(Chapter 5)*

Yet, the Brezhnev regime's search for "scientific" expertise exposed Brezhnev to other perspectives. Georgii Arbatov (head of the Institute of USA and Canada Studies), Aleksandr Bovin, and Fedor Burlatskii (former journalists and Central Committee consultants) all held so-called reformist outlooks. These men, however, worked on the fringe of power and their access to Brezhnev was based on their expertise in foreign affairs dealing with the West. Some Western experts contend they were cool to military interests. The ideologues in the central apparatus dominated policy, however (particularly toward the Third World), and, because Brezhnev was always concerned with maintaining the support of both the military and the influential ideologues, the reformists had only fragmentary influence on foreign policy.

Brezhnev's position on most military issues was greatly affected by his pursuit of political advantage over his rivals. External events, the deteriorating economy, and his previous personal inclinations influenced his decisions, but throughout his regime he usually took the political line of least resistance.

Whether because he truly believed it best or because he found it politically expedient, Brezhnev found he could not simply push for more military spending at the exclusion of other programs. Because he was also ultimately held responsible for keeping the populace fed and under control, Brezhnev advocated two "first priorities": the military and agriculture.

Defense Versus Agriculture

Brezhnev "threw money" at the chronic Soviet agriculture problem without great result. But because the leadership feared the implications of food shortfalls created by bad weather and poor management, Brezhnev's spending continued despite unspectacular results. The leaders had to make cuts elsewhere to fund increases in agricultural and defense spending.

In the Eighth Five-Year Plan (1966-70), the leaders tried to satisfy everyone. Through the late 1960s, they largely succeeded. The standard of living rose and most industries experienced healthy growth. Good weather aided agriculture. The situation worsened in the 1970s. Bad weather created the need to subsidize consumer food prices, which placed a heavy burden on the budget. Adverse demographic trends (a low birthrate in European Russia, high rates of alcoholism and infant mortality; *Chapter 7*) slowed the increase in the labor force. Raw materials, including oil, became more difficult and expensive to procure. Yet the established 3-to-4-percent growth rate for defense spending remained sacrosanct. (Many

Western accounts in the early 1980s revised their estimates of Soviet defense spending upward to 6 percent or higher.) Instead, the leaders slightly cut industrial investment and more severely cut consumer investment. Agricultural spending increased. Overall, the growth of GNP (gross national product) and standard of living improvements slowed. *(Chapter 6)*

Things went from bad to worse in the late 1970s. The regime was forced to sharply reduce investments in both heavy and light industry. Military leaders feared these cutbacks would adversely affect the future of the Soviet military buildup and, in fact, the growth of military spending itself was soon affected to some degree. It would be left to future political leaders to shore up not only the country's economic front but the political relationship with the military as well.

Despite the changes in Politburo personnel over time, the Politburo consensus on military issues and priorities did not change much during the Brezhnev era. Brezhnev's political credentials and military contacts enabled him to benefit from a shift of priorities to the military. He knew many military leaders, most of whom disliked Khrushchev; he never uselessly criticized the military and publicly always appeared supportive of it. He had been the political supervisor for the navy during World War II and had been the party secretary for military industry. Over the years Brezhnev promoted a mythology about his own military experience to justify his self-promotion to marshal of the USSR. Additionally, Brezhnev was able to maintain political consensus and peace with the military because as chairman of the Defense Council he could support the budget requests of his military allies and he had influence over key military appointments. He relied on Defense Minister Grechko, and later Ustinov, for a military show of support on his policies.

Foreign Policy

The newly installed Brezhnev leadership vowed to pursue a moderate course in foreign relations, continuing the Khrushchev-era policy of peaceful coexistence. The twin legacies of Khrushchev's foreign policy were a recently relaxed relationship with the United States and an increasingly bitter quarrel with the People's Republic of China. Moscow's dealings with both nations would be colored by the growing conflict in Vietnam.

Khrushchev's successors continued the relaxation of Moscow-Washington tensions that had begun in 1962 after he backed away from the Cuban missile crisis confrontation with President Kennedy. The two powers had agreed in June 1963 to the installation of a hot line between Washington and Moscow to provide immediate communication and thus lessen the chance of an accidental nuclear war. The same month, on June 10, Kennedy had introduced a new and friendlier tone in U.S. relations toward the Soviets in a speech at American University. This in turn had elicited an amicable response from Moscow.

In his American University speech, Kennedy had announced that the United States, the Soviet Union, and Great Britain would begin talks on a partial nuclear test ban treaty. The treaty was initialed in Moscow July 25 and ratified by the Senate September 24.

Negotiations begun in 1963 resulted in a large wheat sale to the Soviets in 1964. Other 1964 symbols of comity included military budget cuts, efforts to enlarge East-West trade, cutbacks in the production of fissionable uranium by the United States and the Soviet Union, a slight easing in passage between East and West Berlin, and an accord signed February 22 modestly expanding educational, cultural, scientific, and technical exchanges.

The slowly easing tensions were strained anew by American military involvement in two widely separated countries, Vietnam and the Dominican Republic.

Vietnam

The escalating conflict in Vietnam in the mid 1960s posed a dual problem for Soviet leaders. Their hopes for a continuing rapprochement with the United States were jeopardized by Washington's increasing involvement in a war against their socialist ally, North Vietnam. Too much aid and comfort to the North Vietnamese could set back bilateral relations with the United States, or even cause a superpower confrontation; too little support for the Vietnamese "liberation forces" would guarantee an unending stream of invective from China and offer evidence that Moscow had surrendered leadership of the socialist movement.

The optimal solution to the Soviets' Vietnam problem would have been a negotiated peace settlement limiting the U.S. presence in South Vietnam, while enhancing Soviet influence in North Vietnam. But to obtain such a settlement the Soviets needed to convince the independent-minded North Vietnamese to accept major concessions that would likely halt, or at least delay, progress toward their goal of a united Vietnam. Soviet representatives had, indeed, urged Hanoi to go to the bargaining table. But in the wake of U.S. air attacks against North Vietnamese targets on February 7, 1965, Soviet hopes for concessions were reduced. The bombing raids, a response to a Viet Cong assault on the U.S. base at Pleiku, South Vietnam, came while Premier Kosygin was on a state visit to Hanoi, the North Vietnamese capital.

On his way home from Hanoi, Kosygin stopped at Beijing and requested access to Chinese air bases to facilitate shipment of Soviet supplies to North Vietnam. Beijing declined. The *Beijing Review* said in a November 1965 article that "if we were to take united action on the question of Vietnam with the new leaders of the CPSU who are pursuing the Khrushchev revisionist line, wouldn't we be helping them to bring the question of Vietnam within the orbit of Soviet-U.S. collaboration?" The verbal fireworks continued into 1966. The Soviets circulated a highly critical letter and the Chinese refused to attend the 23d Party Congress, renewing their accusations that Moscow cared little for revolution. *(Soviet, Chinese letters, pp. 295, 296)*

These untimely air attacks and the subsequent bombing campaign against North Vietnam that began later in February reduced Soviet flexibility. An attempt by Moscow to pressure Hanoi into a negotiated settlement at that time would have rewarded U.S. aggression, opened up the USSR to further Chinese accusations of a Soviet-American conspiracy, and probably failed, given North Vietnamese resolve. As the war progressed, the Soviets increased their aid to North Vietnam and intensified their condemnations of U.S. behavior in Southeast Asia.

Relations between the USSR and North Vietnam were stable and pragmatic during this period. Hanoi maneuvered to obtain as much aid as possible from Moscow, and Kremlin leaders were forthcoming. Their investment in Vietnam was considerable, yet Southeast Asia was not an area of vital interest for the Soviets in the mid 1960s. Building Soviet influence in Indochina was less important to Moscow than using the situation in Vietnam against the United States and China.

By supplying aid to the North Vietnamese, the USSR enhanced the military capabilities of the communist forces in Vietnam, thereby deepening the quagmire in which the United States found itself. The Soviet Union was careful not to offer weapons or assistance that might have produced a confrontation with the United States. But because Soviet American relations were cool between 1965 and 1968, Moscow did not stand to lose much by supporting Hanoi. U.S. involvement in Vietnam also enabled the Soviet Union to portray the United States to the Third World as an aggressive power willing to use massive force against a small nation to protect its neocolonialist interests.

The Vietnamese conflict gave the Soviet Union an opportunity to outcompete its communist rival China in a Third World arena. The North Vietnamese were primarily interested in obtaining material aid, and the USSR's capacity for delivering economic assistance and quality arms was far greater than China's. Also, Beijing's rejection of the Soviets' plan for a united communist effort against the United States in Vietnam made Chinese accusations that Soviet leaders were not selflessly concerned with Vietnam's struggle sound hypocritical. Finally, Moscow hoped its support of Vietnam would not only solidify its reputation as a defender of Third World national liberation movements, but also produce a cooperative relationship with North Vietnam that would limit Chinese influence in the entire region.

Dominican Republic

Rebellion broke out April 24, 1965, in Santo Domingo, capital of the Dominican Republic, and four days later U.S. troops were sent in to help stem the fighting. The Dominican rebels opposing the military-backed civilian junta of J. Donald Reid Cabral claimed to be fighting to restore the constitutional government under deposed president Juan Bosch.

President Johnson announced April 27 that he had ordered the evacuation of U.S. citizens from Santo Domingo. The following day he disclosed that 400 U.S. Marines had landed to protect and carry out the evacuation of Americans and other nationals caught in the revolution-torn capital. U.S. troops continued to flow into the republic in numbers apparently well beyond those required to protect American citizens. (U.S. troops eventually totaled more than 30,000.) By May the administration was suggesting that the danger of a communist takeover in the Dominican Republic justified the large U.S. force. Newspapers and some members of Congress criticized the intervention, but, mindful of Fidel Castro's takeover in Cuba, many others supported the president's actions. With the backing of Sen. J. William Fulbright, D-Ark., the House endorsed the unilateral use of force by any Western Hemisphere country to prevent a communist takeover anywhere in the hemisphere.

Many Latin American nations voiced strong condemnation of the intervention, which they characterized as a violation of the charter of the Organization of American States. Reaction from the communist world was predictable. The Soviet news agency Tass termed the U.S. action "direct armed intervention" designed to block the "restoration of the constitutional regime." The Cuban communist

newspaper said that U.S. "interference has . . . always been cynical, shameless and monstrous." The Chinese, relating the U.S. move to developments in the Far East, said that "the new intervention on the part of the United States, which came at a moment when United States imperialism was wildly extending its aggression in Vietnam, threw further light on its hideous feature as the international gendarme."

Split in NATO

Throughout the 1960s, the Soviet objective in Europe was to gain worldwide recognition of the status quo as it had been established after World War II — the existence of two German nations and Soviet domination of Eastern Europe. The Soviets began to curry favor with the maverick of Europe, President Charles de Gaulle of France. Reluctant to follow Washington's lead in European affairs, de Gaulle announced in February 1966 that France intended to withdraw from the integrated military command of the North Atlantic Treaty Organization (NATO). De Gaulle subsequently expelled all foreign forces, including Americans, from French soil.

France's withdrawal from the NATO military structure officially occurred in April 1968. (Currently France participates informally as an observer in many NATO meetings and cooperates as an active, but not formal, partner in the alliance.) The hearty welcome extended to de Gaulle on a state visit to the Soviet Union in June 1966 provided ample evidence of Moscow's pleasure at the weakening of the Western alliance. Soviet ambassador to France Valerian Zorin said on March 17 that any reduction in the strength or "aggressive character" of NATO probably would be matched by a similar reduction in the Warsaw Pact alliance. He also said Moscow was ready to conclude a treaty of alliance of nonaggression with France.

Widening Influence

Soviet influence extended beyond Europe to other parts of the world during the 1960s. Adam Ulam writes in *A History of Soviet Russia:*

> For all the formidable internal problems and foreign policy dilemmas, the fiftieth year of the Soviet regime found it in a strong position. Its main rivals were largely incapacitated — the United States by its involvement in Vietnam, China by the travails of the Cultural Revolution. Soviet influence now reached into the areas once the preserve of Western powers, but which the collapse of their empires left in a state of ferment. In practically every corner of the globe, the departure of Western rulers or the eruption of civil strife was followed by offers of aid from the USSR, often the arrival of Soviet advisers, economic "developers," and sometimes military experts. In black Africa's most populous and soon richest state, Nigeria, a civil war [1967-69] pitted the central government dominated by the Moslem north against an attempted secession of an ethnically and linguistically distinct southeast area, Biafra. While public opinion in the West was divided on the Nigerian issue — Biafra's struggle could be construed as a *real* war of national liberation — the Soviet government could throw its support without any com-

punctions to the stronger party. The northern Nigerians' victory enabled the USSR to garner the dividends of increased influence in this oil-rich country. (China expressed its support for Biafra, for no other apparent reason than to be on the opposite side from Russia.) Another civil war in Yemen found two Arab countries supporting rival factions. The Egyptian army, which intervened on behalf of one, found itself unable to prevail over hostile tribesmen aided by Saudi Arabia until helped by Soviet supplies and instructors. With the British about to move out of neighboring Aden, Soviet influence now reached the Red Sea.

India-Pakistan Conflict

The outbreak of major hostilities between India and Pakistan in August 1965 gave Premier Kosygin a chance to play the statesman and increase Soviet prestige and goodwill in the subcontinent. The dispute between India, which had established ties with Moscow, and Pakistan, a friend of Beijing, was mediated by Kosygin in January 1966. Meeting at Tashkent in Soviet Central Asia, the two sides agreed to withdraw their forces to positions held before August 5, 1965. Kosygin's rapid diplomatic intervention blocked Chinese participation in the resolution of a conflict in which Beijing had a strong regional interest.

The dispute between India and Pakistan over Kashmir had flared intermittently since the partition of the state in 1947, following India's and Pakistan's independence from Britain. Fighting in Kashmir continued for more than a year before a cease-fire agreement was negotiated to go into effect January 1, 1949. India was left in control of about two-thirds of the area of Kashmir and Pakistan in control of the other one-third.

Mounting tension between China and India also erupted into war October 20, 1962, when the Chinese opened an offensive that drove back Indian forces in Kashmir. Successful, the Chinese began to withdraw their troops December 1.

In August 1965 India broke the cease-fire line with Pakistan and full-scale Indian-Pakistani hostilities followed. As fighting continued, the United States and Britain halted all military aid shipments to both nations.

In September, India and Pakistan accepted a UN Security Council resolution demanding a cease-fire. The USSR then stepped in and arranged the January negotiating session.

War between India and Pakistan again broke out December 3, 1971, but the Indians, fortified by Soviet military aid and a new 20-year friendship treaty, easily defeated the Pakistanis, who were backed by the Chinese.

Glassboro Summit

Soviet premier Kosygin traveled to New York in 1967 to join the United Nations debate on the Middle East. While in the United States, Kosygin met with President Johnson on June 23 and 25 in Glassboro, New Jersey. Both the nature of the meeting and the site of the impromptu summit conference were in dispute (Kosygin officially was visiting the United Nations, not the United States). The meeting site at Hollybush, home of the president of Glassboro State College, was selected because it allowed Johnson and Kosygin to meet half way between UN headquarters and the White House.

Neither side claimed major gains as a result of the 10 hours of meetings, but the sessions produced a new, although short-lived, feeling of international goodwill — christened the "spirit of Hollybush" or the "spirit of Glassboro." The first session at Glassboro lasted more than five hours and ranged over the Middle East, Vietnam, and

Soviet Premier Aleksei N. Kosygin and President Lyndon B. Johnson at the June 1967 Glassboro, New Jersey, Summit With, From Left, U.S. Secretary of State Dean Rusk, Soviet Foreign Minister Andrei A. Gromyko, and Soviet Ambassador Anatolii F. Dobrynin

the nonproliferation of nuclear arms. After the second meeting it was announced that progress had been made on the nonproliferation issue, but that vast differences still existed over the Middle East and Vietnam. The two world leaders termed the meetings "useful," agreed to meet again some time, and instructed their foreign policy personnel to continue the talks.

Agreements

Another manifestation of slowly relaxing U.S.-Soviet relations in 1967 was the completion of treaties covering consulates and space exploration.

Consular Treaty. On March 16, 1967, the Senate endorsed a controversial three-year-old Consular Convention between the United States and the Soviet Union. The first bilateral treaty between the two nations, it detailed the legal framework and procedures for the operation of consulates in each country, if and when any consulates were established. (Neither country had maintained a consulate in the other for almost 20 years. The Soviet Union established its first consulates in the United States, in San Francisco and New York City, in 1934. The United States set up its first consulate, in Vladivostok, in 1941. Other consulates followed. In August 1948, as East-West relations began to chill, Moscow withdrew its consular missions. The United States followed suit the following month.)

When it was signed in 1964 the treaty had symbolic importance as part of the Johnson administration's effort to improve relations with Moscow. Senate consideration of the treaty was held up until 1967 because of conservative opposition to it. The administration feared that it would not receive the two-thirds Senate majority needed for ratification and that failure to approve the treaty would unnecessarily aggravate U.S.-Soviet relations. The final vote was 66-28, only three votes more than the required two-thirds majority.

Space Treaty. The Senate in 1967 also ratified a treaty governing the peaceful exploration and use of outer space. The multilateral treaty was signed January 27 by the United States, Great Britain, the Soviet Union, and 57 other countries. A key provision obliged signatory nations not to station in space or place in orbit any object carrying nuclear or other weapons of mass destruction (for example, chemical or biological devices).

Trade and Exchanges. Despite tensions caused by the U.S. intervention in Vietnam, relations between the United States and the Soviet Union continued to show signs of improvement in the first half of 1968. The Consular Convention ratified in 1967 formally was concluded January 13 at a White House ceremony. In his 1968 economic report, President Johnson asked for approval of legislation to expand East-West trade. The president June 21 approved the establishment of direct New York-Moscow air service by Pan American World Airways and Aeroflot, the Soviet national airline. Washington and Moscow signed a cultural exchange agreement on July 15.

July 1, two weeks before the exchange agreement was signed, President Johnson announced at the signing of the Non-Proliferation Treaty that the United States and the Soviet Union had agreed to begin talks — to be held some time in the near future — on the limitation and reduction of nuclear arms. The two nations planned to announce in August that talks between President Johnson and Premier Aleksei N. Kosygin would take place September 30 in Leningrad; the Soviet-led invasion of Czechoslovakia August 20 postponed the announcement.

Non-Proliferation Treaty

The Non-Proliferation Treaty, signed July 1, 1968, was the culmination of more than four years of negotiations at the 18-nation Disarmament Conference in Geneva and at the United Nations. The treaty called upon the nuclear powers not to disseminate nuclear devices to nonnuclear nations for at least 25 years and to engage in discussions aimed at halting the arms race. It also pledged nonnuclear nations not to seek to acquire such devices and encouraged cooperation in the peaceful use of nuclear energy. France and the People's Republic of China, the only other nations that, at the time, possessed nuclear weapons, refused to sign the treaty. India, which detonated a nuclear device in May 1974, also refused to sign, as did at least six nations possessing advanced nuclear facilities: Israel, Spain, Argentina, Brazil, Pakistan, and South Africa. By 1985, 130 nations had ratified the Non-Proliferation Treaty.

President Johnson submitted the treaty to the Senate for ratification July 9 and, in the short-lived spirit of détente prevailing before the Czechoslovak invasion, the Senate Foreign Relations Committee took the unprecedented step of beginning consideration of the treaty within 24 hours of its submission. After the Soviet invasion of its neighbor, however, calls arose to postpone ratification to signal U.S. condemnation of the Soviet move. The Senate decided to hold off consideration until the next session. Presidential candidate Richard M. Nixon stated in the 1968 presidential race he strongly opposed ratification at that time for fear of condoning the Czechoslovakian invasion. But in January he called on the Senate to approve the treaty, promising to "implement it in my new administration." The Senate ratified the treaty March 13.

SOVIET INVASION OF CZECHOSLOVAKIA

Soviet troops, accompanied by forces from four Warsaw Pact nations — Poland, Hungary, East Germany, and Bulgaria — invaded Czechoslovakia August 20-21, 1968, to stem a liberal democratic movement that, according to Moscow, threatened Czech socialism. The Soviets reported that the intervention was requested by the "party and government leaders of the Czechoslovak Socialist Republic." In their statement, however, Czech leaders asserted that the invasion occurred "without the knowledge of the President of the Republic, the Chairman of the National Assembly, the Premier or the First Secretary of the Czechoslovak Communist Party Central Committee." The invasion, the Czech statement continued, was "contrary not only to the fundamental principles of relations between Socialist states," but also "contrary to the principles of international law." The statement appealed to the Czechs "to maintain calm and not to offer resistance to the troops on the march. Our army, security corps and people's militia have not received the command to defend the country." (*Excerpts from Czech government statement, Appendix, p. 297*)

Soviet tanks line a street off Old Town Square in Prague following the August 1968 invasion of Czechoslovakia.

The Czech drama began to unfold in December 1962, when the 12th Congress of the Czechoslovak Communist Party decided to "correct" the excesses of the Stalin era, the last of the Eastern bloc nations to do so. The December 1962 decision led to calls for increased personal freedom and to a liberalized economic policy, which produced disappointing results.

Following moderate "corrections" in politics, the 4th Congress of Czechoslovak Writers June 27-29, 1967, adopted a vigorous denunciation of government censorship in literature, culture, and politics. The government expelled from the Communist Party the leaders of the anticensorship movement. But then it exhibited a more relaxed attitude toward foreign relations by signing August 4, 1967, a two-year trade pact with West Germany, despite objections from the Soviets and the East Germans. The most important development, however, occurred in January 1968 when Alexander Dubcek, a reform-minded Slovak, took over the post as party first secretary from the more orthodox Antonin Novotny.

During the "Prague Spring" of 1968, Dubcek and other Czech leaders repeatedly affirmed their intention of moving the country toward "democratic socialism," as contrasted with the party-controlled socialism of the Soviet Union. The Central Committee of the Czechoslovak Communist Party April 15 adopted a program, "Czechoslovakia's Road to Socialism," designed to ensure freedom of speech, the press, assembly, and religion, as well as greater freedom for the country's four noncommunist political parties. Gen. Ludvik Svoboda, who was elected president March 30 following the forced resignation of Novotny from that office, said in May, "We are starting out to create a new type of socialist democracy, a democracy which will lend support to the full development of the human personality."

The first threat of Soviet military intervention developed when Soviet troops, which had moved into Czechoslovakia in June to engage in Warsaw Pact maneuvers, stayed behind when the exercises were completed. A stern word to the Czechs came at a July 14-15 meeting held in Warsaw of officials from Poland, Bulgaria, East Germany, Hungary, and the Soviet Union. The statement warned that "the dangers to the basis of socialism in Czechoslovakia threatens also the common interests of other socialist countries."

Moscow July 19 summoned the Czech leadership to the Soviet Union to discuss Czechoslovakia's "democratic socialism." The Czechs declined but agreed to meet with the Soviet Politburo July 29-August 1 at the Czech border town of Cierna. The Soviet delegation consisted of party chief Brezhnev, Premier Kosygin, President Podgornyi, and 11 other Politburo members. Czechoslovakia's representatives included 16 officials of the party and the government, led by Dubcek. Faced with Czech determination, the Soviets appeared to back down and agreed to remove the USSR troops in Czechoslovakia. The troop withdrawal was announced and an apparent compromise was confirmed at an August 3 meeting in Bratislava attended by representatives of the communist parties of the Soviet Union, Czechoslovakia, Bulgaria, East Germany, Hungary, and Poland.

Yet the relaxation of tension did not last. After a lapse of three weeks, the Soviet Union August 16 resumed criticism of the Czechoslovak press; the party newspaper *Pravda* assailed Czech publications for "fierce and slanderous attacks" on neighboring communist countries. Also on August 16, Dubcek pleaded with the Czechoslovak people not to push liberalization too far or too fast. "We need order in our country," he said, "so that we can be given freedom of action in our democratization process." Four days later, an estimated 400,000 troops, three-fourths of whom were Soviet soldiers, entered Czechoslovakia to put down the "counter-revolution."

The invaders promptly arrested Dubcek and other members of the government; they were flown to Moscow where, under pressure, they agreed to crack down on liberalization. Dubcek remained in power until April 1969, when he was replaced as first secretary by Gustav Husak, a pro-Soviet hard-liner, who oversaw the reinstitution of repressive government.

Widespread Condemnation

World reaction to the invasion of Czechoslovakia generally was severe. Though most of Moscow's satellites supported the move, the two mavericks of Eastern Europe, Romania and Yugoslavia, were critical. Romanian strongman Nicolae Ceausescu charged the invasion was "a great mistake and a grave danger to peace in Europe, to the fate of socialism in the world" and warned that "the entire Romanian people will not allow anybody to violate our land." A Yugoslav statement called the invasion "a significant, historical point of rupture, bearing on the relationship among the socialist countries in general, on the further development of socialism in the world and on the international workers' movement, as well as on peace in Europe and in the world." The communist parties of France and Italy condemned the Soviet action, as did the governments of France, Britain, Italy, India, Canada, and other nations. The Chinese said the invasion was a "shameless act" comparable to Hitler's occupation of the Sudetenland and U.S. involvement in Vietnam.

President Johnson said the invasion "shocks the conscience of the world. The Soviet Union and its allies have invaded a defenseless country to stamp out a resurgence of ordinary human freedom." And Richard Nixon, Republican presidential nominee, remarked, "It's a sad commentary on the nature of the Soviet system that a simple assertion of basic liberties brings repression by the troops of five nations." The platform adopted by the Democratic National Convention said that "the Soviet attack on and invasion of a small country . . . is an ominous reversal of the slow trend toward greater freedom and independence in Eastern Europe. The reimposition of Soviet tyranny raises the spectre of the darkest days of the Stalin era and increases the risk of war in Central Europe, a war that could become a nuclear holocaust."

The Brezhnev Doctrine

In the wake of the international furor over the invasion of Czechoslovakia, the Kremlin formulated a theory, quickly termed the Brezhnev Doctrine, to justify Soviet interference in the affairs of other communist states. The Brezhnev Doctrine was outlined in an article, "Sovereignty and the International Duties of Socialist Countries," published in *Pravda* September 26, 1968:

The weakening of any of the links in the world socialist system directly affects all the socialist countries, which cannot look on indifferently when this happens. Thus, with talk about the right of nations to self-determination the anti-socialist elements in Czechoslovakia actually covered up a demand for so-called neutrality and Czechoslovakia's withdrawal from the socialist community. However, the implementation of "self-determination" of that kind or, in other words, the detaching of Czechoslovakia from the socialist community would have come into conflict with Czechoslovakia's vital interests and would have been detrimental to the other socialist states. Such "self-determination," as a result of which NATO troops would have been able to come up to the Soviet borders, while the community of European socialist countries would have been rent, would have encroached, in actual fact, upon the vital interests of the peoples of these countries and would be in fundamental conflict with the right of these peoples to socialist self-determination.

Brezhnev reiterated the argument in a speech to the Fifth Congress of the Polish Communist Party, November 13, 1968, and in a speech in Moscow made October 28, 1969, to a delegation of Czech officials. He told his Polish audience that "when the internal and external forces hostile to socialism seek to revert the development of any socialist country toward the restoration of the capitalist order, when a threat to the cause of socialism in that country, a threat to the security of the socialist community as a whole emerges, this is no longer a problem of the people of that country but also a common problem, a concern of all socialist countries."

THE ROAD TO NEGOTIATIONS

The invasion of Czechoslovakia in August 1968 stalled but did not reverse the trend toward slowly improving East-West relations. A new administration in Washington, headed by a famous cold warrior, embarked on a course of diplomatic maneuvers that produced a dramatic series of U.S.-Soviet summit meetings, out of which came agreements in several areas, notably the limitation of nuclear weapons.

After its initial successes, however, the Nixon administration's policy of détente came under increasing attack, with critics charging that the Soviets got the best of the bargain and demanding that in return for Western concessions and trade Moscow ease some of its strict internal controls. The succeeding administration of Gerald R. Ford carried on essentially the same policies toward the Soviet Union as had the Nixon administration — and was subjected to the same criticism.

Leonid Brezhnev and his colleagues in the Soviet Union approached détente somewhat differently than did the United States. The Soviets had achieved strategic parity, which granted military superpower status; their military modernization efforts and intensive investments permitted unprecedented forays into the Third World. Unique opportunities brought on by movements for national liberation expanded Soviet involvement around the world. But the Soviets faced technological needs that only détente with the United States could provide.

The Soviet oligarchs recognized that their economy was stagnating but did not act to correct matters. Domestic economic and social difficulties, especially a growing human rights movement, focused unwanted international attention on Soviet internal problems.

Nixon Sets Tone

In his first inaugural address, President Richard Nixon set the tone his administration would adopt toward U.S.-Soviet relations by declaring, "After a period of confrontation, we are entering an era of negotiation." The same day, January 20, 1969, the Soviet Foreign Affairs Ministry announced Moscow was willing to discuss with Washington the "mutual limitation and subsequent reduction of strategic nuclear delivery vehicles, including defensive systems."

At his first presidential news conference, on January 27, 1969, Nixon endorsed arms negotiations and hinted at the "linkage" strategy his administration would later adopt, tying U.S. balance-of-power goals to its problems with the Soviet Union in other areas.

Nixon told reporters, "What I want to do is to see to it that we have strategic arms talks in a way and at a time that will promote, if possible, progress on outstanding political problems at the same time — for example — on the problem of the Mideast and on other outstanding problems in which the United States and the Soviet Union, acting together, can serve the cause of peace."

At the same news conference, Nixon endorsed the Treaty on Non-Proliferation of Nuclear Weapons that had been signed July 1, 1968. In urging the Senate to ratify the treaty, Nixon reminded the Senate that he "opposed ratification of the Treaty last fall in the immediate aftermath of the Soviet invasion of Czechoslovakia. My request at this time in no sense alters my condemnation of that Soviet action." He added, however, "I believe that ratification of the Treaty at this time would advance this administration's policy of negotiation rather than confrontation with the USSR." The Senate consented to the ratification March 13 by an 85-13 roll-call vote.

In adherence to the treaty provision calling for "negotiations in good faith on effective measures relating to cessation of the nuclear arms race at an early date," Nixon on June 19, 1969, invited the Soviet Union to begin strategic arms limitation talks (SALT). The Soviets waited until October 25 to accept. *(Details, Chapter 6)*

European Tensions Eased

Progress toward a nuclear arms limitation agreement went hand-in-hand with a relaxation of acrimony in Europe. The election of a socialist, Willy Brandt, as chancellor of West Germany on October 21, 1969, augured a change in relations between the two Germanies and between West Germany and the Soviet Union. Brandt's government November 28, 1969, signed the Nuclear Non-Proliferation Treaty and then set about to conclude treaties recognizing the de facto borders of postwar Europe. Brandt's *Ostpolitik* (Eastern policy) resulted in agreements in 1970 with the Soviet Union and Poland. The Treaty of Moscow, signed August 12, 1970, recognized existing European frontiers, particularly the Oder-Neisse line between Poland and East Germany. The treaty also held that the Soviet Union and West Germany would not resort to force to settle differences. A similar pact with Poland, the Treaty of Warsaw, was signed December 7.

In 1971 the four powers responsible for Berlin (the United States, France, Great Britain, and the Soviet Union) signed an agreement on September 3 regarding the administration of the divided city. The Soviet Union pledged to refrain from interfering with communication and transportation to West Berlin and all the parties vowed not to attempt to change the status of the city. Moreover, the treaty allowed West Berliners to travel with West German passports and receive West German consular protection abroad, although the four powers did not recognize West Berlin as part of West Germany. In 1972 the two Germanies signed a treaty December 21 that, in effect, recognized their postwar separation.

Exchanging toasts at the 1972 Moscow summit are, from left holding glasses, U.S. president Richard Nixon, Soviet president Nikolai V. Podgornyi, and Communist Party chief Leonid I. Brezhnev. At Nixon's left is interpreter Viktor Sukhodrev.

Nixon on 1972 Summit

"Surprise is another favorite technique of Communist negotiators. After the ceremony on Wednesday afternoon [May 24] when we signed an agreement on cooperation in space exploration, Brezhnev and I walked out of the room together. He began talking about the dinner planned for us at one of the government dachas outside Moscow that evening. As we neared the end of the corridor, he ... said, 'Why don't we go to the country right now so you can see it in the daylight?' ...

"We climbed into the limousine and were on our way while the Secret Service and the others rushed about trying to find cars and drivers to follow us....

"As soon as we arrived at the dacha, Brezhnev suggested that we go for a boat ride on the Moskva River.... Everyone was in a good humor when we got back to the dacha, and Brezhnev suggested that we have a meeting before the dinner, which was scheduled for eight o'clock.... For the next three hours the Soviet leaders pounded me bitterly and emotionally about Vietnam.

"I momentarily thought of Dr. Jekyll and Mr. Hyde when Brezhnev, who had just been laughing and slapping me on the back, started shouting angrily that instead of honestly working to end the war, I was trying to use the Chinese as a means of bringing pressure on the Soviets to intervene with the North Vietnamese. He said that they wondered whether on May 8 [the day increased bombing raids and the mining of North Vietnamese harbors were announced] I had acted out of thoughtless irritation, because they had no doubt that if I really wanted peace I could get a settlement without any outside assistance....

"When Brezhnev finally seemed to run out of steam, Kosygin took up the cudgel.... When Kosygin concluded, Podgorny came to bat....

"After about twenty minutes, Podgorny suddenly stopped and Brezhnev said a few more words. Then there was silence in the room. By this time it was almost eleven o'clock. I felt that before I could let this conversation end, I had to let them know exactly where I stood.

"I pointed out that I had withdrawn over 500,000 men from Vietnam. I had shown the greatest restraint when the North Vietnamese began their massive buildup in March, because I did not want anything to affect the summit. But when the North Vietnamese actually invaded South Vietnam, I had no choice but to react strongly....

"With that we went upstairs, where a lavish dinner was waiting for us.... There was much laughing and joking and storytelling — as if the acrimonious session downstairs had never happened."

—Richard Nixon, *RN: The Memoirs of Richard Nixon* (New York: Grosset & Dunlap, 1978), 612-614.

SALT I TALKS, 1972 MOSCOW SUMMIT

The SALT negotiations, begun November 17, 1969, in Helsinki, were switched to Vienna April 16, 1970. They moved back to Helsinki November 2, 1970. President Nixon announced May 20, 1971, that the United States and the Soviet Union had agreed to concentrate that year on limiting defensive antiballistic missile systems. After they reached agreement on the ABM, a joint communiqué said, the two governments would take up limitation of offensive strategic weapons.

Bargaining continued up through Nixon's trip to the Soviet Union in May 1972. The signing of the SALT accords was the highlight of the Nixon-Brezhnev summit. President Nixon and Communist Party chief Brezhnev reached agreement May 26 on accords prepared by Soviet and American SALT negotiators: a treaty to limit the deployment of ABMs and an executive agreement limiting the number of offensive weapons to those already under construction or deployed when the agreement was signed. The executive agreement also placed limitations on the number of missile-carrying submarines that could be constructed. *(Details, Chapter 6)*

President Nixon's arrival in Moscow on May 22, just three months after his historic trip to China, chalked up another "first." Not only was he the first president to visit China, he was the first to set foot in Soviet Russia. There was speculation immediately preceding the trip that the Soviets might withdraw their invitation as a result of Nixon's decision to thwart a North Vietnamese offensive by increasing air attacks on supply lines in North Vietnam and mining Haiphong harbor and six other ports in the north. That the Kremlin, North Vietnam's main arms supplier, went through with the summit was taken as a sign in the West that Moscow was as eager as Washington to conclude the arms pact and improve relations.

President Nixon and the U.S. delegation, which included Secretary of State William P. Rogers and national security adviser Henry A. Kissinger, arrived in Moscow after a two-day visit to Austria. The Americans were met at the airport by Premier Aleksei Kosygin and President Nikolai V. Podgornyi. Although Nixon was in Moscow to wrap up an arms agreement with Brezhnev, the Communist Party chief did not participate in the welcoming ceremonies because he had no official government post at the time.

President Nixon spent two hours with General Secretary Brezhnev May 22; the two men and their aides met for five hours of discussions the following day. High-level talks continued throughout Nixon's visit, including an unscheduled five-hour session at Brezhnev's dacha outside Moscow. Time also was set aside for ceremonies put on to sign agreements previously concluded. *(Nixon on summit, box, this page)*

The new U.S.-Soviet agreements were:

• An agreement establishing a joint committee on cooperation in the field of environmental protection, signed May 23 by Nixon and Podgornyi.

• A health agreement providing for coordinated research on cancer, heart disease, and environmental health, signed May 23 by Secretary of State Rogers and Boris V. Petrovskii, Soviet minister of public health.

● An agreement on space cooperation that envisioned a joint flight with linked U.S. and Soviet spacecraft in 1975, signed by Nixon and Kosygin May 24. *(Space link-up, box, p. 76)*

● A five-year accord setting up a permanent commission on scientific and technical cooperation, signed May 24 by Nixon and Kosygin.

● An agreement to avoid naval mishaps on the high seas, signed May 25 by U.S. Navy Secretary John W. Warner and Adm. Sergei G. Gorshkov, commander in chief of the Soviet navy. In addition, the parties May 26 reached agreement on a joint commission on trade to discuss a general trade pact. The trade agreement led to the U.S.-Soviet wheat deal announced in July. *(Grain sale, p. 70)*

President Nixon May 27 visited a Leningrad cemetery for the victims of the 1942-43 siege of the city, made a televised address to the Soviet people May 28, and signed a joint declaration of long-range principles with Brezhnev May 29. The joint declaration included an agreement to avoid military confrontations and envisioned total world disarmament. "In the nuclear age," it stated, "there is no alternative to conducting relations on the basis of peaceful coexistence." It pledged that the United States and the Soviet Union would "do their utmost to avoid military confrontations and to prevent the outbreak of nuclear war. They will always exercise restraint in their mutual relations, and will be prepared to negotiate and settle differences by peaceful means."

But an accompanying communiqué, which summarized the summit accords, noted that the two sides had been unable to come to any agreement on Vietnam:

The U.S. side emphasized the need to bring an end to the military conflict as soon as possible and reaffirmed its commitment to the principle that the political future of South Vietnam should be left for the South Vietnamese people to decide for themselves, free from outside interference.

The U.S. side explained its view that the quickest and most effective way to attain the above-mentioned objectives is through negotiations leading to the return of all Americans held captive in the region, the implementation of an internationally supervised, Indochina-wide cease-fire and the subsequent withdrawal of all American forces stationed in South Vietnam within four months, leaving the political questions to be resolved by the Indochinese peoples themselves.

The United States reiterated its willingness to enter into serious negotiations with the North Vietnamese side to settle the war in Indochina on a basis just to all.

The Soviet side stressed its solidarity with the just struggle of the peoples of Vietnam, Laos and Cambodia for their freedom, independence and social progress. Firmly supporting the proposals of the DRV (North Vietnam) and the Provisional Revolutionary Government of the Republic of South Vietnam, which provide a realistic and constructive basis for settling the Vietnam problem, the Soviet Union stands for a cessation of bombings of the DRV, for a complete and unequivocal withdrawal of the troops of the U.S.A. and its allies from South Vietnam, so that the people of Indochina would have the possibility to determine for themselves their fate without any outside interference.

U.S.-Soviet Relations And the 1972 Election

Although the war in Vietnam was the foremost foreign policy issue during the 1972 election, in which President Richard Nixon swamped his opponent, Sen. George McGovern of South Dakota, a liberal Democrat, U.S.-Soviet relations received a great deal of attention as well.

Regarding the Soviet Union, the Democratic platform welcomed the recent improvement in Soviet-American relations but stated that "... in our pursuit of improved relations, America cannot afford to be blind to the continued existence of serious differences between us. In particular, the United States should, by diplomatic contacts, seek to mobilize world opinion to express concern at the denial to the oppressed peoples of Eastern Europe and the minorities of the Soviet Union, including the Soviet Jews, of the right to practice their religion and culture and to leave their respective countries."

The Democratic document also stated that the "SALT agreement should be quickly ratified and taken as a starting point for new agreements," but it warned that the pact "must not be used as an excuse for new 'bargaining chip' military programs or the new round of the arms race."

McGovern proposed January 19, 1972, to cut defense spending by nearly $30 billion over three years.

At a June 15 congressional hearing, McGovern testified: "The plain truth is that the major dangers to American society today are not threats from abroad, but the deterioration of our society from within. We have been so obsessed with the fear of international communism and have spent so much of our energy and resources to feed that fear, that we have robbed and weakened our domestic society."

In contrast, the Republican platform said: "Historians may well regard these years as a golden age of American diplomacy." On relations with the Soviets, the document took note of Nixon's successful summit meeting and added a pledge "to build upon these promising beginnings in reorienting relations between the world's strongest nuclear powers to establish a truly lasting peace."

President Nixon, at a June 27 news conference, urged support of the SALT agreements and his administration's proposals to increase defense spending. "In the event that the United States does not have ongoing [defense] programs, however, there will be no chance that the Soviet Union will negotiate Phase Two of an arms limitation agreement."

National security adviser Kissinger told reporters in Moscow that the Indochina war had been the subject of "long, sometimes difficult and detailed discussions." He said he was unable to predict future Soviet actions in Vietnam.

But the leaders were able to agree that a European security conference should be held soon to discuss the possibility of mutual force reductions on both sides in Central Europe, particularly East and West Germany. Such a conference had long been sought by the Kremlin.

Trade Agreements

The arms limitation agreement was a milestone in U.S.-Soviet relations. As such, it overshadowed another noteworthy achievement of the Nixon-Brezhnev summit meeting — a pledge by both nations to improve and expand trade relations.

The statement on basic principles released at the end of the summit noted that both sides viewed commercial ties "as an important and necessary element in the strengthening of their bilateral relations." In concrete terms, this meant the establishment of a Joint United States-USSR Commercial Commission on May 26, 1972, and the announcement July 8, 1972, that the United States had advanced to Moscow a $500 million line of credit in return for a Soviet pledge to buy $750 million worth of U.S. grain over a three-year period. On July 5 the Soviets had contracted to buy more than 8.5 million tons of U.S. grain. Secretary of Commerce Peter G. Peterson in July led a delegation of American officials to Moscow to discuss further trade accommodations. The discussions were the first formal meeting of the U.S.-Soviet Commercial Commission.

A major stumbling block in the bargaining was settlement of the Soviet Union's World War II lend-lease debts to the United States. Administration officials insisted on settlement of the debts as part of any broad trade agreement. Negotiations culminated October 18 with the signing of a three-year trade pact and an agreement on repayment of the lend-lease debts.

Implementation of the trade agreement hinged on congressional approval of most-favored-nation (MFN) status (nondiscrimination in customs matters) for Soviet production. If MFN status was not granted, the pact would not enter into force and the Soviet Union, in accordance with the second agreement, would not have to repay the balance of its lend-lease debt of $722 million. According to the agreement, the Soviets would remit $48 million by July 1975, but the remaining debt would be deferred until MFN treatment was granted.

Trade Before 1972

As a result of numerous U.S. restrictions on trade made during the Cold War, U.S. trade with communist-bloc nations was substantially less in the postwar era than it was with the same nations before World War II. In 1963, for example, U.S. exports to the communist bloc amounted to only $166.7 million, which equaled just seven-tenths of 1 percent of total U.S. exports of $20.2 billion. In contrast, U.S. exports to the countries that later made up the communist bloc averaged $214 million a year — 4.7 percent of total exports — from 1926 to 1930. (This does not include exports to East Germany, for which separate figures were not then kept.)

Restrictions on trade with communist countries were relaxed with the passage of the Export Administration Act of 1969 (PL 91-184). The act, which replaced the expiring Export Control Act of 1949, contained a provision enabling the United States easily to sell items to communist nations if the items were freely available from other areas or countries, such as Western Europe and Japan. The legislation also recognized that "the unwarranted restrictions of exports from the United States has a serious adverse effect on our balance of payments."

The Nixon administration asked for a simple four-year extension of the 1949 act. But supporters of eased restrictions argued that Cold War hostilities had quieted and that the main effect of the controls in the old act was to deny U.S. exporters access to a growing East European market.

1972 Wheat Sale

The 1972 grain deal proved controversial. As described by the U.S. Agriculture Department, the bulk of the transaction was to consist of feed grains, such as corn, which would be used by the Soviets to bolster their poultry and livestock production. By late summer, however, it became apparent that Soviet interest had shifted to wheat. Agriculture Secretary Earl L. Butz said September 9 that Soviet purchases of wheat alone could reach 400 million bushels in 1972 — more than one-fourth the total U.S. crop. And, Butz added, total U.S. grain sales to the Soviets were approaching $1 billion for the year, far more than the total value originally contemplated over the entire three-year life of the agreement.

In fact, the Soviets bought more than 700 million bushels of grain, including nearly 440 million bushels of wheat. As a result, the government paid more than $300 million in export subsidies to U.S. grain traders. In addition, worldwide prices for grains rose steeply in the wake of the Soviet purchases, which, some critics of the sale said, pushed up consumer costs in the United States.

There was speculation that the large grain traders were aware the Russians were planning to buy an unprecedented amount of grain — which would hike prices — but neglected to share this information with grain farmers before the farmers sold their goods. The Senate Government Operations Permanent Subcommittee on Investigations, in a report issued July 29, 1974, had harsh words for the Agriculture Department's handling of the 1972 grain sales. While the subcommittee lauded the Nixon administration's goals — easing tensions between the United States and Russia, improving America's balance of payments deficit, and allowing U.S. farmers to profitably and usefully dispose of crop surpluses — it concluded that because of inept management and poor judgment in the Department of Agriculture the grain sale resulted in a domestic shortage of farm products, a snarled U.S. transportation system, waste of taxpayers' dollars, "unprecedented" rises in the cost of food, and added inflation.

Memories of the 1972 sale led to an "informal" administration embargo on grain sales to the Soviet Union in 1975 after Moscow again began buying large amounts of grain (9.8 million tons by late July). The embargo was lifted October 20 when a five-year Soviet-American grain agreement was signed in Moscow, pledging the Soviets to buy between 6 million and 8 million tons of grain each year. It was hoped that planned Soviet purchases would cause less disruption of U.S. markets. The grain purchasing arrangement was renegotiated in 1983 to last for five years.

Trade Act of 1973-74

Despite public criticism of the wheat sale and the administration's promotion of expanded U.S.-Soviet trade, President Nixon followed up his commitment made to Kremlin leaders at the Moscow summit by submitting to Congress April 10, 1973, a bill empowering the president to extend most-favored-nation status to the Soviet Union.

When the General Agreement on Tariffs and Trade (GATT) was concluded in Geneva in 1947, the contracting parties agreed to extend MFN treatment to each other. This general rule, a cornerstone of U.S. policy since 1923, required each party to accord equal treatment to the products of all other parties. In the president's trade bill, he requested authority to enter into bilateral commercial arrangements to extend most-favored-nation treatment to products of countries that did not receive such treatment. The president would be authorized to extend the treatment to countries that joined a multilateral trade agreement to which the United States was a party.

The authority to award MFN status was directed primarily at the Soviet Union. Implementation of the October 1972 trade agreement hinged on congressional approval of most-favored-nation treatment for Soviet products. If it was not granted, the pact would not enter into force and the Soviets, in accordance with the other agreement signed in October, would not be obliged to repay the balance of their World War II lend-lease debt.

Extension of MFN treatment was said to be of both material and psychological importance. According to administration officials, it was estimated that such status for Soviet products would result in additional imports from the Soviet Union worth $10 million to $25 million.

Jackson-Vanik Amendment. The bill ran into trouble on Capitol Hill. Anti-Soviet sentiment increased in Congress during 1973 as a result of the Kremlin's role in the Middle East war and the imposition of a tax on Soviet citizens wishing to leave the country.

In August 1972 the Soviets began to levy an exit fee — reportedly up to $30,000 — on holders of advanced academic degrees. Moscow justified the fees as reimbursement for the state's investment in education, the benefits of which would be lost through emigration. But the general effect of the fee was to block the emigration of Soviet Jews to Israel, because Jews were among the most highly educated in the Soviet Union and formed the bulk of those wishing to leave.

In response, Congress proposed to withhold most-favored-nation status from the Soviets. By the end of March 1973, 76 senators and 273 representatives joined in sponsoring an amendment that would bar MFN treatment and the extension of credits, credit guarantees, or investment credits to any nonmarket-economy country denying or taxing emigration. The amendment initiative was led in the Senate by Henry M. Jackson, D-Wash. (who had clashed with the White House over the strategic arms limitation treaty), and in the House by Charles A. Vanik, D-Ohio. Over administration opposition, the House December 11 passed the trade bill containing the restrictive Vanik amendment. During hearings by the House Ways and Means Committee, Secretary of State Rogers argued that better treatment of Soviet Jews "will come not from the confrontation formal legislation would now bring about, but from a steady improvement in our overall relations." The House-passed measure allowed the president to give MFN status to Soviet imports — but only if he certified to Congress that the Soviet government's restrictive emigration policies had been eased — and gave either the House or the Senate power to overrule the president's action.

House consideration of the bill was delayed three times in October and November at the request of President Nixon and Kissinger, who by then had succeeded Rogers as secretary of state. With anti-Soviet, pro-Israeli congressional emotions aroused by the Arab-Israeli war in the Middle East, officials feared that House debate on the trade bill at that time could only increase U.S.-Soviet tensions.

The Senate did not act on the trade bill until late in 1974 as the controversy over Jewish emigration continued. Throughout the year, the Soviets took the position that emigration was an internal matter unrelated to U.S.-Soviet affairs. The administration was forced into negotiating with both the Kremlin and the Senate in an attempt to fashion a compromise that would not alienate the Soviets yet satisfy Congress.

A compromise between the White House and Congress was announced October 18. An exchange of letters between Jackson and Kissinger released that day outlined the conditions the Soviets would have to meet in their emigration policies before the president would certify to Congress that their practices were leading substantially to a free emigration policy. Jackson said the agreement, based on assurances of Soviet leaders, assumed that the annual rate of emigration from the Soviet Union would rise from the 1973 level of about 35,000 and would in the future correspond to the number of applicants, which Jackson said exceeded 130,000. A benchmark of 60,000 annually would be considered a "minimum standard" of compliance, he said.

In testimony before the Senate Finance Committee on December 3, Kissinger said the compromise did not reflect "formal government commitments" between the two countries but was based on "clarifications of Soviet democratic practices from Soviet leaders." He cautioned the committee that any attempt "to nail down publicly" additional details or commitments was "likely to backfire." "If I were to assert here that a formal agreement on emigration from the USSR exists between our governments, that statement would immediately be repudiated by the Soviet government," Kissinger said. He added that no commitments had been made by Soviet leaders on specific numbers of emigrés. The Jackson letter, he said, contained interpretations and elaborations "which were never stated to us by Soviet officials." (*Texts of letters, Appendix, p. 313*)

Soviet Objections. The Soviet Union December 18 issued a statement denying it had given any specific assurances that emigration policies would be eased in return for American trade concessions and replying in particular to Jackson's claim that emigration would increase. It also released the text of an October 26 letter to Kissinger from Foreign Minister Andrei A. Gromyko, criticizing the Jackson-Kissinger letters as a "distorted picture of our position as well as of what we told the American side on that matter." Gromyko called the issue a wholly domestic one and said the Soviet Union expected a decrease, rather than an increase, in the number of persons wishing to emigrate.

Despite the confusion over what exactly had been worked out, Congress passed the bill — the Trade Act of 1974 — December 20, thereby allowing the United States to participate in the worldwide trade negotiations scheduled to begin in February 1975. Soviet reaction came quickly. Kissinger announced January 14, 1975, that the

Kremlin had rejected the terms for trade contained in the Jackson-Vanik amendment and accordingly would not put into force the 1972 trade agreement.

Eximbank Credits

Congress had another opportunity to register disapproval of the Soviet Union during consideration of legislation extending the life of the Export-Import Bank. Congress December 19, 1974, approved a measure satisfying senators' demands for closer congressional oversight of Eximbank's operations, particularly its support for exports to the Soviet Union. Specifically, the legislation:

● Set a $300 million ceiling on total Eximbank loans and guarantees to finance exports to the Soviet Union. The president could set a higher limit if he determined that an increase was in the U.S. national interest, but Congress would have to approve any higher ceiling by concurrent resolution.

● Prohibited use of more than $40 million of that amount to finance exports to the Soviet Union of fossil fuel research or exploration equipment and services, and prohibited any financing of exports intended to develop its fossil fuel resources.

● Required the bank to notify Congress at least 25 days before approving any transaction with any country involving loans, credits, or a combination of financing arrangements that totaled $60 million or more, or any transaction of $25 million or more for fossil fuel projects in the Soviet Union.

1973 SUMMIT OF NIXON, BREZHNEV

Soviet party chief Leonid Brezhnev, in return for Nixon's 1972 trip to Moscow, visited the United States in June 1973. During his stay in Washington June 17-22, Brezhnev met with President Nixon, members of Congress, and business executives. The two world leaders signed several agreements, including a declaration of principles to guide arms limitation negotiations and an agreement on prevention of nuclear war. *(Texts, Appendix, p. 302)*

Nixon June 21 accepted an invitation for a third summit meeting in Moscow in 1974. After leaving Washington, Brezhnev met with the president for two days in San Clemente, California.

The success of the 1973 summit meeting appeared to have been based more on form than substance. While a number of agreements were signed, they generally were minor. Rather than concrete results, the meeting was marked by a new spirit of détente — a feeling promoted by the two leaders that the Cold War in fact had ended.

That spirit was pointed out by Kissinger, Nixon's national security adviser, at a June 25 press briefing in San Clemente. Commenting on the joint communiqué released the same day, Kissinger observed: "One good way of assessing the results of the summit is to compare last year's communiqué with this year's communiqué."

Quoting from the 1972 document, Kissinger concluded that the meeting that year in Moscow had been designed to affirm the concept of peaceful coexistence, while "this year we are speaking of a continuing relationship."

But he added that "as relations between the Soviet Union and United States proceed along the course that was charted last May [1972] ... we cannot expect that these meetings ... will produce a dramatic new departure."

Although Nixon and Brezhnev did not spend much time discussing the lesser agreements signed during the week-long talks, Kissinger said, "the fact that they have determined to give a symbolic expression to this relationship, gives an impetus to negotiations that otherwise would drag on for months, and permits the quick resolution of particular issues which, if left to the expert level, could produce extended stalemate...."

The tenor of the joint communiqué issued just before Brezhnev's June 25 departure for France was reflective of the amicable — almost jovial — mood pervading the entire Brezhnev visit to Washington. *(Communiqué text, Appendix, p. 304)*

Accentuating the positive, the communiqué stressed the prospects of decreasing the dangers of nuclear war, limiting the nuclear arsenals of both countries, and increasing U.S.-Soviet trade.

Agreements

During Brezhnev's visit, the two countries signed documents in which they agreed:

Nuclear War. To avoid actions that could lead them into a nuclear confrontation with each other or a third nation. Both nations agreed "to refrain from the threat or use of force ... in circumstances which may endanger international peace and security" and to enter into "urgent consultations" should the risk of a nuclear conflict occur. No enforcement machinery was provided.

Peaceful Uses of Atomic Energy. To increased cooperation in developing peaceful uses of atomic energy, including construction of joint research facilities "at all stages up to industrial-scale operations."

Transportation. To cooperate in solving problems related to air, sea, and land transportation. The agreement would last five years.

Oceanography. To cooperate in studying the world's oceans. The five-year agreement would extend previous cooperative research and set up a joint committee to implement information exchange and convene annual conferences and seminars.

Cultural Exchange. To expand scientific, cultural, technological, and educational contacts and exchanges. The agreement expanded the existing two-year renewable accords, begun in 1958, to a general accord to last through 1979.

Agriculture. To cooperate in agricultural research, trade, development, production, and processing. The agreement was to remain in force for five years.

Commercial Relations. To discuss the desirability of establishing a U.S.-Soviet chamber of commerce and to expand and improve commercial facilities in Moscow and Washington.

Air Travel. To expand air passenger service between the United States and the Soviet Union.

Taxes. To eliminate double taxation of citizens and companies of one country living or working in the other. This was a treaty requiring Senate ratification. The United States had similar treaties with a number of noncommunist nations.

Arms Limitation Guidelines

Nixon and Brezhnev June 21 signed a declaration of principles to accelerate the strategic arms limitation talks so that a permanent treaty limiting each side's offensive missile and bomber capability could be reached by the end of 1974. The permanent treaty would replace the five-year interim agreement signed in Moscow in 1972.

The declaration, to serve as guidelines for U.S. and Soviet negotiators at the SALT talks in Geneva, said the permanent agreement could apply both to the number and quality of offensive weapons but specified that modernization and replacement of strategic weapons would be permitted under negotiated conditions. Implementation would be subject to verification by "national technical means." The United States previously had insisted on on-site inspection.

Both sides expressed willingness to sign interim agreements in certain areas pending completion of a permanent agreement. *(Chapter 6)*

1974 SUMMIT: DETENTE ATTACKED

Reaction to détente in the United States reached a crescendo in the summer of 1974. The focus of the controversy was President Nixon's June 27-July 3 trip to Moscow. The diplomatic parley came under fire as an attempt by the president to divert attention from mounting domestic difficulties — a faltering economy and the Watergate scandal. (The Watergate crisis culminated in Nixon's resignation August 9.) But critics of détente also objected to the administration's handling of relations with Moscow, some charging that Washington was permitting the Soviets to gain the upper hand militarily, others demanding Soviet concessions (for example, on emigration) in return for improved relations. *(U.S. debate on détente, box, pp. 74-75)*

No Breakthrough

Nixon went to Moscow hoping for a breakthrough on a permanent agreement to limit offensive nuclear weapons. During the week-long meetings, Nixon and General Secretary Brezhnev signed agreements to place further limits on Soviet and American underground nuclear tests and on the number of antiballistic missile sites each country could maintain. The leaders also signed accords in the fields of energy, medicine, and housing. But the sought-after broadening and extension of the five-year SALT treaty eluded the negotiators. Nonetheless, the personal rapport between Nixon and Brezhnev that had marked the 1973 summit meeting again was in evidence at the 1974 session. Soon after it began, Brezhnev disclosed that he had accepted President Nixon's invitation to visit the United States in 1975. *(Summit texts, Appendix, p. 307)*

The leaders signed two nuclear accords and four agreements in the areas of housing, energy, medicine, and trade. But the agreement they failed to reach — on the limitation of strategic arms — took prominence. Secretary of State Kissinger had sought before the summit to discourage optimism that a firm agreement could be reached. But a joint communiqué released July 3 by Brezhnev and Nixon gave surprisingly strong indication that the two sides were further apart in efforts to curb the arms race than had been believed. Although they had pledged at the 1973 summit to try to work out a permanent agreement limiting strategic offensive arms, no such agreement was reached at the 1974 summit. The two leaders also failed to reach a hoped-for limited agreement curbing multiple independently targeted reentry vehicles.

Instead of permanent agreements, they pledged to seek a new interim accord that would cover the period until 1985 and would include both quantitative and qualitative limitations. Agreement on a formula balancing the Soviet missile advantage and the U.S. warhead advantage had proved to be the key stumbling block.

At ceremonies July 3, Nixon and Brezhnev signed a partial test ban treaty on underground nuclear explosions. Because seismic detectors could monitor blasts above the magnitude set by the accord, the agreement could be easily policed. The Soviets continued to oppose policing procedures that required on-site inspections. At the same time, the leaders signed a protocol agreeing to forgo the option of establishing a second antiballistic missile system site as provided for in the ABM treaty signed May 26, 1972. *(Details, Chapter 6)*

Four agreements were signed June 28 and 29 concerning housing, energy, medicine, and trade. They provided for joint projects in housing and construction, particularly residential buildings in earthquake areas; joint research and development programs in nonnuclear forms of energy; cooperation in research and development of artificial hearts; and exchanges of information on economic undertakings and possible cooperation between American companies and Soviet organizations. Other agreements reached involved cooperative environmental research and cultural exchanges.

Little Reaction

The noncontroversial agreements signed at the 1974 summit drew little congressional reaction. One State Department official conceded that most of the accords could have been concluded at lower diplomatic levels. Opposition to the administration's nuclear policy, however, came June 25 from 37 senators, including Senate Majority Leader Mike Mansfield, D-Mont. In a letter to the president, the senators expressed "serious reservations" over a limited test ban that did not ban all tests. Moreover, Nixon's pledge to the Soviets to promote passage of trade reform legislation in Congress that would grant concessions to the Soviet Union provoked criticism from senators Jackson, Jacob K. Javits, R-N.Y., and Abraham Ribicoff, D-Conn. They had told Kissinger before the summit that they would oppose granting trade concessions until the Soviets topped their pledge to permit 45,000 Jews to emigrate each year.

In a speech June 5 to graduates of the U.S. Naval Academy, President Nixon warned against attempts to interfere in Soviet domestic affairs. Declaring that "there are limits to what we can do" to influence the Kremlin's treatment of Soviet citizens, the president asked, "What is our capability to change the domestic structure of other nations? Would a slowdown or reversal of détente help or hurt the positive evolution of other social systems?"

"Not by our choice, but by our capability," Nixon added, "our primary concern in foreign policy must be to

Nixon Pressure for Détente with USSR...

President Richard Nixon's policy of relaxing tensions with the Soviet Union generally received wide public approval as the 1970s got under way. Few observers argued for a return to the days of the Cold War. However, objections to the particulars of détente arose from several quarters.

Opponents of détente were a diverse group. They included:

● American Jewish leaders troubled by Moscow's treatment of Soviet Jews and the USSR role in the Middle East.

● Liberals bent on democratizing Soviet society.

● Conservatives — old-school anticommunists — worried that détente strengthened America's primary adversary.

● Labor leaders, also traditionally anticommunist, fearful that an influx of Soviet goods would fuel U.S. unemployment.

● Pentagon officials and the defense industry concerned that the SALT agreements left the United States seriously weakened.

Journalist Stephen S. Rosenfeld commented on the rise of opponents to détente in the January 1974 issue of *Foreign Affairs:*

The core of the matter is that there is no consensus on what condition we and the Russians ought to be working toward — that is, on what détente means. There is, rather, a debate, one which could not go on while the paramount Soviet-American interest was to reduce the chances of nuclear war and superpower confrontation, but one which cannot be avoided now that that paramount interest has been served. It is characteristic of this debate that each party joining it argues that his cause — first, if not alone — underlies true détente. Some equate détente with trade; others with human rights, emigration and the general "opening" of Soviet society; still others with political settlements and arms control; a few with aid for the world's weak and poor.

Strategic Implications

Military views of détente were aired at hearings on the U.S. defense posture held in February 1974 by the House and Senate Armed Services committees. Adm. Thomas H. Moorer, chairman of the Joint Chiefs of Staff, told the Senate committee the United States and the Soviet Union were "in a state of dynamic equilibrium" in terms of strategic arms, but that the Soviet Union had generated a momentum in offensive weaponry that could upset the balance if SALT negotiations failed.

Détente should not be allowed to weaken U.S.

defenses, Army Chief of Staff Gen. Creighton W. Abrams told the House Armed Services Committee February 14. "Détente may last, but on the other hand it can fade overnight," Abrams said. "It can easily lull us into a false sense of security. American strength made détente attainable, and it is hard to see it continuing unless we maintain that strength."

Critics of the SALT agreement were led on Capitol Hill by Sen. Henry M. Jackson, D-Wash., who contended the 1972 interim agreement had weakened the United States' strategic strength. In an April 22, 1974, speech, Jackson declared that the Soviets were insisting on an arrangement that would widen their strategic margin and that "the response of the administration to this situation has been disappointing in the extreme." He went on to charge that "the administration has concentrated on quick-fix, short-term proposals that can be readied for the forthcoming June summit meeting in Moscow."

The senator's charge evoked a strong response. Secretary of State Henry A. Kissinger told a press conference April 26: "The issues are extremely serious and extremely complicated. And if one uses charged words like 'quick fix' then one really prejudges the answer."

A definition of equality also rose as a point of dispute. "Essential equivalence" — a term used by President Nixon in his 1973 foreign policy message — became the catch-phrase of the administration. In a March 4 appearance on Capitol Hill, Defense Secretary James R. Schlesinger explained: "What it means is, first, that we do not plan to have our side a mirror image of their strategic forces. We do not have to have a match for everything in their arsenal. But in the gross characteristics of the forces, in terms of over-all number and over-all throw weight or payload, there should be some degree of equivalence between the two."

Senate Hearings

After President Nixon's June 1974 summit meeting in Moscow, Kissinger urged a national debate to air the conflicting views on the advantages and disadvantages of the U.S. course toward better relations with the Soviet Union. Such a debate took place at Senate Foreign Relations Committee hearings.

The hearings, begun August 15 and held through the fall, provided a forum for a broad group of détente supporters and opponents. The first witness was W. Averell Harriman, former ambassador to the Soviet Union, who said that Soviet leader Leonid I. Brezhnev had publicly committed himself to détente and would be "politically embarrassed if it ran into a dead end." Harriman, who had met with Brezhnev the previous June, urged passage of the trade bill

... Drew Fire from Diverse U.S. Sources

granting most-favored-nation status to the Soviets. He said that the economic importance of MFN had been exaggerated, but that it was "extremely important psychologically" to the Russians. "Failure to grant [MFN] has become in the Soviet mind a hostile position by the United States," he said.

Testifying August 15, Herbert S. Levine, economics professor at the University of Pennsylvania, said that the Soviet Union stood to gain a great deal in the short run from expanded economic relations with the United States. "What the United States stands to gain is debatable," he continued. Nevertheless, he concluded it was in the U.S. interest to pursue expanded economic ties because of 1) the favorable impact on the U.S. balance of payments, 2) the benefit to U.S. businessmen, 3) the potential for significant additions to U.S. energy supplies from joint development of Soviet resources, and 4) the effect of such ties on increasing the chances for peace.

The United States, said Adam B. Ulam, director of the Russian Research Center at Harvard University, should be "uncompromising and persistent in demanding" that the Soviet Union observe its international obligations and not pursue policies hostile to interests of the United States and its allies.

Marshall D. Shulman, international relations professor at Columbia University, criticized U.S. actions that he said threatened the possibility of ever reaching a plateau of "essential equivalence" in military strength. There was a vicious cycle, he said, of a lengthening U.S. technological lead in weapons programs, with a corresponding Soviet effort to catch up, that then was viewed by the United States as a rationale for more new programs.

Secretary of State Kissinger argued that recent U.S.-Soviet agreements "served to lessen the rigidities of the past and offer hope for a better era. Despite fluctuations a trend has been established; the character of international politics has been markedly changed."

Kissinger added:

But the whole process can be jeopardized if it is taken for granted. As the Cold War recedes in memory, détente can come to seem so natural that it appears safe to levy progressively greater demands on it. The temptation to combine détente with increasing pressure on the Soviet Union will grow. Such an attitude would be disastrous. We would not accept it from Moscow; Moscow will not accept it from us. We will finally wind up again with the Cold War and fail to achieve peace or any humane goal.

George Meany, president of the AFL-CIO, outlined the labor movement's opposition to détente. He said:

'Détente' Defined

"The term 'détente' is frequently used to describe the state of United States-Soviet relations since the Cuban missile crisis of 1962. Harold Nicholson, the noted British diplomat, defined 'détente' as simply a 'relaxation of tension.' The existence of a détente between two powers does not mean that fundamental problems in their relations have been solved. It does not mean that formal, or even informal, agreements have been reached between them. It in no way implies that the relaxed atmosphere is stable or permanent.

"Of course, problems may be solved, agreements reached, and a stable relationship achieved during a period of détente. But if and when these things occur, it is due not to the détente itself, but to the attitudes and skills of those who direct the foreign policies of the nations in question. A détente is a starting-point for conciliation and accommodation, not the product of these processes."

—Stephen S. Anderson, "United States-Soviet Relations: The Path to Accommodation," *Current History*, 55, no. 327 (November 1968): 281.

While détente has produced a silly euphoria in the West, it is viewed with cold calculation in the Soviet Union. While détente has made anti-communism unfashionable in the West — and you know, of course, that anti-communism is out of style with the best people — in the East, détente means an intensification of ideological struggle.

Here's how the Soviet Union sees détente:

Détente is based on U.S. weakness.

Détente means intensification of ideological warfare.

Détente means an undermining of NATO.

Détente means ultimate Soviet military superiority over the West.

Détente means recognition by the West of the Soviet Union's ownership of Eastern Europe.

Détente means withdrawal of American forces from Europe.

help influence the international conduct of nations in the world arena. We would not welcome the intervention of other countries in our domestic affairs, and we cannot expect them to be cooperative when we seek to intervene directly in theirs."

VLADIVOSTOK SUMMIT YIELDS NEW ARMS ACCORD

Gerald Ford assumed the presidency at a time when the office was in disrepute. Congressional displeasure with his predecessor had spurred efforts on Capitol Hill to rein in the executive's authority to chart the nation's foreign policy. Ford himself was not noted for his acumen in international affairs. Yet in his first speech as president to a joint session of Congress, delivered August 12, 1974, Ford declared: "Over the past five and a half years, in Congress and as vice president, I have fully supported the outstanding foreign policy of President Nixon. This I intend to continue."

Ford followed up his pledge with a summit meeting with Soviet chief Brezhnev November 23-24 at Vladivostok, the Siberian port on the Sea of Japan located only 50 miles from the Chinese border. The Vladivostok summit was part of Ford's first overseas presidential trip, which included stops in Japan and South Korea.

Largely engineered by Secretary of State Kissinger, whom Ford had asked to remain in his administration, the summit yielded a surprise tentative agreement to limit the numbers of strategic offensive nuclear weapons and delivery vehicles deployed by the United States and the Soviet Union through 1985.

An unexpectedly lengthy negotiating session November 23, forcing cancellation of a scheduled formal dinner, resulted in the restoration of momentum to the SALT talks, which the leaders announced would resume in Geneva in January 1975. Ford and Brezhnev issued a joint statement November 24 prescribing guidelines to be followed by the delegates. Secretary Kissinger, who had laid the groundwork for the nuclear agreement during talks in October with Brezhnev, said that there was a "very strong possibility" that a final accord on nuclear limitation would be concluded in time for signing during the summer of 1975, when Brezhnev was expected to visit the United States.

The tentative agreement limiting strategic nuclear weapons and delivery vehicles came as a surprise. The administration had not mentioned it in briefings before the visit, which was billed simply as an opportunity for Ford and Brezhnev to become acquainted and to reaffirm the commitment to détente. Kissinger noted November 24 that progress on détente had been hampered during President Nixon's visit to the Soviet Union in June because the Nixon administration had been weakened by the Watergate scandal and by the fact that Nixon was a "lame duck" president. A final communiqué issued November 24 at Vladivostok reaffirmed the determination of the United States and the Soviet Union "to continue, without a loss in momentum, to expand the scale and intensity of their cooperation efforts in all spheres. *(Vladivostok-SALT de-*

Joint Venture in Space

A gesture of international comity occurred 140 miles above the Atlantic Ocean July 17, 1975, when a U.S. Apollo spacecraft docked with a Soviet Soyuz craft. The link-up, telecast live around the world, featured the Apollo commander, Brig. Gen. Thomas P. Stafford of the Air Force, shaking hands with his Soviet counterpart, Col. Aleksei A. Leonov. The astronauts exchanged gifts, listened to messages from the leaders of their two countries, and ate lunch together. The spacecraft remained linked during two days of joint experiments.

In a prepared message read by mission control in Moscow, Soviet party chief Leonid I. Brezhnev said that "The successful docking proved the correctness of the positions which we carried out in joint cooperation and friendship between Soviet and American designers, scientists and cosmonauts."

President Gerald R. Ford, in a telephone conversation with the U.S. and Soviet crews, said, "Your flight is a momentous event and a very great achievement, not only for the five of you but also for the thousands of American and Soviet scientists and technicians who have worked together for three years to ensure the success of this very historic and very successful experiment in international cooperation. It has taken us many years to open this door to useful cooperation in space between our two countries, and I am confident that the day is not far off when space missions made possible by this first joint effort will be more or less commonplace."

Astronaut Thomas P. Stafford and Cosmonaut Aleksei A. Leonov work together in space during the Apollo-Soyuz link-up.

tails, Chapter 6; summit texts, Appendix, p. 314)

But in 1975 the SALT negotiations again stalled over technical issues. Soviet leader Brezhnev's proposed trip to the United States to sign a final pact was pushed back from June to September to November and then to "early 1976" as it became clear that the two nations were at an impasse over two issues not negotiated at Vladivostok: the Soviets' Backfire bomber and the U.S. cruise missile.

Angola

Attention to strategic arms limitation was diverted late in December 1975 by the revelation that Washington and Moscow were backing opposing sides in the newly independent African nation of Angola. Congressional reaction was varied: anger that U.S. aid had been given secretly and with minimal consultation with Congress; fears that relations with other nations in the area would be impaired; alarm that the United States would become involved in another Vietnam-type war in an area of little overriding national interest; and renewed questions about the Soviet commitment to détente.

The administration contended that Soviet and Cuban military assistance to the Popular Movement for the Liberation of Angola (MPLA) amounted to a major new projection of Soviet power beyond the traditional sphere of Soviet influence. In a television interview broadcast January 5, 1976, President Ford said the Soviet action was "destabilizing" and "inconsistent with the aims . . . of détente." As the issue generated debate, Secretary of State Kissinger repeatedly argued that the United States should try to avoid a public confrontation between the superpowers, even though the Soviet involvement demanded an American response. For that reason, he said, the administration chose to support clandestinely the National Front for the Liberation of Angola and the National Union for the Total Independence of Angola, two anti-MPLA factions.

Congress felt otherwise. Both chambers approved an amendment to the fiscal 1976 defense appropriations bill banning the use of any funds contained in the bill for the Angolan civil war. *(Details, update, p. 118)*

Senate Activity

Politics colored Senate consideration of a resolution passed May 5, 1976, calling for continued negotiations between the United States and the Soviet Union on divisive issues so they "do not lead to war." Key language in the so-called prodétente resolution urged both nations to "refrain from seeking advantages by exploiting troubled areas of the world" and to complete a "clearly stated" nuclear arms agreement whose implementation was "verifiable." The resolution also stated that all U.S. initiatives to improve relations with the Soviet Union should be undertaken in "close consultation and cooperation with" U.S. allies.

President Ford and Soviet leader Brezhnev May 28, 1976, signed a treaty governing nuclear explosions for peaceful purposes. But the Senate made no attempt to consider the treaty because election-year politics — especially conservatives' criticism of past Soviet-U.S. nuclear negotiations and the policy of détente, and the concern of liberals with the terms of the treaty — made the treaty unpopular with many senators. (As of April 1986, it had not been ratified.)

According to administration officials, the treaty for the first time allowed on-site inspection of some nuclear blasts.

But the pact's 150-kiloton limitation on the size of explosions from a single nuclear device was called a "wholly inadequate step" by Jimmy Carter, the former governor of Georgia vying for the 1976 Democratic presidential nomination. And the Washington-based Arms Control Association, which counted among its membership former U.S. arms control negotiators who served in the Kennedy and Johnson administrations, May 28 termed the treaty a "disheartening step backward from responsible arms control policies."

The pact was submitted to the Senate July 29 along with a 1974 treaty limiting underground nuclear weapons tests to 150 kilotons. Submission of that treaty had been delayed until agreement was reached on controls governing nuclear explosions for peaceful purposes.

Meanwhile, on the issues of aiding Angola, arms control, and détente as a whole, President Ford needed conservative backing because the 1976 presidential election race was warming up. Ronald Reagan threatened to wrest the GOP nomination from Ford, and Democrat Jimmy Carter was making unexpected gains for his party's nomination. *(1976 election, box, pp. 78-79)*

BREZHNEV AND THE CARTER PRESIDENCY

President Jimmy Carter entered office having pledged to base America's dealings with its allies and foes on a heightened concern for human justice. Carter also had promised to trim the fat from the U.S. military budget, while maintaining a strong defense, and to get the stalled SALT talks moving again. By the time he left office, the use of human rights as a guide to the conduct of foreign relations largely had been discarded, the defense budget had begun to grow, and the SALT II agreement that Carter had pressed for so zealously had been shelved. The Carter team had been replaced by a new administration bent on taking a harder line toward the Soviets.

In the Soviet Union, the communist leaders presided over two key events that triggered a hardened U.S. assessment of Soviet motivations and intentions — the December 1979 invasion of Afghanistan and the December 1981 imposition of martial law by Polish authorities. The Sino-Soviet dispute continued. Moreover, the Kremlin chiefs faced two chronic domestic problems: unrelenting economic troubles and questions surrounding political leadership. The latter was particularly pressing in light of the advancing age of the Soviet leadership and an apparent scarcity of suitable heirs apparent.

Human Rights Policy

The Carter administration ranked human rights practices as a foreign policy priority. "Our commitment to human rights must be absolute," the president said in his January 20, 1977, inaugural address. But the government's application of a human rights standard, critics soon charged, was inconsistent and unproductive.

Carter's expressions of concern for human rights activists in the Soviet Union provoked a sharp response from Brezhnev, who in a March 21 speech accused the United

Ford Gaffe on 'Free' East Europe Nations ...

In the 1976 presidential race, as in 1972, détente was a central issue. But in 1976 the focus had changed. Four years before, détente was the centerpiece of Richard Nixon's carefully crafted statesmanship. In 1976, however, criticism rose from Democrats as well as Republicans about what détente was costing the United States in its competition with the Soviet Union over political and military influence. The continuing Soviet military buildup, Soviet actions in Angola, SALT II, human rights violations, and, late in the campaign season, Soviet domination of East Europe — all were aired at length by candidates of both parties. And as the main architect of détente, Secretary of State Henry A. Kissinger became the whipping boy of the Ford administration's critics.

In November 1975 President Ford announced a shakeup of his cabinet, firing, among others, Defense Secretary James R. Schlesinger, the administration's most vocal critic of détente. Schlesinger's dismissal indicated that the president rejected his calls for a tougher stance toward the Soviets.

Schlesinger during 1975 repeatedly had called for increased U.S. defense spending to offset what he viewed as an alarming buildup of Soviet forces. His outcries were considered increasingly objectionable to Kissinger in his efforts to work out a second-stage arms control agreement with Moscow. Kissinger was thought to be willing to compromise with the Soviets, considering it far more important to reach a SALT II accord promptly than to hold out for a trade-off over the controversial Backfire bomber-cruise missile dispute.

If Schlesinger's departure offended hard-liners, they could take comfort in another major change in the administration: the announcement that moderate Republican Nelson A. Rockefeller, the vice president, would not be Ford's running mate in 1976.

Reagan Campaign

President Ford's main rival for the Republican nomination in the race, former California governor Ronald Reagan, was gaining attention and support for his conservative campaign early in the year. Reagan hammered away at the administration's policy of détente. He spread his view that the trustworthiness of communist leaders was questionable: "There are some who believe that we should grant favors to our adversaries with no strings attached ... in the hope that unilateral concessions will create a 'climate of trust' between the two countries.... History provides very little encouragement for this strategy. The Soviet leaders, from Lenin to Brezhnev, have been realistic, unsentimental bargainers."

As the primary season progressed, the rhetoric heated up. Reagan charged that détente was "a one-way street" that had supplied the United States with benefits no more substantial than "the right to sell Pepsi-Cola in Siberia." Reagan also criticized the Vladivostok agreement, saying that the Soviets were given missile advantages detrimental to U.S. security.

After losing the key Florida primary in March, Reagan began a forceful attack on the president's foreign policy. On March 4, Reagan declared that Ford had shown "neither the vision nor the leadership necessary to halt and reverse the diplomatic and military decline of the United States...." The next day Reagan continued his attack, arguing that the U.S. relationship with China was falling apart under Ford's leadership. He said that the link with China was based on mutual concern for Soviet military power but added, "In place of the determined and confident America the Chinese bargained with four years ago ... they see in Washington today a timid, vacillating and divided leadership attempting to sweet talk the Russians out of their belligerent behavior."

The administration struck back March 11. Kissinger charged that politically motivated criticism of U.S. diplomacy could wreck the nation's foreign policy and declared that there was no alternative to the administration's policy of imposing penalties for Soviet adventurism while offering incentives for restraint. "What do those who speak so glibly about one-way streets or pre-emptive concessions propose concretely that this country do?" Kissinger asked. "What precisely has been given up? What level of confrontation do they seek? What threats would they make? What risks would they run? What precise changes in our defense posture, what level of expenditure over what period of time do they advocate?"

President Ford, for his part, responded to Reagan's charges by emphasizing his determination to "keep cool" in foreign affairs, "keep our powder dry," and avoid "nuclear holocaust," implying that a harder line in foreign policy could have catastrophic effects. He stressed his experience in foreign affairs and lamented that "nitpicking" challenges to the administration's foreign policy were harmful to the nation.

At the same time, Ford hardened his stance. In the Florida primary, for example, he condemned Cuba's Fidel Castro as an "international outlaw" and warned that the United States would take "appropriate measures" if Cuba attempted armed intervention in the Western Hemisphere.

Carter, Ford Nominations

Among the Democratic contenders, the most persistent critic of détente was Sen. Henry M. Jackson of

... Highlighted 1976 Controversy Over Détente

Washington, who termed détente "a coverup for the gross mismanagement of the foreign policy of the United States." Jackson added that the president's "repeated celebrations of the successes of détente are an attempt to sell a false sense of security. He is operating on the premise that Soviet restraint can be purchased by American wheat . . . [and] by American economic largesse and diplomatic passivity."

By the time Democrats gathered in July to nominate their standard bearer, Jackson was long out of contention. The Democrats nominated Carter, who called for a new "moral authority" — a dedication to humanitarian principles and opposition to human injustice abroad — as the guideposts for the United States to follow in mapping relations with other nations. The Democratic platform, which reflected the views of the Carter forces, said the following about human rights and U.S.-Soviet relations:

> Our stance on the issue of human rights and political liberties in the Soviet Union is important to American self-respect and our moral standing in the world. We should continually remind the Soviet Union, by word and conduct, of its commitments in Helsinki to the free flow of people and ideas and of how offensive we and other free people find its violations of the Universal Declaration of Human Rights. As part of our programs of official, technical, trade, cultural and other exchanges with the U.S.S.R., we should press its leaders to open their society to a genuine interchange of people and ideas.

During the primary campaign, Carter said that "The benefits of détente must accrue to both sides, or they are worthless. Their mutual advantage must be apparent, or the American people will not support the policy. . . ."

President Ford had a harder time than his Democratic counterpart in overcoming his primary opposition, but the Ford and Reagan forces made peace after Ford won the nomination at the Republican convention in August.

Presidential Debate

The views of the Democratic and Republican nominees were aired October 6 in a nationally televised debate on foreign policy. Carter, on the offensive, charged that "we've become fearful to compete with the Soviet Union on an equal basis. We talk about détente. The Soviet Union knows what they want in détente, and they've been getting it. We have not known what we've wanted and we've been outtraded in almost every instance."

In response, Ford attacked Carter's proposals for a reduced defense budget, saying, "Let me tell you this straight from the shoulder: You don't negotiate with Mr. Brezhnev from weakness, and the kind of a defense program that Mr. Carter wants will mean a weaker defense and a poor negotiating position."

But the real news that came out of the foreign policy debate centered on the president's remarks concerning East Europe. Discussing the Helsinki accord, Ford said that "There is no Soviet domination of Eastern Europe and there never will be under a Ford administration." He went on to explain, in answer to a follow-up question, that he did not think the Yugoslavs, Romanians, and Poles considered themselves dominated by the Soviets; "each of those countries is independent and autonomous." Carter immediately disputed Ford's claim, saying, "I would like to see Mr. Ford convince the Polish-Americans and the Czech-Americans and the Hungarian-Americans in this country that those countries don't live under the domination of and the supervision of the Soviet Union behind the Iron Curtain."

In the days following the debate, Ford's comments became a major campaign issue with Carter and his running mate, Sen. Walter F. Mondale of Minnesota, trying to capitalize on the president's apparent mistake. Carter October 7 said, "It was a disgrace to our country. It was a very serious blunder for him to say it. The Soviet Union has tank divisions and hundreds of thousands of troops to keep them under domination." Mondale described Ford's statement as "the most incredible and unbelievable ever made by a sitting president since the Iron Curtain clamped down."

Criticism of the president came from other quarters as well. The *London Evening News* said Ford had committed a "major gaffe." And Lev E. Dobriansky, chairman of the National Captive Nations Committee, condemned Ford's statement as "preposterous," insisting that it "blatantly contradicts the brute realities of Russian domination and colonialism in Eastern Europe."

Attempting to clarify his position, Ford said October 7 that he "firmly supports the aspirations for independence of the nations of Eastern Europe. The United States has never conceded and never will concede their domination by the Soviet Union." The president added, "It is our policy to use every peaceful means to assist countries in Eastern Europe in their efforts to become less dependent on the Soviet Union and to establish ties with the West." And at an October 12 meeting with ethnic leaders, the president admitted he had erred. "The original mistake was mine," he said. "I did not express myself clearly; I admit it."

Ford's gaffe undermined his efforts to portray Carter as unqualified in foreign policy matters and may have contributed to Carter's victory.

States of using the issue of human rights to interfere in Soviet internal affairs. He added that it was "unthinkable" that Soviet-American relations could develop normally so long as Carter continued his campaign in support of Soviet dissidents. At a breakfast meeting with members of Congress the next day, Carter said he would not back down on human rights, adding, "Some people are concerned every time Brezhnev sneezes." (Brezhnev speech excerpts, Appendix, p. 316)

The 1978 debate over human rights violators in the Soviet Union focused on the trials of dissidents Anatolii Shcharanskii and Alexander Ginzburg. Many in Congress argued that SALT negotiations with the Soviet Union should be promptly suspended and the U.S. delegates recalled to signal official displeasure.

The Carter administration opposed any interruption in the SALT negotiations and refused to cancel Secretary of State Cyrus R. Vance's meeting with Foreign Minister Gromyko in Geneva as the trials got under way in the Soviet Union in July. "We will persist in our efforts to negotiate a sound SALT II agreement because it is in our national interest to do so," said Vance in a July 8 statement.

The State Department did, however, rescind trips by U.S. environmental and scientific delegations to the USSR in a gesture of protest over the dissidents' treatment. And President Carter July 12 condemned the trials as an "attack on every human being who lives in the world who believes in basic human freedom." The president later unexpectedly revoked the sale of new computer equipment to Tass, the Soviet press agency.

Carter himself said little more about human rights problems during 1978 until December, when he declared that concern about human rights was the "soul" of U.S. foreign policy. "The effectiveness of our human rights policy is now an established fact," Carter said December 6. "It has contributed to an atmosphere of change — sometimes disturbing — but which has encouraged progress in many ways and in many places."

In his December speech, celebrating the 30th anniversary of the United Nations Declaration of Human Rights, Carter singled out seven nations that "continue to practice repression": Cambodia, Chile, Uganda, South Africa, Nicaragua, Ethiopia, and the Soviet Union.

In the year that followed, more pressing issues, particularly the SALT II treaty, the growing strength of Soviet power, and, finally, the Soviet invasion of Afghanistan, made the human rights policy somewhat less than the priority item it had been for U.S.-Soviet relations earlier in the Carter administration.

Soviet Military Buildup

Before Carter took office, reports of the continuing growth of Warsaw Pact military capabilities in the mid-1970s had taken the sheen off détente. President Ford's fiscal 1977 defense budget, which called for more than $7 billion in "real growth" — an increase beyond that necessary to offset inflation — easily won congressional approval. The reason: widespread concern over the rising trend of Soviet military strength and growing suspicion of Soviet diplomatic aims.

Supporters of a beefed-up defense capability pointed to a list of Soviet actions they said justified the Pentagon increase, including the incitement of Arab combatants in the 1973 Middle East war, intransigence toward internal dissidents and Jews wishing to emigrate, and diplomatic and financial support of leftist revolutionary movements in Angola and elsewhere in South Africa.

Carter Budget, Neutron Bomb

During his presidential campaign, Carter had promised "savings" of $5 billion to $7 billion in defense spending. But after the election he and his defense secretary, Harold Brown, explained that the savings would be realized gradually through reductions in the rate at which annual defense spending would increase, rather than from any reduction in the 1977 appropriations. President Carter on February 22, 1977, proposed a Pentagon budget of $120.3 billion for fiscal 1978, $2.8 billion below Ford's figure.

Concern over the military strength of the Soviet Union also was reflected in the discussion of additional weapons for troops of the North Atlantic Treaty Organization (NATO). The debate centered on the "neutron bomb," a highly controversial enhanced-radiation warhead designed to kill enemy soldiers within a restricted area while causing little damage to the surrounding environs. The bomb's main purpose was to destroy the crews of Warsaw Pact tanks, which outnumbered those of NATO members. (Chapter 6)

President Carter asked Congress for permission to go ahead with the production of the weapons. Only after lengthy debate did Congress acquiesce. The basic premise of the Pentagon strategists was that a Soviet attack would be deterred by the threat of weapons that could be used by U.S. troops without causing so much damage as to destroy West Germany in order to save it. Critics, both in the United States and in the other NATO countries, insisted that a Soviet attack on Western Europe would be deterred only by the prospect of U.S. nuclear retaliation against the Russian homeland. They warned that U.S. preparations to fight a "limited" nuclear war in Europe might weaken the deterrent by implying that Washington would not risk Boston to save Bremen.

The Soviet reaction to the radiation weapons debate was to initiate an intense campaign against the neutron bomb. At the Geneva disarmament conference, Moscow proposed a treaty banning radiation weapons, and 31 Soviet scientists wrote Carter that his decision for or against production would test the sincerity of his campaign promises to slow the arms race. In addition, Brezhnev reportedly warned the European NATO governments in strong terms against adding the new weapon to the NATO arsenal.

After all the debate, President Carter on April 7, 1978, announced his decision to defer production of the neutron bomb. He said the "ultimate decision . . . will be influenced by the degree to which the Soviet Union shows restraint in its conventional and nuclear arms programs and force deployments affecting the security of the United States and Western Europe."

On Capitol Hill, critics accused Carter of making, at best, a "nondecision." Many, among them Senator Jackson, also had charged the president with being too "soft" in the SALT negotiations.

SALT II: Unreached Goal

From the early days of his administration, Carter faced a bitter struggle in Congress to win approval for his ideas governing nuclear weapons control. After much haggling, he signed an agreement with Moscow in 1979 and then faced stiff opposition to it in the Senate. A showdown on SALT II was avoided only after the December 1979 Soviet invasion of Afghanistan shelved the issue indefinitely.

Fresh from his victory in having Paul Warnke nominated to head both the arms control agency and the SALT negotiating team, Carter surprised both his critics and his supporters in late March by presenting arms control proposals to the Soviets. The two proposals, discussed between Secretary of State Vance and Soviet leader Brezhnev, were rejected by Moscow. The favored U.S. proposal — the so-called "comprehensive proposal" — called for sizable reductions in strategic arms, particularly by the Soviet Union. The second option — the deferral plan — would simply have involved ratification of the Vladivostok agreement and left the two controversial weapons, the U.S. cruise missile and the Soviet Backfire bomber, for later negotiations. In rejecting the proposals, Soviet foreign minister Gromyko charged on March 31 that the United States was trying to win "unilateral advantages" at the expense of the Soviet Union.

After the Soviets rejected the U.S. SALT proposals, Carter vowed (in a March 30 news conference) to "hang tough" and warned that if, following the meeting of U.S. and Soviet negotiators in Geneva in May, the United States concluded that "the Soviets aren't acting in good faith with us and that an agreement is unlikely, then I would be forced to consider a much more deep commitment to the development and deployment of additional weapons."

The deadlocked talks resumed in May. At the end of the month, negotiators had reached agreement on a new three-part blueprint that would supersede the disputed Vladivostok accord. First, there would be a treaty that would run until 1985, the duration projected in the Vladivostok accord. It would place a ceiling on the number of ballistic missiles for each side. Second, there would be a protocol lasting for three years that would be attached to the treaty expiring in 1985. The protocol would include controversial items such as the cruise missile and Backfire. In other words, the United States would accept constraints on the cruise missile for three years, during which time the two sides would negotiate another treaty with sharp reductions and other limits proposed in Carter's preferred option. Third, there would be a statement of general principles to govern the follow-on negotiations for substantial reductions in strategic arms.

Vance said the three-part framework blended the Soviet and American ideas and that all parts were interdependent, meaning that there would have to be agreement on all three, not just one, aspect. In a May 26 news conference, Carter voiced optimism about the prospects for a SALT II accord, but at the same time cautioned that "there are substantial remaining differences between ourselves and the Soviet Union. No firm proposals were put forward on either side." *(Details, Chapter 6)*

The May and September 1977 agreements involved concessions on both sides. Following their meeting in September 1977, both Secretary of State Vance and Soviet Foreign Minister Gromyko said the two sides had drawn somewhat closer together but avoided forecasts on reaching a new pact.

Speaking before the United Nations October 4, 1977, Carter said that the two superpowers were "within sight of a significant agreement." But none appeared. Meanwhile, the two governments agreed to adhere to the terms of the 1972 accord (which expired October 3, 1977) until a newer one, covering a wider range of weapons, was worked out.

In addition to the military and political complexity of the negotiations themselves, there were several reasons for the slow progress. One was the growing opposition in Congress to several proposed weapons limitations under negotiation. Another was the harsh Soviet reaction to Carter's human rights stand and his outspoken support for Russian dissidents — although the president maintained that his stand should have no effect on the SALT negotiations. "There has been a surprising adverse reaction in the Soviet Union to our stand on human rights," Carter said in a June 1977 interview. "We have never singled them [the Soviets] out. I think I have been quite reticent in trying to publicly condemn the Soviets."

'Linkage' to African Dispute

Early in 1978, prospects for an early SALT II agreement were clouded by the administration's concern over Soviet aid to Ethiopia in that country's conflict with Somalia in the area called the Horn of Africa. At a meeting with reporters March 1, Carter's chief national security adviser, Zbigniew Brzezinski, was asked whether there was a "linkage" between Soviet activities in Africa and the likelihood of reaching a U.S.-Soviet arms control agreement. "We are not imposing any linkages," Brzezinski replied, "but linkages may be imposed by unwarranted exploitation of local conflict for larger international purposes."

Soviet reaction to the comments of Brzezinski and other U.S. officials outlining the same "linkage" concept was swift. In a commentary March 2, *Pravda* labeled the linkage prospect "crude blackmail," "dangerous," and "unacceptable."

On the same day, President Carter moderated Brzezinski's statement. If there is such a link, Carter said in a news conference, it was because the Soviet role in Africa was bound to affect American public opinion in the Senate, which would have to approve any new SALT accord. SALT and the Ethiopia-Somalia dispute are "linked because of actions by the Soviets," Carter said. "We don't initiate the linkage."

The president followed up his news conference comments with a strong speech on defense on March 17, warning that the Soviet military buildup could jeopardize cooperation with the United States. "We are not looking for a one-sided advantage," he said, " but before I sign a SALT agreement on behalf of the United States, I will make sure that it preserves the strategic balance, that we can independently verify Soviet compliance and that we will be at least as strong relative to the Soviet Union as we would be without an agreement."

Reacting with speed and anger, the official Soviet news agency Tass March 17 commented that Carter's speech "actually means a shift of emphasis in American foreign policy, from the earlier proclaimed course towards insuring the national security of the U.S. through negotiations, through limiting the arms race and deepening détente, to a course of threats and a buildup of tension."

Agreement Reached

The SALT negotiations continued through 1978; the administration touted the expected agreement almost exclusively on the argument that military advantages would accrue to the United States if the pact were ratified. Finally, on May 9, 1979, the U.S. and Soviet governments announced that agreement had been reached on all but a handful of technical provisions of SALT II and that Carter and Brezhnev would sign the treaty in Vienna June 15-18.

On the eve of Carter's departure for the summit, Senator Jackson, in his sharpest attack up to that point on Carter's defense policy, expressed the views of many hard-liners against the treaty: It was inequitable, allowing Moscow significant military advantages; and it was politically dangerous, signaling U.S. "appeasement" and distracting Americans from the Soviet threat.

Vienna Summit

The Carter administration had been moving for months to counter any impression that its arms control policy was founded on assumptions of Soviet trust and goodwill. That effort was illustrated by the atmosphere surrounding the Vienna summit. In contrast to the three Nixon-Brezhnev meetings, there were fewer champagne toasts. And there were no routine agreements on peripheral subjects, signed in great ceremony to convey the appearance of broad agreement on issues.

To the contrary, administration spokesmen kept the press informed of sharp exchanges between the two leaders over spiraling defense budgets and U.S. concern with Soviet support of Cuban military intervention in the developing world. Both issues had played a role in undermining U.S. political support for the 1972-style détente. The SALT process had lost much of its allure to congressional moderates, who claimed they had accepted SALT I as part of a package deal that promised a ban on Soviet global adventurism.

Besides highlighting Carter's challenges to Brezhnev on issues of power politics, administration sources also told the press that Carter had wrested concessions from a reluctant Brezhnev on the issue of the Soviet Backfire bomber. To hard-line critics, the plane had become one symbol of the treaty's technical inequities. Although it could strike U.S. targets under certain conditions, the Backfire was not included in the treaty itself because Moscow insisted it would be used only to attack targets in Eurasia and neighboring seas.

But Moscow agreed to a separate statement freezing the plane's production rate and limiting its use in ways that might threaten U.S. targets. Congressional hard-liners dismissed the separate agreement as unenforceable.

The treaty set basic numerical limits on intercontinental missiles and bombers that would be in effect until 1985. Additional restrictions on mobile land-based missiles and cruise missiles launched from land or ships would run only until 1982.

In a June 18 speech presenting the treaty to a joint session of Congress, Carter emphasized its constraints on Soviet strategic programs. "Under this new treaty, the Soviet Union will be held to a third fewer strategic missile launchers and bombers by 1985 than they would have simply by continuing to build at their present rate," he said.

On the other hand, he said, the agreement allowed development of the new mobile, MX intercontinental missile. The Pentagon maintained that a movable missile was necessary to thwart an all-out Soviet missile attack, which in a few years would be able to wipe out the existing stationary U.S. missile launchers, according to U.S. defense officials. And the treaty ensured that the MX would

be militarily viable. "Without the SALT II limits," Carter said, "the Soviet Union could build so many [missile] warheads that any land-based system, fixed or mobile, could be jeopardized."

Cuban Brigade

The Senate Foreign Relations Committee began hearings on the pact July 9, 1979. In the midst of Senate consideration of SALT II, developments in Cuba threatened to block ratification. During the Foreign Relations hearings on the SALT treaty in July, Richard Stone, D-Fla., pressed administration witnesses to comment on rumors that a Soviet combat force was present in Cuba. The administration denied there had been any substantial change in the Soviet presence on the island. But on August 29 committee chairman Frank Church, D-Idaho, told reporters that stepped-up surveillance of Cuba confirmed earlier indications — which the administration said had been ambiguous — that a Soviet brigade was present.

Secretary of State Vance said at a September 5 press conference the force numbered 2,000 to 3,000 men and about 40 tanks. He noted that the force had no airlift or sealift capability that would enable it to attack any other Latin American country. He added that the force had been in Cuba since the mid-1970s, with parts of it there perhaps since the early 1970s.

The brigade's presence was "a very serious matter" running contrary to "long-held American policies," Vance said. He emphasized that it did not pose a direct threat to the United States as had the Russian nuclear missiles sent to Cuba in 1962. But he said: "I will not be satisfied with maintenance of the status quo."

On the other hand, he said that Senate hearings on the SALT treaty should continue since the pact was "a matter of fundamental importance."

In a brief televised statement September 7, Carter reiterated Vance's position that the status quo was "unacceptable." He stressed the need for "calm and a sense of proportion" in formulating the U.S. response. U.S. negotiations with Moscow over the issue would require "firm diplomacy, not panic and not exaggeration," he said, and the public and Congress could aid the process by staying "calm and steady."

Vance had hinted September 5 that the administration might be satisfied with Soviet actions demonstrating that the force was not a threat to U.S. interests. Administration sources cited various roles for which the brigade might be intended, including training Cuban troops and guarding Soviet intelligence installations in Cuba.

But Sen. John Tower, R-Texas, a leading SALT opponent, expressed confidence that the treaty could not be ratified unless the Soviet combat troops were removed from Cuba. Church, who supported the treaty, concurred. "There is no likelihood whatever that the Senate would ratify the SALT treaty as long as Russian combat troops remain in Cuba," he told reporters September 5. The Cuba issue seemed to derive much of its political potency from the fact that Church, who had disclosed the discovery, stated flatly that the treaty could not be ratified while the combat troops remained.

The issue gave SALT opponents a dramatic opportunity to drive home three basic arguments:

● Moscow apparently had gone to great lengths to conceal the fact that its military establishment in Cuba — which was known to U.S. intelligence to number several thousand advisers — included a unit that was organized, equipped, and trained to perform combat missions. That demonstrated the Soviets' fundamental untrustworthiness, SALT foes maintained.

● The Soviet brigade had been operating at least since the mid-1970s, according to administration officials (although former president Ford and officials of his administration insisted there had been no Soviet combat unit in Cuba through 1976). That called into question the quality of U.S. intelligence, SALT critics maintained. If it could not detect a Soviet unit 90 miles from Key West, Florida, how could U.S. intelligence detect relatively subtle improvements in Soviet missiles test-fired in the middle of Asia?, they asked.

● Even more important, according to SALT opponents, was the fact that the deployment demonstrated the unremitting Soviet campaign for political advantage through the use of its military forces. It was that basic premise of Soviet policy that made it dangerous to sign SALT II. Because the treaty did not preclude emerging Soviet advantages in strategic weaponry, it would in effect ratify Soviet military superiority and enhance Moscow's worldwide political leverage, they argued.

Direct U.S.-Soviet negotiations over the status of the Soviet combat unit in Cuba began September 10 when Soviet ambassador Anatolii F. Dobrynin returned to Washington from Moscow. But several meetings apparently produced no significant agreement by week's end. An editorial in *Pravda* the day the talks began insisted the Soviet unit was in Cuba at Havana's invitation and that Washington had no right to object.

Carter addressed the nation on the Cuba issue October 1. The Soviet brigade, he said, "is not a large force, nor an assault force. It presents no direct threat to us . . . . Nevertheless this Soviet brigade in Cuba is a serious matter."

The only progress announced by Carter was Moscow's assurance that the existing character of the force would not be changed. The meaning of that commitment was less than clear because the Soviets insisted the unit was merely a training force.

Except for his statement that the United States would not tolerate any enlargement of the brigade, Carter's speech was a flat rejection of hard-liners' demands that he strike back at Moscow, especially by subordinating SALT II to the U.S.-Soviet political competition.

There were few surprises in Senate reaction to Carter's speech. Sen. Howard H. Baker, Jr., R-Tenn., and Tower maintained that the treaty could not be ratified under the circumstances. But treaty supporters said the speech had put the Cuba episode in its proper perspective — separate from, and less important than, SALT II. In almost daily debates over the Carter speech, SALT backers became progressively more combative in belittling the significance of the Soviet brigade: "It is time to put aside childish things and childish ways," said Alan Cranston, D-Calif.

Casualty of Invasion

The Senate Foreign Relations Committee voted 9-6 on November 9, 1979, to send the treaty to the full Senate for consideration. But, in late December, Soviet troops invaded Afghanistan and President Carter on January 3, 1980, asked the Senate to defer action on the treaty. SALT II was a direct casualty of the invasion. Treaty supporters and opponents agreed that Carter's decision simply reflected the political reality that the pact would not even come close to winning the necessary two-thirds Senate majority in the wake of the Soviet action.

Although there seemed little likelihood that the Senate would return to consideration of SALT II, the president nevertheless continued to express support for strategic arms limitation on its merits, reiterating that it did not depend on Soviet trust. He delayed, but did not formally withdraw, the treaty. At the same time, Carter substantially increased his budget requests for defense spending, asking for $20 billion more in fiscal 1981 than he had requested the previous year. And he promised that subsequent annual increases would average 4.5 percent over inflation through fiscal 1985.

Carter responded quickly against the Soviets because of the invasion. In addition to harsh verbal denunciations, he instituted numerous sanctions against Moscow. Carter lifted a ban on military aid to Pakistan, began aiding the guerrillas fighting the Soviets and the Soviet-backed Afghan government, and pulled the United States out of the upcoming Moscow Olympics. One of his most controversial moves politically was the imposition of an embargo on U.S. grain going to the Soviet Union. His strongest opponent in the upcoming presidential race, Ronald Reagan, later cited the grain embargo as evidence of Carter's mishandling of U.S.-Soviet relations. *(Chapter 5, Afghanistan)*

Carter's difficulties with the Soviets continued to haunt his foreign policy to the last days of his presidency. Trouble brewing in Poland led to his warning in early December that Soviet intervention there would have the "most negative consequences" for U.S.-Soviet relations. In the last weeks of his administration, the White House reported that the Soviets appeared ready to invade Poland. Decisions regarding an appropriate response to Moscow's involvement in Poland's problems were left to the new conservative Republican president, Ronald Reagan.

RELATIONS WITH THE REAGAN PRESIDENCY

President Reagan's hard-line reaction to the events in Poland in 1980 reflected his administration's general approach to U.S.-Soviet relations. In his successful campaign against President Carter, Reagan was widely viewed as the foremost American advocate of a get-tough policy toward Moscow. Reagan characterized the Carter administration's approach to U.S.-Soviet matters as naive.

Reagan opposed the grain embargo and criticized the follow-up actions taken by the Carter administration in the wake of the Afghanistan invasion — including the Olympic boycott — as too little, too late. But he had few specific suggestions for alternatives. Soviet adventurism, as reflected in Afghanistan, was encouraged by American military weakness, he charged.

Concerning the SALT II treaty, Reagan insisted that it favored the Soviet Union. He said that, as president, he would withdraw the treaty and demand that it be renegotiated. Responding to a charge that his position would provoke an arms race, Reagan said in August, "We're already in an arms race, but only the Soviets are racing."

Once in office, the Reagan administration moved to inject a stern tone in U.S. dealings with the Soviets. Secretary of State Alexander M. Haig, Jr., wrote to Foreign Minister Gromyko warning against Soviet interference in Poland. At his first presidential news conference, held January 29, 1981, Reagan commented that the Soviets "reserve unto themselves the right to commit any crime, to lie, to cheat" in order to further their ambitions.

One of the administration's first and most controversial targets was Soviet influence in Central America. Reagan and Haig threw down the gauntlet before the Soviet Union and its ally Cuba and focused attention on El Salvador on February 23, 1981, when they released a "white paper" to document a charge that Soviet-bloc nations had secretly armed leftist insurgents seeking to overthrow El Salvador's government. The administration vowed to support the ruling junta in El Salvador with military aid to help repulse the leftists and economic assistance to help relieve social unrest, despite strong congressional opposition to that policy.

Grain Embargo Lifted

Yet the strident tone of the Reagan administration was not always translated into harsh actions. For example, on April 24 Reagan, fulfilling his campaign promise, lifted Carter's embargo on grain sales to the Soviet Union. "As a presidential candidate," he said, "I indicated my opposition to the curb on sales because American farmers had been unfairly singled out to bear the burden of this ineffective national policy." After he entered office, Reagan continued, "I decided that an immediate lifting of the sales limitation could be misinterpreted by the Soviet Union.... I have determined that our position now cannot be mistaken: The United States, along with the vast majority of nations, has condemned and remains opposed to the Soviet occupation of Afghanistan and other aggressive acts around the world. We will react strongly to acts of aggression wherever they take place. There will never be a weakening of this resolve."

The Reagan administration also exhibited a willingness to talk to the Soviets. The president disclosed in a November 1981 speech that he had been carrying on a correspondence with Soviet leader Brezhnev in which the topic of a Reagan-Brezhnev summit meeting had been raised. The idea of a high-level meeting was first introduced in a January 28, 1981, letter from Gromyko to Haig. It was suggested again by Brezhnev during a speech to the 26th Party Congress in February. Haig, speaking for the administration, said a summit at that time would be "self-defeating in the extreme" without adequate preparation.

The president said in his speech that while he was convalescing from wounds suffered in the March 30 assassination attempt he had written to Brezhnev to ask, "Is it possible that we have permitted ideology, political and economic philosophies and governmental policies to keep us from considering the very real, everyday problems of our peoples?" Brezhnev replied May 25 that "An exchange of correspondence has its limitations, and in this sense a private conversation is better." The notion of a summit meeting officially had been floated.

Conservatives' Displeasure

The Reagan administration's willingness to maintain high-level contact with Moscow despite the imposition of martial law in Poland evoked criticism from conservatives in the United States. It was reported that Reagan's United Nations representative, Jeane J. Kirkpatrick, considered resigning in protest. Others demanded that Washington cut off all relations with Moscow until martial law was lifted in Poland. Perhaps the unkindest cut came from détente's chief architect, former secretary of state Kissinger.

Writing in the *New York Times* on January 17 and 18, Kissinger expressed dismay over the administration's decision to continue high-level discussions with the Soviets. The economic sanctions imposed against Poland, he said, were "of marginal significance" and "not a warning but a reflection of indecision." "How is one to explain a meeting between our Secretary of State and the Soviet Foreign Minister while martial law and concentration camps continue in Poland?" Kissinger asked. "I believe it would have ultimately served the negotiations far better had the United States, early in the Polish crisis, declared a moratorium on high-level contacts with the Soviet Union until martial law was lifted in Poland, the Solidarity leaders were released, and the military rulers began some form of discourse with the Church and the union. Our East-West diplomacy has been confrontational in periods of relative calm and apparently eager to negotiate when challenged. A reversal of these attitudes would serve the prospects of peace better."

Arms Control Issues

The Reagan approach to arms control was characterized by a similar combination of tough talk and a willingness to attempt to resolve differences. The tough talk was most controversially displayed in an October 1981 Defense Department publication entitled *Soviet Military Power*.

Apparently designed to back up administration allegations that the Soviets were building a decisive military lead over the United States, the report said that Moscow was spending 12-14 percent of its annual gross national product on defense, 70 percent more than the United States spent in 1979. "There are no signs of a de-emphasis on military programs," although "the Soviets' own economy is in difficulty and facing competing priorities for scarce resources," it stated. Moscow's "research and development priorities and continued expansion of military industrial production capabilities are keyed to supporting continuing military growth and modernization. In turn, the combined capabilities of the Soviet Ground Forces, Strategic Rocket Forces, Air Forces, Air Defense Forces and Navy are keyed to assisting the projection of Soviet power abroad and the spreading and solidifying of the Soviet Union's political, economic and military influence around the world. This is the challenge we face."

The Soviets released a rebuttal, *Whence the Threat to Peace*, in January 1982. Widely viewed as an effort to convince other governments, notably those in West Europe, that the Reagan administration presented the major threat to world peace, the Soviet booklet alleged that Washington was completing the "development of a so-called first-strike potential in the 1980s.... There is no reason for the United States to rearm because it has never lagged behind the Soviet Union. Rearmament on the pretext of achieving parity is in actual fact a drive for military superiority."

Soviet Foreign Policy

After World War II the Soviet Union had to rebuild not only its domestic economy and military capabilities but its international role as leader of the world communist movement. The Soviets had significantly improved their economy and modernized their military before the 1960s were over. They achieved rough strategic parity with the United States and had demonstrated, in Czechoslovakia, their willingness to use force when necessary to maintain the gains made in the war.

The Soviets' growing military muscle became an underpinning of the global political and ideological struggle with the United States and Western nations. Unlike the West, which provided economic as well as military aid, the Kremlin focused on armaments to assist friends.

The USSR used its military strength to support its argument that history was now favoring communism. The military strength gave the USSR, and nations or groups allied with it, international influence that before World War II had been the exclusive domain of the United States and European colonial nations.

Growing Influence in 1970s

A unique combination of events in the 1970s allowed Moscow to gain considerable influence in the developing nations in Africa, the Middle East, and Latin America. Many newly independent nations emerging from colonial status were rife with rebel movements that sought to overthrow entrenched, often corrupt, governments. The Soviet Union, acting especially through Cuba, was seen for several years as the superpower whose objectives and political history were compatible with these groups' goals of revolution.

The Soviet Union's successes were aided, albeit unintentionally, by the reluctance of the United States to meet directly the Soviets' challenges in many global areas. In the 1970s, following the draining experience of the Vietnam War, U.S. military spending declined and Americans were loath to become involved in limited regional conflicts.

But Soviet activities in the Third World exacted a high price. Significantly, successes in the 1970s contributed to the decline of détente between the superpowers. The SALT II arms control treaty, signed by President Carter and General Secretary Brezhnev, was never ratified by the U.S. Senate, partly because of American displeasure with Soviet worldwide actions. The collapse of détente in the late 1970s

reversed the trends of the previous period. Increased spending for American strategic and conventional armed forces began in the Carter administration in the late 1970s and accelerated rapidly under President Reagan in the early 1980s. The major increases in U.S. armed forces budgets presented new obstacles for the Soviet Union in the superpowers' competition for worldwide influence.

By the end of the Brezhnev regime, Soviet advances around the world were no longer as clear cut as Moscow had earlier hoped. Major rebellions against pro-Soviet governments in Afghanistan, Ethiopia, Nicaragua, Angola, Mozambique, and Kampuchea forced the Soviets to take stock of their gains and reassess their priorities.

Soviet economic problems at home also contributed to Moscow's inability to consolidate the footholds gained during the 1970s. Even if they were so inclined, the Soviets could not afford to give friendly states much economic aid. The economies of many African states with ties to the Soviet Union were in such bad shape that Moscow's traditional method of providing ideological encouragement and arms, but little or no economic assistance, pushed some of those countries toward the West for help. The economies of Angola and Mozambique, for example, were in virtual ruins by the mid-1980s when the leaders of each country made highly publicized visits to the United States seeking aid in 1985 and 1986.

By the mid-1980s, Moscow could claim degrees of success in the Middle East, such as the establishment of diplomatic relations with Oman and the United Arab Emirates near the end of 1985. Although the Kremlin supported Libya's Muammar Qaddafi militarily, the unpredictable Arab leader was unreliable as a stable ally. Syria continued to receive Soviet arms but Moscow did not dictate its policy. Contacts with Saudi Arabia increased in 1985, but the Soviets showed themselves unable to control other events in the Persian Gulf area when fighting broke out between Marxist groups in communist-controlled South Yemen in early 1986. Moscow's hopes of being a major participant in any peace settlement in the Middle East were not close to being realized by early 1986.

First Priority: Close to Home

Moscow pays most attention to those countries nearest its borders. Of foremost concern has been control over Eastern Europe. Social unrest and economic difficulties in

Eastern Europe in the early 1980s, often tied closely to similar problems in the Soviet Union, forced the Kremlin to focus renewed attention on these countries considered the bastion of the empire.

In the Third World, Afghanistan, Iran, China, and Mongolia received the highest priority. The entrenched war in Afghanistan exacted considerable costs for the Soviets — monetarily, in international prestige, and in emerging domestic dismay about the nature of Soviet involvement there.

Relations with the People's Republic of China remained difficult throughout the Brezhnev era. By the time Brezhnev succeeded Nikita Khrushchev, the tenuous alliance between the countries had fallen apart. China had become an independent and sometimes hostile rival for leadership among communist and Third World nations and a developing threat to Soviet security. Near the end of Brezhnev's life Sino-Soviet relations began to improve. But while this improvement was significant, the Soviet Union's presence in Afghanistan, its support of Vietnam's occupation of Kampuchea, and its massive military strength on the Chinese border stood in the way of a comprehensive political settlement between the two nations.

This chapter outlines Soviet involvement in some of the regions most important to the Soviet Union: China and the Far East, Eastern Europe, the Middle East, Latin America, Afghanistan, and Africa.

USSR-EAST EUROPE: UNYIELDING CONTROL

The Soviet Union has been unyielding in its efforts to maintain control over Eastern Europe since World War II. But after several decades of domination, Moscow has become increasingly concerned about its control over the area. The key question concerning future Soviet policy in Eastern Europe is what Soviet leaders will do to preserve their domination and how successful they may be. *(For separate discussion of Poland, see p. 122.)*

Until about 1980, the USSR's growing worldwide interests and capabilities appeared to diminish the importance of Eastern Europe. But the erosion of economic growth rates, alliance cohesion, and Soviet control over events in Eastern Europe in the late 1970s refocused Soviet attention on the region. A combination of destabilizing developments threatened to weaken the economic and political levers the Soviets had used to direct the Eastern bloc. The main question for East European leaders became how much political and economic autonomy the Kremlin would tolerate.

In his article in the book *After Brezhnev*, Andrzej Korbonski of UCLA, expressing the opinions of many experts, said the most important consequence of Poland's crisis during 1980-81 was

the return of Eastern Europe to its earlier status as Moscow's most vital possession and an indispensable part of the Soviet empire. The upheaval in Poland must have convinced the Soviet leaders that they made a serious mistake in failing to pay sufficient attention to internal developments

throughout the region or misunderstanding them. As a result, Eastern Europe has once again become the primary focus of Soviet foreign policy, and its centrality in Soviet decision making remains indisputable in the 1980s.

Soviet Goals, Fears

Moscow has security, political, ideological, and economic interests in Eastern Europe. Following World War II, the Soviets envisioned Eastern Europe as part of an empire whose markets, resources, labor, and knowledge would contribute to Soviet postwar economic reconstruction. The region also was considered a proving ground for the Soviet system and doctrine and a valuable ally against the West. It has not worked out that way for the Kremlin.

Economically, the region has become as much a burden as an asset. Through the 1970s the Soviet Union supplied Eastern Europe with oil and natural gas and other raw materials at prices far below their value on the world market. In return the Soviets were usually paid with manufactured goods of poor quality, as the East Europeans used their best exports to trade for Western goods and technology. During the 1980s, the Soviets raised the price of their energy exports to Eastern Europe and demanded that their allies improve the quality of the goods intended for Soviet consumers. But Eastern Europe continues to be an untraditional "empire" for Moscow, with the costs of credits, subsidies, and defense expenditures for the region outweighing the economic benefits the countries provide to the Soviet Union.

Western Dependence Opposed

Yet regardless of the burden on the Soviet Union's resources created by its special economic relationship with Eastern Europe, the Kremlin hesitates to permit the closer economic ties between East and West Europe that they admit could ease that burden. The Soviets fear Eastern Europe will become too dependent on the West, a situation the Soviet press terms "the imperialist trap." Consequently, they are willing to make economic sacrifices to avoid the possible political hazards of a growth of Western economic influence in Eastern Europe.

Politically, Soviet domination of the region has cost Moscow international prestige and has often been an obstacle to better relations with the West. The Soviet invasions of Hungary in 1956 and Czechoslovakia in 1968 and the Soviet-backed repression of the Polish Solidarity labor movement in the 1980s each prompted Western sanctions and condemnations. These dramatic examples of Moscow's hegemony undercut Soviet claims of being an anti-imperialist power and reinforced Western perceptions that communist control of Eastern Europe had routinely brought human rights abuses and suppression of individual freedoms. Because of Western empathy for Eastern Europe, détente can develop only if the Soviets refrain from military interventions in the region and continue to give East bloc governments some autonomy and their people a degree of cultural freedom. Moscow must consider the consequences of its actions in Eastern Europe on its relations with Western Europe and the United States. Conversely, Moscow must also weigh the effects of improved relations with the West on East European stability. A period of détente would encourage liberalizing forces within the region and allow East European governments to build economic and political bridges to the West. Both developments could make Moscow's task of controlling its allies more difficult.

Militarily, Eastern Europe's contribution to the Warsaw Pact alliance is limited by the questionable reliability of Eastern European troops. In a protracted war, some experts believe more Soviet forces might be needed to ensure Eastern Europe's loyalty than those countries could provide to fight the West.

Consequently, the Soviet Union's deep commitment to domination of Eastern Europe cannot be explained only by its pragmatic interest in maintaining a buffer zone, or *cordon sanitaire*, against the West.

Destabilizing Elements

The Soviet Union and its Eastern European allies face severe economic problems that can be solved only through reforms. Even though the average person in most Eastern European countries is better off economically than the average Soviet citizen, the region's economic problems threaten the political stability of Eastern Europe more than they threaten the Soviet Union.

Improved economic performance will require a shift in growth patterns that will make them more efficient. Workers must be more productive and the countries' economic growth must rely less on energy-intensive, environmentally damaging manufacturing methods, and imported technology and credits.

The reforms necessary to make Eastern European economies more efficient could produce social unrest, particularly if workers believe they are supporting too much of the burden of change. At the same time, postponing change to avoid political problems may produce worse economic crises in the future.

People in Eastern European nations generally have not been overly concerned with the political legitimacy of their ruling regimes so long as their standard of living has been acceptable and the prospect for improvement present. But their expectations, which exceed those of the Soviet working class, make it unlikely they would accept without protest a lengthy and extensive economic decline that damaged their standard of living. Recent education spending cuts may cause unrest if East Europeans think they will hurt chances for individual advancement. Education has been the most important means of upward mobility and has contributed to stability.

Two areas needing reform are the subsidized food supply system and economic investment. Governments traditionally have kept food prices artificially low to help maintain social peace. But this policy has depressed agricultural output and severely strained national budgets. Investment decisions also have produced unwanted results. Housing, health care, and other so-called "nonproductive" areas that do not directly contribute to economic growth have been neglected in favor of investment that brings hard-currency earnings. But the lack of quality housing, health care, and other amenities have impaired labor productivity. Raising food prices (by eliminating subsidies) and neglecting areas of investment that would have raised living standards played a large role in Poland's economic paralysis in the late 1970s.

The Brezhnev to Gorbachev succession in the Soviet Union brought several years of indecisiveness and inertia that weakened Moscow's ability to control events in Eastern Europe. Some experts argue that the evolving succession in the Kremlin encouraged East European governments to test the limits of Soviet tolerance as they sought home-grown, rather than Soviet-imposed, solutions to their problems.

Most Eastern European countries will themselves face succession problems over the rest of the 1980s. Todor Zhivkov of Bulgaria, Gustav Husak of Czechoslovakia, Erich Honecker of East Germany, and Janos Kadar of Hungary are over 70 years old. Soviet influence on past East European successions varied widely, but it restrained full-blown power struggles and promoted neater successions than in the Soviet Union. Experts generally believe there will be deeper Soviet involvement in these upcoming leadership changes.

Soviet Alliance Strategy

After the Eastern bloc was formed in the late 1940s, Stalin sought to bring the region completely under Soviet domination. But since the 1968 Czechoslovakian crisis, in which the Soviets acted militarily to abruptly halt change, and the widening of Soviet global activities in the 1970s, the Kremlin has increasingly accepted a policy of damage limitation in Eastern Europe. According to Angela Stent of Georgetown University, Moscow's main goal in Eastern Europe was to maintain whatever control it could and prevent any further erosion of its power.

One part of that strategy was to make use of East-West détente, which was producing increased trade and transfer of technology financed by Western credit for both the Soviet Union and Eastern Europe. The Soviets also adopted preferential trade policies with their allies. They supplied Eastern Europe with abundant quantities of cheap oil and raw materials in a system of implicit trade subsidies that facilitated Eastern European economic growth at Soviet expense. Simultaneously, Western credits allowed East European governments to import technology and improve the material standard of living of their populations by providing more highly desired Western consumer goods to make the lack of political freedom more palatable.

Major Loans from the West

Most Western analysts and bankers during the early 1970s regarded East European countries as politically stable and generally good credit risks. They believed that the Soviet Union would act as an economic and political umbrella in case of severe problems and would not permit a prolonged crisis "much less economic collapse in one of its Warsaw Pact allies," Sarah M. Terry of Tufts University has commented.

Accordingly, in the era of East-West détente, the West lent Eastern Europe hundreds of millions of dollars. Instead of using the influx of Western credits to modernize their economies, however, the East European governments generally used them to expand industrial capacity (primarily through older energy-intensive technologies) and to increase consumer goods. In some places, notably Hungary, advanced technologies were imported, but even then planning and management changes were not introduced and incentives to increase labor productivity and efficiency were not provided.

Consequently, the East Europeans backed themselves into a corner. Industrial production increasingly required huge amounts of energy because industrial plants were energy intensive and lacked effective conservation practices. Environmental problems, particularly those caused by the use of high-sulphur coal, were ignored. The entire region faces forests denuded by acid rain, contaminated water supplies, and air pollution in many industrial areas that threatens public health. The costs of correcting these problems grow increasingly prohibitive each year.

In the early 1980s, the Soviets began reducing oil shipments to Eastern Europe and charging more for what they did send. To obtain needed energy, East European governments must either deplete their own modest fuel resources or become even more dependent on high-cost imports from the Soviet Union or other world sources. New loans from the West can no longer be counted on to help East European governments take the remedial steps experts believe they should have taken a decade ago. They must use foreign currency earnings from exports to meet energy needs and repay the interest and principal on international loans. Consequently, unless the Eastern European nations can increase their exports, they will not have funds left over to meet rising public demands for consumer goods. Because most of their manufactured products are not of high enough quality to compete on the open world market, the East Europeans will have difficulty increasing their exports. Their financial problems will also limit imports of technology that could improve the quality of their products or begin to solve energy and pollution problems.

Soviet Ideological Leadership

Another part of Soviet strategy for managing the East European alliance during the 1970s, according to Terry, was to reassert Soviet ideological leadership. Rather than impose rigid conformity, however, the Soviets generally tried only to place limits on the amount of diversity allowed in the satellite countries. In particular, Moscow relaxed guidelines concerning economic organization, experiments, and reform and reluctantly left economic initiatives up to the East European leaders. According to Seweryn Bialer of Columbia University, the "Polish case illustrates the independence of the native communist leadership in Eastern Europe with regard to domestic and especially economic questions."

A third aspect of Soviet alliance strategy was to integrate the economies of members of the Council for Mutual Economic Aid (CMEA). But despite Soviet cries to do so (especially since the 1971 Comprehensive Long-Term Target Program and subsequent joint investment plans), economic integration has been limited largely because of East European reluctance. Some experts predict the Soviets will increasingly try to use the CMEA in the 1980s, however, because Western credits have been eliminated.

The Soviets believed all the components of their alliance management strategy complemented one another. They recognized that in the absence of substantial domestic economic reforms in Eastern Europe that were unlikely to be undertaken, their only alternative was to allow substantially increased trade and technology transfer from the West. Moscow, however, also realized it had to take steps to prevent its satellite countries from becoming overly dependent on the West and to prevent popular expectations in those countries from rising beyond manageable proportions.

Failed Strategy

Soviet policy toward Eastern Europe since 1968 preserved Moscow's control over the region but failed in almost every other respect. Eastern European leaders face political and economic instability no matter which course of action — or inaction — they choose. And they must confront the issues of reform in a political and economic environment far less conducive to stable, less painful, change than they would have faced had the issues been addressed in the 1970s.

The Soviets traditionally have selectively applied "economic bandages to ward off the unwanted infection of political change," according to Terry, and have been fortunate that major crises in Eastern Europe have occurred in only one country at a time.

Economic Stringencies

But the Soviets can no longer afford to shore up faltering satellite economies. The costs of doing so have risen considerably. Eastern Europe's debt-service ratios to the West threaten the solvency of Poland and present overwhelming burdens in other East European countries as well. The Soviets may be able, and willing, to continue modest assistance on a selective basis, but "generous rescue packages and the blanket granting of large trade subsidies are clearly a thing of the past," Terry noted in 1984.

Some choices considered politically unacceptable a decade ago might now be reexamined. Warsaw Pact and CMEA organization and burden-sharing are two likely areas where changes may be tried.

On one hand, the Soviets could allow Eastern Europe to reduce its share of defense expenditures within the Warsaw Pact. While Soviet allies do not appear to bear proportionate shares of expenditures in the Warsaw Pact, their relative burdens are significant. In addition, the Soviets have gained international prestige among national liberation movements because of the successful use of East Europeans in the Third World, especially Czech and East German troops and technicians. But East European leaders will face increasing domestic opposition to defense expenditures as their economic fortunes decline. On the other hand, the Soviets will have to decide whether to use their powerful economic leverage to require their allies to continue making these contributions despite the political consequences. Some experts believe Moscow will implement a carrot and stick economic approach to reward those who do contribute significantly and punish those who do not.

Other experts speculate that the USSR might expand the policy-making role of Eastern European officials in the Warsaw Pact alliance to ease dissatisfaction in satellite nations that their leaders have no meaningful participation in decisions. In addition, though less likely, some changes in the command structure of the Western Pact could lend more prestige to the roles of other members. In light of the Polish upheaval, however, the most likely prospect is that the Soviets will tighten control over the alliance by conducting more frequent joint exercises while giving smaller states more formal, but still limited, access to decision-making.

In the CMEA, the Soviet Union may find that current economic conditions are right for greater integration of Eastern Europe. CMEA effectiveness diminished in the 1970s despite official obligation to the Long-Term Target Program. Member countries were far more interested in maintaining strong bilateral ties with the USSR to ensure steady supplies of raw materials than in expanding CMEA commitments. Because of the economic strains created by Moscow's demands for continued Eastern European military expenditures while reducing trade subsidies to those countries, the Kremlin may be able to combine new incentives with tough sanctions to strengthen the CMEA. Experts agree this will be difficult, however, because of the uneven economic strength of member countries and the increasing tendency to promote national interests over alliance goals.

Political Tradeoffs

Terry noted just before the Gorbachev succession that "instead of using economic concessions to maintain political stability and prevent unwanted systemic change," the Soviets could "begin using political concessions as a safety valve for present economic strains." The Soviets have followed this strategy in the past when the potential for bloc instability outweighed the risks of allowing limited nonconformity.

After the NATO missile deployments, for example, the Soviets tolerated limited diversity in views among the East Europeans. There also have been conciliatory gestures to the Catholic church in various countries, most notably Poland. And Poland's unprecedented independent labor movement directed by the nationwide trade union organization called Solidarity, was tolerated at first largely because the Soviets believed it diverted the population's attention from Poland's increasingly dismal economic woes.

Hungary certainly had Moscow's tacit blessing in cautiously increasing domestic reforms (a program called its New Economic Mechanism) and diplomatic contacts with the West. Its citizens also have been granted more political freedom than those in other bloc countries.

East Germany has been eager to maintain its increasingly friendly relations with West Germany and, within limits, has been allowed to do so. Tolerating the German détente has strengthened East Germany's economy and provided technological benefits to the USSR. Yet the intra-German détente displays the costs that the Soviets must accept when they relax controls. The Soviets by the mid-1980s had to contend with an East German peace movement that criticized both superpowers and an East German population exposed daily to West German television. A small peace movement had also developed in Czechoslovakia.

Nonetheless, these concessions to domestic sensitivities have not addressed Eastern Europe's fundamental structural problems.

Multiple Crises

In the future, the Soviets may not have the luxury of dealing with one Eastern European crisis at a time, as in the past. The regional economic malaise is so pervasive that crises could erupt simultaneously, or a crisis in one country could have a ripple effect in other nations. This happened in 1981 when Polish coal exports collapsed and seriously dislocated West German and Czech industrial production. Thus, further integration of CMEA economies, although desirable in many ways, could increase the danger of a crisis spreading from one nation to another.

Because of these problems, Soviet policy in Eastern Europe during the rest of the 1980s probably will stress political stability over economic development. That stability, however, depends ultimately on better economic performance, which, in turn, depends on potentially destabilizing economic reform. To accomplish both their key goals in Eastern Europe — maintaining control and ensuring domestic stability — the Soviets are forced to walk a tightrope between requiring orthodox economic and political conformity among the satellites and encouraging innovation. The Soviets' apparent acceptance of established economic reforms (which the East European populations have accepted) and their consequences illustrates that political considerations are the main influence on Soviet thinking toward the region.

Historical Perspective

Since World War II, it has often been difficult to determine where Moscow's interests in Eastern Europe as an extension of domestic policy making diverge from foreign policy considerations. The Soviet Union's relationship with Eastern Europe has been qualitatively different from relations with any other country or region.

On one level, the Kremlin has treated Eastern Europe as a regional outpost of the Soviet Union, both for security reasons (especially the so-called Iron Triangle of Poland, East Germany, and Czechoslovakia) and because of the dangerous potential for regional instabilities and deviations from the party line to upset the status quo in the Soviet Union.

On the other hand, Moscow often finds it more useful to treat Eastern Europe as nominally sovereign states that can lend international support and generally enhance Soviet legitimacy among other allies or potential allies. Consequently, UCLA's Korbonski has said, in some contexts the Soviets choose

> to consider the individual states as semi-independent actors granted a degree of autonomy, especially in domestic affairs. Hence, in the area of military security as Moscow defines it, there is not much difference between the German Democratic Republic and the Ukraine, whereas in the economic realm Hungary clearly has more room for maneuver than, say, Estonia. These differences help illuminate the inconsistencies, ambiguities, and conflicts in Soviet policy toward the region. They also throw some light on why the USSR has treated some junior partners differently from others, how Soviet policy toward the individual countries has changed over time, and what the nature of Soviet-East European interaction is in specific areas, such as economics, politics, and ideology.

The Soviets since World War II have forced the satellite countries of Eastern Europe to subordinate their security and armed forces to a "dual system of native party supervision and direct control by the Soviet security and military command," according to Columbia University's Bialer. The communications media have been under strict party control and no autonomous political organizations have been permitted to exist, much less challenge the party's monopoly.

Establishing Legitimacy. A pervading concern among both Soviet and East European leaders has been to establish domestic legitimacy for their rule. The Soviets seem to have done so, but the satellite rulers generally have not.

The East Europeans were able to garner elite support but popular support was not forthcoming. Control and intervention by the ever-watchful Soviet Union meant East European governments could not call on the most basic sources of legitimacy — nationalism and free elections. While elite support has been sufficient during periods of stability, it has weakened considerably during crises because those sectors under close Soviet supervision, such as the security and armed forces, communications media, and official trade unions, defer to Soviet policy lines.

Because they benefited from relatively better economic conditions than the rest of the region, East Germany's and Hungary's populations granted a limited and grudging acceptance of the regimes, Bialer stated. Yet, he added:

> The real test of a regime's legitimacy occurs during crises when rulers attempt to mobilize reserves of support. The paucity of such reserves in Eastern Europe demonstrates that satellite governments rely on Soviet power and determination to sustain them and on popular fears of the danger from the East....
>
> The native power elites' dilemma is insoluble. On the one hand, they can gain strong popular support only by advocating the anti-Soviet cause of national independence with the accompanying risks of Soviet military intervention. On the other hand, they can retain power only by ensuring unqualified Soviet support and, if necessary, Soviet military intervention.

Bialer added that the "crucial flaw" of Soviet-controlled communist regimes in Eastern Europe is that those regimes cannot identify themselves with "national interests, nationalism, and independence."

The Eastern Europe intelligentsia also maintains a critical political attitude that is potentially, and in some cases actually, hostile toward the communist leaders. Additionally, many East Europeans are contemptuous of Soviet Russian culture and deeply attached to religion and the church. While the Soviet Union has largely been successful in reducing the role of religion in its society, the Catholic church in Poland, for example, has widespread popular support and has caused the party and government leadership considerable concern.

These and numerous other factors have reduced the communist leadership in Eastern Europe to an "alien and superficial stratum markedly different in stability and effectiveness from its counterpart in the Soviet Union," Bialer contends. Ironically, despite the Soviet Union's preeminence within the alliance, it surpasses Eastern Europe only in military power, not in attributes such as living standards, educational levels, culture, or economic and modern technological development. Even the availability and diversity of food supplies are better in many East European nations than in the Soviet Union.

The Soviet Union's military power has, of course, prevented the dissolution of the Soviet bloc in Eastern Europe and will likely continue to do so. It is the threat of the use of that power which compounds the difficulty in finding solutions to Eastern Europe's problems.

USSR-CHINA: UNNATURAL ALLIES

The announcement October 15, 1964, that Nikita Khrushchev had been removed as premier of the Soviet government and first secretary of the CPSU led many Western analysts to expect an improvement in the Sino-Soviet relationship. The obvious personal dislike Chairman Mao and Premier Khrushchev felt for each other had undoubtedly contributed to the deterioration of relations between their two countries. With Khrushchev absent from the equation, it was reasonable to assume that Moscow and Beijing might find ways to ease the tension created by their growing ideological, geopolitical, and economic disputes. However, the subsequent intensification of the Sino-Soviet rift would demonstrate that it was neither caused nor sustained solely by the personal animosity between Mao and Khrushchev.

Fundamental differences in the histories, cultures, levels of economic development, geographic realities, and goals of the two communist powers had made them unnatural allies, linked only by a common ideology and a common enemy. Regardless of who ruled the USSR in 1964, there was no chance of a return to the close cooperation that existed beween Moscow and Beijing in the early 1950s. The day after Khrushchev's ouster, the Chinese, by coincidence, further complicated the prospects for reconciliation by exploding their first nuclear device. Not only did the test demonstrate China's developing military threat, but it also signaled Chinese resolve to become self-reliant.

But while the continuation of the Sino-Soviet rivalry was certain by 1964, the eventual deterioration of relations to the point of armed conflict was not. The Chinese applauded Khrushchev's ouster and perhaps even saw it as an opportunity to resolve certain contentious issues with the USSR. Immediately following the ouster, Brezhnev and his colleagues communicated their desire to improve relations by ending anti-Chinese propaganda and delaying an international conference of communist parties, so the two communist powers would have a chance to reconcile their differences beforehand. Chou En Lai traveled to Moscow to discuss the future of Sino-Soviet relations. But in spite of the new Soviet regime's goodwill gestures and whatever economic and political concessions it may have offered Chou, the meeting did not produce a reconciliation. The lull in Sino-Soviet polemics began to erode by the spring of 1965, and relations became increasingly hostile during the five-year period (1965-69) that followed.

Vietnam War Focus

The focus of Sino-Soviet differences in the mid-1960s was the Vietnam War. The Chinese accused the Soviets of trying to sell out the North Vietnamese by seeking to arrange a negotiated settlement between Hanoi and Washington. However, following the February 1965 U.S. bombing raids on North Vietnam (which were begun during a visit to Hanoi by Premier Aleksei Kosygin), the Soviets discontinued their efforts to produce a quick settlement of the escalating conflict in Vietnam. Both communist powers increased their efforts to aid the North Vietnamese and the National Liberation Front in South Vietnam against the

United States. The PRC and the USSR funneled large amounts of military and economic aid to North Vietnam, in part to ensure their respective credentials as supporters of national liberation movements.

The issue that split the Chinese and Soviets was whether they should engage in "united action" to get maximum impact from their material support for their Vietnamese allies. Moscow and Hanoi pressed Beijing to agree to united action. In April 1965, the Soviets asked for an agreement that would allow them to ship aid to North Vietnam through China, fly aid over China, and use Chinese airfields and ports near Vietnam. Mao and his supporters rejected all Soviet proposals for extensive united action. They feared that such cooperation could lead to Soviet interference in Chinese internal affairs, a Soviet military presence in China, the growth of Soviet influence in North Vietnam, and a possible extension of U.S. air strikes to Chinese territory. Mao's claims that the Soviets were revisionists who were prepared to sell out North Vietnam to imperialist forces would also have been undercut had he cooperated with Moscow. The Chinese did allow Soviet aid to be transported overland by Chinese workers. But this small show of united action did more harm than good to the Sino-Soviet relationship, since Moscow continually accused the Chinese of obstructing the delivery of aid rather than facilitating it. Instead of uniting behind the North Vietnamese war effort, Moscow and Beijing competed for influence in Hanoi through separate aid programs. The North Vietnamese leaders skillfully played their two supporters off each other to maximize the benefits they could squeeze out of Sino-Soviet competition.

Increasing Differences

Two major developments further exacerbated Sino-Soviet relations in the years following the ouster of Khrushchev. The first was the Chinese Cultural Revolution launched in August 1966. The second was the Soviet military buildup along the Sino-Soviet border.

Cultural Revolution. The chaos within China and its militant attitude toward the outside world during the period of the Cultural Revolution diminished its diplomatic, military, and economic capabilities. The resulting international isolation of the Chinese strengthened Moscow's hand against Beijing among socialist nations.

China's advocacy of a relentlessly militant posture toward perceived enemies of communism had already weakened its standing with more pragmatic communist parties. By the end of 1966 only the Albanian Communist Party considered itself pro-Chinese. The Cultural Revolution also reduced China's already outclassed capacity to compete with Soviet material support of North Vietnam. Yet the unpredictability of Chinese behavior and the growth of anti-Soviet sentiment in China increased Soviet anxieties concerning the dangers presented by their former ally, even as China's power diminished.

The Cultural Revolution was accompanied by escalating propaganda exchanges and the disintegration of meaningful cultural and diplomatic relations between the two nations. In March 1966 the Chinese had ignored their invitation to the 23d Party Congress in Moscow. By doing so they effectively ended party-to-party relations with the Soviet Union. Following the declaration of the Cultural Revolution, even state-to-state relations became difficult to maintain. The first anti-Soviet demonstrations by Chinese students at the Soviet Embassy in Beijing occurred in late August 1966. The following January similar demonstrations became so violent and abusive that the families of Soviet diplomats were evacuated from China, and Soviet diplomats became virtual prisoners in their own compound. During this period the Chinese also harassed the crews of Soviet ships, expelled a number of Soviet journalists and diplomats, and terminated all educational opportunities in China for foreign students. The Soviets responded with similar expulsions and constant radio broadcasts denouncing the Cultural Revolution and urging the Chinese people (especially the ethnic Moslem minorities) to resist Mao's rule.

Soviet Troop Buildup. The second major development that damaged Sino-Soviet relations in the mid-1960s was the Soviet military buildup along the Chinese border.

In 1965, Khrushchev's successors were faced with an "ally" who refused to cooperate with them in the socialist and Third Worlds and brushed aside all their attempts to improve relations. In addition, since 1963, Beijing had openly denounced nineteenth century border treaties between Russia and China as being "unequal." Mao claimed that nearly a million square miles of Soviet territory rightfully belonged to China. Finally, China's emergence as a nuclear power a year earlier added a new dimension to the Chinese threat. Chinese military capabilities would no longer be based solely upon their huge but poorly equipped army.

Consequently, the Soviets began to substantially increase their military strength along the Chinese border during the second half of 1965. In January 1966, the USSR signed a treaty of friendship, cooperation, and mutual aid with Mongolia, which led within a year to the deployment there of 100,000 Soviet troops. The Soviets also took measures to beef up their firepower and troop strength in the Soviet Far East, which included the deployment of battlefield nuclear weapons and the addition of approximately five extra divisions by 1969. This buildup in the late 1960s did appear to be defensive in nature. However, it is likely that Soviet leaders hoped their deployments might pressure the Chinese to adopt a more conciliatory stance toward the USSR, or at least intimidate Beijing from pressing its claims to disputed territories.

The Soviet invasion of Czechoslovakia in August 1968 and the declaration of the "Brezhnev Doctrine" that followed it also contained an implicit warning that Moscow hoped the Chinese would find intimidating. Under the Brezhnev Doctrine the Soviets claimed the right to intervene anywhere in the socialist community to protect the interests of socialism. The relevance of this doctrine for China was obvious. But in the year that followed Chinese leaders did not appear to be intimidated by either the Soviet military buildup or the Brezhnev Doctrine. Rather, Chinese actions became more provocative.

Since 1967, numerous confrontations between Soviet and Chinese troops patrolling in disputed border areas had taken place. These incidents intensified following the Soviet invasion of Czechoslovakia, but until the spring of 1969 both sides had refrained from firing upon the other. On March 2 the situation suddenly exploded into open armed conflict when Chinese forces ambushed a Soviet patrol on Damanskii (Zhenbao) Island in the Ussuri River, which forms part of the border between Manchuria and the USSR. The Soviets responded by returning in force to the island 13 days later to teach the Chinese a lesson. They attacked a numerically inferior force of Chinese and inflicted many casualties. However, in spite of the Soviet military's conventional and nuclear superiority, the Chinese did not curtail their patrols in and near disputed territories.

The March exchange set off a series of border clashes that lasted thoughout the spring and summer. Brezhnev and his colleagues were determined to force the Chinese to back away from their aggressive posture along the Sino-Soviet frontier, but conventional military deployments and threats made little progress. In August and September the Brezhnev Politburo resorted to dropping subtle hints designed to encourage speculation about a possible Soviet preemptive nuclear strike against Chinese nuclear facilities. In the face of this threat, the Chinese backed down and agreed to border negotiations that began October 20. These negotiations produced no significant progress toward a resolution of the border issue. The decade came to an end with China regarding the USSR as its greatest enemy and painfully aware of its diplomatic isolation and vulnerability to a Soviet nuclear attack.

Triangular Diplomacy

As early as 1968, U.S. presidential candidate Richard Nixon indicated his intention to seek improved relations with the China: "We simply cannot afford to leave China forever outside the family of nations, there to nurture its fantasies, cherish its hates and threaten its neighbors. There is no place on this small planet for a billion of its potentially most able people to live in angry isolation."

A long-term relationship with Beijing — drawing it into a constructive role in international affairs — appeared particularly necessary, not only to hasten the end of the Vietnam War, but also to encourage Moscow to moderate its relationship with the West. In the first year of Nixon's term the administration quietly signaled its willingness to improve U.S.-Chinese relations. In July, restrictions on travel to China were eased; in November, naval patrols in the Taiwan Strait were ended; and in December, subsidiaries and affiliates of American companies abroad were granted permission to do extensive business with the Chinese.

These unilateral U.S. initiatives did not produce an immediate Sino-American rapprochement. But China's emergence from the Cultural Revolution, its experience of vulnerability during the Sino-Soviet border crisis of 1969, the beginning of U.S. troop withdrawals from Vietnam, and the continuing Soviet military buildup on the Chinese border created the conditions under which a détente with the United States could begin. China decided to seek an accommodation with a less threatening enemy (the United States) to enhance its security against the USSR.

Nixon Visits China

The thaw in U.S.-Chinese relations took a dramatic step July 15, 1971, when President Nixon announced he would visit Beijing in early 1972 "to seek the normalization of relations between the two countries." Nixon said that his upcoming meeting with the Chinese leaders — the first by a U.S. president — had been arranged during a secret visit to Beijing earlier in the month by his national security adviser, Henry Kissinger.

The initial Soviet reaction to Nixon's announcement was restrained. The Soviet government newspaper

Izvestiia reported July 16 that Nixon and Mao would meet but made no comment. The party newspaper *Pravda* warned July 25, however, that the United States should not use its new relationship with Beijing to pressure the Soviet Union. Privately, Kremlin leaders displayed renewed interest in a summit meeting between Nixon and Brezhnev, a topic that had been under discussion for several months while Washington was secretly negotiating with Beijing. In the wake of the China breakthrough, U.S. and Soviet officials made significant progress on a comprehensive accord concerning the status of Berlin and agreed to a May 1972 summit meeting.

Although Soviet leaders had a variety of reasons for pursuing détente with the West, it was clear that among them was the fear of being left on the wrong side of the U.S.-Soviet-Chinese triangle.

Moscow Efforts Rebuffed

Sino-Soviet hostility in the early 1970s could not easily be repaired, so Moscow sought to convince U.S. and West European leaders that it had more to offer them than Beijing. Indeed, there were areas of cooperation such as arms control and the resolution of the Berlin problem where the Chinese could not compete with the Soviets. But the Soviet Union's growing détente with the West (and Japan) did not stop those nations from engaging in a simultaneous détente with China. Meanwhile the Soviet Union continued its efforts to ensure its own security against the potential Chinese threat by backing India's successful invasion of East Pakistan in late 1971 and further building up its own forces facing China throughout the decade.

The Soviets had hoped that when Mao died his successors might seek to put Sino-Soviet relations on agreeable terms. Accordingly, the USSR signaled its desire to repair Sino-Soviet differences when Mao died in September 1976. But Mao's death brought no more improvement in relations between Beijing and Moscow than Khrushchev's ouster had produced 12 years earlier. The new leaders in Beijing ignored the Soviet cessation of anti-Chinese propaganda and even rejected Brezhnev's note of congratulations to Hua Guofeng for his election to the post of chairman of the Chinese Communist Party. The Soviets' Chinese adversaries were now more flexible, practical, and concerned with economic modernization than Mao had been, but they were no less anti-Soviet.

One manifestation of the new Chinese leadership's anti-Soviet orientation was its emphasis on the "Three Worlds" theory. This theory, supposedly devised by Mao, was first enunciated by Deng Xiaoping April 10, 1974, in his address to the UN General Assembly. However, it achieved additional prominence under the moderate, post-Mao leadership led by Deng. The theory rejected the concept that the world was divided into a capitalist block, a socialist block, and a large group of developing nations. It chose rather to make distinctions between the "First World," consisting of the United States and the USSR; the "Second World," consisting of all other developed nations; and the developing "Third World," of which China itself was a member. The Chinese denied that the Soviet Union should be defined as a socialist nation on the grounds that it behaved more like an imperialistic great power. The theory thus justified China's anti-Soviet policies, including its seeking friends among capitalist nations to act as counterweights to the Soviet threat. The theory also enhanced China's place among Third World, nonaligned nations by setting China up as a kindred Third World country.

Competition in Asia

Sino-Soviet relations in the late 1970s revolved around their respective geopolitical maneuvers in Asia. Both nations sought to enhance their security and influence by strengthening their relationships with various Asian powers. The Chinese and the Soviets both perceived the other as trying to encircle them through treaties and alliances. These perceptions were not unfounded. The Chinese sought to improve their relations with Japan and the United States at the expense of the Soviet Union, while the Soviets conceived of their relationship with the Vietnamese, in part, as a means of surrounding China.

Geopolitical Competition

Sino-Soviet geopolitical competition was most obvious in Southeast Asia. When Saigon fell in 1975, Hanoi enjoyed friendly relations with both the Chinese and the Soviets. In the final years of the Vietnam War, however, the USSR had become the dominant supplier of military and economic assistance to North Vietnam, and Hanoi had grown markedly closer to Moscow. From 1975 to 1977 Hanoi tried to salvage its relationship with the Chinese in spite of disputes over such issues as Hanoi's treatment of the ethnic Chinese living in Vietnam and Beijing's support of the Khmer Rouge in Kampuchea. Even as Sino-Vietnamese tensions grew, Hanoi avoided complete dependence on the USSR and continued making overtures to the Chinese for better relations.

But the events of 1978 ended Hanoi's hopes of sustaining positive relations with Beijing. By the beginning of the year, large-scale hostilities had broken out between Vietnam and Kampuchea along their border. Hanoi, in need of increased military and economic assistance, leaned more heavily on an obliging Moscow, while China threw its full support behind Pol Pot's Kampuchean regime. Beijing also terminated its aid projects in Vietnam and withdrew its advisers and technicians. Faced with the exit of the Chinese, and their own inability to obtain aid from the West, the Vietnamese took a concrete step toward greater cooperation with the Soviet Union by joining the Council for Mutual Economic Aid in June 1978.

Soviet success at strengthening its relationship with Vietnam was mirrored by China's improvement of its relations with Japan. On August 12, 1978, the Sino-Japanese Treaty was signed in Beijing, despite strong warnings from Moscow that the agreement would seriously harm Soviet-Japanese relations. In particular, the Soviets objected to the inclusion in the treaty of Article II, which stated, "The contracting parties declare that neither of them should seek hegemony in the Asia-Pacific region or in any other region and that each is opposed to efforts by any other country or group of countries to establish such hegemony." Since the Chinese constantly accused the Soviets of seeking hegemony, Article II was an obvious reference to the USSR. Japan's agreement to its inclusion signaled Tokyo's choice to improve Sino-Japanese ties at the expense of Soviet-Japanese relations. The Japanese were particularly unhappy with the growth of Soviet military power in the Far East and Soviet unwillingness to return a number of islands northeast of Hokkaido, which the Soviets occupied before the end of World War II. Following the conclusion of the Sino-Japanese treaty, economic and diplomatic cooperation between the two nations grew significantly, while Soviet-Japanese negotiations concerning the disputed Kuril Islands and a possible Soviet-Japanese treaty made no progress. (Similarly, in late 1985 Soviet foreign minister Eduard Shevardnadze made the highest-level Soviet diplomatic trip to Japan in almost a decade to discuss improved relations, especially trade, but the dispute over the islands remained intractable.)

On November 3, 1978, Hanoi and Moscow further solidified their relationship by signing the Soviet-Vietnamese Treaty of Friendship and Cooperation. The agreement was similar to friendship treaties the Soviets had signed with other Third World countries during the 1970s. These treaties neither committed the Soviets to defend the other signatory, nor ensured that a Soviet presence in that nation would last. (For instance, after signing a treaty with Moscow in 1971, Egypt expelled Soviet advisers in 1972 and abrogated the treaty in 1976.) But they did provide the Kremlin with tangible confirmations that Soviet influence and status were indeed growing in the Third World. The Soviet-Vietnamese agreement pledged both sides to cooperate with each other in pursuit of their mutual political, economic, ideological, and security goals. It did not require the Soviet Union to intervene militarily on the side of Vietnam if it came under attack. It did, however, formally pronounce the Soviets' commitment to Vietnam, thereby increasing the likelihood of a strong Soviet response in the event Vietnam's security was threatened.

Vietnam Invades Kampuchea

On Christmas Day 1978 Vietnamese forces invaded Kampuchea, ostensibly in support of Kampuchean opponents to the Khmer Rouge. By January 7, 1979, Phnom Penh had fallen, though communist forces loyal to Pol Pot and supported by China continued to battle the Vietnamese in the countryside. The Soviet leadership applauded the defeat of Pol Pot's regime. Leonid Brezhnev denounced it as "a political system of the Chinese model."

The Vietnamese blitzkrieg into Kampuchea made apparent Hanoi's primary motivation for formalizing its close relationship with the Soviet Union. Just as India had signed a treaty with the Soviets in 1971 prior to their attack on East Pakistan, the Vietnamese had secured an agreement with the Soviets that they hoped would deter the Chinese from militarily intervening on behalf of the Khmer Rouge. There is little doubt that the Soviet leadership knew of the coming Vietnamese invasion of Kampuchea when they signed the treaty, given the level of Vietnamese-Kampuchean tension and the massive numbers of Soviet weapons that were sent to Vietnam during the seven-week period beween the signing of the treaty and the Vietnamese attack. Nevertheless, the invasion appeared to be planned and initiated by the Vietnamese.

As 1979 opened, Beijing's influence in Indochina was being weakened by the events in Kampuchea, but its diplomatic power was being enhanced by its formal establishment of relations with the United States. On December 15, 1978, President Carter announced, "The United States recognizes the government of the People's Republic of China as the sole legal government of China." Full diplomatic relations officially began January 1. While this development was not the harbinger of a Sino-American, anti-Soviet military alliance, it did improve the capability and willingness of China and the United States to cooperate with each other in new ways, including arms sales and technology transfers from the United States to China.

While not condemning the move, Moscow warned against using the continuing Sino-American détente against the USSR. Washington insisted that the establishment of relations with Beijing would not affect U.S.-Soviet relations. The Chinese, however, did not hesitate to call for U.S.-Chinese-Japanese cooperation against the Soviet Union. Deng Xiaoping's statements during his visit to the United States January 29-February 5 were particularly disturbing to the Soviets. He declared: "If we really want to be able to place curbs on the polar bear [the Soviet Union], the only realistic thing for us is to unite." While an anti-Soviet alliance was not forthcoming, Soviet interests in Asia were now opposed by three powerful nations with a shared interest in containing the Soviet Union and a growing potential for anti-Soviet cooperation.

On February 17, 1979, Chinese leaders made good on threats they had been making to teach Hanoi some "necessary lessons." They launched a multipronged armored invasion into northern Vietnam. The Chinese announced that the invasion was a limited, punitive action in response to the Vietnamese invasion of Kampuchea and alleged Vietnamese aggression on the Sino-Vietnamese border.

Brezhnev and his colleagues reacted cautiously to the invasion. They issued vague warnings to the Chinese to get out of Vietnam, but Soviet support for Hanoi was limited to propaganda, resupply efforts, and intelligence assistance. Soviet forces in Asian military districts were not even put on alert. The Brezhnev Politburo appeared unwilling to risk a confrontation with China over Vietnam, in spite of the recently signed Soviet-Vietnamese treaty. The Vietnamese had many of their best troops in Kampuchea but still managed to put up a stiff resistance against the Chinese assault, and Hanoi was never in danger. The Chinese began their withdrawal March 5, declaring that they had achieved their objectives. In the wake of the Chinese invasion, Soviet access to Vietnam, including the naval facilities at Cam Ranh Bay, became more extensive.

Surprisingly, on June 5, only three months after the Chinese withdrawal from Vietnam, Moscow and Beijing announced that negotiations on normalization of relations would take place for the first time since 1964. The talks began September 23 and recessed December 6. But this slight improvement in Sino-Soviet relations did not last. Following the Soviet invasion of Afghanistan in late December, Beijing demanded the withdrawal of Soviet troops and termed the invasion "a threat to China's security." On January 19, 1980, the Chinese Foreign Ministry announced that normalization talks would not be renewed because of the Soviet occupation of Afghanistan.

Relations in the 1980s

In April 1980 the Sino-Soviet treaty of friendship officially expired, although the alliance between the two communist countries had long since ceased to exist in practice. The treaty was a relic of a relatively short period of Sino-Soviet cooperation that is unlikely to be repeated in the foreseeable future.

Numerous divisive issues stand in the way of a reconciliation. The Chinese contend that the Soviets must withdraw from Afghanistan, terminate their support for Vietnamese aggression in Southeast Asia, and reduce their military deployments on the Sino-Soviet border to 1964

levels before progress can be made toward the improvement of relations. In addition, the border between the two countries is still disputed. The Chinese are worried about Soviet SS-20 missile deployments in Asia, while the Soviets voice concern over the sale of weapons and dual-use technology to China by the West. And both nations are suspicious of attempts by the other to expand relations with the United States, Japan, and Western Europe. Ironically, ideological disputes, which were the original source of the Sino-Soviet split, are barely a consideration today. The conflict between China and the Soviet Union has developed into a traditional great power rivalry with the major points of contention involving countervailing alliances, geographic boundaries, military strength, and economic competition.

Despite the many obstacles to a Sino-Soviet reconciliation, the Soviets and Chinese began making an effort in the 1980s to ease tensions between them. Beijing received a Soviet Foreign Ministry official for low-level talks in early 1981, and Soviet anti-Chinese rhetoric softened somewhat. Moscow made several proposals in late 1981 and early 1982 for improved educational and cultural ties, as well as new border negotiations. The Chinese did not accept the proposals, but the intensity of their criticisms of Moscow diminished.

By March of 1982 leaders in both countries had indicated that their ideological differences were not at the center of the conflict, and relations improved gradually throughout the year. On October 5, the two countries opened consultations at the deputy foreign minister level in Beijing on the normalization of relations. The following month, the Chinese used the occasion of Leonid Brezhnev's funeral to send their foreign minister, Huang Hua, to Moscow — a display of good will not seen since the Khrushchev era. Both sides stated their hopes that Sino-Soviet relations would continue to improve.

Yuri Andropov and Konstantin Chernenko adopted Brezhnev's policy of seeking to decrease tensions with Beijing. Additional talks on normalization of relations were held, and Sino-Soviet economic relations expanded. In July 1984, the Chinese concluded a border demarcation agreement with Mongolia, raising speculation that Beijing, if offered the right terms, might be willing to compromise on the border issue with the USSR as well. In December, First Deputy Premier Ivan Arkhipov visited Beijing, becoming the highest ranking Soviet leader to go there since 1969. Then in March 1985, before Konstantin Chernenko died, a Chinese parliamentary delegation traveled to Moscow for the first visit of its kind in more than 20 years.

But while Sino-Soviet relations improved between 1981 and the spring of 1985, the fundamental adversarial relationship between the two countries was not altered. The Soviets made many overtures to the Chinese but were unwilling to make concessions on key issues. Similarly, Chinese insistence that the Soviets withdraw from Afghanistan, end their support for Vietnam, and decrease troop levels on the Chinese border prohibited a more significant improvement of relations.

Reagan Policy Toward China

U.S. policy toward China during President Reagan's first term affected Beijing's willingness to improve relations with Moscow. U.S. arms sales to Taiwan, President Reagan's staunchly pro-Taiwan statements before and after his inauguration, his well-known anticommunist attitudes, and his administration's hesitancy to sell defensive weapons and transfer technology to China caused Beijing to adopt a more balanced approach to the superpowers. Not only did Chinese leaders allow the atmospheric improvement in Sino-Soviet relations, in 1981 the Chinese began frequently criticizing U.S. imperialism along with Soviet hegemonism.

By 1983, however, the Reagan administration had begun to vigorously pursue better relations with the Chinese. Reagan deemphasized the Taiwan issue and sought to establish closer economic and security ties with Beijing. These efforts were climaxed by President Reagan's trip to China April 26-May 1, 1984. Several agreements, including a nuclear technology transfer pact, were signed, and both sides issued cordial statements regarding the state of Sino-American relations.

This improvement of U.S.-Chinese ties, coupled with the intensification of Sino-Vietnamese tensions, had a temporarily negative impact on the Sino-Soviet relationship. First Deputy Premier Ivan Arkhipov's visit to China, scheduled for May 10, was postponed, and both sides intensified their rhetoric during the summer. Yet both the Soviets and the Chinese appeared determined to maintain the improved relationship that had been accomplished during the previous three years. Following meetings in New York between foreign ministers Andrei Gromyko and Wu Xueqian, the Soviets and Chinese resumed their trend toward better relations.

Ties Under Gorbachev

The prospects for continued development of Sino-Soviet ties under Mikhail Gorbachev appear good. Gorbachev advocated "a major improvement of Sino-Soviet relations" and held an extensively publicized meeting with Vice Premier Li Peng following Chernenko's funeral. Since then, the Chinese on occasion have referred to the Soviet Union as a "socialist country" and Mikhail Gorbachev as "comrade." In July 1985, the two countries tangibly improved economic relations by signing a $14 billion trade agreement covering the five-year-period from 1986 to 1990. Under the pact, annual trade will rise to $3.5 billion by 1990, compared with an estimated $1.8 billion in 1985. Moscow also agreed to build seven new factories in China and help modernize selected industrial facilities. In December 1985, political relations appeared to take another step forward when the Soviets and Chinese announced they would exchange foreign ministers in 1986 for the first time in 20 years.

Both communist powers have strong motivations for seeking a deeper rapprochement with the other. Deng Xiaoping has often stated that China must modernize and reinvigorate its economy. The promotion to important leadership posts in 1985 of many younger Chinese officials who support Deng's reforms will likely ensure that modernization will remain a top Chinese priority. To achieve this task, Beijing must avoid expending precious resources on an Asian arms race with the USSR. Also, as evidenced by the July 1985 trade accord, the Chinese believe economic cooperation with the Soviets can aid their modernization drive. Mikhail Gorbachev, like his predecessors, undoubtedly wants to reduce the strategic advantages the United States reaps from the Sino-Soviet rivalry and prevent anti-Soviet security cooperation between China, Japan, and the United States. In addition, the benefits of improved Sino-Soviet economic relations and a stable north Asian arena conducive to the development of Siberia and the Soviet Far East are important to the Soviets.

In conflict with these motivations are constraints working against closer ties that are equally compelling. Less than a month after agreeing to exchange foreign ministers with the Soviet Union, China hardened its position toward Moscow. Vice Foreign Minister Qian Qichen said in a January 6, 1986, interview that while Sino-Soviet technologial and economic cooperation has improved significantly, political relations have not improved. He accused the Soviets of being unwilling to address the issues of Soviet support for the Vietnamese occupation of Kampuchea, Soviet presence in Afghanistan, and Soviet troops along the Chinese border. Qian stated, "It seems the Soviet side has a misconception that it can get around these obstacles or that the obstacles will vanish by themselves. This calculation of the Soviets is unrealistic and unwise."

Even if these obstacles are removed in the future, the Chinese desire to retain their independent international position, and their experience of the withdrawal of Soviet aid and technicians in the early 1960s will make them hesitant to depend too heavily on the USSR again. Chinese independence within the communist world was underscored in February 1986 by their refusal to send a delegation to the 27th Soviet Communist Party Congress. The Soviet Union will continue to be the greatest threat to their security and a less attractive supplier of badly needed technology than Japan and the West. The Soviets, for their part, are not expected to make major concessions soon involving their occupation of Afghanistan or their support of Vietnam. Significant Soviet force reductions in Mongolia and the Soviet Far East are also unlikely given the Soviets' tendency to overensure the security of their frontiers.

Consequently, analysts expect the Soviets to continue their policy of refusing to address the major differences that exist between the Chinese and themselves, while seeking greater economic, scientific, and cultural cooperation with China, as well as a resolution of the border issue and a sustained reduction of polemics. The Chinese are expected to attempt to maintain relatively balanced relations with the Soviet Union and the United States, since Chinese interests would best be served by a foreign policy posture that encourages U.S. technology transfers and economic cooperation, while keeping Sino-Soviet tensions at a low level. Nevertheless, numerous developments could alter this scenario, including internal political changes in China, a dramatic increase in Chinese frustration with Soviet intransigence on the three obstacles, or another Soviet foreign policy move that Beijing perceives as aggressive.

USSR-MIDDLE EAST: STILL AN OUTSIDER

Forty years after World War II began reordering political power in the Middle East, the Soviet Union remained largely an outsider in the region.

Neither the USSR nor the United States has had much success imposing its own strategic international views on the Middle East. But, unlike the United States, the Kremlin has also not enjoyed widespread influence in this region at any time in postwar history.

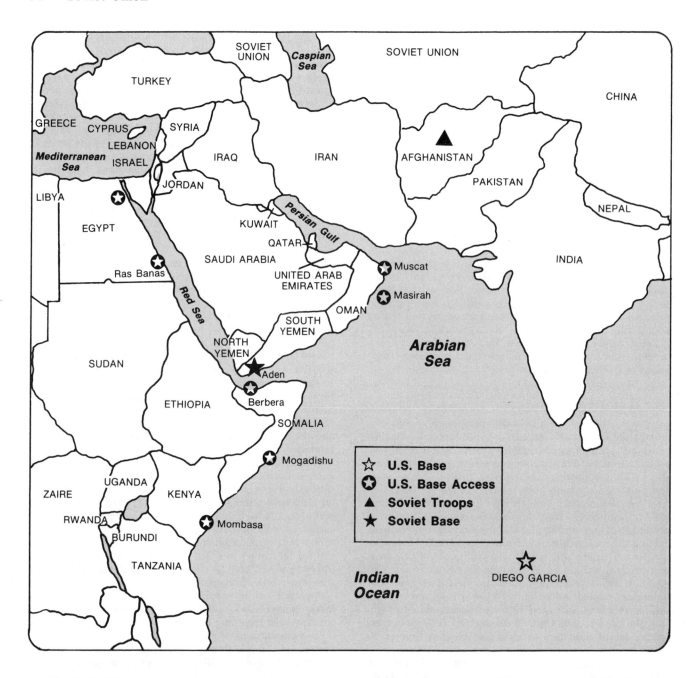

The United States has remained a central figure in the continuing peace process to end 38 years of animosity and war between Israel and its Arab neighbors. The Soviet Union has been largely frozen out of this effort even though it has gained some influence in the region since the mid-1950s. Both the Reagan administration and its counterparts in Moscow have courted Middle East leaders to influence developments or undermine the influence of the other superpower in the region. Neither has been very successful.

Most Middle East nations have not succumbed to the advances of either the United States or the USSR. Although the deficiencies of American policy are apparent enough to Arab eyes because of U.S. support for Israel, many Mideast states harbor deep concern about the ultimate goals of the USSR in the region.

The USSR tried to exploit regional crises to its own benefit and divide Arab states from their Western allies. But in addition to the crucial problem of being on the outside of Middle East peace efforts, it had numerous difficulties of its own. Although generally considered an Arab friend in the cause against Israel, it proved to be an unreliable partner at times and was in no position to pressure Israel for concessions. The USSR heralded the 1979 Iranian revolution as anti-imperialist but could not develop good ties with the Tehran government. Ties to the Iraqi regime of Sadam Hussein slowly deteriorated and relations with Egypt were antagonistic. The Soviet invasion and occupation of Afghanistan was almost universally opposed by the nations in the region. The USSR had an unpredictable ally in Syria and was able to gain little significant advantage among the conservative and oil rich Persian Gulf nations.

Origins of Soviet Involvement

Unlike the United States, which has been involved in the Middle East since the breakup of the Ottoman empire at the end of World War I, the Soviet Union did not have a significant role in the region until the 1950s. In 1955 Egypt became the first Arab country to purchase Soviet-made arms. Historically, Russia was mostly interested in the adjacent northern tier of the Middle East including Iran, Afghanistan, and Turkey. These countries had control over the straits of the Bosporus and the Dardanelles leading into the Aegean Sea from the Black Sea, straits that would give the USSR a warm-water port access. Prior to the 1917 revolution, tsarist Russia considered itself a local power in the region. From 1917 until the mid-1950s, with the exception of its involvement in Iran, the Soviet Union played a minimal role in the area.

Both the United States and the USSR welcomed the creation of Israel in 1948. Without Soviet support in the UN General Assembly, the partition of Palestine would have been difficult to achieve.

The Soviets seemed motivated by numerous factors in their early support for the creation of the Jewish state. The *Yishuv*, the Jewish settlement in Palestine, actively opposed the British mandate and seemed more likely than the Arabs to push the British out. Moreover, most of the Yishuv leadership was socialist in orientation, which the Soviets believed would make them more willing than the British to cooperate with the USSR. Early Soviet backing included not only political and diplomatic support but, through Czechoslovakia, arms to fight for statehood.

Israel said it would remain neutral in the superpower rivalry, apparently eliminating one area of Western influence in the region. However, the USSR's early support for partition of Palestine and the fledgling Jewish state harmed and delayed friendly relations with the Arabs.

Befriending Egypt

The Suez crisis in 1956 helped the Soviets gain a foothold in the Middle East. In that year Egypt, under charismatic leader Gamal Abdel Nasser, seized the Suez Canal from European control. Britain, France, and Israel united in a military attack to regain the waterway, which gave the USSR an opportunity to ally with Arab nationalists against Western influence. Earlier, in 1955, the Soviets supplied Egypt with arms, the beginning of a Soviet-Egyptian alliance that lasted until 1972. However, the United States was not a party to the military actions of its allies, nor even informed of them beforehand. Vigorous U.S. pressure on the three nations to withdraw helped counterbalance Soviet charges of imperialism against the West.

The events of the 1950s helped convince President Dwight Eisenhower of the Soviet threat. Out of this concern came the Eisenhower Doctrine. In January 1957 Eisenhower told Congress that the United States should be prepared to aid any nation requesting help "against armed aggression from any country controlled by international communism." To thwart Soviet expansion, a mutual defense treaty had been formed in 1955 called the Baghdad Pact. It included Britain, Iran, Pakistan, Turkey, and Iraq until that nation withdrew in 1958 after a coup. The organization then was renamed the Central Treaty Organization (CENTO).

The USSR saw tangible threats in CENTO and the Eisenhower Doctrine. To Arab nationalists, such as Egypt's Nasser, they were a rebirth of colonial power in the region, which gave Moscow openings to win support from Nasser and like-minded Arabs.

Soviets Plagued by Obstacles

Nevertheless, Soviet opportunities to gain influence were plagued with problems. Many Arab nationalists, although opposed to Western influence, were unwilling to surrender their independence to the USSR and were not attracted to the atheistic ideology of communism. Most Arab nationalists were secular in their orientation but were not atheists.

At times Moscow found communist parties in Arab countries attacked by regimes it supported. In Egypt, for example, Nasser considered communists a threat and clamped down vigorously, eventually banning them. Soviet allies Syria and Iraq also opposed domestic communist parties and Syria banned them.

Even so, Moscow and its new allies cooperated to keep the West, especially the United States, from gaining influence. Disagreements were subordinated to this goal. At the same time, the Soviets began moving steadily toward the Arab side of the Arab-Israeli conflict.

Soviet Fortunes Change

Soviet Middle East involvement, limited under Nikita Khrushchev, progressed more rapidly after he was deposed. The USSR established itself as a regional power by the mid-1960s. From minimal leverage in the mid-1950s, the Soviets were aggressively seeking to block Western influence by the outbreak of the third Arab-Israeli war in 1967, known as the Six-Day War. But within a decade the Kremlin's influence was headed rapidly downhill.

1967 Six-Day War

The 1967 Six-Day War was a key event for Soviet influence in the area. On June 5, 1967, Israel, provoked by the Egyptian blockade of a key waterway, the strait of Tiran, attacked Arab forces and destroyed much of the armed forces of Egypt, Syria, and Jordan and captured large amounts of Arab territory.

Soviet prestige plummeted when it provided little actual aid and backed a cease-fire while Israel occupied Arab territories. In some ways, the Arab defeat also was a Soviet defeat. The token measure Moscow and its communist allies took was to sever diplomatic ties with Israel.

Nasser charged that U.S. aircraft contributed to Egypt's defeat and broke diplomatic relations with Washington, as did six other Arab states. Partially to atone for inaction during the war, the USSR rebuilt the armed forces of Egypt, Syria, and Jordan. The United States moved to replace the French as the chief arms supplier for Israel.

Militarily defeated and politically humiliated, Nasser moved closer to Moscow. He sought Soviet help with an air defense system to improve Egyptian prestige and halt sporadic Israeli raids, a move that departed from past assistance by permitting Soviet pilots and troops to enter Egypt. An Egyptian-Israeli cease-fire, finally agreed to August 6, 1970, lasted until 1973.

Sadat Takes Power in Egypt

President Nasser died suddenly September 28, 1970, bringing to office Anwar al-Sadat, a relatively obscure and inexperienced man whose view of Egypt's future was not widely known. Unlike Nasser, Sadat was not saddled by guilt over defeat in the 1967 war, but he realized that a no-war and no-peace situation was not in Egypt's long-range interests.

The Soviet Union's problems with Nasser were soon repeated with Sadat. Like Nasser, Sadat opposed attempts by the Egyptian Communist Party to gain control of the government. Sadat also wanted to rebuild Egyptian prestige and Arab pride, while the USSR was more interested in blocking American influence.

Sadat asked repeatedly and unsuccessfully for increased Soviet military aid to prepare for a war with Israel. In 1971 Sadat spoke of a "year of decision" when he would plan to regain the Sinai and other territory lost in 1967. The Soviets continued to press for a peaceful solution of the conflict. When the year ended with no Egyptian decision or action, the Soviets concluded Sadat's statement was a bluff to get more aid.

Soviet-Egyptian differences worsened following a 1972 U.S.-USSR summit between President Richard M. Nixon and Soviet party chief Leonid Brezhnev. The Soviets were more interested in improving relations with the United States than in supporting Sadat's desire to recapture territories. Following the summit, both sides supported peaceful resolution of the Mideast conflict.

Sadat gradually concluded that Egyptian and Soviet goals were incompatible. His increasingly hostile statements reflected anger over the Soviet presence in Egypt and the lack of support in the conflict with Israel. Finally, on July 18, 1972, Sadat ordered all 20,000 Soviet military advisers out of Egypt.

Sadat's action severely damaged the USSR's position in the Middle East. But it much pleased the Nixon administration, which knew that without the largest and most powerful Arab state Soviet influence would be greatly diminished. The USSR then turned elsewhere in the Arab world for support.

Relations with Iraq, which had improved sufficiently to allow a treaty of friendship, continued to get better. The Soviets also courted Syria, although that country, unlike Iraq and Egypt, refused to sign a treaty of friendship. Nevertheless, Syria's president Hafez al-Assad obtained some of the Soviet military equipment he believed was needed to counter Israel. In addition, Moscow's relations with the Palestinian groups began to warm and Soviet arms for the first time went directly to the Palestine Liberation Organization (PLO) rather than through Arab governments. The difficulty Moscow faced then, and to the present, was the rivalries among the member groups in the PLO.

1973 Arab-Israel War

The fourth Arab-Israeli war, in October 1973, further diminished Soviet influence in the area. In joining with the United States to halt the war, the Soviet Union initially was part of the peacemaking process. On October 21, 1973, the two superpowers presented a joint resolution to the United Nations Security Council calling for a cease-fire and implementing Security Council resolution 242, which called for Israeli withdrawal from Arab lands occupied in the 1967 war.

The Soviet Union cosponsored a conference in Geneva in late 1973 to resolve the war issues, but this marked the last time the USSR was deeply involved in Middle East peace negotiations. In addition to the two superpowers, the Geneva conference included Egypt, Israel, and Jordan. Syria boycotted the meeting. The conference lasted two days, ended without success, and never reconvened.

U.S. Secretary of State Henry A. Kissinger in early 1974 began a protracted effort in personal diplomacy, which came to be called shuttle diplomacy because of the many trips he made to Middle East nations. His effort largely excluded the Soviet Union from a role in the peacemaking process. The United States, even with close ties to Israel, impartially negotiated with all the parties and improved its position in the Arab world as a result.

Peace Treaty Excludes Soviets

Sadat in 1977 visited Jerusalem in a historic step toward a peace with Israel. This was followed by the personal negotiations with Israeli leaders at President Carter's retreat in Camp David, Maryland. Eventually a peace treaty with Israel was brokered by Carter and other U.S. officials. Throughout the negotiations, Sadat was repeatedly accused by Arab nations and organizations unalterably opposed to peace with Israel of betraying Arab, particularly Palestinian, rights.

Excluded from the negotiations, the Soviet Union sought to improve relations with the PLO. The Kremlin viewed this group and the Syrians as its only way back into the peace process that was dominated by the United States. The PLO, probably the most anti-American group among the Arabs, welcomed the Soviet support. The Soviets also sought to improve relations with the radical Arab states. There was, on the surface, greater amiability with Syria, Iraq, Libya, and other "rejectionist" nations that opposed any negotiations or settlement with Israel. Contacts between the Soviet Union and Jordan expanded, and the Jordanian media began supporting a strong Soviet role in the peacemaking process.

To many observers, Soviet opposition to the American-engineered Egyptian-Israeli treaty stemmed from being outside the peace process rather than from any real support for its Arab friends. With the United States dominating the peace process, the Soviets were left with improving their own ties with die-hard Arab opponents of a U.S.-backed settlement.

The Soviet Union denounced the peace agreement; Sadat was branded a "traitor" and a "supplicant." The Soviets charged that Israel had no intention of surrendering the West Bank, Gaza, or the Golan Heights, all captured in the 1967 war, and that the United States was forcing a solution giving its Israeli ally all it wanted.

In October 1978 President Assad of Syria, President Houari Boumediene of Algeria, and PLO chairman Yasir Arafat all visited Moscow. During these visits, the Camp David peace formula was denounced and, in return for promises of additional Soviet aid, Assad and Arafat called for a reconvening of the 1973 Geneva conference. The Algerians, along with the Libyans and Iraqis, opposed any direct negotiations with Israel, at Geneva or elsewhere. Soviet condemnation of the agreements continued through 1978 and into 1979. Contacts with Jordan increased, and there even were hints of an improvement in Soviet-Saudi relations.

Compared to the Arab reaction to the peace treaty

itself, Soviet rhetoric was relatively restrained and varied little from the criticism Moscow had voiced ever since the Camp David negotiations. But there were new warnings that the treaty would encourage the United States to form Egyptian-Israeli-American "military pacts" in the region. Israel, the Soviet media argued, would receive a massive increase in U.S. arms, while Egypt would be given enough to become the "policeman" of the Middle East.

Influence Slides in 1980s

Soviet influence, never particularly great in the region, continued to slide in the 1970s and beyond. By the middle of the 1980s, Soviet influence in the region had not progressed beyond that which existed a decade or more earlier, and in fact may have declined. The USSR remained on the outside looking in. Of necessity, it was responding to, rather than leading, events in the region. In certain respects, Soviet policy suffered from the same problems as U.S. policy. Both nations viewed the region as an extension of the superpower conflict and less as an area beset with regional rivalries.

The USSR's problems abounded in the 1980s. It was unable to gain ground in the Persian Gulf, continual war in Lebanon only marginally improved its position in the Arab-Israeli conflict, and it remained unable to create the anti-imperialist alliance it had sought. Most importantly, the USSR was merely an observer in the Arab-Israeli peace process while the United States remained the main negotiator.

Soviet Policy Problems

Soviet policy in the region during the 1980s was hampered by successive leadership changes in the Soviet Union. Soviet goals of expanding its own influence and thwarting America's were not easy to reconcile with the sometimes competing interests of Soviet allies, including Syria and the PLO. The Soviet Union also was harmed by its military involvement in Afghanistan, which cost it credibility in the Mideast region, and was unable to capitalize on Persian Gulf instability brought on by the Iran-Iraq war.

The Soviets continued to seek a resumption of the Geneva conference or another international meeting that would bring them into the peace process. Israel strongly opposed an international conference with Soviet participation because the USSR had not reestablished diplomatic relations that were broken after the 1967 war.

The USSR also continued to tie U.S. actions as closely as possible to Israeli policy. They took this approach in 1981 after Israel bombed and destroyed the nearly completed Ossirak nuclear reactor near Baghdad in Iraq. The Soviets charged that the United States, by providing the planes Israel used, supported the attack. However, the argument failed both to bring the Iraqis closer to the Soviets or expand Soviet influence in the region. The Soviet charge was weakened when the United States sharply criticized the attack and joined in a UN resolution condemning the raid.

Israel's increasing military action against the PLO in Lebanon in the spring of 1981, including Israeli bombing of the PLO headquarters in Beirut, provided the Soviets with another opportunity to exploit. Even though the raid prompted President Reagan to halt deliveries to Israel of sophisticated F-16 planes, the Soviets again sought to create the impression that U.S. and Israeli policies were identical. This strategy served to divert attention from Soviet occupation of Afghanistan and reinforce the view that the main threats to the region were the United States and Israel and not the USSR, as the Reagan administration claimed.

When Israel invaded Lebanon in June 1982, ostensibly to clear a border region of Palestinians who were attacking Israeli villages, the Soviets reacted surprisingly calmly. Except for a few statements critical of the invasion, the Soviets did little until the possibility loomed of a full-scale war between Israel and Syria. Both the Soviet Union and the United States wanted to avoid that. The Soviets pressured the Syrians to accept a cease-fire agreement. The main confrontation between the PLO and Israel continued almost unabated. Significantly, the Soviets delayed resupplying the Syrians after Israel destroyed missile batteries the Syrians had set up within range of Israel.

Soviet reaction to the war that was taking place between Israel and the PLO was quiet in comparison to the previous Arab-Israeli wars. The Soviets did try to exploit the situation, however. Throughout the war, the Soviets continued to claim that the United States supported Israeli actions. They also opposed efforts by the United States to introduce peacekeeping troops and did what they could to undermine American-sponsored negotiations.

Eventually the Soviets clashed with Syria over objectives for Lebanon. Both agreed that a pro-Western government in Lebanon friendly to Israel was undesirable, but the agreement ended there. The Soviets did not want the Lebanese government to become too closely allied with the West. The Syrians had bigger goals: they wanted to become the dominant power in Lebanon. Syria and the Soviets had clashed before over Syrian designs on Lebanon. When the Syrians first invaded Lebanon in 1975, for example, the Soviets opposed the move.

More Soviet-Syrian clashes took place over the PLO. Syria's Assad had a longstanding feud with PLO chairman Arafat. The Soviets had little patience for this feud, viewing it as counterproductive to Soviet goals of diminishing Western influence in the region, and to Arab goals of defeating Israel.

The Soviets did maintain some semblance of their alliance with Syria, which had been formalized in a 1980 bilateral security treaty in 1980. The Soviets criticized stationing of U.S. troops in Lebanon and backed Syrian efforts to undermine the American position in that country. The USSR supported Syrian opposition to the accord reached by Lebanon and Israel, and ultimately backed those forces in Lebanon opposing the government in power there.

Relations with PLO

The Soviet Union has long had difficulty in maintaining stable relations with the Palestine Liberation Organization. In addition to the numerous factions within the PLO, chairman Yasir Arafat has been alternately praised and criticized by the Soviets. His feud with Syria angered the Soviets as did his agreement with Jordan's King Hussein to form a joint negotiating strategy. The Soviets feared this would lead to a shift by Arafat toward the West. After Arafat's attendance at Yuri Andropov's funeral in February 1984, PLO-Soviet relations faltered until it was announced in January 1986 that Arafat would visit Moscow in February, in time for the Soviet Party Congress. Western analysts said the Soviets' move indicated they felt the time was right to improve relations with the PLO.

Persian Gulf

At the beginning of the 1980s the focus of strategic concerns in the Middle East shifted from the Arab-Israeli conflict to the Persian Gulf, containing the world's richest oil reserves. The U.S.-backed shah of Iran was overthrown at the end of 1978 as the Ayatollah Khomeini, preaching Islamic fundamentalism, came to power. In December 1979 the Soviets invaded Afghanistan, giving them a new base from which to project military force in the area. This provided the Soviets with a better military position, but it drew sharp criticism from the Moslem states in the region. The "oil squeezes" in 1973 and 1979 combined with these two events to unveil and expose the concurrent rise in Western vulnerability and Soviet power in the Gulf. A major test of Soviet strength and influence in the Gulf came when Iraq invaded Iran in 1980.

Ties to smaller Gulf states seemingly improved in the fall of 1985, with diplomatic relations established for the first time with Oman and the United Arab Emirates. Until then, only Kuwait among the oil-rich Gulf states had diplomatic relations with the Soviet Union. In the Arabian Peninsula, the Soviet Union had developed its best relations in the Middle East with South Yemen. The stability of that relationship was tested in January 1986 by a coup, but the apparent victors were strongly oriented toward Moscow and Western analysts did not foresee a negative result for the Soviets.

Soviet-Iranian Relations

Moscow was delighted with the turn of events in Iran at the end of 1978. The shah, a staunch American ally, was replaced with a regime extremely hostile to the United States, and the Soviets hoped Iran could be brought into their camp. Many analysts consider Iran the most important Gulf state strategically because of its size and its oil wealth. The Soviet Union had a historical interest in Iran long before oil was discovered in the Persian Gulf, partially because of the significant and growing Moslem population in regions of the USSR adjacent to the Middle East. Additionally, Iran is the only Gulf country that borders the USSR, and control of or friendship with the government there would give Moscow access to a long-sought-after warm-water port. Western petroleum vulnerability simply added a bonus to Iran's potential to serve Soviet interests.

While the Iranian revolution provided opportunities for the Soviets, it also forced the Soviets to make difficult, sometimes contradictory, decisions. The Soviets did not lend immediate support for the Iranian revolution, preferring to wait until the shah's days were obviously numbered before making a commitment to the religious revolutionaries. Initially the Soviets emphasized state-to-state relations after the revolution instead of seeking to expand communist influence; more aggressive moves might have backfired by deepening the Ayatollah Khomeini's suspicions of the USSR. But by 1980 the Soviets had become increasingly pessimistic about the course of their relations with the Iranians.

Despite Iranian rebuffs, the Soviets had attempted to woo the Tehran government in numerous ways. They pledged military, technical, and economic assistance; they offered to help the new regime deal with internal security threats; they blocked UN sanctions against Iran during the American hostage crisis in Tehran; they provided a transit route for goods bound for Iran during the U.S. economic embargo (also a result of the hostage crisis).

The Soviets still made no headway. The Soviet invasion of Afghanistan particularly angered the Iranians and became a major issue between the countries. The Khomeini government repeatedly renounced the 1921 treaty between the Soviet Union and Iran that allowed the Soviets to enter Persia in case of outside intervention. (The shah had also disavowed the pact.) The Soviets had apparently threatened to invoke it during the Iranian revolution in case their embassy in Tehran was threatened. In mid-1979 Iran expelled 18 Soviet representatives for spying; another Soviet embassy officer was expelled in June 1980. The Islamic republic also reduced and limited cultural activities with the Soviet Union while cultivating ties with pro-Western Turkey and Pakistan.

Since the revolution, the Soviets have been broadcasting the National Voice of Iran from the Soviet city of Baku, expressing support for the revolution and warning against "American imperialism." The Soviets even attempted to identify with the revolutionary regime ideologically by claiming, "The liberation struggle can develop under the banner of Islam."

Nonetheless, the Communist Party in Iran — the Tudeh — remained outlawed and its leaders faced increasingly harsh treatment. Many were tried and executed. Iran also increasingly condemned Soviet Middle East policies in the early 1980s and, while fiercely anti-American, had come to view the Soviets as the "lesser Satan."

Iran-Iraq War

The Soviets reacted cautiously to the war between Iran and Iraq that broke out in September 1980, blaming the United States for instigating it and opting ostensibly for a neutral stand.

The war posed a dilemma for the Soviets. Iraq had signed a Treaty of Friendship and Cooperation with the Soviet Union in 1972. Siding with Iran in the war against Iraq would undoubtedly complicate Soviet desires to court both countries and would ultimately force the Soviets to choose one state over the other.

Although officially neutral, Soviet policy initially had a definite Iranian tilt. The Soviet Union cut off arms sales to Iraq while at the same time offering Iran major weapons systems and other forms of assistance. The Iranians rejected the Soviet offer, but Soviet arms and military supplies were provided indirectly by Libya, Syria, North Korea, and East European states. The Kremlin was displeased with Iraq's treatment of the Iraqi Communist Party and with its commercial connections with Western countries. More importantly, however, the installment of a friendly government in Tehran was a far greater prize than good relations with Baghdad. In addition, the Iraqi decision to invade Iran embarrassed the Soviets, primarily because it occurred while Iraqi Deputy Premier and Foreign Minister Tariq Aziz was on an official visit to Moscow, giving the impression that the Soviets supported the invasion, when in fact they did not.

Following Iranian offensives into Iraqi territory in

1982, the Soviets supplied arms to the Iraqis and concluded new arms agreements with them. According to Dennis Ross, executive director of the Berkeley-Stanford Program on Soviet International Behavior, this change in policy occurred for a variety of reasons. First, the Soviets had been rejected by the Iranians and were frustrated by Iranian hostility. Second, it was not necessarily in the Soviet Union's best interests to further the tide of Islamic fundamentalism and the image of an invincible Iran. The threat of a row of Iran-dominated Shi'ite states along the Soviet border must have affected the Soviet outlook. Third, an Iraqi defeat would have embarrassed the Soviets, because Iraq for so long had been a Soviet client.

Additionally, the Soviets seemed to believe that until Khomeini died there was little chance to significantly increase their influence in Iran. They also seemed aware that a decisive victory by either side would not serve Soviet interests. Both Iran and Iraq had demonstrated they were not very receptive to Soviet overtures and a strengthening of either nation's position would not create an opening for Moscow.

During the spring of 1984, although continuing to publicly declare neutrality, the Soviets tilted further toward Iraq. In March the chairman of the State Committee for Foreign Economic Relations of the Soviet Union, Iakov Riabov, traveled to Baghdad and concluded important economic and technical agreements, including an agreement for Soviet construction of a nuclear reactor in Iraq. In April Iraq signed a long-term agreement with the Soviets expanding economic and technical cooperation. The Iraqi foreign minister later indicated that the Soviet Union had extended $2 billion dollars in long-term loans with easy credit terms for Iraqi economic projects. It was also reported that the Soviets had agreed to provide Iraq with surface-to-surface missiles and air-to-ground explosives.

According to Dennis Ross, proof of the Soviet Union's improved ties with Iraq was provided by the Iraqi government. Perhaps the most telling indicator came December 16, 1985, when Iraqi president Saddam Hussein met unexpectedly with Mikhail Gorbachev in Moscow. He met also with Soviet defense minister Sergei Sokolov, indicating discussion of military matters, and President Andrei Gromyko. It was Hussein's first visit to Moscow since 1980. Tass reported the talks were "businesslike, frank, and friendly" and noted that Hussein came at "the invitation of the Soviet leadership."

Earlier, improved relations were presaged when Iraq no longer blamed both superpowers for the continuation of the war. The improved relations between Baghdad and Moscow did not come at the cost of relations between the United States and Iraq because in 1984 the two resumed diplomatic relations that had beeen severed since 1967. Yet in early 1984 Iraqi deputy premier Taha Yasin Ramadan asserted that the West was maintaining Iran's financial and military capabilities to scare Arab states and to force them to seek U.S. support. The Soviet Union, he said, was living up to its treaty agreements.

Even more surprising was an interview in May 1984 by Hussein, who rarely grants interviews. He condemned the United States and referred to "good" relations with the Soviets.

Despite improved relations with the Iraqis, however, the USSR probably wanted to see the war end in some sort of political compromise at the earliest date possible. The continuation of the Iran-Iraq war hurt the Soviet Union for several reasons. The war increased the influence of moderate anti-Soviet Arab nations in the region, such as Saudi Arabia. It facilitated Egypt's return to the Arab community after the isolation caused by the Camp David Accords with Israel. Egyptian support of Iraq was regarded favorably by most Arab states as the threat of Iranian expansionism became a growing fear. Syria, a Soviet ally and longtime rival of Iraq, was alienated because of its support for Iran. Finally, the Iran-Iraq war reduced some of the Arab states' reluctance to allow an American military presence in the region.

South Yemen

The quandary the United States experienced with the fall of the shah of Iran was similar to the crisis the Soviet Union faced with the internal fighting in South Yemen that broke out in January 1986.

Since its independence in 1967 as the People's Republic of Southern Yemen, South Yemen has had a socialist orientation. It is the only communist Arab country. The ruling party, the National Front for the Liberation of South Yemen (NLF), preached "scientific socialism" with a clearly Marxist flavor. President Qahtan al-Sha'bi sought closer ties with the Soviet Union and China as well as with the more radical Arab regimes.

Al-Sha'bi's orientation, however, was not radical enough for some elements of the NLF. In 1969 he was overthrown by a group of militants led by Salim Rubayyi' Ali, and in 1970 the country was renamed the People's Democratic Republic of Yemen. The new regime took extreme steps, including repression and exile, to break traditional patterns of tribalism and religion, and eliminate the vestiges of the bourgeoisie and familial elites.

Externally, relations between North and South Yemen were rocked by political and ideological differences despite mutual advocacy of Yemeni reunification. Saudi Arabia actively opposed the Marxist regime and backed North Yemeni opposition efforts in the south.

Salim Rubayyi' Ali had a powerful rival in the person of Abd al-Fattah Isma'il, secretary general of the NLF (renamed NF). Ali was called a Maoist with pro-China sympathies, whereas Isma'il was thought of as a pragmatic Marxist loyal to Moscow. In June 1978 Isma'il finally seized power and executed Ali. He reorganized the NF into the Yemeni Socialist Party (YSP), became chairman of the Presidium of the People's Supreme Assembly, and named Ali Nasser Muhammad prime minister. In October 1979 Isma'il signed a friendship and cooperation treaty with the USSR.

But Isma'il's fortunes soon changed, and in April 1980 he relinquished his posts as presidium chairman and YSP secretary general. In his place, the YSP Central Committee named Ali Nasser Muhammad.

Poor health had been cited as the reason for Isma'il's resignation, but it appeared to be the result of a power struggle and differences over Aden's foreign policies. Isma'il's intention had been to further cement ties with the Soviet Union and Eastern Europe, and to that extent there was agreement between him and Muhammad. But the latter also wanted to improve relations with Saudi Arabia and other Gulf countries to end South Yemen's isolation in the Arab world and secure new sources of foreign aid. Muhammad also felt that rapprochement with Saudi Arabia would facilitate union between the two Yemens. After his resignation, Isma'il moved to Moscow and lived there until the fall of 1985. He then returned to South Yemen and was elected to the Politburo of the ruling socialist party.

Muhammad began his tenure with visits to the Soviet Union, Saudi Arabia, North Yemen, and other neighboring countries in the Middle East. He signed agreements on economic and technical cooperation with the Soviets, and in late 1980 agreed to a friendship and cooperation treaty with East Germany. The Soviet Union's economic assistance to South Yemen doubled under Muhammad's leadership. The Soviet military presence in South Yemen also increased significantly.

In January of 1986 a coup on the part of those supporting Isma'il escalated to civil war. A combination of ideological differences, tribal rivalries, and personal enmities apparently caused the fighting.

The rebels allied with Isma'il were reportedly displeased with Muhammad's moves to improve relations with South Yemen's neighbors. Although Muhammad was an avowed Marxist, the rebels may have viewed his overtures to the pro-Western Persian Gulf countries as deviations from strict Marxist ideology. The domestic policies pursued by Muhammad also provoked the displeasure of the rebels.

Moscow feared that the fighting in South Yemen could harm its chances of expanding ties with other Gulf countries. The Soviets did not want to jeopardize their recently established diplomatic relations with Oman and the United Arab Emirates.

In addition, the Soviet Union hoped South Yemen would serve as a positive example of what Marxism could mean for other Arab states. The internal instability and bloodshed there became an embarrassment to Moscow.

The Soviets also had to be concerned about the effect the power struggle between Muhammad's supporters and the rebels backing Isma'il would have on their strategically important military bases in Aden and on the South Yemeni island of Socrota in the Arabian Sea. Although both competing factions declared their loyalty to Moscow, the Soviet leadership was careful not to make enemies in South Yemen by taking sides in the civil war.

Kremlin leaders appeared to have blundered when they permitted Isma'il to go back to South Yemen. It is unlikely that they expected his return would precipitate such an internal struggle. The Soviets were caught off-guard by the coup attempt despite the presence in South Yemen of the KGB and other intelligence-gathering agencies of the Soviet Union.

After 12 days of fighting, rebel leaders had gained control of the country. Western sources reported that 10,000 South Yemenis and many top party leaders had been killed. Isma'il had disappeared and was presumed dead, though the new government would not confirm that he had died. His rival, President Muhammad, reportedly fled the country.

Haidar Abu Bakr Attas, the prime minister in Muhammad's government, was abroad when the fighting began. He returned to Aden via Moscow January 25 to become provisional president of the new Marxist coalition government. Contrary to their hard-line credentials, South Yemen's new leaders quickly declared their intention to continue pursuing better relations with neighboring Arab countries. This led analysts to speculate that Moscow encouraged South Yemen to adopt a good neighbor policy as a means of broadening Soviet ties among Arab states and dispelling fears of Soviet subversion and aggression in the Middle East.

Prospects for Future

Soviet influence in the Middle East, which was at a high point in the late 1960s and early 1970s, declined greatly through the mid-1980s. The Soviets found that no matter how they tried to capitalize on strains between the United States and some of the regional players, they were unable to make major gains. This was primarily due to a lack of Soviet understanding of local disputes but also because many local leaders, while welcoming support, remained wary of Soviet intentions. Included in that apprehension was the regional antipathy toward communism. The revolutionary movements in the Middle East have not all been religious but none professed the atheism of communism. This has been a continuing obstacle in the Soviet desire to expand its influence in the Middle East.

Soviet success in establishing diplomatic ties with Oman and the UAE, as important as it is, pales in comparison with the stature of the United States in the region. Soviet relations are good only with the more radical Arab regimes. The Soviets have been unable to make major inroads in establishing ties, let alone having warm ties, with some of the more conservative regimes. The Soviets realize that to gain a larger role in the region they must improve relations with the more conservative regimes, the most important of them being Saudi Arabia.

Even among those states with which it does have diplomatic ties the Soviets have been unable to foster close relations. For example, the Soviet Union reestablished relations with Egypt, but it was unable to strengthen the relationship to anything close to what it was before all Soviet military advisers were ejected in 1972.

The Soviets' problem is the difficulty of maintaining relations with Libya and Syria while trying to establish relations with Saudi Arabia and some of the Persian Gulf nations because of the inter-Arab conflicts that separate these states.

The Soviets can count on resentment toward the West by some regional leaders stemming from the colonial histories of most of the states. But past attempts to exploit this have had only limited success.

In trying to develop a Middle East strategy, the Soviets have had to balance ideological considerations against their need to develop a sphere of influence as a superpower. Some Western experts believe the Kremlin leadership has not abandoned efforts for a larger role in the region through local communist parties, but that they have been unable to blend communism with the religious commitment of most of the region.

USSR-AFGHANISTAN: A SOVIET STALEMATE

U.S.-Soviet relations remained on a relatively even keel for most of 1979. But President Jimmy Carter's hopes for a new era in détente with the Soviet Union were destroyed Christmas Day 1979 when, in a dramatic operation, the Kremlin airlifted into Kabul, Afghanistan's capital, military equipment and several thousand Soviet troops.

Reaction from the United States and many other nations was swift and harsh, although mostly verbal. The

United States was one of the few countries to impose sanctions against the Soviet Union in response, although others joined a U.S. call to boycott the 1980 Moscow Summer Olympics. Neighboring Islamic countries were especially angered and feared the invasion's implications.

Since the December 1979 invasion, however, the Soviets have remained in Afghanistan despite world outcry and increasing costs. The Soviets increased the number of their troops in Afghanistan and brought in more sophisticated weaponry. By the beginning of 1986, there seemed little prospect of Soviet withdrawal soon. But the Soviets have been unable to overcome the determined Afghans in a war that many have termed the "Soviet Union's Vietnam." World outcry diminished somewhat by 1986 but U.S. and other outside support for the rebels fighting the Soviets and Soviet-backed Afghan government remained steady.

Steps to Intervention

On December 27, only a few days after the Soviet airlift began, Hafizullah Amin, the Afghan president placed in power by a Soviet-backed coup in April 1978, was ousted and executed. To replace Amin, the Soviet Union installed as president Babrak Karmal, a former communist leader in Afghanistan who had been living in exile in the Soviet Union.

Reports December 29 confirmed that as many as four Soviet divisions (about 50,000 men), spearheaded by their newest battle tanks, had crossed into Afghanistan from Soviet border towns. By early January 1980 the Soviets had moved an army of 85,000 men into Afghanistan.

Fighting broke out in the streets of Kabul against elements of the Afghan army. Soviet troops reportedly had captured every major town and highway and had consolidated their positions. Rapid deployment of so large a Soviet force indicated to Western military analysts that the Soviets had a strong logistical support system capable of moving quickly and supplying a rapid deployment force for conventional military actions.

Opposition to the takeover continued as Afghan guerrillas in the mountainous countryside fought Soviet troops with weapons that dated from World War II. Some of the guns reportedly were homemade.

Staunchly independent and fiercely anticommunist, the Moslem guerrillas (or *mujahideen*) had been at war with the Kabul government and elements of the politically divided Afghan army since the April 1978 takeover. Although the rebels' insurgency lacked cohesion, it apparently had popular support, in part because of the central government's violence against Afghanistan's minorities and modernization attempts that conflicted with Islamic tradition. The opposition included tens of thousands of troops defecting from the Afghan army.

By pursuing a policy of nonalignment, Afghanistan had received aid from both the United States and the Soviet Union in the 1950s and 1960s. A republic under Mohammed Daoud Khan was established in 1973 when the monarchy was overthrown by the first of many military coups. Soviet influence rose significantly under Daoud, with Moscow increasing its military aid to the Afghan army and training thousands of Afghan officers, mostly in the Soviet Union.

The Soviet-sponsored military coup in 1978 removed Daoud and made Hafizullah Amin first minister and Nur

Sanctions Against Soviets

President Carter imposed numerous, wide-ranging sanctions against the Soviet Union following the 1979 Afghanistan invasion. An embargo on grain sales to the USSR, imposed January 4, 1980, affected all transactions above the 8 million metric tons provided by the 1975 U.S.-Soviet grain agreement. This blocked a previously approved sale of 14.7 million metric tons of corn, wheat, and soybeans. The president also imposed an embargo on the sale of items incorporating "high technology," such as large computers, advanced machine tools, and certain oil and gas production equipment.

The International Longshoremen's Union January 9, 1980, said its workers would not handle cargo on Soviet ships or other Soviet-bound cargos in East and Gulf Coast ports. The United States also suspended a range of economic and cultural contacts with the Soviet Union. Formal contacts with Moscow by any U.S. official at or above the rank of assistant secretary could be made only with the personal approval of President Carter.

The immediate results of this policy included:

● Suspension of plans for a U.S. consulate-general in Kiev, capital of the Soviet Ukraine, and a Soviet consulate-general in New York City. Construction work on the Kiev facility was stopped and the seven U.S. diplomats preparing to set up the office were reassigned. Moscow was asked to withdraw the 17 Soviet diplomats attached to the New York consulate.

● A reduction in flights of Aeroflot, the Soviet airline, to the United States to two from three a week. Aeroflot earlier was told it would get only two flights a week instead of four it sought during the Moscow Olympics. That was in retaliation for Moscow's refusal to lift restrictions on U.S. airlines flying to Moscow during the Olympics.

● Cancellation of scheduled U.S.-Soviet conferences on marine pollution control and on marine navigation systems.

● Deferral of negotiations to renew the U.S.-Soviet cultural exchange agreements which expired December 31.

On January 10, Vice President Walter F. Mondale urged moving the 1980 Summer Olympic Games from Moscow to another city. But many athletes and the U.S. Olympic Committee, over which the U.S. government had no authority, opposed the suggestion.

In the United Nations Security Council, the Soviet Union January 7 vetoed a resolution condemning the Soviet invasion of Afghanistan and demanding the removal of all foreign troops from the country. The UN General Assembly passed the resolution January 14 by a 104-18 vote.

A Chronology of Major Events ...

1839: British march into Afghanistan after deciding that Afghani Durrani Empire is too willing to ally itself with Russians.

1842: By January 1842 British invasion proves a disaster. Retreating British suffer heavy casualties.

1878: After receiving word that Afghans had accepted a Russian mission to Kabul, British invade again in what is called the Second Afghan War.

1919: In what becomes Third Afghan War, Afghans successfully rebel against British, and even attack British India. Although the Afghan foray into Punjab was militarily unsuccessful, it prompted Britain to concede Afghanistan's freedom in both internal and external affairs.

1920s: After Russian Revolution, new Soviet leaders wage war in central Asia against *basmachi* ("bandits") — Uzbek, Tadjhik, and Turkmen kinsmen of northern Afghans unwilling to accept Sovietization. In 1929 Afghan internal upheaval creates room for small Soviet "puppet force" to enter country, although it makes no headway.

1946: Royal Afghan government turns to the United States for modernization assistance. U.S. aid is slow at first but increases over time until Afghan policy and hostile actions toward Pakistan prompt United States to see Afghanistan as strategic threat to favored ally Pakistan.

1950s: Afghan resentment builds as a result of U.S. support of Pakistan. The United States declines to send arms or military advisers to Afghanistan; Soviets swiftly step in to improve relations with Afghanistan and send many Afghan officers to Soviet Union for training.

1953: Mohammed Daoud Khan, cousin of King Zahir Shah, becomes prime minister. Daoud deepens economic dependence on Soviets and allows relations with United States to deteriorate.

1963: King Zahir Shar removes Daoud in effort to better relations with United States.

1965: Nur Mohammed Taraki founds Marxist party, the People's Democratic Party of Afghanistan (PDPA) with Babrak Karmal as his deputy. Hafizullah Amin soon joins. Amin quickly replaces Karmal as Taraki's deputy and becomes leader of party's Khalq ("Masses") faction, named after its newspaper. Karmal had become leader of the Parcham ("Flag") faction.

1973: Bad harvests and political problems undermine government; Daoud takes over in coup.

1978: April military coup overthrows Daoud, who had begun to mend fences with United States.

Amin takes over as first minister, Taraki as president; Amin moves Karmal out of contention by making him ambassador to Prague. Karmal is later exiled and supported in Soviet Union. December 5, the Soviet Union and Afghanistan sign Treaty of Friendship, Good Neighborliness, and Cooperation.

1978-79: Amin institutes repressive measures and tries to place blame on Taraki. Amin promotes coed education and expropriates property, among other reforms. The strongly Islamic Afghan people increasingly oppose repressive, corrupt government and its modernization efforts.

By late 1978 groups opposing Amin operate out of Pakistan and in March 1979 seize city of Herat; rebel groups include large numbers of defectors from Afghan army.

1979: April 5, Soviet general Aleksei Epishev tours Afghanistan with large delegation of senior Soviet officers; meets with Taraki and Amin.

June, Vasilii Safronchuk arrives in Kabul as special representative and deputy to Soviet Ambassador Alexander Puzanov. Safronchuk's apparent goal: convince Taraki and Amin to broaden regime's political base and bring about "radical change" in the leadership. Taraki and Amin decline most Soviet advice.

July, "night letters" (underground pamphlets) begin criticizing Amin but not Taraki. Amin, aware of increasing Soviet displeasure with him, takes de facto control of defense. Serious military mutinies also continue in July. One Soviet battalion arrives in Afghanistan; others increase readiness along border.

August 17, after another serious mutiny, Ivan Pavlovskii, Soviet deputy defense minister and general of the army (head of the ground forces), heads high-powered 63-member military delegation to Afghanistan; the group stays two months. Political contacts through Safronchuk continue; apparently the Soviets consider a progressive noncommunist (or coalition) government to replace Amin if acceptable communists cannot be found. Late August, Taraki attends nonaligned countries' summit in Havana; stops in Moscow on way back and apparently agrees to widen political support and get rid of Amin. Three days after Taraki's fond welcome home, Taraki's security guard unsuccessfully attempts to assassinate Amin, who had purged four key members of the cabinet. After the assassination attempt Amin takes Taraki prisoner.

October 8, Taraki is killed (some accounts say from suffocation by a pillow). Afghan-Soviet differences become more evident in ensuing days and weeks.

... In the History of Afghanistan

Ambassador Puzanov is declared persona non grata and is removed in November. A Soviet Tatar Moslem replaces him. Safronchuk remains. Amin moves to bolster his own position but with little success. Rebel insurgency continues. Amin declines invitation to Moscow but Afghan-Soviet relations continue despite strain. Soviets begin troop call-ups, move some battalions nearer border, and put others on alert. November 28, Soviet Lieutenant General Viktor Paputin arrives in Kabul, presumably to neutralize security police.

December 3, Paputin meets with Amin. December 17, attempt to assassinate Amin fails. December 24-26, three Soviet airborne divisions land (one in Kabul, one at Shindand air base near Herat, one at Qandahar in the south). On evening of December 27, Kabul telephone system is knocked out, Ministry of the Interior is captured, and Tajbeg Palace is attacked. (Amin had moved headquarters to this isolated complex outside Kabul after December 17 incident.) Radio Kabul soon falls. During the night, Amin is killed.

Before Radio Kabul falls, Karmal broadcasts that Amin's regime had fallen. December 28, Karmal is announced as new president of the revolutionary council and general secretary of the PDPA.

Soviets broadcast that Karmal had returned before invasion and that Karmal asked Soviets for military assistance, but this proves false. Also December 28, four Soviet rifle divisions cross border heading for major cities and airfields. Within one month, seven divisions occupy major centers of the country. An estimated 85,000 Soviet personnel are in Afghanistan.

1980: United States and most of world condemns Soviet invasion. United States enacts sanctions against Soviets. *(Sanctions box, p. 103)*

Indigenous resistance to PDPA stiffens immediately, spreading to all 26 provinces. Much of population continues to flee, mostly to Pakistan. By time of invasion an estimated 400,000 had left Amin's regime; by 1985, nearly 4 million are refugees. United States provides covert aid to Afghan guerrilla resistance fighters, who come to be known as *mujahideen* fighting a *jihad* or holy war.

1981: Despite political divisions, resistance groups prevent Soviet victory due to guerrilla fighting, harsh mountainous terrain, and widespread popular support. Afghan army is decimated by defection. Soviets replace many Central Asian conscripts with troops from other parts of country.

1982-83: Soviets become entrenched in Afghanistan with an estimated 115,000 soldiers. Soviets increase air attacks and use of heavy firepower. They change style of warfare to better combat guerrilla methods. Karmal reorganizes Afghan army and several brigades take part in major offensives late in year. A cease-fire agreement with Pakistan covering Panjshir is concluded in early 1983. The Soviets' so-called economic warfare begins; its aim: to drive Afghan people to the cities, where Soviets can control them more effectively.

1984: Soviets extend incursions into Pakistan and move more sophisticated weaponry into Afghanistan. They launch spring offensive in Panjshir, Loghar, and around Herat. Karmal announces Communist Party ranks swell from 5,000 in 1979 to 120,000 in 1984, with about 60 percent of them in the military or security services. Karmal also compromises opposing Khalq faction leaders by bringing them into government.

1985: Soviets increase publicity in USSR about Afghan war, apparently to condition populace to long war. More reports reach West of Soviets taking Afghan youths out of country for education in USSR; an estimated 40,000 leave by late 1985.

June 12, saboteurs among Afghans working at Shindand, Moscow's largest and best-protected air base in Afghanistan, destroy about 20 Soviet jet fighters; the largest loss of aircraft since 1979 invasion. Soviets increase use of Spetsnaz units (counter-insurgency forces).

July, mujahideen push Soviet and Afghan army units from defensive positions near Herat and airport.

September, Soviets hit rebel supply lines; heavy fighting continues through autumn. Rebels claim their supply effort is not substantially disrupted.

October, Afghan government seeks Pakistani involvement in reaching agreement on Soviet troop withdrawal; Pakistan refuses to negotiate directly with Soviet-backed Afghan government and works instead through UN-sponsored efforts.

December, leaders of seven major rebel groups agree to further consolidate alliance as step toward creating resistance government. UN report strongly denounces Soviet human rights abuses in Afghanistan; reportedly bombs and mines in shape of toys have killed and maimed unsuspecting children. Later in December, UN mediators report progress on Afghan-Pakistan treaty. U.S. offers to act as guarantor of Afghan peace settlement to include Soviet troop withdrawal and guarantees to Pakistan.

1986: May, Babrak Karmal resigns May 4 as PDPA head, citing health reasons. Former secret police chief Najibullah replaces him. UN-sponsored Afghan-Pakistan talks resume. Pakistani F-16 jets shoot down an Afghan MiG-21 over Pakistani territory for the first time.

Mohammed Taraki president. The country was renamed the Democratic Republic of Afghanistan.

Taraki had founded the country's Marxist party, the People's Democratic Party of Afghanistan (PDPA) with Karmal in 1965. Amin soon joined them. Amin and Taraki became leaders of the two rival factions of the party: Amin of the Khalq ("Masses"), Taraki of the Parcham ("Flag").

Shortly after the 1978 coup, Amin moved Karmal out of contention for power by making him ambassador to Czechoslovakia and later removing him from that post. Karmal then lived in exile in Moscow until the 1979 invasion and headed the country until being replaced by Najibullah May 4, 1986.

Afghanistan had moved decisively into the Soviet orbit after signing a 20-year friendship treaty with Moscow in December 1978 and adopting a new flag almost indistinguishable from the USSR's. The new regime curtailed relations with Iran and the West. Some Western observers speculated the 1978 coup may have been prompted by Daoud's fence-mending efforts with the United States.

U.S.-Afghan relations had been strained ever since the U.S. ambassador to Afghanistan, Adolph Dubs, was killed by Moslem extremists February 14, 1979, after being abducted in a Kabul hotel. U.S. officials later charged that Afghan authorities ignored pleas not to use force against the terrorists while rescue efforts were under way. In October 1979 Congress suspended all foreign aid to the Kabul government.

Détente Destroyed

Preoccupied with the hostage crisis in Iran, the invasion caught U.S. leaders off guard. Moreover, U.S.-Soviet relations had appeared to be improving. Trade between the two nations was flourishing. President Carter and Soviet President Brezhnev had signed the second Strategic Arms Limitation Treaty (SALT II) at a restrained but cordial ceremony in Vienna. Moscow was prepared to receive thousands of American visitors at the 1980 Summer Olympics. But after the invasion Carter asked the Senate to delay action on the SALT treaty, pulled the United States out of the 1980 Summer Olympics, and halted shipments of grain and high technology goods to the Soviet Union.

Although Afghanistan had been in the Soviet orbit since 1978, the Soviet invasion represented the first time the Soviet Union had intervened with its own troops outside the area the Red Army had occupied in 1945. The invasion raised grave fears in the West that the Soviet Union would make further political and military advances to the Persian Gulf, clashing directly with vital U.S. interests in the region. There also were fears that the Soviets planned to use Afghanistan as a stepping stone to invade Pakistan and thus gain the warm-water port that had long been a Soviet goal.

Carter, Brezhnev Words Fly

The invasion ended more than a decade of détente. Carter and Brezhnev traded some of the harshest accusations by the two countries since the Cold War of the 1950s. Brezhnev implied that the United States was responsible for the political turmoil in Afghanistan. He claimed the Soviets were invited into the country by the Afghan government under terms of a 1978 Soviet-Afghan friendship treaty. The invitation was extended, Brezhnev said, to prevent a takeover by an unnamed third nation — presumably an accusation charging the United States with interfering in Afghan internal affairs.

Carter, in a television news interview December 31, accused Brezhnev of "not telling the facts accurately." He also said that his opinion of the Soviets had "changed [more] drastically in the last week than even the previous two and a half years before that." On NBC's *Meet the Press* January 20, 1980, Carter called the invasion "the most serious threat to peace since the second world war."

National security adviser Zbigniew Brzezinski reaffirmed, in a televised interview on ABC's *Issues and Answers* December 30, that the administration would honor a 1959 agreement with Pakistan. He said the United States would be prepared to respond with military force if the Soviets invaded Pakistan. Several days later Carter requested Congress to lift a ban on arms sales to Pakistan, which it soon did. All U.S. military aid to Pakistan had been halted earlier in 1979 when that country decided to go ahead with efforts to develop nuclear weapons.

On January 2, 1980, Carter recalled Thomas J. Watson, the U.S. ambassador to the Soviet Union, for consultations. The following day administration officials announced that the United States would press the United Nations Security Council to condemn the Soviet invasion — a move the Soviet representative predictably vetoed January 7.

On January 5 Carter announced a series of nonmilitary retaliatory measures against the Soviet Union. He ordered livestock grain sales embargoed, froze the sale of high technology equipment to the Soviet government, and delayed indefinitely the opening of new cultural and economic exchange programs between the United States and the Soviet Union. *(Sanctions, box, p. 103)*

Secretary of Defense Harold Brown visited the People's Republic of China January 5 to discuss with the Chinese senior military establishment "wide cooperation on security matters" between the United States and China. Brown's trip had been scheduled before the Soviet invasion of Afghanistan, but that subject was added to the agenda. The discussion suggested closer Sino-American cooperation on defense matters aimed at halting further Soviet advances.

'Carter Doctrine'

In his January 23, 1980, State of the Union address, President Carter lambasted the Soviets for their "radical and aggressive" invasion of Afghanistan. The president told Congress that the invasion and the hostage crisis in Iran "present a serious challenge to the United States of America and indeed to the other nations of the world. Together, we will meet these threats to peace."

Carter noted that "the Soviet effort to dominate Afghanistan has brought Soviet military forces to within 300 miles of the Indian Ocean and close to the Straits of Hormuz — a waterway through which much of the world's oil must flow. The Soviet Union is now attempting to consolidate a strategic position that poses a grave threat to the free movement of Middle East oil."

Enunciating what came to be known as the "Carter Doctrine," Carter bluntly warned the Kremlin to stay out of the oil-producing nations along the Persian Gulf: "An attempt by any outside force to gain control of the Persian Gulf region will be regarded as an assault on the vital interests of the United States, and such an assault will be repelled by any means necessary, including military force."

In the speech Carter reiterated his call, first made January 20, for a boycott of the Summer Olympics in Moscow unless the Soviets pulled their troops out of Afghanistan. If the troops were not removed, Carter said, "neither the American people nor I will support sending an Olympic team to Moscow." The U.S. government officially announced its boycott of the games February 20; in response, Mikhail A. Suslov, a senior member of the Politburo, said, "The Soviet Union will not be intimidated." Eventually more than 50 nations joined the boycott of the Olympic Games, held July 19-August 3.

The Soviets reacted to the stern tone of Carter's State of the Union address January 24. "It is common knowledge that the United States is the 'outside force' that has concentrated the biggest-ever armada of naval forces" in the Middle East, Tass said. "J. Carter's demagogical call for efforts to 'repel the threat' to the region can only be considered an attempt to distract attention from the imperialist policy of the United States." The press agency called an "absurdity" Carter's claim that an area so distant from the United States was of vital interest.

Reasons for Soviet Actions

Why the Soviet Union invaded Afghanistan has been debated endlessly in the West and numerous reasons have been proposed. Many Western experts believe the Soviets did not want to intervene militarily but did so reluctantly as a last resort after political means to assert Soviet influence failed.

The Soviets viewed Amin as an ambitious ruler and unreliable ally. Some experts have compared this perception with the Soviets' view of former Egyptian president Anwar al-Sadat — someone who would actively seek relations with other powers, even at the expense of the Soviet Union. A failure in Soviet eyes, Amin had disregarded Soviet advice regarding internal reform and severely antagonized much of his own population, which undermined the indigenous communists.

Henry Bradsher in *Afghanistan and the Soviet Union* writes this about Amin: "So long as he remained in charge in Kabul there was no hope of consolidating the grip that Communism had gained ... with the April 1978 coup. There was, instead, the danger of losing it, of having the country fall into a chaotic anti-Communist condition."

In *Détente and Confrontation* Raymond Garthoff argues that improved U.S.-Chinese relations fostered fear among the Soviets that the two countries would act together to fill any vacuum created if Amin fell. The Soviets believed such a vacuum could create an encirclement by a U.S.-NATO-Japan-China alliance.

Also of considerable concern to the Soviets was the large Moslem population in bordering areas of the Soviet Union. Afghan Islamic ethnic groups living north of the Hindu Kush mountain range (the Aimaq, Uzbek, and Tadzhik) all have ties in the Soviet Central Asian republics to the north. According to Garthoff, the Kremlin feared that a "fragmented nationalistic, religious regime in Afghanistan (as well as in Iran) would constitute a hostile and chaotic belt along the border."

Economic investment (over several decades) and political prestige (particularly since the 1978 coup) were also on the line. The Soviets presumably believed that with military intervention and the removal of Amin a more stable socialist regime could be established.

Additionally, the Soviets believed they had a legitimate vital national security interest in ensuring a stable regime in Afghanistan. U.S. involvement in Afghanistan had been nearly nonexistent since the 1978 coup establishing the socialist regime. In fact, the United States had made little outcry over Daoud's removal. Because the Soviets were already in Afghanistan militarily, they presumed criticism from the West would be minimal, especially because of the Soviet view that the United States would recognize its legitimate security needs.

Garthoff claims that on the Afghanistan issue both the Soviet Union and the United States failed "to recognize the perceptions, and motivations, and security interests, of the other side, whether accepting them or not." According to Garthoff, the Soviets believed U.S. reaction to the intervention was really a pretext to

> mobilize American (and to some extent world) opinion in support of an intensified arms race and an anti-Soviet political line of confrontation.... In the Soviet perception, it was the United States that was acting in a manner inconsistent with the implicit code of conduct of détente. The United States was not respecting vital Soviet interests in its security sphere.... The United States was directly challenging them and unnecessarily converting the Afghanistan affair into a broad global political challenge, while discarding the achievements of détente.

U.S. Support Since Invasion

When Ronald Reagan assumed the presidency in 1981, he immediately lifted the Soviet grain embargo imposed by Carter. Reagan had long criticized the embargo as hurting American farmers more than the Soviets. Certain other restrictions imposed on the USSR because of the invasion also were gradually lifted or eased over Reagan's first term. Trade with Afghanistan had slowed to barely a trickle, however, and in early 1986 the president suspended Afghanistan's most-favored-nation trading status.

U.S. humanitarian aid for the mujahideen increased over the years to $15 million in 1985. From 1979 to May 1984, overall U.S. aid (both humanitarian and military) to the guerrillas had surpassed $600 million, according to some estimates. Although there was widespread congressional support for aid to the guerrillas, military aid remained covert. The Central Intelligence Agency (CIA) insisted that its work was best accomplished without the glare of publicity that would accompany open U.S. funding there. Some Afghan assistance groups in the United States maintained that the CIA's tactics were designed not to help the mujahideen win the war but to tie up Soviet forces and drain the Kremlin's military budget.

Aid was also kept covert because of Pakistan's objection to overt U.S. assistance. Most aid passes through Pakistan and must be channeled through Pakistani authorities who relay it to the Afghan resistance fighters.

The Soviets apparently increased pressure on Pakistan in 1985, warning that if the flow of arms through that country did not slow then fighting would worsen. Soviet and Afghan planes and artillery pierced the Pakistan border an estimated 250 times in 1985, triple the amount in any previous year. Nonetheless, arms continued to reach the rebels.

The arms funneling process also brought criticism that only about 20 percent of U.S. military aid reached the rebels. The rest was reportedly diverted to Pakistan's own military interests and the black market.

Soviet Quagmire

More than six years after the Soviet invasion, the military situation in Afghanistan remained stalemated. Varying estimates put the number of Soviet troops there between 110,000 and 130,000 at the end of 1985. The Soviet Union has fought in Afghanistan longer than it fought in World War II. Although Soviet leader Mikhail Gorbachev apparently indicated some willingness at the November 1985 U.S.-Soviet summit to work toward a political settlement of the war, by January 1986 that possibility remained remote. "We're not convinced Gorbachev's really ready to lance the boil and get out," a senior U.S. official was quoted as saying in a January 1986 *Wall Street Journal* article. "He's merely pursuing the war more vigorously without a great increase in troops while leaving the impression of movement in negotiations," the official added. His views were echoed in the months following the summit and after a U.S. offer in December that implied the United States would stop aiding the rebels if Moscow agreed on plans for troop withdrawal. The Soviets declined the offer.

John Keegan, in the November 1985 *Atlantic Monthly*, detailed several reasons why the Soviets have been unable to overcome the Afghans since the invasion:

> [The] structural fragmentation [of the population] ensures that "traditional Soviet methods of control don't work," as the Washington strategic analysts James Curren and Philip Karber have perceptively expressed it. "Infiltration of existing institutions, collectivization of agriculture, restriction of movement, and centralization of everything else can be imposed on a highly interdependent society with a minimum of force." But Afghan society is the opposite of interdependent, and the Afghans have one of the highest tolerances to the use of force of any people on earth. They are not one people but many, and these peoples have an age-old tradition of warring against one another as well as against their common neighbors in the fat lands beyond Afghanistan's borders. The most important of these peoples, the Pathans, cleave to a social canon that can pit tribe against tribe, village against village, neighbor against neighbor, brother against brother.... The Russians are but the most recent of many invaders to have locked horns ...

Aiming at Civilians

During 1982 and 1983, the Soviets changed tactics in dealing with the civilian population. They began so-called economic warfare aimed at driving people to the cities. This made population control easier and more effective. Areas of food production were attacked, and crops were destroyed by napalm and other means, including the smashing of primitive but essential irrigation systems. Food production dropped 20 to 25 percent. Almost every village in the country has been reported damaged, either by direct action or because of disrupted commerce and trade. Many schools, hospitals, and other manifestations of modernization over the past 20 years have been wiped out.

Other efforts to indoctrinate the population into the Soviet way of life include taking thousands of Afghan children and young adults to the Soviet Union for several years of education. By 1985, estimates of the numbers of children and students taken to the Soviet Union ranged from 25,000 to 40,000. According to several Western accounts, the youths (from ages 6 to 30) often were taken without their parents' knowledge.

The Soviet invasion also has disrupted the Afghan education system because thousands of teachers and promising students are among the refugees now in Pakistan and elsewhere. The Soviets have changed school textbooks and curricula to fit Soviet needs. Islamic resistance groups have established some schools (for boys only) as alternatives to the Soviet-run government ones but political rivalry has hampered their effectiveness.

Approximately one-fourth of the Afghan population has fled the country. Of approximately 4 million refugees, about 3 million have gone to Pakistan and about 1 million to Iran.

In 1982 and 1983, the Soviets also began replacing many of their conscripted Central Asian troops with ones from other parts of the country. Concern had apparently increased because of sympathy for the rebels among the soldiers. Reports also increased of Soviet soldiers either going over to the resistance or defecting to the West.

More Publicity in USSR

In the 1980s the Soviets began making the war more visible to their own population, apparently in an effort to prepare them for a long stay. For several years there was no media information given in the USSR about the war beyond the official view that a "limited contingent" of soldiers was performing an "internationalist duty" after being invited by the Afghan government to defend against attacks by imperialist forces. But by late 1985, accounts of the war appeared on television glorifying the role of the Soviet soldier and linking efforts there to the defense of the Soviet motherland. Battle footage was not shown. The guerrillas were portrayed as *basmachis* or *dushmanis*, CIA-backed bandits.

In addition to the perceived concern about preparing the Soviet populace for a long war, another reason for the increased publicity may have been complaints (many in local newspapers) about the lack of war coverage and respect for those fighting in it. Apparently a belief had developed that Afghanistan was not a "real" war, according to

Soviet Infantry Combat Vehicle in Afghanistan

conversations with Soviet citizens relayed in the Western press. Additionally, the magnitude of the Afghan war was mitigated because the odds of a Soviet soldier serving in Afghanistan were relatively small. Fewer than 150,000 troops were there in 1985 out of a military force of 5 million.

Nonetheless, the war has become a morass for the Soviets. They are unable to daunt the elusive, stubborn rebels, unable to stop the flow of arms to them, and unable to control the Afghan population much less the Afghan army. By 1981, the Afghan army had been decimated by defections to the mujahideen, dropping from more than 100,000 troops to fewer than 30,000.

Bloodshed increased. Although the Soviets still refuse to release casualty figures, they did concede in late 1985 that the previous year had seen unprecedented losses. Western sources put the figure at between 10,000 and 30,000 Soviets killed since 1979. Pakistani hospitals, where many wounded resistance fighters are taken, also reported increased numbers of casualties in 1985. Estimates for guerrilla and civilian losses range from a low of 250,000 to a high of 750,000.

A Weapons Testing War

Many Western analysts believed the Soviets had begun to use Afghanistan as a weapons testing war. The Soviets' use and mastery of advanced weaponry in Afghanistan improved. But they still were unable to overcome road supply problems, despite increasingly innovative security efforts likened by some observers to U.S. efforts in Vietnam. Soviet supply convoys were continually attacked, even with the increased use of advanced helicopters, against which the rebels had little protection. Soviet logistical systems were ineffective due largely to the problematic system of centralized control and command of military operations.

By January 1986, however, some accounts reported that calling the situation in Afghanistan a stalemate was misleading. These accounts reported several trends that indicated the Soviets had gained an overall military advantage.

Since about 1984 the mujahideen had obtained heavier weapons, including the Chinese-made 107-mm rocket (apparently through CIA arms pipelines), but Western reports indicated that without proper training the rebels had only limited success with them. And although massive Soviet attempts in the fall of 1985 to cut rebel supply lines failed, they significantly added to the rebels' arms transportation costs.

The Afghan army, after reorganization and politicization efforts, had begun to improve noticeably if not significantly. Their numbers had also begun climbing. According to *Jane's Defence Weekly* November 23, 1985, Afghan forces — including the army, border troops, and troops from the Ministry of Interior (Sarandoy) — totaled more than 56,000 by mid-1985. The Soviets had expanded and improved defenses around the cities. Continuing depopulation of the countryside meant the rebels often no longer had ready food, shelter, and information provided by the civilian population. Additionally, the Soviets increased use of their well-trained *spetsnaz* forces, antiguerrilla commandos who were often dropped in by helicopter to ambush resisters in the mountains.

One of the most important gains for the Soviets, many Western military specialists and resistance commanders have reported, was the expansion of Khad, the KGB-run Afghan secret police. It reportedly employs tens of thousands of people and has infiltrated resistance groups as well as Afghan refugee camps inside and outside the country. Khad has been charged with numerous terrorist activities against the resistance forces. Khad-backed terrorist killings of rebel commanders have been particularly disastrous, some said; since rebel commanders are not easily replaced, the killings threatened to shift the war's stalemate.

In late 1985 the seven major resistance parties agreed to further consolidate their conflict-ridden alliance as a step toward creating a workable government. Although the U.S. State Department reported optimism that the alliance was making significant headway, other experts said longstanding divisions among the groups impeded the transformation of the resistance into a viable political force.

Meanwhile, the UN continued efforts of past years to keep open Afghan-Pakistan peace negotiations. By late 1985 there appeared to be progress in dealing with Afghan refugees in Pakistan but no agreement on Soviet troop withdrawal. Pakistan continued to refuse to negotiate directly with the Soviet-backed Afghan government, believing direct talks would lend legitimacy to the Karmal regime and demoralize resistance fighters.

Some observers believed prospects for a peace settlement improved when Karmal resigned as general secretary of the PDPA May 4, 1986. He had just returned from a month-long medical visit to Moscow and cited health reasons for stepping down. The West was aware of growing Soviet displeasure with Karmal, but his replacement by Najibullah, former head of the Khad, was not expected. Najibullah (who uses no surname) led the Khad until December 1985 and reportedly had made headway infiltrating guerrilla ranks, but it was not known whether he wanted a negotiated settlement or a military victory.

USSR-LATIN AMERICA: CAUTIOUS INVOLVEMENT

Soviet interest and involvement in Latin America and the Caribbean were virtually nonexistent before the Cuban revolution in 1959. The United States has remained the dominant superpower in the region since then, but the consolidation of power by Cuba's revolutionary leader Fidel Castro and subsequent close ties with the USSR suggested that the Soviets could make political inroads in the hemisphere.

But the overthrow of the Marxist government of Salvadore Allende in Chile in 1973 pointed in the other direction. Not until 1979, with the victory of the Sandinista rebels over the ruling regime of Anastasio Somoza in Nicaragua and of Maurice Bishop's leftist New Jewel movement in Grenada, did the USSR start to believe that America's sphere of influence could be challenged effectively.

Historic anti-Americanism aided the USSR's efforts in the Western Hemisphere after World War II. The United States traditionally supported governments that allowed American businesses to operate profitably in their countries. Many of those governments, however, did not extend the benefits of U.S. investment and trade to the majority of their populations. The governments' frequent abuse of human rights and failure to reduce unequal distribution of wealth made these nations ripe for revolution.

In his book *Soviet Strategy In Latin America*, Latin American expert Robert Leiken said U.S. backing of regimes in these nations "lent socialism prestige and cast Cuba and the Soviet Union in a favorable light.... U.S. backing of oppressive regimes in the Third World persuaded many Latin Americans that the United States was the enemy of self-determination and the Soviet Union their natural ally."

Soviet involvement in the Western Hemisphere also is rooted in superpower rivalry. Both nations realize the strategic value to the Soviet Union of access to land in the region. For the United States, the region is both economically and strategically vital. Nearly two-thirds of U.S. trade, movement of U.S. oil and strategic minerals, and shipment of NATO defense supplies to Europe in case of war depend on unihibited use of these Caribbean sea lanes by commercial and naval vessels.

Nevertheless, the USSR has remained cautious in the Western Hemisphere because of geographic distance and fear of conflict with the United States. Soviet leaders also have tried to develop an image as the superpower on the side of oppressed populations rather than on the side of governments they claimed were oppressors.

Relations With Cuba

The evolution of relations with Cuba was crucial to the development of Soviet policy in the region, but the close ties that developed by the late 1960s did not immediately follow the revolution. The USSR was slow to recognize Cuba's revolutionary potential when Fidel Castro came to power in 1959; for some time, he had little involvement with the Soviets.

Cuba and the USSR disagreed in the 1960s about how to implement or force change in Latin America. Cuba supported revolution through armed struggle. The USSR stuck strictly to "the peaceful road to socialism" endorsed at the 20th Soviet Party Congress in February 1956 within the framework of the "peaceful coexistence" policy. Moscow discouraged local communist parties from joining guerrilla movements and encouraged them to back broad electoral fronts while the Soviets sought diplomatic and commercial relations with established governments.

Although Castro criticized the Soviets for this strategy, disagreements were muted in 1968 when the USSR began to view Cuba as a model for revolution in Latin America. In addition, Cuba was an important strategic foothold in the Western Hemisphere and, potentially, a nation that could be an instrument for Soviet policy in other underdeveloped or former colonial nations in the world, especially in Africa. Cuba's differences with the USSR faded in the face of threats of economic sanctions from the Kremlin and Castro began to follow Soviet policy directions in all areas. In 1971 Castro signed a joint communiqué fully endorsing Soviet foreign policy. In 1972 Cuba joined the Council for Mutual Economic Assistance (CMEA), the Soviet bloc's major economic organization.

During this time the Soviets also began modernizing Cuba's military and took advantage of Cuban bases to gradually increase their naval strength in the Caribbean.

By 1982 the USSR was subsidizing Cuba's troubled economy at a cost of $4.9 billion annually, or $8 million to $10 million per day. Much of this aid has come from purchase of Cuban sugar at inflated prices and sale of Soviet oil exported to Cuba at bargain rates. In 1981 the Soviet Union accounted for about 70 percent of Cuba's foreign commerce.

The USSR has also supplied Cuba with extensive weaponry, which made the Cuban military one of the most powerful in Latin America. Total Soviet military assistance to Cuba was estimated to be $3.8 billion during 1961-1979. By the end of 1985 military assistance was approximately $600 million annually, according to U.S. administration sources. According to the same sources there were almost 15,000 Soviet personnel in Cuba, including 2,800 military advisers, a 2,800-man Soviet brigade, and 2,100 individuals running an intelligence facility. There were about 7,000 Soviet civilian advisers in Cuba in 1985.

Although political differences have cropped up between Castro and the USSR, they have never threatened the alliance. Cuba has used its ties to the Soviet Union to achieve its regional and global goals. In return Cuba has been central to the Soviet Union's extension of influence into the traditionally American region of the Western Hemisphere. In addition to Cuban naval bases, the Soviets use Cuban airfields to conduct aerial reconnaissance along the U.S. coastline and over Atlantic sea lanes. Nevertheless, some analysts believe that in a superpower conflict Cuba's defense would be a low priority for the Soviet Union.

Latin American Involvement

The USSR has taken three approaches toward involvement in Latin America. First, the Soviets provide strong support for Cuba, giving essential economic aid to its faltering economy and supplying it with modern weapons. Second, the Soviets have provided less measurable but still enthusiastic support for revolutions in Nicaragua and, before October 1983, Grenada, when a U.S. military invasion toppled the government in that island nation. The Soviets have provided similar support for revolutionary movements elsewhere in Central America, mostly through Cuba and with significantly smaller economic and military commitments. Third, the USSR has established traditional diplomatic and trade relations with the rest of South America and Mexico.

Increased Soviet diplomatic and commercial relations with Latin American states during the 1960s and 1970s coincided with a nationalistic interest in these countries to trade with nations other than the United States. This helped the USSR significantly expand relations with Latin America following the Cuban revolution.

At the beginning of the 1960s the USSR had diplomatic ties with only three Latin American countries: Argentina, Mexico, and Uruguay. U.S. opposition to Soviet involvement in Cuba at first slowed Soviet efforts to expand relations elsewhere in Latin America; only Cuba (in 1960), Brazil (1961), and Chile (1964) established relations. By the late 1960s, however, the USSR had diplomatic relations with Colombia (in 1968); Peru, Ecuador, and Bolivia (1969); and Venezuela and Guyana (1970). By the early 1970s diplomatic ties had been established with Costa Rica, Trinidad and Tobago, Guatemala, Nicaragua, and Jamaica. The USSR had established diplomatic relations with 19 Latin American countries by the end of the 1970s.

Commercial ties also developed. In 1964 the Soviet Union had trade relations with only four Latin American countries; by 1975, 20. Soviet commerce with Latin America, excluding Cuba, increased from $124 million in 1970 to $4.9 billion in 1981, according to some Western experts. Latin American countries also sought technical assistance from the USSR, particularly in the development of hydroelectric resources.

The rise and fall of the Allende government in Chile between 1970 and 1973 was a setback for Moscow. Although Allende came to power peacefully, his downfall reinforced Soviet fears of moving too rapidly toward socialism in developing nations. Allende was overthrown and assassinated just three years after coming to power.

Soviet optimism that USSR influence could be greatly expanded reached its height between 1979 and 1981 with the Sandinista victory in Nicaragua, the leftist victory in Grenada, and the wider and more effective efforts of guerrilla forces in El Salvador.

Nicaragua

After the American-backed Somoza regime was overthrown by armed Sandinista forces in Nicaragua in 1979, the Soviets began to favor military action to replace governments elsewhere in Central America, even though they previously had shunned this approach.

One Soviet expert on Latin America called the Sandinista victory one of "colossal international importance — one of those events that demand re-examination of established concepts."

Cuba was much more deeply involved than the USSR in the early days of the Sandinista movement, primarily because geographically Cuba was much closer to Nicaragua and because politically Cuba believed in the use of armed force rather than peaceful change. Cuba played a major role in reconciling differences among Sandinista factions. Cuba also provided contacts with international arms dealers and sent some weapons directly, often with the help of other countries sympathetic to the Sandinistas' revolutionary goals. In both the Cuban and Nicaraguan revolutions, communist parties loyal to the Soviet Union backed military action late and grudgingly.

The USSR's most direct early role was to force the pro-Soviet Nicaraguan socialist party to switch from opposition to collaboration with the Sandinistas and to favor military over political action. The socialist party formed an armed wing in 1978.

The USSR moved more quickly than it had in Cuba to establish diplomatic, economic, and other relations with the Sandinista regime once it was in power. In March 1980 the first major Sandinista delegation arrived in Moscow and signed economic, technical, scientific, and cultural agreements. The delegation also signed a party-to-party agreement between the Sandinista National Liberation Front (FSLN) and the Soviet Communist Party. This agreement between the parties was important because such agreements are generally taken only when Moscow believes a regime is one of "socialist orientation."

By January 1981 the typical Soviet bloc division of labor was apparent in Nicaragua: the Cubans provided doctors, teachers, military and intelligence specialists, and other advisers to the Sandinista party and to various government ministries; the Soviets, East Germans, Bulgarians, and Cubans handled security; the East Germans assisted with intelligence and communications; the Bulgarians were

Soviet Union Ties To Latin, South America

The status of the Soviet Union's relations with Latin American and the Caribbean nations, as of August 7, 1984, is shown below.

Argentina: Embassy, trade office, Aeroflot scheduled service, 30 to 40 civilian technicians.

Antigua: None.

Bahamas: None.

Barbados: None.

Belize: None.

Bolivia: Embassy, trade office, 26 civilian technicians.

Brazil: Embassy, trade office, 39 civilian technicians.

Chile: None.

Colombia: Embassy, trade office, 17 civilian technicians.

Costa Rica: Embassy, trade office, 1 civilian technician.

Cuba: Embassy, full trade, diplomatic and party relations; substantial military relations.

Dominica: None.

Dominican Republic: None.

Ecuador: Embassy, trade office, 2 civilian technicians.

El Salvador: None.

Grenada: None.

Guyana: Embassy.

Guatemala: None.

Haiti: None.

Honduras: None.

Jamaica: Embassy, Aeroflot scheduled service.

Mexico: Embassy, Aeroflot scheduled service, consulate, trade office.

Nicaragua: Embassy, Aeroflot scheduled service, 140 civilian technicians, 40 military advisers.

Panama: Trade office.

Paraguay: None.

Peru: Embassy, trade office, Aeroflot scheduled service, 30 civilian technicians, 150 military advisers.

St. Lucia, St. Vincent: None.

Suriname: Embassy.

Trinidad and Tobago: Nonresident ambassador.

Uruguay: Embassy.

Venezuela: Embassy, trade office.

Source: James H. Michel, deputy assistant secretary of state for inter-American affairs, in testimony February 28, 1985, before the Subcommittee on Western Hemisphere Affairs of the Committee on Foreign Affairs, House of Representatives.

directing economic planning, finance, and construction; and the Czechoslovaks were providing some military advisers.

Nicaragua has been granted some privileges, such as membership in communist organizations and visits by government leaders to Moscow. However, the instances were too few by early 1986 to accurately judge the Soviet Union's true commitment to the Sandinista regime. In May 1982, Nicaragua joined Intersputnik, the Soviet-sponsored telecommunications organization, the nation's first membership in a multilateral communist organization. In September 1983 the nation became an observer country in the Soviet bloc's CMEA, a position given only to "socialist" or "socialist oriented" nations. Nicaraguans have visited the USSR numerous times, mostly in pursuit of military and economic aid; however, no Soviet leader has visited Nicaragua, an indication of the limits of Soviet enthusiasm toward the Sandinistas.

By the mid-1980s, Soviet bloc literature was available in Nicaraguan bookstores and newsstands and Soviet texts were used in Nicaraguan schools and universities. About 1,000 students were studying in the USSR in late 1984.

U.S. actions toward Nicaragua have affected Soviet military and economic aid to the Sandinistas. The Reagan administration in 1981 sought to block Sandinista arms aid to Salvadoran rebels and to thwart growing ties to Cuba and the Soviet bloc by cutting off a $15 million wheat credit for Nicaragua.

When the wheat credits ended, the USSR and other Soviet bloc countries immediately began wheat shipments — 20,000 tons from the USSR and 60,000 tons from East Germany and Bulgaria. The Soviet bloc shipments more than made up for the U.S. cut-off.

The USSR also provided economic and military aid when the Reagan administration imposed economic sanctions on Nicaragua, pressured multilateral development banks to cut off loans to the Sandinista government, and began providing U.S. aid to the forces fighting the Sandinista government. When these forces attacked Nicaraguan oil storage facilities in late 1983, the Soviet bloc increased its oil shipments. In the first three months of 1984, the Soviets supplied about 60 percent of Nicaragua's oil, replacing Mexico as the major source.

Soviet involvement in Nicaragua has been promoted more by the Sandinista leadership than by the USSR and has not always been successful. Nicaragua showed its loyalty to the Soviets by offering support for Soviet foreign policy positions and risking its nonaligned status. However, when Nicaraguan president Daniel Ortega in June 1984 visited Moscow he returned empty-handed with no new economic or military commitments to his government. The absence of a customary communiqué suggested sharp differences between Ortega and Soviet leader Konstantin Chernenko. It was also reported that the CMEA had turned down Nicaraguan requests for a loan.

The extent of Soviet economic aid to Nicaragua is disputed. Latin America expert Leiken, in an October 1984 article, said Soviet aid fluctuated between $75 million and $150 million annually from 1981 to 1984. He estimated total Soviet bloc aid at between $200 million and $250 million in 1983, a figure he and other observers considered strikingly low considering the continuing deterioration of the Nicaraguan economy. The Soviets by the end of 1985 had not granted Nicaraguan requests for desperately needed foreign exchange. Most Soviet bloc economic aid has been in the form of long-term development aid. The

Soviet bloc also had not become a major trading partner. Although 1984 Soviet foreign trade figures showed overall exports to Nicaragua more than tripled between 1983 and 1984, the figures did not reveal the types of exports.

A change in Soviet leadership may also have brought about a new relationship with Nicaragua. In an April 1985 visit with Soviet leader Mikhail Gorbachev, Ortega obtained new economic aid and Soviet agreement to supply Nicaragua with oil.

Soviet military assistance to Nicaragua substantially increased after 1981, although also with restraint. The increase came as the contras fighting the Sandinista regime increased their activities. Experts have debated whether the substantial Nicaraguan military buildup with the help of the Soviet bloc has been offensive or defensive. According to most reports, arms shipments were about equal in 1981 and 1982, but rose substantially in 1983. U.S. government figures placed the value of arms shipments from 1979 through 1982 at $125 million and the total for 1983 alone at $100 million. U.S. estimates for 1984 placed total shipments at 18,000 tons and reported stepped-up arms deliveries in November 1985. Leiken compared arms shipments to Nicaragua between 1981 and early 1984 — 17,500 metric tons — to Soviet arms shipments to Cuba during a similar threat from insurgents in 1962-64. In 1962 the Soviet Union delivered 250,000 metric tons of arms to Cuba; in 1963, 40,000; and in 1964, 20,000.

The USSR did not provide the MiG fighter planes the Nicaraguans requested, although preparations for using Soviet advanced fighter aircraft in Nicaragua reportedly took place from 1981 on. Nicaraguan pilots received training in Cuba and Bulgaria. In mid-November 1984 there were reports from the U.S. administration that MiG fighters were on their way to Nicaragua on Soviet ships. Although the weapons turned out not to be MiGs, it was the first time the Soviets had sent weapons to Nicaragua under their own flag, rather than through Cuba or Bulgaria. The incident was simultaneously a test of U.S. tolerance for Soviet involvement in the Hemisphere and an indication of Soviet restraint.

The number of Cuban and Soviet military advisers in Nicaragua has a been a source of much dispute. U.S. officials said that 2,500 Cuban military advisers were stationed in Nicaragua as of fall 1985, yet Nicaraguan president Ortega placed that number at fewer than 1,000. U.S. sources placed the number of Soviet military advisers and technicians there at 140 as of February 1985.

El Salvador

The extent of Soviet support for rebels fighting the government of El Salvador was much disputed because of Moscow's low-key role there. The U.S. government accused the USSR of providing political and military support, through Cuba and Nicaragua, for the spread of revolution in El Salvador and in other Central American countries. This became the major issue in growing tension between the United States and Nicaragua. Some experts said it was difficult to evaluate the Soviet role in El Salvador because it was difficult to separate it from Cuba's role.

In an action that was unusual because it strayed from traditional Soviet policy, in January 1980 the pro-Moscow faction of the Salvadoran rebels endorsed revolution through armed struggle. The head of the pro-Soviet Salvadoran Communist Party, Shafik Handal, reportedly led an arms-buying trip to communist nations in June and July

1980. Some analysts said his meeting with a Soviet Communist Party official might have been indirectly responsible for the large amount of military equipment that flowed into El Salvador from Vietnam in early 1981. Leiken has pointed out that the Soviets showed great enthusiasm for the revolution in El Salvador in late 1980 and early 1981. After the failure of an important guerrilla offensive, however, "El Salvador seemed virtually to disappear from the Soviet press," Leiken noted. Leiken also said that Soviet bloc arms transfers to the Salvadoran guerrillas fell off sharply after that offensive.

Another noteworthy point about the Soviet connection to the now-united Salvadoran rebel groups (the FMLN-FDR, the Farabundo Marti National Liberation Front-Democratic Revolutionary Front) was that the three most important guerrilla groups had anti-Soviet origins. According to Leiken, among the Marxist-Leninist guerrillas in El Salvador the organizations that were the greatest distance from the Soviet Union controlled nearly two-thirds of the fighting force. At the same time, it was reported that by early 1982 the USSR had expressly endorsed the guerrilla movement in El Salvador. It was also said that Soviet and Cuban military advisers in Nicaragua were conducting advanced guerrilla training courses for the Salvadoran guerrillas and for leftist guerrillas from other countries in the region.

Grenada

Documents that became available after the U.S. invasion of the Caribbean island of Grenada in October 1983 provided firsthand information about Soviet actions there. Some analysts and policy makers in the United States claimed that Grenada under Maurice Bishop's New Jewel Movement was on its way to becoming a Soviet and Cuban military base in the Caribbean.

Formal Communist Party ties to the New Jewel Movement were initiated by the USSR in May and June 1980. Grenada was designated a state of socialist orientation. In January 1980 Grenada was the only Latin American or Caribbean country to vote with Cuba against the United Nations resolution deploring Soviet intervention in Afghanistan. Nicaragua abstained.

As in Nicaragua, Soviet economic assistance to Grenada was low despite Grenada's great need. The Soviets provided some aid and trade agreements, but Grenada was more important to the USSR politically and militarily. The captured documents revealed a gradual upgrading of Soviet military aid. Three secret military agreements reportedly took place between 1980 and 1983. The Soviets had planned to send $27 million in military equipment to Grenada, and the North Koreans $12 million. The Cubans were to train the armed forces and act as the intermediary in weapons transfers. Cuba had 27 permanent military advisers in Grenada. Grenadian officers also were sent to the USSR for training.

Although Grenada had no Soviet bases at the time of the invasion, some analysts said the island might have been slated by the USSR as a bridge to revolutionary forces in other parts of the region, much like Cuba has been used. A major dispute involved construction of a 9,800-foot runway at an island airport. Grenadians insisted it was needed for tourist-carrying commercial jets, but Americans noted the runway also would handle any Soviet or Cuban military aircraft.

The invasion exposed the limits of Soviet-Cuban power in the face of a concerted U.S. military action, especially in America's strategic backyard. It also illustrated the limits of Soviet support and protection for dependent nations anywhere when action might provoke conflict with the United States. The U.S. invasion of Grenada showed the USSR the parameters of U.S. tolerance in this Hemisphere, reaffirming the concept that spheres of influence would remain inviolable. At a news conference after the invasion, Fidel Castro said that if Nicaragua faced a similar invasion Cuba could not help much against so superior a force.

Relations With South America

Soviet commercial and diplomatic relations with the countries of South America began to expand in the mid-1960s. Argentina became the major trading partner with Brazil the second largest.

The USSR was a chief importer of Argentine grain and meat beginning in the early 1970s. By 1980 the USSR imported 33.7 percent of Argentine exports; grain shipments to the USSR were 60 percent of Argentine grain exports and 22 percent of total trade. In 1981 the Soviets purchased 77 percent of all agricultural commodities exported by Argentina. According to Soviet officials, Argentina became the USSR's most important grain supplier. In January 1986 the two countries reached preliminary agreement on the sale of 4.5 million tons of Argentine grain to the Soviet Union each year for five years. The agreement called for Argentina to purchase $500 million in Soviet industrial products.

The Argentine-Soviet ties developed because of mutual self-interest. For the Soviets, Argentina, the second largest country in South America, is strategically located along sea lanes of the South Atlantic, and is traditionally the most independent-minded state in Latin America. It also has had frequent policy conflicts with the United States. It is a rich source for grain, meat, and wool, and a good market for Soviet machinery. For the Argentines, the USSR has been a major, dependable market for exports and an alternative to the United States. They benefit from Soviet technical assistance, scientific cooperation, and heavy equipment.

The relationship has survived strong ideological differences. The Soviets down-played years of repressive, anti-communist military rule in Argentina. The Argentines have softened criticism of Soviet actions in Afghanistan and Poland. The relationship paid off well in 1980 when Argentina ignored the U.S. grain embargo of the USSR after the invasion of Afghanistan. In the Falklands crisis — provoked by Argentina's seizure of the British owned but disputed Falkland Islands — the USSR sided with Argentina against Britain. This permitted closer ties with Argentina and enhanced Soviet prestige in other Latin American countries sympathetic to the Argentine position.

Military relations have not been substantial although Argentina has indicated interest in purchasing weapons from the Soviets.

As of 1985 Peru was the only South American country with whom the USSR had significant military relations. There were 160 Soviet military advisers stationed there in 1985, including 90 with the Peruvian army. Peru bought $650 million worth of Soviet military equipment in the mid-1970s including tanks, supersonic fighter planes, heavy artillery, and the region's first surface-to-air missiles. In September 1981 the Peruvian armed forces sought permission to buy $200 million worth of new equipment from the Soviets. In February 1985 U.S. government officials reported that Peruvian investment in Soviet military equipment over the years had been more than $1.5 billion.

Limits to Involvement

It is likely the USSR will continue its reach into the Western Hemisphere even though there are limits to its involvement, especially in Central America. The USSR cannot afford to prop up Nicaragua economically as it has Cuba, and will not let that happen even if the Sandinistas pursue it. The USSR has pressed Nicaragua to find new sources of aid and has not provided much-needed foreign exchange even in the face of a U.S. trade embargo in the spring of 1985.

Many experts on Latin America note that Soviet involvement has been just enough to ripple the waters but not enough to cause real conflict. Experts believe this points to a lack of real commitment to the area except to hassle the United States and detract American attention from other locations of superpower confrontation. The USSR, for example, sees little economic value in the region. The Soviets believe it is more beneficial to maintain a low-key approach and exploit the advantage of ingrained anti-Americanism.

There is always the issue of spheres of influence. The USSR equates the U.S. "right" to involvement in Nicaragua with the Soviet Union's "right" to involvement in its backyard — Afghanistan. Leiken has expressed Soviet ambivalence toward Nicaragua (and perhaps the region) this way:

> Moscow appears to be pursuing a wait and see, long term strategy in Nicaragua. It has made minimal economic investments and encourages the Sandinistas to diversify their trading partners and donors.... Moscow provides only enough military aid to make U.S. military intervention costly and save the Soviet "revolutionary" reputation, not enough to guarantee survival or risk confrontation.

Experts such as Leiken have noted that the combination of anti-Americanism and continued hard-line U.S. policy with more subtle Soviet penetration into the area will have the long-term effect of solidifying Soviet influence in the region.

USSR-AFRICA: LIMITED INFLUENCE

The Soviet Union's gains in the sprawling continent of Africa date primarily from the 1970s when growing African nationalism was bringing change in many nations.

Many African nations emerged from Western colonial rule in the years following World War II, often with bitter memories of harsh European exploitation. But even two or more decades later, many remained in embryonic economic development stages and often were rift with political instability as staunchly nationalistic leaders vied for control over their nations.

Soviet interest in Africa arose from different, but often intertwined, factors: superpower rivalry with the West; the desire to advance Soviet ideology; significant deposits of raw materials; and creation of new markets for goods — mostly armaments — with which to earn hard currency.

The continent had never been high on the Kremlin's list of world priorities and — many experts believe — is not high today. But opportunities to gain influence were present:

● Some nations leaned increasingly toward Marxist ideas, believing that the Soviet system was better suited than Western models to problems of developing nations.

● Political vacuums were created in some nations when European colonial powers left, in some cases as late as the 1970s. Rival local factions moved to gain power, bringing confusion and often armed conflict.

● In the southern area of the continent, the continuing struggle between the white-dominated and strongly anti-communist South Africa and neighboring black nationalists offered prime opportunities for the Kremlin to gain new influence among emerging African leaders in revolutionary or insurgency groups.

The USSR attempted to use all of these opportunities to expand its worldwide influence. In Angola in particular, the Soviet-Cuban intervention in 1975-76 became a symbol of the Kremlin's ability and willingness to project its power into far corners of the world; it marked the Soviet Union's emergence as a global power with all the rights and perquisites accompanying that status.

Soviet gains, however, have been anything but an unvarnished success. After developing close ties to a few nations and to a number of insurgency groups in the 1970s, the Soviets became less successful in the mid-1970s and early 1980s. In one case the Kremlin was forced to choose between two warring friends — Ethiopia and Somalia; it sided with Ethiopia at the cost of shattered relations with Somalia. In the southern part of the continent, unexpected negotiations between South Africa and neighboring countries led to concern in the Kremlin that the need for Soviet weapons might be reduced, thereby reducing Soviet influence.

The Soviet's concern highlighted the fact that Soviet inroads throughout the continent were grounded largely in military aid. Economic aid from the Kremlin was extremely limited, but continued to flow in substantial amounts from Western nations, particularly the United States, despite the Marxist ideological leanings of many African nations.

Soviets Extend Global Influence

Soviet interest in Africa was boosted during the 1970s as African leaders became less wary of Soviet intentions. Many nations began reexamining long-standing nonalignment policies and several adopted Marxism-Leninism, including the Congo, Somalia, Angola, Guinea-Bissau, Sao Tome and Principe, Madagascar, and Benin. Pro-Soviet factions gained power in Angola, Ethiopia, and Mozambique.

At the same time, China lost considerable influence in Africa as a result of Soviet policies there in the 1970s, which was one of the Kremlin's goals. In Angola, for example, Soviet-backed forces defeated those backed by the

Western nations and China. China's credibility among the Third World and nonaligned nations was weakened when it was caught aiding forces in Angola that also received aid from South Africa.

In the southern half of the continent, the Soviet Union benefitted from the power vacuum that followed Portugal's withdrawal from its colonial territories in the mid 1970s, and the increased political radicalization among the emerging independent nations.

This southern region was an attractive target for the Kremlin because it is rich with strategic and raw materials and because it borders important sea routes. The sea lanes around the Cape of Good Hope are the world's most heavily trafficked route. Supertankers use the route to travel between the Persian Gulf and ports in Europe and the United States. It also is an important alternate route for Western European-Japanese shipping and is vital to deploying U.S. forces to the Indian Ocean and the Persian Gulf. In addition to obtaining strategic minerals for defense uses, keeping these sea lanes open has been the United States' main strategic interest in the region.

Further north, the Soviets made important strategic gains by developing close ties to Ethiopia, on the Horn of Africa, and nearby South Yemen that allowed the Kremlin to position a sizeable naval force in the region. Ethiopia is located on the Red Sea across from Saudi Arabia and guards the approaches to the Suez Canal and the Indian Ocean. South Yemen is part of the Arabian peninsula, adjacent to Saudi Arabia. The two countries are in key positions to intercept shipping headed from the Persian Gulf or toward the Suez Canal. (Map, p. 96)

The closer ties with Mozambique, farther down the east coast, and especially Angola and Ethiopia demonstrated that the USSR could gain influence in countries beyond those adjacent to its own borders.

Moscow also cultivated relations with some less radical African governments, such as the north-central nations of Nigeria and Morocco, although on a limited basis. In addition, the Soviets developed ties to numerous insurgency groups in Africa such as SWAPO (the Southwest African People's Organization), which was trying to gain independence for Namibia, a southwest territory controlled by neighboring South Africa.

Setbacks Followed Initial Gains

But during the later 1970s and early 1980s, Moscow suffered several political setbacks despite its sharply increased military assistance to Africa. The Soviets were unable to consolidate secure Marxist governments in most nations. Extended Soviet military commitments in southern Africa and the Horn did not produce unchallenged political or military victories among the pro-Soviet governments in the region.

In the first half of the 1980s, the Kremlin sought primarily to consolidate rather than expand its influence. This policy shift was due partly to the shaky leadership in the Politburo from 1980 until the Gorbachev succession. But more importantly, Africa was not so high a priority as were global areas of greater strategic importance. Some analysts said Moscow's reluctance to give more direct assistance to regimes it supports in southern Africa is an indication of the region's low priority among the Kremlin's foreign policy objectives.

A cease-fire between South Africa and Angola over insurgency groups and a nonaggression pact between South Africa and Mozambique in 1984 were further blows to Soviet influence. The agreements with the government in Pretoria held out two prospects for the West:

• Reduced dependency of these nations on the Soviet Union for security needs;

• A better chance that the West could help resolve the issue of Namibia's independence.

Moscow's inability to negotiate with South Africa, the key player in the region, limited Soviet influence in peace negotiations. (This problem was similiar to the Soviet's difficulties in the Middle East where the United States dominated the peace process between Israel and its Arab neighbors and the USSR had little influence.)

In addition to being low on the Soviet priority list, many African nations were not conducive to expanding Soviet influence. Numerous African governments appeared inherently unstable as a result of significant tribal rivalries, continued power struggles, and widespread poverty and economic problems. Nonetheless, while the Soviets only occasionally developed major political clout, the region's continued need for arms meant the Soviets could develop influence through weapons.

Military Aid

Although the African continent remains the most lightly armed part of the world, Soviet military aid to sub-Saharan Africa increased sharply during the 1970s. By the early 1980s, the Soviets were by far the region's largest weapons supplier. From 1975 to 1979 Soviet arms transfers totaled $3.38 billion, according to U.S. Arms Control and Disarmament Agency figures. Approximately $2 billion of that went to Ethiopia and Angola, which continues to receive the bulk of Soviet weapons shipments to Africa. From 1979 to 1983 the Soviets delivered more than 10 times as many weapons to sub-Saharan Africa as did the United States. Nonetheless, arms exports to Africa accounted for less than 11 percent of total Soviet arms deliveries to the Third World over the 1970s and 1980s, according to U.S. government estimates. The Middle East and South Asia received the bulk of Soviet weapons exports.

East Germany and Cuba served Moscow's interests in southern Africa, especially in Ethiopia and Angola. Moscow supplied arms, but Cuba supplied most of the troops and other personnel and East Germany provided security and intelligence services.

The Soviet Union was unable to compete with the ample economic aid flowing from Western states. As a result, experts believe, the Kremlin turned to weapons assistance, which also helps the Soviet Union because approximately 70 to 80 percent of its worldwide arms deliveries are sold for hard currency.

Soviet bloc military personnel in Africa, as well as weapons deliveries, grew considerably over the 1970s and early 1980s. Nearly 37,000 Cuban troops and advisers (mostly in Angola, Ethiopia, and Mozambique) were in Africa in 1981, for example. Cuban troops in Angola peaked at 36,000 in 1976.

Economic Ties

The Soviet Union's position on economic assistance to Africa has changed since the 1950s. Until the Khrushchev era the USSR's ties to Africa were virtually nonexistent. Soviet leader Nikita Khrushchev began economic aid to undermine Western influence in the late 1950s. The Soviets' goals were political, not economic, when they "pumped expensive aid programs into newly independent, radical, non-capitalist states," according to Michael J. Dixon of the Congressional Research Service. After Khrushchev was removed from power in 1964, the USSR under Leonid Brezhnev began realizing the economic advantages African states could provide. The Soviets began importing raw materials and exporting machinery, technology, and expertise. Although Soviet trade with Africa increased significantly by 1975, Western economic influence remained strong.

Western aid dwarfs Soviet assistance programs. The modest Soviet economic aid to sub-Saharan Africa is not likely to grow. Radical African states have pressed the Soviets for more aid and admission to economic trading groups, specifically the CMEA, but Moscow has refused. The Soviets often encourage African states to seek aid in the West or from wealthier, more stable, African countries such as Morocco, Sierra Leone, and Senegal. The Angolan government, as well as its main internal opponent Jonas Savimbi, and Mozambique have all turned to the West for economic aid.

Experts on Africa note that Soviet aid is not designed to compete with Western aid programs but is targeted to succeed in a few selected areas that are most likely to return commensurate benefits. Generally, this has meant commercial ventures and long-term projects that aid Soviet economic plans. For example, $2 billion in aid (out of approximately $3.5 billion total African economic aid over 1975-81) went to Morocco to develop phosphate mining. The phosphate goes to the USSR to produce fertilizer.

In January 1982 the Soviet Union signed a 10-year trade and economic cooperation agreement with Angola worth $2 billion. Soviet advisers apparently are developing coal mining and oil exploration in Mozambique; in Madagascar, the Soviets have committed $42 million for road construction. Madagascar is seen as increasingly aligning itself with Moscow, according to Dixon. Other than these efforts and a small number of similar ones, the Soviets have not tried to reach the poorer African nations.

The Soviets sharply increased the number of nonmilitary personnel in Africa over the 1970s and 1980s. From an estimated 7,200 Soviet and East European economic technicians in sub-Saharan Africa in 1970, the numbers rose to more than 16,000 in the mid-1970s, although somewhat fewer advisers remained in the early 1980s. The USSR extended numerous scholarships to students and military personnel from Africa, hosting more than 30,000 academic students in 1981.

Other Ties to Africa

Cultural diplomacy also played a part in the Soviet Union's efforts to build influence in Africa. The Soviets' two main objectives in this area have been, according to Dixon, to "overcome negative or indifferent impressions of the USSR ... [and] to marshal active support for Soviet policies. Cultural diplomacy (often described as propaganda) is also used to demonstrate that the Soviet revolutionary experience can be successful if applied in Africa and to discredit Western policies in the region." According to Soviet writers in the Moscow journal *International Affairs*, the Soviet Union has always sided with African countries "in their actions in the United Nations aimed against colonialism, racism, and neo-colonialism and in moves to curb aggression and strengthen peace." The Soviets spread considerable amounts of disinformation designed to dis-

credit U.S. policies, such as frequently publicizing U.S. relations to South Africa and accusing the United States of wanting to "perpetuate the apartheid system," and of wanting to install a puppet government in Namibia.

Broadcasting is also a major means of shaping developments in the region. Moscow broadcasts in 10 African languages; the United States broadcasts in only 3 African languages. While other cultural ties had only marginal impact, by 1985 the Soviets had cultural and cooperation agreements with at least 16 African nations, according to Dixon.

South Africa's Role

The strongly anticommunist Republic of South Africa has affected the extent of Soviet gains throughout southern Africa. South Africa's control over Namibia (Southwest Africa) has created intertwined problems for South Africa, Angola, Mozambique, and other surrounding countries as well as for the United States and the Soviet Union.

South Africa, the region's economic and military leader, has controlled Namibia since 1916 but, since 1978, in defiance of UN resolutions calling for Namibia's independence.

Namibia's 330,000 square-mile territory separates Angola and South Africa. South African forces went into southern Angola numerous times in the early 1980s in pursuit of Soviet-supported Southwest African People's Organization guerrillas seeking Namibian independence. Namibia gave the Soviet Union an opportunity to expand its influence if SWAPO eventually took power and adopted a "socialist oriented" government with pro-Soviet leanings, but by early 1986 nothing had come of the Soviets' support. In fact, Angola's apparent willingness in 1985 to negotiate with South Africa over Namibia hinted at a peaceful settlement of the issue and much less need for Soviet military help for SWAPO.

Mozambique and South Africa

Mozambique, South Africa's neighbor to the northeast, also was a frequent target of South African raids in the early 1980s until March 16, 1984, when the two nations signed a nonaggression pact known as the Nkomati Accord. African National Congress (ANC) forces attempting to promote insurgency in South Africa often were chased to their refuges in Mozambique by South African troops. The ANC, the South African black majority's main political party, had been outlawed since the early 1960s. The Soviet Union apparently supports the ANC with arms and funds but many Western diplomats in 1985 doubted the Soviets had any real control over ANC actions, as alleged by South Africa.

In the Nkomati Accord, South Africa agreed it would no longer attack what Pretoria said were ANC bases or support forces rebelling against the Marxist Mozambican government. The Mozambican National Resistance (RENAMO, or NRM) sought to overthrow the governing party, the Liberation Front of Mozambique (FRELIMO) of President Samora Machel. Under the accord, Mozambique was to expel any ANC militants, while South Africa was to discontinue any aid to the Mozambique insurgents. Since then, however, South Africa admitted to breaking the agreement in pursuit of ANC militants.

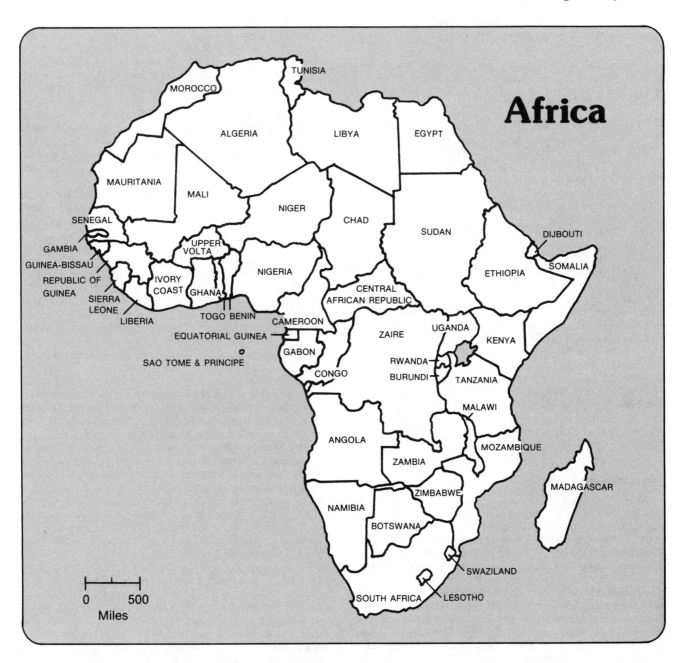

Africa

In the mid-1980s, South Africa stepped up its military campaign against Zimbabwe, Lesotho, and other neighboring countries it accused of harboring ANC guerrillas. Its critics said South Africa's regional policy was really a campaign to destabilize neighboring black governments and thus prevent them from helping opponents of the region's only remaining white government.

Angola and South Africa

South Africa signed a U.S.-mediated cease-fire agreement with Angola in February 1984, but an impasse was reached over the withdrawal of Cuban troops from Angola. South Africa demanded that all Cuban troops leave before it would set a date for Namibian independence and the removal of its own forces from the territory. Angolan presi-

dent José Eduardo dos Santos demanded South Africa first end its aid to guerrilla leader Jonas Savimbi, whose forces were trying to overthrow the government.

Some 2,000 South African troops have been stationed in Namibia and at times have occupied parts of Angola itself, ostensibly to defend the territory from SWAPO. South Africa formally withdrew from Angolan territory in April 1985 but staged at least three raids into the country between then and the end of 1985. After a raid in late December 1985, the Angolan government charged that South African forces were still deep inside the country.

During a 1985 party congress of the Popular Movement for the Liberation of Angola (MPLA), later renamed the MPLA-Party of Labor or MPLA-PT, President dos Santos vowed to keep Cuban troops in Angola as long as South Africa threatened its borders. And despite the international outcry and growing domestic unrest, South Africa showed no sign of weakening on its widely despised policy of apartheid or on its position in Namibia.

The Case of Angola

Like most of its neighbors, Angola has only recently emerged from centuries of exploitation by European colonialists. Angola was established as a Portuguese colony in the fifteenth century, and Portuguese subjugation of Angola's people continued throughout its colonization.

Portugal's treatment of Angola's population spawned widespread resentment and spurred creation of several nationalist groups vying for power. The Popular Movement for the Liberation of Angola, founded under Agostinho Neto in 1956, and the Union of the Populations of North Angola, founded in 1957 by Holden Roberto, who later incorporated it into the FNLA (National Front for the Liberation of Angola), were responsible for anticolonial uprisings in February and March 1961. After the Portuguese crushed these uprisings the groups remained active as guerrilla forces and were eventually joined by Jonas Savimbi's forces, UNITA (National Union for the Total Independence of Angola).

Savimbi had returned to Angola after being educated in Portugal and Switzerland and participated with the FNLA in the 1961 uprising. In 1963 he reportedly split with the FNLA over tribal questions and began organizing UNITA. Savimbi initially went to Egypt, and later China, where he was given small amounts of supplies and provided guerrilla training for several of his followers.

Superpower Intervention

The overthrow of Portugal's government in 1974 marked the end of colonial occupation but not the end of foreign intervention in Angola. When the Portuguese government was deposed, the new government declared that all of Portugal's colonies would be granted independence. The three main Angolan liberation movements were included in a transition government and elections were scheduled for October of that year to determine who would head the first independent Angolan government. However, the nationalist groups could not overcome traditional rivalries. Civil war broke out shortly after the independence agreement was signed in Alvor, and outside powers quickly intervened on behalf of one or more of the three factions.

The MPLA — still headed by Neto — was a European-oriented, Marxist-Leninist group that placed the goal of national liberation above traditional tribal loyalties from its bases in central and western Angola. The MPLA received early support from Cuba, some Western European governments, and Algeria.

Roberto's FNLA based its power largely on tribal allegiances in the north. Roberto, related to the U.S.-backed president of neighboring Zaire, relied heavily on Zairean military support and was the first to receive U.S. covert aid. The most heavily armed of the three groups, the FNLA, also received assistance from China, India, and Romania, as well as the northern African states of Algeria, Morocco, and Tunisia.

Shortly after the independence accord was reached, the Ford administration in the United States authorized the CIA to provide both Savimbi and Roberto armaments to hold off the MPLA until the October elections. In a critical incident in March 1974, Roberto's forces killed some 50 unarmed MPLA activists. It was also during March that the Soviet Union resumed its military assistance to the MPLA, which it had cut off two years before. Separately, Neto also requested, and in early summer received, Cuba's first contingent of 230 military advisers.

By July the MPLA had repelled both the FNLA and UNITA. The turning point in the war came in October, when South African troops joined UNITA and FNLA forces in a thrust on Luanda, the Angolan capital. They were decisively routed by the MPLA with the aid of additional Cuban troops and Soviet arms. Meanwhile, China had abruptly withdrawn its support for UNITA and the FNLA after these groups turned to South Africa for additional aid. China's desire to counter Soviet expansion in the region apparently was outweighed by its reluctance to be associated in any way with the apartheid regime in South Africa.

With Luanda secured, the MPLA declared the People's Republic of Angola in November, while the FNLA and UNITA set up rival governments to the south in Huambo. The FNLA soon dissolved, however, leaving Savimbi's group the only viable opposition force to Angolan president José Eduardo dos Santos.

That same month the Ford administration asked Congress for an additional $28 million in covert CIA funding for the Angola effort. News of the request leaked to the press, prompting critics to warn against U.S. involvement in a distant war that could turn out to be another Vietnam. With that Southeast Asian defeat still fresh in mind, Congress banned all further American assistance for Angola, despite Secretary of State Henry A. Kissinger's exhortation that such a ban would show the world that the United States "is willing to emasculate itself in the face of massive, unprecedented Soviet and Cuban intervention," placing in doubt its credibility as a protector of "global stability."

There is evidence that Kissinger, anxious to prevent Moscow from taking advantage of détente to expand its influence in the Third World, overestimated the extent of Soviet influence in Angola. Not only did the MPLA-PT establish ties with Cuba independently of its backing from the Soviet Union and long before its victory, but Neto successfully repelled a 1977 coup attempt by a rival faction that advocated closer ties with Moscow. "Since then," wrote Soviet analyst Raymond Garthoff in his book *Détente and Confrontation*, "Angolan policy has been based on a general political alignment with the Soviet Union and reliance on the continued presence of Cuban troops to prevent major external attack, but has also included encouragement for diplomatic and trade ties with the West."

In the wake of UNITA's victory in the bloody battle for Cangamba, a large MPLA-PT base in central Angola, the Soviets increased arms shipments and the Cubans augmented their forces. The Soviets also stepped up diplomatic activity by warning South Africa to stop its policies of destabilization. In mid-December 1983, however, South Africa initiated a new offensive into southern Angola against SWAPO.

Unexpectedly, in late January 1984, the South Africans began an intense round of diplomatic activity with the Angolans, with the United States acting as an intermediary. The talks resulted in the February 16 accord signed at Lusaka, Zambia. Writing in *Problems of Communism*, Soviet expert Peter Clement said the agreement "called for the staged withdrawal of South African forces from southern Angola in exchange for Angola's commitment to prevent SWAPO from entering the area. A joint monitoring commission was established to police the area of disengagement and to prevent infiltration of northern Namibia by SWAPO guerrillas." The sides could not reach agreement over the issue of Cuban troop withdrawal. Dos Santos temporarily walked out of the U.S.-mediated talks in November 1985 but the talks resumed in early 1986 and were directed at the troop issue.

Moscow gave grudging approval of the 1984 accord that March. General Secretary Konstantin Chernenko, however, stated March 29 that "no one has the right to turn back the pages of history." According to Western consensus, the speech was a reference to Moscow's belief that Washington was trying to exploit vulnerabilities in Africa and reverse gains the Soviets had made there in the 1970s.

The Lusaka agreement brought mixed results for the Soviets. The cease-fire may have diminished Angola's security threat, Clement argued, thereby giving the Soviets little reason to discourage the continuing Angolan-South African dialogue. And while the Soviets presumably were reluctant to leave SWAPO in the lurch, Clement maintained, the cease-fire would enable Angola and the Cubans to direct their energies to combat UNITA, a much more important long-term goal for the Soviets.

The Kremlin was more concerned about Angola's continued talks with Washington and South Africa on the Namibia issue. The Soviets increased their contacts with SWAPO leaders in the wake of U.S.-Angolan-South African negotiations, apparently trying to preclude them from making a deal with South Africa. Some experts believed the Soviets preferred a military stalemate in Namibia because that would enable them to develop more influence over SWAPO. A peaceful settlement would likely reduce Soviet influence because SWAPO would no longer need as much military aid from Moscow. In addition, the Soviets could not be sure that a SWAPO-led Namibia would not pursue the same pragmatic types of policies as Zimbabwean President Robert Mugabe.

The United States alone among the Western powers does not recognize the MPLA-PT government. Moreover, Angola is the only African country with which the United States does not maintain diplomatic relations. Even China, which had worked so hard to prevent the MPLA-PT from coming to power, maintains diplomatic relations with Angola. Yet Angola is the United States' fourth largest trading partner in Africa and the United States was Angola's largest in 1985.

Angola's economy sharply deteriorated in the 1980s. The costs of trying to overcome Savimbi's growing insurgency and paying for the large Cuban combat force placed a great strain on the Angolan economy, especially after oil prices began declining. Petroleum exports have almost completely replaced minerals and agricultural products as Angola's chief export since the departure of the Portuguese in 1975. Almost 99 percent of Angola's exports to the United States are petroleum, much of which comes from offshore oil fields operated by Gulf Oil Co.

Cuban Connection

Even with the help of Cuban troops in Angola the government had not been able to dislodge Savimbi by 1986. His forces controlled much of the southern and eastern regions of the country and were reported at one time to have held up to two-thirds of the country.

Estimates on Cuban troop levels in Angola ranged from 19,000 to 45,000.

According to Savimbi, Soviet military personnel operating advanced weaponry joined the government offensive that began in the summer of 1985 in an apparent attempt to cut off UNITA from outside assistance. The government forces were stopped deep within UNITA-held territory and only 120 miles from Jamba, Savimbi's capital in the southeastern corner of the country. In a well-publicized visit to Washington that began January 28, 1986, Savimbi asked the United States for military assistance before the end of the rainy season in April or May, when the government offensive was expected to resume.

The visit created substantial controversy. After heated debate in Congress and within the administration and pressure from conservative leaders, the administration announced February 18 that it would send approximately $15 million in "covert" military aid (including antiaircraft and antitank missiles) to Savimbi. The aid would come from CIA funds and therefore would not need congressional approval. There had been considerable opposition in Congress to sending military aid because leaders there believed the aid would hamper chances of achieving a diplomatic solution to the problems in Angola. Savimbi, during his Washington trip, agreed with U.S. officials that the aid, if given, would not permit him to obtain an outright military victory over the Angolan government. Instead, Chester Crocker, U.S. assistant secretary of state for African Affairs, said the aid was meant to prevent the Angolan government from achieving a "military solution" and to put pressure on dos Santos to be more forthcoming in negotiations on withdrawing Cuban troops from Angola and South African troops from Namibia.

The Horn of Africa

Several events in February 1977 converged to precipitate a war between Somalia and Ethiopia into which the superpowers would be drawn and the Soviet Union emerge as the apparent victor.

In Ethiopia, Haile Mengistu Mariam became the new leader February 3 after an internal power struggle. The country had been moving to the left politically since the abdication of Emperor Haile Selassie in 1974 but was not as close to the Soviet Union as was Somalia. Also in February, Somalia made several military incursions into the ethnically Somali desert territory in Ethiopia known as the Ogaden. In late February, President Carter singled out Ethiopia as a violator of human rights and soon barred that country from military grant aid. Mengistu responded to Carter's accusations by expelling U.S. military advisers and closing the American communications and intelligence station in Ethiopia.

In March, Cuban leader Fidel Castro visited Ethiopia after congratulating Mengistu on his assumption of power. The Soviets' warming ties with Ethiopia came at the expense of ties with Somalia, which had been receiving Cuban and Soviet military advisers and Soviet arms for several years. Mengistu flew to Moscow in May of 1977 and signed a major arms assistance agreement, which exacerbated Soviet-Somali tensions.

The Soviets' stepped-up arms shipments to Ethiopia came when Somali irregulars increased operations in the Ogaden. The Soviets strongly urged the Somalis to stop their incursions because they were creating serious problems for the Soviets, who were continuing to supply arms to both sides. In May a small contingent of Cuban military advisers arrived in Ethiopia, which prompted Somali head of state General Mohammed Siad Barre to urgently request new military assistance from President Carter.

The Somalis interpreted Carter's offer to see what he could do as an indication that he would, in fact, provide the arms they sought. This turned out not to be the case, although it was not until August that the United States announced it would send no arms to Somalia. Believing the arms would be forthcoming, the Somalis continued their offensive in the Ogaden and captured almost 90 percent of the region by late September.

The U.S. decision not to supply Somalia came despite the fact that the Soviets had cut off all arms supplies to that nation and had increased arms shipments to Ethiopia. Somalia's Barre had gone to Moscow at the end of August but Brezhnev would not meet with him. Barre learned that the Soviets wanted close ties with Somalia but considered Ethiopia more important. The U.S. refusal to send arms to Somalia came primarily because there was no doubt the Somalis had blatantly invaded Ethiopia and intended to use U.S. arms to incorporate the Ogaden. By not sending the arms, the U.S. not only dealt a blow to the Somalis but, according to Raymond Garthoff,

> also upset U.S. allies and friends who had been urging the Somalis to change course — namely, Saudi Arabia, Sudan, Egypt and Iran. [But] ... it was too late for Somalia to change its commitment to winning the Ogaden by arms, or to change the collision course of Somali-Soviet relations.... The Soviet Union and Cuba, acting in closer concert than they had at the beginning of the civil war in Angola, were determined not to let their new ally be defeated.

More Cuban military advisers and Soviet arms began arriving in November; by the end of the month, Cuban troops and Soviet tanks and other arms were airlifted. According to Garthoff, by February 1978 Cuba had sent between 12,000 and 17,000 troops and the Soviet Union had sent up to $1 billion in arms.

In response to the November actions, Somalia's Barre broke relations with Cuba, expelled all Cuban and Soviet advisers, and abrogated the 1974 friendship treaty with the Soviet Union.

Meanwhile, the United States "in effect wrote off Ethiopia," according to Garthoff. The general consensus in Africa, however, was that the Somali invasion violated the principle of territorial integrity and caused concern about the security of other nations. This was especially true for Sudan and Kenya.

Israel also supported the Ethiopians publicly and, according to Garthoff, continued to send Israeli military counterinsurgency experts there in 1977, despite unwanted publicity about past Israeli-Ethiopian ties. These ties were particularly incongruous because not only the Soviet Union and Cuban but also Libya, South Yemen, and the Palestine Liberation Organization strongly supported Mengistu.

By late January 1978 the Ethiopians began their Soviet- and Cuban-backed counteroffensive. The Somalis were quickly defeated. The Ethiopian army did not, however, cross the border behind the retreating Somalis. Because of both African opinion and continued internal instability in Eritrea (a region where rebels were trying to secede from Ethiopia), the Soviets and Mengistu apparently thought it better to stop at the border. President Carter announced March 9 that the Somalis had withdrawn from the Ogaden, and by mid-March 1978 the war had ended.

During the war with Somalia, Eritrean rebels had gained control of almost the entire region of Eritrea. Although the Soviets, Cubans, and a high-ranking Ethiopian general urged Mengistu to negotiate a settlement with the opposition there, Mengistu refused. The Soviets overcame their preference for a negotiated settlement and helped the Ethiopians launch a major military offensive. Most of Eritrea was recovered. Despite their ties to the Ethiopian government, the Cubans, however, had long aided the Eritrean rebels and, along with the South Yemenis, refused to fight the Eritreans.

Expanding Ties

Soviet and Cuban ties with Ethiopia continued to expand in 1978, and in November Ethiopia signed a treaty of friendship with the Soviet Union. There was still friction, however, because the Soviets wanted Mengistu to establish a legitimate communist party, which he did not want to do because he feared it would threaten his power base. It was not until September 1984 that he finally created a communist party, and even then it was largely made up of close associates.

Cuba continued to have difficulty in its relations with Ethiopia. Cuba secretly arranged for the return to Ethiopia of the leader of the opposition that Mengistu had defeated in his bid for power. When Mengistu discovered this, he expelled the Cuban ambassador and several thousand Cuban troops returned home (about 12,000 remained). Nonetheless, Garthoff pointed out that Cuba's presence in Ethiopia allowed Castro to claim more assistance from the Soviets in light of their sacrifices and it increased Cuba's profile in international affairs. However, the Cuban presence also cost Cuba some goodwill in Africa and increased U.S. concern about the Soviet use of proxies in the Third World.

Soviet reasoning during the war in the Horn of Africa was varied, but rather plain. The conflict between Somalia and Ethiopia was clearly generated locally and the Soviets acted on the opportunity it presented. They took advantage of the new Ethiopian government's decision to break ties with the United States and strongly supported Mengistu, showing him that alliance with the Soviet Union was valuable, Garthoff noted. The Soviets also clearly tried to convince Siad not to invade the Ogaden. The Soviets realized they could not maintain close ties with both countries and they chose the strategically more valuable Ethiopia. The decision was made easier because Ethiopia had a legitimate right to protect its border after the Somali invasion.

Essentially, the United States chose to stay outside the conflict through 1977. It was only after Soviet assistance to Ethiopia increased at the end of 1977 and "especially in early 1978, that the United States became seriously concerned and began to make the matter an issue in American-Soviet relations," according to Garthoff. He added:

> The failure of the United States and the Soviet Union to engage in frank discussions on the unfolding crisis during 1977 was a repeat of the pattern with Angola in 1975, with variations. In

the Horn the United States did not have a favored candidate to win the conflict, as in the case of Angola, while the Soviet Union had an interest in reconciling Somalia and Ethiopian positions and in preventing an open conflict between them. It would therefore appear that a concerted American-Soviet effort to dissuade Somalia from attacking Ethiopia might well have succeeded. But neither the United States nor the Soviet Union was prepared to exercise a joint role of restraint. The Soviet Union was moving to displace American influence in Ethiopia with its own while trying to keep its ties with Somalia as well. For their part, the United States and its Arab friends were trying to turn Somalia from its Soviet alignment, and the United States was unwilling to accept Israel's advice to compete with the Soviet Union to regain the favor of Mengistu's Ethiopia.

The United States provided the bulk of food aid to Ethiopia and the rest of sub-Sahara during the widespread famine and drought in the early 1980s but this did not lead to improved relations with the Reagan administration. Ethiopia remained strongly tied to the Soviet Union despite the fact that Moscow sent little aid to help overcome the crisis.

Other African Nations

Mozambique

The Soviet Union and Mozambique signed a friendship treaty in March 1977. Mozambique President Samora Machel's FRELIMO regime had greatly strengthened Moscow's overall position in the region by maintaining close political ties, although the Soviets had had little involvement in his rise to power. Mozambique had also become more dependent on Moscow in the 1980s after Machel asked for military aid to counter South African raids and the South African-backed RENAMO insurgency.

But disappointed by Moscow's reluctance to match its military support with economic aid — Moscow apparently failed to fulfill aid promises and denied Mozambique membership in the CMEA — Machel turned increasingly to the West for badly needed economic assistance and trade. Machel met with President Reagan in Washington September 19, 1985, seeking U.S. aid. Machel also in the mid-1980s sought U.S. and Western European assistance in pressuring South Africa to stop its aggressive help to RENAMO and UNITA. "Both initiatives [struck] at Moscow's key vulnerabilities — its failure to fulfill its clients' economic needs, and its inability to mediate with South Africa," Clement wrote.

With South Africa's help, RENAMO's strength had increased in 1982. High-ranking Soviet military officials met several times with Mozambican officials throughout the year and declared they would "give every support" to Mozambique's political and military needs. Public support for Machel continued in 1983. That summer, according to Clement, the Soviets suffered their first acknowledged casualties in Mozambique. Two economic technicians were killed and two dozen others were kidnapped by RENAMO forces.

A disastrous famine in 1983 in which the Soviets gave little or no assistance highlighted Machel's frustration with the Soviets. After autumn trips to the West, Machel announced in December that high-level talks had begun with South Africa to ease security problems.

On March 16, 1984, the Nkomati formal nonagression pact was signed between the two countries. Importantly for Mozambique, the accord included agreements on economic and financial assistance in numerous areas. Moscow was clearly dismayed at the accord for many reasons, primarily because it provided room for the West to make inroads in the country and because it seriously weakened the already limited movement of the ANC. Moscow soon acquiesced, however, partly because its stakes in Mozambique were not as significant as in Angola and Soviet prestige was "not so clearly linked" to Machel's fortunes, according to Clement.

In January 1985 the United States announced it would offer approximately $1 million in nonlethal military assistance on top of its $22 million food assistance in 1984. If this trend continued, according to Clement, it would slowly erode Moscow's position in Mozambique.

Zimbabwe

In Zimbabwe, the Soviets supported Joshua Nkomo in his bid for power, but his rival, Robert Mugabe, became prime minister in 1980 and distanced his country from the Soviet Union. But since 1981 the governments signed media, cultural, and trade accords. No military relationship existed, but in late 1985 Mugabe visited Moscow for the first time since he was elected and reportedly requested increased military and economic assistance. Security problems apparently concerned Mugabe as he attempted to establish a one-party state and because of the possibility of unrest in Matabeleland, which would likely draw in South African forces.

Zambia

When Zambia became independent most of its security problems were eliminated, and although President Kenneth Kaunda signed major arms agreements with the Soviets in 1979-80, the agreements did not significantly improve relations between the countries. Kaunda maintained his longstanding nonaligned policies and willingly acted as a peacemaker in negotiations involving South Africa, including the Lusaka accord.

Lesotho

The Soviet Union increased its efforts to maintain good relations with countries in southern Africa after they lost access to the ANC when Mozambique signed the Nkomati accord. Moscow tried to take advantage of former Lesotho prime minister Leabua Jonathan's move to improve ties to the East in 1983, but Jonathan was deposed in January 1986 and the country quickly moved to improve relations with South Africa, which completely surrounds Lesotho. It was not known whether the new government would move to completely cut ties to Moscow.

POLAND:

A Move Toward Liberalization That Failed

A political crisis was triggered in Poland July 1, 1980, when the government removed subsidies from the price of meat. As in 1979 and 1976, when increases in the prices of food and basic goods aroused workers, reaction was explosive. Scattered strikes erupted throughout Poland to protest the price hikes. Workers at the Lenin shipyard in Gdansk, Poland's largest, took over the yard August 14. On August 17 the strikers formed an Interfactory Strike Committee and its leader, 37-year-old unemployed electrician Lech Walesa, announced the group's terms for negotiations. In addition to demands for increased wages and reduced meat prices, the committee called for the formation of independent labor unions, relaxed government censorship, and the right to strike.

After some reluctance, the Polish Communist Party, led by First Secretary Edward Gierek, agreed to negotiate with the strikers. The settlement reached August 30 permitted workers to form unions free of government interference, reduced official censorship, allowed churches and other groups access to the government-controlled news media, and freed imprisoned dissidents who had supported the strike. In addition, the government vowed to increase wages, upgrade medical services, and improve supplies of basic foods.

After strikers returned to work, the party announced September 6 that Gierek had been ousted. Ironically, Gierek had been named first secretary in 1970 after labor unrest caused the downfall of his predecessor, Wladyslaw Gomulka. The new Polish leader, Stanislaw Kania, formerly the head of the country's security forces, pledged to honor the strike settlement and vowed to retain Poland's close ties with the Soviet Union and the Eastern-bloc nations. In early September Moscow agreed to lend Warsaw $100 million and to step up deliveries of food and basic goods.

The situation remained tense for the remainder of 1980 as the strike committee, which took the name Solidarity, accused the Kania regime of failing to fulfill the terms of the settlement. Speculation arose that the Soviet military might intervene in Poland to strengthen Warsaw's control.

President Carter on December 3 warned the Soviets that any intervention in Poland's affairs would have "most negative consequences" and that U.S.-Soviet relations would be "directly and adversely affected." He followed up his warning by dispatching Secretary of State Edmund S. Muskie to Brussels to rally the North Atlantic Treaty Organization behind the U.S. position. In a communiqué issued December 12, the NATO ministers said that Soviet intervention in Poland "would fundamentally alter the entire international situation. The allies would be compelled to react in the manner which the gravity of this development would require."

The problem facing the Kremlin was considerable. If Soviet forces were not sent into Poland, Moscow feared that the momentum of liberalization would threaten the Warsaw government and perhaps spread to other Soviet satellites and into the Soviet Union itself. The control of the Communist Party would weaken and rival centers of power — labor, intellectuals, religious organizations — would encourage political pluralism that is anathema to Moscow. Faced with similar situations in the past, in Hungary and Czechoslovakia, Soviet armies invaded and occupied the states.

In late December, during the last weeks of the Carter administration, the White House reported that Soviet "preparation for possible intervention in Poland appears to have been completed." Meanwhile the Soviet and Eastern-bloc news media kept up a campaign against the "renewal" in Poland and the Solidarity group. Tass, for example, reported in February 1981 that many Poles expected that "measures will be adopted" to turn back the "counter-revolutionary" movement.

Tension Continues

In his 26th Party Congress speech February 23, 1981, Soviet general secretary Leonid Brezhnev, discussing Poland, reiterated the Brezhnev Doctrine. He said the Soviet Union would always stand up for Poland and would "not leave her in the lurch." In Brezhnev's words: "[L]et no one have any doubt about our common determination to secure our interests and defend the peoples' socialist gains." At the same meeting, Polish leader Kania reassured the Soviets that his government was prepared to "prevent a counterrevolution in Poland." *(Brezhnev congress address, p. 323)*

Tension increased after Warsaw Pact military maneuvers in and near Poland were scheduled for March. Moscow stepped up the pressure on the Polish leadership with a June 5 letter stressing measures to block counterrevolution and a July 21 message calling on the Polish Communist Party "to resolutely rebuff anarchy and counterrevolution." Further Warsaw Pact maneuvers were held in early September in the Soviet Union near the Polish border. Throughout the autumn the Soviet press kept up a campaign criticizing Solidarity and charging that the independent labor movement sought to seize power. The Polish government-controlled press joined in the attack on Solidarity in December, apparently in preparation for the military crackdown that occurred December 13.

Martial Law

In the midst of the tense fall of 1981, Polish Communist Party leader Kania was purged and replaced by the prime minister, Gen. Wojciech Jaruzelski. Under Jaruzelski's leadership, the Polish Politburo November 28 ordered the legislature to enact a law banning strikes, thus reversing one of the key elements of the government-Solidarity agreement of August 1980. The Polish authorities December 7 released a tape recording of a Solidarity meeting at which union leader Walesa was heard to call for the overthrow of the government. Walesa admitted that he made the statement, but claimed that he had been quoted out of context. On December 12 Solidarity leaders met in Gdansk to discuss proposals calling for free elections and the establishment of a new government. After the meeting, most top Solidarity officials, including Walesa, were arrested and detained. The government declared martial law, closed the border, and cut off all communications to and from Poland and within Poland itself.

Reaction from Washington was immediate. Secretary of State Alexander M. Haig, Jr., said the United States was "seriously concerned" about events in Poland and repeated Washington's warning to Moscow not to interfere. The Soviets on December 14 said officially that martial law in Poland was "an internal matter." A Tass report December 15 charged the United States with meddling in Polish affairs. The United States, it said, "is trying to prove that the events in Poland in some way concern U.S. security interests. But Poland is a member of the Warsaw Pact treaty organization, a member of the Socialist community of states, and the United States should not look there for any 'security zones,' as Washington is doing practically in all other parts of the globe."

Reagan's Response

Imposition of martial law provided the first test of President Ronald Reagan's handling of U.S.-Soviet relations. In an address televised from the White House, Reagan announced December 23 that the United States would take "concrete political and economic measures" against Moscow if the Polish crackdown continued. The president said, "I want to state tonight that, if the outrages in Poland do not cease, we cannot and will not conduct 'business as usual' with the perpetrators and those who aid and abet them." Reagan added, "The Soviet Union, through its threats and pressures, deserves a major share of blame for the developments in Poland."

The president reported that he had sent a letter to Soviet leader Brezhnev, "urging him to permit the restoration of basic rights in Poland as provided for in the Helsinki Final Act. In it, I informed him that, if this repression continues, the United States will have no choice but take further concrete political and economic measures affecting our relationship."

Seeking to pressure the Polish regime, President Reagan suspended U.S. government shipments of food to Poland, withdrew its line of export credit insurance with the Export-Import Bank, halted Polish airline service in the United States, and withdrew Poland's permission to fish in U.S. waters. Reagan said, "These actions are not directed against the Polish people. They are a warning to the government of Poland that free men cannot and will not stand idly by in the face of brutal repression."

Reagan did not, however, declare Poland's overdue debts to the U.S. government in default, a move that would have severely strained the economy of Poland and possibly of the Soviet Union. With total Polish debt in the West estimated at $27 billion, declaring a default also could have hurt the economies of Western creditor nations, including the United States, West Germany, France, and Britain.

On December 29 Reagan announced sanctions aimed directly at the Soviet Union. Charging that the "Soviet Union bears a heavy and direct responsibility for the repression in Poland," the president:

● Suspended new export licenses for high-technology items, including oil and gas equipment.

● Postponed talks on a maritime pact and a grain agreement. (But Reagan did not renew the grain embargo imposed by President Carter; Reagan lifted the embargo early in his administration.)

● Restricted Soviet access to U.S. ports and withdrew Soviet air service privileges.

● Shut down a Soviet office that arranged purchases of nonagricultural products in the United States.

● Vowed to review all existing energy, science, and technology agreements between Washington and Moscow.

The Reagan administration also embarked on a lobbying effort to convince the NATO allies to impose similar restrictions on contacts with the Soviet Union. But, although he was urged to do so from some quarters, the president declined to cancel either U.S.-Soviet talks on limiting nuclear weapons in Europe or Secretary Haig's January 26, 1982, meeting with Soviet foreign minister Gromyko.

In response to Reagan's sanctions, Tass December 30 said the president was trying "to hurl the world back to the dark times of the cold war" and predicted that the sanctions would have no effect on Soviet or Polish actions. The Tass statement added that Washington wished "to undermine the foundations of Soviet-American relations worked out as a result of huge efforts, and curtail them to a minimum."

Pipeline Sanctions. The most controversial of Reagan's measures intended to punish Moscow were the December 1981 sanctions prohibiting U.S. firms from selling the Soviet Union equipment or technology for oil and gas exploration, production, and refining. The sanctions, costing U.S. companies and their subsidiaries hundreds of millions of dollars' worth of sales, met with stiff opposition from American businesses and Congress. As it became increasingly clear that the sanctions were having no effect on Soviet behavior, Reagan shifted their focus to disrupting construction of a natural gas pipeline from Siberia to Western Europe.

The president believed that the pipeline would make Western Europe overly dependent on the Soviet Union for energy supplies and would provide billions of dollars in hard currency to assist the ailing Soviet economy. The United States also protested the alleged use of forced labor by the Soviet Union at pipeline construction sites.

On June 18, 1982, Reagan extended the sanctions to prohibit foreign subsidiaries of U.S. firms from selling the same equipment and technology and to prohibit overseas firms from selling the Soviets products made under U.S. licenses. European leaders bitterly protested Reagan's action, charging that the ban was "an unacceptable interference" in European economic affairs.

France and Britain defied the ban and ordered their own companies and a U.S. subsidiary to fulfill their contract obligations with the Soviets. West Germany and Italy also soon refused to comply with the ban. Reagan was displeased with the actions by U.S. allies, but was reluctant to pull back the sanctions. He did not want to appear to be retreating from the position of his December 1981 letter to Soviet leader Brezhnev.

Sanctions Lifted. Congressional opposition to the sanctions was so strong that a measure to overturn them was rejected by only three votes in the U.S. House of Representatives September 29. The House vote prompted the administration to reassess its actions. Reagan on November 13 lifted all the sanctions, saying the United States and its allies had finally reached "substantial agreement" on an overall economic strategy toward the Soviet Union that would restrict Soviet trade and commerce more efficiently than the pipeline equipment sanctions.

Although praising Reagan's decision to lift the sanctions, allied leaders made it clear they had agreed only to study future limits on trade with the Soviet Union and had not committed themselves in advance to take specific actions. Many Europeans viewed the agreement as a "face-saving" gesture for the Reagan administration. France promptly refused to acknowledge the new strategy, causing confusion about European acceptance of the deal.

Martial Law Suspended, Lifted

Martial law was "suspended" in Poland at 12 a.m. on December 31, 1982. The conditions in Poland changed only slightly, however, since the government retained restrictive powers that included the right to reimpose martial law at any time.

Reagan did not lift any U.S. sanctions in response to the suspension. Throughout 1983 and 1984, he did remove most of the less important ones. Responding to appeals from Walesa, who had been released November 14, 1982, after 11 months of internment, Reagan restored fishing and certain air carrier rights. He cited the release of political prisoners by the Polish government and the more complete "lifting" of martial law in July 1983, as well as the visit to Poland by Pope John Paul II in June of that year as "positive developments" that encouraged relaxation of additional economic and scientific sanctions. No other sanctions would be lifted, Reagan said, until the Polish government agreed to accept a new U.S. ambassador. One of the more severe economic sanctions kept in place was denial of export commodity credits.

Reagan, however, did withdraw his opposition to Poland's application for membership in the International Monetary Fund (IMF) after Jaruzelski announced a month-long amnesty for political prisoners in 1984. Some observers believed Western members of the IMF would have more control over the situation in Poland if that nation used IMF funds. The Soviet Union at times had opposed Poland's application for membership but apparently had reversed its position. Experts said in early 1986

that Poland's acceptance into the IMF was expected by April 1986.

Subsequent Developments. Since 1984 observers have noted an increase in suppression of Solidarity activists. Three persons in mid-1985 were sentenced to two to three-and-one-half years in prison for planning a 15-minute strike that never took place. The State Department said it was considering retaliatory action against the Polish government, but, by November 1985, none had been taken. In October 1985 and January 1986 more top Solidarity fugitives were arrested, one at a clandestine printing plant. The Underground press remained one of the few thriving remnants of the Solidarity movement.

In October 1985 Solidarity leader Lech Walesa disputed the official results of parliamentary (Sejm) elections held that month and was charged with slander. In what was seen as a conciliatory move, the government dropped the charges in January 1986.

On November 6, 1985, Jaruzelski resigned as premier and the newly elected Sejm elected him president. Jaruzelski, retaining his positions as head of the party and defense council, apparently resigned from his government post to devote more time to party affairs. Numerous other top-level personnel changes came days later; in early 1986 the hard-line ambassador to Moscow, a powerful critic of Jaruzelski, was also removed. Jaruzelski made headlines when he met with French president François Mitterrand in Paris, the first meeting in a Western capital between Jaruzelski and a Western head of state since martial law was imposed in 1981.

Under pressure from a number of groups within the ruling Communist Party in January 1986, Jaruzelski postponed economic reforms and agreed to ease repression of his opposition in hopes of maintaining control over a crucial party congress in June. Soviet leaders had remained relatively silent about the situation in Poland following an April 1985 meeting between Jaruzelski and General Secretary Gorbachev. Jaruzelski apparently was hopeful the Soviets had seen his moves as evidence that Poland was stabilizing politically despite its continued economic straits. The *Wall Street Journal* reported February 20 that Soviet leader Gorbachev had met with Polish prime minister Zbigniew Messner to discuss a program to increase Soviet and intrabloc technological cooperation with Poland but the two apparently disagreed on several points.

The Role of the Military

Military power has become one of the Soviet Union's most critical instruments of foreign policy. Military modernization efforts that began in the late 1950s and expanded rapidly in the 1960s and 1970s thrust the Soviet Union into superpower status, allowing the Kremlin to increase significantly the use of the armed forces for diplomatic purposes. The Soviet military has been called upon to preserve and expand the Kremlin's authority in Eastern Europe and in Afghanistan, for example, as well as to influence other communist regimes and counter actions by the West and China.

While protection of the homeland remains the Soviet military's primary function, nuclear superpower status has enabled the Soviets to wield military force as a tool of foreign policy with more and more assurance of success. In *Diplomacy of Power* Stephen S. Kaplan wrote:

> The Soviet nuclear arsenal, which affords the USSR superpower status, is the principal foundation of the Soviet Union's international position. Without nuclear armaments, Moscow could not orchestrate conventional armed forces with confidence, and Moscow's diplomacy would not be taken as seriously as it is by the United States, China, Western Europe, Japan, and other nations.

By the 1970s the Soviets had obtained rough strategic nuclear parity with the United States. Their headlong rush to reach this status was accomplished by devoting vast amounts of resources to defense, usually at the expense of domestic needs. The capabilities of each of the five Soviet armed forces — the Strategic Rocket Forces, Ground Forces, Air Defense, Air Forces, and Navy — improved considerably. Naval forces, in particular, came to symbolize the USSR's new ability to project power in any part of the globe. Including the Committee for State Security (KGB) and internal security troops, the Soviet Union had more than 5 million men under arms in 1984, according to the most recent Western estimates.

The United States only reluctantly accepted the USSR's increased role in international affairs that came with the Kremlin's greater military capabilities. There was some truth to the Soviet statement in the early 1970s that no major international issue could be decided without their involvement. Further, the United States appeared to many nations to be more fearful than in the past of a conventional confrontation with the other superpower, because of

concern that this could escalate into a nuclear war. This perceived hesitation to get involved in regional crises that could lead to a confrontation between the superpowers led U.S. allies to grow "doubtful about what they could expect from the United States in crises, Soviet allies became more confident, and all nations accorded Soviet positions increased respect," Kaplan noted.

Both the United States and the Soviet Union have long declared interest in and commitment to reducing nuclear weapons and the possibility of war, but superpower arms control negotiations produced only limited, uneven results from the mid-1960s to the mid-1980s. The Strategic Arms Limitation Talks (SALT I and II), the subsequent Strategic Arms Reduction Talks (START), the Intermediate-Range Nuclear Force (INF) talks, and the Mutual and Balanced Force Reduction (MBFR) talks covering Europe all faced substantial barriers throughout the 1970s and early 1980s.

With the demise of détente in 1979, SALT II was delayed in Congress and never ratified. There was no progress on arms control during Ronald Reagan's first term as president. Indeed, after it became clear in late 1983 that NATO missile deployments would begin in Europe, the Soviets walked out of the Geneva talks. No formal arms control talks were held in 1984. Reagan proposed in March 1983 a Strategic Defense Initiative — a space-based anti-ballistic-missile system. The SDI fostered substantial outcry from many parts of the political spectrum, domestically and worldwide. The Soviets refused to negotiate on most arms control issues unless SDI was included, charging SDI would militarize space. The Reagan administration said SDI research was barely beginning, that if it were successful the system would eliminate the need for nuclear weapons, and that the United States needed to match similar efforts already under way in the Soviet Union. For these reasons, the administration maintained that SDI, at least regarding research for it, was nonnegotiable. In the mid-1980s much of the potential progress in arms control negotiations hinged on this divisive issue.

The first part of this chapter outlines the structure and composition of the Soviet Union's armed forces and their position in relation to the Soviet Communist Party and to Soviet society as a whole. The second part discusses arms control efforts between the superpowers, including historical background but emphasizing the period since Ronald Reagan became president.

PARTY FUNCTION
IN MILITARY POLICY

Many Westerners find it difficult to understand how the Soviet Union organizes and commands its armed forces because the system differs vastly from that of the United States and other Western nations. The Soviet Communist Party directs both the military and civilian sides of decision making. The top-level policy-making process works through a dual party-government structure, with the party always the final authority. In essence, the party formulates policy (military and civilian) and the government implements it. In the military realm, the Defense Council reviews policy drafts coming from government organizations involved with security issues (that is, the Ministry of Defense). These policies are then executed by the relevant government agencies.

Command Structure

There are three major bodies in the top Soviet command structure: the USSR Defense Council, the Defense Ministry Collegium, and the General Staff. These organizations constitute the Soviet High Command. There are other important, closely linked, organizations such as the Command and Staff of the Warsaw Pact Forces and the Military-Industrial Commission (which is formally outside the Ministry of Defense). In *The Armed Forces of the USSR*, Harriet Fast Scott and William F. Scott noted that as a group these bodies, especially the Defense Council, "have virtually complete control over the military-economic direction of the Soviet Union."

These high-level organizations always include party members, both civilian and military. This is true even in military bodies because, invariably, high-ranking officers are also party members who are responsive to both party and military orders.

Many ostensibly civilian issues directly influence defense. Even more so than in the United States, it is difficult to pinpoint where military policy diverges from domestic policy. For example, education policy and Russian-language training have direct bearing on the military, and civilian educational agencies work closely with Defense Ministry officials to carry out educational policies that have an impact on defense. The "initial military training" program required of predraft males is carried out by the Ministry of Education, the Ministry of Higher and Specialized Secondary Education, and the State Committee for Vocational and Technical Education. Officials from these agencies work closely with the Defense Ministry's Civilian Military Training Directorate on course syllabi and teaching aids.

Additionally, the Ministry of Defense is involved with civilian activities such as agriculture and construction.

The High Command

The Soviet High Command is the group of the highest-ranking officers who specifically direct military affairs. While the party surely has the final word on most military matters, that does not mean the officers have little control over the daily affairs of the services. As the Scotts noted, the Soviet High Command

represents one of the most experienced bodies of political-military leadership the world has ever seen. All of its members have proved themselves over the course of many years in positions of great responsibility. . . . Many of the senior members of the Soviet high command have been popularized as military leaders. . . . The top Soviet military leadership is much more visible than its counterpart in the United States. . . . [T]hey are closely integrated with the rest of the party, with those at the top wearing two hats: one, that of their military position; and the other, that of their membership on the Central Committee.

The High Command military officers include the minister of defense; three first deputy ministers of defense (who are chief of the General Staff, commander in chief of the Joint Armed Forces of the Warsaw Pact Nations, and usually a general affairs first deputy); several deputy ministers of defense (the commanders in chief of each of the five services, and commanders of several supporting branches such as rear services and armaments); the chief of the Main Political Administration of the Soviet Army and Navy; several commanders of important military districts (including Belorussian, Transbaikal, and Moscow); and a few other high-ranking deputy chiefs. In all, there are about two dozen men uppermost in the Soviet Military High Command. *(Table, p. 129)*

The military services saw numerous changes in 1984 and 1985, changes that initiated a rapid pace of high-level turnover. In September 1984 Chief of the General Staff Nikolai V. Ogarkov was abruptly transferred to "other responsible duties," according to Soviet announcements. In December, longtime defense minister Dmitri F. Ustinov, considered a legendary figure, died. He was replaced by Sergei L. Sokolov, an uncontroversial soldier with no apparent political ambition, during the last months of Konstantin Chernenko's regime.

Sokolov was promoted to candidate Politburo status in April 1985. While this meant a reduced role for the military on the Politburo (in comparison to full membership of recent past defense ministers), it nonetheless ensured continued military representation there. Ogarkov's replacement as chief of the General Staff by Marshal Sergei F. Akhromeev also appeared to smooth party-military relations. While both Akhromeev and Ogarkov were regarded as professionally quite able, they were contrasting personalities. Akhromeev, unlike the outspoken Ogarkov, maintained a remarkably low-key profile. Also unlike some of his predecessors, Akhromeev loyally submitted to party authority in "determining the broad lines of Soviet military doctrine and policy objectives," Robert Hutchinson noted in *Jane's Defense Weekly* October 26, 1985.

Additionally, the commanders of three services were replaced in 1985 and the duties and responsibilities of several high-ranking officers (such as Marshal Viktor G. Kulikov and Army Gen. Mikhail Zaitsev, as well as Marshal Ogarkov) became obscured, at least temporarily.

Defense Council

The most important political-military organization, the USSR Defense Council, illustrates the interconnecting nature of political-military organization and decision making and the supremacy of the party in that process. It also underscores the secretiveness of the Soviets, because Western observers have had to glean most of their information about the Defense Council piecemeal and through arduous efforts at Kremlinology.

Most historians trace the Defense Council to Lenin's Civil War Council of Workers' and Peasants' Defense (which was later named the Council of Labor and Defense, or STO). The more direct predecessor to the Defense Council, however, was the World War II State Committee of Defense, or GKO.

The German attack on the Soviet Union in June 1941 found the Soviet defense structure disastrously unprepared. Within a week Joseph Stalin formed the GKO and was its chairman. Stalin, Viacheslav Molotov, Kliment Voroshilov, Lavrentii Beria, and Georgii Malenkov were the original members. Nikolai Bulganin, Nikolai Voznesenskii, Lazar Kaganovich, and Anastas Mikoian were soon added. These men, in essence, were the war cabinet that ran the nation. The group "settled political and diplomatic questions," directed the entire war economy, "and made all major decisions on the conduct of the war," according to the Scotts. Each member had a special sphere of responsibility. Since the GKO had no administrative personnel or facilities of its own it used existing ones, primarily those of the General Staff. (Description below)

The GKO offered a centralization of control the Soviet leaders found imperative, and Soviet writings since World War II indicate that in a future war it would again have great, perhaps even greater, importance. It is not known whether the Defense Council would remain in its peacetime format or revert to one more similar to the GKO.

The peacetime Defense Council operates, in essence, as an elite subgroup of the Politburo, although it is formally part of the government structure. It determines the country's overall defense posture and ensures the country is prepared for war; that is, it is responsible for strategic military-economic planning. It examines programs to develop and procure new weapons systems and formulates plans to mobilize industry, transportation, and manpower. The Defense Council defines the missions of each of the five services and can create new military districts or change the entire structure of the armed forces.

The Defense Council is responsible for examining proposals from the Ministry of Defense Collegium and the General Staff for both military development and armed forces development; the council makes judgments on those plans and issues decrees for the plans to be implemented. By comparing the structure and duties of defense councils in East European countries, some Western experts have concluded that the Soviet Defense Council also coordinates security activities of the KGB and the Ministry of Internal Affairs (MVD) and reviews key civil defense matters.

In a 1982 account edited by, among others, Boris Ponomarev (then a candidate Politburo member and head of the Central Committee International Information Department), the Defense Council was described as an "organ of political, economic and military leadership" that plays "a most important role in mobilizing all means for maintenance of armed forces combat readiness and ensuring that they have all that is necessary."

It is assumed that the Defense Council presents its recommendations to the Politburo. The council may act on all manner of questions because there is no formal line of

Sergei F. Akhromeev, left, replaced Nikolai V. Ogarkov as chief of the General Staff.

demarcation separating civilian and military issues. There are no published legal parameters guiding the council's membership or authority.

Both civilian and military party members serve on the Defense Council, but there is no evidence of any formal requirements for membership distribution. For example, even though Defense Minister Sergei Sokolov is only a candidate Politburo member, he is likely a member of the council by virtue of his Defense Ministry post. Membership descriptions are only speculative because the Soviets have never published a list as such. The Defense Council itself was not publicly acknowledged until 1976, when *Pravda* noted Leonid Brezhnev as its chairman. Since then, other party general secretaries, including Mikhail Gorbachev, have been publicly pronounced as council chairmen but no other members have been overtly noted.

If it is correct that the council's composition is like that of East European defense councils, this would indicate that members in addition to the general secretary are the defense minister, chairman of the Council of Ministers, chief of the General Staff, and foreign minister. According to Soviet expert Ellen Jones, it is also reasonable to assume that the Central Committee secretaries responsible for national security and the senior Central Committee secretary involved in foreign policy are also members. Jones suggests the head of the Military-Industrial Commission may also be a member. Other individuals are brought in as occasion warrants to give specialized information.

Besides speeches, media statements, and presumed job descriptions, obituary signatures and attendance at military-related occasions have been studied by Kremlinologists to determine council membership. (Top-level officials usually sign obituaries in order according to rank.)

These considerations suggest that the current USSR Defense Council includes several key officials who have been promoted since Mikhail S. Gorbachev assumed the top party post. Egor Ligachev, the secretary in charge of ideology and considered to be the "second secretary" after Gorbachev, is almost certainly a member; and Lev Zaikov, named to the Politburo after the 1986 Party Congress, probably also became a member because of his Central Committee Secretariat defense portfolio. If the presumption is correct that the premier is included, then Nikolai Ryzhkov is also a member.

With Gorbachev's succession, Western experts looked for, but did not necessarily expect, a possible change in political-military relations. Many believed the Defense Council would give higher priority to economic concerns, reflecting Gorbachev's personal ranking of Soviet needs. It will be some time, however, before evidence shows whether Gorbachev's emphasis on economics will cause the Defense Council to usher in significant changes in levels of military funding. And by early 1986 there had been few outward signs of displeasure from the military concerning Gorbachev's actions toward them.

Because he was too young at the time, Gorbachev did not serve in the Great Patriotic War (World War II) in a military or civilian capacity and he has not developed any longstanding ties to the military. But according to Hutchinson of *Jane's Defense Weekly*:

> As a rising Party figure since the early 1960s, Gorbachev will have learnt something of the checks and balances, and the political in-fighting, which shape Party-military relations at all levels. He will, therefore, be in a position to choose men of ability, and of proven technical competence, rather than merely distributing political patronages, in the tradition of Stalin, Khrushchev, and Brezhnev.

But by not promoting Sokolov to full Politburo status, and promoting Akhromeev and other younger men, Gorbachev has asserted his authority over the military and has seemingly ensured that the military will not step out of line for the time being.

Ministry of Defense Collegium

The highest body of the Ministry of Defense is the Collegium. The minister of defense, currently Sergei Sokolov, chairs this advisory group. The defense minister has powers roughly comparable to those of the chairman of the U.S. Joint Chiefs of Staff and the secretary of defense combined.

Other Collegium members include the three first deputy ministers of defense; the head of the Main Political Administration of the Soviet Army and Navy (MPA), Col. Gen. Aleksei Lizichev; the five service commanders; the chief of the General Staff, Sergei Akhromeev; the commander in chief of the Joint Armed Forces of the Warsaw Pact Nations, currently Marshal Kulikov; and various other deputy ministers and branch chiefs.

The Collegium is concerned with problems of the strategic direction and leadership of the armed forces in time of peace. The Collegium resolves professional issues such as interservice rivalries over missions and funds. According to Soviet sources cited in Ellen Jones's *Red Army and Society*, the Collegium "works out solutions to problems relating to the development of the armed forces, their combat and mobilization readiness, the status of combat and political training, selection, placement, and indoctrination of military personnel, and other important issues."

The power and influence of the military leaders are more circumscribed than those of the political leadership. But because the Collegium "frames various proposals that pass through the Defense Council and then to the Politburo," the Collegium "also has a major role in resolving just how the latter's decisions will be implemented," David R. Jones of Dalhousie University noted in *The Soviet Union Today: An Interpretive Guide*.

The Soviets indicate that during war the Collegium would be replaced by Stavka (Headquarters of the Su-

preme High Command), the senior military command that operated during World War II. Stavka assessed and directed all wartime military actions.

As with the wartime GKO, Stavka was not a large organization. There were fewer than a dozen staff members at any one time. Specialists were called in to advise on specific subjects. Stavka could remain small but effective because it could draw on the services of the General Staff. Stavka was abolished after the war and the Collegium eventually reemerged.

During World War II, Stalin had strict, direct control over the entire country and war operations. He was commissar of defense and headed both the GKO and Stavka; he was supreme commander in chief, party general secretary, and head of the government. This provided unity of leadership to the highest degree — politically, economically, and militarily. The late respected Soviet military theorist and strategist, Gen. Vasilii Sokolovskii, said leadership direction in a future war would again be by Stavka to help ensure tight central direction.

General Staff

The General Staff is the largest body in the Soviet High Command. The Soviets have stated that in a future war the "General Staff will be the main agency of the Stavka of Supreme High Command." The United States has no equivalent organization. The General Staff is immediately subordinate to the Defense Minister and, according to the Scotts, "is a major link in the extreme centralization of authority that is characteristic of all activity in the Soviet Union."

The General Staff originated in the early days of Bolshevik rule. Soon after World War II broke out, the General Staff began functioning as Stavka's executive agency. Stalin, as commander in chief and chairman of Stavka, was the only one permitted to give orders to the General Staff. The Staff communicated with Moscow directly from the fronts by telephone or telegraph, and reported daily to Stalin.

Certain of the General Staff's directorates (or divisions) performed tasks unanticipated before the war. For example, war plans assumed that fighting would take place on enemy territory. Detailed maps of the Soviet interior were unavailable. Citing information disclosed in a book by Soviet World War II general S. E. Shtemenko (chief of the General Staff 1948-52), the Scotts wrote: "When forced to fall back toward Moscow, Soviet troops urgently needed maps of their own country. In the first six months of the war, 1.5 million square kilometers had to be resurveyed to provide the required maps."

Strategic Planning. In the 1970s and 1980s the General Staff has been responsible for basic strategic planning. It determines the roles for each of the services (probably in draft form sent to the Defense Council for approval). According to Soviet publications, one of its major tasks is to ensure "the coordinated actions of the main staffs of the services." This includes the staffs of the rear services, civil defense, Ministry of Defense administrations, staffs of military districts, groups abroad, air defense districts, and naval fleets. Because of this coordination responsibility, the services and branches of the armed forces are subordinate to the Ministry of Defense through the General Staff.

Some compare the General Staff to the Pentagon's Joint Staff, but the General Staff's functions are much broader. The General Staff's activities encompass "the

Soviet Military High Command

(March 1986)

Position	Name and Rank
Minister of Defense	Marshal of the Soviet Union Sergei L. Sokolov
First Deputy Minister of Defense, Chief of the General Staff	Marshal of the Soviet Union Sergei F. Akhromeev
First Deputy Minister of Defense, Commander in Chief of Joint Armed Forces of Warsaw Pact Nations	Marshal of the Soviet Union Viktor G. Kulikov
Chief of the Main Political Administration of the Soviet Army and Navy	Col. Gen. Aleksei D. Lizichev
First Deputy Minister of Defense	Marshal of the Soviet Union Vasilii I. Petrov
Deputy Minister of Defense, Commander in Chief of Strategic Rocket Forces	Army Gen. Iurii P. Maksimov
Deputy Minister of Defense, Commander in Chief of Ground Forces	Army Gen. Evgeny F. Ivanovskii
Deputy Minister of Defense, Commander in Chief of Air Forces	Marshal of Aviation Aleksandr N. Efimov
Deputy Minister of Defense, Commander in Chief of Air Defense	Chief Marshal of Aviation Aleksandr I. Koldunov
Deputy Minister of Defense, Commander in Chief of Navy	Admiral of the Fleet Vladimir N. Chernavin
Deputy Minister of Defense, Chief Inspector of the Main Inspectorate	Army Gen. Vladimir L. Govorov
Deputy Minister of Defense, Chief of Rear Services	Marshal of the Soviet Union Semen K. Kurkotkin
Deputy Minister of Defense for Armaments	Army Gen. Vitalii M. Shabanov
Deputy Minister of Defense, Chief of Civil Defense	Army Gen. Aleksandr T. Altunin
Deputy Minister of Defense, Construction and Quartering	Marshal of Engineer Troops Nikolai F. Shestopalov
Deputy Minister of Defense, Cadres	Army Gen. Ivan N. Shkadov
Commander in Chief, Western Theater of Military Operations	Marshal of the Soviet Union Nikolai V. Ogarkov
Commander in Chief, Southern Theater of Military Operations	Army Gen. Mikhail M. Zaitsev
Commander in Chief of Troops of the Far East	Army Gen. Ivan M. Tret'yak
Commander in Chief, Southwestern Theater of Military Operations	Army Gen. Ivan A. Gerasimov
Commander in Chief Group of Soviet Forces, Germany	Army Gen. Petr G. Lushev
Commander, Belorussian Military District	Army Lt. Gen. V. M. Shuralov
Commander, Far East Military District	Army Gen. Dmitri T. Yazov
Commander, Moscow Military District	Army Col. Gen. Vladimir M. Arkhipov
Commander, Transbaikal Military District	Army Col. Gen. Stanislav I. Postnikov

These officers are listed in the generally assumed, but not necessarily authoritative, order of rank and prestige.

Soviet Spetsnaz

Military intelligence in the Soviet Union is controlled by the Main Intelligence Directorate of the Soviet General Staff, or GRU. One GRU department, the Third *Spetsiale Razuedka* or Department of Special Reconnaissance (Spetsnaz), is responsible for carrying out sensitive missions abroad, including assassination and sabotage. Conservative estimates put the size of Spetsnaz forces at about 30,000.

A joint KGB/Spetsnaz force allegedly carried out the killing of Afghan president Hafizullah Amin in December 1979, and Spetsnaz forces under the KGB operated during the 1968 Czechoslovakian invasion.

In peacetime the GRU coordinates reconnaissance programs to provide the intelligence that would be needed in case of war. During a war or crisis Spetsnaz forces are to assassinate political and military leaders, destroy communication and supply lines, and conduct other terrorist operations, according to Jeffrey Richelson, an intelligence specialist. Spetsnaz troops would destroy enemy nuclear facilities or locate them for Soviet aircraft and missiles to attack. Other possible targets would include airfields, naval bases, power stations, and oil and gas storage facilities.

Under Central Committee guidance the KGB coordinates and controls peacetime Spetsnaz missions, but during war the forces apparently would remain under General Staff direction. Spetsnaz forces would operate deep behind enemy lines. They are organized into brigades but would infiltrate and fight as small teams.

Some Spetsnaz forces are attached to the Soviet Navy. According to the Pentagon's *Soviet Military Power*, a brigade-sized unit is attached to each fleet and is trained in parachuting, scuba diving, demolition, sabotage, surveillance, target selection, and languages such as French and English.

possibility of creating automatic systems to direct weapons and troops from a central location. One relatively less sophisticated aspect of cybernetics is the automated battlefield. Theoretically, cybernetics could create a single automated system of planning and command that would allow the General Staff to directly control operations of both theater and strategic forces, obviously a quantum jump in centralization of control.

Although General Staff members come from different services, their promotions depend on work done on the staff and attention to party duties, not on how well they represent service interests. Most General Staff slots are nomenklatura positions. *(Definitions, p. 5)* Key positions go only to graduates of the two-year Voroshilov Academy of the General Staff, the nation's highest professional military school.

Military Intelligence. One of the General Staff's 11 departments, the GRU, is the intelligence branch of the armed forces. Several directorates within GRU cover various types of intelligence collection, including "gathering of open source data, clandestine human collection, satellite and aircraft photographic reconnaissance, and signals intelligence collection," according to Jeffrey Richelson in *Sword and Shield: Soviet Intelligence and Security Apparatus.*

Four directorates are designated by geographical boundaries: Europe and Morocco; North and South America, Australia, New Zealand, United Kingdom; Asia; and Africa. These directorates all conduct human intelligence and report directly to the GRU's first deputy chief, as do the Operational Intelligence Directorate and the Radio, Radio-Technical Intelligence Directorate. The Operational Directorate does not conduct human intelligence itself but directs the activities of the 16 military districts, the 4 groups of forces abroad, and fleet intelligence directorates, according to Richelson.

Four other directorates that report to the first deputy chief are: Moscow; East and West Berlin; National Liberation Movements, Terrorism; Operations from Cuba. Each of these "directions" or branches conducts human intelligence.

The GRU's chief of information has under his control several other directorates, including NATO; Technology; Economics; and Doctrine, Weapons.

Reporting directly to the chief of the GRU, Petr Ivanovich Ivashutin, are directorates and departments such as: Space (or Cosmic) Intelligence; Personnel, and Foreign Relations directorates; Political, Financial, and "Eighth" departments. The Eighth Department "enciphers and deciphers all documents passing into or out of the GRU," according to Richelson.

Military Industrial Committee

The Military Industrial Committee (VPK) is another example of interlocking military and civilian organizations. The VPK is formally part of the Presidium of the Council of Ministers and not part of the High Command. It is, however, an important organization.

A deputy chairman of the Council of Ministers heads the VPK and other members probably include top executives from "the various ministries of defense industry, from the State Planning Commission (Gosplan), from the party, and from the Ministry of Defense and its General Staff," according to David Jones.

The VPK ensures that industrial ministries fulfill the

work of most of the entire Department of Defense in the Pentagon, some of the work of the National Security Council, plus a great many of the activities of the departments of the army, navy, and air force," according to the Scotts.

The General Staff has 11 directorates, according to experts Jeffrey Richelson and Viktor Suvorov: Operations, Intelligence (GRU), Organization-Mobilization, Military Science, Communications, Topography, Armaments, Cryptography, Strategic Deception, Military Assistance (abroad), and Warsaw Pact. The three most important are Operations, Intelligence, and Organization-Mobilization.

Another important General Staff function is the science of cybernetics, the comparative study of complex computers and the human nervous system. This holds out the

Defense Council's plans for production and delivery of arms and that there are sufficient resources to meet those production plans. Consequently, the VPK is a critical link between the military and the industries that serve it.

Although coordinating the overall Soviet effort to acquire Western technology is not the VPK's main mission, it is the part Western experts know most about. According to the Pentagon's *Soviet Military Power, 1985,* the VPK is the "most powerful organization in the defense-research establishment."

Work done for the VPK in its role as a collector of technology for military applications is carried out mostly, but not exclusively, through intelligence channels. Working with the VPK in this regard are, besides the KGB (through its foreign intelligence Directorate T), the military intelligence organization (the Chief Intelligence Directorate of the Soviet General Staff, or GRU, and its counterparts in the Eastern-bloc countries), other national-level organizations such as the Academy of Sciences, Ministry of Foreign Trade, State Committee for Foreign Economic Relations, and the State Committee for Science and Technology.

In France in 1984, for example, the newspaper *Le Monde* published names and types of information acquired from Western sources that apparently came about under VPK auspices. The French government had obtained the information two years earlier and, based on it, expelled 47 Soviet diplomats accused of espionage. The captured documents disclosed that the Soviet Ministry of Aviation Industry's use of Western technology had saved the Soviet Union about $56.5 million in 1979 alone.

General Secretary Gorbachev has expressed dismay over the Soviet failure to develop a computer and electronics industry to supply military needs. The VPK apparently has been held partly to blame for developing a detrimental dependency on Western products (such as mainframe computers) that Gorbachev wants to reduce.

Dzhermen Gvishiani, deputy chairman of the USSR State Committee for Science and Technology (the party's main political adviser on electronics and computing), was overhauling the VPK bureaucracy in the autumn of 1985, according to the October 19, 1985, issue of *Jane's Defense Weekly.* Yevgeny Velikov, the Politburo's main science and technology adviser and expert on the SDI, was guiding the VPK's policy overhaul.

Civil-Military Relations

The Soviet party-military structure in the mid-1980s was much the same as when it was established after the Revolution. The party ensured its control by an intricate web of organizations and individuals throughout all levels of the armed forces. But because high-ranking military officers are invariably also party members, most long-range military interests coincide with those of the civilian leaders. The level of civilian control does not noticeably concern the top military elite, according to Western experts. They work together toward common goals of maintaining party leadership and a strong, modern military; it is somewhat of a symbiotic relationship.

In the past high-ranking military officers, such as Leon Trotsky and Marshal Georgii K. Zhukov, have tried to preempt party leadership, but these failed attempts usually have worked only to reinforce the belief of the civilian leaders that strict control over the military must be maintained. Party-military disagreements surely exist over matters such as resource distribution, but Western analysts have not found that these represent anything more than normal organizational give and take. *(Zhukov, box, p. 132)*

Military Representation

Despite the party's final authority, interlocking party-military membership on prestigious organizations gives the military significant, wide-ranging influence and prestige. The minister of defense and most of his deputies are full Central Committee (CC) members, as are the chief of the MPA and the commanders of the theaters of military operations and a few key military districts. In 1978, 11 of 13 deputies were full members; in 1984, 12 of 14 deputies. At the 27th Party Congress in February 1986, 23 of the 307 full CC members "elected" were from the military. Of the 170 candidate members designated, 15 were military.

Following the Central Committee, the next most prestigious party assignment is to the Central Auditing Commission, which audits party funds. Several military officers historically have served on this body at any given time.

Service in the legislature, the Supreme Soviet, also carries some prestige. Deputies are elected (chosen) for five-year terms. The minister of defense, most deputy ministers of defense, and commanders of forces abroad, military districts, and fleets are automatically elected, as are the MPA chief, his first deputy, and certain other service chiefs. In addition to the Supreme Soviet of the USSR, there are supreme soviets for each of the republics and autonomous republics and military officers serve on all of them.

To a degree, selection to the party congresses held about every five years also confers political-military status. Military delegates form a substantial bloc at the congresses. At the 25th Congress in February 1976, estimated military representation was between 20 and 22 percent. Ten years later at the 27th Congress it was estimated at about the same percentage.

The civil and military sides of the party overlap at the republic or military district level and at even lower levels. Military district commanders may be members of the party executive committees at the union republic level. In reverse, the local party secretary is a member of the military council of his area's military district. Senior military officers often belong to city and oblast party committees. *(Definitions, p. 5)* The civilian and uniformed party members often support each other to obtain further promotions.

Military Councils of Armed Forces. The highest party-military organizations in the Ministry of Defense after the Ministry of Defense Collegium are the military councils of the five services. According to the Scotts, these councils serve as "corporate bodies" for troop control. The Central Committee, and apparently the Main Political Administration, approve the members in each service council. The chief of each service chairs his respective military council. Other members include the senior political worker for that service, the first secretary of the local party committee, as well as other first deputies and commanders.

"Military councils consider and take action on all aspects of military life and activity and are responsible to the Central Committee, the Soviet government, the Ministry of Defense, and 'military councils of higher order' for the state of and combat preparedness of the troops," according to the Scotts. Although these councils are described as colle-

The Party and Zhukov

When Joseph Stalin died in March 1953 Communist Party leaders were concerned that their control over the armed forces might lessen. To extend the party's influence, the Central Committee adopted a resolution in February 1956 requiring military political workers to "participate in and criticize military training," according to Soviet military specialists Harriet Fast Scott and William F. Scott. The resolution said the political officer would now have to combine political and morale concerns with responsibility for the military's combat readiness.

One year later, the Central Committee issued new "Instructions" (formal directives) to armed forces party organizations. These instructions, discussed in the Secretariat, the Presidium (Politburo), and even by a special commission that included party stalwarts Leonid Brezhnev and Mikhail Suslov, confirmed the role of the Main Political Administration of the Soviet Army and Navy (MPA) as the principal agency for party work in the military. The instructions reiterated the MPA's rights as a Central Committee department. (Instructions had been issued only four times in the past, none while Stalin directed the country.) Consequently, the Scotts noted, the 1956 resolution and the 1957 instructions "established a major Party voice in purely military matters."

Marshal Georgii K. Zhukov, who had been named minister of defense in 1955 and promoted from candidate to full Presidium status in June 1957, quietly objected to the interjection of party workers. He felt combat readiness was the exclusive prerogative of the military. In the Scotts' words: "Zhukov wanted to make the professional military officer preeminent in military matters and to restrict the political officers to a minor role. His effort to achieve this was one of the reasons he was removed from office."

Zhukov's opponents accused him of eliminating one-third of the armed forces' political agencies "without any reason," of "drastically reduc[ing]" the number of military-political students, and of preventing the promotions of party workers in the military. Zhukov had taken several steps to limit the political workers' influence. He declared that only a few needed higher educations (which would reduce prestige for the job), and that they could advance only as far as the rank of colonel.

In all likelihood many of the accusations against Zhukov were unfounded. But with his removal in October 1957 the party quickly reestablished control and worked to ensure that it would remain that way. The Soviet military remains subject to party dictates.

gial, discussing and resolving issues by majority vote, it is likely that the councils are mainly deliberative, according to David Jones, "since the commander-in-chief's position easily allows him to achieve a consensus."

Party and Komsomol Organizations. Each service has its own political (party) administration headed by that service's deputy commander for political affairs. The Soviets attempt to portray this individual as a well-trained combat officer as well as a political authority. Each military district, air defense command, and fleet also has a political administration.

The Soviets describe the military's party and Komsomol (Communist Youth League) organizations as among the "most militant detachments of the CPSU." Besides troop combat readiness, party organizations are charged with ensuring that "Communists play the leading role in the sphere of training and service and influence all aspects of life and activity in the unit."

According to the Scotts, one of the main reasons universal military service is required in the USSR may be "to ensure that almost all males receive a firm indoctrination in party affairs." Most conscriptees are in the 14-to-28 age group for Komsomol membership and relatively few resist the intense pressure to join. According to Soviet figures from the 1970s, 80 percent of all nonofficer personnel and 20 percent of the officers are members of the Komsomol. (It is possible to belong to the party and Komsomol at the same time.)

Main Political Administration

The Main Political Administration of the Soviet Army and Navy is the key party-military organization. Besides being part of the Ministry of Defense, the MPA has the legal authority of a Central Committee department, which underscores its importance. Maintaining the ideological purity of the armed forces is the MPA's most important work.

The MPA's highest body is the Bureau of the MPA, about which little is known. Col. Gen. Aleksei D. Lizichev, 57, has headed the MPA since July 1985. Lizichev had held a number of key posts, including some in the Transbaikal Military District in the 1970s when there were considerable Sino-Soviet border problems. He later served (1982-85) as chief of the political administration for the Group of Soviet Forces, Germany.

In addition to Lizichev, leading MPA officials include his assistant chief for Komsomol affairs, the secretary of the Party Commission, the head of the Party-Organization Administration, and the head of the Directorate for Agitation and Propaganda.

General of the Army Aleksei A. Epishev headed the MPA from 1962 until July 1985, shortly before he died at age 77. Epishev had served previously as ambassador to Romania and as a deputy to KGB chief Lavrentii Beria. "His place in the inner circles of the party-military leadership hierarchy appears firmly established. Since at least the early 1960s, [E]pishev has ranked number four in precedence among the Soviet military leaders," the Scotts noted in 1984. It is presumed that Lizichev will retain that prominence. The choice of Lizichev likely indicated Gorbachev's determination to improve overall political indoctrination in the face of a better educated population that is increasingly exposed to Western influence. "It is indeed on the ideological warfare front that both the Party and professional military see the greatest threat to the

Soviet Union in the decade ahead," David Jones commented in late 1983.

Both the minister of defense and the head of the MPA sign basic directives on party-political work. The MPA reports on troop conditions to the Ministry of Defense; directs the military's political, party, and Komsomol organizations; and works to improve troop combat readiness, discipline, and morale. According to Ellen Jones, the MPA "is responsible for directing political socialization, maintaining high morale and discipline, administering cultural and recreational programs, and managing the military's party and Komsomol organizations."

Throughout the military, MPA activities are run by political officers or *zampolit*. Political officers regularly instruct all personnel in Marxism-Leninism. "The contemporary Soviet political officer is part-personnel officer, part-educational or orientation officer, part-socializing agent, and part-chaplain," according to Ellen Jones's description.

The MPA supervises the entire military educational system. Even though it has its own higher education institutes to train future political officers (one for each service), there is a consistent shortage of graduates, according to the Scotts.

The MPA is in charge of all military publications, including Voyenizdat, the Military Publishing House. The MPA has its own party political journal, the *Kommunist vooruzhennykh sil* (Communist of the Armed Forces), as well as publications for the various services. (The daily military newspaper *Kraznaya Zvezda*, or Red Star, is part of the Ministry of Defense; the classified Military Thought is the journal of the General Staff. Both exist only under the strict guidance of the party.) The MPA also has a hand in approving memberships for the various military councils of the five services.

SOVIET SERVICES: A UNIQUE SYSTEM

As with the party-military relationship, the organization of the Soviet armed forces is unlike any other nation's. The Soviet "revolution in military affairs" that began in the 1950s initiated organizational changes that appear to have given the Soviets a more flexible force structure and one more amenable to future war needs. According to the 1983 Soviet *Military Encyclopedic Dictionary*:

> The Armed Forces of the USSR are divided into services: Strategic Rocket Forces (RVSN), Ground Forces (SV), Troops of Air Defense (Voyska PVO), Air Forces (VVS), and Navy (VMF) and also includes the Rear Services of the Armed Forces (Tyl VS), staffs and troops of Civil Defense (GO).... Border Guards and Internal Troops are also part of the Armed Forces USSR.

The Ministry of Defense directly controls the troops of the five services, supporting rear services, and civil defense. Each commander in chief of the five services is a deputy minister of defense.

Border Troops are under the Committee of State Security (KGB) and Internal Troops under the Ministry of Internal Affairs (MVD). Construction and Billeting Troops, Troops of the Tyl, and Troops of Civil Defense are headed by deputy ministers of defense and are not part of any service, according to the Scotts. There are also special engineer, chemical, signal, railroad, and road troops that provide support for each service.

There are no U.S. equivalents of the Border Guards or MVD troops, which numbered approximately 230,000 and 360,000 respectively in 1984. These are generally the first and last military troops visitors to the Soviet Union see, as they collect passports and perform numerous border-control duties. Border Guards are armed with tanks, armored personnel carriers, and light infantry weapons. The many border skirmishes with the Chinese over the past few decades have involved Border Guards, not Ministry of Defense troops.

Overall, the strength of the Soviet armed forces — including the militarized security forces — was estimated at 5.42 million in 1984, according to John M. Collins in *U.S.-Soviet Military Balance 1980-1985*. Only about 10,000 were women. *(Conscription, box, p. 134)*

Nuclear War Planning. Soviet military planning emphasizes that the crucial initial phase of a nuclear war would determine the course of all later actions. Soviet war planners envision a nuclear war fought over vast territories without regular fronts. Thus taking the offensive is essential, with forces relying on mobility and maneuverability. The Soviets believe war could be won only through combined arms warfare, which means coordinating all the efforts of all military capabilities. Considerable efforts have been taken to improve combined, coordinated operations at all levels.

Theaters of Operations. The Soviets have devised large-scale theaters of military operations (TVDs) that would bring together under a single commander the various services and independent units to make most effective use of all forces and weapons. Three major theaters of war have been identified: Western, Southern, and Far Eastern. According to the Pentagon, the theaters have been further broken into TVDs, to include the Far Eastern, Northwestern, Arctic, Atlantic, Western, Southwestern, and Southern TVDs. During war, the TVDs could be combined into the three major theaters of war. Commanders of the four most important TVDs — Far Eastern, Western, Southwestern, and Southern — became full Central Committee members at the 27th Party Congress in 1986.

Military Districts. In peacetime, combat forces (other than the Strategic Rocket Forces and certain other air units) are deployed in 16 military districts, the four groups of forces abroad, and four fleets. *(Map, p. 138)*

Each district has its own commander, political administration, and units of various armed services (including ground, air, and air defense units). District commanders report to the General Staff; the districts are not controlled by any of the five services. The districts vary in importance and are maintained at differing levels of combat readiness. In wartime, they could operate independently if communications were severely disrupted. In peacetime, the districts serve largely as "training and housekeeping components" of the armed forces, according to the Scotts.

Training. As part of the combined arms concept, Soviet military forces are trained and equipped to fight under any contingency — nuclear or conventional; under bacteriologic, chemical, or other environments. During war the five Soviet services would be unified under the General

Conscription: A Fact of Life

The Soviet military is based largely on conscription. Only a small permanent cadre of officers is maintained. The draft provides a steady flow of noncareer personnel for the cadre to train and lead.

For boys, "military-patriotic" training begins in grade school and continues through high school. Girls receive some paramilitary training, although it usually is limited to first aid and political indoctrination. Boys take a 140-hour "Initial Military Training Program." Some predraft males are also assigned to military specialist courses in subjects such as driving, radio-technical communications, and mechanics.

Seventeen-year-old males must register for the draft. At age 18 they begin their two-year mandatory service period. (Navy recruits serve three years.) Few males are exempt; there is no conscientious objector status.

According to Mikhail Tsypkin's article in *The Soviet Union Today: An Interpretive Guide*, "It is only the offspring of the privileged strata in Soviet society who are very reluctant to be drafted, and who literally scramble for college admissions and attendant draft exemptions."

Conscription has been successful in instilling the notion that military service is a part of life, Tyspkin noted.

Besides being useful for political socialization, conscription provides abundant cheap and adaptable labor for priority projects such as the Baikal-Amur Railroad and the Moscow Olympic Village.

Isolation Policy

Draftees are usually sent far from home, both of necessity and because the isolation makes their control easier. This is especially important during civil unrest, when a soldier may be reluctant to threaten his friends and neighbors. Troops stationed in the Warsaw Pact countries are particularly isolated.

Like most Soviet citizens, Soviet conscripts are denied access to Western publications or broadcasts. Their radios are available only on Sundays and holidays. Television sets in barracks of soldiers in East Germany cannot pick up West German programs.

Isolation makes it possible for military commanders to keep troops unaware of or misinformed about their missions or even whereabouts. In Afghanistan, for example, servicemen were told they would be fighting American and Chinese agents. Some participants in the 1968 invasion of Czechoslovakia thought they were in West Germany.

Ethnic diversity makes managing the armed forces difficult. Slavs comprised about 69 percent and Moslems about 18 percent of the draft pool in the mid-1970s. By the mid-1980s the Moslem proportion had climbed to about 24 percent. Some of these conscripts spoke very little Russian, the military's official language.

Conscripts face busy class schedules and exercises in training and strict discipline (with many types of punishment) their entire term of duty. Training is usually by repetition and is characterized by narrow specialization and compartmentalization. According to Tsypkin, the unofficial armed forces motto is: "If you can't do something, we'll teach you; if you don't want to do something, we'll make you."

The two most common discipline violations — going absent without leave (AWOL) or getting drunk — are not believed to affect overall readiness or combat capabilities. Obtaining alcohol requires circumventing rules because liquor stores cannot sell to conscripts, who must be in uniform at all times. Going AWOL is not easy because draftees must hand in internal passports (required of all Soviet citizens) and their civilian clothing is sent home.

Women in Military

The peacetime role of women in the Soviet armed forces is extremely limited. Out of an active force exceeding 5 million in 1986, only about 10,000 were women, according to Soviet military specialist Ellen Jones. But unlike females in most Western countries, Soviet women served in many combat and noncombat roles during World War II.

Nadezhda Durova, a writer and heroine of the 1812 war against Napoleon, was her country's first female officer. She dressed as a man to join a cavalry regiment. According to Jones, Russian women served as nurses in the Crimean War (1853-56) and World War I. Nearly 2,000 women volunteered to form a "Woman's Battalion of Death" in late 1917, but this was an isolated case.

Some of the 66,000 women who served in the Red Army during the Civil War were commanders or political workers, but most were medical, administrative, or communications workers.

During World War II female participation was wider, totaling about 800,000, but again it was largely in support capacities. Many women were traffic controllers, intelligence personnel, and prisoner of war interrogators.

Among women who fought in combat units, according to Jones, many served in bomber regiments and other "special female combat formations." Women also served as "snipers, machine-gunners, and tank crew members" and "were especially prominent in the PVO [air defense] forces...."

Jones noted that the Soviets were in a "far more desperate military situation" than the Western nations in World War II and had more reason to use women in combat roles.

Staff. Steady modernization efforts since the mid-1960s have resulted in reorganized, larger, and better-equipped forces. Nonetheless, Western experts question the ability of conscripted Soviet forces to operate effectively under chaotic wartime conditions. *(Conscription, box, p. 134)*

Strategic Rocket Forces

The Strategic Rocket Forces (RVSN) have since their inception in 1959 been referred to as the "primary service." Their commander in chief takes precedence over commanders of other services; their personnel represent the elite of the services. These forces "are the youngest and most formidable service of the Armed Forces, and compose the basis of the defensive might of our Motherland and are troops of instant combat readiness," the authoritative Soviet *Officer's Handbook* reported. According to Collins's figures, the Strategic Rocket Forces had 322,000 active duty personnel in 1984.

The commander in chief of the Strategic Rocket Forces, Army Gen. Yuri Pavlovich Maksimov, 61, was appointed in July 1985 after Chief Marshal of Artillery Vladimir Fedorovich Tolubko, 71, retired. Tolubko had headed the service since 1972. Maksimov, a senior ground forces officer, rose quickly during the 1970s to command of the Turkestan Military District, a postion he held from 1979 to 1984. Most of the soldiers posted in Afghanistan are apparently trained in the Turkestan District. Like several recently promoted high-ranking officers, Maksimov benefited from his role in the Afghanistan fighting.

Security regarding the Strategic Rocket Forces is so strict the personnel wear the insignia of other forces and are not identified, except for a few senior staff members.

All land-based missiles with ranges exceeding 1,000 kilometers are assigned to this service. Many are not intercontinental ballistic missiles (ICBMs) but are designed to strike Western Europe, the Middle East, and China, the Scotts reported.

Mission. The service's mission has never been clearly explained, but according to a Soviet publication cited by the Scotts the Strategic Rocket Forces are

> the basis of the defense might of the Soviet army and navy.... Strategic Rocket Forces are designated for performing strategic tasks in nuclear war. They are the main and decisive means of achieving the goals of war since they can solve in the shortest period of time the tasks of demolishing the military economic potential of an aggressor, of destroying his strategic means of nuclear missile attack, and of crushing the main [military] groupings.

According to the Pentagon's 1985 edition of *Soviet Military Power*, Strategic Rocket Forces personnel are combat ready at all times and are "regularly trained for the contingencies of preemption, launch-on-tactical warning, or a second strike attack."

An example of the particular secrecy surrounding the Strategic Rocket Forces is seen during arms control negotiations, when the Soviets provide almost no data on their weapons systems. Instead, the United States provides the information. Western negotiators tell their Soviet counterparts how many missiles or types of weapons systems they believe the Soviets possess. If the Soviets do not agree, another figure is given until there is mutual agreement.

Since there is no on-site inspection of Soviet missiles, "national technical means of inspection" (generally, satellite photography) provide most arms control data. The Soviet press openly discusses the advantage this gives, particularly with easily concealed mobile launchers in their vast country. Concern increased in the mid-1980s over development and deployment of the SS-X-24 and SS-X-25 missiles. The United States said the missiles, which could be based in silos or used as mobile missiles, were new; the Soviets said they were modified versions of older missiles. If new, their deployment in the mid-1980s violated SALT II. *(Arms control section, p. 142)*

Space Program. The Strategic Rocket Forces play a major role in the Soviet space program (although the Air Forces apparently have a larger one). Numerous space launchings have improved missile reliability. Because the Soviets try to integrate all types of forces, space is included as part of an overall theater of military operations. According to the Pentagon, space efforts have played a major role in areas such as "antisatellite warfare; intelligence collection; command, control, and communications; meteorological support; navigational support; and targeting." In 1984 a new Soviet auxiliary ship (or AGI), the *Nedelin*, joined several other space and missile support ships. *(Space program, box, p. 137)*

Ground Forces

Until the nuclear age, the Ground Forces were the most important of the services; now they are second. The Ground Forces are still the largest, with just over 3 million personnel in 1984, and many ground force officers are in the upper echelons of the High Command.

Except for troops stationed abroad, all Ground Forces troops are administered by the 16 military districts. Organizational changes in the late 1970s and early 1980s have left the West without a clear picture of the Ground Forces' current structure. The changes apparently were designed at least in part to ensure offensive capability in Eurasian theaters. Considerable modernization has been complemented by improved training, command and control operations, and by employing "innovative operational concepts and tactics," such as the TVDs, according to the Pentagon.

In early 1985 Army Gen. Evgeny F. Ivanovskii replaced Marshal Vasilii I. Petrov as commander in chief of the Ground Forces. Petrov replaced Sokolov as a first deputy minister of defense (in effect becoming the defense minister's senior deputy) in late December 1984.

Ivanovskii, 68, held a number of key ground forces commands, including commanding the Moscow Military District (1968-72), and the Group of Forces, Germany, for eight years until 1980.

The commander in chief of the Joint Armed Forces of Warsaw Pact Nations in 1985 was Viktor G. Kulikov. Soviet Ground Forces in Eastern Europe are divided into four groups, one each in East Germany, Poland, Czechoslovakia, and Hungary. The Group of Soviet Forces, Germany, is the most important individual group of forces abroad.

In July 1985 Army Gen. Mikhail Zaitsev, who replaced Ivanovskii as commander in chief of the group, was in turn succeeded by the fast-rising Gen. Petr Lushev. Zaitsev became commander in chief of the Southern TVD, which includes Afghanistan.

The Soviet Union's Efforts in Space . . .

The Soviet Union opened the space age in 1957 with the launching of Sputnik — the first man-made satellite. Since then Soviet space efforts have continued in what some Western experts call characteristic Soviet fashion: persistence despite mixed results.

The Soviets have had considerable success with their manned space program, which aims to establish the first permanently manned space station, and with planetary exploration. Their record has been spottier with weather, communications, military, and scientific satellites.

Military needs dominate the Soviet space program. According to the Pentagon's 1985 *Soviet Military Power*, 80 percent of all 1984-85 Soviet space launches were purely military, and much of the remaining 20 percent served dual civilian-military purposes.

Surveillance Satellites

Satellites are used to collect five types of intelligence: "imagery, signals intelligence, ocean surveillance, space surveillance, and nuclear detection," according to Jeffrey Richelson in *Sword and Shield: Soviet Intelligence and Security Apparatus.*

Imagery. Soviet spaceborne imagery (photographs and "picturelike representations" from radar and infrared photography) began with the launching of Cosmos 4 in April 1962. According to Richelson, "photographic reconnaissance satellite launches accounted for 82 percent of all satellite launches for intelligence and early warning purposes" between 1962 and 1980 and make up the "largest single element" in the Soviet space program. Imagery can provide information about "war targets, troop deployments, military exercises," and can help monitor U.S. compliance with arms control agreements.

The shorter life spans of Soviet satellites compared with U.S. craft mean the Soviets must put up more in a crisis. But the Soviets have shown they can rapidly launch extra satellites, as during the 1968 Czechoslovakian crisis, the 1973 Middle East war, and the 1983 invasion of Grenada. And the newer photo reconnaissance spacecraft, first launched in 1984, have much longer operating lives.

The USSR has electronic intelligence (ELINT) satellites that can provide information on limitations of ground-based radars and perhaps the general locations of mobile radars.

Ocean Surveillance. Two types of Soviet satellites provide information on U.S./allied naval movements: EORSAT (ELINT Ocean Reconnaissance Satellite) and nuclear-powered RORSAT (Radar Ocean Reconnaissance Satellite). The Pentagon says the United States has no exact counterpart.

EORSATs intercept radar signals from U.S.

ships. RORSATs use their own radar to locate U.S. and allied ships at sea. According to Richelson, the United States has cited RORSATs as a "primary justification for the U.S. Anti-Satellite Program," because they can provide information that can be used "directly against U.S. naval forces."

After completing operations a RORSAT is moved into a higher orbit to wait out the half-life of the highly enriched uranium in its reactor. Two RORSATs failed to reach that higher orbit and eventually crashed to Earth. In 1978 one fell in a sparsely populated area of northern Canada, spreading radioactive debris. (The Soviets eventually paid half of the $6 million clean-up bill the Canadians submitted.) In 1982 the nuclear reactor core of the second burned up reentering the atmosphere but nuclear debris fell into the ocean. Problems with the ocean surveillance program in 1984-85 were confined to nonnuclear EORSATs that fell back to Earth, largely burning up on reentry.

Space Surveillance. To track their own or other space objects the Soviets have several optical devices, signal-shift measuring equipment, and large radars within their borders. Specially equipped surface ships extend their tracking and control network.

According to Richelson, "Any system that tracks strategic missiles also tracks space objects crossing Soviet territory or its near approaches." U.S. officials believed the Soviet radar discovered being built in 1983 at Abalakova (near Krasnoyarsk) was an ABM (antiballistic missile) radar. The Soviets maintained it was for space tracking. The United States claimed it violated the 1972 ABM Treaty because it was neither located on the Soviet periphery nor pointed outward as the treaty requires.

The Pentagon reported in 1985 that the Soviets had a "radar-carrying satellite system" that would map ice formations in polar regions. While the Soviets claim it is for oceanographic research and guiding commercial ships through the ice fields, the Pentagon claims these satellites "will greatly enhance the ability of the Soviet Navy to operate in icebound areas."

Lasers, Early Warning System

The Soviet Union has programs to develop space-based ballistic missile defenses and anti-satellite (ASAT) weapons. The Pentagon stated in 1985 that the Soviets could have prototypes of ground-based laser ASATs by the late 1980s. In 1976 Soviets began testing an antisatellite weapon that was described by Andrew Cockburn in *The Threat: Inside the Soviet Military Machine* as a satellite "designed to maneuver close to an enemy satellite and then explode." More than half the tests by early 1983 had failed, Cockburn reported in 1984.

... Persistence Yields Mixed Results

Particle-beam weapons (ground- and space-based) appear more difficult to develop than lasers but the Soviets also have had particle-beam space development programs under way since the early 1970s.

To supplement ground-based over-the-horizon and phased-array radars, the Soviets have an extensive network of ballistic missile early warning satellites to detect U.S. launches. The Pentagon reported that in 1985 the network could provide "about 30 minutes of warning of any U.S. ICBM launch" and could determine "the general area from which it originated."

Manned Space Program

The first man in orbit was Soviet cosmonaut Iurii Gagarin, in 1961. Since then cosmonauts have set several space endurance records. The current record was set in 1984 by three cosmonauts who spent 237 days aboard Salyut 7, launched in April 1982.

In the spring of 1984 Soviet cosmonauts performed significant on-orbit maintenance and repair of their space station through a series of Extra Vehicular Activities, or space walks, including the first space walk by a woman, Svetlana Savitskaia.

In early 1985 the power supply failed in the then-unmanned Salyut 7 space station and Soviet ground controllers lost contact with the craft. It had been left empty since the 237-day crew returned to the Soviet Union the previous October.

In June 1985 cosmonauts Vladimir Dzhanibekov and Viktor Savinykh piloted their Soyuz T-13 capsule to the ailing Salyut 7. Unable to use Salyut 7's automatic docking aids, they made an unprecedented manual rendezvous with the 47-ton craft. Dzhanibekov later likened the risky maneuver to guiding a truckload of china over ice and into a narrow gate.

The crew then worked 10 days under hazardous conditions to restore power, heat, water, and radio communications to the nearly frozen spacecraft. They eventually added solar panels and helped service a new kind of unmanned free-flying platform spacecraft that docked with the refurbished Salyut 7.

A three-man crew remained on board until November 21, 1985, when the commander became ill and all three cosmonauts returned home.

February and March 1986 saw two big steps for the Soviets' space program. On February 20, they launched the Mir (Russian for world or peace) space station designed to be the hub of a future permanently manned space complex. The Soviet news agency Tass described Mir as about the same size as Salyut 7 but with bigger solar panels, more advanced computers, and better living quarters. It will be bigger than Salyut 7 when all modules are added.

Six docking ports appeared to be Mir's most innovative feature. The ports would permit docking by transport ships as well as expansion of the craft with specialized free-flying modules outfitted for various missions.

Mir's first crew was sent up March 13 from Tyuratam in Central Asian Republic of Kazakhstan. Veteran cosmonauts Leonid Kizim and Vladimir Solovyov, who had been part of the Salyut 7 crew that set the 237-day endurance record, lifted off in the rare live televised launch.

The only other televised launches were the Soyuz mission that joined with the U.S. Apollo in 1975, a mission with a French cosmonaut aboard in 1982, and one with an Indian aboard in 1984. A joint Soviet-U.S. space agreement lapsed in 1982 and has not been renegotiated.

The Soviets admit to having lost five lives in their space efforts. One cosmonaut died in training in 1961; his death was confirmed only in 1986. Another died when his parachute did not operate properly upon reentry, and three cosmonauts died on another mission when their cabin depressurized. Nikita Khrushchev acknowledged in his memoirs a 1960 launch-pad explosion that allegedly killed dozens of people, but the Soviet press has never mentioned the so-called Nedelin accident.

Planetary Exploration

The Soviets have had considerable success with planetary and solar exploration. In December 1985 two Vega (a contraction of the Russian words for Venus and Halley) spacecraft dropped heavily instrumented landers and balloon-carried probes into the Venus atmosphere while on their way toward Halley's Comet.

The Vega I and Vega II provided extensive information about Halley's Comet, including the first detailed photographs of its icy nucleus in March 1986. The second craft passed within 5,000 miles of the nucleus while being battered by dust particles. The Vega mission was part of a multinational project that involved instruments and support from the United States and Europe and other spacecraft from Europe and Japan. Vega itself contained European experiments and used Western equipment.

The Soviets plan to make a complete mineralogical map of the moon, including its uncharted polar regions, when it sends a Lunar Polar Orbiter in 1989 or 1990. A project planned for 1988 is the Mars/Phobos mission, which would survey Mars and its two moons, Phobos and Deimos. The Soviets have invited Western and East European participation.

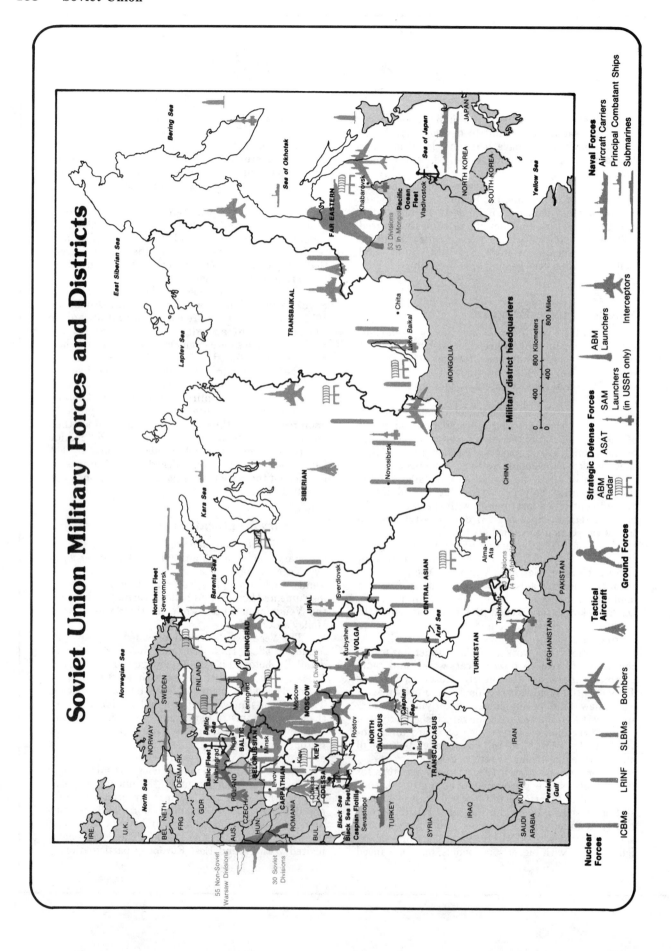

Soviet Union Military Forces and Districts

Lushev's successive promotions after helping Sokolov, then first deputy minister of defense, to plan the Afghanistan invasion have made him a powerful officer. In late 1980 he became commander of the Moscow Military District before replacing Zaitsev.

In the 1970s Soviet sources said the Ground Forces were divided into four basic combat branches: motorized rifle troops, tank troops, rocket troops and artillery, and troops of air defense (PVO). In 1983, however, Soviet publications stated, according to translations by the Scotts, that the Ground Forces were "composed of motorized rifle troops, tank troops, airborne troops, rocket troops and artillery, troops of troop air defense (service branches), army aviation, and also units and subunits of special troops." This, according to the Scotts, indicated that troop air defense and army aviation may "not be organic to the Ground Forces." As of early 1986, Western experts had not come to agreement about the composition of the Ground Forces. Nonetheless, there is still information about the basic combat branches.

Motorized Rifle Troops. Motorized rifle troops make up the largest Ground Forces contingent. They, along with tank troops, have undergone extensive changes in the recent reorganization efforts. Much of their simple yet effective equipment has been combat tested in the Middle East or Southeast Asia. Some items, such as troop combat vehicles, may surpass Western ones in technology and design. But motorized rifle units do not maintain enough vehicles to meet wartime needs. "When required, [civilian] vehicles and reserve drivers simply are called up and move immediately into action," the Scotts noted.

Tank Troops. Tank troops, the primary strike force of the ground troops, carry some protection against chemical, nuclear, and biological weapons. Soviet leaders carefully took stock of tank vulnerability in the 1973 Middle East conflict and apparently made changes that keep Soviet tanks on a par with or superior to U.S. and NATO equipment. Improved antitank defenses have necessitated measures to make tanks less vulnerable, a difficult task.

In 1986 the Soviets had more than 50,000 main battle tanks and, according to Marshall Lee Miller in the January 1986 *Armed Forces Journal*, about 3,000 more tanks are added each year. The United States by comparison, Miller noted, had fewer than 14,000, of which only about 3,000 were in Central Europe. But some Soviet tanks were outmoded because the Soviets routinely keep old equipment on hand.

The legendary mass-produced Soviet T-34 was the best tank in World War II and its mobility and firepower enabled the Soviets to push back the surprised Germans. According to Miller, the Soviets have continued their "pattern of producing vast quantities of robust, heavily-armored but surprisingly light-weight tanks with guns of a larger caliber than their Western contemporaries." Nonetheless, Soviet tank design does have problems, including interior space. According to Miller, tank crew members can be no taller than 5 feet 5 inches.

According to the Scotts, motorized rifle and tank troops may have been combined.

Rocket Troops and Artillery. The Soviets define tactical and operational rockets as those with ranges less than 1,000 kilometers. Two such Soviet rockets, termed Frog and Scud in the West, are being replaced by the SS-21 and SS-23, respectively. These are under Ground Forces' control, while the Strategic Rocket Forces control long-range missiles.

Artillery is divided into organic artillery (which is in the hands of motorized rifle battalions and tank and airborne units, and includes antitank guns and antitank guided missiles) and artillery of the Supreme High Command Reserve (which includes larger guns and mortars). The Soviets gave renewed attention to artillery in the 1970s and early 1980s, especially the development of self-propelled nuclear and conventional artillery.

One Soviet mortar has become a legend of sorts since its use in World War II — the Katyusha. It is really a multiple rocket launcher and is still widely used throughout the world despite its relative inaccuracy because it is inexpensive and expends a heavy volume of fire.

Troops of Troop Air Defense. The air defense troops were created as part of the Ground Forces in 1958. They were equipped with a wide variety of antiaircraft artillery and surface-to-air missiles. In the early 1980s, with the substantial force reorganization, it appeared that the Ground Forces' air defense troops had, for the most part, been transferred. According to the Scotts, "It is believed that troop air defense personnel in the Ground Forces are from the separate service, Troops of Air Defense."

Army Aviation. At the beginning of World War II the Red Army operated bombers, fighters, and other ground support aircraft, but the branch was abolished in 1942. It was not until the early 1980s that army aviation was reintroduced, leading to the belief in the West that certain types of aircraft — combat helicopters, for example — may now be assigned to the Ground Forces.

Airborne Troops. The Airborne Troops (VDV) are a "mini-service, with close ties to the Ground Forces but assigned as a reserve of the High Command," according to the Scotts. It was through this branch, then assigned to the Air Forces, that the Soviets launched mass parachute drops in 1935, years ahead of U.S. Army capability. According to the Pentagon, the Soviet Union has the world's largest airborne force with seven divisions and part of an eighth in Afghanistan. Airborne troops would be dropped into enemy territory in the initial phase of a nuclear war with their primary task being to seize and destroy the enemy's nuclear means, and then to secure key road and rail lines.

Troops of Air Defense

Since World War II the USSR has devoted more attention than the United States to developing protection against aircraft, missile, and satellite attacks. By 1949 the MiG 15 jet fighter was considered a formidable threat to advanced American aircraft, and by the mid-1950s the Soviets had deployed SA-1 ground-to-air missiles around Moscow. Throughout the 1960s, Soviet ground-to-air missiles (SA-2s) proved themselves in Southeast Asia.

More recent efforts to defend against satellites and ballistic missiles have also been significant. The Pentagon said in 1985 that the USSR had begun developing at least three types of high-energy laser weapons and that its strategic defense laser could be operational by the late 1980s.

All these types of defenses come under direction of the Troops of Air Defense (V PVO), as the service has been called since 1981 when the name Troops of National Air Defense (PVO Strany) was dropped. As part of the reorganization, the service gained most (if not all) of the Ground Forces air defense troops (including their military schools) and lost about 45 percent of its aircraft to the Air Forces.

In 1984 the service had an estimated 495,000 personnel. Air Defense units, except for the Moscow Air Defense District, are assigned to the 16 military districts.

Air Defense generally ranks number three in precedence. Marshal of Aviation Aleksandr Ivanovich Koldunov has been its commander in chief since mid-1978.

The three basic Air Defense components are aviation, zenith rocket troops, and radio-technical troops. The aviation component includes fighters such as the MiG-25 Foxhound, and some transports and helicopters. The zenith rocket troops are equipped with surface-to-air missiles (SAMs) of types that have been used in the Middle East. The radio-technical troops operate the massive deployments of radars. Radar density in the Soviet Union far surpasses any other nation's, except perhaps some areas of the Middle East. When new radars are produced, old ones are rarely junked. They are used as backups. Some of the more modern radars are considered superior to NATO equipment.

Other Air Defense units include the PKO (antispace defense) and the PRO (antirocket defense). These terms began showing up in the mid-1960s after two large antiballistic missile (ABM) radars and the Galosh ABM that protects Moscow were prominently displayed. References to these units were quietly dropped after the two superpowers agreed in 1966 not to place nuclear weapons in space.

References to antirocket defense became even more infrequent after 1968, largely because the recently tested U.S. multiple independently targetable reentry vehicles (MIRVs) made the Soviet ABM system ineffective. The new MIRV capabilities and the likely success of the U.S. ABM, the Safeguard, were major factors in the Soviet Union's agreeing to discuss strategic weapons limitation. The Soviets succeeded in getting the United States to delay deployment of the Safeguard until they developed MIRVs themselves. By the early 1980s the Soviets also built long-range early-warning ABM radars, which the United States considered violations of the SALT II agreement. *(Details, arms control section, p. 142)*

Air Forces

The Air Forces are not equivalent to the U.S. Air Force, largely because the USSR has assigned strategic missiles and interceptor aircraft to other services. The Soviet Air Forces had an estimated 530,000 personnel in 1984, according to Collins's figures. Although it was somewhat affected by the early 1980s reorganization, the service continues to have three primary components: long-range aviation, frontal aviation, and military transport aviation. Fighter bombers carry either conventional or nuclear weapons and new models of transport aircraft have been developed. Air transport, both civilian and military, has become a major factor in supporting military actions beyond Soviet borders. In Ethiopia and elsewhere, Soviet airlift capabilities have proven efficient.

The commander in chief of the Air Forces is Marshal of Aviation Aleksandr Nikolaevich Efimov, 63. Efimov was appointed in December 1984 after the death of Chief Marshal of Aviation Pavel Kutakhov, who had commanded the Air Forces since 1969. Efimov had a brilliant wartime record, including participation in the Berlin bombing of March-May 1945.

Long-Range Aviation. The Soviet Union has numerous bombers (including the Bear, Bison, Backfire, Blinder, and Badger), about 450 Fencer SU-24 strike aircraft (similar to the U.S. F-111), and more than 500 tanker, reconnaissance, and electronic warfare aircraft, according to the Scotts. The Blackjack bomber is much larger than the planned B-1 U.S. bomber and was expected to be operational in 1986.

The Soviets refer to bombers as rocket carriers. The main job of long-range aviation is to destroy the "nuclear means" of the enemy, which indicates that ICBMs and nuclear arsenals would be top bomber-targeting priorities. (The Air Forces' strategic bomber fleet is somewhat limited because most intercontinental nuclear strike capabilities have been placed with the Strategic Rocket Forces and on submarines.)

Frontal Aviation. According to the Scotts, Soviet frontal aviation "is roughly equal to tactical aviation in the United States." Its primary mission is to "achieve air superiority and to provide air defense over the battle area or within the TVD."

The Hind helicopter developed specifically to support the Ground Forces in the 1970s substantially improved Soviet frontal aviation capabilities. It carries more firepower than any U.S. attack helicopter.

Soviet forces in Outer Mongolia have frontal aviation units and much fighting in Afghanistan has involved such units. With the Fencer, Flanker, and Fulcrum the Soviets now have substantial advanced fighter capabilities.

Transport Aviation. In the 1950s Soviet transport aircraft were copies of the U.S. DC-3. But the An-12 and the short-lived An-22 were produced in the early 1960s. By the early 1970s the An-76 (similar to the American C-141) was rapidly entering service. By 1976 the wide-bodied but inefficient Il-86 made its initial flight.

The Air Forces also operate helicopters designed especially for special functions such as moving equipment into inaccessible areas.

The civilian airline Aeroflot serves as an important military transport backup under direction of the Ministry of Aviation. Aeroflot carried the first attack forces into Prague in 1968.

The Air Forces have a major role in the Soviet manned space program. Cosmonauts receive Air Forces training and usually wear their uniforms. The official Air Forces magazine is called *Aviation and Cosmonautics*. *(Space program, box, pp. 136-37)*

Navy

The Soviet Navy has become one of the Kremlin's foremost means to project power throughout the world. Largely through the efforts of Commander in Chief and Admiral of the Fleet Sergei G. Gorshkov, who headed the branch from 1955 until late 1985, the Navy expanded from a limited coastal force into a service that supports Soviet interests internationally. By 1984 the Navy had approximately 436,000 personnel.

Gorshkov, 75 when he retired, was replaced by Adm. Vladimir N. Chernavin, 57, the former chief of staff.

The Navy, like the other services, saw several changes after Gorbachev took office. Three commanders of the four fleets (and one flotilla) were replaced in 1985.

In 1983 a Soviet publication said that the Navy consisted of "submarines, surface ships, naval aviation, coastal rocket-artillery troops and naval infantry. . . . The main forces are submarines and aviation." According to Marshal Ogarkov, the main strike forces are nuclear submarines and missile-carrying aviation.

There are four naval fleets: Northern, based at Severomorsk; Baltic, based at Kaliningrad; Black Sea, based at Sevastopol; and Pacific Fleet, based at Vladivostok. There is also a small flotilla based at Baku covering the Caspian Sea. *(Map, p. 138)*

The fleets' wide range exposes them to navigational risks. Soviet ships collided with Turkish and Swedish military vessels in 1985. Five Turkish crew members were killed in the September collision with a Soviet military training ship. In November a Soviet minesweeper rammed a new Swedish naval intelligence ship in Baltic Sea international waters.

Submarines. After World War II the Soviet Union's first large effort was to design and build submarines that could attack aircraft carriers and disrupt sea communications. In a major speech January 14, 1960, Nikita Khrushchev said that the Navy's submarine fleet was acquiring increasing importance. The emphasis continued under Gorbachev, as evidenced by the selection of Admiral Chernavin as commander in chief. Chernavin, a submariner, led the first major cruise of Soviet nuclear submarines under the Artic icecap while he commanded the Northern Fleet.

By the early 1980s the Soviets' general purpose submarine force was the largest in the world. The Pentagon reported in 1985 that the USSR had more than 300 active submarines, about half of them nuclear powered. The submarine force is made up of about 25 classes of torpedo attack, cruise missile, and auxiliary submarines. All but one of the nine classes of submarines the Soviets were testing in the early 1980s were nuclear powered and emphasized quiet and speed. Eighteen new strategic nuclear-powered ballistic missile submarines (SSBNs) were built between the late 1970s and mid-1980s.

The world's largest submarine is the 25,000-ton SSBN Typhoon class, which carries 20 ballistic missiles and can operate under the Arctic Ocean icecap. The Pentagon estimated in 1985 that as many as eight of these submarines could be operating by the early 1990s. The new SSBN class Delta IV has also been deployed and will carry the submarine-launched ballistic missile (SLBM) SN-NX-23, which was being flight tested in 1985.

Some Yankee I ballistic missile submarines have been removed since 1978 to comply with SALT I agreements, but several of these were "reconfigured as attack or cruise missile submarines," according to the Pentagon.

The large force of attack submarines includes the Alpha class, believed to be the world's fastest. Four new classes of nuclear-powered attack submarines have been introduced since 1983. According to the Pentagon, the Soviets move quickly on submarine development, incorporating technological advances "into designs as soon as practical."

The Navy's new cruise missile submarine class Oscar, the largest of the Soviet attack submarines, carries 24 antiship cruise missiles that can be launched while submerged. According to the Pentagon, these are primarily targeted on NATO carrier battle groups.

The U.S. Navy revealed in 1985 that information sold to the Soviets by several active and retired U.S. Navy personnel convicted of spying had enabled the Soviets to

Botched Mutiny

On November 8, 1975, a young, trusted political officer named Capt. Valery Mikailovich Sablin led an attempted mutiny aboard the three-year-old Soviet missile frigate *Storozhevoi*. While most of the officers were in Riga, the ship's home port, celebrating the 58th anniversary of the October Revolution, Sablin and a few remaining crew members quietly slipped the vessel's moorings and headed out to sea toward Sweden.

It was several hours before anyone knew the ship was missing. Sablin, another officer named Markov, and a dozen or so petty officers apparently locked the captain in his cabin, tied up other officers, and ordered the skeleton crew of mostly 18- and 19-year-olds to take the ship to sea.

According to the most authoritative account of the events, by U.S. Navy Lt. Cmdr. Gregory D. Young in the February 1985 issue of *Sea Power*, one sailor jumped ship, apparently unknown to Sablin, and reached shore. It took the sailor more than two hours to reach Riga naval headquarters and convince a duty officer that something was amiss. And it was only after an officer on board managed to untie himself and broadcast an emergency that Soviet authorities realized the magnitude of the situation. By then, the ship had passed through the Gulf of Riga and was steaming toward the Swedish island of Gotland.

Had the mutineers known all they needed to know about operating the ship, they could have made the 200-mile journey before the authorities found them. But because only a few officers on each Soviet vessel are trained in its full operations, Sablin's mutineers apparently were never able to get the ship above half speed.

Riga headquarters sent out search planes. The astonished pilots radioed in Russian, rather than code, that they had found the ship and Swedish military operators overheard them frantically ordering the ship back to Riga. Moscow then ordered the ship stopped at all costs. About 10 planes, half of them TU-95 Bear bombers, were sent out, as was another destroyer from Riga.

After the ship refused to halt, the pilots opened fire, hitting not the *Storozhevoi* but the pursuing destroyer. The mutineers took evasive measures but did not fire back, apparently not knowing how to operate the advanced weapons systems. The *Storozhevoi* eventually stopped about 100 miles outside Swedish waters.

Sablin and about a dozen of the enlisted mutineers were later executed, Young reported. The *Storozhevoi* was repaired, renamed, and transferred from the Baltic Fleet to the Pacific Fleet. The attempted mutiny has never been acknowledged by the Soviets.

substantially improve their submarines.

Several highly publicized Soviet submarine incidents have caused concern among the nation's leaders. On October 27, 1981, a submarine ran aground in Swedish waters. The Swedes later reported the submarine likely had been carrying nuclear weapons because a search of the vessel had detected radiation. In March 1984 a submarine struck an American aircraft carrier while trying to surface.

Surface Vessels. The fourth aircraft carrier of the Kiev class, the largest Soviet surface ship, had become operational by 1986. This class carries cruise missiles that can be targeted beyond the horizon, either by the ship's attack helicopters or by satellite information. This class also carries Forger vertical/short take-off and landing (VSTOL) aircraft that, according to the Pentagon, are "capable of daylight attack, reconnaissance, and intercept missions."

The most technologically advanced Soviet surface vessels appeared in the early 1980s. They were the USSR's first nuclear-powered surface warship, the *Kirov* guided-missile cruiser, and the guided-missile destroyers *Udaloy* and *Sovremennii*.

According to the Pentagon, the introduction of these large surface vessels "illustrates the Soviet Navy's trend toward construction of larger displacement ships with greater firepower, endurance, and sustainability for distant operations."

Other than aircraft carriers, the *Kirov* is the largest warship any country has built since World War II. According to the Pentagon, it carries massive amounts of weaponry, including cruise missiles, air defense weapons, machine guns, torpedoes, and antisubmarine rockets. The second vessel of this class, the *Frunze*, became operational in 1984.

Naval Aviation. Naval aviation aircraft have four main missions according to the Scotts: reconnaissance and surveillance, antiship strike, antisubmarine, and aviation support. Most of the Navy's estimated 1,600 aircraft are land based and are likely to remain so. Strike aircraft, designed primarily to attack carrier forces, include the Badger, Blinder, and the newer supersonic Backfire, which can carry antiship missiles, bombs, or mines. The Backfire entered service in the mid-1970s and is deployed in the Black Sea, Baltic Sea, and Pacific Ocean fleets.

Some Bear turbo-prop long-range reconnaissance aircraft cover the U.S. East Coast from Cuban bases. Bears are also based in Vietnam.

Amphibious Forces. The Soviet Union disbanded its naval infantry (Marines in the United States) after World War II but revived them in the 1960s. By 1985 the naval infantry numbered about 16,000, including about 7,000 in the largest brigade, the Pacific Fleet's. The naval infantry's main job, according to the Pentagon, is to "spearhead amphibious landings for other ground forces — sometimes in concert with airborne troops." The largest amphibious assault ship is the *Ivan Rogov*.

While small in number, the Soviet naval infantry appears especially adapted for use in the Third World. Soviet amphibious ships are routinely deployed throughout the world and have conducted numerous exercises abroad.

Merchant and Fishing Fleets. The Soviet merchant marine and fishing fleets are important components of the Soviet Union's overall maritime forces. The merchant marine had some 1,700 ships in 1985, including at least 40 "roll-on/roll-off" ships that could be used to load tanks and other military vehicles. New fleet ships built since 1965 have increasingly been designed to meet military standards. They are, for the most part, commanded by naval reserve officers and routinely take part in major naval exercises. The fleet also provides a considerable amount of logistic support for the Navy.

According to the Scotts:

> It is difficult to determine whether the collection of intelligence is the primary or secondary function of the fishing fleet. Soviet "fishing" vessels are stationed outside a number of major United States ports and are extremely active during the launches of space vehicles and ballistic missiles.

Soviet naval concepts differ in many ways from the U.S. Navy's. While American strategic planners have long thought in terms of commanding the sea, the Soviet Navy has focused on disrupting enemy sea communications. That is still its main wartime task. But the rapid upgrading of Soviet naval capabilities since the 1960s, the value of projecting force worldwide, and the international environment of the 1980s (including the USSR's continued need to import foodstuffs and the possible future need to import raw materials) may prompt the Soviets to alter their strategic thinking and move to establish their own secure sea communications.

ARMS CONTROL: HISTORICAL PERSPECTIVE

It appeared in the early 1980s that the attitudes of the United States and the Soviet Union toward nuclear weapons and strategic arms limitation had not changed significantly since the first arms control proposals were offered more than three decades earlier.

Despite changes in the strategic balance and the ensuing American shift from a policy of massive retaliation to one of flexible response, the United States tried to maintain its nuclear superiority as the most effective way to contain the Soviet Union. The Kremlin, on the other hand, aimed at parity because Soviet leaders felt that without rough equivalence the USSR would be "subject to coercion based on American strategic nuclear superiority."

Mutual fear and distrust led to massive nuclear weapons buildups and discouraged any substantive effort to limit strategic arms until at least the early 1970s.

Circuitous Negotiations

The difficulties in reaching a strategic arms agreement were evident in the long and arduous negotiations to limit nuclear-weapons testing. Prime Minister Jawaharlal Nehru of India had urged a suspension of tests and the Soviets called for a halt in their disarmament proposals of May 10, 1955. In the years that followed, each superpower temporarily suspended its own testing but there was no international agreement. Public concern about the health hazards of radioactive fallout increased.

Glossary of Arms Control Terms

ABM — Antiballistic missile. Term for weapons designed to destroy enemy ballistic missiles in flight before they reach their targets. Refers to both existing ground-launched interceptor missiles and space-based systems under development.

ASBM — Air-to-surface ballistic missile. An air-launched missile that follows a ballistic, unguided course and has a range of more than 600 km.

CEP — Circular error probable. Measurement of missile accuracy: radius of the circle around a target within which there is a 50 percent probability that a weapon aimed at that target will fall. Naturally, a CEP figure has much uncertainty.

Cruise Missile — Unmanned guided missile propelled by a jet engine and supported by wings, like an airplane, that usually follows the terrain in low-altitude flight. Cruise missiles can be ground-, air-, or sea-launched.

Encryption — In context of SALT II, this term refers to deliberate attempts to alter the manner by which data (telemetry) is transmitted from the testing of a weapon, to complicate the other side's ability to analyze that information.

Heavy Bomber — An airplane that can perform the kind of strategic missions currently performed by the U.S. B-52 and the Soviet Tupelov 95. Also any plane carrying ASBMs or cruise missiles with ranges of more than 600 km.

ICBM — Intercontinental ballistic missile. A ballistic missile with a range of more than 5,500 km. A light ICBM has a launch-weight or a throw-weight no greater than the Soviet SS-19. A heavy ICBM has a launch-weight or a throw-weight greater than the SS-19.

IRBM — Intermediate ballistic missile. Range 2,400-5,500 km. Example: Soviet SS-20.

Kiloton — Measurement of the destructive power of nuclear weapons. One kiloton has the explosive force of 1,000 tons of conventional high explosives. The bomb dropped on Hiroshima had a yield of about 10-15 kilotons. The unratified 1974 Nuclear Weapons Tests Limitation Treaty prohibits the testing of nuclear devices over 150 kilotons.

Launch-Weight — Weight of an ICBM or SLBM when fully loaded with fuel and warheads and ready for launch.

Launcher — Device from which an ICBM or SLBM is launched. The unratified SALT II treaty concentrated on limiting launchers.

LRCM — Long-range cruise missile. Range more than 600 km.

MIRVs — Multiple independently targetable reentry vehicles. Ballistic missile warheads on a single missile capable of dispersing to destroy separate targets.

Mobile ICBM Launcher — Mobile equipment that can launch an ICBM, including vehicles that move on wheels and by rail. Soviet SS-24 and SS-25 missiles may be fired from mobile launchers.

MRBM — Medium-range ballistic missile. Range of 800-2,400 km. Examples: U.S. Pershing II, Soviet SS-4.

National Technical Means of Verification — Electronic and optical devices, including satellites, radar, and radio receivers, with which each country can monitor treaty compliance by others.

Operational-Tactical — Soviet term for missiles having range of less than 1,000 km.

Payload — Weapons and penetration aids carried by a missile or bomber.

Penetration Aids — Radar decoys and other devices carried by a missile to protect its warheads against detection and attack by defensive weapons.

Reentry Vehicle — Section of the ballistic missile that carries the nuclear warhead and reenters Earth's atmosphere during the last part of the missile trajectory.

SALT — Strategic Arms Limitation Talks.

SDI — Strategic Defense Initiative. U.S. research and development program launched in 1983 aimed at producing a space-based defense against Soviet ICBMs. Often referred to as "Star Wars."

SLBM — Submarine-launched ballistic missile.

SRBM — Short-range ballistic missile. Range under 800 km. Examples: U.S. Lance, Soviet SS-23.

SSBN — Strategic nuclear-powered ballistic missile submarine. Examples: U.S. Trident, Poseidon; Soviet Typhoon, Delta.

Strategic Nuclear Weapons — Long-range nuclear weapons, including ICBMs, SLBMs, and heavy bombers, with which nuclear powers can threaten each others' homelands.

START — Strategic Arms Reduction Talks.

Stealth — Technology used to make bombers and cruise missiles less visible to radar, thus enhancing their ability to penetrate enemy defenses.

Tactical Nuclear Weapons — Nuclear weapons with shorter ranges than strategic weapons; designed for use within a theater of operations such as Europe.

Telemetry — Radio-transmitted data from missile flight tests to enable technicians to monitor the weapon's performance during the test.

Throw-Weight — Payload carrying capacity of a ballistic missile. The total weight of the reentry vehicles, MIRV aiming and releasing devices, and penetration aids a missile is capable of carrying over a given range; an index of destructive power.

1963 Test-Ban Treaty

There were several reasons why neither the United States nor the Soviet Union was willing to agree to a test-ban treaty until 1963, and then only to a partial suspension. One was Soviet opposition to on-site inspection. Another was that a ban on testing could be viewed as a back-door approach to total nuclear disarmament. Henry A. Kissinger, then a Harvard professor, took note of this connection in an article in the October 1958 *Foreign Affairs.* "If a cessation of nuclear testing is a 'first step' to anything," he wrote, "it is to an increased campaign to outlaw nuclear weapons altogether."

Missile Gap. Despite overtures from Soviet premier Nikita Khrushchev, American president John F. Kennedy ordered a buildup of ICBMs soon after taking office in 1961. This was partly to counter what he perceived as a "missile gap," a phrase he introduced in his presidential election campaign. It was not until after the Cuban missile crisis of October 1962 that the two sides were able to resume serious negotiations on testing. A limited treaty ending experimental nuclear weapons tests in the atmosphere, outer space, and under water was signed by the United States, the Soviet Union, and Britain in August 1963. More than 110 other countries subsequently signed the test-ban treaty.

Buildups Continue. Regardless of its benefits, the test-ban treaty was hardly a breakthrough in arms control or reduction. Both sides proceeded to conduct their testing underground; the United States carried out more nuclear tests (469) in the 10 years after the test ban than it had in the previous 18 years (424 tests). To win approval of the treaty in the Senate, where the Joint Chiefs of Staff had enlisted several powerful opponents, Kennedy was forced to offer some safeguards.

The American strategic buildup, which began two years before the treaty was signed, continued for the rest of the decade. The number of ICBMs was substantially increased, submarine-launched Polaris missiles were developed, supersonic fighter-bombers were ordered and, by 1965, contracts had been given to the Boeing Company for work on MIRVs. The Soviet reaction was, predictably, an escalation of their own strategic weapons programs.

The Soviet buildup focused on ICBMs and antiballistic missile systems. In 1966, for example, the Soviet Union had about one-third as many ICBMs (250) as the United States. Two years later, according to U.S. estimates, the Soviets had 900. Despite the outcry in the United States, a comparison of strategic arsenals released by Secretary of Defense Clark M. Clifford on October 25, 1968, indicated the United States still enjoyed a sizable overall lead.

Johnson Presidency

A number of factors prevented serious consideration of strategic weapons reduction: the growing American involvement in Vietnam, the Soviet invasion of Czechoslovakia in August 1968, and a large strategic buildup then under way in the Soviet Union. Nevertheless, two multilateral agreements on nuclear weapons were signed in the late 1960s: a 1967 treaty banning the orbiting of devices equipped with nuclear weapons and the 1968 Non-Proliferation Treaty. *(Chapter 4, p. 64)*

During his years in office, President Lyndon Johnson suggested several plans for nuclear arms limitation. Behind many of these proposals was growing American concern about the Soviet ABM program. A Soviet breakthrough in missile defense technology would, if not matched by the West, overcome Washington's advantage in offensive weaponry. By making its territory immune to American missiles, the Soviet Union could attack the United States without fear of retaliation. The choice facing Johnson and later President Richard Nixon was either to begin building a multibillion-dollar ABM system or to persuade the Kremlin to discard its ABM defenses.

At the summit meeting between Johnson and Soviet premier Kosygin in 1967 at Glassboro, New Jersey, Secretary of Defense Robert S. McNamara unsuccessfully urged the Soviet leader to abandon the ABM and hold back an arms race. McNamara opposed the development of American antiballistic missiles as too costly, possibly ineffective, and certain to provoke escalation of the arms race. But faced with the Kremlin's refusal to limit its system, the Pentagon announced late in 1967 that the United States would deploy the limited Sentinel ABM system. Soon after taking office in 1969, President Nixon asked Congress for the Safeguard system.

SALT Begins Under Nixon

President Nixon had urged strategic arms limitation talks with the Soviet Union since June 1969. The talks eventually began November 17, 1969, in Helsinki, Finland. After U.S. and Soviet negotiators had worked arduously to prepare the documents, Nixon and Soviet leader Leonid Brezhnev were set to sign them during a summit in Moscow in May 1972. The strategic arms limitation (SALT) accord signed May 26 was the most important of the documents signed at the summit.

The agreement included both a defensive arms treaty to limit ABM deployments and an executive agreement designed to limit offensive weapons and missile-carrying submarines.

Under the defensive arms treaty, both the United States and the Soviet Union were limited to one ABM site for the defense of their capital cities and one additional site each for the defense of an ICBM installation. (In 1973 Congress prohibited the Defense Department from beginning work on the ABM site to defend Washington; a 1974 protocol between the two nations restricting each to one site was approved by the Senate November 10.)

The five-year interim agreement limiting offensive missile launchers — land-based silos and submarine missile tubes — left the United States 1,710 launchers, of which 1,054 were ICBMs and the remaining 656 were SLBMs (submarine-launched ballistic missiles). The White House estimated the total Soviet strategic missile launcher strength to be 2,358 — 1,618 ICBM launchers and 740 SLBM launchers. (The London-based International Institute for Strategic Studies arrived at a lower estimate.) Besides the numerical edge, the Soviets also had the advantage in throw-weight, estimated at several times that of U.S. capacity. (Throw-weight is the measure of a missile's lift potential and ultimately the number and size of warheads a missile can carry.)

The United States, however, had a numerical advantage in warheads, as well as superiority in strategic bombers — 460 at the time, compared with a Soviet total of 140 — and aircraft that could strike the Soviet Union on one-way missions from European airfields.

Back in the United States for less than half an hour from his overseas mission, Nixon made a televised speech June 1 to a joint session of Congress. He urged the assembled lawmakers to "seize the moment so that our children and the world's children live free of the fears and free of the hatreds that have been the lot of mankind through the centuries." He assured them that "the present and planned strategic forces of the United States are without question sufficient for the maintenance of our security and the protection of our vital interests.... No power on earth is stronger than the United States of America today," he said. "None will be stronger than the United States of America in the future."

As the president urged Congress to approve the accords, the Soviet news agency Tass reported that the Politburo, the Council of Ministers, and the Presidium of the Supreme Soviet all had "entirely approved" the pacts.

The offensive arms agreement required approval by simple majorities in both the House and Senate; the ABM treaty had to be ratified by a two-thirds majority in the Senate. A provision in the 1961 law establishing the U.S. Arms Control and Disarmament Agency, which negotiated the pacts, specified that any agreement to limit U.S. armed forces or armaments required approval by legislation or treaty. Nixon submitted the two accords to Congress in June together with documents explaining U.S.-Soviet agreements and disagreements on interpretations of the accords.

The disagreements concerned mainly the ultimate size of nuclear submarine fleets and the size of certain offensive weapons. The explanation of differences was designed to head off Senate reservations. The explanatory statements, drawn up in Moscow by U.S.-Soviet negotiators, emphasized U.S. concern over development of large Soviet missiles and envisaged future negotiations on nuclear limitations. The document also recorded a unilateral statement, not agreed to by the United States, that the Soviets would increase the number of their nuclear submarines, if Washington's NATO allies increased theirs.

SALT Treaty Controversy

The Senate ratified the ABM treaty 88-2 on August 3, 1972. But the House-passed interim agreement on offensive weapons had some rough moments before it was finally approved, because the Senate attached language demanding a stiff U.S. bargaining stance in future SALT talks.

The hard-line amendment sponsored by Sen. Henry M. Jackson, D-Wash., requested that any future permanent treaty on offensive nuclear arms "not limit the United States to levels of intercontinental strategic forces inferior to" those of the Soviet Union, but rather be based on "the principle of equality." The amendment stipulated that failure to negotiate a permanent treaty limiting offensive arms would be grounds to abrogate the U.S.-Soviet ABM agreement. It also endorsed the maintenance of a vigorous research, development, and modernization program.

Controversy over the Jackson proposal threatened to delay the resumption of SALT talks, then scheduled to begin in Geneva in mid-October. The House September 25 accepted the Senate changes rather than risk further delay.

The Jackson amendment and others added to the measure emphasized congressional disquiet concerning the interim agreement, although they did not affect the accord itself as signed in Moscow.

1973 Summit

When Soviet leader Brezhnev came to the United States to meet with President Nixon in June 1973, the talks were marked by their jovial tenor, not by their substance.

Among several relatively minor agreements, the leaders signed a declaration they hoped would guide U.S. and Soviet negotiators in working toward a permanent strategic arms treaty. The declaration did not go into detail.

Nixon and Brezhnev also signed an agreement pledging each side to avoid nuclear war and said they were willing to sign certain interim agreements until a permanent accord was reached. *(Summit, Chapter 4, p. 72; Summit text, p. 302)*

The details of a permanent strategic arms limitation treaty to replace the earlier interim agreement were left for negotiators to work out. It was not until 1974, when Nixon returned to Moscow, that more arms control agreements were signed.

1974 Summit

Only a month before he would resign from the presidency, Richard Nixon went to Moscow amid considerable domestic criticism seeking a breakthrough in permanent limits on offensive nuclear weapons.

Instead of broadening and extending the five-year-old SALT Treaty, however, the leaders were only able to sign an agreement placing more limits on underground nuclear tests and an agreement limiting the number of ABM sites each country could maintain.

After failing to reach a permanent SALT agreement, the leaders agreed to seek a new interim agreement that would last through 1985. The two agreed that the new interim accord should be concluded as soon as possible — before the October 1977 expiration date of the interim agreement limiting offensive missile launchers reached at the 1972 summit. Negotiators for both sides were scheduled to return to the Geneva bargaining table to begin work on the new agreement. The two leaders were reported to have failed to agree on a mandate on arms limitations for their SALT negotiators. Secretary of State Henry Kissinger said that both sides would formulate new instructions for their delegations "from certain basic principles" agreed on at the Moscow summit.

The main stumbling block had been devising a way to balance the Soviet missile advantage and the U.S. warhead advantage. "It did not prove possible to find a balance between overall numbers and the numbers of missiles with multiple warheads," Kissinger stated in Brussels July 4, 1974. The secretary said that the Soviets could not accept the number of missiles the United States had proposed as the upper limit.

The issue was further complicated by reports of disagreement between Kissinger and the Pentagon over how to approach the arms limitation problem. Kissinger was said to have been willing to conclude a more limited accord on MIRVs, while the Pentagon reportedly wanted a broader agreement covering other strategic weapons.

Besides signing the interim agreement at the July 3 ceremonies in Moscow, the two leaders signed a protocol waiving their option to establish a second ABM site as provided for in the 1972 treaty. The 1972 ABM accord had allowed each country to defend its national capital and maintain one other intercontinental ballistic missile site. But each country had deployed only one system of ABM interceptors by mid-1974; the Americans at Grand Forks,

North Dakota, and the Soviets around Moscow. Under the 1974 accord, each country agreed to limit to one the number of ABM sites within its territory.

Vladivostok Accord

After President Nixon resigned in August 1974, President Gerald R. Ford went to the far eastern Soviet city of Vladivostok to sign accords with Soviet leader Brezhnev. No major agreements were expected from the summit but Ford and Brezhnev surprised officials and the public by announcing a tentative agreement on limiting strategic offensive nuclear weapons and delivery vehicles. The Ford-Brezhnev talks got the stalled SALT talks moving again.

The Vladivostok guidelines called for acceptance of the principle of equivalence in strategic forces — as opposed to the 1972 SALT accord that had set different but counterbalancing quotas. Each country was to be accorded latitude to choose land-based strategic missiles, submarine-launched missiles, or strategic bombers for delivery vehicles. Broad limits were set on the deployment of MIRVs. While mentioning restrictions on the total number of MIRV-equipped vehicles, the agreement left open the number of individual MIRVed warheads that could be deployed.

The Vladivostok guidelines for a SALT II agreement contained these main points:

● Each nation was limited to 2,400 strategic nuclear weapons systems and would have the freedom to mix its ICBMs, submarine-launched ballistic missiles, heavy bombers, and air-launched ballistic missiles (ALBMs) within the ceiling. Excluded from the 2,400 limit were tactical aircraft and medium bombers. Strategic nuclear systems belonging to third countries, such as Britain, France, and China, were not included.

● Construction or enlargement of new ICBM silos or other fixed-site ICBM launchers were restricted, thus imposing a separate ceiling on larger missiles.

● Within the 2,400 limit on launchers of nuclear weapons, up to 1,320 missiles could be equipped with multiple independently targetable reentry vehicles containing several warheads that could strike more than one enemy target.

Kissinger told reporters November 24 that the Soviet Union had made one basic concession to the United States at Vladivostok. It had dropped its earlier insistence that the U.S. total of strategic delivery vehicles include the "forward-based" fighter-bomber systems deployed in Europe.

Differences over the Soviet Backfire bomber and U.S. cruise missiles (which had not been discussed at Vladivostok) stalled SALT negotiation progress in 1975 and forced an extended delay in Brezhnev's planned visit to Washington.

Each side initially insisted that its controversial weapons system should not be counted in the 2,400 ceiling on other strategic arms agreed to at Vladivostok. On September 21, 1975, the United States offered the Soviets a compromise in which cruise missiles and Backfires would be allowed in equal numbers above the ceiling. The plan was rejected by Moscow in late October.

The Soviets insisted that the Backfire's limited range — it was unable to reach the United States and return to the Soviet Union — discounted it as a strategic weapon. The United States countered that the bomber could either be refueled during flight to give it intercontinental capability or could refuel in Cuba or another convenient country after striking targets in the United States. On the other hand, the Soviets demanded that cruise missiles — pilotless planes that could carry nuclear or conventional warheads — be considered strategic weapons if their range exceeded 600 kilometers (370 miles). The dispute was criti-

President Gerald R. Ford and Soviet party leader Leonid I. Brezhnev shake hands after signing arms agreement at Vladivostok in November 1974.

cal because the Soviets, from relatively secure firing positions off the U.S. coasts, could hit half the U.S. population and essential industrial and military targets with their cruise missiles. But because the Soviet heartland is distant from open water only about 5 percent of the Soviet population and a few military-industrial targets were vulnerable to strikes by U.S. submarine-launched cruise missiles having a 600-kilometer range.

Peaceful Explosions Treaty

On May 28, 1976, in the midst of the U.S. presidential election race, President Ford and Soviet leader Brezhnev signed a treaty regarding nuclear explosions for peaceful purposes. The Senate chose not to consider the treaty, which still had not been ratified as of March 1986.

The agreement placed a 150-kiloton limit on the size of explosions from any single nuclear device and provided for some on-site inspection of some nuclear blasts. The agreement was sharply criticized by the Democratic presidential candidate, Jimmy Carter, and by groups such as the Arms Control Association.

Besides imposing a 150-kiloton limitation on the size of an explosion of a single nuclear device for peaceful purposes, the agreement allowed a total nuclear yield of up to 1,500 kilotons from a series of nuclear explosions. If either the Soviet Union or the United States planned to exceed the 150-kiloton level, the pact required on-site inspection by the other.

President Ford called the new agreement a "historic milestone in the history of arms control agreements." But the Arms Control Association said the inspection provisions, which the administration hailed as a "breakthrough," probably never would be implemented because "the science of nuclear test identification has now reached the point where all seismic events which can be detected can also be identified, either as earthquakes or explosions."

The 1974 treaty limiting underground nuclear weapons tests to 150 kilotons was submitted along with the peaceful explosions treaty, but it too was not ratified.

Carter: Continuing Dilemmas

Détente had already begun faltering before Jimmy Carter became president. Continued concern in the United States over the growth of Soviet and Warsaw Pact military capabilities prompted calls for more spending on defense.

Neutron Bomb

Once Carter was in office, his first arms control dilemma arose over the neutron bomb, an enhanced radiation weapon designed to kill Soviet tank crews without widespread property destruction. Proponents saw the weapon as one way to counter the threat of Soviet invasion, particularly a blitzkrieg of tanks and armored personnel carriers rolling into Germany with little or no warning.

Armored vehicles were resistant to the blast and heat of a "regular" nuclear explosion. And Soviet vehicles, unlike their NATO counterparts, were equipped to shield their crews from radioactive fallout. But the radiation warheads could circumvent Soviet defenses. The bombs limited the radius of explosive blast, fire, and fallout. At the same time, they increased the fourth effect of a nuclear detonation: the momentary wave of neutron radiation that kills persons, even in a building or a tank, without harming the structures.

After protracted debate, Congress agreed to Carter's request to approve funding for production of the weapon. Criticism continued at home and among NATO countries, however, and finally, on April 7, 1978, Carter decided to defer the bomb's production. "We will continue to move ahead with our allies to modernize and strengthen our military capabilities, both conventional and nuclear," he said, vowing to consult with NATO allies on the neutron decision and other arms control measures.

Warnke Nomination

Carter's commitment to the goal of nuclear disarmament already had raised eyebrows among hard-liners but the true opening salvo was fired after February 4, 1977, when Carter submitted to the Senate the name of Paul C. Warnke to be chief delegate to the SALT talks and director of the Arms Control and Disarmament Agency. Hard-liners quickly mobilized to oppose Warnke as "too soft" a bargainer. Opponents focused on a 1975 article in which Warnke proposed a six-month moratorium on the development of some strategic weapons to induce a similar gesture from the Soviets.

The mutual hostage relationship between the two superpowers ruled out the use of strategic nuclear arms as levers of political influence, because their use could not credibly be threatened, Warnke argued. Moreover, he said, the United States need not match every Soviet weapon development; it could defer its own arms program, up to a point, without undue risk while seeking arms limitation agreements with Moscow.

The opposite position, held by former defense secretary James R. Schlesinger, among others, insisted that the strategic balance was inherently unstable and that the Soviet Union, if allowed to develop a large lead in the quantity of weapons, could derive massive political advantage.

If they perceived such an advantage, the Soviets according to Schlesinger would be emboldened to pursue a more adventurous course against U.S. allies and nonaligned countries while brandishing the tacit threat of their massive conventional military might. Those nations, believing that the United States could give them no assistance, would cave in to Soviet demands.

Carter's initial decisions in the nuclear arms field went against the hard-liners. In his inaugural address and in press interviews, the president repeatedly placed the highest priority on conclusion of a new SALT agreement. He said he would not let the two outstanding arms control issues, the U.S. cruise missile and the Soviet Backfire bomber, stand in the way.

Against this background, the hard-liners voiced dismay that Warnke was selected to head both the arms control agency and the SALT negotiating team. After occasionally rancorous hearings and four days of debate, the Senate March 9 confirmed Warnke for the SALT job by a 58-40 vote, thanks, in large part, to a strong personal lobbying effort by President Carter.

Proposals Advanced

In late March President Carter presented the Soviets with arms control proposals that surprised his supporters as well as his critics. But the Soviets rejected both the "comprehensive" strategic arms reduction proposal and the "deferral" proposal, which would have ratified the Vladivostok accord while leaving the cruise missile and Backfire for later discussion.

At the SALT talks in Geneva that May, negotiators came up with a three-part blueprint to supersede the disputed Vladivostok agreement. The blueprint included: a treaty placing ceilings on ballistic missiles until 1985; a three-year protocol covering cruise missiles and the Backfire; and a statement of general principles regarding the follow-up negotiations. *(Summit, Chapter 4, p. 82)*

According to U.S. officials, the substance of the agreements, outlined in news reports in September, would place a ceiling of 2,250 on the total of land- and sea-based missiles and long-range bombers, slightly less than a 10 percent reduction from the Vladivostok limits. In addition, three separate ceilings would be placed on weapons armed with multiple warheads, including a limit of 1,320 for land and sea-based missiles and for bombers equipped with cruise missiles. Finally, the large Soviet land-based missiles, the SS-18s, would be restricted to 308. The three-year protocol would place a range restriction of 1,500 miles on cruise missiles launched by bombers and a range limit of 360 miles on the testing and deployment of new weapons for the period of the accord, including mobile ballistic missiles such as the proposed U.S. MX system. (The above figures are approximate and were the subject of continuing negotiation.)

The agreements involved concessions on both sides.

The United States no longer insisted that the Backfire bomber be limited and also allowed the Soviet Union to deploy twice as many SS-18 missiles as the administration originally desired. The United States also accepted temporary range restrictions on cruise missiles. The Soviet Union, for its part, agreed that the 1,200 ceiling on missiles equipped with multiple warheads would not cover aircraft armed with cruise missiles. Moscow also agreed to restrict the number of land-based missiles armed with multiple warheads to 800, a limit it had strongly resisted, and to refrain from increasing production of the Backfire bomber.

Criticism Continues. Between September 1977 and March 1978 congressional criticism of the proposed arms pact mounted and some supporters expressed concern that a new agreement could not secure Senate ratification.

Senate opponents, led by Sen. Jackson, faulted the administration for leaving out the Backfire bomber. They also argued that no limits should be placed on bombers equipped with cruise missiles. Another concern was that the temporary restrictions in the protocol on cruise missiles would become permanent over time. They pointed to the importance that the United States' allies attached to the cruise missile for West European defense. The NATO allies themselves had voiced fears that the United States had conceded too much in the arms talks. Critics also contended that the limits on Soviet land-based missiles were too high. And they questioned whether key features of the agreement could be verified. The Soviets, they said, could make too many improvements in their missiles and could continue development of new weapons too easily.

President Jimmy Carter and Soviet party leader Leonid I. Brezhnev exchange documents after the SALT II signing ceremonies at Vienna's Hofburg Palace, June 19, 1979.

SALT II Agreement: 1986 Status

Provision	Effect on Announced U.S. Programs	Effect on Reported Soviet Programs
Treaty (expired December 31, 1985, but still observed by both parties)		
Ceiling of 2,250 on all strategic launchers (effective as of 1982 — limit was 2,400 until then).	USA as of March 1986 was under total launcher ceiling.	New deployments require compensating scrapping to continue policy of maintaining 1979 launcher level of 2,500.
Ceiling of 820 on ICBMs with MIRVed warheads. No increase in number of MIRV warheads on current ICBM types.	None. With planned deployment of 50 MX missiles, USA will be below ceiling with 600 MIRVed ICBMs (550 Minuteman IIIs). Limits MIRVed warheads to 1,650.	With 818 MIRVed ICBMs as of 1985, would have to dismantle SS-17s, SS-18s, or SS-19s to allow for deployment of 10-warhead SS-24s, scheduled for 1986. Limits MIRVed warheads to 6,176.
Ceiling of 1,200 on ICBMs and SLBMs with MIRVed warheads.	Poseidon submarine dismantling announced June 10, 1985, to allow for deployment of 7th Trident submarine in fall 1985. Eighth Trident deployment scheduled for May 1986; MX, December 1986; 9th Trident, 1988. In each case, SSBNs or MIRVed ICBMs must be dismantled to stay under ceiling.	As of March 1986 USSR was nearing 1,200 ceiling. Planned SLBM modernization and SSBN deployments could force dismantling of 150 SLBMs and of missile-launching sections of 7 SSBNs by 1990. Additional SS-24 deployments would also require compensating scrapping to remain under 1,200 limit.
Ceiling of 1,320 on all MIRVed missiles plus bombers carrying cruise missiles with a range of 600 km or more.	Could limit to 120 the number of B-52s modified to carry cruise missiles unless MIRVed missiles are retired to allow more. The 120th B-52 was scheduled for August 1986 deployment.	None. Soviet cruise missiles, both air- and sea-launched, are not limited because of their short range.
No new land-based launchers for missiles larger than the Soviet SS-19.	None. MX is projected to be slightly smaller than the SS-19. USA will have no missiles the size of the Soviet SS-18.	Freezes SS-18 missiles at 308.
Only one new ICBM tested or deployed that differs from current types by more than 5 percent in size, weight, or throw-weight.	MX was to be deployed in December 1986; treaty could prohibit Midgetman.	With development of SS-24, treaty may prohibit deployment of SS-25.
No circumvention of treaty through third countries.	Soviets charged Pershing II and cruise missile deployments in Europe are violations.	None. Soviets have never stationed nuclear weapons with a range of more than a few hundred miles on their allies' territory.
No coding of radioed missile test data that would be needed to verify compliance with treaty.	None.	Reagan administration charged Soviet data coding impeded U.S. ability to verify treaty compliance.

Alleged Violations

Charges Against Soviets: USA alleges Soviet SS-25 is second type of new ICBM. Soviets designated SS-24 as new type, saying SS-25 is modification of SS-13. USA charges Soviets have encrypted ballistic missile flight test data, impeding treaty compliance verification. Soviets counter their encryption does not violate treaty because USA has overall ability to verify compliance.

Charges Against United States: Soviets claim USA violated noncircumvention provision by deploying Pershing II and cruise missiles in Europe. USA disputes this. USSR charges Midgetman development violates the one new ICBM provision; USA says Midgetman is proportionate response to Soviet SS-25. Soviets allege shelters over Minuteman ICBMs violated ban on use of deliberate concealment measures that impede verification. Soviets charge U.S. GLCM and SLCM deployments violate Protocol of SALT II, which expired in 1981.

The administration countered by saying the agreements contained significant Soviet concessions, were better than the Vladivostok accord, and would provide new sources of stability in the arms race.

They argued that the Backfire's effectiveness had been exaggerated and that the proposed limits on U.S. bombers with cruise missiles were not unduly restrictive. They noted that the protocol would stop the testing and deployment of four new Soviet rockets then in the developmental stage. The administration also defended the verifiability of the proposals. In addition, the administration in February 1978 published an 18-page report defending the record of compliance for SALT I. The report concerned eight challenges raised by the United States against Soviet practices, and Soviet questioning of five American actions. "In each case," the report said, "the activity in question has ceased, or additional information has allayed the concern."

SALT II Agreement

Despite months of criticism, SALT negotiations continued through 1978. In May 1979 the two governments announced a treaty would be ready to sign at the upcoming Vienna summit June 15-18. Carter had said the agreement would give the United States military advantages, but critics such as Sen. Jackson said the treaty was just one more in a long list of gratuitous concessions to Moscow by an administration too eager to maintain the appearance of U.S.-Soviet accord.

While at the ceremonies, Carter avoided making it appear that the two sides were in clear agreement. Administration officials also informed the press that Carter had received Soviet concessions on freezing production and limiting use of the Backfire.

The treaty set basic numerical limits on intercontinental missiles and bombers through 1985:

• Of 2,250 weapons allowed each country (after 1982), no more than 1,320 could be missiles with multiple warheads (MIRVs) or bombers carrying long-range cruise missiles.

• Of those 1,320, no more than 1,200 could be missiles.

• Of those 1,200, no more than 820 could be land-based missiles (ICBMs).

Additional restrictions on mobile land-based missiles and cruise missiles launched from land or ships would run only until 1982.

Ratification Stalled. Once home, Carter ran into significant trouble in trying to get SALT II ratified. A Soviet combat brigade was discovered in Cuba and debates over its significance became daily affairs in Congress.

Finally, in November 1979, the Senate Foreign Relations Committee voted to send the treaty to the full Senate. But after the Soviet Union invaded Afghanistan in December 1979 Carter, knowing the treaty had no chance of passing, asked the Senate to delay its consideration indefinitely.

Reagan and Arms Control

President Reagan came into office in 1981 publicly stating that the United States was strategically inferior to the Soviet Union and that the imbalance needed to be redressed. Administration officials asserted that past arms control agreements, such as the unratified but unofficially

observed SALT II treaty, were hurting American political and military interests rather than serving them. The administration declared that unless the Soviet Union made some unilateral cuts in its nuclear forces, the United States would need to modernize its own forces before it would be ready to negotiate toward mutual reductions. The Soviet Union disagreed and stated that the nuclear arsenals of the two superpowers were roughly equal in strength.

Despite the administration's belief that it was not a propitious time for arms control, three important constituencies — the NATO allies, Congress, and the American public — wanted the United States to vigorously pursue an arms control agreement as soon as possible. West European governments could decide not to abide by the 1979 NATO decision to deploy American Pershing IIs and ground-launched cruise missiles (GLCMs) on their territory; Congress could limit funding for the administration's nuclear weapons modernization program; and many Americans might vote for the Democratic ticket in 1984. Some critics argued that the administration was not truly interested in arms control. Yet because of the leverage these constituencies enjoyed the administration was compelled to promote the perception that it was at least attempting to negotiate. Liberal arms control advocates charged that the administration during Reagan's first term intentionally designed its arms control proposals to be unacceptable to the Soviets.

INF Negotiations

The Intermediate-range Nuclear Forces negotiations were prompted by the Soviet deployment, during the late 1970s, of medium-range SS-20 missiles targeted on Western Europe. Helmut Schmidt, then chancellor of West Germany, sounded the alarm for American action. He feared the European allies were becoming "decoupled" from the U.S. nuclear deterrent and that the large Soviet advantage in intermediate-range nuclear weapons would leave the NATO allies vulnerable to an attack or to political blackmail. If the allies could not counter the Soviet missiles with comparable weapons deployed on their soil, the Kremlin might think it could strike, or credibly threaten to strike, Western Europe, without fearing retaliation from the United States. In December 1979, during the Carter presi-

President Reagan Delivering 'Zero-Option' Speech

NATO-Warsaw Pact
Nuclear Force Comparisons

NATO and weapon category	1972-73 NATO	WP	1979-80 NATO	WP	1985-86 NATO	WP	WARSAW PACT
LAND-BASED							
• Medium, intermediate-range ballistic missiles (older): France SSBS S-2 (S-3 in 1985)	18	500	18	500	18	120	USSR S-4
		100		90		n.a.	USSR S-5 (IRBM)
MRBMs, IRBMs (modern): U.S. Pershing II				120	108	261	USSR SS-20
• Short-range ballistic missiles: NATO	(841)	(900)	(393) [a]	(1,638) [a]	261	1,396	WARSAW
• Long-range cruise missiles: U.S. Tomahawk (GLCM)				(100)	64		USSR SS-N-3
ARTILLERY							
• NATO	n.a.	n.a.	(515)	n.a.	2,544	(3,640)	WARSAW
SEA-BASED [b]							
• Sea-launched ballistic missiles: Britain & France (overall NATO figure in 1979)	86	60	784	1,028	144	(24)	USSR
AIR							
• Land-based aircraft: [c] NATO	n.a.	(1,300)	(640)	(3,650)	1,471	1,845	WARSAW (only USSR in 1972-73)
• Carrier-based aircraft: U.S. & France (only U.S. in 1979-80)	n.a.	—	(100)	—	84	—	USSR

NOTES:

Figures in parentheses are estimated.

n.a.-not available.

No nuclear warheads are known to be held on weapons of Soviet allies; all warheads are in Soviet custody. Therefore, numbers of non-Soviet Warsaw nuclear weapons have only theoretical nuclear capability.

ICBM-range more than 5,500 km   IRBM-2,400-5,500 km
MRBM-800-2,400 km   SRBM-800 km or less
(For explanation of abbreviations, see terms box, p. 143.)

FOOTNOTES:

[a] U.S.-144; Allies-(249). USSR-1,300; Allies-(338)

[b] Table does not include U.S. or Soviet long-range submarine-launched missiles. Sea-launched cruise missiles are also excluded. *(See strategic force chart, p. 155.)*

[c] Assumes two U.S. carriers in European area. Although these planes are nuclear capable many on both sides presumably are assigned nonnuclear missions.

Sources: Arms Control Association; International Institute for Strategic Studies, *The Military Balance, 1985-1986*

dency, NATO decided to adopt a "dual-track" approach. This meant preparing to deploy new intermediate-range nuclear weapons in Europe while simultaneously trying to negotiate with the Soviets to reduce such forces.

In November 1981 President Reagan announced the "zero-option" proposal. Reagan offered to cancel the deployment of U.S. Pershing IIs and GLCMs in Europe if the Soviets would dismantle their SS-20s and their older intermediate range SS-4 and SS-5 missiles. From the Soviet perspective, there were two major problems with this proposal. First, it did not take into account the French and British nuclear missiles targeted on the USSR. Second, the Soviets would be trading operational weapons for U.S. systems that were not yet deployed.

In July 1982 Paul Nitze, the U.S. chief INF negotiator, and his Soviet counterpart, Yuli Kvitsinskii, came up with the so-called "walk-in-the-woods" proposal during an informal meeting. The tentative compromise would have scrapped the U.S. Pershing IIs and decreased the number of GLCMs to be deployed in Europe in exchange for reductions in the SS-20s based west of the Ural Mountains. (The Soviets would also have had to freeze the number of SS-20s based east of the Urals targeted on China, which were mobile and could be moved westward.) It has been reported that to reach numerical equivalence the Soviets would have reduced their SS-20s from 243 to 76 and the United States would have deployed only 57 cruise missile launchers. The Soviets, with three warheads on each SS-20 launcher, and the United States, with four single-warhead GLCMs per launcher, would each have had 228 nuclear warheads deployed on these systems in Europe.

Both Washington and Moscow rejected the walk-in-the-woods proposal. For the United States it would have meant matching the "first-strike" SS-20 ballistic missiles, which can reach their targets in minutes, with slow-flying cruise missiles, which take hours to reach their targets. The United States was not willing to cancel the Pershing II program unless the Soviet Union agreed to dismantle all of its European-based SS-20s. For the Kremlin, accepting the proposal would have contradicted its argument that British and French nuclear forces had to be counted in the INF negotiations. It also would have implicitly acknowledged that it had created an imbalance in Europe that the United States was justified in trying to redress.

In December 1982 Yuri Andropov, Leonid Brezhnev's successor, offered to reduce the number of Soviet missiles aimed at Europe from 243 to 162 (the number deployed by France and Britain) if the United States would abandon its deployment plans. The United States had some serious reservations about this proposal. The United States considers French and British forces independent and not countable in the overall nuclear balance. The United States would not rely on French and British nuclear forces to tip the scales of the nuclear balance in a way that would deter, for example, a Soviet attack on West Germany. The Soviet proposal mentioned nothing about dismantling the SS-20s once they were removed from Europe. This meant the Soviets could simply redeploy their mobile missiles to Asia and then move them back in a crisis. Further, the Andropov proposal was for an equal number of missiles, which created two problems from the American perspective. First, it would have given the Soviets a substantial advantage in warheads. Second, it would have counted other INF weapons, such as bombers, that the United States did not want to include. The United States has never agreed to count its Forward Based Systems (FBS),

such as bombers deployed in Europe, in the U.S.-Soviet nuclear balance, arguing that these systems' missions are primarily for conventional (nonnuclear) contingencies.

Reagan countered Andropov's proposal by saying that the United States would consider any Soviet proposal that would limit to equal numbers the U.S. and Soviet warheads deployed on land-based ballistic missiles in Europe.

In the summer of 1983, Andropov indicated some flexibility on INF, but on September 1 a Soviet pilot shot down a commercial Korean airliner that had strayed into Soviet airspace. All 269 people aboard were killed. The incident exacerbated U.S.-Soviet relations and undermined the chances for progress in arms control negotiations. This unfortunate development underscored the highly political nature of arms control.

On November 23, 1983, after the West German Bundestag voted to accept the deployment of Pershing IIs on its soil, the Soviet INF negotiators walked out of Geneva without setting a date for the resumption of talks.

START Talks

After more than 10 years of the Strategic Arms Limitations Talks (SALT) process, the Reagan administration decided to rename the main forum for arms control negotiations with the Soviet Union. To emphasize the new approach geared to "reductions" rather than just "limitations," Reagan's team came up with the name Strategic Arms Reductions Talks, with the appealing acronym START.

In the START negotiations of 1981-83, U.S. proposals were primarily designed to limit land-based ballistic missiles and throw-weight. Many of the officials who formulated START proposals contended that SALT II's equal limits and sublimits on strategic delivery vehicles — ICBMs, SLBMs, and bombers — did not prevent the Soviets from having an unacceptable advantage in ICBMs. Administration arms control advisers warned that Soviet "heavy" SS-19s and SS-18s, loaded with 6 and 10 warheads respectively, created a "window of vulnerability" in the U.S. deterrent. They maintained that the speed, accuracy, and potency of these missiles made them first-strike weapons capable of knocking out vulnerable U.S. land-based missiles. Conservative hard-liners outlined a grim scenario wherein the Soviets would destroy a high percentage of the U.S. ICBM force in a first strike and then blackmail the American president into capitulation by threatening U.S. cities with a second strike if the president chose to retaliate with his crippled forces. If the Soviets perceived the United States to be vulnerable, they might pursue their foreign policy goals more aggressively, resulting in superpower confrontations in which the United States might have to back down.

Based on this strategic assessment, the U.S. START proposal sought to limit the number of warheads deployed on ICBMs to 2,500. This would have allowed the United States to actually increase the number of multiple independently targetable reentry vehicles (warheads) on its land-based missiles. However, due to the asymmetric nature of the respective nuclear force structures (the Soviets have emphasized land-based ICBMs, while the United States has emphasized submarine-launched missiles and bombers), the Soviet Union would have had to cut the number of warheads on its ICBM forces by more than half. Another related U.S. proposal was to place an equal ceiling on aggregate missile throw-weight substantially below the existing Soviet level. The Soviets, with approximately a 3-to-1 advantage in total throw-weight, found these terms unacceptable. The Soviets proposed percentage reductions in strategic delivery systems based on SALT II limits and also a ban on long-range ground-launched and sea-launched cruise missiles, an area in which the United States had a decided advantage.

Dense Pack. President Reagan's original defense budget had envisioned deploying the 10-warhead MX in a "dense pack" of fortified silos, but Congress turned down dense pack in December 1982. This led the president to appoint a bipartisan commission of defense experts to develop a basing plan for the MX that would meet congressional approval. Thus in January 1983 President Reagan established the Commission on Strategic Forces, headed by retired lieutenant general Brent Scowcroft.

Scowcroft Commission. In April the Scowcroft commission presented its report questioning the "window of vulnerability." The report argued that the U.S. strategic triad was not, for the immediate future, vulnerable to a disarming Soviet first strike. In other words, it was still reasonable to expect that the Soviets would be deterred from a nuclear strike because enough U.S. strategic nuclear warheads would survive a Soviet attack to inflict unacceptable damage on the USSR. It also pointed out that making deep reductions in the number of launchers was not necessarily beneficial. The administration's original START proposal to cut ICBM and SLBM launchers to 850 would have increased the crucial warhead-to-launcher ratio. A MIRVed missile can eliminate several ICBM silos. Therefore, a reduced number of launchers would allow each country to allocate an increased number of warheads for striking each target. The land-based nuclear forces of both countries would, thus, become more vulnerable to a disarming first strike.

The Scowcroft commission recommended that the United States deploy 100 MX missiles in existing ICBM silos, while developing a mobile single-warhead "Midgetman" ICBM. A mobile missile, it was argued, would strengthen deterrence because it would be harder to hit than a fixed one and thus more survivable. A single-warhead missile would be a less attractive target because at best the Soviets would be able to eliminate only one U.S. warhead for each Soviet warhead launched (it is generally believed that at least two strategic warheads are needed to ensure the destruction of one target). It was also suggested that single warhead missiles were less threatening and therefore less likely to provoke a preemptive first strike.

The commission concluded that the controversial MX should be deployed in the interim because it would enhance deterrence, modernize the U.S. ICBM force, alleviate the strategic imbalance, and strengthen the U.S. bargaining position at Geneva. President Reagan, who deemed MX procurement vital to his nuclear weapons strategy, endorsed the commission's recommendation.

Nuclear Freeze; MX Opposition. At this point, the burgeoning nuclear freeze movement was gathering momentum and there was strong opposition to the MX on Capitol Hill. Widespread support for the freeze had grown throughout 1982, reflected in a freeze resolution that was only narrowly defeated in the House in August 1982. Critics charged that the MX would be vulnerable sitting in fixed silos and that its 10 warheads made it an attractive target. They argued that the MX was therefore a destabilizing first-strike weapon designed to be used for an actual attack rather than to deter one.

Build Down. As the vote to release funds for further MX development approached in May 1983, senators William Cohen, R-Maine, Sam Nunn, D-Ga., and Charles Percy, R-Ill., chairman of the Foreign Relations Committee, endorsed a new arms control approach called "build down." With this approach, both countries would dismantle a certain number of warheads for each new warhead deployed. The senators, who opposed the freeze, advocated build down because it allowed for reductions and modernization simultaneously.

They made it clear in a letter to President Reagan that their support for MX procurement was contingent on at least partial incorporation of the build-down approach into the administration's START proposals at Geneva as well as the inclusion of the Scowcroft recommendations for the Midgetman and de-MIRVing. Nine House members, including three representatives who were particularly influential on the MX issue — Les Aspin, D-Wis., Albert Gore, D-Tenn., and Norm Dicks, D-Wash. — also wrote the White House concerning the MX. The representatives warned they would oppose MX deployment unless they were reassured of Reagan's commitment to the entire package of arms control policies recommended by the Scowcroft commission. Reagan approved the build-down concept in principle and indicated that he would modify his START proposal to include the Scowcroft commission's ideas. At the end of the month both the House and the Senate passed the resolution to release the MX funds.

In October, Reagan announced he would incorporate build-down into the U.S. START proposal. Reportedly, the new position called for dismantling two old warheads for the deployment of each new MIRVed ICBM warhead, three old warheads for every two new SLBM warheads, and one old warhead for each new single-warhead ICBM. Such a formula encouraged a force structure emphasizing SLBMs over ICBMs and also provided an inducement for the deployment of single-warhead missiles as the Scowcroft commission had recommended. The proposal also included limits on total warheads, ballistic missile launchers, and throw-weight. The proposed limit on ballistic missile launchers was raised from 850 to 1,250. This new offer, if accepted, would have reduced the ratio of warheads to launchers relative to the result the earlier proposal would have achieved. Thus it too was consistent with the Scowcroft commission's advice.

Nuclear freeze backers criticized the U.S. proposal because it would allow the development of allegedly destabilizing first-strike weapons such as the MX and the Pershing II. The USSR dismissed the offer as biased against ICBMs, which carry approximately 70 percent of Soviet nuclear warheads against only only about 20 percent of American warheads. On October 31, the Senate voted down an amendment supporting a comprehensive nuclear freeze and further debate on the build-down approach was postponed indefinitely.

At the end of the year when the United States began deploying the Euro-missiles, Soviet START negotiators joined the Soviet INF negotiators in leaving the bargaining tables, saying that the strategic balance had been altered and would require a new assessment.

Presidential Race. In the 1984 presidential election campaign, Walter Mondale, the Democratic candidate, tried to exploit President Reagan's record on arms control and U.S.-Soviet relations. In addition to criticizing the president's arms control policies, he charged that Reagan would be the first president since Herbert Hoover not to have met with the Soviet leadership. In 1984 there was a definite softening in the tone of Reagan's public statements about the Soviet Union and many people believed that his more conciliatory rhetoric was a response to this domestic political challenge. In late September, less than two months before the election, President Reagan met with Foreign Minister Andrei Gromyko, in his first encounter with a high Soviet official. Observers suggested that although the Soviets realized this meeting would enhance Reagan's chances of reelection (a result they did not desire), they believed he would win anyway and would probably be more flexible before the election than after.

Debate on Reagan's SDI

During the first half of President Reagan's second term, the issues surrounding arms control were dominated by the debate over the president's Strategic Defense Initiative, commonly referred to as "Star Wars." On March 23, 1983, still during his first term, Reagan gave a speech challenging the scientific community to develop the technology for a space-based antiballistic missile defense that would some day make nuclear weapons "impotent and obsolete."

The initiative sparked tremendous controversy. President Reagan stressed that the deployment of a strategic defense system was a moral imperative because, in contrast to offensive systems, it would destroy weapons rather than people. Supporters argued that SDI might eventually free the people of the world from living under the "terror" of Mutual Assured Destruction (MAD), the doctrine that both superpowers are deterred from starting a nuclear war by the threat of immediate retaliation and devastation.

Other SDI advocates said strategic defense would be a stabilizing factor because it could enhance deterrence. They suggested that an ABM system protecting U.S. ICBM silos would so complicate calculations in Soviet strategic planning that a disarming first strike would be nearly impossible. The Soviets, SDI proponents contended, would never rationally launch a first strike knowing that relatively few ballistic missiles would penetrate the American defense. Supporters also argued that the United States needed a defensive system aside from the Soviet threat. The United States, they pointed out, would need to protect itself from hostile Third World leaders, such as Libya's Muammar Qaddafi or Iran's Ayatollah Khomeini, who could gain access to nuclear weapons.

Critics argued that SDI's development would escalate the arms race because the Soviet Union would upgrade its offensive forces to maintain its ability to penetrate the American defense. They suggested Soviet countermeasures might draw both sides into an "offense-defense spiral." The resulting arms race would be even more dangerous than the existing one.

To underline the likelihood of an intensified arms race, SDI critics cited a historical example. In the 1960s, the Soviet Union was developing a new ABM system. In response, the United States developed MIRVed missiles to saturate and overwhelm the Soviet defense. In 1972 the two countries signed the ABM treaty, limiting missile defense, but no agreement was reached restricting MIRVs and the arms race was ratcheted up another dangerous notch.

Opponents also questioned SDI's cost and efficacy. It has been projected to cost many billions of dollars in research and development and many scientists believe that such a defensive system would never function effectively. In September 1985 the Office of Technological Assessment, a nonpartisan agency of Congress, said that a ballistic missile defense able to ensure the survival of the U.S. population did not appear to be technologically feasible unless the Soviet Union agreed to significant limits on its offensive nuclear weapons. The study suggested that a U.S. effort to develop such a system would probably provoke the Soviet Union to increase its offensive forces.

Skeptics of SDI, including Les Aspin, who became chairman of the House Armed Services Committee in 1984, argued that the deployment of space-based ballistic missile defenses could undermine stability and increase the likelihood of a decision to launch a first strike. If both nations deployed somewhat imperfect systems, the argument ran, each side would have an incentive to launch a preemptive first strike. The side striking first would weaken the retaliatory forces of its adversary, making its own defense more viable and increasing its chances of survival.

Space-based antiballistic missile defense was challenged on the grounds that it could never be tested under realistic circumstances and that, even if it worked, it would not defend the United States against cruise missiles, bombers, and other contingencies such as terrorists or Soviet commandos smuggling in nuclear devices. Further, some argued, a defensive system itself would not be survivable in space, if attacked by offensive space weapons.

The Soviet Union adamantly protested the U.S. development of strategic defense. The Soviets have called it part of a U.S. first-strike strategy that would negate the Soviet Union's ability to maintain a credible nuclear deterrent. The Kremlin maintained that by deploying a strategic defense system the United States might be able to launch a successful surprise attack. U.S. strategic planners might expect that, after wiping out a high percentage of Soviet nuclear weapons, the American defense could repel the remainder of the depleted Soviet strategic forces. Moscow promised that it would take countermeasures, if the United States proceeded with SDI development.

President Reagan steadfastly supported SDI and declared that the research and development program would be nonnegotiable. During Reagan's second term, it was clear that hope for arms control between the superpowers rested on the resolution of the Star Wars issue.

Resumption of Talks

No formal arms control negotiations between the United States and the Soviet Union took place in 1984, but in January 1985 U.S. Secretary of State George Shultz and Gromyko met in Geneva to discuss possibilities for resuming talks. Following the meeting they announced that their respective countries would negotiate on three types of weapons: intercontinental or "strategic" weapons; intermediate-range nuclear forces in Europe; and space weapons. Arms control talks began in March.

There were probably two main reasons for the Soviet decision to return to the bargaining table. First, Moscow wanted to prevent, or at least slow down, the development of SDI. The Soviets generally lag behind the United States in technology, and further competition in space weapons would give the United States an opportunity to exploit that advantage. Also, the Soviet Union would have even greater

U.S.-Soviet Strategic Force Comparison

(December 1985)

	United States	Soviet Union
Launchers		
Intercontinental ballistic missiles (ICBMs)	1,024	1,398
Submarine-launched ballistic missiles (SLBMs)	648	946
Bombers	263	175
Total	1,935	2,519
Warheads		
ICBMs	2,124	6,420
SLBMs	5,760	1,402-2,866[1]
Bombers	3,276-4,476[2]	820
Total	11,160-12,360	8,642-10,106

[1] *Lower number assumes 7 warheads on SSN-20s and 1 warhead on SSN-18s. Higher number assumes 9 warheads on SSN-20s and 7 on SSN-18s.*

[2] *Lower number assumes 12 warheads on B-52Hs and B-52Gs. Higher number assumes 20 warheads on these bombers.*

Source: Arms Control Association, International Institute for Strategic Studies

---

difficulty achieving its objective of greater economic growth if forced to divert more resources from its already-neglected consumer sector to the defense sector. Second, by walking out of the arms control talks, the Soviets had made a costly public relations gaffe in the contest for Western Europe's favorable opinion. The Soviet Union not only failed to prevent the deployment of new American missiles in Western Europe, but it also appeared the more intransigent of the two superpowers when it came to pursuing arms control.

The growing perception that the new negotiations might lead to a beneficial treaty between the United States and the Soviet Union influenced some congressional leaders in their decisions on military spending and procurement of new nuclear weapons systems.

In late March, after intense lobbying by the administration, the House passed a bill to procure 21 more MX missiles for fiscal year 1985. To many, the most compelling argument in the new missile system's favor was that its deployment would indicate American resolve and improve the U.S. bargaining position at Geneva.

President Reagan made use of this rationale successfully in later efforts to engender support in Congress and among the public for SDI and antisatellite weapons.

Summit Posturing

When Konstantin Chernenko died in March 1985, President Reagan sent Vice President George Bush to the funeral in Moscow to present the new Soviet leader, Mikhail Gorbachev, an invitation for a summit. On April 7, Gorbachev indicated he would accept. In addition, Gorbachev announced a moratorium on the deployment of intermediate-range nuclear missiles in Europe, with the hope that the United States would follow suit. President Reagan dismissed the offer as a propaganda ploy that would lock in a Soviet advantage. Such exchanges set the tone for U.S.-Soviet dialogue for the next six months. The resumption of arms control talks and the preparation for the summit between the two leaders, which was eventually set for November 19-20, stimulated a propaganda war between the countries.

'No-Undercut' Policy. Following heated debate within the administration, President Reagan announced June 10 his decision not to "undercut" the terms of the SALT II treaty. To stay under the SALT limit of 1,200 MIRVed ballistic missile launchers, the United States dismantled a Poseidon submarine before deploying a new Trident submarine. Reagan called this action an example of his willingness "to go the extra mile" to eventually achieve a meaningful arms control agreement. In this context, Reagan accused the Soviets of violating SALT II provisions and said that, if necessary, the United States would make "appropriate and proportional responses." Further decisions on adherence that would arise when new MIRVed missile launchers were deployed, such as the next Trident and the MX, would be made on a case-by-case basis in response to Soviet actions.

An alleged Soviet violation, often cited by the Reagan administration, was the Soviet testing and planned deployment of the mobile SS-25 ICBM. The 1979 treaty allowed each country to develop only one new type of ICBM. The Soviets had filled their quota by developing the SS-24, as the United States had by developing the MX. As a response to the deployment of the Soviets' second new ICBM, the SS-25, the United States said that it would be justified in deploying the mobile single-warhead Midgetman ICBM. The Soviets countered that the SS-25 was only a modification of the old SS-13 missile. (Modifications are allowed under the treaty.)

The Soviets dismissed President Reagan's decision to continue adherence to the treaty, arguing that limits on defensive systems, such as those in the ABM treaty, are preconditions for limits on offensive systems. They claimed that development and testing of SDI, which the Soviets said would violate the ABM treaty, precluded stringent restraints on offensive weapons.

Soviet Moratorium. In July, General Secretary Gorbachev declared a Soviet moratorium on the testing of nuclear weapons through the end of 1985, starting on August 6, the 40th anniversary of the bombing of Hiroshima. The United States declined to stop testing, again accusing Gorbachev of a propaganda ploy. The administration said that the Soviets had recently tested their latest nuclear weapons and that a moratorium would hamper the progress of developing American programs needed to catch up. Furthermore, the United States said that such a testing moratorium would be unverifiable, given the Soviet refusal to allow on-site inspections. Instead of declaring a testing moratorium, the administration invited Soviet officials to monitor a U.S. underground nuclear test in Nevada. The Politburo turned down the offer.

U.S. ASAT Test. The U.S. Air Force successfully tested an antisatellite (ASAT) weapon in September amidst great controversy. The Soviets, who had abstained from ASAT testing for two years, accused the United States of escalating the arms race in space and said that they no longer felt bound to their unilateral moratorium. The United States maintained that the test was necessary because the Soviets already had an operational system and an American counterpart could deter its use.

Critics charged that the Soviet Union's ASAT was not capable of destroying U.S. satellites in high orbit where most vital U.S. early warning satellites are deployed. They argued that the U.S. ASAT test would provoke the Soviets to upgrade their relatively primitive system to the extent that it would some day threaten U.S. satellites in high orbit. Opponents asserted that a new test would complicate a future ban on ASATs. Once a system is tested successfully, they claimed, it would be considered operational and then it would be nearly impossible to verify an agreement prohibiting the weapons. Testing can be monitored by national technical means (NTM), such as surveillance satellites, they argued, but once tested the small, concealable weapons could be squirreled away, preventing their detection.

October Soviet Proposal. In late October, Gorbachev presented a new arms control proposal to Reagan through his recently appointed foreign minister, Eduard Shevardnadze. The Soviets offered a 50 percent mutual reduction in strategic offensive weapons, if the United States would scrap its strategic defense program. Four of Moscow's terms were considered especially unacceptable by Washington.

First, the Soviets hinted they wanted to prevent SDI laboratory research as well as testing and deployment. The United States, even if it wanted to concur, believed that such a ban would be nearly impossible to verify.

Second, the Soviets wanted to define "strategic weapons" as any weapons capable of striking each other's territory. This would include U.S. Pershing IIs, GLCMs, and short-range bombers deployed in Europe and Asia and on aircraft carriers, but not Soviet intermediate-range missiles such as the SS-20s targeted on U.S. allies. In November 1974, when Ford and Brezhnev met in Vladivostok to lay out the framework for SALT II, the Soviet Union had informally and tentatively agreed to drop its insistence that American FBS be counted in the "strategic" nuclear weapons balance in return for a commitment from the United States to drop its demand to severely restrict Soviet heavy missiles, such as the SS-18.

Third, the USSR wanted to ban deployment of new weapons systems after a negotiated date. That would probably have allowed the Soviet Union to deploy its new SS-24 and SS-25 mobile ICBMs and Blackjack bomber but prohibited the United States from deploying its Midgetman mobile ICBM, Trident II D-5 SLBM, and Stealth bomber, all of which were only in development stages.

Fourth, Moscow wanted to count "nuclear charges" rather than warheads, which would equate, for example, U.S. gravity bombs on antiquated planes with warheads on Soviet heavy SS-18 ICBMs. Despite these problems, the fact that the Soviets offered a concrete proposal with significant reductions in offensive weapons was considered encouraging.

The Soviet proposal contained additional important provisions. It banned cruise missiles with ranges over 6,000 kilometers, which would have eliminated the U.S. air-launched cruise missile (ALCM) program and limited U.S. submarine-launched cruise missiles (SLCMs). It counted U.S. short-range attack missiles (SRAMs) and bombs carried by U.S. planes in its overall limit of 6,000 nuclear charges, but it did not count weapons carried by the Soviet Backfire bomber, which the United States considers an intercontinental bomber. The United States argues that SRAMs and bombs should not be counted because the Soviets have a relatively strong air defense with which to repel a U.S. bomber attack. The United States has a weaker air defense and the Soviets do not need so many weapons to penetrate it.

In its most promising offer, the Soviet proposal would prohibit either side from placing more than 3,600 warheads on one type of weapon — ICBMs, SLBMs, or bombers. This would have forced the Soviets to make more than a 40 percent cut in the number of warheads on its ICBMs. However, it would allow them to keep all 308 10-warhead SS-18s plus 86 existing 6-warhead SS-19s or 52 10-warhead SS-24s, which were then about to be deployed. These three "hard-target/counterforce" systems reportedly can destroy U.S. hardened silos, threatening the American land-based forces.

The Soviets also proposed in the interim to freeze the

1985 U.S.-Soviet Nuclear Arms Lineup

Following is a breakdown of the strategic force balance between the United States and the Soviet Union as of December 1985. The chart was compiled from figures assembled by the International Institute for Strategic Studies, the Arms Control Association, and other official and private sources.

The numbers do not include several hundred shorter-range planes and missiles in each force that could strike the other side's territory under certain circumstances. The chart also omits British and French planes and missiles that the Soviets say must be counted. Dates in parentheses indicate when initial deployment is expected.

	UNITED STATES			SOVIET UNION		
	Number	Type	Number of Warheads	Number	Type	Number of Warheads
'Prompt Hard-Target Killers'[1]						
Heavy land-based missiles (ICBMs)[2]	0	—	—	308	SS-18	1-10
Other ICBMs	550	Minuteman III[3]	3	360	SS-19[3]	6
		MX *(1986)*	10	18	SS-25[4]	1
		Midgetman *(1990s)*	1		SS-24 *(1986)*	10
Submarine-launched missiles		Trident II *(1989)*	8			
Other ICBMs						
	450	Minuteman II	1	150	SS-17	4
	24	Titan II[5]	1	502	SS-11[6]	1
				60	SS-13	1
Other Submarine-Launched Missiles						
	360	Trident I[4]	8	16	SSN-23[4]	7
	288	Poseidon[7]	10	60	SSN-20[4]	7-9
				224	SSN-18	1-7
					SSN-6[8]	
				634	SSN-8	1
				12	SSN-17	1
Bombers With Long-Range ALCMs						
		B-1 *(1986)*	24	30	Bear H[4]	8
	15	B-52H	20		Blackjack *(1987-89)*	
	98	B-52G	12			
Other Long-Range Bombers						
Heavy Bombers		Stealth *(1990s)*	?	100	Bear	4
	81	B-52H	12-20	45	Bison[9]	4
	69	B-52G	12-20			
	270-307	B-52 hulks[10]	0			
Medium Bombers	63	FB-111	4	260	Backfire	2-3
Homeland Defenses						
Antiballistic Missile Launchers	0			100[11]		
Antiaircraft Missile Launchers	0			12,000 at 1,200 sites		
Antibomber Fighter Planes	270			1,200		

[1] Missiles with the accuracy and explosive power needed to destroy armored underground targets within minutes of launch.
[2] U.S. officials say these missiles need special limits because they have such powerful engines they could be modified to carry 30 to 40 warheads.
[3] U.S. officials now say that the Minuteman III and SS-19 cannot destroy modernized missile silos.
[4] New system still being deployed.
[5] Titan IIs are being scrapped at a rate of about one a month.
[6] SS-11s are being scrapped as SS-25s are deployed.

[7] Poseidons can carry 14 warheads apiece, but according to most sources they carry only 10.
[8] SSN-6s are being scrapped as newer missiles are deployed.
[9] Bisons are being scrapped as newer bombers are deployed.
[10] These are old airplanes that have been stripped of parts — including engines in some cases — but still count as bombers under the rules agreed to in U.S.-Soviet negotiations over SALT II.
[11] Reagan administration officials say that several hundred of the newer types of Soviet antiaircraft missiles can be used against some missile warheads.

number of intermediate-range nuclear forces in Europe. The official offer would have banned U.S. Pershing IIs and GLCMs and reduced the number of Soviet SS-20s to 243, matching British and French force levels. The interim freeze proposal, however, offered hope to the United States for a potential INF agreement, as it implicitly acknowledged acceptance of the U.S. deployment of intermediate-range nuclear forces in Europe up to that time.

ABM Reinterpretation. On October 6, 1985, President Reagan's national security adviser, Robert McFarlane, announced that the administration had reexamined the 1972 Antiballistic Missile Treaty and now interpreted it as allowing SDI development and testing. According to McFarlane, the 1972 agreement barred only deployment of a new ABM system. Article V says, "each party undertakes not to develop, test or deploy ABM systems or components which are sea-based, air-based, space-based or mobile land-based." Agreed statement D, however, upon which the argument for the new, more permissive, interpretation was based, says, "If ABM systems based on other physical principles . . . are created in the future, specific limitations on such systems and their components would be subject to discussion."

SDI supporters suggested that the "other physical principles" clause would allow the United States to test SDI components such as lasers and particle-beam weapons. Gerard Smith, the U.S. chief negotiator for the ABM treaty, disputed the administration's findings.

The new interpretation created an uproar with the NATO allies. The ABM treaty was considered by many to be the cornerstone of arms control, providing a foundation for any agreements limiting offensive weapons. To assuage their concerns, Secretary of State Shultz assured the West Europeans on October 14 that even though the new interpretation was correct the United States would continue to observe the older, more restrictive interpretation.

This incident demonstrated the difficulty the United States had in trying to speak with one coherent voice on arms control policy. The apparent internal conflict suggested that bureaucratic politics — the competition among the agencies for influence with the president — played a key role in shaping his arms control position for the summit.

Krasnoyarsk Offer. Later in October the Soviet Union offered to halt construction on their "phased-array" radar station near Krasnoyarsk in central Siberia, if the United States agreed to forgo modernization of its radar systems in Britain and Greenland. The administration for some time claimed that the Soviet radar station was a violation of the ABM treaty. The treaty allowed early-warning radars to be deployed on the periphery of each nation's territory with their antennas facing outward. The purpose was to prohibit radars based in central areas, such as Siberia, that could be used to track incoming warheads and facilitate the operation of an antiballistic missile system.

The Soviets said the radar station was to be used for space-tracking, allowable under the treaty. However, the Soviet's proposal indicated an implicit acknowledgment that the Krasnoyarsk radar was indeed a violation. The United States, in response to the Soviet offer, refused to abandon modernization of its radar systems in Britain and Greenland. According to administration officials, these two systems existed before the signing of the 1972 treaty and are early-warning radars, allowed by the agreement.

Reagan's Counteroffer. About three weeks before

the summit President Reagan's negotiators offered a counterproposal to Gorbachev's reduction plan. Reagan agreed to the concept of 50 percent cuts but wanted them in ballistic warheads rather than in nuclear charges. The United States continued to stress that extremely accurate and potent ballistic missiles, which can hit their targets in less than 30 minutes, are the most dangerous nuclear weapons and should not be considered equal to slow-flying cruise missiles or bombs delivered by aircraft. The United States proposed a ceiling of 4,500 ballistic warheads, which was 500 fewer than its earlier proposal; and a sublimit on land-based warheads of 3,000, which was 500 more than its earlier proposal (and 600 fewer than the latest Soviet proposal).

The U.S. offer did not yield on President Reagan's commitment to develop and test strategic defense. The proposal also sought a ban on mobile land-based missiles, repudiating the Scowcroft commission's recommendation and angering congressional leaders who had supported the MX in exchange for the administration's backing of Midgetman. Some angry Midgetman supporters in Congress, such as Senator Cohen, charged that Reagan was abandoning the mobile system to generate congressional support for SDI, which could eventually be used to protect the more vulnerable stationary systems.

The administration defended its proposed ban on mobile ICBMs by pointing out that the Soviets would have to scrap their recently deployed SS-24 and SS-25 mobile missiles. It also noted that allowing mobile missile systems would create difficult verification problems and give an advantage to the Soviet Union, which has far more available land on which to deploy these systems. Further arguments against mobile systems included their cost and potentially negative impact on the environment.

The U.S. proposal also called for a limit on throw-weight, which would have forced the Soviets to reduce their existing throw-weight level from approximately 5.7 million kilograms to about 3 million kilograms. The existing U.S. throw-weight level was about 1.9 million kilograms. Another provision called for a ban on the modernization of heavy missiles, which would have denied the Soviets the option of upgrading their 308 SS-18s. Long-range bombers would have been limited to 350 and only 1,500 ALCMs could have been deployed.

For INF, the United States proposed a limit of 140 launchers for each country in Europe and also reductions in Soviet Asian-based SS-20s. This would have allowed the Soviets 140 3-warhead SS-20s, and the United States 36 single-warhead Pershing IIs and 104 GLCMs with 4 single-warhead missiles on each launcher, for 420 and 452 total warheads respectively.

The American offer did not count French and British forces. France and Britain were expected to MIRV their existing single-warhead missiles at the end of the decade, precluding any future deal to include French and British warheads in the balance. If the United States had offered an equal limit on warheads including French and British forces, the Soviets eventually would have been allowed to increase the number of their SS-20s in Europe to compensate for that MIRVing.

Reagan Interview With Soviets. About two weeks before the summit, President Reagan granted an interview with four Soviet journalists and said, "We would not deploy [a strategic defense system] until we sit down with the other nations of the world, and those that have nuclear arsenals, and see if we cannot come to an agreement on which there will be deployment only if there is elimination of the [offensive] nuclear weapons.... We would want it [SDI] for everyone and the terms for getting it, and the terms for our own deployment would be the elimination of the offensive weapons." This indicated that Moscow might have the option to veto SDI deployment. Reagan's aides scrambled to qualify and modify his statement. They said that the president meant there would be a transitional period in which defensive systems were phased in and offensive systems were phased out.

Despite these corrections, the president's "imprecision" raised some disturbing questions. Like his other misstatements, critics charged, it raised further doubt about the president's grasp of arms control issues and the implications of his policies. Skeptics of Reagan's technology-sharing offer pointed out that by the time SDI reached fruition, if ever, Reagan would have long since left the presidency. The Soviets had no guarantee that future U.S. presidents would feel obligated to honor the offer. During the 1984 presidential campaign, Walter Mondale, who was generally perceived to be far less anti-Soviet than Reagan, sharply criticized his opponent's idea of giving U.S. strategic technology to the USSR.

Weinberger Letter. A few days before the summit, a letter from Secretary of Defense Caspar Weinberger to the president was leaked to the *New York Times* and the *Washington Post.* In the letter, Weinberger urged Reagan not to accept an agreement at the meeting in Geneva committing the United States to continue to adhere to the SALT II treaty. Weinberger argued that such an agreement would limit American "options for responding to Soviet [treaty] violations." He also suggested that Reagan not accept a restrictive interpretation of the ABM treaty limiting SDI development and testing.

Weinberger's letter received considerable coverage by the media and some people speculated that the secretary himself had planned for it to be leaked, thereby undermining the prospects for an agreement. Actually, the information divulged was not surprising. Weinberger and his top arms control aide, Richard Perle, had been highly critical of SALT II and had taken a hard-line approach toward dealing with the Soviets.

Presummit Hopes. In the months preceding the summit there had been a degree of optimism that President Reagan and General Secretary Gorbachev could outline the principles for an arms control accord in Geneva, as Ford and Brezhnev had done for SALT II during their 1975 summit in Vladivostok. Despite the asymmetric nature of the force structures of the two countries, many people believed the foundations for an arms control agreement had materialized. Each superpower had complementary programs that the other side wanted to severely limit or reduce. The SDI program, which the Soviets wanted to stop, was geared to defend against the same forces that the United States wanted to reduce: Soviet MIRVed ICBMs. Arms control advocates suggested that the limitation and restriction of one would strengthen the argument for reducing the other.

In addition, both superpower leaders appeared to have strong incentives to reach an agreement. An arms control accord could facilitate the achievement of Gorbachev's domestic goal to build a stronger economy. If he could negotiate a treaty, then the Soviets could channel more resources into capital formation rather than into expanded nuclear weapons programs. Reagan, it had often been reported, wanted to go down in history as a "peacemaker." The

summit would be a great opportunity to start carving that legacy. Reagan also had to contend with a ballooning federal budget deficit, giving him another good reason to try to reach an agreement on limiting arms. In spite of this potential, the administration on the eve of the summit stated that the odds were against a Reagan-Gorbachev joint statement on arms control.

Postsummit Negotiations

After all the media buildup, the summit produced mixed reviews and ambivalence. The two leaders agreed to further meetings and both welcomed the beginning of a new dialogue between the superpowers. They also signed accords expanding cultural exchanges, establishing new consulates, and improving air safety. However, the summit produced no visible progress on major issues. Those who saw the summit results in a positive light expressed satisfaction that Reagan and Gorbachev had conversed amiably and planned to continue talking. This in itself, they said, was a great accomplishment. Those who saw the summit results in a negative light pointed out that arms control, regional, and human rights issues remained unresolved. *(Details, Chapter 9; Summit documents, p. 334)*

Furthermore, Reagan made it clear following the summit that the United States would continue to abide by SALT II after it expired December 31, 1985, if the Soviets did the same. In a December 23 report to Congress, he officially confirmed U.S. intentions to continue complying with SALT II. But at the same time he accused the USSR of new arms control violations.

The administration's commitment to SALT II was to be tested in 1986 when the eighth Trident submarine and the first MX missiles were deployed. The president would again have to decide whether continued observance of the treaty was worth the strategic sacrifice of retiring operational nuclear weapons to stay within SALT II limits.

A December 5, 1985, letter to President Reagan from General Secretary Gorbachev (which was made public December 19) initiated an exchange of offers on nuclear weapons tests that built on the proposals of the previous summer. Gorbachev attempted to counter a primary Reagan administration objection to a mutual moratorium on nuclear testing by offering to allow U.S. inspections of some Soviet nuclear test facilities if the U.S. joined the USSR in an extended testing halt. Gorbachev's proposal for limited on-site verification broke with the usual Soviet pattern of refusing to consider such measures. President Reagan welcomed Gorbachev's offer and proposed technical talks on improving verification of testing agreements. But the administration rejected Gorbachev's moratorium, saying the United States needed testing to maintain the reliability of its arsenal and that the Soviets could not be trusted to honor an extended moratorium. In January 1986 Gorbachev extended the five-month unilateral moratorium on nuclear tests until April, but the United States again refused to join the halt.

On January 15 General Secretary Gorbachev caught the Reagan administration by surprise when he proposed a comprehensive ban on nuclear weapons to be achieved in stages by the year 2000. Gorbachev also called for a comprehensive ban on the production of chemical weapons, a resumption of talks on a comprehensive test ban, and progress on talks on conventional forces and confidence-building measures in Europe. *(Proposal text, p. 342)*

U.S. officials had said they did not expect a new Soviet

proposal until after the Soviet Communist Party Congress ended in early March. Gorbachev's plan incorporated existing Soviet positions but also introduced new ideas. His call for an initial 50 percent reduction in strategic arsenals with each side retaining no more than 6,000 nuclear charges was basically the same offer made by the Soviets in Geneva before the summit. The plan also contained no easing of the Soviet demand that U.S. development of SDI and ASATs be discontinued before any reductions in nuclear weapons. However, with respect to intermediate-range missiles, the Reagan administration was encouraged by what it perceived as shifts in the Soviet position. Gorbachev called for the "complete liquidation" of all U.S. and Soviet intermediate-range missiles in Europe — a statement approaching the original zero-option proposal made by Reagan in 1981. The general secretary also said French and British nuclear weapons would not have to be included in an agreement so long as those countries pledged not to build up their arsenals. Previously, the Soviets had insisted that independent British and French forces be counted.

These changes and Gorbachev's positive statements concerning Soviet willingness to cooperate on verification led U.S. officials to be optimistic about the chances for an INF agreement in 1986. This optimism was reinforced February 6 when Gorbachev told Sen. Edward M. Kennedy, D-Mass., in Moscow that the only conditions for an accord reducing intermediate-range missiles in Europe were a freeze on British and French nuclear arsenals and an agreement that the Western nuclear powers not move weapons to any other country. Gorbachev did not reiterate his January 15 statement that there would be no INF accord until the United States stopped development of space weapons.

The United States formally responded to Gorbachev's arms control plan February 24. In a letter to the general secretary, Reagan said the plan was "clearly not appropriate for consideration at this time." The president stated "the total elimination of nuclear weapons" could be accomplished only if the USSR fully complied with its treaty obligations, reduced its conventional forces in Europe, and cooperated in resolving regional conflicts. He asked that the two sides concentrate their efforts on phasing out intermediate-range nuclear weapons.

Reagan offered two alternative timetables for eliminating intermediate nuclear weapons (including Soviet SS-20s in Asia). He also called for a freeze on deployments of short-range nuclear weapons in Europe. However, Reagan rejected the condition of a freeze on British and French nuclear forces.

General Secretary Gorbachev rebuffed Reagan's offer during his party congress speech February 25. While Gorbachev said Reagan's proposal seemed "to contain some reassuring opinions," he said it was "hard to detect . . . any serious preparedness of the U.S. administration to get down to solving the cardinal problems involved in eliminating the nuclear threat." *(Gorbachev speech excerpts, Appendix, p. 346)*

Gorbachev also suggested that without prior movement on arms control issues he would not take part in another summit with President Reagan. "There is no sense in holding empty talks," he said.

In Geneva, arms control talks ended March 4 with no progress. After the talks had resumed in January there had been hope that advances would be made on medium-range missiles if not on other areas under discussion, a hope based on the joint statement issued at the November summit.

Gorbachev announced March 13 that the Soviet Union had decided to continue its unilateral testing moratorium set to expire at the end of the month. The test-ban extension would remain in effect until the United States carried out a nuclear test. After the United States conducted tests March 22 and April 10, the Soviets announced that they would end the moratorium and resume testing. But following the tragic accident at the Chernobyl nuclear power reactor in April, the Soviets decided to reinstate their testing halt. They had not conducted any tests and their decision would extend their moratorium to a full year. Some Western analysts saw the continuation of the moratorium as an attempt by the Soviet leadership to deflect criticism of their handling of the Chernobyl disaster. Gorbachev said the devastating consequences of even the limited radiation that spewed from Chernobyl convinced the Soviet leadership to reinstate the ban with the hope that the United States would follow its example.

Economy: Perennial Problem

Since World War II the global economy has become increasingly intertwined. Newly independent nations have made established industrial giants vulnerable to outside pressures. But the communist countries occupy a special place within the context of this increasing interdependence.

The centrally planned economies of the Soviet Union and its allies in Eastern Europe, as well as Soviet-supported Third World countries such as Cuba and Vietnam, participate to a far lesser degree in the world economy. This is due to the USSR's abundance of oil and other natural resources, to the Soviet policy of trying to maintain economic self-sufficiency within its own borders, and to the continued dependence of its satellites. As a result of their relative isolation these economies have suffered less directly from the recurrent recessions and oil shocks that have buffeted the capitalist, or market, economies in recent years.

But the communist economies also have benefited less from the stimulus offered by expanding world trade. Their industrial exports are not often competitive on world markets and the Soviets have had difficulty making full use of imported Western technology. Often, high technology has been limited to use in the defense sector, rather than being spread throughout the economy.

Because the Soviet Union and its allies publish few reliable statistics, Western analysis of the communist economies is sketchy and often incomplete. It is clear, however, that central planning has fallen short of expectations. The Soviet Union, which has stood as the principal model of communist economic development since 1917, today presents a lackluster alternative to the free enterprise system. Low industrial productivity, dependence on foreign sources of agricultural commodities, and a dearth of consumer goods are chronic problems.

Raising the low annual rate of economic growth (reportedly only 2 percent in the first quarter of 1985) is but one of several pressures the leadership faces. For years the Soviet economy had relied on *extensive growth* — achieved by putting more capital, labor, energy, and raw materials into the economy. It is widely recognized within the Soviet Union that a shift to *intensive growth* is necessary — that is, using increasingly limited inputs more efficiently and improving technology — but the leadership has been unable, or unwilling, to take appropriate steps to bring it about.

Central Planning System

Central planning is the common denominator of economic activity in all the communist countries, a direct legacy of the Soviet five-year plans first introduced under Joseph Stalin in 1928. Long-range planning, it was reasoned, would not only ensure party control over economic activities but also channel them in an orderly fashion and thus speed industrial development.

The state runs the Soviet economy. All industrial and commercial enterprises are state-owned and state-operated and the state bank (Gosbank) controls all credit. The state planning committee (Gosplan) promulgates the detailed five-year plans that chart the development targets the national economy is expected to meet in the next half decade. (The current plan covers 1986-90.) Production and manufacturing goals are broken down into monthly and yearly quotas for individual industries and factories. Clever factory managers try to keep their quotas as low as possible. Yet problems related to the quota system persist. In *Russia: The People and the Power*, journalist Robert G. Kaiser discusses the practice of "storming," speeding production late in the month to reach the quota:

> The system of "storming" at the end of the month is endemic. The brother-in-law of a friend of mine in Moscow was an executive in a factory, and his wife knew he would never come home during the last four or five days of the month. He would sleep at the plant. The First Secretary of the Party in Azerbaijan said in 1971 that the average factory in his republic produced 10 to 15 percent of its monthly production during the first 10 days of the month and 50 percent during the last 10 days. A prominent Soviet economist, Leonid Kantorovich, winner of the Nobel Prize in 1975, has estimated that the total national income could be increased by *30 to 50 percent* if "storming" could be replaced by efficient use of resources. *(Italics in original)*

Economy Under Brezhnev

Leonid I. Brezhnev, who succeeded Nikita S. Khrushchev in 1964, tinkered with the economy without making much progress. Agricultural production remained stagnant.

After 1970 the country was transformed from an exporter to the world's largest net importer of grain. But the relative domestic calm of the late 1960s and early 1970s was due in part to the Brezhnev regime's commitment to improving the lot of Soviet consumers. The Kremlin, one observer has said, successfully pursued during these years a guns-and-butter policy. Defense expenditures remained steady, but additional attention was paid to increasing the availability of consumer goods.

In the years 1965-72 per capita consumption rose 5 percent; per capita income was up 6.9 percent. In 1960 television sets were owned by only 8 of every 100 families, only 4 of every 100 possessed a refrigerator or a washing machine. By 1977 more than 75 percent of Soviet families had a television set and about 65 percent owned refrigerators and washing machines.

In addition, the government invested in education and health care and reduced the workweek from 48 to 41 hours. Moreover, the Kremlin leaders vowed to increase per capita consumption of meat to levels equal to those in industrialized nations. In 1960 annual meat consumption was 33.3 kilograms (about 73 pounds). By 1970 it had risen to 43 kilograms (nearly 95 pounds; in the United States, meat consumption in 1971 averaged 191 pounds per person).

At the 23d Party Congress in 1966, his first as party chief, Brezhnev pledged "a fuller satisfaction of the material and cultural requirements of all Soviet people" and "a radical improvement of the quality of goods." At the 24th Party Congress in 1971, he again promised consumer improvements.

In his speech opening the 25th Party Congress in 1976, however, Brezhnev admitted that although the government had speeded up the growth rate of heavy industry "we have not learned to accelerate the development" of consumer goods. He mentioned the difficulties the Soviets had experienced trying to improve the quality of consumer goods and reminded his audience of the "unprecedented droughts" of 1972 and 1975 to explain the dismal performance in agriculture. One casualty was Agriculture Minister Dmitri Polianskii; he was dropped from the Politburo in 1976.

Despite the relative gains in the standard of living, the Soviet leaders were aware that their economy, in its existing state, could not fulfill their most cherished goal — equaling the efficiency and production of Western economies. The economy needed outside help. Soviet specialist Marshall D. Shulman wrote in the October 1973 issue of *Foreign Affairs:*

> Rather than face the politically painful choice of instituting substantial economic reforms, the Soviet leadership has opted for a massive effort to overcome its shortcomings by increasing the flow of trade, advanced technology and capital from abroad. To overcome its shortage of hard currency, the Soviet Union seeks help in developing its manufactures for Western markets, and invites Western capital and technology to help exploit Soviet natural resources, such as its large Siberian reserves of natural gas, to be paid for out of the export of these resources. In his meetings with West German and American businessmen, Brezhnev has projected opportunities for vast joint production ventures over periods of 20 to 30 years. The realization of these expectations manifestly requires an international climate of reduced tension.

Problems Set In

Events in the Soviet Union and abroad in the late 1970s posed new problems. The slowing trend in economic growth failed to reverse itself. The Soviets continued to devote a substantial proportion of their gross national product (GNP) — estimates ranged as high as 15 percent — to defense. The productivity of Soviet workers failed to expand as much as the Kremlin chiefs hoped and the growth of the labor force fell from 2 percent annually in 1970-75 to about 1 percent in the late 1970s. In the view of some observers, the fewer workers failed to increase productivity because they lacked sufficient incentives. According to the U.S. Defense Intelligence Agency, "A vicious cycle has appeared; low economic growth requires more capital investment, which reduces consumption, which reduces incentives, which reduces labor productivity, which reduces growth."

Agricultural production was disappointing. A key factor was weather; crops in 1977, 1979, and 1980 were well below target and productivity failed to register the large gains it needed to satisfy consumers. For example, Soviet farmers working on collective farms outnumbered U.S. farmers 5 to 1 in 1980, but productivity was less than one-third American levels. Yet the production record of private plots — small parcels farmed on an individual's free time — was stunning. Although the private plots made up only 3 percent of all Soviet farmland, they accounted for 33 percent of the nation's meat production, 40 percent of the eggs, and 60 percent of the potatoes. Soviet farmers, allowed to keep or market the produce from personal plots, sold their goods at farmers' markets where they could charge prices higher than those set by the state. The government, beset by poor harvests on state farms and huge bills for purchases of foreign grain, began to promote cultivation of private plots in the mid-to-late 1970s to bolster the food supply.

The state of the economy was a major item on the agenda of the November 27, 1979, meeting of the Communist Party Central Committee. During a speech to the committee, General Secretary Brezhnev criticized by name 27 government ministers for "negligence, irresponsibility, or bungling" in handling economic affairs. Brezhnev also called for energy conservation, despite Soviet reserves of oil and natural gas estimated at 223 billion barrels in 1980, the largest reserves in the world. *(Energy resources, p. 168)*

Unmet Goals

The uncertain Soviet economic future resulted in the formulation of a less-than-optimistic Five-Year Plan for the years 1981-85. Unveiled at the 26th Party Congress, held February 23-March 3, 1981, the plan called for the lowest overall growth rate in Soviet history. Industrial output was slated to rise from 5.0 to 5.6 percent annually, down from the projected rate of 6.3 percent in the 1976-80 plan (the actual growth rate for 1976-80 was only 4.7 percent). Stressing the need to improve productivity, Brezhnev told the congress February 23, "Any improvement in the standard of living can be achieved only by hard work on the part of the Soviet people themselves."

Brezhnev also said that exploitation of Siberian natural gas and oil would be the top economic priority. And he pledged to improve the supply of meat and other foods by supporting private farm plots, which he said were "a substantial asset" of Soviet agriculture.

In his economic report to the congress February 27,

Alcohol Abuse: A Soviet Curse

"It is Russia's joy to drink. We cannot do without it," wrote Kiev's Saint Vladimir in the tenth century. That observation apparently holds true in the 1980s as well.

Scientists, journalists, scholars, and public health officials have all bemoaned the number of deaths, workplace accidents, and related health problems caused by alcohol in the Soviet Union. Retardation, infant mortality, miscarriages, and other alcohol-related problems have increased with the significant rise in alcoholism among women. Higher suicide, crime, and divorce rates are attributed to alcoholism, and labor productivity has sharply declined.

The Soviet Union drinks more vodka and other alcoholic beverages than any other nation. Vladimir Treml of Duke University reported in the mid-1980s that consumption of state-produced alcoholic beverages (the only legal source of alcohol) had risen 6.9 percent annually since the early 1960s. According to David Powell in *The Soviet Union Today*, sales of alcohol increased 77 percent between 1970 and 1980, while the population grew by only 9 percent. Teenage and female drinkers account for most of the increase.

In addition to legal alcohol, homemade *samogon*, a low-grade vodka-like beverage, accounts for much of the increase in alcohol-related deaths. Increasing the price of vodka has not resulted in less drinking but in more reliance on the drinking of "after-shave lotion, cleaning fluid, varnish, and industrial alcohol," Treml noted.

According to a study in the 1960s by Boris M. Segal, the Russian Republic had the highest incidence of alcoholism, followed by Belorussia and the Ukraine, and then the Baltic republics. Alcohol consumption and abuse has traditionally been lowest among Jews and Moslems.

The Kremlin has made several efforts to combat alcoholism, but none has proved very effective. In many industries (such as coal mining) workers must take daily sobriety tests. Those picked up by the police for public drunkenness pay fines and are reported to their employers. According to Treml, 12 percent to 15 percent of the adult population spent at least one night in a sobering-up station in 1979.

Western experts believe that crowded living conditions, urbanization, boredom, and a host of other factors cause alcoholism. But Soviet leaders can go only so far in their attempts to curb consumption. More than 10 percent of the Soviet Union's annual revenues come from alcohol taxes.

Nonetheless, in May 1985 General Secretary Mikhail Gorbachev announced several measures to fight alcohol abuse. On June 1 the legal drinking age was raised to 21 from 18 and the opening of liquor stores was delayed for three hours on workdays.

The state also began a gradual reduction in alcohol production. Those caught drunk in public faced stiffer penalties. The fine for driving while intoxicated increased to 100 rubles ($130 at the official exchange rate), and drunk drivers faced the loss of their license for between one and three years.

Prime Minister Nikolai A. Tikhonov urged resumption of U.S.-Soviet trade, which in 1980 amounted to only $1.9 billion, down from $4.5 billion in 1979. Tikhonov neglected to mention Afghanistan as a possible explanation; instead, he blamed the decline on "U.S. policy that is designed to use trade for unseemly political ends foreign to equitable international cooperation." He admitted that the Soviets needed Western technology to improve productivity and the supply of consumer goods, but he termed Western claims that the Soviet economy was faltering "slanderous inventions."

To decrease reliance on imports, Brezhnev in May 1982 introduced the New Food Program, which coupled limited decentralization with greater investment in agriculture. Mikhail Gorbachev was the program's principal architect. Meat and grain output did in fact increase under the program, but demand by a growing urban population largely wiped out these gains. While accounting for only 3 percent of all cultivated land, private plots continued to produce at least a quarter of the nation's food supply, especially meat, dairy products, and fresh fruit and vegetables. Farms run by the military were also said to seldom meet production targets.

Andropov Revises Thinking

Yuri Andropov emphasized economic reform at the outset of his brief tenure as party general secretary (November 1982-February 1984). He encouraged economists to suggest ways to stimulate economic growth, increase resources and consumer goods, and reduce absenteeism and alcoholism among factory and farm workers. *(Alcohol abuse, box, this page)*

Out of the ensuing debate came an unprecedented flow of criticism, some published in Soviet economic journals, some distributed as internal party documents.

Andropov said repeatedly that his "highest priority" was to revive the stagnant economy. He told Central Committee members on November 22, 1982, about the need for increased productivity, realistic planning targets, greater discipline, more independence for farms and factories, and the appointment of "politically mature, competent, and resourceful people." The Soviet Union, Andropov said, should also "take account of the experiences of fraternal countries" as well as "world experience." In sharp contrast to most Soviet leaders, he admitted that "I do not have ready recipes" for solving the country's economic problems.

Thompson R. Buchanan, a former U.S. diplomat with extensive Soviet service, wrote in the summer 1982 *Foreign Policy* that the "most serious question" facing Andropov was "how to motivate a work force that has lost any work ethic and has become demoralized, undisciplined and unresponsive to the familiar Communist techniques of moral exhortation and socialist competition."

In his November 1982 speech, Andropov seemed to offer some "capitalist incentives" for the approximately 147 million civilian Soviet workers. "Shoddy work, inactivity, and irresponsibility should have an immediate and unavoidable effect on the earnings, official status, and moral prestige of workers," he said. He also underlined the need "to extend the independence of amalgamations, enterprises, and collective farms."

According to a widely circulated report by Soviet economists in 1984, known as the Novosibirsk Report, annual economic growth fell from 7.5 percent in the late 1960s to 2.5 percent in the first part of this decade. By the first quarter of 1985 it had sunk to 2.0 percent. The economists said the country's economic problems lay not only in inefficient planning but also in "the outdated nature of the system of industrial organization and economic management, or simply in the inability of the system to ensure complete and efficient utilization of the workers and of the intellectual potential of the society."

Those who believed Andropov would opt for some type of economic decentralization pointed to his experience as ambassador to Hungary at the time of the Soviet invasion in 1956 and to his appointment in 1957 as the Central Committee's specialist on relations with Eastern Europe and other communist nations. Andropov reportedly favored or at least tolerated Hungary's postinvasion program of economic decentralization or "goulash communism." Without making any significant political concessions, Hungarian officials gave managers and workers considerable autonomy in economic matters and this is generally credited with making Hungary the most prosperous of all Eastern-bloc nations.

Hungary, however, was not an appropriate model for Soviet economic reform. Hungary's size, population (in numbers and homogeneity), ingrained work ethic, and level of natural resources are all considerably different from the Soviet Union's.

Additionally, since decentralization requires greater autonomy for industrial and agricultural management, "the first thing the managers will demand is the right to determine the size and composition of their work forces. Millions of people would be fired, creating an unemployment problem for the first time since the 1920s. This would anger provincial party officials who want neither to lose control over economic decision-making nor to have to deal with the unemployed," Soviet expert Dimitri K. Simes wrote in the *Washington Post* November 21, 1982.

But "capitalist incentives" and other decentralization measures were already working in the Soviet Union when Andropov took over and Western observers commented that Andropov would not necessarily have outraged the party elite if he proceeded carefully and gradually to increase both. Brezhnev was not accused of unorthodoxy when he praised and encouraged private farms, for example. In carrying decentralization further, it was expected that Andropov might have been able to enlist the support of the military by arguing that continued high defense outlays require large-scale improvements in the Soviet economy.

Nevertheless, damning assessments of the Stalinist economic system, such as an Academy of Sciences memorandum that was leaked early in Andropov's tenure, were not the norm and Andropov's reforms were far more limited than might have been expected. He called for greater discipline among factory and farm workers — a typical step that produced some short-term results but did not alter the economic structure. Andropov deemphasized the reclamation of marginal lands in favor of improving productivity on already arable lands. Just before his death, Andropov initiated a limited experiment in factory autonomy. Although it was introduced in only a few selected enterprises, the measure was in some ways similar to China's recent industrial reform. Managers were allowed to make their own production decisions, and they had to accept the consequences if they erred. Some Soviet-affairs analysts speculated that these reforms would have been extended to more factories if Andropov had lived.

Chernenko and Agriculture

Western experts did not find it altogether surprising that the USSR condemned China's early 1980s reforms for their "anti-Soviet direction." The Soviet press said that by encouraging foreign investment in its internal economy Beijing was catering to Western, especially American, interests and endangering the socialist economic system.

In a speech before the Politburo November 15, 1984, General Secretary Konstantin U. Chernenko acknowledged the Soviet economy was suffering from some of the same problems China was trying to correct. Chernenko chided workers and managers for poor workmanship and "a tendency to relax." Soviet industry, he said, was not meeting consumers' needs for basic goods such as shoes. Repeating a theme expressed by his predecessor, Yuri Andropov, Chernenko called for greater discipline in the workplace but offered no new plans for achieving this goal.

Chernenko said that Soviet industrial output had grown faster in 1983 and 1984 than it had in 1981 and 1982, and he predicted that real income would rise by 3.3 percent in 1985, a "substantially higher" rate than in recent years. At the same time, Chernenko said, oil and coal production was below target. Annual oil production had leveled off at slightly over 600 million metric tons. Although this was more than enough to satisfy the country's energy requirements, it left little surplus for export, which is the main source of the hard currency the Soviet Union needs to import agricultural goods.

While the Soviet Union appeared to have enjoyed a trade surplus with the West in 1984, reversing the previous year's deficit, it did so not by increasing exports but by cutting imports. The Soviets stepped up borrowing from financial markets in the West, apparently to help finance grain imports. This higher level of borrowing continued in 1985, and Wharton Econometrics estimated that the Soviet gross hard-currency debt could grow by $10 billion between 1985 and 1990.

The most urgent economic problem during Chernenko's tenure was lagging agricultural output. The country suffered its sixth consecutive bad harvest in 1984, due both to poor weather and inefficient farming. Exact statistics were unavailable, but the U.S. Department of Agriculture estimated the Soviet Union produced only 170 million tons of grain in 1984, 70 million tons below its goal.

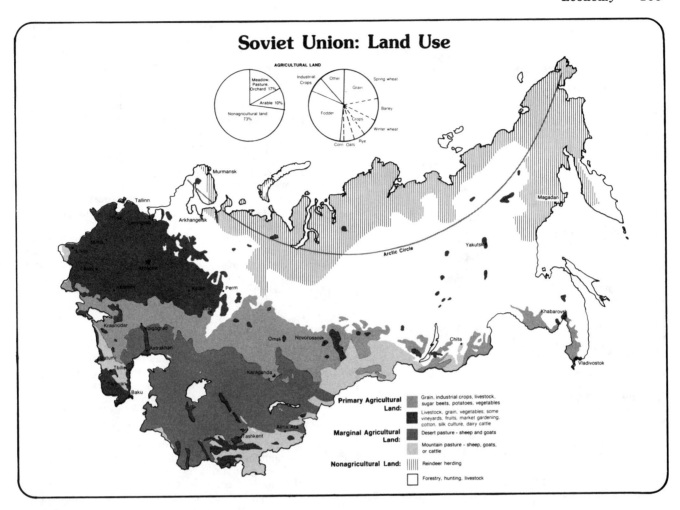

Soviet Union: Land Use

The chronic grain shortage was the subject of an unexpected session of the party's Central Committee October 23, 1984, ironically just three days after the Chinese marked the success of their own agricultural reforms by expanding them to the industrial sector. Chernenko announced that the 1984 harvest had suffered "a substantial shortfall," especially in the feed grains necessary to increase meat production.

The grain shortfall made the Soviet Union increasingly dependent on foreign sources of food. Under a five-year grain purchase agreement signed August 25, 1983, the United States once again became a major supplier of wheat, corn, and soybeans. The agreement was the first major contract concluded since early 1981, when President Reagan lifted the grain embargo Jimmy Carter had imposed in retaliation for the 1979 Soviet invasion of Afghanistan. The Soviet Union's other primary nonsocialist suppliers of grain and food were Argentina, Canada, Australia, and Brazil.

Unlike the Chinese, who increased productivity through decentralization and private incentives, the Soviet leadership offered traditional solutions to the grain shortage. Chernenko and Premier Tikhonov called for the reclamation of new lands — under a program in force since 1966 — to bring the total of drained and irrigated land to between 121 million and 130 million acres by the year 2000. In addition, they cautiously supported a decades-old plan to divert water from the Ob and Irtysh rivers in Siberia

some 1,500 miles southward to open the dry land of Central Asia to cultivation. But under Gorbachev the diversion schemes apparently were dropped.

Gorbachev's Reform Proposals

While the West paid more attention to his diplomatic initiatives, Mikhail Gorbachev's most significant moves during his first year in power dealt with domestic policy. As soon as he was named party chief in March 1985, he began calling for economic reform in more forceful terms than any Soviet leader in recent memory. Within three months he had initiated a nationwide campaign to tighten worker discipline and rid the nation of alcoholism. Gorbachev also announced plans to divert investment from construction of new factories and into retooling of existing facilities as well as machine building. These changes, he predicted, would allow a 4 percent annual growth rate of the economy without cutting back on military or social spending.

Limited Decentralization

Gorbachev also called for decentralization of certain aspects of economic planning. Initially introduced under Andropov in January 1984, the program would reduce the number of specific production targets for individual enter-

Soviet Consumer Goods and Services

(Planned Production Growth, 1986-2000)

	Annual Average Increase	
	1986-1990	1991-2000
All nonfood goods	5.4%	3.3-3.9%
Light industry	3.9	5.3
Textiles	2.6-4.1	1.8-3.1
Knitwear	4.1-4.9	3.7-4.4
Footwear	2.8	1.2
Consumer goods	6.4	3.9-4.4
Radios	3.1-4.8	1.8-3.2
Color TVs	10.9-11.8	3.2-4.1
Refrigerators	1.9-3.5	1.3-2.9
Sewing machines	10.8	3.4
Washing machines	5.1-7.0	0.5-1.6
Printed matter	4.2	3.3
Consumer-purchased services	5.4-7.0	4.1-5.9

Source: Wharton Econometric Forecasting Associates, based on the Soviet Union's *Comprehensive Program for the Development of Consumer Goods Production and the Service Sphere for the Years 1986-2000.*

prises, allow their managers more power to determine wages and investments, and offer extra pay and other inducements for workers to produce more and correct what Gorbachev called an "extremely confused, cumbersome and inefficient" system of incentives.

Decentralization would not, he emphasized, diminish the role of central planning. Gosplan would continue to control decisions regarding investments, prices, and production targets above the enterprise level. Rather, Gorbachev said he would like to reduce the vast bureaucracy known as the *glavki* that lies between the strategic planners in Moscow and the individual enterprises.

Gorbachev's early emphasis on the economy was also reflected in the draft party program announced in October 1985 and ratified by the 27th Party Congress in February 1986. A principal goal was "making the Soviet economy the most sophisticated and powerful in the world." Also in October 1985 the Politburo announced the creation of a new government bureau to oversee machine building, one of the sectors Gorbachev singled out for intensive investment. Another bureaucratic change came in November when five agricultural ministries were merged into the new State Agro-Industrial Committee.

Consumer Goods, Services

Among the plans published in October 1985 by the Central Committee was one to increase investments in nonfood consumer goods and services to raise their quality and variety. The plan envisioned annual growth rates of 5.4 percent in consumer goods and 5.4 to 7.0 percent for consumer-paid services, well over the 4.0 percent growth forecast for national income. *(Table, this page)*

While the program provided few indications as to how this growth was to be achieved, its release shortly before the party congress suggested that this sector would receive greater emphasis and would figure highly in Gorbachev's campaign to raise labor productivity. "If more and better consumer goods and services are available for purchase, the incentive value of wages will increase, and wage policy will be a more effective instrument for increasing labor productivity," Daniel Bond noted in the Wharton Econometric *Centrally Planned Economies Current Analysis* of November 21, 1985.

The draft party program, the first since 1961, later adopted by the 27th Party Congress, presented in general terms the new leadership's economic goals. It called for doubling economic output by the year 2000 — the equivalent of a 4.7 percent annual growth rate — largely by applying new technologies and scientific breakthroughs to Soviet industry and agriculture.

This program was spelled out in detail in the 12th Five-Year Plan, released November 9, 1985. The first draft, drawn up under Chernenko, was returned to the planners that May and rewritten. The current, more optimistic Five-Year Plan bears Gorbachev's stamp. According to the final *Guidelines for the Economic and Social Development of the USSR for 1986-1990 and for the Period Ending in 2000*, the plan's "central objective" was to

... increase the growth rates and efficiency of the economy on the basis of accelerating scientific and technological progress, the technical modernisation and re-equipment of production, intensive utilisation of the created production potential, perfecting the system of management and the economic mechanism and achieving on this basis a further rise in the Soviet people's well-being.

In contrast to recent five-year plans, whose growth targets were lowered to reflect the actual decline in output, the new plan foresaw a slowdown only in industrial output. National income, agricultural production, consumption, and investment were all expected to increase. Investment targets confirmed the party's emphasis on modernization through the "development of electronics, nuclear power engineering, comprehensive automation, production engineering, and the processing of new materials." The plan predicted that high technology would produce "no less than two-thirds of the increment in social labour productivity" to be achieved by 1990. Output in machine building and metalworking — sectors that included computer equipment, robotics, and other automation machinery — were slated to increase by 40 to 45 percent.

Modernization was also expected to raise agricultural production by 14 to 16 percent a year. Considered an overly ambitious target by Western analysts, the gains in food output were to be obtained with better farming techniques and crop improvement through biotechnology and genetic engineering.

First-Year Results

Gorbachev's first-year reforms produced mixed results. The partial decentralization of economic planning and the use of incentives — while far more limited than those introduced in recent years in China and Hungary — began to yield positive results in certain areas and industries, particularly the notoriously inefficient services sector.

It appeared that the declining growth rates had stabilized, although the economy did not noticeably improve. Industrial output for 1985 appeared to come near, if not meet, plan targets — but the plan itself had not demanded much. A good grain harvest in 1985 was another bright spot. The U.S. Department of Agriculture estimated it at 190 million metric tons, which was expected to lead to slightly lower grain imports in 1986.

An especially successful experiment in Gorbachev's first year was the distribution among the workers of all receipts above an enterprise's target, a modified form of profit sharing that Gorbachev indicated at the Party Congress would be used more widely.

But efforts to achieve greater productivity, especially through increased automation and high technology, already had eliminated many jobs. Bureaucratic reorganization had forced out some 3,000 officials by the end of 1985, prompting the first acknowledged use of unemployment insurance in the Soviet Union since the 1930s, when Stalin announced that joblessness had been eradicated. Soviet government economist Vladimir Kostakov, cited by the *New York Times* January 9, 1986, predicted that modernization efforts could cost the jobs of 13 million to 19 million people.

Recent efforts to improve living conditions had begun to pay off by early 1986, according to official accounts. Wages were said to have increased in all sectors, while state subsidies continued to hold down costs of consumer items, housing, transportation, and social services. But the system's ability to meet consumer demands was still limited to essential goods and services. According to one analysis, a loaf of white bread cost about the same for a worker in Moscow as for his counterpart in Washington, D.C., in terms of equivalent work time. The Muscovite enjoyed a clear advantage in terms of rent (one-quarter the Washingtonian's cost) and subway fare (one-half), but a color television or small car cost more than 10 times what it did in Washington, while a bottle of aspirin (not always available) cost 50 times more, according to Mervyn Matthews's article, "Poverty in the Soviet Union," in the autumn 1985 *Wilson Quarterly.*

Potential Opposition to Plans

The 27th Congress ratified both the party program and the Five-Year Plan without major modifications. But the traditional show of approval did not necessarily indicate complete agreement with the new leadership's economic goals.

Ideological conservatives and the military were said to oppose parts of the plan. Since his elevation to the Politburo, Egor Ligachev had countered Gorbachev's enthusiastic predictions of a reinvigorated economy with more conservative pronouncements of his own. In particular, he cautioned that any economic reforms would occur "within the framework of scientific socialism" and would not entail the "shifts toward a market economy or private enterprise" that marked China's recent economic policy, the *New York Times* reported December 23, 1985. Those comments may have been intended to reassure members of the older generation that the new leadership would adhere to the central tenets of Marxism-Leninism; but given Ligachev's second-in-command position some experts construed his remarks as veiled warnings against proceeding too fast on economic reforms.

Some Western experts also believed the Soviet military might take a dim view of Gorbachev's reform proposals because they diverted investment funds from the defense economy. Reagan's space-based weapons program, the Strategic Defense Initiative (SDI), which required esoteric technology the United States had only begun to de-

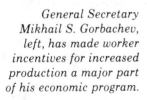

General Secretary Mikhail S. Gorbachev, left, has made worker incentives for increased production a major part of his economic program.

Soviet Union: Oil and Gas Pipelines

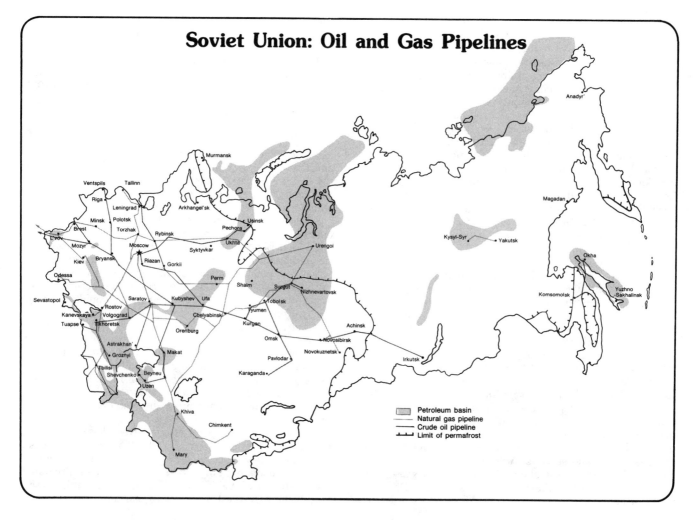

Petroleum basin
Natural gas pipeline
Crude oil pipeline
Limit of permafrost

velop, represented a huge challenge to the Soviet Union's relatively backward technological base. If the United States refused to abandon SDI as part of an arms control agreement, Gorbachev was expected to come under increasing pressure from his own high command to pour more money into defense.

Soviet Energy Resources

The Soviet Union is almost entirely self-sufficient in energy needs. Total energy production from oil and gas, coal, hydroelectricity, and nuclear power was expected by Wharton Econometrics to improve slightly for 1985 over 1984 despite considerable problems in the important oil sector. A long-term energy development program seeks to reduce domestic dependence on oil by conservation and shifting to other energy sources, primarily natural gas and nuclear energy. The Soviet Union has long depended heavily on oil and gas exports to earn foreign currency for vital imports such as machinery and grains. Simultaneous declines in world oil prices and domestic oil production in the mid-1980s meant the Soviets were faced with significant hard-currency losses. According to Wharton Econometrics, about 80 percent of Soviet exports to the developed West and about half of their exports to socialist countries consist of energy sources, mostly oil.

Oil Production, Exports

Soviet oil production began declining after 1983, falling steadily from 4.31 billion barrels to 4.29 billion in 1984 and 4.16 billion in 1985. It was the first time production had fallen since World War II, yet the Soviets remained the world's largest oil producer. Production in 1985 was 226 million barrels below target and in January the Soviets reported they already were almost 3 million barrels behind planned 1986 levels. Western estimates of past oil production were about 12.60 million barrels per day (bpd); 1985 estimates were 11.33 million bpd.

Currency earnings from exports, more than half of which are oil, fell from a $4 billion surplus in 1984 to a deficit of $6 billion in 1985. A drop in oil income meant less money with which to import Western technology needed to modernize the economy and to reach the increasingly inaccessible oil deposits. The currency situation was expected to grow worse through the 1980s. Wharton Econometrics estimated that hard-currency revenues from energy exports in 1985 would drop 10 to 20 percent below 1984's.

The drops in oil production were due to poor management, inadequate transportation facilities, and the depletion of reserves in the Tyumen region of western Siberia, where some 60 percent of the nation's oil is produced. Although Siberian reserves are less accessible than they were in the 1970s, the Soviets announced they would step up drilling by 40 percent nationwide in 1985-86 and by 90 percent in western Siberia, despite the higher investment costs. *(Oil and gas, map, p. 168)*

The decline also hurt the Soviet Union's East European economic partners, who have relied on cheap Soviet oil. Since 1982 the Soviets have curtailed their supply of oil to Eastern Europe, raised the price of the oil they do send, and increased their demand for high-quality finished goods in exchange for Soviet energy and raw materials. By the mid-1980s Western economists predicted that the level of energy cutbacks to Eastern Europe had leveled off and that further curtailments would be to West European customers. In 1985 the harsh winter disrupted and even halted some deliveries to Western Europe, which in 1984 received 15.3 percent of its oil needs from the Soviet Union.

Conservation efforts have been stepped up and could temporarily halt the production decline, although domestic consumption increased slightly in 1985. Consumption had risen 3 percent in the Soviet Union and Eastern Europe between 1979 and 1984, according to *B P Statistical Review of World Energy*. One means of conserving domestic oil use has been to substitute natural gas as much as possible.

To help keep up exports the Soviets also bought more than 20 billion barrels of Middle Eastern oil in 1984, largely in exchange for arms deliveries, and then reexported most of that. Consequently, despite decreased production, the USSR exported more oil in 1984 than in 1983. The Soviets have tried to maintain hard-currency earnings by slashing prices. They could also keep up earnings by selling more of their ample gold reserves and by cutting back loans used to maintain arms exports to less-developed countries. Reduced arms exports have been a byproduct of lower oil prices, because many of the countries that import arms export oil. The Soviets have also increased loans from Western banks; they borrowed approximately $1 billion in 1984 and even more by mid-1985.

Natural Gas

Output of natural gas continued to rise in the mid-1980s and was one of the few bright spots in the Soviet economy. A 10 percent production increase over 1984 was expected for 1985. But with oil more competitive because of lower prices, less revenue from gas was also expected.

Natural gas began taking the place of oil when oil deposits became harder to exploit. According to Vadim Medish of American University, natural gas production was growing faster than "any other branch of the Soviet national economy" in 1984 and at the current rate of growth the Soviet Union could surpass the United States and "become the world's primary natural gas producer" before the end of the 1980s.

The Soviets have had notable success in substituting gas for oil in domestic uses, and according to Wharton Econometrics gas used domestically in 1985 could exceed oil's share for the first time.

Earlier in the decade, the Kremlin hoped to offset some of the outward cash flow spent on imports of Western technology, machinery, and grain with a Siberian natural gas pipeline to Western Europe. According to some estimates, the 3,000-mile Yamal pipeline project could provide up to $10 billion a year in foreign earnings.

The Yamal pipeline, built with Western credits and technology, was opposed by the U.S. government. Washington argued that it would make Western Europe dangerously dependent on the Kremlin (in 1980 Soviet natural gas

The Tash-Kumyrskaya hydroelectric power station on the Naryn River in the Kirgiz Republic was scheduled for its first generator test in December 1985.

accounted for almost 20 percent of West Germany's consumption and nearly half of Austria's). Opponents also contended that it would relieve Moscow's economic pressures and accelerate the Soviet military buildup. In retaliation for alleged Soviet complicity in the military crackdown in Poland in late 1981 the Reagan administration imposed sanctions against the sale of U.S. technology (such as the sale of $175 million worth of U.S.-made gas turbine compressors) intended for the pipeline project. The sanctions did not halt construction, however, and the pipeline was operating successfully by the mid-1980s. *(Martial law in Poland, p. 122)*

Other Energy Resources

Medish noted in *The Soviet Union*, second edition, that "the growth of electric power production is the most important single indicator in the entire Soviet national economy, because it is a prerequisite for further industrialization, urbanization, and modernization of agriculture and transportation." Medish added that electricity production was growing at about 4 percent annually, with total kilowatt production about 60 percent of U.S. production.

Three-quarters of the electricity produced in 1984 was by coal or other thermopower stations; hydropower stations produced about 20 percent. Coal production, although decreasing, is another important energy source. The party program adopted in 1986 said accelerated development of nuclear power was crucial to party energy plans — a cry the Soviets also made in Council of Mutual Economic Assistance meetings. The Soviets have the world's most ambitious nuclear power program, with some 40 to 50 operating reactors, but the number placed on-line during the 1981-85 Five-Year Plan fell far short of the target.

Nuclear power faced an unprecedented setback April 26, 1986, when an accident at the Chernobyl nuclear power station in the Ukraine sent radioactive particles spewing across the USSR and many other countries. Two workers were killed outright. Three weeks later 21 had died and 299 were hospitalized. Eighteen days later Soviet leader Mikhail Gorbachev made his first statement on the disaster and said the reactor had been shut down for regular maintenance when a sudden power surge caused a steam leak, which then led to a hydrogen explosion and a large fire. The explosion blew the roof off the power plant and caused the radiation leak.

The plume of radiation initially drifted northwesterly from Chernobyl, covering eastern Poland, much of Sweden, Denmark, Finland, and Norway. Changing winds then sent the plume back toward the Soviet Union and over other East European countries. In a week's time, nonhazardous radiation increases were reported in Japan and the United States.

Only after Swedish nuclear power workers found abnormal amounts of radiation on their shoes and clothing two days after the accident did the tragedy come to the world's attention. Moscow initially denied Sweden's queries about the possibility of a Soviet nuclear accident. Severe diplomatic distress continued even after the Soviets admitted the accident, because of the sparse information coming from Moscow concerning the radiation leak. Gorbachev's policy of openness had been called sharply into question. An official governmental commission was set up to investigate and, under widespread criticism, the Soviets agreed to share radiation readings from monitoring devices with the International Atomic Energy Agency (IAEA).

The Chernobyl plant is near the town of Pripyat, about 80 miles north of Kiev, and is close to a water reservoir that supplies Kiev's 2.5 million residents. This potentially contaminated water supply concerned officials more than the extensive damage to nearby land. Nonetheless, the European Community (EC) banned the import of agricultural items from the Soviet Union and six East European countries at least through May.

The contamination forced the evacuation of 92,000 people from their homes near the plant — although it was reported later that confused authorities waited 36 hours before beginning evacuations. Evidence mounted through May that local Soviet officials had not realized the extent of the disaster at first. Initially 49,000 people were evacuated, with the zone extending only 6.2 miles from the site. After Prime Minister Nikolai Ryzhkov, Politburo and CC Secretariat member Egor Ligachev, and Ukrainian party chief Vladimir Shcherbitskii visited the area May 3, the zone was extended to 18 miles and another 43,000 persons were evacuated. No panic was evident in Kiev or surrounding areas, but long lines were reported at railway stations as people sought to leave. Kiev schools closed 10 days early so children could leave the city.

More than two weeks after the accident, Soviet officials met with ambassadors of neighboring and Western nations to give more detailed information about what had happened and what was being done to clean up. Westerners were still not entirely satisfied, however, as the information was not complete and seemed designed to minimize governmental embarrassment. Soviet citizens were not told that the Chernobyl meltdown was the most serious nuclear power accident ever. Instead, the Soviet press continued to dwell on Western nuclear accidents and safety records.

An international medical crew, headed by U.S. physician Robert Gale, worked with Soviet doctors conducting bone marrow transplants for some radiation victims. It was reported, however, that many of those patients were not expected to live. The number of persons who will eventually develop cancers and other illnesses from the radiation effects is impossible to predict, but Dr. Gale stated May 18 that 50,000 to 100,000 people have received a radiation dose "that may be of long-term concern."

Outlook for Reform

One approach to economic reform envisioned by some more radical Soviet economists and implemented to various degrees by some East European governments — as well as by the People's Republic of China — is *marketization*. This approach would decentralize much of the planning system and move to alter, among other things, the way items are priced, although pricing would remain under state control. One of the problems with marketization, according to the 1985 *Centrally Planned Economies Outlook* by Wharton Econometrics, is that

> advances made in one area can be neutralized by the unreformed elements in the system.... For example, if enterprises are required to make decisions on the basis of prices, but those prices are still administratively set, there is no guarantee that the enterprises will perform any better than when they are told exactly what to do by the central planning agency. Such partial reforms can even end up being counterproductive.

Soviet leaders will have to believe that the long-term benefits of reform outweigh the costs of planning before even limited marketization can come about.

Modernization, the other commonly cited approach to economic reform, aims to improve or perfect central planning. Entrenched party leaders and government officials find this approach more acceptable because it would require the least effort, could be implemented gradually, and is the least likely to affect the elite's perquisites and power. Most Soviet leaders and economists appear to be convinced that central planning works and that adjustments can correct the system's recognized inefficiencies without altering its basic structure. In pursuing long-range development goals, central planners benefit from an ability to mobilize the country's resources, both manpower and material. "With vast untapped resources in the Siberian and Far East regions, this ability is seen by the leadership as vital for the country's future," explained Daniel Bond of Wharton Econometrics.

Central planning also ensures that the party has control over meeting military needs, and this has made economic reform an even thornier issue. Fulfilling military and strategic production has often been called the "plan within the plan" because of the priority it receives over other targets in the Five-Year Plan.

Modernization also holds an edge because there is a lack of acceptable examples of successful marketization. On the other hand East Germany, the most successful of the satellite countries in Eastern Europe, provides an example of an economy where central planning has proved relatively effective.

But modernization is limited in what it can accomplish and Western experts see it as not being comprehensive enough to achieve the aims Gorbachev has outlined — a fact he apparently recognizes.

People and Society

The population of the Soviet Union is the third largest in the world, after China's and India's. There are approximately 277.9 million Soviet citizens according to July 1985 CIA statistics. More than 170 ethnic groups are represented, the largest of which is the Eastern Slavs. Seventy percent of the Eastern Slavs — who account for about half the Soviet population — are Russians. The remaining 30 percent are Ukrainians and Belorussians. Other groups in the Soviet Union include Turkics, Caucasians, Finno-Ugrics, Baltics, Iranians, Mongolians, and Eskimos. More than 100 nationalities are represented and some 130 languages spoken.

Official 1984 Soviet statistics set the total population at 274.5 million, or about 3.5 million fewer than the CIA estimate. Most Soviet citizens (about 64 percent) live in urban areas, according to the official figures. There are about 2 million more women than men, largely because of the heavy loss of Soviet soldiers in World War II.

According to 1985 CIA statistics, 20 percent of the labor force works in agriculture (compared with only 5 percent in the United States) and 80 percent in industry and nonagricultural labor.

Russians are the dominant ethnic group, making up 52 percent of the population. Although most Russians live in the Russian Soviet Federated Socialist Republic (RSFSR), they have become an important ethnic group in all 15 union republics. Demographers predict, however, that by the year 2000 ethnic Russians will make up only 48 percent of the Soviet population. By the end of the century it is estimated that there will be about 100 million Moslems living in the Tadzhik and other Central Asian regions, constituting more than one-fourth of the entire Soviet population.

As non-Russian ethnic groups increase in size, problems of nationalism may grow even though national antagonism is supposed to give way to international comity according to the principles of communism. Religion, which Karl Marx called "the opiate of the people," is also alleged to be unnecessary under communist rule. Yet both nationalistic pride and religious fervor survive in the Soviet Union and other communist states.

This chapter describes the diverse Soviet society. The health care system and the status of women are examined, as is the plight of Soviet dissidents. Russian and Soviet cultural life and traditions are detailed, with particular emphasis on literature, music, theater, and film.

Language

During World War II Joseph Stalin rallied his country around the concept of "Mother Russia." Nationalism was emphasized over communism. This emphasis has continued, as Soviet leaders attempt to reshape nationalist urges among Soviet ethnic groups into loyalty to the USSR. Russian is the official language, and for the non-Russian population it is considered politic to master and use Russian because it is the language of government, science, the economy, and the military.

The Soviets have made progress in spreading the use of Russian throughout the country. For example, U.S. Census Bureau statistics indicate that the number of Uzbeks claiming Russian as a second language nearly quadrupled from 1970 to 1979. However, that quadrupling, if correct, still represents only 15 percent of the Uzbekistan population. David Heer, a sociologist at the University of Southern California, has projected that the Russian-speaking population in Kazakh is 43.5 percent; Azerbaidzhan, 17.9 percent; Kirgiz, 19.4; Turkmen, 16.2; and Tadzhik, 16. Officially, however, the figures differ. According to the 1979 Soviet census, only 10.8 percent of the Uzbek population speaks Russian. The lowest percentage, according to Soviet statistics, is in Tadhzikistan.

Efforts over the past decade or so to teach young non-Russians the language are succeeding. By 1979, 62 percent declared a command of the Russian language, up from 48.7 percent in 1970.

From the military point of view, the Russian language requirement is extremely important because of the large numbers of recruits from the Asian republics. Ethnic Russians still make up the vast majority of what the Soviets consider the crucial military divisions. As the population of the Asian republics rises, Soviet leaders may be forced to integrate more non-Russians into the political power structure.

The emphasis on the Russian language is one part of the central government's attempt to assimilate the disparate Soviet population. The government also has developed programs to "Russify" the republics, dispatching thousands of ethnic Russians to work in, and sometimes to keep an eye on, ethnically distinct areas. The industrialized Baltic republics (Estonia, Latvia, and Lithuania) have traditionally been highly dissatisfied with the Soviet system. These republics experienced a large postwar influx of Russian migrants who work in the plants, enjoy a higher standard of living than non-Russians, and, some analysts say, maintain a loyal Russian presence in these formerly independent nations.

As part of the effort to expand the Asian republics economically, Moscow has dispatched armies of Russian and other Slavic workers and administrators to operate the industries and agricultural facilities. As a result, by the mid-1970s Russians comprised at least 10 percent of the population in all the republics except Lithuania, Georgia, and Armenia. In the Central Asian republic of Kazakhstan, Russians make up more than half the population.

The number-two government posts in the republics frequently are held by Slavs, usually Russians, and Russians generally head the secret police operations in the republics.

While the Baltics have a somewhat higher living standard, the Central Asian republics are considerably behind the rest of the Soviet Union in economic and social-cultural development. Industrialization has increased, but the Islamic regions are the least urbanized, and accordingly have lower living standards and poorer access to educational and health facilities and other services.

There has been concern that the Islamic upsurge outside the Soviet Union could influence Soviet Moslems. But whether Soviet Moslems will become more radical is hard to calculate.

Women in USSR

The claim of equality for women in Soviet society (Article 35 of the Soviet Constitution) is a source of pride for the Soviets. To a large degree, it is a true claim; however, it has significant qualifications.

For the early Soviet leaders, granting equality to women was pragmatic as well as ideological. Marxist ideology blamed women's exploitation on the bourgeois family and the capitalist economic system. From a practical standpoint, Soviet modernization could not have been accomplished without female participation. By 1926 women constituted 47 percent of the employed population.

This mix of pragmatism and ideology continues today. For most families it is economically necessary for both spouses to work. At the same time, there is a high degree of social pressure for women to be employed.

The statistics on women's education and employment are impressive. According to Vadim Medish in *The Soviet Union*, citing Soviet statistics, 9 of 10 women in the 20-49 age group are employed — a figure higher than in any other industrialized nation. Women comprise more than half the labor force and the student body. They hold 73 percent of the jobs in education; 84 percent of the jobs in public health; and 71 percent of the jobs in the culture and entertainment fields. In addition, women often work in traditionally male occupations such as mine engineering and commercial fishing.

According to Western figures from the 1970s, women in the RSFSR accounted for about 40 percent of the engineers, more than 25 percent of both judges and neurosurgeons, and more than 50 percent of specialists working in research institutes. Additionally, 45 percent of teachers in schools of higher education, 38 percent of principals of secondary schools, and 86 percent of economists and planners were women.

Ironically, it is the equality in the work force that creates the double burden on Soviet women of a full-time job and the responsibility for the housework and child rearing. Virtually all women under retirement age work or study full time. Shopping, usually the task of the woman in a family, is especially difficult because of chronic shortages of consumer goods and long lines.

These demands of the household adversely affect women's professional development. Women have less time for study and other activities that could promote career advancement. To a large degree, women are concentrated in the lower paying sectors of the labor force, and they are underrepresented in professional occupations. Although women make up almost 90 percent of medical workers, they comprise only 60 percent of those who are chief doctors and heads of hospitals.

Fewer than 10 percent of enterprise directors are women, and there are even fewer women at the upper levels of the state and the party, according to Michael P. Sacks in *Contemporary Soviet Society: Sociological Perspectives*. No woman is a member of the Politburo, and until Alexandra Biriukova was named to the Central Committee Secretariat in 1986 only one other woman had been a member of that organization. Moreover, women's opportunities to serve in the armed forces are limited. *(Chapter 6, p. 134)*

The state makes some provisions for women. They receive 16 weeks of maternity leave with full pay and an optional leave of up to one year at half pay to take care of their infants. Usually, however, it is difficult for families to afford this. Women may retire with full pensions at age 55, five years earlier than men. There is an extensive network of nurseries, daycare centers, and kindergartens to help ease the burden of child raising, although there is room for only about 60 percent of the children who need this care.

The difficulties of the double burden make women reluctant to have many children. Birth control, however, is primitive for the most part. This results in another unpleasant reality in the life of the Soviet woman — the use of abortion as a form of birth control. The USSR in 1920 became the first nation to legalize abortion. This decision was reversed in 1936 because of low birth rates but abortion was once again legalized in 1955, although it continues to be discouraged officially. Most Soviet women have multiple abortions, with five or six not unusual.

Church and State

The Soviet state and the religious establishment maintain an uneasy relationship. The USSR is a highly nonreligious society, but some religious groups have been successful in obtaining and retaining members. The regime has grown to tolerate some religion rather than suffer the repercussions of arousing religious dissent and international criticism.

The USSR promotes atheism as an official policy; it was the first nation to proclaim this. The 1977 Constitution (Article 52) states that "USSR citizens are guaranteed freedom of conscience, that is, the right to profess any religion or to profess none, to perform religious worship or to conduct atheistic propaganda." The fact that freedom of religious propaganda is denied makes it possible to declare any openly religious activity illegal, because it might violate the law separating education and church.

The Modern Plight of Soviet Jewry

From tsarist times to the present the USSR has a history of anti-Semitism, and the treatment of Jews there has received much press attention. The nation's Jewish community is the third largest, after the United States' and Israel's. About 15 percent of all Jews live in the Soviet Union.

After the 1967 Arab-Israeli war, the USSR severed relations with Israel. "Anti-Zionism" increased in the Soviet press as did nationalist feelings among Jews, whose dissidents began to emigrate in 1971.

After the 1973 war in Israel, anti-Zionist and anti-Semitic propaganda intensified. In 1974 the U.S. Congress passed the Jackson-Vanik amendment linking U.S. trade with communist countries to improved emigration policies. In 1977 Jewish activist Joseph Begun was sentenced to Siberian exile. The following year Anatolii Shcharanskii, probably the most famous Jew in the Soviet dissident movement, was sentenced to 13 years in prison and labor camp.

In their attempts to get the Jackson-Vanik amendment waived, the Soviets released a record 51,000 Jews in 1979. But the Soviet invasion of Afghanistan the same year ended the liberalization in emigration policy and any chances for a waiver. The number of Jews allowed to emigrate annually dropped to a low of 922 in 1984.

The only reasons that Jews or any other Soviet citizens are allowed to emigrate are for "repatriation" and "reunification of families." An often-used justification for declines in Jewish emigration is that there are no more families to reunite.

A Jew who wants to leave must apply for a visa and obtain an invitation from a relative outside. The applicant must quit his or her job. Applicants who are refused emigration become *refuseniks*. Refuseniks cannot be rehired and often end up performing menial tasks while waiting long periods before being reconsidered for emigration. Applicants are refused for numerous reasons. A common one is that they allegedly possess state secrets.

Although complete freedom to worship and evangelize is denied all believers in the Soviet Union, it is particularly hard for Jews to practice their religion. No printing of the Hebrew Bible or prayer book has been permitted since a 300-copy printing in 1956. There are fewer than 70 official synagogues for 2.5 million Jews. No communication is permitted among synagogues. The teaching of Hebrew, although in theory legal, is prohibited, as is the teaching of religious texts. With increased anti-Semitism, fewer Jews have been admitted to prestigious universities and technological institutions. Many who are active in promoting Jewish culture are arrested, sent to prisons or forced labor camps, or are sentenced to internal exile. Zionism, as defined by the Soviet government, is an evil nearly as deplorable as Nazism, and it is often a focus for government censure and attacks in the press.

Between October 1968 and the end of 1985 nearly 265,000 Jews left the Soviet Union. After 1984, anti-Jewish activity increased dramatically. General Secretary Mikhail Gorbachev may reverse the downward trend in emigration, but the surprise release of Shcharanskii in February 1986 was viewed not as an official change in Kremlin policy but as a temporary response to the November 1985 summit between Gorbachev and President Reagan. (*Famous dissidents, box, pp. 180-181*)

Religion may be practiced only privately — at home or in an officially recognized church. Fewer than 20,000 houses of worship, belonging to 40 denominations, serve 50 million parishioners (20 percent of the population). All churches, clergy, and religious groups must be registered. Association with nonregistered religious activity is punishable as a criminal offense. Religious communities are allowed to train clergy only as replacements for those who die or retire.

The educational system and the mass media treat religious beliefs as superstitious, backward, and old-fashioned. Some observers have pointed to a religious revival among the young, but most worshippers continue to be old women. Many young people with career ambitions fear the risk of attending church.

According to questionable Soviet estimates from the early 1980s, believers represent 15 percent to 20 percent of the adult population, 10 percent to 15 percent of the urban population, and 20 percent to 30 percent of the rural population.

Religion History and Policy

Before 1917 atheism in Russia was unthinkable, but after the Revolution many churches were closed and church officials persecuted. By the late 1930s, officials stated that about half of the population could be considered "believers," two-thirds of them from rural areas.

The antireligious campaign was eased during World War II as Stalin strove to unite the country and allowed the Russian Orthodox church to revive to a certain degree to help foster Russian patriotism. State control again increased under Khrushchev with his official campaigns against religion and "bourgeois nationalism." To the chagrin of the incoming Leonid Brezhnev regime, the crackdown spurred the religious dissident movement of the 1960s and early 1970s. This, combined with international pressure, prompted Brezhnev to ease treatment of believers. Since 1979 their treatment worsened, due partly to the Cold War atmosphere surrounding East-West relations.

The government's tolerance of "domestic" religions

such as Russian and Georgian orthodoxy is greater than toward religions with centers outside the state — Catholicism, Judaism, Islam, and Protestantism. There is little government data on religious affiliation. Most of the following information is based on Western sources.

Russian Orthodox. The most important denomination is the Russian Orthodox church, which controls one-third to one-half of the functioning parishes. It is the largest religious bloc in the Soviet Union, with more than 40 million adherents (according to an official count in 1976), and the largest Eastern Orthodox church in the world. The Russian Orthodoxes are allowed to keep a few monasteries, nunneries, and seminaries. Many Russians are drawn to the Orthodox church as a link with their Russian heritage, and the party, on a restricted level, accepts this.

Islam. Moslems constitute a sizable minority in the Soviet Union — some 50 million people, living in five republics in Soviet Central Asia and in the Volga-Ural region north of the Caspian Sea. This is the so-called "Moslem Crescent" comprised of Azerbaidzhanis, Turkmens, Uzbeks, Tadzhiks, Kirgizians, and Kazakhs. All Moslems share a common historical, cultural, and religious background that distinguishes them from the rest of the Soviet population.

The Soviet Union always has been conscious of the sensitive ethnic, linguistic, and religious ties between its Islamic minority and the peoples of Iran, Afghanistan, and Turkey across its borders. Determined Russification campaigns have ultimately failed. Moslems largely remain outside the mainstream of Soviet life and culture.

Jews. There were approximately 1.81 million Soviet Jews in 1979 (down from 2.15 million in 1970), according to Soviet statistics. Until the early 1970s the Soviet Jewish population was larger than the population of Israel. *(Box, p. 173)*

Roman Catholic. The Roman Catholic church, concentrated on the western frontier, had approximately 2.25 million adherents in Lithuania and as many as 3.5 million in the entire USSR, according to 1977 figures. Lithuanian Catholics have been at the forefront of religious dissent and since 1972 have published a *samizdat* (meaning self-published works, usually mimeographed at clandestine presses in the USSR) journal called *The Chronicle of the Catholic Church in Lithuania.*

Protestants. Soviet Protestants are diverse in composition and number. There are Lutherans (primarily in Latvia and Estonia), Adventists, and even scattered groups of Jehovah's Witnesses. Evangelical Christians and Baptists comprise the largest Protestant group, with about 3 million adherents.

Others. Smaller groups of underground Eastern Rite Catholics (Uniates) operate primarily in the Ukraine. Also existing are the Georgian and Armenian Apostolic churches. There are numerous native Russian religious groups (including Old Believers, who also number in the millions), but generally these groups are fading and being replaced by evangelical protestants. Buddhists number about 50,000, according to 1976 figures.

Health Care

Every Soviet citizen is entitled to free medical care, but the quality is far below Western standards and varies throughout the country. Cities generally have better care than rural areas, and people in the European part of the USSR receive better care than those in East and Central Asia. The Soviet Union has more than double the number of hospital beds and almost twice the number of doctors that the United States has, but these indices apparently represent little more than numbers.

Since 1975 the Kremlin has published few medical statistics, presumably to prevent embarrassment. According to Western demographer Murray Feshbach of Georgetown University, the Soviet Union faced unprecedented reversals in several areas of vital health indicators in the 1970s. These trends continued into the next decade.

Death rates for all citizens are up. Soviet citizens can expect to live shorter lives than Westerners. Most startling is the rise in the infant mortality rate, a situation occurring in no other industrialized nation. Western experts have reported that between 1970 and 1980 the number of children who died before their first birthday rose by approximately 25 percent. This increase came on the heels of steady, significant improvements in infant mortality since the 1917 Revolution. Alcoholism has been a major contributor to increased death rates as well as a contributor to the country's economic difficulties. *(Box, p. 163)*

Heart and circulatory problems have become a major concern of Soviet officials. Deaths from cardiovascular causes (including heart disease) doubled in the Soviet Union from 1960 to 1980, while the numbers in the United States dropped steadily. Despite campaigns against it, cigarette smoking is increasing.

Medical research institutions, sanatoriums, hospitals, and "polyclinics" (medical care centers for average citizens) are administered by the Ministry of Health Protection. The military has its own medical system. The closed health care network for the elite, such as party officials and top scientists, is superior to that serving the general public.

The Soviet Union had about 850,000 doctors and 2.7 million nurses and *fel'dshers*, or paramedics, in the mid-1980s. Physician training begins right out of high school and lasts six years (including internship). Doctors are not accorded high status and do not receive very high salaries. Seventy percent are women.

In an autumn 1985 *Wilson Quarterly* article, sociologist Mark G. Field stated that "medical equipment is scarce and often of 1940's or 1950's vintage. It can take a week or more to obtain simple blood tests and x-rays. There are only a few dozen kidney dialysis machines in the entire nation." Aspirin is often not available.

In his book *Inside Russian Medicine* (1981), internist William A. Knaus reported on the inadequacy of supplies in Moscow's Botkin Hospital, presumably one of the better equipped hospitals because some Westerners are patients. Knaus is one of the few U.S. physicians to have spent a considerable amount of time in Soviet hospitals. Disposable syringes, needles, and other items taken for granted in Western hospitals are in short supply, Knaus noted. Antibiotics, bandages, thermometers, and even iodine are not always readily available. Because sterility requirements are not well enforced, almost one-third of all surgery patients develop postoperative infections, Knaus added.

According to Field, the approximately 2,280 sanatoriums are perhaps "the brightest spot in the Soviet health care system." Citizens usually stay 24 days while receiving individual care for problems such as arthritis, diabetes, and hypertension. Mud baths, mineral water baths, exercise, and drinking mare's milk are part of the standard regimen.

Labor unions control access to sanatoriums. Entrance

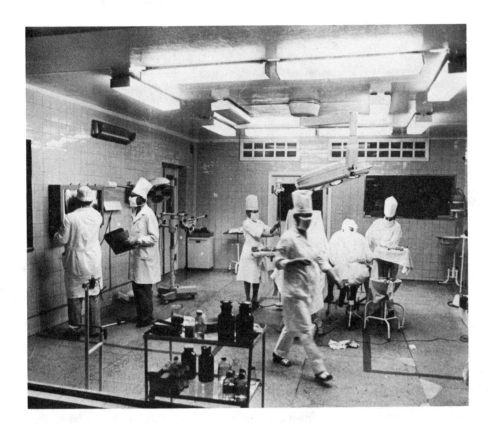

Medical facilities like this operating room at the Republican Microsurgery Center, Moscow, are distributed throughout the Soviet Union.

tickets are highly sought after and often require long waits.

Although Soviet medical scientists lag behind the West in most areas, they have pioneered medical techniques in ultrasound for gallstones and have developed a procedure called radial keratotomy to alleviate severe myopia in eyesight.

THE ARTS: UNDISPUTED LEGACY

Far exceeding the Soviet Union's contribution to medicine is its centuries-old contribution to the arts. Writer Fëdor Dostoevsky, musician Igor Stravinsky, and artist Marc Chagall exemplify the exceptional talent of the Russian people. These famous figures and thousands of less well known artists justify the Soviet Union's undisputed legacy to world culture.

Rich Literary Tradition

The writer in Russian and Soviet society has always held the important role of vanguard of social criticism in a heavily censored world. Revolutionary movements have largely been created by the intelligentsia — the writers. Literature has been viewed by those in power as either a threat to the government or as a useful instrument for maintaining power. Tsar Nicholas I personally censored the verses of Alexander Pushkin because the poet opposed his regime. Writer Nikolai Gogol satirized the corruption of

the nineteenth century provincial bureaucracy. Both during the years of heavy censorship of the nineteenth century and in modern times, fiction and poetry have raised social issues and spurred change. Writers often present new ideas that otherwise would never reach a large audience. Because of this, literature has had more influence on public opinion in Russia than in other countries. *(Writers, box, p. 177)*

Critical Realism

Vissarion G. Belinsky, the famous literary critic of the nineteenth century, popularized the term *critical realism* as a specifically Russian category of literature. Critical realism refers to a socially responsible depiction of life as it really is. It was the writer's duty, according to Belinsky, to illuminate the negative side of life in the hope of encouraging dissatisfaction and thus improvement. The writers of the golden age of Russian literature — Ivan Turgenev, Fëdor Dostoevsky, and Leo Tolstoy — did just that. Their work coincided with the relative leniency of the reign of Alexander II from 1818 to 1881.

In *Sportsman's Sketches* (1847), Turgenev portrayed the suffering of peasants and helped the small educated gentry class identify with their plight. He wrote of the frustrated idealism of radicals unable to bring about change in society.

Tolstoy, a writer as well as a moralist and philosopher, condemned violence, wealth, government repression, and church hypocrisy. Nikolai G. Chernyshevsky's influential novel *What Is to Be Done* (1862) inspired many radicals, including young V. I. Lenin.

By 1914 the writers of the great age of Russian literature were dead. Anton Chekhov represented a link between them and the emerging new writers of the early twentieth century such as Maxim Gorky and Leo Tolstoy. Chekhov described the malaise of the middle-class man. His heroes long for social change but lack the motivation to take action.

The years preceding the 1917 Revolution were revolutionary in literature as well as politics. Indeed, the revolution in the arts helped inspire the political revolt. In the *Futurist Manifesto* of December 1912, writers and artists expressed the mood of the times: "The past is stifling. We must throw Pushkin, Dostoevsky, Tolstoy, etc., from the boat of contemporaneity."

Alexander Blok and Vladimir Mayakovskii became known officially as poets of the revolution. Blok's famous poem *The Twelve* captured the revolutionary spirit, and Mayakovskii's poem *150,000,000* depicted the entire Soviet people as its hero. Between 1918 and 1920 the popular literary journal *Proletarian Culture*, or *Proletkult*, promoted a new literature by and for the proletariat. Studios were set up in Moscow and Leningrad to train new writers, and many famous authors, among them Andrei Bely and Blok, taught there. Two schools of writers, however, emerged: the proletarian writers (those committed to the revolution) and the "fellow travelers" (those who merely accepted the revolution and did not want to produce political art).

During the early twenties, the wartime paper shortage ended, private book publishing facilities resumed operation, and the arts flourished. Authors were free to write and publish what they wished, provided it was not clearly antirevolutionary.

By mid-decade this freedom ended. There could be no neutral art, proletarian writers declared, and they began dictating literary policy through the Association of Proletarian Writers (RAPP). The fellow travelers fell out of favor. The government's first Five-Year Plan was launched in 1928, and all realms of society and the economy were expected to cooperate. Private publishing houses disappeared around 1929, and by 1932 all writers had come under the control of the Union of Soviet Writers.

Socialist Realism

The first All-Union Congress of Soviet Writers in 1934 defined state policy for the arts. Out of Belinsky's concept of critical realism — the writer as social critic — emerged the Soviet doctrine of *socialist realism*. Keynote speaker Maxim Gorky declared:

Party leadership of literature must be strictly purged of all philistine influences. Party members who work in literature must not be only teachers of the ideology that organizes workers of all lands for the final battle for freedom; in all its behavior Party leadership must be a morally authoritative force. This force must above all inculcate in writers a consciousness of their collective responsibility for everything taking place in their midst.... Soviet literature must be ... a mighty weapon of socialist culture.

The task of the social realist was (and is) to produce fictional examples of the New Soviet Man. Realism replaced formalism, or art for art's sake. Literature was to have mass appeal rather than be esoteric, with an optimistic message espousing the party line. Typically the hero is a model worker who contributes in some way to the building of socialism. The "five-year-plan" novel became prominent during the 1930s. Its object was to show how a certain farm

or factory fulfilled or overfulfilled its plans in the face of "wreckers," "saboteurs," and "pessimists."

During World War II socialist realism presented war heroes who bravely fought against the fascists. Often these novels exalted the personality of Joseph Stalin as a caring father figure. Many writers of the prerevolutionary days and early twenties vanished or were silenced. Adherence to socialist realism was strictly enforced, especially between 1946 and Stalin's death in 1953, a period of extreme repression of all the arts.

The 'Thaw'

Stalin's death brought a relaxation of repression in all areas of society, including literature. This period of incredible optimism for writers became known as "the thaw," after Ilya Ehrenburg's novel of the same name written in 1954. Novels critical of the Stalinist way of life began to appear, and writers increasingly expressed individual concerns such as emotions, personal relations, and the trivia of daily existence.

Nikita Khrushchev's 1956 speech at the 20th Congress of the CPSU *(see Appendix p. 279)* marked the real turning point. His denunciation of Stalin's criminal deeds led intellectuals to renew criticism of party control of literature. Vladimir Dudintsev's *Not By Bread Alone* (1956) portrayed a talented and honest individual sentenced to prison by a clique of bureaucrats who saw his innovation as a threat to their interests.

During Khrushchev's leadership of the Soviet Union the kinds of subjects authors were allowed to write about broadened, more foreign works were published in Russian, and some previously condemned authors were rehabilitated such as Anna Akhmatova, Isaac Babel, Mikhail Bulgakov, Osip Mandelshtam, Yuri Olesha, Marina Tsvetaeva, and Mikhail Zoshchenko.

Censorship, however, continued. Boris Pasternak's novel *Dr. Zhivago*, published in Italy in 1957, was banned in the Soviet Union. The novel presented an un-Soviet, although not especially anti-Soviet, view of the 1917 Revolution. Condemned by the Union of Soviet Writers, Pasternak was forced to refuse the Nobel Prize for Literature in 1958.

Four years later, Alexander Solzhenitsyn's powerful novel about the miseries of daily life in a Stalinist labor camp, *One Day in the Life of Ivan Denisovich*, appeared in the literary journal *Novy Mir*. Apparently the novel was published on Khrushchev's instructions after the censors had rejected it. This breakthrough encouraged intellectuals to press for greater freedom of expression.

Brezhnev Era

Since 1964, when Leonid Brezhnev succeeded Khrushchev, literary policy has fluctuated. In 1966 Andrei Siniavskii and Yuli Daniel were tried for publishing abroad under pseudonyms, and a major crackdown on literary freedom ensued. The 1968 Soviet invasion of Czechoslovakia further constrained the intelligentsia.

At the same time the literary underground flourished. It is composed of samizdat and *tamizdat*, works smuggled out, published in the West (*tamizdat* means "over there"), and often smuggled back in.

Despite censorship, a variety of new genres emerged within the bounds of socialist realism. Most popular is *derevshchina*, village prose comparing country life to city

Russian and Soviet Writers

The following are some of the major Russian and Soviet writers and a sampling of their works.

Nineteenth Century

Sergei Aksakov (1791-1859), novels: *Family Chronicle, Recollections of Gogol.*

Alexander Pushkin (1799-1837), father of Russian literature: *Eugene Onegin, A Captain's Daughter, Boris Godunov, Bronze Horseman.*

Nikolai Gogol (1809-52), plays, short stories, novels: *Inspector General, The Overcoat, The Nose, Taras Bulba, Dead Souls.*

Mikhail Lermontov (1814-41), poems, novels: *Death of a Poet, A Hero of Our Time.*

Ivan Turgenev (1818-83), novels, short stories: *Rudin, On the Eve, Fathers and Sons, Smoke, Virgin Soil, Sportsman's Sketches.*

Nikolai Nekrasov (1821-78), radical poet: *Who Lives Well in Russia, Peasant Children.*

Fëdor Dostoevsky (1822-81), novels: *Notes from the Underground, Crime and Punishment, The Gambler, The Idiot, The Possessed, The Brothers Karamazov.*

Aleksandr Ostrovskii (1823-86), first major Russian playwright: *The Storm.*

Mikhail Saltykov-Shchedrin (1826-1889), satire: *Contradictions, A Confused Case, The History of a City, Gentlemen of Tashkent, Provincial Sketches.*

Leo (Lev) Tolstoy (1828-1910), writer and moralist: *War and Peace, Anna Karenina, The Resurrection, Kreutzer Sonata.*

Nikolai Leskov (1831-95), novels, short stories: *Cathedral Folk, The Enchanted Wanderer, The Sealed Angel.*

Anton Chekhov (1860-1904), plays: *Ivanov, Uncle Vanya, The Sea Gull, Three Sisters, The Cherry Orchard.*

Twentieth Century

Maxim Gorky (Aleksei Peshkov) (1868-1936), first major Marxist writer; founded socialist realism: *Mother, The Artamonov Business, Klim Samgin.*

Ivan Bunin (1870-1954), novels; 1933 Nobel Prize: *The Village, The Well of Days, Dark Alleys.*

Leonid Andreev (1871-1919), symbolist: *Darkness, Days of Our Life, He Who Gets Slapped.*

Alexander Blok (1873-1924), symbolist poems: *The Twelve, Scythians.*

Andrei Bely (1880-1934), symbolist: *Petersburg, Kotik Letaev.*

Aleksei Tolstoy (1883-1945), novels: *The Road to Calvary, Peter I, Bread.*

Evgenii Zamiatin (1884-1937), novels, short stories: *We, The Islanders, The Dragon.*

Anna Akhmatova (Gorenko) (1889-1960), poet: *Poem Without a Hero, Courage, Requiem.*

Mikhail Bulgakov (1891-1940), plays, novels: *Heart of a Dog, Master and Margarita.*

Osip Mandelshtam (1892-1938), poems: *The Age, Meganom, The Twilight of Freedom.*

Marina Tsvetaeva (1892-1941), poems: *An Ancient Song, After Russia, An Attempt at Jealousy, The Horn of Roland.*

Vladimir Mayakovskii (1893-1930), plays: *Cloud in Trousers, 150,000,000, The Bathhouse.*

Isaac Babel (1894-1941), short stories: *Red Cavalry, Odessa Tales.*

Sergei Esenin (1895-1925), folk poems: *Autumn, I am the last village poet, Last lines.*

Boris Pasternak (1896-1960), novels, poems; 1958 Nobel Prize: *Doctor Zhivago.*

Ilya Ilf (1897-1937) and Evgenii Petrov (1903-1942), satire: *Twelve Chairs, The Golden Calf.*

Valentin Kataev (1897-1986), novels, plays: *The Embezzlers, Squaring the Circle, Time Forward.*

Leonid Leonov (1899-), novels, plays: *The Thief, Russian Forest, The Orchards of Polovchansk.*

Mikhail Sholokov (1905-), novels; 1965 Nobel Prize: *Quiet Flows the Don, Virgin Soil Upturned.*

Alexander Solzhenitsyn (1918-), novels, short stories; 1970 Nobel Prize: *One Day in the Life of Ivan Denisovich, Cancer Ward, The First Circle, Matryona's Home, The Gulag Archipelago.*

Iurii Nagibin (1920-), novels, short stories: *In Early Spring, The Far and the Near, The Heart of Another, The Bystreets of My Childhood.*

Andrei Siniavskii (1925-), novels: *The Trial Begins, The Icicle, The Makepeace Experiment.*

Iulii Daniel (1925-), short stories: *This is Moscow Speaking, The Flight, Atonement.*

Iurii Trifonov (1927-), novels, short stories: *The Exchange, The House on the Embankment, Students.*

Robert Rozhdestvenskii (1932-), poems: *Winter of Thirty Eight, Nostalgia, They Killed the Lad.*

Vasilii Aksenov (1932-), short stories, novels: *Halfway to the Moon, A Ticket to the Stars, Oranges from Moscow, The Burn, The Island of Crimea.*

Vladimir Voinovich (1932-), short stories, novels: *I Want to Be Honest, The Extraordinary Adventures of Private Ivan Chonkin, In Plain Russian.*

Yevgeny Yevtushenko (1933-), poems, novels, films: *Babi Yar, Dwarf Birches, A Hundred Miles from the Capital City of Hope, Wild Berries, Precocious Autobiography, Kindergarten.*

Bella Akhmadulina (1937-), poems: *String, A Fairytale About Rain, My Genealogy.*

Joseph Brodsky (1940-), poems, essays: *A Stop in the Wilderness, To a Certain Tyrant, Candelmas, A Part of Speech, Less Than One.*

life and extolling the values lost to urbanization and industrialization. Another genre is moral commentary such as Yuri Trifonov's *The Exchange*, about the dilemma of using a dying woman to obtain an extra room in an apartment.

Although the optimism of the fifties had vanished by the end of the 1970s, writers had made gains: communications with foreign countries were less restricted, most established writers visited the West fairly frequently; foreigners were able to travel to the USSR; and cultural exchanges took place. But the delicate balance between permitting free expression of some ideas and quelling dangerous movements of popular opinion remained. In 1979 a group of writers tried to circumvent the censorship process and publish a small-circulation literary collection called *Metropol*. It was suppressed, and soon afterward two of its contributors were expelled from the Union of Soviet Writers.

All writers must be members of the union to legally write as a profession. Once this membership is rescinded (most often because of disagreement with the state), writers may be accused of being "parasites" living off the state.

Those who remain within the literary establishment are greatly rewarded. They enjoy special access to books and archives, housing and country retreats, food stores, medical care, and schooling for children. They get vacations, discounts, theater tickets, and trips abroad. Despite these privileges, the life of a writer in the Soviet Union remains uncertain. State censorship decisions are never predictable. Some works critical of the state may be published because of an author's previous good standing or party connections. And it is often easier to get published in the provinces, as have authors Chingiz Aitmatov and Fazil Iskander.

After Brezhnev

Under general secretaries Yuri Andropov and Konstantin Chernenko, literary policy remained generally the same as under Brezhnev. But Yevgeny Yevtushenko, a solid member of the literary establishment who first gained fame as one of the angry young poets of the 1960s, has been outspoken in pushing for greater openness under new Soviet leader Mikhail Gorbachev. In a bold speech December 12, 1985, to a congress of Soviet writers, Yevtushenko denounced officials and men of letters who keep silent, distort history, and work toward self-promotion. He attacked censorship and the privileges of the elite. Much of his speech was later published in the journal *Literaturnaya Gazeta*, but significant parts were deleted, including his references to Stalin. (*Yevtushenko speech text, p. 340*)

Although Yevtushenko's speech suggested that the Kremlin might be becoming more lenient toward dissent, the Soviet writers' union did not permit the Soviet delegation to attend the 48th international PEN (poets, essayists, and novelists) conference in New York City in January 1986. Soviet writers were not allowed to participate because émigré Soviet authors and other "propagators of hatred" would be there.

Musical Heritage

Russia's musical contribution to world culture is second only to its literary contribution. Mikhail Glinka (1804-57) introduced specifically Russian music that incorporated folk melodies and traditional church music. This movement away from European classical music was continued by Alexander Borodin (1833-87), Modest Mussorgsky (1839-81), and Nikolai Rimsky-Korsakov (1844-1908). Pyotr Tchaikovsky (1840-93) also derived his music from folk melodies, but his works were generally more European.

Igor Stravinsky (1882-71), who composed *Firebird*, *Petrushka*, and *Rite of Spring*, is considered the most important Soviet composer of the twentieth century. Sergei Prokofiev (1891-1953) and Dmitri Shostakovich (1906-75) are also viewed among the greatest of the Soviet composers. They, along with Aram Khachaturian, have gained the most fame outside the USSR. Composers Isaac Dunayesky and Dmitri Kabalevsky are also well known.

Prokofiev, whose famous works include the opera *War and Peace*, the ballets *Romeo and Juliet*, *The Stone Flower*, and *Peter and the Wolf*, and the ballet suite *Scythian Suite*, was censored but never officially disgraced by Stalin because of his universal fame. Harassed under Stalin and condemned in 1936, Shostakovich was rehabilitated in 1956 and became secretary of the RSFSR union of composers in 1960. Shostakovich's well-known works include the operas *The Nose*, *Lady Macbeth of Mtsensk*, the ballet *The Golden Age*, and 11 symphonies.

Stalin's successors launched cultural competitions with the noncommunist world. The most outstanding was the 1956 tour of the United States and West Europe by violinist David F. Oistrakh. Also noteworthy was the Bolshoi Ballet's tour of London in October 1956.

Music Companies

Moscow and other large cities have symphony orchestras, opera and ballet houses, and musical comedy theaters. There were 1,800 official professional composers in the Soviet Union in the early 1980s, and more than 40 opera houses and 300 concert companies. Records and tapes, particularly of classical music, are low priced, making officially sanctioned music accessible.

Opera houses have their own ballet companies. The best known of these are the Moscow Bolshoi Theater and the Leningrad Kirov Theater. Modern music and dance, like modern literature, are criticized for expressing formalism rather than realism. Consequently, while ballet companies and symphony orchestras are impressive technically, they still perform nineteenth century repertoires.

The Leningrad Symphony, the Kirov Ballet, and both the Bolshoi opera and ballet companies were scheduled to appear in the United States in 1986 as part of the cultural exchanges agreed upon at the November 1985 summit. Pianist Vladimir Horowitz returned to the USSR in April 1986 for his first performance there in 61 years.

Popular Music

Authorities have tried without success to undermine the popular music culture in Russia by banning performances, limiting recording opportunities, jamming foreign radio broadcasts, arresting musicians, censoring lyrics, and impeding access to musical instruments and equipment. Denied official recordings, the musical underground thrives on *magnitizdat*, or self-recorded music. Magnitizdat includes all types of unofficial music, but folk, rock, and jazz are the most popular.

Bulat Okudzhava (1924-   ) and Vladimir Vysotsky (1938-80) are the most popular folk poet-musicians. Both gained their fame through magnitizdat. Okudzhava has been tolerated by the Soviet leaders, but since 1970 he has been refused permission to perform abroad. His most popular songs are *Burn, Fire, Burn* and *A Paper Soldier.* Balladeers Mikhail Nozhkin, Yuli Kim, and Alexander Galich (who was forced to emigrate) are also popular.

Vladimir Vysotsky, who died July 25, 1980, at the age of 42, was considered the most listened to and widely revered of the magnitizdat musicians.

While not officially sanctioned, Vysotsky was tolerated. His poems were never officially published, but he remained a leading actor at the Taganka Theater in Moscow and was allowed to perform before small groups. On March 20, 1986, the Soviet news agency Tass announced that a commission of poets and other literary figures had been formed to honor Vysotsky, signaling his rehabilitation. A heavily censored film *Begin at the Beginning* that portrayed his life and featured some of his songs was released just before the commission was announced.

Some American jazz, forbidden under Stalin, is now tolerated. The Ganelin Trio is the best known Soviet jazz group, headed by Viacheslav Ganelin. The first Soviet jazz company allowed to perform in Europe, it was scheduled to tour the United States and Canada in 1986. A few U.S. jazz musicians have played in the Soviet Union, but usually only to closed audiences.

Modern music from the West is considered decadent and for many years could not be obtained except through the black market. As part of an attempt to curtail the black market, the Soviets in the late 1970s and early 1980s allowed limited pressings of works by several rock artists and tours by Western musicians. Soviet rock groups have almost never been allowed to record.

All musicians are required to work through the Philarmonia, a state agency that arranges concerts and television appearances and provides equipment. Unauthorized musical equipment is scarce.

Yuri Andropov forcibly disbanded many rock groups. Komsomol (Communist Youth League) "operational detachment patrols" were sent out to try to halt the black market trade in foreign records. This campaign continued under Konstantin Chernenko, who commented: "On the air waves of pop there swim music groups whose work is of a dubious nature, causing ideological and aesthetic harm to the Soviet Union. We disband such groups without regret."

Time Machine, the Soviet Union's most celebrated rock group, has made things difficult for authorities. The government knows the group is immensely popular and forcing the group to disband would only risk enlarging the already huge underground rock culture.

Other Cultural Areas

The developments in other areas of Soviet culture have been similar to those in literature and music: from modernism and experimentation to strict socialist realism; from a thaw during the 1950s to a general stabilization in the years after Khrushchev.

Theater

Theater is said to be the most liberally treated form of artistic expression in the USSR. But stage plays critical of the state or on taboo subjects are rarely performed and are usually limited to a few avant garde theaters in Moscow. Moscow's major theaters have been allowed to set up "small stages" where they may put on experimental works for audiences of 200 or fewer.

The height of the theatrical tradition in Russia was the collaboration between playwright Chekhov and actor and director Konstantin Stanislavsky, who laid the foundations of modern realistic drama. The theater they founded in 1898 — the Moscow Art Academic Theater — has been one of the world's leading stages. The major playwright of the late nineteenth century was Nikolai Ostrovsky.

At the time of the Revolution, the Bolsheviks recognized the value of the theater as an instrument of mass education and agitation, and they decided to nationalize all theaters. The theaters were placed under the supervision of a division of the People's Commissariat for Enlightenment headed by Vsevolod Meyerhold. Under his direction theater became an experimental medium for proletarian art. Everything that separated the audience from the actors was eliminated. Scenery changes took place in front of the audience. Mass revolutionary productions were staged involving thousands of participants.

The theater is popular in the Soviet Union today. Professional theatrical companies number around 600. The theater is accessible, inexpensive, and performances attract large audiences. Many cities have special theaters for children and young people and some plays are performed in local languages. What appears on the Soviet stage are plays written by contemporary Soviet authors, Russian and foreign classical plays, and works of "progressive" foreign playwrights who often portray negative aspects of life in the United States.

Eduard Radzinsky is the most popular living playwright. His third play, *104 Pages About Love,* has been performed in about 120 Soviet theaters and has been made into a film, an opera, and a ballet. His work also has been seen and produced abroad.

Director Yuri Lyubimov, founder of the well-known Taganka Theater in 1963, was stripped of his citizenship July 11, 1984. The authorities fluctuated in their attitudes toward this playwright. In 1977, after more than 30 of Lyubimov's productions had been staged, *Pravda* published an extremely critical review of his production of Bulgakov's *Master and Margarita;* but four months later Lyubimov was awarded the order of the Red Banner of Labor for his contribution to developing Soviet theater. At the beginning of the 1980s the censors banned three successive productions, and Lyubimov eventually lost his citizenship. Strangely, in September 1984 the Taganka was allowed to stage one of Lyubimov's plays, although works of other individuals in his situation traditionally have been banned.

Western experts cite Lyubimov's treatment as an example of the Soviet system's inconsistency. The authorities apparently allowed the productions because nothing else was as popular.

Film

The first decades of the Soviet regime coincided with the emergence of cinema as a medium. The Bolsheviks saw that it could be more powerful than the written word as a means of agitation. In the 1920s films portrayed the subordination of the individual to the mass, and the great producer Sergei Eisenstein (1898-1948) gave Soviet film international fame. Important films of the time included

Three Famous Soviet Dissidents ...

Three dissidents whose difficulties with the Soviet government have been widely publicized in the West are writer Alexander Solzhenitsyn, physicist Andrei Sakharov, and computer specialist Anatolii Shcharanskii. Only Sakharov remains in the Soviet Union, and he is in internal exile.

Solzhenitsyn

Alexander Solzhenitsyn first gained international acclaim in 1962, when Nikita Khrushchev permitted the literary magazine *Novy Mir* to publish *One Day in the Life of Ivan Denisovich*. Solzhenitsyn's subsequent novels, among them *The First Circle* and *Cancer Ward*, also criticized Stalinist-era abuses. Banned in the Soviet Union but published in the West, they became best-sellers and established Solzhenitsyn's reputation as a writer of the first rank. Although expelled from the official Soviet writers' union in 1969, Solzhenitsyn received the Nobel Prize in Literature the following year, an action that the writers' union said was "deplorable." Solzhenitsyn declined to attend the award ceremonies in Stockholm because he feared he would not be allowed to return home.

Solzhenitsyn's international stature shielded him from arrest during the Kremlin's crackdown on the dissident movement. But the regime mounted a press campaign against him following the December 1973 publication in France of his novel *The Gulag Archipelago, 1918-1956*, an account of terror and death in Joseph Stalin's prison camps. The author announced that if he were arrested he would publish abroad five sequels to *Gulag*, accounts purportedly detailing repression under Khrushchev and Leonid Brezhnev.

Although they dared not arrest and imprison an artistic giant such as Solzhenitsyn, Soviet authorities did settle for banishment. Solzhenitsyn was stripped of his citizenship and sent into exile February 13, 1974, for "performing systematically actions that are incompatible with being a citizen of the USSR."

The most prominent Soviet citizen to be exiled since Leon Trotsky, Solzhenitsyn lived in Switzerland for a year before settling in Cavendish, Vermont, where he continues to criticize the Soviet system and Western willingness to pursue détente. In his first major speech in the West, in Washington, D.C., in June 1975, he urged the United States to "interfere as much as you can" in the internal affairs of the Soviet Union by withholding trade and disarmament agreements, the substance of détente.

Sakharov

After Solzhenitsyn's deportation in 1974, the leader of the dissident movement became Andrei Sa- kharov, a brilliant nuclear physicist who played a major role in developing the Soviet hydrogen bomb. Publication in the West of his essay *Progress, Coexistence and Intellectual Freedom* (1968) first brought him to international attention.

In November 1970 Sakharov and his dissident colleagues founded the Moscow Human Rights Committee to publicize Soviet violations of individual liberties guaranteed by the Soviet Constitution. At a news conference August 21, 1973, Sakharov warned the West that a desire to preserve détente should not foreclose efforts to improve human rights in Soviet society. Sakharov's comments set off a two-week Soviet press campaign to discredit him.

Western critics responded strongly to what they considered undue infringement of individual rights. The National Academy of Sciences, a private U.S. organization responsible for scientific exchanges with the Soviet Union, warned the Soviet Academy of Sciences in a letter September 9 that moves against Sakharov could curtail U.S.-Soviet scientific cooperation. "We think your claims are groundless," the head of the Soviet Academy replied in October.

Sakharov's plight influenced congressional consideration of the Trade Act of 1974, which contained a provision extending most-favored-nation trade status to the Soviet Union. Alluding to the pending legislation, Wilbur D. Mills, D-Ark., chairman of the House Ways and Means Committee, remarked September 9, "I cannot see the United States expanding commercial markets with the Soviet Union if the price is to be paid in the martyrdom of men of genius like Solzhenitsyn and Andrei Sakharov."

By 1975 Sakharov had abandoned his scientific career for a life of protest and political action. That year he was awarded the Nobel Peace Prize, but the Soviet government denied him a visa to receive the award in Oslo, claiming his participation in the hydrogen bomb project made him a security risk. Seventy-two members of the Soviet Academy of Sciences condemned the award, and a Soviet labor newspaper characterized Sakharov, the first Soviet citizen to win the prize, as "Judas" and the prize as "political pornography." Sakharov's wife, Yelena Bonner, accepted the award in his place.

Despite the ever-present threat of arrest, Sakharov continued to draw world attention to repressive conditions in the Soviet Union. In 1977 he wrote to President Jimmy Carter, calling for more pressure on the Soviet government on the human rights issue. In 1980 he opposed the Soviet invasion of Afghanistan and supported an international boycott of the 1980 Moscow Olympic Games. *(Carter, Sakharov letters, Appendix, p. 316)*

... Solzhenitsyn, Sakharov, Shcharanskii

The Kremlin clamped down on the outspoken critic by sending him into internal exile January 22, 1980, for "conducting subversive activities against the Soviet state." Apparently he was sent to Gorkii, about 250 miles east of Moscow, to keep him from issuing public statements in the capital opposing Soviet policy.

Sakharov and his wife successfully used a hunger strike in November 1981 to obtain permission for their daughter-in-law, Yelizaveta Alekseyeva, to join her husband in the United States. She had been married by proxy in the summer of 1981 to Sakharov's stepson, Aleksei Semyonov.

President Ronald Reagan sent a message to Brezhnev, as did 25 prominent American scientists, including 18 Nobel laureates. The U.S. Senate adopted a resolution condemning the "villainous harassment" of the Sakharovs. Seventeen days into their hunger strike, Sakharov and Bonner were told that Alekseyeva would be granted permission to leave the country. The government's reversal was in rare deference to international opinion and the wishes of political dissidents. Alekseyeva left for the United States December 19, 1981.

In the first years of Sakharov's exile, Bonner traveled freely between Gorkii and Moscow and maintained contacts with Soviet and Western supporters. This changed in May 1984 when Sakharov began a hunger strike in support of his wife's efforts to go abroad for medical treatment. Authorities accused her of plotting to take refuge at the U.S. Embassy in Moscow and of using Sakharov's hunger strike to mount an anti-Soviet campaign.

Five days after his hunger strike began, Sakharov was summoned to the Semashko Hospital; on May 11 the hospital began force feeding him. He abandoned the fast May 27 because he was unable to endure the pain of forced feeding, he later reported.

On August 10 Bonner was sentenced to five years of exile in Gorkii. Sakharov was released from the hospital in September and for seven months he and Bonner lived in near total isolation as police watched their apartment around the clock. In October 1984 Sakharov wrote to the Soviet Academy of Sciences threatening to resign by March 1, 1985, if his wife was not allowed to go abroad for treatment. (Sakharov is still a member of the academy and receives full salary, although he was stripped of all other government privileges and awards when he was exiled.)

On April 16, 1985, Sakharov began another hunger strike; five days later he was again taken to Semashko Hospital and fed by force. Bonner heard nothing from him until July 11 when he unexpectedly returned to their apartment. A video tape of the couple's reunion was leaked to the West in June 1985, just before the Helsinki Review Conference in Finland. The tape was part of Soviet attempts to make supporters think all was well with the ailing physicist.

On June 29, Sakharov had written to General Secretary Mikhail Gorbachev asking that Bonner be allowed to travel. He suspended his fast while waiting for a reply. One did not come. July 25 he resumed his fast again, and after two days he was back at the hospital.

A high-ranking KGB official visited Sakharov at the hospital on September 5, 1985, and said that if Bonner agreed in writing not to give news conferences or interviews she could travel to the West. On October 21 Bonner was called to the Gorkii visa office to fill out forms for travel abroad. Two days later Sakharov called off his fast and, victorious, returned home.

Soviet authorities granted Bonner a three-month travel visa for medical purposes. On December 2, 1985, Bonner arrived in Italy to consult an eye specialist. The following month she had heart bypass surgery in the United States.

By permitting Bonner to travel to the West, the Soviets reversed their recent policy of completely isolating Bonner and Sakharov. Political posturing before the Reagan-Gorbachev summit meeting in November 1985 may have prompted the change.

Shcharanskii

Anatolii Shcharanskii, human rights activist and champion of Soviet Jewish emigration, was released to the West February 11, 1985, after eight years in a Soviet prison camp. Shcharanskii's release came as part of an East-West prisoner swap — a result of months of secret negotiations spurred by the November 1985 Geneva summit. In the end, his release was sudden and dramatic. Only one day after Shcharanskii was told he would be freed, he walked across the Gleinicke Bridge separating East and West Germany. He flew to Israel and landed a few hours later among welcoming crowds.

In 1978 Shcharanskii, a 38-year-old computer expert, was imprisoned for espionage, treason, and anti-Soviet agitation. He was sentenced to 13 years in prison and labor camps. The Soviets accused Shcharanskii of spying for the United States, charges both he and the United States denied. Some observers said he became a target for Soviet censure because he talked too much with journalists and politicians from the West.

Shcharanskii married Avital (formerly Natalya Stiglits) in 1974 one day before she was allowed to emigrate to Israel. She expected him to join her soon. When released in 1986, he had not seen his wife in 12 years.

Eisenstein's *The Strike* and *The Battleship Potemkin*; Vsevolod Pudovkin's *Mechanics of the Brain, The End of St. Petersburg,* and *Mother;* and Alexander P. Dovzhenko's *Arsenal* and *The Land.*

The 1953 cultural relaxation led to the release of a number of great films: *Othello* (1955), *Three Men on a Raft* (1954), *The Cranes are Flying,* and *Ballad of a Soldier.* By 1960 the USSR had 59,000 permanent cinemas.

Today films are the most popular art form. The nationalized film industry produces about 160 movies a year. Ticket prices are as low as 55 cents, and an average film reaches about 17 million people. Although a substantial proportion of films are strictly works of socialist realism, a new genre of movies has emerged focusing on family life, infidelity, and the boredom of nine-to-five jobs. A star of this new genre, Andrei Mikhalkov-Konchalovsky, told *Newsweek* in March 1985 that gradual liberalization in the Soviet film industry is inevitable. Andrei Tarkovsky, one of the country's most renowned directors (of *Stalker, Nostalghia,* and *Andrei Roublev*), was less optimistic. He defected in 1984 in search of greater artistic freedom.

Visual Arts

The strong impact of socialist realism on the visual arts gives Soviet painting and sculpture a non-Western character. This is because socialist realism rejects modern abstract art. Current Soviet art reflects a return to the nineteenth century.

The USSR Academy of Arts, headquartered in Moscow, oversees the artistic establishment. There are 15,000 members of the professional artists' union. Most often their products are displayed in public places for the glorification of socialism. In the fall of 1974 a group of unofficial artists (nonmembers of the union) tried to stage an outdoor art show in Moscow of their mildly abstract nonconformist paintings. Plainclothes police harshly dispersed the group when it gathered in an open lot. Some paintings were seized and torn up. The confrontation came to the attention of the international community and, under this pressure, the authorities granted permission for an outdoor exhibition to take place a few weeks later. Unofficial art has declined since the disciplinary crackdowns during Yuri Andropov's tenure as general secretary.

The high point of Soviet art was during the 1920s and 1930s. Avant-garde Soviet artists of this time were at the cutting edge of modern art worldwide. Among the major artists were Kazimir Malevich, Vasilii Kandinsky, Marc Chagall, Vladimir Tatlin, Lyubov Popova, Ivan Kyun, Kliment Rutko, and Aleksandr Rodchenko. Kandinsky and Chagall fled to the West as the avant-garde fell out of favor in the mid-1920s.

The best known Soviet artists today are Alexander Gerassimov (portraits, heroic scenes); Vera Mukhina (sculptures and monuments); Isaac Brodsky (portraits, heroic scenes, historic themes); Alexander Deinida (heroic scenes, historic themes); and Nikolai Rerikh (historic themes, exotic landscapes).

The campaign against formalism in favor of politically edifying art has ended the artistic heyday of the twenties and thirties. Periodic rehabilitations of artists have permitted only some of these early-twentieth-century works to appear publicly in recent decades. The intelligentsia in the 1980s saw no new figures in the arts to replace the early-century innovators or even the artistic challengers of the fifties, sixties, and seventies. On the other hand, the arts are enlivened by the emphasis in Soviet policy on widespread accessibility and on encouraging amateur participation. This has been part of a largely successful effort to keep the arts from becoming a realm exclusively for the elite.

HUMAN RIGHTS, DISSIDENT MOVEMENTS

December 5, 1965, is considered the birthdate of the human rights movement in the USSR. On this day demonstrators in Moscow's Pushkin Square chanted "Respect the Soviet Constitution!" During Khrushchev's tenure as head of the country, the intelligentsia felt a renewed sense of freedom to criticize the government. But after his removal in 1964 they feared a return to Stalinism. The dissident movement began as a response to the arrest in September 1965 of writers Andrei Siniavskii and Yuli Daniel. The men had been charged with "anti-Soviet agitation and propaganda" for publishing their works abroad under the pseudonyms Abram Tertz and Nikolai Arzhak. At their trial in February 1966, both were found guilty and sentenced to labor camps for seven- and five-year terms, respectively. Their arrests, viewed as the first sign of a return to Stalinist methods of repression, produced a nationwide wave of antigovernment demonstrations by members of the intelligentsia, students, workers, ethnic leaders, and others.

Soviet Jews urged fewer restrictions on emigration. Soviet Baptists protested lack of religious freedom. The Ukrainians, Latvians, Lithuanians, and Estonians argued for greater national autonomy. Workers, denied the right to strike, tried without success to form independent labor unions.

After 1965 many Russians were less willing to accept conditions in the Soviet Union, despite improvements in the availability and quality of consumer goods. Dissenters disturbed the relative domestic calm by publicly calling on the government to liberalize social controls. They demanded the right to free speech as proclaimed in the Soviet Constitution and started publicizing aspects of Soviet life either kept quiet or distorted by official information.

Dissent Under Brezhnev

The Kremlin's response to the emerging dissident movement was, in most cases, repressive. At the 23d Party Congress in 1966, General Secretary Leonid Brezhnev said: "There are hack artists who . . . specialize in smearing our system and slandering our heroic people." These "renegades," he continued, "do not care for the interests of our socialist homeland . . . sacred to every Soviet man. It is quite clear that the Soviet people cannot ignore the disgraceful activity of such people. They treat them according to their just desserts." Those remarks set the tone for the Brezhnev regime's harsh treatment of dissidents.

The Soviet invasion of Czechoslovakia in August 1968 aroused a new wave of antigovernment protest. Most prominent in this cause was the former Army major-general Pyotr G. Grigorenko, who, as punishment for an earlier protest in 1964, had been demoted and committed to a

Soviet Defections and Exiles

One measure of the Soviet government's intolerance of dissidents is the long list of notable journalists, performing artists, authors, scientists, and others who have defected or have been stripped of their citizenship and exiled. Prize-winning author Alexander I. Solzhenitsyn was exiled in 1974; world-renowned cellist Mstislav Rostropovich was exiled in 1978; and physicist Andrei Sakharov was forced into internal exile in 1974. *(See Solzhenitsyn-Sakharev-Shcharanskii box, p. 180.)* The Kirov Ballet's leading soloist, Rudolf Nureyev, defected in 1961 and Stalin's daughter, Svetlana Alliluyeva, defected in 1967 and again in 1986, after returning to the USSR in 1984.

Others who have defected include Bolshoi Ballet dancers Sulamith Messerer and her son Mikhail (1981); symphony director Maksim Shostakovich (son of composer Dmitri Shostakovich) and his concert pianist son (1981); Yuri Stepanov, soloist with the Moscow Classical Ballet, and concert violinist Gidon Kremer (1980). Stepanov, who defected in January 1980, was seized on the street in March 1981 and returned to the Soviet Union.

Yuri Lyubimov, theater director and founder of the Taganka Theater, was stripped of his citizenship in 1984. Film director Andrei Tarkovsky defected July 10, 1984, in Italy. In 1983 Tchaikovsky-Prize violinist, Viktoria Mullova, defected in Finland. Pianist Vladimir Ashkenazy left in 1963.

Soloist Alexander Godunov of the Bolshoi Ballet defected with his wife, ballerina Ludmilla Vlasova, August 23, 1979. Vlasova chose to return to the Soviet Union four days later, but in 1980 she applied to return to the United States. Bolshoi Ballet performers Leonid Kozlov and his wife Valentina defected in 1979. Mikhail Baryshnikov, a top dancer with the Kirov Ballet, defected to the United States in 1974. Natalia Makarova, also of the Kirov Ballet, had defected to London four years earlier.

World ice-skating champions Oleg Protopopov and his wife, Ludmilla Belousova, defected to Switzerland in 1979. Gen. Pyotr Grigorenko, the highest-ranking Soviet Army officer to openly join the dissident movement, was exiled in 1978 and received asylum in the United States.

Notable dissident writers and journalists who defected or were expelled include Lev Kopelev, Vladimir Voinovich, Vladimir Maximov, Andrei Amalrik, Joseph Brodsky, Andrei Siniavskii, Anatoli Gladilin, Viktor Nekrasov, and Vasilii Aksenov. Pavel Litvinov and Vladimir Bukovsky were deported in 1976.

Arkady Shevchenko, UN secretary general for political and Security Council affairs, defected in 1978. Viktor Korchnoi, the world's second-ranking chess player, defected in July 1976.

In a rare case, the Soviet Union April 27, 1979, agreed to release Alexander Ginzburg and five other dissidents in return for U.S. release of two convicted Soviet spies. Ginzburg, who came with his family to New York, had been sentenced to hard labor in 1978.

---

psychiatric institution. For his denouncement of the 1968 invasion he was recommitted.

In May 1969 the first human rights association formed in Moscow — the Initiative Group to Defend Human Rights in the USSR. Between 1967 and 1970 the authorities dealt firmly with dissenters and sent many to prison or psychiatric institutions as punishment for "anti-Soviet activities." The Kremlin stepped up its campaign against dissidents in the early 1970s, arresting critics of the regime and sentencing them to hard labor and internal exile.

Many Westerners and émigrés have charged the Soviets with using drugs meant for individuals with mental imbalances on political prisoners. Incarceration in psychiatric hospitals and the use of these drugs led the World Psychiatric Association to call for expulsion of the Soviets from the group. The USSR quit the group before a vote was taken.

As relations with the West improved, repression of Soviet dissidents increased. In fact, some observers have charged that détente permitted large-scale repression of Soviet dissidents; without it, the Kremlin would have been forced to initiate fundamental domestic reforms.

The most important figures to arise during this time were writer Alexander Solzhenitsyn and physicist Andrei Sakharov. *(See box, p. 180.)* They and their fellow dissidents used many methods: protest demonstrations, clandestine publications, and the smuggling of literary works abroad. Samizdat was a crucial element in the rise and spread of information on human rights violations. Another important tool of the dissident movement was the bimonthly publication the *Chronicle of Current Events*. Until its suppression in 1973, the *Chronicle* publicized prison conditions, recent arrests, trials, and letters of protest.

In February 1974 Solzhenitsyn was stripped of his citizenship and the government launched a press campaign against Sakharov. Two years later dissidents Andrei Amalrik, Pavel Litvinov, and Vladimir Bukovsky were deported. Thousands of dissidents were dismissed from their jobs, named enemies of the Soviet state, and placed in labor camps.

The Helsinki Accords

The plight of Solzhenitsyn, Sakharov, and many others (including the geneticist Zhores Medvedev, who was briefly committed to a mental hospital) provoked blistering criticism from the West. To make humane treatment of citizens part of an international code of conduct, Western negotiators incorporated a human rights section in the final document of the Conference on Security and Cooperation in Europe (CSCE) in Helsinki, Finland.

On August 1, 1975, after 22 months of negotiations, the conference reached final agreement on general principles "guiding their mutual relations." These principles were spelled out in a lengthy document known as the Final Act and were signed by the heads of government of the United States, Canada, the Soviet Union, and every other East and West European nation except Albania.

In return for sections implicitly recognizing national boundaries established after World War II, the Soviets agreed to the human rights section of the Final Act. Known as "Basket Three" (the third section of the accord), it was a set of broadly worded measures committing participating states to "take positive action" in the sphere of personal liberties and to promote the free exchange of ideas, people, and information between East and West.

The intent of Basket Three was to relax restrictions on travel and communications for journalists and other individuals, facilitate the reunion of families, and make it easier for persons of one nationality to marry citizens of another.

But the Final Act's effectiveness was open to question. It was nonbinding and had no legal status. Exiled novelist Solzhenitsyn warned that the good intentions expressed in the act were unlikely to ease Soviet policies on human rights.

Crackdown Continues

Incidents occurring after the Helsinki conference seemed to support skeptical views of the CSCE humanitarian clauses. By mid-August 1975 two Soviet citizens had been permitted to join relatives in the United States, according to State Department records, but the records also indicated that as many as 641 individuals known to the U.S. Embassy in Moscow wished to emigrate. Prospects for freer circulation of Western publications behind the Iron Curtain were dimmed by a vigorous Soviet press campaign against their alleged "decadence" and inflammatory character. And critics of the Final Act took the Soviets' refusal to allow Sakharov to travel to Oslo to receive the Nobel Peace Prize as further evidence of Soviet failure to adhere to the provisions of Basket Three.

In May 1976 the Moscow Helsinki Watch Group was founded. It based its activities on the humanitarian provisions of the Helsinki Final Act. Similar groups were formed in other parts of the country. What united all the dissident groups — the human rights groups as well as nationalist and religious dissenters — was their basic commitment to the Helsinki accords. Alarmed by the strengthening ties between these groups, authorities in the late 1970s again cracked down on dissenters. Even fear of criticism from the West did not stop the government from attempting to silence its opponents.

Dissent in the 1980s

The treatment of critics of the regime by Andropov, Brezhnev's successor, and by Chernenko, Andropov's successor, alternated between formal warnings, harassment, intimidation, beatings, imprisonment, hard labor, exile, and expulsion from the USSR. The outlook for human rights under General Secretary Mikhail Gorbachev is unclear, although a thaw in U.S.-Soviet relations after the November 1985 summit portended some improvement. One example of this was the much publicized issue of divided spouses during and immediately after the Geneva summit.

Soviet citizens who marry foreigners must get permission from the state to emigrate to the spouse's country. According to the U.S. State Department, about 80 percent of the requests are approved. The remaining 20 percent either encounter some difficulty, are not granted for years, or never are approved — frequently for unclear reasons.

As a result of the summit, eight long-divided spouses and one son of a U.S. citizen were allowed to go to the United States. Sakharov's wife, Yelena Bonner, was granted permission to travel to the West for medical treatment and human rights activist Anatolii Shcharanskii was released from prison. *(Solzhenitsyn, Sakharov, and Shcharanskii, box, pp. 180-181)*

Despite these signs of good will, the plight of dissidents in the Soviet Union remains bleak. By 1985, 10 years after the height of the dissident movement, public opposition had been virtually silenced and the unity of the movement had largely disintegrated. Most activists had emigrated or were in prison or in exile. Only two of 20 dissidents who formed the unofficial group to monitor Soviet compliance with the Final Act remained free in the USSR.

Changing of the Guard

Leonid Brezhnev's death in 1982 ended years of stagnant leadership and precipitated the long-delayed succession crisis. Would the Kremlin opt for another aging leader who would continue muddling through? Or would it choose a younger man prepared to institute change? Yuri V. Andropov, 68, emerged as a reform-minded leader but his policies produced only minor results before he died in February 1984. Konstantin U. Chernenko, 73, replaced him and began slowing the process of change; he died 13 months later. Mikhail S. Gorbachev and a younger generation intent on reform claimed the helm in March 1985.

But basic changes do not come easily to the Soviet Union. Since the Revolution, the nation's leaders have set widely differing interpretations on communist dogma and have drawn legitimacy from the acceptance of their views by a consensus among the 19 million party members and subgroups they represent. Rulers — whether tsars or communists — must also preserve another claim to legitimacy, that of keeping what former Moscow correspondent Robert G. Kaiser has called "the historic bargain" with the Soviet people. "This bargain is simple," Kaiser explained in the *Washington Post* November 14, 1982:

> The people give up any right to choose their leaders or influence their policies in return for basic security, order and the staples of daily life. An abrupt change in the party line would only raise doubts that the new leaders could make good on their end of the bargain. Abrupt changes would rekindle the ancient Russian fear of disorder or anarchy.

Nikita Khrushchev discovered in 1964 that challenges to the prevailing system would not be lightly tolerated. Leonid Brezhnev did not test the system; instead he chose to pursue stability. Kaiser anticipated in 1982 that these claims to legitimacy would prevent change from coming in the years immediately ahead. But when Andropov was selected as general secretary, former U.S. ambassador to the Soviet Union Malcolm Toon said that "Some measure of reform might be palatable to the old guard ... if carried out under the watchful eye of Andropov." He could, "in the view of the conservatives, be relied upon to use the same ruthlessness he applied to his KGB responsibilities in making sure reforms would not seriously damage the role of the party and thus would not get out of hand," Toon wrote in the *Christian Science Monitor* November 17, 1982.

Changes were expected from Andropov, and indeed he instituted some during his brief tenure. But few expected change from Chernenko. Headed by an interim leader imbued with Brezhnev's legacies, Chernenko's so-called "interregnum" merely prolonged the Brezhnev gerontocracy and seemingly proved Kaiser's belief that change was far down the road.

In his first year as general secretary, Gorbachev demonstrated a firm determination to infuse new life in the ailing Soviet economy and complacent party bureaucracy. But Gorbachev, like his predecessors, has been constrained in his efforts to implement reforms. The bureaucracy's enormous resistance was not overcome merely by Gorbachev's removal of most of the leading members of the old guard. The fear of systemic change remained pervasive.

This final chapter examines the sometimes tentative, sometimes bold alterations of domestic and foreign policy proposed by Andropov, Chernenko, and Gorbachev. All three faced the same dilemma: how to institute necessary economic and social reforms without undermining the Soviet system.

Andropov's Rule

On November 12, 1982, two days after General Secretary Brezhnev's death, Yuri Vladimirovich Andropov was chosen to succeed him as head of the Soviet Communist Party. Within two months Andropov appeared firmly in control of the Soviet Union.

Western assessments focused on Andropov's abilities, intelligence, knowledge, and flexibility. They suggested that he was selected over Brezhnev's personal favorite, Chernenko, because he won the support of the military, the State Security Committee (KGB), and party technocrats who feared that Chernenko would merely continue the stultifyingly stable policies that Brezhnev had pursued. Western experts surmised that the support of Foreign Minister Andrei Gromyko and Defense Minister Dmitri Ustinov was decisive and that the choice of Andropov seemed to indicate a preference for some revitalization in both the economy and foreign relations.

Western observers questioned from the start, however, whether Andropov could institute needed economic reforms without offending the Communist Party bureaucracy that Brezhnev had pampered. Soviet leaders obviously recognized the need for change. But in the centralized bureaucracy of the party structure, large-scale change is exceedingly difficult to implement without infringing on the fiefdoms of national and regional party potentates.

It was not only the corrupt elements of the party bureaucracy that opposed Andropov's moves to clean up the party elite and reinvigorate the economy by limited decentralization. "Many orthodox communists feared system changes on grounds that, once initiated, they could acquire an uncontrollable life of their own," Dusko Doder commented in the *Washington Post* July 28, 1985. The question, Doder added, "was whether the party could hold the society together to make changes smoothly enough, particularly while confronted with President Reagan's rearmament program and Moscow's extended commitments to communist allies and various clients throughout the world."

Adam B. Ulam, director of Harvard University's Russian Research Center, described the "heavy burden" shouldered by Andropov. In the *New Republic* December 6, 1982, Ulam wrote:

> Has the Soviet Union overcommitted itself by trying to subvert and replace the influence of the West in practically every part of the world? Can Moscow reach a real rather than a superficial reconciliation with Peking if it does not constrain its imperialist striving in Southeast Asia, Afghanistan and elsewhere? . . . How long can the present pattern of Soviet domination over Eastern Europe endure, with the Red Army being the sole guarantor of communist rule over some 110 million people, the great majority of whom detest their regimes? Will the ailing economy be able to bear indefinitely the heavy burden of increasing outlays of expenditures and resources that go for armaments?

If Andropov was going to initiate substantive change he would have to act rather quickly, for the new Soviet leader was 68 years old and in dubious health. Andropov's kidneys failed only four months into his tenure, and he had to use a dialysis machine at least twice a week. In September 1983 he was hospitalized when his health deteriorated. In October one kidney was removed. From that point, Andropov was largely confined to a specially equipped apartment inside the Kuntsevo government hospital.

Career History

Despite his poor health, Andropov was able to run the country, seemingly by remote control. As his career history suggests, he was not the prototypical interim leader willing to follow his predecessor's policies until a new generation was ready to take over. As head of the KGB from 1967 until 1982, Andropov oversaw a strong — and effective — campaign against Soviet dissidents. He became a candidate member of the Politburo in 1967 and a full member six years later. Andropov succeeded his patron Mikhail Suslov as the top party ideologist on the Central Committee Secretariat in May 1982; he resigned his KGB post two days afterward.

Like Brezhnev, Andropov became chairman of the important Defense Council after becoming general secretary, but he did not assume the presidency (chairman of the Presidium of the Supreme Soviet) until June 16. Western observers speculated the lengthy vacancy indicated the post's relative unimportance. Some suggested the vacancy meant Andropov had less support than met the eye; still others, however, said the choice was his — that he did not want to burden himself with a time-consuming but relatively powerless job, especially after his illness became more pronounced. This would have been in keeping with the subtle and not-so-subtle ways Andropov discouraged the accumulation of offices and material goods by Soviet party functionaries that Brezhnev lavished on himself and subordinates.

Economic, Personnel Changes

Until his health failed in the fall of 1983, Andropov devoted most attention to revitalizing the sluggish Soviet economy. He openly confronted the party and country about how the bureaucracy stymied change. Calls for labor discipline were emphasized. He opened a debate that unleashed unprecedented criticism of the way the national economy was run. Andropov advocated giving manufacturing and agricultural enterprises more autonomy and introducing incentives for productive workers. In July 1983 he announced a series of economic experiments designed to test all these proposals to reduce central bureaucratic controls.

For his economic reform proposals, Andropov needed all the allies he could find, particularly the help of Defense Minister Ustinov, to whom he was said to be close. To suggest any large-scale reductions in Soviet military spending, necessary for economic reform, would have endangered the support he apparently needed to remain in control. Another factor against cuts in the military budget was the huge increase in military spending by the United States, as was President Reagan's call for a Strategic Defense Initiative (SDI). The Soviet military apparently feared SDI would widen the technological gap between the superpowers. *(Andropov's economic initiatives, Chapter 7)*

After the Korean Air Line tragedy and his health setback in September 1983, Andropov shifted his attention to personnel changes. He retired scores of party and government officials because of their age or ineffectiveness. He pushed Mikhail Gorbachev and numerous other middle-echelon officials into responsible leadership posts. These younger men shared Andropov's concern about the economy's feebleness, and they set the stage for future general secretary Gorbachev's more rapid, extensive personnel changes and economic initiatives.

Nowhere is patronage more important than in the Politburo. At the time of Brezhnev's death, the Politburo had dwindled to only 10 active members, giving Andropov a major voice in the appointment of as many as 5 new members. His first top-level change had been announced November 22, 1982, when Geidar Aliev was elevated to the Politburo. Aliev was a 59-year-old KGB career officer whom Andropov had appointed to oversee the drive against corruption in Azerbaidzhan in the late 1960s. Viktor Chebrikov, who succeeded Andropov as KGB head, was named a candidate Politburo member in December 1983. Mikhail Solomentsev, never a close ally of Brezhnev, was promoted to full Politburo membership, as was Vitalii Vorotnikov. The Central Committee Plenum that approved these promotions also approved the appointment of Egor Ligachev to the Central Committee Secretariat. Andropov's speeches to the Plenum were read by a spokesman in his absence.

Relations With United States

In what was virtually an inaugural address before the Soviet Central Committee November 22, 1982, Andropov said: "The policy of détente is by no means a past stage. The future belongs to this policy." However, U.S.-Soviet relations deteriorated soon after those words were spoken.

Immediately after Brezhnev's death President Reagan and other administration officials had stressed their desire for improved U.S.-Soviet relations. But explicit or implicit in these statements was the caveat that any improvement would require some change in Soviet behavior. "It takes two to tango," President Reagan quipped at a news conference November 11. The English-language *Moscow News* replied November 25 that "asking someone to dance is not generally done by a demand that he or she change their hairdo, let alone thinking."

In a meeting with *Washington Post* editors and reporters November 12, Secretary of State George P. Shultz outlined the steps the Soviet Union must take before better relations could be established: Soviet withdrawal from Afghanistan, Vietnamese withdrawal from Kampuchea (Cambodia), relaxation of tensions in Poland, and progress toward arms reductions. The Soviet reply was hardly unexpected. Andropov, in his speech to the Central Committee November 22, warned that "statements in which the readiness for normalizing relations is linked with the demand that the Soviet Union pay with preliminary concessions in different fields do not sound serious, to say the least. We shall not agree to this."

Arms Control. These and similar comments by the Soviets did not augur well for the most important aspect of U.S.-Soviet relations, arms control.

In a speech November 22, 1982, Reagan proposed the deployment of 100 MX missiles in Wyoming. The new missiles, administration officials argued, would protect U.S. land-based intercontinental ballistic missiles and make it virtually impossible for the Soviets to launch a successful first-strike attack. The administration hoped that the threat would move Kremlin leaders to engage in meaningful arms reduction talks. But MX opponents argued that announcing the decision to deploy the missiles so soon after a new Soviet leader had taken power was hardly the way to convince Andropov that the United States wanted better relations with the Soviet Union.

Moscow denounced the MX decision, saying that it violated existing arms agreements and insisting that the USSR would find "an effective way to reply to Washington" if such provocations continued. The plan to deploy 572 U.S. Pershing II and cruise missiles in Western Europe, beginning in December 1983, also provoked a strong Soviet response. One of Andropov's highest priorities was to prevent the deployment of those missiles.

Andropov offered December 21, 1982, to reduce Soviet intermediate-range missiles to the combined number held by Britain and France if the United States would not deploy its Pershing II and cruise missiles. The United States, Britain, and France rejected the offer on the grounds that it would leave Moscow with a monopoly of intermediate-range missiles in Europe. (*Arms control, Chapter 6, p. 142*)

Andropov closed 1982 by renewing a Soviet proposal for a summit meeting with President Reagan, but the United States showed little initial enthusiasm. Veteran Sovietologist George F. Kennan wrote in the *New York Times* November 14, 1982, that "in the first days following

---

'We Have Been Wrong'

"We have been wrong on just about every major development in the USSR since the Bolshevik revolution. We didn't anticipate the revolution; when it occurred, we didn't think it would succeed; when it was successful, we thought socialism was going to be abandoned; when it wasn't, we thought we wouldn't have to recognize the new Soviet state; when we did, we acted first as if it was like the Western democracies and then as if it was like the Nazis; when the Germans invaded, we thought the Russians could last only six weeks; when they survived the war, we thought they couldn't recover quickly from it; when they recovered quickly, we thought they didn't have the know-how to build missiles, and so on. This record would seem to suggest . . . that perhaps we should not be too positive in other assumptions we have made."

—Fred Warner Neal,
former State Department Soviet affairs officer

---

the change of regime" both the United States and the Soviet Union "have possibilities for conciliatory moves that would involve no significant sacrifice of their own interests but might well represent a turning point in an otherwise strained relationship." But the Reagan administration made it clear that it would continue a large defense buildup; the Soviets made it equally clear that they would counter any effort by their superpower adversary to achieve "nuclear superiority."

Conflicting Advice? It was conceivable that Kremlin strategists were offering Andropov conflicting advice about dealing with the United States. One faction might have argued that, despite the Reagan administration's tough, anti-Soviet rhetoric, the United States, faced with serious economic problems of its own, wanted and needed an arms control agreement. Reagan, it might have been pointed out, lifted the grain embargo and pipeline sanctions and, like his anticommunist predecessor Richard Nixon, could ensure approval of a strategic arms limitation treaty (SALT) or some form of détente. Others might have contended that the Soviet Union should wait for a more accommodating American leader and focus on a weakening of U.S. links with Europe and China.

Trade, Technology. The picture was also unclear regarding conciliatory action in trade and technology transfers. In April 1981 Reagan lifted the grain embargo President Jimmy Carter had imposed in response to the Soviet invasion of Afghanistan in December 1979. And on November 14, 1982, the president ended sanctions against U.S. and foreign companies selling American-made equipment for the Soviet natural gas pipeline to Western Europe. Despite these measures, the United States remained vocal in its opposition to selling military-related equipment to the Soviet Union. The Soviets remained equally vocal in rejecting efforts to use trade as a weapon against them.

The Soviet Union had considerable success in acquiring Western technology and encouraging the peace movement in Western Europe, thereby driving a wedge between the United States and its principal allies. The peace movement did not halt the missile deployments, but U.S.-European relations were strained over how to deal with the Soviets. The "argument with Europe is over how East-West trade can be used, and how the United States can influence East-West trade, to shape Soviet behavior," according to Ed A. Hewett, a Soviet-affairs specialist at the Brookings Institution. "There is strong disagreement ... between European governments who are generally skeptical of the possibility that manipulating trade flows will influence Soviet leaders, and the Reagan administration, which is convinced it can make such a link work," he wrote in the fall 1982 *Brookings Review*.

Other Foreign Policy Concerns

Another priority for Andropov was reconciliation with China. Talks on normalizing relations, which China suspended after the Soviet invasion of Afghanistan, were reconvened a few weeks before Brezhnev's death. During Brezhnev's funeral, the foreign ministers of the two communist giants held the highest-level talks in 13 years, and each side pledged to work toward improved relations. China imposed at least three conditions on a Sino-Soviet reconciliation: a pullback of Soviet troops along the border, Soviet withdrawal from Afghanistan, and an end to Soviet support for Vietnam in Kampuchea. *(Chapter 5, p. 85)*

Western observers noted that the Soviets might find it very much in their interest to withdraw their half-million troops on the Chinese border and the more than 100,000 soldiers bogged down in bloody skirmishes with rebels in Afghanistan. The real problem for Soviet leaders was making a convincing case that they were not acceding to Chinese demands. (Andropov and the KGB, which he headed at the time, reportedly opposed the Soviet invasion, although Andropov was apparently part of the small "quick reaction group" that oversaw operations in Afghanistan once the decision to invade was made.) The adverse publicity from U.S. allegations that the Soviet Union was using chemical warfare in Afghanistan in violation of international treaties perhaps also could have been countered by a Soviet withdrawal.

Andropov might not have been able to withdraw Soviet forces from Afghanistan even if a genuinely neutralist government could have been found to replace the Soviet-imposed regime of Babrak Karmal. Despite the economic, political, and propagandistic benefits of withdrawal it would have been strongly opposed by Soviet party ideologues. No doubt Brezhnev loyalists would have accused Andropov of rejecting the so-called Brezhnev Doctrine.

Andropov perhaps could have relieved the pressure on the Soviet economy somewhat by cutting back on the estimated tens of billions of dollars in aid given to friendly governments and satellites. (It is impossible to determine the extent of Soviet aid because it is given in a variety of ways, including grants, subsidized prices, low-interest loans, and gifts.) But any suggestion to reduce or end assistance to Cuba, Angola, Vietnam, Nicaragua, and particularly Eastern Europe would have sparked at least as much opposition as would have proposals for a withdrawal from Afghanistan. Opponents likely would have argued that an aid reduction would harm Soviet security.

Andropov Disappears

Andropov acted quickly to foster change, and if he had had more time he might have implemented more of his goals. His last public appearance was August 18, 1983, when he received a delegation of nine U.S. senators, at which time he declared a unilateral moratorium on the deployment of Soviet antisatellite weapons. Sen. Patrick Leahy, D-Vt., and the others noted they were impressed with Andropov.

When a Soviet pilot shot down Korean Air Lines flight 007 September 1, 1983, killing all 269 aboard, Andropov was said to be vacationing. Statements on the crisis were made by Soviet diplomatic and military officials, such as Marshal Nikolai Ogarkov. The incident plunged already declining U.S.-Soviet relations to the lowest point since the Cold War, the media noted, but the United States imposed only relatively minor sanctions against the Soviets for the shooting. Most reaction was verbal, such as when Secretary of State Shultz and Foreign Minister Andrei Gromyko exchanged harsh words about the tragedy at their September 8 meeting in Madrid for the Conference on Security and Cooperation in Europe.

Andropov continued to run the country from his closely guarded hospital apartment. In responding to various arms control proposals and in appointing or removing personnel, Andropov relied on the telephone. But by the end of January 1984 his condition had deteriorated markedly. According to most accounts, the government came to a standstill. He died February 10.

Chernenko 'Interregnum'

Konstantin Chernenko's selection as Andropov's successor disappointed many Soviets who privately regarded him as an uneducated professional bureaucrat who rose to positions of power solely because of his association with Brezhnev. This evaluation of the man was truthful but incomplete.

Chernenko had certainly depended on Brezhnev for advancement. He also was uneducated relative to many of his colleagues and was not experienced in foreign policy and defense matters. But Chernenko had other qualities that made his selection less of an aberration. He was a skilled party functionary, a loyal team player, and a leader who knew his limitations. He could be expected to submit to collective leadership and defer to better informed Politburo members on issues outside his expertise.

Chernenko was chosen not for his personal qualities, however, but because, in the Politburo's view, he was the right man for the times. The old guard was not yet ready to turn power over to the next generation of leaders. They wanted a transitional leader — someone who could be trusted to protect the positions of Brezhnev-era appointees and return stability to a bureaucracy shaken by Andropov's personnel changes, but who would not obstruct change in the party hierarchy for years on end. Western scholars have suggested Chernenko was chosen precisely because of his old age and poor health rather than in spite of them. The younger and more progressive leaders promoted by Andropov could accept Chernenko because he would not be around long, while the old guard could cling to their positions and influence a little longer and possibly prepare for retirement. Indeed, not a single member of the Politburo or

Leaders of the Soviet Communist Party

Following are the full and candidate (nonvoting) members of the Politburo and the members of the Central Committee Secretariat as announced

Politburo

Mikhail Gorbachev, party general secretary since March 11, 1985; member since October 1980.

Geidar Aliev, first deputy premier and member since November 1982.

Viktor Chebrikov, State Security Committee (KGB) head; member since April 1985.

Andrei Gromyko, president since April 1985; member since April 27, 1973.

Dinmukhamed Kunaev, Kazakhstan party head; member since April 9, 1971.

Egor Ligachev, party secretary and chief of ideology; member since April 1985.

Nikolai Ryzhkov, premier since September 1985; member since April 1985.

Vladimir Shcherbitskii, Ukraine party head; member since April 9, 1971.

Eduard Shevardnadze, foreign minister and member since July 1985.

Mikhail Solomentsev, party control commission head; member since December 1983.

Vitalii Vorotnikov, premier of Russian Federation; member since December 1983.

Lev Zaikov, party secretary since July 1985; member since March 6, 1986.

Candidate (Nonvoting) Politburo

Petr Demichev, minister of culture; member since November 1, 1964.

Vladimir Dolgikh, party secretary; member since May 1982.

Boris Eltsin, Moscow party head; member since February 18, 1986.

March 6, 1986, in Moscow at the conclusion of the 27th Congress of the Communist Party of the Soviet Union (CPSU):

Nikolai Sliunkov, Belorussian party head; member since March 6, 1986.

Sergei Sokolov, defense minister; member since April 1985.

Iurii Solovev, Leningrad party head; member since March 6, 1986.

Nikolai Talyzin, Gosplan head; member since October 1985.

Central Committee Secretariat

Gorbachev, member since November 1978.

Alexandra Biriukova, trade union official; member since March 6, 1986.

Anatolii Dobrynin, ambassador to United States 1962-86; member since March 6, 1986.

Dolgikh, member since December 1972.

Aleksandr Iakovlev, Central Committee Propaganda Department head since July 1985; member since March 6, 1986.

Ligachev, member since December 1983.

Vadim Medvedev, Central Committee Science and Educational Instititutions Department head; member since March 6, 1986.

Viktor Nikonov, agricultural oversight; member since April 1985.

Georgii Razumovskii, Central Committee Organizational Party Work Department head; member since March 6, 1986.

Zaikov, defense industry oversight; member since July 1985.

Mikhail Zimianin, member since March 6, 1976.

Secretariat lost his job under Chernenko.

But while his selection as general secretary made sense from the perspective of Soviet internal politics, Chernenko was not what the ailing Soviet economy and society needed. He did not possess the strength or will to implement the reforms necessary to substantially improve the lives of Soviet citizens. To his credit, Chernenko endorsed most of the reforms Andropov had been able to push through the system during his 15-month tenure. Chernenko called for the decentralization of selected areas of the economy and greater labor discipline and productivity. But he did not aggressively promote or build on these reforms as Andropov would have done had he lived longer. In some cases, most notably his reversal of Andropov's order to

reduce the bureaucracy by 20 percent, Chernenko actively worked against reform. In addition, Chernenko offered only a few relatively minor domestic initiatives of his own. He backed education reform, a land reclamation project, better representation in constitutional bodies such as the Supreme Soviet, and elimination of some duplication of economic tasks by parallel party and government bodies.

Foreign Policy

Despite Chernenko's lack of foreign policy experience, he succeeded in renewing the arms control dialogue with the United States that had been silenced during Andropov's short tenure. Chernenko's speeches, writings, and loyalty to Brezhnev signaled his support for détente. However, Chernenko's health was too uncertain, his expertise too suspect, and anti-Reagan sentiment in Moscow too strong for him to make many significant changes in the relations between the superpowers. Moreover, during 1984 the Soviets had sought to avoid any action that might contribute to a Reagan-Republican landslide in the November national elections. Thus, even if Chernenko had desired to dramatically redirect U.S.-Soviet relations (which is doubtful), he probably could not have done so.

What he did do was support a return to the Geneva arms control negotiations following Reagan's election. The real architect of this pragmatic shift may have been Gromyko, who was reported to have taken over foreign policy formulation under Chernenko. But Chernenko's backing was critical to the speed with which the policy was implemented and the support it received in Moscow. Only eight days after Reagan's election, Anatolii Dobrynin, then ambassador to the United States, indicated that the Soviet Union was interested in holding umbrella talks on strategic and intermediate nuclear weapons and on weapons in space. The combined talks had initially been proposed by the United States in 1983, but now the Soviets sought to make the proposal their own. On November 22 the superpowers announced that Gromyko and Secretary of State Shultz would meet in Geneva in January to lay the groundwork for the arms control talks. Actual negotiations began March 12, two days after Chernenko's death.

Other areas of Soviet foreign affairs appeared to be on automatic pilot during Chernenko's administration. Using traditional tools of Soviet foreign policy, the Soviets continued many Brezhnev-era policies. Through arms sales they improved their relationship with nonaligned nations such as India and Kuwait. They also continued to seek an elusive military solution to the war in Afghanistan, launching a major offensive in the spring following Chernenko's rise to power.

The summer of 1984 saw a setback in Sino-Soviet relations brought on by President Reagan's April visit to the People's Republic of China and rising tensions on the Sino-Vietnamese border. Nonetheless, the Soviets continued their policy of seeking better relations with the Chinese without offering major concessions. By the end of the year, First Deputy Premier Ivan Arkhipov had signed extensive economic and technological cooperation accords described by Beijing as "the most substantial agreements since relations between our two countries were strained in the 1960s."

Gorbachev's Challenge

Mikhail S. Gorbachev accomplished a great deal in his first year as leader of the Soviet Union. He met with an American president at the first superpower summit in six years and placed his personal stamp on arms control negotiations. He overhauled the Kremlin leadership, replacing older officials with men of his own generation. And he initiated several bureaucratic and economic reforms aimed at improving the country's lagging economy.

Although it was still unclear in early 1986 how substantive Gorbachev's changes would prove to be, he succeeded in creating a different image than his immediate predecessors, who were largely confined to the Kremlin by advanced age or illness. Gorbachev has exploited his rela-tive youth, presenting himself as a vigorous leader capable of improving the Soviet way of life.

Even before he officially succeeded Chernenko as party secretary March 11, 1985, Gorbachev had impressed Western heads of state. But it was his performance at the Geneva summit with Ronald Reagan in November 1985 that firmly established the new Kremlin leader's diplomatic credentials and his abilities as a formidable adversary in the superpower rivalry.

New Faces in the Kremlin

Gorbachev has been called a man in a hurry. The new leader may also be in a hurry to ensure his political survival. Even before his first anniversary at the top, Gorbachev faced a crucial test at the 27th Soviet Communist Party Congress February 25-28, 1986. In angling for support for his domestic and foreign policy initiatives, Gorbachev moved quickly — more quickly than any past general secretary — to realign the leadership.

To reform the economy, Gorbachev must have the allegiance of the officials charged with running it. The most drastic change he brought about during his first year in power was the replacement of dozens of party and government personnel. This gave credence to the comment Foreign Minister Gromyko reportedly made when he nominated Gorbachev to the position of general secretary: "Comrades, this man has a nice smile, but he's got iron teeth." The *Washington Post* reported January 26, 1985, that Gorbachev had replaced 45 of 159 regional party first secretaries and 4 of 15 first secretaries of republics. In addition, 19 of 59 government ministers were replaced, while 37 of 113 seats on the Council of Ministers changed.

The congress in February 1986 elected a new Central Committee of 307 members, and a clear majority supported Gorbachev. This body, responsible for implementing Politburo policy, already had seen greater turnover under Gorbachev than it had during Andropov's 15 months in power or Chernenko's 13 months. By the end of 1985 Gorbachev had retired at least 26 Central Committee members and promoted 30 people to positions that made them eligible for Central Committee membership. (Andropov retired 21 members and named 26 new members, while Chernenko retired just 8 and placed 13 on the Central Committee.)

Many of Gorbachev's targets for retirement were holdovers from the era of Brezhnev, increasingly referred to by the Soviet press as an unnamed "former leader" who allowed corruption to flourish among party and government officials. As another sign of Gorbachev's desire to distance his government from the Brezhnev era, the late leader's son Iurii was demoted from his position in the Ministry of Foreign Trade in January. On the other hand, Gorbachev has rehabilitated many associates of Nikita Khrushchev, Brezhnev's predecessor. Khrushchev was removed from power in 1964 for moving too quickly and radically in attempting reform. No longer anonymous, Khrushchev is "unambiguously extolled as a major contributor to victory in the Soviet-Nazi war," Sidney I. Ploss noted in the spring 1986 issue of *Foreign Policy*. Many of Gorbachev's initiatives are clearly reminiscent of Khrushchev. Ploss also noted the subtle criticism of Stalin in the Soviet press as another indicator of Gorbachev's bias toward reform, as opposed to modernization. Modernization would seek to perfect the system through continued central planning; reform would go further, with at least limited decentralization and moves to realign prices, wages, and other systemic problems.

The most visible evidence of Gorbachev's bloodless purge was the transformation of the Politburo. Just one month after gaining power, Gorbachev added three new members: Egor K. Ligachev, party secretary in charge of high-level appointments and ideology (effectively second in command to Gorbachev); Nikolai I. Ryzhkov, initially charged with setting economic reform policy and later named premier; and Viktor M. Chebrikov, head of the KGB. Like Gorbachev, all three were protégés of Andropov and supported his economic reforms and discipline campaign, which Gorbachev has revived. Ploss noted these three and Gorbachev likely formed the "Big Four" on the Politburo. With support from Aliev, Foreign Minister Eduard A. Shevardnadze, and Russian republic premier Vitalii Vorotnikov, they probably dominate Politburo meetings.

Gromyko's replacement as foreign minister by Shevardnadze was of special interest to the United States. Gromyko, who had presided over the postwar course of U.S.-Soviet relations during 28 years as foreign minister, was named president of the Soviet Union July 2, 1985, at a session of the Supreme Soviet, or parliament. Although his new title carries little weight, Gromyko retains his seat on the Politburo, where he will continue to have a voice in policy making.

Shevardnadze is credited with weeding out corruption when he served as party secretary in his native republic of Georgia. Although he had no previous foreign policy experience, Shevardnadze has impressed Western observers as a capable diplomat whose relaxed demeanor is in keeping with Gorbachev's own style of leadership.

At the same July 1985 session of the Supreme Soviet, Grigorii V. Romanov, the Leningrad party chief and Brezhnev protégé who is thought to have posed the greatest challenge to Gorbachev's rise to power, was retired from the Politburo. Ryzhkov replaced Nikolai A. Tikhonov, the 80-year-old Soviet premier, in October. Moscow party chief Viktor V. Grishin, another member of the old guard, was replaced in December by Boris Eltsin, a Gorbachev ally who has strongly criticized Grishin's handling of city affairs. Eltsin was promoted to candidate Politburo status just one week before the 27th Party Congress.

Numerous other top-level changes came out of the 1986 congress. Lev Zaikov, who had become a Secretariat member in July 1985, was promoted to full Politburo membership. He retained his Secretariat post, making him only the third member of both the Secretariat and the Politburo (in addition to Ligachev and Gorbachev). Zaikov's responsibility for defense industrial issues was presumed to continue.

Two new candidate Politburo members were named, both rather unknown men from the republics: Nikolai Sliunkov, head of the Belorussian party, and Iurii Solovev, who had taken over as head of the Leningrad party when Zaikov was promoted in July 1985 to the Secretariat.

Dobrynin, longtime ambassador to the United States, was named to the Central Committee Secretariat. While his exact position was not known in early April 1986, it was presumed that Dobrynin would assume responsibility on the Secretariat for foreign policy. He was expected to become the key foreign policy administrator, in charge of the International Department and perhaps have oversight of the Department of Liaison with Communist and Workers' Parties of Socialist Countries. The Soviets indicated that Dobrynin would be the main foreign policy adviser and that the Foreign Ministry would be more narrowly charged with implementing policy.

Four other new members were added to the Secretariat, including only the second woman ever to retain a seat there, Alexandra Biriukova, 56. (The first woman was Ekaterina Furtseva, in charge of cultural affairs, who was removed in 1961.) Biriukova has been a leader in the national trade union organization. Also named were Aleksandr Iakovlev, head of the Central Committee's Propaganda Department; Vadim Medvedev, head of the Central Committee's Science and Educational Institutions Department; and Georgii Razumovskii, head of the Central Committee's Organizational Party Work Department.

After the congress, the Politburo had 12 voting members and 7 nonvoting members; the Secretariat rose in membership to 11. One member of the Secretariat, Konstantin Rusakov, was removed and named to a post with the Central Auditing Commission.

Foreign Policy Goals

Some analysts interpreted the replacement of Gromyko with Shevardnadze as a sign that Gorbachev wanted to shift the focus of Soviet foreign policy from U.S.-Soviet relations to a broader approach, with special emphasis on Asia. Gromyko concentrated his efforts on U.S.-Soviet relations to the exclusion of other parts of the world. *(Foreign policy, Chapter 5, p. 85)*

Shevardnadze's trip to Japan in January marked the first time a Soviet foreign minister had visited the Asian economic giant in 10 years. Enemies during World War II, the two countries have never signed a peace treaty because of a dispute over four Soviet-occupied islands north of Japan. Although the visit did not produce a resolution of the territorial dispute or a long-term economic cooperation agreement, it may have opened the way for improved relations between the two countries and increased Soviet access to Japan's advanced technology.

The new Kremlin leadership has also continued the thaw in relations with China initiated by Andropov. Yet the "three obstacles" identified by China to complete normalization of relations, remain: the presence of Soviet troops along the border separating the two nations, the Soviet presence in Afghanistan, and the occupation of Kampuchea by Moscow's ally Vietnam. For their part, the Soviets distrust China's economic modernization campaign and overtures to the West. Because the two nations' communist parties have no official ties, the appearance of a Chinese delegation at the Soviet party congress would have been a sign of reconciliation. But the Chinese chose not to send a delegation, reaffirming their contention that improved ties are primarily trade-related and that those ties do not mean substantial differences have been overcome.

Gorbachev has been less successful on other fronts. Although he maintains good relations with India, neither Indian prime minister Rajiv Gandhi nor other non-Soviet-bloc Asian leaders have shown enthusiasm for a Soviet proposal to form a regional security council. The plan is widely seen as an effort to create tensions between the United States and its Asian allies.

The Kremlin's foreign policy in the Middle East has also had mixed results. To improve its standing among the moderate Arab nations, the Soviet Union established diplomatic relations with the sultanate of Oman and the United Arab Emirates. But a diplomatic setback followed in mid-

January 1986, when civil war broke out in Soviet-backed South Yemen. Although the rebellion was settled by early February with the installation of another Moscow-supported leader, the incident clearly caught the Kremlin by surprise and unprepared to control its closest ally in the region.

Perhaps as a result of his emphasis on domestic issues, Gorbachev seems to have adopted a more cautious foreign policy than his predecessors, especially Brezhnev, who spoke at length at the 1981 Party Congress of Soviet commitment to Third World national liberation movements. Soviet efforts to gain footholds in sub-Saharan Africa and Latin America have proved costly and often ineffective. Gorbachev may have decided that needs closer to home are more pressing. Although Soviet troops in Afghanistan launched a series of offensives against U.S.-supported resistance forces in 1985, Gorbachev told the Supreme Soviet in November that he was seeking a political settlement of the six-year war there and the eventual withdrawal of Soviet forces. In 1986 he called Afghanistan a "bleeding wound."

Military, Trade Status

Because it has received priority treatment in the allocation of resources, the Soviet military is considered to be on a technological par with the West in conventional and nuclear weapons production. Despite Reagan administration claims that the Soviet military has been conducting research on its own version of the Strategic Defense Initiative (SDI), most Western analysts say the development of electronic and laser components needed to construct such a complex "shield" against an offensive nuclear attack would place a tremendous strain on Soviet technological capabilities.

In *East-West Technology Transfer: The Transfer of Western Technology to the USSR*, a report released by the Paris-based Organization for Economic Cooperation and Development (OECD), Morris Bornstein wrote: "There is a striking technological gap between the USSR and the West

in the development of computers. . . . In technical capabilities and performance, currently produced Soviet general-purpose computers are similar to those marketed in the United States a decade earlier."

American trade policy toward the Soviet Union has endeavored to maintain or widen this gap. As a member of the Coordinating Committee for Multilateral Export Controls (CoCom), which includes all NATO members except Iceland and Spain plus Japan, the United States has embargoed or limited the transfer of military items, nuclear reactors, and their components. It has also restricted trade of a wide range of machinery and equipment made for civilian use but having the potential for military application. Computer technology, industrial machinery, and electrical equipment are among the goods that the West tries to keep out of Soviet hands. Moreover, by withholding most-favored-nation status, the United States denies favorable tariff treatment to the USSR and all its Council for Mutual Economic Assistance (CMEA) partners except Hungary and Romania. The Jackson-Vanik amendment bars favorable tariff treatment for the USSR so long as it denies Jews the right to emigrate.

Gorbachev has made relaxation of U.S. trade restrictions with his nation a high-priority item. Addressing a delegation of U.S. business leaders in Moscow to discuss trade, Gorbachev said December 10, 1985, that until the United States lifts its trade restrictions, "there will be no normal development of Soviet-U.S. trade and other economic ties on a large scale. This is regrettable but we are not going to beg the United States for anything." As an example of the American "policy of boycotts, embargoes, 'punishments' and broken contracts," Gorbachev noted that "the volume of U.S. imports from the USSR is roughly equal to what your country imports from the Republic of Ivory Coast."

Despite its growing trade deficit with the world as a whole, the United States has enjoyed a surplus with the Soviet Union. According to the Commerce Department, U.S. imports from the Soviet Union totaled a mere $410 million in 1985, while the United States exported $2.15 billion in goods to the Soviet Union. Most of these exports were agricultural products, particularly corn.

For all Gorbachev's complaints of U.S. unfairness in commerce, the prospect of increased East-West trade presents him with a dilemma. He needs the West's advanced technology to meet his goals, but more trade may expose the Soviet economy to the potentially destabilizing rigors of competition. The nation has carefully guarded against competition by limiting its trade relations largely to the other planned economies of the CMEA. When it comes to economic reform, wrote Jerry Hough, a well-regarded Soviet analyst, ". . . the industrial managers are ambivalent: they would support a change in social policy and a widening of their prerogatives vis-à-vis the workers ('decentralization' is often a code word for this), but they have no desire for the harsh discipline of the market, let alone for the pleasure of competing with Toyota." By broadening commercial ties with the outside world, the leadership also risks losing its grip on Soviet society. "While it would be advantageous to have Tadzhik salesmen selling Soviet computers in Teheran, what ideas would they bring home, especially when they studied the local culture enough to advertise effectively?" Hough queried in the fall 1985 issue of *Foreign Affairs*.

The Reagan administration had announced no plans to request significant changes in trade restrictions by Decem-

U.S.-Soviet Summit Meetings

Date	Place	Leaders	Topic
July-August 1945	Potsdam	President Harry S Truman, Soviet leader Joseph Stalin, British prime ministers Winston Churchill and Clement R. Attlee	Partition and control of Germany
July 1955	Geneva	President Dwight D. Eisenhower, Soviet leader Nikolai A. Bulganin, British prime minister Anthony Eden, French premier Edgar Faure	Reunification of Germany, disarmament, European security
September 1959	Camp David, Md.	President Dwight D. Eisenhower, Soviet leader Nikita S. Khrushchev	Berlin problem
May 1960	Paris	President Dwight D. Eisenhower, Soviet leader Nikita S. Khrushchev, French president Charles de Gaulle, British prime minister Harold Macmillan	U-2 incident
June 1961	Vienna	President John F. Kennedy, Soviet leader Nikita S. Khrushchev	Berlin problem
June 1967	Glassboro, N.J.	President Lyndon B. Johnson, Soviet leader Aleksei N. Kosygin	Middle East
May 1972	Moscow	President Richard Nixon, Soviet leader Leonid I. Brezhnev	SALT I, anti-ballistic missile limitations
June 1973	Washington, D.C.	President Richard Nixon, Soviet leader Leonid I. Brezhnev	Détente
June-July 1974	Moscow and Yalta	President Richard Nixon, Soviet leader Leonid I. Brezhnev	Arms control
November 1974	Vladivostok	President Gerald R. Ford, Soviet leader Leonid I. Brezhnev	Arms control
June 1979	Vienna	President Jimmy Carter, Soviet leader Leonid I. Brezhnev	SALT II
November 1985	Geneva	President Ronald Reagan, Soviet leader Mikhail S. Gorbachev	Arms control, U.S.-Soviet relations

ber 1985, prompting Gorbachev to say then that "if the United States persists in its current policy, we will produce what we need on our own or buy it elsewhere." The search for more cooperative trading partners may explain some foreign policy shifts evident since Gorbachev came to power.

Implications for U.S. Policy

The signs of change emanating from the Kremlin require the United States to make fundamental policy decisions in the areas of trade and arms control. Some observers say the West should do all it can to exacerbate Soviet economic troubles. "... [B]y denying to the Soviet bloc various forms of economic aid, [the West] can help intensify the formidable pressures which are being exerted on their creaky economies," wrote Richard Pipes, of Harvard University and formerly Reagan's top Soviet adviser, in the fall 1984 *Foreign Policy.* "This will push them in the direction of general liberalization as well as accommodation with the West, since this is the only way of reducing military expenditures and gaining access to Western help in modernization."

The Reagan administration has been divided over the issue. Some officials support legislation that would authorize the president to cut off commercial bank loans to Soviet-bloc nations. In December 1985 Secretary of State Shultz accused these officials of "wanting to start an economic war against the Soviet Union." The bill aims to prevent future banking deals with the Soviets. A November 1985 agreement by a group of U.S. lenders extended to the Soviet Union a $400 million, low-interest loan. Earlier in 1985 U.S. banks led international syndicates that lent the Soviets $200 million and East Germany $1.1 billion.

Many analysts support private activity, contending that a more prosperous Soviet Union might lessen the military threat to the West. The United States, wrote author Samuel Pisar in the *Wall Street Journal* December 26, 1985, must decide whether "to make it easier for Russia to evolve into a more modern, open and humane society, or to push it against the wall, hoping it will explode under the weight of its problems and that we will remain unscathed."

Opinions differed widely on arms control policy as well as trade. According to John Kiser, a Washington businessman involved in East-West trade, continuation of research on SDI may have unforeseen effects. In the fall 1985 *Foreign Policy,* he wrote:

> One is that Washington will force the pace of development in Soviet computer technology infrastructure and require Moscow to make a variety of positive organizational changes it might not make otherwise. The United States also may be providing the Soviet leaders with an energizing force from without that the system cannot generate from within.

But it remained unclear whether the Soviet system could accommodate the changes desired by the new leadership. At his first party congress as general secretary, Gorbachev had much to show for a year's work. He made ambitious proposals to improve the economy and, judging from Washington's long silence on the issue, stunned the Western superpower by his sweeping call January 15 to eliminate nuclear arms from the face of Earth by the turn of the century. But judging by the lack of new initiatives proposed at the congress — most of Gorbachev's calls

repeated earlier ones — as well as limited specifics on how to go about the change he desired, most Western observers believed that Gorbachev's power to bring about change was still limited.

U.S.-Soviet Summitry

The glacial silence that characterized superpower relations during the 1980s was broken November 19-21, 1985, when President Reagan and General Secretary Gorbachev met in Geneva. Rarely had the prospect of a summit meeting stirred such widespread interest among politicians, academics, and commentators.

Reagan first proposed the meeting in a letter to Gorbachev delivered March 12 by Vice President George Bush when he attended the funeral of Gorbachev's immediate predecessor, Konstantin U. Chernenko. Gorbachev finally accepted the invitation July 3.

The encounter provided the first direct dialogue between the leaders of the United States and the Soviet Union since June 1979, when President Jimmy Carter met Soviet leader Brezhnev in Vienna to sign the SALT II treaty setting limits on both countries' strategic arsenals. The Geneva summit formally lasted about 15 hours, 8 of them dedicated to substantive dialogue. From the outset, the meeting departed from the announced schedule, with Reagan and Gorbachev spending much more time in private discussions than the 15 minutes initially allocated.

In deciding to go to Geneva, Reagan made an about-face. During his first term he adopted a confrontational tone toward the Soviet Union and dismissed summitry, saying that the Soviets had used past meetings to extract arms control agreements that put the United States at a disadvantage. *(Box, U.S.-Soviet Summit Meetings, p. 193)*

Reagan's decision to engage in superpower summitry was risky — perhaps one reason why the president played down the significance of his tete-à-tete with Gorbachev. In the days leading up to the summit, the White House continued to refer to it as a mere "meeting." One risk arose from Reagan's incomplete grasp of arms control subject matter. But presidential advisers evidently expected the "great communicator" to compensate for any lack of expertise with his conversational talents and flair for simplifying issues.

Reagan's risks paled beside those Gorbachev assumed by going to Geneva only eight months after taking office. Reagan had just three years left to leave his imprint on American diplomacy, but Gorbachev's first summit marked the beginning of his leadership. At 55, Gorbachev could reasonably hope to find himself in charge into the next century. To do so, however, he had to avoid making serious foreign policy blunders.

Propaganda Maneuvering

Both leaders and their respective bureaucracies demonstrated ample skill in the business of public relations. Reagan and Gorbachev tirelessly marketed themselves and their arms control proposals with an eye toward winning support at home, among their opponent's home audience, and the citizens of Western Europe. On July 29, 1985, Gorbachev announced that the Soviet Union, "wishing to set a good example," would "stop unilaterally any nuclear explosions starting from August 6 this year," not coinci-

Gorbachev and Reagan: Accords, Agendas

President Ronald Reagan and Soviet leader Mikhail S. Gorbachev summed up the results of their two-day Geneva summit in a joint communiqué released November 21, 1985. The communiqué provided for: *(Text, p. 334)*

More Meetings. The two leaders announced that Gorbachev would visit Washington in 1986 — although a date was not set — and that Reagan would travel to Moscow in 1987. (By April 1986 plans for Gorbachev's U.S. trip were still on hold.)

They announced plans for "regular meetings" between the U.S. secretary of state and the Soviet foreign minister, and between other department heads of the two governments. They also agreed to regular "exchanges of views on regional issues at the expert level." Among the regional issues are insurgencies in Afghanistan and Nicaragua.

Focused Arms Control. They called for "early progress" toward arms reduction agreements in ongoing Geneva talks, "particularly in areas where there is common ground." Two areas singled out: agreement on a 50 percent reduction in nuclear weapons of the two sides and a separate agreement on medium-range nuclear weapons based in Europe.

The two countries are far apart in publicly defining what kinds of weapons would be covered by those partial accords. Communiqué language that the 50 percent cuts would be "appropriately applied" seemed intended to bridge this disagreement.

The communiqué made no reference to Moscow's previous insistence that agreement to ban space weapons — including Reagan's Strategic Defense Initiative (SDI) — would have to accompany limits on intercontinental and intermediate-range nuclear weapons.

However, in a press conference after the summit's close, Gorbachev seemed to reaffirm the Soviet position that SDI limits would have to be part of any arms deal.

Formal Agreements. Three formal accords were reached:

● Renewing academic and cultural exchanges.

● Authorizing a Soviet consulate in New York City and a U.S. consulate in Kiev, capital of the Ukraine, contingent on restoration of civil air service between the two countries. Reagan stopped the airline flights in 1981, in response to Soviet pressure on Poland. On November 22, negotiators agreed in Moscow to resume flights.

● Formalizing communications arrangements among the United States, the Soviet Union, and Japan to avoid civil airliner incidents in the northwest Pacific, such as the Soviet downing of a Korean Air Lines jet in September 1983. The pact, signed November 19, sets up a communications link between a Soviet air traffic control center and one in Tokyo.

New Efforts. The communiqué announced three new bilateral initiatives:

● A study of "nuclear risk reduction centers" in each country staffed by experts to monitor nuclear weapons activity by third parties, including terrorists.

● Discussions of ways to prevent the proliferation of chemical weapons to other nations.

● "Advocacy" of international cooperation to develop controlled thermonuclear fusion — basically, a controlled hydrogen bomb — as an energy source.

Continuing Agenda. The communiqué also pledged the two countries to continue various ongoing negotiations — or to resume certain efforts that had been suspended. Among these were ongoing talks:

● To reduce conventional military forces in Europe — the mutual and balanced force reduction talks.

● To ban chemical and biological weapons.

● To institute "confidence-building measures" in Europe that would reduce the fear of surprise attack.

They also pledged further efforts on environmental protection and nonproliferation of nuclear weapons.

---

dentally the 40th anniversary of the day the United States dropped the first atomic bomb on Hiroshima, Japan. Continuation of the moratorium past January 1, 1986, Gorbachev said, would depend on whether the United States also stopped nuclear testing.

Unwilling to let the Soviets score easily in the intensifying diplomatic game, the White House dismissed the moratorium as propaganda. The moratorium would not slow Soviet weapons production, the administration said, because the country had accelerated its nuclear testing prior to the announcement and could easily resume tests in January. Experts outside the administration denied that the Soviets had stepped up the pace of testing.

The presummit maneuvering heated up with a visit of a U.S. congressional delegation to Moscow and a surprise interview Gorbachev granted *Time* magazine September 9. On both occasions Gorbachev left the impression of a tough, but reasonable, nonpolemical leader well-versed in foreign affairs and defense issues. He appealed to American public opinion by telling *Time* editors he attached "tremendous importance" to the summit, in contrast to Reagan's cautions against raising "false hopes."

The Kremlin's public relations campaign seemed to catch the White House off guard as it reacted defensively to Gorbachev's assertions. To his appeal for a breakthrough in arms control, the administration said that the Soviet

Union had not offered any concrete proposals. Reagan dismissed Gorbachev's condemnation of the Strategic Defense Initiative, saying categorically that it would not become a "bargaining chip" in Geneva. SDI, Reagan's controversial program to develop a space-based defense against nuclear attack, was already emerging as the central issue on the summit agenda.

The next stage of the Kremlin's "charm offensive" was Soviet foreign minister Shevardnadze's visit to the United States in late September. Shevardnadze addressed the United Nations General Assembly and met with Reagan and Secretary of State Shultz. The trip coincided with the resumption in Geneva of arms control negotiations, which began with great fanfare in March 1985 but by March 1986 had not produced any concrete results.

Like Gorbachev, Shevardnadze presented a striking contrast to the past. Unlike his dour predecessor, Andrei Gromyko, Shevardnadze had a relaxed and friendly air. In his speech to the General Assembly September 24, he continued the verbal assault against SDI, calling for an international space research program of "Star Peace" in contrast to "Star Wars" as SDI is commonly called. Addressing the same forum the previous day, Shultz accused the Soviet Union of making "blatantly one-sided" accusations and invited Moscow to "get down to real business, with the seriousness the subject deserves."

Gorbachev took up Shultz's challenge during a widely publicized visit to Paris in October, his first trip to the West since assuming the Kremlin leadership in March. He used the occasion to publicize the centerpiece of his presummit proposals, an arms reduction proposal Shevardnadze had reportedly presented to Reagan in Washington. If Reagan would give up SDI, Gorbachev said, the Soviet Union would agree to a 50 percent cut in both sides' nuclear weapons, an even deeper reduction in offensive weapons than the United States had previously sought.

Gorbachev's trip to Paris did not reignite the West European peace movement of the early 1980s. His welcome in the French capital was tepid at best, and President François Mitterrand, while highly critical of SDI, refused to join Gorbachev in denouncing the program. France rebuffed Gorbachev's invitation to negotiate a separate arms control agreement, as did Great Britain, the other European nuclear power.

But Gorbachev's failure to win allies in Western Europe did not translate into unconditional support for Reagan. Shortly after his speech to the UN General Assembly October 24 in which he called for a joint U.S.-Soviet initiative to resolve conflicts in five countries where insurgents were challenging Soviet-supported governments, Reagan met with the leaders of five industrialized nations, who told him that arms control remained the most important item on the summit agenda. British prime minister Margaret Thatcher urged Reagan to respond to Gorbachev's arms control proposal in a manner that would break the "deadlock in Geneva." Thatcher and West German chancellor Helmut Kohl later told reporters that they were given to understand that Reagan would offer a counterproposal on arms control before the summit. (The leaders of Britain, West Germany, Japan, Italy, and Canada attended but Mitterrand of France declined Reagan's invitation.)

A minor tempest blew up November 16, the day Reagan and his party left Washington for Geneva, when a letter to Reagan from Defense Secretary Caspar W. Wein-

berger — who was not going to Geneva — was published by the *New York Times*. The letter repeated Weinberger's often-stated skepticism about the value of past arms control agreements and urged Reagan to resist pressures to accept limits on SDI research in return for reductions in Soviet missiles.

Warm Words, Little Agreement

In a joint communiqué released at the end of the summit, Reagan and Gorbachev described their discussions as "frank and useful" while acknowledging that "serious differences remain on a number of critical issues." *(Text, Appendix, p. 334)*

Despite Reagan's last-minute attempt to give high priority to regional conflicts involving the Soviets, arms control issues dominated the meeting. The two leaders pledged to accelerate efforts for an arms reduction agreement in the ongoing Geneva arms talks and singled out two possible areas for early progress: a 50 percent cut in nuclear weapons and a separate agreement to cut intermediate-range forces based in Europe. In both areas, superficial similarities between the U.S. and Soviet positions masked profound disagreements over what weapons the negotiations should cover.

No concrete arms control accords were signed at the summit, but numerous cultural exchange agreements were reached, as were agreements calling for regular high-level meetings, new consulates, air flights, and other cooperative arrangements. *(Accords, box, p. 195)*

President Reagan came home to a warm reception on Capitol Hill. Members of Congress on both sides of the aisle applauded the tone of his and Gorbachev's summit statements, many commenting that they seemed to have put U.S.-Soviet relations back on a businesslike basis, stripped of the confrontational rhetoric that had characterized the previous five years.

Addressing a joint session of Congress on the evening of November 21, Reagan said that the 15 hours of discussion — five of them involving the two leaders accompanied only by translators — marked "a fresh start" in U.S.-Soviet relations.

Tentative plans for a Gorbachev visit to Washington in 1986 and a Reagan trip to Moscow for a third meeting in 1987 also met with approval in Congress. Congressional enthusiasm about the summit was tempered, however, by widespread regret that the meeting produced no concrete accords on arms control.

Gorbachev also stepped up his calls for movement in arms control negotiations. In his address to the 27th Party Congress he stated that, before he would agree to a date for the 1986 summit in Washington, he wanted assurance that progress on arms control would be made there.

The Geneva arms control talks resumed in April, and Secretary of State Shultz and Foreign Minister Shevardnadze were preparing to meet in mid-May, presumably to negotiate a summit date. But after the United States bombed Libya April 14 in retaliation for its alleged ties to terrorist activities, the Kremlin canceled the meeting. Invective continued for weeks. The Kremlin indicated that a 1986 summit, though still possible, was largely dependent on U.S. international behavior. Gorbachev reiterated his position while attending the East German party congress later in April.

Appendix

Biographies

The Politburo, the policy-making body of the Soviet Union, had 12 full members and 7 nonvoting candidate members in April 1986. The Secretariat of the Central Committee had 11 members, several of whom were named in March 1986 after the 27th Party Congress. Biographical information on all Politburo and Secretariat members serving at that time is given below in alphabetical order, following General Secretary Mikhail Gorbachev.

Of the Secretariat members, special emphasis is given to Anatolii Dobrynin, longtime ambassador to the United States, who was named to the Secretariat at the congress. Following the Politburo and Secretariat biographies are biographies of former leaders. Those individuals who were recently removed from power, though perhaps still living, are included in the past leaders' section.

Politburo Members

Mikhail Gorbachev (1931-   )

On March 11, 1985, only five hours after the announcement of Konstantin Chernenko's death, Mikhail Sergeevich Gorbachev, 54, became the youngest general secretary in the Soviet Union's history. He also is the first top Soviet leader to begin his career after Stalin's reign of terror. Gorbachev's accession to the leadership of the Communist Party of the Soviet Union (CPSU) ended an era in Soviet politics dominated by aging leaders and marked by bureaucratic inertia. As general secretary, Gorbachev heads the Defense Council, the coordinating body for Soviet economic-military activity. But unlike his predecessors Leonid Brezhnev, Yuri Andropov, and Chernenko he has not assumed the presidency, a position to which he named senior statesman Andrei Gromyko.

Gorbachev was born March 2, 1931, in the village of Privolnoye in the fertile wheat-growing area of Stavropol Krai in the Russian Soviet Federated Socialist Republic (RSFSR). Of peasant stock, he worked as a youth on an agricultural combine. Gorbachev did not escape the ravages of World War II and the German occupation, during which he lost his father. Although his early education was inter-

rupted by war, Gorbachev entered the prestigious Moscow State University in 1950 at the age of 19. At 21 he became a member of the Communist Party and three years later, in 1955, graduated from the law school at Moscow State University.

Gorbachev's wife, Raisa, has been the subject of much attention in the Western press because of her stylishness and public visibility compared with past Soviet leaders' wives. She studied philosophy at Moscow State University and has lectured on that subject. The couple has a daughter, Irina, and a young granddaughter, Oksana. Irina and her husband are physicians.

Public Career. After graduating from law school, Gorbachev returned to Stavropol where he gained recognition as a leader in the Komsomol (Communist Youth League). He began full-time party work in 1962. He received a degree from the Stavropol Agricultural Institute in 1967. Under the tutelage of Fedor Kulakov, first secretary of the Stavropol Krai Party Committee, he rose quickly through the local party ranks. In 1970, at the relatively young age of 39, he assumed his mentor's post after Kulakov had been promoted to a position in Moscow. Gorbachev's selection to full membership on the CPSU Central Committee in 1971 has been attributed by some to party ideologue Mikhail Suslov, who had strong ties to Stavropol.

In 1978 Kulakov died and Gorbachev, then 47, was called from Stavropol to take his place as the Central Committee secretary responsible for agriculture. Although a series of bad harvests followed, Gorbachev's career did not falter. Indeed, his responsibilities increased rapidly. He became a candidate member of the Politburo in 1979 and a full member in 1980. From 1979 until 1984 he chaired the Legislative Proposals Commission of the Council of the Union of the USSR Supreme Soviet.

Gorbachev continued his rise during the succession battles that followed Brezhnev's death in 1982. Under

Andropov he was given oversight responsibility for the whole economy and lower-level party appointments. In addition, he served as chairman of the Foreign Affairs Commission from early 1984 until July 1985.

After nominating Chernenko as party leader following Andropov's death, Gorbachev effectively became second in command. His responsibilities grew to include oversight of ideology and aspects of foreign affairs. He and his wife made a highly publicized trip to Great Britain in December 1984 that appeared designed to show off the future Soviet leader to the world. Gorbachev made several other trips to the West prior to his selection as general secretary. He had not visited the United States but was slated to go there in 1986 for a summit meeting with President Ronald Reagan.

Analysis. When Andrei Gromyko nominated Gorbachev to succeed Chernenko, he told the Central Committee, "Comrades, this man has a nice smile, but he's got iron teeth." Indeed, during his first year in office Gorbachev displayed both an outwardly gregarious style and a strong will to restructure the Soviet system and advance his country's interests abroad.

Gorbachev's first priority appears to have been to revamp the aging Soviet leadership to pave the way for economic reform. He promoted many younger officials who supported his economic and technological reform proposals. In the process, most surviving Brezhnev-era leaders retired or were ousted within Gorbachev's first year as general secretary. Nevertheless, Gorbachev does not enjoy a free hand in shaping Soviet policy. Various elements of the Soviet power structure including the military, the entrenched bureaucracy, ideological conservatives (such as Egor Ligachev), and those members of the old guard leadership who survived Gorbachev's personnel changes may resist his reforms if they perceive them as coming too quickly or as threatening their interests.

Some Western experts believed in early 1986 that Gorbachev would "move in a genuinely reformist direction when and if he is able to solidify his gains in the Soviet power structure," Sidney Ploss recounted in the spring 1986 *Foreign Policy*. Ploss cited the de facto rehabilitation of Nikita Khrushchev and the "subtle criticism of Stalinism in the Soviet media" as evidence of Gorbachev's reformist bias.

Despite Gorbachev's success at promoting his allies, it is still too early to determine whether the changes produced under his leadership will be of substance or merely style. He has obviously brought a more developed understanding of public relations to his office than his predecessors. His populism, openness, and wit have already altered the way Soviet domestic officials and foreign representatives conduct their business. But Gorbachev's domestic reforms as yet have not been significantly different from those advocated by Andropov and later endorsed by Chernenko. He has sought to decentralize selected areas of the economy, increase worker discipline, and place greater emphasis on the use of new technologies to boost productivity.

Gorbachev has taken firm control of Soviet affairs with other nations despite his relative lack of experience in this area. He appears determined to implement a more outward-looking foreign policy designed to increase Soviet prestige throughout the world instead of focusing on Soviet-U.S. relations. Gorbachev has indicated his desire to create new trading partners and sources of technology that will help the Soviet economy. He also has initiated more cooperative relations with the United States without altering the tough Soviet stance on high-priority issues such as slowing down President Reagan's Strategic Defense Initiative program.

Geidar Aliev (1923-   )

On November 22, 1982, Geidar Alievich Aliev became one of three first deputy chairmen of the USSR Council of Ministers and, after six years as a candidate member, one of the few voting non-Russians on the Politburo. On the council he is responsible for transportation matters and is active in school reform. He has been a deputy to the USSR Supreme Soviet since 1970 and a member of the Central Committee of the CPSU since 1971.

Born May 10, 1923, in Nakhichevan, Azerbaidzhan, into a blue-collar family, Aliev rose to power through the Azerbaidzhan internal security agencies. In 1941 Aliev joined the USSR People's Commissariat of Internal Affairs (NKVD, a forerunner of the Committee for State Security, KGB) and various internal security agencies in Nakhichevan. Between 1950 and 1967 Aliev held increasingly responsible posts in the Azerbaidzhan security apparatus, becoming chairman of the Azerbaidzhan KGB in 1967. From 1969 to 1982 he served as first secretary of the Azerbaidzhan Central Committee and a member of its Politburo.

Aliev, a major general in the Soviet Army, traveled abroad several times in the 1980s, including trips to Mexico, Vietnam, and Syria.

On February 27, 1986, during the 27th Party Congress, Aliev held a press conference. This unusual action by a ruling Politburo member was viewed as part of General Secretary Gorbachev's drive for a more open Soviet leadership.

Viktor Chebrikov (1923-   )

Viktor Mikhailovich Chebrikov has served as chairman of the Committee for State Security since December 1982. He joined the KGB in 1967 after a successful party career in the Dnepropetrovsk region of the Ukraine. He was made a candidate member of the Politburo in December 1983 and a full member in April 1985 following Mikhail Gorbachev's selection as general secretary.

Chebrikov, an ethnic Russian, was born April 27, 1923, into a blue-collar family. During World War II he rose from private to battalion commander in the army. After the war, Chebrikov attended the Dnepropetrovsk Metallurgical Institute. He graduated in 1950 and worked for a year as an engineer. During the 1950s and 1960s he held posts in the Dnepropetrovsk city and oblast (regional) party organizations, including those of secretary of the party committee in a metallurgical factory (1955-58), first secretary of the city party committee (1961-63), and second secretary of the regional party committee (1964-67).

Chebrikov headed the KGB's personnel department until 1968, when he was promoted to deputy chairman under then KGB chief Yuri Andropov. Chebrikov became one of two first deputy chairmen of the KGB in May 1982. He was promoted to the rank of army general in November 1983.

As head of the KGB, Chebrikov has warned in his writings and speeches against the threat to Soviet society from dissent, religion, and consumerism. He also has strongly denounced Western anti-Soviet propaganda and the contaminating effect of Western values on Soviet youth. Chebrikov has made numerous trips to Eastern Europe since becoming KGB chief.

Andrei Gromyko (1909-   )

After 28 years as Soviet foreign minister, 75-year-old Andrei Andreevich Gromyko was elected chairman of the Presidium of the Supreme Soviet (president of the USSR)

on July 2, 1985. He was succeeded as foreign minister by former Georgian party leader Eduard Shevardnadze. Gromyko is formally the highest representative of the Soviet Union in its relations with foreign governments, although the presidency is largely an honorific position. Gromyko hosts foreign delegations in Moscow and presides over the USSR's legislature.

Gromyko, an ethnic Russian of worker-peasant stock, was born July 18, 1909, in Belorussia and grew up on a farm near Minsk. He devoted much of his early adulthood to study and eventually earned a candidate of economics degree in 1936. (Gromyko became a doctor of economics in 1956).

Public Career. Gromyko taught at the Moscow Institute of Economics for three years before being recruited into the foreign service in 1939. Shortly afterward he was assigned to the Soviet Embassy in Washington. In 1943 Joseph Stalin made the 34-year-old diplomat ambassador to the United States, a post he held until 1946. Gromyko later became permanent representative to the United Nations (1946-49) and ambassador to the United Kingdom (1952-53). He served twice as first deputy minister of foreign affairs (1949-52, 1953-57). In 1957 he was appointed minister of foreign affairs under Nikita Khrushchev.

In tandem with his growing status within the government, Gromyko rose steadily in the party. He joined the CPSU in 1931 while still in school. He served as a deputy to the Council of the Union of the Supreme Soviet from 1946 to 1950. In 1952 he became a candidate member of the Central Committee and was promoted to full membership in 1956. He was made a full Politburo member in 1973, and 10 years later he was appointed one of three first deputy prime ministers.

Analysis. As foreign minister Gromyko traveled to more than 40 countries and met most of the major leaders of his era. He headed the Soviet delegation to every session of the UN General Assembly from 1962 until 1984 (except

the 1983 opening following the Soviet downing of a Korean airliner) and participated in every U.S.-Soviet summit until the 1985 meeting between Mikhail Gorbachev and President Reagan.

Gromyko has been known for his intransigence but is respected for his intelligence and knowledge of the West. Gromyko was a loyal and pragmatic implementer of Politburo policy. As his experience and stature grew, so did his power. His 1973 selection to the Politburo signified his growing influence as a policy maker. During Chernenko's tenure as general secretary, Gromyko was believed to dominate the formulation of Soviet foreign policy.

Gromyko also played a key role in Soviet internal politics in the 1980s. Together with Defense Minister Dimitri Ustinov he was instrumental in Yuri Andropov's selection as general secretary over Konstantin Chernenko in 1982. He also supported Mikhail Gorbachev in his bid to succeed Chernenko in 1985 and delivered an eloquent speech nominating Gorbachev for general secretary.

Gromyko's replacement as foreign minister by Shevardnadze, a Georgian party boss with no diplomatic experience, caught Soviet and U.S. diplomats by surprise. Western observers suggested that Gromyko's appointment to the presidency was a reward for both his long service to the Soviet Union and his backing of Gorbachev during the succession process. But many experts also maintained that Gromyko's promotion was a graceful way for Gorbachev to retire Gromyko, thereby strengthening his own control over international affairs.

Dinmukhamed Kunaev (1912-   )

The chief of the Kazakh Communist Party, Dinmukhamed Akhmedovich Kunaev has been a member of the USSR Supreme Soviet Presidium since 1962 and a full member of the Politburo since 1971. Ukranian Vladimir Shcherbitskii is the only other republic leader who is a full member of the Politburo.

A Kazakh from a white-collar family in Alma-Ata, Kunaev was born January 12, 1912. He received a metallurgy degree from the Moscow Institute for Nonferrous Metals and Gold in 1936 and a doctorate of technical sciences in 1969.

Like most Politburo members, Kunaev was a member of the Komsomol while a student. He joined the party in

1939 and almost immediately began to advance through the Kazakh party structure. As deputy chairman of the Kazakh Council of Ministers during World War II, Kunaev was responsible for reorganizing industry behind the front. In 1952 he left this post to become president of the Kazakh Academy of Sciences, where he coordinated academic activities in scientific and technical research until 1955. Kunaev then served as

chairman of the Kazakh Council of Ministers. During this period he became a close associate of Leonid Brezhnev, who from 1954 to 1956 served as second and then first secretary of the Kazakh party. Brezhnev would later be instrumental in Kunaev's rise to national prominence.

In 1960 Kunaev became first secretary of the Kazakh

party. In 1962 he was named chairman of the Kazakh Council of Ministers. Two years later, following Khrushchev's ouster, he returned to his former post as party chief in Kazakhstan. As Brezhnev consolidated his power, Kunaev moved up the party ladder, becoming a candidate Politburo member in 1966 and a full member five years later.

Egor Ligachev (1920-   )

Egor Kuz'mich Ligachev became a full Politburo member in April 1985 when he was promoted to that position, without serving as a candidate member, under Mikhail

Gorbachev. Ligachev is the Central Committee secretary in charge of personnel and is thought to have assumed the important ideological portfolio that is usually the responsibility of the second-highest official in the party hierarchy.

Ligachev's career flourished under Andropov. In April 1983 he was elevated from first secretary of the Tomsk Obkom to head of the Organizational and Party Work Department that oversees the selection and appointment of party functionaries. Just eight months later, in December 1983, Ligachev was promoted to the CPSU Secretariat. Together with Gorbachev, Ligachev supervised election campaigns to the local party committees and the USSR Supreme Soviet during 1983-84.

An ethnic Russian, Ligachev was born in Dubinkina November 29, 1920. He graduated from the Moscow Aviation Institution in 1943 and completed a correspondence program with the Central Committee's Higher Party School in 1951. In the early 1940s he worked as an engineer in Novosibirsk. He joined the CPSU in 1944 and was active in the Novosibirsk Komsomol until 1949. He then held several party posts in Novosibirsk, including those of a department chief of the Oblast Party Committee (Obkom), deputy chairman of the Oblast Executive Committee, and Obkom secretary.

In 1961 Ligachev began working in the Central Committee apparatus. Four years later he was appointed first secretary of the Tomsk Obkom, a post he held until April 1983. Ligachev became a candidate member of the Central Committee in 1966 and a full member in 1976. He has been a deputy to the USSR Supreme Soviet since 1956.

Nikolai Ryzhkov (1929-   )

As chief administrator of the USSR's vast economy, Premier Nikolai Ivanovich Ryzhkov is a key figure in General Secretary Gorbachev's plans to revamp economic planning, streamline the bureaucracy, and promote the development of new technology in Soviet industry.

In April 1985, the month after Gorbachev became party leader, Ryzhkov was elevated directly to full membership in the Politburo, bypassing the usual candidate member stage. The following September Ryzhkov's swift ascent culminated in his appointment to the chairmanship of the USSR Council of Ministers (premier) in place of the aging Nikolai Tikhonov. Ryzhkov relinquished his posi-

tions as Central Committee secretary and Economics Department chief shortly after becoming premier, but he will undoubtedly continue to oversee the Soviet economy from his new post.

Ryzhkov is a Russian national born in the Ukraine September 28, 1929. He is the second-youngest Politburo member after Gorbachev. Ryzhkov graduated from the Kramatorsk Machine Building School in the Ukraine in 1950 and received a degree in engineering from the Ural Polytechnic Institute in 1959. He joined the CPSU in 1956. Between 1950 and 1975 he worked at the Ural Heavy Machine Building Plant in Sverdlovsk, becoming plant director in 1970 and director of the Uralmash production association in 1971. From 1975 until 1979 Ryzhkov was a first deputy minister of heavy and transport machine building. In 1979 he became a deputy chairman of the State Planning Committee (Gosplan), where he primarily was responsible for the heavy industry sector.

Ryzhkov's rapid rise under Gorbachev was set up by his advancement under Andropov, who brought Ryzhkov into the CPSU Secretariat in November 1982. He also became chief of the new Central Committee Economics Department.

Ryzhkov has traveled widely in Eastern Europe and has visited the United States (1975), Vietnam (1983), and Austria (1984). His March 1986 meeting with U.S. secretary of state George P. Shultz in Stockholm following the funeral of Swedish prime minister Olof Palme was an indication that Ryzhkov's leadership role might be expanding beyond economic matters.

Vladimir Shcherbitskii (1918-   )

Vladimir Vasil'evich Shcherbitskii has been a full member of the CPSU Politburo since April 1971 and first secretary of the Ukrainian Communist Party since May 1972. He has survived Mikhail Gorbachev's leadership shuffle despite his age and close association with Leonid Brezhnev. Because his base of power is in the Ukraine he is thought to be a relative outsider to Kremlin politics compared with his Moscow-based colleagues.

Shcherbitskii is regarded as a hard-liner on matters of ideology and dissent. In speeches and articles he has maintained that greater party discipline and control will overcome most socioeconomic problems. His view that the party must strictly manage and control the introduction of new technology was outlined in his 1983 book *Scientific-Technical Progress — a Party Concern.*

Shcherbitskii has traveled widely but has only recently conducted substantive meetings with Western diplomats and government officials. In March 1985 he led a delegation to the United States and met with President Reagan and several members of Congress. His early return to the Soviet Union was one of the first indications that Konstantin Chernenko had died.

Born into a blue-collar family February 17, 1918, Shcherbitskii, like his patron Brezhnev, comes from the Dnepropetrovsk area. He became a member of the Communist Party after graduating from the Dnepropetrovsk Chemical Engineering Institute in 1941. Within months he joined the Red Army and served five years as an officer on the Caucasian front. After the war, he returned to the Dnepropetrovsk region and worked his way up through the Ukrainian party structure. He became chairman of the Ukrainian Council of Ministers (the top government post in that republic) in 1961 and a candidate member of the CPSU Politburo (then called the Presidium) shortly thereafter. Shcherbitskii's career declined in 1963 when then CPSU first secretary Nikita Khrushchev appointed a protégé to head the Ukrainian Communist Party. Not long afterward Shcherbitskii was removed from the Politburo and the chairmanship of the Ukrainian Council of Ministers and demoted to a former job as first secretary of the Dnepropetrovsk Oblast Party Committee. When Brezhnev replaced Khrushchev, he restored Shcherbitskii to his pre-1963 positions on the CPSU Presidium (Politburo) (1964) and in the Ukraine (1965). Shcherbitskii presided over the November 1982 leadership meeting at which Yuri Andropov was chosen as Brezhnev's successor.

Eduard Shevardnadze (1928-   )

A candidate member of the Politburo for seven years and twice passed over for promotion, Eduard Amvrosievich Shevardnadze rocketed to prominence in 1985. He became

a full member of the Politburo July 1 and replaced Andrei Gromyko as minister of foreign affairs July 2.

Shevardnadze was born in Mamati, Georgia, January 25, 1928. He joined the Communist Party in 1948. Shevardnadze holds degrees from the Higher Party School of the Georgian Central Committee and from a pedagogical institute.

He became first secretary of the Georgian Komsomol in 1957. The following year he became a full member of the Central Committee in Georgia. In 1961 he was elected to the bureau of the All-Union Komsomol. After serving in several low-level party posts in Georgia, he was appointed first deputy minister of what is now the Georgian Ministry of Internal Affairs in 1964. From 1965 until 1972 he was minister of that body. As minister, Shevardnadze worked to expose corruption among Georgian party officials. His campaign eventually led to the political demise of Vasilii Mzhavanadze, the republic party chief, whom Shevardnadze succeeded in 1972. In 1976 Shevardnadze was further rewarded with his election to the CPSU Central Committee.

As Georgian party boss until his appointment as foreign minister, he improved the republic's economic performance and instituted agricultural production reforms, a

special interest of Gorbachev. In the USSR Supreme Soviet, to which he has been a deputy since 1974, he serves on the Council of Nationalities.

Shevardnadze had visited only nine nations prior to his appointment as foreign minister. Since then he has become a familiar figure on the world scene. In 1985 he represented the Soviet Union at the Conference on Security and Cooperation in Europe in Helsinki, the 40th UN General Assembly, and the 40th anniversary celebration of the United Nations in New York. He has met with both President Reagan and Secretary of State George Shultz several times and accompanied General Secretary Gorbachev to the 1985 summit in Geneva.

Shevardnadze's replacement of longtime Soviet foreign minister Andrei Gromyko does not appear to have affected the substance of Soviet foreign policy. But the affability and relaxed style of Shevardnadze are in stark contrast to the dour looks and stern rhetoric that marked Gromyko's tenure as foreign minister.

Mikhail Solomentsev (1913-   )

In 1983 Mikhail Sergeevich Solomentsev's career leaped forward: in June he was named to head the CPSU Party Control Committee and in December, after 12 years as a Politburo candidate, he was elected a full member.

From 1971 until he assumed oversight of party discipline, Solomentsev served as chairman of the Russian Soviet Federated Socialist Republic Council of Ministers. He originally was not a supporter of Brezhnev, but he came to adopt a conservative party line during Brezhnev's tenure.

Solomentsev was born November 7, 1913, to a peasant family in the Lipetsk region about 200 miles south of Moscow. In 1940 he joined the CPSU and graduated from the Leningrad Polytechnical Institute. He then spent the next 14 years working his way up to become director of factories in the Chelyabinsk region, where he also began his party work.

During most of the 1960s he worked in Kazakhstan, where he eventually served as a member of that republic's presidium. In 1966 he was named chairman of the Legislative Proposals Commission, Council of the Union, USSR Supreme Soviet, and head of the heavy industries department. He held those positions until he was elevated to the Politburo in 1971.

Vitalii Vorotnikov (1926-   )

Vitalii Ivanovich Vorotnikov was elected a candidate member of the Politburo in June 1983 and became a full member in December 1983. The same year he was appointed chairman of the RSFSR Council of Ministers.

Vorotnikov was born January 20, 1926. During most of the 1940s and 1950s, he worked in a machine-building plant and a mining enterprise in Kubyshev in western Siberia. He graduated from the Kubyshev Higher Aviation Institute and became a member of the CPSU in 1947. He began full-time work in the party in 1960. During the next seven years he advanced from department chief to secretary of the Kubyshev Oblast Party Committee. In 1967 he transferred to the chairmanship of the Soviet Executive Committee, the highest government post in the oblast.

In 1971 Vorotnikov became a full member of the CPSU Central Committee and first secretary of his native Voronezh Oblast. Four years later he moved up to his first Moscow-based job as a first deputy chairman of the RSFSR Council of Ministers. He left that position in 1979 to serve as ambassador to Cuba. Vorotnikov returned to party work in 1982, when he was elected first secretary of the Krasnodar Krai Party Committee.

Lev Zaikov (1923-   )

Lev Nikolaevich Zaikov bypassed candidate Politburo status to become a full member of that body in March 1986, eight months after being elevated to the Secretariat of the Central Committee. Only two other secretaries (General Secretary Gorbachev and Egor Ligachev) also are full Politburo members. Since his promotion to the Secretariat in 1985, Zaikov has spoken at several factories on quality control and the need for labor-saving technologies. In 1985 Gorbachev praised his "Intensification-90" plan, a blueprint for the rapid introduction of modern technology into the production process in the Leningrad region.

A Russian national, Zaikov was born April 3, 1923. In 1963 he graduated from the Leningrad Engineering-Economics Institute with a degree in engineering.

Zaikov began his career as a Leningrad metalworker in 1941. He became a foreman and in 1961 was promoted to factory director. From 1971 to 1976 he served in Leningrad as general director of a scientific production association, an amalgam of related research institutes, design bureaus, and production facilities that work to introduce new technologies into Soviet industry.

A party member since 1957, Zaikov switched to full-time party work in 1976, when he was elected chairman of the Leningrad City Soviet Executive Committee or "mayor." He served in that capacity until 1983, when Grigorii Romanov helped promote him to the position of first secretary of the Leningrad Oblast Party Committee. In 1983 Zaikov also was made a member of the Military Council of the Leningrad Military District. The following year he became a member of the Presidium of the USSR Supreme Soviet.

Zaikov served as a deputy to the RSFSR Supreme Soviet from 1975 to 1980. He has been a deputy on the Council of the Union of the USSR Supreme Soviet since 1979 and a full member of the Central Committee since 1981. He has made several trips to the West including a 1977 visit to the United States.

Candidate Politburo Members

Petr Demichev (1918-   )

Petr Nilovich Demichev has been the minister of culture since 1974 and a candidate member of the Politburo since 1964. A protégé of Nikita Khrushchev, Demichev moved rapidly up the party ladder in Moscow. He became a deputy to the USSR Supreme Soviet in 1958 and first secretary of the Moscow Obkom in 1959. He was made a full member of the CPSU Central Committee in 1961. That year Demichev also was appointed Central Committee secretary responsible for internal ideology, a post he held until he became minister of culture. He was a member of the Presidium of the Supreme Soviet from 1962 to 1966.

Demichev was born January 3, 1918, in Kirov into a blue-collar family. Educated as a chemical technologist, Demichev also developed expertise in Soviet ideology and culture. Between 1965 and 1974 Demichev served on the Central Committee's Ideological Commission. Considered a hard-liner on matters of culture and ideology, Demichev led the party attack on Soviet novelist Alexander Solzhenitsyn. In September 1974, however, he ran into political trouble after he allowed a modern art exhibit to open in Moscow.

Demichev also had ties to former Moscow party chief Viktor Grishin. As minister of culture, Demichev has traveled to most Soviet-bloc countries and several Western nations, including the United States in 1979.

Vladimir Dolgikh (1924-   )

Vladimir Ivanovich Dolgikh, a heavy industry specialist with 20 years of industrial management experience in Siberia, has been a CPSU Central Committee secretary since 1972 and a candidate member of the Politburo since May 1982. When Mikhail Gorbachev became general secretary in 1985, Dolgikh was one of the youngest members of the Kremlin leadership. Some Western observers considered him to be a candidate for premier before Nikolai Ryzhkov was given the position.

Dolgikh was born in Krasnoyarsk Krai, Siberia (the birthplace of his associate, former Soviet leader Konstantin Chernenko), December 5, 1924. His father is believed to have been a high official in the USSR Ministry of Internal Affairs. After graduating from the Mining-Metallurgical Institute in Irkutsk in 1949, Dolgikh served until 1958 as shop superintendent and later chief engineer in Krasnoyarsk. He then was transferred to the Norilsk Mining-Metallurgical Combine near the Arctic Circle, serving as chief engineer (1959-62) and director of the plant (1962-69). A savvy manager, Dolgikh was decorated in 1965 for boosting productivity in Norilsk as he had in Krasnoyarsk.

Dolgikh became a deputy to the USSR Supreme Soviet in 1966. From 1969 to 1972 he served as first secretary of the Krasnoyarsk Krai. He was promoted to full membership on the CPSU Central Committee in 1971. In 1972 he was named to the Central Committee Secretariat and took over responsibility for heavy industry. During 1976-84 he served as chief of the Central Committee's Department of Heavy Industry.

Boris Eltsin (1931-   )

Boris Nikolaevich Eltsin has risen rapidly to the top levels of the CPSU leadership, entering the Secretariat in July 1985, less than three months after his appointment to the Central Committee apparatus. A trained engineer and industrial specialist, he was brought to Moscow in April 1985 — only a few weeks after General Secretary Gorbachev assumed power — to head the Central Committee Construction Department. In December Gorbachev named Eltsin to succeed Viktor Grishin as Communist Party boss of Moscow. A week prior to the 27th Party Congress in February 1986 Eltsin was promoted to candidate Politburo member.

Born February 1, 1931, Eltsin is only six weeks older than Gorbachev. He received a degree in construction engineering from the Ural Polytechnic Institute in Sverdlovsk in 1955. By the late 1960s he had become the director of a housing construction facility. He joined the CPSU in 1961. During 1968-76 he was a department chief, then secretary of the Sverdlovsk Oblast Party Committee (Obkom). In November 1976 he became obkom first secretary. He has been a deputy to the Supreme Soviet since 1974 and a member of its Transportation and Communications Commission since 1979.

Nikolai Sliunkov (1929-   )

The first secretary of the Communist Party in Belorussia, Nikolai Nikitovich Sliunkov, was elected a candidate member of the Politburo on March 6, 1986. Sliunkov, a former deputy chairman of the USSR State Planning Committee (Gosplan), became head of the Belorussian party when the previous first secretary, Tikhon Kiselev, died in January 1983.

A native Belorussian, Sliunkov was born April 26, 1929, in the village of Garadzets. He graduated from a mechanical-technical school in 1950 and began working at the Minsk Tractor Plant, eventually becoming chairman of the factory's trade-union committee. In 1954 he joined the

Communist Party. From 1960 to 1965 he directed the Minsk Spare Parts Plant. Sliunkov graduated from the Belorussian Institute of Mechanization of Agriculture in 1962. He returned to the Minsk Tractor Plant as its director in 1965 and held that job until he switched to party work in 1972.

Sliunkov's initial party post was first secretary of the Minsk City Party Committee. In 1974 he was appointed deputy chairman of Gosplan with special responsibility for machine building. He held this post until he became head of the party in Belorussia.

Sergei Sokolov (1911-   )

In December 1984, the 73-year-old marshal of the Soviet Union, Sergei Leonidovich Sokolov, became minister of defense after almost 18 years as a first deputy defense minister. His predecessor, civilian Dmitri Ustinov, died in office at the age of 76.

A CPSU member since 1937, Sokolov has been a full member of its Central Committee since 1968. In April 1985 he was made a candidate member of the Politburo. Some Western military experts claim Sokolov served as commander in chief of Soviet forces in Afghanistan prior to his appointment as defense minister.

An ethnic Russian, Sokolov was born in the Ukrainian Republic July 1, 1911. He joined the Soviet Army in 1932

and served during World War II as chief of staff of a tank regiment and as commander of the armored and mechanized troops of the 32d Army on the Karelian Front. Sokolov held several command positions after the war and attended the Voroshilov General Staff Academy from 1949 until 1951. During the 1960s he served as chief of staff and first deputy commander of the Moscow Military District and as commander of the Leningrad Military District. Since 1966 he has been a deputy to the USSR Supreme Soviet, where he is a member of the Council of Nationalities. In April 1967 Sokolov was appointed a first deputy minister of defense.

His extensive travels include trips to many African and Middle Eastern countries and to the Warsaw Pact nations. He reportedly has played an important role in negotiating arms sales to Third World countries.

Iurii Solovev (1925-   )

When Grigorii Romanov was promoted to the Central Committee Secretariat in June 1983, many observers expected Iurii Filippovich Solovev, then first secretary of the Leningrad City Party Committee, to succeed him as first secretary of the important Leningrad Obkom. But Solovev was passed over in favor of Lev Zaikov, now a full Politburo

member and Central Committee secretary. But the career setback was only temporary. Solovev was named to head the Leningrad Obkom in July 1985 when Zaikov was promoted, and he became a candidate Politburo member March 6, 1986.

An ethnic Russian, Solovev was born in 1925 and graduated from the Leningrad Institute of Rail Transport in 1951. A veteran of World War II, he worked in various administrative jobs on the construction of the Leningrad subway from 1951 to 1973. He eventually became chief engineer and head administrator of the project.

A party member since 1955, Solovev switched to full-time party work in 1973. He became a secretary of the Leningrad Obkom in 1974 and second secretary in 1975. He was elected to full membership in the CPSU Central Committee in 1976. He left the obkom in 1978 to become first secretary of the Leningrad City Party Committee. He held this post for seven years before returning to the city's obkom as its first secretary.

Nikolai Talyzin (1929-   )

Nikolai Vladimirovich Talyzin replaced the aging Nikolai Baibakov as chairman of the State Planning Committee (Gosplan) October 14, 1985. In addition, he was promoted from deputy chairman (deputy premier) to one of three first deputy chairmen of the Council of Ministers. The following day Talyzin was elected a candidate Politburo member.

Talyzin spent his career in communications engineering until 1980, when he became a deputy chairman of the Council of Ministers and the permanent Soviet representative to the Council for Mutual Economic Assistance. He has been a full member of the CPSU Central Committee since 1981.

Born in Moscow January 28, 1929, Talyzin worked in the electrical industry as a teenager during World War II.

He graduated from the Moscow Electrical Engineering Institute of Communications in 1955 and then joined the State Scientific Research Institute of Radio (NIIR), which was part of the Ministry of Communications. He had worked his way up from engineer to deputy director for scientific research at the institute by the time of his selection as a deputy minister of communications in 1965.

After he became a deputy minister, Talyzin apparently retained some affiliation with NIIR; he received a doctoral degree through the institute for his dissertation on radio communications with satellites in 1970. One year later he was promoted to first deputy minister of communications. He was instrumental in the founding in 1971 of Intersputnik, the Soviet-bloc space communications organization. Talyzin was minister of communications from 1975 until 1980.

He has traveled extensively — often with Nikolai Ryzhkov — in Eastern Europe and has made several trips to other countries, including France, Italy, Algeria, and Afghanistan.

Central Committee Secretariat

Alexandra Biriukova (1929-   )

The only woman in the senior party leadership, Alexandra Pavlovna Biriukova was named to the Secretariat March 6, 1986, at the 27th Party Congress. She reportedly will have special responsibility for light industry and consumer goods production. A full Central Committee member since 1976, she has been deputy chairman of the USSR Central Council of Trade Unions since 1985.

An ethnic Russian, Biriukova was born February 25, 1929. After graduating from the Moscow Textile Institute in 1952, she began working in a Moscow factory as a forewoman and soon rose to management positions. In 1956 she joined the Communist Party. From 1963 to 1968 she was chief engineer of a Moscow collective combine.

In 1968 she was appointed secretary of the USSR Council of Trade Unions, a post she held until 1985 when she became deputy chairman of that body. As Central Committee secretary in charge of light industry, Biriukova likely will focus her efforts on improving the quality and distribution of Soviet consumer goods, a difficult task in an economy that has traditionally stressed heavy industry and defense production.

Anatolii Dobrynin (1919-   )

After 24 years in Washington as the Soviet ambassador to the United States, Anatolii Fedorovich Dobrynin returned to Moscow when named to the Central Committee Secretariat in March 1986 at the 27th Party Congress. A tall, grand-fatherly man who speaks fluent English, Dobrynin is known for his un-Soviet-like wit and affability. He also is known as a tough negotiator when circumstances warrant, but one who seeks to find a solution rather than abandon a problem.

Dobrynin, recognized as one of the Soviet Union's foremost Americanologists, spent much of his working life in the United States, serving in the Soviet Embassy in Washington in the early 1950s, at the United Nations in New York in the late 1950s, and again in Washington after becoming ambassador in 1962. He has traveled to almost every state, taking many reels of home movies, one of his favorite pastimes. He also is an avid chess player and skier.

Dobrynin met his wife, Irina, when both were students in Moscow. They have a daughter and in the 1970s they adopted their granddaughter, who lived with them in

Washington. The Dobrynins mixed more easily in the Washington social circuit than most Soviet diplomats. Dobrynin in 1979 became dean of the Washington diplomatic corps, a largely ceremonial function that required him to attend various events.

Dobrynin was born November 16, 1919, in Krasnaya Gorka, a village less than 100 miles west of Moscow. His father was a plumber. Dobrynin attended the Institute of Aviation in Moscow, becoming an aeronautical engineer. He helped design the Yakovlev, the Russian fighter plane that was equivalent to the British Spitfire.

Public Career. Dobrynin's diplomatic career began in 1944 when he was chosen by a committee set up to find new diplomatic talent. He rose through the ranks at the Soviet Ministry of Foreign Affairs, becoming assistant to the deputy minister in 1949. In 1952 Dobrynin was assigned to Washington as a junior counselor. By the time he returned to Moscow in 1955 he had become the embassy's second-ranking member.

For the next two years Dobrynin was a counselor in the Ministry of Foreign Affairs with the title of ambassador extraordinary and plenipotentiary. He served as an aide to Foreign Minister Dmitri T. Shepilov and participated in a number of international conferences, including one in 1955 that led to the Geneva Convention of 1956 and the London conference in 1956 on the Middle East.

In July 1957 Dobrynin joined the UN Secretariat as an undersecretary without portfolio. He eventually was made undersecretary of the Department of Political and Security Council Affairs, although disarmament issues were removed from his jurisdiction to that of Secretary-General Dag Hammerskjöld.

In February 1960 Dobrynin returned to the Ministry of Foreign Affairs where he became head of the American department. In that post he aided Foreign Minister Andrei Gromyko at the UN Security Council discussions of U.S. U-2 flights over the Soviet Union. Dobrynin also accompanied Soviet premier Nikita Khrushchev to his meetings with President John F. Kennedy in Vienna in 1961.

In March 1962 Dobrynin was named ambassador to the United States, replacing Mikhail A. Menshikov. Little more than six months later Dobrynin faced a diplomatic crisis. A few days before it became evident that the Soviets had placed missiles in Cuba, Dobrynin had assured the Kennedy administration that the Soviets would never do such a thing. Dobrynin retained his credibility because Kennedy and his brother, Attorney General Robert F. Kennedy, were convinced that he was not lying but simply had not been informed about the missiles.

Dobrynin was instrumental during both the Nixon and Carter administrations in developing the two strategic arms limitations treaties and helping to facilitate détente between the two countries.

Before Dobrynin's promotion, the Reagan administration pressed the Soviets to rely less on him in their dealings with Washington and more on the U.S. ambassador to Moscow, Arthur Hartman.

Analysis. Although Dobrynin did not make Soviet policy from his position in Washington, he profoundly influenced the direction of U.S.-Soviet relations during the last 20 years through his extraordinary access to both U.S. and Soviet policy makers.

This access was a sore point with U.S. diplomats in Moscow, who have not enjoyed a similar status. They charged that they were overlooked by their own officials, who instead used Dobrynin to communicate with the Soviet leadership.

A prime example occurred in 1972 when Dobrynin accompanied Secretary of State Henry A. Kissinger on a secret journey to Moscow. Even the U.S. ambassador to the Soviet Union did not know about the trip.

Those who have worked with Dobrynin almost uniformly note his profound understanding of American politics and his ability to translate America to his superiors and, in turn, to make the Soviet leadership's position clear to U.S. leaders. They also observe that he accomplishes this difficult task generally without generating anger or resentment.

In his memoirs Kissinger wrote, "If some day there should come about the genuine relaxation of tensions and dangers which our period demands, Anatoly Dobrynin will have made a central contribution to it."

Dobrynin's promotion at the age of 66, when many other members of his generation are being retired, indicates how highly Mikhail Gorbachev and other top Soviet leaders value his experience and expertise. His affable personal style likely will fit in well with that of Gorbachev's new Kremlin team.

In conjunction with his Secretariat duties, Dobrynin is expected to take charge of both the International Department and the Department of Liaison with Communist and Workers' Parties of Socialist Countries. He would thus become the key foreign policy administrator within the party structure. It is uncertain how Dobrynin's new position will affect the role of Eduard Shevardnadze and the Foreign Ministry, but Soviet sources have hinted that Dobrynin would be primarily responsible for formulating policy and advising the Politburo while the Foreign Ministry would concentrate on implementation.

Aleksandr Iakovlev (1923-   )

The head of the Central Committee's Propaganda Department, Aleksandr Nikolaevich Iakovlev was named to the Central Committee Secretariat March 6, 1986, at the 27th Party Congress. Iakovlev, who appears to have developed a close association with Mikhail Gorbachev, will have responsibility for implementing the general secretary's more open and imaginative propaganda line.

Iakovlev, an ethnic Russian, was born September 2, 1923, in the Yaroslavl region of the RSFSR. He served in the army from 1941 to 1943 and graduated from the Yaroslavl Pedagogical Institute after the war. From 1946 to 1953 he worked in the Yaroslavl Oblast party organization. He then became deputy head of the Department of Science and Culture in Moscow. After attending the Academy of Social Sciences from 1956 to 1960, Iakovlev went to work for the Agitation and Propaganda Department (renamed the Propaganda Department in 1966). He rose through its ranks to become acting head in 1971. In late 1972 he published an article warning against the dangers of growing Russian nationalism in literature and social science. The article reportedly brought Iakovlev into disfavor with the party leadership, and in 1973 he was demoted to the post of ambassador to Canada.

A month after Gorbachev's highly successful visit to Canada in 1983, Iakovlev was brought back to Moscow to head the prestigious Institute of World Economics and International Relations of the USSR Academy of Sciences. In December 1984 Iakovlev accompanied Gorbachev on his trip to Great Britain. The following July Gorbachev named

Iakovlev to head the Central Committee's Propaganda Department.

An expert on the United States, Iakovlev was an exchange student at Columbia University in New York in 1959. He eventually earned a doctor of historical sciences degree in the Soviet Union. Iakovlev has written several monographs on U.S. foreign policy including *From Truman to Reagan: Doctrines and Reality of the Nuclear Age*, published in 1984.

Vadim Medvedev (1929-   )

An academic specialist in science and technology, Vadim Andreevich Medvedev was appointed to the Central Committee Secretariat March 6, 1986, at the 27th Party Congress. He has served since 1983 as the chief of the Central Committee's Science and Educational Institutions Department.

An ethnic Russian, Medvedev was born March 29, 1929, in the Yaroslavl region of the RSFSR. He graduated from Leningrad State University in 1951 and earned a doctor of economic sciences degree in 1968. He held teaching positions at several universities and institutes until 1968 when he became a secretary of the Leningrad Gorkom.

From 1970 to 1978 he was deputy chief of the Central Committee's Department of Propaganda. He then served as rector of the party's Academy of Social Sciences until Yuri Andropov appointed him chief of the Department of Science and Educational Institutions in 1983. Medvedev has traveled widely and written scholarly works on the development of socialism, relations with socialist countries, and economics.

Viktor Nikonov (1929-   )

An agricultural specialist, Viktor Petrovich Nikonov was named in April 1985 to the Central Committee Secretariat with responsibility for agriculture, a post Gorbachev held from 1978 to 1983. Nikonov has been a full member of the CPSU Central Committee since 1976.

Nikonov was born into a Russian peasant family February 28, 1929. He graduated from the Azov-Black Sea Agricultural Institute in 1950 and began his career as an agronomist. He subsequently worked as head of an agricultural school and a machine tractor station. He joined the Communist Party in 1954 and began party work four years later. By 1967 he had risen through the party ranks to become first secretary of the Mary Obkom in Turkmemia. Nikonov's expertise earned him a position as a USSR deputy minister of agriculture from 1979 to 1983. He then became the Minister of Agriculture of the RSFSR, a job he held until he was appointed to the Secretariat.

Nikonov has written extensively on agricultural subjects. He has traveled outside the Eastern bloc to West Germany and several Third World countries.

Georgii Razumovskii (1936-   )

An apparent Gorbachev protégé, Georgii Petrovich Razumovskii was named to the Central Committee Secretariat March 6, 1986, at the 27th Party Congress. He has been the head of the Central Committee's Organizational and Party Work Department since June 1985. In these positions, Razumovskii is responsible for overseeing the appointments of personnel to many key positions.

Razumovskii, an ethnic Russian, was born in the Krasnodar region of southern Russia January 19, 1936. He graduated from the Krasnodar Agricultural Institute in 1958. He was an agronomist on a collective farm until 1959 when he began Komsomol and eventually party work in Krasnodar Krai. In 1971 he was transferred to Moscow to work in the party apparatus. He returned to Krasnodar Krai in 1973 to become chairman of the local Soviet. Then in 1981 he was promoted to chief of the Department of Agro-Industrial Complex of the USSR Council of Ministers. In 1983 he moved back to Krasnodar Kraikom as its first secretary when Vitalii Vorotnikov became chairman of the RSFSR Council of Ministers. Razumovskii was known for his anticorruption campaigns in the region.

Mikhail Zimianin (1914-   )

Mikhail Vasilevich Zimianin, a former chief editor of *Pravda*, has been the Central Committee secretary responsible for internal ideology and propaganda since 1976. He became a full member of the Central Committee and a deputy to the USSR Supreme Soviet in 1966 (he had held both honors in the early 1950s). An experienced diplomat, Zimianin also is deputy chairman of the Foreign Affairs Commission of the Supreme Soviet's Council of Nationalities.

An ethnic Russian, Zimianin was born in Vitebsk, Belorussia, November 21, 1914. His father was a railroad worker, and Zimianin began his working career on the railroad in 1929. In the early 1930s he became a journalist and teacher. After serving in the military from 1936 to 1938, he graduated in 1939 from the Mogilev State Pedigogical Institute and joined the Communist Party.

Zimianin worked his way up through the Belorussian party structure under the patronage of chief of the secret police Lavrentii Beria. In 1953 Zimianin became first secretary of the Belorussian Central Committee, but he lost his party posts that year when Beria fell. Zimianin transferred to the Foreign Ministry, where he held a variety of posts including ambassador to Vietnam (1956-58), chief of the Far Eastern Department (1958-60), ambassador to Czechoslovakia (1960-65), and deputy foreign minister (1965). In 1965 Zimianin returned to party work and became chief editor of *Pravda*, a post he held until he was named to the Secretariat in 1976.

Zimianin is known for his orthodox ideological positions. He reportedly had a close personal friendship with influential party ideologist Mikhail Suslov, who died in 1982.

Past Soviet Leaders

Yuri Andropov (1914-84)

Two days following the death of Leonid Brezhnev on November 10, 1982, Yuri Vladimirovich Andropov was named to succeed Brezhnev as general secretary of the Communist Party. On June 16, 1983, he became chairman of the Presidium of the Supreme Soviet (president), thus continuing a practice begun by Brezhnev of combining the role of head of state with that of party chief.

An ailing 68-year-old when he took over, Andropov died February 10, 1984. Three days later Konstantin Chernenko was chosen as his successor.

The son of a railroad employee, Andropov was born June 15, 1914, in Nagutskaya, now in Stavropol Krai. Andropov never received a degree in higher education al-

though he attended Petrozavodsk University. Between 1930 and 1932 he worked as a telegraph operator, an apprentice film mechanic, and a Volga boatman. Andropov's involvement with the Communist Party began in 1936 with work in the Komsomol. In 1938 he was promoted to regional first secretary of the Komsomol and the following year became a member of the Communist Party.

Public Career. When Germany invaded the Soviet Union in 1941, Andropov was active in party politics in Karelia, near Finland's eastern border. For the next decade he worked alongside Otto Kuusinen, the top party leader in the Karelian Republic and his entrée to power.

With the backing of Kuusinen, Andropov was transferred to Moscow in 1951 to work for the Central Committee of the CPSU. Two years later Soviet leader Joseph Stalin died, Nikita Khrushchev assumed power, and Andropov suffered a career setback: a posting to the Soviet Embassy in Budapest. The switch from inner party politics to diplomacy, however, did not stymie his career. In 1954 he was promoted from counselor to ambassador to Hungary, a post he held until 1957. Andropov played a leading role in suppressing the 1956 Hungarian revolt.

Between 1957 and 1967 he was back in Moscow serving as chief of the party's Department for Liaison with Communist and Workers' Parties of Socialist Countries, where he emphasized the importance of Soviet aid to socialist countries.

Andropov was selected as a candidate member of the Politburo in 1967 when he was named chairman of the USSR Committee for State Security (KGB). He was made a full member of the Politburo in 1973 and thus became the first KGB head to have a vote on the Politburo since Lavrentii Beria was purged in 1953.

As head of the KGB, Andropov worked to destroy the dissident movement that gained momentum during this period. Many prominent Soviet writers, scientists, and others agitating for greater liberalization of the Soviet system were imprisoned or sent into exile under his authority.

In May 1982 Andropov resigned as KGB head and transferred to the Central Committee Secretariat, a better position from which to succeed Brezhnev. By that time he had already gained some key allies, including Foreign Minister Gromyko and Defense Minister Ustinov, who would side with Andropov in the struggle for succession.

Analysis. Although Andropov's administration was brief, only 15 months, it brought significant changes to the Soviet system. During the last 10 years of Brezhnev's life, few changes were made in the composition of the Central Committee. But the complacency of the old guard was shaken by Andropov. He advanced Gorbachev and other younger leaders intent on instituting reforms, and he campaigned against the well-entrenched corruption at the top of the bureaucracy. Were it not for Andropov's domestic initiatives, many experts believe that Gorbachev would not have been able to consolidate his power so quickly. The new optimism and dynamism of the Gorbachev leadership is the legacy not of Chernenko but of Andropov.

Lavrentii Beria (1899-1953)

Lavrentii Pavlovich Beria, political leader and last head of the secret police during the rule of Joseph Stalin, played a key role in the purges of Stalin's enemies.

Beria was born March 29, 1899, in Merkheuli, Georgia. His Georgian heritage endeared him to Stalin, another son of that republic. Soviet sources claim that Beria was born into the family of a "poor peasant" and that he obtained a technical education in a Baku college. Beria joined the Bolshevik Party in 1917 and began his career as a revolutionary worker in the Transcaucasian regions of Georgia and Azerbaidzhan.

Public Career. Stalin visited Georgia as a Politburo representative in June 1921 after Georgia had been incorporated into the Soviet Union. Beria impressed the future dictator, who subsequently appointed him chief of the Georgian Cheka (secret police). In this position Beria became Stalin's "right-hand man" in the Transcaucasus. In 1931 he was appointed to the political leadership of the entire Transcaucasian region.

In July 1938 Stalin summoned Beria to Moscow and appointed him deputy to Nikolai Ivanovich Yezhov, head of the People's Commissariat of Internal Affairs (NKVD) and overseer of the Great Purge. Yezhov was by this time marked by Stalin for execution, and his demise quickly followed.

Beria took command of the entire secret police organization in December 1938. He then investigated NKVD activities and is credited with rehabilitating certain victims and upgrading prison camp conditions.

Beria's ability to magnify Stalin's suspicions of his colleagues and the dictator's great reliance on the secret police enabled Beria to quickly consolidate a powerful position for himself. He became a full Politburo member in 1939.

Beria's responsibilities expanded as World War II approached. He reportedly was involved in the 1940 Katyn forest massacre, a bloody affair during which several thousand Poles, who had been taken prisoner after the Nazi-Soviet partition of Poland a year before, were executed.

When the Germans invaded the Soviet Union in June 1941, Stalin appointed Beria to the State Defense Committee. His duties, in addition to supervising internal security and an international spy network, included the evacuation and resettlement of Soviet industry and later the production of ammunition. For his wartime service Beria was named a marshal of the Soviet Union in 1945.

After the United States dropped atomic bombs on Hiroshima and Nagasaki in August 1945, Stalin assigned Beria to a top-priority atomic research program. The project resulted in a mid-1949 nuclear explosion in the Kazakh/Uzbek desert, although Stalin reportedly was unhappy with the slow progress of the operation.

Upon Stalin's death in 1953, Beria obtained the number-two post under the premiership of Georgii Malenkov. From his powerful position as minister of internal affairs, Beria attempted to make his bid for supreme power. However, the collective leadership, including Malenkov, Viacheslav Molotov, party chief Khrushchev, and others, opposed him.

In June 1953 Beria was arrested for "criminal antiparty and antistate activities." His alleged crimes included involvement with British intelligence and promotion of nationalistic sentiments. In December of that year the party newspaper *Pravda* and the government newspaper *Izvestiia* announced that Beria had been executed for treason.

Analysis. Beria's career is often described as that of an "evil genius" who ingratiated himself to Stalin by effectively eliminating those whom Stalin perceived as enemies. He also is alleged to have approached his work with enthusiasm, personally torturing and killing many prisoners. Khrushchev maintained in his reputed autobiography that Stalin, toward the end of his life, began to fear Beria. In spite of Beria's lifetime association with the security apparatus of the Soviet Union, he proposed many modifications of the system after Stalin's death. In foreign policy Beria supported good relations with Western countries. He intended to restore ties with Yugoslavia's Josip Broz Tito and opposed Russification of non-Russian regions of the Soviet Union. However, he could not garner sufficient power to overcome the combined force of Stalin's heirs, who perceived him as a threat.

Leonid Brezhnev (1906-82)

From the early 1970s until his death November 10, 1982, Leonid Ilich Brezhnev was the unrivaled leader of the Soviet Union. During much of his tenure he was both

general secretary of the Communist Party and chairman of the Presidium of the Supreme Soviet (president).

If Lenin rose to the top because he was a brilliant visionary, Stalin because he had a genius for terror, and Khrushchev because he had an overpowering personality, Brezhnev reached the apex of power because he worked hard and never rocked the boat.

Brezhnev, a Russian, was born December 19, 1906, into a steelworker's family in the Ukrainian town of Kamenskoe (known since 1936 as Dneprodzerzhinsk). In 1915 he entered a school subsidized by the local steel plant where his father worked. When he graduated six years later, Brezhnev — who referred to himself as a "fifth-generation steelman" — went to work as a hired hand, stoker, and fitter in a metallurgical plant.

In 1923 Brezhnev enrolled in the Kursk Technicum for Land Utilization and Reclamation. After graduating in 1927 he spent three years working as a land reclamation specialist in Stalin's collectivization program. He eventually became chief of a district land department and deputy chairman of the executive committee of a soviet, and later the first deputy chief of a regional land administration.

Around 1930 Brezhnev spent a brief period (which often is omitted from official biographies) at the Timiriazev Agricultural Academy in Moscow before returning to his hometown in 1931. He went to work once again as a fitter in the metallurgical plant and studied evenings at

the F. E. Dzerzhinski Metallurgical Institute. Brezhnev, who had been a Komsomol member (1923-29) and had joined the Communist Party in 1931, also served as secretary of the institute's Communist Party committee and chairman of the plant's trade union committee.

Following his graduation from the institute in 1935, he worked as an engineer and briefly served in the Red Army as a political instructor. In 1937-38 he was deputy chairman of the executive committee of the Dneprodzerzhinsk City Workers' Soviet and director of the city's metallurgical technical school.

Public Career. Brezhnev went to work full time for the Communist Party in 1938. Although his switch to party politics came at the time of the Stalinist purges carried out in the Ukraine by Khrushchev, there was no evidence that Brezhnev took part.

Brezhnev's first position was as chief of a department of the Dnepropetrovsk regional party committee. In 1939 he became the committee's secretary for propaganda and the next year secretary for the defense industry. He remained in this post until 1941 when the German army overran the city.

During World War II Brezhnev rose from colonel to major general, serving with the political administration of the Southern and Ukranian fronts and the Carpathian Military District. He fought in the Caucasus, on the Black Sea, in the Crimea, in the Ukraine, and in the liberation of Czechoslovakia.

In 1946 Brezhnev became party first secretary of Zaporozhe and, in 1947, first secretary of Dnepropetrovsk, both important industrial regions in the Ukraine. In 1950, after spending a few months in Moscow working in the Central Committee apparatus, he became first secretary in the union republic of Moldavia. Also in 1950, he was elected a deputy of the Supreme Soviet.

Brezhnev received a major promotion in October 1952. As part of Stalin's move to expand the top leadership, he was named a full member of the Central Committee, one of its 10 secretaries, and a candidate member of its Presidium.

Following Stalin's death in March 1953, most of his 1952 additions to the Secretariat and Presidium — including Brezhnev — were dropped. Brezhnev then spent a year as first deputy chief of the Main Political Administration of the Soviet Army and Navy.

In 1954 Khrushchev, maneuvering for power after Stalin's death, staked his political future on the "virgin lands" program and chose Brezhnev to help carry out the risky venture. From 1954 to 1956 Brezhnev served as second secretary and later as first secretary of the party in the Central Asian Republic of Kazakhstan.

Having displayed his managerial and political skills in the agrarian program, Brezhnev returned in 1956 to Moscow to become once again a secretary of the party's Central Committee (for heavy industry and capital investment; after 1959 for defense and space exploration) and a candidate member of its Presidium.

He supported Khrushchev in his struggle with the so-called "antiparty" group in early 1957, and Brezhnev was among the loyal supporters Khrushchev chose to replace his discredited opponents.

Brezhnev became a full member of the Presidium in 1957, the deputy chairman of the Bureau for the Russian Soviet Federated Socialist Republic (RSFSR) in 1958, and a deputy in the RSFSR Supreme Soviet in 1959.

In a major shakeup the following year, Brezhnev was named chairman of the Presidium of the Supreme Soviet.

The ceremonial post of chief of state served Brezhnev well during his four-year tenure. Traveling abroad as spokesman for the Khrushchev regime's foreign policies, Brezhnev gained needed experience in the noncommunist world.

A few months after his appointment as chief of state, Brezhnev gave up his post as a secretary of the Central Committee. In 1963, however, after Frol Kozlov suffered a stroke, Brezhnev was renamed to the Secretariat.

Brezhnev relinquished the chief of state post in July 1964. Then, as the unofficial second secretary, he turned his full attention to supervising day-to-day party affairs. Only three months later he became first secretary. On October 14, 1964, in a special session of the Central Committee, Khrushchev was abruptly relieved of his two top-level posts. His protégé Brezhnev was chosen to fill his party position and Aleksei Kosygin was named head of the government.

At the 23d Party Congress in March 1966, Brezhnev's title reverted from "first secretary" to the Stalinist-era usage, "general secretary," and the party "Presidium" was renamed the "Politburo," symbolically concluding Khrushchev's de-Stalinization drive.

Initially, the collective leadership seemed to work. Brezhnev concerned himself with party affairs and relations within the international communist movement, and Kosygin with the economy and foreign relations. But by the early 1970s Brezhnev had eclipsed Kosygin. The party leader took over Kosygin's role as the Kremlin's spokesman in international affairs and its chief negotiator with foreign powers. By the time Kosygin resigned in 1980, his influence on economic issues had similarly declined.

In 1976 Brezhnev was named marshal of the Soviet Union, the nation's highest military rank, and his position as chairman of the USSR Defense Council — commander in chief of Soviet armed forces — was publicly acknowledged for the first time.

Brezhnev had his former rival, Nikolai Podgornyi, dismissed in 1977 as chairman of the Presidium of the Supreme Soviet so that he could assume the post. Also in 1977 the Soviet Union adopted a new constitution, which was said to have been largely Brezhnev's work.

Analysis. In 1964, after Khrushchev's fall from power, some Western observers thought Brezhnev would be a transition figure, but he ended up wielding power for 18 years.

Brezhnev was well prepared for the role of Soviet party leader. He brought a broad range of substantive experience to the job that none of his rivals could match. He was experienced in agriculture and industry, had been a party leader in four different republics, had had seven years of political work in the military, and had gained experience in foreign affairs during his four years as chief of state. Brezhnev's military service afforded him the opportunity to renew ties with that important segment of the Soviet establishment.

Brezhnev pursued some apparently contradictory policies during his tenure as Soviet leader. He masterminded Moscow's reconciliation with the West but repeatedly challenged the interests of the West. It was worth the risks and costs, it seemed, to continue an arms buildup, encourage Third World leftist revolutions, invade Afghanistan, and support (if not order) the imposition of martial law in Poland. He also appeared willing to accept Western condemnation of his regime's treatment of dissidents rather than institute liberalizing reforms.

Pragmatist is the word most often used to describe Brezhnev. His regime emphasized a "scientific approach" to decision making, implying a weighing of alternatives, an understanding of limitations, and a reliance on data.

Throughout his career he showed resourcefulness. He knew when to compromise and when to stand firm. He possessed a detailed understanding of power and how to use it. And he managed to come down on the winning side of power struggles in the Soviet Union when it really counted.

Nikolai Bukharin (1888-1938)

The theories of Nikolai Ivanovich Bukharin, a gifted thinker and one of the most popular revolutionary figures in the Soviet Union, remained influential even after he fell from power and was put to death.

Born in Moscow October 9, 1888, Bukharin was attracted to radical philosophies at a young age. In 1908 he joined the Moscow committee of the Bolshevik branch of the Russian Social Democratic Labor Party. Two years later tsarist authorities broke up the Moscow organization, and Bukharin was arrested and exiled to Siberia. He subsequently escaped to Europe, where he began to write theoretical as well as political tracts. He first met Lenin in 1912 in Krakow. During his time abroad, Bukharin was one of the few revolutionary leaders to visit the United States, where he edited a Russian communist newspaper.

Public Career. In 1917 Bukharin returned to Russia and was named an editor of the party newspaper *Pravda* and a member of the Central Committee, which was composed of the most important Bolshevik leaders. He opposed Lenin's positions on several issues, notably the Brest-Litovsk peace treaty with Germany in 1918. Bukharin, however, did not lose his influence with Lenin.

In 1919 Bukharin was elected to the Comintern (Communist International) at its formation. He joined the ruling Politburo in 1924 and enjoyed immense popularity. Following Lenin's death in 1924, he became involved in the power struggle between Leon Trotsky and Joseph Stalin. Although he sided with Stalin, he gradually fell out of favor. Stripped of his Comintern and Politburo posts in 1928, Bukharin submitted to "political self-criticism" and was allowed to continue party work until 1937. However, because he represented a potential source of opposition to Stalin, he fell victim to the Great Purge. In March 1938 he took the witness stand as the main defendant of the third "show trial" in Moscow. The court found the former Politburo member guilty of counterrevolutionary activities, and he was executed immediately after the trial.

Analysis. In his final testament, Lenin called Bukharin "the Party's most eminent and valuable theoretician." Indeed, many experts today consider his writings his most important legacy. They include *World Economy and Imperialism* (1918), *Program of the World Revolution* (1920), *The ABC of Communism* (1921), and *Historical Materialism* (1925).

The evolution of Bukharin's political views charted his development from a revolutionary leftist to a proponent of the gradual spread of socialism. At first Bukharin believed that world upheaval would follow the Russian revolution. He lowered his expectations after the socialist revolution failed in Germany in 1923. He argued that Soviet Russia should slowly build socialism internally. He complemented this notion with the theory that Russia would benefit economically if the assets of the wealthy peasants, or kulaks, could be incorporated without force into the socialist system. Stalin borrowed heavily from Bukharin's ideas in his proposal for building "socialism in one country," but he deviated from them in launching a headlong plunge toward agricultural collectivization by force.

Konstantin Chernenko (1911-85)

On February 13, 1984, Konstantin Ustinovich Chernenko, a party bureaucrat and longtime crony of Leonid Brezhnev, succeeded Yuri Andropov as general secretary of the Communist Party. In addition, he became head of state two months later on April 11, when he was elected chairman of the Presidium of the USSR Supreme Soviet (president).

Chernenko continued what has been called the "graying" of the Kremlin leadership. Vladimir I. Lenin, the founder of the Soviet state, took power when he was 47 years old. Joseph Stalin was the same age when he emerged as the country's sole ruler in 1927. Stalin, in turn, was succeeded by Georgii Malenkov (51), Nikita Khrushchev (60), Brezhnev (58), Andropov (68), and Chernenko (72).

Weak from emphysema when he took office, Chernenko died a little more than a year later on March 11, 1985. A new generation of Kremlin leaders then was ushered in by his successor, 54-year-old Mikhail Gorbachev.

Chernenko was born into a peasant family September 24, 1911, in Novoselovo, Krasnoyarsk Krai. He began his party work in 1929. From 1930 to 1933 he worked as a border guard, duties that were glorified once Chernenko became an important member of the Soviet leadership. He was the only Soviet leader of his generation not to serve in World War II.

Public Career. Chernenko owed much of his party advancement to his associate Brezhnev. From 1948 until 1956 Chernenko served as chief of the Moldavian Central Committee's Propaganda and Agitation Department; for three of those years, 1950-52, Brezhnev was first secretary of the Moldavian Central Committee. In 1956 Chernenko became chief of the Mass Agitation Work Sector of the USSR Central Committee.

When Brezhnev took over the Presidium of the Supreme Soviet in 1960, Chernenko became chief of the Presidium's secretariat. In 1965 he was named head of the USSR Central Committee's General Department, which serves as a secretariat for the party apparatus and which handles citizen complaints and classified documents.

Chernenko was made a secretary of the Central Committee in 1976 and also retained his responsibilities for managing the General Department. He was named a candidate member of the Politburo in 1977 and became a full member in 1978.

Analysis. Chernenko's 13-month administration was largely a stalemate between Brezhnev-era bureaucrats wary of dramatic economic reforms and Andropov's appointees, younger leaders, such as Gorbachev, intent on reconstructing both the Soviet economy and the Soviet image abroad. Gorbachev and the younger generation waited for the ailing Chernenko to die before pressing their claims to power.

During Chernenko's brief tenure, the process of modernization begun by his more activist predecessor was slowed. He reversed one of Andropov's last decisions; namely, to cut the bureaucracy by nearly 20 percent. Chernenko did not bring to a dead halt Andropov's domestic program of economic experimentation or his anticorruption campaign, but he lacked the health, will, and vision to spur modernization and reform. In the area of U.S.-Soviet relations, however, Chernenko took an important step forward by promoting the resumption of arms control talks in Geneva.

Viktor Grishin (1914-   )

Viktor Vasilievich Grishin was one of several "old guard" losers in Gorbachev's shakeup of the Kremlin leadership. After nearly 25 years on the Politburo, he was retired February 18, 1986. He had already been dismissed as head of the Communist Party in Moscow the previous December, a position he held for 18 years (1967-85). Grishin reportedly had joined other veterans on the Politburo in opposing Gorbachev's plans for economic and bureaucratic reform.

The son of a railroad worker, Grishin was born September 18, 1914. He holds degrees as a technical surveyor and as a mechanical engineer. During World War II he converted industries in Serpukhov, his hometown, to arms manufacture. Following the war he became chief of the Machine Building Department in Moscow, rising to head of Soviet trade unions in 1957. Four years later he was made a candidate, or nonvoting, member of the Politburo.

Grishin was politically and personally loyal to Brezhnev, during whose tenure he became a member of the Supreme Soviet Presidium in 1967 and a full member of the Politburo in 1971. In July 1981 Grishin was sent as the Soviet emissary to an emergency session of the Polish Congress. That move was viewed as a ploy to allow Brezhnev and other top leaders in Moscow to dissociate themselves from the results of the emergency session, if need be, and seemed to indicate that Grishin was one of the more expendable Politburo members. That suspicion was reinforced in November 1981 when Grishin did not attend the annual military parade commemorating the 1917 revolution.

Lev Kamenev (1883-1936)

Lev Borisovich Kamenev (Rosenfeld) gained prominence during the Bolsheviks' rise to power as one of Lenin's closest associates.

Born in Moscow on July 22, 1883, Kamenev was the son of parents who had been part of the Russian revolutionary movement of the 1870s. Kamenev initially became involved with Marxist circles during his high school (gymnasium) years. His interest in revolutionary philosophy grew while he studied law at Moscow University, and he was arrested and sent to Siberia in 1902 for his work in the radical student movement. Following his return from exile he traveled to Europe and began working for *Iskra* (The Spark), the revolutionary journal Lenin founded in Paris.

Kamenev's introduction to Lenin and his teachings profoundly influenced his future career. Kamenev continued his underground activity in Europe and later in Russia, staunchly upholding the Bolshevik line during the debates with the Menshevik faction of the Russian Social Democratic Labor Party around 1904. Kamenev, along with

Grigori E. Zinoviev, became one of Lenin's closest literary and political collaborators.

Before Lenin returned to Russia, Kamenev was the principal spokesman for all Bolshevik activities and policies, advocating conditional support of the Provisional Government. Upon his arrival in Petrograd in 1917, Lenin quarreled with Kamenev (and Zinoviev); Kamenev endorsed a seizure of power by a coalition government made up of all socialist parties, while Lenin proposed a Bolshevik-led revolt and regime. These disagreements were smoothed over before the Bolsheviks' November 1917 takeover, and Kamenev was named a member of the first Politburo.

After Lenin's death in 1924, Kamenev joined with Zinoviev and Joseph Stalin against the leader of the "left opposition," Leon Trotsky. Kamenev and his ally, Zinoviev, reversed themselves in 1926, however, supporting Trotsky's ill-fated attempt to thwart Stalin's growing power. Despite later recantations of their alliance with Trotsky, both men lost their important party and government positions. Kamenev was expelled and readmitted to the Communist Party three times between 1927 and 1934. In 1935 he was sentenced to five years in prison for alleged complicity in the murder of the Leningrad party boss, Sergei M. Kirov. The following year, after being retried in the first great "show trial" of Stalin's purge, he was sentenced to death and executed in August.

Aleksandr Kerensky (1881-1970)

Aleksandr Feodorovich Kerensky, a member of the Socialist Revolutionary Party, headed the Russian Provisional Government on the eve of the Bolshevik Revolution in 1917 and later led an unsuccessful effort to overthrow the new regime.

Kerensky was born April 22, 1881, in Simbirsk (now Ulyanovsk), the Volga region of Russia where Lenin was born. (In fact, Kerensky's father was Lenin's high school principal.) While a student in St. Petersburg, Kerensky became active in Populist circles. As a young socialist lawyer, he defended revolutionaries accused of political offenses. The failure of the promised reforms of the 1905 Russian revolution convinced Kerensky that the monarchy should be overthrown.

After the downfall of Tsar Nicholas II in March 1917, the Provisional Government assumed power. Kerensky was the only Social Revolutionary to accept a post in the new regime. He served as minister of justice under Prince Georgi E. Lvov, a liberal aristocrat who was prime minister. Later, Kerensky became minister of war. At the same time he held a post in the Petrograd Soviet and functioned as an intermediary between the Soviet and the Provisional Government.

Kerensky replaced Lvov as prime minister in July 1917, a time when the Bolsheviks gradually were gaining support and the mood of the people was becoming increasingly radical. Kerensky made several unpopular decisions as head of the Provisional Government, including the dismissal of the popular commander in chief of the armed forces, Lavr G. Kornilov, for conspiracy. Kerensky's decision to keep Russia in World War I also provoked wide disapproval.

The "Kornilov affair" demonstrated the military's lack of support for Kerensky's government, which eventually fell to the Bolsheviks in November 1917. Kerensky escaped from St. Petersburg and rallied loyal troops, but his attempts to overthrow the new regime failed. He emigrated and died in New York City on June 11, 1970.

Nikita Khrushchev (1894-1971)

Nikita Sergeevich Khrushchev rose from relative obscurity as an average Communist Party functionary to become one of the most powerful and widely traveled leaders of the Soviet Union. Born April 17, 1894, on the Russo-Ukrainian border in the Kursk province, Khrushchev came from a simple worker's background. Unlike many communist leaders who joined the party as students in their late teens, Khrushchev did not join the Bolsheviks until 1918, when he was 24. He spent the next three years fighting in the civil war. His first wife and two children perished during  the famines of the postwar years. He subsequently married Nina Petrovna, who captured the interest of the American people when she accompanied Khrushchev on a visit to the United States in 1959. The couple had three children.

After the civil war Khrushchev attended an adult technical school and engaged in party work in the Ukraine. He met Joseph Stalin in 1926 as a delegate to a party congress. Transferred to Moscow in 1929, Khrushchev enrolled in the prestigious Industrial Academy where Nadezhda Alliluyeva, Stalin's second wife, was his classmate.

Public Career. Khrushchev's career began to gain momentum in the 1930s. An able and energetic administrator, he played a central role in the Moscow subway construction project. In 1932 he was named to the influential Moscow Communist Party administration. Other promotions followed: the party Central Committee, 1934; the Supreme Soviet, 1937; candidate member of the Politburo, 1938; first secretary of the Ukrainian Communist Party, 1938; full Politburo member, 1939. In less than a decade Khrushchev ranked among the most powerful leaders in the Soviet Union.

Khrushchev's part in the Stalinist purges is unclear, but in all probability his participation was substantial. He supported Stalin against the protests of those in the party who were horrified by the executions, and in doing so probably escaped being purged himself.

With the onset of World War II, Khrushchev was occupied with duties in the Ukraine, notably the annexation of eastern Poland as agreed upon in the 1939 Nazi-Soviet pact. After the outbreak of German-Soviet hostilities in 1941, Khrushchev oversaw the war effort at various field commands throughout the Soviet Union. One of his duties for Stalin was recommending military officers for promotion. These protégés were later instrumental in consolidating Khrushchev's power.

Stalin was displeased with the wartime defense of the Ukraine — the area quickly was overrun by Nazi forces — but he reassigned Khrushchev to head the Ukrainian party in 1944. Devastated by the war, the Ukraine recovered slowly. The party leadership was blamed for the region's postwar difficulties, and Khrushchev in 1947 briefly lost his post as Ukrainian party boss.

In December 1949 Khrushchev returned to Moscow to

serve as a Central Committee secretary. His positions on the Central Committee and the Presidium (the name given the Politburo in 1952; it reverted to the former name in 1966) guaranteed Khrushchev a central role in the power struggle following Stalin's death in 1953. Georgii M. Malenkov emerged as head of the government and party secretary, but Khrushchev replaced him as party boss in a matter of days.

Khrushchev moved quickly to augment his power base by increasing his support within the party apparatus. He upheld the Stalinist line and bolstered the concerns of those in the leadership who opposed Malenkov's bid for power and his new course in domestic and foreign policy. Khrushchev gradually began to place some distance between himself and his Presidium colleagues. He proposed a series of domestic reforms, including the unsuccessful "virgin lands" project to cultivate barren regions in Siberia and Central Asia.

Abroad, Khrushchev improved relations with Yugoslav leader Josip Broz Tito, who broke away from the Soviet bloc early in Stalin's postwar rule. In 1955 he promoted the signing of the Austrian State Treaty and participated in a summit meeting with President Dwight D. Eisenhower.

At home, Khrushchev's political maneuvering brought about Malenkov's downfall in 1955. Khrushchev later would adopt some of the policies Malenkov had endorsed, such as rehabilitation of Stalin's victims and a less hostile stance toward the West.

Khrushchev's speech to the delegates at the 20th Party Congress in February 1956 marked a watershed for Soviet internal and foreign policies. In the "Secret Speech" (so called because it has not been fully published in the Soviet Union), Khrushchev revealed the extent of the Stalinist purge and promised to rehabilitate its victims. Earlier during the congress, he also proposed a policy of peaceful coexistence with the West, reversing the traditional Soviet claim that war was inevitable because the establishment of communism required violent revolution. *(Excerpts from "Secret Speech," Appendix, p. 279)*

This first public denunciation of Stalin shocked the communist community. East European leaders particularly were unnerved because their governments were built on Stalinist principles. Serious disturbances in several countries, notably Poland and Hungary, undermined the USSR's prestige. The People's Republic of China was outraged by Khrushchev's de-Stalinization campaign, which the Chinese termed a "revisionist" act by a leader whose stature could not compare with that of Stalin or of China's own leader, Mao Zedong. Despite these setbacks, Khrushchev's attack on Stalin had the desired effect — it separated him from his rivals for power in the Soviet Union by grouping them together as "Stalin's heirs," and it portrayed Khrushchev as a reformer who refused to follow Stalin's path. Khrushchev continued to consolidate his power by soliciting support for his reform and de-Stalinization policies. In 1957, for example, he unveiled a plan to decentralize economic management.

Khrushchev faced formidable opposition within the Presidium. In mid-1957 a group of high party officials, including Malenkov, Viacheslav M. Molotov, Lazar Kaganovich, and Dmitri Shepilov, conspired to restrict his power. Khrushchev avoided a possible ouster by appealing to the Central Committee for support, thereby outflanking his opponents on the Presidium. The "antiparty" group, as it was dubbed, was expelled from the Central Committee in mid-1957. By 1958 Khrushchev as premier had placed himself at the head of all party, government, and military organs, and, like Stalin, had developed his own "personality cult."

In May 1960 Khrushchev announced the downing of a U.S. spy plane over Sverdlovsk in the Ural Mountains. The "U-2 incident" had several repercussions. A planned summit meeting in Paris on the division of Germany was cancelled and a meeting with President John F. Kennedy in June 1961 was adversely affected. Lack of a solution to the German question led to the erection of the Berlin Wall in 1961. Domestically, the event thwarted Khrushchev's proposed military cutbacks in early 1961.

Khrushchev, in his conduct of foreign affairs, vacillated between threatening gestures toward the West and attempts to thaw out the Cold War. In the fall of 1962 he decided to install Soviet missiles in Cuba to win a political victory over the United States by challenging American military superiority and to silence his critics in Beijing and Moscow. Instead, President Kennedy's ultimatums forced Khrushchev to back down and remove the missiles from Cuba. Less than a year later the superpowers negotiated a treaty providing for a partial ban on nuclear testing.

By 1963 Khrushchev's colleagues were becoming increasingly unhappy with his domestic reforms. Neither his virgin lands program nor his ambitious economic plans came close to achieving their goals, and a disastrous 1963 harvest intensified Soviet economic problems. Although Khrushchev tempered his drive to boost the supply of consumer goods in 1963, conservative Soviet leaders still feared that traditional investments in arms and heavy industry could be threatened. In addition, Khrushchev's bifurcation of the party and government structures into industrial and agricultural branches in 1962 displeased many leaders. These domestic factors, coupled with the erosion of Khrushchev's prestige in Eastern Europe and China and the failure of his plan to put missiles in Cuba, led to his political demise. Following a conspiracy of the Soviet Union's highest officials, it was announced in October 1964 that the 70-year-old Khrushchev would be replaced by Aleksei Kosygin as head of the Soviet government and by Leonid Brezhnev as party first secretary. Khrushchev lived in seclusion after his forced retirement and died September 11, 1971.

Analysis. Khrushchev's achievement in gaining power in the Soviet Union was notable in several respects. He had neither the theoretical brilliance and personal prestige of Lenin nor the secret police machine of Stalin. Instead, Khrushchev attempted to use a comprehensive reform program to secure his power and bring the Soviet Union out of its Stalinist past. Khrushchev did not fear accusations of revisionism so much as a stagnant and outdated Soviet policy at home and abroad. This in part accounted for his acceptance of "different roads to socialism" and his tacit support for the nonaligned socialist movement. Khrushchev can be credited with maintaining relative stability in the Soviet Union even though many of his plans ended in failure. His agricultural reforms proved disastrous, the Soviets were humiliated in the Cuban missile crisis, and relations with China grew increasingly bitter. Yet Khrushchev managed to keep a grip on his power for more than a decade.

Andrei Kirilenko (1906-   )

Andrei Pavlovich Kirilenko, once thought likely to succeed Brezhnev, retired from the Politburo November

22, 1982.

Kirilenko, an ethnic Russian, was born September 8, 1906, in Alekseevka, which was then in the Ukraine but today is in the Belgorod Oblast of the Russian Soviet Federated Socialist Republic. He was the son of an artisan.

After graduating from a professional technical school in 1925, he worked as a fitter in factories and mines. Following his graduation in 1936 from an aviation institute in Rybinsk, he went to work for two years as a design engineer at an aircraft plant in Zaporozhe.

Public Career. Kirilenko joined the Communist Party in 1931 and entered Ukrainian Communist Party politics in 1938, the year Khrushchev arrived in Kiev to carry out the purge of the Ukraine. Kirilenko held a variety of local party posts prior to World War II.

During the war, he served on the Southern Front as a member of the military council of the 18th Ukrainian Army and later as a special representative of the State Defense Committee in a Moscow aircraft plant.

Kirilenko returned to party work in 1944 and three years later was named first secretary of the Nokolaev regional and city committees. In 1950 he succeeded Brezhnev as first secretary of the Dnepropetrovsk regional committee. That same year he became a deputy in the USSR Supreme Soviet. In 1955 he was transferred to the RSFSR, where he was made first secretary of the Sverdlovsk regional committee, one of the most important in the Russian Republic.

He became a full member of the Central Committee in 1956 and the following year was named a candidate member of the Presidium (renamed Politburo after 1966).

Kirilenko mysteriously lost his candidate status on the Presidium in 1961, but Khrushchev reinstated him as a full member in 1962. Kirilenko was also appointed first deputy chairman of the Bureau of the RSFSR, a position he held until 18 months after Brezhnev came to power. Then, in 1966, he became secretary of the Central Committee with responsibility for party work.

Analysis. Kirilenko proved himself to be an effective administrator. His organization and political mobilization of the masses in the Ukraine contributed to the rebuilding of the Ukrainian economy, especially the agricultural sector, after World War II.

He has been described as a prototype political follower, first under Khrushchev and then under Brezhnev. Kirilenko established close personal ties with Brezhnev when they served together on the Southern Front during the war. Their relationship grew several years later, when Brezhnev served as first secretary of the Zaporozhe regional committee while Kirilenko was second secretary. As noted, Kirilenko succeeded Brezhnev in Dnepropetrovsk.

Besides being a full member of the Politburo from 1962 to 1982, Kirilenko also had a position within the Secretariat that placed him strategically in charge of day-to-day party affairs. Until the late 1970s he was generally regarded as the highest-ranking party official after Brezhnev. However, Kirilenko's poor health and an apparent political falling out with Brezhnev destroyed his chances to succeed the general secretary.

Tikhon Kiselev (1917-83)

Until his death January 12, 1983, Tikhon Yakovlevich Kiselev was the only Belorussian on the Politburo. A candidate member since 1980, he also headed the Belorussian Communist Party.

Kiselev was born August 12, 1917. A teacher by profession, he became the chief of the Propaganda and Agitation Schools Supervision Department in Belorussia in 1948, eventually graduating to chief of the entire propaganda department. In 1952 he began moving up through the Belorussian party hierarchy. He served as chairman of the Belorussian Council of Ministers between 1959 and 1978 and as deputy chairman of the USSR Council of Ministers from 1978 until he was named first secretary of the Belorussian party organization in 1980.

Kiselev was considered an able administrator but little was known in the West about his areas of expertise.

Aleksei Kosygin (1904-80)

Aleksei Nikolaevich Kosygin was appointed premier when Khrushchev was ousted in October 1964. Initially he was a coequal with Brezhnev in the collective post-Khrushchev leadership. But by the time Kosygin resigned as premier 16 years later, he had lost much of his authority to party leader Brezhnev.

Kosygin was born February 20, 1904, in St. Petersburg (renamed Petrograd in 1914 and Leningrad in 1924). His father was a lathe operator.

In 1919, at the age of 15, Kosygin volunteered for service in the Red Army and fought in the Civil War until 1921, when he entered a training school for personnel of consumers' cooperatives. Following his graduation from the Leningrad Cooperative Technicum in 1924, he was sent to Siberia to help integrate that region's widespread cooperative movement into the national economy.

Kosygin returned home in 1929 to begin his studies at the Leningrad (later Kirov) Textile Institute. After graduating in 1935 as a textile engineer, he went to work first as a foreman and later as a shop superintendent at the Zhelyabov factory in Leningrad. He served as director of the Oktyabr spinning mill in Leningrad from 1937 to 1938.

Public Career. Kosygin, who previously had been a member of the Komsomol, joined the Communist Party in 1927 when he was in Siberia. During the mid-1930s he was active in party affairs and served on the executive committee of the Vyborg borough party organization. Although he avoided the intraparty conflicts that led to the Leningrad purges, Kosygin benefited from them. Andrei A. Zhdanov, a Stalin favorite who carried out the party purges in Leningrad, brought Kosygin into the depleted ranks of the party hierarchy in 1938. Kosygin went to work for the party full time as the head of the industrial transportation department of the Leningrad regional party committee. Later that year he became chairman of the executive committee of the Leningrad city soviet — in effect, the mayor of Leningrad. He also became a deputy of the USSR Supreme Soviet in 1938.

In 1939 Kosygin became a member of the Central Committee and received his first national government position, that of people's commissar for light industry. From there, he moved up in 1940 to the post of deputy chairman of the Council of People's Commissars (later renamed Council of Ministers), or deputy prime minister. He remained in that position until 1953. From 1943 to 1946 Kosygin also was chairman of the Council of People's Commissars of the Russian Soviet Federated Socialist Republic.

In the early months of World War II Kosygin played an important role in increasing production in the Soviet defense industry. He also was in charge of the evacuation of some 500,000 people from Leningrad in January 1942. After the war he helped to rebuild the Soviet economy in his capacity as the USSR minister of finance, a position he held during most of 1948. He then became the minister of light industry for the remainder of the Stalin period.

He continued his climb up the party ladder as well. After being elected a candidate member of the Politburo in 1946, Kosygin was made a full member in 1948.

But Kosygin's fortunes soon changed. In 1948 his mentor, Zhdanov, died and the following year Stalin began another round of executions and arrests, aimed primarily at the so-called "Leningrad gang," many of whom were Kosygin's former associates. Among the victims was Nikolai A. Voznesenskii, who had been another of Kosygin's sponsors.

Kosygin survived the purge but a shadow had been cast on his career. In 1952, when Stalin expanded the Politburo (which had been renamed the Presidium) from 10 to 25 members, Kosygin was demoted to candidate status. He was the only full member to lose his seat. He did, however, retain his government positions in the Council of Ministers and Ministry of Light Industry.

Following Stalin's death in March 1953, Kosygin lost both his candidate membership in the party Presidium and his government position as a deputy prime minister. He remained in the cabinet as minister of food and light industry (later narrowed down to the Ministry of Industrial Consumer Goods).

Late in 1953 Kosygin became a deputy prime minister once again and within a few months resigned from the consumer goods ministry to devote time to the USSR Council of Ministers. In 1956 he was named deputy chairman of Gosplan (the State Planning Committee) and was temporarily relieved of his post as a deputy prime minister.

In June 1957 Kosygin, as a member of the Central Committee, strongly supported Khrushchev in his confrontation with the so-called "antiparty" group, which was opposed to Khrushchev's economic decentralization plan. Khrushchev won out, and Kosygin was rewarded with candidate membership in the party Presidium once again and was reappointed a deputy prime minister.

In 1959 he was named chairman of Gosplan, thus becoming the country's chief economic planner with responsibility for the allocation of resources, production goals, and pricing. His enhanced position was reaffirmed in 1960 when he was elected a full member of the party Presidium and appointed one of two first deputy prime ministers. In this new position Kosygin traveled frequently in Europe, Asia, and Latin America. In July 1964 he became the sole first deputy prime minister, ranking only behind Khrushchev in the government.

On October 14, 1964, a special session of the Central Committee suddenly removed Khrushchev from power. Kosygin was named to replace him as chairman of the USSR Council of Ministers, or prime minister. Brezhnev assumed Khrushchev's position as first secretary of the Communist Party.

According to the collective leadership scheme, Kosygin was to take care of government affairs, including economic matters and foreign relations, while Brezhnev was to handle party affairs and Soviet relations within the international communist movement. Nikolai V. Podgornyi was moved into the ceremonial position of chief of state.

The division of labor seemed to work at first. While Brezhnev was busy consolidating his power within the party, Kosygin tackled the Soviet Union's economic problems.

In September 1965 he unveiled what was considered a bold economic reform plan that proposed to make profits an index of economic efficiency rather than relying solely on sheer volume of output. He wanted to increase the autonomy of factory managers, who at that time were receiving detailed instructions from Moscow on how to run their businesses.

Kosygin fought hard for his plan against what he called the "conservative" Soviet officials' inability to grasp the spirit of his proposal. But by the late 1960s it was obvious that he had been unable to overcome the opposition of members of the party hierarchy and the central ministries that would have lost power to the local managers.

Kosygin also traveled abroad frequently. He was visiting Hanoi in early 1965 when U.S. President Lyndon B. Johnson ordered bombing raids on North Vietnam. This — and the entire U.S. policy in Southeast Asia — outraged Kosygin and blocked steps toward improved U.S.-Soviet relations for several years. But in 1967, during a visit to the United Nations, Kosygin met with Johnson in Glassboro, New Jersey. Although nothing substantive was resolved, the face-to-face meeting of the two leaders was considered significant.

Kosygin was actively involved in efforts to stem the tide of liberalization in Czechoslovakia in 1968. He favored negotiating and applying economic pressure to bring the Prague government back into line.

Balancing Kosygin's moderate approach was the Soviet military, which favored armed intervention. Brezhnev, who was thought to have been in the middle, playing the role of mediator between the two positions, ultimately sided with the military. The Soviet decision-making process during the Czech crisis was instructive in that it showed the growing dominance of Brezhnev over Kosygin.

By the early 1970s there was no question as to who was running the Soviet Union. Brezhnev met with foreign leaders and conducted high-level summitry. Eventually he came to dominate the economic arena as well.

Kosygin's failing health further accelerated his loss of authority. After he suffered a heart attack in 1976, many of his duties were taken over by Nikolai A. Tikhonov, an ally of Brezhnev who had been named a first deputy prime minister. Kosygin had another heart attack in 1979 and on October 23, 1980, he resigned as prime minister and gave up his seat in the Politburo. In announcing the resignation, Brezhnev offered no praise of Kosygin and his public career of more than 40 years.

Kosygin died December 18, 1980. His life and career were praised lavishly in the official obituary.

Analysis. Kosygin had two traits that probably accounted for much of his success in Soviet politics: He was a top-notch administrator, and he seemed to have no aspirations to the top leadership position. He was extremely competent and posed little threat to incumbent political leaders.

These characteristics may explain, in part, Brezhnev's dominance of his one-time coequal. While Brezhnev consolidated his power, Kosygin was preoccupied with the troubled Soviet economy. He was said to have regarded revitalizing the economy as the major challenge of his career in management. It was a challenge he was unable to meet. Entrenched interests thwarted his pragmatic efforts at reform. At the time of his death, serious problems persisted in Soviet industry and agriculture.

Vasilii Kuznetsov (1901-   )

An expert on China, the United States, and trade unions, Vasilii Vasilievich Kuznetsov served as a candidate member of the Politburo and first deputy chairman of the Presidium, or vice president, from 1977 until March 1986, when, at the age of 85, he was forced to retire as the result of General Secretary Gorbachev's campaign to reinvigorate the Kremlin leadership.

Born February 13, 1901, in Sofilovka near Gorkii, Kuznetsov graduated from Leningrad Polytechnical Institute in 1926 as an engineer. From 1931 until 1933 he was an exchange student in the United States, where he also worked in several steel and automobile plants, including a Ford Motor Company plant near Detroit. He received a master of arts degree in metallurgical sciences in 1933 from Carnegie Institute of Technology in Pittsburgh.

During World War II Kuznetsov served as deputy member for metallurgical questions on the State Committee of Defense. In 1944 he was named chairman of the All-Union Central Council of Trade Unions, a post he held until 1953. During most of that period he served on the World Federation of Trade Unions as a member of the executive committee and general council and later as vice president.

The death of Stalin in 1953 ended Kuznetsov's brief tenure as a full member of the Politburo. His public career then shifted to foreign affairs. He became ambassador to the People's Republic of China in 1953 and is credited with developing plans for China's industrialization. The same year he was made deputy minister of foreign affairs. In 1955 he was promoted to first deputy minister of foreign affairs, a post he held until he was named first deputy chairman of the Presidium in 1977.

Kuznetsov appears to have been somewhat of a trouble-shooter. He was involved in the Cuban missile crisis negotiations of 1962, and he put the Soviet program in place in Czechoslovakia after the 1968 invasion.

Lenin (1870-1924)

Vladimir Ilich Ulyanov was born in the Volga region of Russia on April 22, 1870. Later in life he would adopt a pseudonym, Lenin, to protect himself from tsarist police

persecution. It is by this name that he is known as one of the leading historical figures of the twentieth century. A brilliant theoretician and capable administrator, Lenin was the major force that brought the Russian Revolution of 1917 to fruition.

The family of Vladimir Ilich enjoyed relatively high social status. His father was educational administrator for the entire region of Simbirsk (now Ulyanovsk; the name of the region was changed in 1924 in honor of its most famous son). The first radical in the Ulyanov family was Vladimir's older brother Alexander, who as a student became involved with a populist revolutionary plot to assassinate Tsar Alexander III. He was arrested and executed when Vladimir was 17.

Lenin attended the University of Kazan in 1887 in the juridical program, but soon was expelled for participating in a student demonstration. While temporarily out of school, he spent his time reading radical literature, educating himself, and developing his political views. Increasingly drawn toward Marxism instead of the populist teaching his brother had adopted, Lenin particularly was impressed by two radical tracts: Karl Marx's *Das Kapital* and Georgii V. Plekhanov's *Our Disagreements*. After several years he was readmitted to the university, where he completed studies for a law degree.

In the 1890s Lenin began working for the socialist movement in St. Petersburg. He traveled abroad in 1895 to meet the exiled leaders of Russian socialism, including Plekhanov. At the end of the year Lenin returned to Russia and was arrested for his work on an underground newspaper. Sent to Siberia, he continued writing, maintaining contact with revolutionary circles. He married Nadezhda Krupskaya, another revolutionary, who joined Lenin in Siberia.

Public Career. While Lenin was in exile, the Russian Social Democratic Labor Party (RSDLP) had been formed in 1898 at an illegal congress in Minsk. Lenin approved this development but remained concerned that intraparty groups were deviating from "the true path" of socialism as he perceived it. His ideas were set out in his pamphlet "What Is to Be Done?" published in 1902. Lenin favored a tightly knit, disciplined cadre of full-time revolutionaries who would lead the workers to overthrow the tsarist regime. To support these professionals, Lenin proposed a united and highly centralized party.

By 1900 Lenin had established himself as a leader among the Social Democrats. A target of tsarist police persecution, he fled to Europe where he founded a revolutionary journal *Iskra* (The Spark), with Plekhanov and other prominent revolutionaries. *Iskra*, secretly distributed throughout Russia, became the guiding force of the revolutionary movement for the next several years. Around this time, Lenin dropped his real name, Ulyanov, and began signing articles with his pseudonym.

At the 1903 Congress of the RSDLP, debate over revolutionary methods split the party into two factions. The group that won a slim majority on a vote concerning the composition of the editorial board of *Iskra*, the Bolsheviks (or "majoritarians"), rallied around Lenin's leadership and his avowal of armed insurrection. The Mensheviks (or "minoritarians") included Plekhanov and Leon Trotsky. The Mensheviks, however, regained control of the journal, and Lenin resigned from the editorial board. After the party split, Lenin turned his attention toward underground activity abroad and in Russia. The short-lived 1905 revolution provided no opportunities to seize power and, after a brief stay in Russia, Lenin was forced to immigrate to Europe a second time.

Following the establishment of the Provisional Government in 1917, Lenin secretly returned to Russia in a sealed train provided by the German government. After a tumultuous welcome at Finland Station in Petrograd, Lenin delivered two electrifying speeches before a joint session of Bolsheviks, Mensheviks, and socialists. These speeches, known as the April Theses, represented a call for revolution. In them Lenin inveighed against collaboration with the Provisional Government and support of the war effort.

Instead, he advocated "all power to the soviets," that is, transfer of government authority to the disjointed workers' councils organized in Petrograd, Moscow, and other

Russian cities. Lenin accompanied "all power to the soviets" with another radical proposal, "all land to the peasants." The theses shocked friends and adversaries alike, particularly because they seemed to repudiate the accepted Marxist dogma of revolutionary progression, a step-by-step process that ends with the conferring of power on the workers after the collapse of a highly developed capitalist system. However, his key slogan, "all power to the soviets," indicated that Lenin foresaw the workers' potential as catalysts for revolution.

The year 1917 continued in a confusing pattern of unrest and uprisings, and most of the Bolshevik leaders were forced to flee Petrograd in July. While Lenin was once more away from Russia, he completed "State and Revolution," a pamphlet he had drafted earlier in Europe. Unusually lengthy, it was considered a treatise on anarchy. (Two years after its publication, Lenin, struggling to impose order on the revolutionary society, would criticize his proanarchy comrades.) From Finland Lenin attempted to spur the Bolsheviks into action, while most of the work on the scene was done by Trotsky, who prepared the Bolsheviks for the armed takeover. Lenin returned to Petrograd October 20, just a few weeks before the Bolshevik Revolution in November.

As head of the nascent government with the title of "chairman of the Council of the People's Commissars," Lenin quickly consolidated the Bolsheviks' tenuous control. On the domestic front, civil war broke out between the Bolsheviks and opposition groups. In an attempt to keep industry operative, Lenin imposed "War Communism," a program that centralized the economy and abolished markets, exchange, and money. On the international level, Lenin agreed to a peace with Germany. The March 1918 treaty at Brest-Litovsk was concluded over protests from members of his own government.

Lenin was forced to retreat from his harsh economic policies in 1921. He reinstituted a degree of free enterprise under the "New Economic Policy."

In his early fifties, Lenin began working at a much slower pace. Heart disease and the effects of wounds he suffered in an assassination attempt in 1918 began taking their toll. He suffered a stroke in mid-1922, and his health gradually deteriorated until his death January 21, 1924, in Gorkii.

Analysis. Lenin was not only an administrative and organizational genius, he was a first-rate theoretician. One of his great contributions to the history of political thought was his ability to adapt Marxist theory to conditions in early twentieth-century Russia. Like Marx, Lenin took as his goal the overthrow of capitalism and the establishment of socialism. Unlike Marx, he did not consider it necessary for capitalism to develop before a revolution took place. Another departure from Marxist theory was Lenin's reliance on a professional cadre of revolutionaries to lead the workers into action. Marx envisioned rule by the entire mass of the worker population, but in Lenin's view the Russian proletariat was not ready for such a responsibility. Lenin sought to use any and all means available in his quest for power. He formed an alliance with the peasantry and appealed to Russian nationalism (an expedient departure from socialist internationalism) to rally support for his regime. Despite Lenin's unrivaled position as Soviet leader he was unable to engineer his own succession. In 1923 he advocated Stalin's removal as general secretary, but Lenin's failing health and the lack of a clear successor led to a leadership struggle that brought Stalin to power.

Maksim Litvinov (1876-1951)

A Soviet diplomat well known in the West, Maksim Maksimovich Litvinov served as commissar of foreign affairs from 1930 to 1939 and ambassador to the United States from 1941 to 1943.

Born in Bialystok, Poland, on July 17, 1876, Litvinov (real name, Meir Walach) was attracted to Marxism while a young soldier in the army. His activities in the Kiev Russian Social Democratic Labor Party led to his first arrest in 1901. Litvinov wrote for the revolutionary journal *Iskra* (The Spark) while in jail and continued to work for the journal after he escaped in 1902. Litvinov was forced to emigrate in 1902. He went to Great Britain, where he gained a reputation as a close confidant of Lenin and as a trusted party technician.

After the Bolshevik victory in November 1917, Litvinov was called into service in London as the diplomatic representative of the new government. Arrested by British authorities in October 1918 for allegedly taking part in propaganda activities, he was returned to Russia in exchange for several Britons residing there.

In 1921 Litvinov was appointed deputy commissar of foreign affairs under Georgii V. Chicherin and became a familiar fixture at various European conferences. In 1930 he replaced Chicherin as commissar of foreign affairs.

Litvinov's foreign policies stressed good relations with the West and virulent opposition to fascism. He supported both the entry of the Soviet Union into the League of Nations in 1932 and the establishment of diplomatic relations with the United States the following year.

When Stalin decided to collaborate with Adolf Hitler in 1939, he replaced Litvinov, a Jew opposed to Nazism, with Viacheslav M. Molotov, who concluded a nonaggression pact with Germany. Following the German invasion of the Soviet Union in 1941, Litvinov was appointed ambassador to the United States, a post he held until 1943. Litvinov remained deputy commissar for foreign affairs until his retirement in 1946. He died in Moscow on December 31, 1951.

Litvinov's grandson, Pavel, became a well-known dissident who was arrested in August 1968 for demonstrating against the Soviet government. Expelled from the USSR in March 1974, he took up residence in the United States.

Georgii Malenkov (1902-   )

Georgii Maksimilianovich Malenkov, a member of the ruling "inner circle," succeeded Stalin as premier in 1953, but soon lost the title and his authority in a power struggle with Khrushchev.

Born in Orenburg, Russia, on January 8, 1902, Malenkov was a student during the Bolshevik Revolution of 1917. He joined the Communist Party in 1920 and immediately became an active member. His diligence earned him a place on the Central Committee, where he began his association with Stalin. In 1932 Malenkov became the head of Stalin's personal secretariat. He was one of the main organizers of the purge of Stalin's opposition in the 1930s.

After World War II Malenkov was granted full membership on the Politburo and served as second secretary of the Central Committee and deputy prime minister. In light of his close association with Stalin and official position as second most powerful party member, Malenkov seemed a likely successor to Stalin. His position as heir apparent was reinforced in 1952 when Stalin requested that Malenkov deliver the general report in his place at the 19th Party Congress.

Following Stalin's death in 1953, Malenkov was for a short time both party first secretary and prime minister. He tried to change the course of Soviet foreign and domestic policy, promoting East-West coexistence in the nuclear age and supporting production of consumer goods over traditional reliance on heavy industry. Malenkov also was instrumental in rehabilitating citizens Stalin had accused of crimes.

Malenkov was challenged for supremacy by Khrushchev, who used his power base in the party to force Malenkov to resign as prime minister in 1955. His final defeat came two years later, when Khrushchev attacked Malenkov and other opponents, dubbed the "antiparty group," who had conspired to unseat him. Malenkov was accused of participation in the crimes of Stalin's regime, as well as inept leadership during World War II. He subsequently was expelled from the Central Committee and demoted to the directorship of a power plant in Kazakhstan. Ironically, Khrushchev adopted many policies Malenkov had proposed. In 1964 it was announced that Malenkov was no longer a party member.

Viacheslav Molotov (1890-   )

On July 5, 1984, the Soviet Foreign Ministry announced that former Stalin aide Viacheslav Mikhailovich Molotov had been reinstated in the Communist Party in honor of his 94th birthday March 9, 1984. Molotov became a familiar global figure during World War II as Soviet foreign minister, a post he held from 1939 to 1949 and from 1953 to 1956. He represented the Soviet Union at the wartime conferences and was a vocal proponent of hardline policies toward the West following the war.

Born on March 9, 1890, in the Vyatka Province in Russia, Molotov (real name Skryabin) exhibited an early interest in Bolshevism. He worked in revolutionary organizations as a student and was arrested and sent to prison in 1909. When his exile ended in 1911, Molotov sharpened his propaganda skills in St. Petersburg, where he edited and wrote for *Pravda*. Molotov's role in the 1917 revolution was not crucial, although he was by that time a prominent Bolshevik figure and a senior party organizer.

Molotov became a member of the Central Committee in 1921. He was an early supporter of Stalin (since 1913) and, as Stalin consolidated his power after Lenin's death, Molotov reaped the benefits of their association.

He was appointed to full membership in the Politburo in 1925 and replaced Nikolai I. Bukharin as head of the Comintern in 1929. Molotov's pseudonym means "hammer," which befitted his responsibilities as Stalin's strongman in the 1920s. He worked to strengthen Stalin's position against his opponents, including the Menshevik and Zinovievik factions. By the early 1930s Molotov was one of Stalin's closest associates.

Stalin replaced foreign affairs commissar Maksim M. Litvinov with Molotov in March 1939, a maneuver designed to facilitate closer relations with Adolf Hitler's Germany. Molotov negotiated with the Germans on the Nazi-Soviet Non-Aggression Pact signed in August of 1939. As Stalin's foreign representative, Molotov undertook many other diplomatic missions during and after World War II.

In 1949 Stalin broke up the ranks of his former collaborators in the Foreign Ministry. Molotov seemed on the verge of liquidation, but he survived and after Stalin's death opposed Khrushchev's bid for power. Out-maneuvered and accused of membership in what Khrushchev called the "antiparty group," Molotov was demoted to the obscure post of ambassador to Mongolia. In 1961 Khrushchev disclosed Molotov's alleged complicity in Stalinist-era crimes, and he was expelled from the Communist Party.

Arvid Pel'she (1899-1983)

Born February 7, 1899, Arvid Yanovich Pel'she was the oldest Bolshevik on the Politburo until his death May 29, 1983. A Latvian, Pel'she left Riga in 1915 to escape the tsar's police. He worked as an agitator in northwestern Russian cities for the next three years. In 1919 he returned to Latvia, where he participated in an unsuccessful effort to install Soviet power.

Pel'she then held a series of party jobs in the Soviet Union, largely in the field of agriculture. During this period he organized the Kazakhstan collectivization program, which was marked by violence.

When the Soviets took over Latvia in 1940, Pel'she returned, becoming the Latvian Central Committee's secretary for ideological questions, a post he held until 1958. In 1959 Pel'she was promoted to head the Latvian Communist Party. He joined the Politburo in 1966 and at the same time was made chairman of the Party Control Committee, which served as a court of appeal for those stripped of their party credentials.

Pel'she was a brother-in-law to Mikhail Suslov. The two men attended the Moscow Institute of Red Professors in 1931 and were involved in the takeover of Latvia in 1940. Suslov was instrumental in Pel'she's rise through the party.

Nikolai Podgornyi (1903-83)

Nikolai Viktorovich Podgornyi's lengthy political career ended March 4, 1979, when he was excluded from the newly elected Supreme Soviet. But his real demotion had occurred two years earlier when he was forced to retire as president and ousted from the Politburo and Central Committee. Podgornyi had been a deputy of the 1,500-member Supreme Soviet since 1954, a member of the Central Committee since 1956, and chairman of the Supreme Soviet (the ceremonial head of state) since 1965.

Born February 18, 1903, into the family of a foundry worker in the Ukraine village of Karlovka, Podgornyi had a successful career as an engineer in sugar-beet refineries before he began his rise in the Communist Party, which he joined when he was 27. He died January 12, 1983.

Public Career. Podgornyi's skill in engineering and administration led to his appointment in 1939 as deputy people's commissar of the food industry of the Ukrainian Soviet Socialist Republic. During this time, he met Khrushchev, who was then chairman of the Ukrainian Communist Party. He was to become a Khrushchev protégé.

After serving as head of the Moscow Technological Institute of Food Industry during World War II, Podgornyi returned to his post in the Ukraine. In 1946 Khrushchev appointed him permanent representative of the Ukraine at the Soviet Council of Ministers. During the four years he held that position, Podgornyi undertook the first of many travels abroad that made him a leading Soviet foreign policy expert.

In 1950 he began his rise in the Communist Party apparatus, serving until 1953 as first secretary of the Kharkov Oblast party committee. Between 1953 and 1957 he held a number of posts in the Ukrainian Communist Party and then was appointed first secretary, a position he held until 1963. During this time, Podgornyi attained national prominence. In 1954 he was elected a deputy to the Supreme Soviet; in 1956 he was personally nominated by Khrushchev to become a member of the Central Committee; and in May 1960 he became a member of the Presidium (later renamed Politburo). Three years later, he was appointed a member of the Central Committee Secretariat.

With the ouster of Khrushchev in 1964 and the advent of Leonid Brezhnev as first secretary and Aleksei Kosygin as premier, Podgornyi was widely regarded as the third-ranking leader in the Kremlin. He assumed principal responsibility for party organization and effected major reforms.

When Anastas Mikoian resigned as chairman of the Presidium of the Supreme Soviet (president) in December 1965, Brezhnev nominated Podgornyi to the post. In that capacity he proclaimed all laws and decrees, represented the Soviet Union on official missions abroad, and received foreign dignitaries. Although the post was largely ceremonial, Podgornyi continued to hold powerful party positions.

Podgornyi attended the 15th session of the United Nations General Assembly in 1960, visited Romania in 1963 to outline plans for Eastern Europe economic integration, and made trips to Cuba and France in 1964 and to Turkey and Hungary the following year. Shortly before his ouster from the Politburo in 1977, he undertook an important visit to southern Africa. He was the first top Kremlin official to visit the region. The result of the trip was the signing of a military defense treaty with Mozambique.

Analysis. Podgornyi's ouster from the Politburo in 1977 surprised outside analysts. Podgornyi's age (74) and health may have been factors, but it is also possible Brezhnev wanted to consolidate his power and assume the official title of head of state himself (Brezhnev and Podgornyi had long been rivals). The removal of Podgornyi would clear the way for a revamping of the party hierarchy and adoption of a new constitution, which was approved later in 1977. Observers also pointed to policy differences between the two and Podgornyi's criticisms of the new constitution promoted by Brezhnev.

Boris Ponomarev (1905-   )

Before his replacement as head of the Central Committee International Department in March 1986, Boris Nikolaevich Ponomarev was responsible for the Soviet Union's relations with nonruling communist parties and national liberation movements in the Third World. A key player in shaping Soviet foreign policy for a quarter of a century, Ponomarev became a secretary of the Central Committee in 1961 and a candidate member of the Politburo in 1972.

A Russian born January 17, 1905, to a white-collar family near Moscow, Ponomarev was a teacher of party ideology and held various positions in the International Department before becoming its head. Ponomarev was honored with full membership in the USSR Academy of Sciences in 1962. In 1960 he became chairman of the editorial board for the textbook *Istoriia KPSS* (The History of the Communist Party of the Soviet Union).

Ponomarev was considered an important Soviet leader on matters of ideology. He worked closely with senior party ideologist Mikhail Suslov, who died in 1982.

Sharaf Rashidov (1917-83)

A candidate member of the Politburo from 1961 until his death October 31, 1983, Sharaf Rashidovich Rashidov was head of the Uzbekistan Communist Party.

An Uzbek born November 6, 1917, to a peasant family, Rashidov had degrees as a teacher and philologist. He worked first as a teacher in a secondary school and then in 1937 went to work for the Samarkand provincial newspaper *Lenin yuly* (Lenin's Way). He became chief editor of the paper but left in 1941 to work as a political agitator in the Red Army. He returned to *Lenin yuly* as chief editor from 1943 to 1944, and in 1947 he became chief editor of the republic-wide newspaper, *Kzyl Uzbekistan*. In 1949 he also served as chairman of the Uzbek Union of Writers. In that same year he was named a full member of the Uzbekistan Central Committee and 10 years later he was elevated to head of the republic's party.

Rashidov was respected for his knowledge of Islamic and Afro-Asian cultures and languages. That knowledge, coupled with his high level of education and his writing abilities, apparently aided his rise in the party structure. He established Tashkent in Uzbekistan as a Soviet propaganda center for Afro-Asian countries and was apparently well regarded in noncommunist Asia.

In addition to his nonvoting membership on the Politburo, Rashidov was a deputy of the Supreme Soviet's Council of Nationalities and became a member of the Presidium of the Supreme Soviet in 1970. Rashidov was known as an opponent of nationalism within the Soviet republics.

Grigorii Romanov (1923-   )

When Soviet leader Konstantin Chernenko died March 11, 1985, only two men in the Kremlin were members of both the Politburo and the Secretariat of the Central Committee of the CPSU: Mikhail Gorbachev and Grigorii Vasilievich Romanov. Gorbachev was chosen as Chernenko's successor and on July 1, 1985, he ousted Romanov from both of his positions. The speed with which Gorbachev removed Romanov surprised some Western observers and may have indicated that Romanov had fallen into disfavor with other leaders besides the new general secretary.

Romanov had been a full member of the Politburo since 1976 and a secretary of the Central Committee since 1983. His political base had been Leningrad, where he was stationed during World War II and where he worked as a shipbuilding designer after the war.

Romanov was born February 7, 1923, near Novgorod. He began his party career as secretary of the party committee at the Zhdanov shipbuilding plant, working his way up through the Leningrad city and then the Leningrad regional party system. A strict interpreter of Marxist-Leninist doctrine, he became a full member of the Central Committee in 1966 and a candidate member of the Politburo in 1973.

Romanov was thought to be a protégé of Brezhnev, who reportedly helped Romanov become head of the Leningrad regional party organization by naming the existing head ambassador to China. Romanov left Leningrad for Moscow when he joined the Secretariat in 1983.

Several scandals and indiscretions apparently damaged Romanov's career. In November 1979 he borrowed a dinner setting that had belonged to Catherine the Great from Leningrad's Hermitage Museum to use at his daughter's wedding. The Soviet press reported that several of the dishes were broken and accused him of behaving more like a Romanov, the last imperial rulers, than a communist. More recently he was accused of straying into Finnish waters aboard his yacht; a popular singer was reportedly aboard.

Joseph Stalin (1879-1953)

Joseph Stalin, one of the most powerful and feared world leaders of the twentieth century, had a career that was as complex and mystifying as the personality of the man himself.

Born December 21, 1879, in Georgia, Stalin, unlike many revolutionary leaders, grew up in an impoverished and nonintellectual household. Georgia in the late 1890s was rife with nationalistic sentiment, a topic much discussed at the theological seminary at Tiflis, which Stalin entered in 1893 under his real name, Iosif Vissarionovich Dzhugashvili. While at the seminary Stalin became associated with Georgian nationalistic groups and began to study Marxism. His clandestine lectures on socialism resulted in his expulsion from the seminary in 1899.

Stalin was drawn into propaganda and mass agitation activity for the Russian Social Democratic Labor Party in Tiflis. His connection with the party led to his first arrest and deportation to Siberia in 1901. Prior to the 1917 Revolution, Stalin's life was typical of young revolutionaries of the time. Several times he was arrested and exiled to Siberia for his activities in Georgia, but he always managed to return. Inspired by Lenin's writings, he had become a firm Bolshevik by 1904. Stalin gained a reputation as an efficient organizer during the revolution of 1905.

Public Career. When the Bolsheviks formed their own party in 1912, Lenin sponsored Stalin's membership on the Central Committee. Stalin traveled to Europe as a representative to several radical conferences. Around this time he assumed the pseudonym he retained until the end of his life — Stalin, or the "man of steel." Stalin was arrested once more, in 1913, and remained in Siberia until the February revolution of 1917.

Only after the November Revolution did Stalin gain prominence. He was appointed commissar of nationalities (1917-23) and helped draft the Soviet constitutions of 1918 and 1923; he also served as commissar of the Workers' and Peasants' Inspectorate. As commissar of nationalities, Stalin, with Lenin, drafted "The Declaration of the Rights of the Peoples of Russia." Issac Deutscher wrote in *Stalin:* "The Declaration . . . was one of the documents intended to demonstrate to the world the principles of the revolution. 'The Council of People's Commissars,' it stated, 'has resolved to adopt . . . the following principles as the basis for its activity: 1. the equality and sovereignty of the peoples of Russia; 2. the right of the peoples of Russia to free self-determination, even to the point of separating and forming independent states; 3. the abolition of any and all national and national-religious privileges and disabilities; 4. the free development of national minorities and ethnographic groups inhabiting the territory of Russia.' "

During the civil war Stalin performed military duties, as did most of the Bolshevik leaders. His conduct during the war led to a bitter rivalry with Leon Trotsky, the commissar of war and organizer of the Red Army.

In April 1922 Stalin emerged as general secretary of the Communist Party. After Lenin's death in 1924, he and Trotsky vied for power. Although a brilliant orator and theoretician, Trotsky was no match for the triumvirate of Stalin, Grigori E. Zinoviev, and Lev B. Kamenev, who as the party leaders united against him. Stalin used anti-Trotsky propaganda to weaken his rival's support until he was able to remove Trotsky from his government positions in 1925 and expel him from the Soviet Union four years later. Stalin then turned on Zinoviev and Kamenev, who in 1926 had briefly thrown their support behind Trotsky. Until his power was secure, Stalin forged an alliance with the party's right wing, led by Nikolai I. Bukharin.

Stalin defeated Trotsky partly by winning support for his concept of "socialism in one country." Unlike Trotsky, who promoted world revolution as the Soviet state's first priority, Stalin advocated building Soviet socialism in isolation before spreading the revolution abroad.

His power unchallenged, Stalin next focused his attention on strengthening the USSR's economy and defenses. Under his leadership the Soviet peasantry was brutally collectivized and the Soviet economy was rapidly industrialized. The wealthier peasants (kulaks) who opposed collectivization of their lands were sent to Siberia or killed. As the industrialization campaign reached its peak in the mid-1930s, Stalin began a lengthy and ruthless process of eliminating his perceived enemies. During the "Great Purge," most of the old Bolshevik leaders (including Stalin's former allies Kamenev, Zinoviev, and Bukharin), as well as a large percentage of the military elite and thousands of innocent citizens, were brought to trial and executed. The purge ended in 1938.

The onset of World War II sorely tested the Soviet Union's strength. Stalin's 1939 nonaggression pact with Adolf Hitler kept the USSR out of the fighting for two years, but the German dictator turned against his ally in June 1941. Stalin, who made himself head of the government that year, joined forces with the United States and Britain to fight the Nazi threat.

Under Stalin's leadership the Soviet Union survived severe human losses and property devastation until the tide of the war turned with the Soviet victory at Stalingrad in 1943. Stalin proved to be a cunning bargainer during the wartime allied conferences at Tehran, Yalta, and Potsdam as evidenced by his ability to secure Soviet dominance of Eastern Europe. The establishment of communist regimes there after the war contributed to the growing of distrust and animosity between East and West.

By the end of the war, the "cult of Stalin" permeated every facet of life in the Soviet Union, making the dictator the established authority in government, politics, art, learning, and science. His wisdom and genius were unquestioned. There is evidence that Stalin was planning a second purge in the 1950s, but he died before it was implemented.

Stalin died of a cerebral hemorrhage on March 5, 1953. He was survived by his daughter, Svetlana Alliluyeva, who gained renown in the West when she defected in April 1967. She went back to the Soviet Union in 1984 but in 1986 she defected again and returned to the United States. Stalin's first wife, Ekaterina Svanidze, died around 1905, leaving a son, Yakov, who died in World War II after being taken prisoner by the Germans. Stalin's second wife, Nadezhda Alliluyeva, allegedly was driven to suicide in November 1932. She and Stalin had wed in 1918; they had two childen, Svetlana and a son, Vasili, an alleged alcoholic who, after a corrupt military career, died in 1962.

Analysis. A review of Stalin's career shows him to have been an organizer, a man of action, rather than a theoretician or original thinker. His writings include *Marxism and the National Colonial Question* (1912-13), *Problems of Leninism* (1926), and *Economic Problems of Socialism in the USSR* (1952).

Stalin viewed the industrialization and collectivization drives of the 1930s as absolutely necessary to transform the Soviet Union from a backward nation into a world power. Despite their brutality, Stalin's economic policies achieved his goal of strengthening the Soviet Union.

There is no doubt, however, that Stalin's main goal — and one largely fulfilled — was to gather supreme power for himself. His paranoid pursuit of absolute control left deep scars that have affected Soviet politics to the present day. Since Stalin's death, no Soviet leader has been allowed to become so powerful that he could safely disregard the interests and goals of his fellow leaders.

Mikhail Suslov (1902-82)

At the time of his death in January 1982, Mikhail Andreevich Suslov — a member of both the Politburo and Secretariat — was one of the most powerful Kremlin leaders after Leonid Brezhnev. The death of the party's chief ideologist left a major gap in the Kremlin's ruling elite.

Suslov came from a peasant background. He was born on November 21, 1902, in the village of Shakhovskoe on the Volga in present-day Ulyanovsk Oblast. As a teenager Suslov became politically active and joined the Poor Peasants' Committee, which had been organized by the Bolsheviks to protest tsarist repression and to provide food for the cities and the Red Army. He also became a member of the Komsomol.

In 1921 he joined the Communist Party and went to Moscow to study. Following his graduation from a workers' school in 1924, he studied at the Plekhanov Institute of National Economy until his graduation in 1928. He then attended the prestigious Economics Institute of Red Professors, a school sponsored by the Communist Party. From 1929 to 1931, while attending the institute, he taught at Moscow State University and the Stalin Academy of Industry. Among his students were Nikita Khrushchev and Nadezhda Alliluyeva, Stalin's second wife.

Public Career. In 1931 Suslov received his first responsible positions within the party. He was named to the party's Central Control Commission and to the People's Commissariat of the Workers' and Peasants' Inspection, a combined watchdog group used by Stalin to root out those suspected of having unorthodox views. In 1933-34 he was in charge of purges in the Ural and Chernigov regions.

From there Suslov moved on to hold various regional party posts. In 1937 he was sent to the Rostov region, where he served first as department chief and later as secretary of the regional party organization. In 1939 he became first secretary of the party in Stavropol Territory in the North Caucasus, a post he held until 1944. As chairman of the party's Bureau for Lithuania from 1944 to 1946, Suslov directed the purge in that republic.

From 1941 to 1945, during World War II, he also was a member of the military council on the North Caucasian

Front and chief of staff of the Stavropol Territory partisan forces. In the meantime his activities had not gone unnoticed in Moscow. From 1939 to 1941 he was a member of the Central Auditing Commission of the party and in 1941 he became a full member of the Central Committee.

In 1946 Suslov left his regional duties and returned to Moscow to join the national party apparatus. From 1946 to 1952 he was a member of the Central Committee's Organization Bureau. In 1947 he became a secretary of the Central Committee in charge of the Propaganda and Agitation Department, which was concerned with domestic ideological control.

However, he soon switched from domestic affairs to relations with other communist parties, an area that would remain his prime responsibility throughout his career. He helped to establish the Cominform in 1947 and was a representative of the Soviet Union at the Cominform meeting in June 1948 that expelled Yugoslavia from the organization. Suslov became chairman of the Cominform in August 1948, after the death of A. A. Zhdanov, and held that post until 1953. He was editor-in-chief of the newspaper *Pravda* in 1949-50 but lost his job as a secretary of the Central Committee.

In 1950 he became a member of the Presidium of the Supreme Soviet — his first high post in the government. He remained a member until 1954, the year he became chairman of the Supreme Soviet's Foreign Affairs Commission. In 1952 Suslov, with Stalin's backing, again became a secretary of the Central Committee and remained one until his death. That year he also was made a member of the party's Presidium (renamed Politburo in 1966).

Following Stalin's death in 1953, the Presidium membership was reduced from 25 to 10, and Suslov was one of those dropped. However, in 1955 Khrushchev had Suslov promoted to full membership in the Presidium once again. From then on, his rise in Soviet politics proceeded unimpeded.

Following the ouster of Khrushchev in 1964 — in which Suslov played a key role — Suslov was offered the position of party first secretary. He declined, suggesting that Brezhnev, as a pragmatist, would be more appropriate for the job. Suslov preferred, instead, the role of second secretary.

Analysis. Suslov was considered to be a firm and unyielding Stalinist. Yet, he helped Khrushchev defeat the "antiparty group" of old Bolsheviks in 1957 and aided the de-Stalinization campaign under Khrushchev. By 1964, however, the conservative Suslov thought the campaign had gone too far, and he conspired with other Soviet leaders to oust Khrushchev for "adventurism" at home and abroad. He backed Brezhnev to succeed Khrushchev and was known to have exercised considerable influence over Brezhnev's policies. He was labeled the *éminence grise* of the Brezhnev regime.

From the closing years of the Stalin era until he died January 25, 1982, Suslov was the Soviet Union's spokesman in the international communist movement. He reportedly played a key role in the Kremlin decisions to suppress the Hungarian revolt in 1956, to end the liberalization in Czechoslovakia in 1968 (although some sources indicated he argued against military intervention), and to push Polish authorities to take a harsher line against the independent trade union Solidarity in 1981. He was said to be an unyielding doctrinaire in the Soviet Union's quarrels with Yugoslavia and China.

Nikolai A. Tikhonov (1905-   )

Nikolai Aleksandrovich Tikhonov, a longtime ally of Leonid Brezhnev, became the prime minister of the Soviet Union in 1980 when Aleksei Kosygin resigned. In 1985, 80-year-old Tikhonov resigned for health reasons, and Soviet leader Mikhail Gorbachev named Nikolai Ryzhkov to succeed him. He was reelected, however, to the Central Committee at the 27th Party Congress in February 1986.

Tikhonov, a native Ukrainian, was born into a white-collar family in Kharkov May 14, 1905. He attended the Dnepropetrovsk Railroad Technicum and, after his graduation in 1924, spent a year as an assistant locomotive driver and a mine technician. He soon entered the Dnepropetrovsk Metallurgical Institute and graduated as a metallurgical engineer in 1930. From 1933 to 1947 Tikhonov held a variety of increasingly important industrial management positions.

Public Career. Tikhonov joined the Communist Party in 1940. Ten years later his engineering expertise led him to a position with the government's Ministry of Ferrous Metallurgy. After five years as chief of the main administration for the pipe-rolling and pipe-casting industries, Tikhonov in 1955 was named deputy minister of ferrous metallurgy.

His government career suffered a temporary setback in 1957 when Nikita Khrushchev, under an ill-fated decentralization plan, returned Tikhonov to Dnepropetrovsk to be chairman of an economic council. While there he became a deputy in the USSR Supreme Soviet and in the Ukrainian Supreme Soviet.

But in 1960 he was back in Moscow, this time as deputy chairman of the government's State Scientific and Economic Council. Three years later he became deputy chairman of the State Planning Committee (Gosplan).

Tikhonov was selected to be a deputy chairman of the USSR Council of Ministers — a deputy prime minister — in 1965 and a full member of the Communist Party's Central Committee the following year.

In 1966 Tikhonov was put in charge of coordinating economic relations with East Germany — the Soviet Union's most important economic partner. And in 1975 he became responsible for economic relations with West Germany, when he became vice chairman of the Soviet-West German economic commission.

After becoming a first deputy prime minister in 1976, Tikhonov took over many duties of Prime Minister Kosygin, who was recovering from a heart attack. In 1979, after Kosygin suffered another heart attack, Tikhonov became a full member of the Politburo and virtually ran the Soviet economy. In October 1980 he succeeded Kosygin as chairman of the USSR Council of Ministers, or prime minister, and served in that post until his resignation in 1985.

Analysis. The close personal friendship between Brezhnev and Tikhonov dated back to their days in the Dnepropetrovsk industrial heartland of the Ukraine. Brezhnev promoted Tikhonov to his inner circle, along with other members of what has been tagged the "Dnepropetrovsk mafia" such as Andrei Kirilenko and Konstantin Chernenko. It is possible that Brezhnev advanced Tikhonov to leadership positions within the government to counterbalance Kosygin. When Tikhonov resigned as prime minister in 1985, he was the highest-ranking appointee of Brezhnev in Gorbachev's government. The resignation surprised some observers because senior government posts traditionally have been lifetime appointments.

Leon Trotsky (1879-1940)

Leon Trotsky, one of the greatest theoreticians and orators of early Soviet history, played a significant role in the 1917 Russian revolution and later became Stalin's most important opponent.

Lev Davydovich Bronstein (Trotsky's given name) was born in the Ukraine on October 26, 1879, to a Jewish family. He studied briefly in Odessa and then moved to Nikolaev, where his involvement with workers' circles led to his arrest and deportation to Siberia. During his 1898-1902 jail term, Trotsky became acquainted with Marxism. He escaped from prison in 1902 and subsequently used Trotsky, the name of his jail warden, as a pseudonym. He traveled to Europe and collaborated with Lenin on the revolutionary journal *Iskra* (The Spark). When the Russian Social Democratic Labor Party split into Bolshevik and Menshevik factions in 1903, Trotsky sided with the Mensheviks and became an outspoken opponent of Lenin.

Around 1904 Trotsky developed his "theory of permanent revolution," which looked beyond a revolution in Russia to a worldwide workers' struggle that would overthrow capitalism. For Trotsky, the class struggle was an international phenomenon. He would remain loyal to this theory throughout his life.

Public Career. Active in mass agitation in the 1905 Russian revolution, Trotsky was forced to flee to Europe, where he attempted to unify the badly fractured Social Democratic Labor Party. He was expelled from France in 1916, spent a short time in the United States, and then returned to Russia in May 1917.

Back in Russia, Trotsky joined the Bolshevik Party. Although a late-comer to the party, he was a guiding force behind the events leading to the Bolsheviks' seizure of power in the November revolution. While Lenin was in Finland hiding from the Provisional Government, Trotsky organized the Military Revolutionary Committee, which led the armed insurrection in Petrograd.

After the Bolshevik victory, Trotsky was entrusted with several positions in the new government, notably the commissariats for foreign and military/naval affairs. He established and organized the Red Army and engineered the Bolshevik victory in the civil war, during which his conflict with Stalin developed. As Lenin approached death, Trotsky and Stalin emerged as rivals for leadership of the Communist Party. In the ensuing struggle, Stalin denounced Trotsky's "theory of permanent revolution" as un-Leninist and gathered support for his own doctrine of "socialism in one country." Trotsky was stripped of his government positions in 1925, removed from the Politburo in 1927, and expelled from the Soviet Union in 1929. He spent the remainder of his life in exile in various countries, continuing to oppose Stalin through his writing.

During Stalin's "Great Purge" of the 1930s, Trotsky was named as the main instigator of the counterrevolutionary crimes against the Stalin regime. He was convicted and sentenced to death in absentia.

On August 21, 1940, Trotsky died in Mexico City from wounds inflicted the day before by an assassin reportedly sent to Mexico on Stalin's orders. Trotsky was survived only by his second wife Natasha, who left the Soviet Union with him and their two children in 1929. It is believed that Stalin arranged the deaths of the children, in 1933 and 1938. Stalin already had ordered the execution of Trotsky's first wife and their two children in the Soviet Union.

Of Trotsky's extensive works, many written after his

exile from the Soviet Union, one of the best known is *The History of the Russian Revolution* (1932-33).

Analysis. Lenin called Leon Trotsky "personally perhaps the most capable" in the Central Committee, although he had doubts concerning Trotsky's "excessive liking for the administrative side of things." Trotsky had excellent organizational abilities and his skill for oratory was unmatched among his colleagues. However, he faced formidable obstacles because initially he was not a Bolshevik and also because he had numerous Politburo enemies. Trotsky's concern for his political theories and their relation to world government put him in a vulnerable position against his chief opponent, Stalin, who was not sidetracked from his goal of supreme power.

Dmitri Ustinov (1908-84)

A full member of the Politburo and the nation's defense minister until his death December 10, 1984, Dmitri Fedorovich Ustinov was one of the top administrators of the armaments industry most of his adult life. Born October 30, 1908, in Kubyshev in the Novosibirsk region, Ustinov served as a volunteer in the Red Army during 1922-23. In 1934 he graduated as a mechanical engineer from Leningrad Military Mechanical Institute and went to work as an engineer in Leningrad's Naval Artillery Research Institute. In 1938 he became the director of the Bolshevik Arms Factory in Leningrad.

Ustinov was named USSR People's Commissar of Armaments in 1941. He made a name for himself during World War II when he organized the evacuation of the Soviet arms industry behind the Ural Mountains to escape the invading German army. Ustinov served as minister of armaments until 1953 and as minister of defense industry until 1957. He was deputy chairman of the Council of Ministers from 1957 to 1963 and from 1963 to 1965 was chairman of the Supreme Economic Council. In 1965 Ustinov was named to the Central Committee Secretariat and became a candidate member of the Politburo.

Ustinov was considered an expert on issues of aviation technology and space and was known as an "arms tsar." He was widely regarded as being a leading figure in transforming the Soviet military into a modern fighting force, including having been one of the few party members responsible for ensuring Soviet success in missile production and in space.

Ustinov enjoyed the support of both party leader Leonid Brezhnev (with whom he had worked in the late 1950s) and Premier Aleksei Kosygin. Kosygin recommended Ustinov for defense minister in 1967, but Brezhnev's candidate, Andrei A. Grechko, was elected. When Grechko died in April 1976, Brezhnev turned to Ustinov, who had been promoted to full Politburo status the month before. The appointment of Ustinov, a civilian, may have been intended by Brezhnev to improve his own position in relation to the military.

Shortly after he was named defense minister, Ustinov was also appointed a marshal of the USSR. On his 75th birthday in 1983, Ustinov was awarded his 11th Order of Lenin.

Grigori Zinoviev (1883-1936)

Grigori Evseevich Zinoviev, one of the most prominent Bolsheviks during the Russian revolution, was born in the Ukraine in September 1883. Lacking any formal schooling, Zinoviev became involved with self-education circles, where he received his initial exposure to socialist theory. He joined the Russian Social Democratic Labor Party in 1901, and that same year fled to Europe to escape police persecution for his involvement in economic strikes. He met Lenin in 1903 in Switzerland and supported him when the Social Democrats split into Menshevik and Bolshevik factions later that year.

Zinoviev collaborated closely with Lenin in the years leading to the 1917 revolution. Their only major disagreement occurred over Lenin's commitment to the exclusive seizure of power in Russia by the Bolsheviks. After the revolution Zinoviev joined the five-man Politburo and headed the powerful Petrograd Soviet. From his base in Petrograd, Zinoviev, according to Adam B. Ulam in *The Bolsheviks,* established "his little political kingdom from which he would not be dislodged by Stalin until 1925."

After Lenin's death in 1924, Zinoviev emerged as one of the members of the ruling triumvirate with Lev B. Kamenev and Joseph Stalin. In the ensuing power struggle, Zinoviev and Kamenev briefly joined Leon Trotsky to oppose Stalin. After Stalin consolidated his power, Zinoviev denounced the Trotskyites, but it was too late; he lost his party membership and in 1935 was sentenced to 10 years in jail.

A year later Zinoviev and 15 others were tried in the first "show trial" of the Great Purge. He and Kamenev were convicted of a series of crimes, primarily related to allegedly treasonous and counterrevolutionary activities. Both men were executed immediately after their trial in late August 1936.

Major Events, 1900-63

Following is a chronological listing of major events in Russian and Soviet history from the beginning of the twentieth century through 1963. A more detailed chronology of pertinent domestic and foreign events from 1964 through January 1986 is provided in the next section, which begins on p. 229.

1900. Boxer Rebellion in China; Russian occupation of Manchuria.

1901. University students and workers begin using street demonstrations as a means of protest.

1902. Anglo-Japanese alliance; Vladimir I. Lenin publishes pamphlet, "What Is to Be Done?"

1903. July 30-August 23, Menshevik-Bolshevik split in Social Democratic Labor Party during Second Party Congress. (First Party Congress held March 13-15, 1898.)

1904. Anglo-French Entente Cordiale; February 8, Japan attacks Russian fleet at Port Arthur.

1905. January 22, "Bloody Sunday" — police fire at a large demonstration of workers in St. Petersburg, killing more than 100; April 25-May 10, Third Social Democratic Labor Party Congress; June, crew of battleship *Potemkin* mutinies; Russo-Japanese War is resolved at a peace conference in August in Portsmouth, New Hampshire; workers in St. Petersburg form the Soviet of Workers' Deputies; October Manifesto is issued by the tsar establishing the first *Duma*.

1906. April 23-May 8, Fourth Social Democratic Labor Party Congress; May 10, first Duma meets but is dissolved by Nicholas II July 21.

1907. January 1, Government cancels peasant redemption payments; March 5, second Duma meets but is dissolved June 16; May 13-June 1, Fifth Social Democratic Labor Party Congress; August 31, Russia signs territorial agreement with Britain concerning spheres of influence in Afghanistan (Britain), Persia (divided between Britain and Russia), and Tibet (neutral); emergence of Triple Entente alliance of France, Britain, and Russia opposed to the Triple Alliance of Germany, Austria-Hungary, and Italy; second Hague Peace Conference (first was arranged in 1899 by Nicholas II); November 1, third Duma meets, serves full five-year term.

1908. November, Leon Trotsky becomes editor of recently founded newspaper *Pravda* in Vienna.

1909. February, Duma passes law on inviolability of person.

1910. January, Russia and Japan reject U.S. proposal for "open door" policy in Manchuria.

1911. September 14, assassination of Russian prime minister Pëtr Stolypin; outbreak of Balkan wars.

1912. Fourth Duma elected, remains in session until March 1917.

1913. May 30, Treaty of London ends First Balkan War; Second Balkan War follows, June-August.

1914. June 28, Archduke Francis Ferdinand, heir to the Hapsburg throne, is assassinated; August, World War I begins.

1915. September, Lenin represents Bolsheviks at First International Socialist Conference and advocates transforming imperialist war into civil war.

1916. December 30, assassination of Grigori Rasputin.

1917. March 11, tsar dissolves Duma and orders suppression of demonstrations; March 15, the March revolution results in abdication of Tsar Nicholas II; United States is the first among the great powers to recognize the Provisional Government headed by Prince Georgi Lvov; Petrograd Soviet of Workers' and Soldiers' Deputies formed; April 16, Lenin arrives in Petrograd from Switzerland; May 17, Trotsky reaches Petrograd from United States; June 6-17, All-Russian Congress of Soviets meets; July 16-18, "July Days" mass demonstrations; July 20, Lvov resigns and Aleksandr Kerensky takes over as prime minister; July 26-August 3, Sixth Social Democratic Labor Party Congress; September 9-12, General Kornilov's counterrevolutionary plot fails; October 23, Bolshevik Central Committee advocates armed insurrection; November 7-8, Bolsheviks seize power; November 14, Kerensky's attempt to capture Petrograd fails.

1918. January 8, President Woodrow Wilson issues "Fourteen Points" for postwar settlement, which includes liberal treatment of Russia; March 3, Russia signs Treaty of Brest-Litovsk with Germany; March 6-8, Seventh Russian Communist Party Congress; March, Allied intervention in Russia begins; July 10, first Soviet Constitution is adopted, creating the Russian Soviet Federated Socialist Republic; July 16, tsar and his family are murdered; November 11, World War I ends, Soviets repudiate Treaty of Brest-Litovsk.

1919. March 2, Communist International (Comintern) is founded; March 18-23, Eighth Russian Communist Party Congress; June 28, Treaty of Versailles signed (rejected November 19 by the U.S. Senate); November-December, Red Army scores important victories over White armies.

1920. January, Allies lift coastal blockade of Soviet Union imposed in October 1919; March 29-April 5, Ninth Russian Communist Party Congress; April 25, Polish forces invade Ukraine; July 8, United States imposes trade embargo against Soviet Union, Allied intervention ends.

1921. March 17, Lenin initiates the New Economic Policy; March 8-16, 10th Russian Communist Party Congress; March 18, Treaty of Riga signed, giving Poland many of the lands it wanted and establishing the so-called Curzon Line.

1922. April 3, Joseph Stalin becomes general secretary of the Communist Party; April 16, Soviet Union signs Treaty of Rapallo with Germany; March 27-April 2, 11th Russian Communist Party Congress; May 26, Lenin suffers first of three paralytic strokes; December 24, Lenin writes "Testament" that evaluates his potential successors; December 30, the Union of Soviet Socialist Republics is declared.

1923. January 4, Lenin advocates, in a postscript to his "Testament," replacing Joseph Stalin as general secretary of the Communist Party; April 17-25, 12th Russian Communist Party Congress accepts Stalin's plan to reorganize the party; October 15, "Declaration of the Forty-Six" communist leaders, criticizing the ruling regime, is presented to Central Committee.

1924. January 21, Lenin dies and struggle for power between Stalin and Leon Trotsky intensifies; January 31, USSR Constitution is ratified; February 1, Great Britain recognizes USSR and within one year Italy, Norway, Austria, Sweden, Denmark, Mexico, France, and Japan also extend recognition; May 23-31, 13th Russian Communist Party Congress; November 6, Trotsky publishes *Lessons of October*, attacking Kamenev and Zinoviev; December, Stalin advances theory of "socialism in one country."

1925. May 12, revised Soviet Constitution ratified; December, 18-31, 14th All-Union Communist Party Congress.

1926. October, Trotsky and Kamenev are removed from Politburo, and Zinoviev loses his position in Comintern.

1927. April, USSR and Kuomintang break diplomatic relations; November, Trotsky and Zinoviev are stripped of their party memberships; December, Stalin and followers score decisive victory over Trotskyites, who are expelled from the party December 27 during 15th All-Union Communist Party Congress.

1928. August 27, United States, France, Germany, Britain, Italy, Belgium, Japan, Poland, and Czechoslovakia sign the Kellogg-Briand Peace Pact outlawing war; August 31, Soviet Union announces its support of the pact; October 1, first Five-Year Plan is introduced by Stalin (declared fulfilled December 31, 1932).

1929. January, Trotsky exiled; massive collectivization of peasants under way.

1930. March 2, Stalin's "Dizziness with Success" article blames local party officials for abuses of the initial drive toward collectivization; June 26-July 13, 16th All-Union Communist Party Congress.

1931. June, Stalin proposes a six-point program designed to spur industrialization.

1932. November 29, Soviets and French sign a nonaggression pact; December 31, Soviets declare First Five-Year Plan successfully completed.

1933. November 16, United States and Soviet Union establish diplomatic relations.

1934. January 26-February 10, 17th All-Union Communist Party Congress; September 18, Soviet Union joins the League of Nations; December 1, Sergei Kirov is murdered, setting off the Stalinist purges.

1935. May 2, Soviet-French mutual assistance treaty signed; July 14, Soviet Union and United States sign one-year reciprocal trade agreement.

1936. March 7, Hitler's armies occupy the Rhineland; July 18, Spanish Civil War begins, Soviet Union supports loyalists (war ends March 1939); August 19, first "show trial" opens, and Zinoviev and Kamenev are among the 16 defendants, all of whom are executed; November 17, Germany, Italy, and Japan sign Anti-Comintern Pact; December 5, new Soviet Constitution is adopted.

1937. January, second "show trial" is held, and 13 of 17 defendants are sentenced to death.

1938. March, third and final "show trial" is held, and 18 of 21 defendants, including Nikolai Bukharin, are sentenced to death; March 12, Germany annexes Austria; September, Great Britain and France agree to Germany's annexation of the Sudetenland at conference in Munich.

1939. March 10-21, 18th All-Union Communist Party Congress; August 23, Soviet Union and Nazi Germany conclude a nonaggression pact; September 1, Germany invades Poland, triggering World War II, Soviets subsequently invade Poland; November 1, Supreme Soviet admits Western Ukraine and Western Belorussia into USSR; November 30, Soviet Union invades Finland; December 14, League of Nations expels Soviet Union.

1940. March 12, Soviet-Finnish war ends, with Finland forced to cede territory; August 3-6, Lithuania, Latvia, and Estonia incorporated into the Soviet Union; August 21, Trotsky assassinated in Mexico City.

1941. April 13, Soviet-Japanese neutrality treaty, Germany, Italy, and Romania declare war on the Soviet Union; June 22, Germany invades the Soviet Union; December, first Soviet counteroffensive against the German invasion forces begins; December 7, Japanese attack Pearl Harbor.

1942. January 1, Soviet Union signs United Nations Declaration in Washington; June 11, United States and Soviet Union sign lend-lease agreement providing for reciprocal defense aid.

1943. February 2, battle of Stalingrad ends in defeat of the Germans; May 25, Comintern dissolved; November 28-December 1, U.S. president Franklin D. Roosevelt, British prime minister Winston Churchill, and Soviet premier Stalin meet in Tehran to discuss war and postwar problems.

1944. January 11, Roosevelt denies that "secret treaties or financial commitments" were made at Moscow, Cairo, or Tehran conferences; June 6, Normandy landing by U.S. and other Allies; July 22, conference at Bretton Woods, New Hampshire, closes with Soviet Union agreeing to subscribe $1.2 billion to the proposed International Bank for Reconstruction and Development; October 9, Churchill and Stalin meet, divide Europe hypothetically into "spheres of influence."

1945. February 4-11, Yalta conference of the Allies is held in the Crimea; April 12, Roosevelt dies, Harry S Truman becomes president; May 7, Germany surrenders; June 5, Allies announce assumption of joint control and occupation of Germany; June 25, United Nations charter is approved in San Francisco; August 2, British prime minister Clement Atlee, Stalin, and President Truman issue the

Potsdam Declaration; August 6, U.S. drops an atomic bomb on Hiroshima; August 8, Soviet Union declares war on Japan; August 9, U.S. drops atomic bomb on Nagasaki; August 21, U.S. lend-lease to the Soviet Union ends; September 2, Japan formally surrenders; December 27, Moscow conference of the United States, Britain, and the Soviet Union (the Big Three) ends.

1946. January 10, first session of the United Nations opens; January 19, Iran charges USSR before the UN with illegally occupying its Azerbaidzhan region; January 29, Secretary of State James F. Byrnes confirms existence of secret Roosevelt-Churchill promise at Yalta to give Sakhalin and the Kurile islands to the Soviet Union; March 5, Churchill delivers "Iron Curtain" speech at Fulton, Missouri; May, Soviet troops are withdrawn from Iran; October 27, communist government assumes power in Bulgaria.

1947. March 12, Truman asks for $400 million in funds to aid Greece and Turkey in combating communism (the Truman Doctrine); June 5, Secretary of State George C. Marshall outlines plan for European economic recovery (the Marshall Plan) at Harvard University commencement, but the Soviet Union refuses to participate; July, George Kennan publishes his article "by X" in *Foreign Affairs* outlining the strategy of containment; October 5, Cominform (the Communist Information Bureau, which succeeded the Comintern) is formed; breakdown in December of four-power conference on Germany in London.

1948. February 25, President Eduard Beneś of Czechoslovakia yields to a communist ultimatum to install a pro-Soviet cabinet and join the Soviet bloc; June, the Soviet Union begins the Berlin blockade; June 21, the United States and Britain begin air lift of supplies to Berlin (blockade lifted in May 1949); June 28, Yugoslavia is expelled from the Cominform; August 3, communist Arpad Szakasits becomes president of Hungary.

1949. January 25, Moscow announces formation of six-nation Council for Mutual Economic Assistance (CMEA); April 4, North Atlantic Treaty signed; May 23, constitution of the Federal Republic of Germany (West Germany) approved; September 21, communist leader Mao Zedong proclaims the People's Republic of China; September 23, Truman announces the Soviet Union has exploded an atomic bomb; October 7, German Democratic Republic (East Germany) established.

1950. February 14, Soviet Union and People's Republic of China sign treaty of alliance; June 25, North Korea invades South Korea; June 27, Truman orders U.S. forces under Gen. Douglas MacArthur to help repel North Korean invasion of South Korea; November 26, Chinese communist troops come to the aid of North Korea.

1951. July 10, Korean truce talks begin; November 23, Truman orders withdrawal of all U.S. tariff concessions to the Soviet Union and Poland.

1952. October 5-14, 19th Communist Party of the Soviet Union (CPSU) Congress; November, first U.S. hydrogen bomb is tested.

1953. January 13, disclosure of the arrest of nine Soviet doctors allegedly involved in the "Doctor's Plot"; March 5, Stalin dies and is succeeded by Georgi Malenkov as premier and first secretary of the CPSU; March 14, Malenkov resigns as first secretary and is succeeded by Nikita Khrushchev; April 14, exoneration of the seven surviving doctors accused in "Doctor's Plot"; June 15, Soviet Union and Yugoslavia reestablish diplomatic relations; June 17, East Berlin riots; June 26, chief of secret police Lavrentii Beria is arrested; July 27, Korean War ends;

August 8, Malenkov announces his proconsumer policy before Supreme Soviet; August 12, Soviet Union explodes a hydrogen bomb; December, Beria is tried and executed.

1954. March, Malenkov asserts that war between imperialism and capitalism would mean "the destruction of world civilization"; July 21, Vietnam is partitioned at Geneva conference; October 12, Soviet-Chinese economic and political agreement signed; October 23, West Germany is granted sovereignty and joins NATO.

1955. February 8, Malenkov resigns as prime minister and is replaced by Nikolai Bulganin; May 14, Warsaw Pact, counterpart to NATO, is established; May 15, Austrian state treaty is signed; July 18-23, Geneva summit conference, attended by the United States, Britain, France, and the Soviet Union; September 27, Egypt announces that it will buy arms from Moscow.

1956. February 14-25, 20th CPSU Congress, at which Khrushchev in his "Secret Speech" denounces Stalin and in an earlier speech advocates "peaceful coexistence" with the West; April 18, Cominform is dissolved; June, Tito visits Moscow; June 28-30, strikes in Poland lead to liberalization; July 26, Egypt nationalizes Suez Canal and subsequently Britain, France, and Israel attack Egypt; November 4, Soviet Union crushes Hungarian revolution.

1957. February, Andrei Gromyko becomes foreign minister succeeding Dmitri Shepilov; June, a coalition of Presidium members, including Malenkov, Viacheslav Molotov, and Lazar Kaganovich, demand Khrushchev's resignation, but Khrushchev counters by convening the Central Committee, which supports Khrushchev and removes the "antiparty" group from their government and party positions; August 26, Soviet Union announces successful testing of an intercontinental ballistic missile; October 4, Sputnik, the first space satellite, is launched by the Soviet Union; October 15, Soviet Union and China sign secret agreement pledging the Soviets to help the Chinese develop their own nuclear weapons; October, Khrushchev removes Marshal Georgii Zhukov from the Presidium and as defense minister.

1958. March 27, Khrushchev replaces Bulganin as prime minister and continues as first secretary; October-November, Quemoy-Matsu crisis; October 31, Geneva test-ban conference opens; November 10, Khrushchev sparks Berlin crisis by calling for withdrawal of Allied troops in West Berlin.

1959. January 1, Fidel Castro comes to power in Cuba; January 27-February 5, 21st CPSU Congress; June 20, Soviets rescind their nuclear weapons development agreement with China; July 24, the "kitchen debate" between Vice President Richard Nixon and Khrushchev takes place at a U.S. exhibition in Moscow; September 14, Soviet rocket hits the moon; September 15-27, Khrushchev visits the United States; October 4, December 1, Soviet spacecraft orbits the moon; the United States, the USSR, and 10 other countries sign Antarctica treaty.

1960. January, Khrushchev announces defense cuts; February, Anastas Mikoian visits Cuba to establish diplomatic relations and sign an aid agreement; May 1, Soviets shoot down a U.S. spy plane (a U-2) over the Soviet Union; May 4, Aleksei N. Kosygin becomes a deputy prime minister; May 7, Leonid I. Brezhnev becomes Soviet chief of state; May 17, Paris summit conference attended by President Dwight D. Eisenhower, Khrushchev, French president Charles de Gaulle, and British prime minister Harold Macmillan breaks up after Khrushchev demands apology for U-2 flight; August, Soviet Union withdraws technical experts from China; September 20-October 13, Khrushchev visits the United Nations.

1961. April 12, Soviet Union launches first manned space flight; April 17, U.S.-supported "Bay of Pigs" invasion of Cuba crushed by Castro; May 5, first U.S.-manned space flight; June 3-4, Khrushchev and President John F. Kennedy meet in Vienna but remain deadlocked on key issues; August 13, East Germany seals border between East and West Berlin and begins building Berlin Wall; September 1, Soviet Union resumes nuclear weapons testing, breaking unofficial moratorium; October 17-31, 22d CPSU Congress, which approves Khrushchev's party program; December 10, Soviet Union breaks relations with Albania.

1962. March 14, disarmament conference opens in Geneva, recesses December 24; October 20-November 21, Sino-Indian border war; October 22-November 2, Cuban missile crisis, which ends when Kennedy announces agreement by Moscow to dismantle Soviet missile bases; November, bifurcation of agricultural and industrial branches of Soviet party apparatus.

1963. February 12, Geneva disarmament conference resumes; June 10, President Kennedy's American University speech; June 20, U.S.-Soviet "hot line" established; July 21, talks in Moscow aimed at resolving Sino-Soviet ideological conflict end in failure; July 25, the United States, the Soviet Union, and Britain sign nuclear test-ban treaty (Beijing denounces the treaty); October 9, Kennedy approves sale of wheat to the Soviet Union; November 22, Kennedy assassinated, Lyndon B. Johnson becomes U.S. president.

Chronology of Events, 1964-86

1964

January 2. *USSR Peace Message.* The Soviet Union sends a message of diplomacy to all countries with which it has relations, calling for the renunciation of war as a method of "settling diplomatic disputes." The plan calls for the United States to remove its military forces from Germany, Korea, Vietnam, and China. The Johnson administration terms the communiqué "disappointing."

January 23. *Castro Sides With USSR.* Cuban premier Fidel Castro winds up a visit to the Soviet Union and declares his support for the USSR in its ideological dispute with China.

January 29. *Two U.S. Planes Downed.* A U.S. training plane is shot down over East German airspace by a Soviet aircraft. The Soviet government disavows responsibility for the incident January 31. Both the United States and the Soviet Union attempted to warn the plane during the event, in which three U.S. officers lost their lives. A similar incident occurs March 10 when an unarmed U.S. reconnaissance jet is downed over East Germany and its crew held. Secretary of State Dean Rusk disclaims Soviet accusations of espionage, and the three airmen are released March 27.

February 14. *Khrushchev on Communist Unity.* Premier Nikita S. Khrushchev tells a plenary meeting of the Soviet Communist Party's Central Committee that the USSR is attempting to restore "the monolithic unity of the world socialist system."

March 24. *Soviet Aid to Yemen.* The Soviet Union announces the signing of a five-year treaty of friendship with Yemen and discloses promises of increased economic aid.

April 1. *Khrushchev on the Chinese.* Khrushchev speaks in Budapest, Hungary, blasting the Chinese leadership. On April 3 he calls China's leaders a "great danger"; two days later, while touring Hungary, he says they are "crazy" to try to develop China economically without outside aid.

April 20. *Joint Statement on Nuclear Cooperation.* American president Johnson and Soviet premier Khrushchev declare joint intentions to reduce production of material used in nuclear weapons. The United States will cut back enriched uranium production, and the Soviet Union, among other measures, will not build several reactors for plutonium production.

May 1. *Khrushchev's May Day Speech.* Khrushchev denounces the United States for allegedly flying reconnaissance missions over Cuba. Khrushchev maintains this is not in keeping with the understanding reached between himself and President Kennedy in October 1962 concerning such missions.

May 9. *Khrushchev in Egypt.* Khrushchev arrives in Egypt for nationwide celebrations of the completion of the first stage of the Aswan Dam. Khrushchev is given a tumultuous welcome by the people of Egypt, and in a Cairo rally May 10 states he and Egyptian president Gamal Abdel Nasser will be working together "for the complete eradication of imperialism."

June 12. *Soviet-East German Pact.* Soviet premier Khrushchev and East German president Walter Ulbricht sign a 20-year friendship treaty that "asserts the legal existence of a communist state in Eastern Germany." Although the accord does not affect the 1945 Potsdam agreement, it is denounced by the United States, Britain, and France June 26 as an obstacle to bringing peace to divided Germany.

June 16 - July 4. *Khrushchev in Scandinavia.* Khrushchev tours Scandinavia and meets with heads of state. He reports to the Soviet people July 1 that the trip was an exercise in "peaceful coexistence" that may reap possible trade benefits.

July 13. *Article on Sino-Soviet Split.* Two Chinese communist publications release the ninth and most vituperative article in a series on the Sino-Soviet split. Entitled "On Khrushchev's Phony Communism and its Historical Lessons for the World," the article asserts that the Soviet premier heads a "privileged stratum" in his country that is attempting to restore capitalism while the "masses" are being exploited.

August 7. *Tonkin Gulf Resolution.* In response to evidence of North Vietnamese torpedo boat attacks on U.S. vessels operating in the Gulf of Tonkin, both houses of Congress adopt a resolution authorizing the president to take "all necessary measures to repel any armed attacks against the forces of the United States and to prevent further aggression." Only two senators out of 535 congressional members voted against the resolution. Subsequently the resolution is used by the Johnson administration as evidence of congressional support for its policies in Vietnam.

August 15. *Soviets Respond to Cyprus.* The Soviet Union answers positively to an August 9 appeal from Cyprus for military aid following Turkish air attacks.

September 30. *Cyprus Receives Aid.* The USSR and Cyprus sign an economic and military aid agreement. Cypriot officials declare that the accord contains "no strings or conditions."

October 14-15. *Khrushchev Ousted.* Nikita S. Khrushchev is forced to resign as premier of the Soviet government and first secretary of the Soviet Communist Party. He is replaced as party secretary by Leonid I. Brezhnev, 57, and as premier by Aleksei Kosygin, 60. The Soviet news agency Tass reports October 16 that the Presidium of the Supreme Soviet took the action at Khrushchev's request. The same day, Soviet ambassador to the United States Anatolii F. Dobrynin communicates with President Johnson to extend assurances of the continuation of good U.S.-Soviet relations based on peaceful coexistence. Also October 16, China's leaders extend "warm greetings" to the new Soviet leaders. A *Pravda* editorial October 17 hints Khrushchev's "harebrained scheming" and "hasty decisions" were in part a reason for the ouster. The Soviet announcement of Khrushchev's replacement is followed by numerous requests for a full explanation by East and West European communist parties.

October 16. *China Tests Atomic Device.* China successfully explodes its first atomic device. The same day, the Chinese issue a statement saying, "China cannot remain idle and do nothing in the face of the ever-increasing threat posed by the United States."

October 26. *New Soviet Goals.* The Soviet government newspaper *Izvestiia* publishes an article entitled "A Commonwealth of Equals" in which the new administration outlines its goals for unity of the communist movement with equality and autonomy for each party. On October 30 it is reported in the American and Western European press that a document listing 29 reasons why Khrushchev had been removed had been circulated among party officials. One of the main reasons cited was Khrushchev's poor handling of the Sino-Soviet rift.

November 1. *Soviet Pledge to India.* The Indian minister of information, Indira Gandhi, tells a news conference in New Delhi following her return from Moscow that the new leadership has pledged to continue the policy of giving India both economic and military aid.

November 3. *U.S. Election.* President Johnson is elected in a landslide, leading the Democratic party to its biggest national victory since 1936.

November 6. *47th Anniversary of the Bolshevik Revolution.* Leonid Brezhnev, in a speech to the delegates honoring the anniversary of the Bolshevik Revolution, declares that the new Soviet government will press for improved relations between the communist and capitalist worlds to help prevent war. He urges greater unity within the communist world, more East-West trade, and "ever more democracy for Soviet people."

November 16. *Bifurcation Reversed.* The Central Committee of the CPSU officially reunites the industrial and agricultural bureaus of the party apparatus. The bureaucratic division had been engineered by Khrushchev two years before.

November 17. *Major Shifts in Presidium.* The Soviet government announces major personnel shifts in the Presidium and at the regional/district level of the party.

Alexander N. Shelepin, thought to have had a key role in the Khrushchev ouster, and Petr Y. Shelest are named to full membership in the Presidium.

November 26. *Kosygin Offers Payment.* Soviet premier Aleksei Kosygin hints at a possible payment of a portion of USSR debts from the World War II lend-lease program. The statement is made to a group of visiting U.S. businessmen and reported by the *New York Times.*

December 2. *Rusk-Gromyko Talks.* Secretary of State Dean Rusk and Soviet foreign minister Andrei A. Gromyko confer in New York, reportedly to discuss the financing of United Nations peace-keeping operations.

December 6. *Soviet Involvement in the Congo.* It is reported from Cairo that the USSR has agreed to finance and supply a United Arab Republic/Algerian military airlift to rebels fighting in the Congo.

1965

January 4. *State of the Union Message.* President Johnson in his State of the Union address to Congress invites Soviet leaders to come to the United States to "learn about this country at first hand."

February 5. *Kosygin Abroad.* Soviet premier Aleksei Kosygin receives a cool reception in Beijing, where he stops on his way to Hanoi. On February 7 Kosygin assures a rally in Hanoi that his country will supply North Vietnam with "all necessary assistance if aggressors dare to encroach upon [its] independence and sovereignty." He warns the United States against provoking "acts of war" against North Vietnam.

February 9. *Demonstrations in Moscow.* Following American bombing raids in North Vietnam February 7, the U.S. Embassy in Moscow is attacked by 2,000 demonstrators. The Soviet police do not stop the attack, evoking protests from U.S. ambassador Foy D. Kohler and causing Soviet ambassador Anatolii Dobrynin to be summoned by the State Department.

February 14. *Sino-Soviet Exchange.* China and the Soviet Union exchange messages on the 15th anniversary of the signing of their treaty of mutual assistance and friendship. The Chinese note is far more militant, especially against the United States, than the Soviet message, which does not mention the United States as an enemy or Vietnam as a problem.

March 1-5. *Communist Parties Meet in Moscow.* Delegations from 19 communist parties meet in a Moscow suburb to plan a unity conference of the world's 81 communist parties. The parties of Albania, China, Indonesia, Japan, North Korea, North Vietnam, and Romania turn down invitations to attend. A statement issued March 10 supports the plan for a global conference to reestablish unity in the world communist movement but only after several years of preparation, which would include bilateral party talks and a preliminary meeting of the 81 parties.

March 4. *Moscow Students Mob U.S. Embassy.* Two thousand Russian, Asian (many Chinese), African, and Latin American students break through police barricades in Moscow to storm the U.S. Embassy in protest against American air strikes on North Vietnam. The students break windows and spatter the building with ink; 600 policemen are forced to call in 500 army troops to quell the rioting.

March 4. *Congressional Opposition to Soviet Trade.* Republican congressional leaders Gerald R. Ford and Everett M. Dirksen propose a "no concession-no deal" policy with the Soviets, whereby the United States would refuse to negotiate economic or political agreements while the Soviet Union acts as an aggressor anywhere in the world. Congressional Quarterly reports March 8 that the United States "appears to be on the verge of increasing trade with the Soviet Union and its East European satellites," and that, excepting the GOP leaders, "the only major voice . . . raised against U.S.-Soviet trade had been labor." On March 1 the AFL-CIO had issued a statement criticizing U.S. businessmen seeking trade with the communist world.

March 11-12. *Aftermath of Embassy Incident.* The Soviet government reports that Foreign Minister Andrei Gromyko rejected "on the spot" protests from the Chinese government on the treatment of the Chinese students who participated in the March 4 attack on the U.S. Embassy.

March 26. *Moscow-Hanoi Agreement.* The Soviet Communist Party's Central Committee ratifies a military aid agreement between the Soviet Union and North Vietnam aimed at "repelling aggression on the part of the United States imperialism."

April 10. *Johnson Offer Rejected.* The USSR, China, and North Vietnam soundly reject an offer made by President Johnson April 7 for unconditional talks to end the Vietnam War as well as a U.S.-financed Southeast Asian economic development program. The Soviet response, published in *Pravda*, calls the offer "noisy propaganda" that is inconsistent with the continued "aggression" of the United States. The Soviet Union and North Vietnam issue a joint communiqué April 18 threatening to send Soviet troops to Vietnam if the United States "intensifies" its aggressive military action.

April 24. *U.S. Marines in Dominican Republic.* Following an April 24 coup d'état in the Dominican Republic in which army rebels overthrow the ruling civilian triumvirate, U.S. Marines land in Santo Domingo for the purpose of protecting and evacuating U.S. citizens. The reaction of Tass April 29 is that the United States is guilty of "direct armed intervention."

May 5. *U.S. Increases Forces in Dominican Republic.* U.S. forces in the Dominican Republic are expanded after rumors of communist infiltration into the ranks of rebel troops attempting to take over government control. President Johnson at a meeting of the AFL-CIO on May 3 had said, "We don't propose to sit here in our rocking chair with our hands folded and let the communists set up any government in the Western Hemisphere."

May 6. *Trade Study Findings.* A 12-member committee appointed by President Johnson to assess the possibility of increased trade with the Soviet Union and Eastern Europe recommends easing existing trade restrictions.

May 7. *Soviet-Chinese Thrusts.* At a Moscow rally celebrating the anniversary of V-E Day, Premier Alexsei Kosygin, referring to the Chinese communists, states that "some people contend that only a new world war can bring about the unity and solidarity of the . . . international communist movement." He adds: "We decisively reject such a position. . . ." On May 9 the Beijing *People's Daily* accuses Soviet leaders of "colluding with the United States aggressors and plotting to sell out the basic interests of the people of Vietnam and of all other countries, including the Soviet Union."

June 8. *Vietnam Protest Rally.* Seventeen thousand people gather in New York's Madison Square Garden to protest the war in Vietnam.

July 13. *Preparations for Disarmament Talks.* President Johnson announces that the Soviet Union is once again willing to start disarmament talks in Geneva. The 18-nation UN Disarmament Committee is reconvened in Geneva July 27.

July 28. *Troop Increase.* President Johnson announces that U.S. troop strength in Vietnam will be increased from 75,000 to 125,000. Radio Moscow accuses Johnson of taking "a colossal risk" and causing "escalation of the war."

September 3. *Provisional Government in the Dominican Republic.* A provisional government, sponsored by the Organization of American States, is installed in the Dominican Republic.

September 6. *India Invades Pakistan.* Indian troops invade West Pakistan, ostensibly to relieve pressure from Indian forces fighting on the border at Kashmir.

October 2. *Soviet Economic Changes.* The Supreme Soviet approves a series of domestic economic measures in essence centralizing the administration of the economy and upgrading the importance of the profit motive. The moves are interpreted as an effort to revamp Khrushchev's system of regional economic councils.

October 15-17. *Vietnam Demonstrations.* Student-organized demonstrations against American military involvement in Vietnam flare up across the United States in marches and rallies in 40 cities. Similar protests take place in several capitals of Western Europe and Japan. On October 30 a proadministration demonstration takes place in New York with about 25,000 participants.

December 6. *Kosygin Scores U.S. "Militarism."* In an interview with the *New York Times*, Soviet premier Alexsei Kosygin accuses U.S. government officials of "trying to build up tensions, to create an atmosphere conducive to war" and declares U.S. actions prevent the Soviet Union from reducing its military budget.

December 8. *Protest in Moscow.* U.S. military involvement in Vietnam is protested by thousands of "workers' and citizens' representatives" in Moscow.

December 9. *Mikoian Steps Down.* Anastas I. Mikoian announces his resignation as president of the Presidium of the USSR Supreme Soviet. He is replaced by Nikolai V. Podgornyi. Mikoian requested to step down, citing health problems as a reason.

1966

January 2. *Soviet Reaction to U.S. Peace Drive.* Moscow responds to an intense U.S. campaign begun in late 1965 to achieve a cease-fire and peace in Vietnam. A commentary in the Communist Party newspaper *Pravda* accuses the United States of planning to extend the war into Laos and Cambodia, thereby making the peace effort unbelievable.

January 7-12. *Soviet Delegation in Hanoi.* A five-man delegation headed by Central Committee member Alexander N. Shelepin arrives in Hanoi to confer with North Vietnamese leaders. Shelepin attacks the United

States at a public meeting January 9 and encourages the communist world "to pool their efforts to render all assistance to Vietnam" in its "struggle against the [U.S.] aggressive policy." The visit is followed by an increased flow of military equipment to North Vietnam.

January 10. *Declaration of Tashkent.* Indian prime minister Lal Bahadur Shastri and Pakistani president Mohammed Ayub Khan sign the Declaration of Tashkent ending the four-month border conflict between India and Pakistan. The negotiations, which began January 4, were mediated by Alexsei Kosygin. One day later, while still in the Uzbekian Republic capital, Prime Minister Shastri dies of a heart attack.

February 2. *Chinese Charges.* The Beijing *People's Daily* charges that the Soviet Union is supporting U.S. efforts to achieve the "military encirclement of China." The article claims that Soviet policy on issues concerning Vietnam, India-Pakistan, and Japan "completely conforms with the requirements of U.S. imperialism, especially with the latter's policy of encircling China."

February 17. *Disarmament Conference in Geneva.* The Soviet Union accuses the United States of violating the 1963 nuclear test ban treaty. At a session of the 18-nation disarmament conference, the Soviet delegation cites the crash of a nuclear-bomb-equipped U.S. jet off the coast of Spain, asserting that life-threatening pollution could result. The United States replies to the Soviet claim February 26, defending the necessity of such flights to offset the threat of Moscow's "huge nuclear forces."

March 19. *New Cultural Agreement.* U.S. and Soviet officials sign a new agreement on cultural, scientific, educational, and technical exchanges extending to 1967.

March 22. *Soviet Letter Attacks Chinese Communists.* A letter reportedly written by the Soviet Communist Party's Central Committee to the East European parties is published by the West German newspaper *Die Welt.* An English translation appears two days later in the *New York Times.* The letter states there is "every reason to assert that it is one of the goals of the policy of the Chinese leadership on the Vietnam question to originate a military conflict between the USSR and the United States . . . so that they may, as they say themselves, 'sit on the mountain and watch the fight of the tigers.'" The letter criticizes China on a wide range of topics, from its refusal to join with the USSR in supporting North Vietnam to provoking Sino-Soviet border conflicts.

March 23. *Chinese Refuse Bid to Moscow.* China refuses the Soviet Union's invitation to attend the 23d Congress of the Soviet Communist Party. The Chinese statement, referring to Moscow's anti-Chinese letter, states that "since you have gone so far, the Chinese Communist Party . . . cannot send its delegation to attend this congress of yours."

March 29-April 8. *23d Party Congress.* The 23d Congress of the Communist Party of the Soviet Union convenes in Moscow, the first under the leadership of party chief Leonid Brezhnev. Brezhnev calls for unity even though the Soviets feel China is trying to split the communist movement. China and its allies (the communist parties of Albania, Japan, and New Zealand) boycott the Congress.

Brezhnev announces changes in party nomenclature at the Congress. The Presidium will once again be called the Politburo, and the Communist Party first secretary will revert to the title of general secretary.

Nikolai Podgornyi is replaced on the Secretariat by Brezhnev's close associate Andrei Kirilenko.

Soviet premier Alexsei Kosygin in his speech announces a new Five-Year Plan and outlines goals in Soviet economic development while enumerating advances made since 1928, the date of the First Five-Year Plan under Joseph Stalin. These developments were regarded in the West as a signal that the Soviet leadership had halted de-Stalinization.

April 27. *Gromyko Meets Pope Paul VI.* Soviet foreign minister Andrei A. Gromyko confers with Pope Paul VI in the Vatican, thereby becoming the highest-ranking Soviet official to have a papal audience. Gromyko also meets with Italian heads of state to discuss Italian-Soviet cooperation and issues of world peace and disarmament.

May 7. *Ceausescu on Foreign Policy.* Romanian general secretary Nicolae Ceausescu, speaking on the 45th anniversary of the Romanian communist party, asserts Romania's foreign policy stance of independence and national sovereignty. Ceausescu declares his intention of improving relations with Western European countries and "with all countries regardless of social system." Soviet party chief Brezhnev visits Bucharest May 10-13, reportedly in response to the speech.

May 10-18. *Kosygin in Egypt.* Soviet premier Alexsei Kosygin travels to the United Arab Republic on a state visit and to confer with Egyptian president Gamal Abdel Nasser. The leaders issue a joint communiqué assailing U.S. policy in Lebanon, and Kosygin urges Nasser to improve ties with Syria. Nasser takes an anti-U.S. position throughout Kosygin's visit and May 12 pays tribute to the USSR "for making the miracle of Aswan [Dam] possible."

June 20-July 1. *De Gaulle in USSR.* French president Charles de Gaulle visits the Soviet Union in an attempt to improve Franco-Soviet relations and to reduce postwar tension between East and West. De Gaulle, a highly honored western leader in the USSR, is allowed to stay at the Kremlin.

July 4-6. *Warsaw Pact Summit.* Leaders of the Warsaw Pact countries meet in Bucharest. Two statements are issued on the content of the meeting, the first outlining a promise to send "volunteers" to North Vietnam if so requested by Hanoi. The second concerns a call for a general European conference on security in Europe and increased cooperation among nations, emphasizing that U.S. security protection has "nothing in common with the vital interests of the European peoples." It was not clear whether the United States would be invited to attend the conference.

July 10. *Chinese Accuse Soviets.* Chinese foreign minister Chen Yi charges at a Beijing rally that the Soviet Union is "making military deployments along the Chinese border in coordination with United States imperialist encirclement of China."

August 29. *Anti-Soviet Rally.* Thousands of Red Guards march past the Soviet Embassy in Beijing in an all-day demonstration against "revisionism." Although the parade is well disciplined, Chinese soldiers and police guard the building against possible attack.

October 7. *Johnson on Improved Relations.* President Johnson discusses ways to improve U.S.-Soviet relations. During a speech at the National Editorial Writers' Conference he suggests a reduction of the number of both U.S. and Soviet troops in Germany and an increase of trade with Eastern Europe.

October 9. *Soviets Continue to Protest U.S. Bombing.* The Soviet government scores the U.S. administration's recent initiative to improve relations by stating that the greatest hindrance remains the continued U.S. bombing attacks on North Vietnam.

October 13. *Kosygin Accuses China.* Soviet premier Alexsei Kosygin, in a speech in Sverdlovsk, accuses China of preventing a North Vietnamese victory by blocking efforts of socialist countries to assist North Vietnam.

November 4. *Cooperation in Commercial Aviation.* An agreement is signed by U.S. and Soviet officials providing direct air service between Moscow and New York.

November 21. *Sino-Soviet Border Tension.* The *New York Times* reports that Soviet diplomats openly discussed with American officials the growing concern of Moscow over a nuclear-armed China. According to the *Times* a U.S. official described recent talks between Secretary of State Dean Rusk and Soviet foreign minister Andrei Gromyko as the "most direct, honest, objective, and non-ideological in several years." The official added, "Mr. Gromyko made clear that the break with China is quite fundamental and that Russia is now more interested than ever in settling other outstanding issues."

December 1-9. *Kosygin in France.* Soviet premier Alexsei Kosygin visits France to improve Franco-Soviet cooperation in economic and scientific-technological exchanges. On December 6 he tells reporters in Lyons that he sees a "community of interests" between the United States and the Soviet Union, but he adds: "The United States is bombing defenseless people in Vietnam. We don't see any indication of the way the United States is going to end the war. If it were ended, relations would improve. . . . We want a better understanding with the United States."

December 15. *Soviet Defense Spending Raised.* The Soviet Union announces it will increase its defense spending in 1967 by 8.2 percent due to "aggressive" U.S. policies, especially in Vietnam. On the same day United Press International reports that U.S. officials have indicated "that Russia's increased military budget undoubtedly reflects concern over the situation" along the Sino-Soviet border. Both China and the Soviet Union, the report says, have heavily reinforced the border area "where China still claims 600,000 square miles of Soviet territory."

1967

January 10. *Johnson on U.S.-Soviet Relations.* In his State of the Union message President Johnson urges Congress to increase bilateral trade and approve a new consular convention. He also calls for a slowing of the arms race.

January 24-31. *Podgornyi in Italy.* Soviet president Nikolai V. Podgornyi is the first Soviet head of state to meet with Italian leaders. The visit is intended to strengthen economic relations. Podgornyi also meets Pope Paul VI.

January 25. *Russian-Chinese Clash in Moscow.* The Chinese Embassy in Moscow protests to the Kremlin that Chinese students were attacked "without provocation" by Russian soldiers when they sought to place a wreath at the Lenin Mausoleum in Red Square. The Soviet government accuses the students of provoking the "wild scene." The incident is followed by a massive demonstration outside the Soviet Embassy in Beijing.

January 27. *Outer Space Treaty Signed.* At simultaneous ceremonies in Washington, London, and Moscow,

representatives from 60 countries sign a treaty banning the orbiting of nuclear or other mass-destruction weapons. The treaty came into force October 10, 1967, upon ratification by the United States, the Soviet Union, Great Britain, and eight other countries.

January 28. *Anti-Soviet Demonstrations in Beijing.* Chinese soldiers take part in an enormous demonstration outside the Soviet Embassy in Beijing. The troops wield rifles and bayonets in the third demonstration in as many days. The embassy's walls are plastered with posters reading "Shoot Brezhnev" and "Fry Kosygin." The demonstrators return January 29, resulting in an official protest proclaiming the Soviet government's right to take "necessary measures if the Chinese authorities fail to provide normal conditions for the activity of the Soviet representation." The attacks cease shortly afterward.

January 30. *Kennan on U.S.-Soviet Relations.* Former U.S. ambassador to the Soviet Union George F. Kennan tells the Senate Foreign Relations Committee that the irreparable disunity of the communist world presents the United States with a perfect opportunity to take "greatly exciting" steps to improve U.S.-Soviet relations.

February 4. *Moscow Warns China.* In an official note to Beijing, Moscow demands that China stop vilifying the Soviet Union and humiliating Soviet citizens in Beijing. The Soviet note coincides with an emergency evacuation of most of the Soviet diplomatic staff and their dependents from China. By February 7 it is reported that the remaining diplomats are virtual prisoners within their compound, because of China's refusal to guarantee their safety outside the area.

February 11. *Abrogation of Consular Agreement.* Beijing radio reports termination of the consular agreement between the Soviet Union and China. Travel without visas to and from the two countries no longer is to be permitted. According to a *New York Times* dispatch, Soviet diplomats fear further Chinese measures blocking Soviet aid to North Vietnam. The agreement had guaranteed Soviet specialists freedom of transit through China en route to North Vietnam.

February 19. *Arms to Iran.* Iran and the Soviet Union sign a defense agreement whereby Iran will purchase $110 million in arms and supplies.

March 2. *Soviets Willing on Arms.* President Johnson announces Moscow's willingness to discuss arms limitations by revealing a communiqué from Soviet premier Alexsei Kosygin promising cooperation on this issue.

March 9. *Stalin's Daughter Defects.* The daughter of Joseph Stalin, Svetlana Alliluyeva, defects from the Soviet Union according to the *New York Times*.

March 31. *U.S.-Soviet Consular Treaty Ratified.* President Johnson signs the first U.S.-Soviet bilateral treaty in 50 years. The action follows Senate ratification, by a vote of 66-28, on March 16. The consular treaty specifies the conditions under which each country may set up and operate consulates in the other. The Johnson administration pushed for ratification to improve relations between the two powers. The initial agreement on the treaty was announced in 1964.

April 11. *Grechko Gains Post.* The Soviet news agency Tass announces that Marshal Andrei A. Grechko, 63, is appointed Soviet defense minister. Grechko succeeds Marshal Rodion Y. Malinovskii.

May 18. *Andropov to Head KGB.* Yuri Andropov replaces V. E. Semichastnyi as chairman of the KGB.

May 24-30. *Prelude to War.* Tension increases in the

Middle East as Arab armies are massed along Israel's borders. The United Arab Republic threatens to blockade Israel's shipping in the Gulf of Aqaba. At a UN Security Council emergency session, the Soviet delegate supports the Arab position on the basis of Israel's "provocative" stance.

June 5. *War in the Middle East.* Serious fighting breaks out between Israeli and Arab troops in the Sinai Peninsula and Jerusalem. During the subsequent six-day war, Israeli troops capture all of the Sinai, the Gaza strip, and Jerusalem. During the fighting, the United States pledges to remain neutral while the USSR denounces Israel as the aggressor June 6 and demands the withdrawal of Israeli troops. The crisis ends as Arab nations gradually accept a UN cease-fire. The Middle East war provides the occasion of first use of the Moscow-Washington hot line established in August 1963.

June 10. *USSR Severs Israeli Relations.* The Soviet Union severs diplomatic ties with Israel, pledging assistance to Arab states if Israel refuses to withdraw from conquered territory. By June 13 Bulgaria, Czechoslovakia, Poland, Hungary, and Yugoslavia follow the Soviet lead.

June 14. *Soviet Defeat in the United Nations.* The UN Security Council rejects a Soviet resolution calling for denunciation of Israel and the withdrawal of its troops behind the 1949 armistice lines. On the same date Israeli sources report that Moscow has resumed sending military aid to Egypt and Syria, presumably to replace arms lost during the conflict with Israel.

June 17. *China Explodes Hydrogen Bomb.* Two years and eight months after China's first detonation of a nuclear device, the Xinhua news agency announces detonation of the country's first hydrogen bomb.

June 19. *Johnson and Kosygin on the Middle East.* President Johnson in a nationally televised speech sets forth five points for peace in the Middle East: the right of each country's national existence, fair and just treatment of Arab refugees, freedom of innocent maritime passage, limitation of arms buildup, and guaranteed territorial integrity for each Middle East country. Meanwhile, at the United Nations, Soviet premier Alexsei Kosygin calls for the condemnation of Israel, the withdrawal of Israeli forces from occupied Arab lands, and Israeli reparations to Syria, Jordan, and the UAR for damages incurred during the war.

June 23-25. *Kosygin-Johnson Talks in Glassboro.* Soviet premier Alexsei Kosygin and American president Johnson meet at Glassboro College in New Jersey to discuss the Middle East, Vietnam, arms control, and nuclear proliferation. President Johnson suggested the meeting after Kosygin had arrived in New York June 17 to address a special session of the UN General Assembly. The site was chosen because of its location half way between New York and Washington. The meeting is the first between the two leaders. After the talks Johnson states, "No agreement is readily in sight on the Middle Eastern crisis and our well-known differences over Vietnam continue." Kosygin, at a televised news conference in New York, emphasizes that Israel must withdraw to positions behind the 1949 armistice lines before further progress toward peace in the Middle East can be achieved.

July 9. *Cultural Visit Canceled.* Moscow cancels a U.S. visit by approximately 200 performing artists, including Bolshoi Ballet principals. The action marks the first time since the creation of the cultural exchange agreement of 1958 that such a visit is canceled.

August 11-13. *Sino-Soviet Tension.* The Chinese detain a Soviet freighter for alleged anti-Chinese activities by the crew. The ship is released August 13 after sharp condemnation of China by Soviet premier Alexsei Kosygin. The incident is thought to be an impediment to Sino-Soviet trade.

September 8. *Rusk on Nuclear Weapons.* Secretary of State Dean Rusk emphasizes the importance of U.S.-Soviet cooperation in limiting nuclear missiles, stating that lack of such negotiations may force the United States to build an antiballistic missile defense system.

November 3-7. *50th Anniversary of Bolshevik Revolution.* The USSR engages in a series of festivities marking the 50th anniversary of the Bolshevik Revolution. In a four-and-a-half-hour speech November 3 Communist Party chief Leonid Brezhnev denounces China for disrupting the unity of the world socialist community. Brezhnev calls those in China who resist Mao's policies "the best sons of the Chinese Communist Party." Brezhnev also castigates continued U.S. military involvement in Vietnam. November 7 is highlighted by a Soviet military parade displaying the latest Soviet nuclear missiles.

December 24. *Soviet-Iraqi Cooperation.* Iraq and the Soviet Union agree to cooperate in the development of oil deposits in southern Iraq.

1968

January 5. *Developments in Czechoslovakia.* On the wave of increasing demands for reform, Alexander Dubcek, 46, succeeds Antonin Novotny as first secretary of the Czechoslovak Communist Party.

January 18. *Soviet Warning on Cambodia.* The State Department discloses the contents of a note in which the Soviet government warns that it will "not remain indifferent" if the United States places troops in Cambodia.

January 18. *Draft Nuclear-Weapons Treaty Submitted to United Nations.* Soviet and U.S. delegates to the 18-nation UN Disarmament Committee submit a revised draft treaty to prevent the further spread of nuclear weapons. The joint revision is significant in that it includes provisions for ensuring compliance that were omitted from an earlier draft submitted August 24, 1967.

January 23. *USS Pueblo Seized.* North Korean forces board the U.S. Navy intelligence ship *Pueblo* in the Sea of Japan and take the ship and her 83-man crew into a North Korean port. The Defense Department contends that the *Pueblo* was cruising in international waters. The North Koreans claim the ship had been spying in their territorial waters. The incident is met by serious protest in the United States and an American military buildup ensues in and around South Korea. The U.S. ambassador to the Soviet Union, Llewellyn E. Thompson, tries to enlist Soviet aid in releasing the *Pueblo* January 24 and 26 but is rebuffed. The Soviet government newspaper *Izvestiia* January 26 accuses President Johnson of manipulating the *Pueblo* incident to justify building up military reserves in the area. Eleven months later, on December 23, the 82 surviving crew members are released.

March 23. *East European Summit.* The leaders of Warsaw Pact nations, excluding Romania, convene in Dresden to investigate the increasing liberalization in Czechoslovakia since the ouster of Czech Communist Party head Antonin Novotny. Novotny's successor, Alexander Dubcek, is pressed to reverse the trends of democratization.

March 31. *Johnson Quits Race.* In a televised speech President Johnson announces that he will neither seek nor accept the Democratic nomination for president. Johnson also announces that he has ordered a halt to U.S. bombings of North Vietnam north of the area near the South Vietnamese border where a military buildup was continuing. Tass criticizes Johnson for not completely halting the bombing.

April 2-7. *Kosygin in Iran.* Soviet premier Aleksei N. Kosygin pays a state visit to Iran to promote bilateral economic cooperation. The visit is followed by a communiqué stating that the two nations have "identical or closely approaching views" on Southeast Asia, the Middle East, and European security.

April 4. *King Assassinated.* U.S. civil rights leader Martin Luther King, Jr., is assassinated by a sniper in Memphis, Tennessee. Reaction is widespread, touching off riots in several U.S. cities. The Soviet response appears in a June 6 *Izvestiia* article entitled "The United States is a Nation of Violence and Racism."

April 24. *Moscow Castigates Beijing.* The Soviet theoretical journal *Kommunist* publishes the first of three long articles attacking Chinese party chairman Mao Zedong and the cultural revolution. The articles deal with China's departure from the Marxist-Leninist line, China's alleged attempts to prolong the Vietnam War and incite a confrontation between the United States and the USSR, and an enumeration of the damages that the cultural revolution has brought to China.

June 4. *Johnson in Glassboro.* President Johnson delivers the commencement address at Glassboro State College in New Jersey, site of a June 1967 summit between himself and Soviet premier Aleksei Kosygin. The president appeals to Moscow to join in "the spirit of Glassboro" to work for world peace. Johnson focuses on the progress made in U.S.-Soviet relations, such as the treaty outlawing destructive weapons in space, the nuclear nonproliferation treaty, and the civil air service agreement. On June 12 an *Izvestiia* article belittles the "rosy picture" Johnson drew of U.S.-Soviet relations, contending instead that relations are "frozen" until the United States ceases all involvement in Vietnam.

June 5. *Robert Kennedy Assassinated.* Shortly after midnight Sen. Robert F. Kennedy, D-N.Y., is shot at a hotel party celebrating his victory in the California presidential primary. Reaction is worldwide. *Izvestiia* comments that "a cancer of violence is eating away at the organism of capitalist society."

June 13. *Consular Pact Ceremony.* The instruments of ratification of the U.S.-Soviet consular treaty are formally exchanged in a White House ceremony. The treaty, which is to take effect in 30 days, was ratified by the Presidium of the Supreme Soviet April 26 and by the U.S. Senate March 16, 1967.

July 1. *Nonproliferation Treaty Signed.* Sixty-two nations, including the United States, the Soviet Union, and Great Britain, sign a treaty on the nonproliferation of nuclear weapons in ceremonies in the various capitals. The signing follows ratification of the treaty by the United Nations in June.

July 4-10. *Nasser in Moscow.* United Arab Republic president Gamal Abdel Nasser visits Moscow amid speculation that he is dissatisfied with the level of Soviet mili-

tary assistance to the Arab world. On July 5 Soviet leader Leonid Brezhnev promises at a Kremlin luncheon that the Soviet Union will "always side with the Arab nations for the withdrawal of Israeli troops from all the Arab land occupied as a result of the June [1967] aggression."

July 15. *Air Service Begins.* The first flights take place on the newly inaugurated Moscow-New York commercial airline service. Implementation of the updated agreement, signed November 4, 1966, had been delayed by technical problems and uncertain U.S.-Soviet relations during the interim.

July 14-23. *Tension Mounts Over Czech Liberalization.* The continuing liberalization in Czechoslovakia overseen by Communist Party First Secretary Alexander Dubcek and his supporters is the source of increasing tension between Moscow and Prague. The Soviet Union, along with its hard-line East European allies — East Germany, Hungary, Bulgaria, and Poland — draft a letter following a two-day summit in Warsaw July 14-15, which calls the Czech liberalization "completely unacceptable." A July 22 *Pravda* article demands that Communist Party control be firmly reinstated, in part by reimposing censorship and suppressing "anti-socialist and right-wing" forces. The Soviet Union announces July 23 it plans massive military maneuvers that will continue until August 10. The move is interpreted as a coercive attempt to intimidate Czech authorities to accept Soviet demands.

July 29. *Meeting in Cierna.* At Prague's request, the entire Politburo of the Soviet Communist Party and the Presidium of the Czechoslovak Communist Party meet under tight security in Cierna, Czechoslovakia, to discuss the Czech situation.

August 3. *Meeting in Bratislava.* As a follow-up and ratification of the recent meeting in Cierna, the East European allies of Moscow, along with Soviet and Czechoslovak leaders, meet in Bratislava, Czechoslovakia, and accept the Soviet position that Czechoslovakia be allowed to continue in its liberalization experiment within limits. Immediately preceding the Bratislava meeting the Czechoslovak Foreign Ministry announces that all Soviet troops on maneuvers have left the country. Reportedly, the Czech government made a few concessions to Moscow, including the establishment of an "advisory council" to diminish critical news reporting.

August 8. *Nixon Nominated.* Richard M. Nixon easily wins the Republican nomination for the presidency on the first ballot. In his acceptance speech Nixon states that he will "extend the hand of friendship to all peoples" and specifically to the peoples of the USSR and China.

August 9-11 and 15-17. *Tito and Ceausescu Visit Prague.* Czechoslovakia is visited by Yugoslav president Josip Broz Tito and Romanian president Nicolae Ceausescu. Both leaders endorse Czech Communist Party leader Dubcek and his supporters in their attempt to follow an independent socialist line in spite of Moscow's pressure to reverse liberalization.

August 20-21. *Warsaw Pact Forces Intervene in Czechoslovakia.* The troops of five Warsaw Pact nations (the Soviet Union, East Germany, Poland, Hungary, and Bulgaria) cross the Czechoslovak border and occupy the country. Leading members of the liberalization movement are taken to Moscow, and the number of troops increases from the initial 200,000 to 650,000 during the week. The intervention is met with generally passive resistance on the part of the population, putting an end to the "Prague Spring," the period in which Czechoslovakia experienced a more liberal way of life with fewer ties to Moscow. President Johnson denounces the Warsaw Pact action August 21 but admits that there is no "safe" action the United States can take. The UN Security Council supports a seven-nation resolution condemning the occupation and calling for the removal of Warsaw Pact forces. The resolution is defeated by a USSR veto. The intervention also is protested by the communist parties of France, Italy, Romania, Yugoslavia, and China.

A secret Congress of the Czechoslovak Communist Party is held August 21-22, and a new leadership is elected. The Congress originally had been scheduled for September 9.

August 27. *Changes in Czechoslovakia.* The reversing of liberalization in Czechoslovakia begins with the return to Prague from Moscow of Czech president Ludvik Svoboda and first secretary Dubcek. The leaders announce an agreement with Moscow that results in several actions. On September 1 a new Presidium is elected for the Czech Communist Party, superseding the secret Congress results of August 23. On September 4 press censorship and disbanding of noncommunist organizations are implemented.

September 6. *Kuznetsov in Prague.* Soviet first deputy foreign minister Vasilii V. Kuznetsov visits Prague unexpectedly to mediate differences in the implementation of the Czech-Soviet agreement reached in Moscow August 26. A translation of the agreement is published September 8 in the West by the *New York Times.*

September 11. *Partial Pullout of Soviet Troops.* As part of the second-stage removal of Soviet forces from Czechoslovakia, some troops leave Prague. Troops remain in several parts of the city.

September 17. *Soviet-West German Tension.* Tension between the USSR and West Germany increases as the United States, Britain, and France promise a stern response from NATO in case of a military intervention in West Germany by the Soviet Union. The warnings came in response to a July 5 communiqué from Moscow to Bonn expressing the right to intervene militarily "against the renewal of aggressive policy by a former [World War II] enemy state."

September 26. *Doctrine of "Limited Sovereignty."* The Soviet party newspaper *Pravda* advances a new, ideological argument to justify the invasion of Czechoslovakia by the Warsaw Pact nations. The article says, in effect, that the world socialist community has a right to intervene when socialism comes under attack in a fraternal socialist country and it denies that this in any way violates Czechoslovakia's "real sovereignty." The article asserts that "world socialism is indivisible, and its defense is the common cause of all Communists." The article, written by the publication's ideological specialist, also states that "each Communist party is responsible not only to its own people, but also to all the Socialist countries, to the entire Communist movement." The doctrine of "limited sovereignty" is soon elaborated on by top Soviet officials and subsequently comes to be known as the "Brezhnev Doctrine."

October 3-4. *Czechoslovak Leaders in Moscow.* Czechoslovak leaders travel to Moscow and ultimately succumb to Soviet demands to abolish all remainders of the liberalization program and to allow the indefinite stationing of foreign troops on Czech territory. These actions are taken to break a stalemate in the implementation of the August 26 Moscow agreement.

October 16. *Kosygin in Prague.* Soviet premier Aleksei N. Kosygin flies to Prague to sign a treaty agreed

upon in Moscow October 3-4, authorizing the temporary stationing of Soviet troops in Czechoslovakia. The treaty is ratified by the Czech National Assembly October 18. Moscow continues its pressure on Czech officials October 19 by insisting that party membership be reduced by purging all liberal elements.

October 27. *Czechoslovakia Becomes a Federative Nation.* The Czechoslovak National Assembly passes a bill to create a federative nation of two states (the Czech and Slovak peoples), thereby giving Slovakia greater power over its territory as well as veto power in the National Assembly. The action is expected to go into effect January 1, 1969.

October 28. *Demonstrations in Prague.* Prague witnesses anti-Soviet demonstrations led by a youthful crowd on the 50th anniversary of the Czechoslovak Republic. Sporadic demonstrations continue into November, particularly on the anniversary of the Russian Revolution.

November 1. *Bombing Halted in Vietnam.* President Johnson halts all U.S. bombing in North Vietnam as part of the peace negotiations taking place in Paris.

November 5. *Nixon Elected President.* Richard Nixon narrowly defeats Vice President Hubert H. Humphrey to become the 37th U.S. president. The Soviet reaction is one of hope for better U.S.-Soviet relations and a call for "normalization" of relations between the two powers.

1969

January 20. *Overtures of a New Administration.* President Richard Nixon is sworn into office, stressing a new "era of negotiation" in his inaugural address. On the same day the Soviet Foreign Ministry reaffirms an interest in renewing arms reduction talks that had broken down when Warsaw Pact nations intervened in Czechoslovakia in August 1968.

February 17. *Nixon Invited.* Soviet ambassador Anatolii Dobrynin invites President Nixon to visit Moscow.

February 23-March 2. *Nixon Visits Western Europe.* President Nixon travels to five West European nations to instill a "new spirit of consultation" between the United States and its allies. In a speech to NATO officials in Brussels February 24, Nixon emphasizes that future U.S. negotiations with Moscow will affect Western Europe, and any decisions will be made "on the basis of full consultation and cooperation with our allies, because we recognize that the chances for successful negotiations depend on our unity."

February 26. *Nasser Interviewed.* United Arab Republic president Gamal Abdel Nasser states in a *New York Times* interview that Egypt has not provided naval bases for any country, including the USSR. However, he welcomes Soviet ships in Egyptian territory because the Soviet Union "helped us after the [Israeli] aggression." Nasser says there are fewer than 1,000 Soviet advisers in Egypt but that "I am asking for more."

March 2. *Sino-Soviet Fighting.* Soviet news agency Tass reports that Chinese forces ambushed a Soviet company making a routine patrol of Damanskii Island. In all of 1969 there would be more than 400 skirmishes along the Sino-Soviet border.

March 28. *Anti-Soviet Demonstrations.* Following a Czech victory in a world championship hockey game in Stockholm, anti-Soviet demonstrations erupt in Prague and other Czech cities. Riot police disperse the crowds.

April 17. *Dubcek Resignation.* Alexander Dubcek, main participant in the liberalization program, resigns as Czechoslovak Communist Party first secretary. His successor, Gustav Husak, states that the change in leadership is in the interest of Czech unity. Husak's appointment is welcomed by Moscow.

June 8. *First Vietnam Troop Withdrawal.* President Nixon announces 25,000 U.S. troops are to leave South Vietnam by August 31.

July 10. *Gromyko Stresses Improved Relations.* Soviet foreign minister Andrei A. Gromyko urges closer cooperation with the United States. In a speech to the Supreme Soviet he suggests an exchange of delegations from the Supreme Soviet and the U.S. Congress. Gromyko characterizes Chinese policies toward the Soviet Union, on the other hand, as worse than those "of our most rabid enemies."

August 2-3. *Nixon Visits Romania.* Nixon's visit, a bridge-building effort and the first visit to Romania by a U.S. president, is labeled a propaganda exercise by the Soviet government newspaper *Izvestiia.*

September 3. *Death of Ho Chi Minh.* North Vietnamese leader Ho Chi Minh dies, leaving power in the hands of a collective leadership of the Vietnam Workers' Party.

September 5. *U.S. on Sino-Soviet Split.* Secretary of State Elliott L. Richardson tells the American Political Science Association in New York that the United States will not seek to exploit the Sino-Soviet rift. He says "Soviet apprehensions" will not prevent the United States from "attempting to bring China out of its angry, alienated shell."

September 11. *Kosygin Visits China.* En route to Moscow after attending the funeral of North Vietnamese leader Ho Chi Minh, Soviet premier Kosygin makes a surprise visit to China. His talks with Premier Chou En-lai reduce serious Sino-Soviet tensions caused by months of bloody border skirmishes between Soviet and Chinese forces.

September 18. *President Nixon Addresses the United Nations.* President Nixon in a speech to the UN General Assembly suggests a Middle East arms curb by the big powers. The Soviet Union rebuffs the suggestion.

October 7. *Seabed Pact.* The United States and the Soviet Union submit a joint draft to the UN conference of the Committee on Disarmament in Geneva. The pact bans nuclear and other destructive weapons outside a 12-mile coastal limit as defined in the 1958 Geneva Convention on the Territorial Sea.

October 20. *China-USSR Negotiations.* Chinese and Soviet foreign ministers open negotiations in Beijing on the Sino-Soviet border problems.

November 17. *Preliminary Round of SALT Talks in Helsinki.* The preliminary SALT talks begin, led by Gerard Smith for the United States and Vladimir S. Semenov for the Soviet Union. The talks adjourn December 22. The opening session takes place April 17, 1970, in Vienna.

November 24. *U.S.-Soviet Nuclear Nonproliferation Treaty.* The nuclear nonproliferation treaty is signed by President Nixon and Soviet president Nikolai Podgornyi during separate ceremonies in Washington and Moscow.

December 7. *Upward Turn in Soviet-West German Relations.* The Soviet Union accepts West German chancellor Willy Brandt's offer to negotiate a bilateral treaty normalizing relations between the two countries. The Soviet Union states that conditions for approval of the treaty include recognition of East Germany and the exchange of diplomats.

1970

January 6. *Moscow on Sino-Soviet Split.* The Soviet Communist Party newspaper *Pravda* charges that China is slandering the Soviet Union and preparing for war. The paper also states that Western "imperialists" welcome the differences between the two countries.

January 22. *Nixon on Détente.* In his State of the Union speech President Nixon stresses the importance of dedication to the goal of worldwide peace. He reiterates that the United States is moving from "an era of confrontation to an era of negotiation" with the USSR and China.

February 4. *Nixon Message to Soviets on Middle East.* President Nixon sends a note to Soviet premier Aleksei Kosygin urging cooperation in resolving the Middle East problem. Nixon's communication is in response to a January 31 Kosygin letter that states the USSR would step up arms deliveries to Egypt if the United States persists in giving military aid to Israel.

February 10. *Cultural Exchange.* The signing of the 1970-71 cultural agreement between the Soviet Union and the United States is announced by the State Department.

February 15. *Moscow Denies Planning Attack on China.* The Soviet newspaper *Pravda* criticizes Western press predictions of a Soviet attack on China. The article follows up a statement by the Soviet news agency Tass, which described such predictions as "insinuations" designed to "increase tension" in the relations between the Soviet Union and China.

February 18. *Nixon's Foreign Affairs Message.* President Nixon issues a foreign policy statement entitled "United States Foreign Policy for the '70s: A New Strategy for Peace." Part of the report argues that European security is contingent upon the Soviet Union's willingness to improve relations with the West and moderate its policies toward the Eastern bloc. Nixon criticizes the Soviet Union for lack of cooperation in solving the crises in Vietnam and the Middle East. He contends that the United States will not interfere in East European affairs but will continue to treat each nation as an independent country.

March 19. *Soviet Troops in Egypt.* Diplomatic observers report that a large number of Soviet troops and antiaircraft missiles have arrived in Cairo.

April 17. *SALT Talks Resume in Vienna. (See November 17, 1969.)*

April 21. *Lenin's Centenary.* The communist world celebrates the centenary of Lenin's birth.

April 29. *Missions for Egypt.* The Israeli government says it has evidence to confirm accusations that Soviet planes are flying missions for the Egyptian air force. Soviet sources call the accusations "stupidities."

April 30. *U.S. Invades Cambodia.* President Nixon announces in a televised address that U.S. troops have begun an "incursion" into Cambodia designed to disrupt North Vietnamese sanctuaries in that country. The invasion sparks a public outcry in the United States, with demonstrations on many college campuses. On May 4 four students at Kent State University are killed by Ohio National Guard troops.

June 1. *Antiaircraft Missiles in Egypt. Newsweek* reports the installation of 22 SAM-3 missile sites in Egypt; others are under construction or planned.

June 24. *Soviet Pilots in Egypt.* Foreign intelligence reports received in Washington indicate that Soviet pilots have taken over the air defense of Egypt against Israel and are flying missions south of the Suez Canal.

June 26. *Dubcek Expelled.* Alexander Dubcek is expelled from the Czech Communist Party. The action is regarded as further retaliation against the liberalization effort in Czechoslovakia.

June 29. *United States Withdraws Troops from Cambodia.*

July 1. *Nixon on the Middle East.* President Nixon emphasizes the dangers of a volatile Middle East situation by comparing it with "the Balkans before World War I." He cautions the Soviet Union that a change in the power balance in the Middle East will not be tolerated.

July 10. *Soviets Call for Joint Action.* Soviet SALT negotiators reportedly propose that the United States and the Soviet Union agree to "joint retaliatory action" in response to any "provocative" acts or direct attacks by China. The proposal is not disclosed until 1973 and is denied by the Soviets at that time.

July 17. *Nasser in Moscow.* At the conclusion of United Arab Republic president Gamal Abdel Nasser's visit to Moscow, a joint Soviet-UAR communiqué is issued calling for a political settlement of the Middle East crisis. The communiqué blames Israel for its "aggression against the UAR and other Arab states."

August 12. *West German-Soviet Treaty.* West German chancellor Willy Brandt and Soviet premier Aleksei Kosygin sign a treaty in Moscow renouncing the use of force to settle disputes between their countries. The document includes recognition of the long-disputed Polish-East German border at the Oder-Neisse line.

August 14. *SALT Talks Recess.* SALT negotiators end their current round in Vienna and are scheduled to resume in Helsinki in November.

September 25. *Soviet Activity in Cuba.* The possible building of a strategic submarine base in Cuba is reported by the Defense Department. The suspicions of U.S. officials are aroused when heavy equipment is seen arriving from the Soviet Union. The Soviet Union is warned against such a move, but construction efforts are denied in a September 30 *Pravda* commentary.

September 28. *Death of Nasser.* The president of the United Arab Republic, Gamal Abdel Nasser, dies in Cairo. His death evokes an outpouring of grief throughout the Arab world. Moscow issues a statement September 29 noting that Nasser's position on the Middle East conflict "will continue to enjoy our utmost support." Vice President Anwar al-Sadat is immediately delegated acting president.

September 30 — October 2. *Nixon in Yugoslavia.* In a move designed to improve relations and support Yugoslavia's nonaligned stance, Nixon becomes the first U.S. president to visit that country. Nixon's visit was the first of an eight-day, five-nation European tour.

October 1. *Soviets Protest Harassment.* The Soviet Foreign Ministry protests U.S. government failure to halt attacks against Soviet citizens in the United States. The protest followed a series of incidents involving the Jewish Defense League.

October 8. *Solzhenitsyn Wins Nobel.* Soviet writer Alexander I. Solzhenitsyn wins the 1970 Nobel Prize for Literature. The author's works are banned in the Soviet Union, and the Soviet writers' union October 9 calls the award decision "deplorable."

October 13. *Soviets Deny Cuban Base.* The Soviet Union again denies U.S. reports that a military base is under construction in Cuba. *(See September 25, 1970.)* The incident prompts the departure of Soviet naval vessels.

October 25. *Ceaucescu Visits Washington.* Romanian president Nicolae Ceaucescu confers with President Nixon at the close of his two-week visit to the United States. The expected outcome of the visit is improved trade relations between the two countries.

October 29. *U.S.-Soviet Space Effort.* Soviets and U.S. officials sign the first cooperative space effort agreement. The project involves a joint rendezvous and docking mission in space.

November 2-December 18. *SALT Talks Resume.* Strategic arms limitation talks continue in Helsinki.

November 22. *Sino-Soviet Trade Pact.* The Soviet Union and China sign a trade agreement, the first since 1967. The agreement does not seem to be accompanied by any other lessening of tension between the two countries.

December 15. *Polish Worker Unrest.* Demonstrations by Polish workers against severe increases in food prices end Wladyslaw Gomulka's 14-year career as first secretary of the Polish Communist Party. Edward Gierek replaces him.

1971

January 3. *Trial of Angela Davis.* Fourteen Soviet scientists are invited to the United States to attend the murder trial of communist activist Angela Davis to help ensure a fair trial. The State Department discloses that the invitation was extended December 27, 1970.

January 4. *Disclosure of Soviet Deaths in Egypt.* President Anwar al-Sadat of Egypt announces that six Soviet soldiers died during an Israeli air raid. The soldiers were manning Egyptian missile sites in the Suez Canal area.

January 4. *Aftermath of Harassment of Soviet Citizens.* Following harassment of Soviet officials in the United States, Moscow announces that U.S. citizens will not be given government protection in the Soviet Union. Three days later a small bomb explodes outside the Soviet Embassy in Washington, an incident for which the United States apologizes.

January 15. *Aswan Dam Dedicated.* Egyptian president Anwar al-Sadat and Soviet president Nikolai Podgornyi dedicate the Aswan Dam.

January 15. *Muskie Visits Moscow.* Sen. Edmund S. Muskie, D-Maine, meets with Soviet premier Aleksei N. Kosygin as part of a European tour.

January 23 and 26. *Harassment of U.S. Newsmen.* Two American reporters are accosted in Moscow while keeping appointments with Soviet friends. The incidents are interpreted as efforts to discourage the Western media from making contacts with Soviet citizens and are protested by the U.S. Embassy. Numerous other incidents occur throughout 1971.

January 25. *Chinese Students in Moscow.* About 60 Chinese students clash with Soviet police in front of Lenin's tomb.

February 25. *"Nixon Doctrine."* President Nixon presents his annual State of the World report to the U.S. Congress. The speech is construed as a formal enunciation of the "Nixon Doctrine," namely, that the United States will honor all treaties with its allies, but they will be responsible for supplying their own troops to combat conventional aggression or subversion. Nixon describes U.S.-Soviet relations during his administration as "mixed." He cites positive developments such as advances in SALT talks, the ratification of the seabed and nuclear nonproliferation treaties, negotiations on the Berlin question, and beginnings of joint space cooperation. Obstacles remain over Soviet behavior in the Middle East and Cuba.

March 15. *SALT Talks Resume.* SALT negotiators begin their fourth round in Vienna.

March 17. *Chinese, Soviets Renew Polemics.* On the eve of the 24th Soviet Party Congress, China and the Soviet Union resume their battle of words. China accuses the Soviets of the "most savage and brutal means to deal with revolutionary people," while Moscow warns Beijing against playing a "dangerous game" by trying to improve relations with the United States.

March 30-April 9. *Soviet Party Congress.* Speaking before the 24th Soviet Party Congress in Moscow, Soviet leader Leonid Brezhnev reaffirms a desire for improved relations with the United States. Brezhnev also states that the Soviets oppose Chinese attempts to distort Marxism-Leninism and split the world communist movement.

April 6. *Ping-Pong Diplomacy.* The Chinese government makes a move toward better relations with the United States by inviting the U.S. table tennis team for a visit to begin April 10. A week later President Nixon announces a partial relaxation of the trade embargo with China.

April 18-23. *Vietnam War.* American jets launch a major bombing offensive in North Vietnam.

May 7. *Ceylon Rebellion.* Soviets send a training mission to Ceylon to help the government quash an ultraleftist rebellion.

May 14. *Proposal for Force Reductions in Europe.* In a speech in Tiflis, Soviet leader Brezhnev makes overtures to the West for reducing arms in Central Europe. Washington expresses an interest because State Department officials regard a conference on mutual and balanced force reductions (MBFR) as highly desirable.

May 20. *Progress in SALT Talks.* SALT negotiators announce that a compromise treaty framework has been agreed upon.

May 27. *Egyptian-Soviet Treaty.* Egypt and the Soviet Union sign a 15-year treaty of friendship and cooperation.

June 13. *Pentagon Papers Appear.* The *New York Times* publishes the first installment of the "Pentagon Papers," which sends shock waves through the Nixon administration. National security adviser Henry A. Kissinger later says that such revelations could undo the three most important projects under way in the White House: the opening of relations with China, the strategic arms talks with the Soviet Union, and the peace talks with North Vietnam.

July 4. *Egyptian-Soviet Joint Communiqué.* The United Arab Republic and the Soviet Union issue a joint communiqué declaring that the Suez Canal will be opened only after Israel withdraws all of its forces from Arab territory.

July 15. *Nixon to Visit China.* To continue the normalization of relations, President Nixon accepts an invitation to visit the People's Republic of China in 1972. He emphasizes that the trip will in no way alter existing relations with any other country.

July 16. *USSR on Nixon.* The Soviet government newspaper *Izvestiia* publishes without comment a terse report on the Chinese invitation to President Nixon.

July 25. *Moscow's Response to China Opening.* *Pravda* publishes an article warning the United States that "any schemes to use the contacts between Beijing and Washington for some pressure on the Soviet Union . . . are nothing but the result of a loss of touch with reality."

August 2. *Aftermath of Attempted Coup in the Sudan.* Soviet officials are ordered out of the Sudan following a coup that almost topples from power Premier Mohammed Gaafar Nimeiry. The officials are accused of influencing the coup.

August 9. *India-Soviet Pact.* Soviet foreign minister Andrei Gromyko arrives in New Delhi to sign a 20-year treaty of peace, friendship, and cooperation with India.

August 20. *Soviet Verbal Attacks Escalate.* The Soviet Union begins another extensive press attack against China. *Pravda* contends that China is using the threat of a Soviet invasion as a pretext to improve relations with the West and to erect "fortifications" along the whole length of the Sino-Soviet border.

August 28. *Brezhnev Tolerant.* Soviet leader Brezhnev states that he does not blame China for the fact that the border talks are "going slowly" and promises the Soviets will "continue to display a constructive and patient approach."

August 31. *Jets to Egypt.* The *New York Times* reports that the Soviet Union is sending more jet-pilot squadrons to Egypt. The Soviet foreign affairs weekly *Novoye Vremya* rebukes the Arabs for currying favor with both the Soviet Union and the United States while simultaneously suppressing communist movements in their own countries.

September 11. *Khrushchev Dies.* The former head of the Soviet Union, Nikita S. Khrushchev, dies in Moscow at age 77. His death is ignored by the Soviet press except for one-sentence announcements in *Pravda* and *Izvestiia* two days later.

October 12. *Nixon to Visit USSR.* President Nixon announces a working visit to the Soviet Union planned for May 1972. The visit is welcomed by Soviet officials.

October 20. *Moscow on Two-China Policy.* The Soviet delegate states that the U.S. argument against the expulsion of Nationalist China from the United Nations is an effort to frighten UN members and amounts to "absurd inventions"; he insists that Taiwan is not a state but a "province of China." Five days later the People's Republic of China is admitted to the United Nations.

October 27-November 2. *Tito in the United States.* Josip Broz Tito, president of Yugoslavia, visits the United States. Nixon strongly supports the Yugoslavian nonaligned stance in the world socialist movement.

November 5. *New Grain Deal.* A grain sale of $136

million to the Soviet Union is announced by the U.S. government.

December 3. *India Invades Pakistan.* Fortified by Soviet military aid and a new 20-year treaty of friendship with the Soviet Union, India invades East Pakistan in support of the Bangladesh rebels who had been defeated by Pakistan in April. Beijing radio accuses Moscow of "supporting, encouraging and approving India's aggression against Pakistan." The United States expresses opposition to an increased Soviet naval presence in the area. Hostilities end December 16 with surrender of Pakistani troops and creation of the independent Bangladesh nation.

December 26. *U.S. Resumes Bombing of North Vietnam.* Faced with a massive North Vietnamese buildup, U.S. planes strike at targets in Laos, Cambodia, and North Vietnam. This is the first major U.S. air action in Indochina since 1968.

1972

January 28. *Moscow on Nixon's China Trip.* Soviet foreign minister Andrei A. Gromyko, speaking at a news conference in Tokyo, tells reporters that the Soviet Union does not object to improved Sino-U.S. relations provided they do not "affect adversely the safety and interests of the Soviet Union."

February 9. *Nixon's Third Foreign Policy Statement.* Congress receives President Nixon's foreign policy statement entitled "United States Foreign Policy for the 1970s: The Emerging Structure of Peace." The document describes current relations with the Soviet Union and China and states that the United States is entering an age "where a premium would be placed on compromise and moderation in diplomacy."

February 21. *Nixon Arrives in China.* President Nixon arrives in China for a historic seven-day visit. It is the first time an American head of state has ever visited China, and the visit caps two years of U.S. and Chinese efforts to end the 23-year hostility between the two nations.

February 27. *Shanghai Communiqué Issued.* At the conclusion of the talks in Shanghai between President Nixon and Premier Chou En-lai, the United States and China issue a joint communiqué that pledges both sides to work for a "normalization" of relations. *Pravda* expresses displeasure and contends that the United States is taking advantage of the Sino-Soviet rift. Soviet government sources hint that the Shanghai talks may have been quite different from what was announced in the official statement.

March 30. *North Vietnamese Offensive.* North Vietnam launches a major attack across the demilitarized zone (DMZ) into South Vietnam.

April 6. *U.S. Resumes Bombing.* Faced with a full-scale invasion of South Vietnam by Hanoi, the United States resumes massive air strikes against North Vietnam.

April 11. *U.S.-Soviet Cooperation.* The United States offers to sell grain to the Soviet Union on three-year credit terms. The offer is extended by Secretary of Agriculture Earl Butz in Moscow. On the same day Soviet and U.S. officials sign an agreement extending and augmenting a 14-year-old cultural, educational, and scientific exchange program.

April 20-24. *Kissinger in Moscow.* Henry A. Kissinger, national security adviser to the president, visits Moscow to prepare for Nixon's forthcoming visit.

May 8. *U.S. Mines Haiphong.* President Nixon, faced with a worsening situation in South Vietnam, orders the mining of all North Vietnamese harbors. The move risks a direct confrontation with both China and the Soviet Union, whose ships are supplying Hanoi. The confrontation does not materialize, and President Nixon's upcoming trip to Moscow is not jeopardized, despite indications of internal conflict among the Soviet leadership over the issue of proceeding with the summit.

May 22. *Nixon to Moscow.* President Nixon arrives in Moscow for a summit meeting with Soviet leaders. Among the many topics discussed are a European security conference and mutual balanced force reductions (MBFR) in Eastern Europe.

May 26. *SALT Treaty Signed.* President Nixon and Soviet leader Leonid Brezhnev sign the first Strategic Arms Limitation Treaty (SALT I). On the same day Brezhnev is reported to have assured Nixon that he would press the North Vietnamese to settle the war in Vietnam.

May 28. *Nixon on Soviet Television.* President Nixon says on Soviet television that as "great powers" the Soviet Union and the United States will "sometimes be competitors, but [we] need never be enemies."

June 3. *Quadripartite Berlin Agreement.* The four countries that have responsibility for the divided status of Berlin — the Soviet Union, the United States, France, and Great Britain — sign the final protocol of the four-power agreement. The groundwork was laid in September 1971.

July 8. *U.S.-Soviet Grain Deal.* After months of negotiations, the Soviet Union and the United States agree on a three-year grain deal. It is to date the largest commercial agreement between the two powers and involves approximately $750 million worth of U.S. wheat and other grain.

July 18. *Sadat Expels Soviet Advisers.* President Sadat orders all Soviet military advisers and experts out of Egypt and places all Soviet bases and equipment under Egyptian control. Sadat says in a four-hour speech July 24 that the Soviet Union's reticence in selling arms to Egypt led him to his decision.

July 20 - August 1. *U.S. Trade Officials in Moscow.* The U.S. government dispatches a 30-member delegation, including Secretary of Commerce Peter G. Peterson, to Moscow to initiate discussion on U.S.-Soviet trade.

August 3. *Restrictions on Jewish Emigration.* An exit visa fee for Jewish citizens wishing to emigrate is proclaimed by the Soviet government. According to Soviet officials, the fees are to reimburse the state for educational funds spent on its citizens. Fees range from $4,400 to $37,000, depending on the amount of education received.

August 30. *Debate Over Soviet Grain Sale.* Accusations of violations of conflict-of-interest laws are brought by the Consumers' Union toward the Department of Agriculture. On September 8, Democratic presidential candidate George McGovern charges that the actions of the Nixon administration and large grain exporters resulted in the exploitation of U.S. farmers.

September 5. *Soviet-Syrian Cooperation.* Syria and the Soviet Union agree to new security arrangements. The Soviet Union will improve naval facilities in two Syrian ports for Soviet use, and Syria will receive jet fighters and air defense missiles.

September 9. *Soviets Continue Buildup.* Officials in Washington are quoted as saying the Soviets recently added several mechanized divisions to their troops on the Sino-Soviet border, increasing their strength in the area to nearly one-third of the Soviet army.

September 20. *Nixon Orders Inquiry.* Nixon orders the FBI to investigate the accusation that U.S. grain exporters made "illegal excess profits" from the recent grain sale to the USSR.

September 27. *Jackson on Exit Fees.* Sen. Henry M. Jackson, D-Wash., says he will introduce an amendment to the East-West trade relations act that would link trade concessions to the Soviet Union with "the freedom to emigrate without the payment of prohibitive taxes amounting to ransom." Administration officials maintain that "quiet diplomacy" is the proper route to solve this problem. They reject the "linkage" approach.

October 2-3. *Nixon-Gromyko Talks.* In Washington President Nixon and Soviet foreign minister Andrei Gromyko discuss a wide range of topics. They sign documents that put into effect the SALT I arms accords agreed upon at the Moscow summit in May.

October 4. *Jackson-Vanik Amendment.* Senator Jackson and 75 cosponsors introduce an amendment to the East-West trade bill, barring most-favored-nation status to nations that restrict emigration of their citizens. Rep. Charles A. Vanik, D-Ohio, introduces a similar measure in the House.

October 18. *Signing of U.S.-Soviet Trade Pact.* The trade relations agreement between the U.S. and Soviet governments includes a settlement of the USSR World War II lend-lease debt and a U.S. promise to push for most-favored-nation status for the Soviet Union, despite congressional attempts to link credits with restricted Jewish emigration. President Nixon promises to ask for credits from the Export-Import Bank as well. Trade between the United States and the Soviet Union in the next three years is projected to reach $1.5 billion.

November 1. *Missiles Restored.* Observers report that the USSR will restore missiles to Egypt's air defense system that were removed when the Soviets were ousted in July.

November 7. *Nixon Reelected.* Richard Nixon easily defeats Democrat George McGovern to win another term as president.

November 21. *SALT II Negotiations.* The second set of SALT negotiations begins in Geneva with the purpose of expanding the SALT I agreement.

December 18-30. *Bombing of North Vietnam.* U.S. forces resume bombing North Vietnam above the 20th parallel after peace negotiations in Paris are broken off. The massive air attacks against Hanoi and Haiphong, which caused many casualties and extensive damage, provoke protests both within the United States and abroad. On December 30 the White House announces that the bombings have been halted and peace talks between Henry Kissinger and Le Duc Tho will resume in Paris on January 8, 1973.

December 21-23. *50th Anniversary of Soviet Union.* The 50th anniversary of the founding of the Soviet state is celebrated in Moscow. Party head Leonid Brezhnev delivers a lengthy speech in which he condemns the U.S. bombing in Vietnam. He also accuses China of "undisguised sabotage" of Soviet peace efforts and of attempts to "split" the world communist movement. President Nixon sends a good-will message.

1973

January 27. *Peace Agreements Signed.* Representatives of the United States, North Vietnam, South Vietnam, and the Viet Cong sign a peace agreement in Paris. Although the agreement calls for a cease-fire in Vietnam, it does not end the fighting in Laos or Cambodia. On January 23 President Nixon had announced the completion of an agreement "to end the war and bring peace with honor in Vietnam and Southeast Asia."

February 7. *Watergate Committee Formed.* The Senate votes unanimously to establish a bipartisan select committee to investigate the entire range of activities known as "Watergate."

February 21. *Soviet-U.S. Fishing Agreements.* The governments of the Soviet Union and the United States announce the conclusion of a series of fishing agreements designed to end incidents that occurred off the Pacific and Atlantic coastlines of the United States.

March 11-14. *Soviet-U.S. Trade Talks.* Secretary of the Treasury George P. Shultz discusses U.S.-Soviet trade with Soviet leader Leonid I. Brezhnev in Moscow. On March 15, Sen. Henry M. Jackson, D-Wash., reintroduces the amendment to the East-West trade relations bill to "block trade concessions until free emigration [is] assured."

March 20. *Export-Import Loan Agreements.* The Soviet Union Foreign Trade Bank is granted its first loan from the Export-Import Bank. The Soviet Union receives $101.2 million in direct loans, while American banks promise another $101.2 million for the purchase of U.S. industrial equipment.

March 29. *Vietnam Withdrawal.* North Vietnam releases 67 prisoners of war and the United States withdraws its remaining 2,500 troops from South Vietnam.

April 27. *Politburo Shake-up.* The Central Committee of the Soviet Communist Party publicly endorses Brezhnev's détente policy. In a move viewed as bolstering Brezhnev's authority, several of his conservative critics are ousted from the Politburo. These include Petr Shelest and Gennadii Voronov. Full Politburo membership is granted to Andrei Grechko, defense minister; Andrei Gromyko, foreign minister; and Yuri Andropov, chairman of the Committee for State Security (KGB).

April 30. *White House Reshuffle.* In response to increasing criticism President Nixon announces the resignations of four men implicated in the Watergate cover-up: H. R. Haldeman, White House chief of staff; John D. Ehrlichman, chief adviser for domestic affairs; John W. Dean III, presidential counsel; and Attorney General Richard G. Kleindienst.

May 18-22. *Brezhnev in Bonn.* Soviet leader Leonid Brezhnev visits West Germany and engages in extensive talks with Chancellor Willy Brandt. They sign several accords May 19, including a 10-year economic cooperation agreement.

June 7. *Helsinki Preparatory Talks Close.* The preparatory talks for the European Conference on Security and Cooperation close in Helsinki after the agenda is finalized. Preliminary discussions took six months to complete. The conference agenda includes European security and scientific cooperation. The United States receives reluctant agreement from the Soviet delegation for the inclusion of discussions on "freer exchange of people, ideas, and information."

June 8. *Natural Gas Agreement.* An agreement involving the development of Siberian natural gas fields is reached between the Soviet Trade Ministry, U.S. Occidental Petroleum Co., and El Paso Natural Gas Co. The signed agreements, pending approval by the U.S. government, involve a $10 billion project with eventual daily shipments to the United States of 2 billion cubic feet of gas.

June 16-25. *Brezhnev to U.S. for Summit.* Amidst ongoing Watergate investigations Soviet party leader Leonid Brezhnev arrives in Washington for talks with President Nixon. During the summit the two leaders sign seven agreements concerning cooperation on the development of atomic energy as well as the exchange of information on agriculture, transportation, oceanography, and commerce. The two also pledge to accelerate the SALT talks and complete a new treaty by the end of 1974.

July 3-7. *Opening of CSCE in Helsinki.* The first session of the Conference on Security and Cooperation in Europe — held at the foreign ministers' level — opens in Helsinki.

July 31. *U.S.-Soviet Trade Increases.* U.S.-Soviet trade volume in the first half of 1973 is greater than all of 1972 and totals $694.4 million.

August 15. *U.S. Bombing in Cambodia Ends.* The U.S. combat role in Indochina comes to an end, as American bombers stop their flights over Cambodia. Congress had voted an end to the bombing June 30, and President Nixon promised to honor the vote despite his objections.

August 21. *Sakharov Warnings.* In a discussion with Western media, Andrei Sakharov, a well-known dissident Soviet physicist, warns of the dangers of accepting détente on Soviet terms. Sakharov feels the Jackson-Vanik amendment to the East-West Trade Relations Act does not go far enough to pressure the Soviet Union to improve its human rights policies.

September 9. *U.S. Reaction to Anti-Sakharov Campaign.* In the aftermath of a Soviet press campaign against Andrei Sakharov, the U.S. National Academy of Sciences September 9 announces to its Soviet counterpart that American scientists will not continue in joint research projects unless the harassment is stopped. The Soviet campaign, which consists of a series of accusatory letters in Soviet publications, begins August 29 with a letter written by 39 academicians of the Soviet Academy of Sciences, of which Sakharov is a member. The letter accuses Sakharov of joining "the most reactionary imperialist circles, which actively oppose the course of peaceful coexistence."

September 29. *Nixon-Gromyko Talks.* President Nixon and Soviet foreign minister Andrei Gromyko meet in Washington. Nixon is believed to have assured Gromyko that he would continue to pressure Congress to grant the Soviet Union most-favored-nation status. Mutual balanced force reductions and SALT II are also discussed.

October 1-3. *Shultz in Moscow.* Treasury Secretary George Shultz notes at the conclusion of discussions on bilateral trade in Moscow that expanded trade with the Soviet Union is held up by Congress's refusal to grant most-favored-nation status to Moscow as well as by the Soviets' unwillingness to make further concessions on Jewish emigration.

October 2. *Chinese Attack Détente.* Chinese deputy foreign minister Qiao Guanhua attacks the United States and the Soviet Union before the UN General Assembly.

Qiao criticizes détente, asserting that the two superpowers seek to divide the world into spheres of influence.

October 6. *Yom Kippur War.* War breaks out in the Middle East on the Jewish holy day of Yom Kippur. Egyptian forces cross the Suez Canal and Syria attacks the Golan Heights. Israeli forces counter on October 7, striking back in the Sinai and on the Golan Heights.

October 10. *Agnew Resigns.* Spiro T. Agnew resigns as vice president of the United States. He is replaced two days later by House Minority Leader Gerald R. Ford, R-Mich.

October 17. *Sadat's Peace Proposal.* Egyptian President Anwar al-Sadat, in an open letter to President Nixon, proposes an immediate cease-fire with Israel on the condition that Israel withdraws to pre-1967 boundaries. The same day foreign ministers of four Arab states meet in Washington with President Nixon and Secretary of State Henry A. Kissinger to present a similar peace proposal.

October 18. *Arab Oil Embargo.* Libya cuts off all shipments of crude oil and petroleum products to the United States. The same day Saudi Arabia announces a 10 percent cut in oil production and pledges to cut off all U.S. oil shipments if American support of Israel continues. On October 20 it cuts off all oil exports to the United States.

October 20. *Kissinger in Moscow.* Secretary of State Kissinger arrives in Moscow for talks with Brezhnev on restoring peace to the Middle East.

October 21. *Oil Embargo Widened.* Kuwait, Qatar, Bahrain, and Dubai suspend all oil exports to the United States, theoretically marking the cutoff of all oil from Arab countries to the United States.

October 21. *U.S.-Soviet Joint UN Resolution.* The United States and the Soviet Union present a joint resolution to the UN Security Council calling for a cease-fire in the Middle East and for implementation of a Security Council resolution calling for Israeli withdrawal from lands it has occupied since the 1967 war. The proposal, formulated during Secretary of State Kissinger's trip to Moscow, is adopted by the Security Council October 22.

October 22. *Cease-fire in the Middle East.* A cease-fire takes effect on the Egyptian-Israeli front, but sporadic fighting continues. Jordan accepts the cease-fire proposal, while Iraq and the Palestine Liberation Organization reject it.

October 23. *Security Council Vote.* The UN Security Council votes to reaffirm the Middle East cease-fire, requests Egypt and Israel to return to the cease-fire line established the day before, and asks that UN observers be stationed along the Israeli-Egyptian cease-fire line.

October 24. *Sadat Appeals.* Egyptian president Anwar al-Sadat appeals to the United States and the Soviet Union to send troops for supervision of the cease-fire. The White House announces it will not send forces.

October 25. *U.S. Orders Military Alert.* President Nixon orders a worldwide U.S. military alert as tension mounts over whether the Soviet Union will intervene in the Middle East crisis. Secretary of State Kissinger says in a news conference that the U.S. move is inspired by intelligence reports that the Soviet Union may attempt to airlift troops into Egypt, ostensibly as a peace-keeping force. To avert a U.S.-USSR confrontation in the Middle East, the UN Security Council votes to establish an emergency supervisory force to observe the cease-fire.

October 27. *Direct Negotiations.* The United States announces that Egypt and Israel have agreed to negotiate directly on implementing the cease-fire.

November 11. *Cease-fire Signed.* Israel and Egypt sign a cease-fire accord, drawn up by Secretary of State Kissinger and Egyptian president Anwar al-Sadat November 7 in Cairo. This is the first signing of an important joint document by the two countries since the 1949 armistice ending the first Arab-Israeli war.

December 11. *Trade Bill Passes.* The Houses passes the foreign trade bill, which includes the Jackson-Vanik amendment "barring most-favored-nation treatment for any nation that restricts emigration" for its citizens. The amendment is included over President Nixon's objections. The president, unlike several congressional leaders, opposes the concept of linkage and had virtually assured the Soviet Union of MFN status.

December 21. *Mideast Peace Conference.* The first Arab-Israeli peace conference opens in Geneva, with Israel, Egypt, Jordan, the United States, and the Soviet Union taking part. Syria boycotts the conference.

1974

January 2. *Soviet Condemnation of* Gulag Archipelago. The Soviet news agency Tass responds with virulent criticism after Alexander Solzhenitsyn's book *The Gulag Archipelago, 1918-1956* is published in the West.

January 17. *Suez Disengagement Accords.* Secretary of State Henry A. Kissinger's "shuttle diplomacy" in the Middle East results in the announcement of accords on Suez disengagement. According to the agreement, the Egyptian-Israeli forces along the Suez Canal will be separated to specific disengagement zones. The accords are signed January 18. The pullback to the delineated zones is to be completed in 40 days, with a UN truce force acting as a buffer between Israeli and Egyptian troops.

January 19. *Soviet Diplomats Expelled.* Beijing expels three Soviet diplomats and two of their wives after charging them with espionage and subversion. On January 21 Moscow retaliates by expelling a Chinese diplomat.

February 13. *Solzhenitsyn Expelled.* Soviet author Alexander Solzhenitsyn is expelled to West Germany following his arrest in Moscow. Soviet authorities take action after the widely publicized appearance of Solzhenitsyn's book *Gulag Archipelago* in the West.

February 19. *SALT Talks Resume.* U.S.-Soviet negotiations to reduce strategic arms resume in Geneva. The talks adjourn March 19.

February 28. *U.S.-Egyptian Relations Renewed.* The United States and Egypt renew full diplomatic relations after a seven-year break. President Anwar al-Sadat announces he has invited President Richard Nixon to visit Egypt.

March 1. *Indictment of White House Officials.* Seven former White House and Nixon campaign aides are indicted by Washington grand juries on charges of covering up the Watergate affair. On June 6 it is reported and confirmed that the grand jury had voted unanimously to name President Nixon an unindicted coconspirator.

March 11-23. *Credits to Soviet Union Halted.* A legal technicality causes a temporary cutoff of Export-Import Bank credits to the Soviet Union, Poland, Romania, and Yugoslavia. The action coincides with continuing controversy in the United States over whether to link favorable trade treatment for the Soviets with the Jewish emigration issue.

March 18. *Oil Embargo Partially Lifted.* Arab states meet in Vienna; Saudi Arabia, Algeria, Egypt, Kuwait, Abu Dhabi, Bahrain, and Qatar agree to lift a five-month-old embargo against the United States. Libya and Syria refuse to join in the decision.

March 24-28. *Kissinger in Moscow.* Secretary of State Kissinger holds talks with Soviet leaders in Moscow in anticipation of President Nixon's upcoming visit to the Soviet Union. It is widely reported that the talks fail to achieve Kissinger's aim of "concrete progress" on SALT II and East-West mutual troop reductions.

April 7. *Nixon Meets Podgornyi in Paris.* President Nixon and Soviet president Nikolai Podgornyi discuss the forthcoming Moscow summit and SALT II. Both are in Paris attending the funeral of French president Georges Pompidou.

April 10. *New Chinese Foreign Policy.* Chinese vice premier Deng Xiaoping, in an address to a special session of the UN General Assembly, outlines the basis of a new Chinese foreign policy. Rejecting the existence of a socialist camp because of the Soviet Union's actions as a superpower, Deng argues that there are three "worlds" in existence: the Soviet Union and the United States comprise the First World, all other developed nations are the Second World, and the Third World is made up of all underdeveloped nations. Deng offers China as the leader of the Third World, as Chou En-lai had done in 1954.

April 12. *Gromyko in Washington.* En route to Moscow after an appearance at the United Nations, Soviet foreign minister Andrei Gromyko visits Washington. His discussions with President Nixon and Secretary of State Kissinger focus on the Middle East and SALT II.

April 18. *Egyptian Arms.* President Anwar al-Sadat says Egypt no longer will rely solely on the Soviet Union for arms.

May 9. *Impeachment Hearings Begin.* The House Judiciary Committee formally opens its impeachment hearings against President Nixon.

May 15. *Sino-Soviet Trade Agreement.* Despite an increase in the verbal hostility between the Soviet Union and China, the two nations sign a trade agreement that calls for a 12 percent increase in trade for 1974.

May 18. *India Tests Nuclear Device.* After successfully exploding a nuclear device, India denies any intention to use nuclear technology for military purposes. Prime Minister Indira Gandhi declares, "We are firmly committed only to the peaceful uses of atomic energy."

June 27-July 3. *Third Moscow Summit.* President Nixon and Soviet party chief Leonid I. Brezhnev sign a series of limited agreements on nuclear weapons during their third summit meeting in Moscow. In a Moscow press conference Secretary of State Kissinger blames Watergate for a lack of more substantial negotiations between the two leaders. He charges that Nixon's effectiveness as a leader is being impaired. Nixon returns to the United States July 3. The Soviet Union was the second stop on his trip, which began at a NATO meeting in Brussels June 25-26.

July 8. *Jackson on Normalization.* Following a seven-day visit to China, Sen. Henry M. Jackson, D-Wash., says he told Chinese leaders that China and America are developing a "real" détente, and that, unlike the "untrustworthy Russians," Americans keep their word.

July 15. *Greek-Led Military Coup in Cyprus.* The

Cypriot National Guard commanded by Greek officers overthrows the president of Cyprus, Archbishop Makarios. The new regime reaffirms a desire for an independent Cyprus, and there is no indication that union of Cyprus with Greece will be attempted. However, war threatens between Greece and Turkey as both nations deploy armed forces in an effort to exercise military power over Cyprus. The United States is discreet in its support for Cypriot independence, while the USSR assures Turkey of its support.

July 20. *Turkey Invades Cyprus.* Turkey invades Cyprus by sea and air. A UN-imposed cease-fire begins July 22. The next day the ruling junta in Greece resigns after seven years in power because of its failure to control the Cyprus coup. Civilian rule under former premier Constantine Caramanlis is restored.

August 8. *Nixon Resigns.* In a dramatic television address Richard Nixon announces his resignation from the presidency. Vice President Gerald R. Ford is sworn in as the 38th president the next day. Soviet reaction emphasizes that U.S.-Soviet relations will continue unchanged. Nixon is portrayed in a Moscow television program on August 10 as a victim of political maneuvering and vicious media attacks.

August 30. *Ford on Foreign Policy.* President Ford declares he is looking forward to "new peaceful relationships, not only with the Soviet Union and the People's Republic of China, but with all peoples and every nation if we possibly can."

September 6. *Soviet Pilot Defects.* A lieutenant of the Soviet air force flies his MiG-25 jet to Japan and asks for political asylum.

September 8. *Ford Pardons Nixon.* President Ford grants former president Nixon a "full, free and absolute pardon . . . for all offenses against the United States which he has committed or may have committed" during his years as chief executive. The pardon raises a storm of controversy with Congress and the press.

September 18. *SALT Talks Resume.* Strategic arms limitation talks resume in Geneva; they adjourn November 5.

October 1. *Soviet Criticisms.* On China's National Day Soviet high officials send their greetings and best wishes to the "Chinese people." The message stresses that normalization of ties between the two countries should be achieved through a nonaggression treaty. A commentary in *Pravda* the same day notes the aid that the Soviet Union has given China in the past and charges China's leadership with siding with reactionaries and committing ideological heresy.

October 23. *Kissinger in Moscow.* Secretary of State Kissinger visits Moscow as part of a three-week, worldwide diplomatic tour. Kissinger discusses arms limitation, trade, and the Middle East and reports some progress. But differences remain. The Soviets are annoyed at U.S. publicity surrounding Soviet assurances to increase Jewish emigration. They are also resentful over the cancellation and only partial restoration of a recent grain deal with the United States. President Ford October 4 postponed a sales agreement for the shipment of $3.2 million tons of grain. On October 19 the Treasury Department announced a new agreement that allowed Moscow to purchase 2.2 million tons of U.S. grain through June 1975.

November 23-24. *Vladivostok Summit.* President Ford travels to the Soviet Union to sign a tentative agreement to limit the number of all U.S. and USSR offensive nuclear weapons through 1985.

November 25. *Kissinger to Beijing.* Secretary of State Kissinger arrives in China directly from the summit talks with Soviet leaders at Vladivostok. He briefs Chinese leaders on the Brezhnev-Ford summit and discusses Sino-U.S. relations.

November 26. *Soviets Reject Chinese Offer.* Speaking at a rally in Ulan Bator, Mongolia, Soviet leader Brezhnev rejects the Chinese offer to negotiate the Sino-Soviet border dispute on the ground that there should be no preconditions to any negotiations. The Chinese are demanding the withdrawal of all Soviet troops prior to any discussions.

December 20. *Foreign Trade Bill Passes.* Congress passes the foreign trade bill, which extends greater trade privileges to the Soviet Union in exchange for increased Jewish emigration. The bill is passed despite a December 18 Tass statement denying any agreement to allow freer emigration.

December 30. *Brezhnev Cancels Visit.* Soviet leader Brezhnev calls off his January visit to the Middle East. No official reason is given. Speculation ranges from poor health to serious diplomatic differences between Cairo and Moscow.

1975

January 14. *Soviets Cancel 1972 Trade Agreement.* Secretary of State Henry A. Kissinger announces the Soviet Union's cancellation of the 1972 trade agreement with the United States. The Kremlin objects to recent legislative action in the United States unfavorable to Soviet interests, such as the measure limiting credits to the Soviets and an amendment to the trade reform act that grants trade privileges only if the Soviet Union permits freer Jewish emigration. As a result the Soviet Union will not pay its World War II lend-lease debts, and it will not receive most-favored-nation status or Export-Import Bank loans from the United States.

January 21. *Resumption of SALT II.* The SALT II negotiations resume in Geneva in the wake of the Soviet-U.S. agreements signed in Vladivostok in November 1974. This round of talks adjourns May 7.

February 18. *Egypt Buys Soviet Arms.* Egypt confirms it is receiving Soviet arms for the first time since the 1973 Arab-Israeli war.

March 18. *Soviet Overtures.* Soviet leader Leonid I. Brezhnev reaffirms the need for increased international détente. Speaking at a Hungarian Party Congress, Brezhnev places special emphasis on a successful outcome of the upcoming Conference on Security and Cooperation in Europe. On March 21 the Soviet magazine *Novoye Vremya* (New Times) calls for a successful conclusion to a SALT agreement in 1975.

March 27. *Soviets Rebuff Kissinger on Middle East.* The Soviet Communist Party newspaper *Pravda* publishes an article about Secretary of State Kissinger's peace efforts in the Middle East, saying that they "confirmed the hopelessness of so-called partial solutions to the Near East problem with the aid of 'quiet diplomacy.'" Soviet officials call for the reconvening of the Geneva peace conference, which would assure the Soviet Union maximum input in the peace-making process.

April 10. *Ford's "State of the World" Message.* In his "State of the World" message, President Ford reaffirms the U.S. commitment to détente. He asks Congress to lift existing trade and economic restrictions on the Soviet Union.

April 16. *Removal of Shelepin.* Alexander N. Shelepin, former head of the KGB, is removed from the Politburo. At one time considered a possible challenger to Brezhnev's authority, he had diminished in influence since his demotion from the Secretariat in 1967.

April 30. *South Vietnam Surrenders.* The Vietnam War ends as the South Vietnamese government surrenders to communist forces, and Viet Cong and North Vietnamese troops enter Saigon.

May 12-14. *Capture of the* Mayaguez. The Cambodian government May 12 seizes the American merchant ship *Mayaguez* in the Gulf of Siam. The Ford administration reacts May 14 by sending 200 U.S. Marines, who retake the ship and its crew. Tass describes the U.S. action as "a military intervention to rescue the spy ship *Mayaguez* seized earlier in Cambodian waters."

June 10. *Schlesinger Suspects Somali Base.* Secretary of Defense James R. Schlesinger at a Senate Armed Services Committee hearing accuses the Soviet Union of building naval facilities in the Somalian port of Berbera on the Gulf of Aden. It is thought the base will facilitate Soviet naval exercises in the Indian Ocean. Tass responds June 12, saying that "the American Defense Minister ... must have fallen victim to a mirage...."

June 20. *Soviet Missile Capabilities Increase.* Defense Secretary James R. Schlesinger announces that Moscow has deployed 60 intercontinental ballistic missiles armed with multiple independently targetable warheads in the last six months. Schlesinger adds that these new developments could have a "destabilizing influence" on the balance of strategic weapons.

June 30. *Solzhenitsyn on Détente.* In a speech to the AFL-CIO in Washington, Soviet author Alexander Solzhenitsyn warns of the dangers of détente and of making too many concessions to the Soviets.

July 2. *Ford Refuses to Meet Solzhenitsyn.* President Ford declines to meet with Alexander Solzhenitsyn because of a busy White House schedule. In a news conference July 16 Secretary of State Kissinger discloses that he and other White House aides believed the meeting would damage U.S.-Soviet relations.

July 3. *Sino-Soviet Split Heats Up.* The Chinese Xinhua news agency accuses the Soviet leadership of following in Hitler's footsteps. The commentary accuses Brezhnev of talking peace while preparing for war, militarizing the economy, and invading other countries on absurd pretexts.

July 10-11. *Kissinger-Gromyko Meeting.* Secretary of State Kissinger and Foreign Minister Andrei Gromyko meet in Geneva to discuss U.S.-Soviet relations, in particular the issues that have stalled SALT II negotiations.

July 17. *Successful Apollo-Soyuz Mission.* The first joint Soviet-U.S. space exploration project (called the Apollo-Soyuz Test Project) is capped by the successful rendezvous in space of the Apollo and Soyuz spacecraft.

July 31-August 1. *Conference on Security and Cooperation in Europe.* The largest summit conference in European history, the Conference on Security and Cooperation in Europe (CSCE), convenes in Helsinki. Preparatory talks began in 1972. The conference culminates August 1 with the signing of a 100-page declaration (known as the *Final Act*) by leaders of the 35 participating nations. The Final Act's provisions express a desire for cooperation between nations, a permanent peace for Europe, and respect for the boundaries within the European continent. The Final Act is nonbinding and does not have treaty status. Both President Ford and Soviet party chief Leonid Brezhnev participate in the conference. The Helsinki meeting sparks controversy in the West, primarily because opponents consider the Final Act too conciliatory toward the Soviet Union.

August 14. *Concern Over Events in Portugal.* Secretary of State Kissinger makes an official policy statement in Birmingham, Alabama, on the situation in Portugal. Moderate and conservative forces there oppose Premier Vasco Goncalves and the Communist Party for attempting to impose a communist-led government. Kissinger's comments come in the wake of violent Portuguese demonstrations against these procommunist forces. The United States objects to Soviet support of the Portuguese Communist Party during the crisis. Kissinger states, "The Soviet Union should not assume it has the option, either directly or indirectly, to influence events contrary to the right of the Portuguese people to determine their own future."

August 19. *Soviets Respond to Kissinger.* An article appearing in *Pravda*, understood to reflect the opinions of the Soviet leaders, emphasizes "massive solidarity" with the Communist Party in Portugal.

September 1. *Signing of Sinai Pact.* In separate ceremonies in Jerusalem and Alexandria, Israeli and Egyptian leaders initial the new Sinai Pact. Kissinger initials provisions for stationing U.S. technicians in the Sinai. President Ford asks Congress to approve the new U.S. role in the Middle East.

October 9. *Sakharov Wins Nobel.* Andrei Sakharov, a leading Soviet physicist and dissident, is awarded the Nobel Peace Prize. The action inspires press attacks on Sakharov in the Soviet Union. Moscow denies Sakharov a visa to attend the ceremonies in Oslo, Norway. Sakharov's wife, Yelena Bonner, participates in the Oslo ceremonies December 10 and accepts the Nobel Prize in his name.

October 20. *Soviets Purchase U.S. Grain.* A five-year agreement involving the Soviet purchase of 6 to 8 million tons of American grain annually is announced by the White House. Four days later three U.S. grain corporations announce separate deals, bringing the total amount of grain sales to approximately 11.5 million tons in 1975.

November 2. *Schlesinger Dismissed.* President Ford fires Secretary of Defense James R. Schlesinger, reportedly because of a deepening rift between Schlesinger and Secretary of State Henry A. Kissinger. Part of the reason is that Schlesinger feels Kissinger is too flexible with the Soviets on certain SALT II issues. The Soviet reaction is muted but the Chinese official news agency expresses disapproval. The Schlesinger dismissal is part of a larger administration shake-up.

November 12. *Soviets See No Ideological Détente.* In an attempt to explain Soviet actions in Portugal and Angola, an article in the Soviet military newspaper *Krasnaya Zvezda* states that despite gains toward détente in the political/military sphere, ideological détente between the United States and the Soviet Union is not possible.

November 24. *U.S. Criticizes Soviet Involvement in Angola.* Secretary of State Kissinger protests Soviet and Cuban military involvement in the ongoing Angolan civil war. Speaking in Detroit, Kissinger states that Soviet actions are resulting in "an increasingly skeptical administration view of the Soviet Union's sincerity in improving relations with the United States."

December 16. *Ford's Statement on Angola.* President Ford makes his first public remarks on Angola as criticism of U.S. involvement in the region heats up on Capitol Hill. Ford expresses grave concern about Soviet and Cuban military involvement and calls the situation "not helpful" to détente.

December 23. *Kissinger Follow-Up on Angola.* Secretary of State Kissinger states in a news conference that the Soviets have not directly responded to U.S. requests to end their involvement in Angola and that "there is no question that the United States will not accept Soviet military expansion of any kind." Kissinger expresses his support for continued U.S. aid to the anti-Soviet forces in Angola.

December 24-25. *Soviet Position on Angola.* An article in the Soviet government newspaper *Izvestiia* says that the Soviets are in Angola because "support for the national liberation struggles . . . is one of the most important principles of Soviet foreign policy, as is the consistent struggle for the improvement of international relations and for the further materialization of détente."

1976

January 7. *Soviet Warships Near Angola.* The U.S. government reveals evidence uncovered by intelligence reports that Soviet war ships are heading toward Angola. The allegations are denied by the official Soviet news agency Tass, which defends Soviet support of the Popular Movement for the Liberation of Angola (MPLA).

January 8. *Chou En-lai Dies.* Chinese premier Chou En-lai dies in Beijing. Deputy Premier Hua Guofeng is appointed "acting" premier according to a February 7 Xinhua news agency press release.

January 21-23. *Kissinger in Moscow.* Secretary of State Henry A. Kissinger cites "significant progress" during his discussions with Soviet officials on SALT II. Certain points of contention, including the Soviet Backfire bomber and U.S. cruise missiles, are clarified, and Kissinger states he will return to the United States with new Soviet proposals. Kissinger also attempts to discuss the Angolan situation, but no agreements are achieved.

January 30. *Kissinger Testifies on Angola.* Secretary of State Henry A. Kissinger states in testimony before Congress that the Ford administration will not ask for relaxation of restrictions on U.S. trade with the Soviet Union until its involvement in Angola is ended. Soviet newspapers respond on February 1, accusing President Ford and Kissinger of misrepresenting Soviet policies and intentions in the region.

February 10. *U.S. Embassy in Moscow Bugged.* U.S. officials confirm that the U.S. Embassy in Moscow has warned its employees about potentially dangerous radiation in the building caused by Soviet electronic eavesdropping devices.

February 11. *MPLA Recognized.* The Popular Movement for the Liberation of Angola (MPLA), sup-ported by thousands of Cuban troops, is judged by the Organization of African States to have established sufficient control over Angola and is recognized as its legitimate government. Many West European nations intend to recognize the MPLA by the end of the month.

February 24 - March 5. *Soviet Party Congress.* The 25th Congress of the Communist Party of the Soviet Union convenes in Moscow and, like the 24th Congress, supports the continued leadership of Leonid I. Brezhnev. Brezhnev reaffirms Soviet commitment to détente as well as to an ideological class struggle. He attests to Soviet willingness to end the arms race and defends the Soviet role in Angola as one faithful to "our revolutionary conscience." In discussing relations with China, Brezhnev reproaches Chinese leaders for "frantic efforts to torpedo détente." Two leaders are appointed to full membership in the Politburo — Grigori V. Romanov, head of the Leningrad Communist Party Committee, and Dmitri F. Ustinov, Central Committee secretary responsible for the defense industry.

March 14. *Sadat Abrogates Treaty.* President Anwar al-Sadat moves to end Egypt's 1971 Treaty of Cooperation and Friendship with the Soviet Union.

March 17. *Suslov Attacks West European Communists.* Tass reports a speech by Soviet party ideologist Mikhail Suslov criticizing the independent path of the West European communist parties. He labels those who stray from communist dogma "enemies of Marxism."

March 25. *Brezhnev Visit Unlikely.* The *New York Times* reports that Brezhnev is unlikely to visit the United States because of strained U.S.-Soviet relations over world trouble spots such as Angola.

April 2. *Soviet Concern Over Détente Slowdown.* Americanologist and director of the Soviet Union's Institute of the USA and Canada Georgii Arbatov warns in a Tass commentary that "deep-rooted enemies [in the United States] of the improvement in relations" could have damaging effects on the political atmosphere between the two superpowers. He criticizes President Ford's usage of the phrase "peace through strength" rather than détente.

April 11. *SALT Deadlocked.* The *New York Times* reports that SALT II negotiations are at a stalemate.

April 18. *Egypt and China.* Egyptian vice president Hosni Mubarak arrives in China for an official visit. The trip follows Chinese acclamation of Cairo's abrogation of its treaty of friendship with the Soviet Union and China's statement of its readiness to send military supplies to Egypt.

April 29. *Ford on Minuteman III.* At a Houston press conference President Ford states that the "slowdown" in SALT negotiations is responsible for his decision to continue Minuteman III ICBM production, which was originally scheduled to end June 30.

April 29. *Ustinov Named Defense Head.* Dmitri Ustinov is appointed Soviet defense minister upon the death of his predecessor, Marshal Andrei Grechko.

May 28. *Underground A-Pact Signed.* In joint ceremonies in Washington and Moscow, President Ford and Soviet party chief Brezhnev sign a treaty limiting the size of underground nuclear explosions for peaceful purposes. The treaty, originally scheduled for signing March 13, had been delayed after the United States announced a deferral on May 12 for unspecified reasons. Administration sources later revealed the delay was due to presidential campaign politics. The Ford camp did not want to make the president vulnerable to political attacks from Ronald Reagan supporters who opposed cooperation with the Soviet Union.

June 5. *Soviets on SALT Delay.* An article in *Pravda* accuses the Ford administration of failure to cooperate in stepping up a conclusion of SALT negotiations. Brezhnev reiterates the charge June 29.

July 4. *Bicentennial Greetings.* Soviet president Nikolai Podgornyi sends bicentennial greetings to President Ford in which he expresses the Soviet desire for the growth and strengthening of U.S.-Soviet relations in the interest of securing world peace.

September 9. *Mao Tse-tung Dies.* Chinese Communist Party chairman Mao Tse-tung dies at 82. The Soviet Communist Party sends a telegram to its Chinese counterpart — the first in more than a decade — expressing its "deep condolences." Beijing rejects the telegram September 14.

September 20. *Harriman in Moscow.* Former ambassador to the Soviet Union Averell Harriman meets Soviet leader Brezhnev in Moscow. In a subsequent interview Harriman takes note of Soviet concern over anti-Soviet statements made during the current U.S. presidential election campaign.

September 21. *SALT Talks Resume.* SALT negotiators return to the bargaining table in Geneva. The issue of the inclusion of Soviet long-range bombers and U.S. cruise missiles remains troublesome. Despite an October 2 meeting between Soviet foreign minister Andrei Gromyko and President Ford, no progress on SALT is expected until after the U.S. presidential election.

October 6. *Ford-Carter Second Debate.* In the second of a series of debates between the two main U.S. presidential candidates, Democratic challenger Jimmy Carter focuses his attacks on President Ford's foreign policy achievements. Ford defends his record and the U.S.-Soviet relationship by stating that "... there is no Soviet domination of Eastern Europe and there never will be under a Ford administration." Carter attacks the statement during his campaigning, calling it a "very serious blunder." Ford tries several times after the debate to clarify his statement but admits to a group of ethnic leaders October 12 that he misspoke.

October 10. *Attacks on Moscow Escalate.* The Beijing *People's Daily* publishes a long article strongly reaffirming the anti-Soviet credentials of the new Chinese leadership.

November 2. *Carter Elected.* Democrat Jimmy Carter is elected as the 39th president of the United States by a small margin.

November 12. *MiG Returned to USSR.* The Japanese government ships a Soviet MiG-25 jet fighter back to the Soviet Union in 13 crates; its pilot defected in 1974.

November 21. *U.S. Pact with Romania.* Secretary of Commerce Elliot L. Richardson signs a 10-year trade and economic cooperation pact with Romania in Bucharest. It is the most comprehensive agreement that the United States has negotiated with an East European nation.

November 28. *Sino-Soviet Border Talks Resume.* Leonid Ilyichev, Soviet deputy foreign minister, arrives in Beijing to resume the Sino-Soviet border talks that were suspended for 18 months. There are indications both sides have hardened their positions in the interval.

November 30. *Brezhnev on New Administration.* Soviet leader Leonid Brezhnev tells U.S. businessmen attending the U.S.-USSR Trade and Economic Council in Moscow that SALT should be a top-priority concern of the new Carter administration. President-elect Carter, reportedly in response to Brezhnev's appeal, responds December 3 with a promise to move "aggressively" toward a successful conclusion of the negotiations.

December 27. *Carter to Meet Brezhnev.* President-elect Carter announces that a summit meeting to discuss SALT with Brezhnev is a "likely prospect" before September 1977. Tass reports December 29 that Brezhnev responds favorably to the idea of a summit.

1977

January 26. *State Department Protest.* The State Department protests alleged harassment of Charter 77 members in Czechoslovakia as a violation of the 1975 Helsinki agreements, which call for the protection of human rights. (Charter 77 is an organization of dissidents working for human rights in Czechoslovakia.) It is the first time the United States has publicly accused another nation of violating the Helsinki accords.

January 27. *Sakharov Defended.* The State Department issues a statement in defense of Soviet dissident Andrei Sakharov after he is warned by the Soviet deputy chief prosecutor to cease "hostile and slanderous" activities in his homeland. The occasion marks the first time the United States has publicly championed a Soviet dissident. On January 28 Sakharov writes President Carter, urging him to continue his efforts against human rights violations in the Soviet Union.

February 8. *Carter's First News Conference.* The main topic of Carter's first presidential news conference is an appeal to the Soviet Union to cooperate on SALT II and to discuss other arms issues. Carter outlines his intentions to speak out against human rights violations, but emphasizes that his administration will refrain from "linking" human rights and SALT negotiations.

February 17. *Carter Writes Sakharov.* President Carter writes to Sakharov to assure him that the United States is firm in its commitment to human rights.

February 28. *Sino-Soviet Talks Break Off.* Soviet officials negotiating Sino-Soviet border talks depart for Moscow, marking the end of three months of negotiations. No progress is reported.

March 1. *Carter Receives Bukovsky.* President Carter receives well-known Soviet dissident Vladimir Bukovsky at the White House. Tass comments that Carter "received Bukovsky, a criminal law offender who was expelled from the Soviet Union and is also known as an active opponent of the development of Soviet-American relations."

March 9. *Carter Discusses SALT.* At a news conference President Carter contends that the troublesome Backfire bomber and cruise missile issues should be bypassed to facilitate SALT II negotiations. *Pravda* publishes a response March 13, stating that bypassing those two issues is too radical a departure from the Vladivostok agreement negotiated by the Ford administration. *Pravda* also criticizes the United States for assuming that its censure of Soviet human rights has no bearing on the outcome of arms talks.

March 15. *Shcharanskii Arrest.* Prominent Jewish dissident Anatolii Shcharanskii is arrested after being refused permission to emigrate and after being accused by *Izvestiia* of working for the CIA. Shcharanskii is the fourth dissident arrested since the beginning of February. Alexander I. Ginzburg, an outspoken dissident in charge of a fund aiding political prisoners and their families, was arrested February 4; Ukrainian dissidents Mikola Rudenko and Olexy Tikhy were arrested February 7; and Yuri Orlov, leader of a group unofficially monitoring Soviet compliance with the Helsinki accords, was arrested February 10.

March 21. *Brezhnev Criticizes Carter.* In a speech to the Congress of Trade Unions in Moscow, Soviet leader Leonid Brezhnev criticizes President Carter's recent support of Soviet dissidents. Brezhnev calls Carter's human rights stance "unwarranted interference in our internal affairs." The same day President Carter asks Congress for 28 additional radio transmitters to extend the range of the Voice of America and Radio Free Europe-Radio Liberty broadcasts.

March 28-March 30. *Vance in Moscow.* Secretary of State Cyrus R. Vance visits Moscow in an effort to end the stalemate in SALT II negotiations by resolving the problem of the Backfire bomber and the cruise missile. The talks break down because of Soviet unwillingness to deviate from the Vladivostok agreement and U.S. fears of being placed at a disadvantage. Brezhnev once again expresses displeasure at the U.S. support of Soviet dissidents.

March 31. *USSR-Mozambique Treaty.* During a week-long tour of Africa, Soviet president Nikolai Podgornyi signs a Treaty of Friendship and Cooperation with the government of Mozambique. Podgornyi also visits Tanzania, Zambia, and Somalia.

April 6. *Soviet Commentary on U.S. Policy. Novoye Vremya* (New Times), a Soviet foreign affairs weekly, denies that Soviet rejection of recent SALT proposals by the United States is a reprisal for the U.S. human rights position. The article states that the United States does not fully understand the possible consequences of this "new approach" to foreign policy.

April 11. *Young's Africa Comments.* U.S. ambassador to the United Nations Andrew Young urges the United States to take a more flexible attitude toward communism in Africa. Young says, "...don't get paranoid about a few communists."

May 10. *Carter at NATO Meeting.* President Carter addresses a NATO meeting in London and urges a forceful response to the buildup of Soviet military power in Europe over the last 12 years.

May 16. *U.S.-Soviet Trade.* A report by the U.S. Commercial Office in London states that trade between the two superpowers is down 25 percent in early 1977.

May 18-21. *Vance-Gromyko Meeting.* Secretary of State Cyrus Vance and Soviet foreign minister Andrei Gromyko meet in Geneva to try to end the SALT II stalemate. Several cooperative agreements are signed. Vance states afterward that progress was made toward breaking the deadlock, but Gromyko cautions that "major, serious difficulties remain."

May 22. *Carter at Notre Dame.* Delivering the commencement address at Notre Dame University in South Bend, Indiana, President Carter calls for a more flexible and comprehensive foreign policy to respond to a "a politically awakening world." Carter emphasizes that good relations with Moscow and Beijing are crucial to U.S. foreign policy. He calls détente with the Soviet Union "progress toward peace" but cautions "that progress must be both comprehensive and reciprocal."

May 24. *Podgornyi Ousted.* Soviet president Nikolai Podgornyi is removed from the Politburo. It is speculated that he was forced out because he opposed Brezhnev on the new Soviet Constitution and foreign policy issues.

June 1. *Shcharanskii Charged.* Soviet dissident Anatolii Shcharanskii is charged with treason. Twenty-four members of Congress send a letter of protest to Brezhnev; the White House expresses its concern June 2.

June 4. *New Soviet Constitution Published.* The draft of the new Soviet Constitution is published. The new charter, the fourth in Soviet history, replaces the 1936 document promulgated under Joseph Stalin.

June 8. *Soviets Step Up Criticism.* In apparent anticipation of a battle at the upcoming Belgrade conference to review compliance with the 1975 Helsinki accords, the Soviet press steps up criticism of the Carter administration's stand on human rights. On June 11 Robert Toth of the *Los Angeles Times* is arrested in Moscow by the KGB, which subsequently attempts to link Toth to the activities of dissident Shcharanskii.

June 10. *U.S. to "Challenge" Moscow.* President Carter tells the Magazine Publishers Association that he is inclined "to aggressively challenge, in a peaceful way, of course, the Soviet Union and others for influence in areas of the world we feel are crucial to us now or potentially crucial 15 or 20 years from now."

June 16. *Vance on Jackson-Vanik.* In a press conference Secretary of State Vance expresses the Carter administration's hope that Congress will repeal the Jackson-Vanik amendment. That amendment bars the granting of most-favored-nation trade status and Export-Import Bank credits to communist countries that do not permit freedom of emigration.

June 16. *Brezhnev Elected President.* The Supreme Soviet elects Leonid Brezhnev to the largely ceremonial post of president. He succeeds Nikolai Podgornyi, whose retirement is announced the same day. Brezhnev is the first Soviet leader to hold the positions of party general secretary and president at the same time.

June 23. *Computer Sale Canceled.* The Department of Commerce cancels a planned sale of Cyber 76 computers to the Soviet Union. The sale had been opposed earlier by 65 members of Congress on the ground that the Soviet Union could use the computers' advanced technology for military purposes.

July 4. *Toon Muzzled.* Malcolm Toon, U.S. ambassador to the Soviet Union, is not allowed to deliver his traditional Fourth of July speech on Soviet television because of a reference in the text to human rights. Toon meets with Soviet leader Brezhnev the following day in an allegedly "pointed exchange of views."

July 9. *Soviet Opposition to Neutron Bomb.* Moscow steps up a campaign against the U.S. decision to produce the so-called "neutron bomb," an enhanced-radiation weapon designed to kill tank crews with minimal collateral damage. Soviet commentator Yuri Kornilov declares production of the weapon is incongruent with the professed U.S. desire to promote human rights and may hinder arms control negotiations.

July 21. *Sino-Soviet Trade.* A trade agreement for 1977 is signed in Moscow by Chinese and Soviet officials. It is disclosed that in 1976 Sino-Soviet trade increased $152 million over 1975, despite a recent increase in polemics between the two nations.

July 21. *Carter's Charleston Speech.* President Carter delivers a major foreign policy speech to the Southern Legislative Conference in Charleston, South Carolina, in which he states that U.S. foreign policy is not "designed to heat up the arms race or bring back the Cold War." Carter says the Soviets mistakenly believe that "our concern for human rights is aimed specifically at them or is an attack on their vital interests."

August 3. *Arbatov Response.* In what is perceived as a response to Carter's Charleston speech, American expert and director of Moscow's Institute of the USA and Canada, Georgii Arbatov, criticizes the Carter administration in *Pravda,* although with more moderation than in the past. Arbatov states that détente "has a future" because American public opinion supports it.

August 16. *Unrest in Ethiopia.* Following continued unrest in the Ogaden region of Ethiopia, *Izvestiia* states that Ethiopia is the "victim of an armed invasion." Somalian rebels are fighting Ethiopian forces in an attempt to unite the Ogaden region with Somalia. The Soviet Union supplies both sides with arms, but supports Ethiopia in the current crisis. Western observers August 21 report the arrival of Soviet military aid in Ethiopia.

August 28-29. *South Africa Nuclear Test.* The press reports that the Soviet Union alerted the United States about a nuclear weapons test being prepared by South Africa in the Kalahari Desert. The Soviets requested Western action to prevent the test from taking place. The alert came in an August 6 letter to President Carter from Soviet leader Brezhnev. The Soviet Union could not take direct diplomatic action to persuade South Africa to stop the test because the two countries do not have diplomatic relations.

September 23. *SALT I Extended.* The U.S. announces its intention to continue observing the 1972 SALT I agreement, which is scheduled to expire October 3. Responding September 25, the Soviet Union also promises to abide by the treaty.

October 1. *Joint U.S.-Soviet Statement.* The United States and the Soviet Union issue a joint declaration on a new Middle East peace conference in Geneva, suggesting that talks include discussion of "the legitimate rights of the Palestinian people." On October 2 Israel rejects the statement as "unacceptable."

October 4. *Belgrade Meeting Opens.* Delegates from nations that signed the 1975 Helsinki accords meet in Belgrade for the first formal review conference. The human rights issue, as expected, is a source of disagreement between delegates from Eastern and Western nations.

November 1. *Administration Support for Dissidents.* President Carter and Secretary of State Vance protest the impending trials of Soviet dissidents Anatolii Shcharanskii, Alexander Ginsburg, and Yuri Orlov.

November 2-7. *60th Anniversary of the Bolshevik Revolution.* Soviet leader Leonid Brezhnev addresses the Central Committee and the Supreme Soviet as part of a week-long celebration of the Bolshevik Revolution. Brezhnev stresses Soviet support for détente and the need for better economic performance at home. He expresses concern about Eurocommunism (the independent line taken by some West European communist parties).

November 13. *Moscow Loses African Ally.* In response to Soviet military support of Ethiopia against Somali-backed rebels fighting in the Ogaden region, the Somalian government orders all Soviet advisers to leave the country. The 1974 Somali-Soviet friendship treaty is abrogated and diplomatic relations terminated. Somalia acted

after the Soviet Union stopped the flow of arms to that country October 19.

November 16. *Jackson Attacked. Izvestiia* publishes a commentary attacking attempts by Sen. Henry M. Jackson, D-Wash., to muster congressional opposition to the proposed SALT II treaty.

November 19. *Sadat's Historic Journey.* President Anwar al-Sadat of Egypt arrives in Israel, the first Arab leader to visit that nation since it was established in 1948.

November 21. *Sadat-Begin News Conference.* Egyptian president Anwar al-Sadat and Israeli prime minister Menachem Begin hold a joint news conference in Israel and express their desire for peace.

November 21. *ABM Treaty Successful.* U.S. and Soviet officials issue a report that the 1972 antiballistic missile (ABM) treaty needs no revision.

November 29. *Soviets Attack Sadat.* Soviet foreign minister Andrei Gromyko announces that the USSR will not attend talks in Cairo to arrange the Geneva conference on a Mideast settlement because Egypt has departed "from the common Arab front and sacrifices the interests of the Arab states as a whole." Sadat had also invited the United States and all Middle East countries, including Israel.

December 5. *Egypt Severs Arab Ties.* Egypt severs diplomatic relations with Syria, Iraq, Libya, Algeria, and South Yemen, citing attempts by the hard-line Arab states to disrupt president Anwar al-Sadat's recent peace efforts. The action follows conclusion of a December 2 meeting in Tripoli, Libya, at which the Arab states declared a new "front for resistance and opposition" to thwart Egypt's peace initiatives. Egypt also closes several Soviet cultural centers and consulates in Cairo because of the Soviet Union's endorsement of the Tripoli Declaration.

December 9. *NATO Supports SALT.* A NATO ministerial meeting issues a communiqué at its conclusion supporting the U.S. SALT efforts.

December 14. *Cairo Conference Opens.* The Cairo conference to discuss procedures for reconvening the Geneva Middle East peace talks opens. Delegates from Egypt, Israel, and the United States participate; a UN representative attends as an observer.

December 24. *Scientists' Concern for Shcharanskii.* The National Academy of Sciences announces it sent a cable to Soviet leader Brezhnev asking for permission to send an observer to the trial of Anatolii Shcharanskii. No reply was received to this unusual request.

1978

January 6. *Crown Returned.* Secretary of State Cyrus R. Vance formally returns the crown of St. Stephen to Budapest, Hungary. The crown had been in U.S. possession since 1945 and its return symbolizes the improvement of U.S.-Hungarian relations. Hungary is granted most-favored-nation status by the United States in a ceremony March 3.

January 11. *Syrian-Soviet Arms Deal.* Syria and the Soviet Union sign an arms deal under which Damascus will begin receiving shipments of Soviet planes, tanks, and advanced air-defense missiles.

January 22. *Ethiopian Offensive.* In an attempt to

drive Somali guerrillas from Ethiopia's Ogaden region, Ethiopian troops, aided by the Soviet Union and Cuba, launch an offensive into the Horn of Africa. Secretary of State Vance announces February 10 that Moscow has sent assurances that Ethiopian troops would not cross the Somalia border once the Ogaden region has been cleared.

February 24. *ACDA on ICBMs.* An agreement with Moscow to ban (until September 1980) all land-based intercontinental ballistic missile (ICBM) deployments is announced by the U.S. Arms Control and Disarmament Agency. The agreement will be in effect until after the SALT II negotiations are concluded.

February 25. *U.S. Warning on Ethiopia.* The State Department warns the Soviet Union to halt Soviet-Cuban intervention in Ethiopia or risk harming U.S.-Soviet relations. The statement responds to a February 24 speech in which Soviet president Leonid I. Brezhnev blamed the deadlocked SALT talks on the United States. Soviet officials February 26 term the U.S. perception of Soviet intentions in the Horn of Africa as "premeditated distortion."

February 28. *USSR Compliance Satisfactory.* The State Department releases a Senate Foreign Relations Committee study that finds Soviet compliance with the 1972 SALT treaty satisfactory.

March 9. *Somali Forces Begin Pullout.* President Jimmy Carter announces that Somalia has begun a troop pullout from the Ogaden region of Ethiopia, raising hopes for the possible conclusion of the eight-month skirmish.

March 9. *Belgrade Conference Ends.* The Belgrade Conference of the Commission for Security and Cooperation in Europe (CSCE) ends with the adoption of summary documents and a pledge for a second review conference in Madrid in 1980. Western diplomats admit to difficulties in obtaining any concrete progress on human rights.

March 6-9. *Tito in United States.* Yugoslavian president Josip Broz Tito, on a goodwill visit to the United States, requests U.S. arms.

March 17. *Carter at Wake Forest.* President Carter makes a strong speech at Wake Forest University in North Carolina, warning the Soviet Union about its arms buildup and its military involvement in local disputes. He cites Soviet activity in the Horn of Africa as an example. Carter vows that the United States will not fall behind in military capabilities. Tass publishes a response the same day, scoring the United States for abandoning cooperative efforts and endorsing "a course of threats and a buildup of tension."

March 29. *U.S.-Soviet Trade Declines.* The U.S. Embassy in Moscow reports that U.S.-Soviet trade declined 26.5 percent in 1977 (from $2.5 billion in 1976 to $1.9 billion in 1977), the first decline since the expansion of U.S.-Soviet trade in 1972.

April 7. *Neutron Bombs Deferred.* President Carter announces he has "decided to defer production" of the neutron bomb, stating that the issue's final outcome is dependent on Soviet restraint in arms buildup and force deployment. Tass states April 7 that postponement of the bomb's production is merely a tactic to subdue negative U.S. public opinion.

April 10. *Shevchenko Defects.* Arkady N. Shevchenko, United Nations under secretary general for political and Security Council affairs, defects to the United States. Shevchenko is considered the most important Soviet diplomat to defect to date.

April 20-22. *Vance in Moscow.* Secretary of State Vance meets in Moscow with Soviet foreign minister

Andrei Gromyko and Soviet president Leonid Brezhnev to discuss SALT II. After the discussions both U.S. and Soviet officials report "some progress" in narrowing the differences impeding agreement.

April 27. *Afghanistan Coup.* In a military coup in Afghanistan, President Mohammed Daoud, a neutralist, is killed. His government is replaced by one headed by Nur Mohammed Taraki, a Marxist.

May 28. *Brzezinski on Zaire.* U.S. national security adviser Zbigniew Brzezinski in a television interview accuses the Soviet Union, Cuba, and East Germany of involvement in Zaire's Shaba province, where secessionist rebels attacked Zairian troops on May 18. *Pravda* responds May 30, denying military participation in Zaire and calling Brzezinski an "enemy of détente."

May 31. *Gromyko, Vance in New York.* Foreign Minister Gromyko and Secretary of State Vance confer in New York on the apparent slowdown of SALT II negotiations.

June 7. *Carter in Annapolis.* President Carter, in a commencement address to the U.S. Naval Academy in Annapolis, Maryland, criticizes Soviet foreign and domestic policies. Carter is careful to point out progress in U.S.-Soviet relations on issues such as SALT II, but states: "The Soviet Union can choose either confrontation or cooperation. The United States is adequately prepared to meet either choice." Tass calls the speech "strange, to say the least."

June 8. *MBFR Talks Progress.* Mutual balanced force reduction (MBFR) negotiators report the most substantial progress since the talks opened in 1973. The Soviet Union accepts a common ceiling for both NATO and Warsaw Pact ground troops and a Soviet ceiling of 900,000 on combined ground/air personnel. However, the MBFR talks recess July 19 in a deadlock.

June 8. *Solzhenitsyn's Harvard Address.* Nobel laureate and Soviet dissident Alexander I. Solzhenitsyn delivers the Harvard commencement address on the "decline of courage" in the West.

June 29. *Vietnam Joins COMECON.* Vietnam becomes the tenth full member of the Council for Mutual Economic Assistance (COMECON), the economic assistance organization of the Soviet bloc. The summit is held in Bucharest, Romania.

July 12-13. *Vance, Gromyko Discuss SALT.* Secretary of State Vance and Foreign Minister Gromyko meet in Geneva to discuss the remaining obstacles to a SALT II agreement: the Soviet Backfire bomber and the testing and deployment of missile systems. The discussions are held in a cordial atmosphere despite the ongoing trials of Soviet dissidents Alexander Ginzburg and Anatolii Shcharanskii, which began July 10.

July 13-14. *Ginzburg and Shcharanskii Sentenced.* Ginzburg is sentenced July 13 to eight years in a labor camp for "anti-Soviet agitation and propaganda." Fellow dissident Shcharanskii is sentenced July 14 to three years in prison and ten in a labor camp following his conviction for treason, espionage, and "anti-Soviet agitation." The trial, held under heavy secrecy, focuses on Shcharanskii's association with *Los Angeles Times* reporter Robert Toth, who was accused by the Soviet Union of being an intelligence agent. Shcharanskii defends himself after he refuses a court-appointed lawyer. The trials are vigorously protested in the United States. Both the Senate and House adopted resolutions against the trials amid calls for suspending SALT, abrogating business deals, and moving the 1980 Olympic games from Moscow. On July 11, UN ambassador Andrew Young added to the furor by asserting that "there are hundreds, perhaps thousands of political prisoners in the United States."

July 18. *Computer Sale Banned.* As a result of the conviction of Soviet dissidents Anatolii Shcharanskii and Alexander Ginzburg, the White House cancels the sale of sophisticated Sperry-Univac computers to the Soviet Union and limits the sale of oil technology exports.

August 12. *Sino-Japanese Treaty.* After three years of intermittent negotiations, China and Japan sign a treaty of peace and friendship in Tokyo. The Japanese, who seek good relations with both Beijing and Moscow, had previously resisted signing a treaty that the Soviet Union might find offensive. Tass asserts August 12 that the treaty endangers Soviet-Japanese relations.

August 16. *Hua in Romania.* Chinese Communist Party chairman Hua Guofeng arrives in Romania for an unofficial visit that draws worldwide attention and is generally seen as a challenge to Soviet claims of exclusive influence in this part of Eastern Europe.

August 21. *Hua to Yugoslavia.* Chinese party leader Hua arrives in Yugoslavia for an unprecedented nine-day visit. Hua supports Yugoslavia's efforts to develop its own form of socialism.

August 24. *Moscow Denounces China.* Pravda publishes violent attacks on the August 12 signing of the Sino-Japanese peace treaty and Chairman Hua's August 16 visit to Romania. China is denounced as a country "in the grip of military hysteria."

August 29. *Hua to Iran.* Chairman Hua arrives in Iran for a four-day visit, the first by a ranking Chinese leader to a nonsocialist country.

September 5-17. *Camp David Summit.* Egyptian president Anwar al-Sadat, Israeli premier Menachem Begin, and U.S. president Carter convene in Camp David, Maryland, for a summit on the deadlocked Middle East peace negotiations. Tass denounces the summit September 6 as a "trick" to facilitate greater U.S. influence in the area. After 13 days of negotiations Carter announces the signing of two pacts that offer a framework for a "durable settlement" of Middle East problems. Brezhnev September 22 calls the agreements "a deal worked out behind the backs of the Arabs."

October 11. *Moscow Opposes Arms Sales to China.* Commenting on repeated rumors that various Western governments are contemplating arms sales to China, Tass claims that such sales would "encourage the aggressive militarism of the Maoists." It cautions Britain, which was visited by the Chinese foreign minister October 10-13, that although such a policy is ostensibly aimed at counterbalancing the Soviet Union, it could endanger Britain's own security and jeopardize the SALT II talks.

November 3. *Soviet Treaty With Vietnam.* The Soviet Union signs a treaty of friendship and cooperation with Vietnam.

November 6. *Martial Law in Iran.* The shah of Iran, Mohammed Reza Pahlavi, imposes martial law in an effort to quell the violent antigovernment riots that have shaken Iran since January.

November 19. *Brezhnev on Iran.* Pravda publishes a statement by President Brezhnev warning the United States not to interfere in Iranian affairs and reminding the United States that Iran borders the Soviet Union.

November 20. *Soviet-Ethiopian Agreement.* Brezhnev and Ethiopian head of state Mengistu Haile Mariam sign a 20-year friendship and cooperation pact in Moscow,

climaxing a two-year improvement of relations that saw increased Soviet involvement in the Ethiopian war against secessionist rebels in Eritrea and Ogaden. The pact promises military "consultation" rather than overt assistance.

December 1. *Ceausescu on Military Spending.* In a speech marking the 60th anniversary of the establishment of the country's boundaries, Romanian president Nicolae Ceausescu rejects Soviet-Bloc demands for increased military spending and greater Warsaw Pact integration.

December 5. *Soviet-Afghan Agreement.* Soviet president Brezhnev and Afghan premier Taraki sign a 20-year treaty of friendship and cooperation. The agreement signed in Moscow includes "mutual economic, military and technical assistance" and notes that the Soviet Union "respects the policy of non-alignment" of the Afghan government.

December 11. *Deng Invitation.* U.S. security adviser Brzezinski informs the Chinese Liaison Office in Washington that Vice Premier Deng Xiaoping is being invited to visit the United States. The White House receives word the next day that Deng has accepted.

December 15. *People's Republic of China Recognized.* The governments of China and the United States issue a joint communiqué announcing the establishment of diplomatic relations between them as of January 1, 1979. On December 19 Brezhnev sends President Carter a note that Carter describes as "very positive in tone." Tass December 21 disputes Carter's interpretation, disclosing that Moscow has deep reservations about normalization and particularly about the inclusion of a phrase in the December 15 communiqué condemning "hegemony," a code word the Chinese use to criticize the Soviet Union.

December 21-23. *SALT II Agreement Nears.* Meeting in Geneva, Secretary of State Vance and Foreign Minister Gromyko announce agreement on "most issues," but a SALT treaty is not completed.

December 25. *Vietnam Invades Cambodia.* After months of border fighting, Vietnam launches a massive offensive into Cambodia. Western observers regard the Soviet-Vietnamese treaty signed in November as a measure taken by the Vietnamese to deter the Chinese from intervening on behalf of the pro-Beijing Pol Pot regime. Vietnamese forces capture Phnom Penh January 7.

1979

January 1. *China, U.S. Open Relations.* In ceremonies at the Chinese Liaison Office in Washington and the American Liaison Office in Beijing, full diplomatic relations between the United States and China are established.

January 6. *Civilian Government in Iran.* The shah of Iran officially installs a new civilian government headed by Shahpur Bakhtiar. Shah Mohammed Reza Pahlavi leaves the country January 16 for a vacation that proves to be permanent exile.

January 8. *New Government in Cambodia.* The Vietnamese-sponsored National United Front for National Salvation announces the formation of a People's Revolutionary Government in Cambodia, with Heng Samrin to serve as president of the Revolutionary Council. Soviet leaders January 9 send a congratulatory telegram to the new government.

January 15. *Carter Administration Split.* National security adviser Zbigniew Brzezinski takes a much harder line toward Moscow than Secretary of State Cyrus R. Vance in a talk to business leaders at the State Department. Vance expresses his concern that Moscow might regard the new Sino-U.S. relationship as directed against it and stresses that the United States wants to keep relations with the Soviet Union and China as "evenhanded" as possible. Brzezinski underlines the strategic advantages that would accrue to the United States from its rapprochement with Beijing.

January 15. *Soviet Veto.* The Soviet Union uses its 111th veto to block a UN Security Council resolution that sought the withdrawal of Vietnamese forces from Cambodia.

January 23. *State of the Union Address.* President Carter declares in his State of the Union address to Congress that the completion of SALT II is his main foreign policy goal for the year. Carter requests support for the treaty, which he promises will ensure U.S. military strength and close monitoring of Soviet compliance with the treaty's provisions.

January 28. *Deng in United States.* Vice Premier Deng Xiaoping arrives in the United States for a nine-day visit, the first ever by a senior Chinese communist leader.

February 4. *Soviet Criticism of Deng Visit.* The Soviet Communist Party newspaper *Pravda* criticizes the U.S. government for allowing Vice Premier Deng to denounce the Soviet Union during his U.S. visit. *Pravda* states that "the Soviet public cannot close its eyes to the fact" that Deng "was given a wide podium for slander on the USSR."

February 5. *Soviet Buildup Reported.* The Japanese defense ministry reports that the Soviet Union is building bases and increasing its troop strength on the southernmost Kurile Island, adjacent to the northernmost Japanese island of Hokkaido. Both countries claim the Kurile Islands.

February 9-11. *Revolution in Iran.* Armed revolutionaries and army sympathizers of Ayatollah Ruhollah Khomeini overthrow the government of Shahpur Bakhtiar in Iran. Khomeini, who returned to Iran February 1 from exile in France, installs Mehdi Barzagan as premier of a provisional government. The Soviet Union recognizes the new government on February 12.

February 17. *China Invades Vietnam.* In an action described by the Xinhua news agency as a "counter attack" brought on by repeated Vietnamese border incursions, Chinese troops invade Vietnam. The Soviet government vigorously protests and aids Vietnam with supplies and intelligence. However, Soviet leaders do not offer armed support, and Soviet troops in Asian military districts are neither reinforced nor put on alert. On March 5 the Chinese begin withdrawing their forces after both sides suffer heavy casualties.

March 2. *Brezhnev Address.* Soviet president Leonid Brezhnev addresses the Supreme Soviet on foreign policy issues such as the Chinese invasion of Vietnam, the new government in Iran, and prospects for an agreement on SALT II. Brezhnev expresses confidence in a speedy settlement of outstanding issues.

March 4. *Podgornyi Excluded.* Nikolai V. Podgornyi, former president of the Soviet Union (1965-77), is not reelected to the Supreme Soviet, thereby signifying an end to his political career.

March 26. *Egyptian-Israeli Peace Treaty.* Israeli prime minister Menachem Begin and Egyptian president Anwar al-Sadat sign a peace treaty that formally ends the state of war between their two countries. The ceremony, witnessed by President Carter, takes place on the White House lawn. The Soviet news agency Tass March 22 declared the treaty "a betrayal" of Arab interests.

April 3. *China to End Treaty.* The Xinhua news agency reports that the Chinese government will not renew its 1950 treaty of friendship with the Soviet Union when it expires in 1980.

April 4 and 5. *Brzezinski and Brown on SALT.* On successive days national security adviser Zbigniew Brzezinski and Defense Secretary Harold Brown make public speeches in which they stress the importance of the SALT II treaty for U.S. security.

April 17. *SALT II Compliance.* The *New York Times* publishes a report given by central intelligence director Stansfield Turner in closed Senate testimony and leaked by "congressional sources." Turner states that it would take the United States until 1984 to restore intelligence capability lost in Iran when all monitoring equipment was removed March 1. The Iran monitoring stations, which could observe missile tests, were considered crucial in monitoring Soviet compliance with the SALT II treaty.

April 27. *Soviet Dissidents Exchanged for Spies.* In the first exchange of its kind, five Soviet dissidents are flown to New York's Kennedy Airport and exchanged for two convicted Soviet spies. One of the dissidents released is Alexander Ginzburg, whose conviction in 1978 prompted worldwide protests. The other dissidents are Mark Dymshits and Eduard Kuznetsov, two Soviet Jews convicted of plotting to hijack a plane to Sweden; Valentin Moroz, a historian who advocates Ukrainian independence; and Georgi Vins, convicted for religious activities in the Ukraine.

April 30. *Carter on SALT Verification.* President Carter tries to convince skeptics that SALT II would be adequately verified. Carter stresses in a news conference that the loss of the Iranian monitoring stations does not hinder verification of Soviet compliance.

May 9. *SALT II Draft Treaty Completed.* Secretary of State Vance announces the completion of a SALT II draft treaty with the Soviet Union, thereby clearing the path for a summit meeting between President Brezhnev and President Carter. On May 11 the White House announces that the summit will take place June 16-18 in Vienna.

May 12. *Soviets Praise Proposed Treaty.* The Soviet government newspaper *Izvestiia* publishes a favorable commentary on the completion of a draft SALT II treaty, calling it a "triumph of reason" that will lead to the improvement of U.S.-Soviet relations.

June 2. *Pope Visits Poland.* Pope John Paul II makes a historic nine-day visit to his native Poland to mark the 900th anniversary of the martyrdom of St. Stanislaus, Poland's patron saint. It is the first time a Catholic pope has visited a communist country. A Soviet television broadcast states that "some circles in the Polish church are trying to use [the visit] for anti-state purposes."

June 8. *MX Missile Decision.* The White House announces that President Carter has approved production of the MX mobile intercontinental ballistic missile (ICBM).

June 12. *Jackson Speaks Out.* Sen. Henry M. Jackson, D-Wash., speaks out against SALT II in a speech to the Coalition for a Democratic Majority. Jackson accuses the Carter administration of following a policy of "appeasement" with the Soviet Union parallel to Britain's relationship with Nazi Germany in the 1930s. Secretary of State Vance June 13 criticizes Jackson's remarks as "misguided and simply wrong."

June 16-18. *SALT Summit.* Presidents Carter and Brezhnev meet for the first time at a U.S.-Soviet summit meeting in Vienna, Austria. The conference agenda includes five negotiating sessions and ends with the signing of the second strategic arms limitation treaty between the United States and the Soviet Union. The signing of SALT II concludes seven years of negotiations between the two superpowers.

June 18. *Carter Before Congress.* President Carter returns from the Vienna summit and asks a joint session of Congress for ratification of the SALT II treaty, which he says is "the most detailed, far-reaching, comprehensive treaty in the history of arms control."

June 21. *Chinese Protest.* The Xinhua news agency reports that Deputy Foreign Minister Han Nianlong has lodged an official protest with the USSR following Soviet charges that Beijing is aiding Moslem rebels in Afghanistan, a charge the Chinese repeatedly and forcefully deny.

June 25. *Gromyko Warns Senate.* Soviet foreign minister Andrei Gromyko warns the U.S. Senate against amending the SALT II treaty, stating that it "would be the end of negotiations . . . no matter what amendments would be made." Sen. Barry Goldwater, R-Ariz., responds June 26, stating that "Gromyko should have kept his mouth shut."

July 9. *SALT Hearings Begin.* The Senate Foreign Relations Committee opens three months of hearings on the SALT II treaty. Similar hearings in the Senate Armed Services Committee begin July 23.

July 17. *Somoza Resigns.* Nicaraguan president Anastasio Somoza resigns and flies to the United States. Two days later rebel Sandinista troops overcome disorganized national guard forces and take control of Managua.

August 2. Pravda *Denies Charges.* A *Pravda* article by Chief of Staff Marshal Nikolai Ogarkov attacks U.S. critics of SALT as "crudely distorting the real balance of forces between the USSR and the USA." Moscow had been avoiding comments since June when the debate in the United States over SALT began.

August 29. *Biden Reports on Visit.* Sen. Joseph R. Biden, Jr., D-Del., reports on his visit to the Soviet Union as head of a U.S. Senate delegation to discuss SALT II. He states that Soviet officials seem willing to consider cutbacks of nuclear and conventional weapons in future arms negotiations.

August 31. *Soviet Troops in Cuba.* State Department spokesman Hodding Carter III acknowledges a 2,000- to 3,000-man Soviet combat force in Cuba. Carter claims the troops do not threaten U.S. security. The announcement has a profound effect on the SALT hearings. Frank Church, D-Idaho, chairman of the Senate Foreign Relations Committee, states September 5 that he sees "no likelihood that the Senate would ratify the SALT II treaty as long as Soviet combat troops remain stationed in Cuba."

September 7. *Carter on Troops in Cuba.* In a nationally televised statement President Carter calls the presence of combat troops in Cuba "a very serious matter" but asks for "calm and a sense of proportion" in relation to the situation. On September 8 Carter says in an interview that troops in Cuba should not influence the Senate debate over ratification of SALT II, maintaining that the treaty should be judged "on its own merits."

September 10. *Moscow Response.* In the first Soviet comments on its combat troops in Cuba, a *Pravda* editorial denies the presence of such troops, contending that the issue "is being exploited by those circles in the United States that are trying to prevent the ratification of the SALT II treaty or at least complicate the ratification process." The Soviet news agency Tass states that there has been a training center in Cuba for 17 years, and that its purpose (of training Cuban forces) has not changed.

September 13. *Flights Over Turkey in Doubt.* Both the *New York Times* and the *Sun* (Baltimore) report that Soviet objections have caused the Carter administration to abandon its plans to fly reconnaissance planes over Turkey to ensure Soviet compliance with SALT II.

September 16. *New Government in Afghanistan.* Premier Hafizullah Amin replaces Nur Mohammad Taraki as president of Afghanistan. Officially, Taraki is said to have resigned because of ill health, but it appears that he may have been killed during a government upheaval. Taraki's death is confirmed October 9, but the cause is given as "a severe and prolonged illness."

September 23. *Sino-Soviet Talks.* A Chinese negotiating team arrives in Moscow to begin talks aimed at easing Sino-Soviet tensions. It is the first attempt at such talks since 1964, when the Chinese went to Moscow following the ouster of Soviet leader Nikita S. Khrushchev.

September 23-27. *Vance, Gromyko Confer on Cuba.* The presence of Soviet troops in Cuba is given as the reason for discussions between Secretary of State Vance and Foreign Minister Gromyko in New York. No agreement is reached.

September 26. *Ford on SALT II.* Former president Gerald R. Ford calls for a Senate delay on a SALT II vote until "well into next year." At a speech to the Army War College in Carlisle, Pennsylvania, Ford stresses that a stronger U.S. military posture is needed before the treaty can be approved.

October 1. *Carter on Cuba.* In a nationally televised speech President Carter announces a comprehensive U.S. intelligence effort to survey Cuba and monitor military activity in the Caribbean. Carter stresses that "the brigade issue is certainly no reason for a return to the Cold War" and continues to press for SALT II ratification. Moscow reacts to Carter's speech in an October 2 Tass statement, calling it an example of "gunboat diplomacy" in the Caribbean.

October 3. *Record Grain Sale Approved.* The largest U.S. grain purchase by the Soviet Union is approved by the Agriculture Department. The sale will involve up to 25 million metric tons of grain in the next year.

October 25. *Soviet Union/South Yemen Pact.* Officials of the Soviet Union and South Yemen sign a 20-year friendship pact in Moscow.

November 4. *Crisis in Iran.* Demanding the return of the shah, Iranian students seize the U.S. Embassy in Tehran and take 66 Americans hostage. Thirteen are subsequently freed November 19-20. President Carter blocks sales of military equipment to Iran November 9 and freezes Iranian assets in the United States November 14.

November 6. *Moscow on Nuclear Weapons in Europe.* An appeal from Brezhnev to begin negotiations on nuclear forces in Europe is published in *Pravda*. Brezhnev's appeal comes on the heels of a Soviet campaign against NATO plans to deploy nuclear missiles in Western Europe.

November 9. *Committee Approves SALT.* The Senate Foreign Relations Committee votes 9-6 to recommend the SALT II treaty for ratification.

November 27. *Politburo Changes.* Deputy Prime Minister Nikolai A. Tikhonov is promoted to full membership in the Soviet Politburo while Premier Aleksei Kosygin is recuperating from a heart attack. Mikhail S. Gorbachev is made a candidate (nonvoting) member, becoming the youngest participant at 48.

December 4. *UN Votes on Iran.* The UN Security Council votes to demand an immediate release of the remaining 53 American hostages in Iran. In a *Pravda* article December 5, Moscow supports the UN vote but, citing U.S. naval maneuvers in the Arabian Sea, accuses the United States of attempting to "blackmail Iran by massing forces on its borders" instead of returning the shah.

December 12. *NATO Dual-Track Policy.* NATO members agree to deploy 108 Pershing II and 464 land-based cruise missiles in Europe by 1983. The agreement also calls for engaging Moscow in arms control talks aimed at reducing nuclear weapons in Europe.

December 19. *Concern Over Afghanistan.* The State Department reports an increase in Soviet troops in Afghanistan.

December 20. *Armed Services Committee Rejects SALT.* The Senate Armed Services Committee votes 10-0 to recommend rejection of the SALT II treaty as "not in the national security interest of the United States."

December 24-27. *Soviets Invade Afghanistan.* The Soviet Union begins airlifting troops and supplies into Afghanistan. On December 27 about 20,000 Soviet troops cross the border and invade the country. President Hafizullah Amin is killed. He is succeeded by Babrak Karmal, who returns from exile in Czechoslovakia. By December 31 Soviet troops fan through the country to put down a rebellion by Moslem tribesmen who oppose Marxist rule.

The Soviet Union issues a series of statements December 28-30 supporting the new government, promising necessary assistance, and justifying the military intervention. The first admission of the intervention comes December 30 in a *Pravda* article that states the troops will withdraw when no longer needed.

December 31. *Carter on Afghanistan.* In a televised interview President Carter states that the Soviet intervention in Afghanistan has changed his opinion of the Russians more dramatically than any other event during his administration. By December 31 Soviet troops in Afghanistan allegedly number 50,000.

1980

January 3. *Carter Asks SALT Delay.* Senate Majority Leader Robert C. Byrd, D-W.Va., receives a letter from President Jimmy Carter formally requesting the Senate to delay SALT II ratification in light of the Soviet invasion of Afghanistan.

January 4. *U.S. Response to Afghanistan.* In a nationally televised address, President Carter describes the Soviet intervention in Afghanistan as "an extremely serious threat to peace" and announces a series of retaliatory measures by the United States. These include: a curtailment of U.S. grain sales and export of high technology, restraint of Soviet fishing privileges in U.S. waters, delayed construction of new Soviet and U.S. embassies, and a possible U.S. boycott of the Olympics to be held in Moscow. Soviet sources January 5 call these responses a "flagrant violation" of détente and a return to Cold War policies.

January 6. *Deng on Afghan Crisis.* Chinese vice premier Deng Xiaoping calls the Soviet invasion of Afghanistan "a grave step," repeats Beijing's "firm demand" that the troops be withdrawn, and declares that China will "work together with the Afghan people, and all countries and people . . . to frustrate Soviet acts of aggression and expansion."

January 12. *Brezhnev on Afghanistan.* Soviet president Leonid I. Brezhnev makes his first official statement on the Afghanistan incursion, stating that "aggressive external forces of reaction" necessitated intervention.

January 13. *Iran Resolution Vetoed.* A U.S.-proposed UN Security Council resolution urging economic sanctions against Iran is vetoed by the Soviet Union. The Soviet Union justifies its decision on the grounds that sanctions would have "dealt a blow to the Iranian revolution."

January 14. *U.S. Offers Pakistan Military Aid.* The State Department announces that Pakistan has been offered $400 million in economic/military aid because of the Soviet intervention in neighboring Afghanistan.

January 14. *UN on Afghanistan.* The UN General Assembly approves 104-18 a resolution condemning the Soviet intervention in Afghanistan and demanding a troop withdrawal. The Soviet Union terms the vote as "interference in the internal affairs" of Afghanistan. The Soviet Union vetoed a Security Council resolution on Afghanistan on January 7.

January 15. *"Evenhanded" or "Balanced"?* In an interview published by the *Wall Street Journal,* national security adviser Zbigniew Brzezinski denies that U.S. policy is "evenhanded" treatment for the Soviet Union and China, stating: "[T]he President has very deliberately used the word 'balanced.' . . . The Soviet Union does pose a strategic challenge to the United States, China does not. The Soviet Union does impose regional and strategic strain upon us through its assertive behavior, directly or through proxies. China does not. . . . We therefore cannot pursue an identical policy towards both of these major countries."

January 20. *Carter Sees Danger.* Speaking on NBC's "Meet the Press," President Carter calls the Soviet invasion of Afghanistan the "most serious threat to peace since the Second World War" and warns that the Soviets "cannot invade an innocent country with impunity. They must suffer the consequences."

January 22. *Sakharov Exiled.* Soviet authorities send Nobel prize winning scientist and human rights activist Andrei Sakharov and his wife into internal exile in Gorkii. The Presidium of the Supreme Soviet strips Sakharov of his honors. The Soviet news agency Tass charges that Sakharov "has been conducting subversive activities against the Soviet Union for a number of years." The exiling apparently was prompted by Sakharov's protests against the Soviet invasion of Afghanistan and his support for a Western boycott of the Moscow Summer Olympics.

January 23. *Carter Doctrine.* In what becomes known as the "Carter Doctrine," President Carter in his third State of the Union message declares that the United States will "use any means necessary, including force" to repel any attacks on the oil-producing Persian Gulf region.

January 29. *Gromyko in Syria.* Soviet foreign minister Andrei Gromyko, in a three-day visit to Syria, issues with President Hafez Assad a joint communiqué condemning the Egyptian-Israeli peace treaty signed at Camp David, the occupation of Arab lands by Israel, U.S. military bases in the Middle East, and U.S. retaliatory measures in Iran such as the economic boycott.

January 29. *Senate on Olympics.* The Senate approves 88-4 a U.S. boycott of the Summer Olympics in Moscow. A similar resolution was adopted by the House January 24.

February 2. *Soviets Deny Persian Gulf Designs.* A *Pravda* commentary denies U.S. accusations of Soviet interest in controlling the Persian Gulf: "The Soviet Union has never had and does not have now any intention to push its way to warm seas." On February 4, Soviet leader Brezhnev states that Moscow still wishes to pursue détente with the United States despite tension over Afghanistan.

February 3. *Brzezinski in Pakistan.* National security adviser Brzezinski leads a delegation to Pakistan to discuss security-related matters pertaining to the Afghanistan invasion. Brzezinski assures President Muhammad Zia ul-Haq that U.S. military aid would counter any Soviet attempt to invade Pakistan.

February 12. *IOC Reaffirms Moscow.* The International Olympic Committee (IOC) decides to retain Moscow as the site of the Summer Olympics despite pressure from the U.S. Olympic Committee, which claims Moscow is unsuitable because of the invasion of Afghanistan.

February 22. *Brezhnev on Afghanistan.* Brezhnev states that the need for Soviet involvement in Afghanistan would "cease to exist" if the governments of the United States, Pakistan, and China would end their alleged subversion of the Kabul government.

March 6. *USSR on Poison Gas.* The Soviet Union denies accusations made by Afghan refugees in Pakistan that Moscow is ordering the use of poison gas on Afghan rebels. The denial is made by a Soviet representative to the Geneva Committee on Disarmament.

March 12. *Brzezinski Scores Allies on Afghanistan.* In a speech to the National Press Club, national security adviser Brzezinski presses Western Europe and Japan to take more "tangible action" opposing the Soviet invasion of Afghanistan. Brzezinski was cool to European suggestions supporting Moscow's proposal of a neutral Afghanistan in return for a Soviet troop withdrawal.

March 15. *Carter on SALT.* Following a U.S.-Soviet debate on whether to honor the terms of SALT II pending treaty ratification, President Carter states that if Moscow does not do so, he would consider rejecting SALT II altogether.

April 24-25. *Failed Rescue Mission.* A U.S. commando mission to rescue American hostages in Iran is aborted in the Iranian desert because of equipment failures. Eight commandos are killed in a helicopter-airplane accident that occurs as the rescue team is about to take off. Tass comments April 25 that "the present master of the White House could not care less about his fellow citizens and is prepared to sacrifice their lives for his election interests."

April 28. *Vance Resignation.* Secretary of State Cyrus R. Vance resigns in protest against the Iranian rescue mission. The Senate confirms Vance's successor, Sen. Edmund S. Muskie, D-Maine, May 7. The Soviet Union May 28 praises Vance's commitment to détente and expresses fears that U.S. foreign policy is becoming more militant.

May 4. *Tito Dies.* President Josip Broz Tito of Yugoslavia dies in Ljubljana after a long illness. Under the rotating collective leadership system designed by Tito, Stevan Doronjski becomes chairman of the League of Communists and Vice President Lazar Kolisevski takes over the presidency. Later in May, Cvijetin Mijatovic begins serving a one-year term as president. Moscow, in response to Tito's death, makes no mention of the historically stormy relations between the two nations and does not dwell on Tito's expulsion from the international communist movement in 1948. Instead, the official statement praises Tito as "the outstanding leader of the communists and workers in Yugoslavia and a leading figure of the international communist and workers' movement. The Soviet people deeply mourn his death."

May 9. *Carter on SALT II.* President Carter tells the World Affairs Council that the ratification of SALT II will be sought "at the earliest opportune time" and that "we intend to abide by the treaty's terms as long as the Soviet Union, as observed by us, complies with those terms as well."

May 14. *Shift in NATO Policy.* Foreign and defense ministers of NATO, meeting in Brussels, agree that military preparedness should be augmented in light of the Soviet invasion of Afghanistan. Earlier NATO statements had asserted that the invasion did not affect the East-West strategic balance.

May 16. *Gromyko and Muskie in Vienna.* Secretary of State Muskie meets Foreign Minister Gromyko in Vienna in the first bilateral high-level meeting since the Afghan invasion. The private meeting, the first between the two men, produces no conclusive agreements.

June 6. *Muskie on SALT.* Muskie reaffirms the Carter administration's commitment to the ratification of SALT II by declaring that the treaty is "separable" from the issue of Soviet troops in Afghanistan.

June 9. *Soviet Activity in Yemen.* The Soviet Union steps up its military presence in South Yemen; fighting increases between the North Yemen army and opposition guerrillas in South Yemen.

June 22-23. *Summit in Venice.* Western leaders meet in Venice for an economic summit. President Carter suggests at the conclusion that European leaders become more active in working with the Soviets to resolve the Afghanistan impasse.

June 30-July 1. *Schmidt in Moscow.* West German chancellor Helmut Schmidt confers with Soviet president Brezhnev in Moscow. Schmidt proposes unconditional negotiations on medium-range missiles in Europe and appeals for the Soviet withdrawal of forces in Afghanistan. Moscow and Bonn conclude an industrial/economic agreement and make preliminary plans for a natural gas pipeline project from western Siberia to West Germany.

July 10. *USSR Buys Argentine Wheat.* The Soviet Union concludes a deal to purchase four million tons of grain over a five-year period from Argentina.

July 19. *Moscow Olympics.* The first Olympic games held in a communist country open in Moscow. The 22d Olympics are boycotted by 64 countries; of those, 55 reportedly made their decision to protest the Afghanistan invasion.

August 5. *Presidential Directive 59.* The *New York Times* reports that the previous week President Carter signed Presidential Directive 59, detailing U.S. strategy against the Soviet Union in the event of a nuclear war. PD 59 emphasizes the destruction of the Soviet Union's strategic weapons and its command, control, and communications structure. The document also stresses the need for limited nuclear options and preparations for protracted nuclear war. Tass August 11 calls the document "insanity" developed by persons "who have lost all touch with reality and are prepared to push the world" into nuclear war.

August 14. *Workers Strike in Poland.* A labor crisis in Poland intensifies as 17,000 workers go on strike at the Lenin Shipyards in Gdansk on the Baltic Sea. The strike spreads throughout the region and by August 22 a strikers' committee representing 120,000 Polish workers from northern Poland delivers a request for political and economic reform to the Polish government. On August 21-22, the government arrests 24 leaders of the dissident group that reportedly wrote the demands.

August 20. *Moscow Jams VOA.* The Soviet Union begins jamming Voice of America broadcasts to the USSR, reportedly to prevent news of the labor crisis in Poland from reaching the Soviet population.

August 23. *Concessions to Workers.* The Polish government agrees to negotiate directly with representatives of the striking workers. On August 24, Polish premier Edward Babiuch is ousted as part of a strike-inspired Communist Party and government shake-up. Despite a promise of concessions to the workers, the strike spreads and reportedly involves 300,000 people.

August 27. *Moscow Reacts.* The Soviet Union, in its first direct response to the unrest in Poland, accuses "antisocialist forces" of attempting to disrupt Poland's socialist system. The charge is made after strike leaders in Gdansk reject concessions promised by Polish party leader Edward Gierek.

September 3. *Workers Return.* Most of the striking Polish workers return to their jobs by September 3 after the government announces an agreement allowing free trade unions and the right to strike. The agreement was concluded August 31. On August 21, coal miners in Silesia began their own strike, which lasted until September 3 and in some cases longer.

September 6. *Gierek Replaced.* Polish Communist Party secretary Edward Gierek, reportedly suffering from heart trouble, is replaced by Stanislaw Kania. The Kania government is expected to honor the concessions Gierek made to Polish workers. Kania receives a congratulatory message from Soviet president Brezhnev, who indicates confidence in Kania's ability to "consolidate the position" of party control.

September 7. *Changes in China.* Premier Hua Guofeng formally resigns as head of state but retains the chairmanship of the Chinese Communist Party. Deputy Premier Zhao Ziyang, a protégé of Vice Chairman Deng Xiaoping, is chosen as Hua's successor. The leadership change, a political victory for Deng, stemmed from a new government policy under which political officials are not allowed to hold party and government posts simultaneously.

September 20. *Outbreak of Iraqi-Iranian War.* A dispute between Iraq and Iran escalates into full-scale war. Both sides bomb oil fields; Iraqis invade Iran and threaten to block the strategic Strait of Hormuz. The conflict assumes new proportions September 22 as Iraqi air strikes are mounted against 10 Iranian oil fields.

September 23. *U.S.-Soviet Neutrality.* The USSR and the United States pledge neutrality in the war between Iran and Iraq.

September 24. *Solidarity Formed.* Poland's new independent trade unions register in a Warsaw court as a single nationwide organization called "Solidarity." Solidar-

ity draft statutes are presented by the union's new leader, Lech Walesa.

October 8. *Soviet-Syrian Treaty.* Soviet president Brezhnev and Syrian president Hafez Assad sign a 20-year friendship pact.

October 16. *Muskie Makes Pitch for SALT.* Secretary of State Muskie in a campaign speech for President Carter promises that Carter, if reelected, will press for Senate ratification of SALT II even if Soviet troops remain in Afghanistan. He contrasts Carter's position with that of Republican candidate Ronald Reagan, who he says would "tear up the treaty and embark upon a quest for military superiority."

October 21. *Gorbachev Promoted.* Mikhail S. Gorbachev is promoted from candidate member of the Politburo to full member.

October 23. *Kosygin Resigns.* Aleksei Kosygin resigns as Soviet premier on grounds of ill health. Nikolai A. Tikhonov, 75, an economic planner and Brezhnev protégé, becomes premier. Brezhnev tells the Supreme Soviet that Kosygin also wishes to be excused from his Politburo duties. Kosygin is the first premier to resign while still in good graces with the Soviet leadership.

November 4. *Reagan Elected.* In a landslide election, Reagan defeats Carter for the presidency. Republicans also win control of the Senate and diminish the Democratic majority in the House. Premier Tikhonov cautiously expresses Moscow's hopes that Reagan will assume "a constructive approach" in the area of U.S.-Soviet relations.

November 11. *CSCE Opens in Madrid.* The Conference on Security and Cooperation in Europe (CSCE) meets in Madrid to review the 1975 Helsinki accords. The Soviet Union and its East European allies protest discussion of the human rights issue, preferring more talk on a European disarmament conference. Opening speeches focus on criticism of the Soviet invasion of Afghanistan. The first phase of the meeting closes December 19.

November 21. *Polish Shake-up.* In a major reorganizaiton of the Polish Communist Party and government, four cabinet ministers lose their jobs and a Roman Catholic layman is named as one of six deputy premiers. The move ousts a conservative faction of the leadership that had resisted cooperation with the Polish trade union movement. East European allies of the Soviet Union attack Polish authorities for their inability to control Solidarity. East Germany suspends rail service to Poland November 26, and November 27 the Czech Communist Party newspaper *Rude Pravo* recalls the fate of Czech party leader Alexander Dubcek, who failed in a liberalization attempt in 1968.

December 5. *Summit on Poland.* Leaders of the Soviet Union and East Europe meet in Moscow to discuss the crisis in Poland and to ensure the crisis is solved in accordance "with the socialist path." The meeting is the first emergency summit of the Warsaw Pact nations since the late 1960s. Polish Communist Party secretary Kania attends and proclaims Polish loyalty "to the socialist commonwealth." Simultaneously, reports of Warsaw Pact troop movement increase U.S. fears that the Soviets will invade Poland.

December 12. *NATO on Poland.* At the end of a two-day meeting in Brussels, the foreign ministers of the NATO countries issue a communiqué informing the Soviet Union that any sort of military intervention in Poland will damage East-West détente.

December 17. *Kosygin Death.* Former Soviet premier Kosygin dies of cardiac arrest. His death is not disclosed by Tass until December 20, after the 74th birthday celebrations (December 19) for Soviet leader Leonid Brezhnev.

1981

January 17. *Muskie Protests.* Secretary of State Edmund S. Muskie protests to Soviet ambassador Anatolii Dobrynin after Soviet news sources claim the United States is preparing military maneuvers against Iran even as negotiations for the release of the American hostages appear to be nearing a successful conclusion. White House press secretary Jody Powell calls the reports "an effort to prevent resolution of differences that would bring about the release of 52 innocent diplomats."

January 20. *Iran Frees U.S. Hostages.* The remaining 52 American hostages in Iran are released after U.S. and Iranian negotiators reach an agreement on returning Iran's frozen assets in exchange for the freedom of the hostages. The Americans, who spent 444 days in captivity, fly out of Iran minutes after Ronald Reagan is inaugurated as the 40th president of the United States.

January 29. *Reagan on Détente.* In his first news conference as president, Reagan maintains that "so far, détente's been a one-way street the Soviet Union has used to pursue its own aims," which the president describes as "the promotion of world revolution and a one-world ... communist state...." Reagan also states that in pursuit of their goals the Soviets reserve the "right to commit any crime, to lie, to cheat."

February 9. *Polish Government Shake-up.* Poland's defense minister, Gen. Wojciech Jaruzelski, is named premier following the dismissal of Josef Pinkowski. The government shuffle occurs amid continuing strikes in Poland.

February 14. *Moscow Denies Aid to El Salvador.* The Soviet Embassy denies White House allegations that the Soviet Union is supplying arms to rebels fighting in El Salvador but concedes that Moscow has no restrictions on sending arms to Cuba or Ethiopia, two countries with close ties to the Soviet Union that allegedly provide El Salvadorian rebels with arms. State Department sources February 23 claim "definite evidence" that Cuba and other communist countries have supplied the rebels with military equipment, allegations that the Soviet Union February 25 calls "lies."

February 23. *Brezhnev Proposes Summit.* In an opening speech to the 26th Congress of the Communist Party of the Soviet Union, President Leonid I. Brezhnev proposes a summit meeting with President Reagan in the interest of restoring "normal relations" between the Soviet Union and the United States and lessening the arms race. The Reagan administration responds cautiously. Secretary of State Alexander M. Haig, Jr., tells reporters that the United States is "very interested" in a summit, but that the idea should be considered "very, very carefully."

Brezhnev announces at the end of the congress March 3 that the entire Politburo has been reelected, the first time a party congress has witnessed no change among the top leadership.

March 10. *Soviet Overtures.* Moscow embarks upon a public relations campaign to bolster President Brezhnev's summit proposition. Brezhnev personally corresponds with Western leaders endorsing the summit and a moratorium on nuclear weaponry. Two Soviet Embassy officials appear March 1 and March 8 on U.S. television talk shows — ABC's "Issues and Answers" and CBS's "Face the Nation" — to discuss the summit proposal.

March 19. *Soyuz 81 Maneuvers.* The Polish News Agency (PAP) reports the beginning of Warsaw Pact maneuvers, code-named Soyuz 81, in Poland, the German Democratic Republic, the Soviet Union, and Czechoslovakia. The maneuvers are extended March 26 after Solidarity announces a warning strike for March 27, to be followed by a general strike. The general strike is subsequently canceled.

March 30. *Assassination Attempt.* President Reagan is wounded by a lone gunman outside the Washington Hilton in Washington, D.C. During the president's convalescence he writes President Brezhnev in an effort to improve U.S.-Soviet relations.

April 7. *Brezhnev in Prague.* Speaking to the Czechoslovak Communist Party Congress, Brezhnev states that it is not necessary for Moscow to solve Poland's problems. The Soyuz 81 Warsaw Pact maneuvers end the same day but Western concern over Soviet intentions in Poland continues.

April 13. *Solidarity Criticized.* The Soviet party newspaper *Pravda* publishes criticism of Solidarity from non-Solidarity Polish workers. A group of electronics workers in Warel claims Solidarity members exert "great psychological pressure" on workers to declare strikes.

April 17. *Rural Solidarity Formed.* Representatives of Rural Solidarity sign an agreement with the Polish government granting the organization official recognition. Rural Solidarity claims it represents half of Poland's 3.5 million private farmers.

April 24. *Grain Embargo Lifted.* President Reagan announces in a closed cabinet session that the embargo on grain sales to the Soviet Union will be lifted. President Jimmy Carter imposed the embargo in January 1980 in response to the Soviet intervention in Afghanistan. Reagan had promised during the presidential campaign to lift the embargo.

May 4. *NATO on Moscow.* During a meeting of NATO foreign ministers in Rome, Secretary of State Haig announces that the United States is ready to enter into arms talks with the Soviet Union on the reduction of middle-range nuclear missiles in Europe. At the conclusion of the conference, NATO issues a communiqué that links improved East-West relations with a commitment by Moscow to stop "resorting to force and intimidation and [to] cease exploiting crisis and instability in the Third World."

May 6. *Lebanon Crisis.* The United States and the Soviet Union send officials to Lebanon to help mediate a crisis caused when Syria moves surface-to-air missiles into Lebanon.

May 10. *New French President.* Francois Mitterand is elected president of France under the banner of the Socialist Party.

May 17. *Reagan at Notre Dame.* In a commencement speech at Notre Dame University in South Bend, Indiana, President Reagan declares that "The West will not contain communism; it will transcend communism. We will not bother to denounce it; we'll dismiss it as a sad, bizarre chapter in human history whose last pages are even now being written."

May 24. *Begin on Crisis.* Israeli premier Menachem Begin charges that Soviet advisers are accompanying Syrian army units into Lebanon. Tass May 25 calls Begin's allegation "deliberate and premeditated misinformation designed to delude Arab and world public opinion."

June 16. *Haig on China.* Secretary of State Haig announces at the conclusion of a three-day trip to Beijing that the United States will sell weapons to China, a reversal of previous U.S. policy. Tass responds June 17, charging the United States and China with military expansionism.

July 14-20. *Polish Emergency Congress.* Poland's Communist Party convenes an emergency congress to discuss the political and economic crises buffeting the country. The congress is a watershed because it allows open criticism of party policies and voting by secret ballot. It is the first congress in 60 years to be scheduled before the traditional five-year interval. The Soviet Union protests the inclusion of democratic methods into congress procedures. So that it may dissociate itself from the results of the congress if need be, Moscow sends a less important Politburo member, Viktor V. Grishin, as its representative.

July 15. *Soviet-Brazilian Trade Accord.* Soviet and Brazilian officials sign a $6 billion trade accord in Moscow calling for the Soviet purchase of soybeans and Brazilian acquisition of Soviet oil.

July 20. *Polish Congress Concludes.* The Polish Communist Party emergency congress ends with a large turnover in officials elected to the Central Committee. More than 90 percent had never held a party leadership position. Party boss Stanislaw Kania and Premier Jaruzelski are reelected. Delegates July 15 expel former party first secretary Edward Gierek. Moscow gives the Polish congress perfunctory approval July 21, as Brezhnev sends a cool telegram asserting that the meeting has "set the task of stabilizing" the crisis in Poland. The message warns that internal and external subversive forces are continuing "their subtle attacks on the foundations of the Polish state" and are "providing complications in Poland's relations with its true neighbors." Congratulations to Kania are guarded in contrast to the ebullient terms of praise Moscow sent upon his election in September 1980.

September 5 - October 7. *Solidarity Congress.* In an unprecedented action the Solidarity national congress calls for free parliamentary elections in Poland, thereby defying the leadership position of the Communist Party. The Soviet Union immediately denounces the congress as an "anti-socialist, anti-Soviet orgy" that could develop into "a struggle for power." The congress voted September 9 to urge other East European countries to encourage the development of independent trade unions. Many actions of the congress demonstrate Solidarity's potential as a political organization. Lech Walesa is narrowly reelected as chairman.

September 16. *Polish Authorities Respond.* In the wake of the Solidarity national congress, Polish authorities accuse the trade union of developing into an opposition movement that could push Poland into a "new national tragedy." They charge it with breaking the August/September 1980 agreement with the government.

September 24. *Haig and Gromyko Meeting.* Secretary of State Haig and Foreign Minister Gromyko jointly announce that negotiations concerning the limitation of medium-range nuclear weapons in Europe will begin November 30 in Geneva. The meeting, which began in New York September 23, is the first high-level U.S.-Soviet meeting of the Reagan administration.

October 6. *Sadat Assassinated.* President Anwar al-Sadat of Egypt is assassinated while reviewing a military parade. Vice President Hosni Mubarak officially succeeds Sadat October 13.

October 16. *Reagan on Nuclear War.* In a news briefing President Reagan implies that it may be possible to use tactical nuclear weapons in a confrontation on European soil without igniting a full-scale nuclear war. Reagan's remarks cause a furor over apparent U.S. insensitivity to the fate of Western Europe. The statements cause a major stir in Europe where an increasingly powerful antinuclear movement is gathering momentum. Brezhnev capitalizes on the remarks in an October 20 Tass statement: "The thoughts and efforts of the Soviet leadership . . . are directed at preventing nuclear war altogether, by eliminating the very danger of its outbreak." President Reagan attempts to clarify his remarks on October 21 by denying lack of concern for Western Europe and dispelling the impression that the United States is willing to use nuclear weaponry.

October 18. *Kania Dismissed.* Polish Communist Party head Stanislaw Kania is dismissed as party chief and replaced by Premier Wojciech Jaruzelski. Kania's removal comes in the wake of worsening economic conditions, increasing wildcat strikes, and severe party disagreement on how best to deal with Solidarity. Kania was criticized for being too soft on the powerful trade union federation. Jaruzelski holds supreme power as first secretary of the party, commander of the armed forces, premier, and defense minister.

October 27. *CSCE Reconvenes.* The 35-nation review session of the 1975 Helsinki accords on European security and cooperation reconvenes in Madrid. The session opens with a tirade against the Soviet Union as European delegates repeat earlier accusations of accord violations in the human rights area and condemn Moscow for intervening in Afghanistan and conducting Warsaw Pact maneuvers around Poland. The session ends in a deadlock December 18.

November 2. *Brezhnev Interview.* Soviet president Brezhnev discusses the East-West balance of power, disarmament, and détente in an interview for the German publication *Der Spiegel.* The interview follows widespread demonstrations in Europe October 24-25 protesting NATO plans to deploy medium-range nuclear weapons in Europe. Brezhnev criticizes United States foreign policy as the main factor behind world tension over nuclear weaponry and attempts to lessen impressions of Moscow as a threat to European peace. Secretary of State Haig rejects Brezhnev's statement that "approximate parity" exists in U.S.-Soviet nuclear force deployment in Western Europe.

November 6. *Soviet Sub Released.* Swedish authorities release a Soviet submarine that ran aground in shallow waters near a Swedish naval base October 27.

November 16. *Brezhnev on the Food Supply.* In his address to a Central Committee Plenum, Leonid Brezhnev declares that the Soviet food supply is "economically and politically the central problem of the five-year plan." He pledges development of a new food program that will include more decentralized decision making in the agricultural economy, more incentives for local initiatives, and expanded use of private plots.

November 18. *Reagan's "Zero Option" Proposal.* In a televised speech to the National Press Club, President Reagan announces that the United States will cancel plans for deployment of intermediate-range nuclear weapons in

Europe if the Soviet Union will dismantle its SS-4, SS-5, and SS-20 missiles already in place. Tass calls the speech a "propaganda ploy designed to stalemate disarmament talks."

November 22-25. *Brezhnev in Bonn.* Leonid Brezhnev visits the Federal Republic of Germany and holds extensive talks with Chancellor Helmut Schmidt on arms control and economic and international issues.

November 30. *Negotiations Begin on Medium-Range Nuclear Missiles.* U.S.-Soviet negotiations on the containment of theater nuclear forces in Europe begin in Geneva. The negotiating teams headed by Paul H. Nitze for the United States and Yuli A. Kvitsinsky for the Soviet Union impose a news blackout. The United States bargaining position is Reagan's "zero option" proposal forgoing deployment of medium-range missiles if the Soviets dismantle their intermediate-range missiles already in place. The Soviet team works from a proposal made by President Brezhnev in Bonn during his November 22-25 visit, in which he offered a freeze on medium-range missile deployment. The session recesses December 17.

December 10. *Sakharov Hunger Strike Ends.* Soviet officials confirm the end of a hunger strike by dissident physicist Andrei Sakharov and his wife Yelena Bonner. The Sakharovs began a fast November 22 protesting Moscow's refusal to allow their daughter-in-law, Lisa Alekseyeva, to join her husband, Aleksei Semyonov, in the United States. *Izvestiia* announced December 4 that the Sakharovs had been hospitalized to prevent "complications in the state of their health." The Soviet Union made what is considered an unusual concession by allowing Alekseyeva to emigrate. She arrived in the United States December 20.

December 13. *Martial Law In Poland.* Gen. Jaruzelski declares that Poland is in a state of emergency and imposes martial law. The decree interrupts the operations of the independent trade union federation Solidarity and curtails the civil rights of Polish citizens. Jaruzelski's announcement follows a December 12 decision by Solidarity to call for a nationwide referendum to decide whether to maintain a communist system of government if Polish authorities do not agree to a new series of demands. Jaruzelski declares that "the anti-state subversive action of the forces hostile to socialism had pushed the community to the brink of civil war" and adds "there is no turning back from socialism, there is no turning back to the fake methods and practices before August 1980." Imposition of martial law includes a raid on Solidarity headquarters, detention of Solidarity leaders, a news blackout, and reported troop movements to ensure control. Tass December 14 calls events in Poland an "internal matter."

December 23. *Economic Sanctions Against Poland.* President Reagan in a televised speech announces U.S. economic sanctions against Poland that include suspension of civil aviation and fishing rights and restriction of Export-Import Bank credits, high-technology exports, and export of food products. Reagan places "a major share of the blame" on Moscow for the imposition of martial law. In Poland censored foreign reporting was allowed to resume December 18. Widespread opposition to martial law was reported in the form of strikes and scuffles with military police.

December 29. *Economic Sanctions Against the Soviet Union.* Despite Soviet denials of interference in Poland's internal affairs, the United States imposes economic sanctions against Moscow. These include the suspension of Aeroflot flights to the United States and suspension of scientific exchange agreements. The reaction of U.S. allies is mixed. West Germany in particular questions whether Moscow is indeed the prime mover behind the imposition of martial law in Poland. Tass December 30 assails the sanctions as a move "to hurl the world back into the dark times of the cold war."

1982

January 4-5. *Reagan/Schmidt on Poland.* After meeting for several hours at the White House, President Reagan and Chancellor Helmut Schmidt of West Germany release a joint communiqué expressing agreement on "the responsibility of the Soviet Union for developments in Poland." Schmidt had previously maintained that imposition of martial law and its effect on Poland was a matter of internal concern. Schmidt continues to oppose economic sanctions against the Soviet Union. The Soviet news agency Tass censures Schmidt for joining forces with the United States to criticize the government of Poland but expresses confidence in Schmidt's ability to maintain "his own opinion" in rejecting sanctions against Moscow.

January 11. *NATO on Poland.* Foreign ministers of NATO countries meet in emergency session in Brussels and condemn the Soviet Union for its participation in "the system of repression in Poland." In contrast to the previous stance of West European leaders, the statement calls for Europe to join the United States in imposing economic sanctions against the Soviet Union. Great Britain on February 5 becomes the first NATO country to do so.

January 12. *Arms Talks Reconvene.* U.S. and Soviet negotiators return to Geneva to reconvene discussions on limiting medium-range missiles in Europe.

January 25. *Suslov Dies.* Influential Politburo member and chief Soviet ideologist Mikhail Suslov dies "after a brief illness." The powerful Suslov played a major role in every Soviet regime since V.I. Lenin's.

January 26. *Gromyko and Haig in Geneva.* Secretary of State Alexander M. Haig, Jr., and Soviet foreign minister Andrei Gromyko meet in Geneva in the first high-level meeting of the two countries since September 1981. Following the discussion Haig states that disagreements over the Polish crisis "cast a long, dark shadow over all East-West issues," but he nevertheless terms the discussions "beneficial."

February 9. *New Arms Proposal.* The Soviets offer a new proposal to limit intermediate-range missiles. It calls for reductions by stages throughout 1981 to about 300 weapons for each side. The State Department rejects the plan.

March 5. *Union Leader Dismissed.* It is announced that Aleksei I. Shibayev has been dismissed as chairman of the All-Union Central Council of Trade Unions. The announcement is made just 10 days before a major trade union convention in Moscow. No reason is given. Shibayev is replaced by Stepan A. Shalayev, a government minister with a labor background. Some speculate that Shalayev will try to prevent the sort of trade union activity in the Soviet Union that resulted in Solidarity's formation in Poland.

March 8. *Chemical Warfare.* In testimony before the Senate Foreign Relations Committee, Deputy Secretary of

State Walter J. Stoessel, Jr., states that Soviet troops have been using extensive chemical warfare in Afghanistan.

March 16. *USSR Halts European Missile Deployments.* At a convention of trade unions in Moscow, General Secretary Brezhnev announces that the Soviet Union will not deploy any new SS-20 intermediate-range missiles in the European regions of the USSR. The ban is to stay in effect unless NATO begins its planned deployments of Pershing II and cruise missiles. The Reagan administration immediately dismisses the move as part of the Soviets' propaganda campaign against NATO's nuclear missile modernization program.

March 24. *Brezhnev on China.* Brezhnev delivers a conciliatory speech in Tashkent, Uzbekistan, on Sino-Soviet relations. He urges resumption of border negotiations and emphasizes the Soviets' desire to normalize relations with Beijing.

March 31. *Reagan Asserts Soviet Nuclear Superiority.* In a televised news conference, President Reagan rejects the idea of a mutual nuclear freeze because "The Soviet Union does have a definite margin of superiority — enough so that there is risk." He reaffirms his commitment to arms control but states that under a nuclear freeze the Soviets would have no incentive to negotiate an arms agreement.

April 2. *Argentina Captures Falkland Islands.* Argentine troops seize control of Britain's Falkland, South Georgia, and South Sandwich Islands in the South Atlantic. British prime minister Margaret Thatcher orders a 35-ship naval task force to steam to the islands. The USSR initially declares its neutrality April 7, but as the crisis develops Soviet statements lend increasing support to Argentina.

April 4-5. *Gromyko in Yugoslavia.* Soviet foreign minister Gromyko meets in Belgrade with Yugoslav officials. It is the first visit by a high-level Soviet official since President Tito's death two years before.

April 6. *Haig on "No-First-Use."* Secretary of State Haig in a Washington speech rejects a policy of "no-first-use" of nuclear weapons in Europe. Haig contends that if NATO agreed with the USSR that neither would be the first to use nuclear weapons, deterrence of a Soviet conventional attack would be seriously weakened, thereby necessitating a massive conventional buildup by the West to offset the Soviet threat. Haig also dismisses the wisdom of a nuclear freeze. The speech comes one day before a news conference by four prominent former U.S. officials — McGeorge Bundy, George Kennan, Robert MacNamara, and Gerard Smith — who discuss their forthcoming *Foreign Affairs* article that advocates adoption of a no-first-use policy.

May 9. *Reagan's Eureka College START Proposal.* President Reagan outlines a strategic arms reduction proposal in a speech at his alma mater. His plan calls for a one-third reduction in total warheads, with no more than half being deployed in ICBMs. He also proposes a total ceiling of 850 ICBMs and SLBMs and limits on throw-weight. Reagan makes no mention of possible cuts in bombers and cruise missiles. Brezhnev welcomes Reagan's interest in negotiations May 18 but rejects the specifics of his proposal as "one-sided."

May 10. *Soviet Aid to Nicaragua.* Following an official visit to the USSR by Nicaraguan leader Daniel Ortega, the Soviets announce the signing of a five-year, $166.8 million, economic and technical aid agreement with Nicaragua.

May 13-21. *Unofficial Sino-Soviet Talks.* Mikhail Kapitsa, director of the Soviet Foreign Ministry's Far Eastern Department, on a "private" visit meets in Beijing with Foreign Ministry officials. Following the talks, contacts between the countries increase significantly.

May 24. *Brezhnev Presents Food Program.* In a widely publicized speech to the Central Committee, Brezhnev outlines an expensive new food program designed to ensure reliable supplies of foodstuffs for the Soviet Union through the 1980s.

May 26. *Andropov Leaves KGB for Secretariat.* Following his promotion to the Secretariat May 24, Yuri Andropov resigns as head of the Soviet Committee for State Security (KGB). He is succeeded by Vitalii Fedorchuk.

June 2-11. *Reagan in Europe.* President Reagan travels to Europe to meet with other Western leaders for an economic summit in Versailles, France, June 4-6. The leaders of the seven major industrial democracies agree to "limit their government export credits" to the East bloc, with no specific credit ceiling agreed upon. Following the summit, Reagan visits Rome, Great Britain, Bonn (for the NATO summit), and Berlin. In separate speeches to the British and West German parliaments June 8 and 9, he criticizes Soviet aggression and suppression of freedom and democracy, but he expresses U.S. desires for arms control and East-West cooperation.

June 6. *Israel Invades Lebanon.* The Israeli army launches a major invasion into southern Lebanon, ostensibly to eliminate Palestine Liberation Organization bases. By June 10 Israeli units are within a few miles of Beirut and are engaging in sporadic battles with Syrian peacekeeping troops. On June 9 and 10 the Israeli air force effectively cripples Syria's air defenses by destroying its Soviet-supplied surface-to-air missile batteries and shooting down large numbers of Syrian MiG fighters. The Soviet Union warns Israel June 14 that developments in the Middle East "cannot help affecting the interests of the USSR."

June 12. *Central Park Peace Rally.* More than 500,000 persons gather in New York City's Central Park to support a nuclear freeze. It is the biggest antinuclear rally in U.S. history.

June 14. *British Recapture Falklands.* Argentine forces surrender to the British at Port Stanley, ending the Falkland Islands War begun April 2. The British successfully landed troops on the islands May 21 and proceeded to retake key positions. The USSR maintains intelligence ships in the South Atlantic during the conflict.

June 15. *Gromyko Renounces First-Use.* At the UN General Assembly's special session on disarmament, Foreign Minister Gromyko pledges the Soviet Union will not be the first nation to use nuclear weapons. Two days later President Reagan addresses the special session but does not comment on Gromyko's speech. He emphasizes the U.S. commitment to arms control and accuses the Soviets of being insincere, pursuing a massive military buildup, and seeking to manipulate the peace movement in the West.

June 18. *U.S. Widens Pipeline Sanctions.* President Reagan broadens sanctions aimed at delaying progress of the European-Siberian natural gas pipeline, saying the sanctions are a further response to martial law in Poland. The new measures would prohibit foreign subsidiaries and licensees of U.S. companies from selling equipment for the pipeline. Previous sanctions enacted December 1981 barred only the sale of equipment made in the United States. The

European Economic Community unanimously opposes the U.S. move.

June 19. *Haig on Soviet Missile Tests.* Following two days of negotiations with Foreign Minister Gromyko in New York, Secretary of State Haig accuses the Soviets of recently conducting an "unprecedented" series of missile tests, which included the firing of an antisatellite weapon. Gromyko claimed June 21 that the tests violated no existing treaties and were no different from tests the United States had conducted.

June 29. *START Talks Begin.* The initial round of the Strategic Arms Reduction Talks (START) opens in Geneva, with Edward L. Rowny heading the U.S. negotiating team and Victor P. Karpov, a veteran of SALT II and preliminary INF (intermediate-range nuclear force) talks, heading the Soviet delegation.

July 16. *"Walk-in-the-Woods" Plan.* After weeks of unofficial conversations, U.S. arms negotiator Paul Nitze and his Soviet counterpart at the INF talks, Yuli Kvitsinskii, jointly develop a confidential European arms control package for their respective superiors to consider. The package, drawn up during a private walk in the Jura Mountains near Geneva, is subsequently repudiated by both governments.

July 20. *U.S. Withdraws from Test-Ban Talks.* President Reagan ends U.S. participation in talks on a comprehensive nuclear test ban until verification measures are improved. The three-way negotiations by Great Britain, the USSR, and the United States had been suspended since November 1980. Great Britain and many members of the U.S. Congress express opposition to Reagan's decision. On July 21 Tass accuses the Reagan administration of using verification problems as an excuse to sabotage the talks.

August 20. *U.S.-Soviet Grain Deal Extension.* The Soviet Union renews for another year the one-year grain sale agreement with the United States due to expire September 30. The extension follows a July 30 proposal by President Reagan to continue the current arrangement.

September 1. *Hu on the Superpowers.* Chinese Communist Party chairman Hu Yaobang, in a speech to the 12th Party Congress, claims the United States and USSR pose equal threats to international peace and accuses both of "hegemonism."

September 15. *Brezhnev's Middle East Peace Plan.* In a Kremlin speech General Secretary Brezhnev offers a six-point plan for achieving peace in the Middle East. It calls for Israel to return to its pre-1967 borders and the UN to guarantee a settlement providing for the establishment of a Palestinian state. The plan is similar to one adopted by the Arab League September 9. Brezhnev attacks a September 1 peace proposal by President Reagan for its failure to advocate a completely independent Palestinian state and recognize the Palestine Liberation Organization as the sole legitimate representative of the Palestinian people.

September 17. *Coalition Government Collapses in FRG.* The West German Free Democratic Party ends its alliance with Chancellor Helmut Schmidt's Social Democrats. Schmidt's coalition government falls and Christian Democratic leader Helmut Kohl is elected chancellor October 1.

October 5. *Sino-Soviet Negotiations.* Formal "consultations" between Soviet and Chinese deputy foreign ministers begin in Beijing. It is the first official high-level meeting between the countries since China suspended talks in 1980 following the Soviet invasion of Afghanistan. The talks end October 21 but, as previously agreed, no official statement is released. The parties do agree to hold further consultations, with sessions alternating between Moscow and Beijing.

October 8. *Solidarity Banned.* The Polish Parliament votes to ban Solidarity and all other existing Polish labor organizations. President Reagan responds by announcing October 9 that he plans to end Poland's most-favored-nation trading status.

November 8. *Pope to Visit Poland.* Polish authorities announce that Pope John Paul II will visit Poland June 1983. The trip had previously been scheduled for August 26, 1982, but was canceled by Polish leaders, who claimed a papal visit could disrupt national stability.

November 10. *Brezhnev Dies.* Soviet president and Communist Party general secretary Leonid I. Brezhnev dies of a heart attack at age 75. His death is not announced in the Soviet media until the following day. A four-day period of mourning is declared.

November 11. *Walesa Freed.* The imminent release of Lech Walesa, leader of the outlawed Polish Solidarity labor union, is announced. A government spokesman says Walesa would be free to "do whatever he wants." Walesa had been interned under martial law since December 1981. He arrives home in Gdansk November 14, where he promises his future conduct "will be courageous but also prudent."

November 12. *Andropov Named General Secretary.* The Central Committee unanimously elects 68-year-old Yuri V. Andropov to succeed Brezhnev as general secretary. Andropov, a Politburo member, Central Committee secretary, and former head of the KGB, is nominated by Brezhnev associate Konstantin Chernenko, himself considered a candidate for the post. Andropov does not immediately assume the titular position of president, which Brezhnev also held.

November 13. *Reagan Lifts Pipeline Sanctions.* President Reagan announces he is lifting sanctions designed to prevent U.S. and foreign companies from selling equipment to the Soviet Union for use in the construction of the European-Siberian pipeline. The sanctions (imposed December 1981 and widened June 1982) had caused considerable friction between the United States and its European allies. Reagan maintains the sanctions are no longer necessary due to the allies' new agreement concerning economic strategy toward the Soviet Union "that provides for stronger and more effective measures." However, French president François Mitterand November 15 asserts France has not been a party to any such agreement.

November 15. *Brezhnev's Funeral.* Leonid Brezhnev is buried between the Lenin Mausoleum and the Kremlin wall following a nationally televised ceremony attended by many foreign dignitaries. Yuri Andropov, Brezhnev's successor, delivers the first eulogy. After the funeral Andropov briefly meets with Vice President George Bush, the leader of the U.S. delegation. The talks, attended by U.S. secretary of state George Shultz and Soviet foreign minister Andrei Gromyko, are described by Bush as "frank, cordial and substantive." Andropov also meets with other world leaders in Moscow for Brezhnev's funeral, including Indian prime minister Indira Gandhi, Pakistani leader Zia ul-Haq, Cuban president Fidel Castro, and Afghan leader Babrak Karmal.

November 16. *Gromyko-Huang Discussions.* Soviet foreign minister Gromyko meets with Chinese foreign minister Huang Hua, who had attended Brezhnev's funeral the day before. It is the first time the countries' foreign ministers have met since the 1960s. Western observers regard the meeting, and General Secretary Andropov's warm greeting of Huang the previous day, as concrete signs of an improving Sino-Soviet relationship.

November 22. *Andropov Addresses Central Committee.* Yuri Andropov delivers his first policy speech as general secretary. He expresses his support for détente with the West and improved relations with China, while cautioning that future arms control agreements would require sacrifices by the United States and its allies equal to those made by the USSR. Concerning domestic policy, Andropov advocates more independence for manufacturing and agricultural enterprises and incentives to make workers more productive.

November 23. *Gosplan Estimates Industrial Growth.* Nikolai Baibakov, head of Gosplan, the state planning committee, tells the Supreme Soviet that the industrial growth rate for 1982 is expected to be 2.8 percent, the smallest peacetime growth since the USSR was founded.

December 6. *Ustinov on MX Deployment.* Soviet defense minister Dimitri Ustinov states the USSR will counter the MX missile with a new missile of its own, if the MX is deployed. On November 22 President Reagan had announced his support for an MX missile system deployed in a "dense pack" basing mode.

December 21. *Andropov Missile Proposal.* General Secretary Andropov proposes a reduction in the number of Soviet intermediate-range missiles targeted on Europe to 162, if NATO cancels its planned Pershing II and cruise missile deployments. The proposed figure is equal to the number of missiles deployed by Britain and France, which, along with the United States, immediately reject the offer.

December 27. *Soviet Government Declares Amnesty.* To commemorate the 60th anniversary of the founding of the USSR, the Soviet government declares an amnesty for many prisoners serving sentences for minor crimes.

December 31. *Martial Law Eased in Poland.* The Polish government "suspends" martial law. Communist Party leader Gen. Wojciech Jaruzelski indicates that the government will retain certain restrictive powers while the country gradually returns to normal. President Reagan says the United States will not remove sanctions against Poland unless developments prove the martial law action is more than a "cosmetic change."

1983

January 12. *Podgornyi Dies.* Soviet president from 1965 until 1977 Nikolai Podgornyi, 79, dies in Moscow. Podgornyi had been retired since 1979, when his exclusion from the Supreme Soviet formally ended his political career.

January 16-18. *Gromyko Visits FRG.* Soviet foreign minister Andrei Gromyko campaigns against NATO's planned missile deployments during a three-day visit to West Germany. Gromyko rejects President Reagan's "zero option" proposal, repeats the Soviet offer to reduce the number of intermediate-range missiles targeted on Western Europe to 162, and urges the West Germans not to

accept NATO's 108 Pershing II missiles, due to be deployed in the FRG later in 1983.

January 17. *Soviet Missiles in Syria.* U.S. intelligence officials report that the USSR has provided new surface-to-air missiles to Syria. The long-range SA-5 missiles are expected to significantly improve Syria's air defense capabilities, which were devastated by Israeli warplanes in June 1982.

January 31. *Andropov Visits Factory.* General Secretary Yuri Andropov makes a well-publicized visit to a machine-tool factory in Moscow. Andropov emphasizes the need for greater labor discipline and urges workers to be more productive.

February 10. *Bush Completes European Visit.* Vice President George Bush returns to the United States following a 12-day visit to seven West European nations. Bush's trip was designed to solidify support for NATO's scheduled missile deployments. Before leaving Europe, Bush comments that he has been "reassured" by his meetings but adds that the allies were united in their desire for a flexible approach to arms control negotiations.

February 23. *Andropov Urges Economic Reforms.* In an article in the party journal *Kommunist*, Andropov says he plans to introduce wage incentives in an effort to increase productivity. He also advocates "an invigoration and even wider use of local initiative."

February 25. *FRG Charges Interference.* A West German government spokesman denounces "the massive and hitherto unprecedented manner in which the Soviet Union is interfering in the election and the internal politics of the Federal Republic of Germany." The spokesman cites in particular a German-language radio broadcast by the Soviets that predicted a wave of domestic unrest if Chancellor Helmut Kohl's Christian Democratic Party triumphed in the upcoming elections.

March 6. *Kohl Wins FRG Elections.* Helmut Kohl and his Christian Democratic Party are reelected in West Germany's national parliamentary elections. Their success is regarded as a victory for NATO's current "dual-track" approach to nuclear arms that advocates the deployment of Pershing II and cruise missiles in Europe if an arms control agreement is not reached with the USSR. Kohl supported the dual-track strategy, while his opponent, Social Democrat Hans-Jochen Vogel, criticized it.

March 8. *Reagan's "Evil Empire" Speech.* In a speech to a convention of Protestant evangelicals in Orlando, Florida, President Reagan denounces a nuclear freeze and urges the audience not to "ignore the facts of history and the aggressive impulses of an evil empire [Soviet Union]." Reagan also calls Soviet communism "the focus of evil in the modern world." Tass comments March 9 that the speech shows the Reagan administration "can think only in terms of confrontation and bellicose, lunatic anticommunism."

March 12. *Kohl on "Zero Option" Proposal.* In a *Washington Post* interview West German chancellor Kohl supports the United States' "zero option" negotiating positions on intermediate-range weapons as the optimal solution to the European nuclear arms race. However, Kohl states he doubts it is an obtainable goal.

March 23. *Reagan Calls for ABM Development.* In a nationally televised speech Reagan warns of the Soviet military buildup and defends his record $280.5 billion defense budget request. He calls on American scientists to use their talents to develop an advanced antiballistic missile defense system that would render nuclear ballistic missiles "impotent and obsolete." Reagan declares he is "directing a comprehensive and intensive effort to define a long-term research and development program to begin to achieve our ultimate goal of eliminating the threat posed by strategic nuclear missiles." General Secretary Andropov claims March 26 that Reagan's ABM development plans threaten to cause a runaway arms race.

March 30. *U.S. Modifies INF Position.* Reagan announces a new proposal to limit nuclear weapons in Europe. While affirming the ultimate goal of eliminating all intermediate-range nuclear force (INF) weapons in the European theater, Reagan says the United States would reduce its missile deployments if "the Soviet Union reduced the number of its warheads on longer-range INF missiles to an equal level on a global basis." Gromyko rejects Reagan's offer as "not serious" April 2.

April 1-4. *Easter Weekend Demonstrations.* Numerous demonstrations protesting NATO's planned missile deployments draw large crowds in West Germany and Great Britain.

April 11. *MX Recommendation.* An 11-member commission established January 3, 1983, by President Reagan recommends that 100 MX missiles be deployed in existing Minuteman silos. The panel also supports the development of a smaller, mobile missile that is less vulnerable to a Soviet first strike. Reagan approves the commission's proposal and submits it to Congress April 19.

April 26. *Sweden Claims USSR Sub Incursions.* A Swedish commission charges that Sweden's territorial waters have been repeatedly violated by Soviet submarine patrols. Tass denies the charges April 27.

May 3. *Andropov Offers to Limit Warheads.* Andropov proposes limiting the warheads, missiles, and bombers of the Warsaw Pact and NATO (including French and British forces) to equitable levels. Andropov says the Soviet Union is willing "to have no more missiles and warheads mounted on them than on the side of NATO." U.S. officials welcome the Soviets' new willingness to discuss limitations on warheads but object to Andropov's continued inclusion of French and British nuclear weapons as part of NATO's nuclear arsenal.

May 4. *Iran Disbands Communist Party.* The government of Iran dissolves the Iranian communist Tudeh Party after the head of the party confesses to espionage and treason charges. The government also accuses Soviet Embassy elements of interfering in Iran "by using and establishing links with mercenaries and traitors to the republic" and orders 18 Soviet diplomats to leave the country.

May 9. *Andropov Heads Defense Council.* Defense Minister Dmitri Ustinov discloses in a *Pravda* article that Andropov has assumed the role of chairman of the Defense Council in addition to his general secretary post.

May 16-23. *Gorbachev Visits Canada.* Politburo member and Central Committee secretary Mikhail Gorbachev travels across Canada as leader of a Soviet agricultural delegation. He meets with Prime Minister Pierre Trudeau in Ottawa May 18.

June 8. *Reagan Revises START Proposal.* President Reagan announces alterations in the U.S. negotiating position at the START (Strategic Arms Reduction) talks in Geneva. While the proposed ceiling of 5,000 warheads is to be retained, Reagan says the United States no longer will insist on limiting each side's strategic missiles to 850. He does not propose a specific new missile limit. Reagan also states the United States will relax its demands on limiting the throw-weight of strategic missiles.

June 9. *British Conservatives Reelected.* The Conservative Party, headed by Prime Minister Margaret Thatcher, is decisively returned to power in Britain's national parliamentary elections. The Conservative victory ensures that NATO's scheduled deployments of cruise missiles in Great Britain will take place unless an arms control agreement is concluded with the USSR.

June 16. *Andropov Elected President.* The Supreme Soviet formally elects Communist Party General Secretary Yuri Andropov as president (chairman of the Presidium of the Supreme Soviet). Andropov, who was nominated by Konstantin Chernenko, becomes the only Soviet leader other than Leonid Brezhnev to be president and general secretary simultaneously.

June 16-23. *Pope Visits Poland.* Pope John Paul II travels to his native Poland for a visit that had been postponed by Polish leaders in 1982. In a brief televised speech the pope calls for social reform based on the August 1980 agreements that brought about the Solidarity union. The same day he meets for two hours with Gen. Wojciech Jaruzelski, the leader of the Polish regime. In subsequent speeches to massive crowds, the pope continues to emphasize Polish nationalism and social reform. He holds a private audience with Solidarity leader Lech Walesa June 23 before leaving for Rome.

June 24. *Soviets Reject INF Proposal.* The Reagan administration discloses that the Soviets have rejected the president's March 30 proposal on limiting intermediate-range nuclear weapons in Europe. Secretary of State George Shultz June 26 urges Moscow to make a counteroffer instead of simply rejecting it.

June 26. *Pentecostals to Emigrate.* Seven Soviet Pentecostals who had been living in the U.S. Embassy in Moscow since 1978 are granted permission to emigrate by Soviet authorities.

July 4-7. *Kohl Visits Soviet Union.* West German chancellor Kohl meets in Moscow with Andropov. Andropov reportedly tells Kohl that deployment of NATO missiles in the FRG would endanger West German national security and harm Soviet-West German relations. The two leaders also discuss the issue of German reunification. Kohl stops in Kiev July 7 before returning to Bonn.

July 21. *Poland Ends Martial Law.* Martial law is formally lifted in Poland after 19 months. The government also extends amnesty to many political prisoners. However, the Polish Sejm (Parliament) enacts a series of laws that permits the government to tightly control Poland's economy and social programs. The formal lifting of martial law comes almost seven months after it had been "suspended" December 31, 1982.

July 26. *Experimental Economic Reforms.* The Soviet Union announces economic "experiments" designed to relax central bureaucratic controls. The plan gives factory managers in selected industries greater autonomy over budgets, plant investment, wages, and incentive bonuses. It is scheduled to begin January 1, 1984. Andropov had publicly supported such reforms on several occasions since he became general secretary.

August 18. *Andropov on Antisatellite Weapons.* At a Kremlin meeting with nine visiting U.S. Democratic senators, Andropov declares a unilateral moratorium on the deployment of Soviet antisatellite weapons. He also asks the United States to agree to a treaty "on the elimination of the existing antisatellite systems and the prohibition of the development of new ones."

August 25. *U.S.-Soviet Grain Deal.* A five-year grain sale agreement is signed in Moscow by representatives of the United States and USSR. The pact obligates the Soviet Union to buy 9 million tons of American grain during each of the next five years. The Soviets have the option to buy an additional 3 million tons annually without obtaining further U.S. government approval.

August 26. *Andropov on Liquidation of SS-20s.* Andropov repeats an earlier Soviet offer to conclude an arms agreement reducing SS-20s targeted on Europe to the combined number of French and British missiles. He adds that the missiles to be removed would be dismantled rather than stored or redeployed in Asia.

September 1. *Korean Airliner Shot Down.* A Soviet fighter shoots down Korean Air Lines flight 007 over the Sea of Japan near Sakhalin Island. The Boeing 747, with 269 people on board, had strayed into Soviet airspace for unknown reasons. The Soviets do not admit until September 6 they shot down the plane. They maintain the jetliner was spying for the United States and did not respond to warnings. Chief of the Soviet General Staff Marshal Nikolai Ogarkov tells foreign reporters September 9 that the order to shoot down the plane was "not an accident or an error." Many nations condemn the attack and temporarily restrict civil aviation with the USSR in protest. The Reagan administration strongly denounces the Soviets' action and their denial of responsibility, but it imposes only mild sanctions on the Soviet Union, including the suspension of a bilateral transportation agreement and talks on opening a U.S. consolate in Kiev.

September 8. *Shultz and Gromyko Meet.* U.S. secretary of state Shultz and Soviet foreign minister Gromyko meet in Madrid at the Conference on Security and Cooperation in Europe. Gromyko defends the Soviet downing of KAL flight 007 by saying nobody has "the right to violate with impunity foreign frontiers or the sovereignty of another state." Shultz calls Soviet explanations of the incident "totally unacceptable."

September 15. *Soviet UN Delegation Blocked.* In response to the recent Soviet destruction of a Korean airliner, the governors of New Jersey and New York refuse to allow the Soviet delegation to the UN to land at New York area commercial airports. The governors also question whether they can ensure the Soviet delegation's security. The Reagan administration offers the Soviets the option of landing at a U.S. military airfield. Gromyko cancels the Soviet visit September 17 and attacks the United States for failing to meet its host-country obligations.

September 19. *Lichenstein Statement.* Charles Lichenstein, a U.S. delegate to the United Nations, answers a Soviet accusation concerning U.S. fulfillment of its host-country obligations by saying that if UN members feel unwelcome "then the U.S. strongly encourages such member states seriously to consider removing themselves and this organization from the soil of the United States." Reagan defends Lichenstein's statement September 21, although the White House officially maintains Lichenstein was voicing his personal views.

September 26. *Reagan's UN Speech.* Reagan tells the UN General Assembly that the United States is willing to be flexible in negotiating an arms control agreement with the Soviet Union. He calls on the USSR to accept global limits on intermediate-range missiles and offers to discuss limits on aircraft and a reduction in U.S. Pershing II deployments. Despite Reagan's tone of compromise concerning the INF (intermediate-range nuclear force) talks,

he attacks the USSR for human rights and arms control violations.

September 28. *Andropov Response.* Andropov denounces Reagan's UN speech in a strongly worded Tass statement. He calls Reagan's arms control proposals "mere declarations" and accuses the United States of following "a militant course." Andropov also defends the downing of the Korean airliner and repeats Soviet accusations that the plane was spying for the United States.

October 4. *"Build-Down" Proposal.* In a televised address Reagan proposes that U.S. and Soviet strategic arsenals be reduced through a "build-down" process. The build-down concept, introduced earlier in the year by members of Congress, would require destroying a given number of old warheads for every new warhead deployed. The following day Tass criticizes the build-down plan as meaningless, saying "both sides will get the right to deploy new upgraded systems of mass annihilation as they phase out old, less effective ones."

October 5. *Walesa Awarded Peace Prize.* The head of the outlawed Polish Solidarity union, Lech Walesa, is awarded the Nobel Peace Prize. Walesa announces he will donate the prize money to a charity for Poland's farmers. The Polish government denounces the prize October 6. *Izvestiia*, the Soviet government newspaper, calls Walesa a "low-grade hustler" October 8 but does not mention his Nobel Peace Prize.

October 21. *Sino-Soviet Trade Agreement.* The Soviets and Chinese conclude an agreement to increase annual trade from $800 million to more than $1.6 billion. They also agree to increase cultural, sports, and student exchanges.

October 23. *Antinuclear Rallies.* Demonstrations in European cities against NATO's upcoming missile deployments collectively draw more than 2 million protestors.

October 25. *Invasion of Grenada.* U.S. military forces and troops from six Caribbean states invade Grenada, a small, independently governed island near Venezuela. Reagan justifies the invasion by declaring the United States was acting in response to a "formal request" by the Organization of Eastern Caribbean States (OECS) to help restore order in Grenada. Reagan also cites concern for the safety of American citizens on the island. American troops overcome resistance by local militias and well-armed Cuban "construction workers." The pro-Cuban, hard-line Marxist regime is deposed. The United States declares an end to the fighting November 2. Many nations, including close U.S. allies, criticize the invasion. Tass condemns it as "direct, unprovoked aggression."

October 26. *Soviet INF Concessions.* In a *Pravda* interview Andropov announces that the USSR is willing to reduce the number of SS-20s aimed at Europe to "about 140" and to be more flexible in negotiating limits on medium-range bombers if NATO cancels its upcoming missile deployments. The Soviets previously had offered to reduce their SS-20 force to 162. Andropov also warns that the Soviets will leave the INF negotiations in Geneva if NATO begins deploying missiles. The State Department rejects Andropov's concessions as "vague" and says they were intended to influence Western European public opinion.

November 7. *Andropov Misses Parade.* General Secretary Andropov, who has not been seen in public since August 18, fails to appear at the annual parade in Moscow commemorating the Bolshevik Revolution. Kremlin spokesmen maintain Andropov has a "bad cold," but many Western analysts contend he would have attended the ceremonies were he not seriously ill. Politburo member Konstantin Chernenko takes Andropov's place on the reviewing stand, thus ending recent speculation in the West that he had been demoted.

November 14. *Missiles Arrive in Britain.* The first 16 cruise missiles scheduled for deployment arrive at Greenham Common Air Base in England.

November 18. *USSR Defense Spending Report.* The Joint Economic Committee of Congress releases a report by the Central Intelligence Agency that Soviet defense spending had grown more slowly since 1976 than during the prior decade. The report estimates the growth of Soviet military spending since 1976 at only 2 percent. The report also says the Soviet economy as a whole grew at a 3.5 percent to 4 percent rate during 1983 — a significant improvement over the 2 percent growth the CIA had estimated for 1981 and 1982.

November 22. *FRG Accepts NATO Missiles.* Following a stormy two-day debate, the West German Bundestag (Parliament) votes 286 to 226 to allow NATO missiles to be deployed in the Federal Republic of Germany. The first nine Pershing II missiles arrive in the country the next day.

November 23. *Soviets Leave Talks.* At a brief, final meeting, Yuli Kvitsinskii, head of the Soviet delegation, announces the USSR is withdrawing indefinitely from the INF negotiations in Geneva to protest NATO's missile deployments. Kvitsinskii's American counterpart, Paul Nitze, says the "U.S. is prepared to continue the negotiations at any time" and calls the Soviet decision "as unjustified as it is unfortunate."

November 24. *Soviet Countermeasures.* Andropov issues a tough statement condemning NATO missile deployments and announcing probable Soviet countermeasures. He says the USSR will end its moratorium on additional SS-20 missile deployments in Europe, accelerate the timetable for introducing new tactical nuclear missiles into Czechoslovakia and East Germany, and deploy submarines equipped with cruise missiles or depressed-trajectory ballistic missiles closer to U.S. shores.

December 7. *Wu on Sino-Soviet Talks.* Foreign Minister Wu Xueqian states that China's negotiations on normalizing relations with the USSR are making no progress because of the Soviets' refusal to discuss their presence in Afghanistan, their support of Vietnam's aggression in Kampuchea, and their military maneuvers on the Chinese border.

December 8. *START Talks End.* The Soviet delegation to the START negotiations in Geneva refuses to set a date for another round of talks. The Soviets say they must reexamine their arms control policy in the wake of intermediate-range missile deployments by NATO. The Warsaw Pact also refuses to set a date for resumption of the Mutual and Balanced Force Reduction talks before these negotiations adjourn in Vienna December 15.

December 26. *Kremlin Leadership Changes.* A Central Committee plenum approves promotions of candidate Politburo members Vitalii Vorotnikov and Mikhail Solomentsev to full membership. Although Andropov does not attend the plenum and has not been seen in public since August, many Western observers regard the promotions as evidence that Andropov is still in control. The plenum also approves the appointments of Egor Ligachev to the Central Committee Secretariat and KGB head Viktor Chebrikov to candidate member status on the Politburo.

1984

January 10. *Chemical Weapons Talks Proposed.* The USSR proposes that NATO and the Warsaw Pact hold negotiations on banning chemical weapons in Europe. Western officials welcome the offer but express doubts that the Soviets would agree to adequate verification measures.

January 11. *Report on Central America.* The National Bipartisan Commission on Central America releases its recommendations on U.S. policy in the region. The commission, led by former secretary of state Henry A. Kissinger, had been appointed in July 1983. The report calls for $8 billion in economic aid for Central America, increased military aid to El Salvador linked to human rights progress, and continued support for the Contra rebels in Nicaragua. The commission justifies its recommendations, in part, by citing the threat from Soviet and Cuban supported leftist insurgent groups.

January 12. *INF Negotiators Trade Accusations.* In a *New York Times* article, Yuli Kvitsinskii, head of the Soviet delegation to the INF (intermediate-range nuclear force) talks, blames the United States and Paul Nitze, chief U.S. negotiator, for the breakdown of the talks. Nitze in a January 19 *New York Times* article disputes Kvitsinskii's version of events, including the "walk-in-the-woods" negotiating session of July 1982. Nitze says for Kvitsinskii "the truth or falsity of any statement is only of secondary interest."

January 16. *Reagan on East-West Relations.* President Reagan calls for a resumption of arms negotiations in an address notable for its conciliatory tone. He says the principles of "realism, strength, and dialogue" should determine U.S. policy toward the Soviet Union. "The fact that neither of us likes the other's system," he says, "is no reason to refuse to talk." Tass criticizes the speech as being "of a propaganda nature."

January 17. *Stockholm Conference Opens.* The 35-nation Conference on Confidence and Security-Building Measures and Disarmament in Europe opens in Stockholm with the objective of finding ways to reduce the risk of war. U.S. secretary of state George P. Shultz proposes a six-point NATO plan to lower the possibility of military confrontation. He attacks the Soviet Union's human rights record and its impositions of "an artificial barrier" dividing Europe. In a harshly worded speech January 18, Soviet foreign minister Andrei Gromyko condemns U.S. actions in Lebanon and Grenada and says "the aggressive foreign policy of the United States is the main threat to peace." Shultz and Gromyko meet the same day, but Shultz says January 19 that no progress toward resumption of arms control negotiations had been made.

January 22. *MBFR Talks to Resume.* Secretary Shultz announces the United States has accepted a Soviet proposal to reopen the Mutual and Balanced Force Reduction Talks in Vienna March 16. The Warsaw Pact had refused to set a date for resumption when the last session adjourned December 15.

January 23. *Soviet Arms Violations.* President Reagan sends a classified report to Congress describing alleged Soviet arms control violations. The infractions described in an unclassified synopsis of the report include Soviet use of chemical weapons in Afghanistan, construction of an illegally positioned phased-array radar near Krasnoyarsk, Siberia, and development of a second new ICBM prohibited by the unratified SALT II treaty. The Soviet Union counters with a statement January 29 that dismisses the accusations and charges the United States with many violations of its own.

January 24. *Andropov on East-West Relations.* In a *Pravda* interview carried in advance by Tass, General Secretary Yuri Andropov responds to President Reagan's January 16 speech. Andropov criticizes Reagan for not presenting new ideas or proposals and insisting on negotiating from a position of strength rather than on "an equal footing." He calls on the United States to take "concrete steps" to improve bilateral relations. However, the interview's tone is moderate compared with recent anti-American rhetoric. Western speculation is that the interview was actually a Politburo policy statement issued in the name of Andropov, who is rumored to be seriously ill.

February 9. *Andropov Dies.* Soviet leader Yuri V. Andropov, 69, dies in Moscow of complications caused by acute kidney problems. A bulletin issued February 10 announces Andropov's death and states that he had been receiving kidney dialysis therapy for the last year. Since August 18, 1983, when Andropov was last seen in public, Soviet officials had insisted that he was not ill. Konstantin Chernenko is appointed chairman of Andropov's funeral committee.

February 13. *Chernenko Chosen General Secretary.* Konstantin U. Chernenko, a close ally of Leonid Brezhnev, is unanimously elected general secretary by the Communist Party Central Committee. Premier Nikolai Tikhonov nominated Chernenko, 72, the oldest man to become party leader. Chernenko tells the Central Committee that recent economic reforms should continue. He also calls for "peaceful coexistence of states with different social systems" but warns the West against trying to upset the current military balance. No successor is named to fill the post of president, which Andropov also occupied.

February 14. *Andropov's Funeral.* Andropov is buried behind the Lenin Mausoleum following a televised ceremony in Red Square. Chernenko, Defense Minister Dmitri Ustinov, and Foreign Minister Andrei Gromyko deliver eulogies. Numerous foreign leaders attend the funeral, including Vice President George Bush, who leads the U.S. delegation. He meets with Chernenko for 30 minutes and delivers a letter to the general secretary from Reagan. With regard to improving U.S.-Soviet relations, Bush says the meeting's positive tone "signals that we can go on from there." Vice Premier Wan Li of China also attends, becoming the highest-ranking Chinese leader to visit the Soviet capital in 20 years. East German Communist Party leader Erich Honecker and West German chancellor Helmut Kohl, both in Moscow, use the occasion to meet for the first time February 13.

February 23. *Chernenko Heads Defense Council.* Western military attachés say Marshal Nikolai Ogarkov, chief of the Soviet general staff, referred to General Secretary Chernenko as head of the Defense Council at a Soviet Armed Forces Day reception. Andropov also led the obscure body, which is believed to direct defense policy.

March 2. *Chernenko Address.* Prior to the upcoming Supreme Soviet elections, Chernenko delivers his first policy address as general secretary. He endorses Andropov's economic and anticorruption programs, expresses Soviet desires to normalize relations with the People's Republic of China, and calls for improved East-West relations backed up by new arms control agreements. However, Chernenko seemed to indicate that intermediate-range nuclear force

(INF) and strategic arms reduction (START) talks would not resume unless NATO reversed its decision to deploy intermediate-range missiles in Europe.

March 9. *Indian Arms Purchase.* Following a six-day visit to India by Defense Minister Ustinov, New Delhi officials announce a major purchase of sophisticated Soviet weaponry, including advanced fighter planes. The total cost of the arms package is not disclosed.

March 21. *Collision at Sea.* While surfacing in the Sea of Japan, a Soviet nuclear-powered submarine strikes the U.S. aircraft carrier *Kitty Hawk*. The submarine had been routinely trailing the carrier, which was participating in joint U.S.-South Korean naval exercises. The U.S. Defense Department accuses the submarine of violating several international navigation laws.

April 3-11. *First Indian in Space.* Rakesh Sharma, an Indian air force pilot, joins two Soviet cosmonauts aboard the *Soyuz* T-11 spacecraft to become the first Indian in space. Their eight-day mission includes a rendezvous with the orbiting Soviet *Salyut* 7 space station.

April 11. *Chernenko Elected President.* The Supreme Soviet names Chernenko president (chairman of the Presidium of the Supreme Soviet). The titular post had been vacant since Andropov's death. Politburo member Mikhail Gorbachev formally nominates Chernenko.

April 19. *USSR and Egypt to Restore Ties.* Egypt announces an agreement with Moscow to reestablish diplomatic relations. Egypt had broken off relations in 1981, accusing the Soviet Embassy of promoting unrest among Islamic fundamentalists.

April 21. *Soviet Offensive.* An estimated 20,000 Soviet and Afghan government troops launch a major offensive against rebels operating north of Kabul in the Panjshir Valley of Afghanistan. The campaign is supported by the heaviest Soviet bombings of the conflict to date. Many guerrillas withdraw into side valleys before Soviet and government units can engage them in combat.

April 26-May 1. *Reagan Visits China.* Chinese leaders cordially receive President Reagan during his six-day visit to the People's Republic of China. Several protocols are signed, including a peaceful nuclear cooperation agreement. Reagan is allowed to appear on Chinese television twice, but his implied criticism of the Soviet Union is deleted. During the visit the Soviet press attacks China for its economic and military cooperation with the United States.

May 2. *Sakharov Hunger Strike.* Soviet dissident Andrei Sakharov begins a hunger strike to pressure the government to allow his wife, Yelena Bonner, to receive medical treatment in the West. Bonner reports that Sakharov had been taken to an unknown location by authorities May 7. The Sakharovs' treatment brings widespread condemnation from the West.

May 7. *Soviets Withdraw from Olympics.* The Soviet National Olympic Committee announces that the Soviet team will not attend the summer games in Los Angeles because of "inadequate security." The statement says "chauvinistic sentiments and anti-Soviet hysteria are being whipped up" in the United States. Soviet-bloc nations also pull out, but Romania announces it will participate.

May 9. *Sino-Soviet Talks Postponed.* A May 10 visit to Beijing by Soviet deputy premier Ivan Arkhipov is postponed "by agreement." Arkhipov would have been the highest-ranking Soviet official to visit China since 1969. Western observers speculate that the postponement reflects a worsening of Sino-Soviet relations because of increased U.S.-Chinese cooperation and intensified border hostilities between the PRC and the Soviet Union's ally, Vietnam.

May 20. *Soviet Missile Deployments.* Defense Minister Ustinov says the Soviet navy has increased the number of nuclear missile submarines patrolling off U.S. coasts in response to NATO's INF deployments. He also warns that if NATO's nuclear missile buildup continues the Soviet Union will "accordingly increase the number of SS-20 missiles in the European part of the USSR." President Reagan says May 22 he does not think the new submarine deployments "pose any particular threat at all."

June 11-14. *CMEA Summit.* The 10-nation Council for Mutual Economic Assistance (CMEA) holds a summit in Moscow. The council issues a communiqué June 15 calling for more intra-CMEA cooperation in industrial planning, technological development, and energy conservation. Soviet officials announce June 14 their intention to end the oil pricing system that had brought protests from their allies because it did not reflect the recent drop in world oil prices.

June 14. *Reagan on Summit.* In a televised news conference Reagan says he is "willing to meet and talk any time" with Soviet leaders. Reagan's previous position had been that he would not meet with a Soviet general secretary unless the summit dealt with concrete issues and was carefully prepared.

June 21. *Naval Base Explosion.* U.S. intelligence sources say a huge explosion occurred in mid-May at the USSR northern fleet naval base at Severomorsk. The blast reportedly kills more than 200 people and destroys large stocks of ammunition and conventional missiles. The following day a Kremlin spokesman denies knowledge of the explosion.

June 29. *Space Weapons Talks Proposed.* The Soviet government sends a formal note to Secretary of State Shultz proposing U.S.-Soviet negotiations on banning weapons in space. The United States responds the same day by offering to engage in talks on space weapons if they are linked to negotiations on limiting strategic and intermediate-range nuclear weapons. The Soviets reject the U.S. proposal July 1 but repeat their call for discussions on space weapons.

July 5. *Molotov Reinstated.* Viacheslav M. Mototov, 94, is readmitted to the Soviet Communist Party. Molotov, who had served as prime minister and foreign minister under Joseph Stalin, was removed from power in 1957 by Nikita Khrushchev for being a member of the "antiparty group."

July 11. *Kuwait Buys Soviet Weapons.* Kuwait announces an agreement with the USSR to purchase $327 million in weapons. The deal includes surface-to-air missiles intended to protect Persian Gulf commercial shipping from attacks related to the war between Iran and Iraq. The agreement follows a U.S. refusal to sell Stinger antiaircraft missiles to Kuwait.

July 17. *Hot Line Improved.* U.S. and Soviet officials sign an agreement to modernize the crisis hot line between Washington and Moscow. The new hot line will transmit words three times faster than the current 64-words-per-minute teleprinters.

July 21. *Poland Releases Political Prisoners.* The Polish government announces that 652 political prisoners will be released as part of a larger amnesty for criminals serving short sentences. On August 3 the United States lifts some of the sanctions imposed against Poland in 1981. The

Polish regime demands that all sanctions be lifted.

July 21-August 1. *Space Arms Talks Exchange.* The Soviet Union and the United States exchange proposals and responses regarding possible negotiations on space weapons. The exchange is precipitated by a July 21 Soviet request that the United States agree to a formal statement committing both sides to begin discussions on preventing the militarization of space. No negotiations result, however, because of continuing disagreements over the exact purpose and limits of the talks.

August 11. *Reagan Joke.* During a "voice check" before his regular weekly radio broadcast, President Reagan says, "My fellow Americans, I'm pleased to tell you today that I've signed legislation that will outlaw Russia forever. We begin bombing in five minutes." Although the remark is made off the record as a joke, it prompts a wave of criticism from Reagan's political opponents and U.S. allies. The Soviets sharply condemn Reagan's statement as "unprecedentedly hostile toward the USSR and dangerous to the cause of peace."

August 18. *Friendship '84 Games Begin.* The Soviet Union's sports festival for nations that had pulled out of the Summer Olympics opens in Moscow. Invitations were also sent to selected countries participating in the Los Angeles Olympics.

September 4. *Honecker Visit Postponed.* East German Communist Party leader Erich Honecker indefinitely postpones his scheduled visit to West Germany, which would have been the first visit to that country by an East German leader. The Soviet Union, which recently had intensified its verbal attacks against the West German government and the growing détente between the two Germanies, appeared to have pressured Honecker into the postponement. Chancellor Kohl says Honecker is welcome to visit West Germany in the future.

September 6. *Ogarkov Removed.* Marshal Nikolai Ogarkov is removed as chief of the Soviet general staff and reassigned to unspecified duties. He is succeeded by Marshal Sergei Akhromeev, his deputy. Tass in announcing the move gives no reason for Ogarkov's apparent demotion.

September 21-22. *Gromyko-Wu Talks.* The foreign ministers of the Soviet Union and China, Andrei Gromyko and Wu Xueqian, meet while in New York for the opening of the UN General Assembly. The talks are described in positive terms by both sides and lead to an improvement of relations between the countries.

September 24. *Reagan's UN Speech.* President Reagan omits direct criticism of the Soviet Union from his address to the UN General Assembly. He calls for an overall improvement in U.S.-Soviet relations and negotiations on arms control, regional conflicts, and the militarization of space.

September 26-29. *Gromyko Meetings.* Foreign Minister Gromyko and Secretary of State Shultz talk for three hours in New York September 26 in preparation for Gromyko's meeting with President Reagan. In his address to the United Nations September 27, Gromyko attacks U.S. foreign policy and accuses the Reagan administration of deliberately undermining arms control negotiations. The same day he meets with Democratic presidential nominee Walter F. Mondale. On September 28 Gromyko travels to Washington for a three-and-a-half-hour meeting with President Reagan. It is the first time the president has met with a Soviet leader. No concrete results are reported. Following the meeting Tass issues a Gromyko statement saying the USSR is ready for improved relations with the United

States but that it would require changes in U.S. positions on various issues. Before returning to Moscow, Gromyko meets again with Shultz September 29. Shultz announces the two sides have agreed to "keep in touch."

October 16. *Chernenko Interview.* In a *Washington Post* interview General Secretary Chernenko calls for U.S. ratification of the nuclear test ban treaties signed in 1974 and 1976, a U.S. pledge not to be the first to use nuclear weapons, a mutual nuclear freeze, and a ban on weapons in space. He says progress in some of these areas could allow the resumption of arms control negotiations. Chernenko does not mention the previous Soviet demand for U.S. withdrawal of its new intermediate-range missiles from Western Europe. U.S. officials welcome Chernenko's "positive tone."

October 20. *Chinese Economic Reforms.* The Chinese government announces major economic reforms that further differentiate the Chinese economic system from the Soviet model. The new program is to reduce central control of the nation's economy, force many state-owned enterprises to compete with each other, and allow supply and demand to determine a larger share of market prices.

October 23. *Agricultural Reforms.* The Soviet Central Committee approves a plan to increase significantly the USSR's arable land through reclamation projects. The move is made amidst expectations of a poor 1984 harvest.

November 6. *Reagan Reelected.* Ronald Reagan overwhelmingly defeats Democratic candidate Walter Mondale to win a second term as president.

November 14. *Dobrynin on Arms Talks.* Anatolii Dobrynin, the Soviet ambassador to the United States, expresses Soviet interest in an American proposal made months before to begin talks that would address every aspect of the nuclear arms race. Dobrynin tells reporters at a Soviet Embassy reception that umbrella talks would be unprecedented but that they "must be studied."

November 22. *Arms Talks Announced.* The United States and the USSR announce that Shultz and Gromyko will meet in Geneva January 7-8, 1985, to lay the groundwork for future arms control negotiations. According to the U.S. statement, "the whole range of questions concerning nuclear and outer space arms" would be open for discussion.

November 26. *U.S.-Iraqi Ties Restored.* Iraq, a major recipient of Soviet arms, reestablishes diplomatic relations with the United States that were severed in 1967.

December 15-21. *Gorbachev in Britain.* Politburo member Mikhail Gorbachev and his wife, Raisa, make a highly publicized trip to Great Britain. Gorbachev meets with Prime Minister Margaret Thatcher, who says December 17, "I like Mr. Gorbachev — we can do business together." Gorbachev criticizes the Reagan administration's Strategic Defense Initiative, but speaks positively about the prospects for arms control. He returns to Moscow a day early, December 21, after personally announcing to the West that Defense Minister Dmitri Ustinov had died.

December 20. *Ustinov Dies.* Soviet defense minister and Politburo member Dmitri Ustinov, 76, dies. He had made no public appearances for more than two months. Many Western observers expected Ustinov to be succeeded by Politburo member and Central Committee secretary Grigori Romanov, but Marshal Sergei Sokolov is appointed defense minister. General Secretary Chernenko is absent from Ustinov's December 24 funeral.

December 21-29. *Arkhipov in Beijing.* First Deputy Premier Ivan Arkhipov travels to Beijing for an official visit that had been postponed since May. Arkhipov and Chinese leaders sign accords on economic, scientific, and technological cooperation. They also agree to begin negotiations on a trade pact covering the period from 1986 to 1990. China calls the accords "the most substantial agreements since relations between our two countries were strained in the 1960s."

December 27. *Chernenko Appears.* General Secretary Chernenko, who had missed Dmitri Ustinov's funeral and was believed to be ill, awards several Soviet authors medals for literature. The Soviet media give the ceremony unusually prominent coverage.

1985

January 7-8. *Gromyko and Shultz in Geneva.* Foreign Minister Andrei Gromyko of the Soviet Union and U.S. Secretary of State George Shultz meet in Geneva to discuss the resumption of arms control negotiations. They agree to hold umbrella talks divided into three subgroups: strategic nuclear weapons, intermediate-range nuclear weapons, and weapons in space. The date and site are to be determined later.

January 13. *Gromyko Interview.* In an interview on Soviet television, Gromyko asserts that the U.S. Strategic Defense Initiative (SDI) could be used to "blackmail and pressure" the Soviet Union. He says that without movement toward preventing the militarization of space no progress can be made on limiting strategic weapons.

January 24. *Soviet Economic Statistics.* The Soviet government reports that the economy grew by 2.6 percent in 1984 — the lowest increase since World War II. Industrial production is estimated to have grown 4.2 percent, but the poor performance of the agricultural sector held down overall growth.

January 26. *Arms Talks Set.* The Soviet Union and the United States announce that arms negotiations arranged by Shultz and Gromyko will begin March 12 in Geneva. The Soviet Foreign Ministry also says Viktor Karpov, Yuli Kvitsinskii, and Alexsei Obukhov will be the chief Soviet negotiators. The United States had announced its negotiators — Max Kampelman, John Tower, and Maynard Glitman — January 18. Karpov and Kampelman will lead the delegations.

February 11-14. *Papandreou in Moscow.* Greek premier Andreas Papandreou is warmly received during a four-day visit to the Soviet Union. He and Soviet leaders sign several economic accords and agree to hold regular political consultations. Papandreou's scheduled February 12 meeting with General Secretary Konstantin Chernenko is canceled, fueling speculation that Chernenko is gravely ill.

February 19-20. *Mideast Talks.* Representatives of the United States and the Soviet Union meet in Vienna to discuss the Middle East. The Soviets call for a multilateral conference, as advocated February 11 by Palestine Liberation Organization (PLO) leader Yasir Arafat and King Hussein of Jordan. The United States continues to oppose Soviet involvement, supporting instead direct Arab-Israeli negotiations.

February 20. *Thatcher Endorses SDI.* During a three-day visit to the United States, Prime Minister Margaret Thatcher of Britain endorses President Reagan's SDI in a speech before a joint session of Congress. Her support is preceded by West German chancellor Helmut Kohl's qualified endorsement February 9.

February 21. *Soviets Allow Inspections.* The Soviet Union signs a nuclear safeguards accord with the International Atomic Energy Agency (IAEA), which provides for the opening of some Soviet civilian nuclear power plants to international inspection. Western officials praise Moscow's action as a first step toward establishing effective procedures for verifying Soviet compliance with arms control treaties.

February 24. *Chernenko Appears.* A frail Konstantin Chernenko, supported by an aide, appears briefly before television cameras to cast a ballot at a Moscow polling place. It is the first time Chernenko has been seen in public in more than eight weeks. In contrast, Politburo member Mikhail Gorbachev arrives at another polling place accompanied by his family. He jokes with reporters in front of Western cameras.

February 25-March 1. *Gromyko Trip.* Soviet foreign minister Gromyko repeatedly attacks SDI during state visits to Italy and Spain. While in Rome, Gromyko goes to the Vatican February 27 for his first meeting with Pope John Paul II since 1979.

March 7-10. *Shcherbitskii in U.S.* Politburo member and Ukrainian Communist Party leader Vladimir Shcherbitskii visits the United States as head of a 33-member parliamentary delegation. Shcherbitskii is the first Soviet Politburo member other than Foreign Minister Gromyko to visit the United States since 1973. He tells reporters he tried to persuade President Reagan during their March 7 meeting in Washington that SDI was "not worthwhile." Shcherbitskii returns early to the USSR March 10, apparently after receiving word of Chernenko's death.

March 10. *Chernenko Dies.* General Secretary Konstantin Chernenko, 73, dies in Moscow of heart failure. He had been weakened by a variety of ailments including emphysema, hepatitis, and cirrhosis of the liver. His death is not announced until March 11.

March 11. *Gorbachev Chosen General Secretary.* Mikhail Gorbachev, 54, is elected general secretary of the Communist Party by the Central Committee within hours of the announcement of Chernenko's death. Western observers regard the unusual speed of the succession as evidence that Soviet leaders had agreed to Gorbachev's selection before Chernenko died. In his acceptance speech, Gorbachev promises to continue the policies of the two previous general secretaries, Chernenko and Yuri Andropov, and says economic improvement is his most important goal.

March 12. *Arms Talks Begin.* Despite Chernenko's death, the Geneva arms negotiations begin on schedule. Chief Soviet negotiator Viktor Karpov tells reporters that General Secretary Gorbachev "presided over the Politburo meeting that approved the instructions" for the Soviet negotiating team. Both sides agree to keep the substance of their talks confidential.

March 13. *Chernenko's Funeral.* Konstantin Chernenko is buried near the Kremlin wall following a Red Square ceremony. General Secretary Gorbachev eulogizes Chernenko as a "steadfast fighter for noble communist ideals." Against the advice of several aides, President Reagan does not go to Moscow but sends Vice President George Bush in his stead. However, Reagan does invite Gorbachev to the United States in a letter presented to him by Bush. Gorbachev also meets with many other foreign dignitaries, including Chinese vice premier Li Peng, who delivers an uncharacteristically friendly message to Gorbachev from Chinese general secretary Hu Yaobang.

March 16. *Karpov Accusation.* The leader of the Soviet arms control delegation to Geneva, Viktor Karpov, accuses the United States of trying to "revise the subject and aims" of the talks by refusing to treat SDI as a negotiable issue. Secretary of State Shultz criticizes Karpov's statements as violating the agreement to keep the talks confidential.

March 20. *Belgium Accepts Missiles.* The Belgian Parliament approves the deployment of NATO cruise missiles in Belgium by a 116-93 vote.

March 24. *American Officer Killed.* U.S. Army Maj. Arthur Nicholson, Jr., is shot by a Soviet guard while observing a Soviet military installation in East Germany. Soviet officials claim Nicholson was in a restricted area and failed to heed a warning shot. The United States says he was conducting routine, sanctioned observations in a nonrestricted area in accordance with a 1947 agreement allowing such observations. President Reagan condemns the shooting as an "unwarranted act of violence."

March 28. *MX Funds Appropriated.* Following an intense lobbying effort by President Reagan and direct appeals from U.S. arms control negotiator Max Kampelman, the House of Representatives appropriates $1.5 billion for the production of 21 MX missiles by a 217-210 vote. The Senate had approved the funding earlier in the month, 55-45. The administration had argued the Soviet Union would be unlikely to agree to equitable arms cuts if Congress did not support the MX.

April 7. *Soviet Missile Moratorium.* General Secretary Gorbachev announces Moscow has suspended deployment of intermediate-range missiles in Europe until November and perhaps beyond, if NATO halts its missile deployments. Gorbachev also states he is agreeable to a summit with President Reagan in the near future. The Reagan administration says that, because the USSR holds a ten-to-one missile advantage in Europe, Gorbachev's freeze would not affect the scheduled deployment.

April 23. *Politburo Promotions.* Central Committee secretaries Nikolai Ryzhkov and Egor Ligachev are promoted to full Politburo status along with KGB head Viktor Chebrikov. The Ryzhkov and Ligachev promotions represent dramatic advancements, since they bypassed the traditional step of candidate Politburo membership. Defense Minister Sergei Sokolov is elevated to candidate Politburo status. Viktor Nikonov is named to the Central Committee Secretariat with responsibility for agriculture. Western analysts generally agree the promotions will strengthen Gorbachev's power.

April 25-26. *Warsaw Pact Summit.* Leaders of the seven Warsaw Pact nations meet in Warsaw and approve a 20-year extension of the treaty April 26. Gorbachev attends the summit, making his first foreign trip since becoming general secretary. He stays in Warsaw April 27 for talks with Polish premier Wojciech Jaruzelski.

April 28-29. *Ortega in Moscow.* Nicaraguan president Daniel Ortega Saavedra visits Moscow to discuss Soviet economic assistance. He meets with General Secretary Gorbachev April 29. Although no specific aid is announced, Tass quotes Gorbachev as having promised to continue economic, political, and diplomatic support of Nicaragua.

May 1. *U.S. Embargo.* President Reagan places an embargo on trade with Nicaragua and bans Nicaraguan shipping and air traffic from the United States. In a letter to Congress he says the growing Nicaraguan threat to Central American and U.S. security prompted his action. Tass states May 2 that the embargo is evidence of Reagan's "pathological hatred" of the Sandinista revolution.

May 1. *Reagan in Europe.* President Reagan arrives in Europe for a 10-day visit that includes an economic summit in Bonn May 2-4 and a controversial May 5 stop at Bitburg military cemetery in West Germany, where a number of Nazi SS troops are buried. Reagan had earlier added to his itinerary a trip to Bergen-Belsen concentration camp in hopes of quelling foreign and domestic protests against his Bitburg visit.

May 8. *V-E Day Speeches.* General Secretary Gorbachev and President Reagan deliver speeches on the 40th anniversary of the surrender of Nazi Germany. In Moscow, Gorbachev condemns U.S. "state terrorism" against Nicaragua and aid to Afghan rebels. He also criticizes Reagan's visit to Bitburg cemetery, saying there were political figures at the recent Western summit in Bonn who were "ready to forget or even justify the SS cutthroats and, moreover, pay homage to them." Despite the attacks, Gorbachev calls for a return to détente. Reagan, speaking before the European Parliament in Strasbourg, France, accuses the Soviets of "undermining stability and the basis for nuclear deterrence" by proceeding with plans to deploy a new mobile intercontinental ballistic missile (ICBM) armed with multiple independently targetable warheads.

May 14. *Shultz and Gromyko in Vienna.* Secretary of State Shultz and Foreign Minister Gromyko meet for six hours while in Vienna for ceremonies commemorating the 30th anniversary of the Austrian State Treaty. They discuss arms control and the possibility of a Reagan-Gorbachev summit, but no date or site is announced.

May 16. *Antialcoholism Program.* The Soviet government announces new measures designed to combat drunkenness and alcoholism. Beginning June 1 the legal drinking age will be raised from 18 to 21, liquor store hours shortened, and alcohol production gradually reduced.

May 20. *Walker Arrested.* The FBI arrests John Walker, Jr., a retired U.S. Navy warrant officer, on charges of selling military secrets to the Soviet Union. The case widens during the following two weeks as three other people, including Walker's son and brother, are arrested for spying.

May 20-21. *USA-USSR Trade Talks.* Secretary of Commerce Malcolm Baldrige travels to Moscow for the first meeting of the U.S.-Soviet Joint Commercial Commission since the Soviets invaded Afghanistan. The talks produce only a few minor agreements aimed at improving trade relations, but Baldrige calls the two-day meeting a success because it reestablished "a mechanism for dealing with and resolving commercial and economic problems."

May 22. *Indo-Soviet Economic Pacts.* Prime Minister Rajiv Gandhi of India and General Secretary Gorbachev sign an agreement that provides for $1.2 billion in Soviet credits for construction of industrial and energy projects in India. They also agree to a new 15-year program of economic and technological cooperation. Gandhi is in the USSR on his first official state visit since becoming prime minister in October 1984. At a press conference he praises the Soviet-Indian relationship as a "friendship that is not against anyone."

May 27. *Gorbachev on Arms Talks.* During a meeting with former West German chancellor Willy Brandt, General Secretary Gorbachev says the first round of the Geneva arms talks was "completely fruitless." The second session is set to open May 30.

June 10. *U.S. to Abide by SALT II.* President Reagan announces that the United States will continue to stay within restrictions established by the unratified SALT II treaty. He says that when the next Trident submarine is deployed the Navy will dismantle an older Poseidon submarine to stay within the 1,200 multiple warhead missile limit imposed by the treaty. The Soviets dismiss the action as insignificant.

June 11. *Gorbachev Calls for Reforms.* Speaking before top party and government officials, General Secretary Gorbachev criticizes the draft of the 1986-90 five-year plan and a number of government ministers. He calls for major changes in the Soviet economy, with greater emphasis on market forces, increased production of quality consumer goods, enhancement of the role of local factory managers, and curtailment of central planning in day-to-day factory affairs. He also argues for using capital investment to upgrade existing factories instead of constructing new ones.

June 11-15. *Gandhi in U.S.* Indian prime minister Rajiv Gandhi visits the United States during a five-nation tour. He tells a joint session of Congress May 13 that India supports a political settlement to the conflict in Afghanistan that would ensure that country's "sovereignty, integrity, independence, and non-aligned status."

June 18-19. *Afghanistan Talks.* U.S. and Soviet officials meet in Washington to discuss the conflict in Afghanistan for the first time in three years. The talks are the latest in a recent series of bilateral discussions on regional issues.

July 1-2. *Soviet Leadership Shuffle.* The Central Committee of the CPSU announces that Grigorii Romanov, who had been a rival to Mikhail Gorbachev for the general secretary post, has resigned from the Politburo for health reasons. Western analysts generally agree Romanov was ousted. The Central Committee also promotes Georgian Communist Party leader Eduard Shevardnadze to full Politburo status. On July 2 Shevardnadze is named foreign minister, replacing Andrei Gromyko, who is elected to the vacant office of president (chairman of the Presidium of the Supreme Soviet).

July 2. *Summit Announced.* U.S. officials say the Soviets have agreed to a summit conference between President Reagan and General Secretary Gorbachev in Geneva November 19-20.

July 10. *Sino-Soviet Trade Pact.* Chinese and Soviet representatives sign an agreement that will sharply increase bilateral trade to $14 billion over the five-year period from 1986 to 1990. Annual trade between the countries is expected to rise to $3.5 billion by 1990, compared with a projected $1.8 billion in 1985.

July 17. *Ogarkov Reappointed.* Reports emerge that Nikolai Ogarkov, who was removed as military chief of staff in September 1984, has been appointed commander-in-chief of Warsaw Pact forces and first deputy foreign minister. Ogarkov's comeback is among several unpublicized Soviet high command changes that took place some time in July.

July 29. *Nuclear Test Proposals.* General Secretary Gorbachev declares a unilateral Soviet moratorium on nuclear tests to begin August 6. The moratorium is to continue until the end of the year and will be indefinitely extended if the United States also stops its nuclear tests. U.S. officials quickly reject the proposal, citing a recent spurt of Soviet testing. President Reagan instead invites

Soviet experts to observe a U.S. nuclear test explosion. The Soviets decline but say they will proceed with their unilateral moratorium.

July 30-August 1. *Helsinki Accords Anniversary.* The representatives of 35 nations meet in Helsinki to mark the 10th anniversary of the Helsinki accords. In speeches before the gathering July 30, Secretary of State Shultz criticizes the Soviet Union's human rights record, while Foreign Minister Shevardnadze asserts that the USSR, unlike Western countries, protects its people from poverty, unemployment, and discrimination. The two leaders meet July 31 to discuss the upcoming Reagan-Gorbachev summit.

August 21. *U.S. Alleges Use of Tracking Dust.* The United States accuses the Soviet Union of using a chemical dust thought to be carcinogenic to track American diplomats in Moscow. The Soviets deny the allegation as "absurd" August 22.

August 26. *Gorbachev Interview.* In an interview published in *Time* magazine September 9, General Secretary Gorbachev says he regrets that U.S.-Soviet relations are not improving. He criticizes the Reagan administration for downplaying the upcoming summit and portraying Moscow's recent arms control proposals as propaganda ploys.

September 3. *Senators Meet Gorbachev.* Eight U.S. senators meet in Moscow with General Secretary Gorbachev. They report that Gorbachev indicated he might accept some level of research on space-based antiballistic missile (ABM) systems as part of an arms control agreement.

September 10. *Gorbachev on Chemical Arms.* General Secretary Gorbachev proposes establishing a chemical weapons-free zone in central Europe. The Reagan administration immediately rejects the proposal, saying it wants a "comprehensive verifiable ban" on chemical weapons.

September 12. *Defection Prompts Expulsions.* Great Britain announces that the top KGB agent in Britain, Oleg Gordievskii, has defected. He had been a political counselor at the Soviet Embassy in London. Britain expels 25 Soviets, including diplomats, journalists, and trade representatives, who Gordievskii is said to have named as spies. The Soviet Union retaliates by expelling 25 British citizens September 14. London expels six additional Soviets September 16; Moscow responds by expelling six Britons September 18.

September 13. *U.S. ASAT Test.* An American F-15 fighter plane launches an antisatellite weapon (ASAT) that destroys a U.S. satellite orbiting 290 miles above Earth. The missile test had been announced August 20. On September 4 Tass had warned if the test took place the Soviet Union would "consider itself free of its unilateral commitment" not to deploy ASATs in space.

September 16. *Deng Shakes Up Leadership.* Vice Premier Deng Xiaoping engineers the retirement of many top officials as part of his campaign to reinvigorate China's leadership. Ten of 24 Politburo members step down in favor of younger leaders. Similar turnover occurs at lower levels.

September 17. *Reagan on SDI.* President Reagan states in a press conference that the United States would not negotiate limits on the development and testing of SDI to achieve a nuclear arms control agreement with the Soviets.

September 23-24. *Shultz, Shevardnadze at UN.* Secretary of State Shultz and Foreign Minister Shevardnadze speak on arms control at the opening of the UN General Assembly. Shultz accuses the USSR September 23 of pursuing "the world's most active military space program," while it simultaneously objects to U.S. research on space weapons. On September 24 Shevardnadze portrays SDI as a U.S. attempt to gain military superiority and says the USSR is ready to negotiate an agreement that would achieve "truly radical reductions" in nuclear weapons.

September 26. *KGB Agent Defects.* U.S. officials confirm that Vitalii Yurchenko, a high-ranking KGB agent, has defected. Yurchenko, a counselor with the Soviet Foreign Ministry in Rome, had been taken to Washington for debriefing following his defection and reportedly provided information about Soviet double agents.

September 27. *Ryzhkov Replaces Tikhonov.* Nikolai Tikhonov, 80, retires as chairman of the Council of Ministers (premier), citing health reasons. He is succeeded by Nikolai Ryzhkov, an ally of General Secretary Gorbachev. Ryzhkov, who had been appointed to the Politburo in April, resigns October 15 as a Central Committee secretary.

September 27. *Reagan Meets Shevardnadze.* Following his UN visit Foreign Minister Shevardnadze delivers to President Reagan in Washington a new arms control proposal from General Secretary Gorbachev.

September 30. *Soviet Arms Proposal.* The Soviets formally present a plan at the Geneva arms control talks to substantially cut the nuclear arsenals of both superpowers. Foreign Minister Shevardnadze had outlined the offer during his September 27 meeting with President Reagan. The plan's main feature is a 50 percent reduction in the strategic weapons of both sides. President Reagan said September 28 that he welcomed the Soviet offer and hoped it would provide a basis for discussion. However, senior U.S. administration officials express dissatisfaction with many aspects of the plan, including a provision requiring the United States to halt research on SDI.

September 30. *Soviets Kidnapped.* In two coordinated incidents four Soviet diplomats are kidnapped in West Beirut. The Islamic Liberation Organization (ILO) issues photographs of the Soviet hostages October 1 and threatens to kill them unless the USSR pressures Syria to halt an offensive by Syrian-backed leftist militias against Moslem fundamentalists in Tripoli. One of the hostages is found dead October 2. The Soviet Union evacuates families and nonessential personnel from its West Beirut Embassy October 4. In response to Soviet requests for help in resolving the crisis, Syria negotiates a truce between the warring factions in Tripoli. Syrian troops enter the city October 6 to enforce a cease-fire. The ILO releases the remaining three Soviet hostages unharmed October 30.

October 2-5. *Gorbachev in France.* Mikhail Gorbachev travels to France for his first visit to the West since becoming general secretary. He proposes October 3 that France and Great Britain join the Soviet Union in talks on nuclear weapons in Europe, separate from the Geneva negotiations. France and Britain decline the invitation October 4. Gorbachev says his discussions with President Francois Mitterand were "fruitful and constructive." Western observers point out, however, that the visit did not produce a joint Soviet-French communiqué denouncing SDI, as Gorbachev may have hoped.

October 6. *ABM Interpretation.* U.S. national security adviser Robert McFarlane says that development and testing of space-based ABM weapons would not violate the 1972 ABM Treaty. His statement sets off a dispute within the Reagan administration over how to interpret the treaty. Secretary of State Shultz clarifies the U.S. position October 14, saying the broad interpretation of the treaty enunciated by McFarlane was valid but that the United States would continue to adhere to a restrictive interpretation allowing only research on space-based ABM systems.

October 15. *Gorbachev Presents Programs.* General Secretary Gorbachev presents drafts of the new economic and Communist Party political programs to the Central Committee. The economic program calls for a 150 percent increase in labor productivity and 100 percent increases in national income and industrial output by the year 2000. The new political program is less detailed and more pragmatic than the one adopted in 1961 when Nikita Khrushchev was general secretary.

October 22. *Weinberger on USSR Missile.* American defense secretary Caspar Weinberger says the Soviet Union has begun deploying the SS-25, a new mobile ICBM. He claims its deployment violates the SALT II treaty because the Soviets have also tested the new SS-24 ICBM. The treaty allows each side to develop only one new type of ICBM. Moscow maintains the new missiles do not violate SALT II because they are permissible modifications of older missile types.

October 24. *Reagan, Shevardnadze Before United Nations.* At the UN's 40th anniversary celebration, President Reagan calls for a "fresh start" in U.S.-Soviet relations and asks the Soviets to join the United States in finding ways to end regional conflicts in Afghanistan, Kampuchea, Ethiopia, Angola, and Nicaragua. Foreign Minister Shevardnadze says the arms race must be stopped "from spreading to space."

October 24. *Allies Meet.* President Reagan and the leaders of Great Britain, West Germany, Canada, Japan, and Italy meet in New York to discuss the upcoming summit between Reagan and Gorbachev. President Mitterand of France turned down an invitation to attend.

October 24. *Seaman Jumps Ship.* Soviet seaman Miroslav Medved jumps off a Soviet freighter in the Mississippi River near New Orleans. U.S. border patrol officers attempt to return Medved to his ship but he jumps again. He is interviewed by U.S. officials but returns to his ship after signing a statement saying he does not want to defect. Members of Congress and Ukrainian-American groups claim the episode was mishandled and try to have Medved interviewed again, but his ship is allowed to depart for the USSR November 9.

October 31. *Reagan Interview.* Four Soviet journalists interview President Reagan in Washington. The interview, which focuses on the U.S. role in world affairs and superpower relations, is published November 4 in *Izvestiia*. Several of Reagan's responses are censored, however, and the interview is accompanied by a rebuttal of his statements.

October 31. *Soldier Seeks Refuge.* A Soviet soldier who slips into the U.S. Embassy in Kabul, Afghanistan, indicates he wants to return to the Soviet Union. Afghan government troops November 2 surround the embassy and cut off its power supply to pressure embassy officials to return the soldier. He freely leaves the embassy November 4, after receiving assurances from Soviet authorities in Kabul that he would not be prosecuted.

November 1. *U.S. Arms Offer.* At the Geneva talks the United States proposes a plan for the USSR to forgo deployment of its SS-24 and SS-25 missiles and the United States to stop development of its Midgetman ICBM. Tass

dismisses the offer as containing "old proposals that have been slightly modified and presented in a new wrapping." The Soviets do agree to extend the current round of talks for another week to discuss the proposal.

November 1. *Netherlands Accepts Missiles.* Dutch prime minister Ruud Lubbers, citing increases in the Soviet SS-20 arsenal, announces that the Netherlands will accept 48 U.S. cruise missiles in 1988. The decision originally was to have been made in June 1984. At that time the Dutch government said it would accept the missiles November 1, 1985, unless the Soviets had reduced the number of operational SS-20s from their June 1984 level.

November 2. *U.S. Accepts Soviet Cuts.* President Reagan says in a radio broadcast that the United States favors the idea of a 50 percent reduction in strategic nuclear weapons proposed by the Soviets. Administration officials, however, caution that many differences exist between the negotiating positions of Moscow and Washington.

November 4. *Soviet Arms Shipments.* The Reagan administration claims that in recent weeks there has been a "serious increase" in deliveries of Soviet weapons to the Nicaraguan government.

November 4. *Yurchenko Reversal.* Vitalii Yurchenko, whose defection to the West was announced September 26, declares in a press conference at the Soviet Embassy in Washington that he had been kidnapped in Rome by American agents and held in the United States by the CIA until his recent escape. U.S. officials say Yurchenko defected voluntarily and signed a statement requesting asylum in the United States. They explain that Yurchenko unexpectedly left a Washington restaurant, where he was dining with a CIA agent, and went to the Soviet Embassy. Although they are uncertain whether Yurchenko was a defector who changed his mind or a double agent, U.S. sources maintain he had disclosed valuable information about Soviet agents in the United States. Yurchenko November 5 meets with State Department officials, who determine he freely decided to return to the USSR.

November 4-5. *Moscow Talks.* Secretary of State Shultz and national security adviser Robert McFarlane travel to Moscow for presummit talks with General Secretary Gorbachev. Shultz indicates November 5 that all major issues likely to be addressed were discussed but states, "I can't say anything definitely was settled."

November 15. *Soviets Grant Visas.* The Soviet Foreign Ministry gives the U.S. State Department a list of 10 Soviet citizens with spouses or families in the United States who will be allowed to emigrate from the USSR.

November 16. *Weinberger Letter.* The *New York Times* and *Washington Post* report that Defense Secretary Weinberger gave President Reagan a letter November 13 advising him not to make an agreement at the Geneva summit affirming a restrictive interpretation of the ABM treaty or committing the United States to adhere to the SALT II treaty. The letter is attached to a Pentagon report on Soviet arms control violations.

November 19-21. *Geneva Summit.* President Reagan and General Secretary Gorbachev meet in Geneva for the first summit between a U.S. president and Soviet general secretary since 1979. They achieve no breakthroughs on major issues such as arms control, human rights, or regional conflicts, but both men indicate the meeting was useful. In addition to formal negotiating sessions with aides present, they spend about five hours in private conversation, accompanied only by their interpreters. They sign bilateral agreements November 21 on establishment of consuls in New York and Kiev, resumption of civil aviation ties, air safety in the northern Pacific region, and cultural and scientific exchanges. They also approve extension of numerous other bilateral pacts. At the end of the summit Reagan and Gorbachev issue a joint communiqué that states their mutual intention to accelerate the arms control process to "prevent an arms race in space and to terminate it on Earth, to limit and reduce nuclear arms, and enhance strategic stability." The statement also says both sides favor a 50 percent reduction in nuclear weapons and an interim agreement on intermediate-range nuclear weapons. Reagan and Gorbachev announce they plan to meet again, beginning with a tentative trip to the United States by Gorbachev in 1986. Before leaving Geneva November 21 the general secretary attacks Reagan's inflexibility on SDI and says the USSR would effectively respond to a U.S. space-based ABM system. After the summit, Reagan stops in Brussels to confer with leaders of NATO and Gorbachev stops in Prague to meet with leaders of the Warsaw Pact.

November 22. *SALT II Compliance.* A senior State Department official discloses that the United States informed the Soviets before the Geneva summit that it would continue to abide by the SALT II treaty set to expire at the end of the year. The official says Moscow also was told the United States reserved the right to take appropriate proportional responses to actions that are not permitted by the treaty.

December 2. *Bonner Travels to West.* Yelena Bonner, wife of Soviet dissident Andrei Sakharov, leaves the Soviet Union on a three-month exit visa for medical treatment in the West. She promised Soviet authorities she would not make public statements during her trip. Bonner officially received permission to go abroad October 24. She arrives in the United States December 7, after seeing doctors in Rome.

December 10. *Gorbachev on U.S.-Soviet Trade.* General Secretary Gorbachev tells 400 representatives of U.S. businesses that "there will be no normal development of Soviet-U.S. trade and other economic ties on a large scale" so long as Washington fails to remove political obstacles that hinder economic cooperation. The representatives had come to Moscow with Commerce Secretary Malcolm Baldrige to promote trade between the superpowers. The U.S. denial of most-favored-nation trading status and export-import credits to the Soviet Union are among the obstacles Gorbachev cites.

December 13. *Foreign Minister Exchange.* Soviet officials in Beijing announce that Chinese foreign minister Wu Xueqian will visit Moscow in May 1986 and Soviet foreign minister Shevardnadze will go to Beijing later that year. It will be the first time in 20 years that the countries have exchanged foreign ministers.

December 15-16. *Shultz in East Europe.* During a tour of six European nations, Secretary of State Shultz stops in Romania and Hungary. He warns Romanian president Nicolae Ceaucescu December 15 that the United States might revoke Romania's most-favored-nation trading status if it fails to improve its human rights record. In Hungary December 16 Shultz speaks optimistically about the development of U.S.-Hungarian relations.

December 19. *Soviet Inspections Offer.* The Reagan administration discloses that the president received a letter from General Secretary Gorbachev December 5 offering to allow U.S. technicians to inspect some Soviet nuclear test

facilities if the United States joined the USSR in an extended moratorium on nuclear tests. The White House rejects Gorbachev's call for a moratorium but says December 23 that Reagan sent a message to Gorbachev welcoming his inspection offer.

December 20. *Libyan Missiles.* The State Department discloses that the USSR has provided to Libya long-range, surface-to-air SA-5 missiles that could threaten aircraft over the Mediterranean. The Egyptian newspaper *Al Ahram* reports December 31 that about 2,000 Soviet advisers arrived in Libya in late December.

December 23. *Reagan on SALT II.* President Reagan reports to Congress that the United States will continue to observe the unratified SALT II treaty despite a "continuing pattern of Soviet noncompliance" with arms control agreements.

December 24. *Grishin Removed.* Viktor Grishin, 71, is replaced as first secretary of the Moscow City party committee by Central Committee Secretary Boris N. Eltsin. Western analysts regard the move as part of General Secretary Gorbachev's drive to retire older officials who might obstruct his reforms. Grishin loses his seat on the Politburo January 10, 1986.

December 25. *Jewish Emigration Hinted.* A Soviet diplomat in Washington reportedly tells a representative of an American Jewish organization that he believes Moscow, in February 1986, will restore diplomatic relations with Israel and, prior to the Communist Party Congress, will substantially increase the number of Jews allowed to emigrate.

1986

January 1. *Gorbachev, Reagan Messages.* General Secretary Mikhail Gorbachev and President Ronald Reagan deliver five-minute speeches shown on television in each other's country. Both men express their hopes for peace and say the Geneva summit began a movement toward better relations between their nations. The United States had proposed the exchange prior to the summit; Moscow accepted the idea December 20, 1985.

January 2. *Reagan on Soviet Tactics.* In written responses to questions from a Mexican news agency President Reagan accuses the Soviet Union and Cuba of supporting terrorism and drug trafficking in the Western Hemisphere. He claims the Soviets know that communism "will never be established by choice in this hemisphere, so they resort to subversion and support for terrorism."

January 2. *USSR Targeting Statement.* General Secretary Gorbachev says in a letter to a British Labour Party activist that if Great Britain or any other country dismantles its nuclear weapons and does not allow the United States to base nuclear arms on its soil, the Soviet Union will not consider it a nuclear target. Prime Minister Margaret Thatcher rejects Gorbachev's offer, saying disarmament would make Britain "vulnerable to nuclear blackmail."

January 3. *USSR Protests U.S. Films.* Several Soviet artists and cultural officials hold a press conference to denounce recent U.S. movies for their anti-Soviet themes. The group cites *Rambo: First Blood Part II* and *Rocky IV* as examples. The officials also condemn the ABC television network for planning to produce a miniseries entitled *Amerika*, which depicts the United States after a Soviet takeover. ABC delays production following the Soviet criticism but says January 22 it will proceed with the miniseries despite hints of a Soviet retaliation against ABC's Moscow news bureau.

January 6. *Chinese Accusations.* Chinese vice foreign minister Qian Qichen accuses the USSR of pressing for closer bilateral ties while trying to dodge the issues of Soviet support for the Vietnamese occupation of Kampuchea, Soviet presence in Afghanistan, and Soviet troops along the Chinese border. Qian says the Soviet belief that relations can be improved without addressing these obstacles is "unrealistic and unwise."

January 13. *Civil War in South Yemen.* An attempt by President Ali Nasser Mohammed to have rival Politburo members assassinated precipitates a coup against his rule, which leads to civil war in South Yemen. Thousands of foreigners are evacuated by British and Soviet ships. Western sources report as many as 10,000 killed. Both sides declare their allegiance to Moscow. Radical Marxist opponents of the president gain the upper hand after almost two weeks of fighting. Prime Minister Haider Abu Bakr al-Attas, who was in New Delhi when the fighting erupted, returns to Aden from Moscow January 25 and is named provisional president in a Marxist coalition government. Ali Nasser Mohammed reportedly fled the country.

January 13-16. *Soviets Reinforce Fleet.* Reports emerge that the USSR has expanded its naval presence in the Mediterranean to deter a U.S. or Israeli attack against Libya. The Soviets also deploy the flagship of their Mediterranean fleet in Tripoli Harbor.

January 15. *Gorbachev Arms Plan.* Mikhail Gorbachev proposes a comprehensive global ban on nuclear weapons to be achieved in stages by the year 2000. The Soviet general secretary says the United States must stop development of ASATs (antisatellite weapons) and SDI (the Strategic Defense Initiative) before the plan can be implemented. President Reagan says the United States and its allies will carefully study the proposal. Other U.S. officials assert that much of Gorbachev's offer is not new, but they praise some of its features, most notably its indication of Soviet willingness to cooperate on the issue of verification. Gorbachev also calls for a ban on the production of chemical weapons and announces a three-month extension of the Soviet nuclear test moratorium, which he urges the United States to join.

January 15-19. *Shevardnadze in Tokyo.* Eduard Shevardnadze becomes the first Soviet foreign minister to visit Japan since 1976. He signs several cultural and trade accords and presses the Japanese not to participate in SDI research. Shevardnadze admits he and Japanese leaders discussed the contentious issue of Soviet control of the Japanese-claimed Kuril Islands, but neither side reports progress.

January 28. *Challenger Explodes.* The U.S. space shuttle *Challenger* explodes in flight after takeoff, killing all seven crew members. General Secretary Gorbachev sends a warm message of condolence to President Reagan that is printed on the front page of *Pravda*. Subsequent articles in the Soviet press, however, cite the disaster as an example of the risks of militarizing space.

January 28. *Savimbi in U.S.* Jonas Savimbi, leader of the National Union for the Total Independence of Angola (UNITA), a 30,000-troop guerrilla movement fighting the Soviet- and Cuban-backed Marxist Angolan regime,

begins a two-week visit to the United States. He lobbies for military aid during meetings with President Reagan and other U.S. officials. The administration acknowledges February 18 it plans to provide Savimbi's forces with $15 million in covert military aid from CIA funds.

February 2-4. *Soviet-Iranian Talks.* Soviet first deputy premier Georgii Kornienko travels to Tehran for a three-day visit, which both sides call successful. Kornienko invites the Iranian foreign minister to Moscow and signs an agreement to resume Aeroflot flights to Tehran. Despite the apparent improvement in Soviet-Iranian ties, the Iranian press continues to criticize the Soviet occupation of Afghanistan and Soviet arms sales to Iraq.

February 3. *France Expels Soviets.* The French government expels four Soviet diplomats after accusing them of being Soviet military intelligence (GRU) agents. Moscow retaliates by expelling four French diplomats.

February 6. *Gorbachev Arms Shift.* General Secretary Gorbachev tells U.S. senator Edward M. Kennedy, D-Mass., that the only preconditions for reducing intermediate-range nuclear (INF) missiles in Europe are a freeze on the expansion of British and French nuclear forces and a pledge by the United States not to transfer nuclear weapons to other nations. Gorbachev surprises U.S. officials by not mentioning progress in talks on strategic and space weapons as a requirement for an INF accord. Kennedy, who is in Moscow on a three-day visit, reports that Gorbachev also expressed doubts about the value of a 1986 summit in the absence of an INF agreement.

February 11. *Shcharanskii Freed.* Prominent Soviet Jewish dissident Anatolii Shcharanskii is freed from a Soviet labor camp as part of an East-West spy exchange involving nine people. Shcharanskii, an outspoken critic of the Kremlin's treatment of Soviet Jews, was convicted in 1978 of spying for the West. Upon his release, Shcharanskii flies to Jerusalem, where he is welcomed as a hero and reunited with his wife, Avital.

February 11. *U.S. Rejects Chemical Arms Plan.* The United States dismisses a Soviet proposal for a multilateral agreement that would ban the spread of chemical weapons. General Secretary Gorbachev offered the proposal in his January 15 arms control speech as an interim step toward the elimination of chemical weapons. The Gorbachev plan would have barred the transfer of chemical arms between states and their deployment on the soil of other states. United States officials say guarantees that chemical weapons production will be stopped and existing stockpiles destroyed are needed before an agreement can be reached.

February 15. *Sakharov Letter Revealed.* A letter dated October 15, 1984, from Soviet dissident Andrei Sakharov to Anatolii Aleksandrov, president of the Soviet Academy of Sciences, is made public in the West after being smuggled out of the Soviet Union. It details the forced feeding and other mental and physical abuses that KGB agents inflicted on Sakharov during his four-month incarceration in a Gorkii hospital. Sakharov's relatives and friends in the United States say the letter is authentic. A London newspaper, the *Observer*, publishes the letter February 16 after buying the publication rights.

February 24. *Reagan Arms Response.* President Reagan formally responds to General Secretary Gorbachev's January 15 nuclear arms control proposal by offering two optional three-year timetables for the removal of U.S. and Soviet intermediate-range missiles from Europe and Asia. He says Gorbachev's plan to eliminate all nuclear weapons by the end of the century was "clearly not appropriate for consideration at this time."

February 25-March 6. *27th CPSU Congress.* More than 5,000 Soviet delegates and many foreign representatives attend the 27th Congress of the Communist Party of the Soviet Union in Moscow. General Secretary Gorbachev delivers a five-and-a-half-hour televised keynote address February 25. He indirectly criticizes the policies of the Brezhnev era and calls for numerous economic reforms, including increased autonomy for local managers, revision of the pricing system, and new incentives to increase agricultural production. Gorbachev also advocates a peaceful coexistence policy with the West but denounces President Reagan's February 24 arms control proposal and says progress on arms control will be needed before he will set a date for another superpower summit. On March 5 the congress ratifies the 15-year economic and political programs written under Gorbachev's guidance. Many leadership changes are announced, including the promotions of Central Committee secretary Lev Zaikov to full Politburo membership and longtime ambassador to the United States Anatolii Dobrynin to the Central Committee Secretariat. *(For other leadership changes, see Chapter 9, p. 190.)*

February 27. *Aliev on Privileges.* In an unusually candid interview with Western reporters, Politburo member Geidar Aliev admits Soviet leaders enjoy special privileges such as access to exclusive stores, schools, and hospitals that are not open to ordinary citizens.

February 28. *Moscow Recognizes Aquino Government.* Soviet officials say recognition of the new government of President Corazon Aquino is automatic and that Moscow will maintain relations with the Philippines regardless of who leads it. The Soviet ambassador to Manila had been one of the few foreign envoys to congratulate Ferdinand Marcos on his reelection to the presidency in the disputed February 7 elections. Throughout the Philippine crisis the Soviet press had cautiously supported the Marcos government and portrayed Washington's actions as interventionist.

March 4. *Geneva Talks Adjourn.* The arms control negotiations in Geneva adjourn until May 8. United States negotiators say no progress was made toward an agreement on strategic or space weapons. But they are optimistic about the chances of reaching an agreement on intermediate-range missiles.

March 5. *Reagan on Summit.* President Reagan says he will not visit the Soviet Union in 1987 as planned if General Secretary Gorbachev does not come to the United States for a summit in 1986. The president blames the Kremlin for the difficulty of setting a summit date.

March 6. *Vega Probes Study Comet.* The unmanned Soviet spacecraft Vega 1 takes pictures and gathers data as it passes near Halley's comet. A second Soviet craft, Vega 2, flies even closer to the comet March 9. The Vega probes carry equipment designed by scientists of other nations, and the Soviets participated extensively in the international scientific effort to study Halley's comet.

March 7. *Soviet UN Staff Cuts.* The White House orders the Soviet Union to reduce the combined staffs of the Soviet, Belorussian, and Ukrainian missions to the UN from 275 to 170 officials. Under a 1945 agreement, the Soviet Union gained UN representation for the Belorussian and Ukrainian republics. Reductions are to begin in October 1986. The White House says the large number of Soviet staff members engaged in espionage increases the security threat to the United States. The USSR March 11 protests

the action as "unlawful" and "arbitrary." The same day, the State Department says the move was delayed for six months to avoid disrupting superpower relations.

March 13. *Gorbachev Extends Test Halt.* General Secretary Gorbachev announces the USSR will indefinitely extend its seven-month nuclear testing moratorium set to expire March 31, if the United States joins the halt. The White House rejects the offer and indicates a nuclear test scheduled for March 22 in Nevada will be conducted on schedule. On March 14 Moscow calls for talks on banning nuclear tests.

March 13. *Mir Space Mission.* Two Soviet cosmonauts blast off in a Soyuz spacecraft that carries them to a mission aboard Mir, the orbiting Soviet space station launched February 20. The liftoff is broadcast live on Soviet television, in a departure from Moscow's past practice of televising only those Soviet space missions in which astronauts of other nations are participating.

March 14. *Reagan Verification Proposals.* President Reagan announces he has proposed measures to the Soviets aimed at enhancing verification of nuclear-testing limitations. Reagan asks for bilateral talks on improving verification methods, invites Soviet scientists to witness a nuclear test at a United States facility in April, and offers the Soviets advanced monitoring technology. The same day the White House outlines an ambitious plan for verifying any future treaties limiting intermediate-range missiles. The proposal includes an exchange of inspectors who would count weapons and monitor their production. Tass denounces the verification proposals March 15 as "a political maneuver."

March 15. *Ryzhkov Meets Shultz.* Soviet premier Nikolai Ryzhkov and American secretary of state George Shultz meet in Stockholm following the funeral of Swedish prime minister Olof Palme. They talk for almost two hours on many topics and issue a statement saying neither of their countries is satisfied with the progress of superpower relations since the November summit.

March 18. *U.S. Naval Incursion.* The Kremlin sends a strong note to the U. S. Embassy in Moscow protesting an incursion by two American naval ships into Soviet territorial waters. The incident occurred in the Black Sea during the previous week. The White House confirms that two warships had sailed within six miles of the Soviet coast to exercise the right of innocent passage. Unidentified sources in the Pentagon acknowledge the ships gathered intelligence.

March 20. *Reagan Declines Bonner Meeting.* President Reagan decides not to meet with Yelena Bonner, wife of Soviet dissident Andrei Sakharov. Bonner's visa, which had been set to expire in early March, had been extended by the Soviet government until June. White House officials say the president was concerned that a meeting could jeopardize Bonner's reentry into the Soviet Union and the future release of Soviet citizens seeking to emigrate.

March 24-25. *U.S.-Libyan Clash.* United States ships and warplanes retaliate against Libyan targets after Libya launches Soviet-made missiles at elements of the Sixth Fleet conducting maneuvers in the Gulf of Sidra. American missiles damage or destroy several Libyan ships and a surface-to-air missile radar site near the Libyan coast. General Secretary Gorbachev denounces the U.S. actions as "provocative and threatening" and proposes the withdrawal of all Soviet and U.S. military ships from the Mediterranean. Washington rejects the proposal.

March 29. *Test-Ban Summit Proposal.* General Secretary Gorbachev offers to meet President Reagan in Europe to discuss a nuclear test ban. In spite of the United States' March 22 nuclear test, Gorbachev says the Soviet Union would continue its halt of nuclear testing until the United States conducted another test. President Reagan rejects Gorbachev's summit proposal, saying a meeting should "deal with the entire range" of U.S. relations. Moscow says April 1 that a test ban summit would not necessarily replace a more comprehensive meeting.

March 30. *Soviet Defense Spending.* The CIA says that Soviet spending on arms procurement has barely grown during the past decade and is likely to remain steady or decline during the next five years.

April 8. *Dobrynin Farewell Meeting.* Departing Soviet ambassador to the United States Anatolii Dobrynin and President Reagan discuss a possible 1986 summit. Following the discussions Secretary of State Shultz says he and Foreign Minister Shevardnadze will hold talks in mid-May to prepare for a Reagan-Gorbachev meeting.

April 11. *Soviets End Test Halt.* In response to a U.S. nuclear test conducted April 10 Moscow says it will end its eight-month moratorium on nuclear testing.

April 14. *U.S. Bombs Libya.* U.S. Sixth Fleet naval aircraft and bombers based in England bomb Libya in a massive coordinated air strike. President Reagan says the attack was a response to Col. Muammar Qaddafi's involvement in recent terrorist activities.

April 15. *Soviets Cancel Meeting.* In response to the United States' attack on Libya, Moscow cancels the summit planning meeting scheduled for May 14-16 between Foreign Minister Shevardnadze and Secretary of State Shultz. The Soviet action renders a summer 1986 meeting between Reagan and Gorbachev highly unlikely.

April 16. *Alliluyeva Returns to U.S.* Joseph Stalin's daughter, Svetlana Alliluyeva, returns to the USA and denounces her Soviet citizenship. She defected to the United States in 1967 but returned to the USSR in 1984. She says Mikhail Gorbachev aided her efforts to leave.

April 16-22. *Gorbachev in East Germany.* General Secretary Gorbachev attends the East German Communist Party Congress in East Berlin. In an address April 18 he offers to negotiate troop and arms reductions in Europe. Gorbachev says U.S. nuclear testing and its attack on Libya is undermining East-West relations, but April 20 he says a 1986 summit is still possible.

April 26. *Chernobyl Nuclear Accident.* Just after 1:00 a.m. a fire starts in the Soviet nuclear power station at Chernobyl 80 miles north of Kiev. Complications from the fire quickly cause a meltdown to begin in the reactor's core. Hydrogen gas forms in the overheated reactor and explodes, blowing a hole in the reinforced concrete roof. Huge quantities of radiation escape into the atmosphere. The Soviets do not immediately disclose the accident. Not until the next afternoon do they evacuate nearly 50,000 people from a 6.2-mile radius around the plant.

April 28. *Nuclear Accident Revealed.* Abnormally high levels of radiation are detected in Sweden. Stockholm demands an explanation from Soviet officials after atmospheric analysis reveals the radiation's origin. Tass announces several hours later that a nuclear accident had taken place but says only that "measures are being taken to eliminate the consequences of the accident. Aid is being given to those affected."

April 28. *European Arms Control Plan.* Soviet diplomats hold a press conference in Washington to elaborate on Mikhail Gorbachev's April 18 statement about European arms reductions. They call for new negotiations that would go beyond the existing MBFR talks in Vienna by seeking to reduce tactical nuclear weapons and the military forces of all European nations.

April 29-May 26. *Nuclear Disaster Unfolds.* Radioactivity levels rise throughout much of Europe as Soviet workers attempt to contain the effects of the nuclear meltdown. The Soviets state April 29 that two people were killed at Chernobyl. Some early Western estimates of the dead go as high as 2,000, but later these are proved wrong. By May 29 Moscow reports 21 people had died. Dr. Robert Gale, a U.S. physician, performs bone marrow transplants in Moscow on victims and predicts the death toll will continue to rise. Premier Nikolai Ryzhkov, CC Secretary Egor Ligachev, and Ukrainian party leader Vladimir Shcherbitskii visit the disaster area May 3. The next day the evacuation zone is widened to 18 miles around the reactor. Numerous countries criticize the Soviets for not being more open about the disaster. Eventually Moscow releases films and pictures of the reactor and agrees to provide the IAEA with more information. Many East and West European governments warn of health hazards from food and rainwater affected by the Chernobyl radiation. The European Community May 10 bans all fresh food imports from the Soviet Union and six East European countries at least until the end of May.

May 4. *Karmal Replaced.* Najibullah becomes general secretary of the Afghanistan Communist Party when Babrak Karmal resigns citing poor health. Najibullah formerly headed the Afghan secret police, but analysts speculate the Soviets believe he can attract more support for the Afghan government.

May 13. *Shcharanskii Meets Reagan.* Recently freed Soviet Jewish dissident Anatolii Shcharanskii meets with President Reagan in Washington. White House spokesmen say the president will continue to use quiet diplomacy to advance human rights in the Soviet Union.

May 14. *Gorbachev on Chernobyl.* General Secretary Gorbachev gives a televised address on the Chernobyl nuclear disaster. He says 9 people have died and 299 are hospitalized, but "the worst has passed." He attacks the West for using the accident for anti-Soviet propaganda purposes and denies the USSR withheld timely information on the disaster. Gorbachev renews his offer to meet President Reagan to discuss a nuclear test ban and extends the Soviet moratorium on nuclear testing until August 6.

May 20. *Dubinin Named Ambassador to U.S.* Tass reports that Yuri Dubinin, 55, will become the next Soviet ambassador to the United States. Dubinin had served as the Soviet envoy to the UN since March 1986, but at the time of his May promotion he was not a Central Committee member. Dubinin had been ambassador to Spain for seven years before his UN assignment. A European specialist, he speaks little English and had never been to the United States before 1986. Dubinin's selection surprises Western observers, who expected an American specialist to fill the post. A leading candidate had been Yuli Vorontsov, who was named first deputy foreign minister May 6. He replaced Georgii Kornienko, who was transferred from the Foreign Ministry to become Central Committee secretary Anatolii Dobrynin's deputy.

May 24. *Bonner Leaves for Soviet Union.* Yelena Bonner leaves the United States for Gorkii after a six-month trip to the West for medical treatment.

Selected Documents

Relations between the United States and the Soviet Union since World War II have been documented in a variety of speeches, communiqués, and treaties. In the following section, selected excerpts from these documents trace the relations between the two superpowers from the Cold War of the 1950s and early 1960s through the search for détente in the 1970s, the deterioration of détente that began after the Soviet invasion of Afghanistan in late 1979, and the seeming thaw in tensions after the 1985 Reagan-Gorbachev summit.

WINSTON CHURCHILL'S 'IRON CURTAIN' SPEECH

Following are excerpts from Winston Churchill's "Iron Curtain" speech, delivered March 5, 1946, at Westminster College, Fulton, Missouri. The text is excerpted from The Sinews of Peace: Post-war Speeches by Winston S. Churchill, *ed. Randolph S. Churchill (Boston: Houghton Mifflin Co., 1949).*

... The United States stands at this time at the pinnacle of world power. It is a solemn moment for the American Democracy. For with primacy in power is also joined an awe-inspiring accountability to the future. If you look around you, you must feel not only the sense of duty done but also you must feel anxiety lest you fall below the level of achievement. Opportunity is here now, clear and shining for both our countries. To reject it or ignore it or fritter it away will bring upon us all the long reproaches of the after-time. It is necessary that constancy of mind, persistency of purpose, and the grand simplicity of decision shall guide and rule the conduct of the English-speaking peoples in peace as they did in war. ...

When American military men approach some serious situation they are wont to write at the head of their directive the words "over-all strategic concept". There is wisdom in this, as it leads to clarity of thought. What then is the over-all strategic concept which we should inscribe today? It is nothing less than the safety and welfare, the freedom and progress, of all the homes and families of all the men and women in all the lands.... To give security to these countless homes, they must be shielded from the two giant marauders, war and tyranny.... The awful ruin of Europe, with all its vanished glories, and of large parts of Asia glares us in the eyes.... When I stand here, this quiet afternoon I shudder to visualise what is actually happening to millions now and what is going to happen in this period when famine stalks the earth. None can compute what has been called "the unestimated sum of human pain". Our supreme task and duty is to guard the homes of the common people from the horrors and miseries of another war. We are all agreed on that.

Our American military colleagues, after having proclaimed their "over-all strategic concept" and computed available resources, always proceed to the next step — namely, the method. Here again there is widespread agreement. A world organisation has already been erected for the prime purpose of preventing war. UNO [United Nations Organization], the successor of the League of Nations, with the decisive addition of the United States and all that that means, is already at work. We must make sure that its work is fruitful, that it is a reality and not a sham, that it is a force for action, and not merely a frothing of words, that it is a true temple of peace in which the shields of many nations can some day be hung up, and not merely a cockpit in a Tower of Babel. Before we cast away the solid assurances of national armaments for self-preservation we must be certain that our temple is built, not upon shifting sands or quagmires, but upon the rock. Anyone can see with his eyes open that our path will be difficult and also long, but if we persevere together as we did in the two world wars — though not, alas, in the interval between them — I cannot doubt that we shall achieve our common purpose in the end.

I have, however, a definite and practical proposal to make for action. Courts and magistrates may be set up but they cannot function without sheriffs and constables. The United Nations Organisation must immediately begin to be equipped with an international armed force.... I propose that each of the Powers and States should be invited to delegate a certain number of air squadrons to the service of the world organisation. These squadrons would be trained and prepared in their own countries, but would move around in rotation from one country to another. They would wear the uniform of their own countries but with different badges. They would not be required to act against their own nation, but in other respects they would be directed by the world organisation. This might be started on a modest scale and would grow as confidence grew. I wished to see this done after the first world war, and I devoutly trust it may be done forthwith.

It would nevertheless be wrong and imprudent to entrust the secret knowledge or experience of the atomic bomb, which the United States, Great Britain, and Canada now share, to the world organisation, while it is still in its infancy. It would be criminal madness to cast it adrift in this still agitated and un-united world. No one in any country has slept less well in their beds because this knowledge, and the method and the raw materials to apply it, are at present largely retained in American hands. I do not believe we should all have slept so soundly had the position been reversed and if some Communist or neo-Fascist State monopolised for the time being these dread agencies. The fear of them alone might easily have been used to enforce totalitarian systems upon the free democratic world, with consequences appalling to human imagination. God has willed that this shall not be and we have at least a breathing space to set our house in order before this peril has to be encountered: and even then, if no effort is spared, we should still possess so formidable a superiority as to impose effective deterrents upon its employment, or threat of employment, by others. Ultimately, when the essential brotherhood of man is truly embodied and expressed in a world organisation with all the necessary practical safeguards to make it effective, these powers would naturally be confided to that world organisation.

Now I come to the second danger of these two marauders which threatens the cottage, the home, and the ordinary people — namely, tyranny. We cannot be blind to the fact that the liberties enjoyed by individual citizens throughout the British Empire are not valid in a considerable number of countries, some of which are very powerful. In these States control is enforced upon the common people by various kinds of all-embracing police governments. The power of the State is exercised without restraint, either by dictators or by compact oligarchies operating through a privileged party and a political police. It is not our duty at this time when difficulties are so numerous to interfere forcibly in the internal affairs of countries which we have not conquered in war. But we must never cease to proclaim in fearless tones the great principles of freedom and the rights of man which are the joint inheritance of the English-speaking world and which through Magna Carta, the Bill of Rights, the Habeas Corpus, trial by jury, and the English common law find their most famous expression in the American Declaration of Independence.

'Title Deeds of Freedom'

... Here are the title deeds of freedom which should lie in every cottage home. Here is the message of the British and American peoples to mankind. Let us preach what we practise — let us practise what we preach.

I have now stated the two great dangers which menace the homes of the people: War and Tyranny. I have not yet spoken of poverty and privation which are in many cases the prevailing anxiety. But if the dangers of war and tyranny are removed, there is no doubt that science and co-operation can bring in the next few years to the world, certainly in the next few decades newly taught in the sharpening school of war, an expansion of material well-being beyond anything that has yet occurred in human experience. Now, at this sad and breathless moment, we are plunged in the hunger and distress which are the aftermath of our stupendous struggle; but this will pass and may pass quickly, and there is no reason except human folly or sub-human crime which should deny to all the nations the inauguration and enjoyment of an age of plenty....

Now, while still pursuing the method of realising our overall strategic concept, I come to the crux of what I have travelled here to say. Neither the sure prevention of war, nor the continuous rise of world organisation, will be gained without what I have called the fraternal association of the English-speaking peoples. This means a special relationship between the British Commonwealth and Empire and the United States.... Fraternal association requires not only the growing friendship and mutual understanding between our two vast but kindred systems of society, but the continuance of the intimate relationship between our military advisers, leading to common study of potential dangers.... The United States has already a Permanent Defence Agreement with the Dominion of Canada, which is so devotedly attached to the British Commonwealth and Empire. This Agreement is more effective than many of those which have often been made under formal alliances. This principle should be extended to all British Commonwealths with full reciprocity. Thus, whatever happens, and thus only, shall we be secure ourselves and able to work together for the high and simple causes that are dear to us and bode no ill to any. Eventually there may come — I feel eventually there will come — the principle of common citizenship, but that we may be content to leave to destiny, whose outstretched arm many of us can already clearly see....

A shadow has fallen upon the scenes so lately lighted by the Allied victory. Nobody knows what Soviet Russia and its Communist international organisation intends to do in the immediate future, or what are the limits, if any, to their expansive and proselytising tendencies. I have a strong admiration and regard for the valiant Russian people and for my wartime comrade, Marshal Stalin. There is deep sympathy and goodwill in Britain — and I doubt not here also — towards the peoples of all the Russias and a resolve to persevere through many differences and rebuffs in establishing lasting friendships. We understand the Russian need to be secure on her western frontiers by the removal of all possibility of German aggression. We welcome Russia to her rightful place among the leading nations of the world. We welcome her flag upon the seas. Above all, we welcome constant, frequent and growing contacts between the Russian people and our own people on both sides of the Atlantic. It is my duty however, for I am sure you would wish me to state the facts as I see them to you, to place before you certain facts about the present position in Europe.

'An Iron Curtain Has Descended'

From Stettin in the Baltic to Trieste in the Adriatic, an iron curtain has descended across the Continent. Behind that line lie all the capitals of the ancient states of Central and Eastern Europe. Warsaw, Berlin, Prague, Vienna, Budapest, Belgrade, Bucharest and Sofia, all these famous cities and the populations around them lie in what I must call the Soviet sphere, and all are subject in one form or another, not only to Soviet influence but to a very high and, in many cases, increasing measure of control from Moscow. Athens alone — Greece with its immortal glories — is free to decide its future at an election under British, American and French observation. The Russian-dominated Polish Government has been encouraged to make enormous and wrongful inroads upon Germany, and mass expulsions of millions of Germans on a scale grievous and undreamed of are now taking place. The Communist parties, which were very small in all these Eastern States of Europe, have been raised to pre-eminence and power far beyond their numbers and are seeking everywhere to obtain totalitarian control. Police governments are prevailing in nearly every case, and so far, except in Czechoslovakia, there is no true democracy.

Turkey and Persia are both profoundly alarmed and disturbed at the claims which are being made upon them and at the pressure being exerted by the Moscow Government. An attempt is being made by the Russians in Berlin to build up a quasi-Communist party in their zone of Occupied Germany by showing special favours to groups of left-wing German leaders. At the end of the fighting last June, the American and British Armies withdrew westwards, in accordance with an earlier agreement, to a depth at some points of 150 miles upon a front of nearly four hundred miles, in order to allow our Russian allies to occupy this vast expanse of territory which the Western Democracies had conquered.

If now the Soviet Government tries, by separate action, to build up a pro-Communist Germany in their areas, this will cause new serious difficulties in the British and American zones, and will give the defeated Germans the power of putting themselves up to auction between the Soviets and the Western Democracies. Whatever conclusions may be drawn from these facts — and facts they are — this is certainly not the Liberated Europe we fought to build up. Nor is it one which contains the essentials of permanent peace.

The safety of the world requires a new unity in Europe, from which no nation should be permanently outcast. It is from the quarrels of the strong parent races in Europe that the world wars we have witnessed, or which occurred in former times, have sprung. Twice in our own lifetime we have seen the United States, against their wishes and their traditions, against arguments, the force of which it is impossible not to comprehend, drawn by irresistible forces, into these wars in time to secure the victory of the good cause, but only after frightful slaughter and devastation had occurred. Twice the United States has had to send several millions of its young men across the Atlantic to find the war; but now war can find any nation, wherever it may dwell between dusk and dawn. Surely we should work with conscious purpose for a grand pacification of Europe, within the structure of the United

Nations and in accordance with its Charter. That I feel is an open cause of policy of very great importance.

'Other Causes for Anxiety'

In front of the iron curtain which lies across Europe are other causes for anxiety. In Italy the Communist Party is seriously hampered by having to support the Communist-trained Marshal Tito's claims to former Italian territory at the head of the Adriatic. Nevertheless the future of Italy hangs in the balance. Again one cannot imagine a regenerated Europe without a strong France. All my public life I have worked for a strong France and I never lost faith in her destiny, even in the darkest hours. I will not lose faith now. However, in a great number of countries, far from the Russian frontiers and throughout the world, Communist fifth columns are established and work in complete unity and absolute obedience to the directions they receive from the Communist centre. Except in the British Commonwealth and in the United States where Communism is in its infancy, the Communist parties or fifth columns constitute a growing challenge and peril to Christian civilisation. These are sombre facts for anyone to have to recite on the morrow of a victory gained by so much splendid comradeship in arms and in the cause of freedom and democracy; but we should be most unwise not to face them squarely while time remains.

The outlook is also anxious in the Far East and especially in Manchuria. The Agreement which was made at Yalta, to which I was a party, was extremely favourable to Soviet Russia, but it was made at a time when no one could say that the German war might not extend all through the summer and autumn of 1945 and when the Japanese war was expected to last for a further 18 months from the end of the German war. In this country you are all so well-informed about the Far East, and such devoted friends of China, that I do not need to expatiate on the situation there. . . .

In those days [of the Versailles Treaty] there were high hopes and unbounded confidence that the wars were over, and that the League of Nations would become all-powerful. I do not see or feel that same confidence or even the same hopes in the haggard world at the present time.

On the other hand I repulse the idea that a new war is inevitable; still more that it is imminent. It is because I am sure that our fortunes are still in our own hands and that we hold the power to save the future, that I feel the duty to speak out now that I have the occasion and the opportunity to do so. I do not believe that Soviet Russia desires war. What they desire is the fruits of war and the indefinite expansion of their power and doctrines. But what we have to consider here to-day while time remains, is the permanent prevention of war and the establishment of conditions of freedom and democracy as rapidly as possible in all countries. Our difficulties and dangers will not be removed by closing our eyes to them. They will not be removed by mere waiting to see what happens; nor will they be removed by a policy of appeasement. What is needed is a settlement, and the longer this is delayed, the more difficult it will be and the greater our dangers will become.

From what I have seen of our Russian friends and Allies during the war, I am convinced that there is nothing they admire so much as strength, and there is nothing for which they have less respect than for weakness, especially military weakness. For that reason the old doctrine of a balance of power is unsound. We cannot afford, if we can help it, to work on narrow margins, offering temptations to a trial of strength. If the Western Democracies stand together in strict adherence to the principles of the United Nations Charter, their influence for furthering those principles will be immense and no one is likely to molest them. If however they become divided or falter in their duty and if these all-important years are allowed to slip away then indeed catastrophe may overwhelm us all.

'The Sinews of Peace'

. . . There never was a war in all history easier to prevent by timely action than the one which has just desolated such great areas of the globe. It could have been prevented in my belief without the firing of a single shot, and Germany might be power-ful, prosperous and honoured to-day; but no one would listen and one by one we were all sucked into the awful whirlpool. We surely must not let that happen again. This can only be achieved by reaching now, in 1946, a good understanding on all points with Russia under the general authority of the United Nations Organisation and by the maintenance of that good understanding through many peaceful years, by the world instrument, supported by the whole strength of the English-speaking world and all its connections. There is the solution which I respectfully offer to you in this Address to which I have given the title "The Sinews of Peace".

Let no man underrate the abiding power of the British Empire and Commonwealth. . . . If the population of the English-speaking Commonwealths be added to that of the United States with all that such co-operation implies in the air, on the sea, all over the globe and in science and in industry, and in moral force, there will be no quivering, precarious balance of power to offer its temptation to ambition or adventure. On the contrary, there will be an overwhelming assurance of security. If we adhere faithfully to the Charter of the United Nations and walk forward in sedate and sober strength seeking no one's land or treasure, seeking to lay no arbitrary control upon the thoughts of men; if all British moral and material forces and convictions are joined with your own in fraternal association, the highroads of the future will be clear, not only for us but for all, not only for our time, but for a century to come.

THE 'SECRET SPEECH' OF NIKITA KHRUSHCHEV

Following are excerpts from the so-called "Secret Speech" delivered by Nikita S. Khrushchev February 25, 1956, the last day of the 20th Party Congress, text as supplied by the U.S. Department of State. (Note: Remarks in parentheses describe audience reaction. Explanations and identifying notes in brackets were added by Congressional Quarterly.)

Comrades! In the report of the Central Committee of the party at the 20th Congress, in a number of speeches by delegates to the congress, as also formerly during the plenary CC/CPSU [Central Committee/Communist Party of the Soviet Union] sessions, quite a lot has been said about the cult of the individual and about its harmful consequences.

After Stalin's death the Central Committee of the party began to implement a policy of explaining concisely and consistently that it is impermissible and foreign to the spirit of Marxism-Leninism to elevate one person, to transform him into a superman possessing supernatural characteristics akin to those of a god. Such a man supposedly knows everything, sees everything, thinks for everyone, can do anything, is infallible in his behavior.

Such a belief about a man, and specifically about Stalin, was cultivated among us for many years. . . .

The great modesty of the genius of the revolution, Vladimir Ilyich Lenin, is known. Lenin had always stressed the role of the people as the creator of history, the directing and organizational role of the party as a living and creative organism, and also the role of the Central Committee.

Marxism does not negate the role of the leaders of the workers' class in directing the revolutionary liberation movement.

While ascribing great importance to the role of the leaders and organizers of the masses, Lenin at the same time mercilessly stigmatized every manifestation of the cult of the individual, inexorably combated the foreign-to-Marxism views about a "hero" and a "crowd" and countered all efforts to oppose a "hero" to the masses and to the people.

Lenin taught that the party's strength depends on its indissoluble unity with the masses, on the fact that behind the party follow the people — workers, peasants and intelligentsia. "Only he will win and retain the power," said Lenin, "who believes in the people, who submerges himself in the fountain of the living creativeness of the people.". . .

During Lenin's life the Central Committee of the party was a real expression of collective leadership of the party and of the nation. Being a militant Marxist-revolutionist, always unyielding in matters of principle, Lenin never imposed by force his views upon his co-workers. He tried to convince; he patiently explained his opinions to others. Lenin always diligently observed that the norms of party life were realized, that the party statute was enforced, that the party congresses and the plenary sessions of the Central Committee took place at the proper intervals.

In addition to the great accomplishments of V. I. Lenin for the victory of the working class and of the working peasants, for the victory of our party and for the application of the ideas of scientific communism to life, his acute mind expressed itself also in this, that he detected in Stalin in time those negative characteristics which resulted later in grave consequences. Fearing for the future fate of the party and of the Soviet nation, V. I. Lenin made a completely correct characterization of Stalin, pointing out that it was necessary to consider the question of transferring Stalin from the position of the secretary general because of the fact that Stalin is excessively rude, that he does not have a proper attitude toward his comrades, that he is capricious and abuses his power.

In December 1922 in a letter to the Party Congress Vladimir Ilyich wrote: "After taking over the position of secretary general Comrade Stalin accumulated in his hands immeasurable power and I am not certain whether he will be always able to use this power with the required care."

This letter — a political document of tremendous importance, known in the party history as Lenin's "testament" — was distributed among the delegates to the 20th Party Congress. You have read it, and will undoubtedly read it again more than once. You might reflect on Lenin's plain words, in which expression is given to Vladimir Ilyich's anxiety concerning the party, the people, the state, and the future direction of party policy. . . .

Ths document of Lenin's was made known to the delegates at the 13th Party Congress [May 1924], who discussed the question of transferring Stalin from the position of secretary general. The delegates declared themselves in favor of retaining Stalin in this post, hoping that he would heed the critical remarks of Vladimir Ilyich and would be able to overcome the defects which caused Lenin serious anxiety.

Comrades! The Party Congress should become acquainted with two new documents, which confirm Stalin's character as already outlined by Vladimir Ilyich Lenin in his "testament." These documents are a letter from Nadezhda Konstantinovna Krupskaya [Lenin's wife] to [Lev B.] Kamenev, who was at that time head of the Political Bureau, and a personal letter from Vladimir Ilyich Lenin to Stalin.

I will now read these documents:

"Lev Borisovich!

"Because of a short letter which I had written in words dictated to me by Vladimir Ilyich by permission of the doctors, Stalin allowed himself yesterday an unusually rude outburst directed at me. This is not my first day in the party. During all these thirty years I have never heard from any comrade one word of rudeness. The business of the party and of Ilyich are not less dear to me than to Stalin. I need at present the maximum of self-control. What one can and what one cannot discuss with Ilyich — I know better than any doctor, because I know what makes him nervous and what does not, in any case I know better than Stalin. I am turning to you and to Grigory [Zinoviev] as to much closer comrades of V. I. and I beg you to protect me from rude interference with my private life and from vile invectives and threats. I have no doubt as to what will be the unanimous decision of the Control Commission, with which Stalin sees fit to threaten me; however, I have neither the strength nor the time to waste on this foolish quarrel. And I am a living person and my nerves are strained to the utmost.

"N. Krupskaya"

Nadezhda Konstantinovna wrote this letter on December 23, 1922. After two and a half months, in March 1923, Vladimir Ilyich

Lenin sent Stalin the following letter:

"To Comrade Stalin:

"Copies for: Kamenev and Zinoviev.

"Dear Comrade Stalin!

"You permitted yourself a rude summons of my wife to the telephone and a rude reprimand of her. Despite the fact that she told you that she agreed to forget what was said, nevertheless Zinoviev and Kamenev heard about it from her. I have no intention to forget so easily that which is being done against me, and I need not stress here that I consider as directed against me that which is being done against my wife. I ask you, therefore, that you weigh carefully whether you are agreeable to retracting your words and apologizing or whether you prefer the severance of relations between us.

"Sincerely:
Lenin

"March 5, 1923"

(Commotion in the hall)

Comrades! I will not comment on these documents. They speak eloquently for themselves. Since Stalin could behave in this manner during Lenin's life, could thus behave toward Nadezhda Konstantinovna Krupskaya, whom the party knows well and values highly as a loyal friend of Lenin and as an active fighter for the cause of the party since its creation — we can easily imagine how Stalin treated other people. These negative characteristics of his developed steadily and during the last years acquired an absolutely insufferable character.

As later events have proven, Lenin's anxiety was justified: in the first period after Lenin's death Stalin still paid attention to his [Lenin's] advice, but later he began to disregard the serious admonitions of Vladimir Ilyich.

'Grave Abuse of Power by Stalin'

When we analyze the practice of Stalin in regard to the direction of the party and of the country, when we pause to consider everything which Stalin perpetrated, we must be convinced that Lenin's fears were justified. The negative characteristics of Stalin, which, in Lenin's time, were only incipient, transformed themselves during the last years into a grave abuse of power by Stalin, which caused untold harm to our party.

We have to consider seriously and analyze correctly this matter in order that we may preclude any possibility of a repetition in any form whatever of what took place during the life of Stalin, who absolutely did not tolerate collegiality in leadership and in work, and who practiced brutal violence, not only toward everything which opposed him, but also toward that which seemed to his capricious and despotic character contrary to his concepts.

Stalin acted not through persuasion, explanation, and patient cooperation with people, but by imposing his concepts and demanding absolute submission to his opinion. Whoever opposed this concept or tried to prove his viewpoint, and the correctness of his position, was doomed to removal from the leading collective and to subsequent moral and physical annihilation. This was especially true during the period following the 17th Party Congress [January-February 1934], when many prominent party leaders and rank-and-file party workers, honest and dedicated to the cause of communism, fell victim to Stalin's despotism.

We must affirm that the party had fought a serious fight against the Trotskyites, rightists and bourgeois nationalists, and that it disarmed ideologically all the enemies of Leninism. This ideological fight was carried on successfully, as a result of which the party became strengthened and tempered. Here Stalin played a positive role.

The party led a great political ideological struggle against those in its own ranks who proposed anti-Leninist theses, who represented a political line hostile to the party and to the cause of socialism. . . . Let us consider for a moment what would have happened if in 1928-1929 the political line of right deviation had prevailed among us, or orientation toward "cotton-dress industrialization," or toward the kulak [wealthy peasants], etc. We would not now have a powerful heavy industry, we would not have the *kolkhozes* [collective farms], we would find ourselves disarmed and weak in a capitalist encirclement. . . .

Worth noting is the fact that even during the progress of the furious ideological fight against the Trotskyites, the Zinovievites, the Bukharinites and others, extreme repressive measures were not used against them. The fight was on ideological grounds. But some years later when socialism in our country was fundamentally constructed, ... when the ideological opponents of the party were long since defeated politically — then the repression directed against them began.

It was precisely during this period (1935-1937-1938) that the practice of mass repression through the government apparatus was born, first against the enemies of Leninism — Trotskyites, Zinovievites, Bukharinites, long since politically defeated by the party, and subsequently also against many honest communists, against those party cadres who had borne the heavy load of the civil war and the first and most difficult years of industrialization and collectivization, who actively fought against the Trotskyites and the rightists for the Leninist party line.

Stalin originated the concept "enemy of the people." This term automatically rendered it unnecessary that the ideological errors of a man or men engaged in a controversy be proven; this term made possible the usage of the most cruel repression, violating all norms of revolutionary legality, against anyone who in any way disagreed with Stalin, against those who were only suspected of hostile intent, against those who had bad reputations. This concept, "enemy of the people," actually eliminated the possibility of any kind of ideological fight or the making of one's views known on this or that issue, even those of a practical character. In the main, and in actuality, the only proof of guilt used, against all norms of current legal science, was the "confession" of the accused himself; and, as subsequent probing proved, "confessions" were acquired through physical pressures against the accused. This led to glaring violations of revolutionary legality, and to the fact that many entirely innocent persons, who in the past had defended the party line, became victims.

We must assert that in regard to those persons who in their time had opposed the party line, there were often no sufficiently serious reasons for their physical annihilation. The formula, "enemy of the people," was specifically introduced for the purpose of physically annihilating such individuals.

It is a fact that many persons, who were later annihilated as enemies of the party and people, had worked with Lenin during his life. Some of these persons had made errors during Lenin's life, but, despite this, Lenin benefited by their work, he corrected them and he did everything possible to retain them in the ranks of the party; he induced them to follow him....

'Violence, Mass Repressions, and Terror'

An entirely different relationship with people characterized Stalin. Lenin's traits — patient work with people; stubborn and painstaking education of them; the ability to induce people to follow him without using compulsion, but rather through the ideological influence on them of the whole collective — were entirely foreign to Stalin. He discarded the Leninist method of convincing and educating; he abandoned the method of ideological struggle for that of administrative violence, mass repressions, and terror. He acted on an increasingly larger scale and more stubbornly through punitive organs, at the same time often violating all existing norms of morality and of Soviet laws....

Let us recall some historical facts.

In the days before the October Revolution two members of the Central Committee of the Bolshevik Party — Kamenev and Zinoviev — declared themselves against Lenin's plan for an armed uprising. In addition, on October 18 [1917], they published in the Menshevik newspaper, *Novaya Zhizn,* a statement declaring that the Bolsheviks were making preparations for an uprising and that they considered it adventuristic. Kamenev and Zinoviev thus disclosed to the enemy the decision of the Central Committee to stage the uprising, and that the uprising had been organized to take place within the very near future.

This was treason against the party and against the revolution. In this connection, V. I. Lenin wrote: "Kamenev and Zinoviev revealed the decision of the Central Committee of their party on the armed uprising to [*Duma* president Mikhail] Rodzyanko and [Aleksandr F.] Kerensky [head of the provisional government from

July to October 1917]...." He put before the Central Committee the question of Zinoviev's and Kamenev's expulsion from the party.

However, after the Great Socialist October Revolution, as is known, Zinoviev and Kamenev were given leading positions. Lenin put them in positions in which they carried out most responsible party tasks and participated actively in the work of the leading party and Soviet organs. It is known that Zinoviev and Kamenev committed a number of other serious errors during Lenin's life. In his "testament" Lenin warned that "Zinoviev's and Kamenev's October episode was of course not an accident." But Lenin did not pose the question of their arrest and certainly not their shooting.

Or, let us take the example of the Trotskyites. At present, after a sufficiently long historical period, we can speak about the fight with the Trotskyites with complete calm and can analyze this matter with sufficient objectivity. After all, around Trotsky were people whose origin cannot by any means be traced to bourgeois society. Part of them belonged to the party intelligentsia and a certain part were recruited from among the workers. We can name many individuals who in their time joined the Trotskyites; however, these same individuals took an active part in the workers' movement before the revolution, during the Socialist October Revolution itself, and also in the consolidation of the victory of this greatest of revolutions. Many of them broke with Trotskyism and returned to Leninist positions. Was it necessary to annihilate such people? We are deeply convinced that had Lenin lived such an extreme method would not have been used against many of them.

Such are only a few historical facts. But can it be said that Lenin did not decide to use even the most severe means against enemies of the revolution when this was actually necessary? No, no one can say this. Vladimir Ilyich demanded uncompromising dealings with the enemies of the revolution and of the working class and when necessary resorted ruthlessly to such methods. You will recall only V. I. Lenin's fight with the Socialist Revolutionary organizers of the anti-Soviet uprising, with the counter-revolutionary kulaks in 1918 and with others, when Lenin without hesitation used the most extreme methods against the enemies. Lenin used such methods, however, only against actual class enemies and not against those who blunder, who err, and whom it was possible to lead through ideological influence, and even retain in the leadership....

Stalin, on the other hand, used extreme methods and mass repressions at a time when the revolution was already victorious, when the Soviet state was strengthened, when the exploiting classes were already liquidated and socialist relations were rooted solidly in all phases of national economy, when our party was politically consolidated and had strengthened itself both numerically and ideologically.

It is clear that here Stalin showed in a whole series of cases his intolerance, his brutality and his abuse of power. Instead of proving his political correctness and mobilizing the masses, he often chose the path of repression and physical annihilation, not only against actual enemies, but also against individuals who had not committed any crimes against the party and the Soviet government. Here we see no wisdom but only a demonstration of the brutal force which had once so alarmed V. I. Lenin.

'A Very Ugly Picture'

Lately, especially after the unmasking of the [Lavrentii] Beria gang, the Central Committee has looked into a series of matters fabricated by this gang. This revealed a very ugly picture of brutal willfulness connected with the incorrect behavior of Stalin. As facts prove, Stalin, using his unlimited power, allowed himself many abuses, acting in the name of the Central Committee, not asking for the opinion of the committee members nor even of the members of the Central Committee's Political Bureau; often he did not inform them about his personal decisions concerning very important party and government matters.

Considering the question of the cult of an individual we must first of all show everyone what harm this caused to the interests of our party....

Collegiality of leadership flows from the very nature of our party, a party built on the principles of democratic centralism.

"This means," said Lenin, "that all party matters are accomplished by all party members — directly or through representatives — who without any exceptions are subject to the same rules; in addition, all administrative members, all directing collegia, all holders of party positions are elective, they must account for their activities and are recallable.". . .

During Lenin's life Party Congresses were convened regularly; always, when a radical turn in the development of the party and the country took place, Lenin considered it absolutely necessary that the party discuss at length all the basic matters pertaining to internal and foreign policy and to questions bearing on the development of party and government. . . .

. . . Were our party's holy Leninist principles observed after the death of Vladimir Ilyich?

Whereas during the first few years after Lenin's death Party Congresses and Central Committee plenums took place more or less regularly, later, when Stalin began increasingly to abuse his power, these principles were brutally violated. This was especially evident during the last 15 years of his life. Was it a normal situation when over 13 years elapsed between the 18th [March 1939] and 19th [October 1952] Party Congresses, years during which our party and our country had experienced so many important events? These events demanded categorically that the party should have passed resolutions pertaining to the country's defense during the Patriotic War [World War II] and to peacetime construction after the war. Even after the end of the war a Congress was not convened for over seven years. Central Committee plenums were hardly ever called. It should be sufficient to mention that during all the years of the Patriotic War not a single Central Committee plenum took place. It is true that there was an attempt to call a Central Committee plenum in October 1941, when Central Committee members from the whole country were called to Moscow. They waited two days for the opening of the plenum, but in vain. Stalin did not even want to meet and to talk to the Central Committee members. This fact shows how demoralized Stalin was in the first months of the war and how haughtily and disdainfully he treated the Central Committee members.

In practice Stalin ignored the norms of party life and trampled on the Leninist principle of collective party leadership.

Stalin's willfulness *vis-à-vis* the party and its Central Committee became fully evident after the 17th Party Congress which took place in 1934.

Having at its disposal numerous data showing brutal willfulness toward party cadres, the Central Committee has created a party commission under the control of the Central Committee Presidium; it was charged with investigating what made possible the mass repressions against the majority of the Central Committee members and candidates elected at the 17th Congress of the All-Union Communist Party (Bolsheviks).

The commission has become acquainted with a large quantity of materials in the NKVD [People's Commissariat of Internal Affairs, the name of the secret police from 1934 to 1943; *see box, p. 34*] archives and with other documents and has established many facts pertaining to the fabrication of cases against communists, to false accusations, to glaring abuses of socialist legality — which resulted in the death of innocent people. It became apparent that many party, Soviet and economic activists who were branded in 1937-1938 as "enemies" were actually never enemies, spies, wreckers, etc., but were always honest communists; they were only so stigmatized, and often, no longer able to bear barbaric tortures, they charged themselves (at the order of the investigative judges — falsifiers) with all kinds of grave and unlikely crimes.

The commission has presented to the Central Committee Presidium lengthy and documented materials pertaining to mass repressions against the delegates to the 17th Party Congress and against members of the Central Committee elected at that Congress. These materials have been studied by the Presidium of the Central Committee.

'98 Persons . . . Arrested and Shot'

It was determined that of the 139 members and candidates of the party's Central Committee who were elected at the 17th Congress, 98 persons, i.e., 70 percent, were arrested and shot (mostly in 1937-1938). (Indignation in the hall.). . .

The same fate met not only the Central Committee members but also the majority of the delegates to the 17th Party Congress. Of 1,966 delegates with either voting or advisory rights, 1,108 persons were arrested on charges of anti-revolutionary crimes, i.e., decidedly more than a majority. This very fact shows how absurd, wild and contrary to common sense were the charges of counter-revolutionary crimes made out, as we now see, against a majority of participants at the 17th Party Congress. (Indignation in the hall.)

We should recall that the 17th Party Congress is historically known as the Congress of Victors. Delegates to the Congress were active participants in the building of our socialist state; many of them suffered and fought for party interests during the pre-Revolutionary years in the conspiracy and at the civil war fronts; they fought their enemies valiantly and often nervelessly looked into the face of death.

How then can we believe that such people could prove to be "two-faced" and had joined the camps of the enemies of socialism during the era after the political liquidation of Zinovievites, Trotskyites and rightists and after the great accomplishments of socialist construction? This was the result of the abuse of power by Stalin, who began to use mass terror against the party cadres. . . .

After the criminal murder of S. M. Kirov [Leningrad party boss assassinated December 1, 1934], mass repressions and brutal acts of violation of socialist legality began. On the evening of December 1, 1934, on Stalin's initiative (without the approval of the Political Bureau — which was passed two days later, casually) the Secretary of the Presidium of the Central Executive Committee, [Abel Sofrenovich] Yenukidze, signed the following directive:

"1. Investigative agencies are directed to speed up the cases of those accused of the preparation or execution of acts of terror.

"2. Judicial organs are directed not to hold up the execution of death sentences pertaining to crimes of this category in order to consider the possibility of pardon, because the Presidium of the Central Executive Committee [of the] USSR does not consider as possible the receiving of petitions of this sort.

"3. The organs of the Commissariat of Internal Affairs [NKVD] are directed to execute death sentences against criminals of the above-mentioned category immediately after the passage of sentences."

This directive became the basis for mass acts of abuse against socialist legality. During many of the fabricated court cases the accused were charged with "the preparation" of terroristic acts; this deprived them of any possibility that their cases might be re-examined, even when they stated before the court that their "confessions" were secured by force, and when, in a convincing manner, they disproved the accusations against them.

It must be asserted that to this day the circumstances surrounding Kirov's murder hide many things which are inexplicable and mysterious and demand a most careful examination. There are reasons for the suspicion that the killer of Kirov, [Leonid V.] Nikolayev, was assisted by someone from among the people whose duty it was to protect the person of Kirov.

A month and a half before the killing, Nikolayev was arrested on the grounds of suspicious behavior, but he was released and not even searched. It is an unusually suspicious circumstance that when the Chekist [secret police agent] assigned to protect Kirov was being brought for an interrogation, on December 2, 1934, he was killed in a car "accident" in which no other occupants of the car were harmed. After the murder of Kirov, top functionaries of the Leningrad NKVD were given very light sentences, but in 1937 they were shot. We can assume that they were shot in order to cover the traces of the organizers of Kirov's killing. (Movement in the hall.)

Mass repressions grew tremendously from the end of 1936 after a telegram from Stalin and [Stalin supporter Andrew] Zhdanov, dated from Sochi on September 25, 1936, was addressed to [Lazar] Kaganovich, [Viacheslav] Molotov and other members of the Political Bureau. The content of the telegram was as follows:

"We deem it absolutely necessary and urgent that Comrade [Nikolai] Yeshov be nominated to the post of People's Commissar for Internal Affairs. [Secret police head Genrikh] Yakoda has definitely proved himself to be incapable of unmasking the Trotskyite-Zinovievite bloc. The OGPU [Unified State Political Administration, the name of the secret police from 1922 until 1934] is four years behind in this matter. This is noted by all party workers and by the majority of the representatives of the NKVD."

Strictly speaking we should stress that Stalin did not meet with and therefore could not know the opinion of party workers.

This Stalinist formulation that the "NKVD is four years behind" in applying mass repression and that there is a necessity for "catching up" with the neglected work directly pushed the NKVD workers on the path of mass arrests and executions....

Stalin's report at the February-March Central Committee Plenum in 1937, "Deficiencies of party work and methods for the liquidation of the Trotskyites and of other two-facers," contained an attempt at theoretical justification of the mass terror policy under the pretext that as we march forward toward socialism, class war must allegedly sharpen. Stalin asserted that both history and Lenin taught him this.

Actually Lenin taught that the application of revolutionary violence is necessitated by the resistance of the exploiting classes, and this referred to the era when the exploiting classes existed and were powerful. As soon as the nation's political situation had improved, when in January 1920 the Red Army took Rostov and thus won a most important victory over [White Russian forces led by General Anton] Deniken, Lenin instructed [Felix] Dzerzhinsky [first head of the secret police] to stop mass terror and to abolish the death penalty....

Stalin deviated from these clear and plain precepts of Lenin. Stalin put the party and the NKVD up to the use of mass terror when the exploiting classes had been liquidated in our country and when there were no serious reasons for the use of extraordinary mass terror....

'Brutal Willfulness'

It is known that brutal willfulness was practiced against leading party workers. The party statute, approved at the 17th Party Congress, was based on Leninist principles expressed at the 10th Party Congress. It stated that in order to apply an extreme method such as exclusion from the party against a Central Committee member, against a Central Committee candidate, and against a member of the Party Control Commission, "it is necessary to call a Central Committee Plenum and to invite to the Plenum all Central Committee candidate members and all members of the Party Control Commission"; only if two-thirds of the members of such a general assembly of responsible party leaders find it necessary, only then can a Central Committee member or candidate be expelled.

The majority of the Central Committee members and candidates elected at the 17th Congress and arrested in 1937-1938 were expelled from the party illegally through the brutal abuse of the party statute, because the question of their expulsion was never studied at the Central Committee Plenum.

Now when the cases of some of these so-called "spies" and "saboteurs" were examined it was found that all their cases were fabricated. Confessions of guilt of many arrested and charged with enemy activity were gained with the help of cruel and inhuman tortures....

An example of vile provocation, of odious falsification and of criminal violation of revolutionary legality is the case of the former candidate for the Central Committee Political Bureau, one of the most eminent workers of the party and of the Soviet government, Comrade [Robert I.] Eikhe, who was a party member since 1905. (Commotion in the hall.)

Comrade Eikhe was arrested on April 29, 1938, on the basis of slanderous materials, without the sanction of the prosecutor of the USSR, which was finally received 15 months after the arrest....

Eikhe was forced under torture to sign ahead of time a protocol of his confession prepared by the investigative judges, in which he and several other eminent party workers were accused of anti-Soviet activity.

On October 1, 1939, Eikhe sent his declaration to Stalin in which he categorically denied his guilt and asked for an examination of his case. In the declaration he wrote: "There is no more bitter misery than to sit in the jail of a government for which I have always fought."

A second declaration of Eikhe has been preserved which he sent to Stalin on October 27, 1939; in it he cited facts very convincingly and countered the slanderous accusations made against him, arguing that this provocatory accusation was on the one hand the work of real Trotskyites whose arrests he had sanctioned as First Secretary of the West Siberian Krai [Territory] Party Committee and who conspired in order to take revenge on him, and, on the other hand, the result of the base falsification of materials by the investigative judges....

It would appear that such an important declaration was worth an examination by the Central Committee. This, however, was not done and the declaration was transmitted to Beria while the terrible maltreatment of the Political Bureau candidate, Comrade Eikhe, continued.

On February 4 [1940], Eikhe was shot. (Indignation in the hall.)

It was definitely established now that Eikhe's case was fabricated; he has been posthumously rehabilitated.

Comrade [Yan E.] Rudzutak, candidate member of the Political Bureau, member of the party since 1905, who spent 10 years in a Czarist hard labor camp, completely retracted in court the confession which was forced from him. The protocol of the session of the Collegium of the Supreme Military Court contains the following statement by Rudzutak:

"... The only plea which he places before the court is that the Central Committee of the All-Union Communist Party (Bolsheviks) be informed that there is in the NKVD an as yet not liquidated center which is craftily manufacturing cases, which forces innocent persons to confess; there is no opportunity to prove one's nonparticipation in crimes to which the confessions of various persons testify. The investigative methods are such that they force people to lie and to slander entirely innocent persons in addition to those who already stand accused. He asks the court that he be allowed to inform the Central Committee of the All-Union Communist Party (Bolsheviks) about all this in writing. He assures the Court that he personally had never any evil designs in regard to the policy of our party because he has always agreed with the party policy pertaining to all spheres of economic and cultural activity."

This declaration of Rudzutak was ignored, despite the fact that Rudzutak was in his time the chief of the Central Control commission which was called into being in accordance with Lenin's concept for the purpose of fighting for party unity. In this manner fell the chief of this highly authoritative party organ, a victim of brutal willfulness; he was not even called before the Central Committee's Political Bureau because Stalin did not want to talk to him. Sentence was pronounced on him in 20 minutes and he was shot. (Indignation in the hall.)...

The way in which the former NKVD workers manufactured various fictitious "anti-Soviet centers" and "blocs" with the help of provocatory methods is seen from the confession of Comrade Rozenblum, party member since 1906, who was arrested in 1937 by the Leningrad NKVD.

'Subjected to Terrible Torture'

During the examination in 1955 of the [Nikolai] Komarov [head of the Leningrad Soviet, 1926-29] case Rozenblum revealed the following fact: When Rozenblum was arrested in 1937 he was subjected to terrible torture during which he was ordered to confess false information concerning himself and other persons. He was then brought to the office of [L. M.] Zakovsky [Leningrad secret police head], who offered him freedom on condition that he make before the court a false confession fabricated in 1937 by the NKVD concerning "sabotage, espionage and diversion in a terroristic center in Leningrad." (Movement in the hall.) With unbelievable cynicism Zakovsky told about the vile "mechanism" for the crafty creation of fabricated "anti-Soviet plots."

"In order to illustrate it to me," stated Rozenblum, "Zakovsky gave me several possible variants of the organization of this center and of its branches. After he detailed the organization to me, Zakovsky told me that the NKVD would prepare the case of this center, remarking that the trial would be public.

Before the court were to be brought 4 or 5 members of this

center: [Leningrad second secretary Mikhail] Chudov, [A. I.] Ugarov, [Pyotr] Smorodin, [Boris] Pozern, [Lyndmila] Shaposhnikova (Chudov's wife) and others together with 2 or 3 members from the branches of this center....

"...The case of the Leningrad center has to be built solidly and for this reason witnesses are needed. Social origin (of course, in the past) and the party standing of the witness will play more than a small role.

" 'You, yourself,' said Zakovsky, 'will not need to invent anything. The NKVD will prepare for you a ready outline for every branch of the center; you will have to study it carefully and to remember well all questions and answers which the court might ask. This case will be ready in four-five months, or perhaps a half year. During all this time you will be preparing yourself so that you will not compromise the investigation and yourself. Your future will depend on how the trial goes and on its results. If you begin to lie and to testify falsely, blame yourself. If you manage to endure it, you will save your head and we will feed and clothe you at the government's cost until your death.' "

This is the kind of vile things which were then practiced. (Movement in the hall.)

Even more widely was the falsification of cases practiced in the provinces. The NKVD headquarters of the Sverdlov oblast "discovered" the so-called "Ural uprising staff" — an organ of the bloc of rightists, Trotskyites, socialist Revolutionaries, church leaders — whose chief supposedly was the Secretary of the Sverdlov Oblast Party Committee and member of the Central Committee, All-Union Communist Party (Bolsheviks), [I. D.] Kabakov, who had been a party member since 1914. The investigative materials of that time show that in almost all *krais*, *oblasts* [provinces] and republics there supposedly existed "rightist Trotskyite, espionage-terror and diversionary-sabotage organizations and centers" and that the heads of such organizations as a rule — for no known reason — were first secretaries of *oblast* or republic Communist Party committees or Central Committees. (Movement in the hall.)

Many thousands of honest and innocent Communists have died as a result of this monstrous falsification of such "cases," as a result of the fact that all kinds of slanderous "confessions" were accepted, and as a result of the practice of forcing accusations against oneself and others. In the same manner were fabricated the "cases" against eminent party and state workers — [Politburo member S. V.] Kossior, [Politburo candidate member Vlas Y.] Chubar, Postyshev, [A. V.] Kosarev [head of the Komsomol, the Communist Youth League] and others.

In those years repressions on a mass scale were applied which were based on nothing tangible and which resulted in heavy cadre losses to the party.

The vicious practice was condoned of having the NKVD prepare lists of persons whose cases were under the jurisdiction of the Military Collegium and whose sentences were prepared in advance. [NKVD chief Nikolai] Yezhov would send these lists to Stalin personally for his approval of the proposed punishment. In 1937-1938, 383 such lists containing the names of many thousands of party, Soviet, Komsomol, Army and economic workers were sent to Stalin. He approved these lists.

A large part of these cases are being reviewed now and a great part of them are being voided because they were baseless and falsified. Suffice it to say that from 1954 to the present time the Military Collegium of the Supreme Court has rehabilitated 7,679 persons, many of whom were rehabilitated posthumously.

Mass arrests of party, Soviet, economic and military workers caused tremendous harm to our country and to the cause of socialist advancement....

Only because our party has at its disposal such great moral-political strength was it possible for it to survive the difficult events in 1937-1938 and to educate new cadres. There is, however, no doubt that our march forward toward socialism and toward the preparation of the country's defense would have been much more successful were it not for the tremendous loss in the cadres suffered as a result of the baseless and false mass repressions in 1937-1938. We are justly accusing [NKVD chief Nikolai] Yezhov for the degenerate practices of 1937. But we have to answer these questions:

Could Yezhov have arrested Kossior, for instance, without the knowledge of Stalin? Was there an exchange of opinions or a Political Bureau decision concerning this?

No, there was not, as there was none regarding other cases of this type.

Could Yezhov have decided such important matters as the fate of such eminent party figures?

No, it would be a display of naivete to consider this the work of Yezhov alone. It is clear that these matters were decided by Stalin, and that without his orders and his sanction Yezhov could not have done this....

'Stalin Was ... Sickly Suspicious'

Facts prove that many abuses were made on Stalin's orders without reckoning with any norms of party and Soviet legality. Stalin was a very distrustful man, sickly suspicious; we knew this from our work with him. He could look at a man and say: "Why are your eyes so shifty today?" or "Why are you turning so much today and avoiding to look me directly in the eyes?" The sickly suspicion created in him a general distrust even toward eminent party workers whom he had known for years. Everywhere and in everything he saw "enemies," "two-facers" and "spies."...

When Stalin said that one or another should be arrested, it was necessary to accept on faith that he was an "enemy of the people." Meanwhile, Beria's gang, which ran the organs of state security, outdid itself in proving the guilt of the arrested and the truth of materials which it falsified. And what proofs were offered? The confessions of the arrested, and the investigative judges accepted these "confessions." And how is it possible that a person confesses to crimes which he has not committed? Only in one way — because of application of physical methods of pressuring him, tortures, bringing him to a state of unconsciousness, deprivation of his judgment, taking away of his human dignity. In this manner were "confessions" acquired....

The power accumulated in the hands of one person, Stalin, led to serious consequences during the Great Patriotic War [World War II].

When we look at many of our novels, films and historical "scientific studies," the role of Stalin in the Patriotic War appears to be entirely improbable. Stalin had foreseen everything. The Soviet Army, on the basis of a strategic plan prepared by Stalin long before, used the tactics of so-called "active defense," i.e., tactics which, we know, allowed the Germans to come up to Moscow and Stalingrad. Using such tactics the Soviet Army, supposedly thanks only to Stalin's genius, turned to the offensive and subdued the enemy. The epic victory gained through the armed might of the land of the Soviets, through our heroic people, is ascribed in this type of novel, film and "scientific study" as being completely due to the strategic genius of Stalin....

During the war and after the war Stalin put forward the thesis that the tragedy which our nation experienced in the first part of the war was the result of the "unexpected" attack of the Germans against the Soviet Union. But, Comrades, this is completely untrue. As soon as Hitler came to power in Germany he assigned to himself the task of liquidating Communism. The fascists were saying this openly; they did not hide their plans....

Documents which have now been published show that by April 3, 1941, Churchill, through his ambassador to the USSR, [Sir Stafford] Cripps, personally warned Stalin that the Germans had begun regrouping their armed units with the intent of attacking the Soviet Union....

... However, Stalin took no heed of these warnings. What is more, Stalin ordered that no credence be given to information of this sort, in order not to provoke the initiation of military operations.

We must assert that information of this sort concerning the threat of German armed invasion of Soviet territory was coming in also from our own military and diplomatic sources; however, because the leadership was conditioned against such information, such data was dispatched with fear and assessed with reservation.

Thus, for instance, information sent from Berlin on May 6, 1941, by the Soviet military attaché ... stated: "Soviet citizen Bozer ... communicated to the deputy naval attaché that according to a statement of a certain German officer from Hitler's Headquarters, Germany is preparing to invade the USSR on May 14 through Finland, the Baltic countries and Latvia. At the same time Moscow and Leningrad will be heavily raided and paratroopers landed in border cities...."

In his report of May 22, 1941, the deputy military attaché in Berlin ... communicated that "... the attack of the German army is reportedly scheduled for June 15, but it is possible that it may begin in the first days of June...."

A cable from our London Embassy dated June 18, 1941, stated: "As of now Cripps is deeply convinced of the inevitability of armed conflict between Germany and the USSR which will begin not later than the middle of June. According to Cripps, the Germans have presently concentrated 147 divisions (including air force and service units) along the Soviet borders...."

Despite these particularly grave warnings, the necessary steps were not taken to prepare the country properly for defense and to prevent it from being caught unawares.

Did we have time and the capabilities for such preparations? Yes, we had the time and the capabilities....

Had our industry been mobilized properly and in time to supply the army with the necessary matériel, our wartime losses would have been decidedly smaller. Such mobilization had not been, however, started in time. And already in the first days of the war it became evident that our army was badly armed, that we did not have enough artillery, tanks and planes to throw the enemy back.

Soviet science and technology produced excellent models of tanks and artillery pieces before the war. But mass production of all this was not organized and as a matter of fact we started to modernize our military equipment only on the eve of the war. As a result, at the time of the enemy's invasion of the Soviet land we did not have sufficient quantities either of old machinery which was no longer used for armament production or of new machinery which we had planned to introduce into armament production.

The situation with antiaircraft artillery was especially bad; we did not organize the production of antitank ammunition. Many fortified regions had proven to be indefensible as soon as they were attacked, because the old arms had been withdrawn and new ones were not yet available there.

This pertained, alas, not only to tanks, artillery and planes. At the outbreak of the war we did not even have sufficient numbers of rifles to arm the mobilized manpower. I recall that in those days I telephoned to Comrade [Georgi M.] Malenkov from Kiev and told him, "People have volunteered for the new army and demand arms. You must send us arms."

Malenkov answered me, "We cannot send you arms. We are sending all our rifles to Leningrad and you have to arm yourselves." (Movement in the hall.)

Such was the armament situation.

In this connection we cannot forget, for instance, the following fact: Shortly before the invasion of the Soviet Union by the Hitlerite army, ... [the] Chief of the Kiev Special Military District (he was later killed at the front) wrote to Stalin that the German armies were at the Bug River, were preparing for an attack and in the very near future would probably start their offensive. In this connection ... [he] proposed that a strong defense be organized, that 300,000 people be evacuated from the border areas and that several strong points be organized there: antitank ditches, trenches for the soldiers, etc.

Moscow answered this proposition with the assertion that this would be a provocation, that no preparatory defensive work should be undertaken at the borders, that the Germans were not to be given any pretext for the initiation of military action against us. Thus, our borders were insufficiently prepared to repel the enemy....

And what were the results of this carefree attitude, this disregard of clear facts? The result was that already in the first hours and days the enemy had destroyed in our border regions a large part of our air force, artillery and other military equipment; he annihilated large numbers of our military cadres and disorganized our military leadership; consequently we could not prevent the enemy from marching deep into the country.

Very grievous consequences, especially in reference to the beginning of the war, followed Stalin's annihilation of many military commanders and political workers during 1937-1941 because of his suspiciousness and through slanderous accusations. During these years repressions were instituted against certain parts of military cadres beginning literally at the company and battalion commander level and extending to the higher military centers; during this time the cadre of leaders who had gained military experience in Spain and in the Far East was almost completely liquidated.

The policy of large-scale repression against the military cadres led also to undermined military discipline, because for several years officers of all ranks and even soldiers in the party and Komsomol cells were taught to "unmask" their superiors as hidden enemies. (Movement in the hall.) It is natural that this caused a negative influence on the state of military discipline in the first war period.... All this brought about the situation which existed at the beginning of the war and which was the great threat to our Fatherland.

'This Was the End'

It would be incorrect to forget that after the first severe disaster and defeats at the front, Stalin thought that this was the end. In one of his speeches in those days he said: "All that which Lenin created we have lost forever."

After this Stalin for a long time actually did not direct the military operations and ceased to do anything whatever. He returned to active leadership only when some members of the Political Bureau visited him and told him that it was necessary to take certain steps immediately in order to improve the situation at the front.

Therefore, the threatening danger which hung over our Fatherland in the first period of the war was largely due to the faulty methods of directing the nation and the party by Stalin himself.

However, we speak not only about the moment when the war began, which led to serious disorganization of our army and brought us severe losses. Even after the war began, the nervousness and hysteria which Stalin demonstrated, interfering with actual military operations, caused our army serious damage.

Stalin was very far from an understanding of the real situation which was developing at the front. This was natural because during the whole Patriotic War he never visited any section of the front or any liberated city except for one short ride on the Mozhaisk Highway during a stabilized situation at the front. To this incident were dedicated many literary works full of fantasies of all sorts and so many paintings. Simultaneously, Stalin was interfering with operations and issuing orders which did not take into consideration the real situation at a given section of the front and which could not help but result in huge personnel losses.

I will allow myself in this connection to bring out one characteristic fact which illustrates how Stalin directed operations at the fronts. There is present at this Congress Marshal [Ivan] Bagramyan who was once the chief of operations in the headquarters of the southwestern front and who can corroborate what I tell you.

When there developed an exceptionally serious situation for our Army in 1942 in the Kharkov region, we had correctly decided to drop an operation whose objective was to encircle Kharkov, because the real situation at that time would have threatened our Army with fatal consequences if this operation were continued....

Contrary to common sense, Stalin rejected our suggestion and issued the order to continue the operation aimed at the encirclement of Kharkov, despite the fact that at this time many Army concentrations were themselves actually threatened with encirclement and liquidation....

And what was the result of this? The worst that we had expected. The Germans surrounded our Army concentrations and consequently we lost hundreds of thousands of our soldiers. This is Stalin's military "genius"; this is what it cost us. (Movement in the hall.)...

The tactics on which Stalin insisted without knowing the essence of the conduct of battle operations cost us much blood until we succeeded in stopping the opponent and going over to the offensive.

The military know that already by the end of 1941 instead of great operational maneuvers flanking the opponent and penetrating behind his back, Stalin demanded incessant frontal attacks and the capture of one village after another.

Because of this we paid with great losses — until our generals, on whose shoulders rested the whole weight of conducting the war, succeeded in changing the situation and shifting to flexible-maneuver operations, which immediately brought serious changes at the front favorable to us.

All the more shameful was the fact that after our great victory over the enemy which cost us so much, Stalin began to downgrade many of the commanders who contributed so much to the victory over the enemy, because Stalin excluded every possibility that services rendered at the front should be credited to anyone but himself....

In this connection Stalin very energetically popularized himself as a great leader; in various ways he tried to inculcate in the people the version that all victories gained by the Soviet nation during the Great Patriotic War were due to the courage, daring and genius of Stalin and to no one else. Exactly like Kuzma Kryuchkov [a famous Cossack who performed heroic feats against the Germans] he put one dress on seven people at the same time. (Animation in the hall.)

In the same vein, let us take, for instance, our historical and military films and some literary creations; they make us feel sick. Their true objective is the propagation of the theme of praising Stalin as a military genius. Let us recall the film, *The Fall of Berlin*. Here only Stalin acts; he issues orders in the hall in which there are many empty chairs and only one man approaches him and reports something to him — that is [A. N.] Poskrebyshev [Stalin's secretary and trusted aide], his loyal shield-bearer. (Laughter in the hall.)

And where is the military command? Where is the Political Bureau? Where is the Government? What are they doing and with what are they engaged? There is nothing about them in the film. Stalin acts for everybody; he does not reckon with anyone; he asks no one for advice. Everything is shown to the nation in this false light. Why? In order to surround Stalin with glory, contrary to the facts and contrary to historical truth.

The question arises: And where are the military on whose shoulders rested the burden of the war? They are not in the film; with Stalin in, no room was left for them.

Not Stalin, but the party as a whole, the Soviet government, our heroic Army, its talented leaders and brave soldiers, the whole Soviet nation — these are the ones who assured the victory in the Great Patriotic War. (Tempestuous and prolonged applause.)...

The main role and the main credit for the victorious ending of the war belongs to our Communist Party, to the armed forces of the Soviet Union, and to the tens of millions of Soviet people raised by the party. (Thunderous and prolonged applause.)

Comrades, let us reach for some other facts. The Soviet Union is justly considered as a model of a multinational state because we have in practice assured the equality and friendship of all nations which live in our great Fatherland.

'Mass Deportations'

All the more monstrous are the acts whose initiator was Stalin and which are rude violations of the basic Leninist principles of the nationality policy of the Soviet state. We refer to the mass deportations from their native places of whole nations, together with all Communists and Komsomols without any exception; this deportation action was not dictated by any military considerations.

Thus, already at the end of 1943, when there occurred a permanent breakthrough at the fronts of the Great Patriotic War benefiting the Soviet Union, a decision was taken and executed concerning the deportation of all the Karachai from the lands on which they lived.

In the same period, at the end of December 1943, the same lot befell the whole population of the Autonomous Kalmyk Republic. In March 1944 all the Chechen and Ingush peoples were deported and the Chechen-Ingush Autonomous Republic was liquidated. In April 1944, all Balkars were deported to faraway places from the territory of the Kabardino-Balkar Autonomous Republic and the Republic itself was renamed the Autonomous Kabardin Republic.

The Ukrainians avoided meeting this fate only because there were too many of them and there was no place to which to deport them. Otherwise, he would have deported them also. (Laughter and animation in the hall.)...

After the conclusion of the Patriotic War, the Soviet nation stressed with pride the magnificent victories gained through great sacrifices and tremendous efforts. The country experienced a period of political enthusiasm. The party came out of the war even more united; in the fire of the war party cadres were tempered and hardened. Under such conditions nobody could have even thought of the possibility of some plot in the party.

And it was precisely at this time that the so-called "Leningrad affair" was born. As we have now proven, this case was fabricated. Those who innocently lost their lives included Comrades [Nikolai A.] Voznesensky, [A. A.] Kuznetsov, [Mikhail I.] Rodinov, [Pyotr S.] Popkov, and others.

As is known, Voznesensky and Kuznetsov were talented and eminent leaders. Once they stood very close to Stalin. It is sufficient to mention that Stalin made Voznesensky first deputy to the chairman of the Council of Ministers and Kuznetsov was elected Secretary of the Central Committee. The very fact that Stalin entrusted Kuznetsov with the supervision of the state security organs shows the trust which he enjoyed.

How did it happen that these persons were branded as enemies of the people and liquidated?

Facts prove that the "Leningrad affair" is also the result of willfulness which Stalin exercised against party cadres. Had a normal situation existed in the party's Central Committee and in the Central Committee Political Bureau, affairs of this nature would have been examined there in accordance with party practice, and all pertinent facts assessed; as a result such an affair as well as others would not have happened.

We must state that after the war the situation became even more complicated. Stalin became even more capricious, irritable and brutal; in particular his suspicion grew. His persecution mania reached unbelievable dimensions. Many workers were becoming enemies before his very eyes. After the war Stalin separated himself from the collective even more. Everything was decided by him alone without any consideration for anyone or anything.

This unbelievable suspicion was cleverly taken advantage of by the abject provocateur and vile enemy, Beria, who had murdered thousands of Communists and loyal Soviet people. The elevation of Voznesensky and Kuznetsov alarmed Beria. As we have now proven, it had been precisely Beria who had "suggested" to Stalin the fabrication by him and by his confidants of materials in the form of declarations and anonymous letters, and in the form of various rumors and talks.

The party's Central Committee has examined this so-called "Leningrad affair"; persons who innocently suffered are now rehabilitated and honor has been restored to the glorious Leningrad party organization. [Victor S.] Abakumov [minister of state security, 1947-51] and others who had fabricated this affair were brought before a court; their trial took place in Leningrad and they received what they deserved.

The question arises: Why is it that we see the truth of this affair only now, and why did we not do something earlier, during Stalin's life, in order to prevent the loss of innocent lives? It was because Stalin personally supervised the "Leningrad affair," and the majority of the Political Bureau members did not, at that time, know all of the circumstances in these matters, and could not therefore intervene....

The willfulness of Stalin showed itself not only in decisions concerning the internal life of the country but also in the international relations of the Soviet Union.

The July plenum of the Central Committee studied in detail the reasons for the development of conflict with Yugoslavia. It was a shameful role which Stalin played here. The "Yugoslav affair" contained no problems which could not have been solved through party discussions among comrades. There was no significant basis for the development of this "affair"; it was completely possible to have prevented the rupture of relations with that country. This does not mean, however, that the Yugoslav leaders did not make mistakes or did not have shortcomings. But these mistakes and shortcomings were magnified in a monstrous manner by Stalin, which resulted in a break of relations with a friendly country....

You see to what Stalin's mania for greatness led. He had completely lost consciousness of reality; he demonstrated his suspicion and haughtiness not only in relation to individuals in the USSR, but in relation to whole parties and nations.

We have carefully examined the case of Yugoslavia and have found a proper solution which is approved by the peoples of the Soviet Union and of Yugoslavia as well as by the working masses of all the people's democracies and by all progressive humanity. The liquidation of the abnormal relationship with Yugoslavia was done in the interest of the whole camp of socialism, in the interest of strengthening peace in the whole world.

'Affair of the Doctor-Plotters'

Let us also recall the "affair of the doctor-plotters." (Animation in the hall.) Actually there was no "Affair" outside of the declaration of the woman doctor, [Lydia] Timashuk, who was probably influenced or ordered by someone (after all, she was an unofficial collaborator of the organs of state security) to write Stalin a letter in which she declared that doctors were applying supposedly improper methods of medical treatment.

Such a letter was sufficient for Stalin to reach an immediate conclusion that there were doctor-plotters in the Soviet Union. He issued orders to arrest a group of eminent Soviet medical specialists. He personally issued advice on the conduct of the investigation and the method of interrogation of the arrested persons. He said that the academician [A. I.] Vinogradov should be put in chains, another one should be beaten. Present at this Congress as a delegate is the former Minister of State Security, Comrade [S. D.] Ignatiev. Stalin told him curtly, "If you do not obtain confessions from the doctors we will shorten you by a head." (Tumult in the hall.)

Stalin personally called the investigative judge, gave him instructions, advised him on which investigative methods should be used; these methods were simple — beat, beat and, once again, beat.

Shortly after the doctors were arrested we members of the Political Bureau received protocols with the doctors' confessions of guilt. After distributing these protocols Stalin told us, "You are blind like young kittens; what will happen without me? The country will perish because you do not know how to recognize enemies."

The case was so presented that no one could verify the facts on which the investigation was based. There was no possibility of trying to verify facts by contacting those who had made the confessions of guilt.

We felt, however, that the case of the arrested doctors was questionable. We knew some of these people personally because they had once treated us. When we examined this "case" after Stalin's death, we found it to be fabricated from beginning to end. This ignominious "case" was set up by Stalin; he did not, however, have the time in which to bring it to an end (as he conceived that end), and for this reason the doctors are still alive. Now all have been rehabilitated; they are working in the same places they were working before; they treat top individuals, not excluding members of the government; they have our full confidence; and they execute their duties honestly, as they did before....

Comrades: The cult of the individual acquired such monstrous size chiefly because Stalin himself, using all conceivable methods, supported the glorification of his own person. This is supported by numerous facts. One of the most characteristic examples of Stalin's self-glorification and his lack of even elementary modesty is the edition of his *Short Biography*, which was published in 1948....

We need not give here examples of the loathsome adulation filling this book. All we need to add is that they all were approved and edited by Stalin personally and some of them were added in his own handwriting to the draft text of the book.

What did Stalin consider essential to write into this book? Did

he want to cool the ardor of his flatterers who were composing his *Short Biography*? No! He marked the very places where he thought that the praise of his services was insufficient.

Here are some examples characterizing Stalin's activity, added in Stalin's own hand:

"In this fight against the skeptics and capitulators, the Trotskyites, Zinovievites, Bukharinites and Kamenevites, there was definitely welded together, after Lenin's death, that leading core of the Party ... that upheld the great manner of Lenin, rallied the Party behind Lenin's behests, and brought the Soviet people into the broad road of industrializing the country and collectivizing the rural economy. The leader of this core and the guiding force of the Party and the State was Comrade Stalin."

Thus writes Stalin himself! Then he adds:

"Although he performed his task of leader of the Party and the people with consummate skill and enjoyed the unreserved support of the entire Soviet people, Stalin never allowed his work to be marred by the slightest hint of vanity, conceit or self-adulation."

Where and when could a leader so praise himself? Is this worthy of a leader of the Marxist-Leninist type? No. Precisely against this did Marx and Engels take such a strong position. This also was always sharply condemned by Vladimir Ilyich Lenin....

And one additional fact from the same *Short Biography* of Stalin. As is known, *The Short Course of the History of the All-Union Communist Party (Bolsheviks)* was written by a commission of the party Central Committee.

This book, parenthetically, was permeated with the cult of the individual and was written by a designated group of authors. This fact was reflected in the following formulation on the proof copy of the *Short Biography* of Stalin: "A commission of the Central Committee, All-Union Communist Party (Bolsheviks), under the direction of Comrade Stalin and with his most active personal participation, has prepared a *Short Course of the History of the All-Union Communist Party (Bolsheviks)*."

But even this phrase did not satisfy Stalin; the following sentence replaced it in the final version of the *Short Biography*: "In 1938 appeared the book, *History of the All-Union Communist Party (Bolsheviks), Short Course*, written by Comrade Stalin and approved by a commission of the Central Committee, All Union Communist Party (Bolsheviks)." Can one add anything more? (Animation in the hall.)...

Stalin recognized as the best a text of the national anthem of the Soviet Union which contains not a word about the Communist Party; it contains, however, the following unprecedented praise of Stalin: *"Stalin brought us up in loyalty to the people. He inspired us to great toil and acts."*

In these lines of the anthem is the whole educational, directional and inspirational activity of the great Leninist party ascribed to Stalin. This is, of course, a clear deviation from Marxism-Leninism, a clear debasing and belittling of the role of the party. We should add for your information that the Presidium of the Central Committee has already passed a resolution concerning the composition of a new text of the anthem, which will reflect the role of the people, and the role of the party. (Loud, prolonged applause.)

And was it without Stalin's knowledge that many of the largest enterprises and towns were named after him? Was it without his knowledge that Stalin monuments were erected in the whole country — these "memorials to the living"? It is a fact that Stalin himself had signed on July 2, 1951, a resolution of the USSR Council of Ministers concerning the erection on the Volga-Don Canal of an impressive monument to Stalin; on September 4 of the same year he issued an order making 33 tons of copper available for the construction of this impressive monument. Anyone who has visited the Stalingrad area must have seen the huge statue which is being built there, and that on a site which hardly any people frequent. Huge sums were spent to build it at a time when people of this area had lived since the war in huts. Consider yourself, was Stalin right when he wrote in his biography that "... he did not allow in himself ... even a shadow of conceit, pride, or self-adoration"?

At the same time Stalin gave proofs of his lack of respect for Lenin's memory. It is not a coincidence that, despite the decision taken over 30 years ago to build a Palace of Soviets as a monument to Vladimir Ilyich, this palace was not built, its construction was always postponed, and the project allowed to lapse.

We cannot forget to recall the Soviet Government resolution of August 14, 1925, concerning "the founding of Lenin prizes for educational work." This resolution was published in the press, but until this day there are no Lenin prizes. This, too, should be corrected. (Tumultuous, prolonged applause.)

During Stalin's life, thanks to known methods which I have mentioned, and quoting facts, for instance, from the *Short Biography* of Stalin — all events were explained as if Lenin played only a secondary role, even during the October Socialist Revolution. In many films and in many literary works, the figure of Lenin was incorrectly presented and inadmissibly depreciated.

Stalin loved to see the film *The Unforgettable Year of 1919*, in which he was shown on the steps of an armored train and where he was practically vanquishing the foe with his own saber. Let Kliment Yefremovich [Voroshilov], chairman of the Presidium of the Supreme Soviet, 1953-60], our dear friend, find the necessary courage and write the truth about Stalin; after all, he knows how Stalin had fought. It will be difficult for Comrade Voroshilov to undertake this, but it would be good if he did it. Everyone will approve of it, both the people and the party. Even his grandsons will thank him. (Prolonged applause.)

In speaking about the events of the October Revolution and about the civil war, the impression was created that Stalin always played the main role, as if everywhere and always Stalin had suggested to Lenin what to do and how to do it. However, this is slander of Lenin. (Prolonged applause.)

I will probably not sin against the truth when I say that 99 percent of the persons present here heard and knew very little about Stalin before the year 1924, while Lenin was known to all; he was known to the whole party, to the whole nation, from the children up to the graybeards. (Tumultuous, prolonged applause.)

All this has to be thoroughly revised, so that history, literature, and the fine arts properly reflect V. I. Lenin's role and the great deeds of our Communist Party and of the Soviet people — the creative people. (Applause.)

'The Cult of the Individual'

Comrades! The cult of the individual has caused the employment of faulty principles in party work and in economic activity; it brought about rude violation of internal party and Soviet democracy, sterile administration, deviations of all sorts, covering up of shortcomings and varnishing of reality. Our nation gave birth to many flatterers and specialists in false optimism and deceit.

We should also not forget that due to the numerous arrests of party, Soviet and economic leaders, many workers began to work uncertainly, showed over-cautiousness, feared all which was new, feared their own shadows and began to show less initiative in their work....

Stalin's reluctance to consider life's realities and the fact that he was not aware of the real state of affairs in the provinces can be illustrated by his direction of agriculture.

All those who interested themselves even a little in the national situation saw the difficult situation in agriculture, but Stalin never even noted it. Did we tell Stalin about this? Yes, we told him, but he did not support us. Why? Because Stalin never traveled anywhere, did not meet city and *kolkhoz* workers; he did not know the actual situation in the provinces.

He knew the country and agriculture only from films. And these films had dressed up and beautified the existing situation in agriculture....

Vladimir Ilyich Lenin looked at life differently; he was always close to the people; he used to receive peasant delegates, and often spoke at factory gatherings; he used to visit villages and talk with the peasants.

Stalin separated himself from the people and never went anywhere. This lasted tens of years. The last time he visited a village was in January 1928 when he visited Siberia in connection with grain deliveries. How then could he have known the situation in the provinces?

And when he was once told during a discussion that our situation on the land was a difficult one and that the situation of cattle breeding and meat production was especially bad, a commission was formed which was charged with the preparation of a resolution called, "Means toward further development of animal breeding in *kolkhozes* and *sovkhozes* [state farms]." We worked out this project.

Of course, our propositions of that time did not contain all possibilities, but we did charter ways in which animal breeding on the *kolkhozes* and *sovkhozes* would be raised. We had proposed then to raise the prices of such products in order to create material incentives for the *kolkhoz*, MTS [machine tractor station] and *sovkhoz* workers in the development of cattle breeding. But our project was not accepted and in February 1953 was laid aside entirely.

What is more, while reviewing this project Stalin proposed that the taxes paid by the *kolkhozes* and by the *kolkhoz* workers should be raised by 40 billion rubles; according to him the peasants are well off and the *kolkhoz* worker would need to sell only one more chicken to pay his tax in full.

Imagine what this meant. Certainly 40 billion rubles is a sum which the *kolkhoz* workers did not realize for all the products which they sold to the government. In 1952, for instance, the *kolkhozes* and the *kolkhoz* workers received 26,280 million rubles for all their products delivered and sold to the government.

Did Stalin's position then rest on data of any sort whatever? Of course not....

Comrades! If we sharply criticize today the cult of the individual which was so widespread during Stalin's life and if we speak about the many negative phenomena generated by this cult which is so alien to the spirit of Marxism-Leninism, various persons may ask: How could it be? Stalin headed the party and the country for 30 years and many victories were gained during his lifetime. Can we deny this? In my opinion, the question can be asked in this manner only by those who are blinded and hopelessly hypnotized by the cult of the individual, only by those who do not understand the essence of the revolution and of the Soviet state, only by those who do not understand, in a Leninist manner, the role of the party and of the nation in the development of the Soviet society.

The Socialist Revolution was attained by the working class and by the poor peasantry with the partial support of middle-class peasants. It was attained by the people under the leadership of the Bolshevik Party. Lenin's great service consisted of the fact that he created a militant party of the working class, but he was armed with Marxist understanding of the laws of social development and with the science of proletarian victory in the fight with capitalism, and he steeled this party in the crucible of revolutionary struggle of the masses of the people.

During this fight the party consistently defended the interests of the people, became its experienced leader, and led the working masses to power, to the creation of the first socialist state....

Our historical victories were attained thanks to the organizational work of the party, to the many provincial organizations, and to the self-sacrificing work of our great nation. These victories are the result of the great drive and activity of the nation and of the party as a whole; they are not at all the fruit of the leadership of Stalin, as the situation was pictured during the period of the cult of the individual....

In the last years, when we managed to free ourselves of the harmful practice of the cult of the individual and took several proper steps in the sphere of internal and external policies, everyone saw how activity grew before their very eyes, how the creative activity of the broad working masses developed, how favorably all this acted upon the development of economy and of culture. (Applause.)

Where Was the Political Bureau?

Some comrades may ask us: Where were the members of the Political Bureau of the Central Committee? Why did they not assert themselves against the cult of the individual in time? And why is this being done only now?

First of all we have to consider the fact that the members of the Political Bureau viewed these matters in a different way at different times. Initially, many of them backed Stalin actively because Stalin was one of the strongest Marxists and his logic, his strength and his will greatly influenced the cadres and party work.

It is known that Stalin, after Lenin's death, especially during the first years, actively fought for Leninism against the enemies of Leninist theory and against those who deviated. Beginning with Leninist theory, the party, with its Central Committee at the head, started on a great scale the work of socialist industrialization of the country, agricultural collectivization and the cultural revolution.

At that time Stalin gained great popularity, sympathy and support. The party had to fight those who attempted to lead the country away from the correct Leninist path; it had to fight Trotskyites, Zinovievites and rightists, and the bourgeois nationalists. This fight was indispensable.

Later, however, Stalin, abusing his power more and more, began to fight eminent party and government leaders and to use terroristic methods against honest Soviet people. . . .

It is clear that such conditions put every member of the Political Bureau in a very difficult situation. And when we also consider the fact that in the last years the Central Committee plenary sessions were not convened and that the sessions of the Political Bureau occurred only occasionally, from time to time, then we will understand how difficult it was for any member of the Political Bureau to take a stand against one or another injust or improper procedure, against serious errors and shortcomings in the practices of leadership. . . .

The importance of the Central Committee's Political Bureau was reduced and its work was disorganized by the creation within the Political Bureau of various commissions — the so-called "quintets," "sextets," "septets" and "novenaries." Here is, for instance, a resolution of the Political Bureau of October 3, 1946:

"Stalin's Proposal:

"1. The Political Bureau Commission for Foreign Affairs ("Sextet") is to concern itself in the future, in addition to foreign affairs, also with matters of internal construction and domestic policy.

"2. The Sextet is to add to its roster the Chairman of the State Commission of Economic Planning of the USSR, Comrade Voznesensky, and is to be known as a Septet.

"Signed: Secretary of the Central Committee, J. Stalin."

What a terminology of a card player! (Laughter in the hall.) It is clear that the creation within the Political Bureau of this type of commission — "quintets," "sextets," "septets," and "novenaries" — was against the principle of collective leadership. The result of this was that some members of the Political Bureau were in this way kept away from participation in reaching the most important state matters. . . .

Let us consider the first Central Committee Plenum after the 19th Party Congress when Stalin, in his talk at the Plenum, characterized Vyacheslav Mikhailovich Molotov and Anastas Ivanovich Mikoyan and suggested that these old workers of our party were guilty of some baseless charges. It is not excluded that had Stalin remained at the helm for another several months, Comrades Molotov and Mikoyan would probably have not delivered any speeches at this Congress.

Stalin evidently had plans to finish off the old members of the Political Bureau. He often stated that Political Bureau members should be replaced by new ones.

His proposal, after the 19th Congress, concerning the selection of 25 persons to the Central Committee Presidium, was aimed at the removal of the old Political Bureau members and the bringing in of less experienced persons so that these would extol him in all sorts of ways.

We can assume that this was also a design for the future annihilation of the old Political Bureau members and in this way a cover for all shameful acts of Stalin, acts which we are now considering.

Comrades! In order not to repeat errors of the past, the Central Committee has declared itself resolutely against the cult of the individual. We consider that Stalin was excessively extolled. However, in the past Stalin doubtless performed great services to the party, to the working class, and to the international workers' movement.

This question is complicated by the fact that all this which we have just discussed was done during Stalin's life under his leader-ship and with his concurrence; here Stalin was convinced that this was necessary for the defense of the interests of the working classes against the plotting of the enemies and against the attack of the imperialist camp.

He saw this from the position of the interest of the working class, of the interest of the laboring people, of the interest of the victory of socialism and communism. We cannot say that these were the deeds of a giddy despot. He considered that this should be done in the interest of the party; of the working masses, in the name of the defense of the revolution's gains. In this lies the whole tragedy! . . .

We should in all seriousness consider the question of the cult of the individual. We cannot let this matter get out of the party, especially not to the press. It is for this reason that we are considering it here at a closed Congress session. We should know the limits; we should not give ammunition to the enemy; we should not wash our dirty linen before their eyes. I think that the delegates to the Congress will understand and assess properly all these proposals. (Tumultuous applause.)

Comrades: We must abolish the cult of the individual decisively, once and for all; we must draw the proper conclusions concerning both ideological-theoretical and practical work. It is necessary for this purpose:

First, in a Bolshevik manner to condemn and to eradicate the cult of the individual as alien to Marxism-Leninism and not consonant with the principles of party leadership and the norms of party life, and to fight inexorably all attempts at bringing back this practice in one form or another.

To return to and actually practice in all our ideological work the most important theses of Marxist-Leninist science about the people as the creator of history and as the creator of all material and spiritual good of humanity, about the decisive role of the Marxist party in the revolutionary fight for the transformation of society, about the victory of communism.

In this connection we will be forced to do much work in order to examine critically from the Marxist-Leninist viewpoint and to correct the widely spread erroneous views connected with the cult of the individual in the sphere of history, philosophy, economy and of other sciences, as well as in literature and the fine arts. It is especially necessary that in the immediate future we compile a serious textbook of the history of our party which will be edited in accordance with scientific Marxist objectivism, a textbook of the history of Soviet society, a book pertaining to the events of the civil war and the Great Patriotic War.

Secondly, to continue systematically and consistently the work done by the party's Central Committee during the last years, a work characterized by minute observation in all party organizations, from the bottom to the top, of the Leninist principles of party leadership, characterized, above all, by the main principle of collective leadership, characterized by the observation of the norms of party life described in the statutes of our party, and finally, characterized by the wide practice of criticism and self-criticism.

Thirdly, to restore completely the Leninist principles of Soviet socialist democracy, expressed in the Constitution of the Soviet Union, to fight willfulness of individuals abusing their power. The evil caused by acts violating revolutionary socialist legality which have accumulated during a long time as a result of the negative influence of the cult of the individual has to be completely corrected.

Comrades! The 20th Congress of the Communist Party of the Soviet Union has manifested with a new strength the unshakable unity of our party, its cohesiveness around the Central Committee, its resolute will to accomplish the great task of building communism. (Tumultuous applause.)

And the fact that we present in all their ramifications the basic problems of overcoming the cult of the individual which is alien to Marxism-Leninism, as well as the problem of liquidating its burdensome consequences, is an evidence of the great moral and political strength of our party. (Prolonged applause.)

We are absolutely certain that our party, armed with the historical resolutions of the 20th Congress, will lead the Soviet people along the Leninist path to new successes, to new victories. (Tumultuous, prolonged applause.)

Long live the victorious banner of our party — Leninism! (Tumultuous, prolonged applause ending in ovation. All rise.)

'KITCHEN DEBATE' OF NIXON AND KHRUSHCHEV

Following are excerpts from an exchange between Vice President Richard M. Nixon and Soviet premier Nikita Khrushchev at a U.S. trade exhibition in Moscow, July 24, 1959, as published in The Challenges We Face, *edited and compiled from the speeches and papers of Richard M. Nixon (New York: McGraw-Hill, 1980):*

Khrushchev: "Americans have lost their ability to trade. Now you have grown older and you don't trade the way you used to. You need to be invigorated."

Nixon: "You need to have goods to trade."

Nixon: "There must be a free exchange of ideas.". . .

Khrushchev: "We want to live in peace and friendship with Americans because we are the two most powerful countries, and if we live in friendship, then other countries will also live in friendship. But if there is a country that is too war-minded we could pull its ears a little and say, 'Don't you dare; fighting is not allowed now.' This is a period of atomic armament; some foolish one could start a war and then even a wise one couldn't finish the war. Therefore, we are governed by this idea in our policy, internal and foreign. How long has America existed? Three hundred years?"

Nixon: "More than one hundred and fifty years."

Khrushchev: "More than one hundred and fifty years? Well, then, we will say America has been in existence for 150 years and this is the level she has reached. We have existed not quite forty-two years and in another seven years we will be on the same level as America.

"When we catch you up, in passing you by, we will wave to you. Then if you wish we can stop and say: Please follow up. Plainly speaking, if you want capitalism you can live that way. That is your own affair and doesn't concern us. We can still feel sorry for you, but since you don't understand us, live as you do understand.

"We are all glad to be here at the Exhibition with Vice President Nixon. I personally, and on behalf of my colleagues, express my thanks for the President's message. I have not as yet read it but I know beforehand that it contains good wishes. I think you will be satisfied with your visit and if — I cannot go on without saying it — if you would not take such a position [captive nations resolution passed by Congress July 17] which has not been thought out thoroughly, as was approved by Congress, your trip would be excellent. But you have churned the water yourself — why this was necessary God only knows.

"What happened? What black cat crossed your path and confused you? But that is your affair; we do not interfere with your problems." (Wrapping his arms about a Soviet workman.) "Does this man look like a slave laborer?" (Waving at others.) "With men with such spirit how can we lose?"

Nixon (pointing to American workmen): "With men like that we are strong. But these men, Soviet and American, work together well for peace, even as they have worked together in building this Exhibition. This is the way it should be.

"Your remarks are in the tradition of what we have come to expect — sweeping and extemporaneous. Later on we will both have an opportunity to speak, and consequently I will not comment on the various points that you raised, except to say this — this color television is one of the most advanced developments in communication that we have.

"I can say that if this competition in which you plan to outstrip us is to do the best for both of our peoples and for peoples everywhere, there must be a free exchange of ideas. After all, you don't know everything. . . ."

Khrushchev: "If I don't know everything, you don't know anything about communism except fear of it."

Nixon: "There are some instances where you may be ahead of us; for example, in the development of the thrust of your rockets for the investigation of outer space; there may be some instances in which we are ahead of you — in color television, for instance."

'We Have Bested You'

Khrushchev: "No, we are up with you on this too. We have bested you in one technique and also in the other."

Nixon: "You see, you never concede anything."

Khrushchev: "I do not give up."

Nixon: "Wait till you see the picture. Let's have far more communication and exchange in this very area that we speak of. We should hear you more on our television. You should hear us more on yours."

Khrushchev: "That's a good idea. Let's do it like this. You appear before our people. We will appear before your people. People will see and appreciate this."

Nixon: "There is not a day in the United States when we cannot read what you say. When [Soviet First Deputy Premier Frol R.] Kozlov was speaking in California about peace, you were talking here in somewhat different terms. This was reported extensively in the American press. Never make a statement here if you don't want it to be read in the United States. I can promise you every word you say will be translated into English."

Khrushchev: "I doubt it. I want you to give your word that this speech of mine will be heard by the American people."

Nixon (shaking hands on it): "By the same token, everything I say will be translated and heard all over the Soviet Union?"

Khrushchev: "That's agreed."

Nixon: "You must not be afraid of ideas."

Khrushchev: "We are telling you not to be afraid of ideas. We have no reason to be afraid. We have already broken free from such a situation."

Nixon: "Well, then, let's have more exchange of them. We are all agreed on that. All right? All right?"

Khrushchev: "Fine." (Aside.) "Agreed to what? All right, I am in agreement. But I want to stress what I am in agreement with. I know that I am dealing with a very good lawyer. I also want to uphold my own miner's flag so that the coal miners can say, 'Our man does not concede.' "

Nixon: "No question about that."

Khrushchev: "You are a lawyer for capitalism and I am a lawyer for communism. Let's compete."

Nixon: "The way you dominate the conversation you would make a good lawyer yourself. If you were in the United States Senate you would be accused of filibustering."

Khrushchev: "If your reporters will check on the time, they will see who has talked more."

'You Do All the Talking'

Nixon: "You do all the talking and do not let anyone else talk."

Khrushchev (referring to American model home): "You think the Russian people will be dumbfounded to see this? But I tell you all our modern homes have equipment of this sort, and to get a flat you have only to be a Soviet visitor, not a citizen."

Nixon: "We do not claim to astonish the Russian people. We hope to show our diversity and our right to choose. We do not wish to have decisions made at the top by government officials who say that all homes should be built in the same way. Would it not be better to compete in the relative merits of washing machines than in the strength of rockets? Is this the kind of competition you want?"

Khrushchev: "Yes, that's the kind of competition we want, but your generals say we must compete in rockets. Your generals say they are so powerful they can destroy us. We can also show you something so that you will know the Russian spirit. We are strong; we can beat you. But in this respect we can also show you something."

Nixon: "To me you are strong and we are strong. In some ways, you are stronger than we are. In others, we are stronger, but to me it seems that in this day and age to argue who is the stronger completely misses the point. We are both strong, not only from the standpoint of weapons but also from the standpoint of will and spirit.

"No one should ever use his strength to put another in the position where he in effect has an ultimatum. For us to argue who is the stronger misses the point. If war comes we both lose."

Khrushchev: "For the fourth time I have to say I cannot recognize my friend Mr. Nixon. If all Americans agree with you, then who don't we agree [with]? This is what we want."

Nixon: "Anyone who believes the American government does not reflect the people is not an accurate observer of the American scene. I hope the Prime Minister understands all the implications of what I have just said. When you place either one of the powerful nations or any other nations in a position so that they have no choice but to accept dictation or fight, then you are playing with the most destructive thing in the world.

"This is very important in the present world context. It is very dangerous. When we sit down at a conference table it cannot all be one way. One side cannot put an ultimatum to another. It is impossible. But I shall talk to you about this later."

Khrushchev: "Who is raising an ultimatum?"

Nixon: "We will discuss that later."

Khrushchev: "If you have raised the question, why not go on with it now while the people are listening? We know something about politics, too. Let your correspondents compare watches and see who is filibustering. You put great emphasis on *diktat* [dictation]. Our country has never been guided by *diktat*. *Diktat* is a foolish policy."

Nixon: "I am talking about it in the international sense."

No Threats

Khrushchev: "It sounds to me like a threat. We, too, are giants. You want to threaten — we will answer threats with threats."

Nixon: "That's not my point. We will never engage in threats."

Khrushchev: "You wanted indirectly to threaten me. But we have the means to threaten too."

Nixon: "Who wants to threaten?"

Khrushchev: "You are talking about implications. I have not been. We have the means at our disposal. Ours are better than yours. It is you who want to compete. *Da, da, da.*"

Nixon: "We are well aware that you have the means. To me who is best is not material."

Khrushchev: "You raised the point. We want peace and friendship with all nations, especially with America."

Nixon: "We want peace, too, and I believe that you do also."

Khrushchev: "Yes, I believe that."

Nixon: "I see that you want to build a good life. But I don't think that the cause of peace is helped by reminders that you have greater strength than we do, because this is a threat, too."

Khrushchev: "I was answering your words. You challenged me. Let's argue fairly."

Nixon: "My point was that in today's world it is immaterial which of the two great countries at any particular moment has the advantage. In war, these advantages are illusory. Can we agree on that?"

Khrushchev: "Not quite. Let's not beat around the bush."

Nixon: "I like the way he talks."

Khrushchev: "We want to liquidate all bases from foreign lands. Until that happens we will speak different languages. One who is for putting an end to bases on foreign lands is for peace. One who is against it is for war. We have liquidated our bases, reduced our forces, and offered to make a peace treaty and eliminate the point of friction in Berlin. Until we settle that question, we will talk different languages."

Nixon: "Do you think it can be settled at Geneva?"

Khrushchev: "If we considered it otherwise, we would not have incurred the expense of sending our Foreign Minister to Geneva. [Andrei] Gromyko is not an idler. He is a very good man."

Nixon: "We have great respect for Mr. Gromyko. Some people say he looks like me. I think he is better-looking. I hope it [the Geneva Conference] will be successful."

Khrushchev: "It does not depend on us."

Nixon: "It takes two to make an agreement. You cannot have it all your own way."

Khrushchev: "These are questions that have the same aim. To put an end to the vestiges of war, to make a peace treaty with Germany — that is what we want. It is very bad that we quarrel over the question of war and peace."

Nixon: "There is no question but that your people and you want the government of the United States to be for peace — anyone who thinks that our government is not for peace is not an accurate observer of America. In order to have peace, Mr. Prime Minister, even in an argument between friends, there must be sitting-down around a table. There must be discussion. Each side must find areas where it looks at the other's point of view. The world looks to you today with regard to Geneva. I believe it would be a grave mistake and a blow to peace if it were allowed to fail."

Khrushchev: "This is our understanding as well."

Nixon: "So this is something. The present position is stalemate. Ways must be found to discuss it."

Khrushchev: "The two sides must seek ways of agreement."

KENNEDY, KHRUSHCHEV ON CUBAN MISSILE CRISIS

Following are the texts of President Kennedy's October 22, 1962, television address about Soviet offensive missiles in Cuba and Kennedy's October 27 message to Soviet premier Nikita Khrushchev, and excerpts from Khrushchev's October 27 and October 28 messages to Kennedy and Kennedy's October 28 reply.

Kennedy Speech October 22

Good evening, my fellow citizens:

This Government, as promised, has maintained the closest surveillance of the Soviet military buildup on the island of Cuba. Within the past week, unmistakable evidence has established the fact that a series of offensive missile sites is now in preparation on that imprisoned island. The purpose of these bases can be none other than to provide a nuclear strike capability against the Western Hemisphere.

Upon receiving the first preliminary hard information of this nature last Tuesday morning at 9 a.m., I directed that our surveillance be stepped up. And having now confirmed and completed our evaluation of the evidence and our decision on a course of action, this Government feels obliged to report this new crisis to you in fullest detail.

The characteristics of these new missile sites indicate two distinct types of installations. Several of them include medium range ballistic missiles, capable of carrying a nuclear warhead for a distance of more than 1,000 nautical miles. Each of these missiles, in short, is capable of striking Washington, D.C., the Panama Canal, Cape Canaveral, Mexico City, or any other city in the southeastern part of the United States, in Central America, or in the Caribbean area.

Additional sites not yet completed appear to be designed for intermediate range ballistic missiles — capable of traveling more than twice as far — and thus capable of striking most of the major cities in the Western Hemisphere, ranging as far north as Hudson Bay, Canada, and as far south as Lima, Peru. In addition, jet bombers, capable of carrying nuclear weapons, are now being uncrated and assembled in Cuba, while the necessary air bases are being prepared.

This urgent transformation of Cuba into an important strategic base — by the presence of these large, long-range, and clearly offensive weapons of sudden mass destruction — constitutes an explicit threat to the peace and security of all the Americas, in flagrant and deliberate defiance of the Rio Pact of 1947, the traditions of this Nation and hemisphere, the joint resolution of the 87th Congress, the Charter of the United Nations, and my own public warnings to the Soviets on September 4 and 13. This action also contradicts the repeated assurances of Soviet spokesmen, both publicly and privately delivered, that the arms buildup in Cuba would retain its original defensive character, and that the Soviet Union had no need or desire to station strategic missiles on the territory of any other nation.

The size of this undertaking makes clear that it has been planned for some months. Yet only last month, after I had made clear the distinction between any introduction of ground-to-ground missiles and the existence of defensive antiaircraft missiles, the Soviet Government publicly stated on September 11 that, and I quote, "the armaments and military equipment sent to Cuba are designed exclusively for defensive purposes," that, and I quote the Soviet Government, "there is no need for the Soviet Government to shift its weapons . . . for a retaliatory blow to any other country, for instance Cuba," and that, and I quote their government, "the Soviet Union has so powerful rockets to carry these nuclear warheads that there is no need to search for sites for them beyond the boundaries of the Soviet Union." That statement was false.

Only last Thursday, as evidence of this rapid offensive buildup was already in my hand, Soviet Foreign Minister Gromyko told me in my office that he was instructed to make it clear once again, as he said his government had already done, that Soviet assistance to Cuba, and I quote, "pursued solely the purpose of contributing to the defense capabilities of Cuba," that, and I quote him, "training by Soviet specialists of Cuban nationals in handling defensive armaments was by no means offensive, and if it were otherwise," Mr. Gromyko went on, "the Soviet Government would never become involved in rendering such assistance." That statement also was false.

Neither the United States of America nor the world community of nations can tolerate deliberate deception and offensive threats on the part of any nation, large or small. We no longer live in a world where only the actual firing of weapons represents a sufficient challenge to a nation's security to constitute maximum peril. Nuclear weapons are so destructive and ballistic missiles are so swift, that any substantially increased possibility of their use or any sudden change in their deployment may well be regarded as a definite threat to peace.

For many years, both the Soviet Union and the United States, recognizing this fact, have deployed strategic nuclear weapons with great care, never upsetting the precarious status quo which insured that these weapons would not be used in the absence of some vital challenge. Our own strategic missiles have never been transferred to the territory of any other nation under a cloak of secrecy and deception; and our history — unlike that of the Soviets since the end of world War II — demonstrates that we have no desire to dominate or conquer any other nation or impose our system upon its people. Nevertheless, American citizens have become adjusted to living daily on the bull's-eye of Soviet missiles located inside the U.S.S.R. or in submarines.

In that sense, missiles in Cuba add to an already clear and present danger — although it should be noted the nations of Latin America have never previously been subjected to a potential nuclear threat.

But this secret, swift, and extraordinary buildup of Communist missiles — in an area well known to have a special and historical relationship to the United States and the nations of the Western Hemisphere, in violation of Soviet assurances, and in defiance of American and hemispheric policy — this sudden, clandestine decision to station strategic weapons for the first time outside of Soviet soil — is a deliberately provocative and unjustified change in the status quo which cannot be accepted by this country, if our courage and our commitments are ever to be trusted again by either friend or foe.

The 1930's taught us a clear lesson: aggressive conduct, if allowed to go unchecked and unchallenged, ultimately leads to war. This nation is opposed to war. We are also true to our word.

Our unswerving objective, therefore, must be to prevent the use of these missiles against this or any other country, and to secure their withdrawal or elimination from the Western Hemisphere.

Our policy has been one of patience and restraint, as befits a peaceful and powerful nation, which leads a worldwide alliance. We have been determined not to be diverted from our central concerns by mere irritants and fanatics. But now further action is required — and it is under way; and these actions may only be the beginning. We will not prematurely or unnecessarily risk the costs of worldwide nuclear war in which even the fruits of victory would be ashes in our mouth — but neither will we shrink from that risk at any time it must be faced.

Acting, therefore, in the defense of our own security and of the entire Western Hemisphere, and under the authority entrusted to me by the Constitution as endorsed by the resolution of the Congress, I have directed that the following *initial* steps be taken immediately:

First: To halt this offensive buildup, a strict quarantine on all offensive military equipment under shipment to Cuba is being initiated. All ships of any kind bound for Cuba from whatever nation or port will, if found to contain cargoes of offensive weapons, be turned back. This quarantine will be extended, if needed, to other types of cargo and carriers. We are not at this time, however, denying the necessities of life as the Soviets attempted to do in their Berlin blockade of 1948.

Second: I have directed the continued and increased close surveillance of Cuba and its military buildup. The foreign ministers of the OAS [Organization of American States], in their communique of October 6, rejected secrecy on such matters in this hemisphere. Should these offensive military preparations continue, thus increasing the threat to the hemisphere, further action will be justified. I have directed the Armed Forces to prepare for any eventualities; and I trust that in the interest of both the Cuban people and the Soviet technicians at the sites, the hazards to all concerned of continuing this threat will be recognized.

Third: It shall be the policy of this Nation to regard any nuclear missile launched from Cuba against any nation in the Western Hemisphere as an attack by the Soviet Union on the United States, requiring a full retaliatory response upon the Soviet Union.

Fourth: As a necessary military precaution, I have reinforced our base at Guantanamo, evacuated today the dependents of our personnel there, and ordered additional military units to be on a standby alert basis.

Fifth: We are calling tonight for an immediate meeting of the Organ of Consultation under the Organization of American States, to consider this threat to hemispheric security and to invoke articles 6 and 8 of the Rio Treaty in support of all necessary action. The United Nations Charter allows for regional security arrangements — and the nations of this hemisphere decided long ago against the military presence of outside powers. Our other allies around the world have also been alerted.

Sixth: Under the Charter of the United Nations, we are asking tonight that an emergency meeting of the Security Council be convoked without delay to take action against this latest Soviet threat to world peace. Our resolution will call for prompt dismantling and withdrawal of all offensive weapons in Cuba, under the supervision of U.N. observers, before the quarantine can be lifted.

Seventh and finally: I call upon Chairman Khrushchev to halt and eliminate this clandestine, reckless, and provocative threat to world peace and to stable relations between our two nations. I call upon him further to abandon this course of world domination, and to join in an historic effort to end the perilous arms race and to transform the history of man. He has an opportunity now to move the world back from the abyss of destruction — by returning to his government's own words that it had no need to station missiles outside its own territory, and withdrawing these weapons from Cuba — by refraining from any action which will widen or deepen the present crisis — and then by participating in a search for peaceful and permanent solutions.

This Nation is prepared to present its case against the Soviet threat to peace, and our own proposals for a peaceful world, at any time and in any forum — in the OAS, in the United Nations, or in any other meeting that could be useful — without limiting our freedom of action. We have in the past made strenuous efforts to limit the spread of nuclear weapons. We have proposed the elimination of all arms and military bases in a fair and effective disarmament treaty. We are prepared to discuss new proposals for the removal of tensions on both sides — including the possibilities of a genuinely independent Cuba, free to determine its own destiny. We have no wish to war with the Soviet Union — for we are a peaceful people who desire to live in peace with all other peoples.

'An Atmosphere of Intimidation'

But it is difficult to settle or even discuss these problems in an atmosphere of intimidation. That is why this latest Soviet threat — or any other threat which is made either independently or in response to our actions this week — must and will be met with determination. Any hostile move anywhere in the world against the safety and freedom of peoples to whom we are committed — including in particular the brave people of West Berlin — will be met by whatever action is needed.

Finally, I want to say a few words to the captive people of Cuba, to whom this speech is being directly carried by special radio facilities. I speak to you as a friend, as one who knows of your deep attachment to your fatherland, as one who shares your aspirations for liberty and justice for all. And I have watched and the American people have watched with deep sorrow how your nationalist revolution was betrayed — and how your fatherland fell under foreign domination. Now your leaders are no longer Cuban leaders inspired by Cuban ideals. They are puppets and agents of an international conspiracy which has turned Cuba against your friends and neighbors in the Americas — and turned it into the first Latin American country to become a target for nuclear war — the first Latin American country to have these weapons on its soil.

These new weapons are not in your interest. They contribute nothing to your peace and well-being. They can only undermine it. But this country has no wish to cause you to suffer or to impose any system upon you. We know that your lives and land are being used as pawns by those who deny your freedom.

Many times in the past, the Cuban people have risen to throw out tyrants who destroyed their liberty. And I have no doubt that most Cubans today look forward to the time when they will be truly free — free from foreign domination, free to choose their own leaders, free to select their own system, free to own their own land, free to speak and write and worship without fear or degradation. And then shall Cuba be welcomed back to the society of free nations and to the associations of this hemisphere.

My fellow citizens: let no one doubt that this is a difficult and dangerous effort on which we have set out. No one can foresee precisely what course it will take or what costs or casualties will be incurred. Many months of sacrifice and self-discipline lie ahead — months in which both our patience and our will will be tested — months in which many threats and denunciations will keep us aware of our dangers. But the greatest danger of all would be to do nothing.

The path we have chosen for the present is full of hazards, as all paths are — but it is the one most consistent with our character and courage as a nation and our commitments around the world. The cost of freedom is always high — but Americans have always paid it. And one path we shall never choose, and that is the path of surrender or submission.

Our goal is not the victory of might, but the vindication of right — not peace at the expense of freedom, but both peace *and* freedom, here in this hemisphere, and, we hope, around the world. God willing, that goal will be achieved.

Thank you and good night.

Khrushchev's October 27 Message

...I understand your concern for the security of the United States, Mr. President, because this is the first duty of the president. However, these questions are also uppermost in our minds. The same duties rest with me as chairman of the USSR Council of Ministers. You have been worried over our assisting Cuba with arms designed to strengthen its defensive potential — precisely defensive potential — because Cuba, no matter what weapons it had, could not compare with you since these are different dimensions, the more so given up-to-date means of extermination.

Our purpose has been and is to help Cuba, and no one can challenge the humanity of our motives aimed at allowing Cuba to live peacefully and develop as its people desire. You want to relieve your country from danger and this is understandable. However, Cuba also wants this. All countries want to relieve themselves from danger. But how can we, the Soviet Union and our government, assess your actions which, in effect, mean that you have surrounded the Soviet Union with military bases, surrounded our allies with military bases, set up military bases literally around our country, and stationed your rocket weapons at them? This is no secret. High-placed American officials demonstratively declare this. Your rockets are stationed in Britain and in Italy and pointed at us. Your rockets are stationed in Turkey.

You are worried over Cuba. You say that it worries you because it lies at a distance of 90 miles across the sea from the shores of the United States. However, Turkey lies next to us. Our sentinels are pacing up and down and watching each other. Do you believe that you have the right to demand security for your country and the removal of such weapons that you qualify as offensive, while not recognizing this right for us?

You have stationed devastating rocket weapons, which you call offensive, in Turkey literally right next to us. How then does recognition of our equal military possibilities tally with such unequal relations between our great states? This does not tally at all.

It is good, Mr. President, that you agreed for our representatives to meet and begin talks, apparently with the participation of U.N. Acting Secretary General U Thant. Consequently, to some extent, he assumes the role of intermediary, and we believe that he can cope with the responsible mission if, of course, every side that is drawn into this conflict shows good will.

I think that one could rapidly eliminate the conflict and normalize the situation. Then people would heave a sigh of relief, considering that the statesmen who bear the responsibility have sober minds, an awareness of their responsibility, and an ability to solve complicated problems and not allow matters to slide to the disaster of war.

This is why I make this proposal: We agree to remove those weapons from Cuba which you regard as offensive weapons. We agree to do this and to state this commitment to the United Nations. Your representatives will make a statement to the effect that the United States, on its part, bearing in mind the anxiety and concern of the Soviet state, will evacuate its analogous weapons from Turkey. Let us reach an understanding on what time you and we need to put this into effect.

After this, representatives of the U.N. Security Council could control on-the-spot the fulfillment of these commitments. Of course, it is necessary that the Governments of Cuba and Turkey would allow these representatives to come to their countries and check fulfillment of this commitment, which each side undertakes. Apparently, it would be better if these representatives enjoyed the trust of the Security Council and ours — the United States and the Soviet Union — as well as of Turkey and Cuba. I think that it will not be difficult to find such people who enjoy the trust and respect of all interested sides.

We, having assumed this commitment in order to give satisfaction and hope to the peoples of Cuba and Turkey and to increase their confidence in their security, will make a statement in the Security Council to the effect that the Soviet Government gives a solemn pledge to respect the integrity of the frontiers and the sovereignty of Turkey, not to intervene in its domestic affairs, not to invade Turkey, not to make available its territory as a place d'armes for such invasion, and also will restrain those who would think of launching an aggression against Turkey either from Soviet territory or from the territory of other states bordering on Turkey.

The U.S. Government will make the same statement in the Security Council with regard to Cuba. It will declare that the United States will respect the integrity of the frontiers of Cuba, its sovereignty, undertakes not to intervene in its domestic affairs, not to invade and not to make its territory available as place d'armes for the invasion of Cuba, and also will restrain those who would think of launching an aggression against Cuba either from U.S. territory or from the territory of other places bordering on Cuba.

Of course, for this we would have to reach agreement with you and to arrange for some deadline. Let us agree to give some time, but not to delay, two or three weeks, not more than a month.

The weapons on Cuba, that you have mentioned and which, as you say, alarm you, are in the hands of Soviet officers. Therefore any accidental use of them whatsoever to the detriment of the United States of America is excluded. These means are stationed in Cuba at the request of the Cuban Government and only in defensive aims. Therefore, if there is no invasion of Cuba, or an attack on the Soviet Union, or other of our allies then, of course, these means do not threaten anyone and will not threaten. For they do not pursue offensive aims.

If you accept my proposal, Mr. President, we would send our representatives to New York, to the United Nations, and would give them exhaustive instructions in order to come to terms sooner. If you would also appoint your men and give them appropriate instructions, this problem could be solved soon.

Why would I like to achieve this? Because the entire world is now agitated and expects reasonable actions from us. The greatest pleasure for all the peoples would be an announcement on our agreement, on nipping in the bud the conflict that has arisen. I attach a great importance to such understanding because it might be a good beginning and, specifically, facilitate a nuclear test ban agreement. The problem of tests could be solved simultaneously, not linking one with the other, because they are different problems. However, it is important to reach an understanding to both these problems in order to make a good gift to the people, to let them rejoice in the news that a nuclear test ban agreement has also been reached and thus there will be no further contamination of the atmosphere. Your and our positions on this issue are very close.

All this, possibly, would serve as a good impetus to searching for mutually acceptable agreements on other disputed issues, too, on which there is an exchange of opinion between us. These problems have not yet been solved but they wait for an urgent solution which would clear the international atmosphere. We are ready for this.

These are my proposals, Mr. President.

Respectfully yours,

Nikita Khrushchev
October 27, 1962

Kennedy's October 27 Response

Dear Mr. Chairman:

I have read your letter of October 26th [not made public] with great care and welcomed the statement of your desire to seek a prompt solution to the problem. The first thing that needs to be done, however, is for work to cease on offensive missile bases in Cuba and for all weapons systems in Cuba capable of offensive use to be rendered inoperable, under effective United Nations arrangements.

Assuming this is done promptly, I have given my representatives in New York instructions that will permit them to work out this weekend — in cooperation with the Acting Secretary General and your representative — an arrangement for a permanent solution to the Cuban problem along the lines suggested in your letter of October 26th. As I read your letter, the key elements of your proposals — which seem generally acceptable as I understand them — are as follows:

1. You would agree to remove these weapons systems from Cuba under appropriate United Nations observation and supervision; and undertake, with suitable safeguards, to halt the further introduction of such weapons systems into Cuba.

2. We, on our part, would agree — upon the establishment of adequate arrangements through the United Nations to ensure the carrying out and continuation of these commitments — (a) to remove promptly the quarantine measures now in effect and (b) to give assurances against an invasion of Cuba. I am confident that other nations of the Western Hemisphere would be prepared to do likewise.

If you will give your representative similar instructions, there is no reason why we should not be able to complete these arrangements and announce them to the world within a couple of days. The effect of such a settlement on easing world tensions would enable us to work toward a more general arrangement regarding "other armaments," as proposed in your second letter which you made public. I would like to say again that the United States is very much interested in reducing tensions and halting the arms race; and if your letter signifies that you are prepared to discuss a detente affecting NATO and the Warsaw Pact, we are quite prepared to consider with our allies any useful proposals.

But the first ingredient, let me emphasize, is the cessation of work on missile sites in Cuba and measures to render such weapons inoperable, under effective international guarantees. The continuation of this threat, or a prolonging of this discussion concerning Cuba by linking these problems to the broader questions of European and world security, would surely lead to an intensification of the Cuban crisis and a grave risk to the peace of the world. For this reason I hope we can quickly agree along the lines outlined in this letter and in your letter of October 26th.

John F. Kennedy

Khrushchev's October 28 Message

Dear Mr. President: I have received your message of 27 October. I express my satisfaction and thank you for the sense of proportion you have displayed and for realization of the responsibility which now devolves on you for the preservation of the peace of the world. . . .

In order to eliminate as rapidly as possible the conflict which endangers the cause of peace, to give an assurance to all people who crave peace, and to reassure the American people, who, I am certain, also want peace, as do the people of the Soviet Union, the Soviet Government, in addition to earlier instructions on the discontinuation of further work on weapons construction sites, has given a new order to dismantle the arms which you described as offensive, and to crate and return them to the Soviet Union.

Mr. President, I should like to repeat what I had already written to you in my earlier messages — that the Soviet Government has given economic assistance to the Republic of Cuba, as well as arms, because Cuba and the Cuban people were constantly under the continuous threat of an invasion of Cuba. . . .

The Cuban people want to build their life in their own interests without external interference. This is their right, and they cannot be blamed for wanting to be masters of their own country and disposing of the fruits of their own labor. The threat of invasion of Cuba and all other schemes for creating tension over China are designed to strike the Cuban people with a sense of insecurity, intimidate them, and prevent them from peacefully building their new life.

Mr. President, I should like to say clearly once more that we could not remain indifferent to this. The Soviet Government decided to render assistance to Cuba with means of defense against aggression — only with means for defense purposes. We have supplied the defense means which you describe as offensive means. We have supplied them to prevent an attack on Cuba — to prevent rash acts.

I regard with respect and trust the statement you made in your message of 27 October 1962 that there would be no attack, no invasion of Cuba, and not only on the part of the United States, but also on the part of other nations of the Western Hemisphere, as you said in your same message. Then the motives which induced us to render assistance of such a kind to Cuba disappear.

It is for this reason that we instructed our officers — these means as I had already informed you earlier are in the hands of the Soviet officers — to take appropriate measures to discontinue construction of the aforementioned facilities, to dismantle them, and to return them to the Soviet Union. As I had informed you in the letter of 27 October, we are prepared to reach agreement to enable U.N. representatives to verify the dismantling of these means. Thus in view of the assurances you have given and our instructions on dismantling, there is every condition for eliminating the present conflict. . . .

In conclusion, I should like to say something about a detente between NATO and the Warsaw Treaty countries that you have mentioned. We have spoken about this long since and are prepared to continue to exchange views on this question with you and to find a reasonable solution.

We should like to continue the exchange of views on the prohibition of atomic and thermonuclear weapons, general disarmament, and other problems relating to the relaxation of international tension. . . .

We are confident that the people of all countries, like you, Mr. President, will understand me correctly. We are not threatening. We want nothing but peace. Our country is now on the upsurge. Our people are enjoying the fruits of their peaceful labor. They have achieved tremendous successes since the October Revolution, and created the greatest material, spiritual, and cultural values. Our people are enjoying these values; they want to continue developing their achievements and insure their further development on the way of peace and social progress by their persistent labor.

I should like to remind you, Mr. President, that military reconnaissance planes have violated the borders of the Soviet Union. . . .

[O]n 28 October, . . . one of your reconnaissance planes intruded over Soviet borders in the Chukotka Peninsula area in the north and flew over our territory. The question is, Mr. President: How should we regard this? What is this, a provocation? One of your planes violates our frontier during this anxious time we are both experiencing, when everything has been put into combat readiness. Is it not a fact that an intruding American plane could be easily taken for a nuclear bomber, which might push us to a fateful step; and all the more so since the U.S. Government and Pentagon long ago declared that you are maintaining a continuous nuclear bomber patrol?

Therefore, you can imagine the responsibility you are assuming; especially now, when we are living through such anxious times. I should also like to express the following wish; it concerns the Cuban people. You do not have diplomatic relations. But through my officers in Cuba, I have reports that American planes are making flights over Cuba.

We are interested that there should be no war in the world, and that the Cuban people should live in peace. And besides, Mr. President, it is no secret that we have our people on Cuba. Under a treaty with the Cuban Government we have sent there officers, instructors, mostly plain people: specialists, agronomists, zootechnicians, irrigators, land reclamation specialists, plain workers, tractor drivers, and others. We are concerned about them.

I should like you to consider, Mr. President, that violation of Cuban airspace by American planes could also lead to dangerous consequences. And if you do not want this to happen, it would be better if no cause is given for a dangerous situation to arise. We must be careful now and refrain from any steps which would not be useful to the defense of the states involved in the conflict, which could only cause irritation and even serve as a provocation for a fateful step. Therefore, we must display sanity, reason, and refrain from such steps.

We value peace perhaps even more than other peoples because we went through a terrible war with Hitler. But our people will not falter in the face of any test. Our people trust their government, and we assure our people and world public opinion that the Soviet Government will not allow itself to be provoked. But if the provocateurs unleash a war, they will not evade responsibility and the grave consequences a war would bring upon them. But we are confident that reason will triumph, that war will not be unleashed, and peace and the security of the peoples will be insured. . . .

N. Khrushchev
28 October 1962

Kennedy's October 28 Reply

. . .I consider my letter to you of October twenty-seventh and your reply of today as firm undertakings on the part of both our governments which should be promptly carried out. I hope that the necessary measures can at once be taken through the United Nations, as your message says, so that the United States in turn will be able to remove the quarantine measures now in effect. I have already made arrangements to report all these matters to the Organization of American States, whose members share a deep interest in a genuine peace in the Caribbean area.

You referred in your letter to a violation of your frontier by an American aircraft in the area of the Chukotskiy Peninsula. I have learned that this plane, without arms or photographic equipment, was engaged in an air sampling mission in connection with your nuclear tests. . . . I regret this incident and will see to it that every precaution is taken to prevent recurrence.

Mr. Chairman, both of our countries have great unfinished tasks and I know that your people as well as those of the United States can ask for nothing better than to pursue them free from the fear of war. Modern science and technology have given us the possibility of making labor fruitful beyond anything that could have been dreamed of a few decades ago.

I agree with you that we must devote urgent attention to the problem of disarmament, as it relates to the whole world and also to critical areas. Perhaps now, as we step back from danger, we can together make real progress in this vital field. I think we should give priority to questions relating to the proliferation of nuclear weapons, on earth and in outer space, and to the great effort for a nuclear test ban. But we should also work hard to see if wider measures of disarmament can be agreed and put into operation at an early date. The United States Government will be prepared to discuss these questions urgently, and in a constructive spirit, at Geneva or elsewhere.

John F. Kennedy

SOVIET COMMUNISTS ON SPLIT WITH CHINA

Following are excerpts from the Soviet letter to other Communist parties concerning the Sino-Soviet split, as published by the German newspaper Die Welt *on March 22, 1966:*

The Central Committee of the Communist Party of the Soviet Union [CPSU] deems it necessary to inform you of our position on the new steps taken by the Chinese Communist Party [CCP] that are aimed at strengthening the divisive line in the Socialist community and in the Communist world movement, as well as of the conclusion we draw from these facts. . . .

The CCP leaders are revising the most important guiding principles of Marxist-Leninism. Their line contrasts with the joint course of the international Communist movement in such extremely important questions as war, peace and revolution; the scientific principles and methods of building socialism and communism; the course of development of the young national states; and the principles of international solidarity of the Socialist countries and of the Communist parties. . . .

Since the plenum of October 1964 [which ousted Nikita Khrushchev], the CPSU Central Committee has done everything possible to normalize relations with the CCP and to insure unity of action in the struggle against the common imperialist enemy despite existing differences of view. . . .

In endeavoring to create a favorable political atmosphere, the CPSU Central Committee has unilaterally discontinued open polemics. . . . In early February 1965 the Soviet delegation headed by Comrade A. N. Kosygin . . . made use of a stay in Peking en route to the Democratic Republic of Vietnam [North Vietnam] and the Democratic People's Republic of Korea [North Korea] to establish new contacts with the Chinese leaders. . . .

We submitted an extensive program for normalizing Chinese-Soviet relations at both the party and the state level. This program included proposals on implementing bilateral meetings of delegations of the CPSU and the CCP on the highest level, on the mutual discontinuation of polemics, concrete proposals on extending Chinese-Soviet trade and scientific, technical and cultural cooperation, and on coordinating the foreign policy activities of the CPR [Chinese People's Republic] and the USSR.

Our efforts, however, both failed to meet with understanding and met with obstinate resistance from the Chinese leaders. The CCP Central Committee completely ignored the proposal on a bilateral meeting on the highest level. The CCP leadership failed to accede to an expansion of economic, technical and cultural cooperation and even took additional steps to further curtail such cooperation. In April 1965, the CPR Government officially renounced cooperation with the USSR in constructing a number of industrial projects stipulated in the Chinese-Soviet 1961 agreement. . . .

All this showed that the CCP leadership had embarked on a further deterioration of relations between the CPR and the USSR. The Chinese leadership states more and more frequently that the CCP is waging a political struggle against the Soviet Union. Contrary to common sense they present it as a struggle "of the state of the proletariat against the state of the bourgeoisie."

. . . The Chinese people are made to believe that the Soviet Union is one of their chief enemies. Meetings are being conducted at Chinese offices and enterprises at which every participant is obliged to come up with some criticism of the Soviet Union. The organizing of anti-Soviet rallies has become a system. On March 6, 1965, an anti-Soviet demonstration was even organized in front of the USSR Embassy.

. . . The Peking radio beams articles and materials to the USSR in an attempt to pit various strata of the Soviet people against one another, to obstruct friendship among the peoples of the USSR and to undermine their confidence in the party and in Soviet activists. This is being done to such an extent that direct appeals are being made to engage in political action against the CPSU Central Committee and the Soviet Union. . . .

We should also like to inform you that the Chinese Government refused to resume the negotiations suspended in May 1964, on a precise delimitation of the border. . . .

The official Chinese representative in the bilateral consultations on border questions threatened directly that the CPR authorities would consider "other ways" of settling the territorial questions and stated: "It is not out of the question that we will try to restore historical rights."

But the CPR has no "historical rights." The territories of which the CCP leadership now talks have never belonged to China. The current Soviet-Chinese border has a firm international legal basis; it is stipulated in treaties signed by the governments of the two states.

The attitude of the CPR leadership toward the struggle of the DRV and all Vietnamese people against the United States aggression is currently causing great damage to the joint cause of the countries of socialism and the worldwide liberation movement.

The Soviet Union delivers large amounts of weapons to the DRV, including rocket installations, anti-aircraft artillery, airplanes, tanks, coastal guns, warships and other weapons. . . . Our military aid is being rendered to the extent the Vietnamese leadership itself thinks necessary. . . .

The CPSU has proposed to the Chinese leaders more than once that joint actions [of all Socialist countries] to support Vietnam be organized. But the Chinese leadership opposed such action by the Socialist states. . . .

At the same time, the CCP leadership hindered the implementation of the agreements of the Government of the USSR with the Government of the DRV on an immediate increase in military aid for the DRV. The CCP leaders did not permit Soviet transport planes with weapons to fly over CPR territory. . . .

Then, Chinese personalities also placed obstacles in the way of the transportation of war materiel to Vietnam by rail. . . .

From all this it becomes clear that the Chinese leaders need a lengthy Vietnam war to maintain international tensions, to represent China as a "besieged fortress." There is every reason to assert that it is one of the goals of the policy of the Chinese leadership in the Vietnam question to originate a military conflict between the USSR and the United States. They want a clash of the USSR with the United States so that they may, as they say themselves, "sit on the mountain and watch the fight of the tigers.". . .

Now the role of the ideological-theoretical platform of the Chinese leadership is quite plain. Its exclusive purpose is to serve the nationalistic big-power policy of the Chinese leadership. . . .

The Chinese leaders . . . derive from the whole arsenal of forms of struggle only one — armed revolt, war. They claim that the thesis of Mao Tse-tung concerning "conquest through arms, that is, solution of the problem through war" is the "general" revolutionary principle correct everywhere and at all times. . . .

The emphasis on armed struggle as the only way of revolution . . . is tantamount to denying the historical significance of the building of socialism and communism, its role in the development of the worldwide revolutionary process.

The efforts of the CCP leaders to force all parties of the non-Socialist countries to accept the goal of an immediate revolution independent of actual conditions in effect means to try to force upon the Communist movement putschist, conspiratory tactics. These tactics, however, offer the imperialist bourgeoisie the opportunity to bleed the revolutionary Communist and workers' movement, to expose the leadership and the activists of a number of Communist parties to destruction. . . .

The character of the present ideological-political platform of the CCP leaders consists of military great-power chauvinism and hegemony. Ultrarevolutionary phrasemongering and petty bourgeois revolutionary activities are being used as an instrument to implement the chauvinist, hegemonic course.

In connection with the above, we believe that the hegemonic activities of the Chinese leaders are aimed at subordinating the policy of Socialist countries, the international Communist and workers' movement and the national liberation movement to their great power interests while simultaneously protecting the interests of the CCP and the CPR against particular dangers.

It is not without intention that the Chinese leaders, while criticizing the other fraternal parties and Socialist countries because of their alleged insufficient revolutionary spirit, because of indecisiveness in the fight against imperialism, show extraordinary caution in their own practical deeds, as well as extreme patience toward imperialist powers and their policy, including the policy that is aimed against China itself.

CHINESE REJECTION OF INVITATION TO MOSCOW

Following are excerpts from a March 23, 1966, letter sent to Moscow by the Chinese declining an invitation to attend the 23rd Party Congress:

In normal circumstances it would be considered an indication of friendship for one party to invite another fraternal party to send a delegation to its Congress. But around the time you sent this invitation, you distributed an anti-Chinese document in the Soviet Union, both inside and outside the party, and organized a whole series of anti-Chinese reports from top to bottom, right down to the basic units, whipping up hysteria against China.

Moreover, you sent an anti-Chinese letter to other parties, instigating them to join you in opposing China. You wantonly villified the Communist Chinese party as being "bellicose" and "pseudo-revolutionary," as "refusing to oppose imperialism" and "encouraging United States imperialist aggression," and as being guilty of "adventurism," "splitism," "Trotskyism," "nationalism," "great power chauvinism," "dogmatism," and so on and so forth.

You have also been spreading rumors alleging that China "is obstructing aid to Vietnam" and that "China has been encroaching on Soviet territory." You have gone so far as to state that "China is not a Socialist country.". . . In these circumstances, how can the Chinese Communist party, which you look upon as an enemy, be expected to attend your Congress?

The Chinese Communist party has attended many of the Congresses of the CPSU. Also, we sent delegations to your 20th, 21st and 22nd Congresses, after the Khrushchev revisionist group usurped the leadership of the CPSU. But at the 20th Congress of the CPSU you suddenly lashed out at Stalin. Stalin was a great Marxist-Leninist.

In attacking Stalin, you were attacking Marxism-Leninism, the Soviet Union, Communist parties, China, the people and all the Marxist-Leninists of the world. At the 22nd Party Congress you adopted an out-and-out revisionist program, made a wild public attack on Albania and reproached the Chinese Communist party, so that the head of our delegation had to leave for home while the Congress was only half way through....

Over the last years, we have made a series of efforts in the hope that you would return to the path of Marxism-Leninism. Since Khrushchev's downfall, we have advised the new leaders of the CPSU on a number of occasions to make a fresh start. We have done everything we could, but you have not shown the slightest repentance.

Since coming to power, the new leaders of the CPSU have gone farther and farther down the road of revisionism, splitism and great power chauvinism....

... Despite the tricks you have been playing to deceive people, you are pursuing United States-Soviet collaboration for the domination of the world with your heart and soul. In mouthing a few words against United States imperialism and making a show of supporting anti-imperialist struggles, you are conducting only minor attacks on United States imperialism while rendering it major help.

... Your clamor for "united action," especially on the Vietnam question, is nothing but a trap for the purpose of deceiving the Soviet people and the revolutionary people of the world. You have all along been acting in coordination with the United States in its plot for peace talks, vainly attempting to sell out the struggle of the Vietnamese people against United States aggression and for national salvation and to drag the Vietnam question into the orbit of Soviet-United States collaboration.

You have worked hand in glove with the United States in a whole series of dirty deals inside and outside the United Nations. In close coordination with the counter-revolutionary "global strategy" of United States imperialism, you are now actively trying to build a ring of encirclement around socialist China. Not only have you excluded yourself from the international united front of all peoples against United States imperialism and its lackeys, you have even aligned yourselves with United States imperialism, the main enemy of the people of the world, and establish a holy alliance against China, against the movement and against the Marxist-Leninists....

We are confident that in all parts of the world, including the Soviet Union, the masses of the people, who constitute more than 90 percent of the population, are for revolution and against imperialism and its lackeys. In the ranks of the international Communist movement, including the Communist party of the Soviet Union, more than 90 percent of the Communists and cadres will eventually march along the path of Marxism-Leninism.

... The Soviet people may rest assured that once the Soviet Union meets with imperialist aggression and puts up resolute resistance, China will definitely stand side by side with the Soviet Union and fight against the common enemy.

With fraternal greetings.

CZECH LEADERS
ANNOUNCE INVASION

Following are excerpts from a message broadcast August 21, 1968, by the Czech government reporting the Soviet-led invasion of Czechoslovakia:

To the entire people of the Chechoslovak Socialist Republic:

Yesterday, on August 20, around 2300 [11 a.m.], troops of the Soviet Union, Polish People's Republic, the G.D.R. [East Germany], the Hungarian People's Republic and the Bulgarian People's Republic crossed the frontiers of the Chechoslovak Socialist Republic.

This happened without the knowledge of the President of the Republic, the Chairman of the National Assembly, the Premier or the First Secretary of the Chechoslovak Communist Party Central Committee....

The Chechoslovak Communist Party Central Committee appeals to all citizens of our republic to maintain calm and not to offer resistance to the troops on the march. Our army, security corps and people's militia have not received the command to defend the country.

The Chechoslovak Communist Party Central Committee Presidium regard [sic] this act as contrary not only to the fundamental principles of relations between Socialist states but also as contrary to the principles of international law.

All leading functionaries of the state, the Communist Party and the National Front: Remain in your functions as representatives of the state, elected to the laws of the Chechoslovak Socialist Republic.

Constitutional functionaries are immediately convening a session of the National Assembly of our republic, and the Presidium is at the same time convening a plenum of the Central Committee to discuss the situation that has arisen.

BREZHNEV DOCTRINE
OF LIMITED SOVEREIGNTY

Following are excerpts from Brezhnev's November 13, 1968, speech to the Fifth Congress of the Polish United Workers' Party and his October 28, 1969, address to visiting Czech officials:

Speech to Poles

... The experience of struggle and realistic stocktaking of the situation obtaining in the world with utmost clarity shows that it is vitally necessary for the Communists of the socialist countries to carry high the banner of socialist internationalism, constantly to strengthen the cohesion and solidarity of the countries of socialism. Therein lies one of the main conditions for the successful construction of socialism and communism in each of our countries and the successful struggle of the world system of socialism against imperialism.

The interests of the defence of each socialist country, the interests of its economic, scientific and cultural advance, all this calls for broadest cooperation between the fraternal countries, the all-round development of various contacts between them, genuine internationalism....

The socialist states stand for strict respect for the sovereignty of all countries. We emphatically oppose interference into the affairs of any states, violations of their sovereignty.

At the same time the establishment and defence of the sovereignty of states which have embarked upon the road of building socialism is of particular significance for us, Communists. The forces of imperialism and reaction seek to deprive the people now of ... their sovereign right ... to ensure the prosperity of their country, the well-being and happiness of the broad mass of the working people through building a society free from any oppression and exploitation....

It is common knowledge that the Soviet Union has done much for the real strengthening of the sovereignty and independence of the socialist countries. The CPSU [Communist Party of the Soviet

Union] has always advocated that each socialist country determine the specific forms of its development along the road of socialism with consideration of its specific national conditions. However, it is known, Comrades, that there are also common laws governing socialist construction a deviation from which might lead to a deviation from socialism as such.

And when the internal and external forces hostile to socialism seek to revert the development of any socialist country towards the restoration of the capitalist order, when a threat to the cause of socialism in that country, a threat to the security of the socialist community as a whole emerges, this is no longer only a problem of the people of that country but also a common problem, concern of all socialist countries.

It goes without saying that such an action as military aid to a fraternal country to cut short the threat to the socialist order is an extraordinary, enforced step, it can be sparked off only by direct actions of the enemies of socialism inside the country and beyond its boundaries, actions creating a threat to the common interests of the camp of socialism. . . .

Let all those who are inclined to forget the lessons of history and who would like to engage again in recarving the map of Europe know that the frontiers of Poland, the German Democratic Republic, Czechoslovakia, just as any other member-country of the Warsaw Treaty, are immutable and inviolable. These frontiers are defended by the entire armed might of the socialist community. We advise all who like to encroach upon other peoples' frontiers to remember this well! . . .

Speech to Czechs

. . . Comrades! For almost a year and a half now, the thoughts and feelings of Soviet Communists and all Soviet people, as well as those of people in other socialist countries, have been focused on the events in Czechoslovakia. We had to experience a great deal in this period — anxiety for the destiny of socialism in a fraternal country subjected to the onslaught of the joint forces of internal and external reaction, sentiments of combat solidarity with the principled and staunch Marxists-Leninists in the Communist Party of Czechoslovakia who courageously rose to struggle for the cause of socialism and, last but not least, pride in the successes scored by Czechoslovakia's Communists in this hard struggle. . . .

Hardly can anyone deny now that the forces of socialism have stood this test — test by practice, test by struggle — with honor. The principled stand of Communists, the unity of socialist countries and their international solidarity proved to be stronger than those who wanted to reverse the history of Czechoslovak society and to wrest state power from the hands of the working class, and from the hands of working people. . . .

The CPSU [Communist Party of the Soviet Union] and our entire people had faith that this would be so. We, the allies of Czechoslovakia, did our internationalist duty. . . .

. . . [T]he struggle against the anti-socialist, counter-revolutionary forces in Czechoslovakia raised in all sharpness the question of international responsibility of the Communists for the fate of socialism. There can be only one reply to the attempts of external and internal reaction to weaken the positions of socialism, to impair the socialist community, and that reply is still greater cohesion of the fraternal countries on the basis of socialist internationalism, and mutual support in the struggle against the intrigues of imperialism and for the consolidation of the socialist system.

Our common stand on this issue is clearly expressed in the well-known Bratislava Statement of the fraternal Parties of six socialist countries [issued after an Aug. 3, 1968, meeting of Eastern bloc nations]. It says there, that the support, strengthening and defence of the gains of socialism "are the common international duty of all the socialist countries." And the summing-up document of the recent International Conference of Communist Parties says: "The defence of socialism is the international duty of the Communists." Our invincible strength lies in the close solidarity of the fraternal socialist countries, in the unity of the national detachments of Communists. . . .

NIXON-BREZHNEV 1972 SUMMIT STATEMENTS

Following are the texts of 1) the declaration of basic principles of relations between the United States and the Soviet Union signed May 29, 1972, by President Richard Nixon and Communist Party leader Leonid Brezhnev, 2) a joint communiqué issued by Nixon and Soviet leaders on May 29, and 3) Nixon's address to a joint session of Congress June 1, 1972, immediately on his return from the Moscow summit.

Declaration of Principles

The United States of America and the Union of Soviet Socialist Republics,

Guided by their obligations under the Charter of the United Nations and by a desire to strengthen peaceful relations with each other and to place these relations on the firmest possible basis,

Aware of the need to make every effort to remove the threat of war and to create conditions which promote the reduction of tensions in the world and the strengthening of universal security and international cooperation,

Believing that the improvement of US-Soviet relations and their mutually advantageous development in such areas as economics, science and culture, will meet these objectives and contribute to better mutual understanding and business-like cooperation, without in any way prejudicing the interests of third countries.

Conscious that these objectives reflect the interests of the peoples of both countries.

Have agreed as follows:

First. They will proceed from the common determination that in the nuclear age there is no alternative to conducting their mutual relations on the basis of peaceful coexistence. Differences in ideology and in the social systems of the USA and the USSR are not obstacles to the bilateral development of normal relations based on the principles of sovereignty, equality, non-interference in internal affairs and mutual advantage.

Second. The USA and the USSR attach major importance to preventing the development of situations capable of causing a dangerous exacerbation of their relations. Therefore, they will do their utmost to avoid military confrontations and to prevent the outbreak of nuclear war. They will always exercise restraint in their mutual relations, and will be prepared to negotiate and settle differences by peaceful means. Discussions and negotiations on outstanding issues will be conducted in a spirit of reciprocity, mutual accommodations and mutual benefit.

Both sides recognize that efforts to obtain unilateral advantage at the expense of the other, directly or indirectly, are inconsistent with these objectives. The prerequisites for maintaining and strengthening peaceful relations between the USA and the USSR are the recognition of the security interests of the Parties based on the principle of equality and the renunciation of the use or threat of force.

Third. The USA and the USSR have a special responsibility, as do other countries which are permanent members of the United Nations Security Council, to do everything in their power so that conflicts or situations will not arise which would serve to increase international tensions. Accordingly, they will seek to promote conditions in which all countries will live in peace and security and will not be subject to outside interference in their internal affairs.

Fourth. The USA and the USSR intend to widen the juridical basis of their mutual relations and to exert the necessary efforts so that bilateral agreements which they have concluded and multilateral treaties and agreements to which they are jointly parties are faithfully implemented.

Fifth. The USA and the USSR reaffirm their readiness to continue the practice of exchanging views on problems of mutual interest and, when necessary, to conduct such exchanges at the highest level, including meetings between leaders of the two countries.

The two governments welcome and will facilitate an increase in productive contacts between representatives of the legislative bodies of the two countries.

Sixth. The Parties will continue their efforts to limit armaments on a bilateral as well as on a multilateral basis. They will continue to make special efforts to limit strategic armaments. Whenever possible, they will conclude concrete agreements aimed at achieving these purposes.

The USA and the USSR regard as the ultimate objective of their efforts the achievement of general and complete disarmament and the establishment of an effective system of international security in accordance with the purposes and principles of the United Nations.

Seventh. The USA and the USSR regard commercial and economic ties as an important and necessary element in the strengthening of their bilateral relations and thus will actively promote the growth of such ties. They will facilitate cooperation between the relevant organizations and enterprises of the two countries and the conclusion of appropriate agreements and contracts, including long-term ones.

The two countries will contribute to the improvement of maritime and air communications between them.

Eighth. The two sides consider it timely and useful to develop mutual contacts and cooperation in the fields of science and technology. Where suitable, the USA and the USSR will conclude appropriate agreements dealing with concrete cooperation in these fields.

Ninth. The two sides reaffirm their intention to deepen cultural ties with one another and to encourage fuller familiarization with each other's cultural values. They will promote improved conditions for cultural exchanges and tourism.

Tenth. The USA and the USSR will seek to ensure that their ties and cooperation in all the above-mentioned fields and in any others in their mutual interest are built on a firm and long-term basis. To give a permanent character to these efforts, they will establish in all fields where this is feasible joint commissions or other joint bodies.

Eleventh. The USA and the USSR make no claim for themselves and would not recognize the claims of anyone else to any special rights or advantages in world affairs. They recognize the sovereign equality of all states.

The Development of US-Soviet relations is not directed against third countries and their interests.

Twelfth. The basic principles set forth in this document do not affect any obligations with respect to other countries earlier assumed by the USA and the USSR.

Moscow, May 29, 1972

For the United States of America	For the Union of Soviet Socialist Republics
RICHARD NIXON President of the United States of America	LEONID I. BREZHNEV General Secretary of the Central Committee, CPSU

USA-USSR Joint Communiqué

By mutual agreement between the United States of America and the Union of Soviet Socialist Republics, the President of the United States and Mrs. Richard Nixon paid an official visit to the Soviet Union from May 22 to May 30, 1972. The President was accompanied by Secretary of State William P. Rogers, assistant to the President Dr. H. A. Kissinger, and other American officials. During his stay in the U.S.S.R. President Nixon visited, in addition to Moscow, the cities of Leningrad and Kiev.

President Nixon and L. I. Brezhnev, general secretary of the Central Committee of the Communist Party of the Soviet Union, N. Podgorny, chairman of the Supreme Soviet of the U.S.S.R., and A. N. Kosygin, chairman of the Council of Ministers of the U.S.S.R., conducted talks on fundamental problems of American-Soviet relations and the current international situation.

Also taking part in the conversations were:

On the American side: William P. Rogers, secretary of state, Jacob D. Beam, American ambassador to the U.S.S.R., Dr. Henry A. Kissinger, assistant to the President for national security affairs, Peter M. Flanigan, assistant to the President, and Martin J. Hillenbrand, assistant secretary of state for European affairs.

On the Soviet side: A. A. Gromyko, minister of foreign affairs of the U.S.S.R., N. S. Patolichev, minister of foreign trade, V. V. Kuznetsov, deputy minister of foreign affairs of the U.S.S.R., A. F. Dobrynin, Soviet ambassador to the U.S.A., A. M. Aleksandrov, assistant to the general secretary of the Central Committee, C.P.S.U., G. M. Korniyenko, member of the collegium of the Ministry of Foreign Affairs of the U.S.S.R.

The discussions covered a wide range of questions of mutual interest and were frank and thorough. They defined more precisely those areas where there are prospects for developing greater cooperation between the two countries, as well as those areas where the positions of the two sides are different.

I. Bilateral Relations

Guided by the desire to place U.S.-Soviet relations on a more stable and constructive foundation, and mindful of their responsibilities for maintaining world peace and for facilitating the relaxation of international tension, the two sides adopted a document entitled: "Basic Principles of Mutual Relations Between the United States of America and the Union of Soviet Socialist Republics," signed on behalf of the U.S. by President Nixon and on behalf of the U.S.S.R. by General Secretary Brezhnev.

Both sides are convinced that the provisions of that document open new possibilities for the development of peaceful relations and mutually beneficial cooperation between the U.S.A. and the U.S.S.R.

Having considered various areas of bilateral U.S.-Soviet relations, the two sides agreed that an improvement of relations is possible and desirable. They expressed their firm intention to act in accordance with the provisions set forth in the above-mentioned document.

As a result of progress made in negotiations which preceded the summit meeting, and in the course of the meeting itself, a number of significant agreements were reached. This will intensify bilateral cooperation in areas of common concern as well as in areas relevant to the cause of peace and international cooperation.

Limitation of Strategic Armaments

The two sides gave primary attention to the problem of reducing the danger of nuclear war. They believe that curbing the competition in strategic arms will make a significant and tangible contribution to this cause.

The two sides attach great importance to the treaty on the limitation of anti-ballistic missile systems and the interim agreement on certain measures with respect to the limitation of strategic offensive arms concluded between them.

These agreements, which were concluded as a result of the negotiations in Moscow, constitute a major step towards curbing and ultimately ending the arms race.

They are a concrete expression of the intention of the two sides to contribute to the relaxation of international tension and the strengthening of confidence between states as well as to carry out the obligations assumed by them in the Treaty on the Non-proliferation of Nuclear Weapons Article VI. Both sides are convinced that the achievement of the above agreements is a practical step toward saving mankind from the threat of the outbreak of nuclear war. Accordingly, it corresponds to the vital interests of the American and Soviet peoples as well as to the vital interests of all other peoples.

The two sides intend to continue active negotiations for the limitation of strategic offensive arms and to conduct them in a spirit of good will, respect for each other's legitimate interests and observance of the principle of equal security.

Both sides are also convinced that the agreement on measures to reduce the risk of outbreak of nuclear war between the U.S.A. and the U.S.S.R. signed in Washington Sept. 30, 1971, serves the interest not only of the Soviet and American peoples, but of all mankind.

Commercial and Economic Relations

Both sides agreed on measures designed to establish more favorable conditions for developing commercial and other economic ties between the U.S.A. and the U.S.S.R. They agree that realistic conditions exist for increasing economic ties. These ties should develop on the basis of mutual benefit and in accordance with generally accepted international practice.

Believing that these aims would be served by conclusion of a trade agreement between the U.S.A. and the U.S.S.R., the two sides decided to complete in the near future the work necessary to conclude such an agreement. They agreed on the desirability of credit arrangements to develop mutual trade and of early efforts to resolve other financial and economic issues. It was agreed that a lend-lease settlement will be negotiated concurrently with a trade agreement.

In the interests of broadening and facilitating commercial ties between the two countries, and to work out specific arrangements, the two sides decided to create a U.S.-Soviet joint commercial commission. Its first meeting will be held in Moscow in the summer of 1972.

Each side will promote the establishment of effective working arrangements between organizations and firms of both countries and encouraging the conclusion of long-term contracts.

Maritime Matters, Incidents at Sea

The two sides agreed to continue the negotiations aimed at reaching an agreement on maritime and related matters. They believe that such an agreement would mark a positive step in facilitating the expansion of commerce between the United States and the Soviet Union.

An agreement was concluded between the two sides on measures to prevent incidents at sea and in air space over it between vessels and aircraft of the U.S. and Soviet navies. By providing agreed procedures for ships and aircraft of the two navies operating in close proximity, this agreement will diminish the chances of dangerous accidents.

Cooperation in Science and Technology

It was recognized that the cooperation now under way in areas such as atomic energy research, space research, health and other fields benefits both nations and has contributed positively to their over-all relations. It was agreed that increased scientific and technical cooperation on the basis of mutual benefit and shared effort for common goals is in the interest of both nations and would contribute to a further improvement in their bilateral relations. For these purposes the two sides signed an agreement for cooperation in the fields of science and technology. A U.S.-Soviet joint commission on scientific and technical cooperation will be created for identifying and establishing cooperative programs.

Cooperation in Space

Having in mind the role played by the U.S. and the U.S.S.R. in the peaceful exploration of outer space, both sides emphasized the importance of further bilateral cooperation in this sphere. In order to increase the safety of man's flights in outer space and the future prospects of joint scientific experiments, the two sides agreed to make suitable arrangements to permit the docking of American and Soviet spacecraft and stations. The first joint docking experiment of the two countries' piloted spacecraft, with visits by astronauts and cosmonauts to each other's spacecraft, is contemplated for 1975. The planning and implementation of this flight will be carried out by the U.S. National Aeronautics and Space Administration and the U.S.S.R. Academy of Sciences, according to principles and procedures developed through mutual consultations.

Cooperation in the Field of Health

The two sides concluded an agreement on health cooperation which marks a fruitful beginning of sharing knowledge about, and collaborative attacks on, the common enemies, disease and disability. The initial research efforts of the program will concentrate on health problems important to the whole world — cancer, heart diseases, and the environmental health sciences.

This cooperation subsequently will be broadened to include other health problems of mutual interest. The two sides pledged their full support for the health cooperation program and agreed to continue the active participation of the two governments in the work of international organizations in the health field.

Environmental Cooperation

The two sides agreed to initiate a program of cooperation in the protection and enhancement of man's environment. Through joint research and joint measures, the United States and the U.S.S.R. hope to contribute to the preservation of a healthful environment in their countries and throughout the world. Under the new agreement on environmental cooperation there will be consultations in the near future in Moscow on specific cooperative projects.

Exchanges in the Fields of Science, Technology, Education and Culture

Both sides note the importance of the agreement on exchanges and cooperation in scientific, technical, educational, cultural, and other fields in 1972-1973, signed in Moscow on April 11, 1972. Continuation and expansion of bilateral exchanges in these fields will lead to better understanding and help improve the general state of relations between the two countries. Within the broad framework provided by this agreement the two sides have agreed to expand the areas of cooperation, as reflected in new agreements concerning space, health, the environment and science and technology.

The U.S. side, noting the existence of an extensive program of English-language instruction in the Soviet Union, indicated its intention to encourage Russian-language programs in the United States.

II. International Issues

Europe

In the course of the discussions on the international situation, both sides took note of favorable developments in the relaxation of tensions in Europe.

Recognizing the importance to world peace of developments in Europe, where both world wars originated, and mindful of the responsibilities and commitments which they share with other powers under appropriate agreements, the U.S.A. and the U.S.S.R. intend to make further efforts to ensure a peaceful future for Europe, free of tensions, crises and conflicts.

They agree that the territorial integrity of all states in Europe should be respected.

Both sides view the Sept. 3, 1971, quadripartite agreement relating to the western sectors of Berlin as a good example of fruitful cooperation between the states concerned, including the U.S.A. and the U.S.S.R. The two sides believe that the implementation of that agreement in the near future, along with other steps, will further improve the European situation and contribute to the necessary trust among states.

Both sides welcomed the treaty between the U.S.S.R. and the Federal Republic of Germany signed on Aug. 12, 1970. They noted the significance of the provisions of this treaty as well as of other recent agreements in contributing to confidence and cooperation among the European states.

The U.S.A. and the U.S.S.R. are prepared to make appropriate contributions to the positive trends on the European continent toward a genuine detente and the development of relations of peaceful cooperation among states in Europe on the basis of the principles of territorial integrity and inviolability of frontiers, non-interference in internal affairs, sovereign equality in independence and renunciation of the use or threat of force.

The U.S. and U.S.S.R. are in accord that multilateral consultations looking toward a conference on security and cooperation in Europe could begin after the signature of the final quadripartite protocol of the agreement of Sept. 3, 1971. The two governments agree that the conference should be carefully prepared in order that it may concretely consider specific problems of security and cooperation and thus contribute to the progressive reduction of the underlying causes of tension in Europe. This conference should be convened at a time to be agreed by the countries concerned, but without undue delay.

Both sides believe that the goal of ensuring stability and security in Europe would be served by a reciprocal reduction of armed forces and armaments, first of all in central Europe. Any agreement on this question should not diminish the security of any of the sides. Appropriate agreement should be reached as soon as practicable between the states concerned on the procedures for negotiations on this subject in a special forum.

The Middle East

The two sides set out their positions on this question. They reaffirm their support for a peaceful settlement in the Middle East in accordance with Security Council Resolution 242.

Noting the significance of constructive cooperation of the parties concerned with the special representative of the U.N. secretary general, Ambassador Jarring, the U.S. and the U.S.S.R. confirm their desire to contribute to his mission's success and also declare their readiness to play their part in bringing about a peaceful settlement in the Middle East. In the view of the U.S. and the U.S.S.R., the achievement of such a settlement would open prospects for the normalization of the Middle East situation and would permit, in particular, consideration of further steps to bring about a military relaxation in that area.

Indochina

Each side set forth its respective standpoint with regard to the continuing war in Vietnam and the situation in the area of Indochina as a whole.

The U.S. side emphasized the need to bring an end to the military conflict as soon as possible and reaffirmed its commitment to the principle that the political future of South Vietnam should be left for the South Vietnamese people to decide for themselves, free from outside interference.

The U.S. side explained its view that the quickest and most effective way to attain the above-mentioned objectives is through negotiations leading to the return of all Americans held captive in the region, the implementation of an internationally supervised, Indochina-wide cease-fire and the subsequent withdrawal of all American forces stationed in South Vietnam within four months, leaving the political questions to be resolved by the Indochinese peoples themselves.

The United States reiterated its willingness to enter into serious negotiations with the North Vietnamese side to settle the war in Indochina on a basis just to all.

The Soviet side stressed its solidarity with the just struggle of the peoples of Vietnam, Laos and Cambodia for their freedom, independence and social progress. Firmly supporting the proposals of the DRV (North Vietnam) and the Provisional Revolutionary Government of the Republic of South Vietnam, which provide a realistic and constructive basis for settling the Vietnam problem, the Soviet Union stands for a cessation of bombings of the DRV, for a complete and unequivocal withdrawal of the troops of the U.S.A. and its allies from South Vietnam, so that the people of Indochina would have the possibility to determine for themselves their fate without any outside interference.

Disarmament Issues

The two sides note that in recent years their joint and parallel actions have facilitated the working out and conclusion of treaties which curb the arms race or ban some of the most dangerous types of weapons. They note further that these treaties were welcomed by a large majority of the states in the world, which became parties to them.

Both sides regard the convention on the prohibition of the development, production and stockpiling of bacteriological, biological and toxic weapons and on their destruction, as an essential disarmament measure. Along with Great Britain, they are the depositories for the convention which was recently opened for signature by all states. The U.S.A. and U.S.S.R. will continue their efforts to reach an international agreement regarding chemical weapons.

The U.S.A. and the U.S.S.R., proceeding from the need to take into account the security interests of both countries on the basis of the principle of equality, and without prejudice to the security interests of third countries, will actively participate in negotiations aimed at working out new measures designed to curb and end the arms race. The ultimate purpose is general and complete disarmament, including nuclear disarmament, under strict international control. A world disarmament conference could play a role in this process at an appropriate time.

Strengthening the United Nations

Both sides will strive to strengthen the effectiveness of the United Nations on the basis of strict observance of the U.N. charter.

They regard the United Nations as an instrument for maintaining world peace and security, discouraging conflicts, and developing international cooperation. Accordingly, they will do their best to support United Nations efforts in the interests of international peace.

Both sides emphasized that agreements and understandings reached in the negotiations in Moscow, as well as the contents and nature of these negotiations, are not in any way directed against any other country. Both sides proceed from the recognition of the role, the responsibility and the prerogatives of other interested states, existing international obligations and agreements, and the principles and purposes of the U.N. charter.

Both sides believe that positive results were accomplished in the course of the talks at the highest level. These results indicate that despite the differences between the U.S.A. and the U.S.S.R. in social systems, ideologies, and policy principles, it is possible to develop mutually advantageous cooperation between the peoples of both countries, in the interests of strengthening peace and international security.

Both sides expressed the desire to continue close contact on a number of issues that were under discussion. They agreed that regular consultations on questions of mutual interest, including meetings at the highest level, would be useful.

In expressing his appreciation for the hospitality accorded him in the Soviet Union, President Nixon invited General Secretary L. I. Brezhnev, Chairman N. V. Podgorny and Chairman A. N. Kosygin to visit the United States at a mutually convenient time. This invitation was accepted.

Nixon Address to Congress

... The foundation has been laid for a new relationship between the two most powerful nations on earth. Now it is up to us — to all of us here in this chamber and to all of us across America — to join with other nations in building a new house upon that foundation — one that can be a home for the hopes of mankind and a shelter against the storms of conflict. ...

The pattern of U.S.-Soviet summit diplomacy in the cold war trend is well known. One meeting after another produced a short-lived euphoric mood — the spirit of Geneva, the spirit of Camp David, the spirit of Vienna, the spirit of Glassboro — without producing significant progress on the really difficult issues.

Goal: Concrete Results

Early in this Administration, therefore, I stated that the prospect of concrete results, not atmospherics, would be our criterion for meeting at the highest level. I also announced our intention to pursue negotiations with the Soviet Union across a broad front of related issues, with the purpose of creating a momentum of achievement in which progress in one area could contribute to progress in others.

This is the basis on which we prepared for and conducted last week's talks. This was a working summit. We sought to establish not a superficial spirit of Moscow, but a solid record of progress on solving the difficult issues which for so long have divided our two nations and the world.... I think we have accomplished that goal....

By forming habits of cooperation and strengthening institutional ties in areas of peaceful enterprise, these ... agreements will create on both sides a steadily growing vested interest in the maintenance of good relations between our two countries.

Expanded U.S.-Soviet trade will also yield advantages to both of our nations. When the two largest economies in the world start trading with each other on a much larger scale, living standards in both nations will rise, and the stake which both have in peace will be increased....

Three-fifths of all the people alive in the world today have spent their whole lifetimes under the shadow of a nuclear war which could be touched off by the arms race among the great powers. Last Friday in Moscow we witnessed the beginning of the end of that era which began in 1945. We took the first step toward a new era of mutually agreed restraint and arms limitations between the two principal nuclear powers. With this step we have enhanced the security of both nations....

Must Coexist Peacefully

In addition to the talks which led to the specific agreements ... I also had full, frank and extensive discussions with General Secretary Brezhnev and his colleagues about several parts of the world where American and Soviet interests have come in conflict.

With regard to the reduction of tensions in Europe, we recorded our intention of proceeding later this year with multilateral consultations looking toward a conference on security and cooperation in Europe. We have also jointly agreed to move forward with negotiations on mutual and balanced force reductions in central Europe.

The problem of ending the Vietnam war, which engages the hopes of all Americans, was one of the most extensively discussed subjects of our agenda. It would only jeopardize the search for peace if I were to review here all that was said on that subject. I will simply say this: each side obviously has its own point of view and its own approach to this very difficult issue. But at the same time, both the United States and the Soviet Union share an overriding desire to achieve a more stable peace in the world....

Our summit conversations about the Middle East situation were also full, frank, and extensive. I reiterated the American people's commitment to the survival of Israel and to a settlement just to all the countries in the area....

The final achievement of the Moscow conference was the signing of a landmark declaration entitled "Basic Principles of Mutual Relations Between the United States and the U.S.S.R." As these twelve basic principles are put into practice, they can provide a solid framework for the future development of American-Soviet relations.

They begin with the recognition that two nuclear nations, each of which has the power to destroy humanity, have no alternative but to coexist peacefully — because in a nuclear war there would be no winners, only losers.

The basic principles commit both sides to avoid direct military confrontation and to exercise constructive leadership and restraint with respect to small conflicts which could drag the major powers into war.

They disavow any intention to create spheres of influence or to conspire against the interests of any other nation — a point I would underscore by saying once again tonight that America values its ties with all nations — from our oldest allies in Europe and Asia, as I emphasized by my visit to Iran, to our good friends in the third world, to our new relationship with the People's Republic of China....

However, we must remember that Soviet ideology still proclaims hostility to some of America's most basic values. The Soviet leaders remain committed to that ideology. Like the nation they lead, they are and will continue to be totally dedicated competitors of the United States....

Our successes in the strategic arms talks and in the Berlin negotiations, which opened the road to Moscow, came about because over the past three years we have consistently refused proposals for unilaterally abandoning the ABM, unilaterally pulling back our forces from Europe, and drastically cutting the defense budget. The Congress deserves the appreciation of the American people for having the courage to vote such proposals down and to maintain the strength America needs to protect its interests....

By the same token, we must stand steadfastly with our NATO partners if negotiations leading to a new détente and mutual reduction of forces in Europe are to be productive.... As we seek better relations with those who have been our adversaries, we will not let our friends and allies down.

We must keep our own economy vigorous and competitive if the opening for greater East-West trade is to mean anything.... For America to continue its role of helping to build a more peaceful world, we must keep America number one economically in the world.

We must maintain our own momentum of domestic innovation, growth, and reform if the opportunities for joint action with the Soviets are to fulfill their promise....

Freed From Confrontation

But now in the brief space of four months, these journeys to Peking and to Moscow have begun to free us from perpetual confrontation. We have moved toward better understanding, mutual respect, point-by-point settlement of differences with both of the major Communist powers.

This one series of meetings has not rendered an imperfect world suddenly perfect.... The threat of war has not been eliminated — it has been reduced.... As we continue that effort, our unity of purpose and action will be all-important.

... An unparalleled opportunity has been placed in America's hands. Never has there been a time when hope was more justified or when complacency was more dangerous.... [W]e can make good this opportunity to build a new structure of peace in the world, or let it slip away. Together, therefore, let us seize the moment.... Then the historians of a future age will write of 1972, not that this was the year America went up to the summit and then down to the valley again — but that this was the year when America helped to lead the world up out of the lowlands of constant war, and onto the high plateau of lasting peace.

NIXON-BREZHNEV 1973 SUMMIT STATEMENTS

Following are the texts of 1) the agreement signed June 21, 1973, by President Richard Nixon and Communist Party general secretary Leonid I. Brezhnev concerning the limitation of strategic offensive weapons, 2) a June 22, 1973, agreement between the United States and the Soviet Union on the prevention of nuclear war, and 3) a joint communiqué issued June 25, 1973, at the president's home in San Clemente, California.

Offensive Arms Agreement

The President of the United States of America, Richard Nixon, and the General Secretary of the Central Committee of the CPSU [Communist Party of the Soviet Union], L. I. Brezhnev,

Having thoroughly considered the question of the further limitation of strategic arms, and the progress already achieved in the current negotiations,

Reaffirming their conviction that the earliest adoption of further limitations of strategic arms would be a major contribution in reducing the danger of an outbreak of nuclear war and in strengthening international peace and security,

Have agreed as follows:

First. The two Sides will continue active negotiations in order to work out a permanent agreement on more complete measures on the limitation of strategic offensive arms, as well as their subsequent reduction, proceeding from the Basic Principles of Relations between the United States of America and the Union of Soviet Socialist Republics signed in Moscow on May 29, 1972, and from the Interim Agreement between the United States of America and the Union of Soviet Socialist Republics of May 26, 1972 on Certain Measures with Respect to the Limitation of Strategic Offensive Arms.

Over the course of the next year the two Sides will make serious efforts to work out the provisions of the permanent agreement on more complete measures on the limitation of strategic offensive arms with the objective of signing it in 1974.

Second. New agreements on the limitation of strategic offensive armaments will be based on the principles of the American-Soviet documents adopted in Moscow in May 1972 and the agreements reached in Washington in June 1973; and in particular, both Sides will be guided by the recognition of each other's equal security interests and by the recognition that efforts to obtain unilateral advantage, directly or indirectly, would be inconsistent with the strengthening of peaceful relations between the United States of America and the Union of Soviet Socialist Republics.

Third. The limitations placed on strategic offensive weapons can apply both to their quantitative aspects as well as to their qualitative improvement.

Fourth. Limitations on strategic offensive arms must be subject to adequate verification by national technical means.

Fifth. The modernization and replacement of strategic offensive arms would be permitted under conditions which will be formulated in the agreements to be concluded.

Sixth. Pending the completion of a permanent agreement on more complete measures of strategic offensive arms limitation, both Sides are prepared to reach agreements on separate measures to supplement the existing Interim Agreement of May 26, 1972.

Seventh. Each side will continue to take necessary organizational and technical measures for preventing accidental or unauthorized use of nuclear weapons under its control in accordance with the Agreement of September 30, 1971 between the United States of America and the Union of Soviet Socialist Republics.

Washington, June 21, 1973

For the United States of America:
  Richard Nixon
    President of the United States of America
For the Union of Soviet Socialist Republics:
  L. I. Brezhnev
    General Secretary of the Central Committee, CPSU

Nuclear War Prevention Agreement

The United States of America and the Union of Soviet Socialist Republics, hereinafter referred to as the Parties,

Guided by the objectives of strengthening world peace and international security,

Conscious that nuclear war would have devastating consequences for mankind,

Proceeding from the desire to bring about conditions in which the danger of an outbreak of nuclear war anywhere in the world would be reduced and ultimately eliminated,

Proceeding from their obligations under the Charter of the United Nations regarding the maintenance of peace, refraining from the threat or use of force, and the avoidance of war, and in conformity with the agreements to which either Party has subscribed,

Proceeding from the Basic Principles of Relations between the United States of America and the Union of Soviet Socialist Republics signed in Moscow on May 29, 1972,

Reaffirming that the development of relations between the United States of America and the Union of Soviet Socialist Republics is not directed against other countries and their interests,

Have agreed as follows:

Article I

The United States and the Soviet Union agree that an objective of their policies is to remove the danger of nuclear war and of the use of nuclear weapons.

Accordingly, the Parties agree that they will act in such a manner as to prevent the development of situations capable of causing a dangerous exacerbation of their relations, as to avoid military confrontations, and as to exclude the outbreak of nuclear war between them and between either of the Parties and other countries.

Article II

The Parties agree, in accordance with Article I and to realize the objective stated in that Article, to proceed from the premise that each Party will refrain from the threat or use of force against the other Party, against the allies of the other Party and against other countries, in circumstances which may endanger international peace and security. The Parties agree that they will be guided by these considerations in the formulation of their foreign policies and in their actions in the field of international relations.

Article III

The Parties undertake to develop their relations with each other and with other countries in a way consistent with the purposes of this Agreement.

Article IV

If at any time relations between the Parties or between either Party and other countries appear to involve the risk of a nuclear conflict, or if relations between countries not parties to this Agreement appear to involve the risk of nuclear war between the United States of America and the Union of Soviet Socialist Republics or between either Party and other countries, the United States and the Soviet Union, acting in accordance with the provisions of this Agreement, shall immediately enter into urgent consultations with each other and make every effort to avert this risk.

Article V

Each Party shall be free to inform the Security Council of the United Nations, the Secretary General of the United Nations and the Governments of Allied or other countries of the progress and outcome of consultations initiated in accordance with Article IV of this Agreement.

Article VI

Nothing in this Agreement shall affect or impair:

(a) the inherent right of individual or collective self-defense as envisaged by Article 51 of the Charter of the United Nations,

(b) the provisions of the Charter of the United Nations, including those relating to the maintenance or restoration of international peace and security, and

(c) the obligations undertaken by either Party towards its allies or other countries in treaties, agreements, and other appropriate documents.

Article VII

This Agreement shall be of unlimited duration.

Article VIII

This Agreement shall enter into force upon signature.

Done at Washington on June 22, 1973, in two copies, each in the English and Russian languages, both texts being equally authentic.

For the United States of America:
Richard Nixon
President of the United States of America

For the Union of Soviet Socialist Republics:
L. I. Brezhnev
General Secretary of the Central Committee, CPSU

Nixon-Brezhnev Joint Communiqué

At the invitation of the President of the United States, Richard Nixon, extended during his official visit to the USSR in May 1972, and in accordance with a subsequent agreement, General Secretary of the Central Committee of the Communist Party of the Soviet Union, Mr. Leonid I. Brezhnev, paid an official visit to the United States from June 18 to June 25. Mr. Brezhnev was accompanied by A. A. Gromyko, Minister of Foreign Affairs of the USSR, Member of the Politbureau of the Central Committee, CPSU; N. S. Patolichev, Minister of Foreign Trade; B. Bugayev, Minister of Civil Aviation; G. E. Tsukanov and A. M. Aleksandrov, Assistants to the General Secretary of the Central Committee, CPSU; L. I. Zamyatin, General Director of TASS: E. I. Chazov, Deputy Minister of Public Health of the USSR; G. M. Korniyenko, Member of the Collegium of the Ministry of Foreign Affairs of the USSR; G. A. Arbatov, Director of the USA Institute of the Academy of Sciences of the USSR.

President Nixon and General Secretary Brezhnev held thorough and constructive discussions on the progress achieved in the development of U.S.-Soviet relations and on a number of major international problems of mutual interest.

Also taking part in the conversations held in Washington, Camp David, and San Clemente, were:

On the American side William P. Rogers, Secretary of State; George P. Shultz, Secretary of the Treasury; Dr. Henry A. Kissinger, Assistant to the President for National Security Affairs.

On the Soviet side A. A. Gromyko, Minister of Foreign Affairs of the USSR, Member of the Politbureau of the Central Committee, CPSU; A. F. Dobrynin, Soviet Ambassador to the USA; N. S. Patolichev, Minister of Foreign Trade; B. Bugayev, Minister of Civil Aviation; A. M. Aleksandrov and G. E. Tsukanov, Assistants to the General Secretary of the Central Committee, CPSU; G. M. Korniyenko, Member of the Collegium of the Ministry of Foreign Affairs of the USSR.

I. The General State of U.S.-Soviet Relations

Both Sides expressed their mutual satisfaction with the fact that the American-Soviet summit meeting in Moscow in May 1972, and the joint decisions taken there have resulted in a substantial advance in the strengthening of peaceful relations between the U.S.A. and the U.S.S.R. and have created the basis for the further development of broad and mutually beneficial cooperation in various fields of mutual interest to the peoples of both countries and in the interests of all mankind. They noted their satisfaction with the mutual effort to implement strictly and fully the treaties and agreements concluded between the U.S.A. and the U.S.S.R., and to expand areas of cooperation.

They agreed that the process of reshaping relations between the U.S.A. and the U.S.S.R. on the basis of peaceful coexistence and equal security as set forth in the basic principles of relations between the U.S.A. and the U.S.S.R. signed in Moscow on May 29, 1972, is progressing in an encouraging manner. They emphasized the great importance that each side attaches to these basic principles. They reaffirmed their commitment to the continued scrupulous implementation and the enhancement of the effectiveness of each of the provisions of that document.

Both Sides noted with satisfaction that the outcome of the U.S.-Soviet meeting in Moscow in May 1972, was welcomed by other States and by world opinion as an important contribution to strengthening peace and international security, to curbing the arms race and to developing businesslike cooperation among States with different social systems.

Both Sides viewed the return visit to the USA of the General Secretary of the Central Committee of the CPSU, L. I. Brezhnev, and the talks held during the visit as an expression of their mutual determination to continue the course toward a major improvement in U.S.-Soviet relations.

Both Sides are convinced that the discussions they have just held represent a further milestone in the constructive development of their relations.

Convinced that such a development of American-Soviet relations serves the interests of both of their peoples and all of mankind, it was decided to take further major steps to give these relations maximum stability and to turn the development of friendship and cooperation between their peoples into a permanent factor for worldwide peace.

II. The Prevention of Nuclear War and the Limitation of Strategic Armaments

Issues related to the maintenance and strengthening of international peace were a central point of the talks between President Nixon and General Secretary Brezhnev.

Conscious of the exceptional importance for all mankind of taking effective measures to that end, they discussed ways in which both Sides could work toward removing the danger of war, and especially nuclear war, between the USA and the USSR and between either party and other countries. Consequently, in accordance with the Charter of the United Nations and the Basic Principles of Relations of May 29, 1972, it was decided to conclude an Agreement Between the USA and the USSR on the Prevention of Nuclear War. That Agreement was signed by the President and the General Secretary on June 22, 1973. The text has been published separately.

The President and the General Secretary, in appraising this Agreement, believe that it constitutes a historical landmark in Soviet-American relations and substantially strengthens the foundations of international security as a whole. The United States and the Soviet Union state their readiness to consider additional ways of strengthening peace and removing forever the danger of war, and particularly nuclear war.

In the course of the meetings, intensive discussions were held on questions of strategic arms limitation. In this connection both Sides emphasized the fundamental importance of the Treaty on the Limitation of Anti-Ballistic Missile Systems and the Interim Agreement on Certain Measures with Respect to the Limitation of Strategic Offensive Arms signed between the USA and the USSR in May 1972 which, for the first time in history, placed actual limits on the most modern and most formidable types of armaments.

Having exchanged views on the progress in the implementation of these agreements, both Sides reaffirmed their intention to carry them out and their readiness to move ahead jointly toward an agreement on the further limitation of strategic arms.

Both Sides noted that progress has been made in the negotiations that resumed in November 1972, and that the prospects for reaching a permanent agreement on more complete measures limiting strategic offensive armaments are favorable.

Both Sides agreed that the progress made in the limitation of strategic armaments is an exceedingly important contribution to the strengthening of US-Soviet relations and to world peace.

On the basis of their discussions, the President and the General Secretary signed on June 21, 1973, Basic Principles of Negotiations on the Further Limitation of Strategic Offensive Arms. The text has been published separately.

The USA and the USSR attach great importance to joining with all States in the cause of strengthening peace, reducing the burden of armaments, and reaching agreements on arms limitation and disarmament measures.

Considering the important role which an effective international agreement with respect to chemical weapons would play, the two Sides agreed to continue their efforts to conclude such an agreement in cooperation with other countries.

The two Sides agree to make every effort to facilitate the work of the Committee on Disarmament which has been meeting in Geneva. They will actively participate in negotiations aimed at working out new measures to curb and end the arms race. They reaffirm that the ultimate objective is general and complete disarmament, including nuclear disarmament, under strict international control. A world disarmament conference could play a role in this process at an appropriate time.

III. International Questions: The Reduction of Tensions and Strengthening of International Security

President Nixon and General Secretary Brezhnev reviewed major questions of the current international situation. They gave special attention to the developments which have occurred since the time of the US-Soviet summit meeting in Moscow. It was noted with satisfaction that positive trends are developing in international relations toward the further relaxation of tensions and the strengthening of cooperative relations in the interests of peace. In the opinion of both Sides, the current process of improvement in the international situation creates new and favorable opportunities for reducing tensions, settling outstanding international issues, and creating a permanent structure of peace.

Indochina. The two Sides expressed their deep satisfaction at the conclusion of the Agreement on Ending the War and Restoring Peace in Vietnam, and also at the results of the International Conference on Vietnam which approved and supported that Agreement.

The two Sides are convinced that the conclusion of the Agreement on Ending the War and Restoring Peace in Vietnam, and the subsequent signing of the Agreement on Restoring Peace and Achieving National Concord in Laos, meet the fundamental interests and aspirations of the peoples of Vietnam and Laos and open up a possibility for establishing a lasting peace in Indochina, based on respect for the independence, sovereignty, unity and territorial integrity of the countries of that area. Both Sides emphasized that these agreements must be strictly implemented.

They further stressed the need to bring an early end to the military conflict in Cambodia in order to bring peace to the entire area of Indochina. They also reaffirmed their stand that the political futures of Vietnam, Laos, and Cambodia should be left to the respective peoples to determine, free from outside interference.

Europe. In the course of the talks both Sides noted with satisfaction that in Europe the process of relaxing tensions and developing cooperation is actively continuing and thereby contributing to international stability.

The two Sides expressed satisfaction with the further normalization of relations among European countries resulting from treaties and agreements signed in recent years, particularly between the USSR and the FRG [Federal Republic of Germany, West Germany]. They also welcome the coming into force of the Quadripartite Agreement of September 3, 1971. They share the conviction that strict observance of the treaties and agreements that have been concluded will contribute to the security and well-being of all parties concerned.

They also welcome the prospect of United Nations membership this year for the FRG and the GDR [German Democratic Republic, East Germany] and recall, in this connection, that the USA, USSR, UK and France have signed the Quadripartite Declaration of November 9, 1972, on this subject.

The USA and the USSR reaffirm their desire, guided by the appropriate provisions of the Joint US-USSR Communiqué adopted in Moscow in May 1972, to continue their separate and joint contributions to strengthening peaceful relations in Europe. Both Sides affirm that ensuring a lasting peace in Europe is a paramount goal of their policies.

In this connection satisfaction was expressed with the fact that as a result of common efforts by many States, including the USA and the USSR, the preparatory work has been successfully completed for the Conference on Security and Cooperation in Europe, which will be convened on July 3, 1973. The USA and the USSR hold the view that the Conference will enhance the possibilities for strengthening European security and developing cooperation among the participating States. The USA and the USSR will conduct their policies so as to realize the goals of the Conference and bring about a new era of good relations in this part of the world.

Reflecting their continued positive attitude toward the Conference, both Sides will make efforts to bring the Conference to a successful conclusion at the earliest possible time. Both Sides proceed from the assumption that progress in the work of the Conference will produce possibilities for completing it at the highest level.

The USA and the USSR believe that the goal of strengthening stability and security in Europe would be further advanced if the relaxation of political tensions were accompanied by a reduction of military tensions in Central Europe. In this respect they attach great importance to the negotiations on the mutual reduction of forces and armaments and associated measures in Central Europe which will begin on October 30, 1973. Both Sides state their readiness to make, along with other States, their contribution to the achievement of mutually acceptable decisions on the substance of this problem, based on the strict observance of the principle of the undiminished security of any of the parties.

Middle East. The parties expressed their deep concern with the situation in the Middle East and exchanged opinions regarding ways of reaching a Middle East settlement.

Each of the parties set forth its position on this problem.

Both parties agreed to continue to exert their efforts to promote the quickest possible settlement in the Middle East. This settlement should be in accordance with the interests of all states in the area, be consistent with their independence and sovereignty and should take into due account the legitimate interests of the Palestinian people.

IV. Commercial and Economic Relations

The President and the General Secretary thoroughly reviewed the status of and prospects for commercial and economic ties between the USA and the USSR. Both Sides noted with satisfaction the progress achieved in the past year in the normalization and development of commercial and economic relations between them.

They agreed that mutually advantageous cooperation and peaceful relations would be strengthened by the creation of a permanent foundation of economic relationships.

They recall with satisfaction the various agreements on trade and commercial relations signed in the past year. Both Sides note that American-Soviet trade has shown a substantial increase, and that there are favorable prospects for a continued rise in the exchange of goods over the coming years.

They believe that the two countries should aim at a total of 2-3 billion dollars of trade over the next three years. The Joint US-USSR Commercial Commission continues to provide a valuable mechanism to promote the broad-scale growth of economic relations. The two Sides noted with satisfaction that contacts between American firms and their Soviet counterparts are continuing to expand.

Both Sides confirmed their firm intention to proceed from their earlier understanding on measures directed at creating more favorable conditions for expanding commercial and other economic ties between the USA and the USSR.

It was noted that as a result of the Agreement Regarding Certain Maritime Matters signed in October 1972, Soviet and American commercial ships have been calling more frequently at ports of the United States and the USSR, respectively, and since late May of this year a new regular passenger line has started operating between New York and Leningrad.

In the course of the current meeting, the two Sides signed a Protocol augmenting existing civil air relations between the USA and the USSR providing for direct air services between Washington and Moscow and New York and Leningrad, increasing the frequency of flights and resolving other questions in the field of civil aviation.

In the context of reviewing prospects for further and more permanent economic cooperation, both Sides expressed themselves in favor of mutually advantageous long term projects. They discussed a number of specific projects involving the participation of American companies, including the delivery of Siberian natural gas to the United States. The President indicated that the USA encourages American firms to work out concrete proposals on these projects and will give serious and sympathetic consideration to proposals that are in the interest of both Sides.

To contribute to expanded commercial, cultural and technical relations between the USA and the USSR, the two Sides signed a tax convention to avoid double taxation on income and eliminate, as much as possible, the need for citizens of one country to become involved in the tax system of the other.

A Protocol was also signed on the opening by the end of October 1973 of a Trade Representation of the USSR in Washington and a Commercial Office of the United States in Moscow. In addition a Protocol was signed on questions related to establishing a US-Soviet Chamber of Commerce. These agreements will facilitate the further development of commercial and economic ties between the USA and the USSR.

V. Further Progress in Other Fields of Bilateral Cooperation

The two Sides reviewed the areas of bilateral cooperation in such fields as environmental protection, public health and medicine, exploration of outer space, and science and technology, established by the agreements signed in May 1972 and subsequently. They noted that those agreements are being satisfactorily carried out in practice in accordance with the programs as adopted.

In particular, a joint effort is under way to develop effective means to combat those diseases which are most widespread and dangerous for mankind: cancer, cardiovascular or infectious diseases and arthritis. The medical aspects of the environmental problems are also subjects of cooperative research.

Preparations for the joint space flight of the Apollo and Soyuz spacecraft are proceeding according to an agreed timetable. The joint flight of these spaceships for a rendezvous and docking mission, and mutual visits of American and Soviet astronauts in each other's spacecraft, are scheduled for July 1975.

Building on the foundation created in previous agreements, and recognizing the potential of both the USA and the USSR to undertake cooperative measures in current scientific and technological areas, new projects for fruitful joint efforts were identified and appropriate agreements were concluded.

Peaceful Uses of Atomic Energy. Bearing in mind the great importance of satisfying the growing energy demands in both countries and throughout the world, and recognizing that the development of highly efficient energy sources could contribute to the solution of this problem, the President and General Secretary signed an agreement to expand and strengthen cooperation in the fields of controlled nuclear fusion, fast breeder reactors, and research on the fundamental properties of matter. A Joint Committee on Cooperation in the Peaceful Uses of Atomic Energy will be established to implement this agreement, which has a duration of ten years.

Agriculture. Recognizing the importance of agriculture in meeting mankind's requirement for food products and the role of science in modern agricultural production, the two Sides concluded an agreement providing for a broad exchange of scientific experience in agricultural economics. A US-USSR Joint Committee on Agricultural Cooperation will be established to oversee joint programs to be carried out under the Agreement.

World Ocean Studies. Considering the unique capabilities and the major interest of both nations in the field of world ocean studies, and noting the extensive experience of US-USSR oceanographic cooperation, the two Sides have agreed to broaden their cooperation and have signed an agreement to this effect. In so doing, they are convinced that the benefits from further development of cooperation in the field of oceanography will accrue not only bilaterally but also to all peoples of the world. A US-USSR Joint Committee on Cooperation in World Ocean Studies will be established to coordinate the implementation of cooperative programs.

Transportation. The two Sides agreed that there are opportunities for cooperation between the USA and the USSR in the solution of problems in the field of transportation. To permit expanded, mutually beneficial cooperation in this field, the two Sides concluded an agreement on this subject. The USA and the USSR further agreed that a Joint Committee on Cooperation in Transportation would be established.

Contacts, Exchanges and Cooperation. Recognizing the general expansion of US-USSR bilateral relations and, in particular, the growing number of exchanges in the fields of science, technology, education and culture, and in other fields of mutual interest, the two Sides agreed to broaden the scope of these activities under a new General Agreement on Contacts, Exchanges, and Cooperation, with a duration of six years. The two Sides agreed to this in the mutual belief that it will further promote better understanding between the peoples of the United States and the Soviet Union and will help to improve the general state of relations between the two countries.

Both Sides believe that the talks at the highest level, which were held in a frank and constructive spirit, were very valuable and made an important contribution to developing mutually advantageous relations between the USA and the USSR. In the view of both Sides, these talks will have a favorable impact on international relations.

They noted that the success of the discussions in the United States was facilitated by the continuing consultation and contacts as agreed in May 1972. They reaffirmed that the practice of consultation should continue. They agreed that further meetings at the highest level should be held regularly.

Having expressed his appreciation to President Nixon for the hospitality extended during the visit to the United States, General Secretary Brezhnev invited the President to visit the USSR in 1974. The invitation was accepted.

June 24, 1973

RICHARD NIXON

PRESIDENT OF THE
UNITED STATES
AMERICA

LEONID I. BREZHNEV

GENERAL SECRETARY OF THE
CENTRAL COMMITTEE, CPSU

1974 U.S.-SOVIET ECONOMIC AGREEMENT

Following is the text of the June 29, 1974, Soviet-American agreement on economic, industrial, and technical cooperation, which was renewed for 10 years in June 1985:

Long Term Agreement Between The United States of America and The Union of Soviet Socialist Republics To Facilitate Economic, Industrial, and Technical Cooperation

The United States of America and the Union of Soviet Socialist Republics,

Desiring to promote continuing orderly expansion of economic, industrial, and technical cooperation and the exchange of relevant information to facilitate such cooperation between the two countries and their competent organizations, enterprises, and firms on a long term and mutually beneficial basis,

Guided by the Basic Principles of Relations between the United States of America and the Union of Soviet Socialist Republics of May 29, 1972,[1] the Joint American-Soviet Communiqué of June 24, 1973,[2] and the principles set forth in the Agreement between the Government of the United States of America and the government of the Union of Soviet Socialist Republics Regarding Trade dated October 18, 1972,[3]

Have agreed as follows:

Article I

The Parties shall use their good offices to facilitate economic, industrial, and technical cooperation in keeping with established practices and applicable laws and regulations in the respective countries.

Article II

Cooperation which shall be facilitated as contemplated in Article I shall include:

a. purchases and sales of machinery and equipment for the construction of new enterprises and for the expansion and modernization of existing enterprises in the fields of raw materials, agriculture, machinery and equipment, finished products, consumer goods, and services;

b. purchases and sales of raw materials, agricultural products, finished products, consumer goods, and services;

c. purchases, sales and licensing of patent rights and proprietary industrial know-how, designs, and processes;

d. training of technicians and exchange of specialists; and

e. joint efforts, where appropriate, in the construction of industrial and other facilities in third countries, particularly through supply of machinery and equipment.

Article III

In order to assist relevant organizations, enterprises, and arms of both countries in determining the fields of cooperation most likely to provide a basis for mutually beneficial contracts, a working group of experts convened by the Commission mentioned in Article V shall meet not less frequently than once a year to exchange information and forecasts of basic economic, industrial, and commercial trends.

Article IV

To promote the cooperation foreseen in this Agreement the Parties undertake to facilitate, as appropriate, the acquisition or lease of suitable business and residential premises by organizations, enterprises, and firms of the other party and their employees; the importation of essential office equipment and supplies; the hiring of staffs; the issuance of visas, including multiple entry visas, to qualified officials and representatives of such organizations, enterprises, and firms and to members of their immediate families; and travel by such persons for business purposes in the territory of the receiving country.

Article V

The US-USSR Commercial Commission established pursuant to the Communiqué of May 26, 1972 [4], is authorized and directed to monitor the practical implementation of this Agreement, when necessary jointly with other American-Soviet bodies created by agreement between the Governments of the two countries, with a view to facilitating the cooperation contemplated in this Agreement.

Article VI

This Agreement shall enter into force on the date of its signature, and shall remain in force for 10 years.

The Parties shall agree not later than six months prior to the expiration of the above period upon measures which may be necessary to facilitate further development of economic, industrial, and technical cooperation.

DONE at Moscow on June 29, 1974, in duplicate, in the English and Russian languages, both texts being equally authentic.

FOR THE UNITED STATES
OF AMERICA:
Richard Nixon

President of the
United States of America

FOR THE UNION OF SOVIET
SOCIALIST REPUBLICS:

L. I. Brezhnev

General Secretary of the Central
Committee of the CPSU

Footnotes

1 Department of State Bulletin, June 26, 1972, p. 898.
2 Department of State Bulletin, July 23, 1973, p. 130.
3 Department of State Bulletin, Nov. 20, 1972, p. 595.
4 Weekly Compilation of Presidential Documents, June 5, 1972, p. 924.

NIXON-BREZHNEV 1974 SUMMIT STATEMENTS

Following are the texts of the agreements signed in Moscow on July 2, 1974, by President Richard Nixon and Soviet Communist Party leader Leonid I. Brezhnev concerning limitations on antiballistic missile systems and underground nuclear weapons tests, and a joint communiqué issued July 3:

Limitation of ABM Systems

Protocol to the Treaty Between the United States of America and the Union of Soviet Socialist Republics on the Limitation of Anti-Ballistic Missile Systems.
July 3, 1974

The United States of America and the Union of Soviet Socialist Republics, hereinafter referred to as the Parties,

Proceeding from the Basic Principles of Relations between the United States of America and the Union of Soviet Socialist Republics signed on May 29, 1972,

Desiring to further the objectives of the Treaty between the United States of America and the Union of Soviet Socialist Republics on the Limitation of Anti-Ballistic Missile Systems signed on May 26, 1972, hereinafter referred to as the Treaty,

Reaffirming their conviction that the adoption of further measures for the limitation of strategic arms would contribute to strengthening international peace and security,

Proceeding from the premise that further limitation of antiballistic missile systems will create more favorable conditions for the completion of work on a permanent agreement on more complete measures for the limitation of strategic offensive arms,

Have agreed as follows:

Article I

1. Each Party shall be limited at any one time to a single area out of the two provided in Article III of the Treaty for deployment

of anti-ballistic missile (ABM) systems or their components and accordingly shall not exercise its right to deploy an ABM system or its components in the second of the two ABM system deployment areas permitted by Article III of the Treaty, except as an exchange of one permitted area for the other in accordance with Article II of this Protocol.

2. Accordingly, except as permitted by Article II of this Protocol: the United States of America shall not deploy an ABM system or its components in the area centered on its capital, as permitted by Article III(a) of the Treaty, and the Soviet Union shall not deploy an ABM system or its components in the deployment area of intercontinental ballistic missile (ICBM) silo launchers permitted by Article III(b) of the Treaty.

Article II

1. Each Party shall have the right to dismantle or destroy its ABM system and the components thereof in the area where they are presently deployed and to deploy an ABM system or its components in the alternative area permitted by Article III of the Treaty, provided that prior to initiation of construction, notification is given in accord with the procedure agreed to by the Standing Consultative Commission, during the year beginning October 3, 1977, and ending October 2, 1978, or during any year which commences at five year intervals thereafter, those being the years for periodic review of the Treaty, as provided in Article XIV of the Treaty. This right may be exercised only once.

2. Accordingly, in the event of such notice, the United States would have the right to dismantle or destroy the ABM system and its components in the deployment area of ICBM silo launchers and to deploy an ABM system or its components in an area centered on its capital, as permitted by Article III(a) of the Treaty, and the Soviet Union would have the right to dismantle or destroy the ABM system and its components in the area centered on its capital and to deploy an ABM system or its components in an area containing ICBM silo launchers, as permitted by Article III(b) of the Treaty.

3. Dismantling or destruction and deployment of ABM systems or their components and the notification thereof shall be carried out in accordance with Article VIII of the ABM Treaty and procedures agreed to in the Standing Consultative Commission.

Article III

The rights and obligations established by the Treaty remain in force and shall be complied with by the Parties except to the extent modified by this Protocol. In particular, the deployment of an ABM system or its components within the area selected shall remain limited by the levels and other requirements established by the Treaty.

Article IV

This Protocol shall be subject to ratification in accordance with the constitutional procedures of each Party. It shall enter into force on the day of the exchange of instruments of ratification and shall thereafter be considered an integral part of the Treaty.

Done at Moscow on July 3, 1974, in duplicate, in the English and Russian languages, both texts being equally authentic.

For the United States of America:
Richard Nixon
President of the United States of America

For the Union of Soviet Socialist Republics:
L. I. Brezhnev
General Secretary of the Central Committee of the CPSU

Limitation of Underground Tests

Treaty Between the United States of America and the Union of Soviet Socialist Republics on the Limitation of Underground

Nuclear Weapons Tests.
July 3, 1974

The United States of America and the Union of Soviet Socialist Republics, hereinafter referred to as the Parties,

Declaring their intention to achieve at the earliest possible date the cessation of the nuclear arms race and to take effective measures toward reductions in strategic arms, nuclear disarmament, and general and complete disarmament under strict and effective international control,

Recalling the determination expressed by the Parties to the 1963 Treaty Banning Nuclear Weapon Tests in the Atmosphere, in Outer Space and Under Water in its Preamble to seek to achieve the discontinuance of all test explosions of nuclear weapons for all time, and to continue negotiations to this end,

Noting that the adoption of measures for the further limitation of underground nuclear weapon tests would contribute to the achievement of these objectives and would meet the interests of strengthening peace and the further relaxation of international tension,

Reaffirming their adherence to the objectives and principles of the Treaty Banning Nuclear Weapon Tests in the Atmosphere, in Outer Space and Under Water and of the Treaty on the Non-Proliferation of Nuclear Weapons,

Have agreed as follows:

Article I

1. Each Party undertakes to prohibit, to prevent, and not to carry out any underground nuclear weapon test having a yield exceeding 150 kilotons at any place under its jurisdiction or control, beginning March 31, 1976.

2. Each Party shall limit the number of its underground nuclear weapon tests to a minimum.

3. The Parties shall continue their negotiations with a view toward achieving a solution to the problem of the cessation of all underground nuclear weapon tests.

Article II

1. For the purpose of providing assurance of compliance with the provisions of this Treaty, each Party shall use national technical means of verification at its disposal in a manner consistent with the generally recognized principles of international law.

2. Each Party undertakes not to interfere with the national technical means of verification of the other Party operating in accordance with paragraph 1 of this Article.

3. To promote the objectives and implementation of the provisions of this Treaty the Parties shall, as necessary, consult with each other, make inquiries and furnish information in response to such inquiries.

Article III

The provisions of this Treaty do not extend to underground nuclear explosions carried out by the Parties for peaceful purposes. Underground nuclear explosions for peaceful purposes shall be governed by an agreement which is to be negotiated and concluded by the Parties at the earliest possible time.

Article IV

This Treaty shall be subject to ratification in accordance with the constitutional procedures of each Party. This Treaty shall enter into force on the day of the exchange of instruments of ratification.

Article V

1. This Treaty shall remain in force for a period of five years. Unless replaced earlier by an agreement in implementation of the objectives specified in paragraph 3 of Article I of this Treaty, it shall be extended for successive five-year periods unless either Party notifies the other of its termination no later than six months

prior to the expiration of the Treaty. Before the expiration of this period the Parties may, as necessary, hold consultations to consider the situation relevant to the substance of this Treaty and to introduce possible amendments to the text of the Treaty.

2. Each Party shall, in exercising its national sovereignty, have the right to withdraw from this Treaty if it decides that extraordinary events related to the subject matter of this Treaty have jeopardized its supreme interests. It shall give notice of its decision to the other Party six months prior to withdrawal from this Treaty. Such notice shall include a statement of the extraordinary events the notifying Party regards as having jeopardized its supreme interests.

3. This Treaty shall be registered pursuant to Article 102 of the Charter of the United Nations.

Done at Moscow on July 3, 1974, in duplicate, in the English and Russian languages, both texts being equally authentic.

For the United States of America:
> Richard Nixon
> President of the United States of
> America

For the Union of Soviet Socialist Republics:
> L. I. Brezhnev
> General Secretary of the Central
> Committee of the CPSU

Protocol

To the Treaty Between the United States of America and the Union of Soviet Socialist Republics on the Limitation of Underground Nuclear Weapons Tests

The United States of America and the Union of Soviet Socialist Republics, hereinafter referred to as the Parties,

Having agreed to limit underground nuclear weapon tests,

Have agreed as follows:

1. For the Purpose of ensuring verification of compliance with the obligations of the Parties under the Treaty by national technical means, the Parties shall on the basis of reciprocity, exchange the following data:

a. The geographic coordinates of the boundaries of each test site and of the boundaries of the geophysically distinct testing areas therein.

b. Information on the geology of the testing areas of the sites (the rock characteristics of geological formations and the basic physical properties of the rock, i.e., density, seismic velocity, water saturation, porosity and depth of water table).

c. The geographic coordinates of underground nuclear weapon tests, after they have been conducted.

d. Yield, date, time, depth and coordinates for two nuclear weapon tests for calibration purposes from each geophysically distinct testing area where underground nuclear weapon tests have been and are to be conducted. In this connection the yield of such explosions for calibration purposes should be as near as possible to the limit defined in Article I of the Treaty and not less than one-tenth of that limit. In the case of testing areas where data are not available on two tests for calibration purposes, the data pertaining to one such test shall be exchanged, if available, and the data pertaining to the second test shall be exchanged as soon as possible after a second test having a yield in the above-mentioned range. The provisions of this Protocol shall not require the Parties to conduct tests solely for calibration purposes.

2. The Parties agree that the exchange of data pursuant to subparagraphs a, b, and d of paragraph 1 shall be carried out simultaneously with the exchange of instruments of ratification of the Treaty, as provided in Article IV of the Treaty, having in mind that the Parties shall, on the basis of reciprocity, afford each other the opportunity to familiarize themselves with these data before the exchange of instruments of ratification.

3. Should a party specify a new test site or testing area after the entry into force of the Treaty, the data called for by subparagraphs a and b of paragraph 1 shall be transmitted to the other Party in advance of use of that site or area. The data called for by subparagraph d of paragraph 1 shall also be transmitted in advance of use of that site or area if they are available; if they are not available, they shall be transmitted as soon as possible after they have been obtained by the transmitting Party.

4. The Parties agree that the test sites of each Party shall be located at places under its jurisdiction or control and that all nuclear weapon tests shall be conducted solely within the testing areas specified in accordance with paragraph 1.

5. For the purposes of the Treaty, all underground nuclear explosions at the specified test sites shall be considered nuclear weapon tests and shall be subject to all the provisions of the Treaty relating to nuclear weapon tests. The provisions of Article III of the Treaty apply to all underground nuclear explosions conducted outside of the specified test sites, and only to such explosions.

This Protocol shall be considered an integral part of the Treaty.

Done at Moscow on July 3, 1974.

For the United States of America:
> Richard Nixon
> President of the United States of
> America

For the Union of Soviet Socialist Republics:
> L. I. Brezhnev
> General Secretary of the Central
> Committee of the CPSU

July 3 Joint Communiqué

In accordance with the agreement to hold regular US-Soviet meetings at the highest level and at the invitation, extended during the visit of General Secretary of the Central Committee of the Communist Party of the Soviet Union L. I. Brezhnev to the USA in June 1973, the President of the United States of America and Mrs. Richard Nixon paid an official visit to the Soviet Union from June 27 to July 3, 1974.

During his stay President Nixon visited, in addition to Moscow, Minsk and the Southern Coast of the Crimea.

The President of the United States and the Soviet leaders held a thorough and useful exchange of views on major aspects of relations between the USA and USSR and on the present international situation.

On the Soviet side the talks were conducted by L. I. Brezhnev, General Secretary of the Central Committee of the Communist Party of the Soviet Union; N. V. Podgorny, Chairman of the Presidium of the USSR Supreme Soviet; A. N. Kosygin, Chairman of the USSR Council of Ministers; and A. A. Gromyko, Minister of Foreign Affairs of the USSR.

Accompanying the President of the USA and participating in the talks was Dr. Henry A. Kissinger, US Secretary of State and assistant to the President for National Security Affairs. . . .

The talks were held in a most businesslike and constructive atmosphere and were marked by a mutual desire of both Sides to continue to strengthen understanding, confidence and peaceful cooperation between them and to contribute to the strengthening of international security and world peace.

I. Progress in Improving US-Soviet Relations

Having considered in detail the development of relations between the USA and the USSR since the US-Soviet summit meeting in May 1972, both Sides noted with satisfaction that through their vigorous joint efforts they have brought about over this short period a fundamental turn toward peaceful relations and broad, mutually beneficial cooperation in the interests of the peoples of both countries and of all mankind.

They emphasized the special importance for the favorable development of relations between the USA and the USSR of meetings of their leaders at the highest level, which are becoming established practice. These meetings provide opportunities for effective and responsible discussion, for the solution of fundamental and important bilateral questions, and for mutual contributions to the settlement of international problems affecting the interests of both countries.

Both Sides welcome the establishment of official contacts between the Congress of the US and the Supreme Soviet of the USSR. They will encourage a further development of such contacts, believing that they can play an important role.

Both sides confirmed their mutual determination to continue actively to reshape US-Soviet relations on the basis of peaceful coexistence and equal security, in strict conformity with the spirit and the letter of the agreements achieved between the two countries and their obligations under those agreements. In this connection they noted once again the fundamental importance of the joint documents adopted as a result of the summit meetings in 1972 and 1973, especially of the Basic Principles of Relations Between the USA and the USSR, the Agreement on the Prevention of Nuclear War, the Treaty on the Limitation of Anti-Ballistic Missile Systems, and the Interim Agreement on Certain Measures with Respect to the Limitation of Strategic Offensive Arms.

Both Sides are deeply convinced of the imperative necessity of making the process of improving US-Soviet relations irreversible. They believe that, as a result of their efforts, a real possibility has been created to achieve this goal. This will open new vistas for broad mutually beneficial cooperation, and for strengthening friendship between the American and Soviet peoples, and will thus contribute to the solution of many urgent problems facing the world.

Guided by these worthy goals, both Sides decided to continue steadfastly to apply their joint efforts — in cooperation with other countries concerned, as appropriate — first of all in such important fields as:

—removing the danger of war, including particularly war involving nuclear and other mass-destruction weapons;

—limiting and eventually ending the arms race especially in strategic weapons, having in mind as the ultimate objective the achievement of general and complete disarmament under appropriate international control;

—contributing to the elimination of sources of international tension and military conflict;

—strengthening and extending the process of relaxation of tensions throughout the world;

—developing broad, mutually beneficial cooperation in commercial and economic, scientific-technical and cultural fields on the basis of the principles of sovereignty, equality and noninterference in internal affairs with a view to promoting increased understanding and confidence between the peoples of both countries.

Accordingly, in the course of this summit meeting both Sides considered it possible to take new constructive steps which, they believe, will not only advance further the development of US-Soviet relations but will also make a substantial contribution to strengthening world peace and expanding international cooperation.

II. Further Limitation of Strategic Arms and Other Disarmament Issues

Both sides again carefully analyzed the entire range of their mutual relations connected with the prevention of nuclear war and limitation of strategic armaments. They arrived at the common view that the fundamental agreements concluded between them in this sphere continue to be effective instruments of the general improvement of US-Soviet relations and the international situation as a whole. The USA and the USSR will continue strictly to fulfill the obligations undertaken in those agreements.

In the course of the talks, the two Sides had a thorough review of all aspects of the problem of limitation of strategic arms. They concluded that the Interim Agreement on offensive strategic weapons should be followed by a new agreement between the Soviet Union and the United States on the limitation of strategic arms. They agreed that such an agreement should cover the period until 1985 and deal with both quantitative and qualitative limitations. They agreed that such an agreement should be completed at the earliest possible date, before the expiration of the Interim Agreement.

They hold the common view that such a new agreement would serve not only the interests of the Soviet Union and the United

States but also those of a further relaxation of international tensions and of world peace.

Their delegations will reconvene in Geneva in the immediate future on the basis of instructions growing out of the summit.

Taking into consideration the interrelationship between the development of offensive and defensive types of strategic arms and noting the successful implementation of the Treaty on the Limitation of Anti-Ballistic Missile Systems concluded between them in May 1972, both Sides considered it desirable to adopt additional limitations on the deployment of such systems. To that end they concluded a Protocol providing for the limitation of each Side to a single deployment area for ABM systems instead of two such areas as permitted to each Side by the Treaty.

At the same time, two protocols were signed entitled "Procedures Governing Replacement, Dismantling or Destruction, and Notification Thereof, for Strategic Offensive Arms" and "Procedures Governing Replacement, Dismantling or Destruction, and Notification Thereof, for ABM Systems and their Components." These protocols were worked out by the Standing Consultative Commission which was established to promote the objectives and implementation of the provisions of the Treaty and the Interim Agreement signed on May 26, 1972.

The two Sides emphasized the serious importance which the US and USSR also attach to the realization of other possible measures — both on a bilateral and on a multilateral basis — in the field of arms limitation and disarmament.

Comprehensive Test Ban

Having noted the historic significance of the Treaty Banning Nuclear Weapon Tests in the Atmosphere, in Outer Space and Under Water, concluded in Moscow in 1963, to which the United States and the Soviet Union are parties, both Sides expressed themselves in favor of making the cessation of nuclear weapon tests comprehensive. Desiring to contribute to the achievement of this goal the USA and the USSR concluded, as an important step in this direction, the Treaty on the Limitation of Underground Nuclear Weapon Tests providing for the complete cessation, starting from March 31, 1976, of the tests of such weapons above an appropriate yield threshold, and for confining other underground tests to a minimum.

The Parties emphasized the fundamental importance of the Treaty on the Non-Proliferation of Nuclear Weapons. Having reaffirmed their mutual intention to observe the obligations assumed by them under that Treaty, including Article VI thereof, they expressed themselves in favor of increasing its effectiveness.

A joint statement was also signed in which the US and USSR advocate the most effective measures possible to overcome the dangers of the use of environmental modification techniques for military purposes.

Both Sides reaffirmed their interest in an effective international agreement which would exclude from the arsenals of states such dangerous instruments of mass destruction as chemical weapons. Desiring to contribute to early progress in this direction, the USA and the USSR agreed to consider a joint initiative in the Conference of the Committee on Disarmament with respect to the conclusion, as a first step, of an international Convention dealing with the most dangerous, lethal means of chemical warfare.

Both Sides are convinced that the new important steps which they have taken and intend to take in the field of arms limitation as well as further efforts toward disarmament will facilitate the relaxation of international tensions and constitute a tangible contribution to the fulfillment of the historic task of excluding war from the life of human society and thereby of ensuring world peace. The US and the USSR reaffirmed that a world disarmament conference at an appropriate time can play a positive role in this process.

III. Progress in the Settlement of International Problems

In the course of the meeting detailed discussions were held on major international problems.

Both Sides expressed satisfaction that relaxation of tensions, consolidation of peace, and development of mutually beneficial cooperation are becoming increasingly distinct characteristics of the development of the international situation. They proceed from the assumption that progress in improving the international situation does not occur spontaneously but requires active and purposeful efforts to overcome obstacles and resolve difficulties that remain from the past.

The paramount objectives of all states and peoples should be to ensure, individually and collectively, lasting security in all parts of the world, the early and complete removal of existing international conflicts and sources of tension and the prevention of new ones from arising.

The United States and the Soviet Union are in favor of the broad and fruitful economic cooperation among all states, large and small, on the basis of full equality and mutual benefit.

The United States and the Soviet Union reaffirm their determination to contribute separately and jointly to the achievement of all these tasks.

Europe

Having discussed the development of the situation in Europe since the last American-Soviet summit meeting, both Sides noted with profound satisfaction the further appreciable advances toward establishing dependable relations of peace, good neighborliness and cooperation on the European continent.

Both Sides welcome the major contribution which the Conference on Security and Cooperation in Europe is making to this beneficial process. They consider that substantial progress has already been achieved at the Conference on many significant questions. They believe that this progress indicates that the present stage of the Conference will produce agreed documents of great international significance expressing the determination of the participating states to build their mutual relations on a solid jointly elaborated basis. The US and USSR will make every effort, in cooperation with the other participants, to find solutions acceptable to all for the remaining problems.

Both Sides expressed their conviction that successful completion of the Conference on Security and Cooperation in Europe would be an outstanding event in the interests of establishing a lasting peace. Proceeding from this assumption the USA and the USSR expressed themselves in favor of the final stage of the Conference taking place at an early date. Both Sides also proceed from the assumption that the results of the negotiations will permit the Conference to be concluded at the highest level, which would correspond to the historic significance of the Conference for the future of Europe and lend greater authority to the importance of the Conference's decisions.

Both sides reaffirmed the lasting significance for a favorable development of the situation in Europe of the treaties and agreements concluded in recent years between European states with different social systems.

They expressed satisfaction with the admission to the United Nations of the Federal Republic of Germany and the German Democratic Republic.

Both Sides also stressed that the Quadripartite Agreement of September 3, 1971, must continue to play a key role in ensuring stability and detente in Europe. The US and USSR consider that the strict and consistent implementation of this Agreement by all parties concerned is an essential condition for the maintenance and strengthening of mutual confidence and stability in the center of Europe.

The USA and the USSR believe that, in order to strengthen stability and security in Europe, the relaxation of political tension on this continent should be accompanied by measures to reduce military tensions.

They therefore attach importance to the current negotiations on the mutual reduction of forces and armaments and associated measures in Central Europe, in which they are participating. The two Sides expressed the hope that these negotiations will result in concrete decisions ensuring the undiminished security of any of the parties and preventing unilateral military advantage.

Middle East

Both Sides believe that the removal of the danger of war and tension in the Middle East is a task of paramount importance and

urgency, and therefore, the only alternative is the achievement, on the basis of UN Security Council Resolution 338, of a just and lasting peace settlement in which should be taken into account the legitimate interests of all peoples in the Middle East, including the Palestinian people, and the right to existence of all states in the area.

As Co-Chairmen of the Geneva Peace Conference on the Middle East, the USA and the USSR consider it important that the Conference resume its work as soon as possible, with the question of other participants from the Middle East area to be discussed at the Conference, the achievement of which they will promote in every way, as the establishment of just and stable peace in the Middle East.

They agreed that the USA and USSR will continue to remain in close touch with a view to coordinating the efforts of both countries toward a peaceful settlement in the Middle East.

Indochina

Both sides noted certain further improvements in the situation in Indochina. In the course of the exchange of views on the situation in Vietnam both Sides emphasized that peace and stability in the region can be preserved and strengthened only on the basis of strict observance by all parties concerned of the provisions of the Paris Agreement of January 27, 1973, and the Act of the International Conference on Vietnam of March 2, 1973.

As regards Laos, they noted progress in the normalization of the situation as a result of the formation there of coalition governmental bodies. Both sides also pronounced themselves in favor of strict fulfillment of the pertinent agreements.

Both Sides also stressed the need for an early and just settlement of the problem of Cambodia based on respect of the sovereign rights of the Cambodian people to a free and independent development without any outside interference.

Strengthening the Role of the United Nations

The United States of America and the Soviet Union attach great importance to the United Nations as an instrument for maintaining peace and security and the expansion of international cooperation. They reiterate their intention to continue their efforts toward increasing the effectiveness of the United Nations in every possible way, including in regard to peacekeeping, on the basis of strict observance of the United Nations Charter.

IV. Commercial and Economic Relations

In the course of the meeting great attention was devoted to a review of the status of and prospects for relations between the USA and the USSR in the commercial and economic field.

Both Sides reaffirmed that they regard the broadening and deepening of mutually advantageous ties in this field on the basis of equality and nondiscrimination as an important part of the foundation on which the entire structure of US-Soviet relations is built. An increase in the scale of commercial and economic ties corresponding to the potentials of both countries will cement this foundation and benefit the American and Soviet peoples.

The two Sides noted with satisfaction that since the previous summit meeting US-Soviet commercial and economic relations have on the whole shown an upward trend. This was expressed, in particular, in a substantial growth of the exchange of goods between the two countries which approximated $1.5 billion in 1973. It was noted that prospects were favorable for surpassing the goal announced in the joint US-USSR communique of June 24, 1973, of achieving a total bilateral trade turnover of $2.3 billion during the three-year period 1973-1975. The Joint US-USSR Commercial Commission continues to provide an effective mechanism to promote the broad-scale growth of economic relations.

The two Sides noted certain progress in the development of long-term cooperation between American firms and Soviet organizations in carrying out large-scale projects including those on a compensation basis. They are convinced that such cooperation is an important element in the development of commercial and economic ties between the two countries. The two Sides agreed to encourage the conclusion and implementation of appropriate agreements between American and Soviet organizations and firms.

Taking into account the progress made in a number of specific projects, such as those concerning truck manufacture, the trade center, and chemical fertilizers, the Sides noted the possibility of concluding appropriate contracts in other areas of mutual interest, such as pulp and paper, timber, ferrous and non-ferrous metallurgy, natural gas, the engineering industry, and the extraction and processing of high energy-consuming minerals.

Both Sides noted further development of productive contacts and ties between business circles of the two countries in which a positive role was played by the decisions taken during the previous summit meeting on the opening of a United States commercial office in Moscow and a USSR trade representation in Washington as well as the establishment of a US-Soviet Commercial and Economic Council. They expressed their desire to continue to bring about favorable conditions for the successful development of commercial and economic relations between the USA and the USSR.

Both Sides confirmed their interest in bringing into force at the earliest possible time the US-Soviet trade agreement of October 1972.

Desirous of promoting the further expansion of economic relations between the two countries, the two Sides signed a Long-Term Agreement to Facilitate Economic, Industrial and Technical Cooperation between the USA and the USSR. They believe that a consistent implementation of the cooperation embodied in the Agreement over the ten-year period will be an important factor in strengthening bilateral relations in general and will benefit the peoples of both countries.

Having reviewed the progress in carrying out the Agreement Regarding Certain Maritime Matters concluded in October 1972 for a period of three years, and based on the experience accumulated thus far, the two Sides expressed themselves in favor of concluding before its expiration a new agreement in this field. Negotiations concerning such an agreement will commence this year.

V. Progress in Other Fields of Bilateral Relations

Having reviewed the progress in the implementation of the cooperative agreements concluded in 1972-1973, both Sides noted the useful work done by joint American-Soviet committees and working groups established under those agreements in developing regular contacts and cooperation between scientific and technical organizations, scientists, specialists and cultural personnel of both countries.

The two Sides note with satisfaction that joint efforts by the USA and USSR in such fields of cooperation as medical science and public health, protection and improvement of man's environment, science and technology, exploration of outer space and the world ocean, peaceful uses of atomic energy, agriculture and transportation create conditions for an accelerated solution of some urgent and complicated problems facing mankind.

Such cooperation makes a substantial contribution to the development of the structure of American-Soviet relations, giving it a more concrete positive content.

Both Sides will strive to broaden and deepen their cooperation in science and technology as well as cultural exchanges on the basis of agreements concluded between them.

On the basis of positive experience accumulated in their scientific and technological cooperation and guided by the desire to ensure further progress in this important sphere of their mutual relations, the two Sides decided to extend such cooperation to the following new areas.

Energy

Taking into consideration the growing energy needs of industry, transportation and other branches of the economies of both countries and the consequent need to intensify scientific and technical cooperation in the development of optimal methods of utilizing traditional and new sources of energy, and to improve the understanding of the energy programs and problems of both countries, the two Sides concluded an agreement on cooperation in the field of energy. Responsibility for the implementation of the Agreement is entrusted to a US-USSR Joint Committee on Cooperation in Energy, which will be established for that purpose.

Housing and Other Construction

The two Sides signed an agreement on cooperation in the field of housing and other construction. The aim of this Agreement is to promote the solution by joint effort of problems related to modern techniques of housing and other construction along such lines as the improvement of the reliability and quality of buildings and building materials, the planning and construction of new towns, construction in seismic areas and areas of extreme climatic conditions. For the implementation of this Agreement there will be established a Joint US-USSR Committee on Cooperation in Housing and Other Construction which will determine specific working programs.

For the purpose of enhancing the safety of their peoples living in earthquake-prone areas, the two Sides agreed to undertake on a priority basis a joint research project to increase the safety of buildings and other structures in these areas and, in particular, to study the behavior of prefabricated residential structures during earthquakes.

Artificial Heart Research

In the course of the implementation of joint programs in the field of medical science and public health, scientists and specialists of both countries concluded that there is a need to concentrate their efforts on the solution of one of the most important and humane problems of modern medical science, development of an artificial heart. In view of the great theoretical and technical complexity of the work involved, the two Sides concluded a special agreement on the subject. The US-USSR Joint Committee for Health Cooperation will assume responsibility for this project.

Cooperation in Space

The two Sides expressed their satisfaction with the successful preparations for the first joint manned flight of the American and Soviet spacecraft, Apollo and Soyuz, which is scheduled for 1975 and envisages their docking and mutual visits of the astronauts in each other's spacecraft. In accordance with existing agreements fruitful cooperation is being carried out in a number of other fields related to the exploration of outer space.

Attaching great importance to further American-Soviet cooperation in the exploration and use of outer space for peaceful purposes, including the development of safety systems for manned flights in space, and considering the desirability of consolidating experience in this field, the two Sides agreed to continue to explore possibilities for further joint space projects following the US-USSR space flight now scheduled for July 1975.

Transport of the Future

Aware of the importance of developing advanced modes of transportation, both Sides agreed that high-speed ground systems of the future, including a magnetically levitated train, which can provide economical, efficient, and reliable forms of transportation, would be a desirable and innovative area for joint activity. A working group to develop a joint research cooperation program in this area under the 1973 Agreement on Cooperation in the Field of Transportation will be established at the Fall meeting of the Joint US-USSR Transportation Committee.

Environmental Protection

Desiring to expand cooperation in the field of environmental protection, which is being successfully carried out under the US-USSR Agreement signed on May 23, 1972, and to contribute to the implementation of the "Man and the Biosphere" international program conducted on the initiative of the United Nations Educational, Scientific and Cultural Organization (UNESCO), both Sides agreed to designate in the territories of their respective countries certain natural areas as biosphere reserves for protecting valuable plant and animal genetic strains and ecosystems, and for conducting scientific research needed for more effective actions concerned with global environmental protection. Appropriate work for the implementation of this undertaking will be conducted in conformity with the goals of the UNESCO program and under the auspices of the previously established US-USSR Joint Committee on Cooperation in the Field of Environmental Protection.

Cultural Exchanges

The two Parties, aware of the importance of cultural exchanges as a means of promoting mutual understanding, express satisfaction with the agreement between the Metropolitan Museum of Art of New York City and the Ministry of Culture of the USSR leading to a major exchange of works of art. Such an exchange would be in accordance with the General Agreement on Contacts, Exchanges and Cooperation signed July 19, 1973, under which the parties agreed to render assistance for exchange of exhibitions between the museums of the two countries.

Establishment of New Consulates

Taking into consideration the intensive development of ties between the US and the USSR and the importance of further expanding consular relations on the basis of the US-USSR Consular Convention, and desiring to promote trade, tourism and cooperation between them in various areas, both Sides agreed to open additional Consulates General in two or three cities of each country.

As a first step they agreed in principle to the simultaneous establishment of a United States Consulate General in Kiev and a USSR Consulate General in New York. Negotiations for implementation of this agreement will take place at an early date.

Both Sides highly appreciate the frank and constructive atmosphere and fruitful results of the talks held between them in the course of the present meeting. They are convinced that the results represent a new and important milestone along the road of improving relations between the USA and the USSR to the benefit of the peoples of both countries, and a significant contribution to their efforts aimed at strengthening world peace and security.

Having again noted in this connection the exceptional importance and great practical usefulness of US-Soviet summit meetings, both Sides reaffirmed their agreement to hold such meetings regularly and when considered necessary for the discussion and solution of urgent questions. Both Sides also expressed their readiness to continue their active and close contacts and consultations.

The President extended an invitation to General Secretary of the Central Committee of the CPSU, L. I. Brezhnev, to pay an official visit to the United States in 1975. This invitation was accepted with pleasure.

Richard Nixon
President of the United States of America

L. I. Brezhnev
General Secretary of the Central Committee CPSU

LETTERS ON SOVIET JEWRY

The following are texts of letters released October 18, 1974, between Secretary of State Henry A. Kissinger and Sen. Henry M. Jackson, D-Wash., relating to the Trade Act of 1974 and the emigration of Soviet Jews. Also included is the text of Soviet foreign minister Andrei A. Gromyko's letter to Kissinger reiterating the Soviet position.

Kissinger's Letter

October 18, 1974

Dear Senator Jackson:

I am writing to you, as the sponsor of the Jackson Amendment, in regard to the Trade Bill (H.R. 10710) which is currently before the Senate and in whose early passage the administration is deeply interested. As you know, Title IV of that bill, as it emerged from the House, is not acceptable to the administration. At the same time, the administration respects the objectives with regard to emigration from the U.S.S.R. that are sought by means of the stipulations in Title IV, even if it cannot accept the means employed. It respects in particular your own leadership in this field.

To advance the purposes we share both with regard to passage of the trade bill and to emigration from the U.S.S.R., and on the basis of discussions that have been conducted with Soviet representatives, I should like on behalf of the administration to inform you that we have been assured that the following criteria and practices will henceforth govern emigration from the U.S.S.R.

First, punitive actions against individuals seeking to emigrate from the U.S.S.R. would be violations of Soviet laws and regulations and will therefore not be permitted by the government of the U.S.S.R. In particular, this applies to various kinds of intimidation or reprisal, such as, for example, the firing of a person from his job, his demotion to tasks beneath his professional qualifications, and his subjection to public or other kinds of recrimination.

Second, no unreasonable or unlawful impediments will be placed in the way of persons desiring to make application for emigration, such as interference with travel or communications necessary to complete an application, the withholding of necessary documentation and other obstacles including kinds frequently employed in the past.

Third, applications for emigration will be processed in order of receipt, including those previously filed, and on a nondiscriminatory basis as regards the place of residence, race, religion, national origin and professional status of the applicant. Concerning professional status, we are informed that there are limitations on emigration under Soviet law in the case of individuals holding certain security clearances, but that such individuals who desire to emigrate will be informed of the date on which they may expect to become eligible for emigration.

Fourth, hardship cases will be processed sympathetically and expeditiously; persons imprisoned who, prior to imprisonment, expressed an interest in emigrating, will be given prompt consideration for emigration upon their release; and sympathetic consideration may be given to the early release of such persons.

Fifth, the collection of the so-called emigration tax on emigrants which was suspended last year will remain suspended.

Sixth, with respect to all the foregoing points, we will be in a position to bring to the attention of the Soviet leadership indications that we may have that these criteria and practices are not being applied. Our representations, which would include but not necessarily be limited to the precise matters enumerated in the foregoing points, will receive sympathetic consideration and response.

Finally, it will be our assumption that with the application of the criteria, practices, and procedures set forth in this letter, the rate of emigration from the U.S.S.R. would begin to rise promptly from the 1973 level and would continue to rise to correspond to the number of applicants.

I understand that you and your associates have, in addition, certain understandings incorporated in a letter dated today respecting the foregoing criteria and practices which will henceforth govern emigration from the U.S.S.R. which you wish the President to accept as appropriate guidelines to determine whether the purposes sought through Title IV of the trade bill and further specified in our exchange of correspondence in regard to the emigration practices of non-market economy countries are being fulfilled. You have submitted this letter to me and I wish to advise you on behalf of the President that the understandings in your letter will be among the considerations to be applied by the President in exercising the authority provided for in Sec. 402 of Title IV of the trade bill.

I believe that the contents of this letter represent a good basis, consistent with our shared purposes, for proceeding with an acceptable formulation of Title IV of the trade bill, including procedures for periodic review, so that normal trading relations may go forward for the mutual benefit of the U.S. and the U.S.S.R.

Best regards,

HENRY A. KISSINGER

Jackson's Reply

October 18, 1974

Dear Mr. Secretary:

Thank you for your letter of Oct. 18 which I have now had an opportunity to review. Subject to the further understandings and interpretations outlined in this letter, I agree that we have achieved a suitable basis upon which to modify Title IV by incorporating within it a provision that would enable the President to waive subsections designated (a) and (b) in Sec. 402 of Title IV as passed by the House in circumstances that would substantially promote the objectives of Title IV.

It is our understanding that the punitive actions, intimidation or reprisals that will not be permitted by the government of the U.S.S.R. include the use of punitive conscription against persons seeking to emigrate, or members of their families; and the bringing of criminal actions against persons in circumstances that suggest a relationship between their desire to emigrate and the criminal prosecution against them.

Second, we understand that among the unreasonable impediments that will no longer be placed in the way of persons seeking to emigrate is the requirement that adult applicants receive the permission of their parents or other relatives.

Third, we understand that the special regulations to be applied to persons who have had access to genuinely sensitive classified information will not constitute an unreasonable impediment to emigration. In this connection we would expect such persons to become eligible for emigration within three years of the date on which they last were exposed to sensitive and classified information.

Fourth, we understand that the actual number of emigrants would rise promptly from the 1973 level and would continue to rise to correspond to the number of applicants, and may therefore exceed 60,000 per annum. We would consider a benchmark — a minimum standard of initial compliance — to be the issuance of visas at the rate of 60,000 per annum; and we understand that the President proposes to use the same benchmark as the minimum standard of initial compliance. Until such time as the actual number of emigrants corresponds to the number of applicants the benchmark figure will not include categories of persons whose emigration has been the subject of discussion between Soviet officials and other European governments.

In agreeing to provide discretionary authority to waive the provisions of subsections designated (a) and (b) in Sec. 402 of Title IV as passed by the House, we share your anticipation of good faith in the implementation of the assurances contained in your letter of Oct. 18 and the understandings conveyed by this letter. In particular, with respect to paragraphs three and four of your letter we wish it to be understood that the enumeration of types of punitive action and unreasonable impediments is not and cannot be considered comprehensive or complete, and that nothing in this exchange of correspondence shall be construed as permitting types of punitive action or unreasonable impediments not enumerated therein.

Finally, in order adequately to verify compliance with the standard set forth in these letters, we understand that communication by telephone, telegraph and post will be permitted.

Sincerely yours,

HENRY M. JACKSON

Gromyko's Letter

Dear Mr. Secretary of State:

I believe it necessary to draw your attention to the question concerning the publication in the United States of materials of which you are aware and which touch upon the departure from the Soviet Union of a certain category of Soviet citizens.

I must say straightforwardly that the above-mentioned materials, including the correspondence between you and Senator Jackson, create a distorted picture of our position as well as of what we told the American side on that matter.

When clarifying the actual state of affairs in response to your request, we underlined that the question as such is entirely within the internal competence of our state. We warned at the time that in this matter we had acted and shall act in strict conformity with our present legislation on that score.

But now silence is being kept precisely about this. At the same time, attempts are being made to ascribe to the elucidations that were furnished by us the nature of some assurances and, nearly, obligations on our part regarding the procedure of the departure of Soviet citizens from the U.S.S.R., and even some figures are being quoted as to the supposed number of such citizens, and there is talk about an anticipated increase of that number as compared with previous years.

We resolutely decline such an interpretation. What we said, and you, Mr. Secretary of State, know this well, concerned only and exclusively the real situation in the given question. And when we did mention figures — to inform you of the real situation — the point was quite the contrary, namely about the present tendency toward a decrease in the number of persons wishing to leave the U.S.S.R. and seek permanent residence in other countries.

We believe it important that in this entire matter, considering its principled significance, no ambiguities should remain as regards the position of the Soviet Union.

A. GROMYKO
Minister of Foreign Affairs of the U.S.S.R.

FORD, BREZHNEV SUMMIT AT VLADIVOSTOK

Following are the texts of the U.S.-Soviet joint statement issued November 24, 1974, on the limitation of strategic offensive weapons and the U.S.-Soviet joint communiqué issued November 24 at the end of the summit meeting between President Gerald R. Ford and Soviet party leader Leonid I. Brezhnev:

During their working meeting in the area of Vladivostok on November 23-24, 1974, the President of the USA Gerald R. Ford and General Secretary of the Central Committee of the CPSU [Communist Party of the Soviet Union] L. I. Brezhnev discussed in detail the question of further limitations of strategic offensive arms.

They reaffirmed the great significance that both the United States and the USSR attach to the limitation of strategic offensive arms. They are convinced that a long-term agreement on this question would be a significant contribution to improving relations between the US and the USSR, to reducing the danger of war and to enhancing world peace. Having noted the value of previous agreements on this question, including the Interim Agreement of May 26, 1972, they reaffirm the intention to conclude a new agreement on the limitation of strategic offensive arms, to last through 1985.

As a result of the exchange of views on the substance of such a new agreement the President of the United States of America and the General Secretary of the Central Committee of the CPSU concluded that favorable prospects exist for completing the work on this agreement in 1975.

Agreement was reached that further negotiations will be based on the following provisions.

1. The new agreement will incorporate the relevant provisions of the Interim Agreement of May 26, 1972, which will remain in force until October 1977.

2. The new agreement will cover the period from October 1977 through December 31, 1985.

3. Based on the principle of equality and equal security, the new agreement will include the following limitations:

a. Both sides will be entitled to have a certain agreed aggregate number of strategic delivery vehicles;

b. Both sides will be entitled to have a certain agreed aggregate number of ICBMs and SLBMs equipped with multiple independently targetable warheads (MIRVs).

4. The new agreement will include a provision for further negotiations beginning no later than 1980-1981 on the question of further limitations and possible reductions of strategic arms in the period after 1985.

5. Negotiations between the delegations of the U.S. and USSR to work out the new agreement incorporating the foregoing points will resume in Geneva in January 1975.

November 24, 1974

U.S.-Soviet Joint Communiqué

In accordance with the previously announced agreement, a working meeting between the President of the United States of America Gerald R. Ford and the General Secretary of the Central Committee of the Communist Party of the Soviet Union L. I. Brezhnev took place in the area of Vladivostok on November 23 and 24, 1974. Taking part in the talks were the Secretary of State of the United States of America and assistant to the President for National Security Affairs, Henry A. Kissinger, and Member of the Politburo of the Central Committee of the CPSU, Minister of Foreign Affairs of the U.S.S.R., A. A. Gromyko.

They discussed a broad range of questions dealing with American-Soviet relations and the current international situation.

Also taking part in the talks were:

On the American side Walter J. Stoessel, Jr., Ambassador of the USA to the USSR; Helmut Sonnenfeldt, counselor of the Department of State; Arthur A. Hartman, Assistant Secretary of State for European Affairs; Lieutenant General Brent Scowcroft, Deputy Assistant to the President for National Security Affairs; and William Hyland, official of the Department of State.

On the Soviet side A. F. Dobrynin, Ambassador of the USSR to the USA; A. M. Aleksandrov, Assistant to the General Secretary of the Central Committee of the CPSU; and G. M. Korniyenko, Member of the Collegium of the Ministry of Foreign Affairs of the USSR.

I

The United States of America and the Soviet Union reaffirmed their determination to develop further their relations in the direction defined by the fundamental joint decisions and basic treaties and agreements concluded between the two States in recent years.

They are convinced that the course of American-Soviet relations, directed towards strengthening world peace, deepening the relaxation of international tensions and expanding mutually beneficial cooperation of states with different social systems meets the vital interests of the peoples of both States and other peoples.

Both Sides consider that based on the agreements reached between them important results have been achieved in fundamentally reshaping American-Soviet relations on the basis of peaceful coexistence and equal security. These results are a solid foundation for progress in reshaping Soviet-American relations.

Accordingly, they intend to continue, without a loss in momentum, to expand the scale and intensity of their cooperative efforts in all spheres as set forth in the agreements they have signed so that the process of improving relations between the US and the USSR will continue without interruption and will become irreversible.

Mutual determination was expressed to carry out strictly and fully the mutual obligations undertaken by the US and the USSR in accordance with the treaties and agreements concluded between them.

II

Special consideration was given in the course of the talks to a pivotal aspect of Soviet-American relations: measures to eliminate the threat of war and to halt the arms race.

Both sides reaffirm that the Agreements reached between the US and the USSR on the prevention of nuclear war and the limitation of strategic arms are a good beginning in the process of creating guarantees against the outbreak of nuclear conflict and war in general. They expressed their deep belief in the necessity of promoting this process and expressed their hope that other states would contribute to it as well. For their part the US and the USSR will continue to exert vigorous efforts to achieve this historic task.

A joint statement on the question of limiting strategic offensive arms is being released separately.

Both sides stressed once again the importance and necessity of a serious effort aimed at preventing the dangers connected with the spread of nuclear weapons in the world. In this connection they stressed the importance of increasing the effectiveness of the Treaty on the Non-Proliferation of Nuclear Weapons.

It was noted that, in accordance with previous agreements, initial contacts were established between representatives of the US and of the USSR on questions related to underground nuclear explosions for peaceful purposes, to measures to overcome the dangers of the use of environmental modification techniques for military purposes, as well as measures dealing with the most dangerous lethal means of chemical warfare. It was agreed to continue an active search for mutually acceptable solutions of these questions.

III

In the course of the meeting an exchange of views was held on a number of international issues: special attention was given to negotiations already in progress in which the two Sides are participants and which are designed to remove existing sources of tension and to bring about the strengthening of international security and world peace.

Having reviewed the situation at the Conference on Security and Cooperation in Europe, both Sides concluded that there is a possibility for its early successful conclusion. They proceed from the assumption that the results achieved in the course of the Conference will permit its conclusion at the highest level and thus be commensurate with its importance in ensuring the peaceful future of Europe.

The USA and the USSR also attach high importance to the negotiations on mutual reduction of forces and armaments and associated measures in Central Europe. They agree to contribute actively to the search for mutually acceptable solutions on the basis of principle of undiminished security for any of the parties and the prevention of unilateral military advantages.

Having discussed the situation existing in the Eastern Mediterranean, both Sides state their firm support for the independence, sovereignty and territorial integrity of Cyprus and will make every effort in this direction. They consider that a just settlement of the Cyprus question must be based on the strict implementation of the resolutions adopted by the Security Council and the General Assembly of the United Nations regarding Cyprus.

In the course of the exchange of views on the Middle East both Sides expressed their concern with regard to the dangerous situation in that region. They reaffirmed their intention to make every effort to promote a solution of the key issues of a just and lasting peace in that area on the basis of the United Nations resolution 338, taking into account the legitimate interests of all the peoples of the area, including the Palestinian people, and respect for the right to independent existence of all states in the area.

The Sides believe that the Geneva Conference should play an important part in the establishment of a just and lasting peace in the Middle East, and should resume its work as soon as possible.

IV

The state of relations was reviewed in the field of commercial, economic, scientific and technical ties between the USA and the USSR. Both Sides confirmed the great importance which further progress in these fields would have for Soviet-American relations, and expressed their firm intention to continue the broadening and deepening of mutually advantageous cooperation.

The two Sides emphasized the special importance accorded by them to the development on a long term basis of commercial and economic cooperation, including mutually beneficial large-scale projects. They believe that such commercial and economic cooperation will serve the cause of increasing the stability of Soviet-American relations.

Both Sides noted with satisfaction the progress in the implementation of agreements and in the development of ties and cooperation between the US and the USSR in the fields of science, technology and culture. They are convinced that the continued expansion of such cooperation will benefit the peoples of both countries and will be an important contribution to the solution of world-wide scientific and technical problems.

———————

The talks were held in an atmosphere of frankness and mutual understanding, reflecting the constructive desire of both Sides to strengthen and develop further the peaceful cooperative relationship between the USA and the USSR, and to ensure progress in the solution of outstanding international problems in the interest of preserving and strengthening peace.

The results of the talks provided a convincing demonstration of the practical value of Soviet-American summit meetings and their exceptional importance in the shaping of a new relationship between the United States of America and the Soviet Union.

President Ford reaffirmed the invitation to L. I. Brezhnev to pay an official visit to the United States in 1975. The exact date of the visit will be agreed upon later.

FOR THE UNITED STATES OF AMERICA
    GERALD R. FORD
        President of the United States of America

FOR THE UNION OF SOVIET SOCIALIST REPUBLICS
    L. I. BREZHNEV
        General Secretary of the Central Committee of the CPSU

November 24, 1974

SAKHAROV-CARTER EXCHANGE OF LETTERS

Following are the texts of a January 21, 1977, letter sent by Soviet dissident Andrei D. Sakharov to President Jimmy Carter and Carter's February 5 reply:

Sakharov Letter

It is very important to defend those who suffer because of their non-violent struggle, for openness, for justice, for destroyed rights of other people. Our and your duty is to fight for them. I think that a great deal depends on this struggle — trust between the people, trust in high promises and the final result — international security.

Here we have a hard, almost unbearable situation — not only in the U.S.S.R. but also in all the countries of Eastern Europe.

Now, before the [June 1977] Belgrade meeting [to review the Helsinki accords] and in the conditions of the raising of the struggle for human rights in Eastern Europe and the U.S.S.R., the authorities do not wish to make any concessions to the most vital human rights (freedom of belief, and information, freedom of conscience, freedom of the choice of the country of living, etc.). They are incapable to engage in an honest competition of ideas. They increase repressions and make attempts to compromise the dissidents. They persecute members of the Group for Assistance to Fulfillment of the Helsinki Agreement, in Moscow and the Ukraine. Of special note should be the provocation in the Moscow subway [an explosion Jan. 8, which Sakharov thought had been engineered by the KGB in an attempt to discredit the dissident movement], which should be resisted energetically (we compare it

to the Reichstag fire in 1933 and the killing of [Sergei M.] Kirov in 1934).

It's very important that the U.S. president should continue efforts for the release of those people who are already known to the American public and that these efforts should not be in vain. It is very important to continue the fight for the very sick and for the women — political prisoners. The detailed information about all of them is in Khronika Press [an underground publication].

I have a serious problem with communications. Telephone communications with the West are blocked completely and no telephone calls reach me. It is useless to go to the telephone station as I'm always told that the other party doesn't answer (I'm always closely watched).

We can't cross out any of the names on this list. This is the main list but there are very many others who need the same support.

1. Kovalev; 2. Svetlichny; 3. Romanyuk; 4. Dzhemilev; 5. Gluzman; 6. Ruban; 7. Fyodorov; 8. Vins; 9. Stern; 10. Moroz; 11. Sergeyenko; 12. Makarenko; 13. Pronyuk; 14. Semyonova; 15. Fedorenko.

I also want to ask you especially to raise your voice in defense of Mihajlo Mihajlov (the Yugoslav writer), the authors of Charter 77 in Czechoslovakia [members of a Czech human rights group], the Workers' Defense Committee in Poland [Polish human rights group].

Do you know the truth about the plight of religions in the U.S.S.R.? The humiliated situation of those religions which are allowed by the authorities, about the persecution of Baptists, of the true Orthodox Church, of Pentacostals, of Uniates, and others, about the taking away of children from religious parents (Vins is the best known example) and even about murders (for example, the Baptist, Biblenko).

Terror is applied also to other groups of dissidents. During the last year we know of murders of dissidents that have not been investigated at all. The best known example is the poet and translator, Konstantin Bogatyryov.

The question of communications is principally important for my public activity and for all the human rights movement in this country. I ask you to take some steps on the international level in connection with this.

Carter Reply

I received your letter of Jan. 21, and I want to express my appreciation to you for bringing your thoughts to my personal attention.

Human rights is a central concern of my administration. In my inaugural address I stated: "Because we are free, we can never be indifferent to the fate of freedom elsewhere."

You may rest assured that the American people and our government will continue our firm commitment to promote respect for human rights not only in our country but also abroad.

We shall use our good offices to seek the release of prisoners of conscience, and we will continue our efforts to shape a world response to human aspirations in which nations of differing cultures and histories can live side by side in peace and justice. I am always glad to hear from you, and I wish you well.

BREZHNEV ON HUMAN RIGHTS

Following are excerpts from a speech made March 21, 1977, by Soviet leader Leonid I. Brezhnev to the 16th Congress of Trade Unions, in Moscow:

. . . In our country it is not forbidden to think differently from the majority. We regard the comrades who come out with well-founded criticism, who strive to help the cause, as critics in good faith, and we are grateful to them. Those who criticize erroneously we regard as erring people.

It is another matter when several persons who have broken away from our society actively come out against the socialist system, embark on the road of anti-Soviet activity, violate laws and, having no support inside the country, turn for support abroad, to imperialist subversive centers.

Our people demand that such so-called public figures be treated as opponents of socialism, as persons acting against their own motherland, as accomplices and sometimes agents of imperialism. Quite naturally we have taken and will take measures against them as envisaged by law.

And, in this matter, let no one take offense. To protect the rights, freedoms and security of 260 million Soviet people from the activities of such renegades is not only our right, but our sacred duty.

Now, about Soviet-American relations....

...[T]here are circumstances directly opposed to further improvement of Soviet-American relations. One is the slanderous campaign about a mythical military menace posed by the U.S.S.R.... The other circumstance is the direct attempt by official American bodies to interfere in the internal affairs of the Soviet Union.

Washington's claims to teach others how to live, I believe, cannot be accepted by any sovereign state, not to mention the fact that neither the situation in the United States itself nor United States actions and policies in the world at large give justification to such claims.

The Soviet Union has always firmly upheld and will uphold its sovereign rights, its dignity and its interests. At the same time a constructive, realistic approach by the other side will always encounter our understanding and readiness to reach agreement....

1977 SOVIET CONSTITUTION

Following are excerpts from the draft constitution and excerpts from the constitution ratified by the Supreme Soviet October 7, 1977:

Constitution of the Soviet Union

The Soviet people, guided by the ideas of scientific communism and remaining true to their revolutionary traditions, resting on the great social, economic and political achievements of socialism, striving to further develop socialist democracy, taking into account the international position of the USSR as part of the world socialist system and conscious of their international responsibility, preserving the continuity of the ideas and principles of the 1918 Constitution of the RSFSR, the 1924 Constitution of the USSR and the 1936 Constitution of the USSR, proclaim the aims and principles, define the foundations of the organization of the socialist state of the whole people, and formalize them in this Constitution....

The Political System

Article 1. The Union of Soviet Socialist Republics is a socialist state of the whole people, expressing the will and interests of the working class, the peasantry and the intelligentsia, of all the nations and nationalities in the country.

Article 2. All power in the USSR shall be vested in the people.

The people shall exercise state power through the Soviets of People's Deputies, which constitute the political foundation of the USSR.

All other organs of state shall be under the control of and accountable to the Soviets.

Article 3. The Soviet state shall be organized and shall function in accordance with the principle of democratic centralism: electivity of all organs of state power from top to bottom, their accountability to the people, and mandatory fulfillment of the decisions of higher organs by lower organs. Democratic centralism shall combine single leadership with local initiative and creative activity, with the responsibility of each state organ and each official for the work at hand.

Article 4. The Soviet state, in all its organs, shall function on the basis of socialist legality and ensure the protection of law and order, the interests of society and the rights of citizens. State institutions, public organizations and officials shall observe the Constitution of the USSR and Soviet laws....

Article 6. The Communist Party of the Soviet Union is the leading and guiding force of Soviet society and the nucleus of its political system, of all state and public organizations. The CPSU exists for the people and serves the people.

Armed with the Marxist-Leninist (body of) teaching, the Communist Party shall determine the general perspective of society's development and the guidelines for the internal and external policy of the USSR, give guidance to the great creative endeavor of the Soviet people, and place their struggle for the triumph of communism on a planned, scientific basis....

The Economic System

Article 9. Socialist ownership of the means of production shall be the foundation of the economic system of the USSR. Socialist ownership shall comprise: state property (belonging to the whole people), property of collective farms and other cooperative organizations (collective farm-cooperative property), and property of trade unions and other public organizations.

The state shall protect socialist property and create the conditions for augmenting it.

No one shall have the right to use socialist property for personal gain.

Article 10. State property, i.e., property belonging to the whole people, shall be the principal form of socialist ownership.

The land, its minerals, waters and forests shall be the exclusive property of the state. The state shall be in possession of the basic means of production: industrial, building and agricultural enterprises, means of transport and communication, and also the banks, distributive enterprises and community services and the bulk of urban housing....

Article 13. The free labor of Soviet people shall be the basis of the growth of social wealth and the welfare of the people, of every Soviet citizen.

The state shall control the measure of labor and consumption in accordance with the principle: "From each according to his ability, to each according to his work." It shall determine the rates of the income tax and establish the level of wages exempted from taxes.

Socially useful work and its results shall determine a citizen's status in society. By combining material and moral incentives the state shall help turn labor into the prime need in the life of every Soviet citizen....

Article 15. The economy of the USSR shall be an integral economic complex embracing all the elements of social production, distribution and exchange on the territory of the USSR.

The economy shall be managed on the basis of state plans for economic, social and cultural development with due account taken of the branch and territorial principles, and combining centralized leadership with the economic independence and initiative of enterprises, associations and other organizations. Here active use shall be made of cost accounting, profit and production costs....

Social Development and Culture

Article 19. The Soviet state shall create the conditions for enhancing society's social homogeneity, erasing the essential distinctions between town and countryside and between mental and manual labor, and further developing and drawing together all the nations and nationalities of the USSR.

Article 20. In accordance with the communist ideal, "the free development of each is the condition for the free development of all," the Soviet state shall pursue the aim of expanding the actual possibilities for citizens to develop and apply their creative strength, abilities and talents, for the all-around development of the individual....

Foreign Policy

Article 28. The Soviet state shall consistently pursue the Leninist policy of peace and stand for the consolidation of the security of peoples and broad international cooperation.

The foreign policy of the USSR shall be aimed at ensuring favorable international conditions for the building of communism in the USSR, at strengthening the positions of world socialism, supporting the struggle of peoples for national liberation and social progress, preventing wars of aggression, and consistently implementing the principle of peaceful coexistence of states with different social systems.

In the USSR war propaganda shall be prohibited by law.

Article 29. The relations of the USSR with other states shall be based on the observance of the principle of mutual renunciation of the use or threats of force, and of the principles of sovereign equality, inviolability of frontiers, territorial integrity of states, peaceful settlement of disputes, non-interference in internal affairs, respect for human rights and basic freedoms, equality and the right of peoples to decide their own destiny, cooperation between states, scrupulous fulfillment of commitments emanating from universally recognized principles and norms of international law, and the international treaties signed by the USSR.

Article 30. As part of the world socialist system, of the socialist community, the Soviet Union shall promote and strengthen friendship, cooperation and comradely mutual assistance with the other socialist countries on the basis of socialist internationalism, and shall actively participate in economic integration and in the international socialist division of labor....

The State and the Individual

Article 33. Soviet citizenship shall be uniform for the whole Union of Soviet Socialist Republics. Every citizen of a Union Republic shall be a citizen of the USSR.

The grounds and procedure of acquiring or losing Soviet citizenship shall be established by the law of the USSR.

Citizens of the USSR living abroad shall have the protection and guardianship of the Soviet state.

Article 34. Citizens of the USSR shall be equal before the law, irrespective of origin, social and property status, nationality or race, sex, education, language, attitude to religion, type or character of occupation, domicile, or other particulars.

Equality of rights of citizens of the USSR shall be ensured in all fields of economic, political, social, and cultural life.

Article 35. In the USSR women shall have equal rights with men.

Exercise of these rights shall be ensured by according to women equal opportunities (with men) for education and professional training, for employment, remuneration and promotion, for social, political and cultural activity, and likewise by special measures for the protection of the labor and health of women; by legal protection, material and moral support of mother and child, including paid leaves and other benefits to mothers and expectant mothers, and state aid to unmarried mothers.

Article 36. Soviet citizens of different nationalities and races shall have equal rights.

The exercise of these rights shall be ensured by the policy of all-around development and drawing together of all nations and nationalities of the USSR, education of citizens in the spirit of Soviet patriotism and socialist internationalism, and the opportunity for using their mother tongue as well as the languages of the other peoples of the USSR.

Any and all direct or indirect restrictions of the rights of, or the establishment of direct or indirect privileges for, citizens on grounds of race or nationality, and likewise any advocacy of racial or national exclusiveness, hostility or contempt, shall be punishable by law.

Article 37. In the USSR citizens of other countries and stateless persons shall be guaranteed the rights and freedoms provided for by law, including the right of instituting proceedings in law courts and other state organs in protection of personal, proprietary, family and other rights accorded to them by law.

On the territory of the USSR, citizens of other countries and stateless persons shall be obliged to respect the Constitution of the USSR and to observe Soviet laws.

Article 38. The USSR shall afford the right of asylum to foreign nationals persecuted for upholding the interests of the working people and the cause of peace, or for participating in a revolutionary or national liberation movement, or for progressive social, political, scientific or other creative activity.

Rights, Freedoms and Duties

Article 39. Citizens of the USSR shall enjoy in their entirety the social, economic, political and personal rights and freedoms proclaimed and guaranteed by the Constitution of the USSR and Soviet laws. The socialist system shall ensure extension of rights and freedoms and unintermittent improvement of the conditions of life of citizens relative to the fulfillment of programs of social, economic and cultural development.

Exercise by citizens of rights and freedoms must not injure the interests of society and the state, or the rights of other citizens.

Article 40. Citizens of the USSR shall have the right to work, that is, to guaranteed employment and remuneration for their work in accordance with its quantity and quality, including the right to choice of profession, type of occupation and employment, in accordance with their vocation, abilities, training, education, and with due account taken of the needs of society....

Article 41. Citizens of the USSR shall have the right to rest and leisure....

Article 42. Citizens of the USSR shall have the right to health protection....

Article 43. Citizens of the USSR shall have the right to maintenance in old age, in the event of sickness, and likewise in the event of complete or partial disability or loss of breadwinner....

Article 44. Citizens of the USSR shall have the right to housing. This right shall be ensured by the development and protection of state and public housing, assistance to co-operative and individual house-building, fair distribution under public control of housing, allotted with reference to the implementation of the housing program, and likewise by low rent.

Article 45. Citizens of the USSR shall have the right to education....

Article 46. Citizens of the USSR shall have the right to make use of the achievements of culture....

Article 48. Citizens of the USSR shall have the right to take part in the administration of state and public affairs....

Article 49. Every citizen of the USSR shall have the right to submit to state organs and public organizations proposals for improving their activity, to criticize shortcomings in their work. Officials shall be bound, within terms established by law, to examine proposals and requests made by citizens, reply to them and take due action.

Persecution for criticism shall be prohibited.

Article 50. In conformity with the interests of the working people and for the purpose of strengthening the socialist system, citizens of the USSR shall be guaranteed freedom of speech, press, assembly, meetings, street processions and demonstrations. Exercise of these political freedoms shall be ensured by putting at the disposal of the working people and their organizations public buildings, streets and squares, by broad dissemination of information, and by the opportunity to use the press, television and radio....

Article 52. Freedom of conscience, that is, the right to profess any religion and perform religious rites, or not to profess any religion and to conduct atheistic propaganda, shall be recognized for all citizens of the USSR. Incitement of hostility and hatred on religious grounds shall be prohibited.

The church in the USSR shall be separated from the state, and the school from the church.

Article 53. The family shall be under the protection of the state.

Marriage shall be entered into with the free consent of the

intending spouses; spouses shall be completely equal in their matrimonial relations....

Article 54. Citizens of the USSR shall be guaranteed inviolability of the person. No person shall be subjected to arrest other than by decision of a court of law, or with the sanction of a prosecutor.

Article 55. Citizens of the USSR shall be guaranteed inviolability of the home. No person shall without lawful grounds enter a home against the will of the persons residing in it.

Article 56. The privacy of citizens, of correspondence, telephone conversations and telegraphic messages shall be protected by law.

Article 57. Respect for the individual and protection of the rights and freedoms of Soviet citizens shall be the duty of all state organs, public organizations and officials....

Article 58. Citizens of the USSR shall have the right to lodge complaints against actions of officials in state organs and public organizations. These complaints shall be examined in the manner and within the terms defined by law....

Citizens of the USSR shall have the right to compensation for damage inflicted by unlawful actions of state institutions and public organizations, and likewise by officials in the performance of their duties, in the manner and within the limits defined by law.

Article 59. Exercise of rights and freedoms shall be inseparable from the performance by citizens of their duties....

Article 62. The citizens of the USSR shall be obliged to safeguard the interests of the Soviet state, to contribute to the strengthening of its might and prestige.

Defense of the socialist motherland shall be the sacred duty of every citizen of the USSR.

High treason shall be the gravest crime against the people....

Article 64. It shall be the duty of every citizen of the USSR to respect the national dignity of other citizens, to strengthen the friendship of the nations and nationalities of the Soviet multinational state....

Article 67. Citizens of the USSR shall be obligated to protect nature, to safeguard its wealth.

Concern for the preservation of historical monuments and other cultural values shall be the duty of citizens of the USSR.

Article 68. It shall be the internationalist duty of citizens of the USSR to further the development of friendship and cooperation with the peoples of other countries and the maintenance and consolidation of world peace....

The USSR—A Federal State

Article 69. The Union of Soviet Socialist Republics is an integral federal multinational state formed on the basis of the free self-determination of nations and the voluntary union of equal Soviet Socialist Republics.

The USSR embodies the state unity of the Soviet people and brings all the nations and nationalities together for the joint building of communism....

Article 71. Every Union Republic shall retain the right freely to secede from the USSR....

The Soviets of People's Deputies

Article 88. The Soviets of People's Deputies — the Supreme Soviet of the USSR, the Supreme Soviet of the Union Republics, the Supreme Soviets of the Autonomous Republics, the Territorial and Regional Soviets of People's Deputies, the Soviets of People's Deputies of Autonomous Regions and Autonomous Areas, and the city, district, city district, township and village Soviets of People's Deputies — shall comprise an integral system of organs of state power....

Article 101. Deputies shall be authorized representatives of the people in the Soviets of People's Deputies.

By participating in the work of the Soviets, deputies shall resolve matters related to state, economic, social and cultural development, organize the execution of the decisions of the Soviets, and exercise control over the work of state organs, enterprises, institutions and organizations....

Article 103. A deputy shall have the right to address an inquiry to the appropriate state organs and officials, who shall be obliged to reply to the inquiry at a session of the Soviet.

Deputies shall have the right to address an inquiry to any state or public organ, enterprise, institution or organization on questions within their terms of reference as deputies and to take part in considering the questions thus raised. The heads of the respective state or public organs, enterprises, institutions or organizations shall be obliged to receive deputies without delay and consider their recommendations within the period established by law.

Article 104. Deputies shall be assured conditions for the unobstructed and effective exercise of their rights and duties.

The immunity of deputies, as well as other guarantees of their functions as deputies, shall be defined in the Law on the Status of Deputies and other legislation of the USSR and of the Union and Autonomous Republics....

The Supreme Soviet

Article 106. The Supreme Soviet of the USSR shall be the highest organ of state power in the USSR.

The Supreme Soviet of the USSR shall be empowered to deal with all matters placed within the jurisdiction of the Union of Soviet Socialist Republics by the present Constitution.

The adoption of the Constitution of the USSR and amendments to it, the admission of new Republics to the USSR, approval of the formation of new Autonomous Republics and Autonomous Regions, endorsement of state plans of economic, social and cultural development and of the State Budget of the USSR, and of reports on their execution, and the formation of organs of the USSR accountable to it shall be the exclusive competence of the Supreme Soviet of the USSR.

Laws of the USSR shall be enacted solely by the Supreme Soviet of the USSR.

Article 107. The Supreme Soviet of the USSR shall consist of two chambers: the Soviet of the Union and the Soviet of Nationalities.

The two chambers of the Supreme Soviet of the USSR shall have equal rights.

Article 108. The Soviet of the Union and the Soviet of Nationalities shall have an equal number of deputies.

The Soviet of the Union shall be elected by constituencies with equal populations.

The Soviet of Nationalities shall be elected on the basis of the following quotas: 32 deputies from each Union Republic, 11 deputies from each Autonomous Republic, 5 deputies from each Autonomous Region, and one deputy from each Autonomous Area.

Upon representation by the credentials commissions elected by them, the Soviet of the Union and the Soviet of Nationalities shall recognize the credentials of deputies, and in cases where the election law has been violated, declare the election of individual deputies invalid....

Article 111. The right to initiate legislation in the Supreme Soviet of the USSR shall be exercised by the Soviet of the Union and the Soviet of Nationalities, the Presidium of the Supreme Soviet of the USSR, the Council of Ministers of the USSR, the Union Republics represented by their higher organs of state power, the commissions of the Supreme Soviet of the USSR and the Standing commissions of its chambers, deputies of the Supreme Soviet of the USSR, the Supreme Court of the USSR, and the Prosecutor-General of the USSR.

The right to initiate legislation shall be enjoyed also by mass public organizations represented by their all-Union organs....

Article 117. The Supreme Soviet of the USSR at a joint sitting of the two chambers shall elect the Presidium of the Supreme Soviet of the USSR, the continuously functioning organs of the Supreme Soviet of the USSR accountable to it in all its activities.

Article 118. The Presidium of the Supreme Soviet of the USSR shall be elected from among deputies and shall consist of a President, a First Vice-President, 15 Vice Presidents, i.e., one from each Union Republic, a Secretary of the Presidium, and 21 members of the Presidium of the Supreme Soviet of the USSR....

The Council of Ministers of the USSR

Article 127. The Council of Ministers of the USSR — the Government of the USSR — shall be the highest executive and administrative organ of state power in the USSR.

Article 128. The Council of Ministers of the USSR shall be formed by the Supreme Soviet of the USSR at a joint sitting of the Soviet of the Union and the Soviet of Nationalities and consist of: the Chairman of the Council of Ministers of the USSR, First Vice-Chairmen and Vice-Chairmen of the Council of Ministers of the USSR, the Ministers of the USSR, the Chairmen of state committees of the USSR.

The Council of Ministers of the USSR shall include, by virtue of their office, the Chairmen of the Councils of Ministers of Union Republics.

Upon submission by the Chairman of the Council of Ministers of the USSR, the Supreme Soviet of the USSR may include in the Government of the USSR leaders of other organs and organizations of the USSR.

Article 129. The Council of Ministers of the USSR shall be responsible and accountable to the Supreme Soviet of the USSR, and between sessions of the Supreme Soviet of the USSR to the Presidium of the Supreme Soviet of the USSR, to which it shall be accountable.

The Council of Ministers of the USSR shall regularly report on its work to the Supreme Soviet of the USSR....

Article 131. The Presidium of the Council of Ministers of the USSR, consisting of the Chairman of the Council of Ministers of the USSR and the First Vice-Chairmen and Vice-Chairmen of the Council of Ministers of the USSR, shall function as a permanent organ of the Council of Ministers of the USSR for the purpose of dealing with matters related to the administration of the economy and to other questions of state administration....

Courts of Law and Arbitration

Article 150. In the USSR justice shall be administered exclusively by courts of law.

In the USSR the court system shall consist of the following: the Supreme Court of the USSR, Supreme Courts of Union Republics, Supreme Courts of Autonomous Republics, territorial, regional and city courts, courts of Autonomous Regions, courts of Autonomous Areas, district (city) people's courts, and military tribunals in the Armed Forces.

Article 151. All courts in the USSR shall be formed on the principle of electivity of judges and people's assessors....

The Prosecutor's Office

Article 163. Supreme supervisory power over the precise and uniform execution of laws by all ministries, state committees and departments, enterprises, institutions and organizations, executive and administrative organs of local Soviets of People's Deputies, collective farms, cooperative and other public organizations, officials and citizens, shall be exercised by the Prosecutor General of the USSR and prosecutors subordinate to him.

Article 164. The Prosecutor General of the USSR shall be appointed by the Supreme Soviet of the USSR and shall be responsible and accountable to it, or between sessions of the Supreme Soviet to the Presidium of the Supreme Soviet of the USSR, to which he is accountable....

Amendment of the Constitution of the USSR

Article 172. The Constitution of the USSR shall have supreme legal force. All laws and other acts of state organs shall be issued on the basis of, and in conformity with, the Constitution of the USSR.

The Constitution of the USSR shall be effective from the time of its adoption.

Article 173. Amendment of the Constitution of the USSR shall be by decision of the Supreme Soviet of the USSR, adopted by a majority of not less than two-thirds of the total number of deputies of each of its chambers.

BREZHNEV PROTESTS U.S. NUCLEAR WEAPONS

Following are excerpts from a speech by Soviet Union President Leonid Brezhnev, delivered in Berlin, East Germany, October 6, 1979, on the deployment of new U.S. nuclear weapons in Western Europe:

...The dangerous plans for the deployment of new types of American nuclear-missile weapons in the territory of Western Europe — about which Western propaganda is trumpeting already now — give cause for serious concern. To put it straight, implementation of these designs would change essentially the strategic situation on the continent. Their aim is to upset the balance of forces that has taken shape in Europe and to try to ensure military superiority for the NATO bloc.

As for military superiority — that we shall see. In such a case, the socialist countries would not, of course, watch indifferently the efforts of the NATO militarists. We would have, in such a case, to take the necessary extra steps to strengthen our security. There would be no other way out left for us. But one thing is absolutely clear: Realization of NATO's plans would inevitably aggravate the situation in Europe and vitiate, in many respects, the international atmosphere in general.

It is no secret that the Federal Republic of Germany [West Germany], alongside the USA, is assigned not the least part in the preparation of these dangerous plans.

Frankly speaking, those who shape the policy of that country are facing today a very serious choice. They will have to decide which is best for the FRG: to help strengthen peace in Europe and develop peaceful, mutually beneficial cooperation among European states in the spirit of good-neighborliness and growing mutual confidence, or to contribute to a new aggravation of the situation in Europe and the world by deploying on its territory American nuclear-missile arms spearheaded against the USSR and its allies. It is clear that in this latter case the position of the FRG itself would considerably worsen. It is not hard to see what consequences the FRG would have in store for itself if these new weapons were put to use by their owners one day.

The above-said also applies, of course, to other European NATO countries which would be "lucky" enough to have American medium-range nuclear missiles deployed on their territories.

As for the Soviet Union, I repeat again and again that we do not seek military superiority. We have never intended and do not intend to threaten any state or a group of states. Our strategic doctrine is purely defensive in nature. The assertions that the Soviet Union is building up its military might in the European continent above its defense needs have nothing in common with reality. This is deliberate deception of the broad public.

In Europe, just as in all other parts of our planet, we want peace, a lasting peace. This is the fundamental basis of our foreign policy, its backbone. We are pursuing this policy consistently and undeviatingly.

As Chairman of the Defense Council of the USSR, I am most definitely stating that the number of medium-range carriers of nuclear arms on the territory of the European part of the Soviet Union has not been increased by a single missile, by a single plane during the past 10 years. On the contrary, the number of launchers of medium-range missiles and also the yield of the nuclear charges of these missiles have even been somewhat decreased. The number of medium-range bombers, too, has diminished. As for the territory of other states, the Soviet Union does not deploy such means there at all. For a number of years now we have not increased the number of our troops stationed in Central Europe either.

I will say more. We are prepared to reduce the number of medium-range nuclear means deployed in western areas of the Soviet Union as compared to the present level, but, of course, only if no additional medium-range nuclear means are deployed in Western Europe....

Motivated by a sincere desire to take out of the impasse the efforts of many years to achieve military detente in Europe, to show an example of transition from words to real deeds, we have decided, in agreement with the leadership of the GDR [German Democratic Republic, East Germany] and after consultations with other member states of the Warsaw Treaty, to unilaterally reduce the number of Soviet troops in Central Europe. Up to 20,000 Soviet servicemen, a thousand tanks and also a certain amount of other military hardware will be withdrawn from the territory of the German Democratic Republic in the course of the next 12 months.

We are convinced that this new, concrete manifestation of the peaceableness and good will of the Soviet Union and its allies will be approved by the peoples of Europe and the whole world. We call on the government of NATO countries to properly assess the initiatives of socialist states and to follow our good example.

The Soviet Union comes out for a further expansion of measures of trust in Europe. In particular, we are prepared to reach agreement that notification about large exercises of ground forces, provided for by the Helsinki Final Act, be made even earlier and not from the level of 25,000 men, as is the case now, but from a smaller one, for instance, from the level of 20,000 men. We also are prepared, on the basis of reciprocity, not to conduct military exercises involving more than 40,000 to 50,000 men....

And there is yet another thing that we would like to suggest to the West: In the area defined by the Helsinki act let us give timely notification not only about military exercises, but also about movements of ground forces numbering more than 20,000 men.

Consideration could be given also to other ideas directed at strengthening trust between states, at lessening the danger of the outbreak of war in Europe. We continue to regard a European conference held on the political level as the most suitable place for discussing a broad complex of measures of military detente in Europe. It is a very pressing and, it can be said, a ripe task to prepare and convene such a conference.

Lying ahead, as is known, are also important talks on SALT-III. We are for commencing them immediately after the entry into force of the SALT-II Treaty. Within the framework of these talks we agree to discuss the possibilities of limiting not only intercontinental but also other types of armaments, but with due account, of course, for all related factors and strict observance of the principle of the equal security of the sides.

So the USSR, the GDR and other socialist countries of Europe are offering a clear perspective — to genuinely ensure to all European peoples a life in conditions of security and peace. Now it is up to the Western countries. Their answer will show whether they are prepared to take into consideration the will and vital interests of the peoples. We hope that realism, statesmanship and, finally, just common sense will prevail....

BREZHNEV TASS INTERVIEW

Following is the text of an interview with Soviet Communist Party leader Leonid I. Brezhnev released January 12, 1980, by Tass, the Soviet news agency:

Q: Leonid Ilyich, how do you evaluate the present international situation, especially in the light of the American administration's latest steps?

A: The consistent and creative pursuance by our party of the course of peace, detente and disarmament, of implementing the Peace Program set forth by 24th and 25th Congresses of the Communist Party of the Soviet Union, has made it possible to achieve much. Broadly speaking, the main accomplishment is that we have succeeded in breaking the tragic cycle: world war, brief spell of peace, world war again. We, the Soviet people, our friends

— the peoples of fraternal socialist countries — and all those who have struggled and continue to struggle for peace, for detente, for the peaceful coexistence of states with different social systems have a right to be proud of this historic result.

The situation, unfortunately, has noticeably deteriorated at the junction of the seventies and the eighties, and the peoples must know the truth about who is responsible for this. I will answer without any reservations: The imperialist forces, first of all definite circles in the United States, are to blame for this. The blame is on all those who see in the relaxation of tension an obstacle to their aggressive plans, to the whipping up of militaristic psychosis and to interference in the internal affairs of other peoples. The blame is on those who have a deeply ingrained habit of behaving in a cavalier manner with other states and of acting in the international arena in a way as though everything is permitted them.

It has been clear for some time that the leading circles of the United States and of some other NATO countries have embarked on a course hostile to the cause of detente, a course of spiralling the arms race and leading to a growth of the war danger. The beginning of this was laid already in 1978, at the May session of the NATO Council in Washington, where the automatic growth of the military budgets of NATO member-countries until the end of the 20th century was approved. Lately, militaristic tendencies in the policy of the United States find their expression also in the acceleration of new long-term arms programs, in the creation of new military bases far beyond the United States, including the Middle East and the Indian Ocean area, in the forming of the so-called "quick reaction corps," this instrument of the policy of military interference.

SALT II Treaty

Now, take such an important document as the SALT-II Treaty. Its implementation would have opened the way to big steps in the field of disarmament. As is known, this treaty received support throughout the whole world, including the NATO allies of the United States and broad circles of the international public. And what did the Carter Administration do with it? Hardly was the treaty signed when people in the United States began discrediting it. As for the process of ratification, the opponents of the treaty — not without the connivance of government circles in the United States — actually began using it to complicate the treaty's ratification to the utmost. By his recent decision to freeze indefinitely the debate on the SALT-II Treaty in the Senate, President Carter added one more touch to this unseemly process.

It was the United States that, in December 1979, forced on its NATO allies the decision to deploy in a number of West European countries new, medium-range nuclear missile arms, this leading to a new spiral of the arms race. Washington virtually muzzled those of its allies who inclined to positively respond to the Soviet Union's constructive proposals to hold talks on this matter.

Afghanistan

Today the opponents of peace and detente are trying to speculate on the events in Afghanistan. Mountains of lies are being built up around these events, and a shameless anti-Soviet campaign is being mounted. What has really happened in Afghanistan?

A revolution took place there in April 1978. The Afghan people took their destiny into their hands and embarked on the road of independence and freedom. As it has always been in history, the forces of the past ganged up against the revolution. The people of Afghanistan, of course, could have coped with them themselves. But from the very first days of the revolution it encountered an external aggression and rude interference from outside into their internal affairs.

Thousands and tens of thousands of insurgents, armed and trained abroad, and whole armed units were sent into the territory of Afghanistan. In effect, imperialism, together with its accomplices, launched an undeclared war against revolutionary Afghanistan.

Afghanistan persistently demanded an end to the aggression and that it be allowed to build its new life in peace. Resisting the external aggression, the Afghan leadership, during the lifetime of President [Nur Mohammad] Taraki and then later, repeatedly asked the Soviet Union for assistance. On our part, we warned those concerned that if the aggression did not stop, we would not abandon the Afghan people at a time of trial. As is known, we stand by what we say.

The actions of the aggressors against Afghanistan were assisted by [Hafizullah] Amin, who, upon seizing power, launched cruel repressions against broad segments of Afghan society, against party and military cadres, against representatives of the intelligentsia and the Moslem clergy, that is, exactly against those segments on which the April Revolution relied. And the people under the leadership of the People's Democratic Party headed by Babrak Karmal rose against this Amin tyranny and put an end to it. Now in Washington and some other capitals they are mourning over Amin. This exposes their hypocricy with particular clarity. Where were these mourners when Amin was conducting his mass repressions, when he forcibly removed and unlawfully murdered Taraki, the founder of the new Afghan State?

The unceasing armed intervention, the well advanced plot by external forces of reaction created a real threat that Afghanistan would lose its independence and be turned into an imperialist military bridgehead on our country's southern border. In other words, the time came when we could no longer fail to respond to the request of the government of friendly Afghanistan. To have acted otherwise would have meant leaving Afghanistan prey to imperialism and allowing the aggressive forces to repeat in that country what they had succeeded in doing, for instance, in Chile where the people's freedom was drowned in blood. To act otherwise would have meant to watch passively the origination on our southern border of a seat of serious danger to the security of the Soviet state.

Soviet-Afghan Treaty

When making the request to us, Afghanistan proceeded from clear-cut provisions of the Treaty of Friendship, Good-Neighbourliness and Cooperation, concluded by Afghanistan with the USSR on December 1978, on the right of each state, in accordance with the United Nations Charter, to individual or collective self-defense, a right that other states have exercised more than once.

It was no simple decision for us to send Soviet military contingents to Afghanistan. But the party's Central Committee and the Soviet Government acted in full awareness of their responsibility and took into account the entire sum total of circumstances. The only task given to the Soviet contingents is to assist the Afghans in repulsing the aggression from outside. They will be fully withdrawn from Afghanistan once the causes that made the Afghan leadership request their introduction disappear.

It is deliberately and unscrupulously that the imperialist and also the Peking propaganda distort the Soviet Union's role in Afghan affairs.

It goes without saying that there has been no Soviet "intervention" or "aggression" at all. Oh, there is another thing: We are helping the new Afghanistan, on the request of its government, to defend the national independence, freedom and honor of its country from armed aggressive actions from outside.

The national interests or security of the United States of America and other states are not affected in any way by the events in Afghanistan. All attempts to portray matters otherwise are sheer nonsense. These attempts are being made with ill intent, with the aim of making the fulfillment of their own imperialist plans easier.

False Allegations

Also absolutely false are the allegations that the Soviet Union has some expansionist plans in respect to Pakistan, Iran or other countries of that area. The policy and psychology of colonialists is alien to us. We are not coveting the lands or wealth of others. It is the colonialists who are attracted by the smell of oil.

Outright hypocritical are the attempts to talk at length about the "Soviet threat of peace" and to pose as observers of international morals by those whose record includes the "dirty war" against Vietnam, who did not move a finger when the Chinese aggressors made their armed intrusion into Socialist Vietnam, who for decades have kept a military base on Cuban soil contrary to the will of its people and government, who are engaged in saber-rattling, who are threatening to impose a blockade and are exerting open military pressure on the revolutionary Iranian people by sending to the shores of Iran a naval armada armed with atomic weapons and including a considerable part of the U.S. carrier force.

And one last point must be made in this connection. Interference in the internal affairs of Afghanistan is really taking place, and even such an august and respected institution as the United Nations organization is being used for this. Indeed, can the discussion of the so-called "Afghan question" at the United Nations, contrary to objections by the government of Afghanistan, be described in any other way than a rude flouting of the sovereign rights of the Afghan state?

For the Afghan government and its responsible representative in the United Nations organization are stating for all to hear: Leave us alone; the Soviet military contingents were brought in at our request and in accordance with the Soviet-Afghan Treaty and Article 51 of the United Nations Charter.

Meantime, under the cover of the clamor, assistance is being increased to those elements that are intruding into Afghanistan and perpetrating aggressive actions against the legitimate government. The White House recently openly announced its decision to expand the supply to these elements of military equipment and everything necessary for hostile activities. The Western press reports that during his talks in Peking the U.S. Defense Secretary colluded with the Chinese leadership on the coordination of such actions.

Concluding the Afghan theme, it must be said that there is nothing surprising in the hostile reaction of imperialist forces to the events in Afghanistan. The crux of the matter is that the card on which the imperialists and their accomplices had counted was trumped there.

In short, the events in Afghanistan are not the true cause of the present complication of the international situation. If there were no Afghanistan, certain circles in the United States and in NATO would have surely found another pretext to aggravate the situation in the world.

Cold War Language

Finally, the entire sum total of the American Administration's steps in connection with the events in Afghanistan — the freezing of the SALT-II Treaty, refusal to deliver to the USSR a number of commodities, including grain, in accordance with some already concluded contracts, the termination of talks with the Soviet Union on a number of questions of bilateral relations and so on, shows that Washington again, like decades ago, is trying to speak with us in the language of the Cold War. In this the Carter Administration is displaying contempt for important interstate documents and is disrupting established ties in the field of science, culture and human contacts.

It is difficult even to enumerate the number of treaties, intergovernmental agreements, accords and understandings reached between our two countries on questions of mutual relations in various fields that have been arbitrarily and unilaterally violated lately by the government of President Carter. Of course, we will manage without these ties with the United States. In fact, we never sought these ties as some sort of a favor to us, believing that this is a mutually advantageous matter meeting the mutual interests of the peoples of our countries, first of all in the context of strengthening peace.

But the arrogation by Washington of some sort of a "right" to "reward" or "punish" independent sovereign states raises a question of a principled character. In effect, by such actions the U.S. Government deals a blow at the orderly international system of legal relations among states.

Unreliable Partner

As a result of the Carter Administration's action the impression is increasingly forming in the world of the United States as an absolutely unreliable partner in inter-state ties, as a state whose leadership, prompted by some whim, caprice or emotional outbursts, or by considerations of narrowly understood immediate advantage, is capable at any moment of violating its international obligations and canceling treaties and agreements signed by it. There is hardly any need to explain what a dangerous destabilizing impact this has on the entire international situation, the more so that this is the behavior of the leadership of a big influential power from which the peoples have the right to expect a well-considered and responsible policy.

But, of course, these actions of the U.S. Administration will not inflict on us the damage obviously hoped for by their initiators. The cynical estimates concerning the worsening of the food situation in the Soviet Union as a result of the U.S. refusal to sell us grain are based on nonsensical notions about our economic potential. The Soviet people have sufficient possibilities to live and work calmly, to fulfill our plans, to raise our living standards. In particular, I can assure you that the plans to provide Soviet people with bread and bakery products will not be lessened by a single kilogram.

We can regard the actions of the American Administration only as a poorly weighed attempt to use the events in Afghanistan for blocking international efforts to lessen the military danger, to strengthen peace, to restrict the arms race, in short for blocking the attainment of aims in which humankind is vitally interested.

The unilateral measures taken by the United States are tantamount to serious miscalculations in politics. Like a boomerang, they will hit back at their initiators, if not today then tomorrow.

Now if all these sallies against our policy are intended to check our mettle, this means that the experience of history is totally ignored. When the world's first socialist state was born in 1917, our people did not ask anybody's permission. And now, too, they decide themselves what their way of life is to be. Imperialism tried to put us to test already at the dawn of Soviet government, and everybody remembers what came out of this. The fascist aggressors tried to break us in the bloodiest war ever experienced by humankind. But they suffered a defeat. We were subjected to trials in the years of the Cold War, when the world was being pushed to the brink of the precipice, when one international crisis was engineered after another. But then, too, nobody succeeded in making us waver. It is very useful to remember this today.

Q: What, in your opinion, are the prospects of the development of the situation in Europe?

A: The situation in Europe today is much better than it was, say, in the early 1970s. But, of course, Washington's latest irresponsible actions are making themselves felt here as well. The United States is not content with doing almost everything to poison Soviet-American relations. It would like to spoil also the relations of West European countries with the Soviet Union, relations in which, as is known, many useful things were achieved during the past decade. The United States is trying to undermine the spirit and essence of the Helsinki Final Act, which has become a recognized milestone in strengthening security and developing peaceful cooperation on the continent. Last but not least, by its steps directed at aggravating the international situation, Washington pursues the aim of putting under the European states, first of all its own allies.

But the cardinal interests of the European peoples are unbreakably connected with detente. The Europeans have already come to know its beneficial fruits from their own experience. They are inhabitants of a continent that has been marked more than once by devastating wars, and they are by no means prepared, and we are convinced of this, to embark on a road of ventures at the bidding of politicians from across the ocean. It is impossible to believe that there can be states in Europe that would wish to throw the fruit of detente under the feet of those who are ready to trample them. Western states, and the United States as well, need detente in Europe by no means to a lesser extent than the socialist countries or the Soviet Union.

Future Peace

Much of a constructive nature can be accomplished in Europe for the good of peace in the near future, in particular, in connection with the forthcoming meeting in Madrid and the proposal by Warsaw Treaty countries to hold a conference on military detente and disarmament. We resolutely are for consolidating and multiplying everything positive that has been created over the years in the European continent through the collective efforts of states, big and small. We will further pursue a policy of peace and friendship between peoples.

In stark contrast to Washington's present extremist position, our position is to continue the talks started in recent years along many directions, with the aim of stopping the arms race. This, naturally, also applies to problems of lessening military confrontation in Europe.

I repeat: We are for talks, but for honest and equal talks, for observance of the principle of equal security. It is exactly such talks that we recently proposed to start on the question of medium-range nuclear arms. Nobody can expect the Soviet Union to accept NATO's terms, designed for conducting talks from positions of strength. The present position of NATO countries makes talks on this problem impossible. We formally told the U.S. Government about all this a number of days ago.

We look into the future with optimism. It is a well-founded optimism. We understand that the deliberate aggravation of the international situation by American imperialism expresses its displeasure at the consolidation of the positions of socialism, the upsurge of the national liberation movement, the strengthening of forces coming out for detente and peace. We know that the will of the peoples has cleared, through all obstacles, a road for a positive direction in world affairs that is well expressed by the word "detente." This policy has deep roots. It is supported by mighty forces, and this policy has every chance to remain the leading tendency in relations between states.

Our people and our country are firmly advancing along the road of communist construction, fulfilling the assignments of the Tenth Five-Year Plan, the tasks set by the party. Soviet people and our friends abroad can rest assured that the Leninist foreign policy course is unflagging. It was defined by the decisions of CPSU congresses and is being embodied in all our foreign policy activities. This course combines consistent peaceableness with a firm rebuff to aggression. It has justified itself in past decades and we will adhere to it further. No one will push us off this course.

BREZHNEV ADDRESS TO 26TH PARTY CONGRESS

Following are excerpts from the address by General Secretary Leonid I. Brezhnev to the 26th Congress of the Communist Party of the Soviet Union (CPSU) on February 23, 1981. (Boldface headings in brackets have been added by Congressional Quarterly to highlight the organization of the text.):

... On the international plane, the period under review has been rough and complicated. It has been marked above all by an intensive struggle of two lines in world affairs: the line of bridling the arms race, strengthening peace and detente, and defending the sovereign rights and freedom of nations, on the one hand, and, on the other, the line of disrupting detente, escalating the arms race, of threats and interference in other countries' affairs, and of suppressing the liberation struggle. ...

The sphere of imperialist domination has narrowed. The internal contradictions in capitalist countries and the rivalry between them have grown sharper. The aggressiveness of imperialist policy, notably that of U.S. imperialism, has increased acutely.

When thunderclouds gathered on the international horizon by

the beginning of the eighties, the Soviet Union continued to persevere in efforts to remove the threat of war and to preserve and deepen detente, and acted to expand mutually beneficial cooperation with most countries of the world. . . .

The International Policy of the CPSU

Our struggle to strengthen peace and deepen detente is, above all, designed to secure the requisite external conditions for the Soviet people to carry out its constructive tasks. Thereby we are also solving a problem of a truly global nature. For at present nothing is more essential and more important for any nation than to preserve peace and ensure the paramount right of every human being — the right to life. . . .

There are special cases, too, when friends need urgent aid. This was the case with Vietnam, which became the target of a barbarian aggression by Peking in 1979. The Soviet Union and other countries of the socialist community promptly sent it shipments of food, medical supplies, building materials, and arms. This was also the case with Kampuchea, which had been devastated by the Pol Pot clique of Peking henchmen.

That, comrades, is socialist internationalism in action. Soviet people understand and approve of such action. . . .

It should be noted in general that in recent years our countries have had to deal with their constructive tasks in more complicated conditions. The deterioration of the world economy and spiralling prices have played their part. The slowing of the process of detente and the arms race imposed by the imperialist powers are no small a burden for us as well.

Another thing is the visible sharpening of the ideological struggle. For the West it is not confined to the battle of ideas. It employs a whole system of means designed to subvert or soften up the socialist world.

[Imperialist Hostility to Socialist States]

The imperialists and their accomplices are systematically conducting hostile campaigns against the socialist countries. They malign and distort everything that goes on in them. For them the main thing is to turn people against socialism.

Recent events have shown again and again that our class opponents are learning from their defeats. Their actions against the socialist countries are increasingly refined and treacherous.

And wherever imperialist subversive activity is combined with mistakes and miscalculations in home policy, there arise conditions that stimulate elements hostile to socialism. This is what has happened in fraternal Poland, where opponents of socialism supported by outside forces are, by stirring up anarchy, seeking to channel events into a counter-revolutionary course. As was noted at the latest plenary meeting of the Polish United Workers' Party Central Committee, the pillars of the socialist state in Poland are in jeopardy.

At present, the Polish comrades are engaged in redressing the critical situation. They are striving to enhance the Party's capacity for action and to tighten links with the working class and other working people, and are preparing a concrete programme to restore a sound Polish economy.

Last December's meeting of leaders of the Warsaw Treaty countries in Moscow has rendered Poland important political support. It showed clearly that the Polish Communists, the Polish working class, and the working people of that country can firmly rely on their friends and allies; we will not abandon fraternal, socialist Poland in its hour of need, we will stand by it.

The events in Poland show once again how important it is for the Party, for the strengthening of its leading role, to pay close heed to the voice of the masses, resolutely to combat all signs of bureaucracy and voluntarism, actively to develop socialist democracy, and to conduct a well-considered and realistic policy in foreign economic relations. . . .

[China's Foreign Policy]

Special mention must be made of China. The experience of

the social and economic development of the PRC over the past twenty years is a painful lesson showing what any distortion of the principles and essence of socialism in home and foreign policy leads to.

The present Chinese leaders themselves describe what happened in the period of the so-called cultural revolution in their country as "a most cruel feudal-fascist dictatorship". We have nothing to add to this assessment.

At present, changes are under way in China's internal policy. Time will show what they actually mean. It will show to what extent the present Chinese leadership will manage to overcome the Maoist legacy. But, unfortunately, there are no grounds yet to speak of any changes for the better in Peking's foreign policy. As before, it is aimed at aggravating the international situation, and is aligned with the policy of the imperialist powers. That, of course, will not bring China back to the sound road of development. Imperialists will never be friends of socialism.

The simple reason behind the readiness of the United States, Japan, and a number of NATO countries to expand their military and political ties with China is to use its hostility to the Soviet Union and the socialist community in their own, imperialist interests. That is a hazardous game.

As far as the people of China are concerned, we are deeply convinced that their true interests would be best served by a policy of peace and nothing but a policy of peace and normal relations with other countries.

If Soviet-Chinese relations are still frozen, the reason for this has nothing to do with our position. The Soviet Union has never sought, nor does it now seek any confrontation with the People's Republic of China. We follow the course set by the 24th and 25th Congresses of the CPSU, and would like to build our ties with that country on a good-neighbour basis. Our proposals for normalizing relations with China remain open, and our feelings of friendship and respect for the Chinese people have not changed. . . .

Development of Relations
With the Newly Free Countries

Comrades, among the important results of the Party's international activity in the period under review we can list the visible expansion of cooperation with countries that have liberated themselves from colonial oppression.

These countries are very different. After liberation, some of them have been following the revolutionary-democratic path. In others capitalist relations have taken root. Some of them are following a truly independent policy, while others are today taking their lead from imperialist policy. In a nutshell, the picture is a fairly motley one.

Let me first deal with the socialist-oriented states, that is, states that have opted for socialist development. Their number has increased. Development along the progressive road is not, of course, the same from country to country, and proceeds in difficult conditions. But the main lines are *similar*. These include gradual elimination of the positions of imperialist monopoly, of the local big bourgeoisie and the feudal elements, and restriction of foreign capital. They include the securing by the people's state of commanding heights in the economy and transition to planned development of the productive forces, and encouragement of the cooperative movement in the countryside. They include enhancing the role of the working masses in social life, and gradually reinforcing the state apparatus with national personnel faithful to the people. They include anti-imperialist foreign policy. Revolutionary parties expressing the interests of the broad mass of the working people are growing stronger there.

In the period under review, the Soviet Union has concluded treaties of friendship and cooperation with Angola, Ethiopia, Mozambique, Afghanistan, and the People's Democratic Republic of Yemen. Recently, a treaty of friendship and cooperation was signed with Syria. I am sure that it will serve well to further the Soviet-Syrian friendship and the achievement of a just peace in the Middle East. . . .

Our country does everything it can to help many of the newly-free countries in training personnel — engineers, technicians, skilled workers, doctors, and teachers.

Tens of thousands of Soviet specialists are doing dedicated work on building sites in Asian and African countries, in industry and agriculture, and in hospitals and educational institutions. They are worthy representatives of their great socialist Motherland. We are proud of them, and send them heartfelt wishes of success.

Together with the other socialist countries, we are also helping to strengthen the defence capability of newly-free states if they request such aid. This was the case with, say, Angola and Ethiopia. Attempts were made to crush the people's revolutions in these countries by encouraging domestic counter-revolution or by outside aggression. We are against the export of revolution, and we cannot agree to any export of counter-revolution either.

[Afghanistan and Iran]

Imperialism launched a real undeclared war against the Afghan revolution. This also created a direct threat to the security of our southern frontier. In the circumstances, we were compelled to render the military aid asked for by that friendly country.

The plans of Afghanistan's enemies have collapsed. The well-considered policy of the People's Democratic Party and the government of Afghanistan headed by Comrade Babrak Karmal, which is faithful to the national interests, has strengthened the people's power.

As for the Soviet military contingent, we will be prepared to withdraw it with the agreement of the Afghan government. Before this is done, the infiltration of counter-revolutionary gangs into Afghanistan must be completely stopped. This must be secured in accords between Afghanistan and its neighbours. Dependable guarantees are required that there will be no new intervention. Such is the fundamental position of the Soviet Union, and we keep to it firmly.

The revolution in Iran, which was a major event on the international scene in recent years, is of a specific nature. However complex and contradictory, it is essentially an anti-imperialist revolution, though reaction at home and abroad is seeking to change this feature.

The people of Iran are looking for their own road to freedom and prosperity. We sincerely wish them success in this, and are prepared to develop good relations with Iran on the principles of equality and, of course, reciprocity.

Of late, Islamic slogans are being actively put forward in some countries of the East. We Communists have every respect for the religious convictions of people professing Islam or any other religion. The main thing is what aims are pursued by the forces proclaiming various slogans. The banner of Islam may lead into struggle for liberation. This is borne out by history, including very recent history. But it also shows that reaction, too, manipulates with Islamic slogans to incite counter-revolutionary mutinies. Consequently, the whole thing hinges on the actual content of any movement. . . .

[Recognition of New States]

In Africa, the Caribbean, and Oceania ten new states gained independence in the past five years, and were instantly recognized by the Soviet Union. The birth of the Republic of Zimbabwe, the mounting intensity of the liberation struggle in Namibia, and now also in the Republic of South Africa, are graphic evidence that the rule of "classic" colonialists and racists is approaching its end.

The imperialists are displeased with the fact that the newly-free countries are consolidating their independence. In a thousand ways they are trying to bind these countries to themselves in order to deal more freely with their natural riches, and to use their territory for their strategic designs. In so doing, they make extensive use of the old colonialist method of divide and rule.

Indeed, that is also the Western approach to the Irano-Iraqi war, which has been going on for five months — an absolutely senseless war from the viewpoint of the two countries' interests. But it is of great advantage to imperialism, which is anxious and eager in some way or other to restore its position in that region. We

would like to hope that both Iraq and Iran draw the due conclusions from this.

The Soviet Union firmly calls for an early end to that fratricidal war, and a political settlement of the conflict. In practice, too, we are striving to facilitate this.

[Middle East]

Now about the Middle East problem. In its bid for dominance in the Middle East, the United States has taken the path of the Camp David policy, dividing the Arab world and organizing a separate deal between Israel and Egypt. U.S. diplomacy has failed to turn this separate anti-Arab deal into a broader agreement of a capitulationist type. But it has succeeded in another way: a new deterioration of the situation has occurred in the region. A Middle East settlement was cast back.

What now? As we see it, it is high time to get matters off the ground. It is time to go back to honest collective search of an all-embracing just and realistic settlement. In the circumstances, this could be done, say, in the framework of a specially convened international conference.

The Soviet Union is prepared to participate in such work in a constructive spirit and with good will. We are prepared to do so jointly with the other interested parties — the Arabs (naturally including the Palestine Liberation Organization) and Israel. We are prepared for such search jointly with the United States — and I may remind you that we had some experience in this regard some years ago. We are prepared to cooperate with the European countries and with all those who are showing a sincere striving to secure a just and durable peace in the Middle East.

The U.N., too, could evidently continue to play a useful role in all this.

As for the substance of the matter, we are still convinced that if there is to be real peace in the Middle East, the Israeli occupation of all Arab territories captured in 1967 must be ended. The inalienable rights of the Arab people of Palestine must be secured, up to and including the establishment of their own state. It is essential to ensure the security and sovereignty of all the states of the region, including those of Israel. Those are the basic principles. As for the details, they could naturally be considered at the negotiations. . . .

[Relations With West]

Comrades, in the period under review the USSR continued to pursue Lenin's policy of peaceful coexistence and mutually beneficial cooperation with capitalist states, while firmly repulsing the aggressive designs of imperialism.

A further aggravation of the general crisis of capitalism was witnessed during these years. To be sure, capitalism has not stopped developing. But it is immersed in what is already the third economic recession in the past ten years.

Inflation has grown to unheard-of dimensions. Since 1970 prices in the developed capitalist countries have risen on average by 130 percent and since 1975 by 50 percent. The inflation curve is getting steeper. Not for nothing did the new President of the United States admit in his inaugural address that the United States is suffering from "one of the worst sustained inflations in . . . national history", and that "it threatens to shatter the lives of millions" of Americans.

It is more than obvious that state regulation of the capitalist economy is ineffective. The measures that bourgeois governments take against inflation foster stagnation of production and growth of unemployment; what they do to contain the critical drop in production lends still greater momentum to inflation.

The social contradictions have grown visibly more acute. In capitalist society use of the latest scientific and technical achievements in production turns against the working people, and throws millions of factory workers into the streets. In the past ten years the army of unemployed in the developed capitalist states has doubled. In 1980 it totalled 19 million.

Attempts to dampen the intensity of the class struggle by social reforms of some kind are having no success either. The number of strikers has risen by more than one-third in these ten years, and is even officially admitted to have reached the 250 million mark.

The inter-imperialist contradictions are growing more acute, the scramble for markets and for sources of raw materials and energy is more frantic. Japanese and West European monopolies compete ever more successfully with US capital, and this even in the US domestic market too. In the seventies, the share of the United States in world exports has declined by nearly 20 percent.

The difficulties experienced by capitalism also affect its policy, including foreign policy. The struggle over basic foreign policy issues in the capitalist countries has grown more bitter. Visibly more active of late are the opponents of detente, of limiting armaments, and of improving relations with the Soviet Union and other socialist countries.

Adventurism and a readiness to gamble with the vital interests of humanity for narrow and selfish ends — this is what has emerged in a particularly barefaced form in the policy of the more aggressive imperialist circles. With utter contempt for the rights and aspirations of nations, they are trying to portray the liberation struggle of the masses as "terrorism." Indeed, they have set out to achieve the unachievable — to set up a barrier to the progressive changes in the world, and to again become the rulers of the peoples' destiny.

[Military Spending in Capitalist Countries]

Military expenditures are rising unprecedentedly. In the United States they have climbed to an annual 150,000 million dollars. But even these astronomical figures are not high enough for the U.S. military-industrial complex. It is clamouring for more. The NATO allies of the United States, too, yielding to Washington's demands, have undertaken — though some with great reluctance — to increase military allocations automatically until almost the end of the present century.

A considerable portion of these tremendous sums is being spent on crash development of new types of strategic nuclear arms. Their appearance is accompanied by the advancing of military doctrines dangerous to peace, like the notorious Carter directive. They want people to believe that nuclear war can be limited, they want to reconcile them with the idea that such war is tolerable.

But that is sheer deception of the peoples! A "limited" nuclear war as conceived by the Americans in, say, Europe would from the outset mean the certain destruction of European civilization. And of course the United States, too, would not be able to escape the flames of war. Clearly, such plans and "doctrines" are a grave threat to all nations, including the people of the USA. They are being condemned all over the world. The peoples say an emphatic "No" to them.

Imperialist circles think in terms of domination and compulsion in relation to other states and peoples.

The monopolies need the oil, uranium and non-ferrous metals of other countries, and so the Middle East, Africa and the Indian Ocean are proclaimed spheres of US "vital interests". The US military machine is actively thrusting into these regions, and intends to entrench itself there for a long time to come. Diego Garcia in the Indian Ocean, Oman, Kenya, Somalia, Egypt — where next?

To split the expenses with others and at the same time to tie its NATO partners closer to itself, the United States is seeking to extend the functions of NATO. Washington strategists are obviously eager to involve dozens of other countries in their military preparations, and to enmesh the world in a web of US bases, airfields, and arms depots.

To justify this, Washington is spreading the story of a "Soviet threat" to the oil riches of the Middle East or the oil supply lines. That is a deliberate falsehood, because its authors know perfectly well that the Soviet Union has no intention of impinging on either the one or the other. And in general, it is absurd to think that the oil interests of the West can be "defended" by turning that region into a powder keg.

No, we have completely different views on how peace can really be secured in and around the Persian Gulf. Instead of deploying more and more naval and air armadas, troops and arms

there, we propose that the military threat should be removed by concluding an international agreement. A state of stability and calm can be created in that region by joint effort, with due account for the legitimate interests of all sides. The sovereign rights of the countries there, and the security of maritime and other communications connecting the region with the rest of the world, can be guaranteed. That is the meaning of the proposals made recently by the Soviet Union.

This initiative gained broad support in the world, including a number of Persian Gulf countries. To be sure, there were also opponents of the Soviet proposal, and it is easy to guess in what camp. We would like to express our hope that the governments of the United States and other NATO countries will consider the whole issue calmly and without prejudice, so that we could jointly look for a solution acceptable to all.

Reaching an agreement on this issue could, moreover, give a start to the very important process of reducing the military presence in various regions of the World Ocean.

In our relations with the United States during all these years we have, as before, followed a principled and constructive line. It is only to be regretted that the former administration in Washington put its stakes on something other than developing relations or on mutual understanding. Trying to exert pressure on us, it set to destroying the positive achievements that had been made with no small effort in Soviet-American relations over the preceding years. As a result, our bilateral ties suffered a setback in a number of fields. The entry into force of the SALT-2 treaty was deferred. And negotiations with us on a number of arms limitation issues, such as reducing arms deliveries to third countries, were broken off unilaterally by the United States.

[Military Equilibrium]

Unfortunately, also since the change of leadership in the White House openly bellicose calls and statements have resounded from Washington, as if specially designed to poison the atmosphere of relations between our countries. We would like to hope, however, that those who shape United States policy today will ultimately manage to see things in a more realistic light. The military and strategic equilibrium prevailing between the USSR and the USA, between the Warsaw Treaty and NATO, objectively serves to safeguard world peace. We have not sought, and do not now seek, military superiority over the other side. That is not our policy. But neither will we permit the building up of any such superiority over us. Attempts of that kind and talking to us from a position of strength are absolutely futile.

Not to try and upset the existing balance and not to impose a new, still more costly and dangerous round of the arms race — that would be to display truly wise statesmanship. And for this it is really high time to throw the threadbare scarecrow of a "Soviet threat" out of the door of serious politics.

Let's look at the true state of affairs.

Whether we take strategic nuclear arms or medium-range nuclear weapons in Europe, in both instances there is approximate parity between the sides. In respect of some weapons the West has a certain advantage, and we have an advantage in respect of others. This parity could be more stable if pertinent treaties and agreements were concluded.

There is also talk about tanks. It is true that the Soviet Union has more of them. But the NATO countries, too, have a large number. Besides, they have considerably more anti-tank weapons.

The tale of Soviet superiority in troops strength does not match the facts either. Combined with the other NATO countries, the United States has even slightly more troops than the Soviet Union and the other Warsaw Treaty countries.

So, what talk can there be of any Soviet military superiority?

[Arms Race]

A war danger does exist for the United States, as it does for all the other countries of the world. But the source of the danger is not the Soviet Union, nor any mythical Soviet superiority, but is the arms race and the tension that still prevails in the world. We are prepared to combat this true, and not imaginary, danger hand in hand with the United States, with the countries of Europe, with all countries in the world. To try and outstrip each other in the arms race or to expect to win a nuclear war, is dangerous madness.

It is universally recognized that in many ways the international situation depends on the policy of both the USSR and the USA. As we see it, the state of relations between them at present and the acuteness of the international problems requiring a solution necessitate a dialogue, and an active dialogue, at all levels. We are prepared to engage in this dialogue.

Experience shows that the crucial factor here is meetings at summit level. This was true yesterday, and is still true today.

The USSR wants normal relations with the USA. There is simply no other sensible way from the point of view of the interests of our two nations, and of humanity as a whole....

Speaking of European affairs, we must not ignore the new and serious dangers that have arisen to European peace. This refers first of all to the NATO decision of deploying new U.S. nuclear missiles in Western Europe. This decision is no "response" to any imagined Soviet challenge. Neither is it an ordinary "modernization" of the arsenal, as the West would have us believe. It speaks of an obvious intention to tilt the existing military balance in Europe in NATO's favour.

It must be clearly understood: the deployment in the FRG [Federal Republic of Germany], Italy, Britain, the Netherlands or Belgium of new US missiles, targeted against the USSR and its allies, is bound to affect our relations with these countries, to say nothing of how this will prejudice their own security. So, their governments and parliaments have reason to weigh the whole thing again and again.

The vital interests of the European nations require that Europe should follow a different path — the path blazed in Helsinki.

We believe that the process begun by the all-European conference should be continuous. All forms of talks — multilateral, bilateral — should be used to solve the problems that are troubling Europe.

[Japan, Latin America, and Canada]

Now for relations with Japan. In its foreign-policy course, negative factors are becoming stronger — playing second fiddle to the dangerous plans of Washington and Peking, and a tendency toward militarization. However, we do not think that this is Tokyo's last word, so to speak, and we hope that foresight and an understanding of the country's interests will prevail there. As before, the USSR favors lasting and genuinely good-neighbor relations with Japan.

The role in the world arena of the Latin American states, including Mexico, Brazil, Argentina, Venezuela and Peru, has increased considerably. We note with satisfaction that mutually beneficial ties between the USSR and the Latin American countries have expanded, and we are prepared to continue to develop these ties.

There is considerable potential for the development of relations with Canada. The door for the further expansion of cooperation with that country, as well as with other capitalist states, will remain open. Cooperation of the broadest sort — with governments, parliaments, business circles, cultural figures and public organizations.

Thus, comrades, the policy of peaceful coexistence charted by V. I. Lenin is having an increasingly decisive influence on present-day international relations. The 1970s provided very convincing proof of this.

Life calls for fruitful cooperation among all states to accomplish the peaceful, constructive tasks that confront every people and all mankind.

And this cooperation is not insubstantial utopia. Its first shoots — albeit modest ones so far — are already in evidence. They must be seen, cherished and developed.

Useful cooperation is being developed now, including cooperation within the framework of international organizations and among a large number of states, in such fields as the peaceful use of atomic energy, the fight against epidemic diseases, the elimination of illiteracy, the protection of historical and cultural monuments, and weather-forecasting services. Our country is actively participating in all this.

In short, there is already a proven basis for the further development of practical peaceful cooperation among states. And the need for this is becoming increasingly obvious ...

To Strengthen Peace, Deepen Detente, and Curb the Arms Race

... Let me begin with the problem of limiting nuclear armaments, which are the most dangerous to humanity. All these years, the Soviet Union has worked perseveringly to put an end to the race in such armaments, and to stop their further spread across the world. A tremendous amount of work was done, as you know, in preparing a treaty with the United States on limiting strategic arms. Much was done during the negotiations with the United States and Britain on the complete prohibition of nuclear weapons tests. We made an important move by declaring and reaffirming that we will not use nuclear weapons against non-nuclear countries which do not permit the deployment of such weapons on their territory. But we have also gone further in our proposals: that the manufacture of nuclear weapons be stopped and their stockpiles be reduced until they are completely eliminated.

The Soviet Union has also actively sought the prohibition of all other types of mass destruction weapons. And we have managed to achieve a few things in this field during the period under review. Already operative is a convention banning modification of the environment for military purposes. The basic provisions of a treaty prohibiting radiological weapons have been tentatively agreed upon. Negotiations on removing chemical weapons from the arsenals of states are under way, though at an intolerably slow pace. Action taken by the peace forces secured the suspension of plans for deploying neutron arms in Western Europe. All the greater is the outrage of nations over the new Pentagon attempts to hang the neutron Sword of Damocles over the countries of Europe. For our part, we declare once more that we will not begin manufacturing it if it does not appear in other countries, and that we are prepared to conclude an agreement banning the weapon once and for all....

[Afghanistan]

... It is sometimes said about our Persian Gulf proposals that they should not be divorced from the question of the Soviet military contingent in Afghanistan. What could be said on this score? The Soviet Union is prepared to negotiate the Persian Gulf as an independent problem. It is also prepared, of course, as I have already said, to participate in a separate settlement of the situation around Afghanistan. *But also we do not object to the questions connected with Afghanistan being discussed together with the questions of Persian Gulf security.* Naturally, this applies solely to the international aspects of the Afghan problem, and not to internal Afghan affairs. Afghanistan's sovereignty, like its non-aligned status, must be fully protected.

[Negotiations on Strategic Arms]

Once again, we insistently call for restraint in the field of strategic armaments. It should not be tolerated that the nations of the world live in the shadow of a nuclear war threat.

Limitation and reduction of strategic armaments is a paramount problem. *For our part, we are prepared to continue the relevant negotiations with the United States without delay, preserving all the positive elements that have so far been achieved in this area.* It goes without saying that the negotiations can be conducted only on the basis of equality and equal security. We will not consent to any agreement that gives a unilateral advantage to the USA. There must be no illusions on this score. In our opinion, all the other nuclear powers should join these negotiations at the appropriate time.

The USSR is prepared to negotiate limitation of weapons of all types. At one time we offered to ban the development of the naval Trident missile system in the United States and of a corresponding system in our country. The proposal was not accepted. As a result, the United States has built the new Ohio submarine armed with Trident-1 missiles, while an analogous system, the Typhoon, was built in our country. So, who has stood to gain?

We are prepared to come to terms on limiting the deployment of the new submarines — the Ohio type by the USA, and similar ones by the USSR. We could also agree to banning modernization of existing and development of new ballistic missiles for these submarines.

[Nuclear Forces in Europe]

Now about the nuclear-missile weapons in Europe. An ever more dangerous stockpiling of them is in train. A kind of vicious circle has arisen, with the actions of one side precipitating countermeasures by the other. How to break this chain?

We suggest coming to terms that already now a moratorium should be set on the deployment in Europe of new medium-range nuclear-missile weapons of the NATO countries and the Soviet Union, that is, to freeze the existing quantitative and qualitative level of these weapons, naturally including the U.S. forward-based nuclear weapons in this region. The moratorium could enter into force at once, the moment negotiations begin on this score, and could operate until a permanent treaty is concluded on limiting or, still better, reducing such nuclear weapons in Europe. In making this proposal, we expect the two sides to stop all preparations for the deployment of respective additional weapons, including U.S. Pershing-2 missiles and land-based strategic cruise missiles.

The peoples must know the truth about the destructive consequences for humankind of a nuclear war. *We suggest that a competent international committee should be set up, which would demonstrate the vital necessity of preventing a nuclear catastrophe.* The committee could be composed of the most eminent scientists of different countries. The whole world should be informed of the conclusions they draw.

There are, of course, many other pressing international problems in the world today. Their sensible solution would enable us to slacken the intensity of the international situation, and let the nations breathe with relief. But what is needed here is a far-sighted approach, political will and courage, prestige and influence. That is why it seems to us that it would be *useful to call a special session of the Security Council with the participation of the top leaders of its member-states....*

[Consolidation of Peace]

In sum, comrades, the new measures we are proposing embrace a wide range of issues. They concern conventional as well as nuclear-missile armaments, land forces, and naval and air forces. They touch on the situation in Europe, in the Near East, the Middle East, and the Far East. They deal with measures of a military as well as a political nature. All of them pursue a single aim, our one common aspiration — to do everything possible to relieve the peoples of the danger of a nuclear war, to preserve world peace.

This, if you like, is an organic continuation and development of our Peace Programme in reference to the most burning, topical problems of present-day international life.

To safeguard peace — no task is more important now on the international plane for our Party, for our people and, for that matter, for all the peoples of the world.

By safeguarding peace we are working not only for people who are living today, and not only for our children and grandchildren; we are working for the happiness of dozens of future generations.

If there is peace, the creative energy of the peoples backed by the achievements of science and technology is certain to solve the problems that are now troubling people. To be sure, new, still loftier tasks will then arise before our descendants. But that is the dialectic of progress, the dialectic of life.

Not war preparations that doom the peoples to a senseless squandering of their material and spiritual wealth, but consolidation of peace — that is the clue to the future....

BREZHNEV'S DEATH, EULOGY BY ANDROPOV

Following are texts of the announcement of the death of Soviet leader Leonid I. Brezhnev and a statement to the Soviet people by the CPSU Central Committee, both November 11, 1982, and of the eulogy by Yuri V. Andropov at Brezhnev's funeral, November 15:

Announcement of Death

The Central Committee of the Communist Party of the Soviet Union, the Presidium of the USSR Supreme Soviet and the Council of Ministers of the USSR hereby inform with deep sorrow the party and the entire Soviet people that Leonid Ilyich Brezhnev, General Secretary of the Central Committee of the Communist Party of the Soviet Union and President of the Presidium of the USSR Supreme Soviet, died a sudden death at 8:30 A.M. on November 10, 1982.

The name Leonid Ilyich Brezhnev, a true continuer of Lenin's great cause and an ardent champion of peace and communism, will live forever in the hearts of the Soviet people and all progressive people throughout the world.

Central Committee Statement

Dear comrades,

The Communist Party of the Soviet Union, the entire Soviet people have suffered a grave loss. The true follower of the great cause of Lenin, fiery patriot, outstanding revolutionary and fighter for peace and communism, the most prominent politician and statesman of our times, Leonid Ilyich Brezhnev, has passed away.

All of the diverse activities and the life of L. I. Brezhnev are inseparable from the most important stages in the history of the Land of the Soviets. Collectivization and industrialization, the Great Patriotic War and the postwar rebirth, the opening up of the virgin lands and the organization of space exploration — these are also landmarks in the biography of the glorious son of the working class, Leonid Ilyich Brezhnev. Wherever the party sent him, Leonid Ilyich selflessly, with the energy, persistence, daring and principledness typical of him, struggled for its great ideas.

The Soviet people and our friends all over the world by right associate the consistent assertion of the Leninist norms in party and state life and the perfection of socialist democracy with the name of Comrade Brezhnev and with his tireless work in the posts of General Secretary of the Central Committee of the Communist Party of the Soviet Union and President of the Presidium of the USSR Supreme Soviet. He wisely steered the activities of the Leninist headquarters of the party — its Central Committee, the Politburo of the Central Committee — setting an example of the masterful organization of concerted collective work. He played an outstanding role in drafting and implementing the economic and sociopolitical strategy of the party at the stage of developed socialism, in laying down and pursuing the course of improving the well-being of the people and in the further strengthening of the economic and defense might of our country.

Leonid Brezhnev made an everlasting contribution to the formulation and implementation of the policy of our party on the international scene, a policy of peace, peaceful cooperation, detente, disarmament, giving a strong rebuff to the aggressive intrigues of imperialism and preventing nuclear catastrophe. Great was his contribution to the consolidation of the world socialist community and the development of the international communist movement.

While Leonid Brezhnev's heart was beating, his thoughts and deeds were entirely dedicated to the interests of the working people. He was always linked vitally and inseparably with the masses of working people. He was and remains an embodiment of

Leninist ideological devotion, consistent internationalism, revolutionary optimism and humanism in the minds of Communists and hundreds of millions of people in all continents.

Grave is our loss, profound is our grief. At this hour of mourning the Communists and all the working people of the Soviet Union rally still closer behind the Leninist CPSU Central Committee, its steering nucleus, that was established under the beneficial influence of Leonid Ilyich Brezhnev. The people have faith in the party, its mighty collective reason and will. They wholeheartedly support its domestic and foreign policy. The Soviet people know well that the banner of Lenin, the banner of the October Revolution, under which historic victories of world significance were attained, is in reliable hands.

The party and the people have the grandiose program of communist construction worked out by the 23rd — 26th CPSU Congresses. That program is being steadily implemented. The party will continue doing its utmost to raise the well-being of the people through intensifying production, enhancing its efficiency and quality of work and fulfilling the food program of the USSR.

The party will continue showing great concern for consolidating the alliance of the working class, collective farmers and the intelligentsia, for strengthening the sociopolitical and ideological unity of Soviet society, the fraternal friendship of the peoples of the USSR and for ideologically steeling the working people in the spirit of Marxism-Leninism and proletarian, socialist internationalism.

Invariable is the Soviet people's will for peace. The lodestar leading to tomorrow is not preparations for war, which doom the people to a senseless squandering of their material and spiritual wealth, but consolidation of peace. This noble idea permeates the Peace Program for the 1980s and all the foreign policy activities of the party and the Soviet state.

We see the entire complexity of the international situation, the attempts by the aggressive circles of imperialism to undermine peaceful coexistence, to push the people to the path of enmity and military confrontation. But this cannot shake our resolve to uphold peace. We will do everything necessary for those who are fond of military ventures not to catch the Land of the Soviets unawares, for the potential aggressor to know: A crushing retaliatory strike ineluctably awaits him.

Relying on its might, displaying the greatest vigilance and self-control and retaining invariable loyalty to the peace-loving principles and aims of its foreign policy, the Soviet Union will perseveringly struggle to ward off from humankind the threat of nuclear war and to ensure detente and disarmament.

Together with us in this struggle are the fraternal countries of socialism, the fighters for national and social liberation, the peace-loving countries of all continents, all the upstanding people of the Earth. The policy of peace expresses the fundamental vital interests of humanity, and therefore the future is with this policy.

The Soviet people view the party as their tried and tested collective guide, wise leader and organizer. Serving the working class, the working people — this is the highest goal and meaning of the party's activity. The unshakable unity of the party and the people was and remains a source of the unconquerable strength of Soviet society.

The CPSU cherishes as sacred the trust of the working people and is constantly strengthening its links with the masses. The people have learned in practice that, faced with any turn of developments and any trials, the party is a match for its historical mission. The domestic and foreign policy of the CPSU formulated under the leadership of Leonid Brezhnev will continue to be pursued consistently and purposefully.

The life and work of Leonid Brezhnev will always be an inspiring example of dedicated service to the Communist Party and the Soviet people.

The Central Committee of the Communist Party of the Soviet Union, the Presidium of the USSR Supreme Soviet and the Council of Ministers of the USSR express the confidence that the Communists and all the Soviet people will show a high sense of awareness and organization and ensure by their selfless and creative work under the leadership of the Leninist party the implementation of the plans of communist construction and the further flourishing of our socialist homeland.

Eulogy by Andropov

Comrades, our party, our people and all progressive people on Earth have suffered a heavy loss. Today we are paying our last respects to Leonid Ilyich Brezhnev, a glorious son of our homeland, a fiery Marxist-Leninist, an outstanding leader of the Communist Party and the Soviet state, a prominent leader of the international communist and working class movement, a tireless fighter for peace and friendship of the peoples.

Let me first of all express profound condolences to Leonid Brezhnev's family and relatives.

Leonid Ilyich belonged to the group of political leaders who grew up and were tempered during the years of the Soviet people's selfless struggle for consolidating the gains of the Great October Revolution, for the fulfillment of Lenin's behests, for building socialism in our country and for its freedom and independence.

A worker and soldier, an outstanding organizer and a wise political leader, Leonid Ilyich Brezhnev was flesh of the flesh and bone of the bone of the people and was linked with them by unbreakable bonds. All his life and activities were subordinated to serving the interests of the working people. He devoted all his great talent, all his tremendous energies to the cause of building a society of developed socialism, a society of freedom and social justice, of brotherhood of the working people.

An extremely important period in the history of our party and country was associated with the activities of Leonid Ilyich Brezhnev in the highest positions of authority in the party and the state. It was under his leadership that the party's policy, permeated with constant concern for the working man, for raising the people's welfare, was worked out and consistently translated into life and the Leninist standards for party and state life and a fruitful atmosphere of joint work was firmly established.

Leonid Ilyich Brezhnev will be always remembered by the world as an outstanding fighter for a lasting peace and peaceful cooperation between peoples. He consistently fought, with all the ardor of his soul, for the relaxation of international tension, for delivering humankind from the threat of nuclear war, for strengthening the cohesion of the socialist community and the unity of the international communist movement.

Comrades, at this hour of grief, paying our last homage to Leonid Ilyich Brezhnev, all our party and its Central Committee declare their determination to pursue firmly and consistently the strategic line in domestic and foreign policy, which was worked out under the beneficial influence of Leonid Ilyich Brezhnev.

Rallying still closer round the party, its Leninist Central Committee and its collective leadership, the Soviet people voice their support for the policy of the party and their boundless trust in it. The party will continue to do everything necessary for further raising the living standards of the people, for developing the democratic mainstays of Soviet society, for strengthening the economic and defensive might of the country, for strengthening the friendship of the fraternal peoples of the USSR. The CPSU Central Committee will undeviatingly translate into life the decisions of the 26th Congress of the party and the will of the Soviet people.

We shall do everything possible for further increasing the cohesion of the great community of socialist states and unity in the ranks of Communists throughout the whole world in the struggle for common aims and ideals. We shall guard and develop our solidarity and our cooperation with the countries that have gained freedom from colonial oppression, with the struggle of the peoples for national independence and social progress. We shall always be loyal to the cause of the struggle for peace, for the relaxation of international tension.

In the complicated international situation, as the forces of imperialism are trying to push the peoples onto the road of hostility and military confrontation, the party and the state will firmly uphold the vital interests of our homeland and maintain great vigilance and readiness to give a crushing rebuff to any attempt at aggression. They will redouble their efforts in the struggle for the security of the people and strengthen cooperation with all the peace forces of the world. We are always ready for honest, equal and mutually beneficial cooperation with any state that is willing to cooperate.

In these days of sorrow we are keenly aware of the support and solidarity of the working people of the socialist countries, of the fraternal parties and all fighters for social progress with our party and the Soviet people. We are grateful to the governments and peoples of numerous countries in all continents who paid homage these days to the memory of Leonid Ilyich Brezhnev.

Comrades, the Communist Party of the Soviet Union firmly declares that the cause of the working class, the working people, the cause of communism and peace, to which Leonid Ilyich Brezhnev devoted all his life, will continue to be the supreme aim and meaning behind all its activities.

Farewell, dear Leonid Ilyich. The memory of you will never dim in our hearts. Your cause will be continued in the deeds of our party and people!

I declare the funeral meeting devoted to the memory of Leonid Ilyich Brezhnev open.

ANDROPOV ARMS CONTROL PROPOSALS

Following are excerpts from General Secretary Yuri V. Andropov's first speech outlining arms control proposals, delivered December 21, 1982. (Boldface headings in brackets have been added by Congressional Quarterly to highlight the organization of the text.):

... The war preparations of the United States and the NATO bloc which it leads have grown to an unheard-of, record scale. Official spokesmen in Washington are heard to discourse on the possibility of "limited", "sustained" and other varieties of nuclear war. This is intended to reassure people, to accustom them to the thought that such war is acceptable. Veritably, one has to be blind to the realities of our time not to see that wherever and however a nuclear whirlwind arises, it will inevitably go out of control and cause a worldwide catastrophe.

Our position on this issue is clear: a nuclear war — whether big or small, whether limited or total — must not be allowed to break out. No task is more important today than to stop the instigators of another war. This is required by the vital interests of all nations. That is why the unilateral commitment of the Soviet Union not to use nuclear weapons first was received with approval and hope all over the world. If our example is followed by the other nuclear powers, this will be a truly momentous contribution to the efforts of preventing nuclear war.

It is said that the West cannot take such a commitment because, allegedly, the Warsaw Treaty has an advantage in conventional armaments. To begin with, this is untrue, and the facts and figures bear witness to it. Furthermore, as everybody knows, we are in favour of limiting such armaments as well, and of searching for sensible, mutually acceptable solutions to this end. We are also prepared to agree that the sides should renounce first use of conventional, as well as nuclear arms.

Of course, one of the main avenues leading to a real scaling down of the threat of nuclear war is that of reaching a Soviet-American agreement on limitation and reduction of strategic nuclear arms. We approach negotiations on the matter with the utmost responsibility, and seek an honest agreement that will do no damage to either side and will, at the same time, lead to a reduction of their nuclear arsenals.

So far, unfortunately, we see a different approach by the American side. While calling for "radical reductions" in word, what it really has in mind is essentially a reduction of the Soviet strategic potential. For itself, the United States would like to leave a free hand in building up strategic armaments. It is absurd even to think that we can agree to this. It would, of course, suit the Pentagon, but can on no account be acceptable to the Soviet Union and, for that matter, to all those who have a stake in preserving and consolidating peace.

[Preserving Parity]

Compare to this the proposals of the USSR. They are based on the principle of preserving parity. We are prepared to reduce our strategic arms by more than 25 per cent. US arms, too, must be reduced accordingly, so that the two states have the same number of strategic delivery vehicles. We also propose that the number of nuclear warheads should be substantially lowered and that improvement of nuclear weapons should be maximally restricted.

Our proposals refer to all types of strategic weapons without exception, and envisage reduction of their stockpiles by many hundreds of units. They close all possible channels for any further arms race in this field. And that is only a start: the pertinent agreement would be the point of departure for a still larger mutual reduction of such weapons, which the sides could agree upon, with due account of the general strategic situation in the world.

And while the negotiations are under way, we offer what is suggested by common sense: to freeze the strategic arsenals of the two sides. The US government does not want this, and now everyone can understand why: it has embarked on a new, considerable build-up of nuclear armaments.

Washington's attempts to justify this build-up are obviously irrelevant. The allegation of a "lag" behind the USSR which the Americans must close, is a deliberate untruth. This has been said more than once. And the talk that new weapons systems, such as the MX missile, are meant "to facilitate disarmament negotiations" is altogether absurd.

No programmes of a further arms build-up will ever force the Soviet Union to make unilateral concessions. We will be compelled to counter the challenge of the American side by deploying corresponding weapons systems of our own — an analogous missile to counter the MX missile, and our own long-range cruise missile, which we are now testing, to counter the US long-range cruise missile.

Those are not threats at all. We are wholly averse to any such course of events, and are doing everything to avoid it. But it is essential that those who shape US policy, as well as the public at large, should be perfectly clear on the real state of affairs. Hence, if the people in Washington really believe that new weapons systems will be a "trump" for the Americans at negotiations, we want them to know that these "trumps" are false. Any policy directed to securing military superiority over the Soviet Union has no future and can only heighten the threat of war.

[Confidence-building Measures]

Now a few words about what are known as confidence-building measures. We are serious about them.

Given the swift action and power of modern weapons, the atmosphere of mutual suspicion is especially dangerous. Even a mere accident, miscalculation, or technical failure can have tragic consequences. It is therefore important to take the finger off the trigger, and put a reliable safety catch on all weapons. A few things have already been accomplished to this effect, particularly in the framework of the Helsinki accords. As everybody knows, the Soviet Union is also offering measures of a more far-reaching nature and of broader scope. Our proposals on this score have been tabled at the Soviet-American negotiations in Geneva on limitation and reduction of nuclear armaments.

We are also prepared to consider pertinent proposals made by others, including the recent ones by the US President. But the measures he referred to are not enough to dispel the atmosphere of mutual suspicion, and to restore confidence. Something more is needed: to normalise the situation, and to renounce incitement of hostility and hatred, and propaganda of nuclear war. And, surely, the road to confidence, to preventing any and all wars, including an accidental one, is that of stopping the arms race and going back to calm, respectful relations between states, back to detente.

We consider this important for all regions of the world, and especially for Europe, where a flare-up of any kind may trigger a worldwide explosion.

At present, that continent is beset by a new danger — the prospect of several hundred US missiles being deployed in Western Europe. I must say bluntly: this would make peace still more fragile.

As we see it, the peril threatening the European nations, and, for that matter, the nations of the whole world, can be averted. It is definitely possible to save and strengthen peace in Europe — and this without damage to anyone's security. It is, indeed, for this purpose that we have been negotiating with the United States in Geneva for already more than a year on how to limit and reduce nuclear weapons in the European zone.

[Reduction of Weapons in Europe]

The Soviet Union is prepared to go very far. As everybody knows, we have suggested an agreement renouncing all types of nuclear weapons — both of medium range and tactical — designed to strike targets in Europe. But this proposal has come up against a solid wall of silence. Evidently, they do not want to accept it, but are afraid to reject it openly. I want to reaffirm again that we have not withdrawn this proposal.

We have also suggested another variant: that the USSR and the NATO countries reduce their medium-range weaponry by more than two-thirds. So far, the United States will not have it. For its part, it has submitted a proposal which, as if in mockery, is called a "zero option". It envisages elimination of all Soviet medium-range missiles not only in the European, but also in the Asian part of the Soviet Union, while NATO's nuclear-missile arsenal in Europe is to remain intact and may even be increased. Does anyone really think that the Soviet Union can agree to this? It appears that Washington is out to block an agreement and, citing the collapse of the talks, to station, in one way or another, its missiles on European soil.

The future will show if this is so. We, for our part, will continue to work for an agreement on a basis that is fair to both sides. We are prepared, among other things, to agree that the Soviet Union should retain in Europe only as many missiles as are kept there by Britain and France — and not a single one more. This means that the Soviet Union would reduce hundreds of missiles, including tens of the latest missiles known in the West as SS-20. In the case of the USSR and the USA this would be a really honest "zero" option as regards medium-range missiles. And if, later, the number of British and French missiles were scaled down, the number of Soviet ones would be additionally reduced by as many.

Along with this there must also be an accord on reducing to equal levels on both sides the number of medium-range nuclear-delivery aircraft stationed in this region by the USSR and the NATO countries.

We call on the other side to accept these clear and fair terms, to take this opportunity while it still exists. But let no one delude himself: we will never let our security or the security of our allies be jeopardised. It would also be a good thing if thought were given to the grave consequences that the stationing of new US medium-range weapons in Europe would entail for all further efforts to limit nuclear armaments in general. In short, the ball is now in the court of the USA.

In conclusion, let me say the following. We are for broad, fruitful cooperation among all nations of the world to their mutual advantage and the good of all mankind, free from diktat and interference in the affairs of other countries. The Soviet Union will do everything it can to secure a tranquil, peaceful future for the present and coming generations. That is the aim of our policy, and we shall not depart from it. . . .

ANDROPOV DEATH, SPEECH BY CHERNENKO

Following is the text of the Tass news agency announcement of General Secretary Yuri Andropov's death and excerpts from the February 13, 1984, speech by his successor, Konstantin U. Chernenko. (Boldface headings in brackets have been added by Congressional Quarterly to highlight the organization of the texts.):

Andropov's Death

The Central Committee of the Communist Party of the Soviet Union, the Presidium of the USSR Supreme Soviet and the USSR Council of Ministers with deep sorrow inform the party and the entire Soviet people that Yuri Vladimirovich Andropov, General Secretary of the Central Committee of the Communist Party of the Soviet Union, President of the Presidium of the USSR Supreme Soviet, died after a long illness at 16 hours 50 minutes on February 9, 1984.

The name of Yuri Vladimirovich Andropov, an outstanding leader of the Communist Party and of the Soviet state, a staunch fighter for the ideals of communism and for peace, will always remain in the hearts of the Soviet people and all progressive people.

Chernenko Speech

I cordially thank the members of the Central Committee for the great honor bestowed on me — election as General Secretary of the Central Committee. I fully realize the enormous responsibility which is placed on me. I understand what important and exceptionally difficult work is to be done. I assure the Central Committee and the party that I will exert every effort, use all of my knowledge and experience to live up to this trust, to carry on together with you the principled policy of our party, which has been steadily and persistently implemented by Yuri Vladimirovich Andropov. . . .

The convincing evidence of the correctness of the domestic and foreign policy of the CPSU, its conformity with the requirements and spirit of the times is the ardent countrywide support for this policy. The party firmly marches on the path upon which it embarked — the path of communist creativity and peace. This is how it was in the past. This will always be so!

But we all realize, comrades, that the wish to advance on that path is not enough. We must be able not only to set correct goals, but also to work persistently for their attainment, overcoming any difficulties. It is necessary to evaluate realistically what has been achieved, without exaggerating and also without belittling them. Only this approach prevents mistakes in politics, the temptation to indulge in wishful thinking, makes it possible to see clearly, as Lenin said, "what we have done and what (we) have not . . . yet done."

Yuri Vladimirovich Andropov was destined, comrades, to work at the head of our party and state for a short, painfully short time. We will all miss him. He passed away at the very height of great and intense work aimed at powerfully accelerating the development of the national economy, at overcoming the difficulties which our country encountered at the beginning of the eighties. But we all know what a large amount of work our party has succeeded in doing over that time, how many new and fruitful things have been introduced and reaffirmed in practice. Carrying on and further advancing by collective efforts the work started under the leadership of Yuri Vladimirovich is the best way of paying tribute to his memory and ensuring continuity in politics.

Continuity is not an abstract notion, but a real live cause. And its essence comes down primarily to moving forward, without stopping. This implies advancement relying on everything that has been accomplished earlier, creatively enriching it, concentrating the collective thought and the energy of the communists, the working class and all people on the unresolved tasks, on the key problems of the present and future. All this imposes a deep obligation upon us.

The strength of our party is in its unity, adherence to Marxism-Leninism and ability to develop and guide the creative activity of the masses, to unite them ideologically and organizationally, under the guidance of the tested Leninist principles and methods. You know, comrades, what immense attention our Central Committee, Politburo of the Central Committee and Yuri Vladimirovich Andropov paid recently to the issues of perfecting the work of the state apparatus and improving the style of party leadership.

One of these issues is a clear distinction between the functions of party committees and the tasks of state and economic bodies, eliminating duplication in their performance. This is a major issue of political significance. Frankly speaking, not everything has been properly adjusted here. It happens that workers at Soviets, ministries and enterprises do not display the necessary independence, but leave to party bodies matters which they should handle themselves.... Moreover, this harbors the danger of weakening the role of the party committee as a body of political guidance. For party committees handling economic issues means, above all, being concerned with people engaged in the economy. This must always be borne in mind.

[Economic, Social Issues]

Comrades, a month and a half ago, at the December plenum of the Central Committee, we gave an all-round appraisal of the state of affairs in the country's social and economic development. The resolution it adopted emphasized the importance of maintaining the tempo achieved and general intent to get things going, steadily enhancing the level of party and state guidance over the economy, actively developing positive processes and imparting to them a stable character. It is our direct duty to implement the plenum's instructions in a consistent way.

All of our experience confirms: The most important source of the party's strength were, are and will be its contact with the masses, the civic activity of millions of working people and their practical attitude to production matters and to problems of public life....

The broad response by the country's work collectives to the December plenum's call for raising by one per cent above plan labor productivity and additionally reducing production costs by 0.5 per cent gives rise to profound satisfaction....

I think it is necessary to consider the question of directing all means and resources that will be obtained as a result, and they will not be insignificant, to improving the working and living conditions of Soviet people, medical services and housing construction. This would fully meet the supreme goal of party policy — all-round concern for the benefit of man.

In general, comrades, we must probably think of providing better material and moral incentive to working people for creative initiatives and innovation.

Social justice underlies the very foundation of the Soviet system. This constitutes its immense strength. That is why it is so important that it be strictly observed in everyday affairs, whether the matter concerns salaries or bonuses, distribution of apartments or passes (to a health resort), or awards, in brief, so that everything be fair, in accordance with each person's labor contribution to our common cause....

The question of organization and order is a key, principled one for us. There can be no two views on this. Any slackness or irresponsibility brings to society not only material losses. They inflict serious social and moral damage. We, communists, and millions of Soviet people understand this well. And it is quite natural that the measures adopted by the party with a view to enhancing labor, production, planning and state discipline and strengthening socialist law have evoked countrywide approval.... Yet it would be wrong to believe that everything has already been done. No, comrades, life teaches that by no means should there be any relaxing here.

As far as the guidelines for the development of our economy are concerned, they have been clearly outlined by the party. Intensification, accelerated introduction of the achievements of science and technology into production and the implementation of large-scale comprehensive programs are all designed to raise, in the final analysis, the productive forces of our society to a qualitatively new level.

The system of economic management and our whole economic mechanism need a serious restructuring. Work in this direction has only been started. It includes a large-scale economic experiment for broadening the rights and increasing the responsibility of the enterprises. A search is under way for new forms and methods of management in the field of services. They will undoubtedly be very useful and will help us resolve the strategically important problem of increasing the effectiveness of the entire national economy....

We expect from our economic executives more independence at all levels, a bold search and, if necessary, a well-justified risk in the name of increasing the effectiveness of the economy and ensuring a rise in the living standards of the people.

You know that in the past year the CPSU Central Committee and the government have drawn up and adopted a number of decisions on principled issues of economic development. These decisions have given the party and economic bodies certain levers for increasing the effectiveness of production and accelerating the country's economic development.

The planned measures, and these measures are not only of economic but also of great political significance, will be put into practice only if their implementation becomes the main component of every party organization's and every working person's everyday work....

It is no less important now to ensure an increasingly closer interconnection between the economic, social and intellectual advancement of Soviet society. It is impossible to raise the economy to a qualitatively new level without creating the necessary social and ideological prerequisites for that. It is likewise impossible to resolve pressing problems of the development of socialist consciousness without resting upon a firm foundation of economic and social policy....

[International Relations]

Comrades, in drawing up plans for the further development of our country, we cannot help but take into account the situation now developing in the world. And, as you know, it is now complicated and tense. The correct course of the party and the Soviet state in the sphere of foreign policy acquires still greater significance in these conditions....

It is absolutely clear, comrades, that the success of the effort to preserve and strengthen peace depends in a considerable measure on how great the influence of the socialist countries in the world arena is and how vigorous, purposeful and coordinated their actions will be. Our countries have a vital stake in peace. In the name of this purpose we will strive to broaden cooperation with all the socialist countries.... Addressing the fraternal countries, we say: The Soviet Union will also be your reliable friend and true ally.

One of the fundamentals of our party's and the Soviet state's foreign policy has been and will remain solidarity with the peoples which have shattered the fetters of colonial dependence and embarked on the path of independent development....

Now, about relations with the capitalist countries. The great Lenin bequeathed to us the principle of peaceful coexistence of states with different social systems. We are invariably loyal to this principle. Nowadays, in the age of nuclear weapons and superaccurate missiles, people need it as never before. Deplorably, some leaders of the capitalist countries, to all appearances, do not clearly realize, or do not wish to realize that.

CHERNENKO INTERVIEW BY AMERICAN REPORTER

Following are written questions and answers and an abridged version of the oral interview of Soviet leader Konstantin U. Chernenko given to Dusko Doder of the Washington Post *October 16, 1984:*

Written Exchange

[Q] President Reagan has said that the United States is prepared to resume a dialogue with the Soviet Union on a broad range of questions including arms control. What is the attitude of the Soviet Union toward President Reagan's expression of readiness for talks?

[A] In the past, we have already heard words about the U.S. administration's readiness for talks. But they have never been supported by real deeds that would attest to a genuine desire to reach agreement on a just and mutually acceptable basis at least on one of the essential questions of our relations, particularly in the field of arms limitation and a reduction of the war danger.

Every time we put forward concrete proposals, they would run into a blind wall. Let me give some examples.

Such was the case last March when we identified a whole set of problems. Reaching agreement on them — or at least on some of them — would mean a real shift both in Soviet-U.S. relations and in the international situation as a whole. But what they did was simply to shirk responding to our proposals.

Such was the case when we proposed reaching agreement on preventing the militarization of outer space. This time we were answered, but with what? An attempt was made to substitute the very subject of negotiations. It was proposed to discuss issues related to nuclear weapons, i.e., issues which had previously been discussed at the talks in Geneva that were wrecked by the United States itself.

At the same time, the United States not only refused to remove the obstacles created by the deployment of new U.S. missiles in Western Europe but is going ahead with their deployment.

And what about outer space? Instead of preventing an arms race in space, we were invited to proceed to working out some rules for such a race, and in fact to legalize it. Obviously, we cannot agree to that. Our objective is genuinely peaceful outer space and we shall persistently strive for this objective.

These are the facts.

Turning now to President Reagan's statement which you have referred to. If what the president has said about readiness to negotiate is not merely a tactical move, I wish to state that the Soviet Union will not be found wanting. We have always been prepared for serious and businesslike negotiations and have repeatedly said so.

We are ready to proceed to negotiations with a view to working out and concluding an agreement to prevent the militarization of outer space, including complete renunciation of antisatellite systems, with a mutual moratorium — to be established from the date of the beginning of the talks — on testing and deployment of space weapons. This is precisely the way we formulated our proposal from the outset. Now it is for Washington to respond.

The Soviet proposal that the nuclear powers freeze quantitatively and qualitatively all nuclear weapons at their disposal also remains valid.

Agreement on that matter would mean mutual cessation of the buildup of all components of the existing nuclear arsenals, including delivery vehicles and nuclear warheads. The nuclear arms race would thus be stopped. That would radically facilitate further agreements on reductions in and eventual complete elimination of such weapons.

The White House still has before it our official proposal that the Soviet Union and the United States initially agree to freeze their nuclear weapons, thus setting an example for other nuclear powers.

There is a real opportunity to finalize the agreement on the complete and general prohibition of nuclear weapon tests. Should there be no such tests, these weapons will not be improved, which will put the brakes on the nuclear arms race.

Here, too, the United States could prove in deeds the sincerity of its declarations in favor of nuclear arms limitation. The United States can also prove it by ratifying the Soviet-American treaties on underground nuclear explosions. These treaties were signed as far back as 1974 and 1976. Prove it precisely by ratifying them and not by inviting observers, as suggested by the American side, who would merely dispassionately ascertain the fact of explosion.

The Soviet Union has repeatedly called upon Washington to follow our example in assuming an obligation not to be the first to use nuclear weapons. Every time the answer was "no."

Imagine the reverse situation: the United States assumes an obligation not to be the first to use nuclear weapons and calls upon us to reciprocate while we say "no," this does not suit us and we reserve the right to a first nuclear strike. What would people in the United States think of our intentions in that case? There can be no two views on that score.

I have mentioned several most pressing problems related to the cessation of the arms race and the strengthening of security. There are other important questions which, I believe, the president is well aware of. All of them call for solutions and for making concrete efforts. Unsupported by practical deeds, words about readiness to negotiate remain mere words. I believe the above answers your question.

[Q] A view is widely spread that recently a shift has become discernible which could lead to better Soviet-U.S. relations. What do you think about this and what is your view of the prospects for these relations in the time to come?

[A] Indeed, sentiments in favor of a shift for the better in Soviet-U.S. relations are widely spread in the world. This, in our view, reflects the growing understanding of the importance of these relations, particularly in the current international situation.

Unfortunately, so far there has been no ground to speak of such a shift in Soviet-U.S. relations as a fact of life. It is possible? The resolution of the problems to which I referred earlier would help to bring it about.

I am convinced there is no sound alternative at all to a constructive development of Soviet-U.S. relations. At the same time, we do not overlook the fact that we have different social systems and world outlooks.

But if the responsibility which rests with our two countries is constantly kept in mind, if policy is oriented toward peace and not war, these differences not only do not exclude the search for mutual understanding, but call for it.

I have already said in the past and I wish to stress it once again: we stand for good relations with the U.S.A. and experience shows that they can be such. This requires a mutual desire to build relations as equals, to mutual benefit and for the good of the cause of peace.

Oral Exchange

[Q] I want to use this opportunity to hear your opinion as to what specific steps the Soviet leadership would like to see after the American elections to get out of the current impasse in Soviet-American relations.

[A] First of all, of course, the elections should take place in order to answer what will happen after the elections. The elections are in the future and therefore to determine now, in advance, what, when and where we are going to discuss is obviously too early. But you know our general official point of view.

Whoever is the president in America, our policy — a policy of peace which we are carrying out persistently and systematically — is going, I think, to remain the same. The same. That is why peace is the main question for us, and I think that any president who comes to the White House after the election will, I think, will be thinking about the same question.

As a matter of fact, two great countries can, as we became convinced in the past and are being convinced each day, can do a great deal, in fact they can do everything, in order that flames of another world war do not flare up. This is our objective, this is our direction, our general direction, and we think that any sober-minded person can understand us correctly.

We are doing this not because we . . . like it, but because we experienced in reality what such a war means, war without a hydrogen bomb, without such bombs. And what about a war with atomic bombs? We are now convinced that this is a very terrible weapon and naturally we would like to see in the face of American president a partner in this sacred human task — for peace.

[Q] What about specific measures?

[A] There [in the written answers] is our program on this score.

[Q] Are you optimistic about the present development of Soviet-American relations?

[A] Well, there are considerable possibilities in Soviet-American relations, very considerable possibilities. We have been making attempts, and you know if we enumerate the numbers of our proposals, which we have advanced and which I mentioned in my answers, you can easily see that. . . .

Chernenko's foreign policy adviser Andrei Alexandrov-Agentov: So far, there is no. . . .

Chernenko: No, so far there is no serious shift, businesslike shifts, such moves which could convince people and which could be convincing in themselves. In principle, I am an optimist, an optimist, but that does not mean an endless optimism, since there are limits to everything. I think nevertheless that things are going to get normalized if the American side indeed takes some practical steps in the direction of the struggle for peace. Practical steps.

[Q] And should not both sides take some small steps?

[A] You see, you will find the answers there. And not small steps but big steps that we have made in the direction of peace. But the White House is silent on this question. They are silent and they do not answer. . . . or they do not even simply notice them. Or they consciously do not respond. One thing is clear: there has been no practical shift in the direction of peace by the White House. You can see that yourself.

It is necessary of course to translate those talks, all our agreements, questions and answers onto practical tracks. Here is the essence of the issue. It is not that we lack peace proposals, there are very many of them, but there are no practical solutions, no practical approaches for their resolution.

This is the most important point. And small steps, yes, yes, they only cloud people's eyes. That's it. But I believe that my answers to your questions are also one of our steps, our practical steps, on this important road.

REAGAN-GORBACHEV SUMMIT STATEMENT

Following is the White House text of the joint statement issued November 21, 1985, by President Reagan and Soviet leader Mikhail S. Gorbachev at the conclusion of the U.S.-Soviet summit in Geneva, Switzerland.

By mutual agreement, President of the United States Ronald Reagan and General Secretary of the Central Committee of the Communist Party of the Soviet Union Mikhail Gorbachev met in Geneva November 19-21. Attending the meeting on the U.S. side were Secretary of State George Shultz; Chief of Staff Donald Regan; Assistant to the President Robert McFarlane; Ambassador to the USSR Arthur Hartman; Special Advisor to the President and the Secretary of State for Arms Control Paul H. Nitze; Assistant Secretary of State for European Affairs Rosanne Ridgway; Special Assistant to the President for National Security Affairs Jack Matlock. Attending on the Soviet side were Member of the Politburo of the Central Committee of the CPSU, Minister of Foreign Affairs E. A. Shevardnadze; First Deputy Foreign Minister G. M. Korniyenko; Ambassador to the United States A. F. Dobrynin; Head of the Department of Propaganda of the Central Committee of the CPSU, A. N. Yakovlev; Head of the Department of International Information of the Central Committee of the CPSU, L. M. Zamyatin; Assistant to the General Secretary of the Central Committee of the CPSU, A. M. Aleksandrov.

These comprehensive discussions covered the basic questions of U.S.-Soviet relations and the current international situation. The meetings were frank and useful. Serious differences remain on a number of critical issues.

While acknowledging the differences in their systems and approaches to international issues, some greater understanding of each side's view was achieved by the two leaders. They agreed about the need to improve U.S.-Soviet relations and the international situation as a whole.

In this connection the two sides have confirmed the importance of an ongoing dialogue, reflecting their strong desire to seek common ground on existing problems.

They agreed to meet again in the nearest future. The General Secretary accepted an invitation by the President of the United States to visit the United States of America and the President of the United States accepted an invitation by the General Secretary of the Central Committee of the CPSU to visit the Soviet Union. Arrangements for and timing of the visits will be agreed upon through diplomatic channels.

In their meetings, agreement was reached on a number of specific issues. Areas of agreement are registered on the following pages:

Security

The sides, having discussed key security issues, and conscious of the special responsibility of the USSR and the U.S. for maintaining peace, have agreed that a nuclear war cannot be won and must never be fought. Recognizing that any conflict between the USSR and the U.S. could have catastrophic consequences, they emphasized the importance of preventing any war between them, whether nuclear or conventional. They will not seek to achieve military superiority.

Nuclear and Space Talks

The President and the General Secretary discussed the negotiations on nuclear and space arms.

They agreed to accelerate the work at these negotiations, with a view to accomplishing the tasks set down in the Joint U.S.-Soviet Agreement of January 8, 1985, namely to prevent an arms race in space and to terminate it on Earth, to limit and reduce nuclear arms and enhance strategic stability.

Noting the proposals recently tabled by the U.S. and the Soviet Union, they called for early progress, in particular in areas where there is common ground, including the principle of 50 percent reductions in the nuclear arms of the U.S. and the USSR appropriately applied, as well as the idea of an interim INF [intermediate-range nuclear force] agreement.

During the negotiation of these agreements, effective measures for verification of compliance with obligations assumed will be agreed upon.

Risk Reduction Centers

The sides agreed to study the question at the expert level of centers to reduce nuclear risk taking into account the issues and developments in the Geneva negotiations.

They took satisfaction in such recent steps in this direction as the modernization of the Soviet-U.S. hotline.

Nuclear Non-Proliferation

General Secretary Gorbachev and President Reagan reaffirmed the commitment of the USSR and the U.S. to the Treaty on the Non-Proliferation of Nuclear Weapons and their interest in strengthening together with other countries the non-proliferation regime, and in further enhancing of the Treaty, inter alia by enlarging its membership.

They note with satisfaction the overall positive results of the recent Review Conference of the Treaty on the Non-Proliferation of Nuclear Weapons.

The USSR and the U.S. reaffirm their commitment, assumed by them under the Treaty on the Non-Proliferation of Nuclear Weapons, to pursue negotiations in good faith on matters of nuclear arms limitation and disarmament in accordance with Article VI of the Treaty.

The two sides plan to continue to promote the strengthening of the International Atomic Energy Agency and to support the activities of the Agency in implementing safeguards as well as in promoting the peaceful uses of nuclear energy.

They view positively the practice of regular Soviet-U.S. consultations on non-proliferation of nuclear weapons which have been businesslike and constructive and express their intent to continue this practice in the future.

Chemical Weapons

In the context of discussing security problems, the two sides reaffirmed that they are in favor of a general and complete prohibition of chemical weapons and the destruction of existing stockpiles of such weapons.

They agreed to accelerate efforts to conclude an effective and verifiable international convention in this matter.

The two sides agreed to intensify bilateral discussions on the level of experts on all aspects of such a chemical weapons ban, including the question of verification. They agreed to initiate a dialogue on preventing the proliferation of chemical weapons.

MBFR

The two sides emphasized the importance they attach to the Vienna (MBFR) [mutual balanced force reduction] negotiations and expressed their willingness to work for positive results.

CDE

Attaching great importance to the Stockholm Conference on Confidence and Security Building Measures and Disarmament in Europe [CDE] and noting the progress made there, the two sides stated their intention to facilitate, together with the other participating states, an early and successful completion of the work of the conference. To this end, they reaffirmed the need for a document which would include mutually acceptable confidence and security building measures and give concrete expression and effect to the principle of non-use of force.

Process of Dialogue

President Reagan and General Secretary Gorbachev agreed on the need to place on a regular basis and intensify dialogue at various levels. Along with meetings between the leaders of the two countries, this envisages regular meetings between the USSR Minister of Foreign Affairs and the U.S. Secretary of State, as well as between the heads of other Ministries and Agencies. They agree that the recent visits of the heads of Ministries and Departments in such fields as agriculture, housing and protection of the environment have been useful.

Recognizing that exchanges of views on regional issues on the expert level have proven useful, they agreed to continue such exchanges on a regular basis.

The sides intend to expand the programs of bilateral cultural, educational and scientific-technical exchanges, and also to develop trade and economic ties. The President of the United States and the General Secretary of the Central Committee of the CPSU attended the signing of the Agreement on Contacts and Exchanges in Scientific, Educational and Cultural Fields.

They agreed on the importance of resolving humanitarian cases in the spirit of cooperation.

They believe that there should be greater understanding among our peoples and that to this end they will encourage greater travel and people-to-people contact.

Northern Pacific Air Safety

The two leaders also noted with satisfaction that, in cooperation with the Government of Japan, the United States and the Soviet Union have agreed to a set of measures to promote safety on air routes in the North Pacific and have worked out steps to implement them.

Civil Aviation/Consulates

They acknowledged that delegations from the United States and the Soviet Union have begun negotiations aimed at resumption of air services. The two leaders expressed their desire to reach a mutually beneficial agreement at an early date. In this regard, an agreement was reached on the simultaneous opening of Consulates General in New York and Kiev.

Environmental Protection

Both sides agreed to contribute to the preservation of the environment — a global task — through joint research and practical measures. In accordance with the existing U.S.-Soviet agreement in this area, consultations will be held next year in Moscow and Washington on specific programs of cooperation.

Exchange Initiatives

The two leaders agreed on the utility of broadening exchanges and contacts including some of their new forms in a number of scientific, educational, medical and sports fields (inter alia, cooperation in the development of educational exchanges and software for elementary and secondary school instruction; measures to promote Russian language studies in the United States and English language studies in the USSR; the annual exchange of professors to conduct special courses in history, culture and economics at the relevant departments of Soviet and American institutions of higher education; mutual allocation of scholarships for the best students in the natural sciences, technology, social sciences and humanities for the period of an academic year; holding regular meets in various sports and increased television coverage of sports events). The two sides agreed to resume cooperation in combating cancer diseases.

The relevant agencies in each of the countries are being instructed to develop specific programs for these exchanges. The resulting programs will be reviewed by the leaders at their next meeting.

Fusion Research

The two leaders emphasized the potential importance of the work aimed at utilizing controlled thermonuclear fusion for peaceful purposes and, in this connection, advocated the widest practicable development of international cooperation in obtaining this source of energy, which is essentially inexhaustible, for the benefit of all mankind.

1985 CULTURAL EXCHANGE AGREEMENT

Following are excerpts from the November 21, 1985, summit agreement by President Ronald Reagan and Communist Party General Secretary Mikhail S. Gorbachev on cultural, educational, and other exchanges between their two countries:

THE GENERAL AGREEMENT BETWEEN THE GOVERNMENT OF THE UNITED STATES OF AMERICA AND THE GOVERNMENT OF THE UNION OF SOVIET SOCIALIST REPUBLICS ON CONTACTS, EXCHANGES AND COOPERATION IN SCIENTIFIC, TECHNICAL, EDUCATIONAL, CULTURAL AND OTHER FIELDS

The Government of the United States of America and the Government of the Union of Soviet Socialist Republics;

Desiring to promote better understanding between the peoples of the United States of America and the Union of Soviet

Socialist Republics and to help improve the general state of relations between the two countries;

Referring to the relevant principles, provisions and objectives set forth in the Final Act of the Conference on Security and Cooperation in Europe;

Consistent with the relevant provisions of the Basic Principles of Relations Between the United States of America and the Union of Soviet Socialist Republics, signed at Moscow on May 29, 1972;

Believing that the further expansion of reciprocal and mutually beneficial contacts, exchanges and cooperation will facilitate the achievement of these aims;

Taking into account the positive experience achieved through previous agreements on exchanges in the cultural, educational, scientific and technical fields, and in other fields;

Have agreed as follows:

Article I

1. The Parties will encourage and develop contacts, exchanges and cooperation in the fields of the natural sciences, technology, the humanities and social sciences, education, culture, and in other fields of mutual interest on the basis of equality, mutual benefit, and reciprocity.

2. This General Agreement and implementation of the contacts, exchanges and cooperation under it shall be subject to the Constitution and applicable laws and regulations of the respective countries. Within this framework, the Parties will take all appropriate measures to ensure favorable conditions for such contacts, exchanges and cooperation, and the safety of, and normal working conditions for, those participating in American-Soviet exchanges.

Article II

1. The Parties take note of the following specialized agreements on cooperation in various fields and reaffirm their commitments to achieve their fulfillment and to encourage the renewal or extension of them, when it is considered mutually beneficial:

a. The Agreement on Cooperation in the Field of Environmental Protection between the United States of America and the Union of Soviet Socialist Republics, signed at Moscow on May 23, 1972, and extended until May 23, 1987. . . ;

b. The Agreement . . . on Cooperation in the Field of Medical Science and Public Health, signed at Moscow on May 23, 1972, and extended until May 23, 1987. . . ;

c. The Agreement . . . on Cooperation in the Field of Agriculture, signed at Washington on June 19, 1973, and extended until June 19, 1988. . . ;

d. The Agreement on Cooperation in Studies of the World Ocean, signed at Washington on June 19, 1973, and extended until December 14, 1987. . . ;

e. The Agreement on Scientific and Technical Cooperation in the Field of Peaceful Uses of Atomic Energy, signed at Washington on June 21, 1973, and extended until June 20, 1986. . . ;

f. The Agreement . . . on Cooperation in the Field of Housing and Other Construction, signed at Moscow on June 28, 1974, and extended until June 28, 1989. . . ;

g. The Agreement . . . on Cooperation in Artificial Heart Research and Development, signed at Moscow on June 28, 1974, and extended until June 28, 1987. . . ;

h. The Long Term Agreement . . . to Facilitate Economic, Industrial, and Technical Cooperation, signed at Moscow on June 29, 1974, and extended until June 28, 1994. . . ;

2. When it is considered mutually beneficial, the Parties will encourage within the framework of this Agreement conclusion of specialized agreements, including renewal and mutually agreed amendments between:

a. The National Academy of Sciences of the United States of America and the Academy of Sciences of the Union of Soviet Socialist Republics;

b. The American Council of Learned Societies and the Academy of Sciences of the Union of Soviet Socialist Republics;

c. Institutions of higher education of both countries.

3. The Parties will encourage the conclusion, when it is considered mutually beneficial, of agreements on cooperation in the field of science and technology, and also additional agreements in other specific fields, including the humanities and social sciences, within the framework of this Agreement.

Article III

The Parties will encourage and facilitate, as appropriate, contacts, exchanges and cooperation between organizations of the two countries in the fields of the humanities and social sciences, natural sciences, technology, education, and in other related fields of mutual interest which are not being carried out under specialized agreements concluded between the Parties. These activities may include:

1. The exchange of experts, delegations, scholarly and technical information, the organization of lectures, seminars and symposia, for such experts;

2. The participation of scholars and other specialists in professional congresses, conferences and similar meetings being held in the two countries, and the conducting of specialized exhibits and of joint research work;

3. Other forms of contacts, exchanges and cooperation which may be mutually agreed upon.

Article IV

1. The Parties will encourage and facilitate, as appropriate, contacts, exchanges and cooperation between organizations of the two countries in various fields of education. These activities may include:

a. The exchange of students, graduate students, researchers and faculty members for study and research; the exchange of professors and teachers to lecture, offer instruction, and conduct research; the exchange of specialists and delegations in various fields of education; and, as possible, the organization of lectures, seminars and symposia for such specialists;

b. The exchange of more young researchers preparing dissertations, as well as of young teachers, taking into account the desirability of proper representation of the social sciences, the humanities, and the natural and applied sciences in these exchanges;

c. Making available to students, researchers and teachers appropriate educational, research and open archive materials which are relevant to the agreed topic of research based, as a minimum, upon the agreed preliminary plan of study and, as possible, other resources which may come to light during the course of the researcher's stay;

d. The facilitation of the exchange, by appropriate organizations, of educational and teaching materials (including textbooks, syllabi and curricula), materials on methodology, samples of teaching instruments and audiovisual aids.

2. The Parties will also encourage the study of each other's languages through the development of the exchanges and cooperation listed above and through other mutually agreed measures.

Article V

1. In order to promote better acquaintance with the cultural achievement of each country, the Parties will facilitate the reciprocal development of contacts, exchanges and artistic cooperation in the field of the performing arts. To these ends the Parties will assist exchanges of theatrical, musical, and choreographic ensembles, orchestras, and other performing and artistic groups, as well as individual directors and performers.

Article VI

1. The Parties will encourage the film industries of both countries, as appropriate, to consider means of further expanding the purchase and distribution on a commercial basis of films produced in each country; the joint production of feature, documentary, popular-science, and educational films; and the rendering, upon request, of production and creative assistance by each side for films produced by the other.

2. The Parties will encourage, as appropriate, the exchange

and exhibition of documentary films dealing with science, technology, culture, education and other fields.

3. The Parties will render assistance to the exchange of delegations of creative workers and technical experts in various aspects of film making.

4. The Parties also agree to consider, at the request of organizations or individuals of their own countries, other proposals for the expansion of mutually acceptable exchanges in this field, including holding film premieres and film weeks, and participating in international film festivals held in each country.

Article VII

1. The Parties will, on a mutually acceptable basis, assist contacts and encourage exchanges between organizations of both countries in the field of radio and television, including exchanges of radio programs and television films both for educational purposes and for transmission to local audiences, and in addition exchanges of delegations of creative workers and technical specialists in various fields of radio and television broadcasting. Appearances of representatives of each country on television of the other country can take place in accordance with the existing practices and regulations of each country.

2. The Parties further agree, upon the request of organizations and individuals of their own countries, to consider other proposals in the field of radio and television, including joint production of television films and rendering services in the production of radio and television programs. Each Party, as possible and in accordance with the relevant laws and regulations of the receiving country, will render assistance to the other in the preparation of such programs.

Article VIII

The Parties note that in the pursuit of better mutual understanding, a desirable goal is the greater familiarity of each country's people with the literature and other publications of the other. To this end, the Parties will encourage:

1. The exchange of book exhibits, literary works, magazines, newspapers and other publications devoted to scholarly, technical, cultural, and general educational subjects between libraries, universities and other organizations of each country, as well as the reciprocal distribution of the magazines *Amerika* and *Soviet Life*;

2. Exchanges and visits of journalists, editors and publishers, translators of literary works, as well as their participation in appropriate professional meetings and conferences;

3. Further development of cooperation between publishing houses of the two countries, when such expansion is seen as useful to it by individual publishing houses or their professional organizations.

Article IX

1. The Parties will encourage and facilitate the exchange of exhibitions on various topics of mutual interest. The Parties agree to accord each other the opportunity for two to four circulating exhibitions during the six-year period of this Agreement.

2. The Parties will encourage and facilitate appropriate participation by one Party in exhibitions which may take place in the other's country.

3. The Parties will also render assistance for the exchange of exhibitions between the museums of the two countries.

Article X

The Parties will provide for mutually acceptable exchanges, cooperation and visits of architects, art historians, artists, composers, musicologists, museum specialists, playwrights, theater directors, writers, specialists in various fields of law, including public law and government, and those in other cultural and professional fields, to familiarize themselves with matters of interest to them in their respective fields and to participate in meetings, conferences and symposia.

Article XI

1. The Parties will render assistance to members of the Congress of the United States of America and Deputies of the Supreme Soviet of the Union of Soviet Socialist Republics, as well as to officials of the National Government of both countries making visits to the Union of Soviet Socialist Republics and the United States of America, respectively. Arrangements for such assistance will be agreed upon in advance through diplomatic channels.

2. The Parties will encourage exchanges of representatives of municipal, local and state governments of the United States of America and the Union of Soviet Socialist Republics to study various functions of government at these levels.

Article XII

The Parties will encourage joint undertakings and exchanges between appropriate organizations active in civic and social life, including youth and women's organizations, recognizing that the decision to implement such joint undertakings and exchanges remains a concern of the organizations themselves.

Article XIII

The Parties will encourage the development of contacts in sports through organizing competitions, exchanging delegations, teams, athletes and coaches in the field of physical culture and sports upon agreement between the appropriate sports organizations of both countries.

Article XIV

The Parties will encourage the expansion of tourism between the two countries with the aim of more fully satisfying the requests of tourists to become acquainted with the life, work and culture of the people of each country. In this connection the Parties will encourage, on a mutually acceptable basis, tourist trips, on a group and individual basis, thus to facilitate exchanges between young people, workers, farmers and representatives of other vocations.

Article XV

The Parties will encourage the further development of contacts and cooperation between archival organizations of the two countries. Initial program proposals on these contacts and cooperation will be made through diplomatic channels.

Article XVI

The Parties note that commemorative activities may take place in their countries in connection with the celebration of anniversaries recognized by major international bodies.

Article XVII

The Parties agree that, as necessary, they will hold meetings of their representatives for the general review of the implementation of contacts, exchanges and cooperation in various fields and to consider the possibility of exchanges which are not carried out under specialized agreements between the two Parties. These reviews, which may be requested by either side, will take place usually annually but at least once during the period of each three-year Program.

Article XVIII

The Parties agree that:

1. The programs and itineraries, lengths of stay, dates of arrival, size of delegations, financial and transportation arrangements and other details of exchanges and visits, except as otherwise determined, shall be agreed upon, as a rule, not less than thirty days in advance, through diplomatic channels or between appropriate organizations requested by the Parties to carry out these exchanges;

2. Applications for visas for visitors participating in exchanges and cooperative activities shall be submitted, as a rule, at least ten working days before the estimated time of departure;

3. Unless otherwise provided for in specialized agreements between the Parties, and except where other specific arrangements have been agreed upon, participants in exchanges and cooperative activities will pay their own expenses, including international travel, internal travel and costs of maintenance in the receiving country.

Article XIX

1. In implementation of various provisions of this Agreement, the Parties have established a Program of Cooperation and Exchanges for 1986-88, which is attached and is an integral part of this Agreement. The terms of that Program shall be in force from January 1, 1986, to December 31, 1988, and thereafter, unless and until amended by agreement of the Parties, will provide the basic guidelines for the Program of Cooperation and Exchanges for 1989-1991.

2. The Parties agree that their representatives will meet prior to the end of 1988 to develop the Program of Cooperation and Exchanges for the succeeding three years.

Article XX

1. This Agreement shall enter into force on signature and shall remain in force until December 31, 1991. It may be modified or extended by mutual agreement of the Parties.

2. Nothing in this Agreement shall be construed to prejudice other agreements concluded between the two Parties.

Done at Geneva, this 21st day of November, 1985, in duplicate, in the English and Russian languages, both texts being equally authentic.

FOR THE
GOVERNMENT OF THE
UNITED STATES OF AMERICA:

Ronald Reagan

FOR THE
GOVERNMENT OF THE
UNION OF SOVIET
SOCIALIST REPUBLICS:

Mikhail S. Gorbachev

PROGRAM OF COOPERATION AND EXCHANGES BETWEEN THE UNITED STATES OF AMERICA AND THE UNION OF SOVIET SOCIALIST REPUBLICS FOR 1986-1988

In implementation of various provisions of the General Agreement between the United States of America and the Union of Soviet Socialist Republics on Contacts, Exchanges and Cooperation in Scientific, Technical, Educational, Cultural, and Other Fields signed at Geneva on November 21, 1985, the Parties have agreed on the following Program of Exchanges.

Article I   Higher Education

1. The Parties will exchange annually from each side:

a. For long term advanced research: At least 40 advanced researchers, instructors and professors for study and scholarly research in the humanities and the social, natural and applied sciences for periods of from one semester to one academic year. For the purposes of accounting, two stays of one semester each shall be equivalent to one stay of one academic year.

b. For short-term advanced research: At least ten professors, instructors and advanced researchers to conduct scholarly research in the humanities and the social, natural and applied sciences for periods of between two and five months.

c. At least 30 language teachers and two leaders from universities and other institutions of higher learning to participate in

summer courses of two months to improve their competence in the language of the receiving side.

d. Parallel to the exchanges specified under paragraphs a and b above, the Parties note and encourage the exchange of scholars between the American Council of Learned Societies and the Academy of Sciences of the Union of Soviet Socialist Republics which involves advanced research for up to 60 person-months from each side each academic year.

e. The Parties affirm the reciprocal nature of these programs in which the sending side chooses, at its own discretion, candidates for participation in the exchanges, and the receiving side, at its discretion, agrees to the placement of these candidates.

In this connection, the Parties note that, in the carrying out of the exchanges specified under paragraphs 1a, b and d above, and following the existing practice of mutually acceptable participation in the exchanges of representatives in the humanities, social sciences, and natural and technical sciences, they will strive, as in the past, for such mutually acceptable participation of scholars in the above-mentioned fields.

f. In the practical implementation of these programs, the Parties will strive to maintain the levels of exchange already achieved, where the existing levels exceed the minimum levels given above.

2. In accordance with the wishes of the sending and receiving sides, the Parties will exchange annually at least 15 professors and specialists from universities or other institutions of higher learning from each side. Both sides will attempt to include four lecturers on the languages and literatures of the sending side. The exchanges will be for periods of one to ten months, normally corresponding to the receiving side's academic calendar, to lecture and, as time permits, to teach and conduct research at universities and other institutions of higher learning.

The Parties note that this exchange has involved lecturers from a broad range of fields, corresponding to the needs of both sending and receiving sides. In this connection, the parties will strive to maintain this mutually beneficial exchange in the various fields of the natural and technical sciences, the humanities, and the social sciences.

3. The Parties will exchange during the period of this Program at least two delegations of specialists in higher education consisting of up to five persons from each side for periods of two to three weeks each, including two to three days of seminars with specialists of the other country. The subjects of the seminars and itineraries of the visits will be agreed upon subsequently.

4. The Parties will encourage the conclusion of arrangements for direct exchanges between universities and other institutions of higher learning of the two countries for the purpose of study, research, lecturing, and participating in seminars. These exchanges would take place outside the exchange quotas mentioned in paragraphs 1, 2, and 3 above. They will be the subject of direct separate agreements concluded between the universities or institutes concerned, and the conditions for the exchanges listed above will not necessarily apply to them.

5. The sides agree that the United States will continue to take measures to encourage the study of the Russian language in the United States of America, and the Soviet Union will continue its practice of teaching English language in the Union of Soviet Socialist Republics. In order to realize the above goals, the Parties will encourage the expansion of exchange programs for language study whereby American and Soviet undergraduates can study Russian and English respectively, obtaining academic credits for that study.

6. The Parties agree to continue to exchange information and to conduct appropriate consultations regarding the equivalency of diplomas and scholarly degrees. The Parties expect that the Convention on the Recognition of Studies, Diplomas and Degrees Concerning Higher Education in the States Belonging to the Europe Region, in the elaboration of which the United States of America and the Union of Soviet Socialist Republics have taken part, will lead to closer cooperation in this field.

Article II   Primary and Secondary Education and the Pedagogical Sciences

1. The Parties will exchange annually from each side, groups of language teachers, up to a total of 15 persons, from secondary schools in the United States of America, and from secondary schools or pedagogical institutes in the Union of Soviet Socialist Republics, to participate in summer courses of six weeks duration, including up to two weeks of travel, to improve their competence in the teaching of the Russian and English languages and their knowledge of the Union of Soviet Socialist Republics and the United States of America. Each group of language teachers may be accompanied by a leader.

2. The Parties will exchange one delegation annually of specialists in primary and secondary education of up to five persons from each side for a period of two to three weeks each, including a seminar of normally two to three days with specialists of the other country. The subjects of the seminars, their duration and itineraries of the visits will be agreed upon subsequently.

3. The Parties will encourage the exchange of primary and secondary school textbooks and other teaching materials, and, as is deemed appropriate, the conducting of joint studies on textbooks, between appropriate organizations in the United States of America and the Ministry of Education of the Union of Soviet Socialist Republics.

4. The Parties will encourage the annual exchange of six teachers for periods of three months to conduct practical instruction classes in the English and Russian languages at secondary schools, colleges, universities and pedagogical training institutions of the United States of America and the Union of Soviet Socialist Republics.

Article III   Arts and Culture

1. The Parties agree to facilitate the tours of at least 10 major performing arts groups from each side during the period of this Program. If one Party sends more than 10 major performing arts groups, the other Party will be accorded the opportunity to send a like number of additional groups. The detailed arrangements for tours of these groups will be provided for in contracts to be concluded between the following entities: for tours of American groups, between the Embassy of the United States of America in Moscow or authorized representatives of the groups, and concert organizations of the Union of Soviet Socialist Republics; for tours of Soviet groups, between appropriate organizations or impresarios of the United States of America and concert organizations of the Union of Soviet Socialist Republics. The receiving side, taking into consideration realistic possibilities, will seek to satisfy the wishes of the sending side concerning the timing and the duration of tours and the number of cities visited. The sending side shall provide timely notice in making proposals for performing arts groups to travel to the other country. The receiving side will make every effort to make a decision on each proposal by the sending side as soon as possible.

2. The Parties agree to facilitate the tours of at least 10 individual performers from each side during the period of this Program. If one Party sends more than 10 individual performers, the other Party will be accorded the opportunity to send a like number of additional individual performers. The detailed arrangements for these tours will be provided for in contracts to be concluded between the Embassy of the United States of America in Moscow or authorized representatives for the performers, and concert organizations of the Union of Soviet Socialist Republics; for tours of Soviet performers, between appropriate organizations or impresarios of the United States of America and concert organizations of the Union of Soviet Socialist Republics.

3. For the tours of the groups and individuals specified under paragraphs 1 and 2 above, the Parties will take all appropriate measures, to the extent permitted by applicable laws and regulations, to ensure favorable conditions for these performances and tours, and the safety of, and normal working conditions for, those participating in them.

4. The Parties will render assistance for the exchange of art exhibitions of equal quality or other exhibitions between museums of the two countries, on the basis of reciprocity where possible, and will encourage the establishment and development of direct contacts between these museums with the aim of exchanging informative materials, albums, art monographs and other publications of mutual interest. In the case of art exhibitions, their content and the conditions for conducting them, including questions of financial responsibility of governments in the event of loss or damage, guarantees of appropriate safety precautions and timely return, and immunity from seizure on the part of possible previous owners will be the subject of negotiation between appropriate museums or interested organizations of the United States of America and the Ministry of Culture of the Union of Soviet Socialist Republics, and special agreements between them will be signed in each specific case. Within this process, the possible need for added safety precautions to include additional guards at the exhibit sites will be addressed, as required: in the United States of America by the Indemnity Advisory Panel reporting to the Federal Council on the Arts and Humanities, and in the Union of Soviet Socialist Republics by comparable organizations responsible for the safety of foreign exhibits.

5. The Parties will encourage exchanges of delegations and individual specialists in various fields of art and culture, including, among others, such fields as libraries, museums, music, theater, fine arts, architecture and historic preservation and restoration.

6. The Parties will encourage and facilitate exchanges of theater directors, composers, choreographers, stage designers, performers, musicians and other creative artists for productions and participation in performances, with due concern for, and encouragement of, the production of works of the sending country. The conditions for these exchanges will be agreed upon on a case-by-case basis. Both sides will strive to maintain mutually acceptable exchanges over the course of this Program.

Article IV   Publications

The Parties agree to render practical assistance for the distribution of the magazines *Amerika* in the Union of Soviet Socialist Republics and *Soviet Life* in the United States of America on the basis of reciprocity and to consult as necessary in order to find ways to increase the distribution of these magazines. Upon reaching full distribution of the 62,000 copies of each magazine as currently provided for, the Parties will examine the possibility of expanding the reciprocal distribution of the magazines to 82,000. The Parties will distribute free of charge unsold copies of the magazines among visitors to mutually arranged exhibitions.

Article V   Exhibitions

1. The Parties agree to accord each other the opportunity for 1 to 2 circulating exhibitions during the three-year period of this Program. Each Party will accord the other the opportunity to show its exhibition or exhibitions in 6 to 9 cities in all, with up to 28 showing days in each city. The number of showing days, up to the maxima noted above, will be determined by the sending side. The subjects of the exhibitions will be agreed upon through diplomatic channels. The Parties will discuss in a preliminary fashion the nature and general content of each exhibition and will acquaint each other with the exhibitions before their official opening, in particular through the exchange of catalogues, prospectuses and other information pertinent to the exhibitions. Other conditions for conducting the exhibitions (precise opening and closing dates, size and character of premises, number of personnel, financial terms, etc.) shall be subject to agreement by the Parties. Arrangements for conducting the exhibitions will be concluded no later than five months before their opening.

2. The Parties will agree through diplomatic channels on arrangements for other exhibitions and on participation in national exhibitions which may take place in either country.

Article VI   Other Exchanges

1. The Parties will encourage cooperation between organizations of both countries in the field of radio and television, including exchanges of radio and television programs, the joint production of films and broadcasters, the exchange of delegations and

specialists, and, in addition, at the request of organizations and individuals, will consider other types of activities provided for in Article VII of the General Agreement.

2. The Parties will encourage invitations to journalists for familiarization with the print and broadcast media in the receiving country. To this end the Parties will facilitate the exchange of at least three journalists annually from each side.

3. The Parties will encourage exchanges and contacts in the field of book publishing and translation. Among the desired goals of such exchanges would be mutually acceptable programs which would expand the scope of one country's literature and publications available in translation in the other. Such program decisions would be taken by the appropriate organizations or publishing houses of the two countries.

4. The Parties will encourage the mutually acceptable exchange of films and film specialists, the joint production of films, the rendering of production and creative assistance for films produced by each country and the holding of film premieres, film weeks, seminars and other film events on an annual basis. The Parties will also consider additional proposals aimed at expanding cooperation, as referred to in Article VI of the General Agreement. Conditions for implementing exchanges in this field will be determined by mutual agreement.

5. The Parties recognize the value of visits by other specialists in addition to those noted elsewhere in the Program, for lectures and participation in seminars, meetings and discussions which contribute to better understanding between the peoples of the two countries.

6. In accordance with Article XV of the General Agreement, the Parties will facilitate the development of contacts and cooperation between the archival institutions of the two countries, and will encourage the conclusion of mutually beneficial exchange agreements. In particular, the Parties will encourage the reestablishment of close contacts between the Main Archival Administration under the Council of Ministers of the Union of Soviet Socialist Republics and the National Archives of the United States of America.

7. The Parties will encourage, on a mutually acceptable basis, the expansion of exchanges between young people, workers, farmers and representatives of other vocations.

8. The Parties will encourage continuing contacts between the organizations referred to in Article XII of the General Agreement. Terms of these exchanges will be determined by mutual agreement.

Article VII   General Provisions

1. This Program and the exchanges and visits provided for herein shall be subject to the Constitution and applicable laws and regulations of the two countries. Within this framework, both Parties will take all appropriate measures to ensure favorable conditions for such cooperation, exchanges and visits, and the safety of, and normal working conditions for, those participating in U.S.-Soviet exchanges in accordance with the provisions and objectives of this Program and the General Agreement.

2. The Parties agree to hold periodic meetings of their representatives to discuss the implementation of the Program. The implementation reviews will be held at times and places to be agreed upon through diplomatic channels.

3. Each of the Parties shall have the right to include in delegations interpreters or members of its Embassy, who would be considered as within the agreed total membership of such delegations. The number of such persons shall in each specific case be decided by mutual agreement.

4. This Program is valid from January 1, 1986 through December 31, 1988.

DONE at Geneva, this 21st day of November, 1985, in duplicate, in the English and Russian languages, both texts being equally authentic.

FOR THE   FOR THE
GOVERNMENT OF THE   GOVERNMENT OF THE
UNITED STATES OF AMERICA: UNION OF SOVIET

SOCIALIST REPUBLICS

Ronald Reagan   Mikhail S. Gorbachev

YEVTUSHENKO SPEECH WITH SOVIETS' DELETIONS

Following is the text, as translated by the State Department, of a speech given in December 1985 by poet Yevgeny Yevtushenko to a congress of Soviet writers. The bracketed material in italics was omitted from the version published December 18 by Literaturnaya Gazeta, *a Moscow weekly.*

Two citations. Tolstoy: "The epigraph that I would write for history would say: I conceal nothing. It is not enough not to lie. One should strive not to lie in a negative sense by remaining silent."

Shchedrin: "A system of self-flattery might cause rather pleasant dreams, but at the same time a rather rude awakening."

Not concealing anything and remaining silent about nothing are the cornerstones of civilization, baked to the point where their bottoms are burnt, but one on which Russian literature has stood and will continue to stand.

Lenin was nurtured on Russian classics. *[This ethic enabled him to withstand the test of power and fame, unlike his chosen successor.]* When the country was torn by dislocation and hunger, Lenin was not afraid to attack the newly emerged Soviet bureaucracy and the Communist arrogance, supported Mayakovsky *[— whom he was not fond of]* for his poems that assailed bureaucracy, and putting the interests of the famished nation ahead of ambition and schemes, painlessly transferred the country onto the rails of the New Economic Policy.

Provincial concern about everything that the émigré princesses of Maria Alekseyevna will say was alien to Lenin. Lenin understood that not remaining silent was a self-cleansing force, and that self-flattery was destructive. *[Pasternak brilliantly divined the civic spirit of Lenin. "He governed the flow of thoughts, and only because of this he governed the country."*

A break in the flow of thoughts and in the course of building socialism is impermissible, as it would be equally baneful for building and for thinking. We do not have the right to nihilistically forget the great firsts of industry — Magnitogorsk, the Turksib, the Kuzbas. But we also do not have the right to be silent about the fact that in those same years, contrary to Lenin's legacy, the precious agricultural wisdom of many peasants, undeservedly branded kulaks, was being crushed underfoot, and a merciless purge was under way of the Bolshevik guard, of the best commanders of the Red Army and the industrial cadres, of the leading representatives of Leninist thought.]

Today's long-awaited striving for change for the better in our country gives us profound hopes that self-flattery will be forever rejected, and that nonconcealment will become the norm of civic behavior. We, men of letters, will not be worth a penny if we simply report and laud the social transformations taking place independently of us. We are obliged not only to facilitate these transformations but to prepare the ground for them.

Truly civic writings not only reflect historical events but are themselves historical events. The acceleration of scientific and technical progress is unthinkable without acceleration of the spiritual.

[We will not forget the bitter lesson when cybernetics was branded bourgeois pseudoscience and creative genetics was accused of being reactionary by half-educated persons with titles. This intellectual stagnation stopped short the economic prosperity deserved by our people and reached such limits that in our rich and beautiful land 40 years after the war there still exists in

a number of cities the rationing of butter and meat, and this is morally impermissible. Any sort of closed distribution of foods and goods is morally impermissible, including the special coupons for souvenir kiosks that lie in the pocket of every delegate to this congress, myself included.

[Also morally impermissible are displays of ugly clothing in apparel stores, thousand-people lines for something as simple as sneakers, and the most criminal among all the deficits is the shortage of paper for the books that people read while half the timberlands are being cut down for boring pseudoscholarly brochures.

[We do not have the right to be lulled by the agreeable sight of a forest of upraised hands at meetings if among those who raised their hand something was left unsaid, concealed. Bureaucratic check marks indicating that an undertaking went over smoothly are still not the first signs of the long-awaited changes. Articles rhetorically calling for publicity are not the same as publicity itself.

[Editorials on the need for freshness of thought and language often are written in a language so dry that you involuntarily yawn — was it not for these needs that the greatcoat of the hapless Akaky Akakiyevich was once stolen. When you read Klyuchevsky and Solovyev, you see Russia's real history, complete and unconcealed. But when you read the periodically retouched pages of our modern history, you bitterly see that the pages are interspersed with white spots of silence and concealment, dark spots of obsequious truthstretching and smudges of distortions.

[The fear of a creative analysis of our Revolution has led us to the flagrant, unacceptable fact that in the series of "Lives of Famous People," we still have no book on Lenin. In many textbooks, important names and events are arbitrarily excluded. They not only fail to list the reasons for the disappearance of leading people in the party, but sometimes even the date of their death, as if they were peacefully living on pension.

[How many times in the history of the Great Patriotic War has the origin of victory been assigned to this or that geographical point. It is time people understood that the origin of victory was not a geographical location but in the very heart of Soviet man. How long are we going to go on helping all those foreign Maria Alekseyevnas who happily concoct at least half their poisonous radio menus from things that we hide and hush up?]

A nation that allows itself to analyze its own mistakes and tragedies bravely knocks the ideological weapon out of its enemies' hands, for it is spiritually invincible. Only fearlessness in the face of the past can help to produce a fearless solution to the problems of the present, the only correct solution.

[Marx and Engels have this to say about ideological quacks, about the false civic conscience of cowardly bureaucrats who carelessly carve up the body of literary works: "It is simply a country surgeon who knows but one universal, automatic remedy — the knife. It is a charlatan who drives the rash inside so as not to see it, totally indifferent to the fact that it could affect the internal organs."

[True literary works cannot "rock the ship of state," for they are themselves the masts of this ship.]

Recently, I saw for the first time Aleksei German's film "Road Checks," which impressed me very much with its tragic truth illuminated by the all-purifying flame of the Great Patriotic War. Yet this film lay on the shelf for 15 years, *[covered by the offensive dust of undeserved accusations. To this day Soviet readers have not had access to "The Foundation Pit" or to the whole of "Chevengur," two of the finest civic works by that pure Russian patriot Andrei Platonov.*

[Many perceptive civic writings await constructive criticism and then a meeting with the reading public.] Time itself demands a rejection of the "roadblock" psychology. At the same time an implacable red light should blaze out in front of the false civic conscience of self-deception and self-flattery, in front of the heaps of "useless verses," the bricks of "useless novels," whose authors are content to write better than their neighbor on the same staircase, quite forgetting that in the house of literature, where they are illegally permitted to reside, their immortal neighbors are Pushkin, Tolstoy and Dostoyevsky.

Dostoyevsky wrote of Pushkin: "Take one thing only in Pushkin, just one of his remarkable features, to say nothing of all the others, his ability to be universal, to respond to everything, his all-embracing humanity."

[In literature, as in conscience, there are no provinces. The capital of literature is the writer's heart, which contains within it the whole world.] Belinsky said: "For the poet who wants his genius to be recognized by everyone everywhere, being national is the first, but not the only condition. It is essential that while being national he should also at the same time be universal."

Our literature must continue the "universal response" bequeathed to us by the classics. National responsibility must not turn into national narrowness.

The writer's duty in the ominous shadow of the atomic bomb is to respond to the groans of the prisoners in Chilean prisons, to the stifled gasps from the ruins of Beirut, to the cries of protest from the British women surrounding the rocket base at Greenham Common and to the dying whispers of the starving in Ethiopia. But for us humanity begins with our native land. Only not concealing and not hushing up things in our native land can give us the moral right to be universal. That is what socialist civic conscience is about.

REAGAN, GORBACHEV NEW YEAR'S MESSAGES

Following are the New Year's messages delivered January 1, 1986, by President Reagan and General Secretary Mikhail S. Gorbachev and televised in each other's country. Reagan's transcript is from the White House and Gorbachev's was provided by Tass, the Soviet news agency.

Reagan

Good evening. This is Ronald Reagan, President of the United States of America.

I'm pleased to speak to you on the occasion of the New Year. This is a time for reflection and for hope. As we look back on the year just concluded, and on the year that is to come, I want to share with you my hopes for the new year — hopes for peace, prosperity and good will that the American and Soviet people share.

Just over a month ago, General Secretary Gorbachev and I met for the first time in Geneva. Our purpose was to begin a fresh chapter in the relations between our two countries, and to try to reduce the suspicions and mistrust between us.

I think we made a good beginning. Mr. Gorbachev and I spent many hours together, speaking frankly and seriously about the most important issues of our time — reducing the massive nuclear arsenals on both sides, resolving regional conflicts, ensuring respect for human rights as guaranteed under international agreements, and other questions of mutual interest.

As the elected representative of the American people, I told Mr. Gorbachev of our deep desire for peace, and that the American people do not wish the Soviet people any harm.

While there were many areas on which we did not agree, which was to be expected, we left Geneva with a better understanding of one another and of the goals we each have. We are determined to build on that understanding in the coming months and years.

One of the most important things on which we agreed was the need to reduce the massive nuclear arsenals on both sides. As I have said many times, a nuclear war cannot be won and must never be fought. Therefore, we agreed to accelerate negotiations where there is common ground to reduce and eventually eliminate the means of nuclear destruction.

Our negotiators will soon be returning to the Geneva talks on nuclear and space arms, where Mr. Gorbachev and I agreed, we will seek agreements on the principle of 50 percent reductions in offensive nuclear arms, and an interim agreement on intermediate-range nuclear systems. And it's my hope that one day, we will be able to eliminate these weapons altogether and rely increasingly for our security on defense systems that threaten no one.

Both the United States and the Soviet Union are doing research on the possibilities of applying new technologies to the cause of defense. If these technologies become a reality, it is my dream that — well, to one day free us all from the threat of nuclear destruction.

One of the best ways to build mutual understanding is to allow the American and the Soviet people to get to know one another better.

In Geneva, we signed a new agreement to exchange our most accomplished artists and academics. We also agreed to expand the contacts between our peoples so that students, teachers and young people can get to know each other directly. If people in both countries can visit, study and work together, then we will strengthen the bonds of understanding and build a true foundation for lasting peace.

I also discussed the American people's strong interest in humanitarian issues. Our democratic system is founded on the belief in the sanctity of human life and the rights of the individual — rights such as freedom of speech, of assembly, of movement and of worship. It is a sacred truth to us that every individual is a unique creation of God, with his or her own special talents, abilities, hopes and dreams.

Respect for all people is essential to peace, and as we agreed in Geneva, progress in resolving humanitarian issues in a spirit of cooperation would go a long way to making 1986 a better year for all of us.

A safe and lasting peace also requires finding peaceful settlements to armed conflicts which cause so much human suffering in many parts of the world. I have proposed several concrete steps to help resolve such conflicts. It is my hope that in 1986 we will make progress toward this end. I see a busy year ahead in building on the foundation laid in Geneva. There is much work to be done.

Mr. Gorbachev will visit the United States later this year, and I look forward to showing him our country. In 1987, I plan to visit your country and hope to meet many of you.

On behalf of the American people, I wish you all a happy and healthy new year. Let's work together to make it a year of peace. There is no better goal for 1986 or for any year. Let us look forward to a future of "chistoye nyebo" for all mankind. Thank you, spasibo.

Gorbachev

Dear Americans:

I see a good augury in the way we are beginning the New Year, which has been declared the year of peace. We are starting it with an exchange of direct messages — President Reagan's to the Soviet people and mine to you.

This, I believe, is a hopeful sign of change which, though small, is nonetheless a change for the better in our relations. The few minutes that I will be speaking to you strike me as a meaningful symbol of our mutual willingness to go on moving toward each other, which is what your President and I began doing at Geneva. For a discussion along these lines we had the mandate of our peoples. They want the constructive Soviet-American dialogue to continue uninterrupted and to yield tangible results.

As I face you today, I want to say that the Soviet people are dedicated to peace — that supreme value equal to the gift of life. We cherish the idea of peace, having suffered for it. Together with the pain of unhealing wounds and the agony of irretrievable losses, it has become part and parcel of our flesh and blood. In our country there is not a single family or a single home that has not kept alive the memory of their kith and kin who perished in the flames of war, the war in which the Soviet and American peoples were allies and fought side by side.

I say this because our common quest for peace has its roots in the past, and that means we have a historic record of cooperation which can today inspire our joint efforts for the sake of the future.

The many letters I have received from you and my conversations with your fellow countrymen — senators, congressmen, scientists, businessmen and statesmen — have convinced me that in the United States, too, people realize that our two nations should never be at war, that a collision between them would be the greatest of tragedies.

It is a reality of today's world that it is senseless to seek greater security for oneself through new types of weapons. At present, every step in the arms race increases the danger and the risk for both sides, and for all humankind.

It is the forceful and compelling demand of life itself that we should follow the path of cutting back nuclear arsenals and keeping outer space peaceful. This is what we are negotiating about at Geneva, and we would very much like those talks to be successful this year.

In our efforts for peace we should be guided by an awareness of the fact that today history has willed our two nations to bear an enormous responsibility to the peoples of our two countries and, indeed, the peoples of all countries, for preserving life on Earth. Our duty to all humankind is to offer it a safe prospect of peace, a prospect of entering the third millenium without fear. Let us commit ourselves to doing away with the threat hanging over humanity. Let us not shift that task onto our children's shoulders.

We can hardly succeed in attaining that goal unless we begin saving up, bit by bit, the most precious capital there is — trust among nations and peoples. And it is absolutely essential to start mending the existing deficit of trust in Soviet-American relations.

I believe that one of the main results of my meeting with President Reagan is that, as leaders and as human beings, we were able to take the first steps toward overcoming mistrust and to activate the factor of confidence. The gap dividing us is still wide, to bridge it will not be easy, but we saw in Geneva that it can be done. Bridging that gap would be a great feat — a feat our people are ready to perform for the sake of world peace.

I am reminded of the title of a remarkable work of American literature, the novel "The Winter of Discontent." In that phrase let me just substitute hope for discontent. And may not only this winter but every season of this year and of years to come be full of hope for a better future, a hope that, together, we can turn into reality. I can assure you that we shall spare no effort in working for that.

For the Soviet people, the year 1986 marks the beginning of a new stage in carrying out our constructive plans. Those are peaceful plans; we have made them known to the whole world.

I wish you a Happy New Year. To every American family, I wish good health, peace and happiness.

GORBACHEV PLAN TO BAN NUCLEAR WEAPONS

Following is the text of Mikhail S. Gorbachev's January 15, 1986, statement, as distributed by the Soviet news agency Tass, on elimination of all nuclear weapons:

The new year 1986 has started counting its days. It will be an important year, one can say a turning point in the history of the Soviet state, the year of the 27th Congress of the CPSU. The Congress will chart the guidelines for the political, social, economic and spiritual development of Soviet society in the period up to the next millennium. It will adopt a program for accelerating our peaceful construction.

All efforts of the CPSU are directed towards ensuring a further improvement in the life of the Soviet people.

A turn for the better is also needed in the international arena. This is the expectation and the demand of the peoples of the

Soviet Union and of the peoples throughout the world.

Being aware of this, at the start of the new year the Politburo of the CPSU Central Committee and the Soviet government have adopted a decision on a number of major foreign policy actions of a fundamental nature. They are designed to promote to a maximum degree an improvement in the international situation. They are prompted by the need to overcome the negative, confrontation trends that have been growing in recent years and to clear up ways towards curbing the nuclear arms race on Earth and preventing it in outer space, an overall reduction of the risk of war and trust building as an integral part of relations among states.

I.

Our most important action is a concrete program aimed at the complete elimination of nuclear weapons throughout the world and covering a precisely defined period of time.

The Soviet Union is proposing a step-by-step and consistent process of ridding the Earth of nuclear weapons, to be implemented and completed within the next 15 years, before the end of this century.

The 20th century has given mankind the gift of the energy of the atom. However, this great achievement of human mind can turn into an instrument of self-annihilation of mankind.

Is it possible to solve this contradiction? We are convinced it is. Finding effective ways towards eliminating nuclear weapons is a feasible task, provided it is tackled without delay.

The Soviet Union is proposing a program of ridding mankind of the fear of a nuclear catastrophe to be carried out beginning in 1986. And the fact that this year has been proclaimed by the United Nations The International Year of Peace provides an additional political and moral incentive for this. What is required here is rising above national selfishness, tactical calculations, differences and disputes, whose significance is nothing compared with the preservation of what is most valuable — peace and a safe future. The energy of the atom should be placed at the exclusive service of peace, a goal that our socialist state has invariably advocated and continues to pursue.

It was our country that as early as 1946 was the first to raise the question of prohibiting the production and use of atomic weapons and to make atomic energy serve peaceful purposes for the benefit of mankind.

How does the Soviet Union envisage today in practical terms the process of reducing nuclear weapons, both delivery vehicles and warheads, leading to their complete elimination? Our proposals can be summarized as follows.

Stage One. Within the next 5-8 years the USSR and the USA will reduce by one half the nuclear arms that can reach each other's territory. On the remaining delivery vehicles of this kind each side will retain no more than 6,000 warheads.

It stands to reason that such a reduction is possible only if the USSR and the USA mutually renounce the development, testing and deployment of space strike weapons. As the Soviet Union has repeatedly warned, the development of space strike weapons will dash the hopes for a reduction of nuclear weapons on Earth.

The first stage will include the adoption and implementation of the decision on the complete elimination of intermediate-range missiles of the USSR and the USA in the European zone, both ballistic and cruise missiles, as a first step towards ridding the European continent of nuclear weapons.

At the same time the United States should undertake not to transfer its strategic and medium-range missiles to other countries, while Britain and France should pledge not to build up their respective nuclear arms.

The USSR and the USA should from the very begining agree to stop any nuclear explosions and call upon other states to join in such a moratorium as soon as possible.

We propose that the first stage of nuclear disarmament should concern the Soviet Union and the United States because it is up to them to set an example for the other nuclear powers to follow. We said that very frankly to President Reagan of the United States during our meeting in Geneva.

Stage Two. At this stage, which should start no later than 1990 and last for 5-7 years, the other nuclear powers will begin to

engage in nuclear disarmament. To begin with, they would pledge to freeze all their nuclear arms and not to have them in the territories of other nations.

In this period the USSR and the USA will go on with the reductions agreed upon during the first stage and also carry out further measures designed to eliminate their medium-range nuclear weapons and freeze their tactical nuclear systems.

Following the completion by the USSR and the USA of the 50-percent reduction in their relevant arms at the second stage, another radical step is taken: All nuclear powers eliminate their tactical nuclear arms, namely the weapons having a range (or radius of action) of up to 1,000 KM. At the same stage the Soviet-American accord on the prohibition of space strike weapons would have to become multilateral, with the mandatory participation of major industrial powers in it.

All nuclear powers would stop nuclear-weapons tests.

There would be a ban on the development of non-nuclear weapons based on new physical principles, whose destructive capacity is close to that of nuclear arms or other weapons of mass destruction.

Stage Three will begin no later than 1995. At this stage the elimination of all remaining nuclear weapons will be completed. By the end of 1999 there will be no nuclear weapons on Earth. A universal accord will be drawn up that such weapons should never again come into being.

We have in mind that special procedures will be worked out for the destruction of nuclear weapons as well as the dismantling, re-equipment or destruction of delivery vehicles. In the process, agreement will be reached on the numbers of weapons to be destroyed at each stage, the sites of their destruction and so on.

Verification with regard to the weapons that are destroyed or limited would be carried out both by national technical means and through on-site inspections. The USSR is ready to reach agreement on any other additional verification measures.

The adoption of the nuclear disarmament program that we propose would undoubtedly have a favorable impact on the negotiations conducted at bilateral and multilateral forums. The program would identify specific routes and reference points, establish a specific time-frame for achieving agreements and implementing them and would make the negotiations purposeful and goal-oriented. This would break the dangerous trend whereby the momentum of the arms race is greater than the process of negotiations.

In summary, we propose that we should enter the third millennium without nuclear weapons, on the basis of mutually acceptable and strictly verifiable agreements. If the United States administration is indeed committed to the goal of the complete elimination of nuclear weapons everywhere, as it has repeatedly stated, it is being offered a practical opportunity to begin this in practice. Instead of wasting the next 10-15 years by developing new, extremely dangerous weapons in space, allegedly designed to make nuclear arms useless, would it not be more sensible to start eliminating those arms and finally bring them down to zero? The Soviet Union, I repeat, proposes precisely that.

The Soviet Union calls upon all peoples and states and, naturally, above all nuclear states, to support the program of eliminating nuclear weapons before the year 2000. It is absolutely clear to any unbiased person that if such a program is implemented, nobody would lose and everybody stands to gain. This is a problem common to all mankind and it can and must be solved only through common efforts, and the sooner this program is translated into practical deeds, the safer will be life on our planet.

II.

Guided by the same approach and the desire to make another practical step within the context of the program of nuclear disarmament, the Soviet Union has taken an important decision.

We are extending by 3 months our unilateral moratorium on any nuclear explosions, which expired on December 31, 1985. Such a moratorium will remain in effect even further if the United States for its part also stops nuclear tests. We propose once again to the United States to join this initiative whose significance is evident to practically everyone in the world.

It is clear that adopting such a decision was by no means simple for us. The Soviet Union cannot display unilateral restraint with regard to nuclear tests indefinitely. But the stakes are too high and the responsibility too great for us not to try every possibility of influencing the position of others through the force of example.

All experts, scientists, politicians and military men agree that the cessation of tests would indeed block off the channels for upgrading nuclear weapons. And this task has top priority. A reduction of nuclear arsenals alone, without a prohibition of nuclear-weapons tests, does not offer a way out of the dilemma of nuclear danger, since the remaining weapons would be modernized and there would still remain the possibility of developing increasingly sophisticated and lethal nuclear weapons and evaluating their new types at test ranges.

Therefore, the cessation of tests is a practical step towards eliminating nuclear weapons.

I wish to say the following from the outset. Possible references to verification as an obstacle to the establishment of a moratorium on nuclear explosions would be totally groundless. We declare unequivocally that verification is no problem so far as we are concerned. Should the United States agree to stop all nuclear explosions on a reciprocal basis, appropriate verification of compliance with the moratorium would be fully ensured by national technical means as well as through international procedures — including on-site inspections whenever necessary. We invite the USA to reach agreement to this effect.

The USSR is strongly in favor of the moratorium becoming a bilateral, and later a multilateral action. We are also in favor of resuming the trilateral negotiations involving the USSR, the USA and Great Britain on the complete and general prohibition of nuclear-weapons tests. This could be done immediately, even this month. We are also prepared to begin without delay multilateral test ban negotiations within the framework of the Geneva Conference on Disarmament, with all nuclear powers taking part.

Non-aligned countries are proposing consultations with a view to making the 1963 Moscow treaty banning nuclear weapon tests in the atmosphere, in outer space and under water apply also to the underground tests, which are not covered by the treaty. The Soviet Union is agreeable to this measure too.

Since last summer we have been calling upon the United States to follow our example and stop nuclear explosions. Washington has as yet not done that despite the protests and demands of public opinion, and contrary to the will of most states in the world. By continuing to set off nuclear explosions the U.S. side continues to pursue its elusive dream of military superiority. This policy is futile and dangerous, a policy which is not worthy of the level of civilization that modern society has reached.

In the absence of a positive response from the United States, the Soviet side had every right to resume nuclear tests starting already on January 1, 1986. If one were to follow the usual "logic" of the arms race, that, presumably, would have been the thing to do.

But the point is that it is precisely that notorious logic that has to be resolutely repudiated. We are making yet another attempt in this direction. Otherwise the process of military rivalry will become an avalanche and any control over the course of events would be impossible. To submit to the force of the nuclear arms race is inadmissible. This would mean acting against the voice of reason and the human instinct of self-preservation. What is required are new and bold approaches, a new political thinking and a heightened sense of responsibility for the destinies of the peoples.

The U.S. administration is once again given more time to weigh our proposals on stopping nuclear explosions and to give a positive answer to them. It is precisely this kind of response that people everywhere in the world expect from Washington.

The Soviet Union is addressing an appeal to the United States president and Congress, to the American people. There is an opportunity of halting the process of upgrading nuclear arms and developing new weapons of that kind. It must not be missed. The Soviet proposals place the USSR and the United States in an equal position. These proposals do not attempt to outwit or outsmart the other side. We are proposing to take the road of sensible and responsible decisions.

III.

In order to implement the program of reducing and eliminating nuclear arsenals, the entire existing system of negotiations has to be set in motion and the highest possible efficiency of disarmament machinery ensured.

In a few days the Soviet-American talks on nuclear and space arms will resume in Geneva. When we met with President Reagan last November at Geneva, we had a frank discussion on the whole range of problems that constitute the subject of those negotiations, namely on space, strategic offensive arms and intermediate-range nuclear systems. It was agreed that the negotiations should be accelerated and that agreement must not remain a mere declaration.

The Soviet Delegation in Geneva will be instructed to act in strict compliance with that agreement. We expect the same constructive approach from the U.S. side, above all on the question of space. Space must remain peaceful; strike weapons should not be deployed there. Neither should they be developed. And let there also be a most rigorous control, including opening the relevant laboratories for inspection.

Mankind is at a crucial stage of the new space age. And it is time to abandom the thinking of the Stone Age, when the chief concern was to have a bigger stick or a heavier stone. We are against weapons in space. Our material and intellectual capabilities make it possible for the Soviet Union to develop any weapon if we are compelled to do this. But we are fully aware of our responsibility to the present and future generations. It is our profound conviction that we should approach the third millennium not with the "star wars" program but with large-scale projects of peaceful exploration of space by all minkind. We propose to start practical work on such projects and their implementation. This is one of the major ways of ensuring progress on our entire planet and establishing a reliable system of security for all.

To prevent the arms race from extending into space means to remove the obstacle to deep cuts in nuclear weapons. There is on the negotiating table in Geneva a Soviet proposal on reducing by one half the relevant nuclear arms of the Soviet Union and the United States, which would be an important step towards a complete elimination of nuclear weapons. Barring the possibility of resolving the problem of space means not wanting to stop the arms race on Earth. This should be stated in clear and straightforward terms. It is not by chance that the proponents of the nuclear arms race are also ardent supporters of the "star wars" program. These are the two sides of the same policy, hostile to the interests of people.

Let me turn to the European aspect of the nuclear problem. It is a matter of extreme concern that in defiance of reason and contrary to the national interests of the European peoples, American first-strike missiles continue to be deployed in certain West European countries. This problem has been under discussion for many years now. Meanwhile the security situation in Europe continues to deteriorate.

It is time to put an end to this course of events and cut this Gordian knot. The Soviet Union has for a long time been proposing that Europe should be freed from both intermediate-range and tactical nuclear weapons. This proposal remains valid. As a first radical step in this direction we are now proposing, as I have said, that even at the first stage of our program all intermediate-range ballistic and cruise missiles of the USSR and the USA in the European zone should be eliminated.

Achieving tangible practical results at the Geneva talks would give meaningful material substance to the program designed to totally eliminate nuclear arms by the year 2000, which we are proposing.

IV.

The Soviet Union considers as fully feasible the task of completely eliminating even in this century such barbaric weapons of mass destruction as chemical weapons.

At the talks on chemical weapons within the framework of the Geneva Conference on Disarmament certain signs of progress recently appeared. However, these talks have been unreasonably protracted. We are in favor of intensifying the talks in order to conclude an effective and verifiable international convention prohibiting chemical weapons and destroying the existing stockpiles of those weapons, as agreed with President Reagan at Geneva.

In the matter of banning chemical weapons, just like in other disarmament matters, all participants in the talks should take a fresh look at things. I would like to make it perfectly clear that the Soviet Union is in favor of an early and complete elimination of those weapons and of the industrial base for their production. We are prepared for a timely declaration of the location of enterprises producing chemical weapons and for the cessation of their production and ready to start developing procedures for destroying the relevant industrial base and to proceed, soon after the convention enters into force, to eliminating the stockpiles of chemical weapons. All these measures would be carried out under strict control including international on-site inspections.

A radical solution to this problem would also be facilitated by certain interim steps. For example, agreement could be achieved on a multilateral basis not to transfer chemical weapons to anyone and not to deploy them in the territories of other states. As for the Soviet Union it has always strictly abided by those principles in its practical policies. We call upon other states to follow that example and show equal restraint.

V.

Along with eliminating from the arsenals of states the weapons of mass destruction, the Soviet Union is proposing that conventional weapons and armed forces become subject to agreed reductions.

Reaching agreement at the Vienna negotiations could signal the beginning of progress in this direction. Today it would seem that a framework is emerging for a possible decision to reduce Soviet and U.S. troops and subsequently freeze the level of armed forces of the opposing sides in Central Europe. The Soviet Union and our Warsaw Treaty allies are determined to achieve success at the Vienna talks. If the other side also wants this, 1986 could become a landmark for the Vienna talks too. We proceed from the understanding that a possible agreement on troops reductions would naturally require reasonable verification. We are prepared for it.

As for observing the commitment to freeze the numbers of troops, in addition to national technical means permanent verification posts could be established to monitor any military contingents entering the reduction zone.

Let me now mention such an important forum as the Stockholm Conference on Confidence- and Security-Building Measures and Disarmament in Europe. It is called upon to place barriers against the use of force or covert preparations for war, whether on land, at sea or in the air. The possibilities have now become evident.

In our view, especially in the current situation, it is essential to reduce the numbers of troops participating in major military maneuvers notifiable under the Helsinki Final Act.

It is time to begin dealing effectively with the problems still outstanding at the conference. It is known that the bottleneck there is the issue of notifications regarding major ground force, naval and air force exercises. Of course, those are serious problems and they must be addressed in a serious manner in the interests of building confidence in Europe. However, if their comprehensive solution cannot be achieved at this time, why not explore ways of their partial solution — for instance reach agreement now about notifications of major ground force and air force exercises, postponing the question of naval activities until the next stage of the conference.

It is not an accident that the new Soviet initiatives in their considerable part are directly addressed to Europe. In achieving a radical turn towards the policy of peace, Europe could have a special mission. That mission is erecting a new edifice of detente.

For this Europe has a necessary historical experience, which is often unique. Suffice it to recall that the joint efforts of the Europeans, the United States and Canada produced the Helsinki Final Act. If there is a need for a specific and vivid example of new thinking and political psychology in approaching the problems of peace, cooperation and international trust, that historic document could in many ways serve as such an example.

VI.

Ensuring security in Asia is of vital importance to the Soviet Union, which is a major Asian power. The Soviet program for eliminating nuclear and chemical weapons by the end of the current century is in harmony with the sentiments of the peoples of the Asian continent, for whom the problems of peace and security are no less urgent than for the peoples of Europe. In this context one cannot fail to recall that Japan and its cities Hiroshima and Nagasaki became the victims of nuclear bombing and Vietnam a target hit by chemical weapons.

We highly appreciate the constructive initiatives put forward by the socialist countries of Asia and by India and other members of the non-aligned movement. We view as very important the fact that the two Asian nuclear powers, the USSR and the People's Republic of China, have both undertaken not to be the first to use nuclear weapons.

The implementation of our program would fundamentally change the situation in Asia, rid the nations in that part of the globe, too, of the fear of nuclear and chemical warfare, and bring the security in that region to a qualitatively new level.

We regard our program as a contribution to a search, together with all Asian countries, for an overall comprehensive approach to establishing a system of secure and durable peace in this continent.

VII.

Our new proposals are addressed to the whole world. Initiating active steps to halt the arms race and reduce weapons is a necessary prerequisite for coping with the increasingly acute global problems, those of deteriorating human environment and of the need to find new energy sources and combat economic backwardness, hunger and disease. The pattern imposed by militarism — arms instead of development — must be replaced by the reverse order of things — disarmament for development. The noose of the trillion-dollar foreign debt, which is now strangling dozens of countries and entire continents, is a direct consequence of the arms race. Over two hundred and fifty billion dollars annually siphoned out of the developing countries is the amount practically equal to the size of the mammoth U.S. military budget. Indeed, this coincidence is far from accidental.

The Soviet Union wants each measure limiting and reducing arms and each step towards eliminating nuclear weapons not only to bring nations greater security but also to make it possible to allocate more funds for improving people's lives. It is natural that the peoples seeking to put an end to backwardness and achieve the level of industrially developed countries associate the prospects of freeing themselves from the burden of foreign debt to imperialism, which is draining their economies, with limiting and eliminating weapons, reducing military expenditures and switching resources to the goals of social and economic development. This theme will undoubtedly figure most prominently at the International Conference on Disarmament and Development to be held next summer in Paris.

The Soviet Union is opposed to making the implementation of disarmament measures dependent on the so-called regional conflicts. Behind this is both the unwillingness to follow the path of disarmament and the desire to impose upon sovereign nations what is alien to them and what would make it possible to maintain profoundly unfair conditions whereby some countries live at the expense of others, exploiting their natural, human and spiritual resources for the selfish imperial purposes of certain states or aggressive alliances. The Soviet Union, as before, will continue to oppose this. It will continue consistently to advocate freedom for the peoples, peace, security, and a stronger international legal order. The Soviet Union's goal is not to whip up regional conflicts but to eliminate them through collective efforts on a just basis, and the sooner the better.

Today, there is no shortage of statements professing commitment to peace. What is really in short supply is concrete action to strengthen its foundations. All too often peaceful words conceal war preparations and power politics. Moreover, some statements made from high rostrums are in fact intended to eliminate any trade [sic] of that new "spirit of Geneva" which is having a salutary effect on international relations today. It is not only a matter of statements. There are also actions clearly designed to incite animosity and mistrust and to revive confrontation, which is antithetical to detente.

We reject such a way of acting and thinking. We want 1986 to be not just a peaceful year but one that would enable us to reach the end of the 20th century under the sign of peace and nuclear disarmament. The set of new foreign policy initiatives that we are proposing is intended to make it possible for mankind to approach the year 2000 under peaceful skies and with peaceful space, without fear of nuclear, chemical or any other threat of annihilation and fully confident of its own survival and of the continuation of the human race.

The new resolute measures now taken by the Soviet Union for the sake of peace and of improving the overall international situation give expression to the substance and the spirit of our internal and foreign policies and their organic unity. They reflect the fundamental historic law which was emphasized by Vladimir Ilyich Lenin. The whole world sees that our country is holding high the banner of peace, freedom and humanism raised over our planet by the Great October Revolution.

In the question of preserving peace and saving mankind from the threat of nuclear war, no one should remain indifferent or stand aloof. This concerns all and everyone, each state, large or small, socialist or capitalist, has an important contribution to make. Every responsible political party, every social organization and every person can also make an important contribution.

No task is more urgent, more noble and humane, than uniting all efforts to achieve this lofty goal. This task is to be accomplished by our generation without shifting it onto the shoulders of those who will succeed us. This is the imperative of our time. This, I would say, is the burden of historic responsibility for our decisions and actions in the time remaining until the beginning of the third millennium.

The course of peace and disarmament will continue to be pivotal to the foreign policy of the CPSU and the Soviet State. In actively pursuing this course, the Soviet Union is prepared to engage in wide-ranging cooperation with all those who stand on positions of reason, good will and an awareness of responsibility for assuring mankind a future without wars or weapons.

GORBACHEV SPEECH AT 27TH PARTY CONGRESS

Following are excerpts from the text of General Secretary Mikhail S. Gorbachev's five-and-one-half-hour keynote address to the 27th Party Congress of the CPSU, February 25, 1986:

... It is our task to conceptualise broadly, in Lenin's style, the times we are living in, and to work out a realistic, thoroughly weighed programme ... that will ... blend ... our aims with ... our capabilities. ... [T]he 27th Congress ... is to discuss and adopt a new edition of the programme of the CPSU, amendments to the party rules, and guidelines for economic development in the next five years and the longer term. I need hardly mention what enormous importance these documents have for our party, our state, and our people. Not only do they contain an assessment of the past and a definition of the urgent tasks, but also a glimpse into the future. ...

Soviet society has gone a long way in its development since the now operative party programme was adopted. In substance, we

have built the whole country anew. ... We have blazed the trail into outer space for humanity. We have secured strategic military parity and have thereby substantially restricted imperialism's aggressive plans and capabilities to start a nuclear war. ...

While duly commending the achievements, the leadership of the CPSU considers it to be its duty to tell the party and the people honestly and frankly about the deficiencies in our political and practical activities, the unfavourable tendencies in the economy and the social and moral sphere, and about the reasons for them. For a number of years the deeds and acting of party and government bodies trailed behind the needs of the times and of life. ... The problems in the country's development built up more rapidly than they were being solved. The inertness and stiffness of the forms and methods of administration, the decline of dynamism in our work, and an escalation of bureaucracy — all this was doing no small damage. Signs of stagnation had begun to surface. ...

The situation called for change, but a peculiar psychology — how to improve things without changing anything — took the upper hand in the central bodies and, for that matter, at local level as well. But that cannot be done, comrades. Stop for an instant, as they say, and you fall behind a mile. We must not evade the problems that have arisen. That sort of attitude is much too costly. ... The priority task is to overcome the negative factors in society's socio-economic development as rapidly as possible, to impart to it the essential dynamism and acceleration, to draw to the maximum on the lessons of the past, so that the decisions we adopt for the future should be explicitly clear and considered, and the concrete actions purposeful and effective.

The situation has come to a turning point not only in internal but also in external affairs. ... The situation created by the nuclear confrontation [calls for] new approaches, methods, and forms of relations between the different social systems, states and regions. ... The complexity and acuteness of this moment in history makes it increasingly vital to outlaw nuclear weapons, destroy them and other weapons of mass annihilation completely. ...

The fact that the party has deeply understood the fundamentally new situation ... and that it appreciates its responsibility for the country's future, and has the will and resolve to carry out the requisite change, is borne out by the adoption at the April 1985 plenary meeting of the decision to accelerate the socio-economic development of our society. ...

Any attempt at turning the theory by which we are guided into an assortment of ossified schemes and prescriptions valid everywhere and in all contingencies is most definitely contrary to the essence and spirit of Marxism-Leninism. ...

A far-flung, outspoken and constructive examination of all the crucial problems of our life and of party policy, has taken place during the discussion of the pre-Congress documents. ... We can now see more clearly what has to be done and in what order, and what levers we must set in motion for our progress to acquire the desired acceleration. These days, many things, in fact everything, will depend on how effectively we succeed in using the advantages and possibilities of the socialist system. ...

I. The Contemporary World: Its Main Tendencies and Contradictions

Comrades, the draft programme of the party contains a thorough analysis of the main trends and features of the current development of the world. It is not the purpose of the programme to anticipate the diversity of the concrete developments of the future. That would be a futile occupation. But here is another, no less accurate point: If we want to follow a correct, scientifically grounded policy, we must clearly understand the key tendencies of the current reality. ... Never before has our home on earth been exposed to such great political and physical stresses. Never before has man exacted so much tribute from nature, and never has he been so vulnerable to the forces he himself has created.

... The liberation revolutions triggered by the great October revolution are determining the image of the 20th century. However considerable the achievements of science and technology, and however great the influence on the life of society of the rapid scientific and technological progress, nothing but the social and spiritual emancipation of man can make him truly free. And no matter what difficulties,... the course of history is irreversible....

The way was neither smooth nor simple, it was exceedingly difficult to raise the backward or ruined economy, to teach millions of people to [read and] write, to provide them with a roof over their heads, with food and free medical aid.... Nor were mistakes in politics, and various subjectivist deviations, avoided....

The course of social progress is tied in closely with anti-colonial revolutions, national liberation movements.... Social progress is ... apparent, too, in the stratification of the political forces of the capitalist world, notably the U.S.A., the metropolitan centre of imperialism. Here, progressive tendencies are forcing their way forward through a system of monopolistic totalitarianism ... including their enormous propaganda machine which [looses] avalanches of stupefying misinformation upon people.

... [T]he "enlightened" 20th century is going down in history as a time marked by such imperialist outgrowths as the most devastating wars, an orgy of militarism and fascism, genocide, and the destitution of millions of people. That is the society we are compelled to be neighbours of, looking for ways of cooperation and mutual understanding. Such is the command of history. ...A qualitative leap was registered in humanity's productive forces [with the swift advance of science and technology]. But there was also a qualitative leap in means of destruction....

[In the] capitalism of the 1980s ... militarism is gorging itself on the arms race beyond reason, and also wants to gain control little by little over the political levers of power. It is becoming the ugliest and the most dangerous monster of the 20th century. By its efforts, the most advanced scientific and technical ideas are being converted into weapons of mass destruction.

... It would be wrong to think that the scientific and technological revolution is creating no problems for socialist society.... [T]he scientific and technological revolution not only opens up prospects, but ... it is also a world overloaded with dangers and contradictions.... The first and most important group of contradictions ... is connected with the relations between countries of the two systems.... Capitalism regarded the birth of socialism as an "error" of history which must be "rectified." It was to be rectified at any cost, by any means, irrespective of law and morality: by armed intervention, economic blockade, subversive activity, sanctions and "punishments", or refusal of any and all cooperation. But nothing could interfere with the consolidation of the new system and its historical right to live....

By dint of its social nature, imperialism ceaselessly generates aggressive, adventurist policy. Here we can speak of a whole complex of impelling motives: the predatory appetites of the arms manufacturers and the influential military-bureaucratic groups, the selfish interest of the monopolies in sources of raw materials and sales markets, the bourgeoisie's fear of the ongoing changes, and, lastly, the attempts to resolve its own, snow-balling problems at socialism's expense.

The latter are especially typical of U.S. imperialism. It was nothing but imperial ideology and policy, the wish to create the most unfavourable external conditions for socialism and for the U.S.S.R. that prompted the start of the race of nuclear and other arms after 1945, just when the crushing defeat of fascism and militarism was, it would seem, offering a realistic opportunity for building a world without wars, and a mechanism of international cooperation — the United Nations — had been created for this purpose. But imperialism's nature asserted itself that time again.

Today, too, the right wing of the U.S. monopoly bourgeoisie regards the stoking up of international tensions as something that justifies military allocations, claims to global supremacy, interference in the affairs of other states, and an offensive against the interests and rights of the American working people. No small role seems to be played by the idea of using tensions to exercise pressure on the allies ... to subordinate them to Washington's dictation.

The policy of ... military confrontation has no future.... Socialism has never, of its own free will, related its future to any military solution of international problems. ... [W]e are firmly convinced that pushing revolutions from outside, and doubly so by military [means] is futile and inadmissible....

The myth of a Soviet or communist "threat" that is being circulated today, is meant to justify the arms race and the imperialist countries' own aggressiveness, but it is becoming increasingly clear that the path of war can yield no sensible solutions.... Now that ... the only thing experts argue about is how many times or dozens of times humanity can be destroyed, it is high time to begin an effective withdrawal from the brink of war, from the equilibrium of fear, to normal, civilised forms of relations between the states of the two systems.... It will be a hard and many-sided struggle, because we are dealing with a society whose ruling circles refuse to assess the realities of the world and its perspectives in sober terms.... It is unfortunate when not only the eyesight but also the soul of politicians is blind.

The past period has amply confirmed that the general crisis of capitalism is growing keener.... There is growth of unemployment and deterioration of the entire set of social problems. Militarism ... is applied as the most promising means of enlivening the economy. The crisis of political institutions, of the entire spiritual sphere, is growing. ... True, the present stage of the general crisis does not lead to any absolute stagnation of capitalism and does not rule out possible growth of its economy and the emergence of new scientific and technical trends.... In the 1960s and 70s, with the onset of a favourable economic situation, the working class, and the working people generally, managed to secure a certain improvement of their condition. But from the mid-70s on, ... the working people were flung many years back. Unemployment has reached a postwar high. The condition of peasants and farmers is deteriorating visibly, ... the social stratification is growing deeper and increasingly striking....

Imperialism's ruling circles are doubtlessly aware that such a situation is fraught with social explosions and political destabilisation. But this is not making their policies more considered. On the contrary ... the whole arsenal of means at capitalism's disposal is being put to use. The trade unions are persecuted and economically blackmailed. Anti-labour laws are being enacted. The left and all other progressives are being persecuted. Continuous control or, to be more precise, surveillance of people's state of mind and behaviour has become standard....

The transnational monopoly capital ... is seizing control of, and monopolising, whole branches or spheres of production both on the scale of individual countries and in the world economy as a whole.... The core of the transnational corporations consists of American firms.... [They] are undermining the sovereignty both of developing and of developed capitalist countries.... The U.S. transnational supermonopolies are, as a rule, active conductors of state hegemonism....

The relations between the three main centres of present-day imperialism — the U.S.A., Western Europe and Japan — abound in visible and concealed contradictions. The economic, financial, and technological superiority which the U.S.A. enjoyed over its closest competitors until the end of the 1960s has been put to a serious trial.... Washington is continuously calling on its allies not to waste their gunpowder on internecine strife. But how are the three centres of modern-day imperialism to share one roof if the Americans themselves, manipulating the dollar and the interest rates, are not loath to fatten their economy at the expense of Western Europe and Japan? Wherever the three imperialist centres manage to coordinate their positions, this is more often than not the effect of American pressure or outright dictation.... For the first time, governments of some West European countries ... and the public at large have begun to openly discuss whether ... the United States is going too far in its claims to "leadership"? ...

The liberation of former colonies and semi-colonies was a strong political and ideological blow to the capitalist system. ... To a large extent, the imperialist system is still living off the plunder of the developing countries, off their totally merciless exploitation. The forms and methods are changing, but the essence remains.... The developing countries are being exploited by all the imperialist states, but, unquestionably, U.S. imperialism is doing it with the least consideration for them.... The distressing condition of the developing countries is a major worldwide problem. This and nothing else is the true source of many of the conflicts in Asia, Africa, and Latin America. Such is the truth, however hard the ruling circles of the imperialist powers may invoke the "hand of Moscow" in order to vindicate their neocolonialist policy and global ambitions. . . .

The need for effective international procedures and mechanisms that would make for the rational use of the world's resources as an asset belonging to all humanity, is becoming increasingly apparent. The global problems . . . [call] for cooperation on a worldwide scale. . . . This cooperation must be based on completely equal rights and respect for the sovereignty of each. It must be based on conscientious compliance with accepted commitments and with the standards of international law. . . .

The imperative condition for success in resolving the topical issues of international life is to reduce the time of search for political understandings and to secure the swiftest possible constructive action. We are perfectly well aware that not everything by far is within our power and that much will depend on the West, on its leaders' ability to see things in sober perspective at important cross-roads of history. . . . Will the ruling centres of the capitalist world manage to embark on the path of sober, constructive assessments of what is going on? . . . History denies us the right to make such predictions. . . . We are realists and are perfectly well aware that the two worlds are divided by very many things. . . . But we also see clearly that the need to resolve most vital problems affecting all humanity . . . is the stimulus for solutions commensurate with the realities of our time.

. . . Interaction is essential in order to prevent nuclear catastrophe. . . . It is essential in order that other worldwide problems that are growing more acute should also be resolved jointly in the interests of all concerned. . . .

II. The Strategic Course: Acceleration of the Country's Socio-Economic Development

Comrades, by advancing the strategy of accelerating the country's socio-economic development at the April plenary meeting, the Central Committee of the CPSU adopted a decision of historic significance. . . .

What do we mean by acceleration? First of all, raising the rate of economic growth. But that is not all. In substance it means a new quality of growth: An all-out intensification of production on the basis of scientific and technological progress, a structural reconstruction of the economy, effective forms of management and of organising and stimulating labour.

The policy of acceleration is not confined to changes in the economic field. It envisages an active social policy, a consistent emphasis on the principle of socialist justice. The strategy of acceleration presupposes an improvement of social relations, a renovation of the forms and methods of work of political and ideological institutions, a deepening of socialist democracy, and resolute elimination of inertness, stagnation and conservatism — of everything that is holding back social progress.

The main thing that must ensure us success is the living creativity of the masses. . . . In short, comrades, acceleration of the country's socio-economic development is the key to all our problems: Immediate and long-term, economic and social, political and ideological, internal and external. That is the only way a new qualitative condition of Soviet society can and must be achieved.

A. The Results of Socio-Economic Development and the Need for Its Acceleration

Comrades, . . . in the quarter of a century since the adoption of the third CPSU programme, the Soviet Union has achieved impressive successes. . . . At the same time, difficulties began to build up in the economy in the 1970s, with the rates of economic growth declining visibly. As a result, the targets for economic development . . . were not attained. Neither did we manage to fully carry out the social programme charted for this period. A lag ensued in the material base of science and education, health protection, culture, and everyday services.

Certainly, the state of affairs was affected, among other things, by certain factors beyond our control. But they were not decisive. The main thing was that we had failed to produce a timely political assessment of the changed economic situation, that we failed to apprehend the acute and urgent need for converting the economy to intensive methods of development. . . . There were

many appeals and a lot of talk on this score, but practically no headway was made.

By inertia, the economy continued to develop largely on an extensive basis, with sights set on drawing additional labour and material resources into production. As a result, the rate of growth of labour productivity and certain other efficiency indicators dropped substantially. . . . The economy, which has enormous resources at its disposal, ran into shortages. A gap appeared between . . . the effective demand and the supply of goods.

And though efforts have been made of late, we have not succeeded in wholly remedying the situation. The output of most types of industrial and agricultural goods fell short of the targets set by the 26th Congress of the CPSU and the 11th five-year period. There are serious lags in engineering, the oil and coal industries, the electrical engineering industry, in ferrous metals and chemicals, and in capital construction. Neither have the targets been met for the main indicators of efficiency and the improvement of the people's standard of living. And we, comrades, must draw the most serious lessons from all this.

The first of them may be described as the lesson of truth. A responsible analysis of the past clears the way to the future, whereas a half-truth which shamefully evades the sharp corners holds down the elaboration of realistic policy, and impedes our advance. "Our strength," Lenin said, "lies in stating the truth." That is precisely why the Central Committee deemed it essential to refer once more in the new edition of the party programme to the negative processes that had surfaced in the 70s and the early 80s. That is why, too, [we speak] of them at the Congress today.

The other lesson concerns the sense of purpose and resolve in practical actions. The switchover to intensive development of such an enormous economy as ours is no simple matter and calls for considerable effort, time, and the loftiest sense of responsibility. . . . We must not confine ourselves to half-hearted measures. We must act consistently and energetically, and must not hesitate to take the boldest of steps.

And one more lesson — the main one, I might say. The success of any undertaking depends to a decisive degree on how actively and consciously the masses take part in it. To convince broad sections of the working people that the chosen path is correct, to win their interest morally and materially, and restructure the psychology of the cadre — those are crucial conditions for the acceleration of our growth. . . .

There is no other way. . . . Soviet people must within a short time feel the results of the common effort to cardinally resolve the food problem, to meet the need for high-quality goods and services, to improve the medical services, housing, the conditions of life, and environmental protection.

The acceleration of socio-economic development will enable us to contribute considerably to the consolidation of world socialism, and will raise to a higher level our cooperation with fraternal countries. It will considerably expand our capacity for economic ties with the peoples of the developing countries, and with countries of the capitalist world. In other words, implementation of the policy of acceleration will have far-reaching consequences for the destiny of our motherland.

B. Economic Policy Guidelines

. . . By the end of this century we intend to increase the national income nearly twofold while doubling the production potential and qualitatively transforming it. Labour productivity will go up by 2.3-2.5 times, energy consumption per rouble of national income will drop by 28.6 percent and metal consumption by nearly 50 percent. This will signify a sharp turn towards intensifying production, towards improving quality and effectiveness. . . . The main factors behind this line are scientific and technological progress and a fundamental transformation of society's productive forces. It is impossible to effect cardinal changes with the previous material and technical base. The way out, as we see it, lies in thorough modernisation of the national economy, . . . breakthroughs on the leading avenues of scientific and technological progress, and restructuring of the economic mechanism and management system.

1. Modernisation of the National Economy on the Basis of Scientific and Technological Progress

... However significant though they are, the scales and complexity of the work we carried out in the past cannot be compared with what has to be done in the period ahead to modernise the national economy. What do we need for this? First of all, changing the structural and investment policy.... Shifting the centre of attention from quantitative indices to quality and efficiency, from intermediate results to final results, from building up production assets to renewing them, from expanding fuel and raw material resources to making better use of them, and also to speeding up the development of research-intensive industries and of the production and social infrastructures.

A big step forward is to be made in this direction in the current five-year period. It is intended to allocate upwards of 200 billion roubles of capital investments — more than during the past ten years — for modernising and technically reequipping production. Sizeable though these amounts are, the planning and economic bodies will have to continue the search for additional resources for these purposes.

Large-scale integrated programmes in the strategic areas have been drawn up; and their implementation has begun.... It is clear that the effectiveness of modernisation and also the economic growth rates depend to a crucial degree on machine-building.... Here the foundations are laid for a broad advance to basically new, resource-saving technologies, higher productivity of labour and better quality of the output.... In substance, it is a national modernisation programme for this cardinal sector of industry. A single management body has been set up in it. The machine-building complex has been set the goal of sharply raising the technico-economic level and quality of machines, equipment and instruments by the end of the 12th five-year plan period. The capital investments allocated for modernising this industry will be 90 percent greater than in the previous five years....

Large-scale introduction of computers and overall automation of production will tremendously influence the rate of technical modernisation.... The development of computer software and of management information systems has been put on an industrial footing. The Academy of Sciences ... has set up an information science and computer technologies division to coordinate R&D.

Radical modernisation of the fuel and energy complex is the keynote of the energy programme. The programme puts the emphasis on energy-saving production methods, on the replacement of liquid fuel by natural gas and coal, and on more sophisticated methods of oil refining. Advanced production methods are also to be employed in the extraction industry.... In the course of the current five-year span two and a half times more nuclear power plant generating capacities will be started up than in the previous five years, and outmoded units at thermal power stations will be replaced on a large scale. A great deal will have to be done in the metal-manufacturing and chemical industries....

The party attaches enormous importance to technical reequipment of the production infrastructure, in the first place, in transport and communications. Top [priority will] be given to the development of the light industry and other industries that directly meet consumer demand. Advanced equipment for them is to be manufactured not only by specialised industries but also by other industries.

We will not be able to carry out technical modernisation unless we radically improve capital construction. This calls for raising the entire building industry complex to a new industrial and organisational level, shortening the investment cycle by a minimum of 50 percent both in plant modernisation and in the construction of new facilities. We cannot reconcile ourselves any longer to slow construction rates that freeze enormous sums and retard scientific and technological progress ...

All these tasks, comrades, are gigantic in scale and significance. How they are carried out will, in the final analysis, determine the fulfilment of our plans and the rates of our growth.... The responsibility of the planning and economic bodies for achievement of the planned targets will increase accordingly. Party organisations should also direct their activities toward this.

It is especially important to prevent window dressing and the use of palliatives instead of substantive measures. There are dis-quieting instances, and by no means solitary ones, of ministries and departments erecting new facilities under the guise of modernisation, of stuffing them with outdated equipment, and of drawing up costly projects that do not assure the rise of production to higher technical-economic levels. ... [An] illustration of that approach [is] the Bryansk Engineering Works.... Evidently some comrades have failed to grasp the profound importance of the tasks confronting them. Such examples deserve stern condemnation as undermining the party's policy of modernisation....

The need for modernisation faces scientific research with new tasks. The CPSU will consistently pursue a policy of ... providing scientists with the conditions for fruitful work. However, our country is entitled to expect, from its scientists, discoveries and inventions that will bring about genuinely revolutionary changes in the development of machinery and production methods.... A decision has recently [been] adopted to set up inter-sectoral research-and-technological complexes including large institutes that are the leaders in their respective fields, among them institutes under academies of sciences, design organisations and pilot plants.

Steps are also being taken to improve the functioning of sectoral research institutes and to increase their contribution to faster scientific and technical progress. However, this process is going ahead at an impermissibly slow pace. Many institutes are still an appendage of ministry staffs; not infrequently they support departmental interests and are bogged down in red tape and paper-work.... We must ascertain who is opposing this, what stand the ministries and their party committees take on this issue, and how they are reacting to life's demands.

The research potential of higher educational establishments must also be used more effectively.... The respective departments should draft and submit proposals for strengthening the links between university research and production. The proposals should also take into account the training of the next generation of researchers. Just as a forest cannot live on without undergrowth, the true scientist is inconceivable without pupils. This is a question of the future of science, and, therefore, of our country, too....

In sum, comrades, the orientation of science towards the needs of the national economy should be carried out more energetically. However, it is equally important to orient production towards science.... Regrettably, no few scientific discoveries and major inventions fail to find practical application for years, and sometimes for decades....

We cannot reach our targets in accelerating scientific and technological progress unless we find levers that will guarantee priority only to those research establishments and industrial enterprises whose work collectives actively introduce whatever is new and progressive and seek ways and means of manufacturing articles of high quality and efficacy.

All levels of economic management must change their attitude to the introduction of new methods and technology. This also refers to the State Planning Committee of the U.S.S.R., which should go over more boldly to all-inclusive planning of scientific and technological progress, as well as to the U.S.S.R. State Committee for Science and Technology, which is reorganising its work too slowly. The Academy of Sciences of the U.S.S.R., ministries and departments should pay more attention to basic research and to applying its findings in production. This is a sacred duty of every scientist, engineer, designer, and manager of an enterprise.

... [F]oreign economic contacts must be tied up more closely with the new tasks. There should be a large-scale, forward-looking approach to mutually advantageous economic relations. The member-countries of the Council for Mutual Economic Assistance have worked out a policy of this kind. It presupposes a switchover in economic relations among them from primarily trade relations to deeper specialisation and cooperation in production....

We have no few government departments and organisations that are responsible for separate spheres of foreign economic relations but they do not always coordinate their work. In ... making active use of foreign economic contacts to speed our development we have in mind a step-by-step restructuring of foreign trade, of making our exports and imports more effective.

2. Solving the Food Problem: A Top Priority Task

Comrades, a problem we will have to solve in the shortest time possible is that of fully meeting our country's food needs. This is the aim of the party's present Agrarian Policy. Formulated in the decisions taken by the CPSU Central Committee at its May 1982 plenary meeting and in the food programme of the U.S.S.R. In the period since their adoption a good deal has been done ... but the lag in agriculture is being overcome slowly. A decisive turn is needed ... to improve the food supply.... It is planned to more than double the growth rate of farm production and to ensure a substantial increase in the per capita consumption of meat, milk, vegetables, and fruit.

Can we do this? We can and we must. The party has therefore worked out additional measures to raise the efficiency of all sectors of the agro-industrial complex.... The emphasis is put on economic methods of management, broader autonomy of collective farms and state farms and their higher responsibility for the results of their work.

... We will have to make more effective use of the production potential in the agro-industrial complex and concentrate efforts and resources on the most important sectors providing the highest returns. It is a question, first and foremost, of increasing soil fertility and creating the conditions for stable farming.... [T]he key to success lies in large-scale application of intensive technologies. They yield a tremendous effect. Their application provided, last year alone, an additional 15 million tons of grain and a substantial amount of other produce.

Reducing crop and livestock produce losses during harvesting, transportation, storage, and processing is the most immediate source of augmenting food stocks.... [E]liminating the losses would cost only between a third and one half as much as raising the same amount of produce. Rapid expansion of agricultural machine-building will saturate the collective farms and state farms with highly productive machines capable of performing all the field jobs faster and better. We have also made additional outlays to fortify the manufacture of machinery for the food industry and facilities for the processing and storage of food.... It is equally clear, however, that human beings will, as before, be the mainspring and inspiration of progress.... [A]griculture needs people who want to work actively, who have a high level of professional skill and a feeling for the new. Constant attention to the working and living conditions of the members of the rural community is the best guarantee of all our successes....

... The main idea is to give broad scope to economically viable management methods, to substantially broaden the autonomy of collective farms and state farms, to give them a greater incentive and responsibility for the final results. In substance, ... creatively applying ... Lenin's idea of the food tax.

It is intended to establish fixed plans for the purchase of produce from the collective farms and state farms for each year of the five-year period; these plans will not be altered. Simultaneously, the farms will be given the opportunity to use, as they see fit, all the produce harvested over and above the plan; in the case of fruit and potatoes and other vegetables they will also be able to use a considerable part of the planned produce as they see fit. The farms can sell it ... to the state, ... on the collective-farm market or through cooperative trade outlets, or use it for other needs.

... There is to be a transition to improve planning methods.... The role of cost accounting will be substantially increased.... Neglect of the principles of self-support, material incentives and responsibility for performance led to a deterioration of the financial and economic position of collective farms and state farms and also to their considerable indebtedness. Genuine cost accounting, with the incomes of enterprises depending upon the ultimate results, should become the rule for all links of the agro-industrial complex, and, first and foremost, the collective farms and state farms. The contract and job-by-job systems of payment ... will become widespread.

There will be big opportunities for displaying initiative and resourcefulness. This also presupposes, however, a higher sense of responsibility for meeting the targets of the food programme.... A reliable barrier must be erected in the way of mismanagement and sponging, and an end must be put to excuses such as "objective circumstances," which some collective farms and state farms have been using to cover up their ineptitude, as well as sometimes a lack of desire to work better. The farms will have to use chiefly their

own funds to expand production, increase profits and incomes and provide incentives....

3. Economic Management Must Measure Up to the New Demands

Comrades, ... economic management requires constant improvement. We cannot limit ourselves to partial improvements. A radical reform is needed. The Central Committee of the CPSU and its Political Bureau ... set ourselves the aims of:

• Heightening the efficacy of centralised guidance of the economy, strengthening the role of the centre in implementing the main goals of the party's economic strategy and in determining the rates and proportions of national economic growth.... Simultaneously, the practice of interference by the centre in the daily activities of the other economic links must be overcome;

• Resolutely enlarging the framework of the autonomy of associations and enterprises, increasing their responsibility for attaining the highest ultimate results. Towards this end, to transfer them to genuine cost accounting, self-support and self-financing, and to make the income level of collectives directly dependent on the efficiency of their work;

• Going over to economic methods of guidance at all levels of the national economy, for which purpose to reorganise the system of material and technical supply and improve the system of price formation, financing and crediting, and working out effective incentives to eliminate overexpenditure;

• Introducing modern organisational management structures, taking into account the trends towards concentration, specialisation and cooperation of production. This is a question of setting up complexes of interconnected industries, research and technological inter-sectoral centres, various forms of economic associations and territorial-production formations;

• Ensuring the best possible ... integrated economic and social development of republics and regions; ...

• Carrying out all-round democratisation of management, heightening the part played in it by work collectives, strengthening control from below.... Industrial enterprises are being transferred, in the main, to a two-level system of management. Beginning with the current year, new economic management methods which have gone through experimental testing have been introduced in enterprises and associations that turn out half of the total industrial output. Their introduction in the service sphere, in construction and in transport has begun. Collective forms of work organization and ... economic contract systems, are being applied on an ever wider scale....

Success will depend largely on reorganisation of the work of the central economic bodies, first and foremost, the State Planning Committee of the U.S.S.R. It must indeed become our country's genuine scientific and economic [headquarters], freed from current economic matters. The lion's share of the operational management functions is being delegated directly to the enterprises and associations. The state planning committee and other economic agencies must concentrate their efforts on long-range planning, on ensuring proportional and balanced economic development, on carrying out the structural policy, and on creating the economic wherewithal and incentives for attaining the best final results.... Considerable improvements are needed in the sphere of statistics.

... The financial system does not sufficiently stimulate higher economic efficacy. The defective practice of income redistribution, with the losses of lagging enterprises, ministries and regions covered at the expense of those that operate profitably, has reached a large scale. This undermines cost accounting, promotes dependency and prompts endless demands for assistance from the centre. Crediting no longer serves its purpose.

"Any radical reforms," said Lenin, "will be doomed to failure unless our financial policy is successful." Accordingly, we must radically change the substance, organisation and methods of the work of the financial and credit bodies. Their chief aim is not to carry out petty regulation of the functioning of enterprises but to provide economic incentives and to consolidate money circulation and cost accounting.... [E]verything must be made dependent on the end result....

Prices must become an active factor of economic and social policy. We shall have to carry out a planned readjustment....

Prices must be made more flexible; price levels must be linked up not only with outlays but also with ... their effectiveness and the degree to which products meet the needs of society and consumer demands. Ceiling prices and contract prices are to be employed more widely.... In [the final] analysis, everything ... is aimed at creating conditions for effective functioning of the basic link of the economic system: the association or enterprise.

It is high time to put an end to the practice of ... petty tutelage over enterprises. Ministries should concentrate their attention on technical policy on intra-sectoral proportions, and on meeting the demands of the national economy in high-grade output by their industries. Enterprises and organisations should be given the right to sell to one another, independently, what they produce over and above the plan.... They should also be given the legal right to make such sales to members of the public....

...Moreover, enterprises should be given the possibility — following the example of the Volga Auto Works and the Sumy Engineering Works — to earn, themselves, the funds needed to expand and retool production. It is especially important to give enterprises and organisations greater autonomy in the sphere of consumer goods manufacture and services. Their task is to react quickly to consumer demand....

The time has also come to solve another problem. The sum of an enterprise's payroll should be directly tied in with the returns from the sale of its products. This will help to exclude the manufacture and supply of low-grade goods for which there is no demand, or, as they say, operating for the warehouse.... We can no longer reconcile ourselves to a situation in which the personnel of enterprises producing worthless goods lead an untroubled life, drawing their full pay and receiving bonuses and other benefits.

A well-thought-out approach must also be taken to the question of a rational combination of large, medium and small enterprises. As experience shows, small, well-equipped plants have their own advantages in many cases. They can be quicker and more flexible in taking into account technological innovations and changes in demand....

Our short-term and long-range plans are linked, to a considerable degree, with development of the natural health of Siberia and the Soviet Far East.... Special attention should be paid to providing people there with the conditions for fruitful work and a full-blooded life....

...Comrades, every readjustment of the economic mechanism begins, as you know, with a readjustment of thinking, with a rejection of old stereotypes of thought and actions, with a clear understanding of the new tasks. This refers primarily to the activity of our economic personnel, to the functionaries of the central links of administration. Most of them have a clear idea of the party's initiatives, actively support them, boldly tackle complicated assignments, and seek and find the best ways of carrying them out. This attitude deserves utmost support. It is hard, however, to understand those who take a wait-and-see policy or, who, like the Gogol character that thought up all kinds of fanciful ideas, do not actually do anything or change anything. There will be no reconciliation with the stance taken by functionaries of that kind. We will simply have to part ways with them. All the more so do we have to part ways with those who hope that everything will settle down and return to the old lines. That will not happen, comrades!

...We must not be stopped by long-established ideas, let alone by prejudices.... Unfortunately, there was a widespread view that any change in the economic mechanism should be regarded as being practically a retreat from the principles of socialism. In this connection I should like to emphasise the following: socio-economic acceleration and the concrete consolidation of socialism should be the supreme criterion in the improvement of management and also of the entire system of the socialist relations of production.

The aspects of socialist property as the foundation of our social system acquire great relevance.... We must provide the working people with greater incentives for putting the natural riches to the best possible use and multiplying them.... It would be naive to imagine that the feeling of ownership can be inculcated by words. A person's attitude towards property is shaped, first and foremost, by the actual conditions in which he has been put, by his possibilities of influencing the organisation of production, and the

distribution and use of the results of work. The problem is thus one of further intensifying socialist self-government in the economic sphere.... It is important to carry out unswervingly the principle according to which enterprises and associations are wholly responsible for operating without losses, while the state does not bear any responsibility for their obligations. This is where the substance of cost-accounting lies. You cannot be a master of your country if you are not a real master in your factory or collective farm.... Multiplication of the social wealth, as well as losses, should affect the income level of every member of the collective.

Also, of course, a reliable barrier is needed against all attempts to extract unearned income from the social property. There are still "snatchers", persons who do not consider it a crime to steal from their plant everything that comes their way, and there are also sundry bribe-takers and grabbers who do not stop at using their position for selfish purposes. The full force of the law and of public condemnation should be applied to all of them....

...It is also high time to overcome prejudices regarding commodity-money relations and underestimation of these relations in planned economic guidance. Refusal to recognise that they have an active influence on people's incentives for working better and on production efficiency leads to a weakening of the cost-accounting principle and to other undesirable consequences....

4. Activating Untapped Economic Growth Potentialities

...[T]here follows the need to mobilise all of our untapped potentialities to the maximum. The most sensible things to start with are those that do not require big outlays but yield quick and tangible returns ... making better use of the production capabilities that have been built up, of making the incentives more effective, of improving the level of organisation and tightening discipline, and of eliminating mismanagement....

Failure to meet component delivery obligations is another hindrance. A violation of this kind in one place has a ripple effect throughout the national economy and lowers its efficiency. Jerky production also does tangible damage. It is no secret that at the beginning of the month many plants stand idle longer than they function. But at the end of the month they begin a headlong rush, as a result of which output quality is low. This chronic disease must be eradicated.

...Some economic managers complain of a manpower shortage. I think the complaints are groundless in most cases.... But there is a low level of labour productivity.... I would like to put special emphasis on the problem of output quality standards.... Accelerated scientific and technological progress is impossible today without high quality standards....

C. The Basic Guidelines of Social Policy

...Comrades, questions of social policy, concern for man's welfare, has always stood at the centre of our party's attention.... Social justice ... is embodied in ... the equality of all citizens before the law, the actual equality of nations, respect for the individual....

Lessons of the past, too, require that we pay enhanced attention to social issues.... There was a certain overemphasis on technocratic approaches, blunting attention to the social aspect of production, to everyday life, and leisure.... If private-owner, parasitic sentiments, and levelling tendencies begin to surface, this means that something is wrong about the choice of ways and means in our work, and has got to be rectified....

1. Steady Enhancement of the People's Standard of Living, Consistent Assertion of Social Justice

...In the coming fifteen years, the volume of resources allocated for the improvement of the conditions of life is to be doubled. Real per capita incomes are to go up 60 to 80 percent.... Huge funds are being earmarked for increasing the construction of homes, and of social and cultural facilities. Those are the plans. But we must mention the main thing: These plans will become reality only if every Soviet person works hard and efficiently....

At election meetings and conferences, communists have

rightly raised the question of improving the moral incentives, and, ... greatly enhancing material incentives.... [W]hen equal payments are fixed for the work of a good employee and that of a negligent one — that is a gross violation of our principles....

Rates and salaries in the non-productive sphere will go up.... Many proposals made by working people refer to the role of social consumption funds in enforcing the principle of justice. These funds already account for nearly one-third of the consumed material goods and services. We hold that they are in no way charity. They play an important role in proving equal access ... to education and culture, and in equalising conditions for the raising of children.... The party intends to continue promoting the further growth and more effective use of these public funds. In the 12th five-year period they are to go up by 20 to 23 percent.

Combatting unearned incomes is an important function of the socialist state.... Working people have legitimately raised the question of rooting out such things.... It is considered necessary ... to carry out additional measures against parasites.... We should also give thought to proposals about perfecting our tax policy, including the institution of a progressive inheritance tax. But while combatting unearned incomes, we must not permit any shadow to fall on those who do honest work to earn a supplementary income....

... The objective of enhancing the people's wellbeing will not be attained if we fail to saturate the market with diverse goods and services. That, indeed, is the purpose of the comprehensive programme for the development of the production of consumer goods and services. We must build up an up-to-date services industry as quickly as possible. This applies first of all to services that lighten domestic work and those connected with the improvement and renovation of flats with tourism, and the servicing of cars.... Responding to the proposals of the working people, we are promoting broad expansion of collective gardening and vegetable growing.

The social importance and acuteness of the housing problem has predetermined our earnest attitude to it. To provide every family with a separate flat or house by the year 2000 is, in itself, a tremendous but feasible undertaking....

Comrades, the qualitative changes in the social sphere are impossible without deep-going changes in the content of labour.... [T]he setting of the scientific and technological revolution sets high demands on education.... A reform has been launched of the general and vocational schools.... What is especially urgent is that all pupils should learn the use of computers.

Nothing is more valuable to every person and, for that matter, to society than health.... We must meet the needs of the population in high-quality medical treatment, health protection and pharmaceuticals as quickly as possible....

A fight has been mounted across the country against hard drinking and alcoholism. In the name of the health of society and the individual we have instituted resolute measures and started a battle against traditions that were shaped and cultivated over the centuries. While we should have no illusions about what has been accomplished, we can safely say that drunkenness has been elbowed out of factories and that there is less of it in public places. The situation within families is improving, injuries in production have declined, and order has been tightened. But extensive, persevering and varied efforts are still needed to secure a final break with prevailing habits. There must be no indulgence here!

We face the acute task of ensuring the protection of nature and national use of its resources.... Considerable funds are being allocated for this purpose.... In a number of regions the state of the environment is alarming, and the public, notably our writers, are quite right in calling for a more careful treatment of land, its bowels, lakes and rivers, and the plant and animal world.

2. Improvement of Social-Class Relations and Relations Among the Peoples of the U.S.S.R.

Comrades, analysing problems involved in interrelationship of classes and social groups is of vital importance for a Marxist-Leninist Party....

The problems of consolidating the family are attracting public attention. Our achievements in cultivating the new, socialist type of family are indisputable.... Yet, the formation of the new type

of family is no simple matter.... In particular, although the divorce rate has dropped in the past few years, it is still high. There is still a large number of unhappy families. All this has a negative effect, above all, on the upbringing of children, as well as on the morale of men and women, on their labour and public activity.... More thought should be given to the system of material assistance to newly-weds, above all in solving their housing and everyday problems....

Securing living and working conditions for women that would enable them to successfully combine their maternal duties with active involvement in labour and public activity is a prerequisite for solving many family problems. In the 12th five-year period we are planning to extend the practice of letting women work a shorter day or week, or to work at home. Mothers will have paid leaves until their babies are 18 months old. The number of paid days-off granted to mothers to care for sick children will be increased. The lower-income families with children of up to 12 years of age will receive child allowances. We intend to fully satisfy the people's need for preschool children's institutions within the next few years....

However, our achievements must not create the impression that there are no problems in the national interests.... We are legitimately proud of the achievements of the multinational Soviet socialist culture.... However, the healthy interest in all that is valuable in each national culture must by no means degenerate into attempts to isolate oneself from the objective process by which national cultures interact and come closer together. This applies, among other things, to certain works of literature and art and scholarly writings where, under the guise of national originality, attempts are made to depict in idyllic tones reactionary nationalist and religious survivals contrary to our ideology....

III. Further Democratisation of Society and Promotion of the People's Socialist Self-Government

Comrades, ... the acceleration of society's development is inconceivable and impossible without a further development of all the aspects and manifestations of socialist democracy....

[M]easures aimed at enhancing the democratic character of the socialist system [include] ... steps to invigorate the soviets, the trade unions, the Komsomol, the work collectives and the people's control bodies, and to promote publicity....

[G]overnment should not be the privilege of a narrow circle of professionals.... [T]he socialist system can develop successfully only when the people really run their own affairs.... It is the essence of Soviet power....

That the Supreme Soviet of the U.S.S.R. and the supreme soviets of the union and autonomous republics are becoming increasingly businesslike and effective ... is most welcome.... I should like to draw special attention ... to the activity of local soviets. Today they can and must serve as one of the most effective means of mobilising the masses.... As they receive the electorate's mandate, local government bodies undertake responsibility for all aspects of life on their territory. If someone may be allowed to say, "This is none of my business," this approach is certainly unacceptable to the soviets. Housing and education, public health and consumer goods, trade and the services, public transport and the protection of nature are all paramount concerns of the soviets. Whenever we hear complaints from working people on these subjects, and that is still fairly frequent, it means that they are lacking efficiency and initiative, and that their control is slack. But while making legitimate demands on the soviets, we should not be blind to the fact that for the time being their ability to tackle many of the local problems is limited; there exists excessive centralisation in such matters which are not always clearly visible from the centre and can be much better solved locally.

That is why we have resolutely set our sights on promoting the autonomy and activity of local government bodies. Proposals to this effect are currently being worked out.... Their goal is to make each soviet a full and responsible master in all things related to meeting people's everyday needs and requirements.... We must ... enhance the local bodies' concern for the result of their work.... The Party will continue to see to it that ... the soviet's membership should be systematically renewed....

The development of the people's self-government calls for a further enhancement of democratic principles in administration, in [all] ... government bodies. Most of the people working in them are competent and take what they do close to heart. One should, however, always remember that, even if its executives are masterminds, no apparatus will ever get what it wants unless it relies on the working people's motivated support and participation in government. The times are increasingly exacting and rigid as regards the work of the apparatus. And there are quite a few shortcomings here; one often encounters departmental approach and localism, irresponsibility, red tape and formal indifference to people. One of the main reasons for this is the slackening of control over the activity of the apparatus by the working people, the soviets themselves, and the social organizations.

Bearing all this in mind, the party has sent itself the task of setting in motion all the instruments that actually enable every citizen to actively influence administrative decision-making, verify fulfilment of decisions, and get the requisite information about the activity of the apparatus. This purpose is to be served by a system of regular reports to work collectives and general meetings by all administrative bodies....

In our country, the trade unions are the largest mass organisation. On the whole, they do a lot to satisfy the requirements of factory and office workers and collective farmers, to promote emulation, tighten discipline and heighten labour productivity. Still, trade union committees are in many cases lacking in militancy and resolve when defending the working people's legitimate interests, ensuring labour protection and safety, and constructing and running health-building, sports and cultural facilities. Understandably, such passivity suits those managers for whom production sometimes obscures the people. The trade unions, however, should always give priority to social policy, to promoting to working people's interests. Properly speaking, this is the basic purpose of their activity. The All-Union Central Council of Trade Unions and other trade union bodies enjoy extensive rights and control vast enough funds, both the state's and their own. It is up to them, therefore, to make wide and sure use of them, instead of waiting for somebody else to fulfil the tasks they are charged with.

Comrades, our future largely depends on the young people we are bringing up today. That is the task of the whole party, of the whole people.... [The] Young Communist League, ... the party, government and economic bodies should consistently seek to promote deserving young people to high posts in management, production, science and culture, we say: in our country, all roads are open to young people. That is true. But persistent efforts are needed for these words not to lose lustre....

By and large, the CPSU central committee deems it advisable to take further steps to increase the role of the trade unions, the YCL, the unions of creative workers and the voluntary societies in the system of the people's socialist self-government. In particular, it is planned to extend the range of questions which governmental bodies can settle only with the participation or prior agreement of trade union, YCL or women's organisations and to grant these organisations the right to suspend, in some cases, the implementation of administrative decisions. ... We cannot put up with the still existing instances of workers not knowing the programmes of their own enterprise, of their suggestions not getting due attention and not being taken into account. These instances show that in some places the force of inertia determines the state of affairs, hinders the involvement of factory and office workers in management and impedes the process of fostering among them the feeling that they are full-fledged masters of production....

The law on work collectives adopted two years ago has indisputably stimulated initiatives by work collectives. But we cannot yet say this law is producing the results we expected.... Our conclusion is unambiguous: It is necessary to radically improve the mechanism that enables us to make the democratic principles and norms of the law operative in everyday practice.... [W]e must extend the range of issues on which the work collective's decisions are final ... and raise their responsibility for the implementation of their decisions....

Today the advanced teams which apply the cost-accounting

principle are already becoming primary self-government units that elect their managers.... [I]t appears advisable to spread the electivity principle to all team leaders and then gradually to some other categories of managerial personnel.... [T]his is the direction in which we must look for modern forms of combining centralism and democracy ... in running the national economy.

... Our constitution provides for nation-wide discussions and referendums on major issues of our country's life and for discussions of decisions passed by local soviets. We must expedite the drafting of a law on this highly important question. We must make better use of such reliable channels for ... eliciting public opinion and of making a quick and attentive response to the people's needs and mood.

Broader publicity is a matter of principle to us. It is a political issue. Without publicity there is not, nor can there be, democracy.... When the subject of publicity comes up, calls are sometimes made for exercising greater caution when speaking about the shortcomings, omissions, and difficulties that are inevitable in any ongoing effort. There can only be one answer to this, a Leninist answer: Communists want the truth, always and under all circumstances. The experience of the past year has shown how forcefully Soviet people support an uncompromising appraisal of everything that impedes our advance. But those who have grown used to doing slipshod work, to practising deception, indeed feel really awkward in the glare of publicity, when everything done in the state and in society is under the people's control and is in full public view. Therefore, we must make publicity an unfailingly operative system. It is needed in the centre and no less, perhaps much more, in the localities, wherever people live and work. The citizen wants to know, and should know, not only decisions taken on a country-wide scale but also decisions taken locally....

We must very strictly observe ... the equality of citizens before the law.... [I]t is necessary to take vigorous steps to upgrade the role of the procurators' supervision, to improve the function of courts of law and the bar, and to complete, in the near future, the drafting of a law, as provided for by the constitution, on the procedure of filing appeals in court against unlawful actions by officials that infringe upon the rights of citizens....

In the context of the growing subversive activity by imperialist secret services against the Soviet Union and other socialist countries, greater responsibility devolves upon the state security bodies. Under the party's leadership and scrupulously observing Soviet laws, these bodies are conducting extensive work to expose enemy intrigues, to frustrate all kinds of subversion and to protect our country's sacred frontiers. We are convinced that Soviet security forces and border-guards will always measure up to the demands made of them, will always display vigilance, self-control and tenacity in the struggle against any encroachment on our political and social system.

... [T]he CPSU Central Committee and its Political Bureau pay unflagging attention to our country's defence capability, to the combat might of the armed forces of the U.S.S.R., to the tightening of military discipline.... [W]e can declare with all responsibility that the defence capability of the U.S.S.R. is maintained on a level that reliably protects the peaceful life and labour of the Soviet people....

IV. Basic Aims and Directions of the Party's Foreign Policy Strategy

Comrades, the tasks underlying the country's economic and social development also determine the CPSU's strategy on the world scene. Its main aim is crystal clear — to ensure to the Soviet people the possibility of working under conditions of enduring peace and freedom.... [T]he party's primary programme requirement of our foreign policy ... means, above all, to terminate the material preparations for a nuclear war.

... The CPSU has put forward a coherent programme for the total abolition of weapons of mass destruction before the end of this century, a programme that is historic in terms of its dimensions and significance. ... As you know, we have addressed our proposals not only through the traditional diplomatic channels but also directly to world public opinion, to the peoples. The time has come to have a thorough understanding of the harsh realities of our day: nuclear weapons harbour a hurricane with the potential of sweeping the human race from the face of the Earth....

Socialism unconditionally rejects war as a means of settling state-to-state political and economic contradictions and ideological disputes.... That is why ... the preservation and strengthening of universal peace remains the fundamental direction of the party's activities on the international scene.

There is no alternative to this policy. This is all the more true in periods of tension in international affairs. I would say that never in the decades since the war has the situation in the world been so explosive, and consequently complex and uncongenial as in the first half of the 1980s. The right-wing group that came to power in the U.S.A. and its main NATO fellow-travellers made a steep turn from détente to a policy of military force. They have adopted doctrines that reject good-neighbourly relations and cooperation as a principle of world development.... The administration in Washington remained deaf to our calls for an end to the arms race and an improvement of the situation.

Perhaps it may not be worth churning up the past? Especially today when in Soviet-U.S. relations there seem to be signs of a change for the better, and realistic trends are beginning to resurface in the actions and attitudes of the leadership of some NATO nations. We feel that it is worthwhile, for the drastic frosting of the international climate in the first half of the 1980s was a further reminder that nothing comes of itself, peace has to be fought for, and this has to be a persevering and meaningful fight. We have to look for, find, and use even the smallest opportunity in order — while this is still possible — to halt the trend towards an escalation of the threat of war. Appreciating this, the Central Committee of the CPSU at its plenary meeting once again analysed the character and dimensions of the nuclear threat and defined the practical steps that could lead to an improvement of the situation. We were guided by the following considerations of principle.

First, the character of present-day weaponry leaves no country with any hope of safeguarding itself solely with military and technical means, for example, by building up a defence, even the most powerful. To ensure security is increasingly seen as a political problem, and it can only be resolved by political means. In order to progress along the road of disarmament what is needed is, above all, the will. Security cannot be built endlessly on fear of retaliation. In other words, on the doctrines of "containment" or "deterrence." Apart from the absurdity and amorality of a situation in which the whole world becomes a nuclear hostage, these doctrines encourage an arms race that may sooner or later go out of control.

Second, in the context of the relations between the U.S.S.R. and the U.S.A., security can only be mutual.... It is vital that all should feel equally secure, for the fears and anxieties of the nuclear age generate uncertainty in politics and concrete actions. It is becoming extremely important to take the critical significance of the time factor into account. The appearance of new systems of weapons of mass destruction steadily shortens time and narrows down the possibilities for adopting political decisions on questions of war and peace in crisis situations.

Third, the U.S.A., its military-industrial machine remains the locomotive of militarism, for so far it has no intention of slowing down. This has to be taken into consideration, of course. But we are well aware that the interests and aims of the military-industrial complex are not at all the same as the interests and aims of the American people....

Naturally, the world is much larger than the U.S.A. and its occupation bases on foreign soil. And in world politics one cannot confine oneself to relations with any single, even a very important, country. As we know from experience, this only fosters the arrogance of strength. Needless to say, we attach considerable significance to the state and character of the relations between the Soviet Union and the U.S.A. Our countries have quite a few points of coincidence, and there is the objective needed to live in peace with each other, to cooperate on a basis of equality and mutual benefit, and there is no other basis.

Fourth, the world is in a process of swift changes, and it is not within anybody's power to maintain a perpetual status quo in it.... Countries ... all without exception face a task of fundamental significance, without being blind to social, political, and

ideological differences all have to master the science and art of restraint and circumspection on the international scene, to live in a civilised manner, in other words, under conditions of civil international intercourse and cooperation. But to give this cooperation wide scope there has to be an all-embracing system of international economic security that would in equal measure protect every nation against discrimination, sanctions, and other attributes of imperialist, neocolonialist policy. Alongside disarmament such a system can become a dependable pillar of international security generally.

In short, the modern world has become much too small and fragile for wars and a policy of force.... This means the realisation that it is no longer possible to win an arms race, or nuclear war for that matter.... The situation in the world may become such that it will no longer depend upon the intelligence or will of political leaders. It may become captive to technology, to technocratic military logic. Consequently, not only nuclear war itself but also the preparations for it, in other words, the arms race, the aspiration to win military superiority can, speaking in objective terms, bring no political gain to anybody.

Further, this means understanding that the present level of the balance of the nuclear capabilities of the opposite sides is much too high. For the time being this ensures equal danger to each of them. But only for the time being. Continuation of the nuclear arms race will inevitably heighten this equal threat and may bring it to a point where even parity will cease to be a factor of military-political deterrence. Consequently, it is vital, in the first place, to dramatically reduce the level of military confrontation. In our age, genuine equal security is guaranteed not by an excessively high but by the lowest possible level of strategic parity, from which nuclear and other types of weapons of mass destruction must be totally excluded.

Lastly, this means realising that in the present situation there is no alternative to cooperation and interaction between all countries.... [C]onfrontation between capitalism and socialism can proceed only and exclusively in forms of peaceful competition and peaceful contest.... [I]nternational security ... can only be brought by consistent, methodical, and persevering effort.

Continuity in foreign policy has nothing in common with a simple repetition of what has been done, especially in tackling the problems that have piled up. What is wanted is a high degree of accuracy in assessing one's own possibilities, restraint, and an eminently high sense of responsibility when decisions are made. What is wanted is firmness in upholding principles and postures, tactical flexibility, a readiness for mutually acceptable compromises, and an orientation on dialogue and mutual understanding rather than on confrontation.

As you know, we have made a series of unilateral steps — we put a moratorium on the deployment of intermediate-range missiles in Europe, cut back the number of these missiles, and stopped all nuclear tests. In Moscow and abroad there have been talks with leaders and members of the governments of many countries. The Soviet-Indian, Soviet-French, and Soviet-U.S. summits were necessary and useful steps.

The Soviet Union has made energetic efforts to give a fresh impetus to the negotiations in Geneva, Stockholm, and Vienna.... Negotiations are always a delicate and complex matter. Of cardinal importance here is to lead up to a mutually acceptable balance of interests. To turn weapons of mass destruction into an object of political scheming is, to say the least, immoral, while in political terms this is irresponsible.

Lastly, concerning our statement of January 15 of this year. The Soviet Union offers approaching the problems of disarmament in their totality, for in terms of security they are linked with one another. I am not speaking of rigid linkages or attempts at "backing down" in one direction in order to erect barricades in another. What I am talking about is a plan of concrete actions strictly measured out in terms of time. The U.S.S.R. intends to work perseveringly for its realisation, regarding it as the central direction of our foreign policy for the coming years.

The Soviet military doctrine is also entirely in keeping with the letter and spirit of the initiatives we have put forward. Its orientation is unequivocally defensive.... The U.S.S.R. undertook the the obligation not to be the first to use nuclear weapons and it will abide strictly by that obligation. But it is no secret that scenarios for a nuclear strike against us exist. We have no right to overlook this. The Soviet Union is a staunch adversary of nuclear war in any variant.... [W]e repeat again and again, the Soviet Union lays no claim to more security, but it will not settle for less.

I should like to draw attention to the problem of verification, to which we attach special significance. We have declared on several occasions that the U.S.S.R. is open to verification, that we are interested in it as much as anybody else. All-embracing, strictest verification is perhaps the key element of the disarmament process. The essence of the matter, in our thinking, is that there can be no disarmament without verification and that verification without disarmament makes no sense.

There is yet another matter of principle. We have stated our attitude to Star Wars quite substantively. The U.S.A. has already drawn many of its allies into this programme. There is the danger that things may become irreversible. Before it is too late, it is imperative to find a realistic solution guaranteeing that the arms race does not spread to outer space. The Star Wars programme cannot be permitted to be used as a stimulus for a further arms race or as a road-block to radical disarmament. Tangible progress in what concerns a drastic reduction of nuclear capabilities can be of much help to surmount this obstacle. For that reason the Soviet Union is prepared to make a substantial step in that direction, to resolve the question of intermediate-range missiles in the European zone separately — without a direct link to problems related to strategic armaments and outer space....

The attempts to sow doubt in the Soviet Union's constructive commitment to accelerate ... the destruction of nuclear weapons ... are becoming less and less convincing.... But also it is necessary to take into account the reaction of the centres of power that hold in their hands the keys to the success or failure of disarmament. Of course, the U.S. ruling class, to be more exact its most egotistical groups linked to the military-industrial complex, have other aims that are clearly antipodal to ours. For them disarmament spells out a loss of profits and a political risk, for us it is a blessing in all respects — economically, politically, and morally....

The day before yesterday, we received President Reagan's reply to our statement of January 15. The U.S. side began to set forth its considerations in greater detail at the talks in Geneva. To be sure, we shall closely examine everything the U.S. side has to say on these matters. However, since the reply was received literally on the eve of the Congress, the U.S. administration apparently expects, as we see it, our attitude to the U.S. stand to be made known to the world from this rostrum.

What I can say right away is that the president's letter does not give ground for amending the assessment of the international situation as had been set forth in the report before the reply was received. It says that the elimination of nuclear arms is the goal all the nuclear powers should strive after. In his letter the president agrees in general with some or other Soviet proposals and intentions as regards the issues of disarmament and security. In other words, the reply seems to contain some reassuring opinions and theses.

However, these positive pronouncements are swamped in various reservations, "linkages" and "conditions" which in fact bloc the solution of radical problems of disarmament. Reduction in the strategic nuclear arsenals is made conditional on our consent to the Star Wars programme and reductions, unilateral, by the way, in the Soviet conventional arms. Linked to this are also problems of regional conflicts and bilateral relations. The elimination of nuclear arms in Europe is blocked by the references to the stand taken by Great Britain and France and the demand to weaken our defences in the eastern part of the country with the U.S. military forces retained as they are. The refusal to stop nuclear tests is justified by arguments to the effect that nuclear weapons serve as a factor of "containment." This is in direct contradiction with the purpose reaffirmed in the letter — the need to destroy nuclear weapons. The reluctance of the U.S.A. and its ruling circles to embark on the path of nuclear disarmament manifests itself most clearly in their attitude to nuclear explosions, the termination of which is the demand of the whole world.

To put it in a nutshell, it is hard to detect in the letter we have just received any serious preparedness of the U.S. administration to get down to solving the cardinal problems involved in eliminating the nuclear threat. It looks as if some people in Washington and elsewhere, for that matter, have got used to living side by side with nuclear weapons linking with them their plans in the international arena. However, whether they want it or not, the Western politicians will have to answer the question: Are they prepared to part with nuclear weapons at all?

In accordance with an understanding reached in Geneva there will be another meeting with the U.S. president. The significance that we attach to it is that it ought to produce practical results in key areas of limiting and reducing armaments. There are at least two matters on which an understanding could be reached: the desertion of nuclear tests and the abolition of U.S. and Soviet intermediate-range missiles in the European Zone, and then, as a matter of fact, if there is readiness to seek agreement, the question of the time of the meeting would be resolved of itself: We will accept any suggestion on this count. But there is no sense in holding empty talks. We shall not remain indifferent if the Soviet-U.S. dialogue that was started and inspired some not unfounded hopes of a possibility for changes for the better is used to continue the arms race and the material preparations for war. The Soviet Union is of a firm mind to justify the hopes of the peoples of our two countries and of the whole world who are expecting concrete steps, practical actions, and tangible agreements of the leaders of the U.S.S.R. and the U.S.A. on how to block the arms race. We are prepared for this.

Naturally, like any other country, we attach considerable importance to the security of our frontiers, on land and sea. We have many neighbours, and they are different. We have no territorial claims on any of them. We threaten none of them. But as experience has shown time and again, there are quite a few persons who ... are endeavouring to aggravate the situation on the frontiers of the Soviet Union.

For instance, counter-revolution and imperialism have turned Afghanistan into a bleeding wound. The U.S.S.R. supports that country's efforts to defend its sovereignty. We should like, in the nearest future, to withdraw the Soviet troops stationed in Afghanistan at the request of its government. Moreover, we have agreed with the Afghan side on the schedule for their phased withdrawal as soon as a political settlement is reached that ensures an actual cessation and dependably guarantees the non-resumption of foreign armed interference in the internal affairs of the Democratic Republic of Afghanistan....

The CPSU regards the European direction as one of the main directions of its international activity.... [I]t is important, while preserving the assets that have already been accumulated, to move further: from the initial to a more lasting phase of detente, to mature detente, and then to the building of dependable security on the basis of the Helsinki Process, of a radical reduction of nuclear and conventional weapons.

The significance of the Asian and Pacific direction is growing. In that vast region there are many tangled knots of contradictions and, besides, the political situation in some places is unstable. Here it is necessary, without postponement, to find the relevant solutions and paths. Evidently, this has to begin with ... political settlement of painful problems so as ... to at least take the edge off the military confrontation in various parts of Asia.... This is made all the more urgent by the fact that in Asia and other continents the flashpoints of military danger are not dying down. We are in favour of vitalising collective quests for ways of defusing conflict situations in the Middle East, Central America, South Africa, in all of the planet's turbulent points. This is imperatively demanded by the interests of general security.

Crisis and conflicts are fertile soil also for international terrorism. Undeclared wars, the export of counter-revolution in all forms, political assassination, the taking of hostages, the hijacking of aircraft, and bomb attacks in streets, airports, and railway stations — such is the hideous face of terrorism, which its instigators try to mask with various cynical inventions. The U.S.S.R. rejects terrorism in principle and is prepared to cooperate actively with other states in order to uproot it....

Looking back over the past year one will see that ... the prerequisites for improving the international situation are beginning to form. But prerequisites for a turn are not the turn itself. The arms race continues and the threat of nuclear war remains. However, ... the growth of mass democratic and anti-war movements have significantly enlarged and strengthened the huge potential of peace, reason, and good will. This is a powerful counterbalance to imperialism's aggressive policy.

... We are watched by both friends and foes. We are watched by the huge and heterogeneous world of developing nations. It is looking for its choice, for its road, and what this choice is will depend to a large extent on socialism's successes, on the credibility of its answers to the challenges of time. We are convinced that socialism can resolve the most difficult problems confronting it. ...

Interaction between governing communist parties remains the heart and soul of the political cooperation among these countries. During the past year there has practically been no fraternal countries with whose leaders we have not had meetings and detailed talks. The forms of such cooperation are themselves being updated. A new and perhaps key element, the multilateral working meetings of leaders of fraternal countries is being institutionalised. ...

In the difficult international situation the prolongation of the Warsaw Treaty by a unanimous decision of its signatories was of great significance. ... [I]t is hard to picture world politics as a whole without it. ...

In the economic sphere there now is the comprehensive programme of scientific and technological progress. Its import lies in the transition of the CMEA countries to a coordinated policy in science and technology. ... Vitality, efficiency, and initiative — all these qualities meet the imperatives of the times. ...

The CPSU attaches growing significance to live and broad communication between citizens of socialist countries, between people of different professions and different generations. ... [I]t is especially important to analyse the character of the socialist way of life and understand the processes of perfecting democracy, management methods and personnel policy on the basis of the development of several countries rather than of one country.

... One can say with gratification that there has been a measure of improvement of the Soviet Union's relations with its great neighbour — socialist China. The distinctions in attitudes, in particular, to a number of international problems remain. But we also note something else — that in many cases we can work jointly, cooperate on an equal and principled basis, without prejudice to third countries. There is no need to explain the significance of this. The Chinese Communists called the victory of the U.S.S.R. and the forces of progress in the Second World War a prologue to the triumph of the People's Revolution in China. In turn, the formation of people's China helped to reinforce socialism's positions in the world and disrupt many of imperialism's designs and actions in the difficult postwar years. In thinking of the future, it may be said that the potentialities for cooperation between the U.S.S.R. and China are enormous. They are great because such cooperation is in line with the interests of both countries; because what is dearest to our peoples — socialism and peace — is indivisible.

The CPSU is an inalienable component of the international communist movement. We, the Soviet communists, are well aware that every advance we make in building socialism is an advance of the entire movement. For that reason the CPSU sees its primary internationalist duty in ensuring our country's successful progress along the road opened and blazed by the October Revolution.

The communist movement in the non-socialist part of the world remains the principal target of political pressure and harassment by reactionary circles of the bourgeoisie. All the fraternal parties are constantly under fire from anti-communist propaganda, which does not hold back from the most despicable means and methods. Many parties operate underground, in a situation of unmitigated persecution and repression. Every step the communists take calls for struggle and personal courage. Permit me, comrades, on behalf of the 27th Congress, on behalf of the Soviet communists to express sincere admiration for the dedicated struggle of our comrades, and profound fraternal solidarity with them.

In recent years the communist movement has come face to face with many new realities, tasks, and problems. All the indications are that it has entered upon a qualitatively new phase of development. ... The communist movement's immense diversity

and the tasks that it encounters are likewise a reality. In some cases this leads to disagreements and divergences. The CPSU is not dramatising the fact that complete unanimity among communist parties exists not always and not in everything. ... We do not see the diversity of our movement as a synonym for disunity. ... However, one should look at things realistically: the balance of strength in the struggle against war is shaping in the course of an acute and dynamic confrontation between progress and reaction. An immutable factor is the CPSU's solidarity with the forces of national liberation and social emancipation, and our course towards close interaction with socialist-oriented countries, with revolutionary-democratic parties, and with the nonaligned movement. The Soviet public is prepared to go on promoting links with non-communist movements and organisations, including religious organisations militating against war.

There is also the angle from which the CPSU regards its relations with the social democratic movement. It is a fact that the ideological differences between the communists and the social democrats are deep. ... However, an unbiased look at the standpoints and views of each other is unquestionably useful to both. ...

We see the fundamental principles of this system [of international security] in the following:

1. In the Military Sphere

● Renunciation by the nuclear powers of war — both nuclear and conventional — against each other or against third countries;

● Prevention of an arms race in outer space, cessation of all nuclear weapons tests and the total destruction of such weapons, a ban on and the destruction of chemical weapons, and renunciation of the development of other means of mass annihilation;

● A strictly controlled lowering of the levels of military capabilities of countries to limits of reasonable adequacy;

● Disbandment of military alliances, and as a stage toward this, renunciation of their enlargement and of the formation of new ones;

● Balanced and commensurate reduction of military budgets.

2. In the Political Sphere

● Unconditional respect in international practice for the right of each people to choose the ways and forms of its development independently;

● A just political settlement of international crises and regional conflicts;

● Elaboration of a set of measures aimed at building confidence between states and the creation of effective guarantees against attack from without and of the inviolability of their frontiers;

● Elaboration of effective methods of preventing international terrorism, including the safety of international land, air, and sea communications.

3. In the Economic Sphere

● Exclusion of all forms of discrimination from international practice; renunciation of the policy of economic blockades and sanctions if this is not directly envisaged in the recommendations of the world community;

● Joint quest for ways for a just settlement of the problem of debts;

● Establishment of a new world economic order guaranteeing equal economic security to all countries;

● Elaboration of principles for utilising part of the funds released as a result of a reduction of military budgets for the good of the world community, of developing nations in the first place;

● The pooling of efforts in exploring and making peaceful use of outer space and in resolving global problems on which the destinies of civilisation depend.

4. In the Humanitarian Sphere

● Cooperation in the dissemination of the ideas of peace, disarmament, and international security; greater flow of general objective information and intercourse between peoples for the purpose of learning about one another; reinforcement of the spirit of mutual understanding and concord in the relations between them;

• Extirpation of genocide, apartheid, advocacy of fascism and every other form of racial, national or religious exclusiveness, and also of discrimination against people on this basis;

• Extension — while respecting the laws of each country — of international cooperation in the implementation of the political, social, and personal rights of people;

• Decision in a humane and positive spirit of questions related to the reuniting of families, marriage, and the promotion of contacts between people and between organisations;

• Strengthening of and quests for new forms of cooperation in culture, art, science, education, and medicine.

These principles stem logically from the provisions of the programme of the CPSU. . . . Guided by them it would be possible to make peaceful coexistence the highest principle of state-to-state relations. In our view, these principles could become the point of departure and a sort of guideline for a direct and systematic dialogue between leaders of countries of the world community — both bilateral and multilateral.

And since this concerns the destinies of peace, such a dialogue is particularly important among the permanent members of the security council — the five nuclear powers. They bear the main burden of responsibility for the destinies of humankind. I emphasise — not a privilege, not a foundation for claims to "leadership" in world affairs, but responsibility, about which nobody has the right to forget. Why then should their leaders not gather at a round table and discuss what could and should be done to strengthen peace?

As we see it, the entire existing mechanism of arms limitation negotiations should also start to function at top productivity.

The U.S.S.R. is giving considerable attention to a joint examination of the world economy's problems and prospects, . . . at international forums as well as within the framework of the Helsinki process. We feel that in the future it would be important to convene a world congress on problems of economic security. . . . We are prepared to consider seriously any other proposal aimed at the same direction.

Under all circumstances success must be achieved in the battle to prevent war. . . . The CPSU sees active participation in this battle as the essence of its foreign policy strategy.

V. The Party

Comrades, the magnitude and novelty of what we have to do make exceptionally high demands of the character of the political, ideological, and organisational work conducted by the CPSU, which today has more than 19 million members welded together by unity of purpose, will, and discipline.

. . . Whenever the country faces new problems the party finds ways of resolving them. . . . Last year was special in this respect. As never before there was a need for unity in the party ranks and unity in the CC. We saw clearly that it was no longer possible to evade pressing issues of society's development, to remain reconciled to irresponsibility, laxity, and inertness. Under these conditions the Political Bureau, the CC Secretariat, and the Central Committee decided that the cardinal issues dictated by the times had to be resolved. An important landmark on this road was the April plenary meeting of the CC. We told the people frankly about the difficulties and omissions in our work and about the plans for the immediate future and the long term. . . .

The party can resolve new problems successfully if it is . . . free of the "infallibility" complex, critically assesses the results that have been attained, and clearly sees what has to be done. The new requirements being made of cadres, of the entire style, methods, and character of work are dictated by the magnitude and complexity of the problems and the need to draw lessons from the past without compromise or reservations.

. . . I should like to remind you of Lenin's words: "When the situation has changed and different problems have to be solved, we cannot look back and attempt to solve them by yesterday's methods. Don't try — you won't succeed!"

1. Work in a New Way, Enhance the Role and Responsibility of Party Organisations

The purpose of restructuring party work is that each party organisation — from republican to primary — should vigorously implement the course set by the April plenary meeting. . . .

We are justifiably exasperated by all sorts of shortcomings and by those responsible for them — people who neglect their duties and are indifferent to society's interests: hackworker and idler, grabber and writer of anonymous letters, petty bureaucrat and bribe-taker. But they live and work in a concrete collective. . . . Then who save the collective and the communists should candidly declare that in our working society each person is obliged to work conscientiously and abide strictly by the norms of socialist human association, which are the same for everybody.

This is where the task of enhancing the role of the party organisation rises to its full stature. It does not become us, the communists, to put the blame on anybody. . . . It is not enough to see shortcomings and defects, to stigmatise them. It is necessary to do everything so that they should not exist. . . .

We, the communists, are looked upon as an example in everything — in work and behaviour. We have to live and work in such a way that the working person could say: "Yes, this is a real communist.". . .

. . . The need for restructuring is seen by far from everybody and far from everywhere. . . . We will not move forward a single step if we do not learn to work in a new way, do not put an end to inertness and conservatism in any of their forms, if we lose the courage to assess the situation realistically and see it as it actually is. To make irresponsibility recede into the past, we have to make a rule of calling things by their names, of judging everything openly. It is about time to stop exercises in misplaced tact where there should be exactingness and honesty, a party conscience. Nobody has the right to forget Lenin's stern warning: "False rhetoric and false boastfulness spell moral ruin and lead unfailingly to political extinction."

. . . More urgently than before there is now the need to promote criticism and self-criticism and step up the efforts to remove window-dressing. From the recent past we know that where criticism and self-criticism chokes, where talk about successes is substituted for a party analysis of the actual situation, all party activity is deformed and a situation of complacency, permissiveness, and impunity arises that leads to the most serious consequences. In the localities and even in the centre there appeared quite a few officials who reacted painfully to the critical remarks levelled at them and went so far as to harass people who came up with criticism.

The labour achievements of the people of Moscow are widely known. But . . . as was noted at a city party conference, the leadership of the city committee had evaded decisions on complex problems while parading its successes. This is what generated complacence and was an impediment to making a principled evaluation of serious shortcomings.

Perhaps in their most glaring form negative processes stemming from an absence of criticism and self-criticism manifested themselves in Uzbekistan. Having lost touch with life the republic's former top leadership made it a rule to speak only of successes, paper over shortcomings, and respond irritably to any critical judgments. In the republican party organisation discipline slackened, and persons for whom the sole principle was lack of principles, their own well-being, and careerist considerations were in favour. Toadyism . . . became widespread. . . .

It required intervention by the CPSU Central Committee to normalise the situation. . . . There is something else that causes concern. The shortcomings in the republic did not appear overnight. They piled up over the years, growing from small to big. Officials from All-Union bodies, including the Central Committee, went to Uzbekistan on many occasions and they must have noticed what was happening. Working people of the republic wrote indignant letters to the central bodies about the malignant practices. But these signals were not duly investigated. . . . From this we have to draw the firm conclusion that in the party there neither are nor should be organisations outside the pale of control and closed to criticism, there neither are nor should be leaders fenced off from party responsibility.

. . . [T]he role of party committees of ministries and departments must be enhanced significantly. . . . In improving the forms and methods of leadership, the party is emphatically against confusing the functions of party committees with those of governmental and public bodies. This is not a simple question. In life it is sometimes hard to see the boundary beyond which party control and the organisation of the fulfilment of practical tasks spills over onto petty tutelage or even substitution for governmental and economic bodies. Needless to say, each situation requires a specific approach, and here much is determined by the political culture and maturity of leaders....

2. For Purity and Integrity of the Party Member, for a Principled Personnel Policy

Comrades, the more consistently we draw the party's huge creative potential into the efforts to accelerate the development of Soviet society, the more tangible becomes the profound substantiation of the conclusion drawn by the April plenary meeting about the necessity of enhancing the initiatives and responsibilities of cadres and about the importance of an untiring struggle for the purity and integrity of the party member.

The Communist Party is the political and moral vanguard. During the past five years it has admitted nearly 1,500,000 new members ... but as in any matter, the process of admittance to the party requires further upgrading. Some organisations hasten the growth of the party ranks to the detriment of their quality, and do not set high standards for new members. Our task is to ... close the party to uncommitted people, to those who join it out of careerist or other mercenary considerations....

We bear quite a lot of damage because some communists behave unworthily or perpetrate discrediting acts. Of late a number of senior officials have been discharged from their posts and expelled from the party for various abuses. Some of them have been indicted.... The party will resolutely go on getting rid of all who discredit the name of communist....

The criterion for all promotions and changes boils down to one thing: Political qualities, efficiency, ability, and actual achievements of the person concerned and the attitude to people. I feel it is necessary to emphasise this also because some people have dropped the party traditions of maintaining constant contact with rank-and-file communists, with working people. This is what undermines the very essence of party work.

The person needed today to head each party organisation is one who has close ties to the masses and is ideologically committed, thinks in an innovative way, and is energetic. It is hardly necessary to remind you that with the personality of a leader, of a party leader in the first place, people link all the pros and cons of the concrete, actual life they live....

3. Reinforce Ideology's Link to Life and Enrich People's Intellectual World

... In all its work the CPSU proceeds from the premise that fidelity to the Marxist-Leninist doctrine lies in creatively developing it on the basis of the experience that has been accumulated....

We cannot escape the fact that our philosophy and economics, as indeed our social sciences as a whole, are, I would say, in a state that is some distance away from the imperatives of life. Besides, our economic planning bodies and other departments do not display the proper interest in carrying rational recommendations of social scientists into practice....

But in themselves ideas, however attractive, do not give shape automatically to a coherent and active world view if they are not coupled to the socio-political experience of the masses....

The party defines the basic directions of ideological work in the new edition of the CPSU programme. The most essential thing on which the entire weight of party influence must be focused is that every person should understand the urgency and landmark character of the moment we are living in. Any of our plans would hang in the air if people are left indifferent....

However many lectures we deliver on tact and however much we censure callousness and bureaucracy, this evaporates if a person encounters coarseness in offices, in the street, in a shop.... However many articles we may write about social justice, order, and discipline, they will remain unproductive if they are not accompanied by consistent enforcement of the law....

It is always a complex process to develop the social consciousness, but ... the blackening of socio-economic development was the outcome of serious blunders not only in economic management but also in ideological work.... An essential feature of ideological work is also that it is conducted in a situation marked by a sharp confrontation between socialist and bourgeois ideology.... The psychological warfare unleashed by imperialism cannot be qualified otherwise than as a special form of aggression, of information imperialism.... Naturally, there are no grounds for overestimating the influence of bourgeois propaganda.... We have no right to forget that psychological warfare is a struggle for people's minds.... We are contending with a skillful class adversary....

The insidiousness and unscrupulousness of bourgeois propagandists must be countered with a high standard of professionalism on the part of our ideological workers, by the morality and culture of socialist society....

In our day, which is replete with dynamism and changes, the role of the mass media is growing significantly.... [T]here is a more analytical approach, civic motivation, and sharpness in bringing problems to light and in concrete criticism of shortcomings and omissions.... Changes for the better have clearly appeared here: Television and radio programmes have become more diversified and interesting, and there is a visible aspiration to surmount established stereotypes, to take the diversity of the interests of audiences into account more fully.

But can it be said that our mass media and propaganda are using all their potentials? For the time being, no. There still is much dullness, inertia has not been overcome.... People are dissatisfied with the inadequate promptness in the reporting of news ... [J]ustified censure is evoked by the low standard of some literary works.... There has to be a radical improvement of film distribution and of book and journal publishing. The leadership [must] draw effective conclusions from the innumerable critical remarks from the public....

Society's moral health and the intellectual climate in which people live are in no small measure determined by the state of literature and art.... Neither the party nor the people stand in need of showy verbosity on paper, petty dirty-linen-washing, time-serving, and utilitarianism. What society expects from the writer is artistic innovation and the truth of life, which has always been the essence of real art. But truth is not an abstract concept, it is concrete. It lies in ... life itself, in all its versatility, dramatism, and grandeur. Only a literature that is ideologically motivated, artistic, and committed to the people educates people to be honest, strong in spirit, and capable of shouldering the burden of their time. It is time for literary and art criticism to shake off complacency and servility to rank, ... remembering that criticism is a social matter and not a sphere serving an author's vanity and ambitions....

VI. The Results of the Discussion of the New Edition of the Party Programme and of the Amendments to the Party Rules

Comrades ... the conclusions and provisions of the CPSU programme and rules have met with widespread approval....

The drafts of the new edition of the programme and of the rules have been thoroughly discussed at meetings of primary party organisations, at district, city, area, regional and territorial election conferences, and at congresses of the communist parties of union republics. Since the beginning of the discussion, over six million responses were received to the draft programme alone. They came from workers, collective farmers, scientists, teachers, engineers, doctors, Army and Navy servicemen, communists and non-party people, veterans and young people.... I believe it would be useful to dwell on some of them.

Stressing the novelty of the draft under discussion, the authors of some of the letters suggest adopting it at the congress as the Fourth Party Programme. It will be recalled that the adoption of new party programmes, initially the second and then the third, was necessitated by the fact that the goals set in the preceding programme had been reached. In our case, the situation is different. ... Not all of the estimates and conclusions turned out to be right. Translating the tasks of the full-scale building of communism into direct practical action has proved to be premature.

Certain miscalculations were made, too, in fixing deadlines for the solution of a number of concrete problems. New problems ... have come to the fore and become acute. All this has to be reflected in the party's programme document.

Thus, the assessment of the submitted document as a new edition of the third party programme is justified in reality and is of fundamental importance. It reasserts the main goals of the CPSU, the basic laws governing communist construction, and at the same time shows that the accumulated historical experience has been interpreted in a creative manner, and that the strategy and tactics have been elaborated to suit the specificities of the present turning point.... The main conclusions about modern socialist society confirm that our country has entered the stage of developed socialism. We also show understanding for the task of building developed socialism set down in the programme documents of fraternal parties in the socialist countries. At the same time, it is proper to recall that the ... accents in the interpretation of developed socialism were gradually shifted. Things were not infrequently reduced to just registering successes, while many of the urgent problems ... were not given due attention.... The problems that we have inherited from the preceding stages will be resolved....

Some letters contain proposals for a more precise chronology of the periods that Soviet society will pass through in its advance to communism. According to Lenin's principles of structuring programme documents and the ensuing traditions, the programme should present a full-scale picture of the modern world, the main tendencies and laws governing its development, and a clear, well-argued account of the aims which the party is setting itself and which it is summoning the masses to achieve. At the same time, however, Lenin stressed that the programme must be strictly scientific ... and should not promise more than can be attained....

It seems to me that the submitted edition of the programme is meeting these demands. As for the chronological limits in which the programme targets are to be attained, they do not seem to be needed. The faults of the past are a lesson for us. The only thing we can say definitely today is that the fulfilment of the present programme goes beyond the end of the present century....

In support of the idea of setting communists higher standards some comrades suggest carrying out a purge to free the party of persons whose conduct and way of life contradict our norms and ideals. I do not think there is any need for a special campaign to purge the ranks of the CPSU. Our party is a healthy organism....

What leads us to regard the outlined plans as being feasible? Where is the guarantee that the policy of accelerating socio-economic progress is correct and will be carried out?

First and foremost, the fact that our plans rest on the firm foundation of Marxist-Leninist theory, that they are based on the inexhaustible riches of Lenin's ideas.... At complicated turning points in history the Leninist party has on more than one occasion demonstrated its ability to find correct roads of progress, to inspire, rally and organise the ... working people.... We are confident this will be the case in [the] future, too.

We count on the support of the working class because the party's policy is their policy. We count on the support of the peasantry because the party's policy is their policy. We count on the support of the people's intelligentsia because the party's policy is their policy....

The Soviet people can be confident that the party is profoundly aware of its responsibility for our country's future, for a durable peace on earth, and for the correctness of the charted policy. The main ingredients needed to put it into practice are persistent work, unity of the party and the people, and cohesive actions by all working people.

That is the only way we will be able to carry out the great Lenin's behest to move ever forward with united vigour and resolve. History has not given us any other destiny. But what a wonderful destiny it is, comrades!

Bibliography

CHAPTER 1
The Land and State

Books

Armstrong, John A. *Ideology, Politics, and Government in the Soviet Union: An Introduction.* New York: Praeger Publishers, 1967.

Conquest, Robert. *Soviet Nationalities Policy in Practice.* New York: Praeger Publishers, 1967.

———, ed. *The Soviet Political System.* New York: Praeger Publishers, 1968.

Hazard, John N. *The Soviet System of Government.* Chicago: University of Chicago Press, 1968.

Hough, Jerry F., and Merle Fainsod. *How the Soviet Union Is Governed.* Cambridge: Harvard University Press, 1979.

Hunt, R. N. Carew. *The Theory and Practice of Communism.* New York: Macmillan, 1957.

Katz, Zev, Rosemarie Rogers, and Frederic Harned, eds. *Handbook of Major Soviet Nationalities.* Riverside, N.J.: The Free Press, 1975.

Kulski, W. W. *The Soviet Regime: Communism in Practice.* New York: Syracuse University Press, 1959.

McCagg, William O., Jr., and Brian D. Silver, eds. *Soviet Asian Ethnic Frontiers.* Elmsford, N.Y.: Pergamon, 1979.

Miller, Wright. *Who Are the Russians? A History of the Russian People.* New York: Taplinger, 1973.

Nettl, J. P. *The Soviet Achievement.* New York: Harcourt, Brace & World, 1967.

Ponomaryov, B., et al. *History of Soviet Foreign Policy 1917-1945.* Moscow: Progress Publishers, 1969.

Raymond, Ellsworth. *The Soviet State.* New York: Collier-Macmillan, 1968.

Salisbury, Harrison E., ed. *The Soviet Union: The Fifty Years.* New York: Harcourt, Brace & World, 1967.

Schapiro, Leonard. *The Communist Party of the Soviet Union.* rev. ed. New York: Vintage Books, 1971.

Voslensky, Michael. *Nomenklatura.* New York: Doubleday, 1985.

Articles

Gilison, Jerome M. "New Factors of Stability in Soviet Collective Leadership." *World Politics* (July 1967): 563-81.

Hough, Jerry. "The Soviet Elite: In Whose Hands the Future?" *Problems of Communism* (March/April 1967): 18-25.

Kennan, George F. "The Russian Revolution: Fifty Years After: Its Nature and Consequences." *Foreign Affairs* (Fall 1967): 1-21.

Levi, Arrigo. "The Evolution of the Soviet System." *Problems of Communism* (July/August 1967): 24-29.

Markov, L. "The U.S.S.R. Yesterday and Today." *International Affairs* (November 1967): 271-75.

Petrov, Vladimir. "Formation of Soviet Foreign Policy." *Orbis* (Fall 1973): 819-63.

CHAPTER 2
Imperial Russia and the Revolution

Books

Antonov-Ovseyenko, Anton. *The Time of Stalin: Portrait of a Tyranny.* New York: Harper & Row, 1982.

Anweiler, Oskar, and others. *Revolutionary Russia.* Cambridge: Harvard University Press, 1968.

Bain, Robert N. *First Romanovs, 1613-1725.* New York: Russell & Russell, 1967.

Barghoorn, Frederick C. *The Soviet Image of the United States.* New York: Harcourt, Brace & Co., 1950.

Bashkina, Nina N., ed. *The United States and Russia: The Beginning of Relations, 1765-1815.* Washington, D.C.: Government Printing Office, 1980.

Bauer, Raymond A., Alex Inkeless, and Clyde Kluckhorn. *How the Soviet System Works.* Cambridge: Harvard University Press, 1956.

Beloff, Max. *Soviet Policy in the Far East, 1944-1951.* New York: Oxford University Press, 1953.

Berlin, Isaiah. *Karl Marx: His Life and Environment.* New York: Oxford University Press, 1959.

Bialer, Seweryn, ed. *Stalin and His Generals: Soviet Military Memoirs of World War II.* New York: Pegasus, 1969.

Billington, James H. *The Icon and the Axe.* New York: Random House, 1970.

Black, Cyril Edwin, ed. *Rewriting Russian History.* New York: Praeger Publishers, 1956.

Browder, Robert P. *The Origins of the Soviet-American Diplomacy.* Princeton, N.J.: Princeton University Press, 1953.

Browder, Robert P., and Alexander F. Kerensky, eds. *The Russian Provisional Government Documents.* 3 vols. Stanford, Calif.: Stanford University Press, 1961.

Brzezinski, Zbigniew K. *The Permanent Purge: Politics of Soviet Totalitarianism.* Cambridge: Harvard University Press, 1956.

———. *The Soviet Bloc: Unity and Conflict.* rev. ed. Cambridge: Harvard University Press, 1967.

Budurowycz, Bohdan B. *Polish-Soviet Relations, 1917-1921.* Cambridge: Harvard University Press, 1969.

Carr, Edward H. *A History of Soviet Russia.* 3 vols. New York: Macmillan, 1953.

Chernov, Victor M. *The Great Russian Revolution.* Translated and abridged by Philip E. Moseley. New Haven, Conn.: Yale University Press, 1936.

Clark, Alan. *Barbarossa: The Russian-German Conflict, 1941-45.* New York: William Morrow, 1965.

Clarkson, Jesse D. *History of Russia.* New York: Random House, 1969.

Clemens, Diane Shaver. *Yalta.* New York: Oxford University Press, 1970.

Conquest, Robert. *The Great Terror: Stalin's Purge of the Thirties.* New York: Macmillan, 1968.

Cowles, Virginia. *The Last Tsar.* New York: Putnam, 1977.

Crankshaw, Edward. *The Shadow of the Winter Palace: The Drift to Revolution, 1825-1917.* New York: Penguin Books, 1976.

Curtiss, John S. *Russian Army under Nicholas I.* Durham, N.C.: Duke University Press, 1965.

Dallin, David J. *Soviet Russia's Foreign Policy: 1939-1942.* New Haven, Conn.: Yale University Press, 1942.

Davis, Lynn E. *The Cold War Begins.* Princeton, N.J.: Princeton University Press, 1974.

Deane, John R. *The Strange Alliance: The Story of Our Efforts at Wartime Cooperation with Russia.* New York: Viking, 1947.

Dedjer, Vladimir. *The Battle Stalin Lost: Memoirs of Yugoslavia, 1948-1953.* New York: Viking, 1971.

Deutscher, Isaac. *The Prophet Armed: Trotsky, 1879-1921.* New York: Oxford University Press, 1954.

Djilas, Milovan. *Conversations with Stalin,* trans. Michael B. Petrovich. New York: Harcourt, Brace & World, 1962.

Dmytryshyn, Basil. *Moscow and the Ukraine, 1918-1953.* New York: Bookman, 1956.

——. *USSR: A Concise History.* 4th ed. New York: Charles Scribner's, 1984.

Druks, Herbert. *Harry S. Truman and the Russians, 1945-1953.* New York: Speller & Sons, 1967.

Dukes, P. *Catherine the Great and the Russian Nobility.* New York: Cambridge University Press, 1968.

Fedyshyn, Oleh S. *Germany's Drive to the East and the Ukrainian Revolution, 1917-1918.* New Brunswick, N.J.: Rutgers University Press, 1971.

Feis, Herbert. *Churchill, Roosevelt, Stalin: The War They Waged and the Peace They Sought.* Princeton, N.J.: Princeton University Press, 1957.

Field, Daniel. *Rebels in the Name of the Tsar.* Boston: Houghton Mifflin, 1976.

Filene, Peter G. *Americans and the Soviet Experiment, 1917-1933.* New York: Oxford University Press, 1967.

Fischer, George. *Soviet Opposition to Stalin: A Case Study in World War II.* Cambridge: Harvard University Press, 1952.

Fisher, Alan W. *Russian Annexation of the Crimea, 1772-1773.* New York: Cambridge University Press, 1970.

Fleming, D. F. *The Cold War and Its Origins: 1917-1960.* 2 vols. Garden City, N.Y.: Doubleday, 1961.

Florinsky, Michael T. *The End of the Russian Empire.* New York: Macmillan, 1961.

——. *Russia: A History and an Interpretation.* vol. 2. New York: Macmillan, 1955.

Gaddis, John Lewis. *The United States and the Origins of the Cold War, 1941-1947.* New York: Columbia University Press, 1972.

Graham, Stephen. *Tsar of Freedom: The Life and Reign of Alexander II.* Hamden, Conn.: Shoe String Press, 1968.

Grey, Ian. *The First Fifty Years: Soviet Russia, 1917-1967.* New York: Coward-McCann, 1967.

Harriman, W. Averell, and Elie Abel. *Special Envoy to Churchill and Stalin, 1941-1946.* New York: Random House, 1975.

Hingley, Ronald. *Tsars: From Ivan the Terrible to Nicholas II, 1533-1917.* Urbana: University of Illinois Press, 1968.

Irving, David. *Uprising.* Don Mills, Ontario: Hodder & Stoughton, 1981.

Johnson, Robert E. *Peasant and Proletarian: The Working Class of Moscow at the End of the 19th Century.* New Brunswick, N.J.: Rutgers University Press, 1979.

Kenez, Peter. *Civil War in South Russia, 1918: The First Year of the Volunteer Army.* Berkeley: University of California Press, 1971.

——. *Civil War in South Russia, 1919-1920: The Defeat of the Whites.* Berkeley: University of California Press, 1977.

Kennan, George F. *Russia and the West under Lenin and Stalin.* Boston: Little, Brown, 1961.

——. *Soviet Foreign Policy, 1917-1941.* New York: Van Nostrand, 1960.

Kerensky, Alexander. *The Catastrophe.* New York: Appleton-Century-Crofts, 1929.

Kochan, Miriam L. *The Last Days of Imperial Russia: 1910-1917.* New York: Macmillan, 1976.

——. *Life in Russia under Catherine the Great.* New York: Putnam, 1969.

Kot, Stanislaw. *Conversations with the Kremlin and Dispatches from Russia,* trans. H. C. Stevens. London: Oxford University Press, 1963.

Lane, David. *The Roots of Russian Communism: A Social and Historical Study of Russian Social Democracy, 1898-1907.* University Park: Pennsylvania State University Press, 1975.

Lawrence, John. *A History of Russia.* New York: New American Library, 1978.

Leggett, George. *The Cheka: Lenin's Secret Police.* New York: Oxford University Press, 1981.

Lenin, V. I. *Selected Works.* 12 vols. New York: International Publishers, 1938.

Levytsky, Borys. *The Stalinist Terror in the Thirties.* Stanford, Calif.: Hoover Institution Press, 1974.

Lewin, Moshe. *Lenin's Last Struggle.* New York: Monthly Review Press, 1978.

Lyons, Marvin. *Nicholas II: The Last Tsar.* New York: St. Martin's Press, 1975.

Massie, Robert P. *Nicholas and Alexandra.* New York: Atheneum, 1967.

——. *Peter the Great.* New York: Random House, 1981.

McLane, Charles B. *Soviet Strategies in Southeast Asia: An Exploration of Eastern Policy under Lenin and Stalin.* Princeton, N.J.: Princeton University Press, 1966.

Medvedev, Roy A. *Let History Judge: The Origins and Consequences of Stalinism.* New York: Knopf, 1971.

——. *The October Revolution.* New York: Columbia University Press, 1979.

Mikolajczyk, Stanislaw. *The Pattern of Soviet Domination.* London: Sampson, Low, Marston & Co., 1948.

——. *The Rape of Poland: The Pattern of Soviet Aggression.* New York: McGraw-Hill, 1948.

Moore, Barrington. *Soviet Politics: The Dilemma of Power.* Cambridge: Harvard University Press, 1951.

Mosely, Philip E. *The Kremlin and World Politics: Studies in Soviet Policy and Action.* New York: Vintage Books, 1960.

Mosse, Werner E. *Alexander the Second and the Modernization of Russia.* New York: Macmillan, 1962.

Neil, Grant. *The German-Soviet Pact, August 23, 1939: A Nonaggression Pact.* New York: Franklin Watts, 1975.

Nettl, John P. *The Eastern Zone and Soviet Policy in Germany.* New York: Oxford University Press, 1951.

Neumann, William L. *After Victory: Churchill, Roosevelt, Stalin and the Making of the Peace.* New York: Harper & Row, 1967.

Pares, Sir Bernard. *The Fall of the Russian Monarchy: A Study of the Evidence.* New York: Knopf, 1939.

——. *A History of Russia.* New York: Knopf, 1953.

Paszkiewicz, H. *Origin of Russia.* New York: Gordon Press, 1978.

Pipes, Richard, ed. *Revolutionary Russia.* Cambridge: Harvard University Press, 1968.

Presniakov, Alexander E. *Emperor Nicholas the First of Russia: The Apogee of Autocracy, 1825-1855.* Gulf Breeze, Fla.: Academic International, 1974.

Riasanovsky, Nicholas V. *A History of Russia.* 3d ed. New York: Oxford University Press, 1977.

Salisbury, Harrison E. *Moscow Journal: The End of Stalin.* Chicago: University of Chicago Press, 1961.

——. *The 900 Days: The Siege of Leningrad.* New York: Harper & Row, 1969.

Saul, Norman E. *Sailors in Revolt: The Russian Baltic Fleet in 1917.* Lawrence: University of Kansas Press, 1978.

Seabury, Paul. *The Rise and Decline of the Cold War.* New York: Basic Books, 1967.

Seton-Watson, Hugh. *The Decline of Imperial Russia, 1855-1914.* New York: Praeger Publishers, 1952.

——. *Russian Empire, 1801-1917.* New York: Oxford University Press, 1967.

Shtemenko, General S. M. *The Last Six Months.* New York: Zebra Books, 1978.

Smith, Edward E. *The Young Stalin: The Early Years of an Elusive Revolutionary.* New York: Farrar, Strauss & Giroux, 1967.

Sokol, Edward D. *The Revolt of 1916 in Russian Central Asia.* New York: AMS Press, 1978.

Solzhenitsyn, Alexander. *The Gulag Archipelago, 1918-1956: An Experiment in Literary Investigation.* 2 vols. New York: Harper & Row, 1974.

Sontag, Raymond J., and James S. Beddie, eds. *Nazi-Soviet Relations, 1939-1941: Documents from Archives of German Foreign Office.* Westport, Conn.: Greenwood Press, 1976.

Stalin, J. V. *On the Great Patriotic War of the Soviet Union.* Moscow: Foreign Languages Publishing House, 1945.

Stettinius, Edward R., Jr. *Roosevelt and the Russians: The Yalta Conference.* Garden City, N.Y.: Doubleday, 1949.

Szamuely, Tibor. *The Russian Tradition.* New York: McGraw-Hill, 1975.

Taubman, William. *Stalin's American Policy: From Entente to Détente to Cold War.* New York: W. W. Norton, 1982.

Thomas, Benjamin P. *Russo-American Relations, 1815-1867.* New York: AMS Press, 1978.

Treadgold, Donald W. *Twentieth Century Russia.* 2d. ed. Chicago: Rand McNally, 1964.

Trotsky, Leon. *Trotsky's Diary in Exile, 1935.* Cambridge: Harvard University Press, 1959.

Troyat, Henri. *Catherine the Great.* New York: E. P. Dutton, 1980.

Tucker, Robert C. *The Lenin Anthology.* New York: W. W. Norton, 1975.

——. *Stalin as Revolutionary, 1879-1929: A Study in History and Personality.* New York: W. W. Norton, 1973.

Ulam, Adam B. *The Bolsheviks.* New York: Collier Books, 1968.

——. *Expansion and Coexistence: Soviet Foreign Policy, 1917-73.* 2d ed. New York: Praeger Publishers, 1974.

——. *A History of Soviet Russia.* New York: Praeger Publishers, 1976.

——. *In the Name of the People.* New York: Viking Press, 1977.

——. *Russia's Failed Revolutions: From the Decembrists to the Dissidents.* New York: Basic Books, 1980.

——. *Stalin: The Man and His Era.* New York: Viking Press, 1973.

Umiastowski, R. *Poland, Russia and Great Britain, 1941-1945.* London: Hollis & Carter, 1946.

Vernadsky, George. *A History of Russia.* 6th ed. New Haven, Conn.: Yale University Press, 1969.

Vladimirov, Petr Parfenovic. *The Vladimirov Diaries: Yenan, China, 1942-1945.* Garden City, N.Y.: Doubleday, 1975.

Von Laue, Theodore H. *Why Lenin? Why Stalin? A Reappraisal of the Russian Revolution.* New York: Harper & Row, 1971.

Voznesensky, Nicholas. *Economy of the USSR during World War II.* Washington, D.C.: Public Affairs Press, 1948.

Wittlin, Thaddeus. *Commissar: The Life and Death of Lavrenty Pavlovich Beria.* New York: Macmillan, 1972.

Wolfe, Bertram D. *Three Who Made a Revolution.* New York: Dial Press, 1964.

Wolin, Simon, and Robert M. Slusser, eds. *The Soviet Secret Police.* New York: Praeger Publishers, 1957.

Yanov, Alexander. *The Origins of Autocracy: Ivan the Terrible in Russian History.* Berkeley: University of California Press, 1981.

Articles

Braginskii, B. "The Planning System during the First Post-War Five-Year Plan (1945-1950)." *Problems of Economics* (August 1971): 64-80.

Brzezinski, Zbigniew. "An Analysis of Russia's Domestic Dilemmas and Foreign Policy." *New Leader,* June 27, 1960, 6-8.

——. "How the Cold War Was Played." *Foreign Affairs* (Fall 1972): 181-209.

Dobriansky, Lev E. "Economic Vulnerabilities of the Soviet Union." *Ukrainian Quarterly* (Spring 1960): 26-39.

Ellison, Herbert J., et al. "The Russian Revolution: Some Historical Considerations." *Problems of Communism* (November/December 1967): 1-91.

Fedyshyn, Oleh S. "Khrushchev's Leap Forward: National Assimilation in the USSR after Stalin." *Southwestern Social Science Quarterly* (June 1967): 34-43.

Salisbury, Harrison E. "U.S. and U.S.S.R.: The Dangers Ahead." *Foreign Policy Bulletin,* June 15, 1960, 145-47.

Schapiro, Leonard. "Has Russia Changed?" *Foreign Affairs* (Spring 1960): 391-401.

Schlesinger, Arthur M., Jr. "Origins of the Cold War." *Foreign Affairs* (Fall 1967): 22-52.

Seabury, Paul, and Brian Thomas. "Cold War Origins." *Journal of Contemporary History* (January 1968): 169-98.

Ulam, Adam B. "Forty Years after Yalta." *The New Republic,* February 11, 1985, 18-21.

Voronstov, V. B. "The Liberation Mission of the USSR in the Far East during World War II." *Istoriia USSR.* 4 (July-August 1965): 28-48.

CHAPTER 3
Khrushchev Years: 1953-64

Books

Allison, Graham T. *Essence of Decision: Explaining the Cuban Missile Crisis.* Boston: Little, Brown, 1971.

Armstrong, John A. *The Politics of Totalitarianism.* New York: Random House, 1961.

Bialer, Seweryn. *Stalin's Successors: Leadership, Stability, and Change in the Soviet Union.* New York: Cambridge University Press, 1980.

Breslauer, George W. *Khrushchev and Brezhnev as Leaders: Building Authority in Soviet Politics.* Winchester, Mass.: Allen & Unwin, 1982.

Brzezinski, Zbigniew, and Samuel P. Huntington. *Political Power: USA/USSR.* New York: Viking Press, 1964.

Crankshaw, Edward. *Khrushchev: A Career.* New York: Penguin, 1966.

Dallin, Alexander, ed. *Soviet Conduct in World Affairs.* New York: Columbia University Press, 1960.

Dinerstein, Herbert S. *The Making of a Missile Crisis: October 1962.* Baltimore: Johns Hopkins University Press, 1976.

Dornberg, John. *The New Tsars: Russia Under Stalin's Heirs.* Garden City, N.Y.: Doubleday, 1972.

Garthoff, Raymond L. *Soviet Strategy in the Nuclear Age.* New York: Praeger Publishers, 1958.

Gehlen, Michael P. *The Politics of Coexistence: Soviet Methods and Motives.* Bloomington: Indiana University Press, 1967.

Goldman, Eric. *The Crucial Decade and After, 1945-1960.* New York: Vintage Books, 1960.

Harriman, William Averell. *America and Russia in a Changing World: A Half Century of Personal Observation.* Garden City, N.Y.: Doubleday, 1971.

Horelick, Arnold L., and Myron Rush. *Strategic Power and Soviet Foreign Policy.* Chicago: University of Chicago Press, 1965.

Hyland, William, and Richard W. Shryock. *The Fall of Khrushchev.* New York: Funk & Wagnalls, 1968.

Jones, Goronwy J. *From Stalin to Khrushchev.* London: Linden Press, 1960.

Kennedy, Robert F. *Thirteen Days: A Memoir of the Cuban Missile Crisis.* New York: W. W. Norton, 1971.

Linden, Carl A. *Khrushchev and the Soviet Leadership, 1957-1964.* Baltimore: Johns Hopkins University Press, 1966.

London, Kurt, ed. *The Soviet Union: A Half Century of Communism.* Baltimore: Johns Hopkins University Press, 1968.

McClosky, Herbert, and John E. Turner. *The Soviet Dictatorship.* New York: McGraw-Hill, 1960.

Overstreet, Harry A., and Bonaro Overstreet. *War Called Peace: Khrushchev's Communism.* New York: W. W. Norton, 1961.

Smolansky, Oles. *The Soviet Union and the Arab East under Khrushchev.* Lewisburg, Pa.: Bucknell University Press, 1974.

Talbott, Strobe, ed. *Khrushchev Remembers.* Boston: Little, Brown, 1970.

———. *Khrushchev Remembers: The Last Testament.* Boston: Little, Brown, 1974.

CHAPTER 4
The Brezhnev Era Opens

Books

Amalrik, Andrei. *Will the Soviet Union Survive Until 1984?* New York: Harper & Row, 1970.

Barnet, Richard J. *The Giants: Russia and America.* New York: Simon & Schuster, 1977.

Brzezinski, Zbigniew. *Power and Principle: Memoirs of the National Security Adviser, 1977-1981.* New York: Farrar, Straus, Giroux, 1983.

Conquest, Robert. *Power and Policy in the USSR.* New York: St. Martin's Press, 1961.

Dallin, Alexander, and Thomas H. Larson, eds. *Soviet Politics since Khrushchev.* Englewood Cliffs, N.J.: Prentice-Hall, 1968.

Dawisha, Karen. *Kremlin and the Prague Spring.* Berkeley: University of California Press, 1984.

Dornberg, John. *Brezhnev: The Masks of Power.* New York: Basic Books, 1974.

Dulles, Eleanor L., and Robert D. Crane, eds. *Détente: Cold War Strategies in Transition.* New York: Praeger Publishers, 1965.

Dzirkals, Lilita, Thane Gustafson, and A. Ross Johnson. *The Media and Intra-Elite Communication in the USSR.* R-2869. Santa Monica, Calif.: The Rand Corporation, 1982.

Edmonds, Robin. *Soviet Foreign Policy 1962-1973: The Parody of Super Power.* New York: Oxford University Press, 1975.

Eidlin, Fred. *The Logic of Normalization: The Soviet Intervention in Czechoslovakia of 21 August 1968 and the Czechoslovakia Response.* New York: Columbia University Press, 1980.

Gelman, Harry. *The Brezhnev Politburo and the Decline of Detente.* Ithaca, N.Y.: Cornell University Press, 1984.

Griffith, William E. *The Super Powers and Regional Tensions: The USSR and the U.S. and Europe.* Lexington, Mass.: Lexington Books, 1981.

Hough, Jerry F. *The Soviet Prefects.* Cambridge: Harvard University Press, 1969.

Hyland, William G. *Soviet-American Relations: A New Cold War?* Santa Monica, Calif.: The Rand Corporation, 1981.

Jackson, D. Bruce. *Castro, the Kremlin and Communism in Latin America.* Baltimore: Johns Hopkins University Press, 1969.

Kalb, Marvin, and Bernard Kalb. *Kissinger.* Boston: Little, Brown, 1974.

Kelley, Donald R., ed. *Soviet Politics in the Brezhnev Era.* New York: Praeger Publishers, 1980.

Kissinger, Henry. *White House Years.* Boston: Little, Brown, 1979.

Leites, Nathan. *The Operational Code of the Politburo.* The Rand Corporation. New York: McGraw-Hill, 1951.

Levesque, Jacques. *The USSR and the Cuban Revolution: Soviet Ideological and Strategical Perspectives, 1959-77.* New York: Praeger Publishers, 1981.

London, Kurt, ed. *The Soviet Union in World Politics.* Boulder, Colo.: Westview Press, 1980.

Lyons, Eugene. *Workers' Paradise Lost: Fifty Years of Soviet Communism: A Balance Sheet.* New York: Funk & Wagnalls, 1967.

Nixon, Richard. *RN: The Memoirs of Richard Nixon.* New York: Grosset & Dunlap, 1978.

Petrov, Vladimir. *U.S.-Soviet Détente: Past and Future.* Washington, D.C.: American Enterprise Institute for Public Policy Research, 1975.

Pipes, Richard. *US-Soviet Relations in the Era of Détente.* Boulder, Colo.: Westview Press, 1981.

Simes, Dimitri K. *Détente and Conflict: Soviet Foreign Policy, 1972-1977.* Beverly Hills, Calif.: Sage Publications, 1977.

Simon, Jeffrey. *Ruling Communist Parties and Détente: A Documentary History.* Washington, D.C.: American Enterprise Institute for Public Policy Research, 1975.

Stoessinger, John G. *Nations in Darkness: China, Russia and America.* New York: Random House, 1981.

Strong, John W. *Soviet Union under Brezhnev and Kosygin: The Transition Years.* New York: Van Nostrand Reinhold, 1971.

Tatu, Michel. *Power in the Kremlin from Khrushchev to Kosygin.* New York: Macmillan, 1969.

Ulam, Adam B. *The Rivals: America and Russia Since World War II.* New York: Viking Press, 1971.

———. *Dangerous Relations: The Soviet Union in World Politics, 1970-1982.* New York: Oxford University Press, 1983.

Valenta, Jiri. *Soviet Intervention in Czechoslovakia, 1968.* Baltimore: Johns Hopkins University Press, 1979.

Vance, Cyrus. *Hard Choices: Critical Years in America's Foreign Policy.* New York: Simon & Schuster, 1983.

Yanov, Alexander. *Détente after Brezhnev: The Domestic Roots of Soviet Foreign Policy.* Berkeley: Institute of International Studies, University of California, 1977.

Zeman, Z. A. B. *Prague Spring: A Report on Czechoslovakia.* Baltimore: Penguin Books, 1969.

Articles

Arbatov, Georgii. "The Great Lie of the Opponents of Détente." *Pravda,* February 5, 1977.

Aspaturian, Vernon V. "The Aftermath of the Czech Invasion." *Current History* (November 1968): 263-67.

Blumenfeld, Yorick. "Russia's Diplomatic Offensive." *Editorial Research Reports,* April 5, 1972, 253-70.

Borisov, A. "A Chronicle of Soviet Foreign Policy." *International Affairs* (January 1981): 88-92.

Campbell, John C. "Soviet-American Relations: Conflict and Cooperation." *Current History* (October 1967): 193-202.

Conquest, Robert. "The Limits of Détente." *Foreign Affairs* (Summer 1968): 733-42.

———. "A New Russia? A New World?" *Foreign Affairs* (Spring 1975): 482-97.

Deans, Ralph C. "Trends in U.S.-Soviet Relations." *Editorial Research Reports,* May 25, 1973, 399-416.

Fischer, Benjamin. "The Soviet Political System and Foreign Policy-Making in the Brezhnev Era." Prepared for the Columbia University Research Institute on International Change.

Freedman, Robert O. "The Soviet Image of the Carter Administration's Policy toward the USSR: From the Inauguration to the Invasion of Afghanistan." *Korea and World Affairs* 4, no. 2 (Summer 1980): 224-67.

Gitelman, Zvi. "The Politics of Socialist Restoration in Hungary and Czechoslovakia." *Comparative Politics* (January 1981): 187-210.

Gorbachyov, B. "The Cornerstone of Soviet Foreign Policy." *International Affairs* (August 1981): 21-29.

Hyland, William G. "U.S.-Soviet Relations: The Long Road Back." *Foreign Affairs* (America and the World 1981): 525-50.

Kraft, Joseph. "Letter from Moscow." *New Yorker,* January 31, 1983.

Legvold, Robert. "The Nature of Soviet Power." *Foreign Affairs* (Fall 1977): 49-71.

Leonhard, Wolfgang. "The Domestic Politics of the New Soviet Foreign Policy." *Foreign Affairs* (Fall 1973): 59-74.

Meissner, Boris. "The Soviet Union under Brezhnev and Kosygin." *Modern Age* (Winter 1966/67): 7-23.

Newsom, David. "America Engulfed." *Foreign Policy* 43 (Summer 1981): 17-32.

Pennar, Jaan. "The Arabs, Marxism and Moscow: A Historical Survey." *Middle East Journal* 22, no. 3 (September 1968): 433-47.

Ploss, Sidney. "Politics in the Kremlin." *Problems of Communism* 19, no. 3 (May-June 1970): 1-14.

Rubinstein, Alvin Z. "Soviet-American Relations." *Current History* (October 1974): 145.

Salisbury, Harrison E. "Russia vs. China: Global Conflict?" *Antioch Review* (Winter 1967/1968): 425-39.

Schapiro, Leonard. "The CPSU International Department." *International Journal* 32 (Winter 1966-1967): 41-55.

Shulman, Marshall D. "Toward a Western Philosophy of Coexistence." *Foreign Affairs* (Fall 1973): 35-58.

Sorensen, Theodore C. "Most-Favored-Nation and Less Favorite Nations." *Foreign Affairs* (Winter 1973-74): 273-86.

Tucker, Robert C. "Swollen State, Spent Society: Stalin's Legacy to Brezhnev's Russia." *Foreign Affairs* (Winter 1981-82): 414-35.

Volsky, Dmitry. "Flop or Maneuver." *New Times* (Moscow) 52 (1978): 16-17.

_____. "Vicious Circle." *New Times* (Moscow) 5 (1979): 8-9.

_____. "There Is Light at the End of the Tunnel." *New Times* (Moscow) 49 (1981): 12-13.

CHAPTER 5
Soviet Foreign Policy

Books

Arnold, Anthony. *Afghanistan: The Soviet Invasion in Perspective.* Stanford, Calif.: Hoover Institution Press, 1981.

Becker, A. S., and A. L. Horelick. *Soviet Policy in the Middle East.* Santa Monica, Calif.: The Rand Corporation, 1970.

Bradsher, Henry S. *Afghanistan and the Soviet Union.* 2d ed. Durham, N.C.: Duke University Press, 1983.

Confino, Michael, and Shimon Shamir, eds. *The USSR and the Middle East.* Jerusalem: Israel Universities Press, 1973.

Congressional Research Service. *The Soviet Union in the Third World, 1980-1985, An Imperial Burden or Political Asset?* Report prepared for the Committee on Foreign Affairs of the U.S. House of Representatives. September 23, 1985.

Dawisha, Adeed, and Karen Dawisha. *The Soviet Union in the Middle East: Perspectives & Policies.* New York: Holmes & Meier, 1982.

Donaldson, Robert, ed. *The Soviet Union in the Third World.* Boulder, Colo.: Westview Press, 1981.

Duncan, Raymond W., ed. *Soviet Policy in the Third World.* Elmsford, N.Y.: Pergamon, 1980.

Dupree, Louis. *Afghanistan.* Princeton, N.J.: Princeton University Press, 1978.

_____. *Afghanistan, 1980.* Hanover, N.H.: American Universities Staff, 1980.

Edmonds, Robin. *Soviet Foreign Policy: The Brezhnev Years.* New York: Oxford University Press, 1983.

Freedman, Robert O. *Soviet Policy toward the Middle East since 1970.* 3d ed. New York: Praeger Publishers, 1982.

_____, ed. *World Politics and the Arab-Israeli Conflict.* Elmsford, N.Y.: Pergamon, 1979.

Golan, Galia. *Yom Kippur and after: The Soviet Union and the Middle East Crisis.* New York: Cambridge University Press, 1977.

Hammond, Thomas T. *Red Flag Over Afghanistan: The Communist Coup, the Soviet Invasion, and the Consequences.* Boulder, Colo.: Westview Press, 1984.

Hoffmann, Erik P., and Frederick Fleron, eds. *The Conduct of Soviet Foreign Policy.* Hawthorne, N.Y.: Aldine, 1980.

Hosmer, Stephen T. and Thomas W. Wolfe. *Soviet Policy and Practice Toward Third World Conflicts.* Lexington, Mass.: Heath, 1983.

Hough, Jerry. *The Struggle for the Third World: Soviet Debates and American Options.* Washington, D.C.: Brookings Institution, 1985.

Klieman, Aaron S. *Soviet Russia and the Middle East.* Baltimore: Johns Hopkins Press, 1970.

Klinghoffer, Arthur J. *The Angolan War: A Study in Soviet Foreign Policy in the Third World.* Boulder, Colo.: Westview Press, 1980.

Krammer, Arnold. *The Forgotten Friendship: Israel and the Soviet Bloc 1947-1953.* Urbana: University of Illinois, 1974.

Laqueur, Walter Z. *The Soviet Union and the Middle East.* New York: Praeger Publishers, 1959.

Legvold, Robert. *Soviet Policy in West Africa.* Cambridge: Harvard University Press, 1970.

Leiken, Robert, ed., *Central America, Anatomy of Conflict.* Elmsford, N.Y.: Pergamon, 1984.

Leiken, Robert. *Soviet Strategy in Latin America.* Washington Paper No. 93. New York: Praeger Publishers, 1982.

Lenczowski, George. *Soviet Advances in the Middle East.* Washington, D.C.: American Enterprise Institute for Public Policy Research, 1972.

Nogee, Joseph L., and Robert H. Donaldson. *Soviet Foreign Policy since World War II.* 2d ed. Elmsford, N.Y.: Pergamon, 1984.

Porter, Bruce D. *The USSR in Third World Conflicts.* New York: Cambridge University Press, 1984.

Ro'i, Yaacov, ed. *The Limits to Power: Soviet Policy in the Middle East.* London: Croom Helm, 1979.

Rotberg, Robert I., Henry S. Bienen, Robert Legvold, and Gavin G. Maasdorp, *South Africa and Its Neighbors.* Lexington, Mass.: Lexington Books, 1985.

Rubinstein, Alvin Z. *Soviet Policy Toward Turkey, Iran, and Afghanistan: The Dynamics of Influence.* New York: Praeger Publishers, 1982.

Stockwell, John. *In Search of Enemies: A CIA Story.* New York: W. W. Norton, 1978.

Zagoria, Donald S., ed. *Soviet Policy in East Asia.* New Haven, Conn.: Yale University Press, 1982.

Zimmerman, William, and Robert Axelrod. *The Lesson of Vietnam and Soviet Foreign Policy.* Ann Arbor, Mich.: Institute of Public Policy Studies, 1980.

Articles

Albinski, Henry S. "Chinese and Soviet Policies in the Vietnam Crisis." *Australian Quarterly* (March 1968): 65-74.

Anderson, Richard D., Jr. "Soviet Decisionmaking and Poland." *Problems of Communism* (March-April 1982): 22-36.

Clement, Peter. "Moscow and Southern Africa." *Problems of Communism* (March-April 1985): 29-50.

Dawisha, Adeed I. "Iraq: The West's Opportunity." *Foreign Policy* 41 (Winter 1980-81): 134-53.

Dawisha, Karen. "Moscow's Moves in the Direction of the Gulf — So Near and Yet so Far." *Journal of International Affairs* 34, no. 2 (Fall/Winter 1980-81): 219-33.

Duncan, Raymond W. "Soviet Interests in Latin America: New Opportunities & Old Constraints." *Journal of Interamerican Studies & World Affairs* (May 1984): 163-98.

Freedman, Robert O. "Soviet Policy toward Syria Since Brezhnev." Paper presented at III World Congress of Soviet and East European Studies, Washington, D.C., October 31, 1985.

Freistetter, Franz. "The Battle in Afghanistan: A View from Europe." *Strategic Review* (Winter 1981): 36-43.

Golan, Galia. "The Soviet Union and the Palestine Issue." Paper presented at III World Congress of Soviet and East European Studies, Washington, D.C., October 31, 1985.

_____. "Syria and the Soviet Union since the Yom Kippur War." *Orbis* 21, no. 4 (Winter 1978): 777-801.

Keegan, John. "The Ordeal of Afghanistan." *Atlantic Monthly,* November 1985, 94-105.

Kerr, Malcolm. "The Convenient Marriage of Egypt and Libya." *New Middle East* (London) 48 (September 1972): 4-7.

Khalilzad, Zalmay. "Soviet-Occupied Afghanistan." *Problems of Communism* (November/December 1980): 23-40.

Kridl Valkenier, Elizabeth. "The USSR, the Third World, and the Global Economy." *Problems of Communism* 28 (July-August 1979): 17-32.

Legvold, Robert. "The Super Rivals: Conflict in the Third World." *Foreign Affairs* 57 (Spring 1979): 755-78.

Leiken, Robert. "Fantasies and Facts: The Soviet Union and Nicaragua," *Current History* 83 (October 1984): 314-17+.

Limberg, Wayne P. "The USSR & the Persian Gulf: Continuity vs. Change." Paper presented at III World Congress of Soviet and East European Studies, Washington, D.C., October 31, 1985.

Mirsky, Georgi. "The Middle East: New Factors." *New Times* (Moscow) 48 (1973): 18-19.

Rothenberg, Morris. "Latin America in Soviet Eyes." *Problems of Communism* (September-October 1983): 1-18.

Rubinstein, Alvin. *Soviet Policy toward Turkey, Iran & Afghanistan: The Dynamics of Influence.* New York: Praeger Publishers, 1982.

Savimbi, Jonas, "The War Against Soviet Colonialism," *Policy Review* (Winter 1986): 18-24.

Soviet Posture in the Western Hemisphere. Hearing before the Subcommittee on Western Hemisphere Affairs of the Committee on Foreign Affairs, U.S. House of Representatives. Washington, D.C. February 28, 1985.

Stepanov, A. "Hour of Trial for the Palestinians." *New Times* (Moscow) 42 (1978): 6-7.

Stern, Geoffrey. "The Soviet Union, Afghanistan and East-West Relations." *Millennium* (Autumn 1980): 135-46.

Trofimenko, Henry. "America, Russia and the Third World." *Foreign Affairs* 59 (Summer 1981): 1021-40.

Valenta, Jiri. "From Prague to Kabul: The Soviet Style of Invasion." *International Security* (Fall 1980): 114-41.

——. "The Soviet Invasion of Afghanistan: The Difficulty of Knowing Where to Stop." *Orbis* (Summer 1980): 201-18.

Volsky, Dmitry. "Arab East: Miracles and Realities." *New Times* (Moscow) 24 (1974): 12-13.

——. "Changes in the Sudan." *New Times* (Moscow) 30 (1971): 10-11.

CHAPTER 6
The Role of the Military

Books

Alexander, Arthur J. *Armor Development in the Soviet Union and the United States.* Santa Monica, Calif.: The Rand Corporation, 1976.

Barron, John. *KGB Today: The Hidden Hand.* New York: Reader's Digest Press, 1983.

Berman, Robert P. *Soviet Air Power in Transition.* Washington, D.C.: Brookings Institution, 1978.

Bertram, Christopher. *Prospects of Soviet Power in the 1980s.* Hamden, Conn.: Archon Books, 1980.

Blechman, Barry M., et al. *The Soviet Military Buildup and U.S. Defense Spending.* Washington, D.C.: Brookings Institution, 1977.

Bloomfield, Lincoln P., et al. *Khrushchev and the Arms Race: Soviet Interests in Arms Control and Disarmament, 1954-64.* Cambridge: MIT Press, 1966.

Burt, Richard, ed. *Arms Control and Defense Postures in the 1980s.* Boulder, Colo.: Westview Press, 1981.

Cockburn, Andrew. *The Threat: Inside the Soviet Military Machine.* New York: Random House, 1983.

Colton, Timothy J. *Commissars, Commanders, and Civilian Authority: Structure of Soviet Military Politics.* Cambridge: Harvard University Press, 1979.

——. "The Impact of the Military on Soviet Society." In *The Domestic Context of Soviet Foreign Policy,* ed. Seweryn Bialer, 199-213. Boulder, Colo.: Westview Press, 1981.

Druzhinin, V. V., and D. S. Kontorov. *Concept, Algorithm, Decision.* Moscow: Voyenizday, 1972. English translation part of Soviet Military Thought series (n. 6) published under the auspices of U.S. Air Force. Washington, D.C.: Government Printing Office, 1975.

Gaddis, John Lewis. *Strategies of Containment: A Critical Appraisal of Postwar American National Security Policy.* New York: Oxford University Press, 1982.

Garthoff, Raymond L. *Soviet Military Doctrine.* Glencoe, Ill.: Free Press, 1953.

——. *Soviet Military Policy: A Historical Analysis.* New York: Praeger Publishers, 1966.

Gelman, Harry. *The Soviet Far East Buildup and Soviet Risk-Taking against China.* Santa Monica, Calif.: The Rand Corporation, 1982.

Ginsburgs, George, and Alvin Z. Rubinstein, eds. *Soviet Foreign Policy toward Western Europe.* New York: Praeger Publishers, 1981.

Goure, Leon, Foy D. Kohler, and Mose L. Harvey. *The Role of Nuclear Forces in Current Soviet Strategy.* Miami, Fla.: University of Miami Press, 1974.

Jones, Ellen. *Red Army and Society: A Sociology of the Soviet Military.* Winchester, Mass.: Allen & Unwin, 1985.

Kaplan, Stephen S. *Diplomacy of Power: Soviet Armed Forces as a Political Instrument.* 2d ed. Washington, D.C.: Brookings Institution, 1985.

Katz, Mark N. *The Third World in Soviet Military Thought.* London: Croom Helm, 1982.

Keliber, John G. *The Negotiations on Mutual and Balanced Force Reductions: The Search for Arms Control in Central Europe.* Elmsford, N.Y.: Pergamon, 1980.

Kintner, William R., and Harriett Fast Scott, trans. and eds. *The Nuclear Revolution in Soviet Military Affairs.* Norman: University of Oklahoma Press, 1968.

Kirk, Grayson, and Nils H. Wessell, eds. *The Soviet Threat: Myths and Realities.* New York: The Academy of Political Science, 1978.

Larson, Thomas B. *Disarmament and Soviet Policy, 1964-1968.* Englewood Cliffs, N.J.: Prentice-Hall, 1969.

Leebaert, Derek, ed. *Soviet Military Thinking.* London: Allen & Unwin, 1981.

Lehman, John F., and Seymour Weiss. *Beyond the SALT II Failure.* New York: Praeger Publishers, 1981.

MccGwire, Michael, Ken Booth, and John McDonnell, eds. *Soviet Naval Policy Objectives and Constraints.* New York: Praeger Publishers, 1975.

Newhouse, John. *Cold Dawn: The Story of SALT.* New York: Holt, Rinehart & Winston, 1973.

Payne, Samuel B. *The Soviet Union and SALT.* Cambridge: MIT Press, 1980.

Penkovskiy, Oleg. *The Penkovskiy Papers,* eds. and trans. Peter Deriabin and Frank Gibney. Garden City, N.Y.: Doubleday, 1965.

Potter, William C., ed. *Verification and SALT: The Challenge of Strategic Deception.* Boulder, Colo.: Westview Press, 1980.

Record, Jeffrey. *Sizing Up the Russian Army.* Washington, D.C.: Brookings Institution, 1975.

Richelson, Jeffrey T. *Sword and Shield: Soviet Intelligence and Security Apparatus.* Cambridge, Mass.: Ballinger, 1986.

Schwartz, Harry. *Tsars, Mandarins, and Commissars: A History of Chinese-Russian Relations.* Garden City, N.Y.: Doubleday, 1973.

Scott, Harriet Fast, and William F. Scott. *The Armed Forces of the USSR.* 3d ed. Boulder, Colo.: Westview Press, 1984.

Seaborg, Glenn T., et al. *Kennedy, Khrushchev and the Test Ban.* Berkeley: University of California Press, 1981.

Shavrov, General of the Army I. Ye. *Local Wars: History and the Present.* Moscow: Voyenizdat, 1981.

Shtemenko, S. M. *The General Staff in the Years of the War.* English translation, Moscow: Progress Publishers, 1970; republished in two volumes, Moscow: Voyenizdat, 1981.

Shultz, Richard H., and Roy Godson. *Dezinformatsia: Active Measures in Soviet Strategy.* Washington, D.C.: Pergamon-Brassey's, 1984.

Smith, Gerard. *Doubletalk: The Story of the First Strategic Arms Limitation Talks.* Garden City, N.Y.: Doubleday, 1980.

Sokolovsky, Marshal V. D., ed. *Military Strategy: Soviet Doctrine and Concepts.* New York: Praeger Publishers, 1963.

Suvorov, Viktor. *Soviet Military Intelligence.* London: Hamish Hamilton, 1984.

Talbott, Strobe. *Deadly Gambits*. New York: Random House, 1984.

_____. *Endgame: The Inside Story of SALT II*. New York: Harper & Row, 1980.

U.S. Department of Defense. *Soviet Acquisition of Militarily Significant Western Technology: An Update*. Washington, D.C.: Government Printing Office, 1985.

_____. *Soviet Military Power 1985*. Washington, D.C.: Government Printing Office, 1985.

Ustinov, Dmitri F. *Sluzhim rodine, delu Kommunizma*. Moscow: 1982; English translation, *We Serve the Homeland and the Cause of Communism*. Washington, D.C.: JPRSL/10604, 1982.

Valenta, Jiri, and William C. Potter, eds. *Soviet Decisionmaking for National Security*. London: Allen & Unwin, 1985.

Warner, Edward L. *The Military in Contemporary Soviet Politics*. New York: Praeger Publishers, 1977.

Wolfe, Thomas W. *The SALT Experience*. Cambridge, Mass.: Ballinger, 1979.

Yost, David S. *European Security and the SALT Process*. Beverly Hills, Calif.: Sage Publications, 1981.

Zhukov, Georgii I. *The Memoirs of Marshal Zhukov*. New York: Delacorte, 1971.

Zhukov, Marshal G. *Marshal Zhukov's Greatest Battles*, ed. Harrison E. Salisbury. New York: Harper & Bros., 1969.

Articles

Aspaturian, Vernon V. "The Soviet Military-Industrial Complex: Does It Exist?" *Journal of International Affairs* 26, no. 1 (1972): 1-28.

Boll, Michael M. "Why Do the Soviets Want Détente?" *Military Review* (November 1974): 54-60.

Brady, Linda P. "Negotiating European Security: Mutual and Balanced Force Reductions." *International Security Review* 6 (Summer 1981): 189-208.

Burt, Richard. "Reassessing the Strategic Balance." *International Security* (Summer 1980): 37-52.

Clarke, D. L. "Arms Control and Foreign Policy under Reagan." *Bulletin of the Atomic Scientists* (November 1981): 12-19.

Coffey, J. I. "Soviet ABM Policy: The Implications for the West." *International Affairs* (April 1969): 205-22.

_____. "Strategic Arms Limitations and European Security." *International Affairs* (October 1971): 692-707.

Garn, Jake. "Exploitable Strategic Nuclear Superiority." *International Security Review* (Summer 1980): 173-92.

Gottemoeller, Rose. "Decisionmaking for Arms Limitation in the Soviet Union." In *Decisionmaking for Arms Limitation: Assessments and Prospects*, ed. Hans Guenter Brauch and Duncan L. Clarke, 53-80. Cambridge, Mass.: Ballinger, 1985.

Grechko, A. "The Leading Role of the CPSU in Building the Army of a Developed Socialist Society." *Voprosy istorii KPSS* (Moscow), May 1974.

Hopkins, Mark. "Arms and the Men in Moscow and Washington." *New Leader*, December 29, 1980, 3-6.

Husband, William B. "Soviet Perspectives of U.S. 'Positions-of-Srength' Diplomacy in the 1970s." *World Politics* 31 (July 1979): 495-517.

Jackson, William D. "Soviet Images of the U.S. as Nuclear Adversory, 1969-1979." *World Politics* (July 1981): 614-38.

Jones, Ellen. "Soviet Military Manpower: Prospects in the 1980s." *Strategic Review* (Fall 1981): 65-75.

Kaufman, Richard F. "Causes of the Slowdown in Soviet Defense." *Soviet Economy* 1 (January-March 1985): 9-41.

Kitrinos, Robert W. "International Department of the CPSU," *Problems of Communism* (September-October 1984): 47-75.

Kolkowicz, Roman. "U.S. and Soviet Approaches to Military Strategy: Theory vs. Experience." *Orbis* (Summer 1981): 307-29.

Lambeth, Benjamin S. "Moscow and the Missile Race." *Current History* (October 1971): 215-21.

Mackintosh, Malcolm. "Soviet Foreign Policy." *World Today* (April 1968): 145-50.

_____. "The Soviet Military: Influence on Defense Policymaking." *Problems of Communism* (September-October 1973): 1-12.

Muravchik, Joshua. "Expectations of SALT I: Lessons for SALT II." *World Affairs* (Winter 1980/1981): 278-97.

Ogarkov, N. "Guarding Peaceful Labor." *Kommunist* 10 (1981).

Perlmutter, Amos. "Big Power Games, Small Power Wars." *Transaction* 7, nos. 9-10 (July-August 1970): 79-83.

Pipes, Richard. "Militarism and the Soviet State." *Daedalus* (Fall 1980): 1-12.

Pollack, Jonathan D. "Chinese Global Strategy and Soviet Power." *Problems of Communism* (January/February 1981): 54-69.

Potomov, Y. "The Lebanon Crisis: Who Stands to Gain." *New Times* (Moscow) 26 (1976): 8-9.

Rumyanstev, V. "Syria on the Alert." *New Times* (Moscow) 40 (1972): 8-9.

Scoville, Herbert, Jr. "Beyond SALT One." *Foreign Affairs* (Spring 1972): 488-500.

Singleton, Seth. "The Soviet Invasion of Afghanistan." *Atlantic Community Quarterly* (Summer 1981): 186-200.

Soll, Richard S. "The Soviet Union and Protracted Nuclear War." *Strategic Review* (Fall 1980): 15-28.

_____. "The Soviet Union, 1981." *Current History* (October 1981): 305-46.

Stepanov, A. "Taking Up a Point." *New Times* (Moscow) 17 (1981): 31.

Suvorov, Viktor. "Spetsnaz: The Soviet Union's Special Forces." *Military Review* (March 1984): 30-46.

Ustinov, Marshal Dmitri F., "On Averting the Threat of Nuclear War." *Pravda*, July 12, 1982.

_____. "May 1981 Is Not June 1967." *New Times* (Moscow) 21 (1981): 5-6.

Warnke, Paul C. "Arms-Control Negotiations in a Cold Climate." *Technology Review* (April 1981): 72-74.

CHAPTER 7
Economy: Perennial Problem

Books

Becker, Abraham S. *Guns, Butter and Tools: Tradeoffs in Soviet Resource Allocation*. Santa Monica, Calif.: The Rand Corporation, 1982.

Bornstein, Morris. *East-West Technology Transfer: The Transfer of Western Technology to the USSR*. Paris: OECD, 1985.

_____. *The Soviet Economy: Continuity and Change*. Boulder, Colo.: Westview Press, 1981.

Caldwell, Lawrence T., and William Diebold. *Soviet-American Relations in the 1980s: Superpower Politics and East-West Trade*. New York: McGraw-Hill, 1981.

Centrally Planned Economies Long-Term Projections. Winter 1984/85. Philadelphia: Wharton Econometric Forecasting Associates, 1985.

Centrally Planned Economies Outlook. vol. 6, no. 2. Philadelphia: Wharton Econometrics Forecasting Associates, October 1985.

Denton, M. Elizabeth. "Soviet Consumer Policy: Trends and Prospects." In *Soviet Economy in a Time of Change*. Washington, D.C.: Government Printing Office, 1979.

Goldman, Marshall. *Soviet Foreign Aid*. New York: Praeger Publishers, 1967.

Guidelines for the Economic and Social Development of the USSR for 1986-1990 and for the Period Ending in 2000. Moscow: Novosti Press Agency, 1985.

Hahn, Werner G. *The Politics of Soviet Agriculture, 1960-1970*. Baltimore: Johns Hopkins University Press, 1972.

Hewett, Ed A. *Energy, Economics, and Foreign Policy in the Soviet Union*. Washington, D.C.: Brookings Institution, 1984.

Johnson, D. Gale, and Karen McConnell Brooks. *Prospects for Soviet Agriculture in the 1980s*. Bloomington: Indiana University Press, 1983.

Kanet, Roger, and Donna Bahry, eds. *Soviet Economic and Political Relations with the Developing World*. New York: Praeger Publishers, 1975.

Parrott, Bruce, ed. *Trade, Technology and Soviet-American Relations*. Bloomington: Indiana University Press and Center for Strategic and International Studies, Georgetown, 1985.

Ploss, Sidney. *Conflict and Decision-Making Process in Soviet Russia: A Case Study of Agricultural Policy, 1953-1963*. Princeton, N.J.: Princeton University Press, 1965.

Turpin, William N. *Soviet Foreign Trade*. Lexington, Mass.: Lexington Books, 1977.

Zaleski, Eugene. *Planning Reforms in the Soviet Union, 1962-1966: An Analysis of Recent Trends in Economic Organization and Management*. Chapel Hill: University of North Carolina Press, 1967.

Articles

Bertsch, Gary. "U.S.-Soviet Trade: The Question of Leverage." *Survey* (Spring 1980): 66-80.

Birman, Igor. "Financial Crisis in the U.S.S.R." *Soviet Studies* (January 1980): 84-105.

Bond, Daniel. "Soviet Plan for Consumer Goods and Services." vol. 5, no. 85-86. Washington, D.C.: Wharton Econometrics Centrally Planned Economies Current Analysis, November 21, 1985.

———. "Impact on Soviet Trade of a Sharp Decline in Oil Prices." vol. 5, no. 79-80. Washington, D.C.: Wharton Econometrics Centrally Planned Economies Current Analysis, October 29, 1985.

———. "Soviet Economic Prospects for 1985." vol. 5, no. 63-64. Washington, D.C.: Wharton Econometrics Centrally Planned Economies Current Analysis, September 5, 1985.

CIA Briefing Paper Entitled "USSR: Economic Trends and Policy Developments." In *Allocation of Resources in the Soviet Union and China — 1983*. Hearings before the Subcommittee on International Trade, Finance, and Security Economics of the Joint Economic Committee, 98th Cong. 1st sess. Washington, D.C.: Government Printing Office, 1984.

Costello, Mary. "Soviet Economic Dilemma." *Editorial Research Reports*, February 19, 1982, 127-46.

Gordon, Michael R. "The Grain Embargo: No Great Impact on Either the Farmers or the Soviets." *National Journal*, September 6, 1980, 1480-84.

Lavoie, Louis. "The Limits of Soviet Technology." *Technology Review* (November-December 1985): 69-75.

McIntyre, William R. "American-Soviet Trade." *Editorial Research Reports*, September 2, 1959, 653-70.

Nove, Alec. "A Review of Soviet Economic Progress." *National Institute Economic Review* (November 1959): 37-47.

Paarlberg, Robert L. "Lessons of the Grain Embargo." *Foreign Affairs* (Fall 1980): 144-62.

Root, William A. "Trade Controls That Work." *Foreign Policy* 56 (Fall 1984): 61-80.

Schwartz, Charles A. "Economic Crime in the U.S.S.R.: A Comparison of the Khrushchev and Brezhnev Eras." *International Comparative Law Quarterly* (April 1981): 281-96.

U.S. Department of Commerce. "Foreign Economic Trends and their Implications for the United States." International Marketing Information Series, USSR. Washington, D.C.: Government Printing Office, December, 1985.

Vanous, Jan. "Soviet and East European Trade and Financial Relations with the Middle East." vol. 3, no. 76-78. Washington, D.C.: Wharton Centrally Planned Economies Current Analysis, October 11, 1983.

Vernon, Raymond. "Apparatchiks and Entrepreneurs: U.S. Soviet Economic Relations." *Foreign Affairs* (Winter 1973-74): 249-62.

CHAPTER 8
People and Society

Books

Alexeyeva, Ludmilla. *Soviet Dissent*. Middletown, Conn.: Wesleyan University Press, 1985.

Alliluyeva, Svetlana. *Only One Year*. New York: Harper & Row, 1969.

———. *Twenty Letters to a Friend*. New York: Harper & Row, 1967.

Amalrik, Andrei. *Will the Soviet Union Survive Until 1984?* New York: Harper & Row, 1970.

Babitsky, Paul, and John Rimberg. *The Soviet Film Industry*. New York: Praeger Publishers, 1955.

Brown, Clarence, ed. *The Portable Twentieth-Century Russian Reader*. New York: Viking/Penguin, 1985.

Churchward, L. G. *The Soviet Intelligentsia: An Essay on the Social Structure and Roles of Soviet Intellectuals during the 1960s*. Boston: Routledge & Kegan Paul, 1973.

Feshbach, Murray. *The Soviet Union: Population Trends and Dilemmas*. Population Bulletin, 37, no. 3. Washington, D.C.: Population Reference Bureau, 1982.

Grigorenko, Petr G. *Memoirs*, trans. Thomas P. Whitney. New York: W. W. Norton, 1983.

Kaiser, Robert G. *Russia: The People and Power*. New York: Washington Square Press, 1984.

Leyda, J. *Kino: A History of the Russian and Soviet Film*. New York: Macmillan, 1960.

Matthews, Mervyn. *Education in the Soviet Union: Policies and Institutions Since Stalin*. Winchester, Mass.: Allen and Unwin, 1982.

Medvedev, Zhores A. *Ten Years after Ivan Denisovich*. New York: Vintage, 1974.

Newberg, Paula R., ed. *The Politics of Human Rights*. New York: New York University Press, 1980.

Pankhurst, Jerry G., and Michael Paul Sacks. *Contemporary Soviet Society: Sociological Perspectives*. New York: Praeger Publishers, 1980.

Reddaway, Peter. "Soviet Policy Toward Dissent Since Khrushchev." Radio Free Europe-Radio Liberty, August 21, 1980.

———. *Uncensored Russia*. New York: American Heritage, 1972.

Simis, Konstantin M. *USSR: The Corrupt Society (The Secret World of Soviet Capitalism)*. New York: Simon & Schuster, 1982.

Tökes, Rudolph L., ed. *Dissent in the USSR: Politics, Ideology and People*. Baltimore: Johns Hopkins University Press, 1975.

Triska, Jan F., and Robert M. Slusser. *The Theory, Law and Policy of Soviet Treaties*. Stanford, Calif.: Stanford University Press, 1962.

Utechin, S. V. *A Concise Encyclopaedia of Russia*. New York: E. P. Dutton, 1964.

Vucinich, Alexander. *Science in Russian Culture, 1867-1917*. Stanford, Calif.: Stanford University Press, 1970.

Westwood, J. N. *Endurance and Endeavor: Russian History 1812-1980*. New York: Oxford University Press, 1981.

Willis, David K. *Klass: How Russians Really Live*. New York: St. Martin's Press, 1985.

Articles

Blumenfeld, Yorick. "Dissent in Russia." *Editorial Research Reports*, June 28, 1972, 481-98.

Gibian, George. "New Aspects of Soviet Russian Literature." In *The Soviet Union Since Stalin*, ed. Stephen F. Cohen, Alexander Rabinowitch, Robert Sharlet. Bloomington: Indiana University Press, 1980.

Gidwitz, Betsy. "Labor Unrest in the Soviet Union." *Problems of Communism* (November-December 1982): 25-82.

Gitelman, Zvi. "Moscow and the Soviet Jews: A Parting of the Ways." *Problems of Communism* (January-February 1980): 18-34.

Korey, William. "The Story of the Jackson Amendment, 1973-1975." *Midstream* (March 1975): 7-36.

Proffer, Carl R., and Ellen Dean. "Introduction." *Contemporary Russian Prose*. Ann Arbor, Mich.: Ardis, 1982.

Siniavsky, Andrei. "On Socialist Realism" and introduction by Czeslaw Milosz. Berkeley: University of California Press, 1960.

"Soviet Life, 1985." *Wilson Quarterly*, special supplement (Autumn 1985): 46-87.

Teague, Elizabeth. "Labor Discipline and Legislation in the USSR: 1979-85." Radio Liberty Research Bulletin, October 16, 1985.

CHAPTER 9
Changing of the Guard

Books

Beichman, Arnold, and M. S. Bernstam. *Andropov: New Challenge to the West.* New York: Stein & Day, 1983.

Brown, Archie, and Michael Kaser, eds. *Soviet Policy for the 1980s.* Bloomington: Indiana University Press, 1983.

Byrnes, Robert F., ed. *After Brezhnev: Sources of Soviet Conduct in the 1980s.* Bloomington: Indiana University Press and Georgetown University Center for Strategic and International Studies, 1983.

Crankshaw, Edward. *Putting Up with the Russians; Commentary and Criticism 1947-84.* New York: Viking, 1984.

Dallin, Alexander, and CondoLeezza Rice, eds. *The Gorbachev Era.* Stanford, Calif.: Stanford University Press, 1986.

Ebon, Martin. *The Andropov File.* New York: McGraw-Hill, 1983.

Gorbachev, Mikhail. *A Time for Peace.* New York: Richardson & Steirman, 1986.

Hough, Jerry F. *Soviet Leadership in Transition.* Washington, D.C.: Brookings Institution, 1977.

Medvedev, Zhores A. *Andropov.* New York: W. W. Norton, 1983.

____. *Gorbachev.* New York: W. W. Norton, 1986.

Solovyov, Vladimir, and Elena Klepikova. *Yuri Andropov: A Secret Passage into the Kremlin.* New York: Macmillan, 1983.

Zemtsov, Ilya. *Andropov.* Jerusalem: Israel Research Institute of Contemporary Society, 1983.

Articles

Andropov, Yuri V. "Leninism — The Inexhaustible Source of the Revolutionary Energy and Creativity of the Masses." *Pravda,* April 23, 1982.

Bialer, Seweryn. "The Harsh Decade: Soviet Policies in the 1980s." *Foreign Affairs* (Summer 1981): 999-1020.

Bialer, Seweryn, and Joan Afferica. "Gorbachev's World." *Foreign Affairs* 64, no. 3 (America and the World 1985): 605-44.

Bilinsky, Yaroslav. "Shcherbytskiy, Ukraine, and Kremlin Politics." *Problems of Communism* (July-August 1983): 1-20.

Brown, Archie. "Andropov: Discipline and Reform." *Problems of Communism* (January-February 1983): 18-31.

Caldwell, Lawrence, and Robert Legvold. "Reagan through Soviet Eyes." *Foreign Policy* 52 (Fall 1983): 3-21.

Chernenko, Konstantin U. "Inspired by Lenin, Acting in a Leninist Way." *Pravda,* April 23, 1981.

Costello, Mary. "Russia after Détente." *Editorial Research Reports,* February 6, 1981, 83-104.

Epstein, Edward Jay. "The Andropov File." *New Republic,* February 7, 1983, 18-21.

Floyd, David. "U.S. Negotiations with the U.S.S.R.: The Pattern of Blundering." *Survey* (Spring 1980): 25-31.

Gati, Charles. "Soviet Empire: Alive But Not Well." *Problems of Communism* (March-April 1985): 73-86.

Gelb, Leslie H. "What We Really Know about Russia." *New York Times Magazine,* December 28, 1984, 22-25+.

Gray, Colin. "The Most Dangerous Decade: Historic Mission, Legitimacy, and Dynamics of the Soviet Empire in the 1980s." *Orbis* (Spring 1981): 13-28.

Griffiths, Franklyn. "The Sources of American Conduct: Soviet Perspectives & Their Policy Implications." *International Security* (Fall 1984): 3-50.

Hopkins, Mark. "The Legacy of Leonid Brezhnev." *New Leader,* February 23, 1981, 5-8.

Hough, Jerry F. "Pluralism, Corporatism and the Soviet Union." In *Pluralism in the Soviet Union,* ed. Susan Gross Solomon,

37-60. New York: St. Martin's Press, 1983.

Hyland, William A. "Kto Kogo in the Kremlin." *Problems of Communism* (January-February 1982): 17-26.

Laqueur, Walter. "Reagan and the Russians." *Commentary* (January 1982): 19-26.

Liska, George. "Russia and the West: The Next to the Last Phrase." *SAIS Review* (Summer 1981): 141-53.

Nitze, Paul H. "Strategy in the Decade of the 1980s." *Foreign Affairs* (Fall 1980): 82-101.

Pick, Otto. "Reacting to Reagan: Soviet Fears and Opportunities." *World Today* (July/August 1981): 262-91.

Ploss, Sidney I. "A New Soviet Era?" *Foreign Policy* 62 (Spring 1986): 46-60.

Simes, Dimitri. "America's New Edge," *Foreign Policy* 56 (Fall 1984): 24-43.

____. "National Security under Andropov." *Problems of Communism* (January-February 1983): 32-39.

____. "The New Soviet Challenge." *Foreign Policy* 55 (Summer 1984): 113-31.

Zagoria, Donald. "The Moscow-Beijing Detente." *Foreign Affairs* (Spring 1983): 853-73.

Zlotnik, Marc D. "Chernenko Succeeds." *Problems of Communism* (March-April 1984): 17-31.

General Readings

Bialer, Seweryn, ed. *The Domestic Context of Soviet Foreign Policy.* Studies of the Research Institute on International Change, Columbia University. Boulder, Colo.: Westview Press, 1981.

The Cambridge Encyclopedia of Russia and the Soviet Union, ed. H. T. Willetts, et al. New York: Cambridge University Press, 1981.

Cracraft, James, ed. *The Soviet Union Today: An Interpretive Guide.* Bulletin of the Atomic Scientists, Educational Foundation for Nuclear Science. Chicago: University of Chicago Press, 1983.

Current Digest of the Soviet Press. Weekly compilation of translated Soviet articles; since 1949.

Donaldson, Robert, and Joseph Nogee. *Soviet Foreign Policy since World War II.* Elmsford, N.Y.: Pergamon, 1984.

Foreign Broadcast Information Service. *Daily Report: Soviet Union.*

Garthoff, Raymond L. *Détente and Confrontation: American-Soviet Relations from Nixon to Reagan.* Washington, D.C.: Brookings Institution, 1985.

Hoffmann, Erik P., ed. *The Soviet Union in the 1980s.* New York: The Academy of Political Science, 1984.

Hoffmann, Erik P., and Frederic Fleron, Jr., eds. *The Conduct of Soviet Foreign Policy.* Chicago: Aldine, 1982.

Hoffmann, Erik P., and Robbin F. Laird, eds. *The Soviet Polity in the Modern Era.* New York: Aldine, 1984.

Hough, Jerry F., and Merle Fainsod. *How the Soviet Union Is Governed.* Cambridge: Harvard University Press, 1979.

Kanet, Roger E., ed. *The Behavioral Revolution and Communist Studies.* New York: Free Press, 1971.

Lowenhardt, John. *The Soviet Politburo.* New York: St. Martin's Press, 1982.

Medish, Vadim. *The Soviet Union,* 2d rev. ed. Englewood Cliffs, N.J.: Prentice-Hall, 1985.

Nye, Joseph S., Jr., ed. *The Making of America's Soviet Policy.* New Haven, Conn.: Yale University Press, 1984.

Ovsyany, I. D., et al. *A Study of Soviet Foreign Policy.* Moscow: Progress Publishers, 1975.

Rubinstein, Alvin. *Soviet Foreign Policy since World War II.* Cambridge, Mass.: Little, Brown, 1981.

Scholar's Guide for Washington, D.C. Russian/Soviet Studies, 2d rev. ed. Washington, D.C.: Smithsonian Institution Press, 1983.

Skilling, H. Gordon, and Franklyn Griffiths, eds. *Interest Groups in Soviet Politics.* Princeton, N.J.: Princeton University Press, 1971.

Biographies

Butson, Thomas G. *Gorbachev: A Biography.* New York: Stein & Day, 1985.

Deutscher, Isaac. *Stalin: A Political Biography.* 2d ed. New York: Oxford University Press, 1966.

Haupt, Georges, and Jean-Jaques Marie. *Makers of the Russian Revolution: Biographies of Soviet Leaders.* Ithaca, N.Y.: Cornell University Press, 1974.

Lewytzky, Borys, ed. *Who's Who in the Soviet Union: A biograph-ical encyclopedia of 5,000 leading personalities in the Soviet Union.* Munich: K. G. Saur, 1984.

Radio Liberty Research Bulletin: A Biographic Directory of 100 Leading Soviet Officials, trans. Stelianos Scarlis, compiled by Alexander G. Rahr. Washington, D.C.: Radio Free Europe/Radio Liberty, 1986.

Swearingen, Rodger. *Leaders of the Communist World.* New York: Free Press, 1971.

Zmetsov, Ilya. *Gorbachev: Between Past & Future.* Fairfax, Va.: Hero Books, 1986.

Index